EC/EU Legislation in Ireland

EC/EU
LEGISLATION
IN IRELAND

PATRICIA CONLAN

EDITOR

GILL & MACMILLAN

Published in Ireland by
Gill & Macmillan Ltd
Goldenbridge
Dublin 8

with associated companies throughout the world

© Patricia Conlan 1994

0 7171 2233 6

Print origination by Typeform Repro Ltd, Dublin
Printed by ColourBooks Ltd, Dublin

A catalogue record is available for this book from the British Library.

FOREWORD

It was during my term as Minister for State with responsibility for European Affairs that I first became fully aware of the implications of developments at EC level for this jurisdiction. As Minister for Justice I can see that, with the implementation of the Treaty on European Union, more and more areas of the law are being affected by legal instruments agreed between the Member States of the European Union.

It was more than twenty years ago that Ireland acceded to the European Communities. Indeed many readers of this publication will be students who were born after our accession to the EC and for whom the *acquis communautaire* is an accepted part of our legal structure.

However at one stage the focus of attention was on economic matters and there was a view that unless a lawyer had an interest in competition and the free movement of goods, EC law was of little importance. That certainly is not the case today. The Treaty on European Union and the treaties establishing the European Coal and Steel Community, the European Economic Community, and the European Atomic Energy Community, have been given a special position in our Constitution and the laws adopted in pursuance of these treaties take precedence in our legal system. Neither student of law nor practitioner can afford to ignore the body of EC/EU related law which has grown up. There is now a much greater awareness that our membership of the European Union has implications in a great variety of matters and cannot be ignored. Indeed I understand that the Incorporated Law Society now insists that all potential entrants to the profession of solicitor must have passed an examination in this area.

In addressing any legal issue, it is important to have ready access to the texts of primary and secondary legislation which may be relevant. Dr Patricia Conlan has done a great service in making available to the Irish reader in one comprehensive text the legal instruments relevant to our membership of the European Union.

This commendable publication includes the texts of the treaties themselves, regulations, directives and relevant Irish legislation as well as ancillary instruments. The breadth of the work can be gauged by the fact that it extends to the Acts dealing with the jurisdiction and the enforcement of judgments and the law applicable to contractual obligations. These Acts, which derive from EC related conventions, have had a significant effect on our rules of Private International Law, an area of the law which is increasingly important as our economic and social links with other European countries increase.

I am confident that this publication will be of value to all students of law and will also provide a useful reference book for practising members of the legal profession.

Máire Geoghegan-Quinn, TD
Minister for Justice

PREFACE

Several factors influenced the decision to issue this collection. Not least among them was the fact that the Incorporated Law Society had indicated that as from Michaelmas 1994 it would require European Community law as an exemption subject for entry to the profession. While there are many excellent collections from other jurisdictions dealing with primary and secondary legislation there was none directed specifically at the Irish legal profession. Given the different constitutional requirements in Ireland arising from Bunreacht na hÉireann and the manner in which these have been addressed, as compared to the other Common Law Member States, it seemed opportune to address this gap.

The aim, therefore, has been to take the Incorporated Law Society's requirements as the chief guidelines when deciding on what primary and secondary legislation to include. In addition, to mark the fact that it is a new departure and to provide the user with the most comprehensive collection possible of Irish relevant material, the Accession Treaty, the constitutional amendments and legislation implementing the Treaties have been included as far as practicable. The Competition Act, 1991, the Mergers, Take-overs and Monopolies (Control) Act, 1978 as well as the Jurisdiction of Courts and Enforcement of Foreign Judgments (EC) Act, 1988 and the Contractual Obligations (Applicable Law) Act, 1991 have been included in full to facilitate the student population now that the Incorporated Law Society has indicated that entrants to the profession should have a good knowledge of these statutes.

To the extent that space permitted, some additional secondary legislation has been included. This additional legislation was chosen on the basis of teaching experience at undergraduate and postgraduate level and with a view to broadening the circle beyond the academic world of those who could draw on these useful texts. There were many areas which had equal claims to being included but unfortunately the choices could not be unlimited. To facilitate the user the Official Journal (OJ) and relevant Irish implementing legislation references are given.

One of the most difficult decisions which had to be taken in the course of preparing this collection was that of an appropriate title. The easy option of referring to "Europe" or "European" was discarded in view of the sensibilities of those who (quite rightly) argue that "Europe/European" relates to a wider geographical and historical area than the twelve existing Member States — or even including the four front row aspirant Member States.

When the Incorporated Law Society issued its syllabus the chief concern was the EC. In the interim the Treaty on European Union (TEU) has come into force and with it new policies and forms of cooperation. The Treaty on European Union, on the one hand, establishes a Union (article A, first sentence) founded on the "European Communities, supplemented by the policies and forms of cooperation established by" the Treaty on European Union (article A, third sentence) and on the other marks a "new stage on the process of creating an ever closer union among the peoples of Europe" (article A, second sentence). However, it is the three Communities which continue to enjoy legal personality (ECSCT article 6; ECT article 210; Euratom article 184), whereas the Union does not (Everling, U.: Structure of the Treaty on European Union in CMLRev 29 p. 1059, 1992). Furthermore, the legislative areas of most interest to the intended reader of this collection fall within the scope of application of the EC Treaty. This called for a balance to be struck between the past (EC), the present (EC/EU), and the future (EU). In addition, because the emphasis has been, naturally, on Irish accession to the European Communities, and the constitutional amendments which this necessitated, with the amendments relating to the European Union being of recent origin, these past, present and future changes also had to be identified and accommodated. It is hoped, therefore, that the choice of EC/EU in the title has been a happy one, reflecting both the evolution of Irish membership and the needs of the readership of this collection of documents. Every effort has been taken to have measures adopted up to 30 June, 1994 included.

As is always the case with such a work, thanks are due to many people without whose contribution there would be nothing to celebrate. I am particularly grateful to Finola O'Sullivan, D Rennison Kunz, Gabrielle Noble, Karin Whooley and Mairéad O'Keeffe and their colleagues at Gill & Macmillan, who responded to the idea and against all the odds ensured that the tightest of deadlines was met, to Marie Moore of Devlin Editing who keyed and edited the manuscript with great skill, to Paul Power for his meticulous proof reading and to Harriet Kinahan who was enormously encouraging. Mary Guilfoyle, Marie Dineen and Yvonne Hynes provided the assistance that only those fortunate enough to be able to call on them can fully appreciate. Thanks are due to the Office of Official Publications of the European Communities in Luxembourg and to Government Publications in Dublin for permission to draw on official publications. I am responsible for any shortcomings and would appreciate response from users so that the next edition can address these shortcomings.

Patricia Conlan

University of Limerick

30 June 1994.

CONTENTS

(The IRL graphic appears beside some documents to indicate that an *Implemented in Ireland* reference is listed at the end of those documents.)

PART A. INTRODUCTION

PART B. TREATIES AND ALLIED DOCUMENTS

PART C: DOCUMENTS ON ACCESSION

PART D: AMENDMENTS OF THE CONSTITUTION ACTS

PART E: EUROPEAN COMMUNITIES ACTS

PART F: SECONDARY LEGISLATION

COMPETITION LAW

LABOUR LAW

NOTES

1. The footnotes used in this work do not correspond to the numbering system used in the original documents.

2. The Irish implementing legislation reference ⁺IRL⁺ refers to the statute or, where more appropriate, to the statutory instrument (S.I.).

3. It should be noted that if the four applicant countries (Finland, Norway, Sweden and Austria) do in fact accede to the European Union on 1 January, 1995, as planned, this will have corresponding institutional repercussions most particularly in terms of membership of the Institutions and Bodies.

4. The Treaty establishing a Single Council and a Single Commission of the European Communities (Merger Treaty) signed 1965, into force in 1967 (OJ No 152, 13.7.67) has been omitted from this volume.

5. Except where required (footnoted accordingly) 'European Parliament' has been used instead of 'Assembly' as has 'Commission' instead of 'High Authority' and 'European Community' instead of 'European Economic Community'. These amendments reflect the amendments to the founding treaties.

6. The symbol [preceding an Article indicates that this Article's text has been amended by the Treaty on European Union. All such Articles are also footnoted accordingly.

7. The presentation of the treaties reflects the order of the Treaty on European Union with the three founding treaties (EC, ECSC, Euratom), Titles II, III and IV being incorporated within the body of the Treaty on European Union.

ACKNOWLEDGMENTS

For permission to use extracts from within official European and Irish publications, the editor and publishers wish to acknowledge both the Office for Official Publications of the European Communities in Luxembourg and the Controller, Stationery Office, Office of Public Works in Dublin.

TABLE OF LEGISLATION

TABLE OF TREATIES

TABLE OF PROTOCOLS

Treaty on European Union

TABLE OF DECISIONS

OTHER DOCUMENTS

ABBREVIATIONS

CFI	Court of First Instance
CMLR	Common Market Law Report
CMLRev	Common Market Law Review
EAEC	European Atomic Energy Community
EC	European Community or European Communities
ECB	European Central Bank
ECJ	Court of Justice of the European Communities
ECSC	European Coal and Steel Community
EEA	European Economic Area or Agreement
EEC	European Economic Community
EFTA	European Free Trade Area or Association
EIB	European Investment Bank
EMI	European Monetary Institute
EMS	European Monetary System
EMU	Economic and Monetary Union
ERM	Exchange Rate Mechanism
ESCB	European System of Central Banks
EU	European Union
Euratom	European Atomic Energy Community
GATT	General Agreement on Tariffs and Trade
ILRM	Irish Law Reports Monthly
No	Number
OJ	Official Journal of the European Communities
SEA	Single European Act
S.I.	Statutory Instrument
TEU	Treaty on European Union

PART A

INTRODUCTION

INTRODUCTION

Ireland finally acceded to the European Communities (European Coal and Steel Community, European Economic Community and European Atomic Energy Community) in 1973.

As early as 1961 the then Taoiseach had announced that it was the intention of his government to apply for full membership of the European Economic Community. The reasons lying behind the application included the change in industrial policy at home and, most importantly, the declared intention of the British government to apply for membership. The United Kingdom was Ireland's most important trading partner at that time. In addition, the Irish government wanted to reduce the economic dependence on the United Kingdom and membership of the EEC seemed to present a good alternative. This first application for membership failed in 1963 when General de Gaulle opposed British membership; the application was revived in 1967, never having been officially withdrawn, but it was 1970 before negotiations could begin in earnest. These culminated in the positive outcome to the 1972 constitutional referendum (3rd amendment of the Constitution) followed by ratification of the Treaties and accession (Accession Treaty had been signed on 22 January, 1972) on 1 January, 1973, together with Denmark and the United Kingdom, Norway having failed to carry a referendum allowing for membership.

The Irish people had a second opportunity to cast their votes in a referendum arising from membership of the Communities in May 1987. This was as a result of the Supreme Court decision in Crotty v An Taoiseach ([1987] ILRM 400) that Title III of the Single European Act, 1986 was unconstitutional. The outcome was again positive allowing for ratification of the Single European Act (10th amendment of the Constitution) and the coming into force of the Act, which had been delayed pending the outcome of the Irish referendum, followed on 1 July, 1987.

In June 1992 – some twenty years after the first referendum allowing for accession to the Communities – a referendum (11th amendment of the Constitution) allowed the State to ratify the Treaty on European Union and to become a member of the Union. However, the Treaty on European Union did not come into force until 1 November, 1993, following ratification by Germany in the wake of an unsuccessful constitutional challenge on the Treaty in relation to the German Basic Law.

KEY DATES EC/EU: IRELAND

1951 European Coal and Steel Community Treaty signed in Paris by Belgium, France, Germany, Italy, Luxembourg, Netherlands

1952 European Coal and Steel Community Treaty enters into force

1957 European Economic Community and European Atomic Energy Community Treaties signed in Rome by Belgium, France, Germany, Italy, Luxembourg, Netherlands

1958 European Economic Community and European Atomic Energy Community Treaties enter into force

1961 Announcement by an Taoiseach of intention of Irish government to apply for membership of European Communities

1963 Irish application for membership fails because of French opposition to British membership

1965 Merger Treaty signed

1967 Irish application for membership reactivated

Merger Treaty comes into force

1970 Negotiations on Irish membership begin in earnest

1970 Council Decision on own resources

1972 Accession Treaty signed (by i.a. Ireland)

Referendum (3rd amendment of the Constitution) allowed for accession to the European Communities

1973 Ireland accedes to the European Communities (together with Denmark and the United Kingdom)

1975 Budget Treaty

1978 European Monetary System and Exchange Rate Mechanism

1979 First Direct Elections to European Parliament (Assembly)

1981 Greece accedes to the European Communities

1984 Second direct elections to European Parliament (Assembly)

1985 Greenland leaves the European Communities

Second Decision on own Resources

Commission White Paper on Completing the Internal Market

1986 Portugal and Spain accede to the European Communities

Single European Act signed

Uruguay Round of the GATT launched

1987   Crotty v An Taoiseach: constitutional challenge to the Single
        European Act successful

        Referendum in Ireland (10th amendment of the Constitution)
        allowing for ratification of the Single European Act

        Single European Act enters into force after ratification by
        Ireland

1988   Court of First Instance established

1989   Third direct elections to the European Parliament

1990   Reunification of Germany

1991   European Economic Area Agreement signed between EC and
        EFTA

1992   Treaty on European Union signed

        Referendum in Denmark rejects the Treaty on European Union

        Referendum in Ireland (11th amendment of the Constitution)
        allows for ratification of the Treaty on European Union

        Referendum in France approves of the Treaty on European
        Union

        Referendum in Ireland (13th amendment of the Constitution) on
        the right to travel

        Referendum in Ireland (14th amendment of the Constitution) on
        freedom of information in relation to services

1993   Internal Market to have been achieved (as per SEA)

        Increased jurisdiction for the Court of First Instance

        Referendum in Denmark allows for ratification on the Treaty on
        European Union – taking Decisions and Declarations into
        account

        German constitutional challenge to the Treaty on European
        Union rejected by the Bundesverfassungsgerichtshof allows for
        (final) ratification on the Treaty on European Union

        Treaty on European Union enters into force

        Agreement reached in Uruguay Round of the GATT

1994 European Economic Area Agreement enters into force (excluding Switzerland and Liechtenstein – because of Swiss rejection of the Agreement in a referendum)

Increased jurisdiction for the Court of First Instance

Fourth direct elections to the European Parliament

Final negotiations on accession of Finland, Sweden, Norway and Austria to the European Union

Signing of the Uruguay Round of the GATT

European Parliament votes in favour of the enlargement of the European Union to include Finland, Sweden, Norway and Austria

1995 Anticipated accession of Finland, Sweden, Norway and Austria to the European Union

1996 Intergovernmental Conference to examine revision of certain areas of the Treaty on European Union

PART B

TREATIES AND ALLIED DOCUMENTS

TREATY ON EUROPEAN UNION

'Entered into force: 1.11.1993'

His Majesty the King of the Belgians,

Her Majesty the Queen of Denmark,

The President of the Federal Republic of Germany,

The President of the Hellenic Republic,

His Majesty the King of Spain,

The President of the French Republic,

The President of Ireland,

The President of the Italian Republic,

His Royal Highness the Grand Duke of Luxembourg,

Her Majesty the Queen of the Netherlands,

The President of the Portuguese Republic,

Her Majesty the Queen of the United Kingdom of Great Britain and Northern Ireland,

Resolved to mark a new stage in the process of European integration undertaken with the establishment of the European Communities,

Recalling the historic importance of the ending of the division of the European continent and the need to create firm bases for the construction of the future Europe,

Confirming their attachment to the principle of liberty, democracy and respect for human rights and fundamental freedoms and of the rule of law,

Desiring to deepen the solidarity between their peoples while respecting their history, their culture and their traditions,

Desiring to enhance further the democratic and efficient functioning of the institutions so as to enable them better to carry out, within a single institutional framework, the tasks entrusted to them,

Resolved to achieve the strengthening and the convergence of their economies and to establish an economic and monetary union including, in accordance with the provisions of this Treaty, a single and stable currency,

Determined to promote economic and social progress for their peoples, within the context of the accomplishment of the internal market and of reinforced cohesion and environmental protection, and to implement policies ensuring that advances in economic integration are accompanied by parallel progress in other fields,

Resolved to establish a citizenship common to nationals of their countries,

Resolved to implement a common foreign and security policy including the eventual framing of a common defence policy, which might in time lead to a common defence, thereby reinforcing the European identity and its independence in order to promote peace, security and progress in Europe and in the world,

Reaffirming their objective to facilitate the free movement of persons, while ensuring the safety and security of their peoples, by including provisions on justice and home affairs in this Treaty,

Resolved to continue the process of creating an ever closer union among the peoples of Europe, in which decisions are taken as closely as possible to the citizen in accordance with the principle of subsidiarity,

In view of further steps to be taken in order to advance European integration,

Have decided to establish a European Union and to this end have designated as their plenipotentiaries:

[List omitted]

TITLE I

Common provisions

Article A

By this Treaty, the High Contracting Parties establish among themselves a European Union, hereinafter called 'the Union'.

This Treaty marks a new stage in the process of creating an ever closer union among the peoples of Europe, in which decisions are taken as closely as possible to the citizen.

The Union shall be founded on the European Communities, supplemented by the policies and forms of cooperation established by this Treaty. Its task shall be to organise, in a manner demonstrating consistency and solidarity, relations between the Member States and between their peoples.

Article B

The Union shall set itself the following objectives:

–   to promote economic and social progress which is balanced and sustainable, in particular through the creation of an area without internal frontiers, through the strengthening of economic and social cohesion and through the establishment of economic and monetary union, ultimately including a single currency in accordance with the provisions of this Treaty;

–   to assert its identity on the international scene, in particular through the implementation of a common foreign and security policy including the eventual framing of a common defence policy, which might in time lead to a common defence;

–   to strengthen the protection of the rights and interests of the nationals of its Member States through the introduction of a citizenship of the Union;

–   to develop close cooperation on justice and home affairs;

–   to maintain in full the *acquis communautaire* and build on it with a view to considering, through the procedure referred to in Article N(2), to what extent the policies and forms of cooperation introduced by this Treaty may need to be revised with the aim of ensuring the effectiveness of the mechanisms and the institutions of the Community.

The objectives of the Union shall be achieved as provided in this Treaty and in accordance with the conditions and the timetable set out therein while respecting the principle of subsidiarity as defined in Article 3b of the Treaty establishing the European Community.

Article C

The Union shall be served by a single institutional framework which shall ensure the consistency and the continuity of the activities carried out in order to attain its objectives while respecting and building upon the *acquis communautaire*.

The Union shall in particular ensure the consistency of its external activities as a whole in the context of its external relations, security, economic and development policies. The Council and the Commission shall be responsible for ensuring such consistency. They shall ensure the implementation of these policies, each in accordance with its respective powers.

Article D

The European Council shall provide the Union with the necessary impetus for its development and shall define the general political guidelines thereof.

The European Council shall bring together the Heads of State or Government of the Member States and the President of the Commission. They shall be assisted by the Ministers for Foreign Affairs of the Member States and by a Member of the Commission. The European Council shall meet at least twice a year, under the chairmanship of the Head of State or Government of the Member State which holds the Presidency of the Council.

The European Council shall submit to the European Parliament a report after each of its meetings and a yearly written report on the progress achieved by the Union.

Article E

The European Parliament, the Council, the Commission and the Court of Justice shall exercise their powers under the conditions and for the purposes provided for, on the one hand, by the provisions of the Treaties establishing the European Communities and of the subsequent Treaties and Acts modifying and supplementing them and, on the other hand, by the other provisions of this Treaty.

Article F

1. The Union shall respect the national identities of its Member States, whose systems of government are founded on the principles of democracy.

2. The Union shall respect fundamental rights, as guaranteed by the European Convention for the Protection of Human Rights and Fundamental Freedoms signed in Rome on 4 November 1950 and as they result from the constitutional traditions common to the Member States, as general principles of Community law.

3. The Union shall provide itself with the means necessary to attain its objectives and carry through its policies.

TITLE II

The Treaty establishing the European Economic Community with a view to establishing the European Community

Article G

The Treaty establishing the European Economic Community shall be amended in accordance with the provisions of this Article, in order to establish a European Community.

A – *Throughout the Treaty*:

(1) The term 'European Economic Community' shall be replaced by the term 'European Community'.

B – *In Part One 'Principles'*:

(2) Replaced Article 2.

(3) Replaced Article 3.

(4) Inserted Article 3a.

(5) Inserted Article 3b.

(6) Replaced Article 4.

(7) Inserted Articles 4a-4b.

(8) Deleted Article 6, renamed Article 7 as Article 6 and replaced the second paragraph of the Article.

(9) Renamed Articles 8, 8a, 8b and 8c as Articles 7, 7a, 7b and 7c.

C – *Inserted Part Two, Citizenship of the Union, Articles 8-8e.*

D – *Regrouped Parts Two and Three under Part Three, Community Policies.*

(10) Replaced the first sentence of Article 49.

(11) Replaced Article 54(2).

(12) Replaced Article 56(2).

(13) Replaced Article 57.

(14) Renamed the title of Chapter 4.

(15) Inserted Articles 73a-73h.

(16) Replaced Article 75.

(17) Replaced the title of Title I in Part Three.

(18) Renamed the original point (d) as point (e) and inserted a new point (d) in Article 92(3).

(19) Replaced Article 94.

(20) Replaced Article 99.

(21) Replaced Article 100.

(22) Replaced Article 100a(1).

(23) Inserted Article 100c.

(24) Inserted Article 100d.

(25) Replaced Part Three, Title II, Chapters 1-3 by Title VI, Chapters 1-4, Articles 102a-109m.

(26) Replaced Part Three, Title II, Chapter 4 by Title VII.

(27) Repealed Article 111.

(28) Replaced Article 113.

(29) Repealed Article 114.

(30) Replaced Article 115.

(31) Repealed Article 116.

(32) Replaced Part Three, Title III by Title VIII.

(33) Replaced Article 118a(2), first subparagraph.

(34) Replaced Article 123.

(35) Replaced Article 125.

(36) Inserted Articles 126 and 127.

(37) Inserted Title IX and Article 128.

(38) Replaced Titles IV, V, VI, and VII by Title X-XVII, Articles 129-130y.

(39) Replaced Article 137.

(40) Replaced Article 138(3).

(41) Inserted Articles 138a-138e.

(42) Added a sentence to Article 144, second subparagraph.

(43) Inserted Article 146.

(44) Inserted Article 147.

(45) Repealed Article 149.

(46) Inserted Article 151.

(47) Inserted Article 154.

(48) Inserted Articles 156-165.

(49) Replaced Article 165.

(50) Replaced Article 168a.

(51) Replaced Article 171.

(52) Replaced Article 172.

(53) Replaced Article 173.

(54) Replaced Article 175.

(55) Replaced Article 176.

(56) Replaced Article 177.

(57) Replaced Article 180.

(58) Replaced Article 184.

(59) Inserted Section 5, Articles 188a-188c.

(60) Replaced Article 189.

(61) Inserted Articles 189a-189c.

(62) Replaced Article 190.

(63) Replaced Article 191.

(64) Replaced Article 194.

(65) Replaced Article 196.

(66) Replaced Article 198.

(67) Inserted Chapter 4, Articles 198a-198c.

(68) Inserted Chapter 5, Articles 198d-198e.

(69) Replaced Article 199.

(70) Repealed Article 200.

(71) Replaced Article 201.

(72) Inserted Article 201a.

(73) Replaced Article 205.

(74) Replaced Article 206.

(75) Repealed Articles 206a and 206b.

(76) Replaced Article 209.

(77) Inserted Article 209a.

(78) Replaced Article 215.

(79) Replaced Article 227(2) and (5)(a).

(80) Replaced Article 228.

(81) Inserted Article 228a.

(82) Replaced Article 231.

(83) Repealed Articles 236 and 237.

(84) Replaced Article 238.

E – In Part Five 'Institutions of the Community':

(39) Replaced Article 137.

(40) Replaced paragraph 3 of Article 138.

(41) Inserted Articles 138a-138e.

(42) Supplemented second subparagraph of Article 144.

(43) Inserted Article 146.

(44) Inserted Article 147.

(45) Repealed Article 149.

(46) Inserted Article 151.

(47) Inserted Article 154.

(48) Inserted Articles 156-163.

(49) Replaced Article 165.

(50) Replaced Article 168a.

(51) Replaced Article 171.

(52) Replaced Article 172.

(53) Replaced Article 173.

(54) Replaced Article 175.

(55) Replaced Article 176.

(56) Replaced Article 177.

(57) Replaced Article 180.

(58) Replaced Article 184.

(59) Inserted Section 5, Articles 188a-188c.

(60) Replaced Article 189.

(61) Inserted Articles 189a-189c.

(62) Replaced Article 190.

(63) Replaced Article 191.

(64) Replaced Article 194.

(65) Replaced Article 196.

(66) Replaced Article 198.

(67) Inserted Chapter 4, Articles 198a-198c.

(68) Inserted Chapter 5, Articles 198d-198e.

(69) Replaced Article 199.

(70) Repealed Article 200.

(71) Replaced Article 201.

(72) Inserted Article 201a.

(73) Replaced Article 205.

(74) Replaced Article 206.

(75) Repealed Articles 206a and 206b.

(76) Replaced Article 209.

(77) Inserted Article 209a.

(78) Replaced Article 215.

(79) Amended Article 227: paragraph 2 replaced; paragraph 5, subparagraph (a) replaced.

(80) Replaced Article 228.

(81) Inserted Article 228a.

(82) Replaced Article 231.

(83) Repealed Articles 236 and 237.

(84) Replaced Article 238.

F – In *Annex* III:

(85) Replaced the title.

G – *In the Protocol on the Statute of the European Investment Bank*:

(86) Reference to Articles 129-130 replaced by a reference to Articles 198d-198e.

Text of the Treaty

His Majesty the King of the Belgians, the President of the Federal Republic of Germany, the President of the French Republic, the President of the Italian Republic, Her Royal Highness the Grand Duchess of Luxembourg, Her Majesty the Queen of the Netherlands,

Determined to lay the foundations of an ever closer union among the peoples of Europe,

Resolved to ensure the economic and social progress of their countries by common action to eliminate the barriers which divide Europe,

Affirming as the essential objective of their efforts the constant improvement of the living and working conditions of their peoples,

Recognising that the removal of existing obstacles calls for concerted action in order to guarantee steady expansion, balanced trade and fair competition,

Anxious to strengthen the unity of their economies and to ensure their harmonious development by reducing the differences existing between the various regions and the backwardness of the less favoured regions,

Desiring to contribute, by means of a common commercial policy, to the progressive abolition of restrictions on international trade,

Intending to confirm the solidarity which binds Europe and the overseas countries and desiring to ensure the development of their prosperity, in accordance with the principles of the Charter of the United Nations,

Resolved by thus pooling their resources to preserve and strengthen peace and liberty, and calling upon the other peoples of Europe who share their ideal to join in their efforts,

Have decided to create a [European Community][1] and to this end have designated as their plenipotentiaries:

[List omitted]

Who, having exchanged their Full Powers, found in good and due form, have agreed as follows.

Part One

Principles

Article 1

By this Treaty, the High Contracting Parties establish among themselves a [European Community].[1]

[Article 2

The Community shall have as its task, by establishing a common market and an economic and monetary union and by implementing the common policies or activities referred to in Articles 3 and 3a, to promote throughout the Community a harmonious and balanced development of economic activities, sustainable and non-inflationary growth respecting the environment, a high degree of convergence of economic performance, a high level of employment and of social protection, the raising of the standard of living and quality of life, and economic and social cohesion and solidarity among Member States.][2]

[Article 3

For the purposes set out in Article 2, the activities of the Community shall include, as provided in this Treaty and in accordance with the timetable set out therein:

(a) the elimination, as between Member States, of customs duties and quantitative restrictions on the import and export of goods, and of all other measures having equivalent effect;

(b) a common commercial policy;

(c) an internal market characterised by the abolition, as between Member States, of obstacles to the free movement of goods, persons, services and capital;

(d) measures concerning the entry and movement of persons in the internal market as provided for in Article 100c;

(e) a common policy in the sphere of agriculture and fisheries;

(f) a common policy in the sphere of transport;

(g) a system ensuring that competition in the internal market is not distorted;

(h) the approximation of the laws of Member States to the extent required for the functioning of the common market;

(*i*) a policy in the social sphere comprising a European Social Fund;

(*j*) the strengthening of economic and social cohesion;

(*k*) a policy in the sphere of the environment;

(*l*) the strengthening of the competitiveness of Community industry;

(*m*) the promotion of research and technological development;

(*n*) encouragement for the establishment and development of trans-European networks;

(*o*) a contribution to the attainment of a high level of health protection;

(*p*) a contribution to education and training of quality and to the flowering of the cultures of the Member States;

(*q*) a policy in the sphere of development cooperation;

(*r*) the association of the overseas countries and territories in order to increase trade and promote jointly economic and social development;

(*s*) a contribution to the strengthening of consumer protection;

(*t*) measures in the spheres of energy, civil protection and tourism.][3]

[Article 3a

1. For the purposes set out in Article 2, the activities of the Member States and the Community shall include, as provided in this Treaty and in accordance with the timetable set out therein, the adoption of an economic policy which is based on the close coordination of Member States' economic policies, on the internal market and on the definition of common objectives, and conducted in accordance with the principle of an open market economy with free competition.

2. Concurrently with the foregoing, and as provided in this Treaty and in accordance with the timetable and the procedures set out therein, these activities shall include the irrevocable fixing of exchange rates leading to the introduction of a single currency, the ECU, and the definition and conduct of a single monetary policy and exchange-rate policy the primary objective of both of which shall be to maintain price stability and, without prejudice to this objective, to support the general economic policies in the Community, in accordance with the principle of an open market economy with free competition.

3. These activities of the Member States and the Community shall entail compliance with the following guiding principles: stable prices, sound

public finances and monetary conditions and a sustainable balance of payments.]⁴

[Article 3b

The Community shall act within the limits of the powers conferred upon it by this Treaty and of the objectives assigned to it therein.

In areas which do not fall within its exclusive competence, the Community shall take action, in accordance with the principle of subsidiarity, only if and in so far as the objectives of the proposed action cannot be sufficiently achieved by the Member States and can therefore, by reason of the scale or effects of the proposed action, be better achieved by the Community.

Any action by the Community shall not go beyond what is necessary to achieve the objectives of this Treaty.]⁵

[Article 4

1. The tasks entrusted to the Community shall be carried out by the following institutions:

    –   a European Parliament,

    –   a Council,

    –   a Commission,

    –   a Court of Justice,

    –   a Court of Auditors.

Each institution shall act within the limits of the powers conferred upon it by this Treaty.

2. The Council and the Commission shall be assisted by an Economic and Social Committee and a Committee of the Regions acting in an advisory capacity.]⁶

[Article 4a

A European System of Central Banks (hereinafter referred to as 'ESCB') and a European Central Bank (hereinafter referred to as 'ECB') shall be established in accordance with the procedures laid down in this Treaty; they shall act within the limits of the powers conferred upon them by this Treaty and by the Statute of the ESCB and of the ECB (hereinafter referred to as 'Statute of the ESCB') annexed thereto.]⁷

[*Article 4b*

A European Investment Bank is hereby established, which shall act within the limits of the powers conferred upon it by this Treaty and the Statute annexed thereto.][8]

Article 5

Member States shall take all appropriate measures, whether general or particular, to ensure fulfilment of the obligations arising out of this Treaty or resulting from action taken by the institutions of the Community. They shall facilitate the achievement of the Community's tasks.

They shall abstain from any measure which could jeopardise the attainment of the objectives of this Treaty.

[*Article 6*][9]

Within the scope of application of this Treaty, and without prejudice to any special provisions contained therein, any discrimination on grounds of nationality shall be prohibited.

[The Council, acting in accordance with the procedure referred to in Article 189c, may adopt rules designed to prohibit such discrimination.][10]

[*Article 7*][11]

1. The common market shall be progressively established during a transitional period of twelve years.

This transitional period shall be divided into three stages of four years each; the length of each stage may be altered in accordance with the provisions set out below.

2. To each stage there shall be assigned a set of actions to be initiated and carried through concurrently.

3. Transition from the first to the second stage shall be conditional upon a finding that the objectives specifically laid down in this Treaty for the first stage have in fact been attained in substance and that, subject to the exceptions and procedures provided for in this Treaty, the obligations have been fulfilled.

This finding shall be made at the end of the fourth year by the Council, acting unanimously on a report from the Commission. A Member State may not, however, prevent unanimity by relying upon the non-fulfilment of its own obligations. Failing unanimity, the first stage shall automatically be extended for one year.

At the end of the fifth year, the Council shall make its finding under the same conditions. Failing unanimity, the first stage shall automatically be extended for a further year.

At the end of the sixth year, the Council shall make its finding, acting by a qualified majority on a report from the Commission.

4. Within one month of the last-mentioned vote any Member State which voted with the minority or, if the required majority was not obtained, any Member State shall be entitled to call upon the Council to appoint an arbitration board whose decision shall be binding upon all Member States and upon the institutions of the Community. The arbitration board shall consist of three members appointed by the Council acting unanimously on a proposal from the Commission.

If the Council has not appointed the members of the arbitration board within one month of being called upon to do so, they shall be appointed by the Court of Justice within a further period of one month.

The arbitration board shall elect its own Chairman.

The board shall make its award within six months of the date of the Council vote referred to in the last subparagraph of paragraph 3.

5. The second and third stages may not be extended or curtailed except by a decision of the Council, acting unanimously on a proposal from the Commission.

6. Nothing in the preceding paragraphs shall cause the transitional period to last more than fifteen years after the entry into force of this Treaty.

7. Save for the exceptions or derogations provided for in this Treaty, the expiry of the transitional period shall constitute the latest date by which all the rules laid down must enter into force and all the measures required for establishing the common market must be implemented.

[Article 7a][12]

The Community shall adopt measures with the aim of progressively establishing the internal market over a period expiring on 31 December 1992, in accordance with the provisions of this Article and of Articles [7b, 7c], 13, 28, 57(2), 59, 70(1), 84, 99, 100a and 100b and without prejudice to the other provisions of this Treaty.

The internal market shall comprise an area without internal frontiers in which the free movement of goods, persons, services and capital is ensured in accordance with the provisions of this Treaty.

[*Article 7b*][13]

The Commission shall report to the Council before 31 December 1988 and again before 31 December 1990 on the progress made towards achieving the internal market within the time limit fixed in Article 7a.

The Council, acting by a qualified majority, on a proposal from the Commission, shall determine the guidelines and conditions necessary to ensure balanced progress in all the sectors concerned.

[*Article 7c*][13]

When drawing up its proposals with a view to achieving the objectives set out in Article [7a][12], the Commission shall take into account the extent of the effort that certain economies showing differences in development will have to sustain during the period of establishment of the internal market and it may propose appropriate provisions.

If these provisions take the form of derogations, they must be of a temporary nature and must cause the least possible disturbance to the functioning of the common market.

[Part Two

Citizenship of the Union

Article 8

1. Citizenship of the Union is hereby established.

Every person holding the nationality of a Member State shall be a citizen of the Union.

2. Citizens of the Union shall enjoy the rights conferred by this Treaty and shall be subject to the duties imposed thereby.

Article 8a

1. Every citizen of the Union shall have the right to move and reside freely within the territory of the Member States, subject to the limitations and conditions laid down in this Treaty and by the measures adopted to give it effect.

2. The Council may adopt provisions with a view to facilitating the exercise of the rights referred to in paragraph 1; save as otherwise provided in this Treaty, the Council shall act unanimously on a proposal from the Commission and after obtaining the assent of the European Parliament.

Article 8b

1. Every citizen of the Union residing in a Member State of which he is not a national shall have the right to vote and to stand as a candidate at municipal elections in the Member State in which he resides, under the same conditions as nationals of that State. This right shall be exercised subject to detailed arrangements to be adopted before 31 December 1994 by the Council, acting unanimously on a proposal from the Commission and after consulting the European Parliament; these arrangements may provide for derogations where warranted by problems specific to a Member State.

2. Without prejudice to Article 138(3) and to the provisions adopted for its implementation, every citizen of the Union residing in a Member State of which he is not a national shall have the right to vote and to stand as a candidate in elections to the European Parliament in the Member State in which he resides, under the same conditions as nationals of that State. This right shall be exercised subject to detailed arrangements to be adopted before 31 December 1993 by the Council, acting unanimously on a proposal from the Commission and after consulting the European Parliament; these arrangements may provide for derogations where warranted by problems specific to a Member State.

Article 8c

Every citizen of the Union shall, in the territory of a third country in which the Member State of which he is a national is not represented, be entitled to protection by the diplomatic or consular authorities of any Member State, on the same conditions as the nationals of that State. Before 31 December 1993, Member States shall establish the necessary rules among themselves and start the international negotiations required to secure this protection.

Article 8d

Every citizen of the Union shall have the right to petition the European Parliament in accordance with Article 138d.

Every citizen of the Union may apply to the Ombudsman established in accordance with Article 138e.

Article 8e

The Commission shall report to the European Parliament, to the Council and to the Economic and Social Committee before 31 December 1993 and then every three years on the application of the provisions of this Part. This report shall take account of the development of the Union.

On this basis, and without prejudice to the other provisions of this Treaty, the Council, acting unanimously on a proposal from the Commission and after consulting the European Parliament, may adopt provisions to strengthen or to add to the rights laid down in this Part, which it shall recommend to the Member States for adoption in accordance with their respective constitutional requirements.][14

[Part Three

Community policies][15

Title I

Free movement of goods

Article 9

1. The Community shall be based upon a customs union which shall cover all trade in goods and which shall involve the prohibition between Member States of customs duties on imports and exports and of all charges having equivalent effect, and the adoption of a common customs tariff in their relations with third countries.

2. The provisions of Chapter 1, Section 1, and of Chapter 2 of this Title shall apply to products originating in Member States and to products coming from third countries which are in free circulation in Member States.

Article 10

1. Products coming from a third country shall be considered to be in free circulation in a Member State if the import formalities have been complied with and any customs duties or charges having equivalent effect which are payable have been levied in that Member State, and if they have not benefited from a total or partial drawback of such duties or charges.

2. The Commission shall, before the end of the first year after the entry into force of this Treaty, determine the methods of administrative cooperation to be adopted for the purpose of applying Article 9(2), taking into account the need to reduce as much as possible formalities imposed on trade.

Before the end of the first year after the entry into force of this Treaty, the Commission shall lay down the provisions applicable, as regards trade between Member States, to goods originating in another Member State in whose manufacture products have been used on which the exporting Member State has not levied the appropriate customs duties or charges having equivalent effect, or which have benefited from a total or partial drawback of such duties or charges.

In adopting these provisions, the Commission shall take into account the rules for the elimination of customs duties within the Community and for the progressive application of the common customs tariff.

Article 11

Member States shall take all appropriate measures to enable Governments to carry out, within the periods of time laid down, the obligations with regard to customs duties which devolve upon them pursuant to this Treaty.

Chapter 1

The Customs Union

Section 1

Elimination of customs duties between Member States

Article 12

Member States shall refrain from introducing between themselves any new customs duties on imports or exports or any charges having equivalent effect, and from increasing those which they already apply in their trade with each other.

Article 13

1. Customs duties on imports in force between Member States shall be progressively abolished by them during the transitional period in accordance with Articles 14 and 15.

2. Charges having an effect equivalent to customs duties on imports, in force between Member States, shall be progressively abolished by them during the transitional period. The Commission shall determine by means of directives the timetable for such abolition. It shall be guided by the rules contained in Article 14(2) and (3) and by the directives issued by the Council pursuant to Article 14(2).

Article 14

1. For each product, the basic duty to which the successive reductions shall be applied shall be the duty applied on 1 January 1957.

2. The timetable for the reductions shall be determined as follows:

(*a*) during the first stage, the first reduction shall be made one year after the date when this Treaty enters into force; the second reduction, eighteen months later; the third reduction, at the end of the fourth year after the date when this Treaty enters into force;

(*b*) during the second stage, a reduction shall be made eighteen months after that stage begins; a second reduction, eighteen months after the preceding one; a third reduction, one year later;

(*c*) any remaining reductions shall be made during the third stage; the Council shall, acting by a qualified majority on a proposal from the Commission, determine the timetable therefor by means of directives.

3. At the time of the first reduction, Member States shall introduce between themselves a duty on each product equal to the basic duty minus 10%.

At the time of each subsequent reduction, each Member State shall reduce its customs duties as a whole in such manner as to lower by 10% its total customs receipts as defined in paragraph 4 and to reduce the duty on each product by at least 5% of the basic duty.

In the case, however, of products on which the duty is still in excess of 30%, each reduction must be at least 10% of the basic duty.

4. The total customs receipts of each Member State, as referred to in paragraph 3, shall be calculated by multiplying the value of its imports from other Member States during 1956 by the basic duties.

5. Any special problems raised in applying paragraphs 1 to 4 shall be settled by directives issued by the Council acting by a qualified majority on a proposal from the Commission.

6. Member States shall report to the Commission on the manner in which effect has been given to the preceding rules for the reduction of duties. They shall endeavour to ensure that the reduction made in the duties on each product shall amount:

– at the end of the first stage, to at least 25% of the basic duty;

– at the end of the second stage, to at least 50% of the basic duty.

If the Commission finds that there is a risk that the objectives laid down in Article 13, and the percentages laid down in this paragraph, cannot be attained, it shall make all appropriate recommendations to Member States.

7. The provisions of this Article may be amended by the Council, acting

unanimously on a proposal from the Commission and after consulting the European Parliament.

Article 15

1. Irrespective of the provisions of Article 14, any Member State may, in the course of the transitional period, suspend in whole or in part the collection of duties applied by it to products imported from other Member States. It shall inform the other Member States and the Commission thereof.

2. The Member States declare their readiness to reduce customs duties against the other Member States more rapidly than is provided for in Article 14 if their general economic situation and the situation of the economic sector concerned so permit.

To this end, the Commission shall make recommendations to the Member States concerned.

Article 16

Member States shall abolish between themselves customs duties on exports and charges having equivalent effect by the end of the first stage at the latest.

Article 17

1. The provisions of Articles 9 to 15(1) shall also apply to customs duties of a fiscal nature. Such duties shall not, however, be taken into consideration for the purpose of calculating either total customs receipts or the reduction of customs duties as a whole as referred to in Article 14(3) and (4).

Such duties shall, at each reduction, be lowered by not less than 10% of the basic duty. Member States may reduce such duties more rapidly than is provided for in Article 14.

2. Member States shall, before the end of the first year after the entry into force of this Treaty, inform the Commission of their customs duties of a fiscal nature.

3. Member States shall retain the right to substitute for these duties an internal tax which complies with the provisions of Article 95.

4. If the Commission finds that substitution for any customs duty of a fiscal nature meets with serious difficulties in a Member State, it shall authorise that State to retain the duty on condition that it shall abolish it not later than six years after the entry into force of this Treaty. Such

authorisation must be applied for before the end of the first year after the entry into force of this Treaty.

Section 2

Setting up of the common customs tariff

Article 18

The Member States declare their readiness to contribute to the development of international trade and the lowering of barriers to trade by entering into agreements designed, on a basis of reciprocity and mutual advantage, to reduce customs duties below the general level of which they could avail themselves as a result of the establishment of a customs union between them.

Article 19

1. Subject to the conditions and within the limits provided for hereinafter, duties in the common customs tariff shall be at the level of the arithmetical average of the duties applied in the four customs territories comprised in the Community.

2. The duties taken as the basis for calculating this average shall be those applied by Member States on 1 January 1957.

In the case of the Italian tariff, however, the duty applied shall be that without the temporary 10% reduction. Furthermore, with respect to items on which the Italian tariff contains a conventional duty, this duty shall be substituted for the duty applied as defined above, provided that it does not exceed the latter by more than 10%. Where the conventional duty exceeds the duty applied as defined above by more than 10%, the latter duty plus 10% shall be taken as the basis for calculating the arithmetical average.

With regard to the tariff headings in List A, the duties shown in that List shall, for the purpose of calculating the arithmetical average, be substituted for the duties applied.

3. The duties in the common customs tariff shall not exceed:

(a) 3% for products within the tariff headings in List B;

(b) 10% for products within the tariff headings in List C;

(c) 15% for products within the tariff headings in List D;

(d) 25% for products within the tariff headings in List E; where in respect of such products, the tariff of the Benelux countries contains a duty not exceeding 3%, such duty shall, for the purpose of calculating the arithmetical average, be raised to 12%.

4. List F prescribes the duties applicable to the products listed therein.

5. The Lists of tariff headings referred to in this Article and in Article 20 are set out in Annex I to this Treaty.

Article 20

The duties applicable to the products in List G shall be determined by negotiation between the Member States. Each Member State may add further products to this List to a value not exceeding 2% of the total value of its imports from third countries in the course of the year 1956.

The Commission shall take all appropriate steps to ensure that such negotiations shall be undertaken before the end of the second year after the entry into force of this Treaty and be concluded before the end of the first stage.

If, for certain products, no agreement can be reached within these periods, the Council shall, on a proposal from the Commission, acting unanimously until the end of the second stage and by a qualified majority thereafter, determine the duties in the common customs tariff.

Article 21

1. Technical difficulties which may arise in applying Articles 19 and 20 shall be resolved, within two years of the entry into force of this Treaty, by directives issued by the Council acting by a qualified majority on a proposal from the Commission.

2. Before the end of the first stage, or at latest when the duties are determined, the Council shall, acting by a qualified majority on a proposal from the Commission, decide on any adjustments required in the interests of the internal consistency of the common customs tariff as a result of applying the rules set out in Articles 19 and 20, taking account in particular of the degree of processing undergone by the various goods to which the common tariff applies.

Article 22

The Commission shall, within two years of the entry into force of this Treaty, determine the extent to which the customs duties of a fiscal nature referred to in Article 17(2) shall be taken into account in calculating the arithmetical average provided for in Article 19(1). The Commission shall take account of any protective character which such duties may have.

Within six months of such determination, any Member State may request that the procedure provided for in Article 20 should be applied to the product in question, but in this event the percentage limit provided in that Article shall not be applicable to that State.

Article 23

1. For the purpose of the progressive introduction of the common customs tariff, Member States shall amend their tariffs applicable to third countries as follows:

(*a*) in the case of tariff headings on which the duties applied in practice on 1 January 1957 do not differ by more than 15% in either direction from the duties in the common customs tariff, the latter duties shall be applied at the end of the fourth year after the entry into force of this Treaty;

(*b*) in any other case, each Member State shall, as from the same date, apply a duty reducing by 30% the difference between the duty applied in practice on 1 January 1957 and the duty in the common customs tariff;

(*c*) at the end of the second stage this difference shall again be reduced by 30%;

(*d*) in the case of tariff headings for which the duties in the common customs tariff are not yet available at the end of the first stage, each Member State shall, within six months of the Council's action in accordance with Article 20, apply such duties as would result from application of the rules contained in this paragraph.

2. Where a Member State has been granted an authorisation under Article 17(4), it need not, for as long as that authorisation remains valid, apply the preceding provisions to the tariff headings to which the authorisation applies. When such authorisation expires, the Member State concerned shall apply such duty as would have resulted from application of the rules contained in paragraph 1.

3. The common customs tariff shall be applied in its entirety by the end of the transitional period at the latest.

Article 24

Member States shall remain free to change their duties more rapidly than is provided for in Article 23 in order to bring them into line with the common customs tariff.

Article 25

1. If the Commission finds that the production in Member States of particular products contained in Lists B, C and D is insufficient to supply the demands of one of the Member States, and that such supply traditionally depends to a considerable extent on imports from third countries, the Council shall, acting by a qualified majority on a proposal from the Commission, grant the Member State concerned tariff quotas at a reduced rate of duty or duty free.

Such quotas may not exceed the limits beyond which the risk might arise of activities being transferred to the detriment of other Member States.

2. In the case of the products in List E, and of those in List G for which the rates of duty have been determined in accordance with the procedure provided for in the third paragraph of Article 20, the Commission shall, where a change in sources of supply or shortage of supplies within the Community is such as to entail harmful consequences for the processing industries of a Member State, at the request of that Member State, grant it tariff quotas at a reduced rate of duty or duty free.

Such quotas may not exceed the limits beyond which the risk might arise of activities being transferred to the detriment of other Member States.

3. In the case of the products listed in Annex II to this Treaty, the Commission may authorise any Member State to suspend, in whole or in part, collection of the duties applicable or may grant such Member State tariff quotas at a reduced rate of duty or duty free, provided that no serious disturbance of the market of the products concerned results therefrom.

4. The Commission shall periodically examine tariff quotas granted pursuant to this Article.

Article 26

The Commission may authorise any Member State encountering special difficulties to postpone the lowering or raising of duties provided for in Article 23 in respect of particular headings in its tariff.

Such authorisation may only be granted for a limited period and in respect of tariff headings which, taken together, represent for such State not more than 5% of the value of its imports from third countries in the course of the latest year for which statistical data are available.

Article 27

Before the end of the first stage, Member States shall, in so far as may be necessary, take steps to approximate their provisions laid down by law, regulation or administrative action in respect of customs matters. To this end, the Commission shall make all appropriate recommendations to Member States.

Article 28

Any autonomous alteration or suspension of duties in the common customs tariff shall be decided by the Council acting by a qualified majority on a proposal from the Commission.[16]

Article 29

In carrying out the tasks entrusted to it under this Section the Commission shall be guided by:

(a) the need to promote trade between Member States and third countries;

(b) developments in conditions of competition within the Community in so far as they lead to an improvement in the competitive capacity of undertakings;

(c) the requirements of the Community as regards the supply of raw materials and semi-finished goods; in this connection the Commission shall take care to avoid distorting conditions of competition between Member States in respect of finished goods;

(d) the need to avoid serious disturbances in the economies of Member States and to ensure rational development of production and an expansion of consumption within the Community.

Chapter 2

Elimination of quantitative restrictions between Member States

Article 30

Quantitative restrictions on imports and all measures having equivalent effect shall, without prejudice to the following provisions, be prohibited between Member States.

Article 31

Member States shall refrain from introducing between themselves any new quantitative restrictions or measures having equivalent effect.

This obligation shall, however, relate only to the degree of the liberalisation attained in pursuance of the decisions of the Council of the Organisation for European Economic Cooperation of 14 January 1955. Member States shall supply the Commission, not later than six months after the entry into force of this Treaty, with lists of the products liberalised by them in pursuance of these decisions. These lists shall be consolidated between Member States.

Article 32

In their trade with one another Member States shall refrain from making more restrictive the quotas and measures having equivalent effect existing at the date of the entry into force of this Treaty.

These quotas shall be abolished by the end of the transitional period at the latest. During that period, they shall be progressively abolished in accordance with the following provisions.

Article 33

1. One year after the entry into force of this Treaty, each Member State shall convert any bilateral quotas open to any other Member States into global quotas open without discrimination to all other Member States.

On the same date, Member States shall increase the aggregate of the global quotas so established in such a manner as to bring about an increase of not less than 20% in their total value as compared with the preceding year. The global quota for each product, however, shall be increased by not less than 10%.

The quotas shall be increased annually in accordance with the same rules and in the same proportions in relation to the preceding year.

The fourth increase shall take place at the end of the fourth year after the entry into force of this Treaty; the fifth, one year after the beginning of the second stage.

2. Where, in the case of a product which has not been liberalised, the global quota does not amount to 3% of the national production of the State concerned, a quota equal to not less than 3% of such national production shall be introduced not later than one year after the entry into force of this Treaty. This quota shall be raised to 4% at the end of the second year, and to 5% at the end of the third. Thereafter, the Member State concerned shall increase the quota by not less than 15% annually.

Where there is no such national production, the Commission shall take a decision establishing an appropriate quota.

3. At the end of the tenth year, each quota shall be equal to not less than 20% of the national production.

4. If the Commission finds by means of a decision that during two successive years the imports have been below the level of the quota opened, this global quota shall not be taken into account in calculating the total value of the global quotas. In such case, the Member State shall abolish quota restrictions on the product concerned.

5. In the case of quotas representing more than 20% of the national production of the product concerned, the Council may, acting by a qualified majority on a proposal from the Commission, reduce the minimum percentage of 10% laid down in paragraph 1. This alteration shall not, however, affect the obligation to increase the total value of global quotas by 20% annually.

6. Member States which have exceeded their obligations as regards the degree of liberalisation attained in pursuance of the decisions of the Council of the Organisation for European Economic Cooperation of 14 January 1955 shall be entitled, when calculating the annual total increase of 20% provided for in paragraph 1, to take into account the amount of imports liberalised by autonomous action. Such calculation shall be submitted to the Commission for its prior approval.

7. The Commission shall issue directives establishing the procedure and timetable in accordance with which Member States shall abolish, as between themselves, any measures in existence when this Treaty enters into force which have an effect equivalent to quotas.

8. If the Commission finds that the application of the provisions of this Article, and in particular of the provisions concerning percentages, makes it impossible to ensure that the abolition of quotas provided for in the second paragraph of Article 32 is carried out progressively, the Council may, on a proposal from the Commission, acting unanimously during the first stage and by a qualified majority thereafter, amend the procedure laid down in this Article and may, in particular, increase the percentages fixed.

Article 34

1. Quantitative restrictions on exports, and all measures having equivalent effect, shall be prohibited between Member States.

2. Member States shall, by the end of the first stage at the latest, abolish all quantitative restrictions on exports and any measures having equivalent effect which are in existence when this Treaty enters into force.

Article 35

The Member States declare their readiness to abolish quantitative restrictions on imports from and exports to other Member States more rapidly than is provided for in the preceding Articles, if their general economic situation and the situation of the economic sector concerned so permit.

To this end, the Commission shall make recommendations to the Member States concerned.

Article 36

The provisions of Articles 30 to 34 shall not preclude prohibitions or restrictions on imports, exports or goods in transit justified on grounds of public morality, public policy or public security; the protection of health and life of humans, animals or plants; the protection of national treasures possessing artistic, historic or archaeological value; or the protection of industrial and commercial property. Such prohibitions or restrictions shall not, however, constitute a means of arbitrary discrimination or a disguised restriction on trade between Member States.

Article 37

1. Member States shall progressively adjust any State monopolies of a commercial character so as to ensure that when the transitional period has ended no discrimination regarding the conditions under which goods are procured and marketed exists between nationals of Member States.

The provisions of this Article shall apply to any body through which a Member State, in law or in fact, either directly or indirectly supervises, determines or appreciably influences imports or exports between Member States. These provisions shall likewise apply to monopolies delegated by the State to others.

2. Member States shall refrain from introducing any new measure which is contrary to the principles laid down in paragraph 1 or which restricts the scope of the Articles dealing with the abolition of customs duties and quantitative restrictions between Member States.

3. The timetable for the measures referred to in paragraph 1 shall be harmonised with the abolition of quantitative restrictions on the same products provided for in Articles 30 to 34.

If a product is subject to a State monopoly of a commercial character in only one or some Member States, the Commission may authorise the other Member States to apply protective measures until the adjustment provided for in paragraph 1 has been effected; the Commission shall determine the conditions and details of such measures.

4. If a State monopoly of a commercial character has rules which are designed to make it easier to dispose of agricultural products or obtain for them the best return, steps should be taken in applying the rules contained in this Article to ensure equivalent safeguards for the employment and standard of living of the producers concerned, account being taken of the adjustments that will be possible and the specialisation that will be needed with the passage of time.

5. The obligations on Member States shall be binding only in as far as they are compatible with existing international agreements.

6. With effect from the first stage the Commission shall make recommendations as to the manner in which and the timetable according to which the adjustment provided for in this Article shall be carried out.

Title II

Agriculture

Article 38

1. The common market shall extend to agriculture and trade in agricultural products. 'Agricultural products' means the products of the soil, of stockfarming and of fisheries and products of first-stage processing directly related to these products.

2. Save as otherwise provided in Articles 39 to 46, the rules laid down for the establishment of the common market shall apply to agricultural products.

3. The products subject to the provisions of Articles 39 to 46 are listed in Annex II to this Treaty. Within two years of the entry into force of this Treaty, however, the Council shall, acting by a qualified majority on a proposal from the Commission, decide what products are to be added to this list.

4. The operation and development of the common market for agricultural products must be accompanied by the establishment of a common agricultural policy among the Member States.

Article 39

1. The objectives of the common agricultural policy shall be:

(a) to increase agricultural productivity by promoting technical progress and by ensuring the rational development of agricultural production and the optimum utilisation of the factors of production, in particular labour;

(*b*) thus to ensure a fair standard of living for the agricultural community, in particular by increasing the individual earnings of persons engaged in agriculture;

(*c*) to stabilise markets;

(*d*) to assure the availability of supplies;

(*e*) to ensure that supplies reach consumers at reasonable prices.

2. In working out the common agricultural policy and the special methods for its application, account shall be taken of:

(*a*) the particular nature of agricultural activity, which results from the social structure of agriculture and from structural and natural disparities between the various agricultural regions;

(*b*) the need to effect the appropriate adjustments by degrees;

(*c*) the fact that in the Member States agriculture constitutes a sector closely linked with the economy as a whole.

Article 40

1. Member States shall develop the common agricultural policy by degrees during the transitional period and shall bring it into force by the end of that period at the latest.

2. In order to attain the objectives set out in Article 39 a common organisation of agricultural markets shall be established.

This organisation shall take one of the following forms, depending on the product concerned:

(*a*) common rules on competition;

(*b*) compulsory coordination of the various national market organisations;

(*c*) a European market organisation.

3. The common organisation established in accordance with paragraph 2 may include all measures required to attain the objectives set out in Article 39, in particular regulation of prices, aids for the production and marketing of the various products, storage and carryover arrangements and common machinery for stabilising imports or exports.

The common organisation shall be limited to pursuit of the objectives set out in Article 39 and shall exclude any discrimination between producers or consumers within the Community.

Any common price policy shall be based on common criteria and uniform methods of calculation.

4. In order to enable the common organisation referred to in paragraph 2 to attain its objectives, one or more agricultural guidance and guarantee funds may be set up.

Article 41

To enable the objectives set out in Article 39 to be attained, provision may be made within the framework of the common agricultural policy for measures such as:

(a) an effective coordination of efforts in the spheres of vocational training, of research and of the dissemination of agricultural knowledge; this may include joint financing of projects or institutions;

(b) joint measures to promote consumption of certain products.

Article 42

The provisions of the Chapter relating to rules on competition shall apply to production of and trade in agricultural products only to the extent determined by the Council within the framework of Article 43(2) and (3) and in accordance with the procedure laid down therein, account being taken of the objectives set out in Article 39.

The Council may, in particular, authorise the granting of aid:

(a) for the protection of enterprises handicapped by structural or natural conditions;

(b) within the framework of economic development programmes.

Article 43

1. In order to evolve the broad lines of a common agricultural policy, the Commission shall, immediately this Treaty enters into force, convene a conference of the Member States with a view to making a comparison of their agricultural policies, in particular by producing a statement of their resources and needs.

2. Having taken into account the work of the conference provided for in paragraph 1, after consulting the Economic and Social Committee and within two years of the entry into force of this Treaty, the Commission shall submit proposals for working out and implementing the common

agricultural policy, including the replacement of the national organisations by one of the forms of common organisation provided for in Article 40(2), and for implementing the measures specified in this Title.

These proposals shall take account of the interdependence of the agricultural matters mentioned in this Title.

The Council shall, on a proposal from the Commission and after consulting the European Parliament, acting unanimously during the first two stages and by a qualified majority thereafter, make regulations, issue directives, or take decisions, without prejudice to any recommendations it may also make.

3. The Council may, acting by a qualified majority and in accordance with paragraph 2, replace the national market organisations by the common organisation provided for in Article 40(2) if:

(a) the common organisation offers Member States which are opposed to this measure and which have an organisation of their own for the production in question equivalent safeguards for the employment and standard of living of the producers concerned, account being taken of the adjustments that will be possible and the specialisation that will be needed with the passage of time;

(b) such an organisation ensures conditions for trade within the Community similar to those existing in a national market.

4. If a common organisation for certain raw materials is established before a common organisation exists for the corresponding processed products, such raw materials as are used for processed products intended for export to third countries may be imported from outside the Community.

Article 44

1. In so far as progressive abolition of customs duties and quantitative restrictions between Member States may result in prices likely to jeopardise the attainment of the objectives set out in Article 39, each Member State shall, during the transitional period, be entitled to apply to particular products, in a non-discriminatory manner and in substitution for quotas and to such an extent as shall not impede the expansion of the volume of trade provided for in Article 45(2), a system of minimum prices below which imports may be either:

− temporarily suspended or reduced; or

− allowed, but subjected to the condition that they are made at a price higher than the minimum price for the product concerned.

In the latter case the minimum prices shall not include customs duties.

2. Minimum prices shall neither cause a reduction of the trade existing between Member States when this Treaty enters into force nor form an obstacle to progressive expansion of this trade. Minimum prices shall not be applied so as to form an obstacle to the development of a natural preference between Member States.

3. As soon as this Treaty enters into force the Council shall, on a proposal from the Commission, determine objective criteria for the establishment of minimum price systems and for the fixing of such prices.

These criteria shall in particular take account of the average national production costs in the Member State applying the minimum price, of the position of the various undertakings concerned in relation to such average production costs, and of the need to promote both the progressive improvement of agricultural practice and the adjustments and specialisation needed within the common market.

The Commission shall further propose a procedure for revising these criteria in order to allow for and speed up technical progress and to approximate prices progressively within the common market.

These criteria and the procedure for revising them shall be determined by the Council acting unanimously within three years of the entry into force of this Treaty.

4. Until the decision of the Council takes effect, Member States may fix maximum prices on condition that these are communicated beforehand to the Commission and to the Member States so that they may submit their comments.

Once the Council has taken its decision, Member States shall fix minimum prices on the basis of the criteria determined as above.

The Council may, acting by a qualified majority on a proposal from the Commission, rectify any decisions taken by Member States which do not conform to the criteria defined above.

5. If it does not prove possible to determine the said objective criteria for certain products by the beginning of the third stage, the Council may, acting by a qualified majority on a proposal from the Commission, vary the minimum prices applied to these products.

6. At the end of the transitional period, a table of minimum prices still in force shall be drawn up. The Council shall, acting on a proposal from the Commission and by a majority of nine votes in accordance with the weighting laid down in the first subparagraph of Article 148(2),

determine the system to be applied within the framework of the common agricultural policy.

Article 45

1. Until national market organisations have been replaced by one of the forms of common organisation referred to in Article 40(2), trade in products in respect of which certain Member States:

– have arrangements designed to guarantee national producers a market for their products; and

– are in need of imports,

shall be developed by the conclusion of long-term agreements or contracts between importing and exporting Member States.

These agreements or contracts shall be directed towards the progressive abolition of any discrimination in the application of these arrangements to the various producers within the Community.

Such agreements or contracts shall be concluded during the first stage; account shall be taken of the principle of reciprocity.

2. As regards quantities, these agreements or contracts shall be based on the average volume of trade between Member States in the products concerned during the three years before the entry into force of this Treaty and shall provide for an increase in the volume of trade within the limits of existing requirements, account being taken of traditional patterns of trade.

As regards prices, these agreements or contracts shall enable producers to dispose of the agreed quantities at prices which shall be progressively approximated to those paid to national producers on the domestic market of the purchasing country.

This approximation shall proceed as steadily as possible and shall be completed by the end of the transitional period at the latest.

Prices shall be negotiated between the parties concerned within the framework of directives issued by the Commission for the purpose of implementing the two preceding subparagraphs.

If the first stage is extended, these agreements or contracts shall continue to be carried out in accordance with the conditions applicable at the end of the fourth year after the entry into force of this Treaty, the obligation to increase quantities and to approximate prices being suspended until the transition to the second stage.

Member States shall avail themselves of any opportunity open to them under their legislation, particularly in respect of import policy, to ensure the conclusion and carrying out of these agreements or contracts.

3. To the extent that Member States require raw materials for the manufacture of products to be exported outside the Community in competition with products of third countries, the above agreements or contracts shall not form an obstacle to the importation of raw materials for this purpose from third countries. This provision shall not, however, apply if the Council unanimously decides to make provision for payments required to compensate for the higher price paid on goods imported for this purpose on the basis of these agreements or contracts in relation to the delivered price of the same goods purchased on the world market.

Article 46

Where in a Member State a product is subject to a national market organisation or to internal rules having equivalent effect which affect the competitive position of similar production in another Member State, a countervailing charge shall be applied by Member States to imports of this product coming from the Member State where such organisation or rules exist, unless that State applies a countervailing charge on export.

The Commission shall fix the amount of these charges at the level required to redress the balance; it may also authorise other measures, the conditions and details of which it shall determine.

Article 47

As to the functions to be performed by the Economic and Social Committee in pursuance of this Title, its agricultural section shall hold itself at the disposal of the Commission to prepare, in accordance with the provisions of Articles 197 and 198, the deliberations of the Committee.

Title III

Free movement of persons, services and capital

Chapter 1

Workers

Article 48

1. Freedom of movement for workers shall be secured within the Community by the end of the transitional period at the latest.

2. Such freedom of movement shall entail the abolition of any discrimination based on nationality between workers of the Member States as regards employment, remuneration and other conditions of work and employment.

3. It shall entail the right, subject to limitations justified on grounds of public policy, public security or public health:

(a) to accept offers of employment actually made;

(b) to move freely within the territory of Member States for this purpose;

(c) to stay in a Member State for the purpose of employment in accordance with the provisions governing the employment of nationals of that State laid down by law, regulation or administrative action;

(d) to remain in the territory of a Member State after having been employed in that State, subject to conditions which shall be embodied in implementing regulations to be drawn up by the Commission.

4. The provisions of this Article shall not apply to employment in the public service.

Article 49

[As soon as this Treaty enters into force, the Council shall, acting in accordance with the procedure referred to in Article 189b and after consulting the Economic and Social Committee, issue directives or make regulations setting out the measures required to bring about, by progressive stages, freedom of movement for workers, as defined in Article 48, in particular.][17]

(a) by ensuring close cooperation between national employment services;

(b) by systematically and progressively abolishing those administrative procedures and practices and those qualifying periods in respect of eligibility for available employment, whether resulting from national legislation or from agreements previously concluded between Member States, the maintenance of which would form an obstacle to liberalisation of the movement of workers;

(c) by systematically and progressively abolishing all such qualifying periods and other restrictions provided for either under national legislation or under agreements previously concluded between Member States as imposed on workers of other Member States conditions regarding the free choice of employment other than those imposed on workers of the State concerned;

(*d*) by setting up appropriate machinery to bring offers of employment into touch with applications for employment and to facilitate the achievement of a balance between supply and demand in the employment market in such a way as to avoid serious threats to the standard of living and level of employment in the various regions and industries.

Article 50

Member States shall, within the framework of a joint programme, encourage the exchange of young workers.

Article 51

The Council shall, acting unanimously on a proposal from the Commission, adopt such measures in the field of social security as are necessary to provide freedom of movement for workers; to this end, it shall make arrangements to secure for migrant workers and their dependants:

(*a*) aggregation, for the purpose of acquiring and retaining the right to benefit and of calculating the amount of benefit, of all periods taken into account under the laws of the several countries;

(*b*) payment of benefits to persons resident in the territories of Member States.

Chapter 2

Right of establishment

Article 52

Within the framework of the provisions set out below, restrictions on the freedom of establishment of nationals of a Member State in the territory of another Member State shall be abolished by progressive stages in the course of the transitional period. Such progressive abolition shall also apply to restrictions on the setting up of agencies, branches or subsidiaries by nationals of any Member State established in the territory of any Member State.

Freedom of establishment shall include the right to take up and pursue activities as self-employed persons and to set up and manage undertakings, in particular companies or firms within the meaning of the second paragraph of Article 58, under the conditions laid down for its own nationals by the law of the country where such establishment is effected, subject to the provisions of the Chapter relating to capital.

Article 53

Member States shall not introduce any new restrictions on the right of establishment in their territories of nationals of other Member States, save as otherwise provided in this Treaty.

Article 54

1. Before the end of the first stage, the Council shall, acting unanimously from the Commission and after consulting the Economic and Social Committee and the European Parliament, draw up a general programme for the abolition of existing restrictions on freedom of establishment within the Community. The Commission shall submit its proposal to the Council during the first two years of the first stage.

The programme shall set out the general conditions under which freedom of establishment is to be attained in the case of each type of activity and in particular the stages by which it is to be attained.

[2. In order to implement this general programme or, in the absence of such programme, in order to achieve a stage in attaining freedom of establishment as regards a particular activity, the Council, acting in accordance with the procedure referred to in Article 189b and after consulting the Economic and Social Committee, shall act by means of directives.][18]

3. The Council and the Commission shall carry out the duties devolving upon them under the preceding provisions, in particular:

(a) by according, as a general rule, priority treatment to activities where freedom of establishment makes a particularly valuable contribution to the development of production and trade;

(b) by ensuring close cooperation between the competent authorities in the Member States in order to ascertain the particular situation within the Community of the various activities concerned;

(c) by abolishing those administrative procedures and practices, whether resulting from national legislation or from agreements previously concluded between Member States, the maintenance of which would form an obstacle to freedom of establishment;

(d) by ensuring that workers of one Member State employed in the territory of another Member State may remain in that territory for the purpose of taking up activities therein as self-employed persons, where they satisfy the conditions which they would be required to satisfy if they were entering that State at the time when they intended to take up such activities;

(e) by enabling a national of one Member State to acquire and use land and buildings situated in the territory of another Member State, in so far as this does not conflict with the principles laid down in Article 39(2);

(f) by effecting the progressive abolition of restrictions on freedom of establishment in every branch of activity under consideration, both as regards the conditions for setting up agencies, branches or subsidiaries in the territory of a Member State and as regards the subsidiaries in the territory of a Member State and as regards the conditions governing the entry of personnel belonging to the main establishment into managerial or supervisory posts in such agencies, branches or subsidiaries;

(g) by coordinating to the necessary extent the safeguards which, for the protection of the interests of members and others, are required by Member States of companies or firms within the meaning of the second paragraph of Article 58 with a view to making such safeguards equivalent throughout the Community;

(h) by satisfying themselves that the conditions of establishment are not distorted by aids granted by Member States.

Article 55

The provisions of this Chapter shall not apply, so far as any given Member State is concerned, to activities which in that State are connected, even occasionally, with the exercise of official authority.

The Council may, acting by a qualified majority on a proposal from the Commission, rule that the provisions of this Chapter shall not apply to certain activities.

Article 56

1. The provisions of this Chapter and measures taken in pursuance thereof shall not prejudice the applicability of provisions laid down by law, regulation or administrative action providing for special treatment for foreign nationals on grounds of public policy, public security or public health.

[2. Before the end of the transitional period, the Council shall, acting unanimously on a proposal from the Commission and after consulting the European Parliament, issue directives for the coordination of the abovementioned provisions laid down by law, regulation or administrative action. After the end of the second stage, however, the Council shall, acting in accordance with the procedure referred to in Article 189b, issue directives for the coordination of such provisions as, in each Member State, are a matter for regulation or administrative action.][19]

[Article 57

1. In order to make it easier for persons to take up and pursue activities as self-employed persons, the Council shall, acting in accordance with the procedure referred to in Article 189b, issue directives for the mutual recognition of diplomas, certificates and other evidence of formal qualifications.

2. For the same purpose, the Council shall, before the end of the transitional period, issue directives for the coordination of the provisions laid down by law, regulation or administrative action in Member States concerning the taking up and pursuit of activities as self-employed persons. The Council, acting unanimously on a proposal from the Commission and after consulting the European Parliament, shall decide on directives the implementation of which involves in at least one Member State amendment of the existing principles laid down by law governing the professions with respect to training and conditions of access for natural persons. In other cases the Council shall act in accordance with the procedure referred to in Article 189b.

3. In the case of the medical and allied and pharmaceutical profession, the progressive abolition of restrictions shall be dependent upon coordination of the conditions for their exercise in the various Member States.][20]

Article 58

Companies or firms formed in accordance with the law of a Member State and having their registered office, central administration or principal place of business within the Community shall, for the purposes of this Chapter, be treated in the same way as natural persons who are nationals of Member States.

'Companies or firms' means companies or firms constituted under civil or commercial law, including cooperative societies, and other legal persons governed by public or private law, save for those which are non-profit making.

Chapter 3

Services

Article 59

Within the framework of the provisions set out below, restrictions on freedom to provide services within the Community shall be progressively abolished during the transitional period in respect of nationals of Member States who are established in a State of the Community other than that of the person for whom the services are intended.

The Council may, acting by a qualified majority on a proposal from the Commission, extend the provisions of the Chapter to nationals of a third country who provide services and who are established within the Community.

Article 60

Services shall be considered to be 'services' within the meaning of this Treaty where they are normally provided for remuneration, in so far as they are not governed by the provisions relating to freedom of movement for goods, capital and persons.

'Services' shall in particular include:

(a) activities of an industrial character;

(b) activities of a commercial character;

(c) activities of craftsmen;

(d) activities of the professions.

Without prejudice to the provisions of the Chapter relating to the right of establishment, the person providing a service may, in order to do so, temporarily pursue his activity in the State where the service is provided, under the same conditions as are imposed by that State on its own nationals.

Article 61

1. Freedom to provide services in the field of transport shall be governed by the provisions of the Title relating to transport.

2. The liberalisation of banking and insurance services connected with movements of capital shall be effected in step with the progressive liberalisation of movement of capital.

Article 62

Save as otherwise provided in this Treaty, Member States shall not introduce any new restrictions on the freedom to provide services which have in fact been attained at the date of the entry into force of this Treaty.

Article 63

1. Before the end of the first stage, the Council shall, acting unanimously on a proposal from the Commission and after consulting the Economic and Social Committee and the European Parliament, draw up a general programme for the abolition of existing restrictions on freedom to provide services within the Community. The Commission shall submit its proposal to the Council during the first two years of the first stage.

The programme shall set out the general conditions under which and the stages by which each type of service is to be liberalised.

2. In order to implement this general programme or, in the absence of such programme, in order to achieve a stage in the liberalisation of a specific service, the Council shall, on a proposal from the Commission and after consulting the Economic and Social Committee and the European Parliament, issue directives acting unanimously until the end of the first stage and by a qualified majority thereafter.

3. As regards the proposals and decisions referred to in paragraphs 1 and 2, priority shall as a general rule be given to those services which directly affect production costs or the liberalisation of which helps to promote trade in goods.

Article 64

The Member States declare their readiness to undertake the liberalisation of services beyond the extent required by the directives issued pursuant to Article 63(2), if their general economic situation and the situation of the economic sector concerned so permit.

To this end, the Commission shall make recommendations to the Member States concerned.

Article 65

As long as restrictions on freedom to provide services have not been abolished, each Member State shall apply such restrictions without distinction on grounds of nationality or residence to all persons providing services within the meaning of the first paragraph of Article 59.

Article 66

The provisions of Articles 55 to 58 shall apply to the matters covered by this Chapter.

Chapter 4

Capital [and payments] [21]

Article 67

1. During the transitional period and to the extent necessary to ensure the proper functioning of the common market, Member States shall progressively abolish between themselves all restrictions on the movement of capital belonging to persons resident in Member States and any discrimination based on the nationality or on the place of residence of the parties or on the place where such capital is invested.

2. Current payments connected with the movement of capital between Member States shall be freed from all restrictions by the end of the first stage at the latest.

Article 68

1. Member States shall, as regards the matters dealt with in this Chapter, be as liberal as possible in granting such exchange authorisations as are still necessary after the entry into force of this Treaty.

2. Where a Member State applies to the movements of capital liberalised in accordance with the provisions of this Chapter the domestic rules governing the capital market and the credit system, it shall do so in a non-discriminatory manner.

3. Loans for the direct or indirect financing of a Member State or its regional or local authorities shall not be issued or placed in other Member States unless the States concerned have reached agreement thereon. This provision shall not preclude the application of Article 22 of the Protocol on the Statute of the European Investment Bank.

Article 69

The Council shall, on a proposal from the Commission, which for this purpose shall consult the Monetary Committee provided for in Article 105, issue the necessary directives for the progressive implementation of the provisions of Article 67, acting unanimously during the first two stages and by a qualified majority thereafter.

Article 70

1. The Commission shall propose to the Council measures for the progressive coordination of the exchange policies of Member States in respect of the movement of capital between those States and third countries. For this purpose the Council shall issue directives, acting by a qualified majority. It shall endeavour to attain the highest possible degree of liberalisation. Unanimity shall be required for measures which constitute a step back as regards the liberalisation of capital movements.[22]

2. Where the measures taken in accordance with paragraph 1 do not permit the elimination of differences between the exchange rules of Member States and where such differences could lead persons resident in one of the Member States to use the freer transfer facilities within the Community which are provided for in Article 67 in order to evade the rules of one of the Member States concerning the movement of capital to or from third countries, that State may, after consulting the other Member States and the Commission, take appropriate measures to overcome these difficulties.

Should the Council find that these measures are restricting the free movement of capital within the Community to a greater extent than is required for the purpose of overcoming the difficulties, it may, acting by a qualified majority on a proposal from the Commission, decide that the State concerned shall amend or abolish these measures.

Article 71

Member States shall endeavour to avoid introducing within the Community any new exchange restrictions on the movement of capital and current payments connected with such movements, and shall endeavour not to make existing rules more restrictive.

They declare their readiness to go beyond the degree of liberalisation of capital movements provided for in the preceding Articles in so far as their economic situation, in particular the situation of their balance of payments, so permits.

The Commission may, after consulting the Monetary Committee, make recommendations to Member States on this subject.

Article 72

Member States shall keep the Commission informed of any movements of capital to and from third countries which come to their knowledge. The Commission may deliver to Member States any opinions which it considers appropriate on this subject.

Article 73

1. If movements of capital lead to disturbances in the functioning of the capital market in any Member State, the Commission shall, after consulting the Monetary Committee, authorise that State to take protective measures in the field of capital movements, the conditions and details of which the Commission shall determine.

The Council may, acting by a qualified majority, revoke this authorisation or amend the conditions or details thereof.

2. A Member State which is in difficulties may, however, on grounds of secrecy or urgency, take the measures mentioned above, where this proves necessary, on its own initiative. The Commission and the other Member States shall be informed of such measures by the date of their entry into force at the latest. In this event the Commission may, after consulting the Monetary Committee, decide that the State concerned shall amend or abolish the measures.

[Article 73a

As from 1 January 1994, Articles 67 to 73 shall be replaced by Articles 73b, c, d, e, f and g.

Article 73b

1. Within the framework of the provisions set out in this Chapter, all restrictions on the movement of capital between Member States and between Member States and third countries shall be prohibited.

2. Within the framework of the provisions set out in this Chapter, all restrictions on payments between Member States and between Member States and third countries shall be prohibited.

Article 73c

1. The provisions of Article 73b shall be without prejudice to the application to third countries of any restrictions which exist on 31 December 1993 under national or Community law adopted in respect of the movement of capital to or from third countries involving direct investment – including investment in real estate – establishment, the provision of financial services or the admission of securities to capital markets.

2. Whilst endeavouring to achieve the objective of free movement of capital between Member States and third countries to the greatest extent possible and without prejudice to the other Chapters of this Treaty, the Council may, acting by a qualified majority on a proposal from

the Commission, adopt measures on the movement of capital to or from third countries involving direct investment – including investment in real estate – establishment, the provision of financial services or the admission of securities to capital markets. Unanimity shall be required for measures under this paragraph which constitute a step back in Community law as regards the liberalisation of the movement of capital to or from third countries.

Article 73d

1. The provisions of Article 73d shall be without prejudice to the right of Member States:

(a) to apply the relevant provisions of their tax law which distinguish between tax-payers who are not in the same situation with regard to their place of residence or with regard to the place where their capital is invested;

(b) to take all requisite measures to prevent infringements of national law and regulations, in particular in the field of taxation and the prudential supervision of financial institutions, or to lay down procedures for the declaration of capital movements for purposes of administrative or statistical information, or to take measures which are justified on grounds of public policy or public security.

2. The provisions of this Chapter shall be without prejudice to the applicability of restrictions on the right of establishment which are compatible with this Treaty.

3. The measures and procedures referred to in paragraphs 1 and 2 shall not constitute a means of arbitrary discrimination or a disguised restriction on the free movement of capital and payments as defined in Article 73b.

Article 73e

By way of derogation from Article 73b, Member States which, on 31 December 1993, enjoy a derogation on the basis of existing Community law, shall be entitled to maintain, until 31 December 1995 at the latest, restrictions on movements of capital authorised by such derogations as exist on that date.

Article 73f

Where in exceptional circumstances, movements of capital to or from third countries cause, or threaten to cause, serious difficulties for the operation of economic and monetary union, the Council, acting by a qualified majority on a proposal from the Commission and after consulting the ECB, may take safeguard measures with regard to third countries for a period not exceeding six months if such measures are strictly necessary.

Article 73g

1. If, in the cases envisaged in Article 228a, action by the Community is deemed necessary, the Council may, in accordance with the procedure provided for in Article 228a, take the necessary urgent measures on the movement of capital and on payments as regards the third countries concerned.

2. Without prejudice to Article 224 and as long as the Council has not taken measures pursuant to paragraph 1, a Member State may, for serious political reasons and on grounds of urgency, take unilateral measures against a third country with regard to capital movements and payments. The Commission and the other Member States shall be informed of such measures by the date of their entry into force at the latest.

The Council may, acting by a qualified majority on a proposal from the Commission, decide that the Member State concerned shall amend or abolish such measures. The President of the Council shall inform the European Parliament of any such decision taken by the Council.

Article 73h

Until 1 January 1994, the following provisions shall be applicable:

(1) Each Member State undertakes to authorise, in the currency of the Member State in which the creditor or the beneficiary resides, any payments connected with the movement of goods, services or capital, and any transfers of capital and earnings, to the extent that the movement of goods, services, capital and persons between Member States has been liberalised pursuant to this Treaty.

The Member States declare their readiness to undertake the liberalisation of payments beyond the extent provided in the preceding subparagraph, in so far as their economic situation in general and the state of their balance of payments in particular so permit.

(2) In so far as movements of goods, services and capital are limited only by restrictions on payments connected therewith, these restrictions shall be progressively abolished by applying, *mutatis mutandis*, the provisions of this Chapter and the Chapters relating to the abolition of quantitative restrictions and to the liberalisation of services.

(3) Member States undertake not to introduce between themselves any

new restrictions on transfers connected with the invisible transactions listed in Annex III to the Treaty.

The progressive abolition of existing restrictions shall be effected in accordance with the provisions of Articles 63 to 65, in so far as such abolition is not governed by the provisions contained in paragraphs 1 and 2 or by the other provisions of this Chapter.

(4) If need be, Member States shall consult each other on the measures to be taken to enable the payments and transfers mentioned in this Article to be effected; such measures shall not prejudice the attainment of the objectives set out in this Treaty.][23]

Title IV

Transport

Article 74

The objectives of this Treaty shall, in matters governed by this Title, be pursued by Member States within the framework of a common transport policy.

[Article 75

1. For the purpose of implementing Article 74, and taking into account the distinctive features of transport, the Council shall, acting in accordance with the procedure referred to in Article 189c and after consulting the Economic and Social Committee, lay down:

(a) common rules applicable to international transport to or from the territory of a Member State or passing across the territory of one or more Member States;

(b) the conditions under which non-resident carriers may operate transport services within a Member State;

(c) measures to improve transport safety;

(d) any other appropriate provisions.

2. The provisions referred to in (a) and (b) of paragraph 1 shall be laid down during the transitional period.

3. By way of derogation from the procedure provided for in paragraph 1, where the application of provisions concerning the principles of the regulatory system for transport would be liable to have a serious effect on the standard of living and on employment in certain areas and on the operation of transport facilities, they shall be laid down by the Council

acting unanimously on a proposal from the Commission, after consulting the European Parliament and the Economic and Social Committee. In so doing, the Council shall take into account the need for adaptation to the economic development which will result from establishing the common market.][24]

Article 76

Until the provisions referred to in Article 75(1) have been laid down, no Member State may, without the unanimous approval of the Council, make the various provisions governing the subject when this Treaty enters into force less favourable in their direct or indirect effect on carriers of other Member States as compared with carriers who are nationals of that State.

Article 77

Aids shall be compatible with this Treaty if they meet the needs of coordination of transport or if they represent reimbursement for the discharge of certain obligations inherent in the concept of a public service.

Article 78

Any measures taken within the framework of this Treaty in respect of transport rates and conditions shall take account of the economic circumstances of carriers.

Article 79

1. In the case of transport within the Community, discrimination which takes the form of carriers charging different rates and imposing different conditions for the carriage of the same goods over the same transport links on grounds of the country of origin or of destination of the goods in question, shall be abolished, at the latest, before the end of the second stage.

2. Paragraph 1 shall not prevent the Council from adopting other measures in pursuance of Article 75(1).

3. Within two years of the entry into force of this Treaty, the Council shall, acting by a qualified majority on a proposal from the Commission and after consulting the Economic and Social Committee, lay down rules for implementing the provisions of paragraph 1.

The Council may in particular lay down the provisions needed to enable the institutions of the Community to secure compliance with the rule laid down in paragraph 1 and to ensure that users benefit from it to the full.

4. The Commission shall, acting on its own initiative or on application by a Member State, investigate any cases of discrimination falling within paragraph 1 and, after consulting any Member State concerned, shall take the necessary decisions within the framework of the rules laid down in accordance with the provisions of paragraph 3.

Article 80

1. The imposition by a Member State, in respect of transport operations carried out within the Community, of rates and conditions involving any element of support or protection in the interest of one or more particular undertakings or industries shall be prohibited as from the beginning of the second stage, unless authorised by the Commission.

2. The Commission shall, acting on its own initiative or on application by a Member State, examine the rates and conditions referred to in paragraph 1, taking account in particular of the requirements of an appropriate regional economic policy, the needs of underdeveloped areas and the problems of areas seriously affected by political circumstances on the one hand, and of the effects of such rates and conditions on competition between the different modes of transport on the other.

After consulting each Member State concerned, the Commission shall take the necessary decisions.

3. The prohibition provided for in paragraph 1 shall not apply to tariffs fixed to meet competition.

Article 81

Charges or dues in respect of the crossing of frontiers which are charged by a carrier in addition to the transport rates shall not exceed a reasonable level after taking the costs actually incurred thereby into account.

Member States shall endeavour to reduce these costs progressively.

The Commission may make recommendations to Member States for the application of this Article.

Article 82

The provisions of this Title shall not form an obstacle to the application of measures taken in the Federal Republic of Germany to the extent that such measures are required in order to compensate for the economic disadvantages caused by the division of Germany to the economy of certain areas of the Federal Republic affected by that division.

Article 83

An Advisory Committee consisting of experts designated by the Governments of Member States, shall be attached to the Commission. The Commission, whenever it considers it desirable, shall consult the Committee on transport matters without prejudice to the powers of the transport section of the Economic and Social Committee.

Article 84

1. The provisions of this Title shall apply to transport by rail, road and inland waterway.

2. The Council may, acting by a qualified majority, decide whether, to what extent and by what procedure appropriate provisions may be laid down for sea and air transport.[25]

The procedural provisions of Article 75(1) and (3) shall apply.[26]

[Title V

Common rules on competition, taxation and approximation of laws] [27]

Chapter 1

Rules on competition

Section 1

Rules applying to undertakings

Article 85

1. The following shall be prohibited as incompatible with the common market: all agreements between undertakings, decisions by associations of undertakings and concerted practices which may affect trade between Member States and which have as their object or effect the prevention, restriction or distortion of competition within the common market, and in particular those which:

(a) directly or indirectly fix purchase or selling prices or any other trading conditions;

(b) limit or control production, markets, technical development, or investment;

(c) share markets or sources of supply;

(d) apply dissimilar conditions to equivalent transactions with other trading parties, thereby placing them at a competitive disadvantage;

(e) make the conclusion of contracts subject to acceptance by the other parties of supplementary obligations which, by their nature or according to commercial usage, have no connection with the subject of such contracts.

2. Any agreements or decisions prohibited pursuant to this Article shall be automatically void.

3. The provisions of paragraph 1 may, however, be declared inapplicable in the case of:

- any agreement or category of agreements between undertakings;

- any decision or category of decisions by associations of undertakings;

- any concerted practice or category of concerted practices;

which contributes to improving the production or distribution of goods or to promoting technical or economic progress, while allowing consumers a fair share of the resulting benefit, and which does not:

(a) impose on the undertakings concerned restrictions which are not indispensable to the attainment of these objectives;

(b) afford such undertakings the possibility of eliminating competition in respect of a substantial part of the products in question.

Article 86

Any abuse by one or more undertakings of a dominant position within the common market or in a substantial part of it shall be prohibited as incompatible with the common market in so far as it may affect trade between Member States.

Such abuse may, in particular, consist in:

(a) directly or indirectly imposing unfair purchase or selling prices or other unfair trading conditions;

(b) limited production, markets or technical development to the prejudice of consumers;

(c) applying dissimilar conditions to equivalent transactions with other trading parties, thereby placing them at a competitive disadvantage;

(d) making the conclusion of contracts subject to acceptance by the other parties of supplementary obligations which, by their nature or according to commercial usage, have no connection with the subject of such contracts.

Article 87

1. Within three years of the entry into force of this Treaty the Council shall, acting unanimously on a proposal from the Commission and after consulting the European Parliament, adopt any appropriate regulations or directives to give effect to the principles set out in Articles 85 and 86.

If such provisions have not been adopted within the period mentioned, they shall be laid down by the Council, acting by a qualified majority on a proposal from the Commission and after consulting the European Parliament.

2. The regulations or directives referred to in paragraph 1 shall be designed in particular:

(a) to ensure compliance with the prohibitions laid down in Article 85(1) and in Article 86 by making provision for fines and periodic penalty payments;

(b) to lay down detailed rules of the application of Article 85(3), taking into account the need to ensure effective supervision on the one hand, and to simplify administration to the greatest possible extent on the other;

(c) to define, if need be, in the various branches of the economy, the scope of the provisions of Articles 85 and 86;

(d) to define the respective functions of the Commission and of the Court of Justice in applying the provisions laid down in this paragraph;

(e) to determine the relationship between national laws and the provisions contained in this Section or adopted pursuant to this Article.

Article 88

Until the entry into force of the provisions adopted in pursuance of Article 87, the authorities in Member States shall rule on the admissibility of agreements, decisions and concerted practices and on abuse of a dominant position in the common market in accordance with the law of their country and with the provisions of Article 85, in particular paragraph 3, and of Article 86.

Article 89

1. Without prejudice to Article 88, the Commission shall, as soon as it takes up its duties, ensure the application of the principles laid down in Articles 85 and 86. On application by a Member State or on its own initiative, and in cooperation with the competent authorities in the Member States, who shall give it their assistance, the Commission shall investigate cases of suspected infringement of these principles. If it finds that there has been an infringement, it shall propose appropriate measures to bring it to an end.

2. If the infringement is not brought to an end, the Commission shall record such infringement of the principles in a reasoned decision. The Commission may publish its decision and authorise Member States to take the measures, the conditions and details of which it shall determine, needed to remedy the situation.

Article 90

1. In the case of public undertakings and undertakings to which Member States grant special or exclusive rights, Member States shall neither enact nor maintain in force any measure contrary to the rules contained in this Treaty, in particular to those rules provided for in Article 6 and Articles 85 to 94.

2. Undertakings entrusted with the operation of services of general economic interest or having the character of a revenue-producing monopoly shall be subject to the rules contained in this Treaty, in particular to the rules on competition, in so far as the application of such rules does not obstruct the performance, in law or in fact, of the particular tasks assigned to them. The development of trade must not be affected to such an extent as would be contrary to the interests of the Community.

3. The Commission shall ensure the application of the provisions of this Article and shall, where necessary, address appropriate directives or decisions to Member States.

Section 2

Dumping

Article 91

1. If during the transitional period, the Commission, on application by a Member State or by any other interested party, finds that dumping is being practised within the common market, it shall address

recommendations to the person or persons with whom such practices originate for the purpose of putting an end to them.

Should the practices continue, the Commission shall authorise the injured Member State to take protective measures, the conditions and details of which the Commission shall determine.

2. As soon as this Treaty enters into force, products which originate in or are in free circulation in one Member State and which have been exported to another Member State shall, on reimportation, be admitted into the territory of the first-mentioned State free of all customs duties, quantitative restrictions or measures having equivalent effect. The Commission shall lay down appropriate rules for the application of this paragraph.

Section 3

Aids granted by States

Article 92

1. Save as otherwise provided in this Treaty, any aid granted by a Member State or through State resources in any form whatsoever which distorts or threatens to distort competition by favouring certain undertakings or the production of certain goods shall, in so far as it affects trade between Member States, be incompatible with the common market.

2. The following shall be compatible with the common market:

(a) aid having a social character, granted to individual consumers, provided that such aid is granted without discrimination related to the origin of the products concerned;

(b) aid to make good the damage caused by natural disasters or exceptional occurrences;

(c) aid granted to the economy of certain areas of the Federal Republic of Germany affected by the division of Germany, in so far as such aid is required in order to compensate for the economic disadvantages caused by that division.

3. The following may be considered to be compatible with the common market:

(a) aid to promote the economic development of areas where the standard of living is abnormally low or where there is serious underemployment;

(b) aid to promote the execution of an important project of common European interest or to remedy a serious disturbance in the economy of a Member State;

(c) aid to facilitate the development of certain economic activities or of certain economic areas, where such aid does not adversely affect trading conditions to an extent contrary to the common interest. However, the aids granted to shipbuilding as of 1 January 1957 shall, in so far as they serve only to compensate for the absence of customs protection, be progressively reduced under the same conditions as apply to the elimination of customs duties, subject to the provisions of this Treaty concerning common commercial policy towards third countries;

[(d) aid to promote culture and heritage conservation where such aid does not affect trading conditions and competition in the Community to an extent that is contrary to the common interest;][28]

[(e)][29] such other categories of aid as may be specified by decision of the Council acting by a qualified majority on a proposal from the Commission.

Article 93

1. The Commission shall, in cooperation with Member States, keep under constant review all systems of aid existing in those States. It shall propose to the latter any appropriate measures required by the progressive development or by the functioning of the common market.

2. If, after giving notice to the parties concerned to submit their comments, the Commission finds that aid granted by a State or through State resources is not compatible with the common market having regard to Article 92, or that such aid is being misused, it shall decide that the State concerned shall abolish or alter such aid within a period of time to be determined by the Commission.

If the State concerned does not comply with this decision within the prescribed time, the Commission or any other interested State may, in derogation from the provisions of Articles 169 and 170, refer the matter to the Court of Justice direct.

On application by a Member State the Council may, acting unanimously, decide that aid which that State is granting or intends to grant shall be considered to be compatible with the common market, in derogation from the provisions of Article 92 or from the regulations provided for in Article 94, if such a decision is justified by exceptional circumstances. If, as regards the aid in question, the Commission has already initiated the procedure provided for in the first subparagraph of this paragraph, the fact that the State concerned has made its application to the Council shall have the effect of suspending that procedure until the Council has made its attitude known.

If, however, the Council has not made its attitude known within three months of the said application being made, the Commission shall give its decision on the case.

3. The Commission shall be informed, in sufficient time to enable it to submit its comments, of any plans to grant or alter aid. If it considers that any such plan is not compatible with the common market having regard to Article 92, it shall without delay initiate the procedure provided for in paragraph 2. The Member State concerned shall not put its proposed measures into effect until this procedure has resulted in a final decision.

[*Article* 94

The Council, acting by a qualified majority on a proposal from the Commission and after consulting the European Parliament, may make any appropriate regulations for the application of Articles 92 and 93 and may in particular determine the conditions in which Article 93(3) shall apply and the categories of aid exempted from this procedure.][30]

Chapter 2

Tax provisions

Article 95

No Member State shall impose, directly or indirectly, on the products of other Member States any internal taxation of any kind in excess of that imposed directly or indirectly on similar domestic products.

Furthermore, no Member State shall impose on products of other Member States any internal taxation of such a nature as to afford indirect protection to other products.

Member States shall, not later than at the beginning of the second stage, repeal or amend any provisions existing when this Treaty enters into force which conflict with the preceding rules.

Article 96

Where products are exported to the territory of any Member State, any repayment of internal taxation shall not exceed the internal taxation imposed on them whether directly or indirectly.

Article 97

Member States which levy a turnover tax calculated on a cumulative multi-stage tax system may, in the case of internal taxation imposed by them on imported products or of repayments allowed by them on exported products, establish average rates for products or groups of products, provided that there is no infringement of the principles laid down in Articles 95 and 96.

Where the average rates established by a Member State do not conform to these principles, the Commission shall address appropriate directives or decisions to the State concerned.

Article 98

In the case of charges other than turnover taxes, excise duties and other forms of indirect taxation, remissions and repayments in respect of exports to other Member States may not be granted and countervailing charges in respect of imports from Member States may not be imposed unless the measures contemplated have been previously approved for a limited period by the Council acting by a qualified majority on a proposal from the Commission.

[Article 99

The Council shall, acting unanimously on a proposal from the Commission and after consulting the European Parliament and the Economic and Social Committee, adopt provisions for the harmonisation of legislation concerning turnover taxes, excise duties and other forms of indirect taxation to the extent that such harmonisation is necessary to ensure the establishment and the functioning of the internal market within the time-limit laid down in Article 7a.][31]

[Article 100

The Council shall, acting unanimously on a proposal from the Commission and after consulting the European Parliament and the Economic and Social Committee, issue directives for the approximation of such laws, regulations or administrative provisions of the Member States as directly affect the establishment or functioning of the common market.][32]

Article 100a

[1. By way of derogation from Article 100 and save where otherwise provided in this Treaty, the following provisions shall apply for the achievement of the objectives set out in Article 7a. The Council shall, acting in accordance with the procedure referred to in Article 189b and after consulting the Economic and Social Committee, adopt the measures for the approximation of the provisions laid down by law, regulation or administrative action in Member States which have as their object the establishment and functioning of the internal market.][33]

2. Paragraph 1 shall not apply to fiscal provisions, to those relating to the free movement of persons nor to those relating to the rights and interest of employed persons.

3. The Commission, in its proposals envisaged in paragraph 1 concerning health, safety, environmental protection and consumer protection, will take as a base a high level of protection.

4. If, after the adoption of a harmonisation measure by the Council acting by a qualified majority, a Member State deems it necessary to apply national provisions on grounds of major needs referred to in Article 36, or relating to protection of the environment or the working environment, it shall notify the Commission of these provisions.

The Commission shall confirm the provisions involved after having verified that they are not a means of arbitrary discrimination or a disguised restriction on trade between Member States.

By way of derogation from the procedure laid down in Articles 169 and 170, the Commission or any Member State may bring the matter directly before the Court of Justice if it considers that another Member State is making improper use of the powers provided for in this Article.

5. The harmonisation measures referred to above shall, in appropriate cases, include a safeguard clause authorising the Member States to take, for one or more of the non-economic reasons referred to in Article 36, provisional measures subject to a Community control procedure.

Article 100b

1. During 1992, the Commission shall, together with each Member State, draw up an inventory of national laws, regulations and administrative provisions which fall under Article 100a and which have not been harmonised pursuant to that Article.

The Council, acting in accordance with the provisions of Article 100a, may decide that the provisions in force in a Member State must be recognised as being equivalent to those applied by another Member State.

2. The provisions of Article 100a(4) shall apply by analogy.

3. The Commission shall draw up the inventory referred to in the first

subparagraph of paragraph 1 and shall submit appropriate proposals in good time to allow the Council to act before the end of 1992.

[Article 100c

1. The Council, acting unanimously on a proposal from the Commission and after consulting the European Parliament, shall determine the third countries whose nationals must be in possession of a visa when crossing the external borders of the Member States.

2. However, in the event of an emergency situation in a third country posing a threat of a sudden inflow of nationals from that country into the Community, the Council, acting by a qualified majority on a recommendation from the Commission, may introduce, for a period not exceeding six months, a visa requirement for nationals from the country in question. The visa requirement established under this paragraph may be extended in accordance with the procedure referred to in paragraph 1.

3. From 1 January 1996, the Council shall adopt the decisions referred to in paragraph 1 by a qualified majority. The Council shall, before that date, acting by a qualified majority on a proposal from the Commission and after consulting the European Parliament, adopt measures relating to a uniform format for visas.

4. In the areas referred to in this Article, the Commission shall examine any request made by a Member State that it submit a proposal to the Council.

5. This Article shall be without prejudice to the exercise of the responsibilities incumbent upon the Member States with regard to the maintenance of law and order and the safeguarding of internal security.

6. This Article shall apply to other areas if so decided pursuant to Article K.9 of the provisions of the Treaty on European Union which relate to cooperation in the fields of justice and home affairs, subject to the voting conditions determined at the same time.

7. The provisions of the conventions in force between the Member States governing areas covered by this Article shall remain in force until their content has been replaced by directives or measures adopted pursuant to this Article.][34]

[Article 100d

The Coordinating Committee consisting of senior officials set up by Article K.4 of the Treaty on European Union shall contribute, without prejudice to the provisions of Article 151, to the preparation of the proceedings of the Council in the fields referred to in Article 100c.][35]

Article 101

Where the Commission finds that a difference between the provisions laid down by law, regulation or administrative action in Member States is distorting the conditions of competition in the common market and that the resultant distortion needs to be eliminated, it shall consult the Member States concerned.

If such consultation does not result in an agreement eliminating the distortion in question, the Council shall, on a proposal from the Commission, acting unanimously during the first stage and by a qualified majority thereafter, issue the necessary directives. The Commission and the Council may take any other appropriate measures provided for in this Treaty.

Article 102

1. Where there is reason to fear that the adoption or amendment of a provision laid down by law, regulation or administrative action may cause distortion within the meaning of Article 101, a Member State desiring to proceed therewith shall consult the Commission. After consulting the Member States, the Commission shall recommend to the States concerned such measures as may be appropriate to avoid the distortion in question.

2. If a State desiring to introduce or amend its own provisions does not comply with the recommendation addressed to it by the Commission, other Member States shall not be required, in pursuance of Article 101, to amend their own provisions in order to eliminate such distortion. If the Member State which has ignored the recommendation of the Commission causes distortion detrimental only to itself, the provisions of Article 101 shall not apply.

[Title VI

Economic and monetary policy

Chapter 1

Economic policy

Article 102a

Member States shall conduct their economic policies with a view to contributing to the achievement of the objectives of the Community, as defined in Article 2, and in the context of the broad guidelines referred to in Article 103(2). The Member States and the Community shall act in accordance with the principle of an open market economy with free competition, favouring an efficient allocation of resources, and in compliance with the principles set out in Article 3a.

Article 103

1. Member States shall regard their economic policies as a matter of common concern and shall coordinate them within the Council, in accordance with the provisions of Article 102a.

2. The Council shall, acting by a qualified majority on a recommendation from the Commission, formulate a draft for the broad guidelines of the economic policies of the Member States and of the Community, and shall report its findings to the European Council.

The European Council shall, acting on the basis of the report from the Council, discuss a conclusion on the broad guidelines of the economic policies of the Member States and of the Community.

On the basis of this conclusion, the Council shall, acting by a qualified majority, adopt a recommendation setting out these broad guidelines. The Council shall inform the European Parliament of its recommendation.

3. In order to ensure closer coordination of economic policies and sustained convergence of the economic performances of the Member States, the Council shall, on the basis of reports submitted by the Commission, monitor economic developments in each of the Member States and in the community as well as the consistency of economic policies with the broad guidelines referred to in paragraph 2, and regularly carry out an overall assessment.

For the purpose of this multilateral surveillance, Member States shall forward information to the Commission about important measures taken by them in the field of their economic policy and such other information as they deem necessary.

4. Where it is established, under the procedure referred to in paragraph 3, that the economic policies of a Member State are not consistent with the broad guidelines referred to in paragraph 2 or that they risk jeopardising the proper functioning of economic and monetary union, the Council may, acting by a qualified majority on a recommendation from the Commission, make the necessary recommendations to the Member State concerned. The Council may, acting by a qualified majority on a proposal from the Commission, decide to make its recommendations public.

The President of the Council and the Commission shall report to the

European Parliament on the results of multilateral surveillance. The President of the Council may be invited to appear before the competent Committee of the European Parliament if the Council has made its recommendations public.

5. The Council, acting in accordance with the procedure referred to in Article 189c, may adopt detailed rules for the multilateral surveillance procedure referred to in paragraphs 3 and 4 of this Article.

Article 103a

1. Without prejudice to any other procedures provided for in this Treaty, the Council may, acting unanimously on a proposal from the Commission, decide upon the measures appropriate to the economic situation, in particular if severe difficulties arise in the supply of certain products.

2. Where a Member State is in difficulties or is seriously threatened with severe difficulties caused by exceptional occurrences beyond its control, the Council may, acting unanimously on a proposal from the Commission, grant, under certain conditions, Community financial assistance to the Member State concerned. Where the severe difficulties are caused by natural disasters, the Council shall act by qualified majority. The President of the Council shall inform the European Parliament of the decision taken.

Article 104

1. Overdraft facilities or any other type of credit facility with the ECB or with central banks of the Member States (hereinafter referred to as 'national central banks') in favour of Community institutions or bodies, central governments, regional, local or other public authorities, other bodies governed by public law, or public undertakings of Member States shall be prohibited, as shall the purchase directly from by the ECB or national central banks of debt instruments.

2. Paragraph 1 shall not apply to publicly owned credit institutions which, in the context of the supply of reserves by central banks, shall be given the same treatment by national central banks and the ECB as private credit institutions.

Article 104a

1. Any measure, not based on prudential considerations, establishing privileged access by Community institutions or bodies, central governments, regional, local or other public authorities, other bodies governed by public law, or public undertakings of Member States to financial institutions shall be prohibited.

2. The Council, acting in accordance with the procedure referred to in Article 189c, shall, before 1 January 1994, specify definitions for the application of the prohibition referred to in paragraph 1.

Article 104b

1. The Community shall not be liable for or assume the commitments of central governments, regional, local or other public authorities, other bodies governed by public law, or public undertakings of any Member State, without prejudice to mutual financial guarantees for the joint execution of a specific project. A Member State shall not be liable for or assume the commitments of central governments, regional, local or other public authorities, other bodies governed by public law or public undertakings of another Member State, without prejudice to mutual financial guarantees for the joint execution of a specific project.

2. If necessary, the Council, acting in accordance with the procedure referred to in Article 189c, may specify definitions for the application of the prohibitions referred to in Article 104 and in this Article.

Article 104c

1. Member States shall avoid excessive government deficits.

2. The Commission shall monitor the development of the budgetary situation and of the stock of government debt in the Member States with a view to identifying gross errors. In particular it shall examine compliance with budgetary discipline on the basis of the following two criteria:

(a) whether the ratio of the planned or actual government deficit to gross domestic product exceeds a reference value, unless

- either the ratio has declined substantially and continuously and reached a level that comes close to the reference value;

- or, alternatively, the excess over the reference value is only exceptional and temporary and the ratio remains close to the reference value;

(b) whether the ratio of government debt to gross domestic product exceeds a reference value, unless the ratio is sufficiently diminishing and approaching the reference value at a satisfactory pace.

The reference values are specified in the Protocol on the excessive deficit procedure annexed to this Treaty.

3. If a Member State does not fulfil the requirements under one or both of these criteria, the Commission shall prepare a report. The report of

the Commission shall also take into account whether the government deficit exceeds government investment expenditure and take into account all other relevant factors, including the medium-term economic and budgetary position of the Member State.

The Commission may also prepare a report if, notwithstanding the fulfilment of the requirements under the criteria, it is of the opinion that there is a risk of an excessive deficit in a Member State.

4. The Committee provided for in Article 109c shall formulate an opinion on the report of the Commission.

5. If the Commission considers that an excessive deficit in a Member State exists or may occur, the Commission shall address an opinion to the Council.

6. The Council shall, acting by a qualified majority on a recommendation from the Commission, and having considered any observations which the Member State concerned may wish to make, decide after an overall assessment whether an excessive deficit exists.

7. Where the existence of an excessive deficit is decided according to paragraph 6, the Council shall make recommendations to the Member State concerned with a view to bringing that situation to an end within a given period. Subject to the provisions of paragraph 8, these recommendations shall not be made public.

8. Where it establishes that there has been no effective action in response to its recommendations within the period laid down, the Council may make its recommendations public.

9. If a Member State persists in failing to put into practice the recommendations of the Council, the Council may decide to give notice to the Member State to take, within a specified time-limit, measures for the deficit reduction which is judged necessary by the Council in order to remedy the situation.

In such a case, the Council may request the Member State concerned to submit reports in accordance with a specific timetable in order to examine the adjustment efforts of that Member State.

10. The rights to bring actions provided for in Articles 169 and 170 may not be exercised within the framework of paragraphs 1 to 9 of this Article.

11. As long as a Member State fails to comply with a decision taken in accordance with paragraph 9, the Council may decide to apply or, as the case may be, intensify one or more of the following measures:

– to require the Member State concerned to publish additional information, to be specified by the Council, before issuing bonds and securities;

- to invite the European Investment Bank to reconsider its lending policy towards the Member State concerned;

- to require the Member State concerned to make a non-interest-bearing deposit of an appropriate size with the Community until the excessive deficit has, in the view of the Council, been corrected;

- to impose fines of an appropriate size.

The President of the Council shall inform the European Parliament of the decisions taken.

12. The Council shall abrogate some or all of its decisions referred to in paragraphs 6 to 9 and 11 to the extent that the excessive deficit in the Member State concerned has, in the view of the Council, been corrected. If the Council has previously made public recommendations, it shall, as soon as the decision under paragraph 8 has been abrogated, make a public statement that an excessive deficit in the Member State concerned no longer exists.

13. When taking the decision referred to in paragraphs 7 to 9, 11 and 12, the Council shall act on a recommendation from the Commission by a majority of two-thirds of the votes of its members weighted in accordance with Article 148(2), excluding the votes of the representative of the Member State concerned.

14. Further provisions relating to the implementation of the procedure described in this Article are set out in the Protocol on the excessive deficit procedure annexed to this Treaty.

The Council shall, acting unanimously on a proposal from the Commission and after consulting the European Parliament and the ECB, adopt the appropriate provisions which shall then replace the said Protocol.

Subject to the other provisions of this paragraph the Council shall, before 1 January 1994, acting by a qualified majority on a proposal from the Commission and after consulting the European Parliament, lay down detailed rules and definitions for the application of the provisions of the said Protocol.

Chapter 2

Monetary policy

Article 105

1. The primary objective of the ESCB shall be to maintain price stability. Without prejudice to the objective of price stability, the ESCB shall support the general economic policies in the Community with a view to contributing to the achievement of the objectives of the Community as laid down in Article 2. The ESCB shall act in accordance with the principle of an open market economy with free competition, favouring an efficient allocation of resources, and in compliance with the principles set out in Article 3a.

2. The basic tasks to be carried out through the ESCB shall be:

–   to define and implement the monetary policy of the Community;

–   to conduct foreign-exchange operations consistent with the provisions of Article 109;

–   to hold and manage the official foreign reserves of the Member States;

–   to promote the smooth operation of payment systems.

3. The third indent of paragraph 2 shall be without prejudice to the holding and management by the governments of Member States of foreign-exchange working balances.

4. The ECB shall be consulted:

–   on any proposed Community act in its fields of competence;

–   by national authorities regarding any draft legislative provision in its fields of competence, but within the limits and under the conditions set out by the Council in accordance with the procedure laid down in Article 106(6).

The ECB may submit opinions to the appropriate Community institutions or bodies or to national authorities on matters in its fields of competence.

5. The ESCB shall contribute to the smooth conduct of policies pursued by the competent authorities relating to the prudential supervision of credit institutions and the stability of the financial system.

6. The Council may, acting unanimously on a proposal from the Commission and after consulting the ECB and after receiving the assent of the European Parliament, confer upon the ECB specific tasks

concerning policies relating to the prudential supervision of credit institutions and other financial institutions with the exception of insurance undertakings.

Article 105a

1. The ECB shall have the exclusive right to authorise the issue of banknotes within the Community. The ECB and the national central banks may issue such notes. The banknotes issued by the ECB and the national central banks shall be the only such notes to have the status of legal tender within the Community.

2. Member States may issue coins subject to approval by the ECB of the volume of the issue. The Council may, acting in accordance with the procedure referred to in Article 189c and after consulting the ECB, adopt measures to harmonise the denominations and technical specifications of all coins intended for circulation to the extent necessary to permit their smooth circulation within the Community.

Article 106

1. The ESCB shall be composed of the ECB and of the national central banks.

2. The ECB shall have legal personality.

3. The ESCB shall be governed by the decision-making bodies of the ECB which shall be the Governing Council and the Executive Board.

4. The Statute of the ESCB is laid down in a Protocol annexed to this Treaty.

5. Articles 5.1, 5.2, 5.3, 17, 18, 19.1, 22, 23, 24, 26, 32.2, 32.3, 32.4, 32.6, 33.1(a) and 36 of the Statute of the ESCB may be amended by the Council, acting either by a qualified majority on a recommendation from the ECB and after consulting the Commission or unanimously on a proposal from the Commission and after consulting the ECB. In either case, the assent of the European Parliament shall be required.

6. The Council, acting by a qualified majority either on a proposal from the Commission and after consulting the European Parliament and the ECB or on a recommendation from the ECB and after consulting the European Parliament and the Commission, shall adopt the provisions referred to in Articles 4, 5.4, 19.2, 20, 28.1, 29.2, 30.4 and 34.3 of the Statute of the ESCB.

Article 107

When exercising the powers and carrying out the tasks and duties conferred upon them by this Treaty and the Statute of the ESCB, neither the ECB, nor a national central bank, nor any member of their decision-making bodies shall seek or take instructions from Community institutions or bodies, from any government of a Member State or from any other body. The Community institutions and bodies and the governments of the Member States undertake to respect this principle and not to seek to influence the members of the decision-making bodies of the ECB or of the national central banks in the performance of their tasks.

Article 108

Each Member State shall ensure, at the latest at the date of the establishment of the ESCB, that its national legislation including the statutes of its national central bank is compatible with this Treaty and the Statute of the ESCB.

Article 108a

1. In order to carry out the tasks entrusted to the ESCB, the ECB shall, in accordance with the provisions of this Treaty and under the conditions laid down in the Statute of the ESCB:

– make regulations to the extent necessary to implement the tasks defined in Article 3.1, first indent, Articles 19.1, 22 and 25.2 of the Statute of the ESCB and in cases which shall be laid down in the acts of the Council referred to in Article 106(6);

– take decisions necessary for carrying out the tasks entrusted to the ESCB under this Treaty and the Statute of the ESCB;

– make recommendations and deliver opinions.

2. A regulation shall have general application. It shall be binding in its entirety and directly applicable to all Member States.

Recommendations and opinions shall have no binding force.

A decision shall be binding in its entirety upon those to whom it is addressed.

Articles 190 to 192 shall apply to regulations and decisions adopted by the ECB.

The ECB may decide to publish its decisions, recommendations and opinions.

3. Within the limits and under the conditions adopted by the Council under the procedure laid down in Article 106(6), the ECB shall be entitled

to impose fines or periodic penalty payments on undertakings for failure to comply with obligations under its regulations and decisions.

Article 109

1. By way of derogation from Article 228, the Council may, acting unanimously on a recommendation from the ECB or from the Commission, and after consulting the ECB in an endeavour to reach a consensus consistent with the objective of price stability, after consulting the European Parliament, in accordance with the procedure in paragraph 3 for determining the arrangements, conclude formal agreements on an exchange-rate system for the ECU in relation to non-Community currencies. The Council may, acting by a qualified majority on a recommendation from the ECB or from the Commission, and after consulting the ECB in an endeavour to reach a consensus consistent with the objective of price stability, adopt, adjust or abandon the central rates of the ECU within the exchange-rate system. The President of the Council shall inform the European Parliament of the adoption, adjustment or abandonment of the ECU central rates.

2. In the absence of an exchange-rate system in relation to one or more non-Community currencies as referred to in paragraph 1, the Council, acting by a qualified majority either on a recommendation from the Commission and after consulting the ECB or on a recommendation from the ECB, may formulate general orientations for exchange-rate policy in relation to these currencies. These general orientations shall be without prejudice to the primary objective of the ESCB to maintain price stability.

3. By way of derogation from Article 228, where agreements concerning monetary or foreign-exchange regime matters need to be negotiated by the Community with one or more States or international organisations, the Council, acting by a qualified majority on a recommendation from the Commission and after consulting the ECB, shall decide the arrangements for the negotiation and for the conclusion of such agreements. These arrangements shall ensure that the Community expresses a single position. The Commission shall be fully associated with the negotiations.

Agreements concluded in accordance with this paragraph shall be binding on the institutions of the Community, on the ECB and on Member States.

4. Subject to paragraph 1, the Council shall, on a proposal from the Commission and after consulting the ECB, acting by a qualified majority decide on the position of the Community at international level as regards issues of particular relevance to economic and monetary union and,

acting unanimously, decide its representation in compliance with the allocation of powers laid down in Articles 103 and 105.

5. Without prejudice to Community competence and Community agreements as regards economic and monetary union, Member States may negotiate in international bodies and conclude international agreements.

Chapter 3

Institutional provisions

Article 109a

1. The Governing Council of the ECB shall comprise the members of the Executive Board of the ECB and the Governors of the national central banks.

2. (a) The Executive Board shall comprise the President, the Vice-President and four other members.

(b) The President, the Vice-President and the other members of the Executive Board shall be appointed from among persons of recognised standing and professional experience in monetary or banking matters by common accord of the governments of the Member States at the level of Heads of State or Government, on a recommendation from the Council, after it has consulted the European Parliament and the Governing Council of the ECB.

Their term of office shall be eight years and shall not be renewable.

Only nationals of the Member States may be members of the Executive Board.

Article 109b

1. The President of the Council and a member of the Commission may participate, without having the right to vote, in meetings of the Governing Council of the ECB.

The President of the Council may submit a motion for deliberation to the Governing Council of the ECB.

2. The President of the ECB shall be invited to participate in Council meetings when the Council is discussing matters relating to the objectives and tasks of the ESCB.

3. The ECB shall address an annual report on the activities of the ESCB and on the monetary policy of both the previous and current year to the

European Parliament, the Council and the Commission, and also to the European Council. The President of the ECB shall present this report to the Council and to the European Parliament, which may hold a general debate on that basis.

The President of the ECB and the other members of the Executive Board may, at the request of the European Parliament or on their own initiative, be heard by the competent Committees of the European Parliament.

Article 109c

1. In order to promote coordination of the policies of Member States to the full extent needed for the functioning of the internal market, a Monetary Committee with advisory status is hereby set up.

It shall have the following tasks:

- to keep under review the monetary and financial situation of the Member States and of the Community and the general payments system of the Member States and to report regularly thereon to the Council and to the Commission;

- to deliver opinions at the request of the Council or of the Commission, or on its own initiative for submission to those institutions;

- without prejudice to Article 151, to contribute to the preparation of the work of the Council referred to in Articles 73f, 73g, 103(2), (3), (4) and (5), 103a, 104a, 104b, 104c, 109e(2), 109f(6), 109h, 109i, 109j(2) and 109k(1);

- to examine, at least once a year, the situation regarding the movement of capital and the freedom of payments, as they result from the application of this Treaty and of measures adopted by the Council; the examination shall cover all measures relating to capital movements and payments; the Committee shall report to the Commission and to the Council on the outcome of this examination.

The Member States and the Commission shall each appoint two members of the Monetary Committee.

2. At the start of the third stage, an Economic and Financial Committee shall be set up. The Monetary Committee provided for in paragraph 1 shall be dissolved.

The Economic and Financial Committee shall have the following tasks:

- to deliver opinions at the request of the Council or of the Commission, or on its own initiative for submission to those institutions;

- to keep under review the economic and financial situation of the Member States and of the Community and to report regularly thereon to the Council and to the Commission, in particular on financial relations with third countries and international institutions;

- without prejudice to Article 151, to contribute to the preparation of the work of the Council referred to in Articles 73f, 73g, 103(2), (3), (4), and (5), 103a, 104a, 104b, 104c, 105(6), 105a(2), 106(5) and (6), 109, 109h, 109i(2) and (3), 109k(2), 109l(4) and (5), and to carry out other advisory and preparatory tasks assigned to it by the Council;

- to examine, at least once a year, the situation regarding the movement of capital and the freedom of payments, as they result from the application of this Treaty and of measures adopted by the Council; the examination shall cover all measures relating to capital movements and payments; the Committee shall report to the Commission and to the Council on the outcome of this examination.

The Member States, the Commission and the ECB shall each appoint no more than two members of the Committee.

3. The Council shall, acting by a qualified majority on a proposal from the Commission and after consulting the ECB and the Committee referred to in this Article, lay down detailed provisions concerning the composition of the Economic and Financial Committee. The President of the Council shall inform the European Parliament of such a decision.

4. In addition to the tasks set out in paragraph 2, if and as long as there are Member States with a derogation as referred to in Articles 109k and 109l, the Committee shall keep under review the monetary and financial situation and the general payments system of those Member States and report regularly thereon to the Council and to the Commission.

Article 109d

For matters within the scope of Articles 103(4), 104c with the exception of paragraph 14, 109, 109j, 109k and 109l(4) and (5), the Council or a Member State may request the Commission to make a recommendation or a proposal, as appropriate. The Commission shall examine this request and submit its conclusions to the Council without delay.

Chapter 4

Transitional provisions

Article 109e

1. The second stage for achieving economic and monetary union shall begin on 1 January 1994.

2. Before that date

(a) each Member State shall:

- adopt, where necessary, appropriate measures to comply with the prohibitions laid down in Article 73b, without prejudice to Article 73e, and in Articles 104 and 104a(1);

- adopt, if necessary, with a view to permitting the assessment provided for in subparagraph (b), multiannual programmes intended to ensure the lasting convergence necessary for the achievement of economic and monetary union, in particular with regard to price stability and sound public finances;

(b) the Council shall, on the basis of a report from the Commission, assess the progress made with regard to economic and monetary convergence, in particular with regard to price stability and sound public finances, and the progress made with the implementation of Community law concerning the internal market.

3. The provisions of Articles 104, 104a(1), 104b(1) and 104c with the exception of paragraphs 1, 9, 11 and 14 shall apply from the beginning of the second stage.

The provisions of Articles 103a(2), 104c(1), (9) and (11), 105, 105a, 107, 109, 109a, 109b and 109c(2) and (4) shall apply from the beginning of the third stage.

4. In the second stage, Member States shall endeavour to avoid excessive government deficits.

5. During the second stage, each Member State shall, as appropriate, start the process leading to the independence of its central bank, in accordance with Article 108.

Article 109f

1. At the start of the second stage, a European Monetary Institute (hereinafter referred to as 'EMI') shall be established and take up its duties; it shall have legal personality and be directed and managed by a

Council, consisting of a President and the Governors of the national central banks, one of whom shall be Vice-President.

The President shall be appointed by common accord of the governments of the Member States at the level of Heads of State or Government, on a recommendation from, as the case may be, the Committee of Governors of the central banks of the Member States (hereinafter referred to as 'Committee of Governors') or the Council of the EMI, and after consulting the European Parliament and the Council. The President shall be selected from among persons of recognised standing and professional experience in monetary or banking matters. Only nationals of Member States may be President of the EMI. The Council of the EMI shall appoint the Vice-President.

The Statute of the EMI is laid down in a Protocol annexed to this Treaty.

The Committee of Governors shall be dissolved at the start of the second stage.

2. The EMI shall:

- strengthen cooperation between the national central banks;

- strengthen the coordination of the monetary policies of the Member States, with the aim of ensuring price stability;

- monitor the functioning of the European Monetary System;

- hold consultations concerning issues falling within the competence of the national central banks and affecting the stability of financial institutions and markets;

- take over the tasks of the European Monetary Cooperation Fund, which shall be dissolved; the modalities of dissolution are laid down in the Statute of the EMI;

- facilitate the use of the ECU and oversee its development, including the smooth functioning of the ECU clearing system.

3. For the preparation of the third stage, the EMI shall:

- prepare the instruments and the procedures necessary for carrying out a single monetary policy in the third stage;

- promote the harmonisation, where necessary, of the rules and practices governing the collection, compilation and distribution of statistics in the areas within its field of competence;

- prepare the rules for operations to be undertaken by the national central banks within the framework of the ESCB;

- promote the efficiency of cross-border payments;

– supervise the technical preparation of ECU banknotes.

At the latest by 31 December 1996, the EMI shall specify the regulatory, organisational and logistical framework necessary for the ESCB to perform its tasks in the third stage. This framework shall be submitted for decision to the ECB at the date of its establishment.

4. The EMI, acting by a majority of two-thirds of the members of its Council, may:

– formulate opinions or recommendations on the overall orientation of monetary policy and exchange-rate policy as well as on related measures introduced in each Member State;

– submit opinions or recommendations to governments and to the Council on policies which might affect the internal or external monetary situation in the Community and, in particular, the functioning of the European Monetary System;

– make recommendations to the monetary authorities of the Member States concerning the conduct of their monetary policy.

5. The EMI, acting unanimously, may decide to publish its opinions and its recommendations.

6. The EMI shall be consulted by the Council regarding any proposed Community act within its field of competence.

Within the limits and under the conditions set out by the Council, acting by a qualified majority on a proposal from the Commission and after consulting the European Parliament and the EMI, the EMI shall be consulted by the authorities of the Member States on any draft legislative provision within its field of competence.

7. The Council may, acting unanimously on a proposal from the Commission and after consulting the European Parliament and the EMI, confer upon the EMI other tasks for the preparation of the third stage.

8. Where this Treaty provides for a consultative role for the ECB, references to the ECB shall be read as referring to the EMI before the establishment of the ECB.

Where this Treaty provides for a consultative role for the EMI, references to the EMI shall be read, before 1 January 1994, as referring to the Committee of Governors.

9. During the second stage, the term 'ECB' used in Articles 173, 175, 176, 177, 180 and 215 shall be read as referring to the EMI.

Article 109g

The currency composition of the ECU basket shall not be changed.

From the start of the third stage, the value of the ECU shall be irrevocable fixed in accordance with Article 109l(4).

Article 109h

1. Where a Member State is in difficulties or is seriously threatened with difficulties as regards its balance of payments either as a result of an overall disequilibrium in its balance of payments, or as a result of the type of currency at its disposal, and where such difficulties are liable in particular to jeopardise the functioning of the common market or the progressive implementation of the common commercial policy, the Commission shall immediately investigate the position of the State in question and the action which, making use of all the means at its disposal, that State has taken or may take in accordance with the provisions of this Treaty. The Commission shall state what measures it recommends the State concerned to take.

If the action taken by a Member State and the measures suggested by the Commission do not prove sufficient to overcome the difficulties which have arisen or which threaten, the Commission shall, after consulting the Commission referred to in Article 109c, recommend to the Council the granting of mutual assistance and appropriate methods therefor.

The Commission shall keep the Council regularly informed of the situation and of how it is developing.

2. The Council, acting by a qualified majority, shall grant such mutual assistance; it shall adopt directives or decisions laying down the conditions and details of such assistance, which may take such forms as:

(a) a concerted approach to or within any other international organisations to which Member States may have recourse;

(b) measures need to avoid deflection of trade where the State which is in difficulties maintains or reintroduces quantitative restrictions against third countries;

(c) the granting of limited credits by other Member States, subject to their agreement.

3. If the mutual assistance recommended by the Commission is not granted by the Council or if the mutual assistance granted and the measures taken are insufficient, the Commission shall authorise the

State which is in difficulties to take protective measures, the conditions and details of which the Commission shall determine.

Such authorisation may be revoked and such conditions and details may be changed by the Council acting by a qualified majority.

4. Subject to Article 109k(6), this Article shall cease to apply from the beginning of the third stage.

Article 109i

1. Where a sudden crisis in the balance of payments occurs and a decision within the meaning of Article 109h(2) is not immediately taken, the Member State concerned may, as a precaution, take the necessary protective measures. Such measures must cause the least possible disturbance in the functioning of the common market and must not be wider in scope than is strictly necessary to remedy the sudden difficulties which have arisen.

2. The Commission and the other Member States shall be informed of such protective measures not later than when they enter into force. The Commission may recommend to the Council the granting of mutual assistance under Article 109h.

3. After the Commission has delivered an opinion and the Committee referred to in Article 109c has been consulted, the Council may, acting by a qualified majority, decide that the State concerned shall amend, suspend or abolish the protective measures referred to above.

4. Subject to Article 109k(6), this Article shall cease to apply from the beginning of the third stage.

Article 109j

1. The Commission and the EMI shall report to the Council on the progress made in the fulfilment by the Member States of their obligations regarding the achievement of economic and monetary union. These reports shall include an examination of the compatibility between each Member State's national legislation, including the statutes of its national central bank, and Articles 107 and 108 of this Treaty and the Statute of the ESCB. The reports shall also examine the achievement of a high degree of sustainable convergence by reference to the fulfilment by each Member State of the following criteria:

- the achievement of a high degree of price stability; this will be apparent from a rate of inflation which is close to that of, at most, the three best performing Member States in terms of price stability;

- the sustainability of the government financial position; this will be apparent from having achieved a government budgetary position without a deficit that is excessive as determined in accordance with Article 104c(6);

- the observance of the normal fluctuation margins provided for by the exchange-rate mechanism of the European Monetary System, for at least two years, without devaluing against the currency of any other Member State;

- the durability of convergence achieved by the Member State and of its participation in the exchange-rate mechanism of the European Monetary System being reflected in the long-term interest-rate levels.

The four criteria mentioned in this paragraph and the relevant periods over which they are to be respected are developed further in a Protocol annexed to this Treaty. The reports of the Commission and the EMI shall also take account of the development of the ECU, the results of the integration of markets, the situation and development of the balances of payments on current account and an examination of the development of unit labour costs and other price indices.

2. On the basis of these reports, the Council, acting by a qualified majority on a recommendation from the Commission, shall assess:

- for each Member State, whether it fulfils the necessary conditions for the adoption of a single currency;

- whether a majority of the Member States fulfil the necessary conditions for the adoption of a single currency,

and recommend its findings to the Council, meeting in the composition of the Heads of State or Government. The European Parliament shall be consulted and forward its opinion to the Council, meeting in the composition of the Heads of State or Government.

3. Taking due account of the reports referred to in paragraph 1 and the opinion of the European Parliament referred to in paragraph 2, the Council, meeting in the composition of Heads of State or Government, shall, acting by a qualified majority, not later than 31 December 1996:

- decide, on the basis of the recommendations of the Council referred to in paragraph 2, whether a majority of the Member States fulfil the necessary conditions for the adoption of a single currency;

- decide whether it is appropriate for the Community to enter the third stage,

and if so

– set the date for the beginning of the third stage.

4. If by the end of 1997 the date for the beginning of the third stage has not been set, the third stage shall start on 1 January 1999. Before 1 July 1998, the Council, meeting in the composition of Heads of State or Government, after a repetition of the procedure provided for in paragraphs 1 and 2, with the exception of the second indent of paragraph 2, taking into account the reports referred to in paragraph 1 and the opinion of the European Parliament, shall, acting by a qualified majority and on the basis of the recommendations of the Council referred to in paragraph 2, confirm which Member States fulfil the necessary conditions for the adoption of a single currency.

Article 109*k*

1. If the decision has been taken to set the date in accordance with Article 109j(3), the Council shall, on the basis of its recommendations referred to in Article 109j(2), acting by a qualified majority on a recommendation from the Commission, decide whether any, and if so which, Member States shall have a derogation as defined in paragraph 3 of this Article. Such Member States shall in this Treaty be referred to as 'Member States with a derogation'.

If the Council has confirmed which Member States fulfil the necessary conditions for the adoption of a single currency, in accordance with Article 109j(4), those Member States which do not fulfil the conditions shall have a derogation as defined in paragraph 3 of this Article. Such Member States shall in this Treaty be referred to as 'Member States with a derogation'.

2. At least once every two years, or at the request of a Member State with a derogation, the Commission and the ECB shall report to the Council in accordance with the procedure laid down in Article 109j(1). After consulting the European Parliament and after discussion in the Council, meeting in the composition of the Heads of State or Government, the Council shall, acting by a qualified majority on a proposal from the Commission, decide which Member States with a derogation fulfil the necessary conditions on the basis of the criteria set out in Article 109j(1), and abrogate the derogations of the Member States concerned.

3. A derogation referred to in paragraph 1 shall entail that the following Articles do not apply to the Member State concerned: Articles 104c(9) and (11), 105(1), (2), (3) and (5), 105a, 108a, 109 and 109a(2)(*b*). The exclusion of such a Member State and its national central bank from rights and obligations within the ESCB is laid down in Chapter IX of the Statute of the ESCB.

4. In Articles 105(1), (2) and (3), 105a, 108a, 109 and 109a(2)(*b*), 'Member States' shall be read as 'Member States without a derogation'.

5. The voting rights of Member States with a derogation shall be suspended for the Council decisions referred to in the Articles of this Treaty mentioned in paragraph 3. In that case, by way of derogation from Articles 148 and 189a(1), a qualified majority shall be defined as two-thirds of the votes of the representatives of the Member States without a derogation weighted in accordance with Article 148(2), unanimity of those Member States shall be required for an act requiring unanimity.

6. Articles 109h and 109i shall continue to apply to a Member State with a derogation.

Article 109*l*

1. Immediately after the decision on the date for the beginning of the third stage has been taken in accordance with Article 109j(3), or, as the case may be, immediately after 1 July 1998:

– the Council shall adopt the provisions referred to in Article 106(6);

– the governments of the Member States without a derogation shall appoint, in accordance with the procedure set out in Article 50 of the Statute of the ESCB, the President, the Vice-President and the other members of the Executive Board of the ECB. If there are Member States with a derogation, the number of members of the Executive Board may be smaller than provided for in Article 11.1 of the Statute of the ESCB, but in no circumstances shall it be less than four.

As soon as the Executive Board is appointed, the ESCB and the ECB shall be established and shall prepare for their full operation as described in this Treaty and the Statute of the ESCB. The full exercise of their powers shall start from the first day of the third stage.

2. As soon as the ECB is established, it shall, if necessary, take over tasks of the EMI. The EMI shall go into liquidation upon the establishment of the ECB; the modalities of liquidation are laid down in the Statute of the EMI.

3. If and as long as there are Member States with a derogation, and without prejudice to Article 106(3) of this Treaty, the General Council of the ECB referred to in Article 45 of the Statute of the ESCB shall be constituted as a third decision-making body of the ECB.

4. At the starting date of the third stage, the Council shall, acting with the unanimity of the Member States without a derogation, on a proposal from the Commission and after consulting the ECB, adopt the conversion rates at which their currencies shall be irrevocably fixed and

at which irrevocably fixed rate the ECU shall be substituted for these currencies, and the ECU will become a currency in its own right. This measure shall by itself not modify the external value of the ECU. The Council shall, acting according to the same procedure, also take the other measures necessary for the rapid introduction of the ECU as the single currency of those Member States.

5. If it is decided, according to the procedure set out in Article 109k(2), to abrogate a derogation, the Council shall, acting with the unanimity of the Member States without a derogation and the Member State concerned, on a proposal from the Commission and after consulting the ECB, adopt the rate at which the ECU shall be substituted for the currency of the Member State concerned, and take the other measures necessary for the introduction of the ECU as the single currency in the Member State concerned.

Article 109m

1. Until the beginning of the third stage, each Member State shall treat its exchange-rate policy as a matter of common interest. In so doing, Member States shall take account of the experience acquired in cooperation within the framework of the European Monetary System (EMS) and in developing the ECU, and shall respect existing powers in this field.

2. From the beginning of the third stage and for as long as a Member State has a derogation, paragraph 1 shall apply by analogy to the exchange-rate policy of that Member State.][36]

[Title VII

Common commercial policy][37]

Article 110

By establishing a customs union between themselves Member States aim to contribute, in the common interest, to the harmonious development of world trade, the progressive abolition of restrictions on international trade and the lowering of customs barriers.

The common commercial policy shall take into account the favourable effect which the abolition of customs duties between Member States may have on the increase in the competitive strength of the undertakings in those States.

Article 111

Repealed by the Treaty on European Union, Title II, Article G,D(27).

Article 112

1. Without prejudice to obligations undertaken by them within the framework of other international organisations, Member States shall, before the end of the transitional period, progressively harmonise the systems whereby they grant aid for exports to third countries, to the extent necessary to ensure that competition between undertakings of the community is not distorted.

On a proposal from the Commission, the Council, shall, acting unanimously until the end of the second stage and by a qualified majority thereafter, issue any directives needed for this purpose.

2. The preceding provisions shall not apply to such drawback of customs duties or charges having equivalent effect nor to such repayment of indirect taxation including turnover taxes, duties and other indirect taxes as is allowed when goods are exported from a Member State to a third country, in so far as such drawback or repayment does not exceed the amount imposed, directly or indirectly, on the products exported.

[Article 113

1. The common commercial policy shall be based on uniform principles particularly in regard to changes in tariff rates, the conclusion of tariff and trade agreements, the achievement of uniformity in measures of liberalisation, export policy and measures to protect trade such as those to be taken in the event of dumping or subsidies.

2. The Commission shall submit proposals to the Council for implementing the common commercial policy.

3. Where agreements with one or more States or international organisations need to be negotiated, the Commission shall make recommendations to the Council, which shall authorise the Commission to open the necessary negotiations.

The Commission shall conduct these negotiations in consultation with a special committee appointed by the Council to assist the Commission in this task and within the framework of such directives as the Council may issue to it.

The relevant provisions of Article 228 shall apply.

4. In exercising the powers conferred upon it by this Article, the Council shall act by a qualified majority.][38]

Article 114

Repealed by the Treaty on European Union, Title II, Article G,D(29).

[Article 115

In order to ensure that the execution of measures of commercial policy taken in accordance with this Treaty by any Member State is not obstructed by deflection of trade, or where differences between such measures lead to economic difficulties in one or more Member States, the Commission shall recommend the methods for the requisite cooperation between Member States. Failing this, the Commission may authorise Member States to take the necessary protective measures, the conditions and details of which it shall determine.

In case of urgency, Member States shall request authorisation to take the necessary measures themselves from the Commission, which shall take a decision as soon as possible; the Member States concerned shall then notify the measures to the other Member States. The Commission may decide at any time that the Member States concerned shall amend or abolish the measures in question.

In the selection of such measures, priority shall be given to those which cause the least disturbance to the functioning of the common market.][39]

Article 116

Repealed by the Treaty on European Union, Title II, Article G,D(31).

[Title VIII

Social policy, education, vocational training and youth][40]

Chapter 1

Social provisions

Article 117

Member States agree upon the need to promote improved working conditions and an improved standard of living for workers, so as to make possible their harmonisation while the improvement is being maintained.

They believe that such a development will ensue not only from the functioning of the common market, which will favour the harmonisation of social systems, but also from the procedures provided for in this

Treaty and from the approximation of provisions laid down by law, regulation or administrative action.

Article 118

Without prejudice to the other provisions of this Treaty and in conformity with its general objectives, the Commission shall have the task of promoting close cooperation between Member States in the social field, particularly in matters relating to:

- employment;
- labour law and working conditions;
- basic and advanced vocational training;
- social security;
- prevention of occupational accidents and diseases;
- occupational hygiene;
- the right of association, and collective bargaining between employers and workers.

To this end, the Commission shall act in close contact with Member States by making studies, delivering opinions and arranging consultations both on problems arising at national level and on those of concern to international organisations.

Before delivering the opinions provided for in this Article, the Commission shall consult the Economic and Social Committee.

Article 118a

1. Member States shall pay particular attention to encouraging improvements, especially in the working environment, as regards the health and safety of workers, and shall set as their objective the harmonisation of conditions in this area, while maintaining the improvements made.

[2. In order to help achieve the objective laid down in the first paragraph, the Council, acting in accordance with the procedure referred to in Article 189c and after consulting the Economic and Social Committee, shall adopt by means of directives, minimum requirements for gradual implementation, having regard to the conditions and technical rules obtaining in each of the Member States.][41]

Such directives shall avoid imposing administrative, financial and legal constraints in a way which would hold back the creation and development of small and medium-sized undertakings.

3. The provisions adopted pursuant to this Article shall not prevent any Member State from maintaining or introducing more stringent measures for the protection of working conditions compatible with this Treaty.

[Article 118*b*

The Commission shall endeavour to develop the dialogue between management and labour at European level which could, if the two sides consider it desirable, lead to relations based on agreement.][42]

Article 119

Each Member State shall during the first stage ensure and subsequently maintain the application of the principle that men and women should receive equal pay for equal work.

For the purpose of this Article, 'pay' means the ordinary basic or minimum wage or salary and any other consideration, whether in cash or in kind, which the worker receives, directly or indirectly, in respect of his employment from his employer.

Equal pay without discrimination based on sex means:

(*a*) that pay for the same work at piece rates shall be calculated on the basis of the same unit of measurement;

(*b*) that pay for work at time rates shall be the same for the same job.

Article 120

Member States shall endeavour to maintain the existing equivalence between paid holiday schemes.

Article 121

The Council may, acting unanimously and after consulting the Economic and Social Committee, assign to the Commission tasks in connection with the implementation of common measures, particularly as regards social security for the migrant workers referred to in Articles 48 to 51.

Article 122

The Commission shall include a separate chapter on social developments within the Community in its annual report to the European Parliament.

The European Parliament may invite the Commission to draw up reports on any particular problems concerning social conditions.

Chapter 2

The European Social Fund

[Article 123

In order to improve employment opportunities for workers in the internal market and to contribute thereby to raising the standard of living, a European Social Fund is hereby established in accordance with the provisions set out below; it shall aim to render the employment of workers easier and to increase their geographical and occupational mobility within the Community, and to facilitate their adaptation to industrial changes and to changes in production systems, in particular through vocational training and retraining.][43]

Article 124

The Fund shall be administered by the Commission.

The Commission shall be assisted in this task by a Committee presided over by a member of the Commission and composed of representatives of Governments, trades unions and employers' organisations.

[Article 125

The Council, acting in accordance with the procedure referred to in Article 189c and after consulting the Economic and Social Committee, shall adopt implementing decisions relating to the European Social Fund.][44]

[Chapter 3

Education, vocational training and youth

Article 126

1. The Community shall contribute to the development of quality education by encouraging cooperation between Member States and, if necessary, by supporting and supplementing their action, while fully respecting the responsibility of the Member States for the content of teaching and the organisation of education systems and their cultural and linguistic diversity.

2. Community action shall be aimed at:

– developing the European dimension in education, particularly through the teaching and dissemination of the languages of the Member States;

- encouraging mobility of students and teachers, *inter alia* by encouraging the academic recognition of diplomas and periods of study;

- promoting cooperation between educational establishments;

- developing exchanges of information and experience on issues common to the education systems of the Member States;

- encouraging the development of youth exchanges and of exchanges of socio-educational instructors;

- encouraging the development of distance education.

3. The Community and the Member States shall foster cooperation with third countries and the competent international organisations in the field of education, in particular the Council of Europe.

4. In order to contribute to the achievement of the objectives referred to in this Article, the Council:

- acting in accordance with the procedure referred to in Article 189b, after consulting the Economic and Social Committee and the Committee of the Regions, shall adopt incentive measures, excluding any harmonisation of the laws and regulations of the Member States;

- acting by a qualified majority on a proposal from the Commission, shall adopt recommendations.

Article 127

1. The Community shall implement a vocational training policy which shall support and supplement the action of the Member States, while fully respecting the responsibility of the Member States for the content and organisation of vocational training.

2. Community action shall aim to:

- facilitate adaptation to industrial changes, in particular through vocational training and retraining;

- improve initial and continuing vocational training in order to facilitate vocational integration and reintegration into the labour market;

- facilitate access to vocational training and encourage mobility of instructors, and trainees and particularly young people;

- stimulate cooperation on training between educational or training establishments and firms;

- develop exchanges of information and experience on issues common to the training systems of the Member States.

3. The Community and the Member States shall foster cooperation with third countries and the competent international organisations in the sphere of vocational training.

4. The Council, acting in accordance with the procedure referred to in Article 189c and after consulting the Economic and Social Committee, shall adopt measures to contribute to the achievement of the objectives referred to in this Article, excluding any harmonisation of the laws and regulations of the Member States.][45]

[Title IX

Culture

Article 128

1. The Community shall contribute to the flowering of the cultures of the Member States, whilst respecting their national and regional diversity and at the same time bringing the common cultural heritage to the fore.

2. Action by the Community shall be aimed at encouraging cooperation between Member States and, if necessary, supporting and supplementing their action in the following areas:

- improvement of the knowledge and dissemination of the culture and history of the European peoples;

- conservation and safeguarding of cultural heritage of European significance;

- non-commercial cultural exchanges;

- artistic and literary creation, including in the audiovisual sector.

3. The Community and the Member States shall foster cooperation with third countries and the competent international organisations in the sphere of culture, in particular the Council of Europe.

4. The Community shall take cultural aspects into account in its action under other provisions of this Treaty.

5. In order to contribute to the achievement of the objectives referred to in this Article, the Council:

- acting in accordance with the procedure referred to in Article 189b and after consulting the Committee of the Regions, shall adopt incentive measures, excluding any harmonisation of the laws and regulations of the Member States. The Council shall act unanimously throughout the procedures referred to in Article 189b;

– acting unanimously on a proposal from the Commission, shall adopt recommendations.][46]

[Title X

Public health

Article 129

1. The Community shall contribute towards ensuring a high level of human health protection by encouraging cooperation between the Member States and, if necessary, lending support to their action.

Community action shall be directed towards the prevention of diseases, in particular the major health scourges, including drug dependence, by promoting research into their causes and their transmission as well as health information and education.

Health protection requirements shall form a constituent part of the Community's other policies.

2. Member States shall, in liaison with the Commission, coordinate among themselves their policies and programmes in the areas referred to in paragraph 1. The Commission may, in close contact with the Member States, take any useful initiative to promote such coordination.

3. The Community and the Member States shall foster cooperation with third countries and the competent international organisations in the sphere of public health.

4. In order to contribute to the achievement of the objectives referred to in this Article, the Council:

– acting in accordance with the procedure referred to in Article 189b, after consulting the Economic and Social Committee and the Committee of the Regions, shall adopt incentive measures, excluding any harmonisation of the laws and regulations of the Member States;

– acting by a qualified majority on a proposal from the Commission, shall adopt recommendations.

Title XI

Consumer protection

Article 129a

1. The Community shall contribute to the attainment of a high level of consumer protection through:

(*a*) measures adopted pursuant to Article 100a in the context of the completion of the internal market;

(*b*) specific action which supports and supplements the policy pursued by the Member States to protect the health, safety and economic interests of consumers and to provide adequate information to consumers.

2. The Council, acting in accordance with the procedure referred to in Article 189b and after consulting the Economic and Social Committee, shall adopt the specific action referred to in paragraph 1(*b*).

3. Action adopted pursuant to paragraph 2 shall not prevent any Member State from maintaining or introducing more stringent protective measures. Such measures must be compatible with this Treaty. The Commission shall be notified of them.

Title XII

Trans-European networks

Article 129b

1. To help achieve the objectives referred to in Articles 7a and 130a and to enable citizens of the Union, economic operators and regional and local communities to derive full benefit from the setting up of an area without internal frontiers, the Community shall contribute to the establishment and development of trans-European networks in the areas of transport, telecommunications and energy infrastructures.

2. Within the framework of a system of open and competitive markets, action by the Community shall aim at promoting the interconnection and interoperability of national networks as well as access to such networks. It shall take account in particular of the need to link island, landlocked and peripheral regions with the central regions of the Community.

Article 129c

1. In order to achieve the objectives referred to in Article 129b, the Community:

– shall establish a series of guidelines covering the objectives, priorities and broad lines of measures envisaged in the sphere of trans-European networks; these guidelines shall identify projects of common interest;

– shall implement any measures that may prove necessary to ensure the interoperability of the networks, in particular in the field of technical standardisation;

– may support the financial efforts made by the Member States for projects of common interest financed by Member States, which are identified in the framework of the guidelines referred to in the first indent, particularly through feasibility studies, loan guarantees or interest-rate subsidies; the Community may also contribute, through the Cohesion Fund to be set up no later than 31 December 1993 pursuant to Article 130d, to the financing of specific projects in Member States in the area of transport infrastructure.

The Community's activities shall take into account the potential economic viability of the projects.

2. Member States shall, in liaison with the Commission, coordinate among themselves the policies pursued at national level which may have a significant impact on the achievement of the objectives referred to in Article 129b. The Commission may, in close cooperation with the Member States, take any useful initiative to promote such coordination.

3. The Community may decide to cooperate with third countries to promote projects of mutual interest and to ensure the interoperability of networks.

Article 129d

The guidelines referred to in Article 129c(1) shall be adopted by the Council, acting in accordance with the procedure referred to in Article 189b and after consulting the Economic and Social Committee and the Committee of the Regions.

Guidelines and projects of common interest which relate to the territory of a Member State shall require the approval of the Member State concerned.

The Council, acting in accordance with the procedure referred to in Article 189c and after consulting the Economic and Social Committee and the Committee of the Regions, shall adopt the other measures provided for in Article 129c(1).

Title XIII

Industry

Article 130

1. The Community and the Member States shall ensure that the conditions necessary for the competitiveness of the Community's industry exist.

For that purpose, in accordance with a system of open and competitive markets, their action shall be aimed at:

– speeding up the adjustment of industry to structural changes;

– encouraging an environment favourable to initiative and to the development of undertakings throughout the Community, particularly small and medium-sized undertakings;

– encouraging an environment favourable to cooperation between undertakings;

– fostering better exploitation of the industrial potential of policies of innovation, research and technological development.

2. The Member States shall consult each other in liaison with the Commission and, where necessary, shall coordinate their action. The Commission may take any useful initiative to promote such coordination.

3. The Community shall contribute to the achievement of the objectives set out in paragraph 1 through the policies and activities it pursues under other provisions of this Treaty. The Council, acting unanimously on a proposal from the Commission, after consulting the European Parliament and the Economic and Social Committee, may decide on specific measures in support of action taken in the Member States to achieve the objectives set out in paragraph 1.

This Title shall not provide a basis for the introduction by the Community of any measure which could lead to a distortion of competition.

Title XIV

Economic and social cohesion

Article 130a

In order to promote its overall harmonious development, the Community shall develop and pursue its actions leading to the strengthening of its economic and social cohesion.

In particular, the Community shall aim at reducing disparities between the levels of development of the various regions and the backwardness of the least favoured regions, including rural areas.

Article 130b

Member States shall conduct their economic policies and shall coordinate them in such a way as, in addition, to attain the objectives set out in Article 130a. The formulation and implementation of the Community's policies and actions and the implementation of the internal market shall take into account the objectives set out in Article 130a and shall contribute to their achievement. The Community shall also support the achievement of these objectives by the action it takes through the structural Funds (European Agricultural Guidance and Guarantee Fund – Guidance Section; European Social Fund; European Regional Development Fund), the European Investment Bank and the other existing financial instruments.

The Commission shall submit a report to the European Parliament, the Council, the Economic and Social Committee and the Committee of the Regions every three years on the progress made towards achieving economic and social cohesion and on the manner in which the various means provided for in this Article have contributed to it. This report shall, if necessary, be accompanied by appropriate proposals.

If specific actions prove necessary outside the Funds and without prejudice to the measures decided upon within the framework of the other Community policies, such actions may be adopted by the Council acting unanimously on a proposal from the Commission and after consulting the European Parliament, the Economic and Social Committee and the Committee of the Regions.

Article 130c

The European Regional Development Fund is intended to help to redress the main regional imbalances in the Community through participation in the development and structural adjustment of regions whose development is lagging behind and in the conversion of declining industrial regions.

Article 130d

Without prejudice to Article 130e, the Council, acting unanimously on a proposal from the Commission and after obtaining the assent of the European Parliament and consulting the Economic and Social Committee and the Committee of the Regions, shall define the tasks, priority objectives and the organisation of the structural Funds, which may involve grouping the Funds. The Council, acting by the same procedure, shall also define the general rules applicable to them and the provisions necessary to ensure their effectiveness and the coordination of the Funds with one another and with the existing financial instruments.

The Council, acting in accordance with the same procedure, shall before 31 December 1993 set up a Cohesion Fund to provide a financial contribution to projects in the fields of environment and trans-European networks in the area of transport infrastructure.

Article 130e

Implementing decisions relating to the European Regional Development Fund shall be taken by the Council, acting in accordance with the procedure referred to in Article 189c and after consulting the Economic and Social Committee and the Committee of the Regions.

With regard to the European Agricultural Guidance and Guarantee Fund – Guidance Section, and the European Social Fund, Articles 43 and 125 respectively shall continue to apply.

Title XV

Research and technological development

Article 130f

1. The Community shall have the objective of strengthening the scientific and technological bases of Community industry and encouraging it to become more competitive at international level, while promoting all the research activities deemed necessary by virtue of other Chapters of this Treaty.

2. For this purpose the Community shall, throughout the Community, encourage undertakings, including small and medium-sized undertakings, research centres and universities in their research and

technological development activities of high quality; it shall support their efforts to cooperate with one another, aiming, notably, at enabling undertakings to exploit the internal market potential to the full, in particular through the opening up of national public contracts, the definition of common standards and the removal of legal and fiscal obstacles to that cooperation.

3. All Community activities under this Treaty in the area of research and technological development, including demonstration projects, shall be decided on and implemented in accordance with the provisions of this Title.

Article 130g

In pursuing these objectives, the Community shall carry out the following activities, complementing the activities carried out in the Member States:

(a) implementation of research, technological development and demonstration programmes, by promoting cooperation with and between undertakings, research centres and universities;

(b) promotion of cooperation in the field of Community research, technological development and demonstration with third countries and international organisations;

(c) dissemination and optimisation of the results of activities in Community research, technological development and demonstration;

(d) stimulation of the training and mobility of researchers in the Community.

Article 130h

1. The Community and the Member States shall coordinate their research and technological development activities so as to ensure that national policies and Community policy are mutually consistent.

2. In close cooperation with the Member States, the Commission may take any useful initiative to promote the coordination referred to in paragraph 1.

Article 130i

1. A multiannual framework programme, setting out all the activities of the Community, shall be adopted by the Council, acting in accordance with the procedure referred to in Article 189b after consulting the

Economic and Social Committee. The Council shall act unanimously throughout the procedures referred to in Article 189b.

The framework programme shall:

- establish the scientific and technological objectives to be achieved by the activities provided for in Article 130g and fix the relevant priorities;

- indicate the broad lines of such activities;

- fix the maximum overall amount and the detailed rules for Community financial participation in the framework programme and the respective shares in each of the activities provided for.

2. The framework programme shall be adapted or supplemented as the situation changes.

3. The framework programme shall be implemented through specific programmes developed within each activity. Each specific programme shall define the detailed rules for implementing it, fix its duration and provide for the means deemed necessary. The sum of the amounts deemed necessary, fixed in the specific programmes, may not exceed the overall maximum amount fixed for the framework programme and each activity.

4. The Council, acting by a qualified majority on a proposal from the Commission and after consulting the European Parliament and the Economic and Social Committee, shall adopt the specific programmes.

Article 130j

For the implementation of the multiannual framework programme the Council shall:

- determine the rules of the participation of undertakings, research centres and universities;

- lay down the rules governing the dissemination of research results.

Article 130k

In implementing the multiannual framework programme, supplementary programmes may be decided on involving the participation of certain Member States only, which shall finance them subject to possible Community participation.

The Council shall adopt the rules applicable to supplementary programmes, particularly as regards the dissemination of knowledge and access by other Member States.

Article 130*l*

In implementing the multiannual framework programme the Community may make provision, in agreement with the Member States concerned, for participation in research and development programmes undertaken by several Member States, including participation in the structures created for the execution of those programmes.

Article 130*m*

In implementing the multiannual framework programme the Community may make provision for cooperation in Community research, technological development and demonstration with third countries or international organisations.

The detailed arrangements for such cooperation may be the subject of agreements between the Community and the third parties concerned, which shall be negotiated and concluded in accordance with Article 228.

Article 130*n*

The Community may set up joint undertakings or any other structure necessary for the efficient execution of Community research, technological development and demonstration programmes.

Article 130*o*

The Council, acting unanimously on a proposal from the Commission and after consulting the European Parliament and the Economic and Social Committee, shall adopt the provisions referred to in Article 130n.

The Council, acting in accordance with the procedure referred to in Article 189c and after consulting the Economic and Social Committee, shall adopt the provisions referred to in Articles 130j to l. Adoption of the supplementary programmes shall require the agreement of the Member States concerned.

Article 130*p*

At the beginning of each year the Commission shall send a report to the European Parliament and the Council. The report shall include information on research and technological development activities and the dissemination of results during the previous year, and the work programme for the current year.

Title XVI

Environment

Article 130r

1. Community policy on the environment shall contribute to pursuit of the following objectives:

−   preserving, protecting and improving the quality of the environment;

−   protecting human health;

−   prudent and rational utilisation of natural resources;

−   promoting measures at international level to deal with regional or worldwide environmental problems.

2. Community policy on the environment shall aim at a high level of protection taking into account the diversity of situations in the various regions of the Community. It shall be based on the precautionary principle and on the principles that preventive action should be taken, that environmental damage should as a priority be rectified at source and that the polluter should pay. Environmental protection requirements must be integrated into the definition and implementation of other Community policies.

In this context, harmonisation measures answering these requirements shall include, where appropriate, a safeguard clause allowing Member States to take provisional measures, for non-economic environmental reasons, subject to a Community inspection procedure.

3. In preparing its policy on the environment, the Community shall take account of:

−   available scientific and technical data;

−   environmental conditions in the various regions of the Community;

−   the potential benefits and costs of action or lack of action;

−   the economic and social development of the Community as a whole and the balanced development of its regions.

4. Within their respective spheres of competence, the Community and the Member States shall cooperate with third countries and with the competent international organisations. The arrangements for Community cooperation may be the subject of agreements between the Community and the third parties concerned, which shall be negotiated and concluded in accordance with Article 228.

The previous subparagraph shall be without prejudice to Member States' competence to negotiate in international bodies and to conclude international agreements.

Article 130s

1. The Council, acting in accordance with the procedure referred to in Article 189c and after consulting the Economic and Social Committee, shall decide what action is to be taken by the Community in order to achieve the objectives referred to in Article 130r.

2. By way of derogation from the decision-making procedure provided for in paragraph 1 and without prejudice to Article 100a, the Council, acting unanimously on a proposal from the Commission and after consulting the European Parliament and the Economic and Social Committee, shall adopt:

– provisions primarily of a fiscal nature;

– measures concerning town and country planning, land use with the exception of waste management and measures of a general nature, and management of water resources;

– measures significantly affecting a Member State's choice between different energy sources and the general structure of its energy supply.

The Council may, under the conditions laid down in the preceding subparagraph, define those matters referred to in this paragraph on which decisions are to be taken by a qualified majority.

3. In other areas, general action programmes setting out priority objectives to be attained shall be adopted by the Council, acting in accordance with the procedure referred to in Article 189b and after consulting the Economic and Social Committee.

The Council, acting under the terms of paragraph 1 or paragraph 2 according to the case, shall adopt the measures necessary for the implementation of these programmes.

4. Without prejudice to certain measures of a Community nature, the Member States shall finance and implement the environment policy.

5. Without prejudice to the principle that the polluter should pay, if a measure based on the provisions of paragraph 1 involves costs deemed disproportionate for the public authorities of a Member State, the Council shall, in the act adopting that measure, lay down appropriate provisions in the form of:

– temporary derogations, and/or

- financial support from the Cohesion Fund to be set up no later than 31 December 1993 pursuant to Article 130d.

Article 130t

The protective measures adopted pursuant to Article 130s shall not prevent any Member State from maintaining or introducing more stringent protective measures. Such measures must be compatible with this Treaty. They shall be notified to the Commission.

Title XVII

Development cooperation

Article 130u

1. Community policy in the sphere of development cooperation, which shall be complementary to the policies pursued by the Member States, shall foster:

- the sustainable economic and social development of the developing countries and more particularly the most disadvantaged among them;
- the smooth and gradual integration of the developing countries into the world economy;
- the campaign against poverty in the developing countries.

2. Community policy in this area shall contribute to the general objective of developing and consolidating democracy and the rule of law, and to that of respecting human rights and fundamental freedoms.

3. The Community and the Member States shall comply with the commitments and take account of the objectives they have approved in the context of the United Nations and other competent international organisations.

Article 130v

The Community shall take account of the objectives referred to in Article 130u in the policies that it implements which are likely to affect developing countries.

Article 130w

1. Without prejudice to the other provisions of this Treaty the Council, acting in accordance with the procedure referred to in Article 189c, shall adopt the measures necessary to further the objectives referred to in

Article 130u. Such measures may take the form of multiannual programmes.

2. The European Investment Bank shall contribute, under the terms laid down in its Statute, to the implementation of the measures referred to in paragraph 1.

3. The provisions of this Article shall not affect cooperation with the African, Caribbean and Pacific countries in the framework of the ACP-EEC Convention.

Article 130x

1. The Community and the Member States shall coordinate their policies on development cooperation and shall consult each other on their aid programmes, including in international organisations and during international conferences. They may undertake joint action. Member States shall contribute if necessary to the implementation of Community aid programmes.

2. The Commission may take any useful initiative to promote the coordination referred to in paragraph 1.

Article 130y

Within their respective spheres of competence, the Community and the Member States shall cooperate with third countries and with the competent international organisations. The arrangements for Community cooperation may be the subject of agreements between the Community and the third parties concerned, which shall be negotiated and concluded in accordance with Article 228.

The previous paragraph shall be without prejudice to Member States' competence to negotiate in international bodies and to conclude international agreements.][47]

Part Four

Association of the overseas countries and territories

Article 131

The Member States agree to associate with the Community the non-European countries and territories which have special relations with Belgium, Denmark, France, Italy, the Netherlands and the United Kingdom. These countries and territories (hereinafter called the 'countries and territories') are listed in Annex IV to this Treaty.

The purpose of association shall be to promote the economic and social development of the countries and territories and to establish close economic relations between them and the Community as a whole.

In accordance with the principles set out in the Preamble to this Treaty, association shall serve primarily to further the interests and prosperity of the inhabitants of these countries and territories in order to lead them to the economic, social and cultural development to which they aspire.

Article 132

Association shall have the following objectives:

1. Member States shall apply to their trade with the countries and territories the same treatment as they accord each other pursuant to this Treaty.

2. Each country or territory shall apply to its trade with Member States and with the other countries and territories the same treatment as that which it applies to the European State with which it has special relations.

3. The Member States shall contribute to the investments required for the progressive development of these countries and territories.

4. For investments financed by the Community, participation in tenders and supplies shall be open on equal terms to all natural and legal persons who are nationals of a Member State or of one of the countries and territories.

5. In relations between Member States and the countries and territories the right of establishment of nationals and companies or firms shall be regulated in accordance with the provisions and procedures laid down in the Chapter relating to the right of establishment and on a non-discriminatory basis, subject to any special provisions laid down pursuant to Article 136.

Article 133

1. Customs duties on imports into the Member States of goods originating in the countries and territories shall be completey abolished in conformity with the progressive abolition of customs duties between Member States in accordance with the provisions of this Treaty.

2. Customs duties on imports into each country or territory from Member States or from the other countries or territories shall be progressively abolished in accordance with the provisions of Articles 12, 13, 14, 15 and 17.

3. The countries and territories may, however, levy customs duties which meet the needs of their development and industrialisation or produce revenue for their budgets.

The duties referred to in the preceding subparagraph shall nevertheless be progressively reduced to the level of those imposed on imports of products from the Member State with which each country or territory has special relations. The percentages and the timetable of the reductions provided for under this Treaty shall apply to the difference between the duty imposed on a product coming from the Member State which has special relations with the country or territory concerned and the duty imposed on the same product coming from within the Community on entry into the importing country or territory.

4. Paragraph 2 shall not apply to countries and territories which, by reason of the particular international obligations by which they are bound, already apply a non-discriminatory customs tariff when this Treaty enters into force.

5. The introduction of or any change in customs duties imposed on goods imported into the countries and territories shall not, either in law or in fact, give rise to any direct or indirect discrimination between imports from the various Member States.

Article 134

If the level of the duties applicable to goods from a third country on entry into a country or territory is liable, when the provisions of Article 133(1) have been applied, to cause deflections of trade to the detriment of any Member State, the latter may request the Commission to propose to the other Member States the measures needed to remedy the situation.

Article 135

Subject to the provisions relating to public health, public security or public policy, freedom of movement within Member States for workers from the countries and territories, and within the countries and territories for workers from Member States, shall be governed by agreements to be concluded subsequently with the unanimous approval of Member States.

Article 136

For an initial period of five years after the entry into force of this Treaty, the details of and procedure for the association of the countries and territories with the Community shall be determined by an Implementing Convention annexed to this Treaty.

Before the Convention referred to in the preceding paragraph expires, the Council shall, acting unanimously, lay down provisions for a further period, on the basis of the experience acquired and of the principles set out in this Treaty.

Article 136a

The provisions of Articles 131 to 136 shall apply to Greenland, subject to the specific provisions for Greenland set out in the Protocol on special arrangements for Greenland, annexed to this Treaty.

Part Five

Institutions of the Community

Title I

Provisions governing the institutions

Chapter 1

The institutions

Section 1

The European Parliament

[Article 137

The European Parliament, which shall consist of representatives of the peoples of the States brought together in the Community, shall exercise the powers conferred upon it by this Treaty.][48]

Article 138

(*Paragraphs 1 and 2 lapsed on 17 July 1979 in accordance with Article 14 of the Act concerning the election of the representatives of the European Parliament*)

[*See Article 1 of that Act which reads as follows*:

1. The representatives in the European Parliament of the peoples of the States brought together in the Community shall be elected by direct universal suffrage.]

[Article 2 of that Act is replaced by Decision 93/691/Euratom/ECSC/EEC]

[*Article 2*

The number of representatives elected in each Member State shall be as follows:

Belgium	25
Denmark	16
Germany	99
Greece	25
Spain	64
France	87
Ireland	15
Italy	87
Luxembourg	6
Netherlands	31
Portugal	25
United Kingdom	87][49]

[3. The European Parliament shall draw up proposals for elections by direct universal suffrage in accordance with a uniform procedure in all Member States.

The Council shall, acting unanimously after obtaining the assent of the European Parliament, which shall act by a majority of its component members, lay down the appropriate provisions, which it shall recommend to the Member States for adoption in accordance with their respective constitutional requirements.][50]

[*Article 138a*

Political parties at European level are important as a factor for integration within the Union. They contribute to forming a European awareness and to expressing the political will of the citizens of the Union.

Article 138b

In so far as provided in this Treaty, the European Parliament shall participate in the process leading up to the adoption of Community acts by exercising its powers under the procedures laid down in Articles 189b and 189c and by giving its assent or delivering advisory opinions.

The European Parliament may, acting by a majority of its members, request the Commission to submit any appropriate proposal on matters on which it considers that a Community act is required for the purpose of implementing this Treaty.

Article 138c

In the course of its duties, the European Parliament may, at the request of a quarter of its members, set up a temporary Committee of Inquiry to investigate, without prejudice to the powers conferred by this Treaty on other institutions or bodies, alleged contraventions or maladministration in the implementation of Community law, except where the alleged facts are being examined before a court and while the case is still subject to legal proceedings.

The temporary Committee of Inquiry shall cease to exist on the submission of its report.

The detailed provisions governing the exercise of the right of inquiry shall be determined by common accord of the European Parliament, the Council and the Commission.

Article 138d

Any citizen of the Union, and any natural or legal person residing or having his registered office in a Member State, shall have the right to address, individually or in association with other citizens or persons, a petition to the European Parliament on a matter which comes within the Community's fields of activity and which affects him directly.

Article 138e

1. The European Parliament shall appoint an Ombudsman empowered to receive complaints from any citizen of the Union or any natural or legal person residing or having his registered office in a Member State concerning instances of maladministration in the activities of the community institutions or bodies, with the exception of the Court of Justice and the Court of First Instance acting in their judicial role.

In accordance with his duties, the Ombudsman shall conduct inquiries for which he finds grounds, either on his own initiative or on the basis of complaints submitted to him direct or through a member of the European Parliament, except where the alleged facts are or have been the subject of legal proceedings. Where the Ombudsman establishes an instance of maladministration, he shall refer the matter to the institution concerned, which shall have a period of three months in which to inform him of its views. The Ombudsman shall then forward a report to the European Parliament and the institution concerned. The person lodging the complaint shall be informed of the outcome of such inquiries.

The Ombudsman shall submit an annual report to the European Parliament on the outcome of his inquiries.

2. The Ombudsman shall be appointed after each election of the European Parliament for the duration of its term of office. The Ombudsman shall be eligible for reappointment.

The Ombudsman may be dismissed by the Court of Justice at the request of the European Parliament if he no longer fulfils the conditions required for the performance of his duties or if he is guilty of serious misconduct.

3. The Ombudsman shall be completely independent in the performance of his duties. In the performance of those duties he shall neither seek nor take instructions from any body. The Ombudsman may not, during his term of office, engage in any other occupation, whether gainful or not.

4. The European Parliament shall, after seeking an opinion from the Commission and with the approval of the Council acting by a qualified majority, lay down the regulations and general conditions governing the performance of the Ombudsman's duties.][51]

Article 139

The European Parliament shall hold an annual session. It shall meet, without requiring to be convened, on the second Tuesday in March.[52] [53]

The European Parliament may meet in extraordinary session at the request of a majority of its members or at the request of the Council or of the Commission.

Article 140

The European Parliament shall elect its President and its officers from among its members.

Members of the Commission may attend all meetings and shall, at their request, be heard on behalf of the Commission.

The Commission shall reply orally or in writing to questions put to it by the European Parliament or by its members.

The Council shall be heard by the European Parliament in accordance with the conditions laid down by the Council in its rules of procedure.

Article 141

Save as otherwise provided in this Treaty, the European Parliament shall act by an absolute majority of the votes cast.

The rules of procedure shall determine the quorum.

Article 142

The European Parliament shall adopt its rules of procedure, acting by a majority of its members.

The proceedings of the European Parliament shall be published in the manner laid down in its rules of procedure.

Article 143

The European Parliament shall discuss in open session the annual general report submitted to it by the Commission.

Article 144

If a motion of censure on the activities of the Commission is tabled before it, the European Parliament shall not vote thereon until at least three days after the motion has been tabled and only by open vote.

If the motion of censure is carried by a two-thirds majority of the votes cast, representing a majority of the members of the European Parliament, the members of the Commission shall resign as a body. They shall continue to deal with current business until they are replaced in accordance with Article 158. [In this case, the term of office of the members of the Commission appointed to replace them shall expire on the date on which the term of office of the members of the Commission obliged to resign as a body would have expired.][54]

Section 2

The Council

Article 145

To ensure that the objectives set out in this Treaty are attained, the Council shall, in accordance with the provisions of this Treaty:

— ensure coordination of the general economic policies of the Member States;

— have power to take decisions;

— confer on the Commission, in the acts which the Council adopts, powers for the implementation of the rules which the Council lays down. The Council may impose certain requirements in respect of the exercise of these powers. The Council may also reserve the right, in specific cases, to exercise directly implementing powers itself. The procedures referred to above must be consonant with principles and rules to be laid down in advance by the Council, acting unanimously on a proposal from the Commission and after obtaining the Opinion of the European Parliament.

[*Article* 146

The Council shall consist of a representative of each Member State at ministerial level, authorised to commit the government of that Member State.

The office of President shall be held in turn by each Member State in the Council for a term of six months, in the following order of Member States:

- for a first cycle of six years: Belgium, Denmark, Germany, Greece, Spain, France, Ireland, Italy, Luxembourg, Netherlands, Portugal, United Kingdom;

- for the following cycle of six years: Denmark, Belgium, Greece, Germany, France, Spain, Italy, Ireland, Netherlands, Luxembourg, United Kingdom, Portugal.][55]

[*Article* 147

The Council shall meet when convened by its President on his own initiative or at the request of one of its members or of the Commission.][56]

Article 148

1. Save as otherwise provided in this Treaty, the Council shall act by a majority of its members.

2. Where the Council is required to act by a qualified majority, the votes of its members shall be weighted as follows:

Belgium	5
Denmark	3
Germany	10
Greece	5
Spain	8
France	10
Ireland	3
Italy	10
Luxembourg	2
Netherlands	5
Portugal	5
United Kingdom	10

For their adoption, acts of the Council shall require at least:

- fifty-four votes in favour where this Treaty requires them to be adopted on a proposal from the Commission,

- fifty-four votes in favour, cast by at least eight members, in other cases.

3. Abstentions by members present in person or represented shall not prevent the adoption by the Council of acts which require unanimity.

Article 149

Repealed by the Treaty on European Union, Title II, Article G,E(45).

Article 150

Where a vote is taken, any member of the Council may also act on behalf of not more than one other member.

[Article 151]

1. A committee consisting of the Permanent Representatives of the Member States shall be responsible for preparing the work of the Council and for carrying out the tasks assigned to it by the Council.

2. The Council shall be assisted by a General Secretariat, under the direction of a Secretary-General. The Secretary-General shall be appointed by the Council acting unanimously.

The Council shall decide on the organisation of the General Secretariat.

3. The Council shall adopt its rules of procedure.][57]

Article 152

The Council may request the Commission to undertake any studies the Council considers desirable for the attainment of the common objectives, and to submit to it any appropriate proposals.

Article 153

The Council shall after receiving an opinion from the Commission, determine the rules governing the committees provided for in this Treaty.

[Article 154

The Council shall, acting by a qualified majority, determine the salaries, allowances and pensions of the President and members of the Commission, and of the President, Judges, Advocates-General and

Registrar of the Court of Justice. It shall also, again by a qualified majority, determine any payment to be made instead of remuneration.][58]

Section 3

The Commission

Article 155

In order to ensure the proper functioning and development of the common market, the Commission shall:

- ensure that the provisions of this Treaty and the measures taken by the institutions pursuant thereto are applied;

- formulate recommendations or deliver opinions on matters dealt with in this Treaty, if it expressly so provides or if the Commission considers it necessary;

- have its own power of decision and participate in the shaping of measures taken by the Council and by the European Parliament in the manner provided for in this Treaty;

- exercise the powers conferred on it by the Council for the implementation of the rules laid down by the latter.

[Article 156

The Commission shall publish annually, not later than one month before the opening of the session of the European Parliament, a general report on the activities of the Community.

Article 157

1. The Commission shall consist of 17 members, who shall be chosen on the grounds of their general competence and whose independence is beyond doubt.

The number of members of the Commission may be altered by the Council acting unanimously.

Only nationals of Member States may be members of the Commission.

The Commission must include at least one national of each of the Member States, but may not include more than two members having the nationality of the same State.

2. The members of the Commission shall, in the general interest of the Community, be completely independent in the performance of their duties.

In the performance of these duties, they shall neither seek nor take instructions from any government or from any other body. They shall refrain from any action incompatible with their duties. Each Member State undertakes to respect this principle and not to seek to influence the members of the Commission in the performance of their tasks.

The members of the Commission may not, during their term of office, engage in any other occupation, whether gainful or not. When entering upon their duties they shall give a solemn undertaking that, both during and after their term of office, they will respect the obligations arising therefrom and in particular their duty to behave with integrity and discretion as regards the acceptance, after they have ceased to hold office, of certain appointments or benefits. In the event of any breach of these obligations, the Court of Justice may, on application by the Council or the Commission, rule that the member concerned be, according to the circumstances, either compulsorily retired in accordance with Article 160 or deprived of his right to a pension or other benefits in its stead.

Article 158

1. The members of the Commission shall be appointed, in accordance with the procedure referred to in paragraph 2, for a period of five years, subject, if need be, to Article 144.

Their term of office shall be renewable.

2. The governments of the Member States shall nominate by common accord after consulting the European Parliament, the person they intend to appoint as President of the Commission.

The governments of the Member States shall, in consultation with the nominee for President, nominate the other persons whom they intend to appoint as members of the Commission.

The President and the other members of the Commission thus nominated shall be subject as a body to a vote of approval by the European Parliament. After approval by the European Parliament, the President and the other members of the Commission shall be appointed by common accord of the governments of the Member States.

3. Paragraphs 1 and 2 shall be applied for the first time to the President and the other members of the Commission whose term of office begins on 7 January 1995.

The President and the other members of the Commission whose term of office begins on 7 January 1993 shall be appointed by common accord of the governments of the Member States. Their term of office shall expire on 6 January 1995.

Article 159

Apart from normal replacement, or death, the duties of a member of the Commission shall end when he resigns or is compulsorily retired.

The vacancy thus caused shall be filled for the remainder of the member's term of office by a new member appointed by common accord of the governments of the Member States. The Council may, acting unanimously, decide that such a vacancy need not be filled.

In the event of resignation, compulsory retirement or death, the President shall be replaced for the remainder of his term of office. The procedure laid down in Article 158(2) shall be applicable for the replacement of the President.

Save in the case of compulsory retirement under Article 160, members of the Commission shall remain in office until they have been replaced.

Article 160

If any member of the Commission no longer fulfils the conditions required for the performance of his duties or if he has been guilty of serious misconduct, the Court of Justice may, on application by the Council or the Commission, compulsorily retire him.

Article 161

The Commission may appoint a Vice-President or two Vice-Presidents from among its members.

Article 162

1. The Council and the Commission shall consult each other and shall settle by common accord their methods of cooperation.

2. The Commission shall adopt its rules of procedure so as to ensure that both it and its departments operate in accordance with the provisions of this Treaty. It shall ensure that these rules are published.

Article 163

The Commission shall act by a majority of the number of members provided for in Article 157.

A meeting of the Commission shall be valid only if the number of members laid down in its rules of procedure is present.][59]

Section 4

The Court of Justice

Article 164

The Court of Justice shall ensure that in the interpretation and application of this Treaty the law is observed.

[Article 165

The Court of Justice shall consist of 13 Judges.

The Court of Justice shall sit in plenary session. It may, however, form chambers, each consisting of three or five Judges, either to undertake certain preparatory inquiries or to adjudicate on particular categories of cases in accordance with rules laid down for these purposes.

The Court of Justice shall sit in plenary session when a Member State or a Community institution that is a party to the proceedings so requests.

Should the Court of Justice so request, the Council may, acting unanimously, increase the number of Judges and make the necessary adjustments to the second and third paragraphs of this Article and to the second paragraph of Article 167.][60]

Article 166

The Court of Justice shall be assisted by six Advocates-General.

It shall be the duty of the Advocates-General, acting with complete impartiality and independence, to make, in open court, reasoned submissions on cases brought before the Court of Justice, in order to assist the Court in the performance of the task assigned to it in Article 164.

Should the Court of Justice so request, the Council may, acting unanimously, increase the number of Advocates-General and make the necessary adjustments to the third paragraph of Article 167.

Article 167

The Judges and Advocates-General shall be chosen from persons whose independence is beyond doubt and who possess the qualifications required for appointment to the highest judicial offices in their respective countries or who are jurisconsults of recognised competence; they shall be appointed by common accord of the Governments of the Member States for a term of six years.

Every three years there shall be a partial replacement of the Judges. Seven and six Judges shall be replaced alternately.

Every three years there shall be a partial replacement of the Advocates-General. Three Advocates-General shall be replaced on each occasion.

Retiring Judges and Advocates-General shall be eligible for reappointment.

The Judges shall elect the President of the Court of Justice from among their number for a term of three years. He may be re-elected.

Article 168

The Court of Justice shall appoint its Registrar and lay down the rules governing his service.

[Article 168a

1. A Court of First Instance shall be attached to the Court of Justice with jurisdiction to hear and determine at first instance, subject to a right of appeal to the Court of Justice on points of law only and in accordance with the conditions laid down by the Statute, certain classes of action or proceeding defined in accordance with the conditions laid down in paragraph 2. The Court of First Instance shall not be competent to hear and determine questions referred for a preliminary ruling under Article 177.

2. At the request of the Court of Justice and after consulting the European Parliament and the Commission, the Council, acting unanimously, shall determine the classes of action or proceeding referred to in paragraph 1 and the composition of the Court of First Instance and shall adopt the necessary adjustments and additional provisions to the Statute of the Court of Justice. Unless the Council decides otherwise, the provisions of this Treaty relating to the Court of Justice, in particular the provisions of the Protocol on the Statute of the Court of Justice, shall apply to the Court of First Instance.

3. The members of the Court of First Instance shall be chosen from persons whose independence is beyond doubt and who possess the ability required for appointment to judicial office; they shall be appointed by common accord of the governments of the Member States for a term of six years. The membership shall be partially renewed every three years. Retiring members shall be eligible for reappointment.

4. The Court of First Instance shall establish its rules of procedure in agreement with the Court of Justice. Those rules shall require the unanimous approval of the Council.][61]

Article 169

If the Commission considers that a Member State has failed to fulfil an obligation under this Treaty, it shall deliver a reasoned opinion on the matter after giving the State concerned the opportunity to submit its observations.

If the State concerned does not comply with the opinion within the period laid down by the Commission, the latter may bring the matter before the Court of Justice.

Article 170

A Member State which considers that another Member State has failed to fulfil an obligation under this Treaty may bring the matter before the Court of Justice.

Before a Member State brings an action against another Member State for an alleged infringement of an obligation under this Treaty, it shall bring the matter before the Commission.

The Commission shall deliver a reasoned opinion after each of the States concerned has been given the opportunity to submit its own case and its observations on the other party's case both orally and in writing.

If the Commission has not delivered an opinion within three months of the date on which the matter was brought before it, the absence of such opinion shall not prevent the matter from being brought before the Court of Justice.

[Article 171

1. If the Court of Justice finds that a Member State has failed to fulfil an obligation under this Treaty, the State shall be required to take the necessary measures to comply with the judgment of the Court of Justice.

2. If the Commission considers that the Member State concerned has not taken such measures it shall, after giving that State the opportunity to submit its observations, issue a reasoned opinion specifying the points on which the Member State concerned has not complied with the judgment of the Court of Justice.

If the Member State concerned fails to take the necessary measures to comply with the Court's judgment within the time-limit laid down by the Commission, the latter may bring the case before the Court of Justice. In so doing it shall specify the amount of the lump sum or penalty payment to be paid by the Member State concerned which it considers appropriate in the circumstances.

If the Court of Justice finds that the Member State concerned has not complied with its judgment it may impose a lump sum or penalty payment on it.

This procedure shall be without prejudice to Article 170.][62]

[Article 172

Regulations adopted jointly by the European Parliament and the Council, and by the Council, pursuant to the provisions of this Treaty, may give the Court of Justice unlimited jurisdiction with regard to the penalties provided for in such regulations.][63]

[Article 173

The Court of Justice shall review the legality of acts adopted jointly by the European Parliament and the Council, of acts of the Council, of the Commission and of the ECB, other than recommendations and opinions, and of acts of the European Parliament intended to produce legal effects *vis-à-vis* third parties.

It shall for this purpose have jurisdiction in actions brought by a Member State, the Council or the Commission on grounds of lack of competence, infringement of an essential procedural requirement, infringement of this Treaty or of any rule of law relating to its application, or misuse of powers.

The Court shall have jurisdiction under the same conditions in actions brought by the European Parliament and by the ECB for the purpose of protecting their prerogatives.

Any natural or legal person may, under the same conditions, institute proceedings against a decision addressed to that person or against a decision which, although in the form of a regulation or a decision addressed to another person, is of direct and individual concern to the former.

The proceedings provided for in this Article shall be instituted within two months of the publication of the measure, or of its notification to the plaintiff, or, in the absence thereof, of the day on which it came to the knowledge of the latter, as the case may be.][64]

Article 174

If the action is well founded, the Court of Justice shall declare the act concerned to be void.

In the case of a regulation, however, the Court of Justice shall, if it considers this necessary, state which of the effects of the regulation which it has declared void shall be considered as definitive.

[Article 175

Should the European Parliament, the Council or the Commission, in infringement of this Treaty, fail to act, the Member States and the other institutions of the Community may bring an action before the Court of Justice to have the infringement established.

The action shall be admissible only if the institution concerned has first been called upon to act. If, within two months of being so called upon, the institution concerned has not defined its position, the action may be brought within a further period of two months.

Any natural or legal person may, under the conditions laid down in the preceding paragraphs, complain to the Court of Justice that an institution of the Community has failed to address to that person any act other than a recommendation or an opinion.

The Court of Justice shall have jurisdiction, under the same conditions, in actions or proceedings brought by the ECB in the areas falling within the latter's field of competence and in actions or proceedings brought against the latter.][65]

[Article 176

The institution or institutions whose act has been declared void or whose failure to act has been declared contrary to this Treaty shall be required to take the necessary measures to comply with the judgment of the Court of Justice.

This obligation shall not affect any obligation which may result from the application of the second paragraph of Article 215.

This Article shall also apply to the ECB.][66]

[Article 177

The Court of Justice shall have jurisdiction to give preliminary rulings concerning:

(a) the interpretation of this Treaty;

(b) the validity and interpretation of acts of the institutions of the Community and of the ECB;

(c) the interpretation of the statutes of bodies established by an act of the Council, where those statutes so provide.

Where such a question is raised before any court or tribunal of a Member

State, that court or tribunal may, if it considers that a decision on the question is necessary to enable it to give judgment, request the Court of Justice to give a ruling thereon.

Where any such question is raised in a case pending before a court or tribunal of a Member State against whose decisions there is no judicial remedy under national law, that court or tribunal shall bring the matter before the Court of Justice.][67]

Article 178

The Court of Justice shall have jurisdiction in disputes relating to compensation for damage provided for in the second paragraph of Article 215.

Article 179

The Court of Justice shall have jurisdiction in any dispute between the Community and its servants within the limits and under the conditions laid down in the Staff Regulations or the Conditions of Employment.

[Article 180

The Court of Justice shall, within the limits hereinafter laid down, have jurisdiction in disputes concerning:

(a) the fulfilment by Member States of obligations under the Statute of the European Investment Bank. In this connection, the Board of Directors of the Bank shall enjoy the powers conferred upon the Commission by Article 169;

(b) measures adopted by the Board of Governors of the European Investment Bank. In this connection, any Member State, the Commission or the Board of Directors of the Bank may institute proceedings under the conditions laid down in Article 173;

(c) measures adopted by the Board of Directors of the European Investment Bank. Proceedings against such measures may be instituted only by Member States or by the Commission, under the conditions laid down in Article 173, and solely on the grounds of non-compliance with the procedure provided for in Article 21(2), (5), (6) and (7) of the Statute of the Bank;

(d) the fulfilment by national central banks of obligations under this Treaty and the Statute of the ESCB. In this connection the powers of the Council of the ECB in respect of national central banks shall be the same as those conferred upon the Commission in respect of Member States by Article 169. If the Court of Justice finds that a national central bank has failed to fulfil an obligation under this Treaty, that bank shall be required to take the necessary measures to comply with the judgment of the Court of Justice.][68]

Article 181

The Court of Justice shall have jurisdiction to give judgment pursuant to any arbitration clause contained in a contract concluded by or on behalf of the Community, whether that contract be governed by public or private law.

Article 182

The Court of Justice shall have jurisdiction in any dispute between Member States which relates to the subject matter of this Treaty if the dispute is submitted to it under a special agreement between the parties.

Article 183

Save where jurisdiction is conferred on the Court of Justice by this Treaty, disputes to which the Community is a party shall not on that ground be excluded from the jurisdiction of the courts or tribunals of the Member States.

[Article 184

Notwithstanding the expiry of the period laid down in the fifth paragraph of Article 173, any party may, in proceedings in which a regulation adopted jointly by the European Parliament and the Council, or a regulation of the Council, of the Commission, or of the ECB is at issue, plead the grounds specified in the second paragraph of Article 173 in order to invoke before the Court of Justice the inapplicability of that regulation.][69]

Article 185

Actions brought before the Court of Justice shall not have suspensory effect. The Court of Justice may, however, if it considers that circumstances so require, order that application of the contested act be suspended.

Article 186

The Court of Justice may in any cases before it prescribe any necessary interim measures.

Article 187

The judgments of the Court of Justice shall be enforceable under the conditions laid down in Article 192.

Article 188

The Statute of the Court of Justice is laid down in a separate Protocol.

The Council may, acting unanimously at the request of the Court of Justice and after consulting the Commission and the European Parliament, amend the provisions of Title III of the Statute.

The Court of Justice shall adopt its rules of procedure. These shall require the unanimous approval of the Council.

[Section 5

The Court of Auditors

Article 188a

The Court of Auditors shall carry out the audit.

Article 188b

1. The Court of Auditors shall consist of 12 members.

2. The members of the Court of Auditors shall be chosen from among persons who belong or have belonged in their respective countries to external audit bodies or who are especially qualified for this office. Their independence must be beyond doubt.

3. The members of the Court of Auditors shall be appointed for a term of six years by the Council, acting unanimously after consulting the European Parliament.

However, when the first appointments are made, four members of the Court of Auditors, chosen by lot, shall be appointed for a term of office of four years only.

The members of the Court of Auditors shall be eligible for reappointment.

They shall elect the President of the Court of Auditors from among their number for a term of three years. The President may be re-elected.

4. The members of the Court of Auditors shall, in the general interest of the Community, be completely independent in the performance of their duties.

In the performance of these duties, they shall neither seek nor take instructions from any government or from any other body. They shall refrain from any action incompatible with their duties.

5. The members of the Court of Auditors may not, during their term of office engage in any other occupation, whether gainful or not. When entering upon their duties they shall give a solemn undertaking that, both during and after their term of office, they will respect the obligations arising therefrom and in particular their duty to behave with integrity and discretion as regards the acceptance, after they have ceased to hold office, of certain appointments or benefits.

6. Apart from normal replacement, or death, the duties of a member of the Court of Auditors shall end when he resigns, or is compulsorily retired by a ruling of the Court of Justice pursuant to paragraph 7.

The vacancy thus caused shall be filled for the remainder of the member's term of office.

Save in the case of compulsory retirement, members of the Court of Auditors shall remain in office until they have been replaced.

7. A member of the Court of Auditors may be deprived of his office or of his right to a pension or other benefits in its stead only if the Court of Justice, at the request of the Court of Auditors, finds that he no longer fulfils the requisite conditions or meets the obligations arising from his office.

8. The Council, acting by a qualified majority, shall determine the conditions of employment of the President and the members of the Court of Auditors and in particular their salaries, allowances and pensions. It shall also, by the same majority, determine any payment to be made instead of remuneration.

9. The provisions of the Protocol on the Privileges and Immunities of the European Communities applicable to the Judges of the Court of Justice shall also apply to the members of the Court of Auditors.

Article 188c

1. The Court of Auditors shall examine the accounts of all revenue and expenditure of the Community. It shall also examine the accounts of all revenue and expenditure of all bodies set up by the Community in so far as the relevant constituent instrument does not preclude such examination.

The Court of Auditors shall provide the European Parliament and the Council with a statement of assurance as to the reliability of the accounts and the legality and regularity of the underlying transactions.

2. The Court of Auditors shall examine whether all revenue has been received and all expenditure incurred in a lawful and regular manner and whether the financial management has been sound.

The audit of revenue shall be carried out on the basis both of the amounts established as due and the amounts actually paid to the Community.

The audit of expenditure shall be carried out on the basis both of commitments undertaken and payments made.

These audits may be carried out before the closure of accounts for the financial year in question.

3. The audit shall be based on records and, if necessary, performed on the spot in the other institutions of the Community and in the Member States. In the Member States the audit shall be carried out in liaison with the national audit bodies or, if these do not have the necessary powers, with the competent national departments. These bodies or departments shall inform the Court of Auditors whether they intend to take part in the audit.

The other institutions of the Community and the national audit bodies or, if these do not have the necessary powers, the competent national departments, shall forward to the Court of Auditors, at its request, any document or information necessary to carry out its task.

4. The Court of Auditors shall draw up an annual report after the close of each financial year. It shall be forwarded to the other institutions of the Community and shall be published, together with the replies of these institutions to the observations of the Court of Auditors, in the *Official Journal of the European Communities*.

The Court of Auditors may also, at any time, submit observations, particularly in the form of special reports, on specific questions and deliver opinions at the request of one of the other institutions of the Community.

It shall adopt its annual reports, special reports or opinions by a majority of its members.

It shall assist the European Parliament and the Council in exercising their powers of control over the implementation of the budget.][70]

Chapter 2

Provisions common to several institutions

[*Article* 189

In order to carry out their task and in accordance with the provisions of this Treaty, the European Parliament acting jointly with the Council, the Council and the Commission shall make regulations and issue directives, take decisions, make recommendations or deliver opinions.

A regulation shall have general application. It shall be binding in its entirety and directly applicable in all Member States.

A directive shall be binding, as to the result to be achieved, upon each Member State to which it is addressed, but shall leave to the national authorities the choice of form and methods.

A decision shall be binding in its entirety upon those to whom it is addressed.

Recommendations and opinions shall have no binding force.][71]

[*Article* 189*a*

1. Where, in pursuance of this Treaty, the Council acts on a proposal from the Commission, unanimity shall be required for an act constituting an amendment to that proposal, subject to Article 189b(4) and (5).

2. As long as the Council has not acted, the Commission may alter its proposal at any time during the procedures leading to the adoption of a Community act.

Article 189*b*

1. Where reference is made in this Treaty to this Article for the adoption of an act, the following procedure shall apply.

2. The Commission shall submit a proposal to the European Parliament and the Council.

The Council, acting by a qualified majority after obtaining the opinion of the European Parliament, shall adopt a common position. The common position shall be communicated to the European Parliament. The Council shall inform the European Parliament fully of the reasons which led it to adopt its common position. The Commission shall inform the European Parliament fully of its position.

If, within three months of such communication, the European Parliament:

(*a*) approves the common position, the Council shall definitely adopt the act in question in accordance with that common position;

(*b*) has not taken a decision, the Council shall adopt the act in question in accordance with its common position;

(*c*) indicates, by an absolute majority of its component members, that it intends to reject the common position, it shall immediately inform the Council. The Council may convene a meeting of the Conciliation Committee referred to in paragraph 4 to explain further its position. The European Parliament shall thereafter either confirm, by an absolute majority of its component members, its rejection of the common position, in which event the proposed act shall be deemed not to have been adopted, or propose amendments in accordance with subparagraph (*d*) of this paragraph;

(*d*) proposes amendments to the common position by an absolute majority of its component members, the amended test shall be forwarded to the Council and to the Commission, which shall deliver an opinion on those amendments.

3. If, within three months of the matter being referred to it, the Council, acting by a qualified majority, approves all the amendments of the European Parliament, it shall amend its common position accordingly and adopt the act in question; however, the Council shall act unanimously on the amendments on which the Commission has delivered a negative opinion. If the Council does not approve the act in question, the President of the Council, in agreement with the President of the European Parliament, shall forthwith convene a meeting of the Conciliation Committee.

4. The Conciliation Committee, which shall be composed of the members of the Council or their representatives and an equal number of representatives of the European Parliament, shall have the task of reaching agreement on a joint text, by a qualified majority of the members of the Council or their representatives and by a majority of the representatives of the European Parliament. The Commission shall take part in the Conciliation Committee's proceedings and shall take all the necessary initiatives with a view to reconciling the positions of the European Parliament and the Council.

5. If, within six weeks of its being convened, the Conciliation Committee approves a joint text, the European Parliament, acting by an absolute majority of the votes cast, and the Council, acting by a qualified majority, shall have a period of six weeks from that approval in which to adopt the act in question in accordance with the joint text. If one of the two

institutions fails to approve the proposed act, it shall be deemed not to have been adopted.

6. Where the Conciliation Committee does not approve a joint text, the proposed act shall be deemed not to have been adopted unless the Council, acting by a qualified majority within six weeks of expiry of the period granted to the Conciliation Committee, confirms the common position to which it agreed before the conciliation procedure was initiated, possibly with amendments proposed by the European Parliament. In this case, the act in question shall be finally adopted unless the European Parliament, within six weeks of the date of confirmation by the Council, rejects the text by an absolute majority of its component members, in which case the proposed act shall be deemed not to have been adopted.

7. The periods of three months and six weeks referred to in this Article may be extended by a maximum of one month and two weeks respectively by common accord of the European Parliament and the Council. The period of three months referred to in paragraph 2 shall be automatically extended by two months where paragraph 2(c) applies.

8. The scope of the procedure under this Article may be widened, in accordance with the procedure provided for in Article N(2) of the Treaty on European Union, on the basis of a report to be submitted to the Council by the Commission by 1996 at the latest.

Article 189c

Where reference is made in this Treaty to this Article for the adoption of an act, the following procedure shall apply:

(a) The Council, acting by a qualified majority on a proposal from the Commission and after obtaining the opinion of the European Parliament shall adopt a common position.

(b) The Council's common position shall be communicated to the European Parliament. The Council and the Commission shall inform the European Parliament fully of the reasons which led the Council to adopt its common position and also of the Commission's position.

If, within three months of such communication, the European Parliament approves this common position or has not taken a decision within that period the Council shall definitively adopt the act in question in accordance with the common position.

(c) The European Parliament may, within the period of three months referred to in subparagraph (b), by an absolute majority of its component members propose amendments to the Council's common position. The European Parliament may also, by the same majority, reject the Council's common position. The result of the proceedings shall be transmitted to the Council and the Commission.

If the European Parliament has rejected the Council's common position, unanimity shall be required for the Council to act on a second reading.

(d) The Commission shall, within a period of one month, re-examine the proposal on the basis of which the Council adopted its common position, by taking into account the amendments proposed by the European Parliament.

The Commission shall forward to the Council, at the same time as its re-examined proposal, the amendments of the European Parliament which it has not accepted, and shall express its opinion on them. The Council may adopt these amendments unanimously.

(e) The Council, acting by a qualified majority, shall adopt the proposal as re-examined by the Commission.

Unanimity shall be required for the Council to amend the proposal as re-examined by the Commission.

(f) In the cases referred to in subparagraphs (c), (d) and (e), the Council shall be required to act within a period of three months. If no decision is taken within this period, the Commission proposal shall be deemed not to have been adopted.

(g) The periods referred to in subparagraphs (b) and (f) may be extended by a maximum of one month by common accord between the Council and the European Parliament.][72]

[Article 190

Regulations, directives and decisions adopted jointly by the European Parliament and the Council, and such acts adopted by the Council or the Commission, shall state the reasons on which they are based and shall refer to any proposals or opinions which were required to be obtained pursuant to this Treaty.][73]

[Article 191

1. Regulations, directives and decisions adopted in accordance with the procedure referred to in Article 189b shall be signed by the President of the European Parliament and by the President of the Council and published in the *Official Journal of the European Communities*. They shall enter into force on the date specified in them or, in the absence thereof, on the 20th day following that of their publication.

2. Regulations of the Council and of the Commission, as well as directives of those institutions which are addressed to all Member States, shall be published in the *Official Journal of the European Communities*. They shall enter into force on the date specified in them or, in the absence thereof, on the 20th day following that of their publication.

3. Other directives, and decisions, shall be notified to those to whom they are addressed and shall take effect upon such notification.][74]

Article 192

Decisions of the Council or of the Commission which impose a pecuniary obligation on persons other than States, shall be enforceable.

Enforcement shall be governed by the rules of civil procedure in force in the State in the territory of which it is carried out. The order for its enforcement shall be appended to the decision, without other formality than verification of the authenticity of the decision, by the national authority which the Government of each Member State shall designate for this purpose and shall make known to the Commission and to the Court of Justice.

When these formalities have been completed on application by the party concerned, the latter may proceed to enforcement in accordance with the national law, by bringing the matter directly before the competent authority.

Enforcement may be suspended only by a decision of the Court of Justice. However, the courts of the country concerned shall have jurisdiction over complaints that enforcement is being carried out in an irregular manner.

Chapter 3

The Economic and Social Committee

Article 193

An Economic and Social Committee is hereby established. It shall have advisory status.

The Committee shall consist of representatives of the various categories of economic and social activity, in particular, representatives of producers, farmers, carriers, workers, dealers, craftsmen, professional occupations and representatives of the general public.

[*Article* 194

The number of members of the Economic and Social Committee shall be as follows:

Belgium	12
Denmark	9
Germany	24
Greece	12
Spain	21
France	24
Ireland	9
Italy	24
Luxembourg	6
Netherlands	12
Portugal	12
United Kingdom	24

The members of the Committee shall be appointed by the Council, acting unanimously, for four years. Their appointments shall be renewable.

The members of the Committee may not be bound by any mandatory instructions. They shall be completely independent in the performance of their duties, in the general interest of the Community.

The Council, acting by a qualified majority, shall determine the allowances of members of the Committee.][75]

Article 195

1. For the appointment of the members of the Committee, each Member State shall provide the Council with a list containing twice as many candidates as there are seats allotted to its nationals.

The composition of the Committee shall take account of the need to ensure adequate representation of the various categories of economic and social activity.

2. The Council shall consult the Commission. It may obtain the opinion of European bodies which are representative of the various economic and social sectors to which the activities of the Community are of concern.

[Article 196

The Committee shall elect its chairman and officers from among its members for a term of two years.

It shall adopt its rules of procedure.

The Committee shall be convened by its chairman at the request of the Council or of the Commission. It may also meet on its own initiative.][76]

Article 197

The Commission shall include specialised sections for the principal fields covered by this Treaty.

In particular, it shall contain an agricultural section and a transport section, which are the subject of special provisions in the Titles relating to agriculture and transport.

These specialised sections shall operate within the general terms of reference of the Committee. They may not be consulted independently of the Committee.

Sub-committees may also be established within the Committee to prepare on specific questions or in specific fields, draft opinions to be submitted to the Committee for its consideration.

The rules of procedure shall lay down the methods of composition and the terms of reference of the specialised sections and of the sub-committees.

[Article 198

The Committee must be consulted by the Council or by the Commission where this Treaty so provides. The Committee may be consulted by these institutions in all cases in which they consider it appropriate. It may issue an opinion on its own initiative in cases in which it considers such action appropriate.

The Council or the Commission shall, if it considers it necessary, set the Committee, for the submission of its opinion, a time-limit which may not be less than one month from the date on which the chairman receives notification to this effect. Upon expiry of the time-limit, the absence of an opinion shall not prevent further action.

The opinion of the Committee and that of the specialised section, together with a record of the proceedings, shall be forwarded to the Council and to the Commission.][77]

[Chapter 4

The Committee of the Regions

Article 198a

A committee consisting of representatives of regional and local bodies, hereinafter referred to as 'the Committee of the Regions', is hereby established with advisory status.

The number of members of the Committee of the Regions shall be as follows:

Belgium	12
Denmark	9
Germany	24
Greece	12
Spain	21
France	24
Ireland	9
Italy	24
Luxembourg	6
Netherlands	12
Portugal	12
United Kingdom	24

The members of the Committee and an equal number of alternate members shall be appointed for four years by the Council acting unanimously on proposals from the respective Member States. Their term of office shall be renewable.

The members of the Committee may not be bound by any mandatory instructions. They shall be completely independent in the performance of their duties, in the general interest of the Community.

Article 198b

The Committee of the Regions shall elect its chairman and officers from among its members for a term of two years.

It shall adopt its rules of procedure and shall submit them for approval to the Council, acting unanimously.

The Committee shall be convened by its chairman at the request of the Council or of the Commission. It may also meet on its own initiative.

Article 198c

The Committee of the Regions shall be consulted by the Council or by the Commission where this Treaty so provides and in all other cases in which one of these two institutions considers it appropriate.

The Council or the Commission shall, if it considers it necessary, set the Committee, for the submission of its opinion, a time-limit which may not be less than one month from the date on which the chairman receives notification to this effect. Upon expiry of the time-limit, the absence of an opinion shall not prevent further action.

Where the Economic and Social Committee is consulted pursuant to Article 198, the Committee of the Regions shall be informed by the Council or the Commission of the request for an opinion. Where it considers that specific regional interests are involved, the Committee of the Regions may issue an opinion on the matter.

It may issue an opinion on its own initiative in cases in which it considers such action appropriate.

The opinion of the Committee, together with a record of the proceedings, shall be forwarded to the Council and to the Commission.][78]

[Chapter 5

The European Investment Bank

Article 198d

The European Investment Bank shall have legal personality.

The members of the European Investment Bank shall be the Member States.

The Statute of the European Investment Bank is laid down in a Protocol annexed to this Treaty.

Article 198e

The task of the European Investment Bank shall be to contribute, by having recourse to the capital market and utilising its own resources, to the balanced and steady development of the common market in the interest of the Community. For this purpose the Bank shall, operating on a non-profit-making basis, grant loans and give guarantees which facilitate the financing of the following projects in all sectors of the economy:

(*a*) projects for developing less-developed regions;

(*b*) projects for modernising or converting undertakings or for developing fresh activities called for by the progressive establishment of the common market, where these projects are of such a size or nature that they cannot be entirely financed by the various means available in the individual Member States;

(*c*) projects of common interest to several Member States which are of such a size or nature that they cannot be entirely financed by the various means available in the individual Member States.

In carrying out its task, the Bank shall facilitate the financing of investment programmes in conjunction with assistance from the structural Funds and other Community financial instruments.][79]

Title II

Financial provisions

[*Article* 199

All items of revenue and expenditure of the Community, including those relating to the European Social Fund, shall be included in estimates to be drawn up for each financial year and shall be shown in the budget.

Administrative expenditure occasioned for the institutions by the provisions of the Treaty on European Union relating to common foreign and security policy and to cooperation in the fields of justice and home affairs shall be charged to the budget. The operational expenditure occasioned by the implementation of the said provisions may, under the conditions referred to therein, be charged to the budget.

The revenue and expenditure shown in the budget shall be in balance.][80]

Article 200

Repealed by the Treaty on European Union, Title II, Article G,E(70).

[*Article* 201

Without prejudice to other revenue, the budget shall be financed wholly from own resources.

The Council, acting unanimously on a proposal from the Commission and after consulting the European Parliament, shall lay down provisions relating to the system of own resources of the Community, which it shall recommend to the Member States for adoption in accordance with their respective constitutional requirements.][81]

[*Article* 201*a*]

With a view to maintaining budgetary discipline, the Commission shall not make any proposal for a Community act, or alter its proposals, or adopt any implementing measure which is likely to have appreciable implications for the budget without providing the assurance that that proposal or that measure is capable of being financed within the limit of the Community's own resources arising under provisions laid down by the Council pursuant to Article 201.][82]

Article 202

The expenditure shown in the budget shall be authorised for one financial year, unless the regulations made pursuant to Article 209 provide otherwise.

In accordance with conditions to be laid down pursuant to Article 209, any appropriations, other than those relating to staff expenditure, that are unexpended at the end of the financial year may be carried forward to the next financial year only.

Appropriations shall be classified under different chapters grouping items of expenditure according to their nature or purpose and subdivided, as far as may be necessary, in accordance with the regulations made pursuant to Article 209.

The expenditure of the European Parliament, the Council, the Commission and the Court of Justice shall be set out in separate parts of the budget, without prejudice to special arrangements for certain common items of expenditure.

Article 203

1. The financial year shall run from 1 January to 31 December.

2. Each institution of the Community shall, before 1 July, draw up estimates of its expenditure. The Commission shall consolidate these estimates in a preliminary draft budget. It shall attach thereto an opinion which may contain different estimates.

The preliminary draft budget shall contain an estimate of revenue and an estimate of expenditure.

3. The Commission shall place the preliminary draft budget before the Council not later than 1 September of the year preceding that in which the budget is to be implemented.

The Council shall consult the Commission and, where appropriate, the other institutions concerned whenever it intends to depart from the preliminary draft budget.

The Council, acting by a qualified majority, shall establish the draft budget and forward it to the European Parliament.

4. The draft budget shall be placed before the European Parliament not later than 5 October of the year preceding that in which the budget is to be implemented.

The European Parliament shall have the right to amend the draft budget, acting by a majority of its members, and to propose to the Council, acting by an absolute majority of the votes cast, modifications to the draft budget relating to expenditure necessarily resulting from this Treaty or from acts adopted in accordance therewith.

If, within 45 days of the draft budget being placed before it, the European Parliament has given its approval, the budget shall stand as finally adopted. If within this period the European Parliament has not amended the draft budget nor proposed any modifications thereto, the budget shall be deemed to be finally adopted.

If within this period the European Parliament has adopted amendments or proposed modifications, the draft budget together with the amendments or proposed modifications shall be forwarded to the Council.

5. After discussing the draft budget with the Commission and, where appropriate, with the other institutions concerned, the Council shall act under the following conditions:

(a) The Council may, acting by a qualified majority, modify any of the amendments adopted by the European Parliament;

(b) With regard to the proposed modifications:

     − where a modification proposed by the European Parliament does not have the effect of increasing the total amount of the expenditure of an institution, owing in particular to the fact that the increase in expenditure which it would involve would be expressly compensated by one or more proposed modifications correspondingly reducing expenditure, the Council may, acting by a qualified majority, reject the proposed modification. In the absence of a decision to reject it, the proposed modification shall stand as accepted;

     − where a modification proposed by the European Parliament has the effect of increasing the total amount of the expenditure of an institution, the Council may, acting by a qualified majority, accept this proposed modification. In the absence of a decision to accept it, the proposed modification shall stand as rejected;

- where, in pursuance of one of the two preceding subparagraphs, the Council has rejected a proposed modification, it may, acting by a qualified majority, either retain the amount shown in the draft budget or fix another amount.

The draft budget shall be modified on the basis of the proposed modifications accepted by the Council.

If, within 15 days of the draft being placed before it, the Council has not modified any of the amendments adopted by the European Parliament and if the modifications proposed by the latter have been accepted, the budget shall be deemed to be finally adopted. The Council shall inform the European Parliament that it has not modified any of the amendments and that the proposed modifications have been accepted.

If within this period the Council has modified one or more of the amendments adopted by the European Parliament or if the modifications proposed by the latter have been rejected or modified, the modified draft budget shall again be forwarded to the European Parliament. The Council shall inform the European Parliament of the results of its deliberations.

6. Within 15 days of the draft budget being placed before it, the European Parliament, which shall have been notified of the action taken on its proposed modifications, may, acting by a majority of its members and three-fifths of the votes cast, amend or reject the modifications to its amendments made by the Council and shall adopt the budget accordingly. If within this period the European Parliament has not acted, the budget shall be deemed to be finally adopted.

7. When the procedure provided for in this Article has been completed, the President of the European Parliament shall declare that the budget has been finally adopted.

8. However, the European Parliament, acting by a majority of its members and two-thirds of the votes cast, may, if there are important reasons, reject the draft budget and ask for a new draft to be submitted to it.

9. A maximum rate of increase in relation to the expenditure of the same type to be incurred during the current year shall be fixed annually for the total expenditure other than that necessarily resulting from this Treaty or from acts adopted in accordance therewith.

The Commission shall, after consulting the Economic Policy Committee, declare what this maximum rate is as it results from:

- the trend, in terms of volume, of the gross national product within the Community;

- the average variation in the budgets of the Member States;

and

- the trend of the cost of living during the preceding financial year.

The maximum rate shall be communicated, before 1 May, to all the institutions of the Community. The latter shall be required to conform to this during the budgetary procedure, subject to the provisions of the fourth and fifth subparagraphs of this paragraph.

If, in respect of expenditure other than that necessarily resulting from this Treaty or from acts adopted in accordance therewith, the actual rate of increase in the draft budget, established by the Council is over half the maximum rate, the European Parliament may, exercising its right of amendment, further increase the total amount of that expenditure to a limit not exceeding half the maximum rate.

Where the European Parliament, the Council or the Commission consider that the activities of the Communities require that the rate determined according to the procedure laid down in this paragraph should be exceeded, another rate may be fixed by agreement between the Council, acting by a qualified majority, and the European Parliament, acting by a majority of its members and three-fifths of the votes cast.

10. Each institution shall exercise the powers conferred upon it by this Article, with due regard for the provisions of the Treaty and for acts adopted in accordance therewith, in particular those relating to the Communities' own resources and to the balance between revenue and expenditure.

Article 204

If at the beginning of a financial year, the budget has not yet been voted, a sum equivalent to not more than one-twelfth of the budget appropriations for the preceding financial year may be spent each month in respect of any chapter or other subdivision of the budget in accordance with the provisions of the Regulations made pursuant to Article 209; this arrangement shall not, however, have the effect of placing at the disposal of the Commission appropriations in excess of one-twelfth of those provided for in the draft budget in course of preparation.

The Council may, acting by a qualified majority, provided that the other conditions laid down in the first subparagraph are observed, authorise expenditure in excess of one-twelfth.

If the decision relates to expenditure which does not necessarily result from this Treaty or from acts adopted in accordance therewith, the Council shall forward it immediately to the European Parliament; within 30 days the European Parliament, acting by a majority of its members and three-fifths of the votes cast, may adopt a different decision on the expenditure in excess of the one-twelfth referred to in the first subparagraph. This part of the decision of the Council shall be suspended until the European Parliament has taken its decision. If within the said period the European Parliament has not taken a decision which differs from the decision of the Council, the latter shall be deemed to be finally adopted.

The decisions referred to in the second and third subparagraphs shall lay down the necessary measures relating to resources to ensure application of this Article.

[Article 205

The Commission shall implement the budget, in accordance with the provisions of the regulations made pursuant to Article 209, on its own responsibility and within the limits of the appropriations, having regard to the principles of sound financial management.

The regulations shall lay down detailed rules for each institution concerning its part in effecting its own expenditure.

Within the budget, the Commission may, subject to the limits and conditions laid down in the regulations made pursuant to Article 209, transfer appropriations from one chapter to another or from one subdivision to another.][83]

Article 205a

The Commission shall submit annually to the Council and to the European Parliament the accounts of the preceding financial year relating to the implementation of the budget. The Commission shall also forward to them a financial statement of the assets and liabilities of the Community.

[Article 206

1. The European Parliament, acting on a recommendation from the Council which shall act by a qualified majority, shall give a discharge to the Commission in respect of the implementation of the budget. To this end, the Council and the European Parliament in turn shall examine the accounts and the financial statement referred to in Article 205a, the annual report by the Court of Auditors together with the replies of the

institutions under audit to the observations of the Court of Auditors and any relevant special reports by the Court of Auditors.

2. Before giving a discharge to the Commission, or for any other purpose in connection with the exercise of its powers over the implementation of the budget, the European Parliament may ask to hear the Commission give evidence with regard to the execution of expenditure or the operation of financial control systems. The Commission shall submit any necessary information to the European Parliament at the latter's request.

3. The Commission shall take all appropriate steps to act on the observations in the decisions giving discharge and on other observations by the European Parliament relating to the execution of expenditure, as well as on comments accompanying the recommendations on discharge adopted by the Council.

At the request of the European Parliament or the Council, the Commission shall report on the measures taken in the light of these observations and comments and in particular on the instructions given to the departments which are responsible for the implementation of the budget. These budgets shall also be forwarded to the Court of Auditors.][84]

Article 206a

Repealed by the Treaty on European Union, Title II, Article G,E(75).

Article 206b

Repealed by the Treaty on European Union, Title II, Article G,E(75).

Article 207

The budget shall be drawn up in the unit of account determined in accordance with the provisions of the regulations made pursuant to Article 209.

The financial contributions provided for in Article 200(1) shall be placed at the disposal of the Community by the Member States in their national currencies.

The available balances of these contributions shall be deposited with the Treasuries of Member States or with bodies designated by them. While on deposit, such funds shall retain the value corresponding to the parity, at the date of deposit, in relation to the unit of account referred to in the first paragraph.

The balances may be invested on terms to be agreed between the Commission and the Member State concerned.

The regulations made pursuant to Article 209 shall lay down the technical conditions under which financial operations relating to the European Social Fund shall be carried out.

Article 208

The Commission may, provided it notifies the competent authorities of the Member States concerned, transfer into the currency of one of the Member States its holdings in the currency of another Member State, to the extent necessary to enable them to be used for purposes which come within the scope of this Treaty. The Commission shall as far as possible avoid making such transfers if it possesses cash or liquid assets in the currencies which it needs.

The Commission shall deal with each Member State through the authority designated by the State concerned. In carrying out financial operations the Commission shall employ the services of the bank of issue of the Member State concerned or of any other financial institution approved by that State.

[Article 209

The Council, acting unanimously on a proposal from the Commission and after consulting the European Parliament and obtaining the opinion of the Court of Auditors, shall:

(a) make Financial Regulations specifying in particular the procedure to be adopted for establishing and implementing the budget and for presenting and auditing accounts;

(b) determine the methods and procedure whereby the budget revenue provided under the arrangements relating to the Community's own resources shall be made available to the Commission, and determine the measures to be applied, if need be, to meet cash requirements;

(c) lay down rules concerning the responsibility of financial controllers, authorising officers and accounting officers, and concerning appropriate arrangements for inspection.][85]

[Article 209a

Member States shall take the same measures to counter fraud affecting the financial interests of the Community as they take to counter fraud affecting their own financial interests.

Without prejudice to other provisions of this Treaty, Member States shall coordinate their action aimed at protecting the financial interests of the Community against fraud. To this end they shall organise, with the help of the Commission, close and regular cooperation between the competent departments of their administrations.][86]

Part Six

General and final provisions

Article 210

The Community shall have legal personality.

Article 211

In each of the Member States, the Community shall enjoy the most extensive legal capacity accorded to legal persons under their laws; it may, in particular, acquire or dispose of movable and immovable property and may be a party to legal proceedings. To this end, the Community shall be represented by the Commission.

Article 212

(Article repealed by Article 24 of the Merger Treaty)

[See Article 24(1) of the Merger Treaty, which reads as follows:

1. The officials and other servants of the European Coal and Steel Community, the European Economic Community and the European Atomic Energy Community shall, at the date of entry into force of this Treaty, become officials and other servants of the European Communities and form part of the single administration of those Communities.

The Council shall, acting by a qualified majority on a proposal from the Commission and after consulting the other institutions concerned, lay down the Staff Regulations of the officials of the European Communities and the Conditions of Employment of other servants of those Communities.]

Article 213

The Commission may, within the limits and under conditions laid down by the Council in accordance with the provisions of this Treaty, collect any information and carry out any checks required for the performance of the tasks entrusted to it.

Article 214

The members of the institutions of the Community, the members of the committees, and the officials and other servants of the Community shall be required, even after their duties have ceased, not to disclose information of the kind covered by the obligation of professional secrecy, in particular information about undertakings, their business relations or their cost components.

[Article 215

The contractual liability of the Community shall be governed by the law applicable to the contract in question.

In the case of non-contractual liability, the Community shall, in accordance with the general principles common to the laws of the Member States, make good any damage caused by its institutions or by its servants in the performance of their duties.

The preceding paragraph shall apply under the same conditions to damage caused by the ECB or by its servants in the performance of their duties.

The personal liability of its servants towards the Community shall be governed by the provisions laid down in their Staff Regulations or in the Conditions of Employment applicable to them.][87]

Article 216

The seat of the institutions of the Community shall be determined by common accord of the Governments of the Member States.

Article 217

The rules governing the languages of the institutions of the Community shall, without prejudice to the provisions contained in the rules of procedure of the Court of Justice, be determined by the Council, acting unanimously.

Article 218

(Article repealed by the second paragraph of Article 28 of the Merger Treaty)

[See the first paragraph of Article 28 of the Merger Treaty, which reads as follows:

The European Communities shall enjoy in the territories of the Member States such privileges and immunities as are necessary for the performance of their tasks, under the conditions laid down in the

Protocol annexed to this Treaty. The same shall apply to the European Investment Bank.]

Article 219

Member States undertake not to submit a dispute concerning the interpretation or application of this Treaty to any method of settlement other than those provided for therein.

Article 220

Member States shall, so far as is necessary, enter into negotiations with each other with a view to securing for the benefit of their nationals:

-   the protection of persons and the enjoyment and protection of rights under the same conditions as those accorded by each State to its own nationals;

-   the abolition of double taxation within the Community;

-   the mutual recognition of companies or firms within the meaning of the second paragraph of Article 48, the retention of legal personality in the event of transfer of their seat from one country to another, and the possibility of mergers between companies or firms governed by the laws of different countries;

-   the simplification of formalities governing the reciprocal recognition and enforcement of judgments of courts or tribunals and of arbitration awards.

Article 221

Within three years of the entry into force of this Treaty, Member States shall accord nationals of the other Member States the same treatment as their own nationals as regards participation in the capital of companies or firms within the meaning of Article 58, without prejudice to the application of the other provisions of this Treaty.

Article 222

This Treaty shall in no way prejudice the rules in Member States governing the system of property ownership.

Article 223

1. The provisions of this Treaty shall not preclude the application of the following rules:

(a) No Member State shall be obliged to supply information the disclosure of which it considers contrary to the essential interests of its security;

(*b*) Any Member State may take such measures as it considers necessary for the protection of the essential interests of its security which are connected with the production of or trade in arms, munitions and war material; such measures shall not adversely affect the conditions of competition in the common market regarding products which are not intended for specifically military purposes.

2. During the first year after the entry into force of this Treaty, the Council shall, acting unanimously, draw up a list of products to which the provisions of paragraph 1(*b*) shall apply.

3. The Council may, acting unanimously on a proposal from the Commission, make changes in this list.

Article 224

Member States shall consult each other with a view to taking together the steps needed to prevent the functioning of the common market being affected by measures which a Member State may be called upon to take in the event of serious internal disturbances affecting the maintenance of law and order, in the event of war, serious international tension constituting a threat of war, or in order to carry out obligations it has accepted for the purpose of maintaining peace and international security.

Article 225

If measures taken in the circumstances referred to in Articles 223 and 224 have the effect of distorting the conditions of competition in the common market, the Commission shall, together with the State concerned, examine how these measures can be adjusted to the rules laid down in this Treaty.

By way of derogation from the procedure laid down in Articles 169 and 170, the Commission or any Member State may bring the matter directly before the Court of Justice if it considers that another Member State is making improper use of the powers provided for in Articles 223 and 224. The Court of Justice shall give its ruling *in camera*.

Article 226

1. If, during the transitional period, difficulties arise which are serious and liable to persist in any sector of the economy or which could bring about serious deterioration in the economic situation of a given area, a Member State may apply for authorisation to take protective measures

in order to rectify the situation and adjust the sector concerned to the economy of the common market.

2. On application by the State concerned, the Commission shall, by emergency procedure, determine without delay the protective measures which it considers necessary, specifying the circumstances and the manner in which they are to be put into effect.

3. The measures authorised under paragraph 2 may involve derogations from the rules of this Treaty, to such an extent and for such periods as are strictly necessary in order to attain the objectives referred to in paragraph 1. Priority shall be given to such measures as will least disturb the functioning of the common market.

Article 227

1. This Treaty shall apply to the Kingdom of Belgium, the Kingdom of Denmark, the Federal Republic of Germany, the Hellenic Republic, the Kingdom of Spain, the French Republic, Ireland, the Italian Republic, the Grand Duchy of Luxembourg, the Kingdom of the Netherlands, the Portuguese Republic and the United Kingdom of Great Britain and Northern Ireland.

[2. With regard to the French overseas departments, the general and particular provisions of this Treaty relating to:

- the free movement of goods;

- agriculture, save for Article 40(4);

- the liberalisation of services;

- the rules on competition;

- the protective measures provided for in Articles 109h, 109i and 226;

- the institutions,

shall apply as soon as this Treaty enters into force.

The conditions under which the other provisions of this Treaty are to apply shall be determined, within two years of the entry into force of this Treaty, by decisions of the Council, acting unanimously on a proposal from the Commission.

The institutions of the Community will, within the framework of the procedures provided for in this Treaty, in particular Article 226, take care that the economic and social development of these areas is made possible.][88]

3. The special arrangements for association set out in Part Four of this

Treaty shall apply to the overseas countries and territories listed in Annex IV to this Treaty.

This Treaty shall not apply to those overseas countries and territories having special relations with the United Kingdom of Great Britain and Northern Ireland which are not included in the aforementioned list.[89]

4. The provisions of this Treaty shall apply to the European territories for whose external relations a Member State is responsible.

5. Notwithstanding the preceding paragraphs:

[(a) this Treaty shall not apply to the Faroe Islands.][90]

(b) This Treaty shall not apply to the Sovereign Base Areas of the United Kingdom of Great Britain and Northern Ireland in Cyprus.

(c) This Treaty shall apply to the Channel Islands and the Isle of Man only to the extent necessary to ensure the implementation of the arrangements for those islands set out in the Treaty concerning the accession of the new Member States to the European Economic Community and to the European Atomic Energy Community signed on 22 January 1972.

[Article 228

1. Where this Treaty provides for the conclusion of agreements between the Community and one or more States or international organisations, the Commission shall make recommendations to the Council, which shall authorise the Commission to open the necessary negotiations. The Commission shall conduct these negotiations in consultation with special committees appointed by the Council to assist it in this task and within the framework of such directives as the Council may issue to it.

In exercising the powers conferred upon it by this paragraph, the Council shall act by a qualified majority, except in the cases provided for in the second sentence of paragraph 2, for which it shall act unanimously.

2. Subject to the powers vested in the Commission in this field, the agreements shall be concluded by the Council, acting by a qualified majority on a proposal from the Commission. The Council shall act unanimously when the agreement covers a field for which unanimity is required for the adoption of internal rules, and for the agreements referred to in Article 238.

3. The Council shall conclude agreements after consulting the European Parliament, except for the agreements referred to in Article 113(3), including cases where the agreement covers a field for which the procedure referred to in Article 189b or that referred to in Article 189c is

required for the adoption of internal rules. The European Parliament shall deliver its opinion within a time-limit which the Council may lay down according to the urgency of the matter. In the absence of an opinion within that time-limit, the Council may act.

By way of derogation from the previous subparagraph, agreements referred to in Article 238, other agreements establishing a specific institutional framework by organising cooperation procedures, agreements having important budgetary implications for the Community and agreements entailing amendment of an act adopted under the procedure referred to in Article 189b shall be concluded after the assent of the European Parliament has been obtained.

The Council and the European Parliament may, in an urgent situation, agree upon a time-limit for the assent.

4. When conducting an agreement, the Council may, by way of derogation from paragraph 2, authorise the Commission to approve modifications on behalf of the Community where the agreement provides for them to be adopted by a simplified procedure or by a body set up by the agreement; it may attach specific conditions to such authorisation.

5. When the Council envisages concluding an agreement which calls for amendments to this Treaty, the amendments must first be adopted in accordance with the procedure laid down in Article N of the Treaty on European Union.

6. The Council, the Commission or a Member State may obtain the opinion of the Court of Justice as to whether an agreement envisaged is compatible with the provisions of this Treaty. Where the opinion of the Court of Justice is adverse, the agreement may enter into force only in accordance with Article N of the Treaty on European Union.

7. Agreements concluded under the conditions set out in this Article shall be binding on the institutions of the Community and on Member States.][91]

[Article 228a

Where it is provided, in a common position or in a joint action adopted according to the provisions of the Treaty on European Union relating to the common foreign and security policy, for an action by the Community to interrupt or to reduce, in part or completely, economic relations with one or more third countries, the Council shall take the necessary urgent measures. The Council shall act by a qualified majority on a proposal from the Commission.][92]

Article 229

It shall be for the Commission to ensure the maintenance of all appropriate relations with the organs of the United Nations, of its specialised agencies and of the General Agreement on Tariffs and Trade.

The Commission shall also maintain such relations as are appropriate with all international organisations.

Article 230

The Community shall establish all appropriate forms of cooperation with the Council of Europe.

[Article 231

The Community shall establish close cooperation with the Organisation for Economic Cooperation and Development, the details of which shall be determined by common accord.][93]

Article 232

1. The provisions of this Treaty shall not affect the provisions of the Treaty establishing the European Coal and Steel Community, in particular as regards the rights and obligations of Member States, the powers of the institutions of that Community and the rules laid down by that Treaty for the functioning of the common market in coal and steel.

2. The provisions of this Treaty shall not derogate from those of the Treaty establishing the European Atomic Energy Community.

Article 233

The provisions of this Treaty shall not preclude the existence or completion of regional unions between Belgium and Luxembourg, or between Belgium, Luxembourg and the Netherlands, to the extent that the objectives of these regional unions are not attained by application of this Treaty.

Article 234

The rights and obligations arising from agreements concluded before the entry into force of this Treaty between one or more Member States on the one hand, and one or more third countries on the other, shall not be affected by the provisions of this Treaty.

To the extent that such agreements are not compatible with this Treaty, the Member State or States concerned shall take all appropriate steps to eliminate the incompatibilities established. Member States shall, where necessary, assist each other to this end and shall, where appropriate, adopt a common attitude.

In applying the agreements referred to in the first paragraph, Member States shall take into account the fact that the advantages accorded under this Treaty by each Member State form an integral part of the establishment of the Community and are thereby inseparably linked with the creation of common institutions, the conferring of powers upon them and the granting of the same advantages by all the other Member States.

Article 235

If action by the Community should prove necessary to attain, in the course of the operation of the common market, one of the objectives of the Community and this Treaty has not provided the necessary powers, the Council shall, acting unanimously on a proposal from the Commission and after consulting the European Parliament, take the appropriate measures.

Article 236

Repealed by the Treaty on European Union, Title II, Article G,E(83).

Article 237

Repealed by the Treaty on European Union, Title II, Article G,E(83).

[Article 238

The Community may conclude with one or more States or international organisations agreements establishing an association involving reciprocal rights and obligations, common action and special procedures.][94]

Article 239

The Protocols annexed to this Treaty by common accord of the Member States shall form an integral part thereof.

Article 240

This Treaty is concluded for an unlimited period.

Setting up of the institutions

Article 241

The Council shall meet within one month of the entry into force of this Treaty.

Article 242

The Council shall, within three months of its first meeting, take all appropriate measures to constitute the Economic and Social Committee.

Article 243

The Assembly[95] shall meet within two months of the first meeting of the Council, having been convened by the President of the Council, in order to elect its officers and draw up its rules of procedure. Pending the election of its officers, the oldest member shall take the chair.

Article 244

The Court of Justice shall take up its duties as soon as its members have been appointed. Its first President shall be appointed for three years in the same manner as its members.

The Court of Justice shall adopt its rules of procedure within three months of taking up its duties.

No matter may be brought before the Court of Justice until its rules of procedure have been published. The time within which an action must be brought shall run only from the date of this publication.

Upon his appointment, the President of the Court of Justice shall exercise the powers conferred upon him by this Treaty.

Article 245

The Commission shall take up its duties and assume the responsibilities conferred upon it by this Treaty as soon as its members have been appointed.

Upon taking up its duties, the Commission shall undertake the studies and arrange the contacts needed for making an overall survey of the economic situation of the Community.

Article 246

1. The first financial year shall run from the date on which this Treaty enters into force until 31 December following. Should this Treaty, however, enter into force during the second half of the year, the first financial year shall run until 31 December of the following year.

2. Until the budget for the first financial year has been established, Member States shall make the Community interest-free advances which

shall be deducted from their financial contributions to the implementation of the budget.

3. Until the Staff Regulations of officials and the Conditions of Employment of other servants of the Community provided for in Article 212 have been laid down, each institution shall recruit the Staff it needs and to this end conclude contracts of limited duration.

Each institution shall examine together with the Council any question concerning the number, remuneration and distribution of posts.

Final provisions

Article 247

This Treaty shall be ratified by the High Contracting Parties in accordance with their respective constitutional requirements. The instruments of ratification shall be deposited with the Government of the Italian Republic.

This Treaty shall enter into force on the first day of the month following the deposit of the instrument of ratification by the last signatory State to take this step. If, however, such deposit is made less than fifteen days before the beginning of the following month, this Treaty shall not enter into force until the first day of the second month after the date of such deposit.

Article 248

This Treaty, drawn up in a single original in the Dutch, French, German and Italian languages, all four texts being equally authentic, shall be deposited in the archives of the Government of the Italian Republic, which shall transmit a certified copy to each of the Governments of the other signatory States.

In witness whereof, the undersigned plenipotentiaries have signed this Treaty.

Done at Rome this twenty-fifth day of March in the year one thousand nine hundred and fifty-seven.

[List omitted]

EDITORIAL NOTE

For Protocols and Declarations not included in this volume see: Office for Official Publications of the European Communities, Treaties establishing the European Communities: Treaties amending these Treaties, 1987, volume I; and, ditto European Union selected instruments taken from the Treaties Books I and II, volumes I and II (Book I, volume I 1993, Luxembourg; others to be published).

FOOTNOTES

1. Replaced by the Treaty on European Union, Title II, Article G,A(1), previously 'European Economic Community'.
2. Article 2 replaced by the Treaty on European Union, Title II, Article G,B(2).
3. Article 3 replaced by the Treaty on European Union, Title II, Article G,B(3).
4. Article 3a inserted by the Treaty on European Union, Title II, Article G,B(4).
5. Article 3b inserted by the Treaty on European Union, Title II, Article G,B(5).
6. Article 4 replaced by the Treaty on European Union, Title II, Article G,B(6).
7. Article 4a inserted by the Treaty on European Union, Title II, Article G,B(7).
8. Article 4b inserted by the Treaty on European Union, Title II, Article G,B(7).
9. Article 6 deleted and Article 7 renamed Article 6 by the Treaty on European Union, Title II, Article G,B(8).
10. Replaced by the Treaty on European Union, Title II, Article G,B(8).
11. Article 8 renamed Article 7 by the Treaty on European Union, Title II, Article G,B(9).
12. Article 8a renamed Article 7a by the Treaty on European Union, Title II, Article G,B(9).
13. Articles 7b and 7c renamed by the Treaty on European Union, Title II, Article G,B(9), previously '8b' and '8c'.
14. Part Two inserted by the Treaty on European Union, Title II, Article G,C.
15. Parts Two and Three regrouped under heading of Part Three by the Treaty on European Union, Title II, Article G,D.
16. Article as replaced by Article 16(1) of the SEA. OJ No 152, 13.7.67.
17. Replaced by the Treaty on European Union, Title II, Article G,D(10).
18. Replaced by the Treaty on European Union, Title II, Article G,D(11).
19. Replaced by the Treaty on European Union, Title II, Article G, D(12).
20. Article 57 replaced by the Treaty on European Union, Title II, Article G,D(13).
21. Words added to heading by the Treaty on European Union, Title II, Article G,D(14).
22. Paragraph 1, excepting the first sentence, as amended by Article 16(4) of the SEA.
23. Articles 73a to 73h inserted by the Treaty on European Union, Title II, Article G,D(15).
24. Article 75 replaced by the Treaty on European Union, Title II, Article G,D(16).
25. First subparagraph of paragraph 2 as amended by Article 16(5) of the SEA.
26. Second subparagraph of paragraph 2 as amended by Article 16(6) of the SEA.
27. Replaced by the Treaty on European Union, Title II, Article G,D(17), previously 'Title I Common rules'.
28. Inserted by the Treaty on European Union, Title II, Article G,D(18).
29. Point (d) renamed (e) by the Treaty on European Union, Title II, Article G,D(18).
30. Article 94 replaced by the Treaty on European Union, Title II, Article G,D(19).
31. Article 99 replaced by the Treaty on European Union, Title II, Article G,D(20).
32. Article 100 replaced by the Treaty on European Union, Title II, Article G,D(21).
33. Article 100a(1) replaced by the Treaty on European Union, Title II, Article G,D(22).
34. Article 100c replaced by the Treaty on European Union, Title II, Article G,D(23).
35. Article 100d replaced by the Treaty on European Union, Title II, Article G,D(24).
36. Title II, Chapters 1, 2 and 3 replaced by the Treaty on European Union, Title II, Article G,D(25).
37. Title replaced by the Treaty on European Union, Title II, Article G,D(26).
38. Article 113 replaced by the Treaty on European Union, Title II, Article G,D(28).
39. Article 115 replaced by the Treaty on European Union, Title II, Article G,D(30).
40. Title replaced by the Treaty on European Union, Title II, Article G,D(32).

41. Replaced by the Treaty on European Union, Title II, Article G,D(33).
42. Article 118b added by Article 22 of the SEA.
43. Article 123 replaced by the Treaty on European Union, Title II, Article G,D(34).
44. Article 125 replaced by the Treaty on European Union, Title II, Article G,D(35).
45. Chapter 3, Articles 126, 127 and 128 replaced by the Treaty on European Union, Title II, Article G,D(36).
46. Title IX, Article 128 inserted by the Treaty on European Union, Title II, Article G,D(37).
47. Articles 128 to 130y inserted by the Treaty on European Union, Title II, Article G,D(38).
48. Article 137 replaced by the Treaty on European Union, Title II, Article G,E(39).
49. OJ No L 33, 9.2.93, p.15.
50. Paragraph 3 replaced by the Treaty on European Union, Title II, Article G,E(40).
51. Articles 138a to 138e inserted by the Treaty on European Union, Title II, Article G,E(41).
52. First paragraph as amended by Article 27(1) of the Merger Treaty.
53. As regards the second sentence of this Article see also Article 10(3) of the Act concerning the election of the representatives of the European Parliament.
54. Inserted by the Treaty on European Union, Title II, Article G,E(42)
55. Article 146 inserted by the Treaty on European Union, Title II, Article G,E(43).
56. Article 147 inserted by the Treaty on European Union, Title II, Article G,E(44).
57. Article 151 inserted by the Treaty on European Union, Title II, Article G,E(46).
58. Article 154 inserted by the Treaty on European Union, Title II, Article G,E(47).
59. Articles 156 to 163 inserted by the Treaty on European Union, Title II, Article G,E(48).
60. Article 165 replaced by the Treaty on European Union, Title II, Article G,E(49).
61. Article 168a replaced by the Treaty on European Union, Title II, Article G,E(50).
62. Article 171 replaced by the Treaty on European Union, Title II, Article G,E(51).
63. Article 172 replaced by the Treaty on European Union, Title II, Article G,E(52).
64. Article 173 replaced by the Treaty on European Union, Title II, Article G,E(53).
65. Article 175 replaced by the Treaty on European Union, Title II, Article G,E(54).
66. Article 176 replaced by the Treaty on European Union, Title II, Article G,E(55).
67. Article 177 replaced by the Treaty on European Union, Title II, Article G,E(56).
68. Article 180 replaced by the Treaty on European Union, Title II, Article G,E(57).
69. Article 184 replaced by the Treaty on European Union, Title II, Article G,E(58).
70. Articles 188a to 188c inserted by the Treaty on European Union, Title II, Article G,E(59).
71. Article 189 replaced by the Treaty on European Union, Title II, Article G,E(60).
72. Articles 189a to 189c inserted by the Treaty on European Union, Title II, Article G,E(61).
73. Article 190 replaced by the Treaty on European Union, Title II, Article G,E(62).
74. Article 191 replaced by the Treaty on European Union, Title II, Article G,E(63).
75. Article 194 replaced by the Treaty on European Union, Title II, Article G,E(64).
76. Article 196 replaced by the Treaty on European Union, Title II, Article G,E(65).
77. Article 198 replaced by the Treaty on European Union, Title II, Article G,E(66).
78. Chapter 4 inserted by the Treaty on European Union, Title II, Article G,E(67).
79. Chapter 5 inserted by the Treaty on European Union, Title II, Article G,E(68).
80. Article 199 replaced by the Treaty on European Union, Title II, Article G,E(69).
81. Article 201 replaced by the Treaty on European Union, Title II, Article G,E(71).
82. Article 201a inserted by the Treaty on European Union, Title II, Article G,E(72).

83. Article 205 replaced by the Treaty on European Union, Title II, Article G,E(73).
84. Article 206 replaced by the Treaty on European Union, Title II, Article G,E(74).
85. Article 209 replaced by the Treaty on European Union, Title II, Article G,E(76).
86. Article 209a inserted by the Treaty on European Union, Title II, Article G,E(77).
87. Article 215 replaced by the Treaty on European Union, Title II, Article G,E(78).
88. Article 227 paragraph 2 replaced by the Treaty on European Union, Title II, Article G,E(79)(a).
89. Article 227 second subparagraph of paragraph 3 added by Article 26(2) of the Act of Accession DK/IRL/UK.
90. Article 227 paragraph 5(a) replaced by the Treaty on European Union, Title II, Article G,E(79)(b).
91. Article 228 replaced by the Treaty on European Union, Title II, Article G,E(80).
92. Article 228a inserted by the Treaty on European Union, Title II, Article G,E(81).
93. Article 231 replaced by the Treaty on European Union, Title II, Article G,E(82).
94. Article 238 replaced by the Treaty on European Union, Title II, Article G,E(84).
95. Editorial Note: Notwithstanding the provisions of Article 3 of the SEA, and for historical reasons, the term 'Assembly' has not been replaced by the terms 'European Parliament'.

Annex I

[Lists A to G referred to in Articles 19 and 20 of this Treaty]

Annex II

[List referred to in Article 38 of this Treaty]

Annex III

[List of invisible transactions referred to in Article 73h of this Treaty][1]

- Maritime freights, including chartering, harbour expenses, disbursements for fishing vessels, etc.

- Inland waterway freights, including chartering.

- Road transport: passengers and freights, including chartering.

- Air transport: passengers and freights, including chartering.

  Payment by passengers of international air tickets and excess charges; payment of international air freight charges and flights.

  Receipts from the sale of international air tickets, charges, international air freight charges, and chart vices

- For all means of transport of maritime transport

(bunkering and provisioning, maintenance, repairs, expenses for crews, etc).

For all means of inland waterway transport: harbour services (bunkering and provisioning, maintenance and minor repairs of equipment, expenses for crews, etc).

For all means of commercial road transport: fuel, oil, minor repairs, garaging, expenses for drivers and crews, etc.

For all means of air transport: operating costs and general overheads, including repairs to aircraft and to air transport equipment.

- Warehousing and storage charges, customs clearance.

- Customs duties and fees.

- Transit charges.

- Repair and assembly charges.

Processing, finishing, processing of work under contract, and other services of the same nature.

- Repair of ships.

Repair of means of transport other than ships and aircraft.

- Technical assistance (assistance relating to the production and distribution of goods and services at all stages, given over a period limited according to the specific purpose of such assistance, and including e.g. advice or visits by experts, preparation of plans and blueprints, supervision of manufacture, market research, training of personnel).

- Commission and brokerage.

Profits arising out of transit operations or sales of transhipment.

Banking commissions and charges.

Representation expenses.

Advertising by all media.

Business travel.

Participation by subsidiary companies and branches in overhead expenses of parent companies situated abroad and vice-versa.

Contracting (construction and maintenance of buildings, roads, ports, etc carried out by specialised firms, and, generally, at prices after open tender).

- Differences, margins and deposits due in respect of operations on commodity terminal markets in conformity with normal *bona fide* commercial practice.

- Tourism.

- Travel for private reasons (education).

- Travel for private reasons (health).

- Travel for private reasons (family).

- Subscriptions to newspapers, periodicals, books, musical publications.

  Newspapers, periodicals, books, musical publications and records.

- Printed films, commercial, documentary, educational, etc (rentals, dues, subscriptions, reproduction and synchronization fees, etc).

- Membership fees.

- Current maintenance and repair of private property abroad.

- Government expenditure (official representation abroad, contributions to international organisations).

- Taxes, court expenses, registration fees for patents and trade marks.

  Claims for damages.

  Refunds in the case of cancellation of contracts and refunds of uncalled-for payments.

  Fines.

- Periodical settlements in connection with public transport and postal, telegraphic and telephone services.

- Exchange authorisations granted to own or foreign national emigrating.

  Exchange authorisation granted to own or foreign nationals returning to their country of origin.

- Salaries and wages (of frontier or seasonal workers and of other non-residents, without prejudice to the right of a country to regulate terms of employment of foreign nationals).

- Emigrants' remittances (without prejudice to the right of a country to regulate immigration).

- Fees.

- Dividends and shares in profits.

- Interest on debentures, mortgages, etc.

- Rent.
- Contractual amortization (with the exception of transfers in connection with amortization having the character either of anticipated repayments or of the discharge of accumulated arrears).
- Profits from business activity.
- Authors' royalties.

  Patents, designs, trade marks and inventions (the assignment and licensing of patent rights, designs, trade marks and inventions, whether or not legally protected, and transfers arising out of such assignment or licensing).
- Consular receipts.
- Pensions and other income of a similar nature.

  Maintenance payments resulting from a legal obligation or from a decision of a court and financial assistance in cases of hardship.

  Transfers by instalments of assets deposited in one member country by persons residing in another member country whose personal income in that country is not sufficient to cover their living expenses.
- Transactions and transfers in connection with direct insurance.
- Transactions and transfers in connection with reinsurance and retrocession.
- Opening and reimbursement of commercial or industrial credits.
- Transfers of minor amounts abroad.
- Charges for documentation of all kinds incurred on their own account by authorised dealers in foreign exchange.
- Sports prizes and racing earnings.
- Inheritances.
- Dowries.

FOOTNOTE

1. Replaced by the Treaty on European Union, Title II, Article G,F(85).

Annex IV

Overseas countries and territories to which the provisions of Part Four of this Treaty apply [1,2,3]

French West Africa: Senegal, French Sudan, French Guinea, Ivory Coast, Dahomey, Mauritania, Niger and Upper Volta;[4]

French Equatorial Africa: Middle Congo, Ubangi-Shari, Chad and Gabon;[4]

Saint Pierre and Miquelon,[5] the Comoro Archipelago,[6] Madagascar[4] and dependencies,[4] French Somaliland,[4] New Caledonia and dependencies, French Settlements in Oceania,[7] Southern and Antarctic Territories;[8]

The autonomous Republic of Togoland;[4]

The trust territory of the Cameroons under French administration;[4]

The Belgian Congo and Ruanda-Urundi;[4]

The trust territory of Somaliland under Italian administration;[4]

Netherlands New Guinea;[4]

The Netherlands Antilles;[9]

Anglo-French Condominium of the New Hebrides;[4]

The Bahamas;[4]

Bermuda;[10]

Brunei;[11]

Associated States in the Caribbean: Antigua, Dominica, Grenada, St Lucia, St Vincent, St Christopher, Nevis, Anguilla;[12]

British Honduras;[4]

Cayman Islands;

Falkland Islands and Dependencies;[13]

Gilbert and Ellice Islands;[4]

Central and Southern Line Islands;[10]

British Solomon Islands;[4]

Turks and Caicos Islands;

British Virgin Islands;

Monserrat;

Pitcairn;

St Helena and Dependencies;

The Seychelles;[4]

British Antarctic Territory;

British Indian Ocean Territory;

Greenland.[14]

EDITORIAL NOTES [ORIGINAL]:

1. As amended by
   - Article 1 of the Convention of 13 November 1962 amending the Treaty establishing the European Community, (OJ No 150, 1.10.64, p.2414) and
   - Article 24(2) of the Act of Accession DK/IRL/UK, modified by Article 13 of the AD AA DK/IRL/UK,
   - The Treaty of 13 March 1984 amending, with regard to Greenland, the Treaties establishing the European Communities (OJ No L 29, 1.2.85).
2. Council Decision 86/283/EEC of 30 June 1986 on the association of the overseas countries and territories with the European Community (OJ No L 175, 1.7.86) contains a list of overseas countries and territories to which the provisions of Part Four of the Treaty apply.
3. The provisions of Part Four of the Treaty applied to Surinam, by virtue of a Supplementary Act of the Kingdom of the Netherlands to complete its instruments of ratification, from 1 September 1962 to 16 July 1976.
4. The provisions of Part Four of the Treaty no longer apply to these countries and territories, which have become independent and whose names may have been changed.
   The relations between the European Community and certain African States and Madagascar were the subject of the Conventions of Association signed at Yaoundé on 20 July 1963 and 29 July 1969. The relations with certain African, Caribbean and Pacific States were subsequently the subject of:
   - the ACP-EEC Convention of Lomé, signed on 28 February 1975 (OJ No L 25, 30.1.76), which entered into force on 1 April 1976,
   - the Second ACP-EEC Convention, signed at Lomé on 31 October 1979 (OJ No L 347, 22.12.80), which entered into force on 1 January 1981,
   - the Third ACP-EEC Convention, signed at Lomé on 8 December 1984 (OJ No L 86, 31.3.86), which entered into force on 1 May 1986.
5. Has become a French overseas department.
6. The provisions of Part Four of the Treaty no longer apply to this Archipelago, except for the territorial collectivity of Mayotte which has remained on the list of overseas countries and territories (see footnote 2).
7. New name: Overseas territory of French Polynesia.
   Overseas territory of the Wallis and Futuna Islands.
8. New name: French Southern and Antarctic Territories.
9. New name: Overseas countries of the Kingdom of the Netherlands:
   - Aruba
   - the Netherlands Antilles
     - Bonaire,
     - Curaçao,
     - Saba,
     - Sint Eustatius,
     - Sint Maarten.
10. These territories are not included in the overseas countries and territories covered by Council Decision 86/283/EEC of 30 June 1986 (see footnote 2).
11. The provisions of Part Four of the Treaty no longer apply to this territory, which became independent on 31 December 1983.
12. The associated States, as a constitutional group, no longer exist. All the component territories have become independent, except Anguilla, to which the provisions of Part Four of the Treaty continue to apply.

13. The dependencies of the Falkland Islands changed their name to South Georgia and the South Sandwich Islands on 3 October 1985 on ceasing to be dependencies of the Falkland Islands.
14. Entry added by Article 4 of the Greenland Treaty.

Protocols

Protocol on the Statute of the European Investment Bank

The High Contracting Parties,

Desiring to lay down the Statute of the European Investment Bank provided for in Article [198d][1] of this Treaty,

Have agreed upon the following provisions, which shall be annexed to this Treaty:

Article 1

The European Investment Bank established by Article [198d][1] of this Treaty (hereinafter called the 'Bank') is hereby constituted; it shall perform its functions and carry on its activities in accordance with the provisions of this Treaty and of this Statute.

The seat of the Bank shall be determined by common accord of the Governments of the Member States.

Article 2

The task of the Bank shall be that defined in Article [198e][1] of this Treaty.

Article 3[2]

In accordance with Article [198d][1] of this Treaty, the following shall be members of the Bank:

- the Kingdom of Belgium;
- the Kingdom of Denmark;
- the Federal Republic of Germany;
- the Hellenic Republic;
- the Kingdom of Spain;
- the French Republic;
- Ireland;
- the Italian Republic;
- the Grand Duchy of Luxembourg;
- the Kingdom of the Netherlands;

– 	the Portuguese Republic;
– 	the United Kingdom of Great Britain and Northern Ireland.

Article 4

1. The capital of the Bank shall be twenty-eight thousand eight hundred million ECU, subscribed by the Member States as follows:

Germany	5 508 725 000
France	5 508 725 000
Italy	5 508 725 000
United Kingdom	5 508 725 000
Spain	2 024 928 000
Belgium	1 526 980 000
Netherlands	1 526 980 000
Denmark	773 154 000
Greece	414 190 000
Portugal	266 922 000
Ireland	193 288 000
Luxembourg	38 658 000 [3]

The unit of account shall be defined as being the ECU used by the European Communities.[4] The Board of Governors, acting unanimously on a proposal from the Board of Directors, may alter the definition of the unit of account.[5]

The Member States shall be liable only up to the amount of their share of the capital subscribed and not paid up.

2. The admission of a new member shall entail an increase in the subscribed capital corresponding to the capital brought in by the new member.

3. The Board of Governors may, acting unanimously, decide to increase the subscribed capital.

4. The share of a member in the subscribed capital may not be transferred, pledged or attached.

Article 5

1. The subscribed capital shall be paid in by Member States to the extent of 9.01367457% on average of the amounts laid down in Article 4(1).[6]

2. In the event of an increase in the subscribed capital, the Board of

Governors, acting unanimously, shall fix the percentage to be paid up and the arrangements for payment.[7]

3. The Board of Directors may require payment of the balance of the subscribed capital, to such extent as may be required for the Bank to meet its obligations towards those who have made loans to it.

Each Member State shall make this payment in proportion to its share of the subscribed capital in the currencies required by the Bank to meet these obligations.[8]

Article 6

1. The Board of Governors may, acting by a qualified majority on a proposal from the Board of Directors, decide that Member States shall grant the Bank special interest-bearing loans if and to the extent that the Bank requires such loans to finance specific projects and the Board of Directors shows that the Bank is unable to obtain the necessary funds on the capital markets on terms appropriate to the nature and purpose of the projects to be financed.

2. Special loans may not be called for until the beginning of the fourth year after the entry into force of this Treaty. They shall not exceed 400 million units of account in the aggregate or 100 million units of account per annum.

3. The term of special loans shall be related to the term of the loans or guarantees which the Bank proposes to grant by means of the special loans; it shall not exceed twenty years. The Board of Governors may, acting by a qualified majority on a proposal from the Board of Directors, decide upon the prior repayment of special loans.

4. Special loans shall bear interest at 4% per annum, unless the Board of Governors, taking into account the trend and level of interest rates on the capital markets, decides to fix a different rate.

5. Special loans shall be granted by Member States in proportion to their share in the subscribed capital; payment shall be made in national currency within six months of such loans being called for.

6. Should the Bank go into liquidation, special loans granted by Member States shall be repaid only after the other debts of the Bank have been settled.

Article 7[9]

1. Should the value of the currency of a Member State in relation to the unit of account defined in Article 4 be reduced, that State shall adjust

the amount of its capital share paid in its own currency in proportion to the change in value by making a supplementary payment to the Bank.

2. Should the value of the currency of a Member State in relation to the unit of account defined in Article 4 be increased, the Bank shall adjust the amount of the capital share paid in by that State in its own currency in proportion to the change in value by making a repayment to that State.

3. For the purpose of this Article, the value of the currency of a Member State in relation to the unit of account, defined in Article 4, shall correspond to the rate for converting the unit of account into this currency and vice versa based on market rates.

4. The Board of Governors, acting unanimously on a proposal from the Board of Directors, may alter the method of converting sums expressed in units of account into national currencies and vice versa.

Furthermore, acting unanimously on a proposal from the Board of Directors, it may define the method for adjusting the capital referred to in paragraphs 1 and 2 of this Article; adjustment payments must be made at least once a year.

Article 8

The Bank shall be directed and managed by a Board of Governors, a Board of Directors and a Management Committee.

Article 9

1. The Board of Governors shall consist of the Ministers designated by the Member States.

2. The Board of Governors shall lay down general directives for the credit policy of the Bank, with particular reference to the objectives to be pursued as progress is made in the attainment of the common market.

The Board of Governors shall ensure that these directives are implemented.

3. The Board of Governors shall in addition:

(a) decide whether to increase the subscribed capital in accordance with Article 4(3) and Article 5(2);[10]

(b) exercise the powers provided in Article 6 in respect of special loans;

(c) exercise the powers provided in Articles 11 and 13 in respect of the appointment and the compulsory retirement of the members of the

Board of Directors and of the Management Committee, and those powers provided in the second subparagraph of Article 13(1);[10]

(d) authorise the derogation provided for in Article 18(1);

(e) approve the annual report of the Board of Directors;

(f) approve the annual balance sheet and profit and loss account;

(g) exercise the powers and functions provided in Articles 4, 7, 14, 17, 26 and 27;[11]

(h) approve the rules of procedure of the Bank.

4. Within the framework of this Treaty and this Statute, the Board of Governors shall be competent to take, acting unanimously, any decisions concerning the suspension of the operations of the Bank and, should the event arise, its liquidation.

Article 10[12]

Save as otherwise provided in this Statute, decisions of the Board of Governors shall be taken by a majority of its members. This majority must represent at least 45% of the subscribed capital. Voting by the Board of Governors shall be in accordance with the provisions of Article 148 of this Treaty.

Article 11

1. The Board of Directors shall have sole power to take decisions in respect of granting loans and guarantees and raising loans; it shall fix the interest rates on loans granted and the commission on guarantees; it shall see that the Bank is properly run; it shall ensure that the Bank is managed in accordance with the provisions of this Treaty and of this Statute and with the general directives laid down by the Board of Governors.

At the end of the financial year the Board of Directors shall submit a report to the Board of Governors and shall publish it when approved.

2. The Board of Directors shall consist of 22 directors and 12 alternates.[13]

The directors shall be appointed by the Board of Governors for five years as shown below:

– three directors nominated by the Federal Republic of Germany,

– three directors nominated by the French Republic,

– three directors nominated by the Italian Republic,

- three directors nominated by the United Kingdom of Great Britain and Northern Ireland,
- two directors nominated by the Kingdom of Spain,
- one director nominated by the Kingdom of Belgium,
- one director nominated by the Kingdom of Denmark,
- one director nominated by the Hellenic Republic,
- one director nominated by Ireland,
- one director nominated by the Grand Duchy of Luxembourg,
- one director nominated by the Kingdom of the Netherlands,
- one director nominated by the Portuguese Republic,
- one director nominated by the Commission.[13]

The alternates shall be appointed by the Board of Governors for five years as shown below:

- two alternates nominated by the Federal Republic of Germany,
- two alternates nominated by the French Republic,
- two alternates nominated by the Italian Republic,
- two alternates nominated by the United Kingdom of Great Britain and Northern Ireland,
- one alternate nominated by common accord of the Kingdom of Denmark, the Hellenic Republic and Ireland,
- one alternate nominated by common accord of the Benelux countries,
- one alternate nominated by common accord of the Kingdom of Spain and the Portuguese Republic,
- one alternate nominated by the Commission.[13]

The appointments of the directors and the alternates shall be renewable.[14]

Alternates may take part in the meetings of the Board of Directors. Alternates nominated by a State, or by common accord of several States, or by the Commission, may replace directors nominated by that State, by one of those States or by the Commission respectively. Alternates shall have no right of vote except where they replace one director or more than one director or where they have been delegated for this purpose in accordance with Article 12(1).[14]

The President of the Management Committee or, in his absence, one of the Vice-Presidents, shall preside over meetings of the Board of Directors but shall not vote.

Members of the Board of Directors shall be chosen from persons whose independence and competence are beyond doubt; they shall be responsible only to the Bank.

3. A director may be compulsorily retired by the Board of Governors only if he no longer fulfils the conditions required for the performance of his duties; the Board must act by a qualified majority.

If the annual report is not approved, the Board of Directors shall resign.

4. Any vacancy arising as a result of death, voluntary resignation, compulsory retirement or collective resignation shall be filled in accordance with paragraph 2. A member shall be replaced for the remainder of his term of office, save where the entire Board of Directors is being replaced.

5. The Board of Governors shall determine the remuneration of members of the Board of Directors. The Board of Governors shall, acting unanimously, lay down what activities are incompatible with the duties of a director or an alternate.

Article 12

1. Each director shall have one vote on the Board of Directors. He may delegate his vote in all cases, according to procedures to be laid down in the rules of procedure of the Bank.[15]

2. Save as otherwise provided in this Statute, decisions of the Board of Directors shall be taken by a simple majority of the members entitled to vote. A qualified majority shall require fifteen votes in favour.[16] The rules of procedure of the Bank shall lay down how many members of the Board of Directors constitute the quorum needed for the adoption of decisions.

Article 13

1. The Management Committee shall consist of a President and six Vice-Presidents appointed for a period of six years by the Board of Governors on a proposal from the Board of Directors. Their appointments shall be renewable.[17]

The Board of Governors, acting unanimously, may vary the number of members on the Management Committee.[18]

2. On a proposal from the Board of Directors adopted by a qualified

majority, the Board of Governors may, acting in its turn by a qualified majority, compulsorily retire a member of the Management Committee.

3. The Management Committee shall be responsible for the current business of the Bank, under the authority of the President and the supervision of the Board of Directors.

It shall prepare the decisions of the Board of Directors, in particular decisions on the raising of loans and the granting of loans and guarantees; it shall ensure that these decisions are implemented.

4. The Management Committee shall act by a majority when delivering opinions on proposals for raising loans or granting loans and guarantees.

5. The Board of Governors shall determine the remuneration of members of the Management Committee and shall lay down what activities are incompatible with their duties.

6. The President or, if he is prevented, a Vice-President shall represent the Bank in judicial and other matters.

7. The officials and other employees of the Bank shall be under the authority of the President. They shall be engaged and discharged by him. In the selection of staff, account shall be taken not only of personal ability and qualifications but also of an equitable representation of nationals of Member States.

8. The Management Committee and the staff of the Bank shall be responsible only to the Bank and shall be completely independent in the performance of their duties.

Article 14

1. A Committee consisting of three members, appointed on the grounds of their competence by the Board of Governors, shall annually verify that the operations of the Bank have been conducted and its books kept in a proper manner.

2. The Committee shall confirm that the balance sheet and profit and loss account are in agreement with the accounts and faithfully reflect the position of the Bank in respect of its assets and liabilities.

Article 15

The Bank shall deal with each Member State through the authority designated by that State. In the conduct of financial operations the Bank shall have recourse to the bank of issue of the Member State concerned or to other financial institutions approved by that State.

Article 16

1. The Bank shall cooperate with all international organisations active in fields similar to its own.

2. The Bank shall seek to establish all appropriate contacts in the interests of cooperation with banking and financial institutions in the countries to which its operations extend.

Article 17

At the request of a Member State or of the Commission, or on its own initiative, the Board of Governors shall, in accordance with the same provisions as governed their adoption, interpret or supplement the directives laid down by it under Article 9 of this Statute.

Article 18

1. Within the framework of the task set out in Article 130 of this Treaty, the Bank shall grant loans to its members or to private or public undertakings for investment projects to be carried out in the European territories of Member States, to the extent that funds are not available from other sources on reasonable terms.

However, by way of derogation authorised by the Board of Governors, acting unanimously on a proposal from the Board of Directors, the Bank may grant loans for investment projects to be carried out, in whole or in part, outside the European territories of Member States.

2. As far as possible, loans shall be granted only on condition that other sources of finance are also used.

3. When granting a loan to an undertaking or to a body other than a Member State, the Bank shall make the loan conditional either on a guarantee from the Member State in whose territory the project will be carried out or on other adequate guarantees.

4. The Bank may guarantee loans contracted by public or private undertakings or other bodies for the purpose of carrying out projects provided for in Article 130 of this Treaty.

5. The aggregate amount outstanding at any time of loans and guarantees granted by the Bank shall not exceed 250% of its subscribed capital.

6. The Bank shall protect itself against exchange risks by including in contracts for loans and guarantees such clauses as it considers appropriate.

Article 19

1. Interest rates on loans to be granted by the Bank and commission on guarantees shall be adjusted to conditions prevailing on the capital market and shall be calculated in such a way that the income therefrom shall enable the Bank to meet its obligations, to cover its expenses and to build up a reserve fund as provided for in Article 24.

2. The Bank shall not grant any reduction in interest rates. Where a reduction in the interest rate appears desirable in view of the nature of the project to be financed, the Member State concerned or some other agency may grant aid towards the payment of interest to the extent that this is compatible with Article 92 of this Treaty.

Article 20

In its loan and guarantee operations, the Bank shall observe the following principles:

1. It shall ensure that its funds are employed as rationally as possible in the interests of the Community.

It may grant loans or guarantees only:

(a) where, in the case of projects carried out by undertakings in the production sector, interest and amortisation payments are covered out of operating profits or, in other cases, either by a commitment entered into by the State in which the project is carried out or by some other means; and

(b) where the execution of the project contributes to an increase in economic productivity in general and promotes the attainment of the common market.

2. It shall neither acquire any interest in an undertaking nor assume any responsibility in its management unless this is required to safeguard the rights of the Bank in ensuring recovery of funds lent.

3. It may dispose of its claim on the capital market and may, to this end, require its debtors to issue bonds or other securities.

4. Neither the Bank nor the Member States shall impose conditions requiring funds lent by the Bank to be spent within a specified Member State.

5. The Bank may make its loans conditional on international invitations to tender being arranged.

6. The Bank shall not finance, in whole or in part, any project opposed by the Member State in whose territory it is to be carried out.

Article 21

1. Applications for loans or guarantees may be made to the Bank either through the Commission or through the Member State in whose territory the project will be carried out. An undertaking may also apply direct to the Bank for a loan or guarantee.

2. Applications made through the Commission shall be submitted for an opinion to the Member State in whose territory the project will be carried out. Applications made through a Member State shall be submitted to the Commission for an opinion. Applications made direct by an undertaking shall be submitted to the Member State concerned and to the Commission.

The Member State concerned and the Commission shall deliver their opinions within two months. If no reply is received within this period, the Bank may assume that there is no objection to the project in question.

3. The Board of Directors shall rule on applications for loans or guarantees submitted to it by the Management Committee.

4. The Management Committee shall examine whether applications for loans or guarantees submitted to it comply with the provisions of this Statute, in particular with Article 20. Where the Management Committee is in favour of granting the loan or guarantee, it shall submit the draft contract to the Board of Directors; the Committee may make its favourable opinion subject to such conditions as it considers essential. Where the Management Committee is against granting the loan or guarantee, it shall submit the relevant documents together with its opinion to the Board of Directors.

5. Where the Management Committee delivers an unfavourable opinion, the Board of Directors may not grant the loan or guarantee concerned unless its decision is unanimous.

6. Where the Commission delivers an unfavourable opinion, the Board of Directors may not grant the loan or guarantee concerned unless its decision is unanimous, the director nominated by the Commission abstaining.

7. Where both the Management Committee and the Commission deliver an unfavourable opinion, the Board of Directors may not grant the loan or guarantee.

Article 22

1. The Bank shall borrow on the international capital markets the funds necessary for the performance of its tasks.

2. The Bank may borrow on the capital market of a Member State either in accordance with the legal provisions applying to internal issues or, if there are no such provisions in a Member State, after the Bank and the Member State concerned have conferred together and reached agreement on the proposed loan.

The competent authorities in the Member State concerned may refuse to give their assent only if there is reason to fear serious disturbances on the capital market of that State.

Article 23

1. The Bank may employ any available funds which it does not immediately require to meet its obligations in the following ways:

(a) it may invest on the money markets;

(b) it may, subject to the provisions of Article 20(2), buy and sell securities issued by itself or by those who have borrowed from it;

(c) it may carry out any other financial operation linked with its objectives.

2. Without prejudice to the provisions of Article 25, the Bank shall not, in managing its investments, engage in any currency arbitrage not directly requiring to carry out its lending operations or fulfil commitments arising out of loans raised or guarantees granted by it.

3. The Bank shall, in the fields covered by this Article, act in agreement with the competent authorities or with the bank of issue of the Member State concerned.

Article 24

1. A reserve fund of up to 10% of the subscribed capital shall be built up progressively. If the state of the liabilities of the Bank should so justify, the Board of Directors may decide to set aside additional reserves. Until such time as the reserve fund has been fully built up, it shall be fed by:

(a) interest received on loans granted by the Bank out of sums to be paid up by the Member States pursuant to Article 5;

(b) interest received on loans granted by the Bank out of funds derived from repayment of the loans referred to in (a);

to the extent that this income is not required to meet the obligations of the Bank or to cover its expenses.

2. The resources of the reserve fund shall be so invested as to be available at any time to meet the purpose of the fund.

Article 25

1. The Bank shall at all times be entitled to transfer its assets in the currency of one Member State into the currency of another Member State in order to carry out financial operations corresponding to the task set out in Article 130 of this Treaty, taking into account the provisions of Article 23 of this Statute. The Bank shall, as far as possible, avoid making such transfers if it has cash or liquid assets in the currency required.

2. The Bank may not convert its assets in the currency of a Member State into the currency of a third country without the agreement of the Member State concerned.

3. The Bank may freely dispose of that part of its capital which is paid up in gold or convertible currency and of any currency borrowed on markets outside the Community.

4. The Member States undertake to make available to the debtors of the Bank the currency needed to repay the capital and pay the interest on loans or commission on guarantees granted by the Bank for projects to be carried out in their territory.

Article 26

If a Member State fails to meet the obligations of membership arising from this Statute, in particular the obligation to pay its share of the subscribed capital, to grant its special loans or to service its borrowings, the granting of loans or guarantees to that Member State or its nationals may be suspended by a decision of the Board of Governors, acting by a qualified majority.

Such decision shall not release either the State or its nationals from their obligations towards the Bank.

Article 27

1. If the Board of Governors decides to suspend the operations of the Bank, all its activities shall cease forthwith, except those required to ensure the due realisation, protection and preservation of its assets and the settlement of its liabilities.

2. In the event of liquidation, the Board of Governors shall appoint the liquidators and give them instructions for carrying out the liquidation.

Article 28

1. In each of the Member States, the Bank shall enjoy the most extensive legal capacity accorded to legal persons under their laws; it may, in

particular, acquire or dispose of movable or immovable property and may be a party to legal proceedings.

(*Second subparagraph repealed by the second paragraph of Article 28 of the Merger Treaty*)

[*See the first paragraph of Article 28 of the Merger Treaty, which reads as follows*:

The European Communities shall enjoy in the territories of the Member States such privileges and immunities as are necessary for the performance of their tasks, under the conditions laid down in the Protocol annexed to this Treaty. The same shall apply to the European Investment Bank.][19]

2. The property of the Bank shall be exempt from all forms of requisition or expropriation.

Article 29

Disputes between the Bank on the one hand, and its creditors, debtors or any other person on the other, shall be decided by the competent national courts, save where jurisdiction has been conferred on the Court of Justice.

The Bank shall have an address for service in each Member State. It may, however, in any contract, specify a particular address for service or provide for arbitration.

The property and assets of the Bank shall not be liable to attachment or to seizure by way of execution except by decision of a court.

Done at Rome this twenty-fifth day of March in the year one thousand nine hundred and fifty-seven.

[List omitted]

EDITORIAL NOTE

See Treaty amending certain provisions of the Protocol on the Statute of the European Investment Bank (OJ No L 91, 6.4.78) and the Act amending the Protocol on the Statute of the European Investment Bank (OJ No 173, 7.7.94, p.1).

FOOTNOTES

1. Replaced by the Treaty on European Union, Title II, Article G,G(86).
2. Text as replaced by Article 1 of Protocol No 1 annexed to the Act of Accession ESP/PORT.
3. First subparagraph of paragraph 1 as replaced by Article 2 of Protocol No 1 annexed to the Act of Accession ESP/PORT.
4. Second subparagraph of paragraph 1 as amended by the Decision of the Board of Governors of 13 May 1981 (OJ No L 311, 30.10.81).
5. Second subparagraph of paragraph 1 as supplemented by Article 1 of the Treaty amending the Protocol on the Statute of the Bank.

6. Paragraph 1 as replaced by Article 3 of Protocol No 1 annexed to the Act of Accession ESP/PORT.
7. Paragraph 2 as replaced by Article 3 of Protocol No 1 annexed to the Act of Accession DK/IRL/UK.
8. Paragraph 3 as replaced by Article 3 of Protocol No 1 annexed to the Act of Accession DK/IRL/UK.
9. Article as amended by Article 3 of Protocol No 1 annexed to the Act of Accession GR.
10. Subparagraphs (a) and (c) as amended by Article 4 of Protocol No 1 annexed to the Act of Accession DK/IRL/UK.
11. Subparagraph (g) as amended by Article 3 of the Treaty amending the Protocol on the Statute of the Bank.
12. Article as amended by Article 4 of Protocol No 1 annexed to the Act of Accession ESP/PORT.
13. First, second and third subparagraphs of paragraph 2 as amended by Article 5 of Protocol No 1 annexed to the Act of Accession ESP/PORT.
14. Fourth and fifth subparagraphs of paragraph 2 as amended by Article 6 of Protocol No 1 annexed to the Act of Accession DK/IRL/UK in the version resulting from Article 37 of the AD AA DK/IRL/UK.
15. Paragraph 1 as amended by Article 7 of Protocol No 1 annexed to the Act of Accession DK/IRL/UK.
16. Second sentence of paragraph 2 as amended by Article 6 of Protocol No 1 annexed to the Act of Accession ESP/PORT.
17. First subparagraph of paragraph 1 as amended by Article 7 of Protocol No 1 annexed to the Act of Accession ESP/PORT.
18. Second subparagraph of paragraph 1 as amended by Article 9 of Protocol No 1 annexed to the Act of Accession DK/IRL/UK.
19. Text of Merger Treaty not included in this volume. See OJ No 152, 13.7.67.

Protocol on German internal trade and connected problems

[Text omitted]

Protocol on certain provisions relating to France

[Text omitted]

Protocol on Italy

[Text omitted]

Protocol on the Grand Duchy of Luxembourg

[Text omitted]

Protocol on goods originating in and coming from certain countries and enjoying special treatment when imported into a Member State

The High Contracting Parties,

Desiring to define in greater detail the application of this Treaty to certain goods originating in and coming from certain countries and enjoying special treatment when imported into a Member State,

Have agreed upon the following provisions, which shall be annexed to this Treaty:

1. The application of the Treaty establishing the European Community shall not require any alteration in the customs treatment applicable, at the time of the entry into force of this Treaty, to imports:

(a) into the Benelux countries of goods originating in and coming from Surinam[1] or the Netherlands Antilles;[2]

(b) into France of goods originating in and coming from Morocco, Tunisia, the Republic of Vietnam, Cambodia or Laos. This shall also apply to the French Settlements in the Condominium of the New Hebrides;[3]

(c) into Italy of goods originating in and coming from Libya or the Trust Territory of Somaliland currently under Italian administration.[4]

2. Goods imported in a Member State and benefiting from the treatment referred to above shall not be considered to be in free circulation in that State within the meaning of Article 10 of this Treaty when re-exported to another Member State.

3. Before the end of the first year after the entry into force of this Treaty, Member States shall communicate to the Commission and to the other Member States their rules governing the special treatment referred to in this Protocol, together with a list of the goods entitled to such treatment.

They shall also inform the Commission and the other Member States of any changes subsequently made in those lists or in the treatment.

4. The Commission shall ensure that the application of these rules cannot be prejudicial to other Member States; to this end it may take any appropriate measures as regards relations between Member States.

Done at Rome this twenty-fifth day of March in the year one thousand nine hundred and fifty-seven.

[List omitted]

FOOTNOTES

1. Editorial note [original]: These provisions of Part Four of the Treaty were applied to Surinam, by virtue of a Supplementary Act of the Kingdom of the Netherlands to complete its instrument of ratification, from 1 September 1962 to 16 July 1976.

2. In accordance with Article 1 of the Convention of 13 November 1962 amending the Treaty establishing the European Community (OJ No 150, 1.10.64, p.2414), the protocol no longer applies to the Netherlands Antilles.
3. See Annex IV of the Treaty.
4. These two countries have become independent.

Protocol on the treatment to be applied to products within the province of the European Coal and Steel Community in respect of Algeria and the Overseas Departments of the French Republic

The High Contracting Parties,

Conscious of the fact that the provisions of this Treaty relating to Algeria and the overseas departments of the French Republic raise the problem of the treatment to be applied, in respect of Algeria and those departments, to products covered by the Treaty establishing the European Coal and Steel Community.

Desiring to seek an appropriate solution in harmony with the principles of the two Treaties,

Undertake to settle this problem in a spirit of mutual cooperation within the shortest possible time and not later than the first revision of the Treaty establishing the European Coal and Steel Community.

Done at Rome this twenty-fifth day of March in the year one thousand nine hundred and fifty-seven.

[List omitted]

Protocol on mineral oils and certain of their derivatives

The High Contracting Parties,

Have agreed upon the following provisions, which shall be annexed to this Treaty:

1. Each Member State may, for a period of six years after this Treaty enters into force, maintain in regard to other Member States and third countries the customs duties and charges having equivalent effect applied to products falling within headings Nos 27.09, 27.10, 27.11, 27.12 and ex 27.13 (paraffin wax, microcrystalline wax, slack wax and scale wax) of the Brussels Nomenclature on 1 January 1957 or, if lower, on the date when this Treaty enters into force. The duty to be maintained on crude oils shall not, however, be such as to result in an increase of more than 5% in the difference existing on 1 January 1957 between the duties on crude oils and those on the derivatives referred to above. Where no such difference exists, any difference subsequently introduced

shall not exceed 5% of the duty which applied on 1 January 1957 to products falling within heading No 27.09. If, before the end of this period of six years, a reduction is made in the customs duties or charges having equivalent effect in respect of products falling within heading No 27.09, a corresponding reduction shall be made in any customs duties or charges having equivalent effect imposed on the other products referred to above.

At the end of this period, the duties maintained in accordance with the preceding subparagraph shall be completely abolished in respect of other Member States. At the same time, the common customs tariff shall be applicable to third countries.

2. Any aids to the production of mineral oils falling within heading No 27.09 of the Brussels Nomenclature shall, where such aids prove necessary in order to bring the price of crude oils down to the world market price cif European port of a Member State, be governed by Article 92(3)(c) of this Treaty. The Commission shall, during the first two stages, make use of the powers provided under Article 93 only to the extent required to prevent such aids being misused.

Done at Rome this twenty-fifth day of March in the year one thousand nine hundred and fifty-seven.

[List omitted]

Protocol on the application of the Treaty establishing the European Community to the non-European parts of the Kingdom of the Netherlands

The High Contracting Parties,

Anxious, at the time of signature of the Treaty establishing the European Community, to define the scope of the provisions of Article 227 of this Treaty in respect of the Kingdom of the Netherlands,

Have agreed upon the following provisions, which shall be annexed to this Treaty:

The Government of the Kingdom of the Netherlands, by reason of constitutional structure of the Kingdom resulting from the Statute of 29 December 1954, shall, by way of derogation from Article 227, be entitled to ratify the Treaty on behalf of the Kingdom in Europe and Netherlands New Guinea only.

Done at Rome this twenty-fifth day of March in the year one thousand nine hundred and fifty-seven.

[List omitted]

Protocol on the Statute of the Court of Justice of the [European Communities][1]

The High Contracting Parties to the Treaty establishing the European Community,

Desiring to lay down the Statute of the Court provided for in Article 188 of this Treaty,

Have designated as their plenipotentiaries for this purpose:

[List omitted]

Who, having exchanged their Full Powers, found in good and due form,

Have agreed upon the following provisions, which shall be annexed to the Treaty establishing the European Community.

Article 1

The Court established by Article 4 of this Treaty shall be constituted and shall function in accordance with the provisions of this Treaty and of this Statute.

Title I

Judges and Advocates-General

Article 2

Before taking up his duties each Judge shall, in open court, take an oath to perform his duties impartially and conscientiously and to preserve the secrecy of the deliberations of the Court.

Article 3

The Judges shall be immune from legal proceedings. After they have ceased to hold office, they shall continue to enjoy immunity in respect of acts performed by them in their official capacity including words spoken or written.

The Court, sitting in plenary session, may waive the immunity.

Where immunity has been waived and criminal proceedings are instituted against a Judge, he shall be tried, in any of the Member States, only by the Court competent to judge the members of the highest national judiciary.

Article 4

The Judges may not hold any political or administrative office.

They may not engage in any occupation, whether gainful or not, unless exemption is exceptionally granted by the Council.

When taking up their duties, they shall give a solemn undertaking that, both during the after their term of office, they will respect the obligations arising therefrom in particular the duty to behave with integrity and discretion as regards the acceptance, after they have ceased to hold office, of certain appointments or benefits.

Any doubt on this point shall be settled by decision of the Court.

Article 5

Apart from normal replacement, or death, the duties of a Judge shall end when he resigns.

Where a Judge resigns, his letter of resignation shall be addressed to the President of the Court for transmission to the President of the Council. Upon this notification a vacancy shall arise on the bench.

Save where Article 6 applies, a Judge shall continue to hold office until his successor takes up his duties.

Article 6

A Judge may be deprived of his office or of his right to a pension or other benefits in its stead only if, in the unanimous opinion of the Judges and Advocates-General of the Court, he no longer fulfils the requisite conditions or meets the obligations arising from his office. The Judge concerned shall not take part in any such deliberations.

The Registrar of the Court shall communicate the decision of the Court to the President of the European Parliament and to the President of the Commission and shall notify it to the President of the Council.

In the case of a decision depriving a Judge of his office, a vacancy shall arise on the bench upon this latter notification.

Article 7

A Judge who is to replace a member of the Court whose term of office has not expired shall be appointed for the remainder of his predecessor's term.

Article 8

The provisions of Articles 2 to 7 shall apply to the Advocates-General.

Title II

Organisation

Article 9

The registrar shall take an oath before the Court to perform his duties impartially and conscientiously and to preserve the secrecy of the deliberations of the Court.

Article 10

The Court shall arrange for replacement of the Registrar on occasions when he is prevented from attending the Court.

Article 11

Officials and other servants shall be attached to the Court to enable it to function. They shall be responsible to the Registrar under the authority of the President.

Article 12

On a proposal from the Court, the Council may, acting unanimously, provide for the appointment of Assistant Rapporteurs and lay down the rules governing their service. The Assistant Rapporteurs may be required, under conditions laid down in the rules of procedure, to participate in preparatory inquiries in cases pending before the Court and to cooperate with the Judge who acts as Rapporteur.

The Assistant Rapporteurs shall be chosen from persons whose independence is beyond doubt and who possess the necessary legal qualifications; they shall be appointed by the Council. They shall take an oath before the Court to perform their duties impartially and conscientiously and to preserve the secrecy of the deliberations of the Court.

Article 13

The Judges, the Advocates-General and the Registrar shall be required to reside at the place where the Court has its seat.

Article 14

The Court shall remain permanently in session. The duration of the judicial vacations shall be determined by the Court with due regard to the needs of its business.

Article 15[2]

Decisions of the Court shall be valid only when an uneven number of its members is sitting in the deliberations. Decisions of the full Court shall be valid if seven members are sitting. Decisions of the Chambers shall be valid only if three Judges are sitting; in the event of one of the Judges of a Chamber being prevented from attending, a Judge of another Chamber may be called upon to sit in accordance with conditions laid down in the rules of procedure.

Article 16

No Judge or Advocate-General may take part in the disposal of any case in which he has previously taken part as agent or adviser or has acted for one of the parties, or in which he has been called upon to pronounce as a Member of a court or tribunal, of a commission of inquiry or in any other capacity.

If, for some special reason, any Judge or Advocate-General considers that he should not take part in the judgment or examination of a particular case, he shall so inform the President. If, for some special reason, the President considers that any Judge or Advocate-General should not sit or make submissions in a particular case, he shall notify him accordingly.

Any difficulty arising as to the application of this Article shall be settled by decision of the Court.

A party may not apply for a change in the composition of the Court or of one of its Chambers on the grounds of either the nationality of a judge or the absence from the Court or from the Chamber of a Judge of the nationality of that party.

Title III

Procedure

Article 17

The States and the institutions of the Community shall be represented before the Court by an agent appointed for each case; the agent may be assisted by an adviser or by a lawyer entitled to practise before a court of a Member State.

Other parties must be represented by a lawyer entitled to practise before a court of a Member State.

Such agents, advisers and lawyers shall, when they appear before the Court, enjoy the rights and immunities necessary to the independent exercise of their duties, under conditions laid down in the rules of procedure.

As regards such advisers and lawyers who appear before it, the Court shall have the powers normally accorded to courts of law, under conditions laid down in the rules of procedure.

University teachers being nationals of a Member State whose law accords them a right of audience shall have the same rights before the Court as are accorded by this Article to lawyers entitled to practise before a court of a Member State.

Article 18

The procedure before the Court shall consist of two parts: written and oral.

The written procedure shall consist of the communication to the parties and to the institutions of the Community whose decisions are in dispute, of applications, statements of case, defences and observations, and of replies, if any, as well as of all papers and documents in support or of certified copies of them.

Communications shall be made by the Registrar in the order and within the time laid down in the rules of procedure.

The oral procedure shall consist of the reading of the report presented by a Judge acting as Rapporteur, the hearing by the Court of agents, advisers and lawyers entitled to practise before a court of a Member State and of the submissions of the Advocate-General, as well as the hearing, if any, of witnesses and experts.

Article 19

A case shall be brought before the Court by a written application addressed to the Registrar. The application shall contain the applicant's name and permanent address and the description of the signatory, the name of the party against whom the application is made, the subject matter of the dispute, the submissions and a brief statement of the grounds on which the application is based.

The application shall be accompanied, where appropriate, by the measure the annulment of which is sought or, in the circumstances referred to in Article 175 of this Treaty, by documentary evidence of the date on which an institution was, in accordance with that Article, requested to act. If the documents are not submitted with the application, the Registrar shall ask the party concerned to produce them within a reasonable period, but in that event the rights of the party shall not lapse even if such documents are produced after the time limit for bringing proceedings.

Article 20

In the cases governed by Article 177 of this Treaty, the decision of the court or tribunal of a Member State which suspends its proceedings and refers a case to the Court shall be notified to the Court by the court or tribunal concerned. The decision shall then be notified by the Registrar of the Court to the parties, to the Member States and to the Commission, and also to the Council if the act the validity or interpretation of which is in dispute originates from the Council.

Within two months of this notification, the parties, the Member State, the Commission and, where appropriate, the Council, shall be entitled to submit statements of case or written observations to the Court.

Article 21

The Court may require the parties to produce all documents and to supply all information which the Court considers desirable. Formal note shall be taken of any refusal.

The Court may also require the Member States and institutions not being parties to the case to supply all information which the Court considers necessary for the proceedings.

Article 22

The Court may at any time entrust any individual, body, authority, committee or other organisation it chooses with the task of giving an expert opinion.

Article 23

Witnesses may be heard under conditions laid down in the rules of procedure.

Article 24

With respect to defaulting witnesses the Court shall have the powers generally granted to courts and tribunals and may impose pecuniary penalties under conditions laid down in the rules of procedure.

Article 25

Witnesses and experts may be heard on oath taken in the form laid down in the rules of procedure or in the manner laid down by the law of the country of the witness or expert.

Article 26

The Court may order that a witness or expert be heard by the judicial authority of his place of permanent residence.

The order shall be sent for implementation to the competent judicial authority under conditions laid down in the rules of procedure. The documents drawn up in compliance with the letters rogatory shall be returned to the Court under the same conditions.

The Court shall defray the expenses, without prejudice to the right to charge them, where appropriate, to the parties.

Article 27

A Member State shall treat any violation of an oath by a witness or expert in the same manner as if the offence had been committed before one of its courts with jurisdiction in civil proceedings. At the instance of the Court, the Member State concerned shall prosecute the offender before its competent court.

Article 28

The hearing in court shall be public, unless the Court, of its own motion or on application by the parties, decides otherwise for serious reasons.

Article 29

During the hearings the Court may examine the experts, the witnesses and the parties themselves. The latter, however, may address the Court only through their representatives.

Article 30

Minutes shall be made of each hearing and signed by the President and the Registrar.

Article 31

The case list shall be established by the President.

Article 32

The deliberations of the Court shall be and shall remain secret.

Article 33

Judgments shall state the reasons on which they are based. They shall contain the names of the Judges who took part in the deliberations.

Article 34

Judgments shall be signed by the President and the Registrar. They shall be read in open court.

Article 35

The Court shall adjudicate upon costs.

Article 36

The President of the Court may, by way of summary procedure, which may, in so far as necessary, differ from some of the rules contained in this Statute and which shall be laid down in the rules of procedure, adjudicate upon applications to suspend execution, as provided for in Article 185 of this Treaty, or to prescribe interim measures in pursuance of Article 186, or to suspend enforcement in accordance with the last paragraph of Article 192.

Should the President be prevented from attending, his place shall be taken by another Judge under conditions laid down in the rules of procedure.

The ruling of the President or of the Judge replacing him shall be provisional and shall in no way prejudice the decision of the Court on the substance of the case.

Article 37

Member States and institutions of the Community may intervene in cases before the Court.

The same right shall be open to any other person establishing an interest in the result of any case submitted to the Court, save in cases between Member States, between institutions of the Community or between Member States and institutions of the Community.

Submissions made in an application to intervene shall be limited to supporting the submissions of one of the parties.

Article 38

Where the defending party, after having been duly summoned, fails to file written submissions in defence, judgment shall be given against that party by default. An objection may be lodged against the judgment within one month of it being notified. The objection shall not have the effect of staying enforcement of the judgment by default unless the Court decides otherwise.

Article 39

Member States, institutions of the Community and any other natural or legal persons may, in cases and under conditions to be determined by the rules of procedure, institute third-party proceedings to contest a judgment rendered without their being heard, where the judgment is prejudicial to their rights.

Article 40

If the meaning or scope of a judgment is in doubt, the Court shall construe it on application by any party or any institution of the Community establishing an interest therein.

Article 41

An application for revision of a judgment may be made to the Court only on discovery of a fact which is of such a nature as to be a decisive factor, and which, when the judgment was given, was unknown to the Court and to the party claiming the revision.

The revision shall be opened by a judgment of the Court expressly recording the existence of a new fact, recognising that it is of such a character as to lay the case open to revision and declaring the application admissible on this ground.

No application for revision may be made after the lapse of ten years from the date of the judgment.

Article 42

Periods of grace based on considerations of distance shall be determined by the rules of procedure.

No right shall be prejudiced in consequence of the expiry of a time limit if the party concerned proves the existence of unforeseeable circumstances or of *force majeure*.

Article 43

Proceedings against the Community in matters arising from non-contractual liability shall be barred after a period of five years from the occurrence of the event giving rise thereto. The period of limitation shall be interrupted if proceedings are instituted before the Court or if prior to such proceedings an application is made by the aggrieved party to the relevant institution of the Community. In the latter event the proceedings must be instituted within the period of two months provided for in Article 173; the provisions of the second paragraph of Article 175 shall apply where appropriate.

[Title IV

The Court of First Instance of the European Communities

Article 44

Articles 2 to 8, and 13 to 16 of this Statute shall apply to the Court of First Instance and its members. The oath referred to in Article 2 shall be taken before the Court of Justice and the decisions referred to in Articles 3, 4 and 6 shall be adopted by that Court after hearing the Court of First Instance.

Article 45

The Court of First Instance shall appoint its Registrar and lay down the rules governing his service. Articles 9, 10 and 13 of this Statute shall apply to the Registrar of the Court of First Instance *mutatis mutandis*.

The President of the Court of Justice and the President of the Court of First Instance shall determine, by common accord, the conditions under which officials and other servants attached to the Court of Justice shall render their services to the Court of First Instance to enable it to function. Certain officials or other servants shall be responsible to the Registrar of the Court of First Instance under the authority of the President of the Court of First Instance.

Article 46

The procedure before the Court of First Instance shall be governed by Title III of this Statute, with the exception of Article 20.

Such further and more detailed provisions as may be necessary shall be laid down in the Rules of Procedure established in accordance with Article 168a(4) of the Treaty.

Notwithstanding the fourth paragraph of Article 18 of this Statute, the Advocate-General may make his reasoned submissions in writing.

Article 47

Where an application or other procedural document addressed to the Court of First Instance is lodged by mistake with the Registrar of the Court of Justice it shall be transmitted immediately by that Registrar to the Registrar of the Court of First Instance; likewise, where an application or other procedural document addressed to the Court of Justice is lodged by mistake with the Registrar of the Court of First Instance, it shall be transmitted immediately by that Registrar to the Registrar to the Court of Justice.

Where the Court of First Instance finds that it does not have jurisdiction to hear and determine an action in respect of which the Court of Justice has jurisdiction, it shall refer that action to the Court of Justice; likewise, where the Court of Justice finds that an action falls within the jurisdiction of the Court of First Instance, it shall refer that action to the Court of First Instance, whereupon that Court may not decline jurisdiction.

Where the Court of Justice and the Court of First Instance are seised of cases in which the same relief is sought, the same issue or interpretation is raised or the validity of the same act is called in question, the Court of First Instance may, after hearing the parties, stay the proceedings before it until such time as the Court of Justice shall have delivered judgment. Where applications are made for the same act to be declared void, the Court of First Instance may, after hearing the parties, stay the proceedings before it until such time as the Court of Justice shall have delivered judgment. Where applications are made for the same act to be declared void, the Court of First Instance may also decline jurisdiction in order that the Court of Justice may rule on such applications. In the cases referred to in this subparagraph, the Court of Justice may also decide to stay the proceedings before it; in that event, the proceedings before the Court of First Instance shall continue.

Article 48

Final decisions of the Court of First Instance, decisions disposing of the substantive issues in part only or disposing of a procedural issue concerning a plea of lack of competence or inadmissibility, shall be notified by the Registrar of the Court of First Instance to all parties as well as all Member States and the Community institutions even if they have not intervened in the case before the Court of First Instance.

Article 49

An appeal may be brought before the Court of Justice, within two months of the notification of the decision appealed against, against final decisions of the Court of First Instance and decisions of that Court disposing of the substantive issues in part only or disposing of a procedural issue concerning a plea of lack of competence or inadmissibility.

Such an appeal may be brought by any party which has been unsuccessful, in whole or in part, in its submissions. However, interveners other than the Member States and the Community institution may bring such an appeal only where the decision of the Court of First Instance directly affects them.

With the exception of cases relating to disputes between the Communities and their servants, an appeal may also be brought by Member States and Community institutions which did not intervene in the proceedings before the Court of First Instance. Such Member States and institutions shall be in the same position as Member States or institutions which intervened at first instance.

Article 50

Any person whose application to intervene has been dismissed by the Court of First Instance may appeal to the Court of Justice within two weeks by the notification of the decision dismissing the application.

The parties to the proceedings may appeal to the Court of Justice against any decision of the Court of First Instance made pursuant to Article 185 or 186 or the fourth paragraph of Article 192 of the Treaty within 2 months from their notification.

The appeal referred to in the first two paragraphs of this article shall be heard and determined under the procedure referred to in Article 36 of this Statute.

Article 51

An appeal to the Court of Justice shall be limited to points of law. It shall lie on the grounds of lack of competence of the Court of First Instance, a breach of procedure before it which adversely affects the interest of the appellant as well as the infringement of Community law by the Court of First Instance.

No appeal shall lie regarding only the amount of the costs or the party ordered to pay them.

Article 52

Where an appeal is brought against a decision of the Court of First

Instance, the procedure before the Court of Justice shall consist of a written part and an oral part. In accordance with conditions laid down in the Rules of Procedure the Court of Justice, having heard the Advocate-General and the parties, may dispense with the oral procedure.

Article 53

Without prejudice to Articles 185 and 186 of the Treaty, an appeal shall have suspensory effect.

By way of derogation from Article 187 of the Treaty, decisions of the Court of First Instance declaring a regulation to be void shall take effect only as from the date of expiry of the period referred to in the first paragraph of Article 49 of this Statute or, if an appeal shall have been brought within that period, as from the date of dismissal of the appeal, without prejudice, however, to the right of a party to apply to the Court of Justice, pursuant to Articles 185 and 186 of this Treaty, for the suspension of the effects of the regulation which has been declared void or for the prescription of any other interim measure.][3]

[Article 54][4]

The rules of procedure of the Court provided for in Article 188 of this Treaty shall contain, apart from the provisions contemplated by this Statute, any other provisions necessary for applying and, where required, supplementing it.

[Article 55][5]

The Council may, acting unanimously, make such further adjustments to the provisions of this Statute as may be required by reason of measures taken by the Council in accordance with the last paragraph of Article 165 of this Treaty.

[Article 56][6]

Immediately after the oath has been taken, the President of the Council shall proceed to choose by lot the Judges and the Advocates-General whose terms of office are to expire at the end of the first three years in accordance with the second and third paragraphs of Article 167 of this Treaty.

In witness whereof, the undersigned plenipotentiaries have signed this Protocol.

Done at Brussels this seventeenth day of April in the year one thousand nine hundred and fifty-seven.

[List omitted]

EDITORIAL NOTE

The Protocols on the Statute of the Court of Justice of the ECSC/EAEC have been omitted from this volume.

FOOTNOTES

1. 'European Economic Community' replaced by 'European Community' by the Treaty on European Union, Title II, Article G,A(1).
2. Text as amended by Article 20 of the Act of Accession DK/IRL/UK.
3. Title IV, Articles 44 to 53 inserted by Decision 88/591, ECSC, EEC, Euratom, OJ No L 319, 25.11.88, p.1.
4. Article 44 renamed Article 54 by Decision 88/591, ECSC, EEC, Euratom, OJ No L 319, 25.11.88, p.1.
5. Article 45 renamed Article 55 by Decision 88/591, ECSC, EEC, Euratom, OJ No L 319, 25.11.88, p.1.
6. Article 46 renamed Article 56 by Decision 88/591, ECSC, EEC, Euratom, OJ No L 319, 25.11.88, p.1.

Protocol concerning imports into the [European Community]¹ of petroleum products refined in the Netherlands Antilles²

The High Contracting Parties,

Being desirous of giving fuller details about the system of trade applicable to imports into the [European Community]¹ of petroleum products refined in the Netherlands Antilles,

Have agreed on the following provisions to be appended to that Treaty:

Article 1

This Protocol is applicable to petroleum products coming under the Brussels Nomenclature numbers 27.10, 27.11, 27.12, ex 27.13 (paraffin wax, petroleum or shale wax and paraffin residues) and 27.14, imported for use in Member States.

Article 2

Member States shall undertake to grant to petroleum products refined in the Netherlands Antilles the tariff preferences resulting from the association of the latter with the Community, under the conditions provided for in this Protocol. These provisions shall hold good whatever may be the rules of origin applied by the Member States.

Article 3

1. When the Commission, at the request of a Member State or on its own initiative, establishes that imports into the Community of petroleum

products refined in the Netherlands Antilles under the system provided for in Article 2 above are giving rise to real difficulties on the market of one or more Member States, it shall decide that customs duties on the said imports shall be introduced, increased or re-introduced by the Member States in question, to such an extent and for such a period as may be necessary to meet that situation. The rates of the customs duties thus introduced, increased or re-introduced may not exceed the customs duties applicable to third countries for these same products.

2. The provisions of paragraph 1 can in any case be applied when imports into the Community of petroleum products refined in the Netherlands Antilles reach two million metric tonnes a year.

3. The Council shall be informed of decisions taken by the Commission in pursuance of paragraph 1 and 2, including those directed at rejecting the request of a Member State. The Council shall, at the request of any Member State, assume responsibility for the matter and may at any time amend or revoke them by a decision taken by a qualified majority.

Article 4

1. If a Member State considers that the imports of petroleum products refined in the Netherlands Antilles, made either directly or through another Member State under the system provided for in Article 2 above, are giving rise to real difficulties on its market and that immediate action is necessary to meet them, it may on its own initiative decide to apply customs duties to such imports, the rate of which may not exceed those of the customs duties applicable to third countries in respect of the same products. It shall notify its decision to the Commission which shall decide within one month whether the measures taken by the State should be maintained or must be amended or cancelled. The provisions of Article 3(3) shall be applicable to such decision of the Commission.

2. When the quantities of petroleum products refined in the Netherlands Antilles imported either directly or through another Member State, under the system provided for in Article 2 above, into a Member State or States of the EEC exceed during a calendar year the tonnage shown in the Annex to this Protocol, the measures taken in pursuance of paragraph 1 by that or those Member States for the current year shall be considered to be justified; the Commission shall, after assuring itself that the tonnage fixed has been reached, formally record the measures taken. In such a case the other Member States shall abstain from formally placing the matter before the Council.

Article 5

If the Community decides to apply quantitative restrictions to petroleum products, no matter whence they are imported, these restrictions may also be applied to imports of such products from the Netherlands Antilles. In such a case preferential treatment shall be granted to the Netherlands Antilles as compared with third countries.

Article 6

1. The provisions of Articles 2 to 5 shall be reviewed by the Council, by unanimous decision, after consulting the European Parliament and the Commission, when a common definition of origin for petroleum products from third countries and associated countries is adopted, or when decisions are taken within the framework of a common commercial policy for the products in question or when a common energy policy is established.

2. When such revision is made, however, equivalent preferences must in any case be maintained in favour of the Netherlands Antilles in a suitable form and for a minimum quantity of 2½ million metric tonnes of petroleum products.

3. The Community's commitments in regard to equivalent preferences as mentioned in paragraph 2 of this Article may, if necessary, be broken down country by country taking into account the tonnage indicated in the Annex to this Protocol.

Article 7

For the implementation of this Protocol, the Commission is responsible for following the pattern of imports into Member States of petroleum products refined in the Netherlands Antilles. Member States shall communicate to the Commission, which shall see that it is circulated, all useful information to that end in accordance with the administrative conditions recommended by it.

In witness whereof the undersigned plenipotentiaries have placed their signatures below this Protocol.

[List omitted]

Done at Brussels the thirteenth day of November in the year one thousand nine hundred and sixty-two.

Annex to the Protocol

For the implementation of Article 4(2) of the Protocol concerning imports into the [European Community][1] of petroleum products refined in the Netherlands Antilles, the High Contracting Parties have decided that the quantity of 2 million metric tonnes of petroleum products from the Antilles shall be allocated among the Member States as follows:

Germany	625 000 metric tonnes
Belgo/Luxembourg Economic Union	200 000 metric tonnes
France	75 000 metric tonnes
Italy	100 000 metric tonnes
Netherlands	1 000 000 metric tonnes

FOOTNOTES

1. 'European Economic Community' replaced by 'European Community' by the Treaty on European Union, Title II, Article G,A(1).
2. Added by Article 2 of the Convention of 13 November 1962 amending the Treaty establishing the European Community (OJ No 150, 1.10.64).

Protocol[1] on special arrangements for Greenland

Article 1

1. The treatment on import into the Community of products subject to the common organisation of the market in fishery products, originating in Greenland, shall, while complying with the mechanisms of the common market organisation, involve exemption from customs duties and charges having equivalent effect and the absence of quantitative restrictions or measures having equivalent effect if the possibilities for access to Greenland fishing zones granted to the Community pursuant to an agreement between the Community and the authority responsible for Greenland are satisfactory to the Community.

2. All measures relating to the import arrangements for such products, including those relating to the adoption of such measures, shall be adopted in accordance with the procedure laid down in Article 43 of the Treaty establishing the European Community.

Article 2

The Commission shall make proposals to the Council, which shall act by a qualified majority, for the transitional measures which it considers necessary, by reason of the entry into force of the new arrangements, with regard to the maintenance of rights acquired by natural or legal persons during the period when Greenland was part of the Community and the regularisation of the situation with regard to financial assistance granted by the Community to Greenland during that period.

Article 3

The following text shall be added to Annex I to the Council Decision of 16 December 1980 on the association of the overseas countries and territories with the European Community:

'6. Distinct community of the Kingdom of Denmark:

– Greenland.'

Protocol on the Privileges and Immunities of the European Community

[Repealed by the second paragraph of Article 28 of the Merger Treaty: see Protocol on the Privileges and Immunities of European Communities]

Implementing Convention on the association of the overseas countries and territories with the Community[2]

[Text of the Implementing Convention and Protocols omitted: of historical interest only]

Final Act

The Intergovernmental Conference on the Common Market and Euratom, convened in Venice on 29 May 1956 by the Ministers for Foreign Affairs of the Kingdom of Belgium, the Federal Republic of Germany, the French Republic, the Italian Republic, the Grand Duchy of Luxembourg and the Kingdom of the Netherlands, having continued its deliberations in Brussels and having, on concluding them, met in Rome on 25 March 1957, has adopted the following texts:

I

1. The Treaty establishing the [European Community][3], and the Annexes thereto,

2. The Protocol on the Statute of the European Investment Bank,

3. The Protocol on German internal trade and connected problems,

4. The Protocol on certain provisions relating to France,

5. The Protocol on Italy,

6. The Protocol on the Grand Duchy of Luxembourg,

7. The Protocol on goods originating in and coming from certain

countries and enjoying special treatment when imported into a Member State,

8. The Protocol on the treatment to be applied to products within the province of the European Coal and Steel Community in respect of Algeria and the Overseas Departments of the French Republic,

9. The Protocol on mineral oils and certain of their derivatives,

10. The Protocol on the application of the Treaty establishing the [European Community][3] to the non-European parts of the Kingdom of the Netherlands,

11. The Implementing Convention on the association of the overseas countries and territories with the Community, and the Annexes thereto,

12. The Protocol on the tariff quota for imports of bananas,

13. The Protocol on the tariff quota for imports of raw coffee.

II

1. The Treaty establishing the European Atomic Energy Community, and the Annexes thereto,

2. The Protocol on the application of the Treaty establishing the European Atomic Energy Community to the non-European parts of the Kingdom of the Netherlands.

III

The Convention on certain institutions common to the European Communities

At the time of signature of these texts, the Conference adopted the declarations listed below and annexed to this Act:

1. A joint declaration on cooperation with the Member States of international organisations,

2. A joint declaration on Berlin,

3. A declaration of intent on the association of the independent countries of the Franc area with the [European Community][3],

4. A declaration of intent on the association of the Kingdom of Libya with the [Economic Community][3],

5. A declaration of intent on the Trust Territory of Somaliland currently under the administration of the Italian Republic,

6. A declaration of intent on the association of Surinam and the Netherlands Antilles with the [European Community][3].

The Conference further took note of the declarations listed below and annexed to this Act:

1. A declaration by the Government of the Federal Republic of Germany on the definition of the expression 'German national',

2. A declaration by the Government of the Federal Republic of Germany on the application of the Treaties to Berlin,

3. A declaration by the Government of the French Republic on applications for patents covering information to be kept secret for defence reasons,

Finally, the Conference decided to draw up at a later date:

1. The Protocol on the Statute of the Court of Justice of the [European Community][3],

2. The Protocol on the privileges and immunities of the [European Community][3],

3. The Protocol on the Statute of the Court of Justice of the European Atomic Energy Community,

4. The Protocol on the privileges and immunities of the European Atomic Community (sic).

Protocols 1 and 2 shall be annexed to the Treaty establishing the [European Community][3]; Protocols 3 and 4 shall be annexed to the Treaty establishing the European Atomic Energy Community.

In witness whereof, the undersigned plenipotentiaries have signed this Final Act.

Done at Rome this twenty-fifth day of March in the year one thousand nine hundred and fifty-seven.

[List omitted]

FOOTNOTES

1. Article 3 of the Greenland Treaty provides that this Protocol, attached to the latter Treaty, shall be annexed to the Treaty establishing the European Community (OJ No L 29, 1.2.85).
2. This Implementing Convention, which was concluded for a period of five years, expired on 31 December 1962.
3. 'European Economic Community' replaced by 'European Community' by the Treaty on European Union, Title II, Article G,A(1).

Joint Declaration

on cooperation with the States members of international organisations.

The Governments of the Kingdom of Belgium, the Federal Republic of Germany, the French Republic, the Italian Republic, the Grand Duchy of Luxembourg and the Kingdom of the Netherlands,

At the time of signature of the Treaties establishing the [European Community][1] and the European Atomic Energy Community,

Conscious of the responsibilities which they are assuming for the future of Europe by combining their markets, bringing their economies closer together and laying down the principles and details of a common policy in this field;

Recognising that, by setting up a customs union and working closely together on the peaceful development of nuclear energy, they will be ensuring economic and social progress and thus contributing not only to their own prosperity but also to that of other countries,

Anxious that these countries should share in the prospects of expansion afforded thereby,

Declare their readiness to conclude, a soon as these Treaties enter into force, agreements with other countries, particularly within the framework of the international organisations to which they belong, in order to attain these objectives of common interest and to ensure the harmonious development of trade in general.

Joint Declaration

on Berlin.

[Text omitted]

Declaration of intent

on the association of the independent countries of the Franc Area with the [European Community][1].

The Governments of the Kingdom of Belgium, the Federal Republic of Germany, the French Republic, the Italian Republic, the Grand Duchy of Luxembourg and the Kingdom of the Netherlands,

Taking into consideration the economic, financial and monetary agreements and conventions concluded between France and the other independent countries of the Franc Area,

Anxious to maintain and intensify the traditional trade flows between the Member States of the [European Community] and these independent countries and to contribute to the economic and social development of the latter,

Declare their readiness, as soon as this Treaty enters into force, to propose to these countries the opening of negotiations with a view to concluding conventions for economic association with the Community.

FOOTNOTE

1. 'European Economic Community' replaced by 'European Community' by the Treaty on European Union, Title II, Article G,A(1).

Declaration of intent

on the association of the Kingdom of Libya with the [European Community][1].

[Text omitted]

FOOTNOTE

1. 'European Economic Community' replaced by 'European Community' by the Treaty on European Union, Title II, Article G,A(1).

Declaration of intent

on the Trust Territory of Somaliland[1] currently under the administration of the Italian Republic.

[Text omitted]

EDITORIAL NOTE

1. The country has become independent.

Declaration of intent

on the association of Surinam and the Netherlands Antilles with the [European Community][1].

The Governments of the Kingdom of Belgium, the Federal Republic of Germany, the French Republic, the Italian Republic, the Grand Duchy of Luxembourg and the Kingdom of the Netherlands,

Taking into consideration the close ties which unite the several parts of the Kingdom of the Netherlands,

Anxious to maintain and intensify the traditional trade flows between the Member States of the [European Community][1] on the one hand and Surinam and the Netherlands Antilles on the other, and to contribute to the economic and social development of these countries,

Declare their readiness, as soon as this Treaty enters into force, to open negotiations at the request of the Kingdom of the Netherlands, with a view to concluding conventions for the economic association of Surinam and the Netherlands Antilles with the Community.

FOOTNOTE

1. 'European Economic Community' replaced by 'European Community' by the Treaty on European Union, Title II, Article G,A(1).

Declaration by the Government of the Federal Republic of Germany

on the definition of the expression 'German national'.

At the time of signature of the Treaty establishing the [European Community][1] and the Treaty establishing the European Atomic Energy Community, the Government of the Federal Republic of Germany makes the following declaration:

'All Germans as defined in the Basic Law for the Federal Republic of Germany shall be considered nationals of the Federal Republic of Germany.'

FOOTNOTE

1. 'European Economic Community' replaced by 'European Community' by the Treaty on European Union, Title II, Article G,A(1).

Declaration by the Government of the Federal Republic of Germany

on the application of the Treaties to Berlin.

[Text omitted]

Declaration by the Government of the French Republic

on applications for patents covering information to be kept secret for defence reasons.

The Government of the French Republic,

Taking into account the provisions of Articles 17 and 25(2) of the Treaty establishing the European Atomic Energy Community,

Declares its readiness to take such administrative measures and to propose to the French Parliament such legislative measures as may be necessary to ensure that, as soon as this Treaty enters into force, applications for patents covering secret information result, following the normal procedure, in the grant of patents subject to temporary prohibition of publication.

TITLE III

The Treaty establishing the European Coal and Steel Community

Article H

The Treaty establishing the European Coal and Steel Community shall be amended in accordance with the provisions of this Article.

(1) Replaced Article 7.

(2) Replaced Articles 9-13.

(3) Replaced Article 16.

(4) Inserted Article 17.

(5) Added a subparagraph to Article 18.

(6) Inserted Articles 20a-20d.

(7) Replaced Article 21(3).

(8) Replaced Article 24.

(9) Inserted Articles 27-27a.

(10) Inserted Articles 29-30.

(11) Replaced Article 32.

(12) Replaced Article 32d.

(13) Replaced Article 33.

(14) Inserted Chapter V, Articles 45a-45c.

(15) Replaced Article 78c.

(16) Repealed Articles 78e and 78f.

(17) Replaced Article 78g.

(18) Replaced Article 78h.

(19) Inserted Article 78i.

(20) Replaced Article 79a.

(21) Repealed Articles 96 and 98.

Text of the Treaty

[List omitted]

Considering that world peace can be safeguarded only by creative efforts commensurate with the dangers that threaten it,

Convinced that the contribution which an organised and vital Europe can make to civilisation is indispensable to the maintenance of peaceful relations,

Recognising that Europe can be built only through practical achievements which will first of all create real solidarity, and through the establishment of common bases for economic development,

Anxious to help, by expanding their basic production, to raise the standard of living and further the works of peace,

Resolved to substitute for age-old rivalries the merging of their essential interests; to create, by establishing an economic community, the basis for a broader and deeper community among peoples long divided by bloody conflicts; and to lay the foundations for institutions which will give direction to a destiny henceforward shared,

Have decided to create a European Coal and Steel Community and to this end have designated as their plenipotentiaries:

[List omitted]

Who, having exchanged their Full Powers, found in good and due form, have agreed as follows.

Title One

The European Coal and Steel Community

Article 1

By this Treaty, the High Contracting Parties establish among themselves a European Coal and Steel Community, founded upon a common market, common objectives and common institutions.

Article 2

The European Coal and Steel Community shall have as its task to contribute, in harmony with the general economy of the Member States and through the establishment of a common market as provided in Article 4, to economic expansion, growth of employment and a rising standard of living in the Member States.

The Community shall progressively bring about conditions which will of themselves ensure the most rational distribution of production at the highest possible level of productivity, while safeguarding continuity of employment and taking care not to provoke fundamental and persistent disturbances in the economies of Member States.

Article 3

The institutions of the Community shall, within the limits of their respective powers, in the common interest:

(a) ensure an orderly supply to the common market, taking into account the needs of third countries;

(b) ensure that all comparably placed consumers in the common market have equal access to the sources of production;

(c) ensure the establishment of the lowest prices under such conditions that these prices do not result in higher prices charged by the same undertakings in other transactions or in a higher general price level at another time, while allowing necessary amortization and normal return on investment capital;

(d) ensure the maintenance of conditions which will encourage undertakings to expand and improve their production potential and to promote a policy of using natural resources rationally and avoiding their unconsidered exhaustion;

(e) promote improved working conditions and an improved standard of living for the workers in each of the industries for which it is responsible, so as to make possible their harmonisation while the improvement is being maintained;

(f) promote the growth of international trade and ensure that equitable limits are observed in export pricing;

(g) promote the orderly expansion and modernisation of production, and the improvement of quality, with no protection against competing industries that is not justified by improper action on their part or in their favour.

Article 4

The following are recognised as incompatible with the common market for coal and steel and shall accordingly be abolished and prohibited within the Community, as provided in this Treaty:

(a) import and export duties, or charges having equivalent effect, and quantitative restrictions on the movement of products;

(b) measures or practices which discriminate between producers, between purchasers or between consumers, especially in prices and delivery terms or transport rates and conditions, and measures or practices which interfere with the purchaser's free choice of supplier;

(c) subsidies or aids granted by States, or special charges imposed by States, in any form whatsoever;

(d) restrictive practices which tend towards the sharing or exploiting of markets.

Article 5

The Community shall carry out its task in accordance with this Treaty, with a limited measure of intervention.

To this end the Community shall:

— provide guidance and assistance for the parties concerned, by obtaining information, organising consultations and laying down general objectives;

— place financial resources at the disposal of undertakings for their investment and bear part of the cost of readaptation;

— ensure the establishment, maintenance and observance of normal competitive conditions and exert direct influence upon production or upon the market only when circumstances so require;

– publish the reasons for its actions and take the necessary measures to ensure the observance of the rules laid down in this Treaty.

The institutions of the Community shall carry out these activities with a minimum of administrative machinery and in close cooperation with the parties concerned.

Article 6

The Community shall have legal personality.

In international relations, the Community shall enjoy the legal capacity it requires to perform its functions and attain its objectives.

In each of the Member States, the Community shall enjoy the most extensive legal capacity accorded to legal persons constituted in that State; it may, in particular, acquire or dispose of movable and immovable property and may be a party to legal proceedings.

The Community shall be represented by its institutions, each within the limits of its powers.

Title Two

The institutions of the Community

[Article 7

The institutions of the Community shall be:

– a High Authority (hereinafter referred to as 'the Commission');

– a Common Assembly (hereinafter referred to as 'the European Parliament');

– a Special Council of Ministers (hereinafter referred to as 'the Council');

– a Court of Justice;

– a Court of Auditors.

The Commission shall be assisted by a Consultative Committee.][1]

Chapter I

The [Commission][2]

Article 8

It shall be the duty of the [Commission][2] to ensure that the objectives set out in this Treaty are attained in accordance with the provisions thereof.

[Article 9

1. The Commission shall consist of 17 members, who shall be chosen on the grounds of their general competence and whose independence is beyond doubt.

The number of members of the Commission may be altered by the Council, acting unanimously.

Only nationals of the Member States may be members of the Commission.

The Commission must include at least one national of each of the Member States, but may not include more than two members having the nationality of the same State.

2. The members of the Commission shall, in the general interest of the Community, be completely independent in the performance of their duties.

In the performance of these duties, they shall neither seek nor take instructions from any government or from any other body. They shall refrain from any action incompatible with their duties. Each Member State undertakes to respect this principle and not to seek to influence the members of the Commission in the performance of their tasks.

The members of the Commission may not, during their term of office, engage in any other occupation, whether gainful or not. When entering upon their duties they shall give a solemn undertaking that, both during and after their term of office, they will respect the obligations arising therefrom and in particular their duty to behave with integrity and discretion as regards the acceptance, after they have ceased to hold office, of certain appointments or benefits. In the event of any breach of these obligations, the Court of Justice may, on application by the Council or the Commission, rule that the member concerned be, according to the circumstances, either compulsorily retired in accordance with Article 12a or deprived of his right to a pension or other benefits in its stead.

Article 10

1. The members of the Commission shall be appointed, in accordance with the procedure referred to in paragraph 2, for a period of five years, subject, if need be, to Article 24.

Their term of office shall be renewable.

2. The governments of the Member States shall nominate by common accord, after consulting the European Parliament, the person they intend to appoint as President of the Commission.

The governments of the Member States shall, in consultation with the nominee for President, nominate the other persons whom they intend to appoint as members of the Commission.

The President and the other members of the Commission thus nominated shall be subject as a body to a vote of approval by the European Parliament. After approval by the European Parliament, the President and the other members of the Commission shall be appointed by common accord of the governments of the Member States.

3. Paragraphs 1 and 2 shall be applied for the first time to the President and the other members of the Commission whose term of office begins on 7 January 1995.

The President and the other members of the Commission whose term of office begins on 7 January 1993 shall be appointed by common accord of the governments of the Member States. Their term of office shall expire on 6 January 1995.

Article 11

The Commission may appoint a Vice-President or two Vice-Presidents from among its members.

Article 12

Apart from normal replacement, or death, the duties of a member of the Commission shall end when he resigns or is compulsorily retired.

The vacancy thus caused shall be filled for the remainder of the member's term of office by a new member appointed by common accord of the governments of the Member States. The Council may, acting unanimously, decide that such a vacancy need not be filled.

In the event of resignation, compulsory retirement or death, the President shall be replaced for the remainder of his term of office. The procedure laid down in Article 10(2) shall be applicable for the replacement of the President.

Save in the case of compulsory retirement under Article 12a, members of the Commission shall remain in office until they have been replaced.

Article 12a

If any member of the Commission no longer fulfils the conditions required for the performance of his duties or if he has been guilty of serious misconduct, the Court of Justice may, on application by the Council or the Commission, compulsorily retire him.

Article 13

The Commission shall act by a majority of the number of members provided for in Article 9.

A meeting of the Commission shall be valid only if the number of members laid down in its rules of procedure is present.][3]

Article 14

In order to carry out the tasks assigned to it the [Commission][2] shall, in accordance with the provisions of this Treaty, take decisions, make recommendations or deliver opinions.

Decisions shall be binding in their entirety.

Recommendations shall be binding as to the aims to be pursued but shall leave the choice of the appropriate methods for achieving these aims to those to whom the recommendations are addressed.

Opinions shall have no binding force.

In cases where the [Commission][2] is empowered to take a decision, it may confine itself to making a recommendation.

Article 15

Decisions, recommendations and opinions of the [Commission][2] shall state the reasons on which they are based and shall refer to any opinions which were required to be obtained.

Where decisions and recommendations are individual in character, they shall become binding upon being notified to the party concerned.

In all other cases, they shall take effect by the mere fact of publication.

The [Commission][2] shall determine the manner in which this Article is to be implemented.

[*Article* 16

The Commission shall make all appropriate administrative arrangements for the operation of its departments.

It may set up study committees, including an economic study committee.

The Council and the Commission shall consult each other and shall settle by common accord their methods of cooperation.

The Commission shall adopt its rules of procedure so as to ensure that both it and its departments operate in accordance with the provisions of this Treaty. It shall ensure that these rules are published.][4]

[*Article* 17

The Commission shall publish annually, not later than one month before the opening of the session of the European Parliament, a general report on the activities of the Community.][5]

Article 18

A Consultative Committee shall be attached to the [Commission][2]. It shall consist of not less than seventy-two and not more than ninety-six members and shall comprise equal numbers of producers, of workers and of consumers and dealers.

The members of the Consultative Committee shall be appointed by the Council.

In the case of the producers and workers, the Council shall designate representative organisations among which it shall allocate the seats to be filled. Each organisation shall be required to draw up a list containing twice as many names as there are seats allotted to it. Appointment shall be made from this list.

The members of the Consultative Committee shall be appointed in their personal capacity for two years. They shall not be bound by any mandate or instructions from the organisations which nominated them.

The Consultative Committee shall elect its chairman and officers from among its members for a term of one year. The Committee shall adopt its rules of procedure.

[Text omitted][6]

[The Council shall, acting by a qualified majority, determine any payment to be made instead of remuneration.][7]

Article 19

The [Commission]² may consult the Consultative Committee in all cases in which it considers this appropriate. It must do so whenever such consultation is prescribed by this Treaty.

The [Commission]² shall submit to the Consultative Committee the general objectives and the programmes drawn up under Article 46 and shall keep the Committee informed of the broad lines of its action under Articles 54, 65 and 66.

Should the [Commission]² consider it necessary, it may set the Consultative Committee a time limit for the submission of its opinion. The period allowed may not be less than ten days from the date on which the chairman receives notification to this effect.

The Consultative Committee shall be convened by its chairman, either at the request of the [Commission]² or at the request of a majority of its members, for the purpose of discussing a specific question.

The minutes of the proceedings shall be forwarded to the [Commission]² and to the Council at the same time as the opinions of the Committee.

Chapter II

The European Parliament

Article 20

The European Parliament, which shall consist of representatives of the peoples of the States brought together in the Community, shall exercise the supervisory powers which are conferred upon it by this Treaty.

[Article 20a

The European Parliament may, acting by a majority of its members, request the Commission to submit any appropriate proposal on matters on which it considers that a Community act is required for the purpose of implementing this Treaty.

Article 20b

in the course of its duties, the European Parliament may, at the request of a quarter of its members, set up a temporary Committee of Inquiry to investigate, without prejudice to the powers conferred by this Treaty on other institutions or bodies, alleged contraventions or maladministration in the implementation of Community law, except where the alleged facts are being examined before a court and while the case is still subject to legal proceedings.

The temporary Committee of Inquiry shall cease to exist on the submission of its report.

The detailed provisions governing the exercise of the right of inquiry shall be determined by common accord of the European Parliament, the Council and the Commission.

Article 20c

Any citizen of the Union, and any natural or legal person residing or having its registered office in a Member State, shall have the right to address, individually or in association with other citizens or persons, a petition to the European Parliament on a matter which comes within the Community's fields of activity and which affects him, her or it directly.

Article 20d

1. The European Parliament shall appoint an Ombudsman empowered to receive complaints from any citizen of the Union or any natural or legal person residing or having its registered office in a Member State concerning instances of maladministration in the activities of the Community institutions or bodies, with the exception of the Court of Justice and the Court of First Instance acting in their judicial role.

In accordance with his duties, the Ombudsman shall conduct inquiries for which he finds grounds, either on his own initiative or on the basis of complaints submitted to him direct or through a member of the European Parliament, except where the alleged facts are or have been the subject of legal proceedings. Where the Ombudsman establishes an instance of maladministration, he shall refer the matter to the institution concerned, which shall have a period of three months in which to inform him of its views. The Ombudsman shall then forward a report to the European Parliament and the institution concerned. The person lodging the complaint shall be informed of the outcome of such inquiries.

The Ombudsman shall submit an annual report to the European Parliament on the outcome of his inquiries.

2. The Ombudsman shall be appointed after each election of the European Parliament for the duration of its term of office. The Ombudsman shall be eligible for reappointment.

The Ombudsman may be dismissed by the Court of Justice at the request of the European Parliament if he no longer fulfils the conditions required for the performance of his duties or if he is guilty of serious misconduct.

3. The Ombudsman shall be completely independent in the performance of his duties. In the performance of those duties he shall neither seek nor take instructions from any body. The Ombudsman may not, during his term of office, engage in any other occupation, whether gainful or not.

4. The European Parliament shall, after seeking an opinion from the Commission and with the approval of the Council acting by a qualified majority, lay down the regulations and general conditions governing the performance of the Ombudsman's duties.][8]

Article 21

(*Paragraphs 1 and 2 lapsed on 17 July 1979 in accordance with Article 14 of the Act concerning the election of the representatives of the European Parliament*).

[*See Article 1 of that Act which reads as follows*:

1. The representatives in the European Parliament of the peoples of the States brought together in the Community shall be elected by direct universal suffrage.]

[Article 2 of that Act replaced by Decision 93/81/Euratom/ECSC/EEC[9]

Article 2

The number of representatives elected in each Member State shall be as follows:

Belgium	25
Denmark	16
Germany	99
Greece	25
Spain	64
France	87
Ireland	15
Italy	87
Luxembourg	6
Netherlands	31
Portugal	25
United Kingdom	87][9]

[3. The European Parliament shall draw up proposals for elections by direct universal suffrage in accordance with a uniform procedure in all Member States.

The Council shall, acting unanimously after obtaining the assent of the European Parliament, which shall act by a majority of its component members, lay down the appropriate provisions, which it shall recommend to Member States for adoption in accordance with their respective constitutional requirements.][10]

Article 22

The European Parliament shall hold an annual session. It shall meet, without requiring to be convened, on the second Tuesday in March.

The European Parliament may be convened in extraordinary session at the request of the Council in order to deliver an opinion on such questions as may be put to it by the Council.

It may also meet in extraordinary session at the request of a majority of its members or of the [Commission].[2]

Article 23

The European Parliament shall elect its President and its officers from among its members.

Members of the [Commission][2] may attend all meetings. The President of the [Commission][2] or such of its members as it may designate shall be heard at their request.

The [Commission][2] shall reply orally or in writing to questions put to it by the European Parliament or its members.

The members of the Council may attend all meetings and shall be heard at their request.

[Article 24

The European Parliament shall discuss in open session the general report submitted to it by the Commission.

If a motion of censure on the activities of the Commission is tabled before it, the European Parliament shall not vote thereon until at least three days after the motion has been tabled and only by open vote.

If a motion of censure is carried by a two-thirds majority of the votes cast, representing a majority of the members of the European Parliament, the members of the Commission shall resign as a body. They shall continue to deal with current business until they are replaced in accordance with Article 10. In this case, the term of office of the members of the Commission appointed to replace them shall expire on the date on which the term of office of the members of the Commission obliged to resign as a body would have expired.][11]

Article 25

The European Parliament shall adopt its rules of procedure, acting by a majority of its members.

The proceedings of the European Parliament shall be published in the manner laid down in its rules of procedure.

Chapter III

The Council

Article 26

The Council shall exercise its powers in the cases provided for and in the manner set out in this Treaty, in particular in order to harmonise the action of the [Commission][2] and that of the Governments, which are responsible for the general economic policies of their countries.

To this end, the Council and the [Commission][2] shall exchange information and consult each other.

The Council may request the [Commission][2] to examine any proposals or measures which the Council may consider appropriate or necessary for the attainment of the common objectives.

[Article 27

The Council shall consist of a representative of each Member State at ministerial level, authorised to commit the government of that Member State.

The office of President shall be held in turn by each Member State in the Council for a term of six months, in the following order of Member States:

– for a first cycle of six years: Belgium, Denmark, Germany, Greece, Spain, France, Ireland, Italy, Luxembourg, Netherlands, Portugal, United Kingdom;

– for the following cycle of six years: Denmark, Belgium, Greece, Germany, France, Spain, Ireland, Netherlands, Luxembourg, United Kingdom, Portugal.

Article 27a

The Council shall meet when convened by its President on his own initiative or at the request of one of its members or of the Commission.][12]

Article 28

When the Council is consulted by the [Commission][2], it shall consider the matter without necessarily taking a vote. The minutes of its proceedings shall be forwarded to the [Commission][2].

Wherever this Treaty requires that the assent of the Council be given, that assent shall be considered to have been given if the proposal submitted by the [Commission][2] receives the approval:

– of an absolute majority of the representatives of the Member States, including the votes of the representatives of two Member States which each produce at least one ninth of the total value of the coal and steel output of the Community; or

– in the event of an equal division of votes and if the [Commission][2] maintains its proposal after a second discussion, of the representatives of three Member States which each produce at least one ninth of the total value of the coal and steel output of the Community.

Wherever this Treaty requires a unanimous decision or unanimous assent, such decision or assent shall have been duly given if all the members of the Council vote in favour. However, for the purposes of applying Articles 21, 32, 32a, 78e and 78h of this Treaty, and Article 16, the third paragraph of Article 20, the fifth paragraph of Article 28 and Article 44 of the Protocol on the Statute of the Court of Justice, abstention by members present in person or represented shall not prevent the adoption by the Council of acts which require unanimity.

Decisions of the Council, other than those for which a qualified majority or unanimity is required, shall be taken by a vote of the majority of its members; this majority shall be considered to be attained if it represents an absolute majority of the representatives of two Member States, including the votes of the representatives of two Member States which each produce at least one ninth of the total value of the coal and steel output of the Community. However, for the purpose of applying Articles 78, 78b and 78e of this Treaty which require a qualified majority, the votes of the members of the Council shall be weighted as follows:

Belgium	5
Denmark	3
Germany	10
Greece	5
Spain	8

France	10
Ireland	3
Italy	10
Luxembourg	2
Netherlands	5
Portugal	5
United Kingdom	10

For their adoption, acts shall require at least 54 votes in favour, cast by not less than eight members.

Where a vote is taken, any member of the Council may act on behalf of not more than one other member.

The Council shall deal with the Member States through its President.

The acts of the Council shall be published in such a manner as it may decide.

[Article 29

The Council shall, acting by a qualified majority, determine the salaries, allowances and pensions of the President and members of the Commission, and of the President, Judges, Advocates-General and Registrar of the Court of Justice. It shall also, again by a qualified majority, determine any payment to be made instead of remuneration.

Article 30

1. A committee consisting of the Permanent Representatives of the Member States shall be responsible for preparing the work of the Council and for carrying out the tasks assigned to it by the Council.

2. The Council shall be assisted by a General Secretariat, under the direction of a Secretary-General. The Secretary-General shall be appointed by the Council acting unanimously.

The Council shall decide on the organisation of the General Secretariat.

3. The Council shall adopt its rules of procedure.][13]

Chapter IV

The Court

Article 31

The Court shall ensure that in the interpretation and application of this Treaty, and of rules laid down for the implementation thereof, the law is observed.

[Article 32

The Court of Justice shall consist of 13 Judges.

The Court of Justice shall sit in plenary session. It may, however, form Chambers, each consisting of three or five Judges, either to undertake certain preparatory inquiries or to adjudicate on particular categories of cases in accordance with the rules laid down for these purposes.

The Court of Justice shall sit in plenary session when a Member State or a Community institution that is a party to the proceedings so requests.

Should the Court of Justice so request, the Council may, acting unanimously increase the number of Judges and make the necessary adjustments to the second and third paragraphs of this Article and to the second paragraph of Article 32b.][14]

Article 32a

The Court of Justice shall be assisted by six Advocates-General.

It shall be the duty of the Advocate-General acting with complete impartiality and independence, to make, in open court, reasoned submissions on cases brought before the Court, in order to assist the Court in the performance of the task assigned to it in Article 31.

Should the Court so request, the Council may, acting unanimously, increase the number of Advocates-General and make the necessary adjustments to the third paragraph of Article 32b.

Article 32b

The Judges and Advocates-General shall be chosen from persons whose independence is beyond doubt and who possess the qualifications required for appointment to the highest judicial offices in their respective countries or who are jurisconsults of recognised competence; they shall be appointed by common accord of the Governments of the Member States for a term of six years.

Every three years there shall be a partial replacement of the Judges. Seven and six Judges shall be replaced alternately.

Every three years there shall be a partial replacement of the Advocates-General. Three Advocates-General shall be replaced on each occasion.

Retiring Judges and Advocates-General shall be eligible for reappointment.

The Judges shall elect the President of the Court from among their number for a term of three years. He may be re-elected.

Article 32c

The Court shall appoint its Registrar and lay down the rules governing his service.

[Article 32d

1. A Court of First Instance shall be attached to the Court of Justice with jurisdiction to hear and determine at first instance, subject to a right of appeal to the Court of Justice on points of law only and in accordance with the conditions laid down by the Statute, certain classes of action or proceeding defined in accordance with the conditions laid down in paragraph 2. The Court of First Instance shall not be competent to hear and determine questions referred for a preliminary ruling under Article 41.

2. At the request of the Court of Justice and after consulting the European Parliament and the Commission, the Council, acting unanimously, shall determine the classes of action or proceeding referred to in paragraph 1, and the composition of the Court of First Instance and shall adopt the necessary adjustments and additional provisions to the Statute of the Court of Justice. Unless the Council decides otherwise, the provisions of this Treaty relating to the Court of Justice, in particular the provisions of the Protocol on the Statute of the Court of Justice, shall apply to the Court of First Instance.

3. The members of the Court of First Instance shall be chosen from persons whose independence is beyond doubt and who possess the ability required for appointment to judicial office; they shall be appointed by common accord of the governments of the Member States for a term of six years. The membership shall be partially renewed every three years. Retiring members shall be eligible for re-appointment.

4. The Court of First Instance shall establish its rules of procedure in agreement with the Court of Justice. Those rules shall require the unanimous approval of the Council.][15]

[*Article* 33

The Court of Justice shall have jurisdiction in actions brought by a Member State or by the Council to have decisions or recommendations of the Commission declared void on grounds of lack of competence, infringement of an essential procedural requirement, infringement of this Treaty or of any rule of law relating to its application, or misuse of powers. The Court of Justice may not, however, examine the evaluation of the situation, resulting from economic facts or circumstances, in the light of which the Commission took its decisions or made its recommendations, save where the Commission is alleged to have misused its powers or to have manifestly failed to observe the provisions of this Treaty or any rule of law relating to its application.

Undertakings or associations referred to in Article 48 may, under the same conditions, institute proceedings against decisions or recommend-ations concerning them which are individual in character or against general decisions or recommendations which they consider to involve a misuse of powers affecting them.

The proceedings provided for in the first two paragraphs of this Article shall be instituted within one month of the notification or publication, as the case may be, of the decision or recommendation.

The Court of Justice shall have jurisdiction under the same conditions in actions brought by the European Parliament for the purpose of protecting its prerogatives.][16]

Article 34

If the Court declares a decision or recommendation void, it shall refer the matter back to the [Commission][2]. The [Commission][2] shall take the necessary steps to comply with the judgment. If direct and special harm is suffered by an undertaking or group of undertakings by reason of a decision or recommendation held by the Court to involve a fault of such a nature as to render the Community liable, the [Commission][2] shall, using the powers conferred upon it by this Treaty, take steps to ensure equitable redress for the harm resulting directly from the decision or recommendation declared void and, where necessary, pay appropriate damages.

If the [Commission][2] fails to take within a reasonable time the necessary steps to comply with the judgment, proceedings for damages may be instituted before the Court.

Article 35

Wherever the [Commission][2] is required by this Treaty, or by rules laid down for the implementation thereof, to take a decision or make a recommendation and fails to fulfil this obligation, it shall be for States, the Council, undertakings or associations, as the case may be, to raise the matter with the [Commission][2].

The same shall apply if the [Commission][2], where empowered by this Treaty, or by rules laid down for the implementation thereof, to take a decision or make a recommendation, abstains from doing so and such abstention constitutes a misuse of powers.

If at the end of two months the [Commission][2] has not taken any decision or made any recommendation, proceedings may be instituted before the Court within one month against the implied decision of refusal which is to be inferred from the silence of the [Commission][2] on the matter.

Article 36

Before imposing a pecuniary sanction or ordering a periodic penalty payment as provided for in this Treaty, the [Commission][2] must give the party concerned the opportunity to submit its comments.

The Court shall have unlimited jurisdiction in appeals against pecuniary sanctions and periodic penalty payments imposed under this Treaty.

In support of its appeal, a party may, under the same conditions as in the first paragraph of Article 33 of this Treaty, contest the legality of the decision or recommendation which that party is alleged not to have observed.

Article 37

If a Member State considers that in a given case action or failure to act on the part of the [Commission][2] is of such a nature as to provoke fundamental and persistent disturbances in its economy, it may raise the matter with the [Commission][2].

The [Commission][2], after consulting the Council, shall, if there are grounds for so doing, recognise the existence of such a situation and decide on the measures to be taken to end it, in accordance with the provisions of this Treaty, while at the same time safeguarding the essential interests of the Community.

When proceedings are instituted in the Court under this Article against such a decision or against an express or implied decision refusing to recognise the existence of the situation referred to above, it shall be for the Court to determine whether it is well founded.

If the Court declares the decision void, the [Commission][2] shall, within the terms of the judgment of the Court, decide on the measures to be taken for the purposes indicated in the second paragraph of this Article.

Article 38

The court may, on application by a Member State or the [Commission][2], declare an act of the European Parliament or of the Council to be void.

Application shall be made within one month of the publication of the act of the European Parliament or the notification of the act of the Council to the Member States or to the [Commission][2].

The only grounds for such application shall be lack of competence or infringement of an essential procedural requirement.

Article 39

Actions brought before the Court shall not have suspensory effect.

The Court may, however, if it considers that circumstances so require, order that application of the contested decision or recommendation be suspended.

The Court may prescribe any other necessary interim measures.

Article 40

Without prejudice to the first paragraph of Article 34, the Court shall have jurisdiction to order pecuniary reparation from the Community, on application by the injured party, to make good any injury caused in carrying out this Treaty by a wrongful act or omission on the part of the Community in the performance of its functions.

The Court shall also have jurisdiction to order the Community to make good any injury caused by a personal wrong by a servant of the Community in the performance of his duties. The personal liability of its servants towards the Community shall be governed by the provisions laid down in their Staff Regulations or the Conditions of Employment applicable to them.

All other disputes between the Community and persons other than its servants to which the provisions of this Treaty or the rules laid down for the implementation thereof do not apply shall be brought before national courts or tribunals.

Article 41

The court shall have sole jurisdiction to give preliminary rulings on the validity of acts of the [Commission][2] and of the Council where such validity is in issue in proceedings brought before a national court or tribunal.

Article 42

The Court shall have jurisdiction to give judgment pursuant to any arbitration clause contained in a contract concluded by or on behalf of the Community, whether that contract be governed by public or private law.

Article 43

The Court shall have jurisdiction in any other case provided for by a provision supplementing this Treaty.

It may also rule in all cases which relate to the subject matter of this Treaty where jurisdiction is conferred upon it by the law of a Member State.

Article 44

The judgments of the Court shall be enforceable in the territory of Member States under the conditions laid down in Article 92.

Article 45

The Statute of the Court is laid down in a Protocol annexed to this Treaty.

The Council may, acting unanimously at the request of the Court of Justice and after consulting the Commission and the European Parliament, amend the provisions of Title III of the Statute.

[Chapter V

The Court of Auditors

Article 45a

The Court of Auditors shall carry out the audit.

Article 45b

1. The Court of Auditors shall consist of 12 members.

2. The members of the Court of Auditors shall be chosen from among persons who belong or have belonged in their respective countries to external audit bodies or who are especially qualified for this office. Their independence must be beyond doubt.

3. The members of the Court of Auditors shall be appointed for a term

of six years by the Council, acting unanimously after consulting the European Parliament.

However, when the first appointments are made, four members of the Court of Auditors, chosen by lot, shall be appointed for a term of office of four years only.

The members of the Court of Auditors shall be eligible for reappointment.

They shall elect the President of the Court of Auditors from among their number for a term of three years. The President may be re-elected.

4. The members of the Court of Auditors shall, in the general interest of the Community, be completely independent in the performance of their duties.

In the performance of these duties, they shall neither seek nor take instructions from any government or from any other body. They shall refrain from any action incompatible with their duties.

5. The members of the Court of Auditors may not, during their term of office, engage in any other occupation whether gainful or not. When entering upon their duties they shall give a solemn undertaking that, both during and after their term of office, they will respect the obligations arising therefrom and in particular their duty to behave with integrity and discretion as regards the acceptance, after they have ceased to hold office, of certain appointments or benefits.

6. Apart from normal replacement, or death, the duties of a member of the Court of Auditors shall end when he resigns, or is compulsorily retired by a ruling of the Court of Justice pursuant to paragraph 7.

The vacancy thus caused shall be filled for the remainder of the member's term of office.

Save in the case of compulsory retirement, members of the Court of Auditors shall remain in office until they have been replaced.

7. A member of the Court of Auditors may be deprived of his office or of his right to a pension or other benefits in its stead only if the Court of Justice, at the request of the Court of Auditors, finds that he no longer fulfils the requisite conditions or meets the obligations arising from his office.

8. The Council, acting by a qualified majority, shall determine the conditions of employment of the President and the members of the Court of Auditors and in particular their salaries, allowances and pensions. It shall also, by the same majority, determine any payment to be made instead of remuneration.

9. The provisions of the Protocol on the Privileges and Immunities of the European Communities applicable to the Judges of the Court of Justice shall also apply to the members of the Court of Auditors.

Article 45c

1. The Court of Auditors shall examine the accounts of all revenue and expenditure of the Community. It shall also examine the accounts of all revenue and expenditure of all bodies set up by the Community in so far as the relevant constituent instrument does not preclude such examination.

The Court of Auditors shall provide the European Parliament and the Council with a statement of assurance as to the reliability of the accounts and the legality and regularity of the underlying transactions.

2. The Court of Auditors shall examine whether all revenue referred to in paragraph 1 has been received and all expenditure referred to in that paragraph has been incurred in a lawful and regular manner and whether the financial management has been sound.

The audit of revenue shall be carried out on the basis of the amounts established as due and the amounts actually paid to the Community.

The audit of expenditure shall be carried out on the basis both of commitments undertaken and payments made.

These audits may be carried out before the closure of accounts for the financial year in question.

3. The audit shall be based on records and, if necessary, performed on the spot in the other institutions of the Community and in the Member States. In the Member States the audit shall be carried out in liaison with the national audit bodies or, if these do not have the necessary powers, with the competent national departments. These bodies or departments shall inform the Court of Auditors whether they intend to take part in the audit.

The other institutions of the Community and the national audit bodies or, if these do not have the necessary powers, the competent national departments, shall forward to the Court of Auditors, at its request, any document or information necessary to carry out its task.

4. The Court of Auditors shall draw up an annual report after the close of each financial year. It shall be forwarded to the other institutions of the Commission and shall be published, together with the replies of these institutions to the observations of the Court of Auditors, in the *Official Journal of the European Communities*.

The Court of Auditors may also, at any time, submit observations, particularly in the form of special reports, on specific questions and deliver opinions at the request of one of the other institutions of the Community.

It shall adopt its annual reports, special reports or opinions by a majority of its members.

It shall assist the European Parliament and the Council in exercising their powers of control over the implementation of the budget.

5. The Court of Auditors shall also draw up a separate annual report stating whether the accounting other than that for the expenditure and revenue referred to in paragraph 1 and the financial management by the Commission relating thereto have been effected in a regular manner. It shall draw up this report within six months of the end of the financial year to which the accounts refer and shall submit it to the Commission and the Council. The Commission shall forward it to the European Parliament.][17]

Title Three

Economic and social provisions

Chapter I

General provisions

Article 46

The [Commission][2] may at any time consult Governments, the various parties concerned (undertakings, workers, consumers and dealers) and their associations, and any experts.

Undertakings, workers, consumers and dealers, and their associations, shall be entitled to present any suggestions or comments to the [Commission][2] on questions affecting them.

To provide guidance, in line with the tasks assigned to the Community, on the course of action to be followed by all concerned, and to determine its own course of action, in accordance with the provisions of this Treaty, the [Commission][2] shall, in consultation as provided above:

1. conduct a continuous study of market and price trends;

2. periodically draw up programmes indicating foreseeable developments in production, consumption, exports and imports;

3. periodically lay down general objectives for modernisation, long-term planning of manufacture and expansion of productive capacity;

4. take part, at the request of the Governments concerned, in studying the possibilities for re-employing, in existing industries or through the creation of new activities, workers made redundant by market developments or technical changes;

5. obtain the information it requires to assess the possibilities for improving working conditions and living standards for workers in the industries within its province, and the threats to those standards.

The [Commission][2] shall publish the general objectives and the programmes after submitting them to the Consultative Committee.

It may publish the studies and information mentioned above.

Article 47

The [Commission][2] may obtain the information it requires to carry out its tasks. It may have any necessary checks made.

The [Commission][2] must not disclose information of the kind covered by the obligation of professional secrecy, in particular information about undertakings, their business relations or their cost components. Subject to this reservation, it shall publish such data as could be useful to Governments or to any other parties concerned.

The [Commission][2] may impose fines or periodic penalty payments on undertakings which evade their obligations under decisions taken in pursuance of this Article or which knowingly furnish false information. The maximum amount of such fines shall be 1 per cent of the annual turnover, and the maximum amount of such penalty payments shall be 5 per cent of the average daily turnover for each day's delay.

Any breach of professional secrecy by the [Commission][2] which has caused damage to an undertaking may be the subject of an action for compensation before the Court, as provided in Article 40.

Article 48

The right of undertakings to form associations shall not be affected by this Treaty. Membership of such associations must be voluntary. Associations may engage in any activity which is not contrary to the provisions of this Treaty or to the decisions or recommendations of the [Commission].[2]

Where this Treaty requires the Consultative Committee to be consulted, any association shall have the right to submit to the [Commission][2], within such time as the latter may set, the comments of its members on the proposed course of action.

To obtain information which it requires, or to facilitate the performance of the tasks entrusted to it, the [Commission]² shall normally call upon producers' associations on condition either that they provide for accredited representatives of workers and consumers to sit on their governing bodies or on advisory committees attached to them, or that they make satisfactory provision in some other way in their organisation for the interests of workers and consumers to be voiced.

The associations referred to in the preceding paragraphs shall furnish the [Commission]² with such information on their activities as it may consider necessary. The comments referred to in the second paragraph of this Article and the information furnished in pursuance of this paragraph shall also be forwarded by those associations to the Government concerned.

Chapter II

Financial provisions

Article 49

The [Commission]² is empowered to procure the funds it requires to carry out its tasks:

- by imposing levies on the production of coal and steel;

- by contracting loans.

It may receive gifts.

Article 50

1. The levies are intended to cover:

- the administrative expenditure provided for in Article 78;

- the non-repayable aid towards readaptation provided for in Article 56;

- in the case of the financing arrangements provided for in Articles 54 and 56, and after recourse to the reserve fund, any portion of the amounts required for servicing loans raised by the [Commission]² which may not be covered by receipts from the servicing of loans granted by it, and any payments to be made under guarantees granted by the [Commission]² on loans contracted directly by undertakings;

– expenditure on the promotion of technical and economic research as provided for in Article 55(2).

2. The levies shall be assessed annually on the various products according to their average value; the rate thereof shall not, however, exceed 1 per cent unless previously authorised by the Council, acting by a two-thirds majority. The mode of assessment and collection shall be determined by a general decision of the [Commission]² taken after consulting the Council; cumulative imposition shall be avoided as far as possible.

3. The [Commission]² may impose upon undertakings which do not comply with decisions taken by it under this Article surcharges of not more than 5 per cent for each quarter's delay.

Article 51

1. The [Commission]² may not use the funds obtained by borrowing except to grant loans.

The issue of loans by the [Commission]² on the markets of Member States shall be subject to the rules and regulations in force on these markets.

If the [Commission]² considers the guarantee of Member States necessary in order to contract certain loans, it shall approach the Government or Governments concerned after consulting the Council; no State shall be obliged to give its guarantee.

2. The [Commission]² may, as provided in Article 54, guarantee loans granted direct to undertakings by third parties.

3. The [Commission]² may so determine its conditions for loans or guarantees as to enable a reserve fund to be built up for the sole purpose of reducing whatever amounts may have to be paid out of the levies in accordance with the third subparagraph of Article 50(1); the sums thus accumulated must not, however, be used for any form of lending to undertakings.

4. The [Commission]² shall not itself engage in the banking operations which its financial tasks entail.

Article 52

Member States shall make all appropriate arrangements to enable transfers of funds derived from the levies, from pecuniary sanctions and periodic penalty payments and from the reserve fund to be effected within the territories referred to in the first paragraph of Article 79 in accordance with the procedure for commercial payments, to the extent necessary to make it possible for them to be used for the purposes intended by this Treaty.

The procedure for effecting transfers, both between Member States and to third countries, arising out of other financial operations carried out or guaranteed by the [Commission]², shall be determined by agreement between the [Commission]² and the Member States concerned or the appropriate agencies; there shall, however, be no obligation upon any Member State which applies exchange controls to permit transfers where it has not expressly undertaken to do so.

Article 53

Without prejudice to the provisions of Article 58 or Chapter V of Title III, the [Commission]² may:

(a) after consulting the Consultative Committee and the Council, authorise the making, on conditions which it shall determine and under its supervision, of any financial arrangements common to several undertakings which it recognises to be necessary for the performance of the tasks set out in Article 3 and compatible with this Treaty, and in particular with Article 65;

(b) with the unanimous assent of the Council, itself make any financial arrangements serving the same purposes.

Similar arrangements made or maintained by Member States shall be notified to the [Commission]², which, after consulting the Consultative Committee and the Council, shall make the necessary recommendations to the States concerned where such arrangements are inconsistent, in whole or in part, with the application of this Treaty.

Chapter III

Investment and financial aid

Article 54

The [Commission]² may facilitate the carrying out of investment programmes by granting loans to undertakings or by guaranteeing other loans which they may contract.

With the unanimous assent of the Council, the [Commission]² may by the same means assist the financing of works and installations which contribute directly and primarily to increasing the production, reducing the production costs or facilitating the marketing of products within its jurisdiction.

In order to encourage coordinated development of investment, the [Commission][2] may, in accordance with Article 47, require undertakings to inform it of individual programmes in advance, either by a special request addressed to the undertaking concerned or by a decision stating what kind and scale of programme must be communicated.

The [Commission][2] may, after giving the parties concerned full opportunity to submit their comments, deliver a reasoned opinion on such programmes within the framework of the general objectives provided for in Article 46. If application is made by the undertaking concerned, the [Commission][2] must deliver a reasoned opinion. The [Commission][2] shall notify the opinion to the undertaking concerned and shall bring the opinion to the attention of its Government. Lists of such opinions shall be published.

If the [Commission][2] finds that the financing of a programme or the operation of the installations therein planned would involve subsidies, aids, protection or discrimination contrary to this Treaty, the adverse opinion delivered by it on these grounds shall have the force of a decision within the meaning of Article 14 and the effect of prohibiting the undertaking concerned from drawing on resources other than its own funds to carry out the programme.

The [Commission][2] may impose on undertakings which disregard the prohibition referred to in the preceding paragraph fines not exceeding the amounts improperly devoted to carrying out the programme in question.

Article 55

1. The [Commission][2] shall promote technical and economic research relating to the production and increased use of coal and steel and to occupational safety in the coal and steel industries. To this end it shall organise all appropriate contacts among existing research bodies.

2. After consulting the Consultative Committee, the [Commission][2] may initiate and facilitate such research:

(a) by inducing joint financing by the undertakings concerned; or

(b) by allotting for that purpose any funds received as gifts; or

(c) with the assent of the Council, by allotting for that purpose funds derived from the levies provided for in Article 50; the limit laid down in paragraph 2 of that Article must not, however, be exceeded.

The results of research financed as provided in subparagraphs (b) and (c) shall be made available to all concerned in the Community.

3. The [Commission][2] shall deliver any opinions which serve to make technical improvements more widely known, particularly with regard to the exchange of patents and the granting of licences for using them.

Article 56

1. If the introduction, within the framework of the general objectives of the [Commission][2], of new technology processes or equipment should lead to an exceptionally large reduction in labour requirements in the coal or the steel industry, making it particularly difficult in one or more areas to re-employ redundant workers, the [Commission][2], on application by the Governments concerned:

(a) shall obtain the opinion of the Consultative Committee;

(b) may facilitate, in the manner laid down in Article 54, either in the industries within its jurisdiction or, with the assent of the Council, in any other industry, the financing of such programmes as it may approve for the creation of new and economically sound activities capable of reabsorbing the redundant workers into productive employment;

(c) shall provide non-repayable aid towards:

- the payment of tideover allowances to workers;

- the payment of resettlement allowances to workers;

- the financing of vocational retraining for workers having to change their employment.

The [Commission][2] shall make the provision of non-repayable aid conditional upon payment by the State concerned of a special contribution of not less than the amount of that aid, unless an exception is authorised by the Council, acting by a two-thirds majority.

2.[18] If the fundamental changes, not directly connected with the establishment of the common market, in market conditions for the coal or the steel industry should compel some undertakings permanently to discontinue, curtail or change their activities, the [Commission][2], on application by the Governments concerned:

(a) may facilitate, in the manner laid down in Article 54, either in the industries within its jurisdiction or, with the assent of the Council, in any other industry, the financing of such programmes as it may approve for the creation of new and economically sound activities or for the conversion of existing undertakings capable of reabsorbing the redundant workers into productive employment;

(b) may provide non-repayable aid towards:

- the payment of tideover allowances to workers;

- the payment of allowances to undertakings to enable them to continue paying such of their workers as may have to be temporarily laid off as a result of the undertakings' change of activity;

- the payment of resettlement allowances to workers;

- the financing of vocational retraining for workers having to change their employment.

The [Commission]² shall make the provision of non-repayable aid conditional upon payment by the State concerned of a special contribution of not less than the amount of that aid, unless an exception is authorised by the Council, acting by a two-thirds majority.

Chapter IV

Production

Article 57

In the sphere of production, the [Commission]² shall give preference to the indirect means of action at its disposal, such as:

- cooperation with Governments to regularise or influence general consumption, particularly that of the public services;

- intervention in regard to prices and commercial policy as provided for in this Treaty.

Article 58

1. In the event of a decline in demand, if the [Commission]² considers that the Community is confronted with a period of manifest crisis and that the means of action provided for in Article 57 are not sufficient to deal with this, it shall, after consulting the Consultative Committee and with the assent of the Council, establish a system of production quotas, accompanied to the necessary extent by the measures provided for in Article 74.

If the [Commission]² fails to act, a Member State may bring the matter before the Council, which may, acting unanimously, require the [Commission]² to establish a system of quotas.

2. The [Commission]² shall, on the basis of studies made jointly with undertakings and associations of undertakings, determine the quotas on an equitable basis, taking account of the principles set out in Articles 2,

3 and 4. It may in particular regulate the level of activity of undertakings by appropriate levies on tonnages exceeding a reference level set by a general decision.

The funds thus obtained shall be used to support undertakings whose rate of production has fallen below that envisaged, in order, in particular, to maintain employment in these undertakings as far as possible.

3. The system of quotas shall be ended on a proposal made to the Council by the [Commission]² after consulting the Consultative Committee, or by the Government of a Member State, unless the Council decides otherwise, acting unanimously if the proposal emanates from the [Commission]² or by a simple majority if the proposal emanates from a Government. An announcement on the ending of the quota system shall be made by the [Commission]².

4. The [Commission]² may impose upon undertakings which do not comply with decisions taken by it under this Article fines not exceeding the value of the tonnages produced in disregard thereof.

Article 59

1. If, after consulting the Consultative Committee, the [Commission]² finds that the Community is confronted with a serious shortage of any or all of the products within its jurisdiction, and that the means of action provided for in Article 57 are not sufficient to deal with this, it shall bring the situation to the attention of the Council and shall, unless the Council, acting unanimously, decides otherwise, propose to it the necessary measures.

If the [Commission]² fails to act, a Member State may bring the matter before the Council, which may, acting unanimously, recognise that the situation in question does in fact exist.

2. The Council shall, acting unanimously on a proposal from and in consultation with the [Commission]², establish consumption priorities and determine the allocation of the coal and steel resources of the Community to the industries within its jurisdiction, to export and to other sectors of consumption.

On the basis of the consumption priorities thus established, the [Commission]² shall, after consulting the undertakings concerned, draw up the production programmes with which the undertakings shall be required to comply.

3. If the Council does not reach a unanimous decision on the measures referred to in paragraph 2, the [Commission]² shall itself allocate the

resources of the Community among the Member States on the basis of consumption and exports, irrespective of the place of production.

Within each of the Member States allocation of the resources assigned by the [Commission][2] shall be carried out on the responsibility of the Government, provided that the deliveries scheduled to be supplied to other Member States are not affected and that the [Commission][2] is consulted concerning the portions to be allotted to export and to the operation of the coal and steel industries.

If the portion allotted by a Government to export is less than the amount taken as the basis for calculating the total tonnage to be assigned to the Member State concerned, the [Commission][2] shall, to the necessary extent, at the next allocation, redivide among the Member States the resources thus made available for consumption.

If the portion allotted by a Government to the operation of the coal and steel industries is similarly less and the result is a decrease in Community production of one of these, the tonnage assigned to the Member State concerned shall, at the next allocation, be reduced by the amount of the decrease in production so caused.

4. In all cases, the [Commission][2] shall be responsible for allocating equitably among undertakings the quantities assigned to the industries within its jurisdiction, on the basis of studies made jointly with undertakings and associations of undertakings.

5. Should the situation provided for in paragraph 1 of this Article arise, the [Commission][2] may, in accordance with Article 57, after consulting the Consultative Committee and with the assent of the Council, decide that restrictions on exports to third countries shall be imposed in all the Member States, or, if the [Commission][2] fails to act, the Council may, acting unanimously, so decide on a proposal from a Government.

6. The [Commission][2] may end the arrangements made under this Article after consulting the Consultative Committee and the Council. It shall not do so if the Council unanimously dissents.

If the [Commission][2] fails to act, the Council may, acting unanimously, itself end the arrangements.

7. The [Commission][2] may impose upon undertakings which do not comply with decisions taken under this Article fines not exceeding twice the value of prescribed production or deliveries either not effected or diverted from their proper use.

Chapter V

Prices

Article 60

1. Pricing practices contrary to Articles 2, 3 and 4 shall be prohibited, in particular:

— unfair competitive practices, especially purely temporary or purely local price reductions tending towards the acquisition of a monopoly position within the common market;

— discriminatory practices involving, within the common market, the application by a seller of dissimilar conditions to comparable transactions, especially on grounds of the nationality of the buyer.

The [Commission]² may define the practices covered by this prohibition by decisions taken after consulting the Consultative Committee and the Council.

2. For these purposes:

(a) the price lists and conditions of sale applied by undertakings within the common market must be made public to the extent and in the manner prescribed by the [Commission]² after consulting the Consultative Committee. If the [Commission]² finds that an undertaking's choice of point on which it bases its price lists is abnormal and in particular makes it possible to evade the provisions of subparagraph (b), it shall make appropriate recommendations to that undertaking;

(b) the methods of quotation used must not have the effect that prices charged by an undertaking in the common market, when reduced to their equivalent at the point chosen for its price lists, result in:

— increases over the price shown in the price list in question for a comparable transaction; or

— reductions below that price the amount of which exceeds either:

— the extent enabling the quotation to be aligned on the price list, based on another point which secures the buyer the most advantageous delivered terms; or

— the limits fixed, by decision of the [Commission]² after the Consultative Committee has delivered its opinion, for each category of product, with due regard, where appropriate, for the origin and destination of products.

Such decisions shall be taken when found necessary, to avoid disturbances in the whole or any part of the common market or disequilibria resulting from a difference between the methods of quotation used for a product and for materials involved in making it. Such decisions shall not preclude undertakings from aligning their quotations on those of undertakings outside the Community, on condition that the transactions are notified to the [Commission][2], which may, in the event of abuse, restrict or abrogate the right of the undertakings concerned to take advantage of this exception.

Article 61

On the basis of studies made jointly with undertakings and associations of undertakings, in accordance with the first paragraph of Article 46 and the third paragraph of Article 48, and after consulting the Consultative Committee and the Council as to the advisability of so doing and the price level to be so determined, the [Commission][2] may, for one or more of the products within its jurisdiction:

(a) fix maximum prices within the common market, if it finds that such a decision is necessary to attain the objectives set out in Article 3, and particularly in paragraph (c) thereof;

(b) fix minimum prices within the common market, if it finds that a manifest crisis exists or is imminent and that such a decision is necessary to attain the objectives set out in Article 3;

(c) after consulting the associations to which the undertakings concerned belong, or the undertakings themselves, fix, by methods appropriate to the nature of the export markets, minimum or maximum export prices, if such an arrangement can be effectively supervised and is necessary both in view of the dangers to the undertakings resulting from the state of the market and in order to secure the acceptance in international economic relations of the objective set out in Article 3(f); any fixing of minimum prices shall be without prejudice to the measures provided for in the last subparagraph of Article 60(2).

In fixing prices, the [Commission][2] shall take into account the need to ensure that the coal and steel industries and the consumer industries remain competitive, in accordance with the principles laid down in Article 3(c).

If in these circumstances the [Commission][2] fails to act, the Government of a Member State may bring the matter before the Council, which may, acting unanimously, call upon [Commission][2] to fix such maximum or minimum prices.

Article 62

If the [Commission][2] considers this the most appropriate way of preventing coal from being priced at the level of the production costs of the mines which have the highest costs but which it is recognised should be temporarily maintained in service in order that the tasks laid down in Article 3 may be performed, it may, after consulting the Consultative Committee, authorise equalisation payments:

- between undertakings in the same coalfield to which the same price lists apply;

- after consulting the Council, between undertakings in different coalfields.

These equalisation payments may, moreover, be instituted as provided in Article 53.

Article 63

1. If the [Commission][2] finds that discrimination is being systematically practised by purchasers, in particular under provisions governing contracts entered into by bodies dependent on a public authority, it shall make appropriate recommendations to the Governments concerned.

2. Where the [Commission][2] considers it necessary, it may decide that:

(a) undertakings must frame their conditions of sale in such a way that their customers and commission agents acting on their behalf shall be under an obligation to comply with the rules made by the [Commission][2] in application of this Chapter;

(b) undertakings shall be held responsible for infringements of this obligation by their direct agents or by commission agents acting on their behalf.

In the event of an infringement of this obligation by a purchaser, the [Commission][2] may restrict or, should the infringement be repeated, temporarily prohibit dealings with that purchaser by Community undertakings. If this is done, the purchaser shall have the right, without prejudice to Article 33, to bring an action before the Court.

3. In addition, the [Commission][2] is empowered to make to the Member State concerned any appropriate recommendations to ensure that the rules laid down for the application of Article 60(1) are duly observed by all distributive undertakings and agencies in the coal and steel sectors.

Article 64

The [Commission][2] may impose upon undertakings which infringe the provisions of this Chapter or decisions taken thereunder fines not exceeding twice the value of the sales effected in disregard thereof. If the infringement is repeated, this maximum shall be doubled.

Chapter VI

Agreements and Concentrations

Article 65

1. All agreements between undertakings, decisions by associations of undertakings and concerted practices tending directly or indirectly to prevent, restrict or distort normal competition within the common market shall be prohibited, and in particular those tending:

(*a*) to fix or determine prices;

(*b*) to restrict or control production, technical development or investment;

(*c*) to share markets, products, customers or sources or supply.

2. However the [Commission][2] shall authorise specialisation agreements or joint-buying or joint-selling agreements in respect of particular products if it finds that:

(*a*) such specialisation or such joint-buying or -selling will make for a substantial improvement in the production or distribution of those products;

(*b*) the agreement in question is essential in order to achieve these results and is not more restrictive than is necessary for that purpose; and

(*c*) the agreement is not liable to give the undertakings concerned the power to determine the prices, or to control or restrict the production or marketing, of a substantial part of the products in question within the common market, or to shield them against effective competition from other undertakings within the common market.

If the [Commission][2] finds that certain agreements are strictly analogous in nature and effect to those referred to above, having particular regard to the fact that this paragraph applies to distributive undertakings it shall authorise them also when satisfied that they meet the same requirements.

Authorisations may be granted subject to specified conditions and for limited periods. In such cases the [Commission][2] shall renew an authorisation once or several times if it finds that the requirements of subparagraphs (*a*) to (*c*) are still met at the time of renewal.

The [Commission][2] shall revoke or amend an authorisation if it finds that as a result of a change in circumstances the agreement no longer meets these requirements, or that the actual results of the agreement or of the application thereof are contrary to the requirements for its authorisation.

Decisions granting, renewing, amending, refusing or revoking an authorisation shall be published together with the reasons therefor; the restrictions imposed by the second paragraph of Article 47 shall not apply thereto.

3. The [Commission][2] may, as provided in Article 47, obtain any information needed for the application of this Article, either by making a special request to the parties concerned or by means of regulations stating the kinds of agreement, decision or practice which must be communicated to it.

4. Any agreement or decision prohibited by paragraph 1 of this Article shall be automatically void and may not be relied upon before any court or tribunal in the Member States.

The [Commission][2] shall have sole jurisdiction, subject to the right to bring actions before the Court, to rule whether any such agreement or decision is compatible with this Article.

5. On any undertaking which has entered into an agreement which is automatically void, or has enforced or attempted to enforce, by arbitration, penalty, boycott or any other means, an agreement or decision which is automatically void or an agreement for which authorisation has been refused or revoked, or has obtained an authorisation by means of information which it knew to be false or misleading, or has engaged in practices prohibited by paragraph 1 of this Article, the [Commission][2] may impose fines or periodic penalty payments not exceeding twice the turnover on the products which were the subject of the agreement, decision or practice prohibited by this Article; if, however, the purpose of the agreement, decision or practice is to restrict production, technical development or investment, this maximum may be raised to 10 per cent of the annual turnover of the undertakings in question in the case of fines, and 20 per cent of the daily turnover in the case of periodic penalty payments.

Article 66

1. Any transaction shall require the prior authorisation of the [Commission][2], subject to the provisions of paragraph 3 of this Article, if

it has in itself the direct or indirect effect of bringing about within the territories referred to in the first paragraph of Article 79, as a result of action by any person or undertaking or group of persons or undertakings, a concentration between undertakings at least one of which is covered by Article 80, whether the transaction concerns a single product or a number of different products, and whether it is effected by merger, acquisition of shares or parts of the undertaking or assets, loan, contract or any other means of control. For the purpose of applying these provisions, the [Commission]² shall, by regulations made after consulting the Council, define what constitutes control of an undertaking.

2. The [Commission]² shall grant the authorisation referred to in the preceding paragraph if it finds that the proposed transaction will not give to the persons or undertakings concerned the power, in respect of the product or products within its jurisdiction:

– to determine prices, to control or restrict production or distribution or to hinder effective competition in a substantial part of the market for those products; or

– to evade the rules of competition instituted under this Treaty, in particular by establishing an artificially privileged position involving a substantial advantage in access to supplies or markets.

In assessing whether this is so, the [Commission]² shall, in accordance with the principle of non-discrimination laid down in Article 4(*b*), take account of the size of like undertakings in the Community, to the extent it considers justified in order to avoid or correct disadvantages resulting from unequal competitive conditions.

The [Commission]² may make its authorisation subject to any conditions which it considers appropriate for the purposes of this paragraph.

Before ruling on a transaction concerning undertakings at least one of which is not subject to Article 80, the [Commission]² shall obtain the comments of the Governments concerned.

3. The [Commission]² shall exempt from the requirement of prior authorisation such classes of transactions as it finds should, in view of the size of the assets or undertakings concerned, taken in conjunction with the kind of concentration to be effected, be deemed to meet the requirements of paragraph 2. Regulations made to this effect, with the assent of the Council, shall also lay down the conditions governing such exemption.

4. Without prejudice to the application of Article 47 to undertakings within its jurisdiction, the [Commission]² may, either by regulations made

after consultation with the Council stating the kind of transaction to be communicated to it or by a special request under these regulations to the parties concerned, obtain from the natural or legal persons who have acquired or regrouped or are intending to acquire or regroup the rights or assets in question any information needed for the application of this Article concerning transactions liable to produce the effect referred to in paragraph 1.

5. If a concentration should occur which the [Commission][2] finds has been effected contrary to the provisions of paragraph 1 but which nevertheless meets the requirements of paragraph 2, the [Commission][2] shall make its approval of that concentration subject to payment by the persons who have acquired or regrouped the rights or assets in question of the fine provided for in the second subparagraph of paragraph 6; the amount of the fine shall not be less than half of the maximum determined in that subparagraph should it be clear that authorisation ought to have been applied for. If the fine is not paid, the [Commission][2] shall take the steps hereinafter provided for in respect of concentrations found to be unlawful.

If a concentration should occur which the [Commission][2] finds cannot fulfil the general or specific conditions to which an authorisation under paragraph 2 would be subject, the [Commission][2] shall, by means of a reasoned decision, declare the concentration unlawful and, after giving the parties concerned the opportunity to submit their comments, shall order separation of the undertakings or assets improperly concentrated or cessation of joint control, and any other measures which it considers appropriate to return the undertakings or assets in question to independent operation and restore normal conditions of competition. Any person directly concerned may institute proceedings against such decisions, as provided in Article 33. By way of derogation from Article 33, the Court shall have unlimited jurisdiction to assess whether the transaction effected is a concentration within the meaning of paragraph 1 and of regulations made in application thereof. The institution of proceedings shall have suspensory effect. Proceedings may not be instituted until the measures provided for above have been ordered, unless the [Commission][2] agrees to the institution of separate proceedings against the decision declaring the transaction unlawful.

The [Commission][2] may at any time, unless the third paragraph of Article 39 is applied, take or cause to be taken such interim measures of protection as it may consider necessary to safeguard the interests of competing undertakings and of third parties, and to forestall any step which might hinder the implementation of its decisions. Unless the Court decides otherwise, proceedings shall not have suspensory effect in respect of such interim measures.

The [Commission][2] shall allow the parties concerned a reasonable period in which to comply with its decisions, on expiration of which it may impose daily penalty payments not exceeding one tenth of one per cent of the value of the rights or assets in question.

Furthermore, if the parties concerned do not fulfil their obligations, the [Commission][2] shall itself take steps to implement its decision; it may in particular suspend the exercise, in undertakings within its jurisdiction, of the rights attached to the assets acquired irregularly, obtain the appointment by the judicial authorities of a receiver of such assets, organise the forced sale of such assets subject to the protection of the legitimate interests of their owners, and annul with respect to natural or legal persons who have acquired the rights or assets in question through the unlawful transaction, the acts, decisions, resolutions or proceedings of the supervisory and managing bodies or undertakings over which control has been obtained irregularly.

The [Commission][2] is also empowered to make such recommendations to the Member States concerned as may be necessary to ensure that the measures provided for in the preceding subparagraphs are implemented under their own law.

In the exercise of its powers, the [Commission][2] shall take account of the rights of third parties which have been acquired in good faith.

6. The [Commission][2] may impose fines not exceeding:

- 3 per cent of the value of the assets acquired or regrouped or to be acquired or regrouped, on natural or legal persons who have evaded the obligations laid down in paragraph 4;

- 10 per cent of the value of the assets acquired or regrouped, on natural or legal persons who have evaded the obligations laid down in paragraph 1; this maximum shall be increased by one twenty-fourth for each month which elapses after the end of the twelfth month following completion of the transaction until the [Commission][2] establishes that there has been an infringement;

- 10 per cent of the value of the assets acquired or regrouped or to be acquired or regrouped, on natural or legal persons who have obtained or attempted to obtain authorisation under paragraph 2 by means of false or misleading information;

- 15 per cent of the value of the assets acquired or regrouped, on undertakings within its jurisdiction which have engaged in or been party to transactions contrary to the provisions of this Article.

Persons fined under this paragraph may appeal to the Court as provided in Article 36.

7. If the [Commission][2] finds that public or private undertakings which, in law or in fact, hold or acquire in the market for one of the products within its jurisdiction a dominant position shielding them against effective competition in a substantial part of the common market are using that position for purposes contrary to the objectives of this Treaty, it shall make to them such recommendations as may be appropriate to prevent the position from being so used. If these recommendations are not implemented satisfactorily within a reasonable time, the [Commission][2] shall, by decisions taken in consultation with the Government concerned, determine the prices and conditions of sale to be applied by the undertaking in question or draw up production or delivery programmes with which it must comply, subject to liability to the penalties provided for in Articles 58, 59 and 64.

Chapter VII

Interference with conditions of competition

Article 67

1. Any action by a Member State which is liable to have appreciable repercussions on conditions of competition in the coal or the steel industry shall be brought to the knowledge of the [Commission][2] by the Government concerned.

2. If the action is liable, by substantially increasing differences in production costs otherwise than through changes in productivity, to provoke a serious disequilibrium, the [Commission][2], after consulting the Consultative Committee and the Council, may take the following steps:

–   if the action taken by that State is having harmful effects on the coal or steel undertakings within the jurisdiction of that State, the [Commission][2] may authorise it to grant aid to these undertakings, the amount, conditions and duration of which shall be determined in agreement with the [Commission][2]. The same shall apply in the case of any change in wages and working conditions which would have the same effects, even if not resulting from any action by that State;

–   if the action taken by that State is having harmful effects on the coal or steel undertakings within the jurisdiction of other Member States, the [Commission][2] shall make a recommendation to that State with a view to remedying these effects by such measures as that State may consider most compatible with its own economic equilibrium.

3. If the action taken by that State reduces differences in production costs by allowing special benefits to or imposing special charges on the coal or steel undertakings within its jurisdiction in comparison with the

other industries in the same country, the [Commission][2] is empowered to make the necessary recommendations to that State after consulting the Consultative Committee and the Council.

Chapter VIII

Wages and movement of workers

Article 68

1. The methods used for fixing wages and welfare benefits in the several Member States shall not, in the case of the coal and steel industries, be affected by this Treaty, subject to the following provisions.

2. If the [Commission][2] finds that one or more undertakings are charging abnormally low prices because they are paying abnormally low wages compared with the wage level in the same area, it shall, after consulting the Consultative Committee, make appropriate recommendations to them. If the abnormally low wages are the result of governmental decisions, the [Commission][2] shall confer with the Government concerned, and failing agreement it may, after consulting the Consultative Committee, make a recommendation to that Government.

3. If the [Commission][2] finds that wage reduction entails a lowering of the standard of living of workers and at the same time is being used as a means for the permanent economic adjustment of undertakings or as a means of competition between them, it shall, after consulting the Consultative Committee, make a recommendation to the undertaking or Government concerned with a view to securing, at the expense of the undertakings, benefits for the workers in order to compensate for the reductions.

This provision shall not apply to:

(a) overall measures taken by a Member State to restore its external equilibrium, without prejudice in such case to any action under Article 67;

(b) wage reductions resulting from the application of a sliding scale established by law or by contract;

(c) wage reductions resulting from a fall in the cost of living;

(d) wage reductions to correct abnormal increases that occurred previously in exceptional circumstances which no longer obtain.

4. Save in the cases referred to in paragraph 3(a) and (b), any wage reduction affecting all or a substantial number of the workers in an undertaking shall be notified to the [Commission][2].

5. The recommendations provided for in the preceding paragraphs may be made by the [Commission]² only after consulting the Council, unless they are addressed to undertakings smaller than a minimum size to be defined by the [Commission]² in agreement with the Council.

If in one of the Member States a change in the arrangements for the financing of social security or for dealing with unemployment and its effects, or a change in wages, produces the effects referred to in Article 67(2) or (3), the [Commission]² is empowered to take the steps provided for in that Article.

6. The [Commission]² may impose upon undertakings which do not comply with recommendations made to them under this Article fines and periodic penalty payments not exceeding twice the amount of the saving in labour costs improperly effected.

Article 69

1. Member States undertake to remove any restriction based on nationality upon the employment in the coal and steel industries of workers who are nationals of Member States and have recognised qualifications in a coalmining or steelmaking occupation, subject to the limitations imposed by the basic requirements of health and public policy.

2. For the purpose of applying this provision, Member States shall draw up common definitions of skilled trades and qualifications therefor, shall determine by common accord the limitations provided for in paragraph 1, and shall endeavour to work out arrangements on a Community-wide basis for bringing offers of employment into touch with applications for employment.

3. In addition, with regard to workers not covered by paragraph 2, they shall, should growth of coal or steel production be hampered by a shortage of suitable labour, adjust their immigration rules to the extent needed to remedy this state of affairs; in particular, they shall facilitate the re-employment of workers from the coal and steel industries of other Member States.

4. They shall prohibit any discrimination in remuneration and working conditions between nationals and migrant workers, without prejudice to special measures concerning frontier workers; in particular, they shall endeavour to settle among themselves any matters remaining to be dealt with in order to ensure that social security arrangements do not inhibit labour mobility.

5. The [Commission]² shall guide and facilitate action by Member States in applying this Article.

6. This Article shall not affect the international obligations of Member States.

Chapter IX

Transport

Article 70

It is recognised that the establishment of the common market necessitates the application of such rates and conditions for the carriage of coal and steel as will afford comparable price conditions to comparably placed consumers.

Any discrimination in rates and conditions of carriage of every kind which is based on the country of origin or destination of products shall be prohibited in traffic between Member States. For the purpose of eliminating such discrimination it shall in particular be obligatory to apply to the carriage of coal and steel to or from another country of the Community the scales, rates and all other tariff rules of every kind which are applicable to the internal carriage of the same goods on the same route.

The scales, rates and all other tariff rules of every kind applied to the carriage of coal and steel within each Member State and between Member States shall be published or brought to the knowledge of the [Commission][2].

The application of special internal rates and conditions in the interest or one or more coal- or steel-producing undertakings shall require the prior agreement of the [Commission][2], which shall verify that they are in accordance with the principles of this Treaty; it may make its agreement temporary or conditional.

Subject to the provisions of this Article, and to the other provisions of this Treaty, transport policy, including the fixing and altering of rates and conditions of carriage of every kind and the making of rates on a basis calculated to secure for the transport undertakings concerned a properly balanced financial position, shall continue to be governed by the laws or regulations of the individual Member States, as shall measures relating to coordination or competition between different modes of transport or different routes.

Chapter X

Commercial policy

Article 71

The powers of the Governments of Member States in matters of commercial policy shall not be affected by this Treaty, save as otherwise provided therein.

The powers conferred on the Community by this Treaty in matters of commercial policy towards third countries may not exceed those accorded to Member States under international agreements to which they are parties, subject to the provisions of Article 75.

The Governments of Member States shall afford each other such mutual assistance as is necessary to implement measures recognised by the [Commission][2] as being in accordance with this Treaty and with existing international agreements. The [Commission][2] is empowered to propose to the Member States concerned the methods by which this mutual assistance may be provided.

Article 72

Minimum rates below which Member States undertake not to lower their customs duties on coal and steel as against third countries, and maximum rates above which they undertake not to raise them, may be fixed by decision of the Council, acting unanimously on a proposal from the [Commission][2] made on the latter's own initiative or at the request of a Member State.

Within the limits so fixed each Government shall determine its tariffs according to its own national procedure. The [Commission][2] may, on its own initiative or at the request of a Member State, deliver an opinion suggesting amendment of the tariffs of the State.

Article 73

The administration of import and export licences for trade with third countries shall be a matter for the Government in whose territory the place of destination for imports or the place of origin for exports is situated.

The [Commission][2] is empowered to supervise the administration and verification of these licences with respect to coal and steel. Where necessary it shall, after consulting the Council, make recommendations to Member States to ensure that the arrangements in this connection are not more restrictive than the circumstances governing their adoption or retention require, and to secure the coordination of measures taken under the third paragraph of Article 71 or under Article 74.

Article 74

In the cases set out below, the [Commission][2] is empowered to take any measures which is in accordance with this Treaty, and in particular with the objectives set out in Article 3, and to make to Governments any recommendation which is in accordance with the second paragraph of Article 71:

1. if it is found that countries not members of the Community or undertakings situated in such countries are engaging in dumping or other practices condemned by the Havana Charter;

2. if a difference between quotations by undertakings outside and by undertakings within the jurisdiction of the Community is due solely to the fact that those of the former are based on conditions of competition contrary to this Treaty;

3. if one of the products referred to in Article 81 of this Treaty is imported into the territory of one or more Member States in relatively increased quantities and under such conditions that these imports cause or threaten to cause serious injury to production within the common market of like or directly competing products.

However, recommendations for the introduction of quantitative restrictions under subparagraph 2 may be made only with the assent of the Council, and under subparagraph 3 only under the conditions laid down in Article 58.

Article 75

The Member States undertake to keep the [Commission][2] informed of proposed commercial agreements or arrangements having similar effect where these relate to coal and steel or to the importation of other raw materials and specialised equipment needed for the production of coal and steel in Member States.

If a proposed agreement or arrangement contains clauses which would hinder the implementation of this Treaty, the [Commission][2] shall make the necessary recommendations to the State concerned within ten days of receiving notification of the communication addressed to it; in any other case it may deliver opinions.

Title Four

General provisions

Article 76

(*Article repealed by the second paragraph of Article 28 of the Merger Treaty*)

[*See Merger Treaty, first paragraph of Article 28, which reads as follows*:

The European Communities shall enjoy in the territories of the Member States such privileges and immunities as are necessary for the performance of their tasks, under the conditions laid down in the Protocol annexed to this Treaty. The same shall apply to the European Investment Bank.]

Article 77

The seat of the institutions of the Community will be determined by common accord of the Governments of the Member States.

Article 78

1. The financial year shall run from 1 January to 31 December.

The administrative expenditure of the Community shall comprise the expenditure of the [Commission]², including that relating to the functioning of the Consultative Committee, and that of the European Parliament, the Council, and of the Court of Justice.

2. Each institution of the Community shall, before 1 July, draw up estimates of its administrative expenditure. The [Commission]² shall consolidate these estimates in a preliminary draft administrative budget. It shall attach thereto an opinion which may contain different estimates.

The preliminary draft budget shall contain an estimate of revenue and an estimate of expenditure.

3. The [Commission]² shall place the preliminary draft administrative budget before the Council not later than 1 September of the year preceding that in which the budget is to be implemented.

The Council shall consult the [Commission]² and, where appropriate, the other institutions concerned whenever it intends to depart from the preliminary draft budget.

The Council shall, acting by a qualified majority, establish the draft administrative budget and forward it to the European Parliament.

4. The draft administrative budget shall be placed before the European

Parliament not later than 5 October of the year preceding that in which the budget is to be implemented.

The European Parliament shall have the right to amend the draft administrative budget, acting by a majority of its members and to propose to the Council, acting by an absolute majority of the votes cast, modifications to the draft budget relating to expenditure necessarily resulting from this Treaty or from acts adopted in accordance therewith.

If, within 45 days of the draft administrative budget being placed before it, the European Parliament has given its approval, the administrative budget shall stand as finally adopted. If within this period the European Parliament has not amended the draft administrative budget nor proposed any modifications thereto, the administrative budget shall be deemed to be finally adopted.

If within this period the European Parliament has adopted amendments or proposed modifications, the draft administrative budget together with the amendments or proposed modifications shall be forwarded to the Council.

5. After discussing the draft administrative budget with the [Commission][2] and, where appropriate, with the other institutions concerned, the Council shall act under the following conditions:

(a) the Council may, acting by a qualified majority, modify any of the amendments adopted by the European Parliament;

(b) with regard to the proposed modifications:

- where a modification proposed by the European Parliament does not have the effect of increasing the total amount of the expenditure of an institution, owing in particular to the fact that the increase in expenditure which it would involve would be expressly compensated by one or more proposed modifications correspondingly reducing expenditure, the Council may, acting by a qualified majority, reject the proposed modification. In the absence of a decision to reject it, the proposed modification shall stand as accepted,

- where a modification proposed by the European Parliament has the effect of increasing the total amount of the expenditure of an institution, the Council may, acting by a qualified majority, accept this proposed modification. In the absence of a decision to accept it, the proposed modification shall stand as rejected,

- where, in pursuance of one of the two preceding subparagraphs, the Council has rejected a proposed modification, it may, acting by a qualified majority, either retain the amount shown in the draft administrative budget or fix another amount.

The draft administrative budget shall be modified on the basis of the proposed modifications accepted by the Council.

If, within 15 days of the draft administrative budget being placed before it, the Council has not modified any of the amendments adopted by the European Parliament and if the modifications proposed by the latter have been accepted, the administrative budget shall be deemed to be finally adopted. The Council shall inform the European Parliament that it has not modified any of the amendments and that the proposed modifications have been accepted.

If within this period the Council has modified one or more of the amendments adopted by the European Parliament or if the modifications proposed by the latter have been rejected or modified, the modified draft administrative budget shall again be forwarded to the European Parliament. The Council shall inform the European Parliament of the results of its deliberations.

6. Within 15 days of the draft administrative budget being placed before it, the European Parliament, which shall have been notified of the action taken on its proposed modification, may, acting by a majority of its members and three-fifths of the votes cast, amend or reject the modifications to its amendments made by the Council and shall adopt the administrative budget accordingly. If within this period the European Parliament has not acted, the administrative budget shall be deemed to be finally adopted.

7. When the procedure provided for in this Article has been completed, the President of the European Parliament shall declare that the administrative budget has been finally adopted.

8. However, the European Parliament, acting by a majority of its members and two-thirds of the votes cast, may, if there are important reasons, reject the draft administrative budget and ask for a new draft to be submitted to it.

9. A maximum rate of increase in relation to the expenditure of the same type to be incurred during the current year shall be fixed annually for the total expenditure other than that necessarily resulting from this Treaty or from acts adopted in accordance therewith.

The [Commission][2] shall, after consulting the Economic Policy Committee, declare what this maximum is as it results from:

– the trend, in terms of volume, of the gross national product within the Community,

– the average variation in the budgets of the Member States, and

– the trend of the cost of living during the preceding financial year.

The maximum rate shall be communicated, before 1 May, to all the institutions of the Community. The latter shall be required to conform to this during the budgetary procedure, subject to the provisions of the fourth and fifth subparagraphs of this paragraph.

If, in respect of expenditure other than that necessarily resulting from this Treaty or from acts adopted in accordance therewith, the actual rate of increase on the draft administrative budget established by the Council is over half the maximum rate, the European Parliament may, exercising its right of amendment, further increase the total amount of that expenditure to a limit not exceeding half the maximum rate.

Where the European Parliament, the Council or the [Commission][2] considers that the activities of the Communities require that the rate determined according to the procedure laid down in this paragraph should be exceeded, another rate may be fixed by agreement between the Council, acting by a qualified majority, and the European Parliament, acting by a majority of its members and three-fifths of the votes cast.

10. Each institution shall exercise the powers conferred upon it by this Article, with due regard for the provisions of this Treaty and for acts adopted in accordance therewith, in particular those relating to the Communities' own resources and to the balance between revenue and expenditure.

11. Final adoption of the administrative budget shall have the effect of authorising and requiring the [Commission][2] to collect the corresponding revenue in accordance with the provisions of Article 49.

Article 78a

The administrative budget shall be drawn up in the unit of account determined in accordance with the provisions of the regulations made pursuant to Article 78h.

The expenditure shown on the budget shall be authorised for one financial year, unless the regulations made pursuant to Article 78h provide otherwise.

In accordance with conditions to be laid down pursuant to Article 78h any appropriations, other than those relating to staff expenditure, that are unexpended at the end of the financial year may be carried forward to the next financial year only.

Appropriations shall be classified under different chapters grouping items of expenditure according to their nature or purpose and subdivided, as far as may be necessary, in accordance with the regulations made pursuant to Article 78h.

The expenditure of the European Parliament, the Council, the [Commission][2] and the Court shall be set out in separate parts of the administrative budget, without prejudice to special arrangements for certain common items of expenditure.

Article 78b

1. If, at the beginning of a financial year, the administrative budget has not yet been voted, a sum equivalent to not more than one-twelfth of the budget appropriations for the preceding financial year may be spent each month in respect of any chapter or other subdivision of the administrative budget in accordance with the provisions of the regulations made pursuant to Article 78h; this arrangement shall not, however, have the effect of placing at the disposal of the [Commission][2] appropriations in excess of one-twelfth of those provided for in the draft administrative budget in course of preparation.

The [Commission][2] is authorised and required to impose the levies up to the amount of the appropriations for the preceding financial year, but shall not thereby exceed the amount which would have resulted from the adoption of the draft administrative budget.

2. The Council may, acting by a qualified majority, provided that the other conditions laid down in paragraph 1 are observed, authorise expenditure in excess of one-twelfth. The authorisation and requirement to impose the levies may be adjusted accordingly.

If the decision relates to expenditure which does not necessarily result from this Treaty or from acts adopted in accordance therewith, the Council shall forward it immediately to the European Parliament; within 30 days the European Parliament, acting by a majority of its members and three-fifths of the votes cast, may adopt a different decision on the expenditure in excess of the one-twelfth referred to in paragraph 1. This part of the decision of the Council shall be suspended until the European Parliament has taken its decision. If within the said period the European Parliament has not taken a decision which differs from the decision of the Council, the latter shall be deemed to be finally adopted.

[Article 78c

The Commission shall implement the administrative budget, in accordance with the provisions of the regulations made pursuant to

Article 78h, on its own responsibility and within the limits of the appropriations, having regard to the principles of sound financial management.

The regulations shall lay down detailed rules for each institution concerning its part in effecting its own expenditure.

Within the administrative budget, the Commission may, subject to the limits and conditions laid down in the regulations made pursuant to Article 78h, transfer appropriations from one chapter to another or from one subdivision to another.][19]

Article 78d [20, 21]

The [Commission][2] shall submit annually to the Council and to the European Parliament the accounts of the preceding financial year relating to the implementation of the administrative budget. The [Commission][2] shall also forward to them a financial statement of the assets and liabilities of the Community in the field covered by that budget.

Article 78e

Repealed by the Treaty on European Union, Title III, Article H(16).

Article 78f

Repealed by the Treaty on European Union, Title III, Article H(16).

[Article 78g

1. The European Parliament, acting on a recommendation from the Council, which shall act by a qualified majority, shall give a discharge to the Commission in respect of the implementation of the administrative budget. To this end, the Council and the European Parliament in turn shall examine the accounts and the financial statement referred to in Article 78d, the annual report by the Court of Auditors together with the replies of the institutions under audit to the observations of the Court of Auditors, and any relevant special reports by the Court of Auditors.

2. Before giving a discharge to the Commission, or for any other purpose in connection with the exercise of its powers over the implementation of the administrative budget, the European Parliament may ask to hear the Commission give evidence with regard to the execution of the expenditure or the operation of financial control systems. The Commission shall submit any necessary information to the European Parliament at the latter's request.

3. The Commission shall take all appropriate steps to act on the observations in the decisions giving discharge and on other observations by the European Parliament relating to the execution of expenditure, as well as on comments accompanying the recommendations on discharge adopted by the Council.

At the request of the European Parliament or the Council, the Commission shall report on the measures taken in the light of these observations and comments and in particular on the instructions given to the departments which are responsible for the implementation of the administrative budget. These reports shall also be forwarded to the Court of Auditors.][22]

[Article 78h

The Council, acting unanimously on a proposal from the Commission and after consulting the European Parliament and obtaining the opinion of the Court of Auditors, shall:

(a) make financial regulations specifying in particular the procedure to be adopted for establishing and implementing the administrative budget and for presenting and auditing accounts;

(b) determine the methods and procedure whereby the budget revenue provided under the arrangements relating to the Communities' own resources shall be made available to the Commission, and determine the measures to be applied, if need be, to meet cash requirements:

(c) lay down rules concerning the responsibility of financial controllers, authorising officers and accounting officers, and concerning appropriate arrangements for inspection.][23]

[Article 78i

Member States shall take the same measures to counter fraud affecting the financial interests of the Community as they take to counter fraud affecting their own financial interests.

Without prejudice to other provisions of this Treaty, Member States shall coordinate their action aimed at protecting the financial interests of the Community against fraud. To this end they shall organise, with the help of the Commission, close and regular cooperation between the competent departments of their administrations.][24]

Article 79

This Treaty shall apply to the European territories of the High Contracting Parties. It shall also apply to European territories for whose external relations a signatory State is responsible; as regards the Saar, an exchange of letters between the Governments of the Federal Republic of Germany and the Government of the French Republic is annexed to this Treaty.

Notwithstanding the preceding paragraph:

[(a) This Treaty shall not apply to the Faroe Islands.][25]

(b) This Treaty shall not apply to the Sovereign Base Areas of the United Kingdom of Great Britain and Northern Ireland in Cyprus.

(c) This Treaty shall apply to the Channel Islands and the Isle of Man only to the extent necessary to ensure the implementation of the arrangements for those islands set out in the Decision of the Council of the European Communities of 22 January 1972 concerning the accession of new Member States to the European Coal and Steel Community.

Each High Contracting Party undertakes to extend to the other Member States the preferential treatment which it enjoys with respect to coal and steel in the non-European territories under its jurisdiction.

Article 80

For the purposes of this Treaty, 'undertaking' means any undertaking engaged in production in the coal or the steel industry within the territories referred to in the first paragraph of Article 79, and also, for the purposes of Articles 65 and 66 and of information required for their application and proceedings in connection with them, any undertaking or agency regularly engaged in distribution other than sale to domestic consumers or small craft industries.

Article 81

The expressions 'coal' and 'steel' are defined in Annex I to the Treaty.

Additions to the lists in that Annex may be made by the Council, acting unanimously.

Article 82

The turnover taken as the basis for calculating any fines and periodic penalty payments imposed on undertakings under this Treaty shall be the turnover on products within the jurisdiction of the [Commission][2].

Article 83

The establishment of the Community shall in no way prejudice the system of ownership of the undertakings to which this Treaty applies.

Article 84

For the purposes of this Treaty, the words 'this Treaty' mean the provisions of the Treaty and its Annexes, of the Protocols annexed thereto and of the Convention on the Transitional Provisions.

Article 85

The initial and transitional measures agreed by the High Contracting Parties to enable the provisions of this Treaty to be applied are laid down in a Convention annexed to this Treaty.

Article 86

Member States undertake to take all appropriate measures, whether general or particular, to ensure fulfilment of the obligations resulting from decisions and recommendations of the institutions of the Community and to facilitate the performance of the Community's tasks.

Member States undertake to refrain from any measures incompatible with the common market referred to in Articles 1 and 4.

They shall make all appropriate arrangements, as far as lies within their powers, for the settlement of international accounts arising out of trade in coal and steel within the common market and shall afford each other mutual assistance to facilitate such settlements.

Officials of the [Commission]² entrusted by it with tasks of inspection shall enjoy in the territories of Member States, to the full extent required for the performance of their duties, such rights and powers as are granted by the laws of these States to their own revenue officials. Forthcoming visits of inspection and the status of the officials shall be· duly notified to the State concerned. Officials of that State may, at its request or at that of the [Commission]², assist the [Commission's]² officials in the performance of their task.

Article 87

The High Contracting Parties undertake not to avail themselves of any treaties, conventions or declarations made between them for the purpose of submitting a dispute concerning the interpretation or application of this Treaty to any method of settlement other than those provided for therein.

Article 88

If the [Commission]² considers that a State has failed to fulfil an obligation under this Treaty, it shall record this failure in a reasoned decision after giving the State concerned the opportunity to submit its comments. It shall set the State a time limit for the fulfilment of its obligation.

The State may institute proceedings before the Court within two months of notification of the decision; the Court shall have unlimited jurisdiction in such cases.

If the State has not fulfilled its obligations by the time limit set by the [Commission]², or if it brings an action which is dismissed, the [Commission]² may, with the assent of the Council acting by a two-thirds majority:

(a) suspend the payment of any sums which it may be liable to pay to the State in question under this Treaty;

(b) take measures, or authorise the other Member States to take measures, by way of derogation from the provisions of Article 4, in order to correct the effects of the infringement of the obligation.

Proceedings may be instituted before the Court against decisions taken under subparagraphs (a) and (b) within two months of their notification; the Court shall have unlimited jurisdiction in such cases.

If these measures prove ineffective, the [Commission]² shall bring the matter before the Council.

Article 89

Any dispute between Member States concerning the application of this Treaty which cannot be settled by another procedure provided for in this Treaty may be submitted to the Court on application by one of the States which are parties to the dispute.

The Court shall also have jurisdiction in any dispute between Member States which relates to the subject matter of this Treaty, if the dispute is submitted to it under a special agreement between the parties.

Article 90

If failure to fulfil an obligation under this Treaty on the part of an undertaking also constitutes an infringement of its obligations under the law of its State and judicial or administrative action is being taken under that law against the undertaking, the State in question shall so inform the [Commission]², which may defer its decision.

If the [Commission]² defers its decision, it shall be kept informed of the progress of the action taken by national authorities and shall be permitted to produce all relevant documents and expert and other evidence. It shall also be informed of the final decision on the case and shall take account of this decision in determining any penalty it may itself impose.

Article 91

If an undertaking does not pay by the time limit set a sum which it is liable to pay to the [Commission]² either under this Treaty or rules laid down for the implementation thereof or in discharge of a pecuniary sanction or periodic penalty imposed by the [Commission]², the [Commission]² may suspend payment of sums which it is liable to pay to that undertaking, up to the amount of the outstanding payment.

Article 92

Decisions of the [Commission]² which impose a pecuniary obligation shall be enforceable.

Enforcement in the territory of Member States shall be carried out by means of the legal procedure in force in each State, after the order for enforcement in the form in use in the State in whose territory the decision is to be enforced has been appended to the decision, without other formality than verification of the authenticity of the decision. This formality shall be carried out at the instance of a Minister designated for this purpose by each of the Governments.

Enforcement may be suspended only by a decision of the Court.

Article 93

The [Commission]² shall maintain all appropriate relations with the United Nations and the Organisation for European Economic Cooperation and shall keep these organisations regularly informed of the activities of the Community.

Article 94

Relations shall be maintained between the institutions of the Community and the Council of Europe as provided in a Protocol annexed to this Treaty.

Article 95

In all cases not provided for in this Treaty where it becomes apparent that a decision or recommendation of the [Commission]² is necessary to attain, within the common market in coal and steel and in accordance with Article 5, one of the objectives of the Community set out in Articles 2, 3 and 4, the decision may be taken or the recommendation made with the unanimous assent of the Council and after the Consultative Committee has been consulted.

Any decision so taken or recommendation so made shall determine what penalties, if any, may be imposed.

If, after the end of the transitional period provided in the Convention on the Transitional Provisions, unforeseen difficulties emerging in the light of experience in the application of this Treaty, or fundamental economic or technical changes directly affecting the common market in coal and steel, make it necessary to adapt the rules for the [Commission's][2] exercise of its powers, appropriate amendments may be made; they must not, however, conflict with the provisions of Articles 2, 3 and 4 or interfere with the relationship between the powers of the [Commission][2] and those of the other institutions of the Community.

These amendments shall be proposed jointly by the [Commission][2] and the Council, acting by a ten-twelfths majority of its members, and shall be submitted to the Court for its opinion. In considering them, the Court shall have full power to assess all points of fact and of law. If as a result of such consideration it finds the proposals compatible with the provisions of the preceding paragraph, they shall be forwarded to the European Parliament and shall enter into force if approved by a majority of three quarters of the votes cast and two thirds of the members of the European Parliament.

Article 96

Repealed by the Treaty on European Union, Title III, Article H(21).

Article 97

This Treaty is concluded for a period of fifty years from its entry into force.

Article 98

Repealed by the Treaty on European Union, Title III, Article H(21).

Article 99

This Treaty shall be ratified by all the Member States in accordance with their respective constitutional requirements; the instruments of ratification shall be deposited with the Government of the French Republic.

This Treaty shall enter into force on the date of the deposit of the instrument of ratification by the last signatory State to take this step.

If all the instruments of ratification have not been deposited within six months of the signature of this Treaty, the Governments of the States which have deposited their instruments shall consult each other on the measures to be taken.

Article 100

This Treaty, drawn up in a single original, shall be deposited in the archives of the Government of the French Republic, which shall transmit a certified copy thereof to each of the Governments of the other signatory States.

In witness whereof, the undersigned plenipotentiaries have signed this Treaty and affixed thereto their seals.

Done at Paris this eighteenth day of April in the year one thousand nine hundred and fifty-one.

[List omitted]

EDITORIAL NOTES

For Protocols and Declarations not included in this volume see: Office for Official Publications of the European Communities, Treaties establishing the European Communities: Treaties amending these Treaties, 1987, volume I; and, ditto European Union selected instruments taken from the Treaties, Books I and II, volumes I and II (Book I, volume I 1993, Luxembourg; others – to be published).

Relating to Articles 33.2, 35, 40.1, 40.2 and 74: see Decision 94/149 ECSC, EC, in OJ No L 66, 10.3.94, p.29 amending the jurisdiction of the Court of First Instance of the EC.

FOOTNOTES

1. Substituted by the Treaty on European Union, Title III, Article H(1).
2. Substituted by Article 7 which was substituted by the Treaty on European Union, Title III, Article H(1).
3. Inserted by the Treaty on European Union, Title III, Article H(2).
4. Replaced by the Treaty on European Union, Title III, Article H(3).
5. Inserted by the Treaty on European Union, Title III, Article H(4).
6. Repealed by the Merger Treaty, Article 19.
7. Added by the Treaty on European Union, Title III, Article H(5).
8. Inserted by the Treaty on European Union, Title III, Article H(6).
9. OJ No L 33, 9.2.93, p.15.
10. Replaced by the Treaty on European Union, Title III, Article H(7).
11. Replaced by the Treaty on European Union, Title III, Article H(8).
12. Inserted by the Treaty on European Union, Title III, Article H(9).
13. Inserted by the Treaty on European Union, Title III, Article H(10).
14. Article 32 replaced by the Treaty on European Union, Title III, Article H(11).
15. Article 32d replaced by the Treaty on European Union, Title III, Article H(12).
16. Article 33 replaced by the Treaty on European Union, Title III, Article H(13).
17. Chapter V inserted by the Treaty on European Union, Title III, Article H(14).

18. Paragraph (2) added in accordance with the procedure under the third and fourth paragraphs of Article 95 of this Treaty (OJ No 33, 16.5.60).
19. Replaced by the Treaty on European Union, Title III, Article H(15).
20. Text as amended by Article 5 of the Treaty amending Certain Financial Provisions.
21. Text as amended by Article 6 of the Treaty amending Certain Financial Provisions.
22. Article 78g replaced by the Treaty on European Union, Title III, Article H(17).
23. Article 78h replaced by the Treaty on European Union, Title III, Article H(18).
24. Article 78i inserted by the Treaty on European Union, Title III, Article H(19).
25. Article 79(a) replaced by the Treaty on European Union, Title III, Article H(20).

Annex I

Definition of the expressions 'coal' and 'steel'

1. The expressions 'coal' and 'steel' cover the products listed below.

2. In the exercise of its functions in relation to special steels, coke and scrap the [Commission][1] shall take account of the special features of production of these materials or of trade in them.

3. The [Commission][1] shall exercise its functions in relation to gas coke, and to brown coal other than for the making of briquettes and semi-coke, only where this is necessary by reason of appreciable disturbances caused by these products on the market in fuels.

4. The [Commission][1] shall take account of the fact that the production of some of the products listed is directly linked with the production of by-products which are not listed but whose selling prices may influence those of the principal products.

OEEC Code No (for reference)	Product
3000	FUELS
3100	Hard coal
3200	Hard coal briquettes
3300	Coke, excluding electrode and petroleum coke
	Semi-coke derived from hard coal
3400	Brown coal briquettes
3500	Run-of-mine brown coal
	Semi-coke derived from brown coal
4000	IRON AND STEEL
4100[2]	Raw materials for iron and steel production[3]

Iron ore (except pyrites)

Sponge iron and steel[4]

Ferrous scrap

Manganese ore

4200　　*Pig iron and ferro-alloys*

Pig iron for steelmaking

Foundry and other pig iron

Spiegeleisen and high-carbon ferro-manganese[5]

4300　　*Crude and semi-finished products of iron, ordinary steel or special steel, including products for re-use and re-rolling*

Liquid steel cast or not cast into ingots, including ingots for forging[6]

Semi-finished products: blooms, billets and slabs; sheet bars and tinplate bars; hot-rolled wide coils (other than coils classed as finished products)

4400　　*Hot finished products of iron, ordinary steel or special steel*[7]

Rails, sleepers, fishplates, soleplates, joists, heavy sections 80mm and over, sheet piling

Bars and sections of less than 80mm and flats of less than 150mm

Wire rod

Tube rounds and squares

Hot-rolled hoop and strip (including tube strip)

Hot-rolled sheet under 3 mm (coated or uncoated)

Plates and sheets of 3 mm thickness and over, universal plates of 150mm and over

4500　　*End products of iron, ordinary steel or special steel*[8]

Tinplate, terneplate, blackplate, galvanised sheets, other coated sheets

Cold-rolled sheets under 3mm

Electrical sheets

Strip for tinplate

Cold-rolled plate, in coil and in strips, of a thickness of 3mm or more[9]

FOOTNOTES

1. Substituted by Article 7 which was substituted by the Treaty on European Union, Title III, Article H(1).
2. Text of heading as amended by Article 1 of the Decision of the Council of the European Coal and Steel Community (OJ No 129, 6.12.62, p.2810).
3. Not including the raw materials under OEEC Code No 4190 ('Other raw materials not elsewhere classified for iron and steel production') which are not contained in this list. Not including refractories.
4. Including sponge iron proper or in briquetted form, Renn balls and similar products.
5. Not including other ferro-alloys.
6. The [Commission][1] shall concern itself with production of liquid steel for castings only where this is to be regarded as an activity of the steel industry proper.
   Any other production of liquid steel for castings, such as that at small and medium-sized independent foundries, shall be subject to statistical coverage only, such coverage not to give rise to any discriminatory action in respect thereof.
7. Not including steel castings, forgings and powder metallurgy products.
8. Not including steel tubes (seamless or welded), cold-rolled strip less than 500mm in width (other than for tinplating), wire and wire products, bright bars and iron castings (tubes, pipes and fittings, and other iron castings).
9. Text of the heading as supplemented by the Single Article of the Council Decision of 21 February 1983 adding a number of products to the list in Annex I to the ECSC Treaty (OJ No L 56, 3.3.83).

Annex II

Scrap

The provisions of this Treaty shall apply to ferrous scrap, but account shall be taken of the following practical arrangements necessitated by the special features of the recovery of and trade in scrap:

(a) any prices fixed by the [Commission][1] under Chapter V of Title III shall apply to purchases by Community undertakings; Member States shall cooperate with the [Commission][1] in ensuring that sellers comply with the decisions taken;

(b) Article 59 shall not apply to:

- cast iron scrap usable only in foundries outside the jurisdiction of the Community;

- undertakings' own arisings, availabilities of which shall, however, be taken into account in calculating the bases for allocations of bought scrap;

(c) for the application of Article 59 to bought scrap, the [Commission][1] shall, in cooperation with the Governments of Member States, obtain the necessary information on availabilities and requirements, including exports to third countries.

On the basis of the information thus obtained, the [Commission][1] shall allocate availabilities among Member States in accordance with Article 59, in such a way to enable the most efficient use to be made of them and taking into account all the operating and supply conditions in the different parts of the steel industry within its jurisdiction.

To ensure that shipments of scrap so allocated from one Member State to another, or purchases by undertakings in one Member State of the tonnages to which they are entitled on the market of another Member State, will not involve discrimination harmful to undertakings in either State, the following measures shall be taken:

1. Each Member State shall authorise the shipment from its territory to other Member States of tonnages in accordance with the allocation made by the [Commission][1]; in return, each Member State shall be authorised to effect the necessary checks to establish that outgoing shipments are not in excess of the amounts provided for. The [Commission][1] is empowered to ensure that the arrangements made are not more restrictive than is necessary for this purpose.

2. The allocation among Member States shall be reviewed at as frequent intervals as may be necessary to maintain a relation fair both to local purchasers and to purchasers from other Member States between the recorded availabilities in each Member State and the tonnages it is required to ship to other Member States.

3. The [Commission][2] shall ensure that the regulations made by each Member State concerning sellers within its jurisdiction do not lead to the application of dissimilar conditions to comparable transactions, especially on grounds of the nationality of the buyers.

FOOTNOTE

1. Substituted by Article 7 which was substituted by the Treaty on European Union, Title III, Article H(1).

Annex III

Special steels

Special steels and high carbon steels, as defined in the draft European customs nomenclature finalised by the Tariff Committee at its meeting in Brussels on 15 July 1950, shall be treated according to which of the following groups they fall within:

(a) special steels commonly called structural steels, containing less than 0.6 per cent of carbon and not more than 8 per cent of two or more alloying elements taken together or 5 per cent of a single alloying element;[1]

(b) high carbon steels, containing between 0.6 and 1.6 per cent of carbon; special steels other than those defined in (a) above, containing less than 40 per cent of two or more alloying elements taken together or 20 per cent of a single alloying element;[1]

(c) special steels not covered by (a) or (b).

Products in groups (a) and (b) shall come within the jurisdiction of the [Commission][2], but to enable study to be made of appropriate arrangements for the application of this Treaty to them, given the special features of their production and of trade in them, the date for the abolition of import and export duties or equivalent charges and of all quantitative restrictions on their movement within the Community shall be deferred until one year after the date of the establishment of the common market in steel.

As to products in group (c), the [Commission][2] shall, upon taking up its duties, enter into a series of studies to determine appropriate arrangements for the application of the Treaty to them, taking into account the special features of their production and of trade in them; as and when the findings are forthcoming, and within three years of the establishment of the common market at the latest, the arrangements suggested for each of the products in question shall be submitted by the [Commission][2] to the Council, which shall pronounce upon them in accordance with Article 81. During this period products in group (c) shall be subject only to statistical checks by the [Commission][2].

FOOTNOTES

1. Sulphur, phosphorus, silicon and manganese in the amounts normally accepted in ordinary steels are not counted as alloying elements.
2. Substituted by Article 7 which was substituted by the Treaty on European Union, Title III, Article H(1).

Protocols

Protocol on the Statute of the Court of Justice of the European Coal and Steel Community

See Protocol on the Statute of the Court of Justice of the European Community – editorial note

Privileges and Immunities of the European Coal and Steel Community

Repealed by the second paragraph of Article 28 of the Merger Treaty: see Protocol on the Privileges and Immunities of European Communities – editorial note

Protocol on relations with the Council of Europe

The High Contracting Parties,

Fully aware of the need to establish ties as close as possible between the European Coal and Steel Community and the Council of Europe, particularly between the European Parliament and the Consultative Assembly of the Council of Europe,

Taking note of the recommendations of the Assembly of the Council of Europe,

Have agreed upon the following provisions:

Article 1

The Governments of the Member States are invited to recommend to their respective Parliaments that the members of the Assembly[1] whom these Parliaments are called upon to designate should preferably be chosen from among the representatives to the Consultative Assembly of the Council of Europe.

Article 2

The European Parliament of the Community shall forward each year to the Consultative Assembly of the Council of Europe a report on its activities.

Article 3

The [Commission][2] shall communicate each year to the Committee of Ministers and to the Consultative Assembly of the Council of Europe the general report provided for in Article 17 of this Treaty.

Article 4

The [Commission]² shall inform the Council of Europe of the action which it has been able to take on any recommendations that may have been sent to it by the Committee of Ministers of the Council of Europe under Article 15(*b*) of the Statute of the Council of Europe.

Article 5

The present Treaty establishing the European Coal and Steel Community and the Annexes thereto shall be registered with the Secretariat of the Council of Europe.

Article 6

Agreements between the Community and the Council of Europe may, among other things, provide for any other type of mutual assistance and cooperation between the two organisations and indicate the appropriate forms thereof.

Done at Paris this eighteenth day of April in the year one thousand nine hundred and fifty-one.

[List omitted]

EDITORIAL NOTE

1. Notwithstanding the provisions of Article 3 of the SEA, and for historical reasons, the term 'Assembly' has not been replaced by the terms 'European Parliament'.

FOOTNOTE

2. Substituted by Article 7 which was substituted by the Treaty on European Union, Title III, Article H(1).

Exchange of letters between the Government of the Federal Republic of Germany and the Government of the French Republic concerning the Saar

[Translation]

The Federal Chancellor
and
Minister for Foreign Affairs

Paris, 18 April 1951

His Excellency President Robert Schuman,
Minister for Foreign Affairs,
Paris

Sir,

The representatives of the Federal Government have several times declared in the course of the negotiations on the European Coal and Steel Community that the status of the Saar can be finally settled only by the Peace Treaty or a similar Treaty. Furthermore, they have declared in the course of the negotiations that in signing the Treaty the Federal Government is not expressing recognition of the present status of the Saar.

I would repeat this declaration and would ask you to confirm that the French Government agrees with the Federal Government that the status of the Saar can be finally settled only by the Peace Treaty or a similar Treaty and that the French Government does not view the Federal Government's signature of the European Coal and Steel Community Treaty as recognition by the Federal Government of the present status of the Saar.

I am, Sir,

(*Signed*) **Adenauer**

[*Translation*]

Paris, 18 April 1951

Sir,

In reply to your letter of 18 April 1951, the French Government notes that the Federal Government in signing the Treaty establishing the European Coal and Steel Community does not intend recognition of the present status of the Saar.

The French Government declares, in accordance with its own point of view, that it is acting on behalf of the Saar by virtue of the present status of the latter but does not view the Federal Government's signature of the Treaty as recognition by the Federal Government of the present status of the Saar. It is not its understanding that the Treaty establishing the European Coal and Steel Community prejudges the final status of the Saar, which is a matter for the Peace Treaty or a Treaty in place thereof.

I am, Sir,

(*Signed*) **Schuman**

Dr Konrad Adenauer,
Chancellor and Minister for Foreign Affairs
of the Federal Republic of Germany.

Convention on the Transitional Provisions

[Text omitted]

TITLE IV

The Treaty establishing the European Atomic Energy Community

Article I

The Treaty establishing the European Atomic Energy Community shall be amended in accordance with the provisions of this Article.

(1) Replaced Article 3.

(2) Inserted Articles 107a-107d.

(3) Replaced Article 108(3).

(4) Supplemented the second subparagraph to Article 114.

(5) Inserted Articles 116-117.

(6) Inserted Article 121.

(7) Inserted Article 123.

(8) Inserted Articles 125-132.

(9) Repealed Article 133.

(10) Replaced Article 137.

(11) Replaced Article 140a.

(12) Replaced Article 143.

(13) Replaced Article 146.

(14) Inserted Section V, Articles 160a-160c.

(15) Replaced Article 166.

(16) Replaced Article 168.

(17) Replaced Article 170.

(18) Repealed Article 172(1)-(3).

(19) Replaced Article 173.

(20) Inserted Article 173a.

(21) Replaced Article 179.

(22) Repealed Articles 180 and 180a.

(23) Replaced Article 180b.

(24) Replaced Article 183.

(25) Inserted Article 183a.

(26) Replaced Article 198(a).

(27) Replaced Article 201.

(28) Repealed Articles 204-205.

(29) Replaced Article 206.

Text of the Treaty

His Majesty the King of the Belgians, the President of the Federal Republic of Germany, the President of the French Republic, the President of the Italian Republic, Her Royal Highness the Grand Duchess of Luxembourg, Her Majesty the Queen of the Netherlands,

Recognising that nuclear energy represents an essential resource for the development and invigoration of industry and will permit the advancement of the cause of peace,

Convinced that only a joint effort undertaken without delay can offer the prospect of achievements commensurate with the creative capacities of their countries,

Resolved to create the conditions necessary for the development of a powerful nuclear industry which will provide extensive energy resources, lead to the modernisation of technical processes and contribute, through its many other applications, to the prosperity of their peoples,

Anxious to create the conditions of safety necessary to eliminate hazards to the life and health of the public,

Desiring to associate other countries with their work and to cooperate with international organisations concerned with the peaceful development of atomic energy,

Have decided to create a European Atomic Energy Community (Euratom) and to this end have designated as their plenipotentiaries:

[List omitted]

Who, having exchanged their Full Powers, found in good and due form, have agreed as follows.

Title One

The tasks of the Community

Article 1

By this Treaty the High Contracting Parties establish among themselves a European Atomic Energy Community (Euratom).

It shall be the task of the Community to contribute to the raising of the standard of living in the Member States and to the development of relations with the other countries by creating the conditions necessary for the speedy establishment and growth of nuclear industries.

Article 2

In order to perform its task, the Community shall, as provided in this Treaty:

(a) promote research and ensure the dissemination of technical information;

(b) establish uniform safety standards to protect the health of workers and of the general public and ensure that they are applied;

(c) facilitate investment and ensure, particularly by encouraging ventures on the part of undertakings, the establishment of the basic installations necessary for the development of nuclear energy in the Community;

(d) ensure that all users in the Community receive a regular and equitable supply of ores and nuclear fuels;

(e) make certain, by appropriate supervision, that nuclear materials are not diverted to purposes other than those for which they are intended;

(f) exercise the right of ownership conferred upon it with respect to special fissile materials;

(g) ensure wide commercial outlets and access to the best technical facilities by the creation of a common market in specialised materials and equipment, by the free movement of capital for investment in the field of nuclear energy and by freedom of employment for specialists within the Community;

(h) establish with other countries and international organisations such relations as will foster progress in the peaceful uses of nuclear energy.

[Article 3

1. The tasks entrusted to the Community shall be carried out by the following institutions:

- a European Parliament,
- a Council,
- a Commission,
- a Court of Justice,
- a Court of Auditors.

Each institution shall act within the limits of the powers conferred upon it by this Treaty.

2. The Council and the Commission shall be assisted by an Economic and Social Committee acting in an advisory capacity.]¹

Title Two

Provisions for the encouragement of progress in the field of nuclear energy

Chapter I

Promotion of research

Article 4

1. The Commission shall be responsible for promoting and facilitating nuclear research in the Member States and for complementing it by carrying out a Community research and training programme.

2. The activity of the Commission in this respect shall be carried out within the fields listed in Annex I to the Treaty.

This list may be amended by the Council, acting by a qualified majority on a proposal from the Commission. The latter shall consult the Scientific and Technical Committee established under Article 134.

Article 5

For purposes of coordinating and complementing research undertaken in Member States, the Commission shall, either by a specific request addressed to a given recipient and conveyed to the Government concerned, or by a general published request, call upon Member States, persons or undertakings to communicate to it their programmes relating to the research which it specified in the request.

After giving those concerned full opportunity to comment, the Commission may deliver a reasoned opinion on each of the programmes communicated to it. The Commission shall deliver such an opinion if the State, person or undertaking which has communicated the programme so requests.

By such opinions the Commission shall discourage unnecessary duplication and shall direct research towards sectors which are insufficiently explored. The Commission may not publish these programmes without the consent of the State, person or undertaking which has communicated them.

The Commission shall publish at regular intervals a list of those sectors of nuclear research which it considers to be insufficiently explored.

The Commission may bring together representatives of public and private research centres as well as any experts engaged in research in the same or related fields for mutual consultation and exchanges of information.

Article 6

To encourage the carrying out of research programmes communicated to it the Commission may:

(a) provide financial assistance within the framework of research contracts, without, however, offering subsidies;

(b) supply, either free of charge or against payment, for carrying out such programmes, any source materials or special fissile materials which it has available;

(c) place installations, equipment or expert assistance at the disposal of Member States, persons or undertakings, either free of charge or against payment;

(d) promote joint financing by the Member States, persons or undertakings concerned.

Article 7

Community research and training programmes shall be determined by the Council, acting unanimously on a proposal from the Commission, which shall consult the Scientific and Technical Committee.

These programmes shall be drawn up for a period of not more than five years.

The funds required for carrying out these programmes shall be included each year in the research and investment budget of the Community.

The Commission shall ensure that these programmes are carried out and shall submit an annual report thereon to the Council.

The Commission shall keep the Economic and Social Committee informed of the broad outlines of Community research and training programmes.

Article 8

1. After consulting the Scientific and Technical Committee, the Commission shall establish a Joint Nuclear Research Centre.

This Centre shall ensure that the research programmes and other tasks assigned to it by the Commission are carried out.

It shall also ensure that a uniform nuclear terminology and a standard system of measurements are established.

It shall set up a central bureau for nuclear measurements.

2. The activities of the Centre may, for geographical or functional reasons, be carried out in separate establishments.

Article 9

1. After obtaining the opinion of the Economic and Social Committee the Commission may, within the framework of the Joint Nuclear Research Centre, set up schools for the training of specialists, particularly in the fields of prospecting for minerals, the production of high-purity nuclear materials, the processing of irradiated fuels, nuclear engineering, health and safety and the production and use of radioisotopes.

The Commission shall determine the details of such training.

2. An institution of university status shall be established; the way in which it will function shall be determined by the Council, acting by a qualified majority on a proposal from the Commission.

Article 10

The Commission may, by contract, entrust the carrying out of certain parts of the Community research programme to Member States, persons or undertakings, or to third countries, international organisations or nationals of third countries.

Article 11

The Commission shall publish the research programmes referred to in Articles 7, 8 and 10, and also regular progress reports on their implementation.

Chapter II

Dissemination of information

Section I

Information over which the Community has power of disposal

Article 12

Member States, persons or undertakings shall have the right, on application to the Commission, to obtain non-exclusive licences under patents, provisionally protected patent rights, utility models or patent applications owned by the Community, where they are able to make effective use of the inventions covered thereby.

Under the same conditions, the Commission shall grant sub-licences under patents, provisionally protected patent rights, utility models or patent applications, where the Community holds contractual licences conferring power to do so.

The Commission shall grant such licences or sub-licences on terms to be agreed with the licensees and shall furnish all the information required for their use. These terms shall relate in particular to suitable remuneration and, where appropriate, to the right of the licensee to grant sub-licences to third parties and to the obligation to treat the information as a trade secret.

Failing agreement on the terms referred to in the third paragraph, the licensees may bring the matter before the Court of Justice so that appropriate terms may be fixed.

Article 13

The Commission shall communicate to Member States, persons and undertakings information acquired by the Community which is not covered by the provisions of Article 12, whether such information is derived from its own research programme or communicated to the Commission with authority to make free use of it.

The Commission may, however, make the disclosure of such information conditional on its being treated as confidential and not passed on to third parties.

The Commission may not disclose information which has been acquired subject to restrictions on its use or dissemination – such as information known as classified information – unless it ensures compliance with these restrictions.

Section II

Other information

(a) Dissemination by amicable agreement

Article 14

The Commission shall endeavour, by amicable agreement, to secure both the communication of information which is of use to the Community in the attainment of its objectives and the granting of licences under patents, provisionally protected patent rights, utility models or patent applications covering such information.

Article 15

The Commission shall establish a procedure by which Member States, persons and undertakings may use it as an intermediary for exchanging provisional or final results of their research, in so far as these results have not been acquired by the Community under research contracts awarded by the Commission.

This procedure must be such as to ensure the confidential nature of the exchange. The results communicated may, however, be transmitted by the Commission to the Joint Nuclear Research Centre for documentation purposes; this shall not entail any right of use to which the communicating party has not agreed.

(b) Compulsory communication to the Commission

Article 16

1. As soon as an application for a patent or a utility model relating to a specifically nuclear subject is filed with a Member State, that State shall ask the applicant to agree that the contents of the application be communicated to the Commission forthwith.

If the applicant agrees, this communication shall be made within three months of the date of filing the application. If the applicant does not agree, the Member State shall, within the same period, notify the Commission of the existence of the application.

The Commission may require a Member State to communicate the contents of an application of whose existence it has been notified.

The Commission shall make any such request within two months of the date of notification. Any extension of this period shall entail a corresponding extension of the period referred to in the sixth subparagraph of this paragraph.

On receiving such a request from the Commission, the Member State shall again ask the applicant to agree to communication of the contents of the application. If the applicant agrees, communication shall be made forthwith.

If the applicant does not agree, the Member State shall nevertheless be required to make this communication to the Commission within eighteen months of the date on which the application was filed.

2. Member States shall inform the Commission, within eighteen months

of the filing date, of the existence of any as yet unpublished application for a patent or utility model which seems to them, *prima facie*, to deal with a subject which, although not specifically nuclear, is directly connected with and essential to the development of nuclear energy in the Community.

If the Commission so requests, the contents of the application shall be communicated to it within two months.

3. In order that publication may take place as soon as possible, Member States shall reduce to a minimum the time taken to process applications for patents or utility models relating to subjects referred to in paragraphs 1 and 2 concerning which a request has been made by the Commission.

4. The Commission shall treat the above-mentioned communications as confidential. They may only be made for documentation purposes. The Commission may, however, make use of the inventions communicated to it, either with the consent of the applicant or in accordance with Articles 17 to 23.

5. The provisions of this Article shall not apply when an agreement concluded with a third State or an international organisation precludes communication.

(c) Grant of licences by arbitration or under compulsory powers

Article 17

1. Failing amicable agreement, non-exclusive licences may be granted either by arbitration or under compulsory powers in accordance with Articles 18 to 23:

(a) to the Community or to Joint Undertakings accorded this right under Article 48 in respect of patents, provisionally protected patent rights or utility models relating to inventions directly connected with nuclear research, where the granting of such licences is necessary for the continuance of their own research or indispensable to the operation of their installations.

If the Commission so requests, such licences shall include the right to authorise third parties to make use of the invention, where they are carrying out work for or orders placed by the Community or Joint Undertakings;

(b) to persons or undertakings which have applied to the Commission for them in respect of patents, provisionally protected patent rights or utility models relating to inventions directly connected with and essential to the development of nuclear energy in the Community, provided that all the following conditions are fulfilled:

(i) At least four years have elapsed since the filing of the patent application, save in the case of an invention relating to a specifically nuclear subject;

(ii) The requirements arising out of the development of nuclear energy, in the Commission's conception of such development, in the territory of a Member State where an invention is protected, are not being met with regard to that invention;

(iii) The proprietor, having been called upon to meet such requirements either himself or through his licensees, has not complied with this request;

(iv) The persons or undertakings applying for licences are in a position to meet such requirements effectively by making use of the invention.

Member States may not, in order to meet such requirements, take any coercive measures provided for in their national legislation which will limit the protection accorded to the invention, save at the prior request of the Commission.

2. A non-exclusive licence may not be granted as provided for in paragraph 1 where the proprietor can establish the existence of legitimate reasons, in particular that he has not had sufficient time at his disposal.

3. The granting of a licence pursuant to paragraph 1 shall confer a right to full compensation, the amount of which shall be agreed between the proprietor of the patent, provisionally protected patent right or utility model and the licensee.

4. The provisions of this Article shall not affect those of the Paris Convention for the Protection of Industrial Property.

Article 18

An Arbitration Committee is hereby established for the purposes provided for in this Section. The Council shall appoint the members and lay down the rules of procedure of this Committee, acting on a proposal from the Court of Justice.

An appeal, having suspensory effect, may be brought by the parties before the Court of Justice against a decision of the Arbitration Committee within one month of notification thereof. The Court of Justice shall confine its examination to the formal validity of the decision and to the interpretation of the provisions of this Treaty by the Arbitration Committee.

The final decisions of the Arbitration Committee shall have the force of *res judicata* between the parties concerned. They shall be enforceable as provided in Article 164.

Article 19

Where, failing amicable agreement, the Commission intends to secure the granting of licences in one of the cases provided for in Article 17, it shall give notice of its intention to the proprietor of the patent, provisionally protected patent right, utility model or patent application, and shall specify in such notice the name of the applicant for and the scope of the licence.

Article 20

The proprietor may, within one month of receipt of the notice referred to in Article 19, propose to the Commission and, where appropriate, to the applicant that they conclude a special agreement to refer the matter to the Arbitration Committee.

Should the Commission or the applicant refuse to enter into such an agreement, the Commission shall not require the Member State or its appropriate authorities to grant the licence or cause it to be granted.

If, when the matter is referred to it under a special agreement, the Arbitration Committee finds that the request from the Commission complies with the provisions of Article 17, it shall give a reasoned decision containing a grant of the licence to the applicant and laying down the terms of the licence and the remuneration therefor, to the extent that the parties have not reached agreement on these points.

Article 21

If the proprietor does not propose that the matter be referred to the Arbitration Committee, the Commission may call upon the Member State concerned or its appropriate authorities to grant the licence or cause it to be granted.

If, having heard the proprietor's case, the Member State, or its appropriate authorities, considers that the conditions of Article 17 have not been complied with, it shall notify the Commission of its refusal to grant the licence or to cause it to be granted.

If it refuses to grant the licence or to cause it to be granted, or if, within four months of the date of the request, no information is forthcoming with regard to the granting of the licence, the Commission shall have two months in which to bring the matter before the Court of Justice.

The proprietor must be heard in the proceedings before the Court of Justice.

If the judgment of the Court of Justice establishes that the conditions of Article 17 have been complied with, the Member State concerned, or its appropriate authorities, shall take such measures as enforcement of that judgment may require.

Article 22

1. If the proprietor of the patent, provisionally protected patent right or utility model and the licensee fail to agree on the amount of compensation, the parties concerned may conclude a special agreement to refer the matter to the Arbitration Committee.

By doing so, the parties waive the right to institute any proceedings other than those provided for in Article 18.

2. If the licensee refuses to conclude a special agreement, the licence he has been granted shall be deemed void.

If the proprietor refuses to conclude a special agreement, the compensation referred to in this Article shall be determined by the appropriate national authorities.

Article 23

After the lapse of one year, the decisions of the Arbitration Committee or the appropriate national authorities may, if there are new facts to justify it, be revised with respect to the terms of the licence.

Such revision shall be a matter for the body which gave the decision.

Section III

Security provisions

Article 24

Information which the Community acquires as a result of carrying out its research programme, and the disclosure of which is liable to harm the defence interests of one or more Member States, shall be subject to a security system in accordance with the following provisions.

1. The Council shall, acting on a proposal from the Commission, adopt

security regulations which, account being taken of the provisions of this Article, lay down the various security gradings to be applied and the security measures appropriate to each grading.

2. Where the Commission considers that the disclosure of certain information is liable to harm the defence interests of one or more Member States, it shall provisionally apply to that information the security grading required in that case by the security regulations.

It shall communicate such information forthwith to the Member States, which shall provisionally ensure its security in the same manner.

Member States shall inform the Commission within three months whether they wish to maintain the grading provisionally applied, substitute another or declassify the information.

Upon the expiry of this period, the highest grading of those requested shall be applied. The Commission shall notify the Member States accordingly.

At the request of the Commission or of a Member State, the Council may, acting unanimously, at any time apply another grading or declassify the information. The Council shall obtain the opinion of the Commission before taking any action on a request from a Member State.

3. The provisions of Articles 12 and 13 shall not apply to information subject to a security grading.

Nevertheless, provided that the appropriate security measures are observed,

(a) the information referred to in Articles 12 and 13 may be communicated by the Commission:

   (i) to a Joint Undertaking;

   (ii) to a person or undertaking other than a Joint Undertaking, through the Member State in whose territory that person or undertaking operates;

(b) the information referred to in Article 13 may be communicated by a Member State to a person or to an undertaking other than a Joint Undertaking, operating in the territory of that State, provided that the Commission is notified of this communication;

(c) each Member State has, however, the right to require the Commission to grant a licence under Article 12 to meet the needs of that State or those of a person or undertaking operating in its territory.

Article 25

1. A Member State notifying the existence or communicating the contents of an application for a patent or utility model relating to a subject specified in Article 16(1) or (2) shall, where appropriate, draw attention to the need to apply a given security grading for defence reasons, at the same time stating the probable duration of such grading.

The Commission shall pass on to the other Member States all communications received in accordance with the preceding sub-paragraph. The Commission and the Member States shall take those measures which, under the security regulations, correspond to the grading required by the State or origin.

2. The Commission may also pass on these communications to Joint Undertakings or, through a Member State, to a person or to an undertaking other than a Joint Undertaking operating in the territory of that State.

Inventions which are the subject of applications referred to in paragraph 1 may be used only with the consent of the applicant or in accordance with Articles 17 to 23.

The communications and, where appropriate, the use referred to in this paragraph shall be subject to the measures which, under the security regulations, correspond to the security grading required by the State of origin.

The communications shall in all cases be subject to the consent of the State of origin. Consent to communication and use may be withheld only for defence reasons.

3. At the request of the Commission or of a Member State, the Council may, acting unanimously, at any time apply another grading or declassify the information. The Council shall obtain the opinion of the Commission before taking any action on a request from a Member State.

Article 26

1. Where information covered by patents, patent applications, provisionally protected patent rights, utility models or applications for utility models has been classified in accordance with Articles 24 and 25, the States which have applied for such classification may not refuse to allow corresponding applications to be filed in the other Member States.

Each Member State shall take the necessary measures to maintain the security of such rights and applications in accordance with the procedure laid down in its own laws and regulations.

2. No application relating to information classified in accordance with Article 24 may be filed outside the Member States except with the unanimous consent of the latter. Should Member States fail to make known their attitude, their consent shall be deemed to have been obtained on the expiry of six months from the date on which the information was communicated to the Member States by the Commission.

Article 27

Compensation for any damage suffered by the applicant as a result of classification for defence reasons shall be governed by the provisions of the national laws of the Member States and shall be the responsibility of the State which applied for such classification or which either obtained the upgrading or extension of the classification or caused the filing of applications outside the Community to be prohibited.

Where several Member States have either obtained the upgrading or extension of the classification or caused the filing of applications outside the Community to be prohibited, they shall be jointly responsible for making good any damage arising out of their action.

The Community may not claim any compensation under this Article.

Section IV

Special provisions

Article 28

Where, as a result of their communication to the Commission, unpublished applications for patents or utility models, or patents or utility models classified for defence reasons, are improperly used or come to the knowledge of an unauthorised person, the Community shall make good the damage suffered by the party concerned.

Without prejudice to its own rights against the person responsible for the damage, the Community shall, to the extent that it has made good such damage, acquire any rights of action enjoyed by those concerned against third parties. This shall not affect the right of the Community to take action against the person responsible for the damage in accordance with the general provisions in force.

Article 29

Where an agreement or contract for the exchange of scientific or industrial information in the nuclear field between a Member State, a person or an undertaking on the one hand, and a third State, an international organisation or a national of a third State on the other, requires, on either part, the signature of a State acting in its sovereign capacity, it shall be concluded by the Commission.

Subject to the provisions of Articles 103 and 104, the Commission may, however, on such conditions as it considers appropriate, authorise a Member State, a person or an undertaking to conclude such agreements.

Chapter III

Health and Safety

Article 30

Basic standards shall be laid down within the Community for the protection of the health of workers and the general public against the dangers arising from ionizing radiations.

The expression 'basic standards' means:

(a) maximum permissible doses compatible with adequate safety;

(b) maximum permissible levels of exposure and contamination;

(c) the fundamental principles governing the health surveillance of workers.

Article 31

The basic standards shall be worked out by the Commission after it has obtained the opinion of a group of persons appointed by the Scientific and Technical Committee from among scientific experts, and in particular public health experts, in the Member States. The Commission shall obtain the opinion of the Economic and Social Committee on these basic standards.

After consulting the European Parliament the Council shall, on a proposal from the Commission, which shall forward to it the opinions obtained from these Committees, establish the basic standards; the Council shall act by a qualified majority.

Article 32

At the request of the Commission or of a Member State, the basic standards may be revised or supplemented in accordance with the procedure laid down in Article 31.

The Commission shall examine any request made by a Member State.

Article 33

Each Member State shall lay down the appropriate provisions, whether by legislation, regulation or administrative action, to ensure compliance with the basic standards which have been established and shall take the necessary measures with regard to teaching, education and vocational training.

The Commission shall make appropriate recommendations for harmonising the provisions applicable in this field in the Member States.

To this end, the Member States shall communicate to the Commission the provisions applicable at the date of entry into force of this Treaty and any subsequent draft provisions of the same kind.

Any recommendations the Commission may wish to issue with regard to such draft provisions shall be made within three months of the date on which such draft provisions are communicated.

Article 34

Any Member State in whose territories particularly dangerous experiments are to take place shall take additional health and safety measures, on which it shall first obtain the opinion of the Commission.

The assent of the Commission shall be required where the effects of such experiments are liable to affect the territories of the other Member States.

Article 35

Each Member State shall establish the facilities necessary to carry out continuous monitoring of the level of radioactivity in the air, water and soil and to ensure compliance with the basic standards.

The Commission shall have the right of access to such facilities; it may verify their operation and efficiency.

Article 36

The appropriate authorities shall periodically communicate information on the checks referred to in Article 35 to the Commission so that it is kept informed of the level of radioactivity to which the public is exposed.

Article 37

Each Member State shall provide the Commission with such general data relating to any plan for the disposal of radioactive waste in whatever form as will make it possible to determine whether the implementation of such plan is liable to result in the radioactive contamination of the water, soil or airspace of another Member State.

The Commission shall deliver its opinion within six months, after consulting the group of experts referred to in Article 31.

Article 38

The Commission shall make recommendations to the Member States with regard to the level of radioactivity in the air, water and soil.

In cases of urgency, the Commission shall issue a directive requiring the Member State concerned to take, within a period laid down by the Commission, all necessary measures to prevent infringement of the basic standards and to ensure compliance with regulations.

Should the State in question fail to comply with the Commission directive within the period laid down, the Commission or any Member State concerned may forthwith, by way of derogation from Articles 141 and 142, bring the matter before the Court of Justice.

Article 39

The Commission shall set up within the framework of the Joint Nuclear Research Centre, as soon as the latter has been established, a health and safety documentation and study section.

This section shall in particular have the task of collecting the documentation and information referred to in Articles 33, 36 and 37 and of assisting the Commission in carrying out the tasks assigned to it by this Chapter.

Chapter IV

Investment

Article 40

In order to stimulate action by persons and undertakings and to facilitate coordinated development of their investment in the nuclear field, the Commission shall periodically publish illustrative programmes indicating in particular nuclear energy production targets and all the types of investment required for their attainment.

The Commission shall obtain the opinion of the Economic and Social Committee on such programmes before their publication.

Article 41

Persons and undertakings engaged in the industrial activities listed in Annex II to this Treaty shall communicate to the Commission investment projects relating to new installations, and also to replacements or conversions which fulfil the criteria as to type and size laid down by the Council on a proposal from the Commission.

The list of industrial activities referred to above may be altered by the Council, acting by a qualified majority on a proposal from the Commission, which shall first obtain the opinion of the Economic and Social Committee.

Article 42

The projects referred to in Article 41 shall be communicated to the Commission and, for information purposes, to the Member State concerned not later than three months before the first contracts are concluded with the suppliers or, if the work is to be carried out by the undertaking with its own resources, three months before the work begins.

The Council may, acting on a proposal from the Commission, alter this time limit.

Article 43

The Commission shall discuss with the persons or undertakings all aspects of investment projects which relate to the objectives of this Treaty.

It shall communicate its views to the Member State concerned.

Article 44

The Commission may, with the consent of the Member States, persons and undertakings concerned, publish any investment projects communicated to it.

Chapter V

Joint Undertakings

Article 45

Undertakings which are of fundamental importance to the development of the nuclear industry in the Community may be established as Joint

Undertakings within the meaning of this Treaty, in accordance with the following Articles.

Article 46

1. Every project for establishing a Joint Undertaking, whether originating from the Commission, a Member State or any other quarter, shall be the subject of an inquiry by the Commission.

For this purpose, the Commission shall obtain the views of Member States and of any public or private body which in its opinion can usefully advise it.

2. The Commission shall forward to the Council any project for establishing a Joint Undertaking, together with its reasoned opinion.

If the Commission delivers a favourable opinion on the need for the proposed Joint Undertaking, it shall submit proposals to the Council concerning:

(a) location;

(b) statutes;

(c) the scale of and timetable for financing;

(d) possible participation by the Community in the financing of the Joint Undertaking;

(e) possible participation by a third State, an international organisation or a national of a third State in the financing or management of the Joint Undertaking;

(f) the conferring of any or all of the advantages listed in Annex III to this Treaty.

The Commission shall attach a detailed report on the project as a whole.

Article 47

The Council may, when the matter has been submitted to it by the Commission, request the latter to supply such further information or to undertake such further inquiries as the Council may consider necessary.

If the Council, acting by a qualified majority, considers that a project forwarded by the Commission with an unfavourable opinion should nevertheless be carried out, the Commission shall submit to the Council the proposals and the detailed report referred to in Article 46.

Where the opinion of the Commission is favourable or in the case referred to in the preceding paragraph, the Council shall act by a qualified majority on each of the proposals from the Commission.

The Council shall, however, act unanimously in respect of:

(a) participation by the Community in the financing of the Joint Undertaking;

(b) participation by a third State, an international organisation or a national of a third State in the financing or management of the Joint Undertaking.

Article 48

The Council may, acting unanimously on a proposal from the Commission, make applicable to each Joint Undertaking any or all of the advantages listed in Annex III to this Treaty; each Member State shall for its part ensure that these advantages are conferred.

The Council may, in accordance with the same procedure, lay down the conditions governing the conferment of these advantages.

Article 49

Joint Undertakings shall be established by Council decision.

Each Joint Undertaking shall have legal personality.

In each of the Member States, it shall enjoy the most extensive legal capacity accorded to legal persons under their respective national laws; it may, in particular, acquire or dispose of movable and immovable property and may be a party to legal proceedings.

Save as otherwise provided in this Treaty or in its own statutes, each Joint Undertaking shall be governed by the rules applying to industrial or commercial undertakings; its statutes may make subsidiary reference to the national laws of the Member States.

Save where jurisdiction is conferred upon the Court of Justice by this Treaty, disputes in which Joint Undertakings are concerned shall be determined by the appropriate national courts or tribunals.

Article 50

The statutes of Joint Undertakings shall be amended, where necessary in accordance with the special provisions which they contain for this purpose.

Such amendments shall not, however, enter into force until they have been approved by the Council, acting in accordance with the procedure laid down in Article 47 on a proposal from the Commission.

Article 51

The Commission shall be responsible for carrying out all decisions of the Council relating to the establishment of Joint Undertakings until the bodies responsible for the operation of such Undertakings have been set up.

Chapter VI

Supplies

Article 52

1. The supply of ores, source materials and special fissile materials shall be ensured, in accordance with the provisions of this Chapter, by means of a common supply policy on the principle of equal access to sources of supply.

2. For this purpose and under the conditions laid down in this Chapter:

(a) all practices designed to secure a privileged position for certain users shall be prohibited;

(b) an Agency is hereby established; it shall have a right of option on ores, source materials and special fissile materials produced in the territories of Member States and an exclusive right to conclude contracts relating to the supply of ores, source materials and special materials coming from inside the Community or from outside.

The Agency may not discriminate in any way between users on grounds of the use which they intend to make of the supplies requested unless such use is unlawful or is found to be contrary to the conditions imposed by suppliers outside the Community on the consignment in question.

Section 1

The Agency

Article 53

The Agency shall be under the supervision of the Commission, which shall issue directives to it, possess a right of veto over its decisions and appoint its Director-General and Deputy Director-General.

Any act, whether implied or expressed, performed by the Agency in the exercise of its right of option or of its exclusive right to conclude supply contracts, may be referred by the parties concerned to the Commission, which shall give a decision thereon within one month.

Article 54

The Agency shall have legal personality and financial autonomy.

The Council shall lay down the statutes of the Agency, acting by a qualified majority on a proposal from the Commission.

The statutes may be amended in accordance with the same procedure.

The statutes shall determine the Agency's capital and the terms upon which it is to be subscribed. The major part of the capital shall always belong to the Community and to the Member States. The contributions to the capital shall be determined by common accord of the Member States.

The rules for the commercial management of the activities of the Agency shall be laid down in the statutes. The latter may provide for a charge on transactions to defray the operating expenses of the Agency.

Article 55

The Member States shall communicate or cause to be communicated to the Agency all the information necessary to enable it to exercise its right of option and its exclusive right to conclude supply contracts.

Article 56

The Member States shall be responsible for ensuring that the Agency may operate freely in their territories.

They may establish one or more bodies having authority to represent, in relations with the Agency, producers and users in the non-European territories under their jurisdiction.

Section II

Ores, source materials and special fissile materials coming from inside the Community

Article 57

1. The right of option of the Agency shall cover:

(a) the acquisition of rights to use and consume materials owned by the Community under the provisions of Chapter VIII;

(b) the acquisition of the right of ownership in all other cases.

2. The Agency shall exercise its right of option by concluding contracts with producers of ores, source materials and special fissile materials.

Subject to Articles 58, 62 and 63, every producer shall offer to the Agency the ores, source materials or special fissile materials which he produces within the territories of Member States before they are used, transferred or stored.

Article 58

Where a producer carries out several stages of production from extraction of the ore up to and including production of the metal, he may offer the product to the Agency at whichever stage of production he chooses.

The same shall apply to two or more connected undertakings, where the connection has been duly communicated to the Commission and discussed with it in accordance with the procedures laid down in Articles 43 and 44.

Article 59

If the Agency does not exercise its right of option on the whole or any part of the output of a producer, the latter

(a) may, either by using his own resources or under contract, process or cause to be processed the ores, source materials or special fissile materials, provided that he offers to the Agency the product of such processing;

(b) shall be authorised by a decision of the Commission to dispose of his available production outside the Community, provided that the terms he offers are not more favourable than those previously offered to the Agency. However, special fissile materials may be exported only through the Agency and in accordance with the provisions of Article 62.

The Commission may not grant such authorisation if the recipients of the supplies fail to satisfy it that the general interests of the Community will be safeguarded or if the terms and conditions of such contracts are contrary to the objectives of this Treaty.

Article 60

Potential users shall periodically inform the Agency of the supplies they require, specifying the quantities, the physical and chemical nature, the place of origin, the intended use, delivery dates and price terms, which are to form the terms and conditions of the supply contract which they wish to conclude.

Similarly, producers shall inform the Agency of offers which they are able to make, stating all the specifications, and in particular the duration of contracts, required to enable their production programmes to be drawn up. Such contracts shall be of not more than ten year's duration save with the agreement of the Commission.

The Agency shall inform all potential users of the offers and of the volume of applications which it has received and shall call upon them to place their orders by a specified time limit.

When the Agency has received all such orders, it shall make known the terms on which it can meet them.

If the Agency cannot meet in their entirety all the orders received, it shall, subject to the provisions of Articles 68 and 69, share out the supplies proportionately among the orders relating to each offer.

Agency rules, which shall require approval by the Commission, shall determine the manner in which demand is to be balanced against supply.

Article 61

The Agency shall meet all orders unless prevented from so doing by legal or material obstacles.

When concluding a contract, the Agency may, while complying with the provisions of Article 52, require users to make appropriate advance payments either as security or to assist in meeting the Agency's own long-term commitments to producers where these are essential to carrying out the order.

Article 62

1. The Agency shall exercise its right of option on special fissile materials produced in the territories of Member States in order

(a) to meet demand from users within the Community in accordance with Article 60; or

(b) to store such materials itself; or

(c) to export such materials with the authorisation of the Commission which shall comply with the second subparagraph of Article 59(b).

2. Nevertheless, while continuing to be subject to the provisions of Chapter VII, such materials and any fertile wastes shall be left in the possession of the producer, so that he may

(*a*) store them with the authorisation of the Agency; or

(*b*) use them within the limits of his own requirements; or

(*c*) make them available to undertakings in the Community, within the limits of their requirements, where for carrying out a programme duly communicated to the Commission, these undertakings have with the producer a direct connection which has neither the aim nor the effect of limiting production, technical development or investment or of improperly creating inequalities between users in the Community.

3. The provisions of Article 89(1)(*a*) shall apply to special fissile materials which are produced in the territories of Member States and on which the Agency has not exercised its right of option.

Article 63

Ores, source materials and special fissile materials produced by Joint Undertakings shall be allotted to users in accordance with the rules laid down in the statutes or agreements of such Undertakings.

Section III

Ores, source materials and special fissile materials coming from outside the Community

Article 64

The Agency, acting where appropriate within the framework of agreements concluded between the Community and a third State or an international organisation shall, subject to the exceptions provided for in this Treaty, have the exclusive right to enter into agreements or contracts whose principal aim is the supply of ores, source materials or special fissile materials coming from outside the Community.

Article 65

Article 60 shall apply applications from users and to contracts between users and the Agency relating to the supply of ores, source materials or special fissile materials coming from outside the Community.

The Agency may, however, decide on the geographical origin of supplies provided that conditions which are at least as favourable as those specified in the order are thereby secured for the user.

Article 66

Should the Commission find, on application by the users concerned, that the Agency is not in a position to deliver within a reasonable period of time all or part of the supplies ordered, or that it can only do so at excessively high prices, the users shall have the right to conclude directly contracts relating to supplies from outside the Community, provided that such contracts meet in essential respects the requirements specified in their orders.

This right shall be granted for a period of one year; it may be extended if the situation which justified its granting continues.

Users who avail themselves of the right provided for in this Article shall communicate to the Commission the direct contracts which they propose to conclude. The Commission may, within one month, object to the conclusion of such contracts if they are contrary to the objectives of this Treaty.

Section IV

Prices

Article 67

Save where exceptions are provided for in this Treaty, prices shall be determined as a result of balancing supply against demand as provided in Article 60; the national regulations of the Member States shall not contravene such provisions.

Article 68

Pricing practices designed to secure a privileged position for certain users in violation of the principle of equal access laid down in the provisions of this Chapter shall be prohibited.

If the Agency finds that any such practices are being employed it shall report them to the Commission.

The Commission may, if it accepts the findings, set the prices of the offers in issue at a level compatible with the principle of equal access.

Article 69

The Council may fix prices, acting unanimously on a proposal from the Commission.

When the Agency lays down, in pursuance of Article 60, the terms on which orders can be met, it may propose to the users who have placed orders that prices be equalised.

Section V

Provisions relating to supply policy

Article 70

Within the limits set by the budget of the Community, the Commission may, on such conditions as it shall determine, give financial support to prospecting programmes in the territories of Member States.

The Commission may make recommendations to the Member States with a view to the development of prospecting for and exploitation of mineral deposits.

The Member States shall submit annually to the Commission a report on the development of prospecting and production, on probable reserves and on investment in mining which has been made or is planned in their territories. The reports shall be submitted to the Council, together with an opinion from the Commission which shall state in particular what action has been taken by Member States on recommendations made to them under the preceding paragraph.

If, when the matter has been submitted to it by the Commission, the Council finds by a qualified majority that, although the prospects for extraction appear economically justified on a long-term basis, prospecting activities and the expansion of mining operations continue to be markedly inadequate, the Member State concerned shall, for as long as it has failed to remedy this situation, be deemed to have waived, both for itself and for its nationals, the right of equal access to other sources of supply within the Community.

Article 71

The Commission shall make all appropriate recommendations to Member States with regard to revenue or mining regulations.

Article 72

The Agency may, from material available inside or outside the Community, build up the necessary commercial stocks to facilitate supplies to or normal deliveries by the Community.

The Commission may, where necessary, decide to build up emergency stocks. The method of financing such stocks shall be approved by the Council, acting by a qualified majority on a proposal from the Commission.

Section VI

Special provisions

Article 73

Where an agreement or contract between a Member State, a person or an undertaking on the one hand, and a third State, an international organisation or a national of a third State on the other, provides *inter alia* for delivery of products which come within the province of the Agency, the prior consent of the Commission shall be required for the conclusion or renewal of that agreement or contract, as far as delivery of the products is concerned.

Article 74

The Commission may exempt from the provisions of this Chapter the transfer, import or export of small quantities of ores, source materials or special fissile materials such as are normally used in research.

The Agency shall be notified of every transfer, import or export operation effected by virtue of this provision.

Article 75

The provisions of this Chapter shall not apply to commitments relating to the processing, conversion or shaping of ores, source materials or special fissile materials and entered into,

(a) by several persons or undertakings, where the material is to return to the original person or undertaking after being processed, converted or shaped; or

(b) by a person or undertaking and an international organisation or a national of a third State, where the material is processed, converted or shaped outside the Community and then returned to the original person or undertaking; or

(c) by a person or undertaking and an international organisation or a national of a third State, where the material is processed, converted or shaped inside the Community and is then returned either to the original organisation or national or to any other consignee likewise outside the Community designated by such organisation or national.

The persons and undertakings concerned shall, however, notify the Agency of the existence of such commitments and, as soon as the contracts are signed, of the quantities of material involved in the movements. The Commission may prevent the commitments referred to in subparagraph (*b*) from being undertaken if it considers that the conversion or shaping cannot be carried out efficiently and safely and without the loss of material to the detriment of the Community.

The materials to which such commitments relate shall be subject in the territories of the Member States to the safeguards laid down in Chapter VII. The provisions of Chapter VIII shall not, however, be applicable to special fissile materials covered by the commitments referred to in subparagraph (*c*).

Article 76

On the initiative of a Member State or of the Commission, and particularly if unforeseen circumstances create a situation of general shortage, the Council may, acting unanimously on a proposal from the Commission and after consulting the European Parliament, amend the provisions of this Chapter. The Commission shall inquire into any request made by a Member State.

Seven years after the entry into force of this Treaty, the Council may confirm these provisions in their entirety. Failing confirmation, new provisions relating to the subject matter of this Chapter shall be adopted in accordance with the procedure laid down in the preceding paragraph.

Chapter VII

Safeguards

Article 77

In accordance with the provisions of this Chapter, the Commission shall satisfy itself that, in the territories of Member States,

(*a*) ores, source materials and special fissile materials are not diverted from their intended uses as declared by the users;

(*b*) the provisions relating to supply and any particular safeguarding obligations assumed by the Community under an agreement concluded with a third State or an international organisation are complied with.

Article 78

Anyone setting up or operating an installation for the production, separation or other use of source materials or special fissile materials or for the processing of irradiated nuclear fuels shall declare to the Commission the basic technical characteristics of the installations, to the extent that knowledge of these characteristics is necessary for the attainment of the objectives set out in Article 77.

The Commission must approve the techniques to be used for the chemical processing of irradiated materials, to the extent necessary to attain the objectives set out in Article 77.

Article 79

The Commission shall require that operating records be kept and produced in order to permit accounting for ores, source materials and special fissile materials used or produced. The same requirement shall apply in the case of the transport of source materials and special fissile materials.

Those subject to such requirements shall notify the authorities of the Member State concerned of any communications they make to the Commission pursuant to Article 78 and to the first paragraph of this Article.

The nature and the extent of the requirements referred to in the first paragraph of this Article shall be defined in a regulation made by the Commission and approved by the Council.

Article 80

The Commission may require that any excess special fissile materials recovered or obtained as by-products and not actually being used or ready for use shall be deposited with the Agency or in other stores which are or can be supervised by the Commission.

Special fissile materials deposited in this way must be returned forthwith to those concerned at their request.

Article 81

The Commission may send inspectors into the territories of Member States. Before sending an inspector on his first assignment in the territory of a Member State, the Commission shall consult the State concerned; such consultation shall suffice to cover all future assignments of this inspector.

On presentation of a document establishing their authority, inspectors shall at all times have access to all places and data and to all persons who, by reason of their occupation, deal with materials, equipment or installations subject to the safeguards provided for in this Chapter, to the extent necessary in order to apply such safeguards to ores, source materials and special fissile materials and to ensure compliance with the provisions of Article 77. Should the State concerned so request, inspectors appointed by the Commission shall be accompanied by representatives of the authorities of that State; however, the inspectors shall not thereby be delayed or otherwise impeded in the performance of their duties.

If the carrying out of an inspection is opposed, the Commission shall apply to the President of the Court of Justice for an order to ensure that the inspection be carried out compulsorily. The President of the Court of Justice shall give a decision within three days.

If there is danger in delay, the Commission may itself issue a written order, in the form of a decision, to proceed with the inspection. This order shall be submitted without delay to the President of the Court of Justice for subsequent approval.

After the order or decision has been issued, the authorities of the State concerned shall ensure that the inspectors have access to the places specified in the order or decision.

Article 82

Inspectors shall be recruited by the Commission.

They shall be responsible for obtaining and verifying the records referred to in Article 79. They shall report any infringement to the Commission.

The Commission may issue a directive calling upon the Member State concerned to take, by a time limit set by the Commission, all measures necessary to bring such infringement to an end; it shall inform the Council thereof.

If the Member State does not comply with the Commission directive by the time limit set, the Commission or any Member State concerned may, in derogation from Articles 141 and 142, refer the matter to the Court of Justice direct.

Article 83

1. In the event of an infringement on the part of persons or undertakings of the obligations imposed on them by this Chapter, the Commission may impose sanctions on such persons or undertakings.

These sanctions shall be in order of severity:

(a) a warning;

(b) the withdrawal of special benefits such as financial or technical assistance;

(c) the placing of the undertaking for a period not exceeding four months under the administration of a person or board appointed by common accord of the Commission and the State having jurisdiction over the undertaking;

(d) total or partial withdrawal of source materials or special fissile materials.

2. Decisions taken by the Commission in implementation of paragraph 1 and requiring the surrender of materials shall be enforceable.

They may be enforced in the territories of Member States in accordance with Article 164.

By way of derogation from Article 157, appeals brought before the Court of Justice against decisions of the Commission which impose any of the sanctions provided for in paragraph 1 shall have suspensory effect. The Court of Justice may, however, on application by the Commission or by any Member State concerned, order that the decision be enforced forthwith.

There shall be an appropriate legal procedure to ensure the protection of interests that have been prejudiced.

3. The Commission may make any recommendations to Member States concerning laws or regulations which are designed to ensure compliance in their territories with the obligations arising under this Chapter.

4. Member States shall ensure that sanctions are enforced and, where necessary, that the infringements are remedied by those committing them.

Article 84

In the application of the safeguards, no discrimination shall be made on grounds of the use for which ores, source materials and special fissile materials are intended.

The scope of and procedure for the safeguards and the powers of the bodies responsible for their application shall be confined to the attainment of the objectives set out in this Chapter.

The safeguards may not extend to materials intended to meet defence requirements which are in the course of being specially processed for this purpose or which, after being so processed, are, in accordance with an operational plan, placed or stored in a military establishment.

Article 85

Where new circumstances so require, the procedures for applying the safeguards laid down in this Chapter may, at the request of a Member State or of the Commission, be adapted by the Council, acting unanimously on a proposal from the Commission and after consulting the European Parliament. The Commission shall examine any such request made by a Member State.

Chapter VIII

Property Ownership

Article 86

Special fissile materials shall be the property of the Community.

The Community's right of ownership shall extend to all special fissile materials which are produced or imported by a Member State, a person or an undertaking and are subject to the safeguards provided for in Chapter VII.

Article 87

Member States, persons or undertakings shall have the unlimited right of use and consumption of special fissile materials which have properly come into their possession, subject to the obligations imposed on them by this Treaty, in particular those relating to safeguards, the right of option conferred on the Agency and health and safety.

Article 88

The Agency shall keep a special account in the name of the Community, called 'Special Fissile Materials Financial Account'.

Article 89

1. In the Special Fissile Materials Financial Account:

(a) the value of special fissile materials left in the possession of or put at the disposal of a Member State, person or undertaking shall be credited to the Community and debited to that Member State, person or undertaking;

(b) the value of special fissile materials which are produced or imported by a Member State, person or undertaking and become the property of the Community shall be debited to the Community and credited to that Member State, person or undertaking. A similar entry shall be made when a Member State, person or undertaking restores to the Community special fissile materials previously left in the possession of or put at the disposal of that State, person or undertaking.

2. Variations in value affecting the quantities of special fissile material shall be expressed for accounting purposes in such a way as not to give rise to any loss or gain to the Community. Any loss or gain shall be borne by or accrue to the holder.

3. Balances arising from the transactions referred to above shall become payable forthwith upon the request of the creditor.

4. Where the Agency undertakes transactions for its own account, it shall, for the purposes of this Chapter, be deemed to be an undertaking.

Article 90

Where new circumstances so require, the provisions of this Chapter relating to the Community's right of ownership may, at the request of a Member State or of the Commission, be adjusted by the Council, acting unanimously on a proposal from the Commission and after consulting the European Parliament. The Commission shall examine any such request made by a Member State.

Article 91

The system of ownership applicable to all objects, materials and assets which are not vested in the Community under this Chapter shall be determined by the law of each Member State.

Chapter IX

The Nuclear Common Market

Article 92

The provisions of this Chapter shall apply to the goods and products specified in the Lists forming Annex IV to this Treaty.

These Lists may, at the request of the Commission or of a Member State, be amended by the Council, acting on a proposal from the Commission.

Article 93

Member States shall abolish between themselves, one year after the entry into force of this Treaty, all customs duties on imports and exports or charges having equivalent effect, and all quantitative restrictions on imports and exports, in respect of:

(a) products in List A^1 and A^2;

(b) products in List B if subject to a common customs tariff and accompanied by a certificate issued by the Commission stating that they are intended to be used for nuclear purposes.

Non-European territories under the jurisdiction of a Member State may, however, continue to levy import and export duties or charges having equivalent effect where they are of an exclusively fiscal nature. The rates of such duties and charges and the system governing them shall not give rise to any discrimination between that State and the other Member States.

Article 94

The Member States shall set up a common customs tariff in accordance with the following provisions:

(a) With regard to products specified in List A^1, the common customs tariff shall be fixed at the level of the lowest tariff in force in any Member State on 1 January 1957;

(b) With regard to products specified in List A^2, the Commission shall take all appropriate measures to ensure that negotiations between Member States shall begin within three months of the entry into force of this Treaty. If, on some of these products, no agreement can be reached within one year of the entry into force of this Treaty, the Council shall, acting by a qualified majority on a proposal from the Commission, determine the applicable duties in the common customs tariff;

(c) The common customs tariff on the products specified in Lists A^1 and A^2 shall be applied from the end of the first year following the entry into force of this Treaty.

Article 95

The Council may, acting unanimously on a proposal from the Commission, decide on the earlier application of the duties in the common customs tariff on products in List B where such a measure would tend to contribute to the development of nuclear energy in the Community.

Article 96

The Member States shall abolish all restrictions based on nationality affecting the right of nationals of any Member State to take skilled employment in the field of nuclear energy, subject to the limitations resulting from the basic requirements of public policy, public security or public health.

After consulting the European Parliament, the Council may, acting by a qualified majority on a proposal from the Commission, which shall first request the opinion of the Economic and Social Committee, issue directives for the application of this Article.

Article 97

No restrictions based on nationality may be applied to natural or legal persons, whether public or private, under the jurisdiction of a Member State, where they desire to participate in the construction of nuclear installations of a scientific or industrial nature in the Community.

Article 98

Member States shall take all measures necessary to facilitate the conclusion of insurance contracts covering nuclear risks.

Within two years of the entry into force of this Treaty, the Council, acting by a qualified majority on a proposal from the Commission, which shall first request the opinion of the Economic and Social Committee, shall, after consulting the European Parliament, issue directives for the application of this Article.

Article 99

The Commission may make any recommendations for facilitating movements of capital intended to finance the industrial activities listed in Annex II to this Treaty.

Article 100

Each Member State undertakes to authorise, in the currency of the Member State in which the creditor or the beneficiary resides, any payments connected with the movement of goods, services or capital, and any transfers of capital and earnings, to the extent that the movement of goods, services, capital and persons between Member States has been liberalised pursuant to this Treaty.

Chapter X

External relations

Article 101

The Community may, within the limits of its powers and jurisdiction, enter into obligations by concluding agreements or contracts with a third State, an international organisation or a national of a third State.

Such agreements or contracts shall be negotiated by the Commission in accordance with the directives of the Council: they shall be concluded by the Commission with the approval of the Council, which shall act by a qualified majority.

Agreements or contracts whose implementation does not require action by the Council and can be effected within the limits of the relevant budget shall, however, be negotiated and concluded solely by the Commission; the Commission shall keep the Council informed.

Article 102

Agreements or contracts concluded with a third State, an international organisation or a national of a third State to which, in addition to the Community, one or more Member States are parties, shall not enter into force until the Commission has been notified by all the Member States concerned that those agreements or contracts have become applicable in accordance with the provisions of their respective national laws.

Article 103

Member States shall communicate to the Commission draft agreements or contracts with a third State, an international organisation or a national of a third State to the extent that such agreements or contracts concern matters within the purview of this Treaty.

If a draft agreement or contract contains clauses which impede the application of this Treaty, the Commission shall, within one month of receipt of such communication, make its comments known to the State concerned.

The State shall not conclude the proposed agreement or contract until it has satisfied the objections of the Commission or complied with a ruling by the Court of Justice, adjudicating urgently upon an application from the State, on the compatibility of the proposed clauses with the provisions of this Treaty. An application may be made to the Court of Justice at any time after the State has received the comments of the Commission.

Article 104

No person or undertaking concluding or renewing an agreement or contract with a third State, an international organisation or a national of a third State after the entry into force of this Treaty may invoke that agreement or contact in order to evade the obligations imposed by this Treaty.

Each Member State shall take such measures as it considers necessary in order to communicate to the Commission, at the request of the latter, all information relating to agreements or contracts concluded after the entry into force of this Treaty, within the purview thereof, by a person or undertaking with a third State, an international organisation or a national of a third State. The Commission may require such communication only for the purpose of verifying that such agreements or contracts do not contain clauses impeding the implementation of this Treaty.

On application by the Commission, the Court of Justice shall give a ruling on the compatibility of such agreements or contracts with the provisions of this Treaty.

Article 105

The provisions of this Treaty shall not be invoked so as to prevent the implementation of agreements or contracts concluded before its entry into force by a Member State, a person or an undertaking with a third State, an international organisation or a national of a third State where such agreements or contracts have been communicated to the Commission not later than 30 days after the entry into force of this Treaty.

Agreements or contracts concluded between the signature and the entry into force of this Treaty by a person or an undertaking with a third State, an international organisation or a national of a third State shall not, however, be invoked as grounds for failure to implement this Treaty if, in the opinion of the Court of Justice, ruling on an application from the Commission, one of the decisive reasons on the part of either of the parties in concluding the agreement or contract was an intention to evade the provisions of this Treaty.

Article 106

Member States which, before the entry into force of this Treaty, have concluded agreements with third States providing for cooperation in the field of nuclear energy shall be required to undertake jointly with the Commission the necessary negotiations with these third States in order to ensure that the rights and obligations arising out of such agreements shall as far as possible be assumed by the Community.

Any new agreement ensuing from such negotiations shall require the consent of the Member State or States signatory to the agreements referred to above and the approval of the Council, which shall act by a qualified majority.

Title Three

Provisions governing the institutions

Chapter I

The institutions of the Community

Section I

The European Parliament

Article 107

The European Parliament which shall consist of representatives of the peoples of the States brought together in the Community, shall exercise the advisory and supervisory powers which are conferred upon it by this Treaty.

[Article 107a

The European Parliament may, acting by a majority of its members, request the Commission to submit any appropriate proposal on matters on which it considers that a Community act is required for the purpose of implementing this Treaty.

Article 107b

In the course of its duties, the European Parliament may, at the request of a quarter of its members, set up a temporary Committee of Inquiry to investigate, without prejudice to the powers conferred by this Treaty on other institutions or bodies, alleged contraventions or maladministration in the implementation of Community law, except where the alleged facts are being examined before a court and while the case is still subject to legal proceedings.

The temporary Committee of Inquiry shall cease to exist on the submission of its report.

The detailed provisions governing the exercise of the right of inquiry shall be determined by common accord of the European Parliament, the Council and the Commission.

Article 107c

Any citizen of the Union, and any natural or legal person residing or having its registered office in a Member State, shall have the right to address, individually or in association with other citizens or persons, a petition to the European Parliament on a matter which comes within the Community's fields of activity and which affects him, her or it directly.

Article 107d

1. The European Parliament shall appoint an Ombudsman empowered to receive complaints from any citizen of the Union or any natural or legal person residing or having its registered office in a Member State concerning instances of maladministration in the activities of the Community institutions or bodies, with the exception of the Court of Justice and the Court of First Instance acting in their judicial role.

In accordance with his duties, the Ombudsman shall conduct inquiries for which he finds grounds, either on his own initiative or on the basis of complaints submitted to him direct or through a member of the European Parliament, except where the alleged facts are or have been the subject of legal proceedings. Where the Ombudsman establishes an instance of maladministration, he shall refer the matter to the institution concerned, which shall have a period of three months in which to inform him of its views. The Ombudsman shall then forward a report to the European Parliament and the institution concerned. The person lodging the complaint shall be informed of the outcome of such inquiries.

The Ombudsman shall submit an annual report to the European Parliament on the outcome of his inquiries.

2. The Ombudsman shall be appointed after each election of the European Parliament for the duration of its term of office. The Ombudsman shall be eligible for reappointment.

The Ombudsman may be dismissed by the Court of Justice at the request of the European Parliament if he no longer fulfils the conditions required for the performance of his duties or if he is guilty of serious misconduct.

3. The Ombudsman shall be completely independent in the performance of his duties. In the performance of those duties he shall neither seek nor take instructions from any body. The Ombudsman may not, during his term of office, engage in any other occupation, whether gainful or not.

4. The European Parliament shall, after seeking an opinion from the Commission and with the approval of the Council acting by a qualified majority, lay down the regulations and general conditions governing the performance of the Ombudsman's duties.][2]

Article 108

(*Paragraphs 1 and 2 lapsed on 17 July 1979 in accordance with Article 14 of the Act concerning the election of the representatives of the European Parliament*)

[*See Article 1 of that Act which reads as follows:*

1. The representatives in the European Parliament of the peoples of the States brought together in the Community shall be elected by direct universal suffrage.]

[*Article 2 of that Act amended by Decision 93/81 Euratom/ECSC/EEC:*[3]

2. The number of representatives elected in each Member State shall be as follows:

Belgium	25
Denmark	16
Germany	99
Greece	25
Spain	64
France	87
Ireland	15
Italy	87
Luxembourg	6
Netherlands	31
Portugal	25
United Kingdom	87]

[3. The European Parliament shall draw up proposals for elections by direct universal suffrage in accordance with a uniform procedure in all Member States.

The Council shall, acting unanimously after obtaining the assent of the European Parliament, which shall act by a majority of its component members, lay down the appropriate provisions, which it shall recommend to Member States for adoption in accordance with their respective constitutional requirements.][4]

Article 109

The European Parliament shall hold an annual session. It shall meet, without requiring to be convened, on the second Tuesday in March.[5, 6]

The European Parliament may meet in extraordinary session at the request of a majority of its members or at the request of the Council or of the Commission.

Article 110

The European Parliament shall elect its President and its officers from among its members.

Members of the Commission may attend all meetings and shall, at their request, be heard on behalf of the Commission.

The Commission shall reply orally or in writing to questions put to it by the European Parliament or by its members.

The Council shall be heard by the European Parliament in accordance with the conditions laid down by the Council in its rules of procedure.

Article 111

Save as otherwise provided in this Treaty, the European Parliament shall act by an absolute majority of the votes cast.

The rules of procedure shall determine the quorum.

Article 112

The European Parliament shall adopt its rules of procedure, acting by a majority of its members.

The proceedings of the European Parliament shall be published in the manner laid down in its rules of procedure.

Article 113

The European Parliament shall discuss in open session the annual general report submitted to it by the Commission.

Article 114

If a motion of censure on the activities of the Commission is tabled before it, the European Parliament shall not vote thereon until at least three days after the motion has been tabled and only by open vote.

If the motion of censure is carried by a two-thirds majority of the votes cast, representing a majority of the members of the European Parliament, the members of the Commission shall resign as a body. They shall continue to deal with current business until they are replaced in accordance with Article 127.

[In this case, the term of office of the members of the Commission appointed to replace them shall expire on the date on which the term of office of the members of the Commission obliged to resign as a body would have expired.][7]

Section II

The Council

Article 115

The Council shall carry out its duties and exercise its powers of decision in accordance with the provisions of this Treaty.

It shall take all measures within its powers to coordinate the actions of the Member States and of the Community.

[Article 116

The Council shall consist of a representative of each Member State at ministerial level, authorised to commit the government of that Member State.

The office of President shall be held in turn by each Member State in the Council for a term of six months, in the following order of Member States:

– for a first cycle of six years: Belgium, Denmark, Germany, Greece, Spain, France, Ireland, Italy, Luxembourg, Netherlands, Portugal, United Kingdom;

– for the following cycle of six years: Denmark, Belgium, Greece, Germany, France, Spain, Italy, Ireland, Netherlands, Luxembourg, United Kingdom, Portugal.

Article 117

The Council shall meet when convened by its President on his own initiative or at the request of one of its members or of the Commission.][8]

Article 118

1. Save as otherwise provided in this Treaty, the Council shall act by a majority of its members.

2. Where the Council is required to act by a qualified majority, the votes of its members shall be weighted as follows:

Belgium	5
Denmark	3

Germany	10
Greece	5
Spain	8
France	10
Ireland	3
Italy	10
Luxembourg	2
Netherlands	5
Portugal	5
United Kingdom	10

For their adoption, acts of the Council shall require at least:

- fifty-four votes in favour where this Treaty requires them to be adopted on a proposal from the Commission,

- fifty-four votes in favour, cast by at least eight members, in other cases.[9]

3. Abstentions by members present in person or represented shall not prevent the adoption by the Council of acts which require unanimity.

Article 119

Where, in pursuance of this Treaty, the Council acts on a proposal from the Commission, unanimity shall be required for an act constituting an amendment to that proposal.

As long as the Council has not acted, the Commission may alter its original proposal, in particular where the European Parliament has been consulted on that proposal.

Article 120

Where a vote is taken, any member of the Council may also act on behalf of not more than one other member.

[Article 121

1. A committee consisting of the Permanent Representatives of the Member States shall be responsible for preparing the work of the Council and for carrying out the tasks assigned to it by the Council.

2. The Council shall be assisted by a General Secretariat, under the direction of a Secretary-General. The Secretary-General shall be appointed by the Council acting unanimously.

The Council shall decide on the organisation of the General Secretariat.

3. The Council shall adopt its rules of procedure.][10]

Article 122

The Council may request the Commission to undertake any studies which the Council considers desirable for the attainment of the common objectives and to submit to it any appropriate proposals.

[Article 123

The Council shall, acting by a qualified majority, determine the salaries, allowances and pensions of the President and members of the Commission, and of the President, Judges, Advocates-General and Registrar of the Court of Justice. It shall also, again by a qualified majority, determine any payment to be made instead of remuneration.][11]

Section III

The Commission

Article 124

In order to ensure the development of nuclear energy within the Community, the Commission shall:

- ensure that the provisions of this Treaty and the measures taken by the institutions pursuant thereto are applied;

- formulate recommendations or deliver opinions in the fields covered by this Treaty, if the Treaty expressly so provides or if the Commission considers it necessary;

- have its own power of decision and participate in the shaping of measures taken by the Council and by the European Parliament in the manner provided for in this Treaty;

- exercise the powers conferred on it by the Council for the implementation of the rules laid down by the latter.

[Article 125

The Commission shall publish annually, not later than one month before the opening of the session of the European Parliament, a general report on the activities of the Community.

Article 126

1. The Commission shall consist of 17 members, who shall be chosen on

the grounds of their general competence and whose independence is beyond doubt.

The number of members of the Commission may be altered by the Council, acting unanimously.

Only nationals of the Member States may be members of the Commission.

The Commission must include at least one national of each of the Member States, but may not include more than two members having the nationality of the same State.

2. The members of the Commission shall, in the general interest of the Community, be completely independent in the performance of their duties.

In the performance of these duties, they shall neither seek nor take instructions from any government or from any other body. They shall refrain from any action incompatible with their duties. Each Member State undertakes to respect this principle and not to seek to influence the members of the Commission in the performance of their tasks.

The members of the Commission may not, during their term of office, engage in any other occupation, whether gainful or not. When entering upon their duties they shall give a solemn undertaking that, both during and after their term of office, they will respect the obligations arising therefrom and in particular their duty to behave with integrity and discretion as regards the acceptance, after they have ceased to hold office, of certain appointments or benefits. In the event of any breach of these obligations, the Court of Justice may, on application by the Council or the Commission, rule that the member concerned be, according to the circumstances, either compulsorily retired in accordance with Article 129 or deprived of his right to a pension or other benefits in its stead.

Article 127

1. The members of the Commission shall be appointed in accordance with the procedure referred to in paragraph 2, for a period of five years, subject, if need be, to Article 114.

Their term of office shall be renewable.

2. The governments of the Member States shall nominate by common accord, after consulting the European Parliament, the person they intend to appoint as President of the Commission.

The governments of the Member States shall, in consultation with the nominee for President, nominate the other persons whom they intend to appoint as members of the Commission.

The President and the other members of the Commission thus nominated shall be subject as a body to a vote of approval by the European Parliament. After approval by the European Parliament, the President and the other members of the Commission shall be appointed by common accord of the governments of the Member States.

3. Paragraphs 1 and 2 shall be applied for the first time to the President and the other members of the Commission whose term of office begins on 7 January 1995.

The President and the other members of the Commission whose term of office begins on 7 January 1993 shall be appointed by common accord of the governments of the Member States. Their term of office shall expire on 6 January 1995.

Article 128

Apart from normal replacement, or death, the duties of a member of the Commission shall end when he resigns or is compulsorily retired.

The vacancy thus caused shall be filled for the remainder of the member's term of office by a new member appointed by common accord of the governments of the Member States. The Council may, acting unanimously, decide that such a vacancy need not be filled.

In the event of resignation, compulsory retirement or death, the President shall be replaced for the remainder of his term of office. The procedure laid down in Article 127(2) shall be applicable for the replacement of the President.

Save in the case of compulsory retirement under Article 129, members of the Commission shall remain in office until they have been replaced.

Article 129

If any member of the Commission no longer fulfils the conditions required for the performance of his duties or if he has been guilty of serious misconduct, the Court of Justice may, on application by the Council or the Commission, compulsorily retire him.

Article 130

The Commission may appoint a Vice-President or two Vice-Presidents from among its members.

Article 131

The Council and the Commission shall consult each other and shall settle by common accord their methods of cooperation.

The Commission shall adopt its rules of procedure so as to ensure that both it and its departments operate in accordance with the provisions of this Treaty. It shall ensure that these rules are published.

Article 132

The Commission shall act by a majority of the number of members provided for in Article 126.

A meeting of the Commission shall be valid only if the number of members laid down in its rules of procedure is present.][12]

[Article 133

Repealed by the Treaty on European Union, Article I(9).]

Article 134

1. A Scientific and Technical Committee is hereby set up; it shall be attached to the Commission and shall have advisory status.

The Committee must be consulted where this Treaty so provides. The Committee may be consulted in all cases in which the Commission considers this appropriate.

2. The Committee shall consist of 33 members, appointed by the Council after consultation with the Commission.

The members of the Committee shall be appointed in their personal capacity for five years. Their appointment shall be renewable. They shall not be bound by any mandatory instructions.

The Scientific and Technical Committee shall each year elect its chairman and officers from among its members.

Article 135

The Commission may undertake any consultations and establish any study groups necessary to the performance of its tasks.

Section IV

The Court of Justice

Article 136

The Court of Justice shall ensure that in the interpretation and application of this Treaty the law is observed.

[*Article* 137

The Court of Justice shall consist of 13 Judges.

The Court of Justice shall sit in plenary session. It may, however form Chambers, each consisting of three or five Judges, either to undertake certain preparatory inquiries or to adjudicate on particular categories of cases in accordance with the rules laid down for these purposes.

The Court of Justice shall sit in plenary session when a Member State or a Community institution that is a party to the proceedings so requests.

Should the Court of Justice so request, the Council may, acting unanimously, increase the number of Judges and make the necessary adjustments to the second and third paragraphs of this Article and to the second paragraph of Article 139.][13]

Article 138

The Court of Justice shall be assisted by six Advocates-General.[14]

It shall be the duty of the Advocate-General, acting with complete impartiality and independence, to make, in open court, reasoned submissions on cases brought before the Court of Justice, in order to assist the Court in the performance of the task assigned to it in Article 136.

Should the Court of Justice so request, the Council may, acting unanimously, increase the number of Advocates-General and make the necessary adjustments to the third paragraph of Article 139.

Article 139

The Judges and Advocates-General shall be chosen from persons whose independence is beyond doubt and who possess the qualifications required for appointment to the highest judicial offices in their respective countries or who are jurisconsults of recognised competence; they shall be appointed by common accord of the Governments of the Member States for a term of six years.

Every three years there shall be a partial replacement of the Judges. Seven and six Judges shall replaced alternately.[15]

Every three years there shall be a partial replacement of the Advocates-General. Three Advocates-General shall be replaced on each occasion.[15]

Retiring Judges and Advocates-General shall be eligible for reappointment.

The Judges shall elect the President of the Court of Justice from among their number for a term of three years. He may be re-elected.

Article 140

The Court of Justice shall appoint its Registrar and lay down the rules governing his service.

[Article 140a

1. A Court of First Instance shall be attached to the Court of Justice with jurisdiction to hear and determine at first instance, subject to a right of appeal to the Court of Justice on points of law only and in accordance with the conditions laid down by the Statute, certain classes of action or proceeding defined in accordance with the conditions laid down in paragraph 2. The Court of First Instance shall not be competent to hear and determine questions referred for a preliminary ruling under Article 150.

2. At the request of the Court of Justice and after consulting the European Parliament and the Commission, the Council, acting unanimously, shall determine the classes of action or proceeding referred to in paragraph 1 and the composition of the Court of First Instance and shall adopt the necessary adjustments and additional provisions to the Statute of the Court of Justice. Unless the Council decides otherwise, the provisions of this Treaty relating to the Court of Justice, in particular the provisions of the Protocol on the Statute of the Court of Justice, shall apply to the Court of First Instance.

3. The members of the Court of First Instance shall be chosen from persons whose independence is beyond doubt and who possess the ability required for appointment to judicial office; they shall be appointed by common accord of the governments of the Member States for a term of six years. The membership shall be partially renewed every three years. Retiring members shall be eligible for re-appointment.

4. The Court of First Instance shall establish its rules of procedure in agreement with the Court of Justice. Those rules shall require the unanimous approval of the Council.][16]

Article 141

If the Commission considers that a Member State has failed to fulfil an obligation under this Treaty, it shall deliver a reasoned opinion on the matter after giving the State concerned the opportunity to submit its observations.

If the State concerned does not comply with the opinion within the period laid down by the Commission, the latter may bring the matter before the Court of Justice.

Article 142

A Member State which considers that another Member State has failed to fulfil an obligation under this Treaty may bring the matter before the Court of Justice.

Before a Member State brings an action against another Member State for an alleged infringement of an obligation under this Treaty, it shall bring the matter before the Commission.

The Commission shall deliver a reasoned opinion after each of the States concerned has been given the opportunity to submit its own case and its observations on the other party's case both orally and in writing.

If the Commission has not delivered an opinion within three months of the date on which the matter was brought before it, the absence of such opinion shall not prevent the matter from being brought before the Court of Justice.

[Article 143

1. If the Court of Justice finds that a Member State has failed to fulfil an obligation under this Treaty, the State shall be required to take the necessary measures to comply with the judgment of the Court of Justice.

2. If the Commission considers that the Member State concerned has not taken such measures it shall, after giving that State the opportunity to submit its observations, issue a reasoned opinion specifying the points on which the Member State concerned has not complied with the judgment of the Court of Justice.

If the Member State concerned fails to take the necessary measures to comply with the Court's judgment within the time-limit laid down by the Commission, the latter may bring the case before the Court of Justice. In so doing it shall specify the amount of the lump sum or penalty payment to be paid by the Member State concerned which it considers appropriate in the circumstances.

If the Court of Justice finds that the Member State concerned has not complied with its judgment it may impose a lump sum or penalty payment on it.

This procedure shall be without prejudice to Article 142.][17]

Article 144

The Court of Justice shall have unlimited jurisdiction in:

(a) proceedings instituted under Article 12 to have the appropriate terms fixed for the granting by the Commission of licences or sub-licences;

(b) proceedings instituted by persons or undertakings against sanctions imposed on them by the Commission under Article 83.

Article 145

If the Commission considers that a person or undertaking has committed an infringement of this Treaty to which the provisions of Article 83 do not apply, it shall call upon the Member State having jurisdiction over that person or undertaking to cause sanctions to be imposed in respect of the infringement in accordance with its national law.

If the State concerned does not comply with such a request within the period laid down by the Commission, the latter may bring an action before the Court of Justice to have the infringement of which the person or undertaking is accused established.

[Article 146

The Court of Justice shall review the legality of acts of the Council and of the Commission, other than recommendations and opinions, and of acts of the European Parliament intended to produce legal effects vis-à-vis third parties.

It shall for this purpose have jurisdiction in actions brought by a Member State, the Council or the Commission on grounds of lack of competence, infringement of an essential procedural requirement, infringement of this Treaty or of any rule of law relating to its application, or misuse of powers.

The Court shall have jurisdiction under the same conditions in actions brought by the European Parliament for the purpose of protecting its prerogatives.

Any natural or legal person may, under the same conditions, institute proceedings against a decision addressed to that person or against a decision which, although in the form of a regulation or a decision addressed to another person, is of direct and individual concern to the former.

The proceedings provided for in this Article shall be instituted within two months of the publication of the measure, or of its notification to the plaintiff, or, in the absence thereof, of the day on which it came to the knowledge of the latter, as the case may be.][18]

Article 147

If the action is well founded, the Court of Justice shall declare the act concerned to be void.

In the case of a regulation, however, the Court of Justice shall, if it considers this necessary, state which of the effects of the regulation which it has declared void shall be considered as definitive.

Article 148

Should the Council or the Commission, in infringement of this Treaty, fail to act, the Member States and the other institutions of the Community may bring an action before the Court of Justice to have the infringement established.

The action shall be admissible only if the institution concerned has first been called upon to act. If, within two months of being so called upon, the institution concerned has not defined its position, the action may be brought within a further period of two months.

Any natural or legal person may, under the conditions laid down in the preceding paragraphs, complain to the Court of Justice that an institution of the Community has failed to address to that person any act other than a recommendation or an opinion.

Article 149

The institution whose act has been declared void or whose failure to act has been declared contrary to this Treaty shall be required to take the necessary measures to comply with the judgment of the Court of Justice.

This obligation shall not affect any obligation which may result from the application of the second paragraph of Article 188.

Article 150

The Court of Justice shall have jurisdiction to give preliminary rulings concerning:

(a) the interpretation of this Treaty;

(b) the validity and interpretation of acts of the institutions of the Community;

(c) the interpretation of the statutes of bodies established by an act of the Council, save where those statutes provide otherwise.

Where such a question is raised before any court or tribunal of a Member State, that court or tribunal may, if it considers that a decision on the question is necessary to enable it to give judgment, request the Court of Justice to give a ruling thereon.

Where any such question is raised in a case pending before a court or tribunal of a Member State, against whose decisions there is no judicial remedy under national law, that court or tribunal shall bring the matter before the Court of Justice.

Article 151

The Court of Justice shall have jurisdiction in disputes relating to the compensation for damage provided for in the second paragraph of Article 188.

Article 152

The Court of Justice shall have jurisdiction in any dispute between the Community and its servants within the limits and under the conditions laid down in the Staff Regulations or the Conditions of Employment.

Article 153

The Court of Justice shall have jurisdiction to give judgment pursuant to any arbitration clause contained in a contract concluded by or on behalf of the Community, whether that contract be governed by public or private law.

Article 154

The Court of Justice shall have jurisdiction in any dispute between Member States which relates to the subject matter of this Treaty if the dispute is submitted to it under a special agreement between the parties.

Article 155

Save where jurisdiction is conferred on the Court of Justice by this Treaty, disputes to which the Community is a party shall not on that ground be excluded from the jurisdiction of the courts or tribunals of the Member States.

Article 156

Notwithstanding the expiry of the period laid down in the third paragraph of Article 146, any party may, in proceedings in which a regulation of the Council or of the Commission is in issue, plead the grounds specified in the first paragraph of Article 146, in order to invoke before the Court of Justice the inapplicability of that regulation.

Article 157

Save as otherwise provided in this Treaty, actions brought before the Court of Justice shall not have suspensory effect. The Court of Justice may, however, if it considers that circumstances so require, order that application of the contested act be suspended.

Article 158

The Court of Justice may in any cases before it prescribe any necessary interim measures.

Article 159

The judgments of the Court of Justice shall be enforceable under the conditions laid down in Article 164.

Article 160

The Statute of the Court of Justice is laid down in a separate Protocol.

The Council may, acting unanimously at the request of the Court of Justice and after consulting the Commission and the European Parliament, amend the provisions of Title III of the Statute.

The Court of Justice shall adopt its rules of procedure. These shall require the unanimous approval of the Council.[19]

[Section V

The Court of Auditors

Article 160a

The audit shall be carried out by the Court of Auditors.

Article 160b

1. The Court of Auditors shall consist of 12 members.

2. The members of the Court of Auditors shall be chosen from among persons who belong or have belonged in their respective countries to external audit bodies or who are especially qualified for this office. Their independence must be beyond doubt.

3. The members of the Court of Auditors shall be appointed for a term of six years by the Council, acting unanimously after consulting the European Parliament.

However, when the first appointments are made, four members of the Court of Auditors, chosen by lot, shall be appointed for a term of office of four years only.

The members of the Court of Auditors shall be eligible for reappointment.

They shall elect the President of the Court of Auditors from among their number for a term of three years. The President may be re-elected.

4. The members of the Court of Auditors shall, in the general interest of the Community, be completely independent in the performance of their duties.

In the performance of these duties, they shall neither seek nor take instructions from any government or from any other body. They shall refrain from any action incompatible with their duties.

5. The members of the Court of Auditors may not, during their term of office, engage in any other occupation, whether gainful or not. When entering upon their duties they shall give a solemn undertaking that, both during and after their term of office, they will respect the obligations arising therefrom and in particular their duty to behave with integrity and discretion as regards the acceptance, after they have ceased to hold office, of certain appointments or benefits.

6. Apart from normal replacement, or death, the duties of a member of the Court of Auditors shall end when he resigns, or is compulsorily retired by a ruling of the Court of Justice pursuant to paragraph 7.

The vacancy thus caused shall be filled for the remainder of the member's term of office.

Save in the case of compulsory retirement, members of the Court of Auditors shall remain in office until they have been replaced.

7. A member of the Court of Auditors may be deprived of his office or of his right to a pension or other benefits in its stead only if the Court of Justice, at the request of the Court of Auditors, finds that he no longer fulfils the requisite conditions or meets the obligations arising from his office.

8. The Council, acting by a qualified majority, shall determine the conditions of employment of the President and the members of the Court of Auditors and in particular their salaries, allowances and pensions. It shall also, by the same majority, determine any payment to be made instead of remuneration.

9. The provisions of the Protocol on the Privileges and Immunities of the European Communities applicable to the Judges of the Court of Justice shall also apply to the members of the Court of Auditors.

Article 160c

1. The Court of Auditors shall examine the accounts of all revenue and expenditure of the Community. It shall also examine the accounts of all revenue and expenditure of all bodies set up by the Community in so far as the relevant constituent instrument does not preclude such examination.

The Court of Auditors shall provide the European Parliament and the Council with a statement of assurance as to the reliability of the accounts and the legality and regularity of the underlying transactions.

2. The Court of Auditors shall examine whether all revenue has been received and all expenditure incurred in a lawful and regular manner and whether the financial management has been sound.

The audit of revenue shall be carried out on the basis of the amounts established as due and the amounts actually paid to the Community.

The audit of expenditure shall be carried out on the basis both of commitments undertaken and payments made.

These audits may be carried out before the closure of accounts for the financial year in question.

3. The audit shall be based on records and, if necessary, performed on the spot in the other institutions of the Community and in the Member States. In the Member States the audit shall be carried out in liaison with

the national audit bodies or, if these do not have the necessary powers, with the competent national departments. These bodies or departments shall inform the Court of Auditors whether they intend to take part in the audit.

The other institutions of the Community and the national audit bodies or, if these do not have the necessary powers, the competent national department, shall forward to the Court of Auditors, at its request, any document or information necessary to carry out its task.

4. The Court of Auditors shall draw up an annual report after the close of each financial year. It shall be forwarded to the other institutions of the Community and shall be published, together with the replies of these institutions to the observations of the Court of Auditors, in the *Official Journal of the European Communities*.

The Court of Auditors may also, at any time, submit observations, particularly in the form of special reports, on specific questions and deliver opinions at the request of one of the other institutions of the Community.

It shall adopt its annual report, special reports or opinions by a majority of its members.

It shall assist the European Parliament and the Council in exercising their powers of control over the implementation of the budget.][20]

Chapter II

Provisions common to several institutions

Article 161

In order to carry out their task the Council and the Commission shall, in accordance with the provisions of this Treaty, make regulations, issue directives, take decisions, make recommendations or deliver opinions.

A regulation shall have general application. It shall be binding in its entirety and directly applicable in all Member States.

A directive shall be binding, as to the result to be achieved, upon each Member State to which it is addressed, but shall leave to the national authorities the choice of form and methods.

A decision shall be binding in its entirety upon those to whom it is addressed.

Recommendations and opinions shall have no binding force.

Article 162

Regulations, directives and decisions of the Council and of the Commission shall state the reasons on which they are based and shall refer to any proposals or opinions which were required to be obtained pursuant to this Treaty.

Article 163

Regulations shall be published in the *Official Journal of the European Communities*. They shall enter into force on the date specified in them or, in the absence thereof, on the twentieth day following their publication.

Directives and decisions shall be notified to those to whom they are addressed and shall take effect upon each notification.

Article 164

Enforcement shall be governed by the rules of civil procedure in force in the State in the territory of which it is carried out. The order for its enforcement shall be appended to the decision, without other formality than verification of the authenticity of the decision, by the national authority which the Government of each Member State shall designate for this purpose and shall make known to the Commission, to the Court of Justice and to the Arbitration Committee set up by Article 18.

When these formalities have been completed on application by the party concerned, the latter may proceed to enforcement in accordance with the national law, by bringing the matter directly before the competent authority.

Enforcement may be suspended only by a decision of the Court of Justice. However, the courts of the country concerned shall have jurisdiction over complaints that enforcement is being carried out in an irregular manner.

Chapter III

The Economic and Social Committee

Article 165

An Economic and Social Committee is hereby established. It shall have advisory status.

The Committee shall consist of representatives of the various categories of economic and social activity.

Article 166

The number of members of the Economic and Social Committee shall be as follows:

Belgium	12
Denmark	9
Germany	24
Greece	12
Spain	21
France	24
Ireland	9
Italy	24
Luxembourg	6
Netherlands	12
Portugal	12
United Kingdom	24

The members of the Committee shall be appointed by the Council, acting unanimously, for four years. Their appointments shall be renewable.

The members of the Committee may not be bound by any mandatory instructions. They shall be completely independent in the performance of their duties, in the general interest of the Community.

The Council, acting by a qualified majority, shall determine the allowances of members of the Committee.][21]

Article 167

1. For the appointment of the members of the Committee, each Member State shall provide the Council with a list containing twice as many candidates as there are seats allotted to its nationals.

The composition of the Committee shall take account of the need to ensure adequate representation of the various categories of economic and social activity.

2. The Council shall consult the Commission. It may obtain the opinion of European bodies which are representative of the various economic and social sectors to which the activities of the Community are of concern.

[*Article* 168

The Committee shall elect its chairman and officers from among its members for a term of two years.

It shall adopt its rules of procedure.

The Committee shall be convened by its chairman at the request of the Council or of the Commission. It may also meet on its own initiative.][22]

Article 169

The Committee may be divided into specialised sections.

These specialised sections shall operate within the general terms of reference of the Committee. They may not be consulted independently of the Committee.

Subcommittees may also be established within the Committee to prepare, on specific questions or in specific fields, draft opinions to be submitted to the Committee for its consideration.

The rules of procedure shall lay down the methods of composition and the terms of reference of the specialised sections and of the subcommittees.

[*Article* 170

The Committee must be consulted by the Council or by the Commission where this Treaty so provides. The Committee may be consulted by these institutions in all cases in which they consider it appropriate. It may issue an opinion on its own initiative in cases in which it considers such action appropriate.

The Council or the Commission shall, if it considers it necessary, set the Committee, for the submission of its opinion, a time-limit which may not be less than one month from the date on which the chairman receives notification to this effect. Upon expiry of the time-limit, the absence of an opinion shall not prevent further action.

The opinion of the Committee and that of the specialised section, together with a record of the proceedings, shall be forwarded to the Council and to the Commission.][23]

Title Four

Financial provisions

Article 171

1. Estimates shall be drawn up for each financial year of all revenue and expenditure of the Community, other than those of the Agency and the

Joint Undertakings, and such revenue and expenditure shall be shown either in the operating budget or in the research and investment budget.

The revenue and expenditure shown in each budget shall be in balance.

2. The revenue and expenditure of the Agency, which shall operate in accordance with commercial principles, shall be budgeted for in a special account.

The manner of estimating, implementing and auditing such revenue and expenditure shall be laid down, with due regard to the statutes of the Agency, in financial regulations made pursuant to Article 183.

3. The estimates of revenue and expenditure, together with the operating accounts and the balance sheets of the Joint Undertakings for each financial year, shall be placed before the Commission, the Council and the European Parliament in accordance with the statutes of those Undertakings.

Article 172

4[24]. Loans for the financing of research or investment shall be raised on terms fixed by the Council in the manner provided for in Article 177(5).

The Community may borrow on the capital market of a Member State, either in accordance with the legal provisions applying to internal issues, or, if there are no such provisions in a Member State, after the Member State concerned and the Commission have conferred together and have reached agreement upon the proposed loan.

The competent authorities of the Member State concerned may refuse to give their assent only if there is reason to fear serious disturbances on the capital market of that State.

[Article 173

Without prejudice to other revenue, the budget shall be financed wholly from own resources.

The Council, acting unanimously on a proposal from the Commission and after consulting the European Parliament, shall lay down provisions relating to the system of own resources of the Community, which it shall recommend to the Member States for adoption in accordance with their respective constitutional requirements.][25]

[Article 173a

With a view to maintaining budgetary discipline, the Commission shall not make any proposal for a Community act, or alter its proposals, or adopt any implementing measure which is likely to have appreciable implications for the budget without providing the assurance that that proposal or that measure is capable of being financed within the limit of the Community's own resources arising under provisions laid down by the Council pursuant to Article 173.][26]

Article 174

1. The expenditure shown in the operating budget shall include in particular:

(a) administrative expenditure;

(b) expenditure relating to safeguards and to health and safety.

2. The expenditure shown in the research and investment budget shall include in particular:

(a) expenditure relating to the implementation of the Community research programme;

(b) any participation in the capital of the Agency and in its investment expenditure;

(c) expenditure relating to the equipment of training establishments;

(d) any participation in Joint Undertakings or in certain joint operations.

Article 175

The expenditure shown in the operating budget shall be authorised for one financial year, unless the regulations made pursuant to Article 183 provide otherwise.

In accordance with conditions to be laid down pursuant to Article 183, any appropriations, other than those relating to staff expenditure, that are unexpended at the end of the financial year may be carried forward to the next financial year only.

Appropriations to cover expenditure shall be classified under different chapters grouping items of expenditure according to their nature or purpose and subdivided, as far as may be necessary, in accordance with the regulations made pursuant to Article 183.

The expenditure of the European Parliament, the Council, the Commission and the Court of Justice shall be set out in separate parts of the budget, without prejudice to special arrangements for certain common items of expenditure.

Article 176

1. Subject to the limits resulting from programmes or decisions involving expenditure which, in pursuance of this Treaty, require the unanimous approval of the Council, allocations for research and investment expenditure shall include:

(a) commitment appropriations, covering a series of items which constitute a separate unit and form a coherent whole;

(b) payment appropriations which represent the maximum amount payable each year in respect of the commitments entered into under subparagraph (a).

2. The schedule of due dates for commitments and payments shall be annexed to the corresponding draft budget proposed by the Commission.

3. Appropriations for research and investment shall be classified under different chapters grouping items of expenditure according to their nature or purpose and subdivided, as far as may be necessary, in accordance with the regulations made pursuant to Article 183.

4. Unused payment authorisations shall be carried forward to the next financial year by decisions of the Commission, unless the Council decides otherwise.

Article 177

1. The financial year shall run from 1 January to 31 December.

Within the meaning of this Article, 'budget' shall include the operating budget and the research and investment budget.

2. Each institution of the Community shall, before 1 July, draw up estimates of its expenditure. The Commission shall consolidate these estimates in a preliminary draft budget. It shall attach thereto an opinion which may contain different estimates.

The preliminary draft budget shall include an estimate of revenue and an estimate of expenditure.

3. The Commission shall place the preliminary draft budget before the Council not later than 1 September of the year preceding that in which the budget is to be implemented.

The Council shall consult the Commission and, where appropriate, the other institutions concerned whenever it intends to depart from the preliminary draft budget.

The Council shall, acting by a qualified majority, establish the draft budget and forward it to the European Parliament.

4. The draft budget shall be placed before the European Parliament not later than 5 October of the year preceding that in which the budget is to be implemented.

The European Parliament shall have the right to amend the draft budget acting by a majority of its members, and to propose to the Council, acting by an absolute majority of the votes cast, modifications to the draft budget relating to the expenditure necessarily resulting from this Treaty or from acts adopted in accordance therewith.

If, within 45 days of the draft budget being placed before it, the European Parliament has given its approval, the budget shall stand as finally adopted. If within this period the European Parliament has not amended the draft budget or proposed any modifications thereto, the budget shall be deemed to be finally adopted.

If within this period the European Parliament has adopted amendments or proposed modifications, the draft budget together with the amendments or proposed modifications shall be forwarded to the Council.

5. After discussing the draft budget with the Commission and, where appropriate, with the other institutions concerned, the Council shall act under the following conditions:

(a) the Council may, acting by a qualified majority, modify any of the amendments adopted by the European Parliament;

(b) with regard to the proposed modifications:

    – where a modification proposed by the European Parliament does not have the effect of increasing the total amount of the expenditure of an institution, owing in particular to the fact that the increase in expenditure which it would involve would be expressly compensated by one or more proposed modifications correspondingly reducing expenditure, the Council may, acting by a qualified majority, reject the proposed modification. In the absence of a decision to reject it, the proposed modification shall stand as accepted,

    – where a modification proposed by the European Parliament has the effect of increasing the total amount of the expenditure of an institution, the Council may, acting by a qualified majority, accept this proposed modification. In the absence of a decision to accept it, the proposed modification shall stand as rejected,

–   where, in pursuance of the two preceding subparagraphs, the Council has rejected a proposed modification, it may, acting by a qualified majority, either retain the amount shown in the draft budget or fix another amount.

The draft shall be modified on the basis of the proposed modifications accepted by the Council.

If, within 15 days of the draft budget being placed before it, the Council has not modified any of the amendments adopted by the European Parliament and if the modifications proposed by the latter have been accepted, the budget shall be deemed to be finally adopted. The Council shall inform the European Parliament that it has not modified any of the amendments and that the proposed modifications have been accepted.

If within this period the Council has modified one or more of the amendments adopted by the European Parliament or if the modifications proposed by the latter have been rejected or modified, the modified draft budget shall again be forwarded to the European Parliament. The Council shall inform the European Parliament of the results of its deliberations.

6. Within 15 days of the draft budget being placed before it, the European Parliament, which shall have been notified of the action taken on its proposed modifications may, acting by a majority of its members and three-fifths of the votes cast, amend or reject the modifications to its amendments made by the Council and shall adopt the budget accordingly. If within this period the European Parliament has not acted, the budget shall be deemed to be finally adopted.

7. When the procedure provided for in this Article has been completed, the President of the European Parliament shall declare that the budget has been finally adopted.

8. However, the European Parliament, acting by a majority of its members and two-thirds of the votes cast may, if there are important reasons, reject the draft budget and ask for a new draft to be submitted to it.

9. A maximum rate of increase in relation to the expenditure of the same type to be incurred during the current year shall be fixed annually for the total expenditure other than that necessarily resulting from this Treaty or from acts adopted in accordance therewith.

The Commission shall, after consulting the Economic Policy Committee, declare what this maximum rate is, as it results from:

–   the trend in terms of volume, of the gross national product within the Community,

– the average variation in the budgets of the Member States, and

– the trend of the cost of living during the preceding financial year.

The maximum rate shall be communicated, before 1 May, to all the institutions of the Community. The latter shall be required to conform to this during the budgetary procedure, subject to the provisions of the fourth and fifth subparagraphs of this paragraph.

If, in respect of expenditure other than that necessarily resulting from this Treaty or from acts adopted in accordance therewith, the actual rate of increase in the draft budget established by the Council is over half the maximum rate, the European Parliament may, exercising its right of amendment, further increase the total amount of that expenditure to a limit not exceeding half the maximum rate.

Where the European Parliament, the Council or the Commission considers that the activities of the Communities require that the rate determined according to the procedure laid down in this paragraph should be exceeded, another rate may be fixed by agreement between the Council, acting by a qualified majority, and the European Parliament, acting by a majority of its members and three-fifths of the votes cast.

10. Each institution shall exercise the powers conferred upon it by this Article, with due regard for the provisions of the Treaty and for acts adopted in accordance therewith, in particular those relating to the Communities' own resources and to the balance between revenue and expenditure.

Article 178

If, at the beginning of a financial year, the budget has not yet been voted, a sum equivalent to not more than one-twelfth of the budget appropriations for the preceding financial year may be spent each month in respect of any chapter or other subdivision of the budget in accordance with the provisions of the Regulations made pursuant to Article 183; this arrangement shall not, however, have the effect of placing at the disposal of the Commission appropriations in excess of one-twelfth of those provided for in the draft budget in the course of preparation.

The Council may, acting by a qualified majority, provided that the other conditions laid down in the first subparagraph are observed, authorise expenditure in excess of one-twelfth.

If the decision relates to expenditure which does not necessarily result from this Treaty or from acts adopted in accordance therewith, the

Council shall forward it immediately to the European Parliament; within 30 days the European Parliament, acting by a majority of its members and three-fifths of the votes cast, may adopt a different decision on the expenditure in excess of the one-twelfth referred to in the first subparagraph. This part of the decision of the Council shall be suspended until the European Parliament has taken its decision. If, within this period, the European Parliament has not taken a decision which differs from the decision of the Council, the latter shall be deemed to be finally adopted.

The decisions referred to in the second and third subparagraphs shall lay down the necessary measures relating to resources to ensure application of this Article.

[Article 179

The Commission shall implement the budgets, in accordance with the provisions of the regulations made pursuant to Article 183, on its own responsibility and within the limits of the appropriations, having regard to the principles of sound financial management.

The regulations shall lay down detailed rules for each institution concerning its part in effecting its own expenditure.

Within the budgets, the Commission may, subject to the limits and conditions laid down in the regulations made pursuant to Article 183, transfer appropriations from one chapter to another or from one subdivision to another.][27]

Article 179a

The Commision shall submit annually to the Council and to the European Parliament the accounts of the preceding financial year relating to the implementation of the budget. The Commission shall also forward to them a financial statement of the assets and liabilities of the Community.

Article 180

Repealed by the Treaty on European Union, Article I(22).

Article 180a

Repealed by the Treaty on European Union, Article I(22).

[Article 180b

1. The European Parliament, acting on a recommendation from the Council which shall act by a qualified majority, shall give a discharge to

the Commission in respect of the implementation of the budget. To this end, the Council and European Parliament in turn shall examine the accounts and the financial statement referred to in Article 179a, the annual report by the Court of Auditors together with the replies of the institutions under audit to the observations of the Court of Auditors, and of any relevant special reports by the Court of Auditors.

2. Before giving a discharge to the Commission, or for any other purpose in connection with the exercise of its powers over the implementation of the budget, the European Parliament may ask to hear the Commission give evidence with regard to the execution of expenditure of the operation of financial control systems. The Commission shall submit any necessary information to the European Parliament at the latter's request.

3. The Commission shall take all appropriate steps to act on the observations in the decisions giving discharge and on other observations by the European Parliament relating to the execution of expenditure, as well as on comments accompanying the recommendations on discharge adopted by the Council.

At the request of the European Parliament or the Council, the Commission shall report on the measures taken in the light of these observations and comments and in particular on the instructions given to the departments which are responsible for the implementation of the budgets. These reports shall also be forwarded to the Court of Auditors.][28]

Article 181

The budgets and the account provided for in Article 171(1) and (2) shall be drawn up in the unit of account determined in accordance with the provisions of the financial regulations made pursuant to Article 183.

The financial contributions provided for in Article 172 shall be placed at the disposal of the Community by the Member States in their national currencies.

The available balances of these contributions shall be deposited with the Treasuries of Member States or with bodies designated by them. While on deposit, such funds shall retain the value corresponding to the parity, at the date of deposit, in relation to the unit of account referred to in the first paragraph.

The balances may be invested on terms to be agreed between the Commission and the Member State concerned.

Article 182

1. The Commission may, provided it notifies the competent authorities of the Member States concerned, transfer into the currency of one of the Member States its holdings of currency of another Member State, to the extent necessary to enable them to be used for purposes which come within the scope of this Treaty. The Commission shall as far as possible avoid making such transfers if it possesses cash or liquid assets in the currencies which it needs.

2. The Commission shall deal with each Member State through the authority designated by the State concerned. In carrying out financial operations the Commission shall employ the services of the bank of issue of the Member State concerned or any other financial institutions approved by that State.

3. As regards expenditure which the Community has to incur in the currencies of third countries, the Commission shall, before the budgets are finally adopted, submit to the Council a programme indicating anticipated revenue and expenditure in the different currencies.

This programme shall be approved by the Council, acting by a qualified majority. It may be modified in the course of the financial year in accordance with the same procedure.

4. Member States shall provide the Commission with the currency of third countries needed for the expenditure shown in the programme provided for in paragraph 3 according to the scales laid down in Article 172. Amounts collected by the Commission in the currency of third countries shall be transferred to Member States in accordance with the same scales.

5. The Commission may freely make use of any amounts in the currency of third countries derived from loans it has raised in such countries.

6. The Council may, acting unanimously on a proposal from the Commission apply, in whole or in part, to the Agency and to Joint Undertakings the exchange arrangements provided for in the preceding paragraphs, and, where appropriate, adapt these arrangements to their operational requirements.

[Article 183

The Council acting unanimously on a proposal from the Commission and after consulting the European Parliament and obtaining the opinion of the Court of Auditors, shall:

(a) make financial regulations specifying in particular the procedure to be adopted for establishing and implementing the budget and for presenting and auditing accounts;

(b) determine the methods and procedure whereby the budget revenue provided under the arrangements relating to the Community's own resources shall be made available to the Commission, and determine the measures to be applied, if need be, to meet cash requirements;

(c) lay down rules concerning the responsibility of financial controllers, authorising officers and accounting officers, and concerning appropriate arrangements for inspection.][29]

[Article 183a

Member States shall take the same measures to counter fraud affecting the financial interests of the Community as they take to counter fraud affecting their own financial interests.

Without prejudice to other provisions of this Treaty, Member States shall coordinate their actions aimed at protecting the financial interests of the Community against fraud. To this end they shall organise, with the help of the Commission, close and regular cooperation between the competent departments of their administrations.][30]

Title Five

General provisions

Article 184

The Community shall have legal personality.

Article 185

In each of the Member States, the Community shall enjoy the most extensive legal capacity accorded to legal persons under their laws; it may, in particular, acquire or dispose of movable and immovable property and may be a party to legal proceedings. To this end, the Community shall be represented by the Commission.

Article 186

(Article repealed by Article 24(2) of the Merger Treaty)

[See Article 24(1) of the Merger Treaty which reads as follows:

1. The officials and other servants of the European Coal and Steel Community, the European Economic Community and the European Atomic Energy Community shall, at the date of entry into force of this

Treaty, become officials and other servants of the European Communities and form part of the single administration of these Communities.

The Council shall, acting by a qualified majority on a proposal from the Commission and after consulting the other institutions concerned, lay down the Staff Regulations of officials of the European Communities and the Conditions of Employment of other servants of these Communities.]

Article 187

The Commission may, within the limits and under the conditions laid down by the Council in accordance with the provisions of this Treaty, collect any information and carry out any checks required for the performance of the tasks entrusted to it.

Article 188

The contractual liability of the Community shall be governed by the law applicable to the contract in question.

In the case of non-contractual liability, the Community shall, in accordance with the general principles common to the laws of the Member States, make good any damage caused by its institutions or by its servants in the performance of their duties.

The personal liability of its servants towards the Community shall be governed by the provisions laid down in the Staff Regulations or in the Conditions of Employment applicable to them.

Article 189

The seat of the institutions of the Community shall be determined by common accord of the Governments of the Member States.

Article 190

The rules governing the languages of the institutions of the Community shall, without prejudice to the provisions contained in the rules of procedure of the Court of Justice, be determined by the Council, acting unanimously.

Article 191

(Article repealed by the second paragraph of Article 28 of the Merger Treaty)

[See the first paragraph of Article 28 of the Merger Treaty which reads as follows:

The European Communities shall enjoy in the territories of the Member

States such privileges and immunities as are necessary for the performance of their tasks, under the conditions laid down in the Protocol annexed to this Treaty. The same shall apply to the European Investment Bank.]

Article 192

Member States shall take all appropriate measures, whether general or particular, to ensure fulfilment of the obligations arising out of this Treaty or resulting from action taken by the institutions of the Community. They shall facilitate the achievement of the Community's tasks.

They shall abstain from any measures which could jeopardise the attainment of the objectives of this Treaty.

Article 193

Member States undertake not to submit a dispute concerning the interpretation or application of this Treaty to any method of settlement other than those provided for therein.

Article 194

1. The members of the institutions of the Community, the members of committees, the officials and other servants of the Community and any other persons who by reason of their duties or their public or private relations with the institutions or installations of the Community or with Joint Undertakings are called upon to acquire or obtain cognizance of any facts, information, knowledge, documents or objects which are subject to a security system in accordance with provisions laid down by a Member State or by an institution of the Community, shall be required, even after such duties or relations have ceased, to keep them secret from any unauthorised person and from the general public.

Each Member State shall treat any infringement of this obligation as an act prejudicial to its rules on secrecy and as one falling, both as to merits and jurisdiction, within the scope of its laws relating to acts prejudicial to the security of the State or to disclosure of professional secrets. Such Member State shall, at the request of any Member State concerned or of the Commission, prosecute anyone within its jurisdiction who commits such an infringement.

2. Each Member State shall communicate to the Commission all provisions regulating within its territories the classification and secrecy of information, knowledge, documents or objects covered by this Treaty.

The Commission shall ensure that these provisions are communicated to the other Member States.

Each Member State shall take all appropriate measures to facilitate the gradual establishment of as uniform and comprehensive a security system as possible. The Commission may, after consulting the Member States concerned, make recommendations for this purpose.

3. The institutions of the Community, their installations and also the Joint Undertakings shall be required to apply the rules of the security system in force in the territory in which each of them is situated.

4. Any authorisation granted either by an institution of the Community or by a Member State to a person carrying out his activities within the field covered by this Treaty to have access to facts, information, documents or objects covered by this Treaty which are subject to a security system, shall be recognised by every other institution and every other Member State.

5. The provisions of this Article shall not prevent application of special provisions resulting from agreements concluded between a Member State and a third State or an international organisation.

Article 195

The institutions of the Community, the Agency and the Joint Undertakings shall, in applying this Treaty, comply with the conditions of access to ores, source materials and special fissile materials laid down in national rules and regulations made for reasons of public policy or public health.

Article 196

For the purposes of this Treaty, save as otherwise provided therein:

(a) 'person' means any natural person who pursues all or any of his activities in the territories of Member States within the field specified in the relevant chapter of this Treaty;

(b) 'undertaking' means any undertaking or institution which pursues all or any of its activities in the territories of Member States within the field specified in the relevant Chapter of this Treaty, whatever its public or private legal status.

Article 197

For the purposes of this Treaty:

1. 'Special fissile materials' means plutonium-239; uranium-233; uranium enriched in uranium-235 or uranium-233; and any substance containing one or more of the foregoing isotopes and such other fissile materials as may be specified by the Council, acting by a qualified

majority on a proposal from the Commission; the expression 'special fissile materials' does not, however, include source materials.

2. 'Uranium enriched in uranium-235 or uranium-233' means uranium containing uranium-235 or uranium-233 or both in an amount such that the abundance ratio of the sum of these isotopes to isotope 238 is greater than the ratio of isotope 235 to isotope 238 occurring in nature.

3. 'Source materials' means uranium containing the mixture of isotopes occurring in nature; uranium whose content in uranium-235 is less than normal; thorium; any of the foregoing in the form of metal, alloy, chemical compound or concentrate; any other substance containing one or more of the foregoing in such a concentration as shall be specified by the Council, acting by a qualified majority on a proposal from the Commission.

4. 'Ores' means any ore containing, in such average concentrations as shall be specified by the Council acting by a qualified majority on a proposal from the Commission, substances from which the source materials defined above may be obtained by the appropriate chemical and physical processing.

Article 198

Save as otherwise provided, this Treaty shall apply to the European territories of Member States and to non-European territories under their jurisdiction.

It shall also apply to the European territories for whose external relations a Member State is responsible.

Notwithstanding the previous paragraphs:

[(a) This Treaty shall not apply to the Faroe Islands.][31]

(b) This Treaty shall not apply to the Sovereign Base Areas of the United Kingdom of Great Britain and Northern Ireland in Cyprus.

(c) This Treaty shall not apply to those overseas countries and territories having special relations with the United Kingdom of Great Britain and Northern Ireland which are not listed in Annex IV to the Treaty establishing the European Economic Community.

(d) This Treaty shall apply to the Channel Islands and the Isle of Man only to the extent necessary to ensure the implementation of the arrangements for those islands set out in the Treaty concerning the accession of New Member States to the European Economic Community and to the European Atomic Energy Community signed on 22 January 1972.

Article 199

It shall be for the Commission to ensure the maintenance of all appropriate relations with the organs of the United Nations, of its specialised agencies and of the General Agreement on Tariffs and Trade.

The Commission shall also maintain such relations as are appropriate with all international organisations.

Article 200

The Community shall establish all appropriate forms of cooperation with the Council of Europe.

[Article 201

The Community shall establish close cooperation with the Organisation for Economic Cooperation and Development, the details of which shall be determined by common accord.][32]

Article 202

The provisions of this Treaty shall not preclude the existence or completion of regional unions between Belgium and Luxembourg, or between Belgium, Luxembourg and the Netherlands, to the extent that the objectives of these regional unions are not attained by application of this Treaty.

Article 203

If action by the Community should prove necessary to attain one of the objectives of the Community and this Treaty has not provided the necessary powers, the Council shall, acting unanimously on a proposal from the Commission and after consulting the European Parliament, take the appropriate measures.

Article 204

Repealed by the Treaty on European Union, Article I(28).

Article 205

Repealed by the Treaty on European Union, Article I(28).

[Article 206

The Community may conclude with one or more States or international organisations agreements establishing an association involving reciprocal rights and obligations, common action and special procedures.

These agreements shall be concluded by the Council, acting unanimously after consulting the European Parliament.

Where such agreements call for amendments to this Treaty, these amendments shall first be adopted in accordance with the procedure laid down in Article N of the Treaty on European Union.][33]

Article 207

The Protocols annexed to this Treaty by common accord of the Member States shall form an integral part thereof.

Article 208

This Treaty is concluded for an unlimited period.

Title Six

Provisions relating to the initial period

Section I

Setting up of the institutions

Article 209

The Council shall meet within one month of the entry into force of this Treaty.

Article 210

The Council shall, within three months of its first meeting, take all appropriate measures to constitute the Economic and Social Committee.

Article 211

The Assembly[34] shall meet within two months of the first meeting of the Council, having been convened by the President of the Council, in order to elect its officers and draw up its rules of procedure. Pending the election of its officers, the oldest member shall take the chair.

Article 212

The Court of Justice shall take up its duties as soon as its members have been appointed. Its first President shall be appointed for three years in the same manner as its members.

The Court of Justice shall adopt its rules of procedure within three months of taking up its duties.

No matter may be brought before the Court of Justice until its rules of procedure have been published. The time within which an action must be brought shall run only from the date of this publication.

Upon his appointment, the President of the Court of Justice shall exercise the powers conferred upon him by this Treaty.

Article 213

The Commission shall take up its duties and assume the responsibilities conferred upon it by this Treaty as soon as its members have been appointed.

Upon taking up its duties, the Commission shall undertake the studies and arrange the contacts with Member States, undertakings, workers and consumers needed for making an overall survey of the situation of nuclear industries in the Community. The Commission shall submit a report on this subject to the European Parliament within six months.

Article 214

1. The first financial year shall run from the date when this Treaty enters into force until 31 December following. Should this Treaty, however, enter into force during the second half of the year, the first financial year shall run until 31 December of the following year.

2. Until the budgets for the first financial year have been established, Member States shall make the Community interest-free advances which shall be deducted from their financial contributions to the implementation of these budgets.

3. Until the Staff Regulations of officials and the Conditions of Employment of other servants of the Community provided for in Article 186 have been laid down, each institution shall recruit the staff it needs and to this end conclude contracts of limited duration.

Each institution shall examine together with the Council any question concerning the number, remuneration and distribution of posts.

Section II

Provisions for the initial application of this Treaty

Article 215

1. An initial research and training programme, which is set out in Annex V to this Treaty and the cost of which shall not, unless the Council unanimously decides otherwise, exceed 215 million EPU units of account, shall be carried out within five years of the entry into force of this Treaty.

2. A breakdown of the expenditure necessary for the implementation of this programme is set out by way of illustration under main subdivisions in Annex V.

The Council may, acting by a qualified majority on a proposal from the Commission, modify this programme.

Article 216

The Commission proposals on the way in which the institution of university status referred to in Article 9 is to function shall be submitted to the Council within one year of the entry into force of this Treaty.

Article 217

The security regulations provided for in Article 24 concerning the security gradings applicable to the dissemination of information shall be adopted by the Council within six months of the entry into force of this Treaty.

Article 218

The basic standards shall be determined in accordance with the provisions of Article 31 within one year of entry into force of this Treaty.

Article 219

Provisions laid down by law, regulation or administrative action to ensure the protection of the health of the general public and of workers in the territories of Member States against the dangers arising from ionizing radiations shall, in accordance with Article 33, be communicated to the Commission by these States within three months of the entry into force of this Treaty.

Article 220

The Commission proposals relating to the statutes of the Agency which are provided for in Article 54 shall be submitted to the Council within three months of the entry into force of this Treaty.

Section III

Transitional provisions

Article 221

The provisions of Articles 14 to 23 and of Articles 25 to 28 shall apply to patents, provisionally protected patent rights and utility models, and also to patent and utility model applications in existence before the entry into force of this Treaty, under the following conditions:

1. When assessing the period of time referred to in Article 17(2), allowance shall be made, in favour of the owner, for the new situation created by the entry into force of this Treaty.

2. With regard to the communication of an invention which is not secret, where either or both of the periods of three and eighteen months referred to in Article 16 have expired at the date on which this Treaty enters into force, a further period of six months shall run from that date.

If either or both of those periods remain unexpired at that date, they shall be extended by six months from the date of their normal expiry.

3. The same provisions shall apply to the communication of a secret invention in accordance with Article 16 and Article 25(1); in such case, however, the date of entry into force of the security regulations referred to in Article 24 shall be the date taken as the starting point for the new period or for the extension of a current period.

Article 222

During the period between the date of entry into force of this Treaty and the date fixed by the Commission on which the Agency takes up its duties, agreements and contracts for the supply of ores, source materials or special fissile materials shall be concluded or renewed only with the prior approval of the Commission.

The Commission shall refuse to approve the conclusion or renewal of any agreements and contracts which it considers would prejudice the implementation of this Treaty. It may in particular make its approval dependent upon the insertion in agreements and contracts of clauses permitting the Agency to take part in carrying them out.

Article 223

By way of derogation from the provisions of Article 60, reactors installed in the territories of a Member State which may go critical before the expiry of a period of seven years from the date of entry into force of this Treaty shall, during a period of not more than 10 years from that date, in order to take account of work and studies already initiated, be granted priority which may be exercised in respect both of supplies of ores or source materials coming from the territories of that State and also of supplies of source materials or special fissile materials which are the subject of a bilateral agreement concluded before the entry into force of this Treaty and communicated to the Commission in accordance with Article 105.

The same priority shall be granted during the same period of 10 years in respect of supplies for any isotope separation plant, whether or not it constitutes a Joint Undertaking, which comes into operation in the territory of a Member State before the expiry of a period of seven years from the date of entry into force of this Treaty.

The Agency shall conclude the appropriate contracts, after the Commission has ascertained that the conditions for the exercise of the right of priority have been fulfilled.

Final provisions

Article 224

This Treaty shall be ratified by the High Contracting Parties in accordance with their respective constitutional requirements. The instruments of ratification shall be deposited with the Government of the Italian Republic.

This Treaty shall enter into force on the first day of the month following the deposit of the instrument of ratification by the last signatory State to take this step. If, however, such deposit is made less than 15 days before the beginning of the following month, this Treaty shall not enter into force until the first day of the second month after the date of such deposit.

Article 225

This Treaty, drawn up in a single original in the Dutch, French, German and Italian languages, all four texts being equally authentic, shall be deposited in the archives of the Government of the Italian Republic, which shall transmit a certified copy to each of the Governments of the other signatory States.

In witness whereof, the undersigned plenipotentiaries have signed this Treaty.

Done at Rome this twenty-fifth day of March in the year one thousand nine hundred and fifty-seven.

[List omitted]

EDITORIAL NOTE

For Protocols and Declarations not included in this volume see: Office for Official Publications of the European Communities, Treaties establishing the European Communities: Treaties amending these Treaties, 1987, volume I; and, ditto European Union selected instruments taken from the Treaties, Books I and II, volumes I and II (Book I, volume I 1993, Luxembourg; others – to be published).

FOOTNOTES

1. Article 3 replaced by the Treaty on European Union, Title IV, Article I(1).
2. Articles 107a to 107d inserted by the Treaty on European Union,Title IV, Article I(2).
3. OJ No L 33, 9.2.93, p.15.
4. Paragraph 3 replaced by the Treaty on European Union, Title IV, Article I(3).
5. First paragraph as amended by Article 27(1) of the Merger Treaty.
6. For the second sentence of this paragraph, see also Article 10(3) of the Act concerning the election of the representatives of the European Parliament.
7. Paragraph 3 inserted by the Treaty on European Union, Title IV, Article I(4).
8. Articles 116 and 117 inserted by the Treaty on European Union, Title IV, Article I(5).
9. Paragraph 2 as amended by Article 14 of the Act of Accession ESP/PORT.
10. Article 121 inserted by the Treaty on European Union, Title IV, Article I(6).
11. Article 123 inserted by the Treaty on European Union, Title IV, Article I(7).
12. Articles 125 to 132 inserted by the Treaty on European Union, Title IV, Article I(8).
13. Article 137 replaced by the Treaty on European Union, Title IV, Article I(10).
14. First paragraph as amended by Article 18 of the Act of Accession ESP/PORT.
15. Second and third paragraphs as amended by Article 19 of the Act of Accession ESP/PORT.
16. Article 140a replaced by the Treaty on European Union, Title IV, Article I(11).
17. Article 143 replaced by the Treaty on European Union, Title IV, Article I(12).
18. Article 146 replaced by the Treaty on European Union, Title IV, Article I(13).
19. See the Statute of the Court of Justice of the EC.
20. Section V, Articles 160a to 160c inserted by the Treaty on European Union, Title IV, Article I(14).
21. Article 166 replaced by the Treaty on European Union, Title IV, Article I(15).
22. Article 168 replaced by the Treaty on European Union, Title IV, Article I(16).
23. Article 170 replaced by the Treaty on European Union, Title IV, Article I(17).
24. Paragraphs 1 to 3 repealed by the Treaty on European Union, Title IV, Article I(18).
25. Article 173 replaced by the Treaty on European Union, Title IV, Article I(19).
26. Article 173a inserted by the Treaty on European Union, Title IV, Article I(20).
27. Article 179 replaced by the Treaty on European Union, Title IV, Article I(21).
28. Article 180b replaced by the Treaty on European Union, Title IV, Article I(23).
29. Article 183 replaced by the Treaty on European Union, Title IV, Article I(24).

30. Article 183a inserted by the Treaty on European Union, Title IV, Article I(25).
31. Paragraph (*a*) replaced by the Treaty on European Union, Title IV, Article I(26).
32. Article 201 replaced by the Treaty on European Union, Title IV, Article I(27).
33. Article 206 replaced by the Treaty on European Union, Title IV, Article I(29).
34. Editorial Note: Notwithstanding the provisions of Article 3 of the SEA, and for historical reasons, the term 'Assembly' has not been replaced by the terms 'European Parliament'.

Annexes

(not included in this volume – editorial note)

Protocols

Protocol on the application of the Treaty establishing the European Atomic Energy Community to the non-European parts of the Kingdom of the Netherlands

The High Contracting Parties,

Anxious, at the time of signature of the Treaty establishing the European Atomic Energy Community, to define the scope of the provisions of Article 198 of this Treaty in respect of the Kingdom of the Netherlands,

Have agreed upon the following provisions, which shall be annexed to this Treaty:

The Government of the Kingdom of the Netherlands, by reason of the constitutional structure of the Kingdom resulting from the Statute of 29 December 1954, shall, by way of derogation from Article 198, be entitled to ratify this Treaty either on behalf of the Kingdom of the Netherlands in its entirety or on behalf of the Kingdom in Europe and Netherlands New Guinea. In the event of ratification being limited to the Kingdom in Europe and Netherlands New Guinea, the Government of the Kingdom of the Netherlands may at any time, by notification to the Government of the Italian Republic as depositary of the instruments of ratification, declare this Treaty also applicable either to Surinam, or to the Netherlands Antilles, or to both Surinam and the Netherlands Antilles.

Done at Rome this twenty-fifth day of March in the year one thousand nine hundred and fifty-seven.

[List omitted]

Protocol on the Statute of the Court of Justice of the European Atomic Energy Community

(See Protocol on the Court of Justice of the European Community – editorial note)

Protocol on the Privileges and Immunities of the European Atomic Energy Community

(Repealed by the second paragraph of Article 28 of the Merger Treaty: see Protocol on the Privileges and Immunities of the European Communities – editorial note)

TITLE V

Common Foreign and Security Policy

Article J

A common foreign and security policy is hereby established which will be governed by the following provisions.

Article J.1

1. The Union and its Member States shall define and implement a common foreign and security policy, governed by the provisions of this Title and covering all areas of foreign and security policy.

2. The objectives of the common foreign and security policy shall be:

- to safeguard the common values, fundamental interests and independence of the Union;

- to strengthen the security of the Union and its Member States in all ways;

- to preserve peace and strengthen international security, in accordance with the principles of the United Nations Charter as well as the principles of the Helsinki Final Act and the objectives of the Paris Charter;

- to promote international cooperation;

- to develop and consolidate democracy and the rule of law, and respect for human rights and fundamental freedoms.

3. The Union shall pursue these objectives:

- by establishing systematic cooperation between Member States in the conduct of policy, in accordance with Article J.2;

- by gradually implementing, in accordance with Article J.3, joint action in the areas in which the Member States have important interests in common.

4. The Member States shall support the Union's external and security

policy actively and unreservedly in a spirit of loyalty and mutual solidarity. They shall refrain from any action which is contrary to the interests of the Union or likely to impair its effectiveness as a cohesive force in international relations. The Council shall ensure that these principles are complied with.

Article J.2

1. Member States shall inform and consult one another within the Council on any matter of foreign and security policy of general interest in order to ensure that their combined influence is exerted as effectively as possible by means of concerted and convergent action.

2. Whenever it deems it necessary, the Council shall define a common position.

Member States shall ensure that their national policies conform to the common positions.

3. Member States shall coordinate their action in international organisations and at international conferences. They shall uphold the common positions in such forums.

In international organisations and at conferences where not all the Member States participate, those which do take part shall uphold the common positions.

Article J.3

The procedure for adopting joint action in matters covered by the foreign and security policy shall be the following:

1. The Council shall decide, on the basis of general guidelines from the European Council, that a matter should be the subject of joint action.

Whenever the Council decides on the principle of joint action, it shall lay down the specific scope, the Union's general and specific objectives in carrying out such action, if necessary its duration, and the means, procedures and conditions for its implementation.

2. The Council shall, when adopting the joint action and at any stage during its development, define those matters on which decisions are to be taken by a qualified majority.

Where the Council is required to act by a qualified majority pursuant to the proceeding subparagraph, the votes of its members shall be weighted in accordance with Article 148(2) of the Treaty establishing the European Community, and for their adoption, acts of the Council shall require at least 54 votes in favour, cast by at least eight members.

3. If there is a change in circumstances having a substantial effect on a question subject to joint action, the Council shall review the principles and objectives of that action and take the necessary decisions. As long as the Council has not acted, the joint action shall stand.

4. Joint actions shall commit the Member States in the positions they adopt and in the conduct of their activity.

5. Whenever there is any plan to adopt a national position or take national action pursuant to a joint action, information shall be provided in time to allow, if necessary, for prior consultations within the Council. The obligation to provide prior information shall not apply to measures which are merely a national transposition of Council decisions.

6. In cases of imperative need arising from changes in the situation and failing a Council decision, Member States may take the necessary measures as a matter of urgency having regard to the general objectives of the joint action. The Member State concerned shall inform the Council immediately of any such measures.

7. Should there be any major difficulties in implementing a joint action, a Member State shall refer them to the Council which shall discuss them and seek appropriate solutions. Such solutions shall not run counter to the joint action or impair its effectiveness.

Article J.4

1. The common foreign and security policy shall include all questions related to the security of the Union, including the eventual framing of a common defence policy, which might in time lead to a common defence.

2. The Union requests the Western European Union (WEU), which is an integral part of the development of the Union, to elaborate and implement decisions and actions of the Union which have defence implications. The Council shall, in agreement with the institutions of the WEU, adopt the necessary practical arrangements.

3. Issues having defence implications dealt with under this Article shall not be subject to the procedures set out in Article J.3.

4. The policy of the Union in accordance with this Article shall not prejudice the specific character of the security and defence policy of certain Member States and shall respect the obligations of certain Member States under the North Atlantic Treaty and be compatible with the common security and defence policy established within that framework.

5. The provisions of this Article shall not prevent the development of closer cooperation between two or more Member States on a bilateral

level, in the framework of the WEU and the Atlantic Alliance, provided such cooperation does not run counter to or impede that provided for in this Title.

6. With a view to furthering the objective of this Treaty, and having in view the date of 1988 in the context of Article XII of the Brussels Treaty, the provisions of this Article may be revised as provided for in Article N(2) on the basis of a report to be presented in 1996 by the Council to the European Council, which shall include an evaluation of the progress made and the experience gained until then.

Article J.5

1. The Presidency shall represent the Union in matters coming within the common foreign and security policy.

2. The Presidency shall be responsible for the implementation of common measures; in that capacity it shall in principle express the position of the Union in international organisations and international conferences.

3. In the tasks referred to in paragraphs 1 and 2, the Presidency shall be assisted if need be by the previous and next Member States to hold the Presidency. The Commission shall be fully associated in these tasks.

4. Without prejudice to Article J.2(3) and Article J.3(4), Member States represented in international organisations or international conferences where not all the Member States participate shall keep the latter informed of any matter of common interest.

Member States which are also members of the United Nations Security Council will concert and keep the other Member States fully informed. Member States which are permanent members of the Security Council will, in the execution of their functions, ensure the defence of the positions and the interests of the Union, without prejudice to their responsibilities under the provisions of the United Nations Charter.

Article J.6

The diplomatic and consular missions of the Member States and the Commission Delegations in third countries and international conferences, and their representations to international organisations, shall cooperate in ensuring that the common positions and common measures adopted by the Council are complied with and implemented.

They shall step up cooperation by exchanging information, carrying out joint assessments and contributing to the implementation of the provisions referred to in Article 8c of the Treaty establishing the European Community.

Article J.7

The Presidency shall consult the European Parliament on the main aspects and the basic choices of the common foreign and security policy and shall ensure that the views of the European Parliament are duly taken into consideration. The European Parliament shall be kept regularly informed by the Presidency and the Commission of the development of the Union's foreign and security policy.

The European Parliament may ask questions of the Council or make recommendations to it. It shall hold an annual debate on progress in implementing the common foreign and security policy.

Article J.8

1. The European Council shall define the principles of and general guidelines for the common foreign and security policy.

2. The Council shall take the decisions necessary for defining and implementing the common foreign and security policy on the basis of the general guidelines adopted by the European Council. It shall ensure the unity, consistency and effectiveness of action by the Union.

The Council shall act unanimously, except for procedural questions and in the case referred to in Article J.3(2).

3. Any Member State or the Commission may refer to the Council any question relating to the common foreign and security policy and may submit proposals to the Council.

4. In cases requiring a rapid decision, the Presidency, of its own motion, or at the request of the Commission or a Member State, shall convene an extraordinary Council meeting within 48 hours or, in an emergency, within a shorter period.

5. Without prejudice to Article 151 of the Treaty establishing the European Community, a Political Committee consisting of Political Directors shall monitor the international situation in the areas covered by common foreign and security policy and contribute to the definition of policies by delivering opinions to the Council at the request of the Council or on its own initiative. It shall also monitor the implementation of agreed policies, without prejudice to the responsibility of the Presidency and the Commission.

Article J.9

The Commission shall be fully associated with the work carried out in the common foreign and security policy field.

Article J.10

On the occasion of any review of the security provisions under Article J.4, the Conference which is convened to that effect shall also examine whether any other amendments need to be made to provisions relating to the common foreign and security policy.

Article J.11

1. The provisions referred to in Articles 137, 138, 139 to 142, 146, 147, 150 to 153, 157 to 163 and 217 of the Treaty establishing the European Community shall apply to the provisions relating to the areas referred to in this Title.

2. Administrative expenditure which the provisions relating to the areas referred to in this Title entail for the institutions shall be charged to the budget of the European Communities.

The Council may also:

– either decide unanimously that operational expenditure to which the implementation of those provisions gives rise is to be charged to the budget of the European Communities; in that event, the budgetary procedure laid down in the Treaty establishing the European Community shall be applicable;

– or determine that such expenditure shall be charged to the Member States, where appropriate in accordance with a scale to be decided.

TITLE VI

Provisions on cooperation in the fields of justice and home affairs

Article K

Cooperation in the fields of justice and home affairs shall be governed by the following provisions.

Article K.1

For the purposes of achieving the objectives of the Union, in particular the free movement of persons, and without prejudice to the powers of the European Community, Member States shall regard the following areas as matters of common interest:

1. asylum policy;

2. rules governing the crossing by persons of the external borders of the Member States and the exercise of controls thereon;

3. immigration policy and policy regarding nationals of third countries:

(a) conditions of entry and movement by nationals of third countries on the territory of Member States;

(b) conditions of residence by nationals of third countries on the territory of Member States, including family reunion and access to employment;

(c) combating unauthorised immigration, residence and work by nationals of third countries on the territory of Member States;

4. combating drug addiction in so far as this is not covered by (7) to (9);

5. combating fraud on an international scale in so far as this is not covered by 7 to 9;

6. judicial cooperation in civil matters;

7. judicial cooperation in criminal matters;

8. customs cooperation;

9. police cooperation for the purposes of preventing and combating terrorism, unlawful drug trafficking and other serious forms of international crime, including if necessary certain aspects of customs cooperation, in connection with the organisation of a Union-wide system for exchanging information within a European Police Office (Europol).

Article K.2

1. The matters referred to in Article K.1 shall be dealt with in compliance with the European Convention for the Protection of Human Rights and Fundamental Freedoms of 4 November 1950 and the Convention relating to the Status of Refugees of 28 July 1951 and having regard to the protection afforded by Member States to persons persecuted on political grounds.

2. This Title shall not affect the exercise of the responsibilities incumbent upon Member States with regard to the maintenance of law and order and the safe-guarding of internal security.

Article K.3.

1. In areas referred to in Article K.1, Member States shall inform and consult one another within the Council with a view to coordinating their action. To that end, they shall establish collaboration between the relevant departments of their administrations.

2. The Council may:

— on the initiative of any Member State or of the Commission, in the areas referred to in Article K.1(1) to (6);

— on the initiative of any Member State, in the areas referred to in Article K.1(7) to (9):

   (a) adopt joint positions and promote, using the appropriate form and procedures, any cooperation contributing to the pursuit of the objectives of the Union;

   (b) adopt joint action in so far as the objectives of the Union can be attained better by joint action by the Member States acting individually on account of the scale or effects of the action envisaged; it may decide that measures implementing joint action are to be adopted by a qualified majority;

   (c) without prejudice to Article 220 of the Treaty establishing the European Community, draw up conventions which it shall recommend to the Member States for adoption in accordance with their respective constitutional requirements.

Unless otherwise provided by such conventions, measures implementing them shall be adopted within the Council by a majority of two-thirds of the High Contracting Parties.

Such conventions may stipulate that the Court of Justice shall have jurisdiction to interpret their provisions and to rule on any disputes regarding their application, in accordance with such arrangements as they may lay down.

Article K.4

1. A Coordinating Committee shall be set up consisting of senior officials. In addition to its coordinating role, it shall be the task of the Committee to:

— give opinions for the attention of the Council, either at the Council's request or on its own initiative;

— contribute, without prejudice to Article 151 of the Treaty establishing the European Community, to the preparation of the Council's discussions in the areas referred to in Article K.1 and, in accordance with the conditions laid down in Article 100d of the Treaty establishing the European Community, in the areas referred to in Article 100c of that Treaty.

2. The Commission shall be fully associated with the work in the areas referred to in this Title.

3. The Council shall act unanimously, except on matters of procedure and in cases where Article K.3 expressly provides for other voting rules.

Where the Council is required to act by a qualified majority, the votes of its members shall be weighted as laid down in Article 148(2) of the Treaty establishing the European Community, and for their adoption, acts of the Council shall require at least 54 votes in favour, cast by at least eight members.

Article K.5

Within international organisations and at international conferences in which they take part, Member States shall defend the common positions adopted under the provisions of this Title.

Article K.6

The Presidency and the Commission shall regularly inform the European Parliament of discussions in the areas covered by this Title.

The Presidency shall consult the European Parliament on the principal aspects of activities in the areas referred to in this Title and shall ensure that the views of the European Parliament are duly taken into consideration.

The European Parliament may ask questions of the Council or make recommendations to it. Each year, it shall hold a debate on the progress made in implementation of the areas referred to in this Title.

Article K.7

The provisions of this Title shall not prevent the establishment or development of closer cooperation between two or more Member States in so far as such cooperation does not conflict with, or impede, that provided for in this Title.

Article K.8

1. The provisions referred to in Articles 137, 138, 139 to 142, 146, 147, 150 to 153, 157 to 163 and 217 of the Treaty establishing the European

Community shall apply to the provisions relating to the areas referred to in this Title.

2. Administrative expenditure which the provisions relating to the areas referred to in this Title entail for the institutions shall be charged to the budget of the European Communities.

The Council may also:

- either decide unanimously that operational expenditure to which the implementation of those provisions gives rise is to be charged to the budget of the European Communities; in that event, the budgetary procedure laid down in the Treaty establishing the European Community shall be applicable;

- or determine that such expenditure shall be charged to the Member States, where appropriate in accordance with a scale to be decided.

Article K.9

The Council, acting unanimously on the initiative of the Commission or a Member State, may decide to apply Article 100c of the Treaty establishing the European Community to action in areas referred to in Article K.1(1) to (6), and at the same time determine the relevant voting conditions relating to it. It shall recommend the Member States to adopt that decision in accordance with their respective constitutional requirements.

TITLE VII

Final provisions

Article L

The provisions of the Treaty establishing the European Community, the Treaty establishing the European Coal and Steel Community and the Treaty establishing the European Atomic Energy Community concerning the powers of the Court of Justice of the European Communities and the exercise of those powers shall apply only to the following provisions of this Treaty:

(a) provisions amending the Treaty establishing the European Economic Community with a view to establishing the European Community, the Treaty establishing the European Coal and Steel Community and the European Atomic Energy Community;

(b) the third subparagraph of Article K.3(2)(c);

(c) Articles L to S.

Article M

Subject to the provisions amending the Treaty establishing the European Economic Community with a view to establishing the European Community, the Treaty establishing the European Coal and Steel Community and the Treaty establishing the European Atomic Energy Community, and to these final provisions, nothing in this Treaty shall affect the Treaties establishing the European Communities or the subsequent Treaties and Acts modifying or supplementing them.

Article N

1. The government of any Member State of the Commission may submit to the Council proposals for the amendment of the Treaties on which the Union is founded.

If the Council, after consulting the European Parliament and, where appropriate, the Commission, delivers an opinion in favour of calling a conference of representatives of the governments of the Member States, the conference shall be convened by the President of the Council for the purpose of determining by common accord the amendments to be made to those Treaties. The European Central Bank shall also be consulted in the case of institutional changes in the monetary area.

The amendments shall enter into force after being ratified by all the Member States in accordance with their respective constitutional requirements.

2. A conference of representatives of the government of the Member States shall be convened in 1996 to examine those provisions of this Treaty for which revision is provided, in accordance with the objectives set out in Articles A and B.

Article O

Any European State may apply to become a Member of the Union. It shall address its application to the Council, which shall act unanimously after consulting the Commission and after receiving the assent of the European Parliament, which shall act by an absolute majority of its component members.

The conditions of admission and the adjustments to the Treaties on which the Union is founded which such admission entails shall be subject of an agreement between the Member States and the applicant State. This agreement shall be submitted for ratification by all the contracting States in accordance with their respective constitutional requirements.

Article P

1. Articles 2 to 7 and 10 to 19 of the Treaty establishing a Single Council and a Single Commission of the European Communities, signed in Brussels on 8 April 1965, are hereby repealed.

2. Article 2, Article 3(2) and Title III of the Single European Act signed in Luxembourg on 17 February 1986 and in The Hague on 28 February 1986 are hereby repealed.

Article Q

This Treaty is concluded for an unlimited period.

Article R

1. This Treaty shall be ratified by the High Contracting Parties in accordance with their respective constitutional requirements. The instruments of ratification shall be deposited with the government of the Italian Republic.

2. This Treaty shall enter into force on 1 January 1993, provided that all the instruments of ratification have been deposited or, failing that, on the first day of the month following the deposit of the instrument of ratification by the last signatory State to take this step.

Article S

This Treaty, drawn up in a single original in the Danish, Dutch, English, French, German, Greek, Irish, Italian, Portuguese and Spanish languages, the texts in each of these languages being equally authentic, shall be deposited in the archives of the government of the Italian Republic, which will transmit a certified copy to each of the governments of the signatory States.

In witness whereof the undersigned plenipotentiaries have signed this Treaty.

Done at Maastricht on the seventh day of February in the year one thousand nine hundred and ninety-two.

[List omitted].

PROTOCOLS

Protocol on the acquisition of property in Denmark

The High Contracting Parties,

Desiring to settle certain particular problems relating to Denmark,

Have agreed upon the following provision, which shall be annexed to the Treaty establishing the European Community:

Notwithstanding the provisions of this Treaty, Denmark may maintain the existing legislation on the acquisition of second homes.

Protocol concerning Article 119 of the Treaty establishing the European Community

The High Contracting Parties,

Have agreed upon the following provision, which shall be annexed to the Treaty establishing the European Community:

For the purposes of Article 119 of this Treaty, benefits under occupational social security schemes shall not be considered as remuneration if and in so far as they are attributable to periods of employment prior to 17 May 1990, except in the case of workers or those claiming under them who have before that date initiated legal proceedings or introduced an equivalent claim under the applicable national law.

Protocol on the Statute of the European System of Central Banks and of the European Central Bank

The High Contracting Parties,

Desiring to lay down the Statute of the European System of Central Banks and of the European Central Bank provided for in Article 4a of the Treaty establishing the European Community,

Have agreed upon the following provisions, which shall be annexed to the Treaty establishing the European Community:

Chapter I

Constitution of the ESCB

Article 1

The European System of Central Banks

1.1. The European System of Central Banks (ESCB) and the European Central Bank (ECB) shall be established in accordance with Article 4a of this Treaty; they shall perform their tasks and carry on their activities in accordance with the provisions of this Treaty and of this Statute.

1.2. In accordance with Article 106(1) of this Treaty, the ESCB shall be composed of the ECB and of the central banks of the Member States ('national central banks'). The Institut monétaire luxembourgeois will be the central bank of Luxembourg.

Chapter II

Objectives and tasks of the ESCB

Article 2

Objectives

In accordance with Article 105(1) of this Treaty, the primary objective of the ESCB shall be to maintain price stability. Without prejudice to the objective of price stability, it shall support the general economic policies in the Community with a view to contributing to the achievement of the objectives of the Community as laid down in Article 2 of this Treaty. The ESCB shall act in accordance with the principle of an open market economy with free competition, favouring an efficient allocation of resources, and in compliance with the principles set out in Article 3a of this Treaty.

Article 3

Tasks

3.1. In accordance with Article 105(2) of this Treaty, the basic tasks to be carried out through the ESCB shall be:

– to define and implement the monetary policy of the Community;

– to conduct foreign-exchange operations consistent with the provisions of Article 109 of this Treaty;

– to hold and manage the official foreign reserves of the Member States;

– to promote the smooth operation of payment systems.

3.2. In accordance with Article 105(3) of this Treaty, the third indent of Article 3.1 shall be without prejudice to the holding and management by the governments of Member States of foreign-exchange working balances.

3.3. In accordance with Article 105(5) of this Treaty, the ESCB shall contribute to the smooth conduct of policies pursued by the competent authorities relating to the prudential supervision of credit institutions and the stability of the financial system.

Article 4

Advisory functions

In accordance with Article 105(4) of this Treaty:

(*a*) the ECB shall be consulted:

- – on any proposed Community act in its fields of competence;
- – by national authorities regarding any draft legislative provision in its fields of competence, but within the limits and under the conditions set out by the Council in accordance with the procedure laid down in Article 42;

(*b*) the ECB may submit opinions to the appropriate Community institutions or bodies or to national authorities on matters in its fields of competence.

Article 5

Collection of statistical information

5.1. In order to undertake the tasks of the ESCB, the ECB, assisted by the national central banks, shall collect the necessary statistical information either from the competent national authorities or directly from economic agents. For these purposes it shall cooperate with the Community institutions or bodies and with the competent authorities of the Member States or third countries and with international organisations.

5.2. The national central banks shall carry out, to the extent possible, the tasks described in Article 5.1.

5.3. The ECB shall contribute to the harmonisation, where necessary, of the rules and practices governing the collection, compilation and distribution of statistics in the areas within its fields of competence.

5.4. The Council, in accordance with the procedure laid down in Article 42, shall define the natural and legal persons subject to reporting requirements, the confidentiality regime and the appropriate provisions for enforcement.

Article 6

International cooperation

6.1. In the field of international cooperation involving the tasks entrusted to the ESCB, the ECB shall decide how the ESCB shall be represented.

6.2. The ECB and, subject to its approval, the national central banks may participate in international monetary institutions.

6.3. Articles 6.1 and 6.2 shall be without prejudice to Article 109(4) of this Treaty.

Chapter III

Organisation of the ESCB

Article 7

Independence

In accordance with Article 107 of this Treaty, when exercising the powers and carrying out the tasks and duties conferred upon them by this Treaty and this Statute, neither the ECB, nor a national central bank, nor any member of their decision-making bodies shall seek or take instructions from Community institutions or bodies, from any government of a Member State or from any other body. The Community institutions and bodies and the governments of the Member States undertake to respect this principle and not to seek to of influence the members of the decision-making bodies of the ECB or of the national central banks in the performance of their tasks.

Article 8

General principle

The ESCB shall be governed by the decision-making bodies of the ECB.

Article 9

The European Central Bank

9.1. The ECB which, in accordance with Article 106(2) of this Treaty, shall have legal personality, shall enjoy in each of the Member States the most extensive legal capacity accorded to legal persons under its law; it may, in particular, acquire or dispose of movable and immovable property and may be a party to legal proceedings.

9.2. The ECB shall ensure that the tasks conferred upon the ESCB under Article 105(2),(3) and (5) of this Treaty are implemented either by its own activities pursuant to this Statute or through the national central banks pursuant to Articles 12.1 and 14.

9.3. In accordance with Article 106(3) of this Treaty, the decision-making bodies of the ECB shall be the Governing Council and the Executive Board.

Article 10

The Governing Council

10.1. In accordance with Article 109a(1) of this Treaty, the Governing Council shall comprise the members of the Executive Board of the ECB and the Governors of the national central banks.

10.2. Subject to Article 10.3, only members of the Governing Council present in person shall have the right to vote. By way of derogation from this rule, the Rules of Procedure referred to in Article 12.3 may lay down that members of the Governing Council may cast their vote by means of teleconferencing. These rules shall also provide that a member of the Governing Council who is prevented from voting for a prolonged period may appoint an alternate as a member of the Governing Council.

Subject to Articles 10.3 and 11.3, each member of the Governing Council shall have one vote. Save as otherwise provided for in this Statute, the Governing Council shall act by a simple majority. In the event of a tie, the President shall have the casting vote.

In order for the Governing Council to vote, there shall be a quorum of two-thirds of the members. If the quorum is not met, the President may convene an extraordinary meeting at which decisions may be taken without regard to the quorum.

10.3. For any decisions to be taken under Articles 28, 29, 30, 32, 33 and 51, the votes in the Governing Council shall be weighted according to the national central banks' shares in the subscribed capital of the ECB. The weights of the votes of the members of the Executive Board shall be zero. A decision requiring a qualified majority shall be adopted if the votes cast in favour represent at least two-thirds of the subscribed capital of the ECB and represent at least half of the shareholders. If a Governor is unable to be present, he may nominate an alternate to cast his weighted vote.

10.4. The proceedings of the meetings shall be confidential. The Governing Council may decide to make the outcome of its deliberations public.

10.5. The Governing Council shall meet at least 10 times a year.

Article 11

The Executive Board

11.1. In accordance with Article 109a(2)(a) of this Treaty, the Executive Board shall comprise the President, the Vice-President and four other members.

The members shall perform their duties on a full-time basis. No member shall engage in any occupation, whether gainful or not, unless exemption is exceptionally granted by the Governing Council.

11.2. In accordance with Article l09a(2)(b) of this Treaty, the President, the Vice-President and the other Members of the Executive Board shall be appointed from among persons of recognised standing and professional experience in monetary or banking matters by common accord of the governments of the Member States at the level of the Heads of State or Government, on a recommendation from the Council after it has consulted the European Parliament and the Governing Council.

Their term of office shall be eight years and shall not be renewable.

Only nationals of Member States may be members of the Executive Board.

11.3. The terms and conditions of employment of the members of the Executive Board, in particular their salaries, pensions and other social security benefits shall be the subject of contracts with the ECB and shall be fixed by the Governing Council on a proposal from a Committee comprising three members appointed by the Governing Council and three members appointed by the Council. The members of the Executive Board shall not have the right to vote on matters referred to in this paragraph.

11.4. If a member of the Executive Board no longer fulfils the conditions required for the performance of his duties or if he has been guilty of serious misconduct, the Court of Justice may, on application by the Governing Council or the Executive Board, compulsorily retire him.

11.5. Each member of the Executive Board present in person shall have the right to vote and shall have, for that purpose, one vote. Save as otherwise provided, the Executive Board shall act by a simple majority of the votes cast. In the event of a tie, the President shall have the casting vote. The voting arrangements shall be specified in the Rules of Procedure referred to in Article 12.3.

11.6. The Executive Board shall be responsible for the current business of the ECB.

11.7. Any vacancy on the Executive Board shall be filled by the appointment of a new member in accordance with Article 11.2.

Article 12

Responsibilities of the decision-making bodies

12.1. The Governing Council shall adopt the guidelines and make the decisions necessary to ensure the performance of the tasks entrusted to the ESCB under this Treaty and this Statute. The Governing Council shall formulate the monetary policy of the Community including, as appropriate, decisions relating to intermediate monetary objectives, key interest rates and the supply of reserves in the ESCB, and shall establish the necessary guidelines for their implementation.

The Executive Board shall implement monetary policy in accordance with the guidelines and decisions laid down by the Governing Council. In doing so the Executive Board shall give the necessary instructions to national central banks. In addition the Executive Board may have certain powers delegated to it where the Governing Council so decides.

To the extent deemed possible and appropriate and without prejudice to the provisions of this Article, the ECB shall have recourse to the national central banks to carry out operations which form part of the tasks of the ESCB.

12.2. The Executive Board shall have responsibility for the preparation of meetings of the Governing Council.

12.3. The Governing Council shall adopt the Rules of Procedure which determine the internal organisation of the ECB and its decision-making bodies.

12.4. The Governing Council shall exercise the advisory functions referred to in Article 4.

12.5. The Governing Council shall take the decisions referred to in Article 6.

Article 13

The President

13.1. The President or, in his absence, the Vice-President shall chair the Governing Council and the Executive Board of the ECB.

13.2. Without prejudice to Article 39, the President or his nominee shall represent the ECB externally.

Article 14

National central banks

14.1. In accordance with Article 108 of this Treaty, each Member State shall ensure, at the latest at the date of the establishment of the ESCB, that its national legislation, including the statutes of its national central bank, is compatible with this Treaty and this Statute.

14.2. The statutes of the national central banks shall, in particular, provide that the term of office of a Governor of a national central bank shall be no less than five years.

A Governor may be relieved from office only if he no longer fulfils the conditions required for the performance of his duties or if he has been guilty of serious misconduct. A decision to this effect may be referred to the Court of Justice by the Governor concerned or the Governing Council on grounds of infringement of this Treaty or of any rule of law relating to its application. Such proceedings shall be instituted within two months of the publication of the decision or of its notification to the plaintiff or, in the absence thereof, of the day on which it came to the knowledge of the latter, as the case may be.

14.3. The national central banks are an integral part of the ESCB and shall act in accordance with the guidelines and instructions of the ECB. The Governing Council shall take the necessary steps to ensure compliance with the guidelines and instructions of the ECB, and shall require that any necessary information be given to it.

14.4. National central banks may perform functions other than those specified in this Statute unless the Governing Council finds, by a majority of two thirds of the votes cast, that these interfere with the objectives and tasks of the ESCB. Such functions shall be performed on the responsibility and liability of national central banks and shall not be regarded as being part of the functions of the ESCB.

Article 15

Reporting commitments

15.1. The ECB shall draw up and publish reports on the activities of the ESCB at least quarterly.

15.2. A consolidated financial statement of the ESCB shall be published each week.

15.3. In accordance with Article 109b(3) of this Treaty, the ECB shall address an annual report on the activities of the ESCB and on the monetary policy of both the previous and the current year to the European Parliament, the Council and the Commission, and also to the European Council.

15.4. The reports and statements referred to in this Article shall be made available to interested parties free of charge.

Article 16

Banknotes

In accordance with Article 105a(1) of this Treaty, the Governing Council shall have the exclusive right to authorise the issue of banknotes within the Community. The ECB and the national central banks may issue such notes. The banknotes issued by the ECB and national central banks shall be the only such notes to have the status of legal tender within the Community.

The ECB shall respect as far as possible existing practices regarding the issue and design of banknotes.

Chapter IV

Monetary functions and operations of the ESCB

Article 17

Accounts with the ECB and the national central banks

In order to conduct their operations, the ECB and the national central banks may open accounts for credit institutions, public entities and other market participants and accept assets, including book-entry securities, as collateral.

Article 18

Open market and credit operations

18.1. In order to achieve the objectives of the ESCB and to carry out its tasks, the ECB and the national central banks may:

-   operate in the financial markets by buying and selling outright (spot and forward) or under repurchase agreements and by lending or borrowing claims and marketable instruments, whether in Community or in non-Community currencies, as well as precious metals;

– conduct credit operations with credit instructions and other market participants with lending being based on adequate collateral.

18.2. The ECB shall establish general principles for open market and credit operations carried out by itself or the national central banks, including for the announcement of conditions under which they stand ready to enter into such transactions.

Article 19

Minimum reserves

19.1. Subject to Article 2, the ECB may require credit institutions established in Member States to hold minimum reserves on accounts with the ECB and national central banks in pursuance of monetary policy objectives. Regulations concerning the calculation and determination of the required minimum reserves may be established by the Governing Council. In cases of non-compliance the ECB shall be entitled to levy penalty interest and to impose other sanctions with comparable effect.

19.2. For the application of this Article, the Council shall, in accordance with the procedure laid down in Article 42, define the basis for minimum reserves and the maximum permissible ratios between those reserves and their basis, as well as the appropriate sanctions in cases of non-compliance.

Article 20

Other instruments of monetary control

The Governing Council may, by the majority of two-thirds of the votes cast, decide upon the use of such other operational methods of monetary control as it sees fit, respecting Article 2.

The Council shall, in accordance with the procedure laid down in Article 42, define the scope of such methods if they impose obligations on third parties.

Article 21

Operations with public entities

21.1. In accordance with Article 104 of this Treaty, overdrafts or any other type of credit facility with the ECB or with the national central banks in favour of Community institutions or bodies, central governments, regional, local or other public authorities, other bodies governed by public law, or public undertaking of Member States shall be prohibited, as shall the purchase directly from them by the ECB or national central banks of debt instruments.

21.2. The ECB and national central banks may act as fiscal agents for the entities referred to in Article 21.1.

21.3. The provisions of this Article shall not apply to publicly-owned credit institutions which, in the context of the supply of reserves by central banks, shall be given the same treatment by national central banks and the ECB as private credit institutions.

Article 22

Clearing and payment systems

The ECB and national central banks may provide facilities, and the ECB may make regulations, to ensure efficient and sound clearing and payment systems within the Community and with other countries.

Article 23

External operations

The ECB and national central banks may:

- establish relations with central banks and financial institutions in other countries and, where appropriate, with international organisations;

- acquire and sell spot and forward all types of foreign exchange assets and precious metals; the term 'foreign exchange asset' shall include securities and all other assets in the currency of any country or units of account and in whatever form held;

- hold and manage the assets referred to in this Article;

- conduct all types of banking transactions in relations with third countries and international organisations, including borrowing and lending operations.

Article 24

Other operations

In addition to operations arising from their tasks, the ECB and national central banks may enter into operations for their administrative purposes or for their staff.

Chapter V

Prudential supervision

Article 25

Prudential supervision

25.1. The ECB may offer advice to and be consulted by the Council, the Commission and the competent authorities of the Member States on the scope and implementation of Community legislation relating to the prudential supervision of credit institutions and to the stability of the financial system.

25.5. In accordance with any decision of the Council under Article 105(6) of this Treaty, the ECB may perform specific tasks concerning policies relating to the prudential supervision of credit institutions and other financial institutions with the exception of insurance undertakings.

Chapter VI

Financial provisions of the ESCB

Article 26

Financial accounts

26.1. The financial year of the ECB and national central banks shall begin on the first day of January and end on the last day of December.

26.2. The annual accounts of the ECB shall be drawn up by the Executive Board, in accordance with the principles established by the Governing Council. The accounts shall be approved by the Governing Council and shall thereafter be published.

26.3. For analytical and operational purposes, the Executive Board shall draw up a consolidated balance sheet of the ESCB, comprising those assets and liabilities of the national central banks that fall within the ESCB.

26.4. For the application of this Article, the Governing Council shall establish the necessary rules for standardising the accounting and reporting of operations undertaken by the national central banks.

Article 27

Auditing

27.1. The accounts of the ECB and national central banks shall be audited by independent external auditors recommended by the Governing Council and approved by the Council. The auditors shall have full power to examine all books and accounts of the ECB and national central banks and obtain full information about their transactions.

27.2. The provisions of Article 188c of this Treaty shall only apply to an examination of the operational efficiency of the management of the ECB.

Article 28

Capital of the ECB

28.1. The capital of the ECB, which shall become operational upon its establishment, shall be ECU 5000 million. The capital may be increased by such amounts as may be decided by the Governing Council acting by the qualified majority provided for in Article 10.3, within the limits and under the conditions set by the Council under the procedure laid down in Article 42.

28.2. The national central banks shall be the sole subscribers to and holders of the capital of the ECB. The subscription of capital shall be according to the key established in accordance with Article 29.

28.3. The Governing Council, acting by the qualified majority provided for in Article 10.3, shall determine the extent to which and the form in which the capital shall be paid up.

28.4. Subject to Article 28.5, the shares of the national central banks in the subscribed capital of the ECB may not be transferred, pledged or attached.

28.5. If the key referred to in Article 29 is adjusted, the national central banks shall transfer among themselves capital shares to the extent necessary to ensure that the distribution of capital shares corresponds to the adjusted key. The Governing Council shall determine the terms and conditions of such transfers.

Article 29

Key for capital subscription

29.1. When in accordance with the procedure referred to in Article 1091(*l*) of this Treaty the ESCB and the ECB have been established, the key for subscription of the ECB's capital shall be established. Each national central bank shall be assigned a weighting in this key which shall be equal to the sum of:

−   50% of the share of its respective Member State in the population of the Community in the penultimate year preceding the establishment of the ESCB;

−   50% of the share of its respective Member State in the gross domestic product at market prices of the Community as recorded in the last five years preceding the penultimate year before the establishment of the ESCB;

The percentages shall be rounded up to the nearest multiple of 0.05 percentage points.

29.2. The statistical data to be used for the application of this Article shall be provided by the Commission in accordance with the rules adopted by the Council under the procedure provided for in Article 42.

29.3. The weightings assigned to the national central banks shall be adjusted every five years after the establishment of the ESCB by analogy with the provisions laid down in Article 29.1. The adjusted key shall apply with effect from the first day of the following year.

29.4. The Governing Council shall take all other measures necessary for the application of this Article.

Article 30

Transfer of foreign reserve assets to the ECB

30.1. Without prejudice to Article 28, the ECB shall be provided by the national central banks with foreign reserve assets other than Member State's currencies, ECUs, IMF reserve positions and SDRs, up to the amount equivalent to ECU 50 000 million. The Governing Council shall decide upon the proportion to be called up by the ECB following its establishment and the amounts called up at later dates. The ECB shall have the full right to hold and manage the foreign reserves that are transferred to it and to use them for the purposes set out in this Statute.

30.2. The contributions of each national central bank shall be fixed in proportion to its share in the subscribed capital of the ECB.

30.3. Each national central bank shall be credited by the ECB with a claim equivalent to its contribution. The Governing Council shall determine the denomination and remuneration of such claims.

30.4. Further calls of foreign reserve assets beyond the limit set in

Article 30.1 may be effected by the ECB, in accordance with Article 30.2, within the limits and under the conditions set by the Council in accordance with the procedure laid down in Article 42.

30.5. The ECB may hold and manage IMF reserve positions and SDRs and provide for the pooling of such assets.

30.6. The Governing Council shall take all other measures necessary for the application of this Article.

Article 31

Foreign reserve assets held by national central banks

31.1. The national central banks shall be allowed to perform transactions in fulfilment of their obligations towards international organisations in accordance with Article 23.

31.2. All other operations in foreign reserve assets remaining with the national central banks after the transfers referred to in Article 30, and Member States' transactions with their foreign exchange working balances shall, above a certain limit to be established within the framework of Article 31.3, be subject to approval by the ECB in order to ensure consistency with the exchange rate and monetary policies of the Community.

31.3. The Governing Council shall issue guidelines with a view to facilitating such operations.

Article 32

Allocation of monetary income of national central banks

32.1. The income accruing to the national central banks in the performance of the ESCB's monetary policy function (hereinafter referred to as 'monetary income') shall be allocated at the end of each financial year in accordance with the provisions of this Article.

32.2. Subject to Article 32.3, the amount of each national central bank's monetary income shall be equal to its annual income derived from its assets held against notes in circulation and deposit liabilities to credit institutions. These assets shall be earmarked by national central banks in accordance with guidelines to be established by the Governing Council.

32.3. If, after the start of the third stage, the balance sheet structures of the national central banks do not, in the judgment of the Governing Council, permit the application of Article 32.2, the Governing Council, acting by a qualified majority, may decide that, by way of derogation from Article 32.2, monetary income shall be measured according to an alternative method for a period of not more than five years.

32.4. The amount of each national central bank's monetary income shall be reduced by an amount equivalent to any interest paid by that central bank on its deposit liabilities to credit institutions in accordance with Article 19.

The Governing Council may decide that national central banks shall be indemnified against costs incurred in connection with the issue of banknotes or in exceptional circumstances for specific losses arising from monetary policy operations undertaken for the ESCB. Indemnification shall be in a form deemed appropriate in the judgment of the Governing Council; these amounts may be offset against the national central banks' monetary income.

32.5. The sum of the national central banks' monetary income shall be allocated to the national central banks in proportion to their paid-up shares in the capital of the ECB, subject to any decision taken by the Governing Council pursuant to Article 33.2.

32.6. The clearing and settlement of the balances arising from the allocation of monetary income shall be carried out by the ECB in accordance with guidelines established by the Governing Council.

32.7. The Governing Council shall take all other measures necessary for the application of this Article.

Article 33

Allocation of net profits and losses of the ECB

33.1. The net profit of the ECB shall be transferred in the following order:

(a) an amount to be determined by the Governing Council, which may not exceed 20% of the net profit, shall be transferred to the general reserve fund subject to a limit equal to 100% of the capital;

(b) the remaining net profit shall be distributed to the shareholders of the ECB in proportion to their paid-up shares.

33.2. In the event of a loss incurred by the ECB, the shortfall may be offset against the general reserve fund of the ECB and, if necessary, following a decision by the Governing Council, against the monetary income of the relevant financial year in proportion and up to the amounts allocated to the national central banks in accordance with Article 32.5.

Chapter VII

General provisions

Article 34

Legal acts

34.1. In accordance with Article 108a of this Treaty, the ECB shall:

– make regulations to the extent necessary to implement the tasks
  defined in Article 3.1, first indent, Articles 19.1, 22 or 25.2 and in
  cases which shall be laid down in the acts of the Council referred to
  in Article 42;

– take decisions necessary for carrying out the tasks entrusted to the
  ESCB under this Treaty and this Statute;

– make recommendations and deliver opinions.

34.2. A regulation shall have general application. It shall be binding in
its entirety and directly applicable in all Member States.

Recommendations and opinions shall have no binding force.

A decision shall be binding in its entirety upon those to whom it is
addressed.

Articles 190 to 192 of this Treaty shall apply to regulations and decisions
adopted by the ECB.

The ECB may decide to publish its decisions, recommendations and
opinions.

34.3. Within the limits and under the conditions adopted by the Council
under the procedure laid down in Article 42, the ECB shall be entitled to
impose fines or periodic penalty payments on undertakings for failure to
comply with obligations under its regulations and decisions.

Article 35

Judicial control and related matters

35.1. The acts or omissions of the ECB shall be open to review or
interpretation by the Court of Justice in the cases and under the
conditions laid down in this Treaty. The ECB may institute proceedings in
the cases and under the conditions laid down in this Treaty.

35.2. Disputes between the ECB, on the one hand, and its creditors,
debtors or any other person, on the other, shall be decided by the

competent national courts, save where jurisdiction has been conferred upon the Court of Justice.

35.3. The ECB shall be subject to the liability regime provided for in Article 215 of this Treaty. The national central banks shall be liable according to their respective national laws.

35.4. The Court of Justice shall have jurisdiction to give judgment pursuant to any arbitration clause contained in a contract concluded by or on behalf of the ECB, whether that contract be governed by public or private law.

35.5. A decision of the ECB to bring an action before the Court of Justice shall be taken by the Governing Council.

35.6. The Court of Justice shall have jurisdiction in disputes concerning the fulfilment by a national central bank of obligations under this Statute. If the ECB considers that a national central bank has failed to fulfil an obligation under this Statute, it shall deliver a reasoned opinion on the matter after giving the national central bank concerned the opportunity to submit its observations. If the national central bank concerned does not comply with the opinion within the period laid down by the ECB, the latter may bring the matter before the Court of Justice.

Article 36

Staff

36.1. The Governing Council, on a proposal from the Executive Board, shall lay down the conditions of employment of the staff of the ECB.

36.2. The Court of Justice shall have jurisdiction in any dispute between the ECB and its servants within the limits and under the conditions laid down in the conditions of employment.

Article 37

Seat

Before the end of 1992, the decision as to where the seat of the ECB will be established shall be taken by common accord of the governments of the Member States at the level of Heads of State or Government.

Article 38

Professional secrecy

38.1. Members of the governing bodies and the staff of the ECB and the national central banks shall be required, even after their duties have ceased, not to disclose information of the kind covered by the obligation of professional secrecy.

38.2. Persons having access to data covered by Community legislation imposing an obligation of secrecy shall be subject to such legislation.

Article 39

Signatories

The ECB shall be legally committed to third parties by the President or by two members of the Executive Board or by the signatures of two members of the staff of the ECB who have been duly authorised by the President to sign on behalf of the ECB.

Article 40

Privileges and immunities

The ECB shall enjoy in the territories of the Member States such privileges and immunities as are necessary for the performance of its tasks, under the conditions laid down in the Protocol on the Privileges and Immunities of the European Communities annexed to the Treaty establishing a Single Council and a Single Commission of the European Communities.

Chapter VIII

Amendment of the Statute and Complementary Legislation

Article 41

Simplified amendment procedure

41.1. In accordance with Article 106(5) of this Treaty, Articles 5.1, 5.2, 5.3, 17, 18, 19.1, 22, 23, 24, 26, 32.2, 32.3, 32.4, 32.6, 33.1(a) and 36 of this Statute may be amended by the Council, acting either by a qualified majority on a recommendation from the ECB and after consulting the Commission, or unanimously on a proposal from the Commission and after consulting the ECB. In either case the assent of the European Parliament shall be required.

41.2. A recommendation made by the ECB under this Article shall require a unanimous decision by the Governing Council.

Article 42

Complementary legislation

In accordance with Article 106(6) of this Treaty, immediately after the decision on the date for the beginning of the third stage, the Council, acting by qualified majority either on a proposal from the Commission and after consulting the European Parliament and the ECB or on a recommendation from the ECB and after consulting the European Parliament and the Commission, shall adopt the provisions referred to in Articles 4, 5.4, 19.2, 20, 28.1, 29.2, 30.4 and 34.3 of this Statute.

Chapter IX

Transitional and other provision for the ESCB

Article 43

General provisions

43.1. A derogation as referred to in Article 109k(1) of this Treaty shall entail that the following Articles of this Statute shall not confer any rights or impose any obligations on the Member State concerned: 3, 6, 9.2, 12.1, 14.3, 16, 18, 19, 20, 22, 23, 26.2, 27, 30, 31, 32, 33, 34, 50 and 52.

43.2. The central banks of Members States with a derogation as specified in Article 109k(1) of this Treaty shall retain their powers in the field of monetary policy according to national law.

43.3. In accordance with Article 109k(4) of this Treaty, 'Member States' shall be read as 'Member States without a derogation' in the following Articles of this Statute: 3, 11.2, 19, 34.2 and 50.

43.4. 'National central banks' shall be read as 'central banks of Member States without a derogation' in the following Articles of this Statute: 9.2, 10.1, 10.3, 12.1, 16, 17, 18, 22, 23, 27, 30, 31, 32, 33.2 and 52.

43.5. 'Shareholders' shall be read as 'central banks of Member States without a derogation' in Articles 10.3 and 33.1.

43.6. 'Subscribed capital of the ECB' shall be read as 'capital of the ECB subscribed by the central banks of Member States without a derogation' in Articles 10.3 and 30.2.

Article 44

Transitional tasks of the ECB

The ECB shall take over those tasks of the EMI which, because of the derogations of one or more Member States, still have to be performed in the third stage.

The ECB shall give advice in the preparations for the abrogation of the derogations specified in Article 109k of this Treaty.

Article 45

The General Council of the ECB

45.1. Without prejudice to Article 106(3) of this Treaty, the General Council shall be constituted as a third decision-making body of the ECB.

45.2. The General Council shall comprise the President and Vice-President of the ECB and the Governors of the national central banks. The other members of the Executive Board may participate, without having the right to vote, in meetings of the General Council.

45.3. The responsibilities of the General Council are listed in full in Article 47 of this Statute.

Article 46

Rules of procedure of the General Council

46.1. The President or, in his absence, the Vice-President of the ECB shall chair the General Council of the ECB.

46.2. The President of the Council and a member of the Commission may participate, without having the right to vote, in meetings of the General Council.

46.3. The President shall prepare the meetings of the General Council.

46.4. By way of derogation from Article 12.3, the General Council shall adopt its Rules of Procedure.

46.5. The Secretariat of the General Council shall be provided by the ECB.

Article 47

Responsibilities of the General Council

47.1. The General Council shall:

–   perform the tasks referred to in Article 44;

– contribute to the advisory functions referred to in Articles 4 and 25.1.

47.2. The General Council shall contribute to:

– the collection of statistical information as referred to in Article 5;

– the reporting activities of the ECB as referred to in Article 15;

– the establishment of the necessary rules for the application of Article 26 as referred to in Article 26.4;

– the taking of all other measures necessary for the application of Article 29 as referred to in Article 29.4;

– the laying down of the conditions of employment of the staff of the ECB as referred to in Article 36.

47.3. The General Council shall contribute to the necessary preparations for irrevocably fixing the exchange rates of the currencies of Member States with a derogation against the currencies, or the single currency, of the Member States without a derogation, as referred to in Article 109*l*(5) of this Treaty.

47.4. The General Council shall be informed by the President of the ECB of decisions of the Governing Council.

Article 48

Transitional provisions for the capital of the ECB

In accordance with Article 29.1 each national central bank shall be assigned a weighting in the key for subscription the ECB's capital. By way of derogation from Article 28.3, central banks of Member States with a derogation shall not pay up their subscribed capital unless the General Council, acting by a majority representing at least two-thirds of the subscribed capital of the ECB and at least half of the shareholders, decides that a minimal percentage has to be paid up as a contribution to the operational costs of the ECB.

Article 49

Deferred payment of capital, reserves and provisions of the ECB

49.1. The central bank of a Member State whose derogation has been abrogated shall pay up its subscribed share of the capital of the ECB to the same extent as the central banks of other Member States without a derogation, and shall transfer to the ECB foreign reserve assets in accordance with Article 30.1. The sum to be transferred shall be determined by multiplying the ECU value at current exchange rates of the foreign reserve assets which have already been transferred to the ECB in accordance with Article 30.1, by the ratio between the number of shares subscribed by the national central bank concerned and the number of shares already paid up by the other national central banks.

49.2. In addition to the payment to be made in accordance with Article 49.1, the central bank concerned shall contribute to the reserves of the ECB, to those provisions equivalent to reserves, and to the amount still to be appropriated to the reserves and provisions corresponding to the balance of the profit and loss account as at 31 December of the year prior to the abrogation of the derogation. The sum to be contributed shall be determined by multiplying the amount of the reserves, as defined above and as stated in the approved balance sheet of the ECB, by the ratio between the number of shares subscribed by the central bank concerned and the number of shares already paid up by the other central banks.

Article 50

Initial appointment of the members of the Executive Board

When the Executive Board of the ECB is being established, the President, the Vice-President and the other members of the Executive Board shall be appointed by common accord of the governments of the Member States at the level of Heads of State or Government, on a recommendation from the Council and after consulting the European Parliament and the Council of the EMI. The President of the Executive Board shall be appointed for eight years. By way of derogation from Article 11.2, the Vice-President shall be appointed for four years and the other members of the Executive Board for terms of office of between five and eight years. No term of office shall be renewable. The number of members of the Executive Board may be smaller than provided for in Article 11.1, but in no circumstance shall it be less than four.

Article 51

Derogation from Article 32

51.1. If, after the start of the third stage, the Governing Council decides that the application of Article 32 results in significant changes in national central banks' relative income positions, the amount of income to be allocated pursuant to Article 32 shall be reduced by a uniform percentage which shall not exceed 60% in the first financial year after the start of the third stage and which shall decrease by at least 12 percentage points in each subsequent financial year.

51.2. Article 51.1 shall be applicable for not more than five financial years after the start of the third stage.

Article 52

Exchange of banknotes in Community currencies

Following the irrevocable fixing of exchange rates, the Governing Council shall take the necessary measures to ensure that banknotes denominated in currencies with irrevocably fixed exchange rates are exchanged by the national central banks at their respective par values.

Article 53

Applicability of the transitional provisions

If and as long as there are Member States with a derogation Articles 43 to 48 shall be applicable.

Protocol on the Statute of the European Monetary Institute

The High Contracting Parties,

Desiring to lay down the Statute of the European Monetary Institute,

Have agreed upon the following provisions, which shall be annexed to the Treaty establishing the European Community:

Article 1

Constitution and name

1.1. The European Monetary Institute (EMI) shall be established in accordance with Article 109f of this Treaty; it shall perform its functions and carry out its activities in accordance with the provisions of this Treaty and of this Statute.

1.2. The members of the EMI shall be the central banks of the Member States ('national central banks'). For the purposes of this Statute, the Institut monétaire luxembourgeois shall be regarded as the central bank of Luxembourg.

1.3. Pursuant to Article 109f of this Treaty, both the Committee of Governors and the European Monetary Cooperation Fund (EMCF) shall be dissolved. All assets and liabilities of the EMCF shall pass automatically to the EMI.

Article 2

Objectives

The EMI shall contribute to the realisation of the conditions necessary for the transition to the third stage of economic and monetary union, in particular by:

-   strengthening the coordination of monetary policies with the view to ensuring price stability;

-   making the preparations required for the establishment of the European System of Central Banks (ESCB), and for the conduct of a single monetary policy and the creation of a single currency in the third stage;

-   overseeing the development of the ECU.

Article 3

General principles

3.1. The EMI shall carry out the tasks and functions conferred upon it by this Treaty and this Statute without prejudice to the responsibility of the competent authorities for the conduct of the monetary policy within the respective Member States.

3.2. The EMI shall act in accordance with the objectives and principles stated in Article 2 of the Statute of the ESCB.

Article 4

Primary tasks

4.1. In accordance with Article 109f(2) of this Treaty, the EMI shall:

-   strengthen cooperation between the national central banks;

-   strengthen the coordination of the monetary policies of the Member States with the aim of ensuring price stability;

-   monitor the functioning of the European Monetary System (EMS);

-   hold consultations concerning issues falling within the competence of the national central banks and affecting the stability of financial institutions and markets;

-   take over the tasks of the EMCF; in particular it shall perform the functions referred to in Articles 6.1, 6.2 and 6.3;

- facilitate the use of the ECU and oversee its development, including the smooth functioning of the ECU clearing system.

The EMI shall also:

- hold regular consultations concerning the course of monetary policies and the use of monetary policy instruments;

- normally be consulted by the national monetary authorities before they take decisions on the course of monetary policy in the context of the common framework for *ex ante* coordination.

4.2. At the latest by 31 December 1996, the EMI shall specify the regulatory, organisational and logistical framework necessary for the ESCB to perform its tasks in the third stage, in accordance with the principle of an open market economy with free competition. The framework shall be submitted by the Council of the EMI for decision to the ECB at the date of its establishment.

In accordance with Article 109f(3) of this Treaty, the EMI shall in particular:

- prepare the instruments and the procedures necessary for carrying out a single monetary policy in the third stage;

- promote the harmonisation, where necessary, of the rules and practices governing the collection, compilation and distribution of statistics in the areas within its field of competence;

- prepare the rules for operations to be undertaken by the national central banks in the framework of the ESCB;

- promote the efficiency of cross-border payments;

- supervise the technical preparation of ECU banknotes.

Article 5

Advisory functions

5.1. In accordance with Article 109f(4) of this Treaty, the Council of the EMI may formulate opinions or recommendations on the overall orientation of monetary policy and exchange-rate policy as well as on related measures introduced in each Member State. The EMS may submit opinions or recommendations to governments and to the Council on policies which might affect the internal or external monetary situation in the Community and, in particular, the functioning of the EMS.

5.2. The Council of the EMI may also make recommendations to the monetary authorities of the Member States concerning the conduct of their monetary policy.

5.3. In accordance with Article 109f(6) of this Treaty, the EMI shall be consulted by the Council regarding any proposed Community act within its field of competence.

Within the limits and under the conditions set out by the Council acting by a qualified majority on a proposal from the Commission and after consulting the European Parliament and the EMI, the EMI shall be consulted by the authorities of the Member States on any draft legislative provision within its field of competence in particular with regard to Article 4.2.

5.4. In accordance with Article 109f(5) of this Treaty, the EMI may decide to publish its opinions and its recommendations.

Article 6

Operational and technical functions

6.1. The EMI shall:

– provide for the multilateralisation of positions resulting from interventions by the national central banks in community currencies and the multilateralisation of intra-Community settlements;

– administer the very short-term financing mechanism provided for by the Agreement of 13 March 1979 between the central banks of the Member States of the European Economic Community laying down the operating procedures for the European Monetary System (hereinafter referred to as 'EMS Agreement') and the short-term monetary support mechanism provided for in the Agreement between the central banks of the Member States of the European Economic Community of 9 February 1970, as amended;

– perform the functions referred to in Article 11 of Council Regulation (EEC) No 1969/88 of 24 June 1988 establishing a single facility providing medium-term financial assistance for Member States' balances of payments.

6.2. The EMI may receive monetary reserves from the national central banks and issue ECUs against such assets for the purpose of implementing the EMS Agreement. These ECUs may be used by the EMI and the national central banks as a means of settlement and for transactions between them and the EMI. The EMI shall take the necessary administrative measures for the implementation of this paragraph.

6.3. The EMI may grant to the monetary authorities of third countries and to international monetary institutions the status of 'other holders' of ECUs and fix the terms and conditions under which such ECUs may be acquired, held or used by other holders.

6.4. The EMI shall be entitled to hold and manage foreign exchange reserves as an agent for and at the request of national central banks. Profits and losses regarding these reserves shall be for the account of the national central bank depositing the reserves. The EMI shall perform this function on the basis of bilateral contracts in accordance with rules laid down in a decision of the EMI. These rules shall ensure that transactions with these reserves shall not interfere with the monetary policy and exchange-rate policy of the competent monetary authority of any Member State and shall be consistent with the objectives of the EMI and the proper functioning of the exchange-rate mechanism of the EMS.

Article 7

Other tasks

7.1. Once a year the EMI shall address a report to the Council on the state of the preparations for the third stage. These reports shall include an assessment of the progress towards convergence in the Community, and cover in particular the adaptation of monetary policy instruments and the preparation of the procedures necessary for carrying out a single monetary policy in the third stage, as well as the statutory requirements to be fulfilled for national central banks to become an integral part of the ESCB.

7.2. In accordance with the Council decisions referred to in Article 109f(7) of this Treaty, the EMI may perform other tasks for the preparation of the third stage.

Article 8

Independence

The members of the Council of the EMI who are the representatives of their institutions shall, with respect to their activities, act according to their own responsibilities. In exercising the powers and performing the tasks and duties conferred upon them by this Treaty and this Statute, the Council of the EMI may not seek or take any instructions from Community institutions or bodies or governments of Member States. The Community institutions and bodies as well as the governments of the Member States undertake to respect this principle and not to seek to influence the Council of the EMI in the performance of its tasks.

Article 9

Administration

9.1. In accordance with Article 109f(1) of this Treaty, the EMI shall be directed and managed by the Council of the EMI.

9.2. The Council of the EMI shall consist of a President and the Governors of the national central banks, one of whom shall be Vice-President. If a Governor is prevented from attending a meeting, he may nominate another representative of his institution.

9.3. The President shall appoint by common accord of the governments of the Member States at the level of Heads of State or Government, on a recommendation from, as the case may be, the Committee of Governors or the Council of the EMI, and after consulting the European Parliament and the Council. The President shall be selected from among persons of recognised standing and professional experience in monetary or banking matters. Only nationals of Member States may be President of the EMI. The Council of the EMI shall appoint the Vice-President. The President and Vice-President shall be appointed for a period of three years.

9.4. The President shall perform his duties on a full-time basis. He shall not engage in any occupation, whether gainful or not, unless exemption is exceptionally granted by the Council of the EMI.

9.5. The President shall:

– prepare and chair the meetings of the Council of the EMI;

– without prejudice to Article 22, present the views of the EMI externally;

– be responsible for the day-to-day management of the EMI.

In the absence of the President, his duties shall be performed by the Vice-President.

9.6. The terms and conditions of employment of the President, in particular his salary, pension and other social security benefits, shall be the subject of a contract with the EMI and shall be fixed by the Council of the EMI on a proposal from a Committee comprising three members appointed by the Committee of Governors or the Council of the EMI, as the case may be, and three members appointed by the Council. The President shall not have the right to vote on matters referred to in this paragraph.

9.7. If the President no longer fulfils the condition required for the performance of his duties or if he has been guilty of serious misconduct, the Court of Justice may, on application by the Council of the EMI, compulsorily retire him.

9.8. The Rules of Procedure of the EMI shall be adopted by the Council of the EMI.

Article 10

Meetings of the Council of the EMI and voting procedures

10.1. The Council of the EMI shall meet at least 10 times a year. The proceedings of Council meetings shall be confidential. The Council of the EMI may, acting unanimously, decide to make the outcome of its deliberations public.

10.2. Each member of the Council of the EMI or his nominee shall have one vote.

10.3. Save as otherwise provided for in this Statute, the Council of the EMI shall act by a simple majority of its members.

10.4. Decisions to be taken in the context of Articles 4.2, 5.4, 6.2 and 6.3 shall require unanimity of the members of the Council of the EMI.

The adoption of opinions and recommendations under Articles 5.1 and 5.2, the adoption of decisions under Articles 6.4, 16 and 23.6 and the adoption of guidelines under Article 15.3 shall require a qualified majority of two thirds of the members of the Council of the EMI.

Article 11

Inter-institutional cooperation and reporting requirements

11.1. The President of the Council and a member of the Commission may participate, without having the right to vote, in meetings of the Council of the EMI.

11.2. The President of the EMI shall be invited to participate in Council meetings when the Council is discussing matters relating to the objectives and tasks of the EMI.

11.3. At a date to be established in the Rules of Procedure, the EMI shall prepare an annual report on its activities and on monetary and financial conditions in the Community. The annual report, together with the annual accounts of the EMI, shall be addressed to the European Parliament, the Council and the Commission and also to the European Council.

The President of the EMI may, at the request of the European Parliament or on his own initiative, be heard by the competent Committees of the European Parliament.

11.4. Reports published by the EMI shall be made available to interested parties free of charge.

Article 12

Currency denomination

The operations of the EMI shall be expressed in ECUs.

Article 13

Seat

Before the end of 1992, the decision as to where the seat of the EMI will be established shall be taken by common accord of the governments of the Member States at the level of Heads of State or Government

Article 14

Legal capacity

The EMI, which in accordance with Article 109f(1) of this Treaty, shall have legal personality, shall enjoy in each of the Member States the most extensive legal capacity accorded to legal persons under their law; it may, in particular, acquire or dispose of moveable or immovable property and may be a party to legal proceedings.

Article 15

Legal acts

15.1. In the performance of its tasks, and under the conditions laid down in this Statute, the EMI shall:

– deliver opinions;

– make recommendations;

– adopt guidelines, and take decisions, which shall be addressed to the national central banks.

15.2. Opinions and recommendations of the EMI shall have no binding force.

15.3. The Council of the EMI may adopt guidelines laying down the methods for the implementation of the conditions necessary for the

ESCB to perform its functions in the third stage. EMI guidelines shall have no binding force; they shall be submitted for decision to the ECB.

15.4. Without prejudice to Article 3.1, a decision of the EMI shall be binding in its entirety upon those to whom it is addressed. Articles 190 and 191 of this Treaty shall apply to these decisions.

Article 16

Financial resources

16.1. The EMI shall be endowed with its own resources. The size of the resources of the EMI shall be determined by the Council of the EMI with a view to ensuring the income deemed necessary to cover the administrative expenditure incurred in the performance of the tasks and functions of the EMI.

16.2. The resources of the EMI determined in accordance with Article 16.1 shall be provided out of contributions by the national central banks in accordance with the key referred to in Article 29.1 of the Statute of the ESCB and be paid up at the establishment of the EMI. For this purpose, the statistical data to be used for the determination of the key shall be provided by the Commission, in accordance with the rules adopted by the Council, acting by a qualified majority on a proposal from the Commission and after consulting the European Parliament, the Committee of Governors and the Committee referred to in Article 109c of this Treaty.

16.3. The Council of the EMI shall determine the form in which contributions shall be paid up.

Article 17

Annual accounts and auditing

17.1. The financial year of the EMI shall begin on the first day of January and end on the last day of December.

17.2. The Council of the EMI shall adopt an annual budget before the beginning of each financial year.

17.3. The annual accounts shall be drawn up in accordance with the principles established by the Council of the EMI. The annual accounts shall be approved by the Council of the EMI and shall thereafter be published.

17.4. The annual accounts shall be audited by independent external auditors approved by the Council of the EMI. The auditors shall have full power to examine all books and accounts of the EMI and to obtain full information about its transactions.

The provisions of Article 188c of this Treaty shall only apply to an examination of the operational efficiency of the management of the EMI.

17.5. Any surplus of the EMI shall be transferred in the following order:

(a) an amount to be determined by the Council of the EMI shall be transferred to the general reserve fund of the EMI;

(b) any remaining surplus shall be distributed to the national central banks in accordance with the key referred to in Article 16.2.

17.6. In the event of a loss incurred by the EMI, the shortfall shall be offset against the general reserve fund of the EMI. Any remaining shortfall shall be made good by contributions from the national central banks, in accordance with the key as referred to in Article 16.2.

Article 18

Staff

18.1. The Council of the EMI shall lay down the conditions of employment of the staff of the EMI.

18.2. The Court of Justice shall have jurisdiction in any dispute between the EMI and its servants within the limits and under the conditions laid down in the conditions of employment.

Article 19

Judicial control and related matters

19.1. The acts or omissions of the EMI shall be open to review or interpretation by the Court of Justice in the cases and under the conditions laid down in this Treaty. The EMI may institute proceedings in the cases and under the conditions laid down in this Treaty.

19.2. Disputes between the EMI, on the one hand, and its creditors, debtors or any other person, on the other, shall fall within the jurisdiction of the competent national courts, save where jurisdiction has been conferred upon the Court of Justice.

19.3. The EMI shall be subject to the liability regime provided for in Article 215 of this Treaty.

19.4. The Court of Justice shall have jurisdiction to give judgment pursuant to any arbitration clause contained in a contract concluded by or on behalf of the EMI, whether that contract be governed by public or private law.

19.5. A decision of the EMI to bring an action before the Court of Justice shall be taken by the Council of the EMI.

Article 20

Professional secrecy

20.1. Members of the Council of the EMI and the staff of the EMI shall be required, even after their duties have ceased, not to disclose information of the kind covered by the obligation of professional secrecy.

20.2. Persons having access to data covered by Community legislation imposing an obligation of secrecy shall be subject to such legislation.

Article 21

Privileges and immunities

The EMI shall enjoy in the territories of the Member States such privileges and immunities as are necessary for the performance of its tasks, under the conditions laid down in the Protocol on the Privileges and Immunities of the European Communities annexed to the Treaty establishing a Single Council and a Single Commission of the European Communities.

Article 22

Signatories

The EMI shall be legally committed to third parties by the President or the Vice-President or by the signatures of two members of the staff of the EMI who have been duly authorised by the President to sign on behalf of the EMI.

Article 23

Liquidation of the EMI

23.1. In accordance with Article 109*l* of this Treaty, the EMI shall go into liquidation on the establishment of the ECB. All assets and liabilities of the EMI shall then pass automatically to the ECB. The latter shall liquidate the EMI according to the provisions of this Article. The liquidation shall be completed by the beginning of the third stage.

23.2. The mechanism for the creation of ECUs against gold and US dollars as provided for by Article 17 of the EMS Agreement shall be unwound by the first day of the third stage in accordance with Article 20 of the said Agreement.

23.3. All claims and liabilities arising from the very short-term financing mechanism and the short-term monetary support mechanism, under the Agreements referred to in Article 6.1, shall be settled by the first day of the third stage.

23.4. All remaining assets of the EMI shall be disposed of and all remaining liabilities of the EMI shall be settled.

23.5. The proceeds of the liquidation described in Article 23.4 shall be distributed to the national central banks in accordance with the key referred to in Article 16.2.

23.6. The Council of the EMI may take the measures necessary for the application of Articles 23.4 and 23.5.

23.7. Upon the establishment of the ECB, the President of the EMI shall relinquish his office.

Protocol on the excessive deficit procedure

The High Contracting Parties,

Desiring to lay down the details of the excessive deficit procedure referred to in Article 104c of the Treaty establishing the European Community,

Have agreed upon the following provisions, which shall be annexed to the Treaty establishing the European Community:

Article 1

The reference values referred to in Article 104c(2) of this Treaty are:

– 3% for the ratio of the planned or actual government deficit to gross domestic product at market prices;

– 60% for the ratio of government debt to gross domestic product at market prices.

Article 2

In Article 104c of this Treaty and in this Protocol:

– government means general government, that is central government, regional or local government and social security funds, to the exclusion of commercial operations, as defined in the European System of Integrated Economic Accounts;

- deficit means net borrowing as defined in the European System of Integrated Economic Accounts;

- investment means gross fixed capital formation as defined in the European System of Integrated Economic Accounts;

- debt means total gross debt at nominal value outstanding at the end of the year and consolidated between and within the sectors of general government as defined in the first indent.

Article 3

In order to ensure the effectiveness of the excessive deficit procedure, the governments of the Member States shall be responsible under this procedure for the deficits of general government as defined in the first indent of Article 2. The Member States shall ensure that national procedures in the budgetary area enable them to meet their obligations in this area deriving from this Treaty. The Member States shall report their planned and actual deficits and the levels of their debt promptly and regularly to the Commission.

Article 4

The statistical data to be used for the application of this Protocol shall be provided by the Commission.

Protocol on the convergence criteria referred to in Article 109j of the Treaty establishing the European Community

The High Contracting Parties,

Desiring to lay down the details of the convergence criteria which shall guide the Community in taking decisions on the passage to the third stage of economic and monetary union, referred to in Article 109j(1) of this Treaty,

Have agreed upon the following provisions, which shall be annexed to the Treaty establishing the European Community:

Article 1

The criterion on price stability referred to in the first indent of Article 109j(1) of this Treaty shall mean that a Member State has a price performance that is sustainable and an average rate of inflation, observed over a period of one year before the examination, that does not exceed by more than 1½ percentage points that of, at most, the three best performing Member States in terms of price stability. Inflation shall be measured by means of the consumer price index on a comparable basis, taking into account differences in national definitions.

Article 2

The criterion on the government budgetary position referred to in the second indent of Article 109j(1) of this Treaty shall mean that at the time of the examination the Member State is not the subject of a Council decision under Article 104c(6) of this Treaty that an excessive deficit exists.

Article 3

The criterion on participation in the exchange-rate mechanism of the European Monetary System referred to in the third indent of Article 109j(1) of this Treaty shall mean that a Member State has respected the normal fluctuation margins provided for by the exchange-rate mechanism of the European Monetary System without severe tensions for at least the last two years before the examination. In particular, the Member State shall not have devalued its currency's bilateral central rate against any other Member State's currency on its own initiative for the same period.

Article 4

The criterion on the convergence of interest rates referred to in the fourth indent of Article 109j(1) of this Treaty shall mean that, observed over a period of one year before the examination, a Member State has had an average nominal long-term interest rate that does not exceed by more than two percentage points that of, at most, the three best performing Member States in terms of price stability. Interest rates shall be measured on the basis of long-term government bonds or comparable securities, taking into account differences in national definitions.

Article 5

The statistical data to be used for the application of this Protocol shall be provided by the Commission.

Article 6

The Council shall, acting unanimously on a proposal from the Commission and after consulting the European Parliament, the EMI or the ECB as the case may be, and the Committee referred to in Article 109c, adopt appropriate provisions to lay down the details of the convergence criteria referred to in Article 109j of this Treaty, which shall then replace this Protocol.

Protocol amending the Protocol on the Privileges and Immunities of the European Communities

The High Contracting Parties,

Considering that, in accordance with Article 40 of the Statute of the European System of Central Banks and of the European Central Bank and Article 21 of the Statute of the European Monetary Institute, the European Central Bank and the European Monetary Institute shall enjoy in the territories of the Member States such privileges and immunities as are necessary for the performance of their tasks,

Have agreed upon the following provisions, which shall be annexed to the Treaty establishing the European Community:

Sole Article

The Protocol on the Privileges and Immunities of the European Communities, annexed to the Treaty establishing a Single Council and a Single Commission of the European Communities, shall be supplemented by the following provisions:

'Article 23

This Protocol shall also apply to the European Central Bank, to the members of its organs and to its staff, without prejudice to the provisions of the Protocol on the Statute of the European System of Central Banks and the European Central Bank.

The European Central Bank shall, in addition, be exempt from any form of taxation or imposition of a like nature on the occasion of any increase in its capital and from the various formalities which may be connected therewith in the State where the Bank has its seat. The activities of the Bank and of its organs carried on in accordance with the Statute of the European System of Central Banks and of the European Central Bank shall not be subject to any turnover tax.

The above provisions shall also apply to the European Monetary Institute. Its dissolution or liquidation shall not give rise to any imposition.'

Protocol on Denmark

The High Contracting Parties,

Desiring to settle certain particular problems relating to Denmark,

Have agreed upon the following provisions, which shall be annexed to the Treaty establishing the European Community:

The provisions of Article 14 of the Protocol on the Statute of the European System of Central Banks and of the European Central Bank shall not affect the right of the National Bank of Denmark to carry out its existing tasks concerning those parts of the Kingdom of Denmark which are not part of the Community.

Protocol on Portugal

The High Contracting Parties,

Desiring to settle certain particular problems relating to Portugal,

Have agreed upon the following provisions, which shall be annexed to the Treaty establishing the European Community:

1. Portugal is hereby authorised to maintained the facility afforded to the Autonomous Regions of the Azores and Madeira to benefit from an interest-free credit facility with the Banco de Portugal under the terms established by existing Portuguese Law.

2. Portugal commits itself to pursue its best endeavours in order to put an end to the abovementioned facility as soon as possible.

Protocol on the transition to the third stage of Economic and Monetary Union

The High Contracting Parties,

Declare the irreversible character of the Community's movement to the third stage of economic and monetary union by signing the new Treaty provisions on the economic and monetary union.

Therefore all Member States shall, whether they fulfil the necessary conditions for the adoption of a single currency or not, respect the will for the Community to enter swiftly into the third stage, and therefore no Member State shall prevent the entering into the third stage.

If by the end of 1997 the date of the beginning of the third stage has not been set, the Member States concerned, the Community institutions and other bodies involved shall expedite all preparatory work during 1998, in order to enable the Community to enter the third stage irrevocably on 1 January 1999 and to enable the ECB and the ESCB to state their full functioning from this date.

This Protocol shall be annexed to the Treaty establishing the European Community.

Protocol on certain provisions relating to the United Kingdom of Great Britain and Northern Ireland

The High Contracting Parties,

Recognising that the United Kingdom shall not be obliged or committed to move to the third stage of economic and monetary union without a separate decision to do so by its government and Parliament,

Noting the practice of the government of the United Kingdom to fund its borrowing requirement by the sale of debt to the private sector,

Have agreed the following provisions, which shall be annexed to the Treaty establishing the European Community:

1. The United Kingdom shall notify the Council whether it intends to move to the third stage before the Council makes its assessment under Article 109j(2) of this Treaty.

Unless the United Kingdom notifies the Council that it intends to move to the third stage, it shall be under no obligation to do so.

If no date is set for the beginning of the third stage under Article 109j(3) of this Treaty, the United Kingdom may notify its intention to move to the third stage before 1 January 1998.

2. Paragraphs 3 to 9 shall have effect if the United Kingdom notifies the Council that it does not intend to move to the third stage.

3. The United Kingdom shall not be included among the majority of Member States which fulfil the necessary conditions referred to in the second indent of Article 109j(2) and the first indent of Article 109j(3) of this Treaty.

4. The United Kingdom shall retain its powers in the field of monetary policy according to national law.

5. Articles 3a(2), 104c(1), (9) and (11), 105(1) to (5), 105a, 107, 108, 108a, 109, 109a(1) and(2)(b) and 109l(4) and (5) of this Treaty shall not apply to the United Kingdom. In these provisions references to the Community or the Member States shall not include the United Kingdom and references to national central banks shall not include the Bank of England.

6. Articles 109e(4) and 109h and i of this Treaty shall continue to apply to the United Kingdom. Articles 109c(4) and 109m shall apply to the United Kingdom as if it had a derogation.

7. The voting rights of the United Kingdom shall be suspended in respect of acts of the Council referred to in the Articles listed in paragraph 5. For this purpose the weighted votes of the United Kingdom shall be excluded from any calculation of a qualified majority under Article 109k(5) of this Treaty.

The United Kingdom shall also have no right to participate in the appointment of the President, the Vice-President and the other members of the Executive Board of the ECB under Articles 109a(2)(b) and 109*l*(1) of this Treaty.

8. Articles 3, 4, 6, 7, 9.2, 10.1, 10.3, 11.2, 12.1, 14, 16, 18 to 20, 22, 23, 26, 27, 30 to 34, 50 and 52 of the Protocol on the Statute of the European System of Central Banks and of the European Central Bank ('the Statute') shall not apply to the United Kingdom.

In those Articles references to the Community or the Member States shall not include the United Kingdom and references to national central banks or shareholders shall not include the Bank of England.

References in Articles 10.3 and 30.2 of the Statute to 'subscribed capital of the ECB' shall not include capital subscribed by the Bank of England.

9. Article 109*l*(3) of this Treaty and Articles 44 to 48 of the Statute shall have effect, whether or not there is any Member State with a derogation, subject to the following amendments:

(*a*) References in Article 44 to the tasks of the ECB and the EMI shall include those tasks that still need to be performed in the third stage owing to any decision of the United Kingdom not to move to that stage.

(*b*) In addition to the tasks referred to in Article 47 the ECB shall also give advice in relation to and contribute to the preparation of any decision of the Council with regard to the United Kingdom taken in accordance with paragraphs 10(a) and 10(c).

(*c*) The Bank of England shall pay up its subscription to the capital of the ECB as a contribution to its operational costs on the same basis as national central banks of Member States with a derogation.

10. If the United Kingdom does not move to the third stage, it may change its notification at any time after the beginning of that stage. In that event:

(*a*) The United Kingdom shall have the right to move to the third stage provided only that it satisfies the necessary conditions. The Council, acting at the request of the United Kingdom and under the conditions and in accordance with the procedure laid down in Article 109k(2) of this Treaty, shall decide whether it fulfils the necessary conditions.

(*b*) The Bank of England shall pay up its subscribed capital, transfer to the ECB foreign reserve assets and contribute to its reserves on the same basis as the national central bank of a Member State whose derogation has been abrogated.

(*c*) The Council, acting under the conditions and in accordance with the procedure laid down in Article 109*l*(5) of this Treaty, shall take all other necessary decisions to enable the United Kingdom to move to the third stage.

If the United Kingdom moves to the third stage pursuant to the provisions of this Protocol, paragraphs 3 to 9 shall cease to have effect.

11. Notwithstanding Articles 104 and 109e(3) of this Treaty and Article 21.1 of the Statute, the government of the United Kingdom may maintain its 'ways and means' facility with the Bank of England if and so long as the United Kingdom does not move to the third stage.

Protocol on certain provisions relating to Denmark

The High Contracting Parties,

Desiring to settle, in accordance with general objectives of the Treaty establishing the European Community, certain particular problems existing at the present time,

Taking into account that the Danish Constitution contains provisions which may imply a referendum in Denmark prior to Danish participation in the third stage of economic and monetary union,

Have agreed on the following provisions, which shall be annexed to the Treaty establishing the European Community:

1. The Danish Government shall notify the Council of its position concerning participation in the third stage before the Council makes its assessment under Article 109j(2) of this Treaty.

2. In the event of a notification that Denmark will not participate in the third stage, Denmark shall have an exemption. The effect of the exemption shall be that all Articles and provisions of this Treaty and the Statute of the ESCB referring to a derogation shall be applicable to Denmark.

3. In such case, Denmark shall not be included among the majority of Member States which fulfil the necessary conditions referred to in the second indent of Article 109j(2) and in the first indent of Article 109j(3) of this Treaty.

4. As for the abrogation of the exemption, the procedure referred to in Article 109k(2) shall only be initiated at the request of Denmark.

5. In the event of abrogation of the exemption status, the provisions of this Protocol shall cease to apply.

Protocol on France

The High Contracting Parties,

Desiring to take into account a particular point relating to France,

Have agreed upon the following provisions, which shall be annexed to the Treaty establishing the European Community:

France will keep the privilege of monetary emission in its overseas territories under the terms established by its national laws, and will be solely entitled to determine the parity of the CFP franc.

Protocol on social policy

The High Contracting Parties,

Noting that 11 Member States, that is to say the Kingdom of Belgium, the Kingdom of Denmark, the Federal Republic of Germany, the Hellenic Republic, the Kingdom of Spain, the French Republic, Ireland, the Italian Republic, the Grand Duchy of Luxembourg, the Kingdom of the Netherlands and the Portuguese Republic, wish to continue along the path laid down in the 1989 Social Charter; that they have adopted among themselves an Agreement to this end; that this Agreement is annexed to this Protocol; that this Protocol and the said Agreement are without prejudice to the provisions of this Treaty, particularly those relating to social policy which constitute an integral part of the *acquis communautaire*.

1. Agree to authorise those 11 Member States to have recourse to the institutions, procedures and mechanisms of the Treaty for the purposes of taking among themselves and applying as far as they are concerned the acts and decisions required for giving effect to the abovementioned Agreement.

2. The United Kingdom of Great Britain and Northern Ireland shall not take part in the deliberations and the adoption by the Council of Commission proposals made on the basis of this Protocol and the abovementioned Agreement.

By way of derogation from Article 148(2) of the Treaty, acts of the Council which are made pursuant to this Protocol and which must be adopted by a qualified majority shall be deemed to be so adopted if they have received at least 44 votes in favour. The unanimity of the Council, with the exception of the United Kingdom of Great Britain and Northern Ireland, shall be necessary for acts of the Council which must be adopted unanimously and for those amending the Commission proposal.

Acts adopted by the Council and any financial consequences other than administrative costs entailed for the institutions shall not be applicable to the United Kingdom of Great Britain and Northern Ireland.

3. This Protocol shall be annexed to the Treaty establishing the European Community.

Agreement

on Social Policy concluded between the Member States of the European Community with the exception of the United Kingdom of Great Britain and Northern Ireland

The undersigned 11 High Contracting Parties, that is to say the Kingdom of Belgium, the Kingdom of Denmark, the Federal Republic of Germany, the Hellenic Republic, the Kingdom of Spain, the French Republic, Ireland, the Italian Republic, the Grand Duchy of Luxembourg, the Kingdom of the Netherlands and the Portuguese Republic (hereinafter referred to as 'the Member States'),

Wishing to implement the 1989 Social Charter on the basis of the *acquis communautaire*.

Considering the Protocol on social policy,

Have agreed as follows:

Article 1

The Community and the Member States shall have as their objectives the promotion of employment, improved living and working conditions, proper social protection, dialogue between management and labour, the development of human resources with a view to lasting high employment and the combating of exclusion. To this end the Community and the Member States shall implement measures which take account of the diverse forms of national practices in particular in the field of contractual relations, and the need to maintain the competitiveness of the Community economy.

Article 2

1. With a view to achieving the objectives of Article 1, the Community shall support and complement the activities of the Member States in the following fields:

- improvement in particular of the working environment to protect the workers' health and safety;

- working conditions;

- the information and consultation of workers;

- equality between men and women with regard to labour market opportunities and treatment at work;

- the integration of persons excluded from the labour market, without prejudice to Article 127 of the Treaty establishing the European Community (hereinafter referred to as 'the Treaty').

2. To this end, the Council may adopt, by means of directives, minimum requirements for gradual implementation, having regard to the conditions and technical rules obtaining in each of the Member States. Such directives shall avoid imposing administrative, financial and legal constraints in a way which would hold back the creation and development of small and medium-sized undertakings.

The Council shall act in accordance with the procedure referred to in Article 189c of the Treaty after consulting the Economic and Social Committee.

3. However, the Council shall act unanimously on a proposal from the Commission, after consulting the European Parliament and the Economic and Social Committee, in the following areas:

- social security and social protection of workers;

- protection of workers where their employment contract is terminated;

- representation and collective defence of the interests of workers and employers, including co-determination, subject to paragraph 6;

- conditions of employment for third-country nationals legally residing in Community territory;

- financial contributions for promotion of employment and job-creation, without prejudice to the provisions relating to the Social Fund.

4. A Member State may entrust management and labour, at their joint request, with the implementation of directives adopted pursuant to paragraphs 2 and 3.

In this case, it shall ensure that, no later than the date on which a directive must be transposed in accordance with Article 189, management and labour have introduced the necessary measures by agreement, the Member State concerned being required to take any necessary measure enabling it at any time to be in a position to guarantee the results imposed by that directive.

5. The provisions adopted pursuant to this Article shall not prevent any

Member State from maintaining or introducing more stringent protective measures compatible with the Treaty.

6. The provisions of this Article shall not apply to pay, the right of association, the right to strike or the right to impose lock-outs.

Article 3

1. The Commission shall have the task of promoting the consultation of management and labour at Community level and shall take any relevant measure to facilitate their dialogue by ensuring balanced support for the parties.

2. To this end, before submitting proposals in the social policy field, the Commission shall consult management and labour on the possible direction of Community action.

3. If, after such consultation, the Commission considers Community action advisable, it shall consult management and labour on the content of the envisaged proposal. Management and labour shall forward to the Commission an opinion or, where appropriate, a recommendation.

4. On the occasion of such consultation, management and labour may inform the Commission of their wish to initiate the process provided for in Article 4. The duration of the procedure shall not exceed nine months, unless the management and labour concerned and the Commission decide jointly to extend it.

Article 4

1. Should management and labour so desire, the dialogue between them at Community level may lead to contractual relations, including agreements.

2. Agreements concluded at Community level shall be implemented either in accordance with the procedures and practices specific to management and labour and the Member States or, in matters covered by Article 2, at the joint request of the signatory parties, by a Council decision on a proposal from the Commission.

The Council shall act by qualified majority, except where the agreement in question contains one or more provisions relating to one of the areas referred to in Article 2(3), in which case it shall act unanimously.

Article 5

With a view to achieving the objectives of Article 1 and without prejudice to the other provisions of the Treaty, the Commission shall encourage cooperation between the Member States and facilitate the coordination of their action in all social policy fields under this Agreement.

Article 6

1. Each Member State shall ensure that the principle of equal pay for male and female workers for equal work is applied.

2. For the purpose of this Article, 'pay' means the ordinary basic or minimum wage or salary and any other consideration, whether in cash or in kind, which the worker receives directly or indirectly, in respect of his employment, from his employer.

Equal pay without discrimination based on sex means:

(a) that pay for the same work at piece rates shall be calculated on the basis of the same unit of measurement;

(b) that pay for work at time rates shall be the same for the same job.

3. This Article shall not prevent any Member State from maintaining or adopting measures providing for specific advantages in order to make it easier for women to pursue a vocational activity or to prevent or compensate for disadvantages in their professional careers.

Article 7

The Commission shall draw up a report each year on progress in achieving the objectives of Article 1, including the demographic situation in the Community. It shall forward the report to the European Parliament, the Council and the Economic and Social Committee.

The European Parliament may invite the Commission to draw up reports on particular problems concerning the social situation.

Declarations

1. Declaration on Article 2(2)

The 11 High Contracting Parties note that in the discussions on Article 2(2) of the Agreement it was agreed that the Community does not intend, in laying down minimum requirements for the protection of the safety and health of employees to discriminate in a manner unjustified by the circumstances against employees in small and medium-sized undertakings.

2. Declaration on Article 4(2)

The 11 High Contracting Parties declare that the first of the arrangements for application of the agreements between management and labour at Community Level – referred to in Article 4(2) – will consist in developing, by collective bargaining according to the rules of each Member State, the content of the agreements, and that consequently this arrangement implies no obligation on the Member States to apply the agreements directly or to work out rules for their transposition, nor any obligation to amend national legislation in force to facilitate their implementation.

Protocol on economic and social cohesion

The High Contracting Parties,

Recalling that the Union has set itself the objective of promoting economic and social progress, *inter alia*, through the strengthening of economic and social cohesion,

Recalling that Article 2 of the Treaty establishing the European Community includes the task of promoting economic and social cohesion and solidarity between Member States and that the strengthening of economic and social cohesion figures among the activities of the Community listed in Article 3,

Recalling that the provisions of Part Three, Title XIV, on economic and social cohesion as a whole provide the legal basis for consolidating and further developing the Community's action in the field of economic and social cohesion, including the creation of a new fund,

Recalling that the provisions of Part Three, Title XII on trans-European networks and Title XVI on environment envisage a Cohesion Fund to be set up before 31 December 1993,

Stating their belief that progress towards economic and monetary union will contribute to the economic growth of all Member States,

Noting that the Community's structural Funds are being doubled in real terms between 1987 and 1993, implying large transfers, especially as a proportion of GDP of the less prosperous Member States,

Noting that the European Investment Bank is lending large and increasing amounts for the benefit of the poorer regions,

Noting the desire for greater flexibility in the arrangements for allocations from the structural Funds,

Noting the desire for modulation of the levels of Community participation in programmes and projects in certain countries,

Noting the proposal to take greater account of the relative prosperity of Member States in the system of own resources,

Reaffirm that the promotion of economic and social cohesion is vital to the full development and enduring success of the Community, and underline the importance of the inclusion of economic and social cohesion in Article 2 and 3 of this Treaty,

Reaffirm their conviction that the structural Funds should continue to play a considerable part in the achievement of Community objectives in the field of cohesion,

Reaffirm their conviction that the European Investment Bank should continue to devote the majority of its resources to the promotion of economic and social cohesion, and declare their willingness to review the capital needs of the European Investment Bank as soon as this is necessary for that purpose,

Reaffirm the need for a thorough evaluation of the operation and effectiveness of the structural Funds in 1992, and the need to review, on that occasion, the appropriate size of these Funds in the light of the tasks of the Community in the area of economic and social cohesion,

Agree that the Cohesion Fund to be set up before 31 December 1993 will provide Community financial contributions to projects in the fields of environment and trans-European networks in Member States with a per capita GNP of less than 90% of the Community average which have a programme leading to the fulfilment of the conditions of economic convergence as set out in Article 104c,

Declare their intention of allowing a greater margin of flexibility in allocating financing from the structural Funds to specific needs not covered under the present structural Funds regulations,

Declare their willingness to modulate the levels of Community participation in the context of programmes and projects of the structural Funds, with a view to avoiding excessive increases in budgetary expenditure in the less prosperous Member States,

Recognise the need to monitor regularly the progress made towards achieving economic and social cohesion and state their willingness to study all necessary measures in this respect,

Declare their intention of taking greater account of the contributive capacity of individual Member States in the system of own resources, and of examining means of correcting, for the less prosperous Member States, regressive elements existing in the present own resources system,

Agree to annex this Protocol to the Treaty establishing the European Community.

Protocol on the Economic and Social Committee and the Committee of the Regions

The High Contracting Parties

Have agreed upon the following provision, which shall be annexed to this Treaty establishing the European Community:

The Economic and Social Committee and the Committee of the Regions shall have a common organisational structure.

Protocol annexed to the Treaty on European Union and to the Treaties establishing the European Communities

The High Contracting Parties,

Have agreed upon the following provision, which shall be annexed to the Treaty on European Union and to the Treaties establishing the European Communities:

Nothing in the Treaty on European Union, or in the Treaties establishing the European Communities, or in the Treaties or Acts modifying or supplementing those Treaties, shall affect the application in Ireland of Article 40.3.3 of the Constitution of Ireland.

FINAL ACT

1. The Conferences of the Representatives of the Governments of the Member States convened in Rome on 15 December 1990 to adopt by common accord the amendments to be made to the Treaty establishing the European Economic Community with a view to the achievement of political union and with a view to the final stages of economic and monetary union, and those convened in Brussels on 3 February 1992 with a view to amending the Treaties establishing respectively the European Coal and Steel Community and the European Atomic Energy Community as a result of the amendments envisaged for the Treaty establishing the European Economic Community have adopted the following texts:

I.

The Treaty on European Union

II.

Protocols

1. Protocol on the acquisition of property in Denmark

2. Protocol concerning Article 119 of the Treaty establishing the European Community

3. Protocol on the Statute of the European System of Central Banks and of the European Central Bank

4. Protocol on the Statute of the European Monetary Institute

5. Protocol on the excessive deficit procedure

6. Protocol on the convergence criteria referred to in Article 109j of the Treaty establishing the European Community

7. Protocol amending the Protocol on the privileges and immunities of the European Communities

8. Protocol on Denmark

9. Protocol on Portugal

10. Protocol on the transition to the third stage of economic and monetary union

11. Protocol on certain provisions relating to the United Kingdom of Great Britain and Northern Ireland

12. Protocol on certain provisions relating to Denmark

13. Protocol on France

14. Protocol on social policy, to which is annexed an agreement concluded between the Member States of the European Community with the exception of the United Kingdom of Great Britain and Northern Ireland, to which two declarations are attached

15. Protocol on economic and social cohesion

16. Protocol on the Economic and Social Committee and the Committee of the Regions

17. Protocol annexed to the Treaty on European Union and to the Treaties establishing the European Communities

The Conferences agreed that the Protocols referred to in 1 to 16 above will be annexed to the Treaty establishing the European Community and that the Protocol referred to in 17 above will be annexed to the Treaty on European Union and to the Treaties establishing the European Communities.

2. At the time of signature of these texts, the Conferences adopted the declarations listed below and annexed to this Final Act:

III.

Declarations

1. Declaration on civil protection, energy and tourism

2. Declaration on nationality of a Member State

3. Declaration on Part Three, Titles III and VI, of the Treaty establishing the European Community

4. Declaration on Part Three, Title VI, of the Treaty establishing the European Community

5. Declaration on monetary cooperation with non-Community countries

6. Declaration on monetary relations with the Republic of San Marino, the Vatican City and the Principality of Monaco

7. Declaration on Article 73d of the Treaty establishing the European Community

8. Declaration on Article 109 of the Treaty establishing the European Community

9. Declaration on Part Three, Title XVI, of the Treaty establishing the European Community

10. Declaration on Articles 109, 130r and 130y of the Treaty establishing the European Community

11. Declaration on the Directive of 24 November 1988 (Emissions)

12. Declaration on the European Development Fund

13. Declaration on the role of national parliaments in the European Union

14. Declaration on the Conference of the Parliaments

15. Declaration on the number of members of the Commission and of the European Parliament

16. Declaration on the hierarchy of Community Acts

17. Declaration on the right of access to information

18. Declaration on estimated costs under Commission proposals

19. Declaration on the implementation of Community law

20. Declaration on assessment of the environmental impact of Community measures

21. Declaration on the Court of Auditors

22. Declaration on the Economic and Social Committee

23. Declaration on cooperation with charitable associations

24. Declaration on the protection of animals

25. Declaration on the representation of the interests of the overseas countries and territories referred to in Article 227(3) and (5)(a) and (b) of the Treaty establishing the European Community

26. Declaration on the outermost regions of the Community

27. Declaration on voting in the field of the common foreign and security policy

28. Declaration on practical arrangements in the field of the common foreign and security policy

29. Declaration on the use of languages in the field of the common foreign and security policy

30. Declaration on Western European Union

31. Declaration on asylum

32. Declaration on police cooperation

33. Declaration on disputes between the ECB and the EMI and their servants

Done at Maastricht this seventh day of February in the year one thousand nine hundred and ninety-two.

Declaration on civil protection, energy and tourism

The Conference declares that the question of introducing into the Treaty establishing the European Community Titles relating to the spheres referred to in Article 3(t) of that Treaty will be examined, in accordance with the procedure laid down in Article N(2) of the Treaty on European Union, on the basis of a report which the Commission will submit to the Council by 1996 at the latest.

The Commission declares that Community action in those spheres will be pursued on the basis of the present provisions of the Treaties establishing the European Communities.

Declaration on nationality of a Member State

The Conference declares that, wherever in the Treaty establishing the European Community reference is made to nationals of the Member States, the question whether an individual possesses the nationality of a Member State shall be settled solely by reference to the national law of the Member State concerned. Member States may declare, for information, who are to be considered their nationals for Community purposes by way of a declaration lodged with the Presidency and may amend any such declaration when necessary.

Declaration on Part Three, Titles III and VI, of the Treaty establishing the European Community

The Conference affirms that, for the purpose of applying the provisions set out in Part Three, Title III, Chapter 4 on capital and payments, and Title VI on economic and monetary policy, of this Treaty, the usual practice, according to which the Council meets in the composition of Economic and Finance Ministers, shall be continued, without prejudice to Article 109j(2) to (4) and Article 109k(2).

Declaration on Part Three, Title VI, of the Treaty establishing the European Community

The Conference affirms that the President of the European Council shall invite the Economic and Finance Ministers to participate in European Council meetings when the European Council is discussing matters relating to economic and monetary union.

Declaration on monetary cooperation with non-Community countries

The Conference affirms that the Community shall aim to contribute to stable international monetary relations. To this end the Community shall be prepared to cooperate with other European countries and with those non-European countries with which the Community has close economic ties.

Declaration on monetary relations with the Republic of San Marino, the Vatican City and the Principality of Monaco

The Conference agrees that the existing monetary relations between Italy and San Marino and the Vatican City and between France and Monaco remain unaffected by the Treaty establishing the European Community until the introduction of the ECU as the single currency of the Community.

The Community undertakes to facilitate such renegotiations of existing arrangements as might become necessary as a result of the introduction of the ECU as a single currency.

Declaration on Article 73d of the Treaty establishing the European Community

The Conference affirms that the right of Member States to apply the relevant provisions of their tax law as referred to in Article 73d(1)(a) of this Treaty will apply only with respect to the relevant provisions which exist at the end of 1993. However, this Declaration shall apply only to capital movements between Member States and to payments effected between Member States.

Declaration on Article 109 of the Treaty establishing the European Community

The Conference emphasises that use of the term 'formal agreements' in Article 109(1) is not intended to create a new category of international agreement within the meaning of Community law.

Declaration on Part Three, Title XVI, of the Treaty establishing the European Community

The Conference considers that, in view of the increasing importance of nature conservation at national, Community and international level, the Community should, in exercising its powers under the provisions of Part Three, Title XVI, take account of the specific requirements of this area.

Declaration on Articles 109, 130r and 130y of the Treaty establishing the European Community

The Conference considers that the provisions of Article 109(5), Article 130r(4), second subparagraph, and Article 130y do not affect the principles resulting from the judgment handed down by the Court of Justice in the AETR case.

Declaration on the Directive of 24 November 1988 (Emissions)

The Conference declares that changes in Community legislation cannot undermine the derogations granted to Spain and Portugal until 31 December 1999 under the Council Directive of 24 November 1988 on the limitation of emissions of certain pollutants into the air from large combustion plants.

Declaration on the European Development Fund

The Conference agrees that the European Development Fund will continue to be financed by national contributions in accordance with the current provisions.

Declaration on the role of National Parliaments in the European Union

The Conference considers that it is important to encourage greater involvement of national parliaments in the activities of the European Union.

To this end, the exchange of information between national parliaments and the European Parliament should be stepped up. In this context, the governments of the Member States will ensure, *inter alia*, that national parliaments receive Commission proposals for legislation in good time for information or possible examination.

Similarly, the Conference considers that it is important for the contacts between the national parliaments and the European Parliament to be stepped up, in particular through the granting of appropriate reciprocal facilities and regular meetings between members of Parliament interested in the same issues.

Declaration on the Conference of the Parliaments

The Conference invites the European Parliament and the national parliament to meet as necessary as a Conference of the Parliaments (or 'assises').

The Conference of the Parliaments will be consulted on the main features of the European Union, without prejudice to the powers of the European Parliament and the rights of the national parliaments. The President of the European Council and the President of the Commission will report to each session of the Conference of the Parliaments on the state of the Union.

Declaration on the number of members of the Commission and of the European Parliament

The Conference agrees that the Member States will examine the questions relating to the number of members of the Commission and the number of members of the European Parliament no later than at the end of 1992, with a view to reaching an agreement which will permit the establishment of the necessary legal basis for fixing the number of members of the European Parliament in good time for the 1994 elections. The decisions will be taken in the light, *inter alia*, of the need to establish the overall size of the European Parliament in an enlarged Community.

Declaration on the hierarchy of Community acts

The Conference agrees that the Intergovernmental Conference to be convened in 1996 will examine to what extent it might be possible to review the classification of Community acts with a view to establishing an appropriate hierarchy between the different categories of act.

Declaration on the right of access to information

The Conference considers that transparency of the decision-making process strengthens the democratic nature of the institutions and the public's confidence in the administration. The Conference accordingly recommends that the Commission submit to the Council no later than 1993 a report on measures designed to improve public access to the information available to the institutions.

Declaration on estimated costs under Commission proposals

The Conference notes that the Commission undertakes, by basing itself where appropriate on any consultations it considers necessary and by strengthening its system for evaluating Community legislation, to take account in its legislative proposals of costs and benefits to the Member States' public authorities and all the parties concerned.

Declaration on the implementation of Community law

1. The Conference stresses that it is central to the coherence and unity of the process of European construction that each Member State should fully and accurately transpose into national law the Community Directives addressed to it within the deadlines laid down therein.

Moreover, the Conference, while recognising that it must be for each Member State to determine how the provisions of Community law can best be enforced in the light of its own particular institutions, legal system and other circumstances, but in any event in compliance with Article 189 of the Treaty establishing the European Community, considers it essential for the proper functioning of the Community that the measures taken by the different Member States should result in Community law being applied with the same effectiveness and rigour as in the application of their national law.

2. The Conference calls on the Commission to ensure, in exercising its powers under Article 155 of this Treaty, that Member States fulfil their obligations. It asks the Commission to publish periodically a full report for the Member States and the European Parliament.

Declaration on assessment of the environmental impact of Community measures

The Conference notes that the Commission undertakes in its proposals, and that the Member States undertake in implementing those proposals, to take full account of their environmental impact and of the principle of sustainable growth.

Declaration on the Court of Auditors

The Conference emphasises the special importance it attaches to the task assigned to the Court of Auditors by Articles 188a, 188b, 188c and 206 of the Treaty Establishing the European Community.

It requests the other Community institutions to consider, together with the Court of Auditors, all appropriate ways of enhancing the effectiveness of its work.

Declaration on the Economic and Social Committee

The Conference agrees that the Economic and Social Committee will enjoy the same independence with regard to its budget and staff management as the Court of Auditors has enjoyed hitherto.

Declaration on cooperation with charitable associations

The Conference stresses the importance, in pursuing the objectives of Article 117 of the Treaty establishing the European Community, of cooperation between the latter and charitable associations and foundations as institutions responsible for social welfare establishments and services.

Declaration on the protection of animals

The Conference calls upon the European Parliament, the Council and the Commission, as well as the Member States, when drafting and implementing Community legislation on the common agricultural policy, transport, the internal market and research, to pay full regard to the welfare requirements of animals.

Declaration on the representation of the interests of the overseas countries and territories referred to in Article 227(3) and (5)(a) and (b) of the Treaty establishing the European Community

The Conference, noting that in exceptional circumstances divergencies may arise between the interests of the Union and those of the overseas countries and territories referred to in Article 227(3) and (5)(a) and (b), agrees that the Council will seek to reach a solution which accords with the position of the Union. However, in the event that this proves impossible, the Conference agrees that the Member State concerned may act separately in the interests of the said overseas countries and territories, without this affecting the Community's interests. The Member State concerned will give notice to the Council and the Commission where such a divergence of interests is likely to occur and, when separate action proves unavoidable, make it clear that it is acting in the interests of an overseas territory mentioned above.

This declaration also applies to Macao and East Timor.

Declaration on the outermost regions of the Community

The Conference acknowledges that the outermost regions of the Community (the French overseas departments, Azores and Madeira and Canary Islands) suffer from major structural backwardness compounded by several phenomena (remoteness, island status, small size, difficult topography and climate, economic dependence on a few products), the permanence and combination of which severely restrain their economic and social development.

It considers that, while the provisions of the Treaty establishing the European Community and secondary legislation apply automatically to the outermost regions, it is none the less possible to adopt specific measures to assist them inasmuch and as long as there is an objective need to take such measures with a view to the economic and social development of those regions. Such measures should have as their aim both the completion of the internal market and a recognition of the regional reality to enable the outermost regions to achieve the average economic and social level of the Community.

Declaration on voting in the field of the common foreign and security policy

The Conference agrees that, with regard to Council decisions requiring unanimity, Member States will, to the extent possible, avoid preventing a unanimous decision where a qualified majority exists in favour of that decision.

Declaration on practical arrangements in the field of the common foreign and security policy

The Conference agrees the division of work between the Political Committee and the Committee of Permanent Representatives will be examined at a later stage, as will the practical arrangements for merging the Political Cooperation Secretariat with the General Secretariat of the Council and for cooperation between the latter and the Commission.

Declaration on the use of languages in the field of the common foreign and security policy

The Conference agrees that the use of languages shall be in accordance with the rules of European Communities.

For Coreu communications, the current practice of European political cooperation will serve as a guide for the time being.

All common foreign and security policy texts which are submitted to or adopted at meetings of the European Council and of the Council as well as all texts which are to be published are immediately and simultaneously translated into all the official Community languages.

Declaration on Western European Union

The Conference notes the following declarations:

I. Declaration

by Belgium, Germany, Spain, France, Italy, Luxembourg,
the Netherlands, Portugal and the United Kingdom of Great Britain and
Northern Ireland, which are members of the Western European Union
and also members of the European Union on

the role of the Western European Union and its relations with the
European Union and with the Atlantic Alliance

Introduction

1. WEU Member States agree on the need to develop a genuine European security and defence identity and a greater European responsibility on defence matters. This identity will be pursued through a gradual process involving successive phases. WEU will form an integral part of the process of the development of the European Union and will enhance its contribution to solidarity within the Atlantic Alliance. WEU Member States agree to strengthen the role of WEU, in the longer term perspective of a common defence policy within the European Union which might in time lead to a common defence, compatible with that of the Atlantic Alliance.

2. WEU will be developed as the defence component of the European Union and as a means to strengthen the European pillar of the Atlantic Alliance. To this end, it will formulate common European defence policy and carry forward its concrete implementation through the further development of its own operational role.

WEU Member States take note of Article J.4 relating to the common foreign and security policy of the Treaty on European Union which reads as follows:

'1. *The common foreign and security policy shall include all questions related to security of the Union, including the eventual framing of a common defence policy, which might in time lead to a common defence.*

2. *The Union requests the Western European Union (WEU), which is an integral part of development of the Union, to elaborate and implement decisions and actions of the Union which have defence implications. The Council shall, in agreement with the institutions of the WEU, adopt the necessary practical arrangements.*

3. *Issues having defence implications dealt with under this Article shall not be subject to the procedures set out in Article J.3.*

4. *The policy of the Union in accordance with this Article shall not prejudice the specific character of the security and defence policy of certain Member States and shall respect the obligations of certain Member States under the North Atlantic Treaty and be compatible with the common security and defence policy established within that framework.*

5. *The provisions of this Article shall not prevent the development of closer cooperation between two or more Member States on a bilateral level, in the framework of the WEU and the Atlantic Alliance, provided such cooperation does not run counter to or impede that provided for in this Title.*

6. *With a view to furthering the objective of this Treaty, and having in view the date of 1998 in context of Article XII of the Brussels Treaty, the provisions of this Article may be revised as provided for in Article N(2) on the basis of a report to be presented in 1996 by the Council to the European Council, which shall include an evaluation of the progress made and the experience gained until then.'*

A – WEU's relations with European Union

3. The objective is to build up WEU in stages as the defence component of the European Union. To this end, WEU is prepared, at the request of the European Union, to elaborate and implement decisions and actions of the Union which have defence implications.

To this end, WEU will take the following measures to develop a close working relationship with the Union:

–   as appropriate, synchronisation of the dates and venues of meeting and harmonisation of working methods;

–   establishment of close cooperation between the Council and Secretariat-General of WEU on the one hand, and the Council of the Union and General Secretariat of the Council on the other;

- consideration of the harmonisation of the sequence and duration of the respective Presidencies;

- arranging for appropriate modalities so as to ensure that the Commission of the European Communities is regularly informed and, as appropriate, consulted on WEU activities in accordance with the role of the Commission in the common foreign and security policy as defined in the Treaty on European Union;

- encouragement of closer cooperation between the Parliamentary Assembly of WEU and the European Parliament;

The WEU Council shall, in agreement with the competent bodies of the European Union, adopt the necessary practical arrangements.

B – WEU's relations with the Atlantic Alliance

4. The objective is to develop WEU as a means to strengthen the European pillar of the Atlantic Alliance. Accordingly WEU is prepared to develop further the close working links between WEU and the Alliance and to strengthen the role, responsibilities and contributions of WEU Member States in the Alliance. This will be undertaken on the basis of the necessary transparency and complementarity between the emerging European security and defence identity and the Alliance. WEU will act in conformity with the positions adopted in the Atlantic Alliance.

- WEU Member States will intensify their coordination on Alliance issues which represent an important common interest with the aim of introducing joint positions agreed in WEU into the process of consultation in the Alliance which will remain the essential forum for consultation among its members and the venue for agreement on policies bearing on the security and defence commitments of Allies under the North Atlantic Treaty.

- Where necessary, dates and venues of meetings will be synchronised and working methods harmonised.

- Close cooperation will be established between the Secretariats-General of WEU and NATO.

C – Operational role of WEU

5. WEU's operational role will be strengthened by examining and defining appropriate missions, structures and means, covering in particular:

- WEU planning cell;

- closer military cooperation complementary to the Alliance in particular in the fields of logistics, transport, training and strategic surveillance;

– meetings of WEU Chiefs of Defence Staff;

– military units answerable to WEU.

Other proposals will be examined further, including:

– enhanced cooperation in the field of armaments with the aim of creating a European armaments agency;

– development of the WEU Institute into a European Security and Defence Academy.

Arrangements aimed at giving WEU a stronger operational role will be fully compatible with the military dispositions necessary to ensure the collective defence of all Allies.

D – Other measures

6. As a consequence of the measures set out above, and in order to facilitate the strengthening of WEU's role, the seat of the WEU Council and Secretariat will be transferred to Brussels.

7. Representation on the WEU Council must be such that the Council is able to exercise its functions continuously in accordance with Article VIII of the modified Brussels Treaty. Member States may draw on a double-hatting formula, to be worked out, consisting of their representatives to the Alliance and to the European Union.

8. WEU notes that, in accordance with the provisions of Article J.4(6) concerning the common foreign and security policy of the Treaty on European Union, the Union will decide to review the provisions of this Article with a view to furthering the objective to be set by it in accordance with the procedure defined. The WEU will re-examine the present provisions in 1996. This re-examination will take account of the progress and experience acquired and will extend to relations between WEU and the Atlantic Alliance.

II. Declaration

by Belgium, Germany, Spain, France, Italy, Luxembourg, the Netherlands, Portugal and the United Kingdom of Great Britain and Northern Ireland which are members of the Western European Union

'The Member States of WEU welcome the development of the European security and defence identity. They are determined, taking into account the role of WEU as the defence component of the European Union and as the means to strengthen the European pillar of the Atlantic Alliance, to put the relationship between WEU and *the other European States on a new basis for the sake of stability and security in Europe. In this spirit, they propose the following:*

States which are members of the European Union are invited to accede to WEU on conditions to be agreed in accordance with Article XI of the modified Brussels Treaty, or to become observers if they so wish. Simultaneously, other European Member States of NATO are invited to become associate members of WEU in a way which will give them the possibility of participating fully in the activities of WEU.

The Member States of WEU assume that treaties and agreements corresponding with the above proposals will be concluded before 31 December 1992.'

Declaration on asylum

1. The Conference agrees that, in context of the proceedings provided for in Articles K.1 and K.3 of the provisions on cooperation in the fields of justice and home affairs, the Council will consider as a matter of priority questions concerning Member States' asylum policies, with the aim of adopting, by the beginning of 1993, common action to harmonise aspects of them, in the light of the work programme and timetable contained in the report on asylum drawn up at the request of the European Council meeting in Luxembourg on 28 and 29 June 1991.

2. In this connection, the Council will also consider, by the end of 1993, on the basis of a report, the possibility of applying Article K.9 to such matters.

Declaration on police cooperation

The Conference confirms the agreement of the Member States on the objectives underlying the German delegation's proposals at the European Council meeting in Luxembourg on 28 and 29 June 1991.

For the present, the Member States agree to examine as a matter of priority the drafts submitted to them, on the basis of the work programme and timetable agreed upon in the report drawn up at the request of the Luxembourg European Council, and they are willing to envisage the adoption of practical measures in the areas such as those suggested by the German delegation, relating to the following functions in the exchange of information and experience:

–   support for national criminal investigation and security authorities, in particular in the coordination of investigations and search operations;

–   creation of database;

–   central analysis and assessment of information in order to take stock of the situation and identify investigative approaches;

– collection and analysis of national prevention programmes for forwarding to Member States and for drawing up European-wide prevention strategies;

– measures relating to further training, research, forensic matters and criminal records departments.

Member States agree to consider on the basis of a report, during 1994 at the latest, whether the scope of such cooperation should be extended.

Declaration on disputes between the ECB and the EMI and their servants

The Conference considers it proper that the Court of First Instance should hear this class of action in accordance with Article 168a of the Treaty establishing the European Community. The Conference therefore invites the institutions to adapt the relevant rules accordingly.

Done at Maastricht on the seventh day of February in the year one thousand nine hundred and ninety-two.

[List of signatories omitted]

Declaration of 1 May 1992

of the High Contracting Parties to the Treaty on European Union

On 1 May 1992, in Guimarães (Portugal), the High Contracting Parties to the Treaty on European Union adopted the following Declaration:

The High Contracting Parties to the Treaty on European Union signed at Maastricht on the seventh day of February 1992,

Having considered the terms of Protocol No 17 to the said Treaty on European Union which is annexed to that Treaty and to the Treaties establishing the European Communities,

Hereby give the following legal interpretation:

That it was and is their intention that the Protocol shall not limit freedom to travel between Member States or, in accordance with conditions which may be laid down, in conformity with Community law, by Irish legislation, to obtain or make available in Ireland information relating to services lawfully available in Member States.

At the same time the High Contracting Parties solemnly declare that, in the event of a future constitutional amendment in Ireland which concerns the subject matter of Article 40.3.3 of the Constitution of Ireland and which does not conflict with the intention of the High Contracting Parties hereinbefore expressed, they will, following the entry into force of the Treaty on European Union, be favourably disposed to amending the said Protocol so as to extend its application to such constitutional amendment if Ireland so requests.

 IRL Implemented in Ireland: European Communities Acts 1972-1993; S.I. 331/72; S.I. 341/72; S.I. 170/87; S.I. 170S/87; S.I. 304S/93; S.I. 91S/94; S.I. 122S/94

EDITORIAL NOTE

For Protocols and Declarations relating to the EC, ECSC, EAEC not included in this volume see Office for Official Publications of the European Communities, Treaties establishing the European Communities: Treaties amending these Treaties, Volume I, 1987: ditto European Union: Selected instruments taken from the Treaties, Book I, Volumes I (1993) and II (not yet published).

Denmark and the Treaty on European Union [1]

(92/C 348/01)

(OJ No C 348, 31.12.92, p.1)

The European Council recalled that the entry into force of the Treaty signed in Maastricht requires ratification by all the twelve Member States in accordance with their respective constitutional requirements, and reaffirmed the importance of concluding the process as soon as possible, without reopening the present text, as foreseen in Article R of the Treaty.

The European Council noted that Denmark has submitted to Member States on 30 October a document entitled 'Denmark in Europe', which sets out the following points as being of particular importance:

- the defence policy dimension,
- the third stage of Economic and Monetary Union,
- citizenship of the Union,
- cooperation in the fields of justice and home affairs,
- openness and transparency in the Community's decision-making process,
- the effective application of the principle of subsidiarity,
- promotion of cooperation between the Member States to combat unemployment.

Against this background, the European Council has agreed on the following set of arrangements, which are fully compatible with the Treaty, are designed to meet Danish concerns, and therefore apply exclusively to Denmark and not to other existing or acceding Member States:

(a) Decision concerning certain problems raised by Denmark on the Treaty on European Union (Annex 1). This Decision will take effect on the date of entry into force of the Treaty on European Union;

(b) the declaration in Annex 2.

The European Council has also taken cognisance of the unilateral declarations in Annex 3, which will be associated with the Danish act of ratification of the Treaty on European Union.

Annex 1

Decision of the Heads of State and Government, meeting within the European Council, concerning certain problems raised by Denmark on the Treaty on European Union

The Heads of State and Government, meeting within the European Council, whose Governments are signatories of the Treaty on European Union, which involves independent and sovereign States having freely decided, in accordance with the existing Treaties, to exercise in common some of their competences,

– desiring to settle, in conformity with the Treaty on European Union, particular problems existing at the present time specifically for Denmark and raised in its memorandum 'Denmark in Europe' of 30 October 1992,

– having regard to the conclusions of the Edinburgh European Council on subsidiarity and transparency,

– noting the declarations of the Edinburgh European Council relating to Denmark,

– taking cognisance of the unilateral declarations of Denmark made on the same occasion which will be associated with its act of ratification,

– noting that Denmark does not intend to make use of the following provisions in such a way as to prevent closer cooperation and action among Member States compatible with the Treaty and within the framework of the Union and its objectives,

Have agreed on the following decision:

Section A

Citizenship

The provisions of Part Two of the Treaty establishing the European Community relating to citizenship of the Union give nationals of the Member States additional rights and protection as specified in that Part. They do not in any way take the place of national citizenship. The question whether an individual possesses the nationality of a Member State will be settled solely by reference to the national law of the Member State concerned.

Section B

Economic and Monetary Union

1. The Protocol on certain provisions relating to Denmark attached to the Treaty establishing the European Community gives Denmark the right to notify the Council of the European Communities of its position concerning participation in the third stage of Economic and Monetary Union. Denmark has given notification that it will not participate in the third stage. This notification will take effect upon the coming into effect of this decision.

2. As a consequence, Denmark will not participate in the single currency, will not be bound by the rules concerning economic policy which apply only to the Member States participating in the third stage of Economic and Monetary Union, and will retain its existing powers in the field of monetary policy according to its national laws and regulations, including powers of the National Bank of Denmark in the field of monetary policy.

3. Denmark will participate fully in the second stage of Economic and Monetary Union and will continue to participate in exchange-rate cooperation within the European Monetary System (EMS).

Section C

Defence Policy

The Heads of State and Government note that, in response to the invitation from the Western European Union (WEU), Denmark has become an observer to that organisation. They also note that nothing in the Treaty on European Union commits Denmark to become a member of the WEU. Accordingly, Denmark does not participate in the elaboration and the implementation of decisions and actions of the Union which have defence implications, but will not prevent the development of closer cooperation between Member States in this area.

Section D

Justice and Home affairs

Denmark will participate fully in cooperation on Justice and Home Affairs on the basis of the provisions of Title VI of the Treaty on European Union.

Section E

Final provisions

1. This decision will take effect on the date of entry into force of the Treaty on European Union; its duration shall be governed by Articles Q and N(2) of that Treaty.

2. At any time Denmark may, in accordance with its constitutional requirements, inform other Member States that it no longer wishes to avail itself of all or part of this decision. In that event, Denmark will apply in full all relevant measures then in force taken within the framework of the European Union.

Annex 2

Declarations of the European Council

Declaration on social policy, consumers, environment, distribution of income

1. The Treaty on European Union does not prevent any Member State from maintaining or introducing more stringent protection measures compatible with the EC Treaty:

- in the field of working conditions and in social policy (Article 118A(3) of the EC Treaty and Article 2(5) of the Agreement on social policy concluded between the Member States of the European Community with the exception of the United Kingdom),

- in order to attain a high level of consumer protection (Article 129A(3) of the EC Treaty),

- in order to pursue the objectives of protection of the environment (Article 130T of the EC Treaty).

2. The provisions introduced by the Treaty on European Union, including the provisions on Economic and Monetary Union, permit each Member State to pursue its own policy with regard to distribution of income and maintain or improve social welfare benefits.

Declaration on defence

The European Council takes note that Denmark will renounce its right to exercise the Presidency of the Union in each case involving the elaboration and the implementation of decisions and actions of the Union which have defence implications. The normal rules for replacing the President, in the case of the President being indisposed, shall apply.

These rules will also apply with regard to the representation of the Union in international organisations, international conferences and with third countries.

Annex 3

Unilateral declarations of Denmark, to be associated to the Danish Act of Ratification of the Treaty on European Union and of which the eleven other Member States will take cognizance

Declaration on citizenship of the Union

1. Citizenship of the Union is a political and legal concept which is entirely different from the concept of citizenship within the meaning of the Constitution of the Kingdom of Denmark and of the Danish legal system. Nothing in the Treaty on European Union implies or foresees an undertaking to create a citizenship of the Union in the sense of citizenship of a nation-state. The question of Denmark participating in any such development does, therefore, not arise.

2. Citizenship of the Union in no way in itself gives a national of another Member State the right to obtain Danish citizenship or any of the rights, duties, privileges or advantages that are inherent in Danish citizenship by virtue of Denmark's constitutional, legal and administrative rules. Denmark will fully respect all specific rights expressly provided for in the Treaty and applying to nationals of the Member States.

3. Nationals of the other Member States of the European Community enjoy in Denmark the right to vote and to stand as a candidate at municipal elections, foreseen in Article 8b of the European Community Treaty. Denmark intends to introduce legislation granting nationals of the other Member States the right to vote and to stand as a candidate for elections to the European Parliament in good time before the next elections in 1994. Denmark has no intention of accepting that the detailed arrangements foreseen in paragraphs 1 and 2 of this Article could lead to rules detracting from the rights already given in Denmark in that matter.

4. Without prejudice to the other provisions of the Treaty establishing the European Community, Article 8e requires the unanimity of all the Member States of the Council of the European Communities, i.e. all Member States, for the adoption of any provision to strengthen or to add to the rights laid down in Part Two of the EC Treaty. Moreover, any unanimous decision of the Council, before coming into force, will have to be adopted in each Member State, in accordance with its

constitutional requirements. In Denmark, such adoption will, in the case of a transfer of sovereignty, as defined in the Danish Constitution, require either a majority of ⅚ of Members of the Folketing or both a majority of the Members of the Folketing and a majority of voters in a referendum.

Declaration on cooperation in the fields of justice and home affairs

Article K9 of the Treaty on European Union requires that unanimity of all the Members of the Council of the European Union, i.e. all Member States, to the adoption of any decision to apply Article 100C of the Treaty establishing the European Community to action in areas referred to in Article K1(1) to (6). Moreover, any unanimous decision of the Council, before coming into force, will have to be adopted in each Member State, in accordance with its constitutional requirements. In Denmark, such adoption will, in the case of a transfer of sovereignty, as defined in the Danish Constitution, require either a majority of ⅚ of Members of the Folketing or both a majority of the Members of the Folketing and a majority of voters in a referendum.

Final Declaration

The Decision and Declarations above are a response to the result of the Danish referendum of 2 June 1992 on ratification of the Maastricht Treaty. As far as Denmark is concerned, the objectives of that Treaty in the four areas mentioned in sections A to D of the Decision are to be seen in the light of these documents, which are compatible with the Treaty and do not call its objectives into question.

FOOTNOTE

1. European Council, Edinburgh, 11 and 12 December 1992; Conclusions of the Presidency, Part B.

PROTOCOL ON THE PRIVILEGES AND IMMUNITIES OF THE EUROPEAN COMMUNITIES[1]

The High Contracting Parties

Considering that, in accordance with Article 28 of the Treaty establishing a Single Council and a Single Commission of the European Communities, these Communities and the European Investment Bank shall enjoy in the territories of the Member States such privileges and immunities as are necessary for the performance of their tasks,

Have agreed upon the following provisions, which shall be annexed to this Treaty:

Chapter I

Property, funds, assets and operations of the European Communities

Article 1

The premises and buildings of the Communities shall be inviolable. They shall be exempt from search, requisition, confiscation or expropriation. The property and assets of the Communities shall not be the subject of any administrative or legal measure of constraint without the authorisation of the Court of Justice.

Article 2

The archives of the Communities shall be inviolable.

Article 3

The Communities, their assets, revenues and other property shall be exempt from all direct taxes.

The Governments of the Member States shall, wherever possible, take the appropriate measures to remit or refund the amount of indirect taxes or sales taxes included in the price of movable or immovable property, where the Communities make, for their official use, substantial purchases the price of which includes taxes of this kind. These provisions shall not be applied, however, so as to have the effect of distorting competition within the Communities.

No exemption shall be granted in respect of taxes and dues which amount merely to charges for public utility services.

Article 4

The Communities shall be exempt from all customs duties, prohibitions and restrictions on imports and exports in respect of articles intended for their official use: articles so imported shall not be disposed of, whether or not in return for payment, in the territory of the country into which they have been imported, except under conditions approved by the Government of that country.

The Communities shall also be exempt from any customs duties and any prohibitions and restrictions on imports and exports in respect of their publications.

Article 5

The European Coal and Steel Community may hold currency of any kind and operate accounts in any currency.

Chapter II

Communications and *laissez-passer*

Article 6

For their official communications and the transmission of all their documents, the institutions of the Communities shall enjoy in the territory of each Member State the treatment accorded by that State to diplomatic missions.

Official correspondence and other official communications of the institutions of the Communities shall not be subject to censorship.

Article 7

1. *Laissez-passer* in a form to be prescribed by the Council, which shall be recognised as valid travel documents by the authorities of the Member States, may be issued to members and servants of the institutions of the Communities by the Presidents of these institutions. These *laissez-passer* shall be issued to officials and other servants under conditions laid down in the Staff Regulations of officials and the Conditions of Employment of other servants of the Communities.

The Commission may conclude agreements for these *laissez-passer* to be recognised as valid travel documents within the territory of third countries.

2. The provisions of Article 6 of the Protocol on the Privileges and Immunities of the European Coal and Steel Community shall, however,

remain applicable to members and servants of the institutions who are at the date of entry into force of this Treaty in possession of the *laissez-passer* provided for in that Article, until the provisions of paragraph 1 of this Article are applied.

Chapter III

Members of the European Parliament

Article 8

No administrative or other restriction shall be imposed on the free movement of members of the European Parliament travelling to or from the place of meeting of the European Parliament.

Members of the European Parliament shall, in respect of customs and exchange control, be accorded:

(*a*) by their own Government, the same facilities as those accorded to senior officials travelling abroad on temporary official missions;

(*b*) by the Governments of other Member States, the same facilities as those accorded to representatives of foreign Governments on temporary official missions.

Article 9

Members of the European Parliament shall not be subject to any form of inquiry, detention or legal proceedings in respect of opinions expressed or votes cast by them in the performance of their duties.

Article 10

During the sessions in the European Parliament, its members shall enjoy:

(*a*) in the territory of their own State, the immunities accorded to members of their parliament;

(*b*) in the territory of any other Member State, immunity from any measure of detention and from legal proceedings.

Immunity shall likewise apply to members while they are travelling to and from the place of meeting of the European Parliament.

Immunity cannot be claimed when a member is found in the act of committing an offence and shall not prevent the European Parliament from exercising its right to waive the immunity of one of its members.

Chapter IV

Representatives of Member States taking part in the work of the institutions of the European Communities

Article 11

Representatives of Member States taking part in the work of the institutions of the Communities, their advisers and technical experts shall, in the performance of their duties and during their travel to and from the place of meeting, enjoy the customary privileges, immunities and facilities.

This Article shall also apply to members of the advisory bodies of the Communities.

Chapter V

Officials and other servants of the European Communities

Article 12

In the territory of each Member State and whatever their nationality, officials and other servants of the Communities shall:

(a) subject to the provisions of the Treaties relating, on the one hand, to the rules on the liability of officials and other servants towards the Communities and, on the other hand, to the jurisdiction of the Court in disputes between the Communities and their officials and other servants, be immune from legal proceedings in respect of acts performed by them in their official capacity, including their words spoken or written. They shall continue to enjoy this immunity after they have ceased to hold office;

(b) together with their spouses and dependent members of their families, not be subject to immigration restrictions or to formalities for the registration of aliens;

(c) in respect of currency or exchange regulations, be accorded the same facilities as are customarily accorded to officials of international organisations;

(d) enjoy the right to import free of duty their furniture and effects at the time of first taking up their post in the country concerned, and the right to re-export free of duty their furniture and effects, on termination of their duties in that country, subject in either case to the conditions considered to be necessary by the Government of the country in which this right is exercised;

(e) have the right to import free of duty a motor car for their personal use, acquired either in the country of their last residence or in the country of which they are nationals on the terms ruling in the home market in that country, and to re-export it free of duty, subject in either case to the conditions considered to be necessary by the Government of the country concerned.

Article 13

Officials and other servants of the Communities shall be liable to a tax for the benefit of the Communities on salaries, wages and emoluments paid to them by the Communities, in accordance with the conditions and procedure laid down by the Council, acting on a proposal from the Commission.

They shall be exempt from national taxes on salaries, wages and emoluments paid by the Communities.

Article 14

In the application of income tax, wealth tax and death duties and in the application of conventions on the avoidance of double taxation concluded between Member States of the Communities, officials and other servants of the Communities who, solely by reason of the performance of their duties in the service of the Communities, establish their residence in the territory of a Member State other than their country of domicile for tax purposes at the time of entering the service of the Communities, shall be considered, both in the country of their actual residence and in the country of domicile for tax purposes, as having maintained their domicile in the latter country provided that it is a member of the Communities. This provision shall also apply to a spouse, to the extent that the latter is not separately engaged in a gainful occupation, and to children dependent on and in the care of the persons referred to in this Article.

Movable property belonging to persons referred to in the preceding paragraph and situated in the territory of the country where they are staying shall be exempt from death duties in that country; such property shall, for the assessment of such duty, be considered as being in the country of domicile for tax purposes, subject to the rights of third countries and to the possible application of provisions of international conventions on double taxation.

Any domicile acquired solely by reason of the performance of duties in the service of other international organisations shall not be taken into consideration in applying the provisions of this Article.

Article 15

The Council shall, acting unanimously on a proposal from the Commission, lay down the scheme of social security benefits for officials and other servants of the Communities.

Article 16

The Council shall, acting on a proposal from the Commission and after consulting the other institutions concerned, determine the categories of officials and other servants of the Communities to whom the provisions of Article 12, the second paragraph of Article 13, and Article 14 shall apply, in whole or in part.

The names, grades and addresses of officials and other servants included in such categories shall be communicated periodically to the Governments of the Member States.

Chapter VI

Privileges and immunities of missions of third countries accredited to the European Communities

Article 17

The Member State in whose territory the Communities have their seat shall accord the customary diplomatic immunities and privileges to missions of third countries accredited to the Communities.

Chapter VII

General provisions

Article 18

Privileges, immunities and facilities shall be accorded to officials and other servants of the Communities solely in the interests of the Communities.

Each institution of the Communities shall be required to waive the immunity accorded to an official or other servant wherever that institution considers that the waiver of such immunity is not contrary to the interest of the Communities.

Article 19

The institutions of the Communities shall, for the purpose of applying this Protocol, cooperate with the responsible authorities of the Member States concerned.

Article 20

Articles 12 to 15 and Article 18 shall apply to members of the Commission.

Article 21

Articles 12 to 15 and Article 18 shall apply to the Judges, the Advocates-General, the Registrar and the Assistant Rapporteurs of the Court of Justice, without prejudice to the provisions of Article 3 of the Protocols on the Statute of the Court of Justice concerning immunity from legal proceedings of Judges and Advocates-General.

Article 22

This Protocol shall also apply to the European Investment Bank, to the members of its organs, to its staff and to the representatives of the Member States taking part in its activities, without prejudice to the provisions of the Protocol on the Statute of the Bank.

The European Investment Bank shall in addition be exempt from any form of taxation or imposition of a like nature on the occasion of any increase in its capital and from the various formalities which may be connected therewith in the State where the Bank has its seat. Similarly, its dissolution or liquidation shall not give rise to any imposition. Finally, the activities of the Bank and of its organs carried on in accordance with its Statute shall not be subject to any turnover tax.

In witness whereof, the undersigned plenipotentiaries have signed this Protocol.

Done at Brussels this eighth day of April in the year one thousand nine hundred and sixty-five.[2]

[List omitted]

FOOTNOTES

1. OJ No 152, 13.7.67.
2. Editorial note: This Protocol is annexed to the Treaty establishing a Single Council and a Single Commission of the European Communities (Merger Treaty). This Treaty is omitted from this volume but is to be found in OJ No 152, 13.7.67.

 Implemented in Ireland: European Communities Act, 1972.

SINGLE EUROPEAN ACT, 1986

His Majesty the King of the Belgians,

Her Majesty the Queen of Denmark,

The President of the Federal Republic of Germany,

The President of the Hellenic Republic,

His Majesty the King of Spain,

The President of the French Republic,

The President of Ireland,

The President of the Italian Republic,

His Royal Highness the Grand Duke of Luxembourg,

Her Majesty the Queen of the Netherlands,

The President of the Portuguese Republic,

Her Majesty the Queen of the United Kingdom of Great Britain and Northern Ireland,

Moved by the will to continue the work undertaken on the basis of the Treaties establishing the European Communities and to transform relations as a whole among their States into a European Union, in accordance with the Solemn Declaration of Stuttgart of 19 June 1983,

Resolved to implement this European Union on the basis, firstly, of the Communities operating in accordance with their own rules and, secondly, of European Cooperation among the Signatory States in the sphere of foreign policy and to invest this union with the necessary means of action,

Determined to work together to promote democracy on the basis of the fundamental rights recognised in the constitutions and laws of the Member States, in the Convention for the Protection of Human Rights and Fundamental Freedoms and the European Social Charter, notably freedom, equality and social justice,

Convinced that the European idea, the results achieved in the fields of economic integration and political cooperation, and the need for new developments correspond to the wishes of the democratic peoples of Europe, for whom the European Parliament, elected by universal suffrage, is an indispensable means of expression,

Aware of the responsibility incumbent upon Europe to aim at speaking ever increasingly with one voice and to act with consistency and solidarity in order more effectively to protect its common interests and independence, in particular to display the principles of democracy and compliance with the law and with human rights to which they are attached, so that together they may make their own contribution to the preservation of international peace and security in accordance with the undertaking entered into by them within the framework of the United Nations Charter,

Determined to improve the economic and social situation by extending common policies and pursuing new objectives, and to ensure a smoother functioning of the Communities by enabling the institutions to exercise their powers under conditions most in keeping with Community interests,

Whereas at their Conference in Paris from 19 to 21 October 1972 the Heads of State or of Government approved the objective of the progressive realisation of economic and monetary union;

Having regard to the Annex to the conclusions of the Presidency of the European Council in Bremen on 6 and 7 July 1978 and the Resolution of the European Council in Brussels on 5 December 1978 on the introduction of the European Monetary System (EMS) and related questions, and noting that in accordance with that Resolution, the Community and the Central Banks of the Member States have taken a number of measures intended to implement monetary cooperation,

Have decided to adopt this Act and to this end have designated as their plenipotentiaries:

[List omitted]

Who, having exchanged their full powers, found in good and due form, have agreed as follows:

Title I

Common provisions

Article 1

The European Communities and European Political Cooperation shall have as their objective to contribute together to making concrete progress towards European unity.

The European Communities shall be founded on the Treaties establishing the European Coal and Steel Community, the European Economic Community, the European Atomic Energy Community and on the subsequent Treaties and Acts modifying or supplementing them.

Political Cooperation shall be governed by Title III. The provisions of the Title shall confirm and supplement the procedures agreed in the reports of Luxembourg (1970), Copenhagen (1973), London (1981), the Solemn Declaration on European Union (1983) and the practices gradually established among the Member States.

Article 2

The European Council shall bring together the Heads of State or of Government of the Member States and the President of the Commission of the European Communities. They shall be assisted by the Ministers for Foreign Affairs and by a Member of the Commission.

The European Council shall meet at least twice a year.

Article 3

1. The institutions of the European Communities, henceforth designated as referred to hereafter, shall exercise their powers and jurisdiction under the conditions and for the purposes provided for by the Treaties establishing the Communities and by the subsequent Treaties and Acts modifying or supplementing them and by the provisions of Title II.

2. The institutions and bodies responsible for European Political Cooperation shall exercise their powers and jurisdiction under the conditions and for the purposes laid down in Title III and in the documents referred to in the third paragraph of Article 1.

Title II

Provisions amending the Treaties establishing the European Communities

[Text included in Treaties as amendments]

Title III

Provisions on European cooperation in the sphere of foreign policy

Article 30

European Cooperation in the sphere of foreign policy shall be governed by the following provisions:

1. The High Contracting Parties, being members of the European Communities, shall endeavour jointly to formulate and implement a European foreign policy.

2. (a) The High Contracting Parties undertake to inform and consult each

other on any foreign policy matters of general interest so as to ensure that their combined influence is exercised as effectively as possible through coordination, the convergence of their positions and the implementation of joint action.

(b) Consultations shall take place before the High Contracting Parties decide on their final position.

(c) In adopting its positions and in its national measures each High Contracting Party shall take full account of the positions of the other partners and shall give due consideration to the desirability of adopting and implementing common European positions.

In order to increase their capacity for joint action in the foreign policy field, the High Contracting Parties shall ensure that common principles and objectives are gradually developed and defined.

The determination of common positions shall constitute a point of reference for the policies of the High Contracting Parties.

(d) The High Contracting Parties shall endeavour to avoid any action or position which impairs their effectiveness as a cohesive force in international relations or within international organisations.

3. (a) The Ministers for Foreign Affairs and a member of the Commission shall meet at least four times a year within the framework of European Political Cooperation. They may also discuss foreign policy matters within the framework of Political Cooperation on the occasion of meetings of the Council of the European Communities.

(b) The Commission shall be fully associated with the proceedings of Political Cooperation.

(c) In order to ensure the swift adoption of common positions and the implementation of joint action, the High Contracting Parties shall, as far as possible, refrain from impeding the formation of a consensus and the joint action which this could produce.

4. The High Contracting Parties shall ensure that the European Parliament is closely associated with European Political Cooperation. To that end the Presidency shall regularly inform the European Parliament of the foreign policy issues which are being examined within the framework of Political Cooperation and shall ensure that the views of the European Parliament are duly taken into consideration.

5. The external policies of the European Community and the policies agreed in European Political Cooperation must be consistent.

The Presidency and the Commission, each within its own sphere of competence, shall have special responsibility for ensuring that such consistency is sought and maintained.

6. (a) The High Contracting Parties consider that closer cooperation on questions of European security would contribute in an essential way to the development of a European identity in external policy matters. They are ready to coordinate their positions more closely on the political and economic aspects of security.

(b) The High Contracting Parties are determined to maintain the technological and industrial conditions necessary for their security. They shall work to that end both at national level and, where appropriate, within the framework of the competent institutions and bodies.

(c) Nothing in this Title shall impede closer cooperation in the field of security between certain of the High Contracting Parties within the framework of the Western European Union or the Atlantic Alliance.

7. (a) In international institutions and at international conferences which they attend, the High Contracting Parties shall endeavour to adopt common positions on the subjects covered by this Title.

(b) In international institutions and at international conferences in which not all the High Contracting Parties participate, those who do participate shall take full account of positions agreed in European Political Cooperation.

8. The High Contracting Parties shall organise a political dialogue with third countries and regional groupings whenever they deem it necessary.

9. The High Contracting Parties and the Commission, through mutual assistance and information, shall intensify cooperation between their representations accredited to third countries and to international organisations.

10. (a) The Presidency of European Political Cooperation shall be held by the High Contracting Party which holds the Presidency of the Council of the European Communities.

(b) The Presidency shall be responsible for initiating action and coordinating and representing the positions of the Member States in relations with third countries in respect of European Political Cooperation activities. It shall also be responsible for the management of Political Cooperation and in particular for drawing up the timetable of meetings and for convening and organising meetings.

(c) The Political Directors shall meet regularly in the Political Committee in order to give the necessary impetus, maintain the continuity of European Political Cooperation and prepare Ministers' discussions.

(d) The Political Committee or, if necessary, a ministerial meeting shall convene within forty-eight hours at the request of at least three Member States.

(e) The European Correspondents' Group shall be responsible, under the direction of the Political Committee, for monitoring the implementation of European Political Cooperation and for studying general organisational problems.

(f) Working groups shall meet as directed by the Political Committee.

(g) A Secretariat based in Brussels shall assist the Presidency in preparing and implementing the activities of European Political Cooperation and in administrative matters. It shall carry out its duties under the authority of the Presidency.

11. As regards privileges and immunities, the members of the European Political Cooperation Secretariat shall be treated in the same way as members of the diplomatic missions of the High Contracting Parties based in the same place as the Secretariat.

12. Five years after the entry into force of this Act the High Contracting Parties shall examine whether any revision of Title III is required.

Title IV

General and final provisions

Article 31

The provisions of the Treaty establishing the European Coal and Steel Community, the Treaty establishing the European Economic Community and the Treaty establishing the European Atomic Energy Community concerning the powers of the Court of Justice of the European Communities and the exercise of those powers shall apply only to the provisions of Title II and to Article 32; they shall apply to those provisions under the same conditions as for the provisions of the said Treaties.

Article 32

Subject to Article 3(1), to Title II and to Article 31, nothing in this Act shall affect the Treaties establishing the European Communities or any subsequent Treaties and Acts modifying or supplementing them.

Article 33

1. This Act will be ratified by the High Contracting Parties in accordance with their respective constitutional requirements. The instruments of ratification will be deposited with the Government of the Italian Republic.

2. This Act will enter into force on the first day of the month following that in which the instrument of ratification is deposited of the last Signatory State to fulfil that formality.

Article 34

This Act, drawn up in a single original in the Danish, Dutch, English, French, German, Greek, Irish, Italian, Portuguese and Spanish languages, the texts in each of these languages being equally authentic, will be deposited in the archives of the Government of the Italian Republic, which will remit a certified copy to each of the Governments of the other Signatory States.

In witness whereof, the plenipotentiaries have signed this Act.

Done at Luxembourg, 17 February 1986, and at The Hague, 28 February 1986.

Final Act

The Conference of the Representatives of the Governments of the Member States convened at Luxembourg on 9 September 1985,

which carried on its discussions in Luxembourg and Brussels and which met at the end thereof in Luxembourg on 17 February 1986 and in The Hague on 28 February 1986, has adopted the following text.

At the time of signing this text, the Conference adopted the declarations listed hereinafter and annexed to this Final Act:

1. Declaration on the powers of implementation of the Commission

2. Declaration on the Court of Justice

3. Declaration on Article 8A of the EEC Treaty

4. Declaration on Article 100A of the EEC Treaty

5. Declaration on Article 100B of the EEC Treaty

6. General Declaration on Articles 13 to 19 of the Single European Act

7. Declaration on Article 118A(2) of the EEC Treaty

8. Declaration on Article 130D of the EEC Treaty

9. Declaration on Article 130R of the EEC Treaty

10. Declaration by the High Contracting Parties on Title III of the Single European Act

11. Declaration on Article 30(10)(9) of the Single European Act.

The Conference also notes the declarations listed hereinafter and annexed to this Final Act:

1. Declaration by the Presidency on the time limit within which the Council will give its opinion following a first reading (Article 149(2) of the EEC Treaty)

2. Political Declaration by the Governments of the Member States on the free movement of persons

3. Declaration by the Government of the Hellenic Republic on Article 8A of the EEC Treaty

4. Declaration by the Commission on Article 28 of the EEC Treaty

5. Declaration by the Government of Ireland on Article 57(2) of the EEC Treaty

6. Declaration by the Government of the Portuguese Republic on Articles 59, second paragraph, and 84 of the EEC Treaty

7. Declaration by the Government of the Kingdom of Denmark on Article 100A of the EEC Treaty

8. Declaration by the Presidency and the Commission on the monetary capacity of the Community

9. Declaration by the Government of the Kingdom of Denmark on European Political Cooperation.

Declaration on the powers of implementation of the Commission

The Conference asks the Community authorities to adopt, before the Act enters into force, the principles and rules on the basis of which the Commission's powers of implementation will be defined in each case.

In this connection the Conference requests the Council to give the Advisory Committee procedure in particular a predominant place in the interests of speed and efficiency in the decision-making process, for the exercise of the powers of implementation conferred on the Commission within the field of Article 100A of the EEC Treaty.

Declaration on the Court of Justice

The Conference agrees that the provisions of Article 32d(1) of the ECSC Treaty, Article 168A(1) of the EEC Treaty and Article 140A(1) of the EAEC Treaty do not prejudge any conferral of judicial competence likely to be provided for in the context of agreements concluded between the Member States.

Declaration on Article 8A of the EEC Treaty

The Conference wishes by means of the provisions in Article 8A to express its firm political will to take before 1 January 1993 the decisions necessary to complete the internal market defined in those provisions, and more particularly the decisions necessary to implement the Commission's programme described in the White Paper on the Internal Market.

Setting the date of 31 December 1992 does not create an automatic legal effect.

Declaration on Article 100A of the EEC Treaty

In its proposals pursuant to Article 100A(1) the Commission shall give precedence to the use of the instrument of a directive if harmonisation involves the amendment of legislative provisions in one or more Member States.

Declaration on Article 100B of the EEC Treaty

The Conference considers that, since Article 8C of the EEC Treaty is of general application, it also applies to the proposals which the Commission is required to make under Article 100B of that Treaty.

General declaration on Articles 13 to 19 of the Single European Act

Nothing in these provisions shall affect the right of Member States to take such measures as they consider necessary for the purpose of controlling immigration from third countries, and to combat terrorism, crime, the traffic in drugs and illicit trading in works of art and antiques.

Declaration on Article 118A(2) of the EEC Treaty

The Conference notes that in the discussions on Article 118A(2) of the EEC Treaty it was agreed that the Community does not intend, in laying down minimum requirements for the protection of the safety and health of employees, to discriminate in a manner unjustified by the circumstances against employees in small and medium-sized undertakings.

Declaration on Article 130D of the EEC Treaty

In this context the Conference refers to the conclusions of the European Council in Brussels in March 1984, which read as follows:

'The financial resources allocated to aid from the Funds, having regard to the IMPs, will be significantly increased in real terms within the limits of financing possibilities.'

Declaration on Article 130R of the EEC Treaty:

Re paragraph 1, third indent

The Conference confirms that the Community's activities in the sphere of the environment may not interfere with national policies regarding the exploitation of energy resources.

Re paragraph 5, second subparagraph

The Conference considers that the provisions of Article 130R(5), second subparagraph do not affect the principles resulting from the judgment handed down by the Court of Justice in the AETR case.

Declaration by the High Contracting Parties on Title III of the Single European Act

The High Contracting Parties to Title III on European Political Cooperation reaffirm their openness to other European nations which share the same ideals and objectives. They agree in particular to strengthen their links with the member countries of the Council of Europe and with other democratic European countries with which they have friendly relations and close cooperation.

Declaration on Article 30(10)(g)

The Conference considers that the provisions of Article 30(10)(g) do not affect the Decision of the Representatives of the Governments of the Member States of 8 April 1965 on the provisional location of certain institutions and departments of the Communities.

Declaration by the Presidency on the time limit within which the Council will give its opinion following a first reading (Article 149(2) of the EEC Treaty)

As regards the declaration by the European Council in Milan, to the effect that the Council must seek ways of improving its decision-making procedures, the Presidency states its intention of completing the work in question as soon as possible.

Political declaration by the Governments of the Member States on the free movement of persons

In order to promote the free movement of persons, the Member States shall cooperate, without prejudice to the powers of the Community, in particular as regards the entry, movement and residence of nationals of third countries. They shall also cooperate in the combating of terrorism, crime, the traffic in drugs and illicit trading in works of art and antiques.

Declaration by the Government of the Hellenic Republic on Article 8A of the EEC Treaty

Greece considers that the development of Community policies and actions, and the adoption of measures on the basis of Articles 70(1) and 84, must both take place in such a way as not to harm sensitive sectors of Member States' economies.

Declaration by the Commission on Article 28 of the EEC Treaty

With regard to its own internal procedures, the Commission will ensure that the changes resulting from the amendment of Article 28 will not lead to delays in responding to urgent requests for the alteration or suspension of Common Customs Tariff duties.

Declaration by the Government of Ireland on Article 57(2) of the EEC Treaty

Ireland, in confirming its agreement to qualified majority voting under Article 57(2), wishes to recall that the insurance industry in Ireland is a particularly sensitive one and that special arrangements have had to be made by the Government of Ireland for the protection of insurance-policy holders and third parties. In relation to harmonisation of legislation on insurance, the Government of Ireland would expect to be able to rely on a sympathetic attitude from the Commission and from the other Member States of the Community should Ireland later find itself in a situation where the Government of Ireland considers it necessary to have special provision made for the position of the industry in Ireland.

Declaration by the Government of the Portuguese Republic on Articles 59, second paragraph, and 84 of the EEC Treaty

Portugal considers that as the change from unanimous to qualified majority voting in Articles 59, second paragraph, and 84 was not contemplated in the negotiations for the accession of Portugal to the Community and substantially alters the Community *acquis*, it must not damage sensitive and vital sectors of the Portuguese economy, and, wherever necessary, appropriate and specific transitional measures should be introduced to forestall the adverse consequences that could ensue for these sectors.

Declaration by the Government of the Kingdom of Denmark on Article 100A of the EEC Treaty

The Danish Government notes that in cases where a Member State is of the opinion that measures adopted under Article 100A do not safeguard higher requirements concerning the working environment, the protection of the environment or the needs referred to in Article 36, the provisions of Article 100A(4) guarantee that the Member State in question can apply national provisions. Such national provisions are to be taken to fulfil the abovementioned aim and may not entail hidden protectionism.

Declaration by the Presidency and the Commission on the monetary capacity of the Community

The Presidency and the Commission consider that the provisions inserted in the EEC Treaty with reference to the Community's monetary capacity are without prejudice to the possibility of further development within the framework of the existing powers.

Declaration by the Government of the Kingdom of Denmark on European Political Cooperation

The Danish Government states that the conclusion of Title III on European Political Cooperation in the sphere of foreign policy does not affect Denmark's participation in Nordic cooperation in the sphere of foreign policy.

Implemented in Ireland: S.I. 170S/87. (Editorial note: European Communities (Amendment) Act, 1986 implemented certain aspects of SEA in Ireland.)

EUROPEAN ECONOMIC AREA AGREEMENT

The European Economic Community,

The European Coal and Steel Community,

The Kingdom of Belgium,

The Kingdom of Denmark,

The Federal Republic of Germany,

The Hellenic Republic,

The Kingdom of Spain,

The French Republic,

Ireland,

The Italian Republic,

The Grand Duchy of Luxembourg,

The Kingdom of the Netherlands,

The Portuguese Republic,

The United Kingdom of Great Britain and Northern Ireland,

and

The Republic of Austria,

The Republic of Finland,

The Republic of Iceland,

The Principality of Liechtenstein,

The Kingdom of Norway,

The Kingdom of Sweden,

The Swiss Confederation

hereinafter referred to as the Contracting Parties;

Convinced of the contribution that a European Economic Area will bring to the construction of a Europe based on peace, democracy and human rights;

Reaffirming the high priority attached to the privileged relationship between the European Community, its Member States and the EFTA States, which is based on proximity, long-standing common values and European identity;

Determined to contribute, on the basis of market economy, to world-wide trade liberalisation and cooperation, in particular in accordance with the provisions of the General Agreement on Tariffs and Trade and the Convention on the Organisation for Economic Cooperation and Development;

Considering the objective of establishing a dynamic and homogeneous European Economic Area, based on common rules and equal conditions of competition and providing for the adequate means of enforcement including at the judicial level, and achieved on the basis of equality and reciprocity and of an overall balance of benefits, rights and obligations for the Contracting Parties;

Determined to provide for the fullest possible realisation of the free movement of goods, persons, services and capital within the whole European Economic Area, as well as for strengthened and broadened cooperation in flanking and horizontal policies;

Aiming to promote a harmonious development of the European Economic Area and convinced of the need to contribute through the application of this Agreement to the reduction of economic and social regional disparities;

Desirous of contributing to the strengthening of the cooperation between the members of the European Parliament and of the Parliaments of the EFTA States, as well as between the social partners in the European Community and in the EFTA States;

Convinced of the important role that individuals will play in the European Economic Area through the exercise of the rights conferred on them by this Agreement and through the judicial defence of these rights;

Determined to preserve, protect and improve the quality of the environment and to ensure a prudent and rational utilisation of natural resources on the basis, in particular, of the principle of sustainable development, as well as the principle that precautionary and preventive action should be taken;

Determined to take, in the further development of rules, a high level of protection concerning health, safety and the environment as a basis;

Noting the importance of the development of the social dimension, including equal treatment of men and women, in the European Economic Area and wishing to ensure economic and social progress and to promote conditions for full employment, an improved standard of living and improved working conditions within the European Economic Area;

Determined to promote the interests of consumers and to strengthen their position in the market place, aiming at a high level of consumer protection;

Attached to the common objectives of strengthening the scientific and technological basis of European industry and of encouraging it to become more competitive at the international level;

Considering that the conclusion of this Agreement shall not prejudge in any way the possibility of EFTA States to accede to the European Communities;

Whereas, in full deference to the independence of the courts, the objective of the Contracting Parties is to arrive at, and maintain, a uniform interpretation and application of this Agreement and those provisions of Community legislation which are substantially reproduced in this Agreement and to arrive at an equal treatment of individuals and economic operators as regards the four freedoms and the conditions of competition;

Whereas this Agreement does not restrict the decision-making autonomy or the treaty-making power of the Contracting Parties, subject to the provisions of this Agreement and the limitations set by public international law;

Have decided to conclude the following Agreement:

PART I

Objectives and principles

Article 1

1. The aim of this Agreement of association is to promote a continuous and balanced strengthening of trade and economic relations between the Contracting Parties with equal conditions of competition, and the respect of the same rules, with a view to creating a homogeneous European Economic Area, hereinafter referred to as the EEA.

2. In order to attain the objectives set out in paragraph 1, the association shall entail, in accordance with the provisions of this Agreement:

(a) the free movement of goods;

(b) the free movement of persons;

(c) the free movement of services;

(d) the free movement of capital;

(e) the setting up of a system ensuring that competition is not distorted and that the rules thereon are equally respected; as well as

(f) closer cooperation in other fields, such as research and development, the environment, education and social policy.

Article 2

For the purposes of this Agreement:

(a) the term 'Agreement' means the main Agreement, its Protocols and Annexes as well as the acts referred to therein;

(b) the term 'EFTA States' means the Contracting Parties, which are members of the European Free Trade Association;

(c) the term 'Contracting Parties' means, concerning the Community and the EC Member States, the Community and the EC Member States, or the Community, or the EC Member States. The meaning to be attributed to this expression in each case is to be deduced from the relevant provisions of this Agreement as they follow from the Treaty establishing the European Economic Community and the Treaty establishing the European Coal and Steel Community.

Article 3

The Contracting Parties shall take all appropriate measures, whether general or particular, to ensure fulfilment of the obligations arising out of this Agreement.

They shall abstain from any measure which could jeopardise the attainment of the objectives of this Agreement.

Moreover, they shall facilitate cooperation within the framework of this Agreement.

Article 4

Within the scope of application of this Agreement, and without prejudice to any special provisions contained therein, any discrimination on grounds of nationality shall be prohibited.

Article 5

A Contracting Party may at any time raise a matter of concern at the level of the EEA Joint Committee or the EEA Council according to the modalities laid down in Articles 92(2) and 89(2), respectively.

Article 6

Without prejudice to future developments of case-law, the provisions of this Agreement, in so far as they are identical in substance to corresponding rules of the Treaty establishing the European Economic Community and the Treaty establishing the European Coal and Steel Community and to acts adopted in application of these two Treaties, shall, in their implementation and application, be interpreted in conformity with the relevant rulings of the Court of Justice of the European Communities given prior to the date of signature of this Agreement.

Article 7

Acts referred to or contained in the Annexes to this Agreement or in decisions of the EEA Joint Committee shall be binding upon the Contracting Parties and be, or be made, part of their internal legal order as follows:

(a) an act corresponding to an EEC regulation shall as such be made part of the internal legal order of the Contracting Parties;

(b) an act corresponding to an EEC directive shall leave to the authorities of the Contracting Parties the choice of form and method of implementation.

PART II

Free movement of goods

Chapter 1

Basic principles

Article 8

1. Free movement of goods between the Contracting Parties shall be established in conformity with the provisions of this Agreement.

2. Unless otherwise specified, Articles 10 to 15, 19, 20 and 25 to 27 shall apply only to products originating in the Contracting Parties.

3. Unless otherwise specified, the provisions of this Agreement shall apply only to:

(a) products falling within Chapters 25 to 97 of the Harmonised Commodity Description and Coding System, excluding the products listed in Protocol 2;

(b) products specified in Protocol 3, subject to the specific arrangements set out in that Protocol.

Article 9

1. The rules of origin are set out in Protocol 4. They are without prejudice to any international obligations which have been, or may be, subscribed to by the Contracting Parties under the General Agreement on Tariffs and Trade.

2. With a view to developing the results achieved in this Agreement, the Contracting Parties will continue their efforts in order further to improve and simplify all aspects of rules of origin and to increase cooperation in customs matters.

3. A first review will take place before the end of 1993. Subsequent reviews will take place at two-yearly intervals. On the basis of these reviews, the Contracting Parties undertake to decide on the appropriate measures to be included in this Agreement.

Article 10

Customs duties on imports and exports, and any charges having equivalent effect, shall be prohibited between the Contracting Parties. Without prejudice to the arrangements set out in Protocol 5, this shall also apply to customs duties of a fiscal nature.

Article 11

Quantitative restrictions on imports and all measures having equivalent effect shall be prohibited between the Contracting Parties.

Article 12

Quantitative restrictions on exports and all measures having equivalent effect shall be prohibited between the Contracting Parties.

Article 13

The provisions of Articles 11 and 12 shall not preclude prohibitions or restrictions on imports, exports or goods in transit justified on grounds of public morality, public policy or public security; the protection of health and life of humans, animals or plants; the protection of national treasures possessing artistic, historic or archaeological value; or the protection of industrial and commercial property. Such prohibitions or restrictions shall not, however, constitute a means of arbitrary discrimination or a disguised restriction on trade between the Contracting Parties.

Article 14

No Contracting Party shall impose, directly or indirectly, on the products of other Contracting Parties any internal taxation of any kind in excess of that imposed directly or indirectly on similar domestic products.

Furthermore, no Contracting Party shall impose on the products of other Contracting Parties any internal taxation of such a nature as to afford indirect protection to other products.

Article 15

Where products are exported to the territory of any Contracting Party, any repayment of internal taxation shall not exceed the internal taxation imposed on them whether directly or indirectly.

Article 16

1. The Contracting Parties shall ensure that any State monopoly of a commercial character be adjusted so that no discrimination regarding the conditions under which goods are procured and marketed will exist between nationals of EC Member States and EFTA States.

2. The provisions of this Article shall apply to any body through which the competent authorities of the Contracting Parties, in law or in fact, either directly or indirectly supervise, determine or appreciably influence imports or exports between Contracting Parties. These provisions shall likewise apply to monopolies delegated by the State to others.

Chapter 2

Agricultural and fishery products

Article 17

Annex I contains specific provisions and arrangements concerning veterinary and phytosanitary matters.

Article 18

Without prejudice to the specific arrangements governing trade in agricultural products, the Contracting Parties shall ensure that the arrangements provided for in Articles 17 and 23(a) and (b), as they apply to products other than those covered by Article 8(3), are not compromised by other technical barriers to trade. Article 13 shall apply.

Article 19

1. The Contracting Parties shall examine any difficulties that might arise in their trade in agricultural products and shall endeavour to seek appropriate solutions.

2. The Contracting Parties undertake to continue their efforts with a view to achieving progressive liberalisation of agricultural trade.

3. To this end, the Contracting Parties will carry out, before the end of 1993 and subsequently at two-yearly intervals, reviews of the conditions of trade in agricultural products.

4. In the light of the results of these reviews, within the framework of their respective agricultural policies and taking into account the results of the Uruguay Round, the Contracting Parties will decide, within the framework of this Agreement, on a preferential, bilateral or multilateral, reciprocal and mutually beneficial basis, on further reductions of any type of barriers to trade in the agricultural sector, including those resulting from State monopolies of a commercial character in the agricultural field.

Article 20

Provisions and arrangements that apply to fish and other marine products are set out in Protocol 9.

Chapter 3

Cooperation in customs-related matters and trade facilitation

Article 21

1. In order to facilitate trade between them, the Contracting Parties shall simplify border controls and formalities. Arrangements for this purpose are set out in Protocol 10.

2. The Contracting Parties shall assist each other in customs matters in order to ensure that customs legislation is correctly applied. Arrangements for this purpose are set out in Protocol 11.

3. The Contracting Parties shall strengthen and broaden cooperation with the aim of simplifying the procedures for trade in goods, in particular in the context of Community programmes, projects and actions aimed at trade facilitation, in accordance with the rules set out in Part VI.

4. Notwithstanding Article 8(3), this Article shall apply to all products.

Article 22

A Contracting Party which is considering the reduction of the effective level of its duties or charges having equivalent effect applicable to third countries benefiting from most-favoured-nation treatment, or which is considering the suspension of their application, shall, as far as may be practicable, notify the EEA Joint Committee not later than 30 days before such reduction or suspension comes into effect. It shall take note of any representations by other Contracting Parties regarding any distortions which might result therefrom.

Chapter 4

Other rules relating to the free movement of goods

Article 23

Specific provisions and arrangements are laid down in:

(*a*) Protocol 12 and Annex II in relation to technical regulations, standards, testing and certification;

(*b*) Protocol 47 in relation to the abolition of technical barriers to trade in wine;

(*c*) Annex III in relation to product liability.

They shall apply to all products unless otherwise specified.

Article 24

Annex IV contains specific provisions and arrangements concerning energy.

Article 25

Where compliance with the provisions of Articles 10 and 12 leads to:

(*a*) re-export towards a third country against which the exporting Contracting Party maintains, for the product concerned, quantitative export restrictions, export duties or measures or charges having equivalent effect; or

(*b*) a serious shortage, or threat thereof, of a product essential to the exporting Contracting Party;

and where the situations referred to above give rise, or are likely to give rise, to major difficulties for the exporting Contracting Party, that Contracting Party may take appropriate measures in accordance with the procedures set out in Article 113.

Article 26

Anti-dumping measures, countervailing duties and measures against illicit commercial practices attributable to third countries shall not be applied in relations between the Contracting Parties, unless otherwise specified in this Agreement.

Chapter 5

Coal and steel products

Article 27

Provisions and arrangements concerning coal and steel products are set out in Protocols 14 and 25.

PART III

Free movement of persons, services and capital

Chapter 1

Workers and self-employed persons

Article 28

1. Freedom of movement for workers shall be secured among EC Member States and EFTA States.

2. Such freedom of movement shall entail the abolition of any discrimination based on nationality between workers of EC Member States and EFTA States as regards employment, remuneration and other conditions of work and employment.

3. It shall entail the right, subject to limitations justified on grounds of public policy, public security or public health:

(a) to accept offers of employment actually made;

(b) to move freely within the territory of EC Member States and EFTA States for this purpose;

(c) to stay in the territory of an EC Member State or an EFTA State for the purpose of employment in accordance with the provisions governing the employment of nationals of that State laid down by law, regulation or administrative action;

(d) to remain in the territory of an EC Member State or an EFTA State after having been employed there.

4. The provisions of this Article shall not apply to employment in the public service.

5. Annex V contains specific provisions on the free movement of workers.

Article 29

In order to provide freedom of movement for workers and self-employed persons, the Contracting Parties shall, in the field of social security, secure, as provided for in Annex VI, for workers and self-employed persons and their dependants, in particular:

(a) aggregation, for the purpose of acquiring and retaining the right to benefit and of calculating the amount of benefit, of all periods taken into account under the laws of the several countries;

(b) payment of benefits to persons resident in the territories of Contracting Parties.

Article 30

In order to make it easier for persons to take up and pursue activities as workers and self-employed persons, the Contracting Parties shall take the necessary measures, as contained in Annex VII, concerning the mutual recognition of diplomas, certificates and other evidence of formal qualifications, and the coordination of the provisions laid down by law, regulation or administrative action in the Contracting Parties concerning the taking up and pursuit of activities by workers and self-employed persons.

Chapter 2

Right of establishment

Article 31

1. Within the framework of the provisions of this Agreement, there shall be no restrictions on the freedom of establishment of nationals of an EC Member State or an EFTA State in the territory of any other of these States. This shall also apply to the setting up of agencies, branches or subsidiaries by nationals of any EC Member State or EFTA State established in the territory of any of these States.

Freedom of establishment shall include the right to take up and pursue activities as self-employed persons and to set up and manage undertakings, in particular companies or firms within the meaning of Article 34, second paragraph, under the conditions laid down for its own nationals by the law of the country where such establishment is effected, subject to the provisions of Chapter 4.

2. Annexes VIII to XI contain specific provisions on the right of establishment.

Article 32

The provisions of this Chapter shall not apply, so far as any given Contracting Party is concerned, to activities which in that Contracting Party are connected, even occasionally, with the exercise of official authority.

Article 33

The provisions of this Chapter and measures taken in pursuance thereof shall not prejudice the applicability of provisions laid down by law, regulation or administrative action providing for special treatment for foreign nationals on grounds of public policy, public security or public health.

Article 34

Companies or firms formed in accordance with the law of an EC Member State or an EFTA State and having their registered office, central administration or principal place of business within the territory of the Contracting Parties shall, for the purposes of this Chapter, be treated in the same way as natural persons who are nationals of EC Member States or EFTA States.

'Companies or firms' means companies or firms constituted under civil or commercial law, including cooperative societies, and other legal persons governed by public or private law, save for those which are non-profit-making.

Article 35

The provisions of Article 30 shall apply to the matters covered by this Chapter.

Chapter 3

Services

Article 36

1. Within the framework of the provisions of this Agreement, there shall be no restrictions on freedom to provide services within the territory of

the Contracting Parties in respect of nationals of EC Member States and EFTA States who are established in an EC Member State or an EFTA State other than that of the person for whom the services are intended.

2. Annexes IX to XI contain specific provisions on the freedom to provide services.

Article 37

Services shall be considered to be 'services' within the meaning of this Agreement where they are normally provided for remuneration, in so far as they are not governed by the provisions relating to freedom of movement for goods, capital and persons.

'Services' shall in particular include:

(a) activities of an industrial character;

(b) activities of a commercial character;

(c) activities of craftsmen;

(d) activities of the professions.

Without prejudice to the provisions of Chapter 2, the person providing a service may, in order to do so, temporarily pursue his activity in the State where the service is provided, under the same conditions as are imposed by that State on its own nationals.

Article 38

Freedom to provide services in the field of transport shall be governed by the provisions of Chapter 6.

Article 39

The provisions of Articles 30 and 32 to 34 shall apply to the matters covered by this Chapter.

Chapter 4

Capital

Article 40

Within the framework of the provisions of this Agreement, there shall be no restrictions between the Contracting Parties on the movement of capital belonging to persons resident in EC Member States or EFTA States and no discrimination based on the nationality or on the place of residence of the parties or on the place where such capital is invested. Annex XII contains the provisions necessary to implement this Article.

Article 41

Current payments connected with the movement of goods, persons, services or capital between Contracting Parties within the framework of the provisions of this Agreement shall be free of all restrictions.

Article 42

1. Where domestic rules governing the capital market and the credit system are applied to the movements of capital liberalised in accordance with the provisions of this Agreement, this shall be done in a non-discriminatory manner.

2. Loans for the direct or indirect financing of an EC Member State or an EFTA State or its regional or local authorities shall not be issued or placed in other EC Member States or EFTA States unless the States concerned have reached agreement thereon.

Article 43

1. Where differences between the exchange rules of EC Member States and EFTA States could lead persons resident in one of these States to use the freer transfer facilities within the territory of the Contracting Parties which are provided for in Article 40 in order to evade the rules of one of these States concerning the movement of capital to or from third countries, the Contracting Party concerned may take appropriate measures to overcome these difficulties.

2. If movements of capital lead to disturbances in the functioning of the capital market in any EC Member State or EFTA State, the Contracting Party concerned may take protective measures in the field of capital movements.

3. If the competent authorities of a Contracting Party make an alteration in the rate of exchange which seriously distorts conditions of competition, the other Contracting Parties may take, for a strictly limited period, the necessary measures in order to counter the consequences of such alteration.

4. Where an EC Member State or an EFTA State is in difficulties, or is seriously threatened with difficulties, as regards its balance of payments either as a result of an overall disequilibrium in its balance of payments, or as a result of the type of currency at its disposal, and where such difficulties are liable in particular to jeopardise the functioning of this

Agreement, the Contracting Party concerned may take protective measures.

Article 44

The Community, on the one hand, and the EFTA States, on the other, shall apply their internal procedures, as provided for in Protocol 18, to implement the provisions of Article 43.

Article 45

1. Decisions, opinions and recommendations related to the measures laid down in Article 43 shall be notified to the EEA Joint Committee.

2. All measures shall be the subject of prior consultations and exchange of information within the EEA Joint Committee.

3. In the situation referred to in Article 43(2), the Contracting Party may, however, on the grounds of secrecy and urgency take the measures, where this proves necessary, without prior consultations and exchange of information.

4. In the situation referred to in Article 43(4), where a sudden crisis in the balance of payments occurs and the procedures set out in paragraph 2 cannot be followed, the Contracting Party concerned may, as a precaution, take the necessary protective measures. Such measures must cause the least possible disturbance in the functioning of this Agreement and must not be wider in scope than is strictly necessary to remedy the sudden difficulties which have arisen.

5. When measures are taken in accordance with paragraphs 3 and 4, notice thereof shall be given at the latest by the date of their entry into force, and the exchange of information and consultations as well as the notifications referred to in paragraph 1 shall take place as soon as possible thereafter.

Chapter 5

Economic and monetary policy cooperation

Article 46

The Contracting Parties shall exchange views and information concerning the implementation of this Agreement and the impact of the integration on economic activities and on the conduct of economic and monetary policies. Furthermore, they may discuss macroeconomic situations, policies and prospects. This exchange of views and information shall take place on a non-binding basis.

Chapter 6

Transport

Article 47

1. Articles 48 to 52 shall apply to transport by rail, road and inland waterway.

2. Annex XIII contains specific provisions on all modes of transport.

Article 48

1. The provisions of an EC Member State or an EFTA State, relative to transport by rail, road and inland waterway and not covered by Annex XIII, shall not be made less favourable in their direct or indirect effect on carriers of other States as compared with carriers who are nationals of that State.

2. Any Contracting Party deviating from the principle laid down in paragraph 1 shall notify the EEA Joint Committee thereof. The other Contracting Parties which do not accept the deviation may take corresponding countermeasures.

Article 49

Aid shall be compatible with this Agreement if it meets the needs of coordination of transport or if it represents reimbursement for the discharge of certain obligations inherent in the concept of a public service.

Article 50

1. In the case of transport within the territory of the Contracting Parties, there shall be no discrimination which takes the form of carriers charging different rates and imposing different conditions for the carriage of the same goods over the same transport links on the grounds of the country of origin or of destination of the goods in question.

2. The competent authority according to Part VII shall, acting on its own initiative or on application by an EC Member State or an EFTA State, investigate any cases of discrimination falling within this Article and take the necessary decisions within the framework of its internal rules.

Article 51

1. The imposition, in respect of transport operations carried out within the territory of the Contracting Parties, of rates and conditions involving

any element of support or protection in the interest of one or more particular undertakings or industries, shall be prohibited unless authorised by the competent authority referred to in Article 50(2).

2. The competent authority shall, acting on its own initiative or on application by an EC Member State or an EFTA State, examine the rates and conditions referred to in paragraph 1, taking account in particular of the requirements of an appropriate regional economic policy, the needs of underdeveloped areas and the problems of areas seriously affected by political circumstances, on the one hand, and of the effects of such rates and conditions on competition between the different modes of transport, on the other.

The competent authority shall take the necessary decisions within the framework of its internal rules.

3. The prohibition provided for in paragraph 1 shall not apply to tariffs fixed to meet competition.

Article 52

Charges or dues in respect of the crossing of frontiers which are charged by a carrier in addition to transport rates shall not exceed a reasonable level after taking the costs actually incurred thereby into account. The Contracting Parties shall endeavour to reduce these costs progressively.

PART IV

Competition and other common rules

Chapter 1

Rules applicable to undertakings

Article 53

1. The following shall be prohibited as incompatible with the functioning of this Agreement: all agreements between undertakings, decisions by associations of undertakings and concerted practices which may affect trade between Contracting Parties and which have as their object or effect the prevention, restriction or distortion of competition within the territory covered by this Agreement, and in particular those which:

(a) directly or indirectly fix purchase or selling prices or any other trading conditions;

(b) limit or control production, markets, technical development, or investment;

(c) share markets or sources of supply;

(d) apply dissimilar conditions to equivalent transactions with other trading parties, thereby placing them at a competitive disadvantage;

(e) make the conclusion of contracts subject to acceptance by the other parties of supplementary obligations which, by their nature or according to commercial usage, have no connection with the subject of such contracts.

2. Any agreements or decisions prohibited pursuant to this Article shall be automatically void.

3. The provisions of paragraph 1 may, however, be declared inapplicable in the case of:

– any agreement or category of agreements between undertakings;

– any decision or category of decisions by associations of undertakings;

– any concerted practice or category of concerted practices;

which contributes to improving the production or distribution of goods or to promoting technical or economic progress, while allowing consumers a fair share of the resulting benefit, and which does not:

(a) impose on the undertakings concerned restrictions which are not indispensable to the attainment of these objectives;

(b) afford such undertakings the possibility of eliminating competition in respect of a substantial part of the products in question.

Article 54

Any abuse by one or more undertakings of dominant position within the territory covered by this Agreement or in a substantial part of it shall be prohibited as incompatible with the functioning of this Agreement in so far as it may affect trade between Contracting Parties.

Such abuse may, in particular, consist in:

(a) directly or indirectly imposing unfair purchase or selling prices or other unfair trading conditions;

(b) limiting production, markets or technical development to the prejudice of consumers;

(c) applying dissimilar conditions to equivalent transactions with other trading parties, thereby placing them at a competitive disadvantage;

(d) making the conclusion of contracts subject to acceptance by the other parties of supplementary obligations which, by their nature or according to commercial usage, have no connection with the subject of such contracts.

Article 55

1. Without prejudice to the provisions giving effect to Articles 53 and 54 as contained in Protocol 21 and Annex XIV of this Agreement, the EC Commission and the EFTA Surveillance Authority provided for in Article 108(1) shall ensure the application of the principles laid down in Articles 53 and 54.

The competent surveillance authority, as provided for in Article 56, shall investigate cases of suspected infringement of these principles, on its own initiative, or on application by a State within the respective territory or by the other surveillance authority. The competent surveillance authority shall carry out these investigations in cooperation with the competent national authorities in the respective territory and in cooperation with the other surveillance authority, which shall give it its assistance in accordance with its internal rules.

If it finds that there has been an infringement, it shall propose appropriate measures to bring it to an end.

2. If the infringement is not brought to an end, the competent surveillance authority shall record such infringement of the principles in a reasoned decision.

The competent surveillance authority may publish its decision and authorise States within the respective territory to take the measures, the conditions and details of which it shall determine, needed to remedy the situation. It may also request the other surveillance authority to authorise States within the respective territory to take such measures.

Article 56

1. Individual cases falling under Article 53 shall be decided upon by the surveillance authorities in accordance with the following provisions:

(a) individual cases where only trade between EFTA States is affected shall be decided upon by the EFTA Surveillance Authority;

(b) without prejudice to subparagraph (c), the EFTA Surveillance Authority decides, as provided for in the provisions set out in Article 58, Protocol 21 and the rules adopted for its implementation, Protocol 23 and Annex XIV, on cases where the turnover of the undertakings concerned in the territory of the EFTA States equals 33% or more of their turnover in the territory covered by this Agreement;

(c) the EC Commission decides on the other cases as well as on cases under (b) where trade between EC Member States is affected, taking into account the provisions set out in Article 58, Protocol 21, Protocol 23 and Annex XIV.

2. Individual cases falling under Article 54 shall be decided upon by the surveillance authority in the territory of which a dominant position is found to exist. The rules set out in paragraph 1(b) and (c) shall apply only if dominance exists within the territories of both surveillance authorities.

3. Individual cases falling under subparagraph (c) of paragraph 1, whose effects on trade between EC Member States or on competition within the Community are not appreciable, shall be decided upon by the EFTA Surveillance Authority.

4. The terms 'undertaking' and 'turnover' are, for the purposes of this Article, defined in Protocol 22.

Article 57

1. Concentrations the control of which is provided for in paragraph 2 and which create or strengthen a dominant position as a result of which effective competition would be significantly impeded within the territory covered by this Agreement or a substantial part of it, shall be declared incompatible with this Agreement.

2. The control of concentrations falling under paragraph 1 shall be carried out by:

(a) the EC Commission in cases falling under Regulation (EEC) No 4064/89 in accordance with that Regulation and in accordance with Protocols 21 and 24 and Annex XIV to this Agreement. The EC Commission shall, subject to the review of the EC Court of Justice, have sole competence to take decisions on these cases;

(b) the EFTA Surveillance Authority in cases not falling under subparagraph (a) where the relevant thresholds set out in Annex XIV are fulfilled in the territory of the EFTA States in accordance with Protocols 21 and 24 and Annex XIV. This is without prejudice to the competence of EC Member States.

Article 58

With a view to developing and maintaining a uniform surveillance throughout the European Economic Area in the field of competition and to promoting a homogeneous implementation, application and interpretation of the provisions of this Agreement to this end, the competent authorities shall cooperate in accordance with the provisions set out in Protocols 23 and 24.

Article 59

1. In the case of public undertakings and undertakings to which EC Member States or EFTA States grant special or exclusive rights, the Contracting Parties shall ensure that there is neither enacted nor maintained in force any measure contrary to the rules contained in this Agreement, in particular to those rules provided for in Articles 4 and 53 to 63.

2. Undertakings entrusted with the operation of services of general economic interest or having the character of a revenue-producing monopoly shall be subject to the rules contained in this Agreement, in particular to the rules on competition, in so far as the application of such rules does not obstruct the performance, in law or in fact, of the particular tasks assigned to them. The development of trade must not be affected to such an extent as would be contrary to the interests of the Contracting Parties.

3. The EC Commission as well as the EFTA Surveillance Authority shall ensure within their respective competence the application of the provisions of this Article and shall, where necessary, address appropriate measures to the States falling within their respective territory.

Article 60

Annex XIV contains specific provisions giving effect to the principles set out in Articles 53, 54, 57 and 59.

Chapter 2

State aid

Article 61

1. Save as otherwise provided in this Agreement, any aid granted by EC Member States, EFTA States or through State resources in any form whatsoever which distorts or threatens to distort competition by favouring certain undertakings or the production of certain goods shall, in so far as it affects trade between Contracting Parties, be incompatible with the functioning of this Agreement.

2. The following shall be compatible with the functioning of this Agreement:

(a) aid having a social character, granted to individual consumers, provided that such aid is granted without discrimination related to the origin of the products concerned;

(b) aid to make good the damage caused by natural disasters or exceptional occurrences;

(c) aid granted to the economy of certain areas of the Federal Republic of Germany affected by the division of Germany, in so far as such aid is required in order to compensate for the economic disadvantages caused by that division.

3. The following may be considered to be compatible with the functioning of this Agreement:

(a) aid to promote the economic development of areas where the standard of living is abnormally low or where there is serious underemployment;

(b) aid to promote the execution of an important project of common European interest or to remedy a serious disturbance in the economy of an EC Member State or an EFTA State;

(c) aid to facilitate the development of certain economic activities or of certain economic areas, where such aid does not adversely affect trading conditions to an extent contrary to the common interest;

(d) such other categories of aid as may be specified by the EEA Joint Committee in accordance with Part VII.

Article 62

1. All existing systems of State aid in the territory of the Contracting Parties, as well as any plans to grant or alter State aid, shall be subject to constant review as to their compatibility with Article 61. This review shall be carried out:

(a) as regards the EC Member States, by the EC Commission according to the rules laid down in Article 93 of the Treaty establishing the European Economic Community;

(b) as regards the EFTA States, by the EFTA Surveillance Authority according to the rules set out in an agreement between the EFTA States establishing the EFTA Surveillance Authority which is entrusted with the powers and functions laid down in Protocol 26.

2. With a view to ensuring a uniform surveillance in the field of State aid throughout the territory covered by this Agreement, the EC Commission and the EFTA Surveillance Authority shall cooperate in accordance with the provisions set out in Protocol 27.

Article 63

Annex XV contains specific provisions on State aid.

Article 64

1. If one of the surveillance authorities considers that the implementation by the other surveillance authority of Articles 61 and 62 of this Agreement and Article 5 of Protocol 14 is not in conformity with the maintenance of equal conditions of competition within the territory covered by this Agreement, exchange of views shall be held within two weeks according to the procedure of Protocol 27, paragraph (f).

If a commonly agreed solution has not been found by the end of this two-week period, the competent authority of the affected Contracting Party may immediately adopt appropriate interim measures in order to remedy the resulting distortion of competition.

Consultations shall then be held in the EEA Joint Committee with a view to finding a commonly acceptable solution.

If within three months the EEA Joint Committee has not been able to find such a solution, and if the practice in question causes, or threatens to cause, distortion of competition affecting trade between the Contracting Parties, the interim measures may be replaced by definitive measures, strictly necessary to offset the effect of such distortion. Priority shall be given to such measures that will least disturb the functioning of the EEA.

2. The provisions of this Article will also apply to State monopolies, which are established after the date of signature of the Agreement.

Chapter 3

Other common rules

Article 65

1. Annex XVI contains specific provisions and arrangements concerning procurement which, unless otherwise specified, shall apply to all products and to services as specified.

2. Protocol 28 and Annex XVII contain specific provisions and arrangements concerning intellectual, industrial and commercial property, which, unless otherwise specified, shall apply to all products and services.

PART V

Horizontal provisions relevant to the Four Freedoms

Chapter 1

Social policy

Article 66

The Contracting Parties agree upon the need to promote improved working conditions and an improved standard of living for workers.

Article 67

1. The Contracting Parties shall pay particular attention to encouraging improvements, especially in the working environment, as regards the health and safety of workers. In order to help achieve this objective, minimum requirements shall be applied for gradual implementation, having regard to the conditions and technical rules obtaining in each of the Contracting Parties. Such minimum requirements shall not prevent any Contracting Party from maintaining or introducing more stringent measures for the protection of working conditions compatible with this Agreement.

2. Annex XVIII specifies the provisions to be implemented as the minimum requirements referred to in paragraph 1.

Article 68

In the field of labour law, the Contracting Parties shall introduce the measures necessary to ensure the good functioning of this Agreement. These measures are specified in Annex XVIII.

Article 69

1. Each Contracting Party shall ensure and maintain the application of the principle that men and women should receive equal pay for equal work.

For the purposes of this Article, 'pay' means the ordinary basic or minimum wage or salary and any other consideration, whether in cash or in kind, which the worker receives, directly or indirectly, in respect of his employment from his employer.

Equal pay without discrimination based on sex means:

- research and technological development,
- information services,
- the environment,
- education, training and youth,
- social policy,
- consumer protection,
- small and medium-sized enterprises,
- tourism,
- the audiovisual sector, and
- civil protection,

in so far as these matters are not regulated under the provisions of other Parts of this Agreement.

Article 79

1. The Contracting Parties shall strengthen the dialogue between them by all appropriate means, in particular through the procedures provided for in Part VII, with a view to identifying areas and activities where closer cooperation could contribute to the attainment of their common objectives in the fields referred to in Article 78.

2. They shall, in particular, exchange information and, at the request of a Contracting Party, hold consultations within the EEA Joint Committee in respect of plans or proposals for the establishment or amendment of framework programmes, specific programmes, actions and projects in the fields referred to in Article 78.

3. Part VII shall apply *mutatis mutandis* with regard to this Part whenever the latter or Protocol 31 specifically provides therefor.

Article 80

The cooperation provided for in Article 78 shall normally take one of the following forms:

- participation by EFTA States in EC framework programmes, specific programmes, projects or other actions;
- establishment of joint activities in specific areas, which may include concentration or coordination of activities, fusion of existing activities and establishment of *ad hoc* joint activities;
- the formal and informal exchange or provision of information;

– common efforts to encourage certain activities throughout the territory of the Contracting Parties;

– parallel legislation, where appropriate, of identical or similar content;

– coordination, where this is of mutual interest, of efforts and activities via, or in the context of, international organisations, and of cooperation with third countries.

Article 81

Where cooperation takes the form of participation by EFTA States in an EC framework programme, specific programme, project or other action, the following principles shall apply:

(a) The EFTA States shall have access to all parts of a programme.

(b) The status of the EFTA States in the committees which assist the EC Commission in the management or development of a Community activity to which EFTA States may be contributing financially by virtue of their participation shall take full account of that contribution.

(c) Decisions by the Community, other than those relating to the general budget of the Community, which affect directly or indirectly a framework programme, specific programme, project or other action, in which EFTA States participate by a decision under this Agreement, shall be subject to the provisions of Article 79(3). The terms and conditions of the continued participation in the activity in question may be reviewed by the EEA Joint Committee in accordance with Article 86.

(d) At the project level, institutions, undertakings, organisations and nationals of EFTA States shall have the same rights and obligations in the Community programme or other action in question as those applicable to partner institutions, undertakings, organisations and nationals of EC Member States. The same shall apply *mutatis mutandis* to participants in exchanges between EC Member States and EFTA States, under the activity in question.

(e) EFTA States, their institutions, undertakings, organisations and nationals shall have the same rights and obligations with regard to dissemination, evaluation and exploitation of results as those applicable to EC Member States, their institutions, undertakings, organisations and nationals.

(f) The Contracting Parties undertake, in accordance with their respective rules and regulations, to facilitate the movement of participants in the programme and other action to the extent necessary.

Article 82

1. When the cooperation envisaged under the present Part involves a financial participation of the EFTA States, this participation shall take one of the following forms:

(*a*) The contribution of the EFTA States, arising from their participation in Community activities, shall be calculated proportionally:

- to the commitment appropriations; and

- to the payment appropriations;

entered each year for the Community in the general budget of the Community for each budgetary line corresponding to the activities in question.

The 'proportionality factor' determining the participation of the EFTA States shall be the sum of the ratios between, on the one hand, the gross domestic product at market prices of each of the EFTA States and, on the other hand, the sum of the gross domestic products at market prices of the EC Member States and of that EFTA State. This factor shall be calculated, for each budgetary year, on the basis of the most recent statistical data.

The amount of the contribution of the EFTA States shall be additional, both in commitment appropriations and in payment appropriations, to the amounts entered for the Community in the general budget on each line corresponding to the activities concerned.

The contributions to be paid each year by EFTA States shall be determined on the basis of the payment appropriations.

Commitments entered into by the Community prior to the entry into force, on the basis of this Agreement, of the participation of the EFTA States in the activities in question – as well as the payments which result from this – shall give rise to no contribution on the part of the EFTA States.

(*b*) The financial contribution of the EFTA States deriving from their participation in certain projects or other activities shall be based on the principle that each Contracting Party shall cover its own costs, with an appropriate contribution which shall be fixed by the EEA Joint Committee to the Community's overhead costs.

(*c*) The EEA Joint Committee shall take the necessary decisions concerning the contribution of the Contracting Parties to the costs of the activity in question.

2. The detailed provisions for the implementation of this Article are set out in Protocol 32.

Article 83

Where cooperation takes the form of an exchange of information between public authorities, the EFTA States shall have the same rights to receive, and obligations to provide, information as EC Member States, subject to the requirements of confidentiality, which shall be fixed by the EEA Joint Committee.

Article 84

Provisions governing cooperation in specific fields are set out in Protocol 31.

Article 85

Unless otherwise provided for in Protocol 31, cooperation already established between the Community and individual EFTA States in the fields referred to in Article 78 on the date of entry into force of this Agreement shall thereafter be governed by the relevant provisions of this Part and of Protocol 31.

Article 86

The EEA Joint Committee shall, in accordance with Part VII, take all decisions necessary, for the implementation of Articles 78 to 85 and measures derived therefrom, which may include, *inter alia*, supplementing and amending the provisions of Protocol 31, as well as adopting any transitional arrangements required by way of implementation of Article 85.

Article 87

The Contracting Parties shall take the necessary steps to develop, strengthen or broaden cooperation in the framework of the Community's activities in fields not listed in Article 78, where such cooperation is considered likely to contribute to the attainment of the objectives of this Agreement, or is otherwise deemed by the Contracting Parties to be of mutual interest. Such steps may include the amendment of Article 78 by the addition of new fields to those listed therein.

Article 88

Without prejudice to provisions of other Parts of this Agreement, the provisions of this Part shall not preclude the possibility for any Contracting Party to prepare, adopt and implement measures independently.

PART VII

Institutional provisions

Chapter 1

The structure of the association

Section 1

The EEA Council

Article 89

1. An EEA Council is hereby established. It shall, in particular, be responsible for giving the political impetus in the implementation of this Agreement and laying down the general guidelines for the EEA Joint Committee.

To this end, the EEA Council shall assess the overall functioning and the development of the Agreement. It shall take the political decisions leading to amendments of the Agreement.

2. The Contracting Parties, as to the Community and the EC Member States in their respective fields of competence, may, after having discussed it in the EEA Joint Committee, or directly in exceptionally urgent cases, raise in the EEA Council any issue giving rise to a difficulty.

3. The EEA Council shall by decision adopt its rules of procedure.

Article 90

1. The EEA Council shall consist of the members of the Council of the European Communities and members of the EC Commission, and of one member of the Government of each of the EFTA States.

Members of the EEA Council may be represented in accordance with the conditions to be laid down in its rules of procedure.

2. Decisions by the EEA Council shall be taken by agreement between the Community, on the one hand, and the EFTA States, on the other.

Article 91

1. The office of President of the EEA Council shall be held alternately, for a period of six months, by a member of the Council of the European Communities and a member of the Government of an EFTA State.

2. The EEA Council shall be convened twice a year by its President. The EEA Council shall also meet whenever circumstances so require, in accordance with its rules of procedure.

Section 2

The EEA Joint Committee

Article 92

1. An EEA Joint Committee is hereby established. It shall ensure the effective implementation and operation of this Agreement. To this end, it shall carry out exchanges of views and information and take decisions in the cases provided for in this Agreement.

2. The Contracting Parties, as to the Community and the EC Member States in their respective fields of competence, shall hold consultations in the EEA Joint Committee on any point of relevance to the Agreement giving rise to a difficulty and raised by one of them.

3. The EEA Joint Committee shall by decision adopt its rules of procedure.

Article 93

1. The EEA Joint Committee shall consist of representatives of the Contracting Parties.

2. The EEA Joint Committee shall take decisions by agreement between the Community, on the one hand, and the EFTA States speaking with one voice, on the other.

Article 94

1. The office of President of the EEA Joint Committee shall be held alternately, for a period of six months, by the representative of the Community, i.e. the EC Commission, and the representative of one of the EFTA States.

2. In order to fulfil its functions, the EEA Joint Committee shall meet, in principle, at least once a month. It shall also meet on the initiative of its President or at the request of one of the Contracting Parties in accordance with its rules of procedure.

3. The EEA Joint Committee may decide to establish any subcommittee or working group to assist it in carrying out its tasks. The EEA Joint Committee shall in its rules of procedure lay down the composition and mode of operation of such subcommittees and working groups. Their tasks shall be determined by the EEA Joint Committee in each individual case.

4. The EEA Joint Committee shall issue an annual report on the functioning and the development of this Agreement.

Section 3

Parliamentary cooperation

Article 95

1. An EEA Joint Parliamentary Committee is hereby established. It shall be composed of equal numbers of, on the one hand, members of the European Parliament and, on the other, members of Parliaments of the EFTA States. The total number of members of the Committee is laid down in the Statute in Protocol 36.

2. The EEA Joint Parliamentary Committee shall alternately hold sessions in the Community and in an EFTA State in accordance with the provisions laid down in Protocol 36.

3. The EEA Joint Parliamentary Committee shall contribute, through dialogue and debate, to a better understanding between the Community and the EFTA States in the fields covered by this Agreement.

4. The EEA Joint Parliamentary Committee may express its views in the form of reports or resolutions, as appropriate. It shall, in particular, examine the annual report of the EEA Joint Committee, issued in accordance with Article 94(4), on the functioning and the development of this Agreement.

5. The President of the EEA Council may appear before the EEA Joint Parliamentary Committee in order to be heard by it.

6. The EEA Joint Parliamentary Committee shall adopt its rules of procedure.

Section 4

Cooperation between economic and social partners

Article 96

1. Members of the Economic and Social Committee and other bodies representing the social partners in the Community and the corresponding bodies in the EFTA States shall work to strengthen contacts between them and to cooperate in an organised and regular manner in order to enhance the awareness of the economic and social aspects of the growing interdependence of the economies of the Contracting Parties and of their interests within the context of the EEA.

2. To this end, an EEA Consultative Committee is hereby established. It shall be composed of equal numbers of, on the one hand, members of the Economic and Social Committee of the Community and, on the other, members of the EFTA Consultative Committee. The EEA Consultative Committee may express its views in the form of reports or resolutions, as appropriate.

3. The EEA Consultative Committee shall adopt its rules of procedure.

Chapter 2

The decision-making procedure

Article 97

This Agreement does not prejudge the right for each Contracting Party to amend, without prejudice to the principle of non-discrimination and after having informed the other Contracting Parties, its internal legislation in the areas covered by this Agreement:

– if the EEA Joint Committee concludes that the legislation as amended does not affect the good functioning of this Agreement; or

– if the procedures referred to in Article 98 have been completed.

Article 98

The Annexes to this Agreement and Protocols 1 to 7, 9 to 11, 19 to 27, 30 to 32, 37, 39, 41 and 47, as appropriate, may be amended by a decision of the EEA Joint Committee in accordance with Articles 93(2), 99, 100, 102 and 103.

Article 99

1. As soon as new legislation is being drawn up by the EC Commission in a field which is governed by this Agreement, the EC Commission shall informally seek advice from experts of the EFTA States in the same way as it seeks advice from experts of the EC Member States for the elaboration of its proposals.

2. When transmitting its proposal to the Council of the European Communities, the EC Commission shall transmit copies thereof to the EFTA States.

At the request of one of the Contracting Parties, a preliminary exchange of views takes place in the EEA Joint Committee.

3. During the phase preceding the decision of the Council of the European Communities, in a continuous information and consultation process, the Contracting Parties consult each other again in the EEA Joint Committee at the significant moments at the request of one of them.

4. The Contracting Parties shall cooperate in good faith during the information and consultation phase with a view to facilitating, at the end of the process, the decision-taking in the EEA Joint Committee.

Article 100

The EC Commission shall ensure experts of the EFTA States as wide a participation as possible according to the areas concerned, in the preparatory stage of draft measures to be submitted subsequently to the committees which assist the EC Commission in the exercise of its executive powers. In this regard, when drawing up draft measures the EC Commission shall refer to experts of the EFTA States on the same basis as it refers to experts of the EC Member States.

In the cases where the Council of the European Communities is seized in accordance with the procedure applicable to the type of committee involved, the EC Commission shall transmit to the Council of the European Communities the views of the experts of the EFTA States.

Article 101

1. In respect of committees which are covered neither by Article 81 nor by Article 100 experts from EFTA States shall be associated with the work when this is called for by the good functioning of this Agreement.

These committees are listed in Protocol 37. The modalities of such an association are set out in the relevant sectoral Protocols and Annexes dealing with the matter concerned.

2. If it appears to the Contracting Parties that such an association should be extended to other committees which present similar characteristics, the EEA Joint Committee may amend Protocol 37.

Article 102

1. In order to guarantee the legal security and the homogeneity of the EEA, the EEA Joint Committee shall take a decision concerning an amendment of an Annex to this Agreement as closely as possible to the adoption by the Community of the corresponding new Community legislation with a view to permitting a simultaneous application of the latter as well as of the amendments of the Annexes to the Agreement. To this end, the Community shall, whenever adopting a legislative act on an issue which is governed by this Agreement, as soon as possible inform the other Contracting Parties in the EEA Joint Committee.

2. The part of an Annex to this Agreement which would be directly affected by the new legislation is assessed in the EEA Joint Committee.

3. The Contracting Parties shall make all efforts to arrive at an agreement on matters relevant to this Agreement.

The EEA Joint Committee shall, in particular, make every effort to find a mutually acceptable solution where a serious problem arises in any area which, in the EFTA States, falls within the competence of the legislator.

4. If, notwithstanding the application of the preceding paragraph, an agreement on an amendment of an Annex to this Agreement cannot be reached, the EEA Joint Committee shall examine all further possibilities to maintain the good functioning of this Agreement and take any decision necessary to this effect, including the possibility to take notice of the equivalence of legislation. Such a decision shall be taken at the latest at the expiry of a period of six months from the date of referral to the EEA Joint Committee or, if that date is later, on the date of entry into force of the corresponding Community legislation.

5. If, at the end of the time-limit set out in paragraph 4, the EEA Joint Committee has not taken a decision on an amendment of an Annex to this Agreement, the affected part thereof, as determined in accordance with paragraph 2, is regarded as provisionally suspended, subject to a decision to the contrary by the EEA Joint Committee. Such a suspension shall take effect six months after the end of the period referred to in paragraph 4, but in no event earlier than the date on which the corresponding EC act is implemented in the Community. The EEA Joint Committee shall pursue its efforts to agree on a mutually acceptable solution in order for the suspension to be terminated as soon as possible.

6. The practical consequences of the suspension referred to in

paragraph 5 shall be discussed in the EEA Joint Committee. The rights and obligations which individuals and economic operators have already acquired under this Agreement shall remain. The Contracting Parties shall, as appropriate, decide on the adjustments necessary due to the suspension.

Article 103

1. If a decision of the EEA Joint Committee can be binding on a Contracting Party only after the fulfilment of constitutional requirements, the decision shall, if a date is contained therein, enter into force on that date, provided that the Contracting Party concerned has notified the other Contracting Parties by that date that the constitutional requirements have been fulfilled.

In the absence of such a notification by that date, the decision shall enter into force on the first day of the second month following the last notification.

2. If upon the expiry of a period of six months after the decision of the EEA Joint Committee such a notification has not taken place, the decision of the EEA Joint Committee shall be applied provisionally pending the fulfilment of the constitutional requirements unless a Contracting Party notifies that such a provisional application cannot take place. In the latter case, or if a Contracting Party notifies the non-ratification of a decision of the EEA Joint Committee, the suspension provided for in Article 102(5) shall take effect one month after such a notification but in no event earlier than the date on which the corresponding EC act is implemented in the Community.

Article 104

Decisions taken by the EEA Joint Committee in the cases provided for in this Agreement shall, unless otherwise provided for therein, upon their entry into force be binding on the Contracting Parties which shall take the necessary steps to ensure their implementation and application.

Chapter 3

Homogeneity, surveillance procedure and settlement of disputes

Section 1

Homogeneity

Article 105

1. In order to achieve the objective of the Contracting Parties to arrive at as uniform an interpretation as possible of the provisions of the Agreement and those provisions of Community legislation which are substantially reproduced in the Agreement, the EEA Joint Committee shall act in accordance with this Article.

2. The EEA Joint Committee shall keep under constant review the development of the case-law of the Court of Justice of the European Communities and the EFTA Court. To this end judgments of these Courts shall be transmitted to the EEA Joint Committee which shall act so as to preserve the homogeneous interpretation of the Agreement.

3. If the EEA Joint Committee within two months after a difference in the case-law of the two Courts has been brought before it, has not succeeded to preserve the homogeneous interpretation of the Agreement, the procedures laid down in Article 111 may be applied.

Article 106

In order to ensure as uniform an interpretation as possible of this Agreement, in full deference to the independence of courts, a system of exchange of information concerning judgments by the EFTA Court, the Court of Justice of the European Communities and the Court of First Instance of the European Communities and the Courts of last instance of the EFTA States shall be set up by the EEA Joint Committee. This system shall comprise:

(a) transmission to the Registrar of the Court of Justice of the European Communities of judgments delivered by such courts on the interpretation and application of, on the one hand, this Agreement or, on the other hand, the Treaty establishing the European Economic Community and the Treaty establishing the European Coal and Steel Community, as amended or supplemented, as well as the acts adopted in pursuance thereof in so far as they concern provisions which are identical in substance to those of this Agreement;

(b) classification of these judgments by the Registrar of the Court of Justice of the European Communities including, as far as necessary, the drawing up and publication of translations and abstracts;

(c) communications by the Registrar of the Court of Justice of the European Communities of the relevant documents to the competent national authorities, to be designated by each Contracting Party.

Article 107

Provisions on the possibility for an EFTA State to allow a court or tribunal to ask the Court of Justice of the European Communities to decide on the interpretation of an EEA rule are laid down in Protocol 34.

Section 2

Surveillance procedure

Article 108

1. The EFTA States shall establish an independent surveillance authority (EFTA Surveillance Authority) as well as procedures similar to those existing in the Community including procedures for ensuring the fulfilment of obligations under this Agreement and for control of the legality of acts of the EFTA Surveillance Authority regarding competition.

2. The EFTA States shall establish a court of justice (EFTA Court).

The EFTA Court shall, in accordance with a separate agreement between the EFTA States, with regard to the application of this Agreement be competent, in particular, for:

(a) actions concerning the surveillance procedure regarding the EFTA States;

(b) appeals concerning decisions in the field of competition taken by the EFTA Surveillance Authority;

(c) the settlement of disputes between two or more EFTA States.

Article 109

1. The fulfilment of the obligations under this Agreement shall be monitored by, on the one hand, the EFTA Surveillance Authority and, on the other, the EC Commission acting in conformity with the Treaty establishing the European Economic Community, the Treaty establishing the European Coal and Steel Community and this Agreement.

2. In order to ensure a uniform surveillance throughout the EEA, the

EFTA Surveillance Authority and the EC Commission shall cooperate, exchange information and consult each other on surveillance policy issues and individual cases.

3. The EC Commission and the EFTA Surveillance Authority shall receive any complaints concerning the application of this Agreement. They shall inform each other of complaints received.

4. Each of these bodies shall examine all complaints falling within its competence and shall pass to the other body any complaints which fall within the competence of that body.

5. In case of disagreement between these two bodies with regard to the action to be taken in relation to a complaint or with regard to the result of the examination, either of the bodies may refer the matter to the EEA Joint Committee which shall deal with it in accordance with Article 111.

Article 110

Decisions under this Agreement by the EFTA Surveillance Authority and the EC Commission which impose a pecuniary obligation on persons other than States, shall be enforceable. The same shall apply to such judgments under this Agreement by the Court of Justice of the European Communities, the Court of First Instance of the European Communities and the EFTA Court.

Enforcement shall be governed by the rules of civil procedure in force in the State in the territory of which it is carried out. The order for its enforcement shall be appended to the decision, without other formality than verification of the authenticity of the decision, by the authority which each Contracting Party shall designate for this purpose and shall make known to the other Contracting Parties, the EFTA Surveillance Authority, the EC Commission, the Court of Justice of the European Communities, the Court of First Instance of the European Communities and the EFTA Court.

When these formalities have been completed on application by the party concerned, the latter may proceed to enforcement, in accordance with the law of the State in the territory of which enforcement is to be carried out, by bringing the matter directly before the competent authority.

Enforcement may be suspended only by a decision of the Court of Justice of the European Communities, as far as decisions by the EC Commission, the Court of First Instance of the European Communities or the Court of Justice of the European Communities are concerned, or by a decision of the EFTA Court as far as decisions by the EFTA Surveillance Authority or the EFTA Court are concerned. However, the courts of the States concerned shall have jurisdiction over complaints that enforcement is being carried out in an irregular manner.

Section 3

Settlement of disputes

Article 111

1. The Community or an EFTA State may bring a matter under dispute which concerns the interpretation or application of this Agreement before the EEA Joint Committee in accordance with the following provisions.

2. The EEA Joint Committee may settle the dispute. It shall be provided with all information which might be of use in making possible an in-depth examination of the situation, with a view to finding an acceptable solution. To this end, the EEA Joint Committee shall examine all possibilities to maintain the good functioning of the Agreement.

3. If a dispute concerns the interpretation of provisions of this Agreement, which are identical in substance to corresponding rules of the Treaty establishing the European Economic Community and the Treaty establishing the European Coal and Steel Community and to acts adopted in application of these two Treaties and if the dispute has not been settled within three months after it has been brought before the EEA Joint Committee, the Contracting Parties to the dispute may agree to request the Court of Justice of the European Communities to give a ruling on the interpretation of the relevant rules.

If the EEA Joint Committee in such a dispute has not reached an agreement on a solution within six months from the date on which this procedure was initiated or if, by then, the Contracting Parties to the dispute have not decided to ask for a ruling by the Court of Justice of the European Communities, a Contracting Party may, in order to remedy possible imbalances,

– either take a safeguard measure in accordance with Article 112(2) and following the procedure of Article 113;

– or apply Article 102 *mutatis mutandis*.

4. If a dispute concerns the scope or duration of safeguard measures taken in accordance with Article 111(3) or Article 112, or the proportionality of rebalancing measures taken in accordance with Article 114, and if the EEA Joint Committee after three months from the date when the matter has been brought before it has not succeeded to resolve the dispute, any Contracting Party may refer the dispute to

arbitration under the procedures laid down in Protocol 33. No question of interpretation of the provisions of this Agreement referred to in paragraph 3 may be dealt with in such procedures. The arbitration award shall be binding on the parties to the dispute.

Chapter 4

Safeguard measures

Article 112

1. If serious economic, societal or environmental difficulties of a sectorial or regional nature liable to persist are arising, a Contracting Party may unilaterally take appropriate measures under the conditions and procedures laid down in Article 113.

2. Such safeguard measures shall be restricted with regard to their scope and duration to what is strictly necessary in order to remedy the situation. Priority shall be given to such measures as will least disturb the functioning of this Agreement.

3. The safeguard measures shall apply with regard to all Contracting Parties.

Article 113

1. A Contracting Party which is considering taking safeguard measures under Article 112 shall, without delay, notify the other Contracting Parties through the EEA Joint Committee and shall provide all relevant information.

2. The Contracting Parties shall immediately enter into consultations in the EEA Joint Committee with a view to finding a commonly acceptable solution.

3. The Contracting Party concerned may not take safeguard measures until one month has elapsed after the date of notification under paragraph 1, unless the consultation procedure under paragraph 2 has been concluded before the expiration of the stated time-limit. When exceptional circumstances requiring immediate action exclude prior examination, the Contracting Party concerned may apply forthwith the protective measures strictly necessary to remedy the situation.

For the Community, the safeguard measures shall be taken by the EC Commission.

4. The Contracting Party concerned shall, without delay, notify the

measures taken to the EEA Joint Committee and shall provide all relevant information.

5. The safeguard measures taken shall be the subject of consultations in the EEA Joint Committee every three months from the date of their adoption with a view to their abolition before the date of expiry envisaged, or to the limitation of their scope of application.

Each Contracting Party may at any time request the EEA Joint Committee to review such measures.

Article 114

1. If a safeguard measure taken by a Contracting Party creates an imbalance between the rights and obligations under this Agreement, any other Contracting Party may towards that Contracting Party take such proportionate rebalancing measures as are strictly necessary to remedy the imbalance. Priority shall be given to such measures as will least disturb the functioning of the EEA.

2. The procedure under Article 113 shall apply.

PART VIII

Financial mechanism

Article 115

With a view to promoting a continuous and balanced strengthening of trade and economic relations between the Contracting Parties, as provided for in Article 1, the Contracting Parties agree on the need to reduce the economic and social disparities between their regions. They note in this regard the relevant provisions set out elsewhere in this Agreement and its related Protocols, including certain of the arrangements regarding agriculture and fisheries.

Article 116

A Financial Mechanism shall be established by the EFTA States to contribute, in the context of the EEA and in addition to the efforts already deployed by the Community in this regard, to the objectives laid down in Article 115.

Article 117

Provisions governing the Financial Mechanism are set out in Protocol 38.

PART IX

General and final provisions

Article 118

1. Where a Contracting Party considers that it would be useful in the interests of all the Contracting Parties to develop the relations established by this Agreement by extending them to fields not covered thereby, it shall submit a reasoned request to the other Contracting Parties within the EEA Council. The latter may instruct the EEA Joint Committee to examine all the aspects of this request and to issue a report.

The EEA Council may, where appropriate, take the political decisions with a view to opening negotiations between the Contracting Parties.

2. The agreements resulting from the negotiations referred to in paragraph 1 will be subject to ratification or approval by the Contracting Parties in accordance with their own procedures.

Article 119

The Annexes and the acts referred to therein as adapted for the purposes of this Agreement as well as the Protocols shall form an integral part of this Agreement.

Article 120

Unless otherwise provided in this Agreement and in particular in Protocols 41, 43 and 44, the application of the provisions of this Agreement shall prevail over provisions in existing bilateral or multilateral agreements binding the European Economic Community, on the one hand, and one or more EFTA States, on the other, to the extent that the same subject matter is governed by this Agreement.

Article 121

The provisions of this Agreement shall not preclude cooperation:

(a) within the framework of the Nordic cooperation to the extent that such cooperation does not impair the good functioning of this Agreement;

(b) within the framework of the regional union between Switzerland and Liechtenstein to the extent that the objectives of this union are not attained by the application of this Agreement and the good functioning of this Agreement is not impaired;

(c) within the framework of cooperation between Austria and Italy concerning Tyrol, Vorarlberg and Trentino-South Tyrol/Alto Adige, to the extent that such cooperation does not impair the good functioning of this Agreement.

Article 122

The representatives, delegates and experts of the Contracting Parties, as well as officials and other servants acting under this Agreement shall be required, even after their duties have ceased, not to disclose information of the kind covered by the obligation of professional secrecy, in particular information about undertakings, their business relations or their cost components.

Article 123

Nothing in this Agreement shall prevent a Contracting Party from taking any measures:

(a) which it considers necessary to prevent the disclosure of information contrary to its essential security interests;

(b) which relate to the production of, or trade in, arms, munitions and war materials or other products indispensable for defence purposes or to research, development or production indispensable for defence purposes, provided that such measures do not impair the conditions of competition in respect of products not intended for specifically military purposes;

(c) which it considers essential to its own security in the event of serious internal disturbances affecting the maintenance of law and order, in time of war or serious international tension constituting threat of war or in order to carry out obligations it has accepted for the purpose of maintaining peace and international security.

Article 124

The Contracting Parties shall accord nationals of EC Member States and EFTA States the same treatment as their own nationals as regards participation in the capital of companies or firms within the meaning of Article 34, without prejudice to the application of the other provisions of this Agreement.

Article 125

This Agreement shall in no way prejudice the rules of the Contracting Parties governing the system of property ownership.

Article 126

1. The Agreement shall apply to the territories to which the Treaty establishing the European Economic Community and the Treaty establishing the European Coal and Steel Community is applied and under the conditions laid down in those Treaties, and to the territories of the Republic of Austria, the Republic of Finland, the Republic of Iceland, the Principality of Liechtenstein, the Kingdom of Norway, the Kingdom of Sweden and the Swiss Confederation.

2. Notwithstanding paragraph 1, this Agreement shall not apply to the Åland Islands. The Government of Finland may, however, give notice, by a declaration deposited when ratifying this Agreement with the Depositary, which shall transmit a certified copy thereof to the Contracting Parties, that the Agreement shall apply to those Islands under the same conditions as it applies to other parts of Finland subject to the following provisions:

(*a*)   The provisions of this Agreement shall not preclude the application of the provisions in force at any given time on the Åland Islands on:

   (i)   restrictions on the right for natural persons who do not enjoy regional citizenship in Åland, and for legal persons, to acquire and hold real property on the Åland Islands without permission by the competent authorities of the Islands;

   (ii) restrictions on the right of establishment and the right to provide services by natural persons who do not enjoy regional citizenship in Åland, or by any legal person, without permission by the competent authorities of the Åland Islands.

(*b*) The rights enjoyed by Ålanders in Finland shall not be affected by this Agreement.

(*c*) The authorities of the Åland Islands shall apply the same treatment to all natural and legal persons of the Contracting Parties.

Article 127

Each Contracting Party may withdraw from this Agreement provided it gives at least 12 months' notice in writing to the other Contracting Parties.

Immediately after the notification of the intended withdrawal, the other Contracting Parties shall convene a diplomatic conference in order to envisage the necessary modifications to bring to the Agreement.

Article 128

1. Any European State becoming a member of the Community shall, or becoming a member of EFTA may, apply to become a Party to this Agreement. It shall address its application to the EEA Council.

2. The terms and conditions for such participation shall be the subject of an agreement between the Contracting Parties and the applicant State. That agreement shall be submitted for ratification or approval by all Contracting Parties in accordance with their own procedures.

Article 129

1. This Agreement is drawn up in a single original in the Danish, Dutch, English, Finnish, French, German, Greek, Icelandic, Italian, Norwegian, Portuguese, Spanish and Swedish languages, each of these texts being equally authentic.

The texts of the acts referred to in the Annexes are equally authentic in Danish, Dutch, English, French, German, Greek, Italian, Portuguese and Spanish as published in the *Official Journal of the European Communities* and shall for the authentication thereof be drawn up in the Finnish, Icelandic, Norwegian and Swedish languages.

2. This Agreement shall be ratified or approved by the Contracting Parties in accordance with their respective constitutional requirements.

It shall be deposited with the General Secretariat of the Council of the European Communities by which certified copies shall be transmitted to all other Contracting Parties.

The instruments of ratification or approval shall be deposited with the General Secretariat of the Council of the European Communities which shall notify all other Contracting Parties.

3. This Agreement shall enter into force on 1 January 1993, provided that all Contracting Parties have deposited their instruments of ratification or approval before that date. After that date this Agreement shall enter into force on the first day of the second month following the last notification. The final date for such a notification shall be 30 June 1993. After that date the Contracting Parties shall convene a diplomatic conference to appreciate the situation.

In Witness Whereof the undersigned Plenipotentiaries have signed this Agreement.

Done at Oporto on the second day of May in the year one thousand nine hundred and ninety-two.

FINAL ACT

The plenipotentiaries of:

The European Economic Community,

The European Coal and Steel Community,

hereinafter referred to as 'the Community', and of:

The Kingdom of Belgium,

The Kingdom of Denmark,

The Federal Republic of Germany,

The Hellenic Republic,

The Kingdom of Spain,

The French Republic,

Ireland,

The Italian Republic,

The Grand Duchy of Luxembourg,

The Kingdom of the Netherlands,

The Portuguese Republic,

The United Kingdom of Great Britain and Northern Ireland,

Contracting Parties to the Treaty establishing the European Economic Community and the Treaty establishing the European Coal and Steel Community,

hereinafter referred to as 'the EC Member States',

and

the plenipotentiaries of:

The Republic of Austria,

The Republic of Finland,

The Republic of Iceland,

The Principality of Liechtenstein,

The Kingdom of Norway,

The Kingdom of Sweden,

The Swiss Confederation,

hereinafter referred to as 'the EFTA States',

meeting at Oporto, this second day of May in the year one thousand nine hundred and ninety-two for the signature of the Agreement on the European Economic Area, hereinafter referred to as the EEA Agreement, have adopted the following texts:

I. the Agreement on the European Economic Area;

II. the texts listed below which are annexed to the Agreement on the European Economic Area:

A. Protocol 1   on horizontal adaptations

Protocol 2   on products excluded from the scope of the Agreement in accordance with Article 8(3)(a)

Protocol 3   concerning products referred to in Article 8(3)(b) of the Agreement

Protocol 4   on rules of origin

Protocol 5   on customs duties of a fiscal nature (Switzerland/Liechtenstein)

Protocol 6   on the building up of compulsory reserves by Switzerland and Liechtenstein

Protocol 7   on quantitative restrictions which Iceland may retain

Protocol 8   on State monopolies

Protocol 9   on trade in fish and other marine products

Protocol 10   on simplification of inspections and formalities in respect of carriage of goods

Protocol 11   on mutual assistance in customs matters

Protocol 12   on conformity assessment agreements with third countries

Protocol 13   on the non-application of anti-dumping and countervailing measures

Protocol 14   on trade in coal and steel products

Protocol 15   on transitional periods on the free movement of persons (Switzerland and Liechtenstein)

The plenipotentiaries of the EC Member States and of the Community and the plenipotentiaries of the EFTA States have adopted the joint declarations listed below and annexed to this Final Act:

1. Joint Declaration concerning the preparation of joint reports under paragraph 5 of Protocol 1 on horizontal adaptations;

2. Joint Declaration on mutual recognition and protection agreements for the designations of wine and spirituous beverages;

3. Joint Declaration on a transitional period concerning the issuing or making out of documents relating to the proof of origin;

4. Joint Declaration concerning Articles 10 and 14(1) of Protocol 11 to the Agreement;

5. Joint Declaration on electro-medical equipment;

6. Joint Declaration concerning nationals of the Republic of Iceland who hold a diploma in specialised medicine, specialised dentistry, veterinary medicine, pharmacy, general medical practice or architecture conferred in a third country;

7. Joint Declaration concerning nationals of the Republic of Iceland who hold higher-education diplomas awarded on completion of professional education and training of at least three years' duration conferred in a third country;

8. Joint Declaration on transport of goods by road;

9. Joint Declaration concerning rules on competition;

10. Joint Declaration on Article 61(3)(b) of the Agreement;

11. Joint Declaration on Article 61(3)(c) of the Agreement;

12. Joint Declaration on aid through the EC Structural Funds or other financial instruments;

13. Joint Declaration on paragraph (c) of Protocol 27 to the Agreement;

14. Joint Declaration on shipbuilding;

15. Joint Declaration on applicable procedures in cases where, by virtue of Article 76 and Part VI of the Agreement and corresponding Protocols, EFTA States participate fully in EC committees;

16. Joint Declaration on cooperation in cultural affairs;

17. Joint Declaration on cooperation against illegal traffic in cultural goods;

18. Joint Declaration on the association of Community experts with the work of committees among the EFTA States or set up by the EFTA Surveillance Authority;

19. Joint Declaration on Article 103 of the Agreement;

20. Joint Declaration on Protocol 35 to the Agreement;

21. Joint Declaration concerning the Financial Mechanism;

22. Joint Declaration on the relation between the EEA Agreement and existing agreements;

23. Joint Declaration on the agreed interpretation of Article 4(1) and (2) of Protocol 9 on trade in fish and other marine products;

24. Joint Declaration concerning the application of tariff concessions for certain agricultural products;

25. Joint Declaration on plant health issues;

26. Joint Declaration on mutual assistance between control authorities in the area of spirit drinks;

27. Joint Declaration on Protocol 47 on the abolition of technical barriers to trade in wine;

28. Joint Declaration on modification of tariff concessions and on special treatment of Spain and Portugal;

29. Joint Declaration on animal welfare;

30. Joint Declaration on the Harmonised System.

The plenipotentiaries of the EC Member States and the plenipotentiaries of the EFTA States have adopted the declarations listed below and annexed to this Final Act:

1. Declaration by the Governments of the Member States of the EC and the EFTA States on the facilitation of border controls;

2. Declaration by the Governments of the Member States of the EC and the EFTA States on political dialogue.

The plenipotentiaries of the EC Member States and of the Community and the plenipotentiaries of the EFTA States have also taken note of the arrangement regarding the functioning of a High-Level Interim Group during the period preceding the entry into force of the EEA Agreement which is annexed to this Final Act. They have further agreed that the High-Level Interim Group shall, at the latest by the entry into force of the EEA Agreement, decide on the authentication of texts of the EC acts referred to in the Annexes to the EEA Agreement which have been drawn up in the Finnish, Icelandic, Norwegian and Swedish languages.

The plenipotentiaries of the EC Member States and of the Community and the plenipotentiaries of the EFTA States have further taken note of the arrangement regarding the publication of EEA relevant information which is annexed to this Final Act.

Further, the plenipotentiaries of the EC Member States and of the Community and the plenipotentiaries of the EFTA States have taken note of the arrangements regarding the publication of EFTA notices on procurement which is annexed to this Final Act.

Furthermore, the plenipotentiaries of the EC Member States and of the Community and the plenipotentiaries of the EFTA States have adopted the Agreed Minutes from the negotiations which are annexed to this Final Act. The Agreed Minutes shall have a binding character.

Finally, the plenipotentiaries of the EC Member States and of the Community and the plenipotentiaries of the EFTA States have taken note of the declarations listed below and annexed to this Final Act:

1. Declaration by the Governments of Finland, Iceland, Norway and Sweden on alcohol monopolies;

2. Declaration by the Governments of Liechtenstein and Switzerland on alcohol monopolies;

3. Declaration by the European Community on mutual assistance in customs matters;

4. Declaration by the Governments of the EFTA States on free circulation of light duty commercial vehicles;

5. Declaration by the Government of Liechtenstein on product liability;

6. Declaration by the Government of Liechtenstein on the specific situation of the country;

7. Declaration by the Government of Austria on safeguards;

8. Declaration by the European Community;

9. Declaration by the Government of Iceland on the use of safeguard measures under the EEA Agreement;

10. Declaration by the Government of Switzerland on safeguard measures;

11. Declaration by the European Community;

12. Declaration by the Government of Switzerland on the introduction of post-diploma studies in architecture at the higher technical colleges;

13. Declaration by the Governments of Austria and Switzerland on audiovisual services;

14. Declaration by the Governments of Liechtenstein and Switzerland on administrative assistance;

15. Declaration by the European Community;

16. Declaration by the Government of Switzerland on the use of the safeguard clause in connection with capital movements;

17. Declaration by the European Community;

18. Declaration by the Government of Norway on the direct enforceability of decisions by the EC institutions regarding pecuniary obligations addressed to enterprises located in Norway;

19. Declaration by the European Community;

20. Declaration by the Government of Austria on the enforcement on its territory of decisions by EC institutions regarding pecuniary obligations;

21. Declaration by the European Community;

22. Declaration by the European Community on shipbuilding;

23. Declaration by the Government of Ireland concerning Protocol 28 on intellectual property – international conventions;

24. Declaration by the Governments of the EFTA States on the Charter of the Fundamental Social Rights of Workers;

25. Declaration by the Government of Austria on the implementation of Article 5 of Directive 76/207/EEC in respect of night-work;

26. Declaration by the European Community;

27. Declaration by the European Community on the rights for the EFTA States before the EC Court of Justice;

28. Declaration by the European Community on the rights of lawyers of the EFTA States under Community law;

29. Declaration by the European Community on the participation of the EFTA States' experts in EEA relevant EC committees in application of Article 100 of the Agreement;

30. Declaration by the European Community on Article 103 of the Agreement;

31. Declaration by the Governments of the EFTA States on Article 103(1) of the Agreement;

32. Declaration by the European Community on transit in the fisheries sector;

33. Declaration by the European Community and the Governments of Austria, Finland, Liechtenstein, Sweden and Switzerland on whale products;

34. Declaration by the Government of Switzerland concerning customs duties of a fiscal nature;

35. Declaration by the European Community on bilateral agreements;

36. Declaration by the Government of Switzerland on the Agreement between the EEC and the Swiss Confederation on the carriage of goods by road and rail;

37. Declaration by the Government of Austria on the Agreement between the EEC and the Republic of Austria on the transit of goods by road and rail;

38. Declaration by the Governments of the EFTA States concerning the EFTA financial mechanism;

39. Declaration by the Governments of the EFTA States concerning a court of first instance.

 Implemented in Ireland: European Communities (Amendment) Act 1993; S.I. 415S/93; S.I. 91S/94

TREATY
AMENDING CERTAIN PROVISIONS OF THE PROTOCOL ON THE STATUTE OF THE EUROPEAN INVESTMENT BANK

(OJ No L 91, 6.4.78)

[List omitted]

Having regard to Article 236 of the Treaty establishing the European Economic Community,

Whereas the Protocol on the Statute of the European Investment Bank which is annexed to the Treaty establishing the European Economic Community is an integral part thereof;

Whereas the definition of the unit of account and the methods of conversion as between this unit and the currencies of the Member States contained in the present text of the second subparagraph of Article 4(1), and in Article 7(3) and (4) of the Statute of the Bank are no longer entirely in keeping with the circumstances of international monetary relations;

Whereas the future evolution of the international monetary system cannot be foreseen; whereas, consequently, rather than adopting immediately a new definition of the unit of account in the Statute of the Bank, it is desirable, particularly taking into account the position of the Bank in relation to capital markets, to give the Bank the means to adapt the definition of the unit of account and the methods of conversion to changes, where necessary and on appropriate conditions;

Whereas in order to permit this rapid and flexible adaptation it is appropriate to give the Board of Governors of the Bank powers to alter, if necessary, the definition of the unit of account and the methods of conversion as between the unit of account and the various currencies;

Have decided to amend certain provisions of the Protocol on the Statute of the European Investment Bank, hereinafter called 'the Protocol', and to this end have designated as their Plenipotentiaries:

[List omitted]

Who, having exchanged their Full Powers, found in good and due form,

Have agreed as follows:

Article 1

The following sentence shall be added to the second subparagraph of Article 4(1) of the Protocol:

'The Board of Governors, acting unanimously on a proposal from the Board of Directors, may alter the definition of the unit of account.'

Article 2

The following sentence shall be added to Article 7(4) of the Protocol:

'Furthermore it may, acting unanimously on a proposal from the Board of Directors, alter the method of converting sums expressed in units of account into national currencies and vice versa.'

Article 3

Article 9(3)(g) of the Protocol shall be replaced by the following:

'(g) exercise the powers and functions provided for in Articles 4, 7, 14, 17, 26 and 27;'

Article 4

This Treaty will be ratified by the High Contracting Parties in accordance with their respective constitutional requirements. The instruments of ratification will be deposited with the Government of the Italian Republic.

Article 5

This Treaty shall enter into force on the first day of the month following the deposit of the instrument of ratification by the last signatory State to take this step.

Article 6

This Treaty, drawn up in a single original in the Danish, Dutch, English, French, German, Irish and Italian languages, all seven texts being authentic, shall be deposited in the archives of the Government of the Italian Republic, which will transmit a certified copy to each of the Governments of the other signatory States.

In witness whereof, the undersigned plenipotentiaries have affixed their signatures below this Treaty.

Done at Brussels on the tenth day of July in the year one thousand nine hundred and seventy five.

[List omitted]

Notice regarding the entry into force of the Treaty amending certain provisions of the Protocol on the Statute of the European Investment Bank, signed on Brussels on 10 July 1975

The necessary conditions for the entry into force of the Treaty amending certain provisions of the Protocol on the Statute of the European Investment Bank, signed in Brussels on 10 July 1975, were fulfilled on 1 September 1977 and the Treaty therefore entered into force, in accordance with Article 5 thereof, on 1 October 1977.

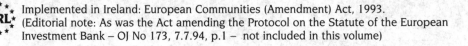 Implemented in Ireland: European Communities (Amendment) Act, 1993.
(Editorial note: As was the Act amending the Protocol on the Statute of the European Investment Bank – OJ No 173, 7.7.94, p.1 – not included in this volume)

Part C
Documents on Accession

TREATY

between

the Kingdom of Belgium,

the Federal Republic of Germany,

the French Republic,

the Italian Republic,

the Grand Duchy of Luxembourg,

the Kingdom of the Netherlands,

    Member States of the European Communities,

the Kingdom of Denmark,

Ireland,

the Kingdom of Norway,

and the United Kingdom of Great Britain and Northern Ireland

concerning the accession of the Kingdom of Denmark, Ireland, the Kingdom of Norway and the United Kingdom of Great Britain and Northern Ireland to the European Economic Community and to the European Atomic Energy Community

His Majesty the King of the Belgians, Her Majesty the Queen of Denmark, The President of the Federal Republic of Germany, The President of the French Republic, The President of Ireland, The President of the Italian Republic, His Royal Highness The Grand Duke of Luxembourg, Her Majesty the Queen of the Netherlands, His Majesty the King of Norway, Her Majesty The Queen of the United Kingdom of Great Britain and Northern Ireland,

United in their desire to pursue the attainment of the objectives of the Treaty establishing the European Economic Community and the Treaty establishing the European Atomic Energy Community,

Determined in the spirit of those Treaties to construct an ever closer union among the peoples of Europe on the foundations already laid,

Considering that Article 237 of the Treaty establishing the European Economic Community and Article 205 of the Treaty establishing the European Atomic Energy Community afford European States the opportunity of becoming members of these Communities,

Considering that the Kingdom of Denmark, Ireland, the Kingdom of Norway and the United Kingdom of Great Britain and Northern Ireland have applied to become members of these Communities,

Considering that the Council of the European Communities, after having obtained the Opinion of the Commission, has declared itself in favour of the admission of these States,

Have decided to establish by common agreement the conditions of admission and the adjustments to be made to the Treaties establishing the European Economic Community and the European Atomic Energy Community, and to this end have designated as their plenipotentiaries:

[List omitted]

Who, having exchanged their Full Powers found in good and due form, have agreed as follows:

Article 1

1. The Kingdom of Denmark, Ireland, the Kingdom of Norway and the United Kingdom of Great Britain and Northern Ireland hereby become members of the European Economic Community and of the European Atomic Energy Community and Parties to the Treaties establishing these Communities as amended or supplemented.

2. The conditions of admission and the adjustments to the Treaties establishing the European Economic Community and the European Atomic Energy Community necessitated thereby are set out in the Act annexed to this Treaty. The provisions of that Act concerning the European Economic Community and the European Atomic Energy Community shall form an integral part of this Treaty.

3. The provisions concerning the rights and obligations of the Member States and the powers and jurisdiction of the institutions of the Communities as set out in the Treaties referred to in paragraph 1 shall apply in respect of this Treaty.

Article 2

This Treaty will be ratified by the High Contracting Parties in accordance with their respective constitutional requirements. The instruments of ratification will be deposited with the Government of the Italian Republic by 31 December 1972 at the latest.

This Treaty will enter into force on 1 January 1973, provided that all the instruments of ratification have been deposited before that date and that all the instruments of accession to the European Coal and Steel Community are deposited on that date.

If, however, the States referred to in Article 1(1) have not all deposited their instruments of ratification and accession in due time, the Treaty shall enter into force for those States which have deposited their instruments. In this case, the Council of the European Communities, acting unanimously, shall decide immediately upon such resulting adjustments as have become indispensable, to Article 3 of this Treaty, and to Articles 14, 16, 17, 19, 20, 23, 129, 142, 143, 155 and 160 of the Act concerning the Conditions of Accession and the Adjustments to the Treaties, to the provisions of Annex I to that Act concerning the composition and functioning of various committees, and to Articles 5 and 8 of the Protocol on the Statute of the European Investment Bank; acting unanimously, it may also declare that those provisions of the aforementioned Act which refer expressly to a State which has not deposited its instruments of ratification and accession have lapsed, or it may adjust them.

Article 3[1]

This Treaty, drawn up in a single original in the Danish, Dutch, English, French, German, Irish, Italian and Norwegian languages, the Danish, Dutch, English, French, German, Irish and Italian texts all being equally authentic, will be deposited in the archives of the Government of the Italian Republic, which will transmit a certified copy to each of the Governments of the other signatory States.

In witness whereof, the undersigned plenipotentiaries have affixed their signatures below this Treaty.

Done at Brussels, on this twenty-second day of January in the year one thousand nine hundred and seventy-two.

[List omitted]

ACT

concerning the conditions of accession and the adjustments to the Treaties

PART ONE

Principles

Article 1

For the purposes of this Act:

– the expression 'original Treaties' means the Treaty establishing the

European Coal and Steel Community, the Treaty establishing the European Economic Community and the Treaty establishing the European Atomic Energy Community, as supplemented or amended by treaties or other acts which entered into force before accession; the expressions 'ECSC Treaty', 'EEC Treaty' and 'Euratom Treaty' mean the relevant original Treaties thus supplemented or amended;

— the expression 'original Member States' means the Kingdom of Belgium, the Federal Republic of Germany, the French Republic, the Italian Republic, the Grand Duchy of Luxembourg and the Kingdom of the Netherlands;

the expression 'new Member States' means the Kingdom of Denmark, Ireland and the United Kingdom of Great Britain and Northern Ireland.[2]

Article 2

From the date of accession, the provisions of the original Treaties and the acts adopted by the institutions of the Communities shall be binding on the new Member States and shall apply in those States under the conditions laid down in those Treaties and in this Act.

Article 3

1. The new Member States accede by this Act to the decisions and agreements adopted by the Representatives of the Governments of the Member States meeting in Council. They undertake to accede from the date of accession to all other agreements concluded by the original Member States relating to the functioning of the Communities or connected with their activities.

2. The new Member States undertake to accede to the conventions provided for in Article 220 of the EEC Treaty, and to the protocols on the interpretation of those conventions by the Court of Justice, signed by the original Member States and to this end they undertake to enter into negotiations with the original Member States in order to make the necessary adjustments thereto.

3. The new Member States are in the same situation as the original Member States in respect of declarations or resolutions of, or other positions taken up by, the Council and in respect of those concerning the European Communities adopted by common agreement of the Member States; they will accordingly observe the principles and guidelines deriving from those declarations, resolutions or other positions and will take such measures as may be necessary to ensure their implementation.

Article 4

1. The agreements or conventions entered into by any of the Communities with one or more third States, with an international organisation or with a national of a third State, shall, under the conditions laid down in the original Treaties and in this Act, be binding on the new Member States.

2. The new Member States undertake to accede, under the conditions laid down in this Act, to agreements or conventions concluded by the original Member States and any of the Communities, acting jointly, and to agreements concluded by the original Member States which are related to those agreements or conventions. The Community and the original Member States shall assist the new Member States in this respect.

3. The new Member States accede by this Act and under the conditions laid down therein to the internal agreements concluded by the original Member States for the purpose of implementing the agreements or conventions referred to in paragraph 2.

4. The new Member States shall take appropriate measures, where necessary, to adjust their positions in relation to international organisations and international agreements to which one of the Communities or to which other Member States are also parties, to the rights and obligations arising from their accession to the Communities.

Article 5

Article 234 of the EEC Treaty and Articles 105 and 106 of the Euratom Treaty shall apply, for the new Member States, to agreements or conventions concluded before accession.

Article 6

The provisions of this Act may not, unless otherwise provided herein, be suspended, amended or repealed other than by means of the procedure laid down in the original Treaties enabling those Treaties to be revised.

Article 7

Acts adopted by the institutions of the Communities to which the transitional provisions laid down in this Act relate shall retain their status in law; in particular, the procedures for amending those acts shall continue to apply.

Article 8

Provisions of this Act the purpose or effect of which is to repeal or amend acts adopted by the institutions of the Communities, otherwise than as a transitional measure, shall have the same status in law as the provisions which they repeal or amend and shall be subject to the same rules as those provisions.

Article 9

1. In order to facilitate the adjustment of the new Member States to the rules in force within the Communities, the application of the original Treaties and acts adopted by the institutions shall, as a transitional measure, be subject to the derogations provided for in this Act.

2. Subject to the dates, time limits and special provisions provided for in this Act, the application of the transitional measures shall terminate at the end of 1977.

PART TWO

Adjustments to the Treaties

Title I

Provisions governing the institutions

Chapter 1

The European Parliament

Article 10[3]

The following shall be substituted for Article 21(2) of the ECSC Treaty, Article 138(2) of the EEC Treaty and Article 108(2) of the Euratom Treaty:

'The number of these delegates shall be as follows:

Belgium	14
Denmark	10
Germany	36
France	36
Ireland	10
Italy	36

Luxembourg   6
Netherlands   14
United Kingdom   36.'

Chapter 2

The Council

Article 11[4]

The following shall be substituted for the second paragraph of Article 2 of the Treaty establishing a Single Council and a Single Commission of the European Communities:

'The office of President shall be held for a term of six months by each member of the Council in turn, in the following order of Member States: Belgium, Denmark, Germany, France, Ireland, Italy, Luxembourg, Netherlands, United Kingdom.'

Article 12[5]

The following shall be substituted for Article 28 of the ECSC Treaty:

'*Article* 28

When the Council is consulted by the High Authority, it shall consider the matter without necessarily taking a vote. The minutes of its proceedings shall be forwarded to the High Authority.

Wherever this Treaty requires that the assent of the Council be given, that assent shall be considered to have been given if the proposal submitted by the High Authority receives the approval:

–   of an absolute majority of the representatives of the Member States, including the votes of the representatives of two Member States which each produce at least one-eighth of the total value of the coal and steel output of the Community; or

–   in the event of an equal division of votes and if the High Authority maintains its proposal after a second discussion of the representatives of three Member States which each produce at least one-eighth of the total value of the coal and steel output of the Community.

Wherever this Treaty requires a unanimous decision or unanimous assent, such decision or assent shall have been duly given if all the members of the Council vote in favour. However, for the purposes of applying Articles 21, 32, 32a, 78d and 78f of this Treaty, and Article

16, the third paragraph of Article 20, the fifth paragraph of Article 28 and Article 44 of the Protocol on the Statute of the Court of Justice, abstention by members present in person or represented shall not prevent the adoption by the Council of acts which require unanimity.

Decisions of the Council, other than those for which a qualified majority or unanimity is required, shall be taken by a vote of the majority of its members; this majority shall be considered to be attained if it represents an absolute majority of the representatives of the Member States, including the votes of the representatives of two Member States which each produce at least one-eighth of the total value of the coal and steel output of the Community. However, for the purpose of applying those provisions of Articles 78, 78b and 78d of this Treaty which require a qualified majority, the votes of the members of the Council shall be weighted as follows: Belgium 5, Denmark 3, Germany 10, France 10, Ireland 3, Italy 10, Luxembourg 2, Netherlands 5, United Kingdom 10. For their adoption, acts shall require at least 41 votes in favour, cast by not less than six members.

Where a vote is taken, any member of the Council may act on behalf of not more than one other member.

The Council shall deal with the Member States through its President.

The acts of the Council shall be published in such a manner as it may decide.'

Article 13[6]

The following shall be substituted for the fourth paragraph of Article 95 of the ECSC Treaty:

'These amendments shall be proposed jointly by the High Authority and the Council, acting by an eight-ninths majority of its members, and shall be submitted to the Court for its opinion. In considering them, the Court shall have full power to assess all points of fact and of law. If as a result of such consideration it finds the proposals compatible with the provisions of the preceding paragraph, they shall be forwarded to the European Parliament and shall enter into force if approved by a majority of three-quarters of the votes cast and two-thirds of the members of the European Parliament.'

Article 14[7]

The following shall be substituted for Article 148(2) of the EEC Treaty and Article 118(2) of the Euratom Treaty:

'Where the Council is required to act by a qualified majority, the votes of its members shall be weighted as follows:

Belgium	5
Denmark	3
Germany	10
France	10
Ireland	3
Italy	10
Luxembourg	2
Netherlands	5
United Kingdom	10

For their adoption, acts of the Council shall require at least:

- forty-one votes in favour where this Treaty requires them to be adopted on a proposal from the Commission,

- forty-one votes in favour, cast by at least six members, in other cases.'

Chapter 3

The Commission

Article 15[8]

The following shall be substituted for the first subparagraph of Article 10(1) of the Treaty establishing a Single Council and a Single Commission of the European Communities:

'The Commission shall consist of 14 members, who shall be chosen on the grounds of their general competence and whose independence is beyond doubt.'

Article 16

The following shall be substituted for the first paragraph of Article 14 of the Treaty establishing a Single Council and a Single Commission of the European Communities:

'The President and the five Vice-Presidents of the Commission shall be appointed from among its members for a term of two years in accordance with the same procedure as that laid down for the appointment of members of the Commission. Their appointments may be renewed.'

Chapter 4

The Court of Justice

Article 17[9]

The following shall be substituted for the first paragraph of Article 32 of the ECSC Treaty, the first paragraph of Article 165 of the EEC Treaty and the first paragraph of Article 137 of the Euratom Treaty:

'The Court of Justice shall consist of nine Judges.'

Article 18[10]

The following shall be substituted for the first paragraph of Article 32a of the ECSC Treaty, the first paragraph of Article 166 of the EEC Treaty and the first paragraph of Article 138 of the Euratom Treaty:

'The Court of Justice shall be assisted by three Advocates-General.'

Article 19[11, 12]

The following shall be substituted for the second and third paragraphs of Article 32b of the ECSC Treaty, the second and third paragraphs of Article 167 of the EEC Treaty and the second and third paragraphs of Article 139 of the Euratom Treaty:

'Every three years there shall be a partial replacement of the Judges. Five and four Judges shall be replaced alternately.

Every three years there shall be a partial replacement of the Advocates-General. One and two Advocates-General shall be replaced alternately.'

Article 20

The following shall be substituted for the second paragraph of Article 18 of the Protocol on the Statute of the Court of Justice of the European Coal and Steel Community, Article 15 of the Protocol on the Statute of the Court of Justice of the European Economic Community and Article 15 of the Protocol on the Statute of the Court of Justice of the European Atomic Energy Community:

'Decisions of the Court shall be valid only when an uneven number of its members is sitting in the deliberations. Decisions of the full Court shall be valid if seven members are sitting. Decisions of the Chambers shall be valid only if three Judges are sitting; in the event of one of the Judges of a Chamber being prevented from attending, a Judge of another Chamber may be called upon to sit in accordance with the conditions laid down in the rules of procedure.'

Chapter 5

The Economic and Social Committee

Article 21[13]

The following shall be substituted for the first paragraph of Article 194 of the EEC Treaty and the first paragraph of Article 166 of the Euratom Treaty:

'The number of members of the Committee shall be as follows:

Belgium	12
Denmark	9
Germany	24
France	24
Ireland	9
Italy	24
Luxembourg	6
Netherlands	12
United Kingdom	24.'

Chapter 6

The ECSC Consultative Committee

Article 22

The following shall be substituted for the first paragraph of Article 18 of the ECSC Treaty:

'A Consultative Committee shall be attached to the High Authority. It shall consist of not less than 60 and not more than 84 members and shall comprise equal numbers of producers, of workers and of consumers and dealers.'

Chapter 7

The Scientific and Technical Committee

Article 23[14]

The following shall be substituted for the first subparagraph of Article 134(2) of the Euratom Treaty:

'The Committee shall consist of 27 members, appointed by the Council after consultation with the Commission.'

Title II

Other Adjustments

Article 24[15]

1. The United Kingdom shall be added to the Member States specified in the first sentence of Article 131 of the EEC Treaty.

2. The following countries and territories shall be added to the list in Annex IV to the EEC Treaty:

Anglo-French Condominium of the New Hebrides

The Bahamas

Bermuda

British Antarctic Territory

British Honduras

British Indian Ocean Territory

British Solomon Islands

British Virgin Islands

Brunei

Associated States in the Caribbean: Antigua, Dominica, Grenada, St Lucia, St Vincent, St Kitts-Nevis-Anguilla

Cayman Islands

Central and Southern Line Islands

Falkland Islands and Dependencies

Gilbert and Ellice Islands

Montserrat

Pitcairn

St Helena and Dependencies

The Seychelles

Turks and Caicos Islands.

Article 25[16]

The following paragraph shall be added after the first paragraph of Article 79 of the ECSC Treaty:

'Notwithstanding the preceding paragraph:

(a) This Treaty shall not apply to the Faroe Islands. The Government of the Kingdom of Denmark may, however, give notice, by a declaration deposited by 31 December 1975 at the latest with the Government of the French Republic, which shall transmit a certified copy thereof to each of the Governments of the other Member States, that this Treaty shall apply to those islands. In that event, this Treaty shall apply to those islands from the first day of the second month following the deposit of the declaration.

(b) This Treaty shall not apply to the Sovereign Base Areas of the United Kingdom of Great Britain and Northern Ireland in Cyprus.

(c) This Treaty shall apply to the Channel Island and the Isle of Man only to the extent necessary to ensure the implementation of the arrangements for those islands set out in the Council decision of 22 January 1972 concerning the accession of new Member States to the European Coal and Steel Community.'

Article 26

1.[17] The following shall be substituted for Article 227(1) of the EEC Treaty:

'1. This Treaty shall apply to the Kingdom of Belgium, the Kingdom of Denmark, the Federal Republic of Germany, the French Republic, Ireland, the Italian Republic, the Grand Duchy of Luxembourg, the Kingdom of the Netherlands and the United Kingdom of Great Britain and Northern Ireland.'

2. The following subparagraph shall be added to Article 227(3) of the EEC Treaty:

'This Treaty shall not apply to those overseas countries and territories having special relations with the United Kingdom of Great Britain and Northern Ireland which are not included in the aforementioned list.'

3.[18] The following paragraph shall be added to Article 227 of the EEC Treaty:

'5. Notwithstanding the preceding paragraphs:

(a) This Treaty shall not apply to the Faroe Islands. The Government of the Kingdom of Denmark may, however, give notice, by a declaration deposited by 31 December 1975 at the latest with the Government of the Italian Republic, which shall transmit a certified copy thereof to each of the Governments of the other Member States, that this Treaty shall apply to those islands. In that event this Treaty shall apply to those islands from the first day of the second month following the deposit of the declaration.

(b) This Treaty shall not apply to the Sovereign Base Areas of the United Kingdom of Great Britain and Northern Ireland in Cyprus.

(c) This Treaty shall apply to the Channel Islands and the Isle of Man only to the extent necessary to ensure the implementation of the arrangements for those islands set out in the Treaty concerning the accession of new Member States to the European Economic Community and to the European Atomic Energy Community signed on 22 January 1972.'

Article 27[19]

The following paragraph shall be added to Article 198 of the Euratom Treaty:

'Notwithstanding the previous paragraphs:

(a) This Treaty shall not apply to the Faroe Islands. The Government of the Kingdom of Denmark may, however, give notice, by a declaration deposited by 31 December 1975 at the latest, with the Government of the Italian Republic, which shall transmit a certified copy thereof to each of the Governments of the other Member States, that this Treaty shall apply to those islands. In that event, this Treaty shall apply to those islands from the first day of the second month following the deposit of the declaration.

(b) This Treaty shall not apply to the Sovereign Base Areas of the United Kingdom of Great Britain and Northern Ireland in Cyprus.

(c) This Treaty shall not apply to those overseas countries and territories having special relations with the United Kingdom of Great Britain and Northern Ireland which are not listed in Annex IV to the Treaty establishing the European Economic Community.

(d) This Treaty shall apply to the Channel Islands and the Isle of Man only to the extent necessary to ensure the implementation of the arrangements for those islands set out in the Treaty concerning the accession of new Member States to the European Economic Community and to the European Atomic Energy Community signed on 22 January 1972.'

Article 28

Acts of the institutions of the Community relating to the products in Annex II to the EEC Treaty and the products subject, on importation into the Community, to specific rules as a result of the implementation of the common agricultural policy, as well as the acts on the harmonisation of legislation of Member States concerning turnover taxes, shall not apply to Gibraltar unless the Council, acting unanimously on a proposal from the Commission, provides otherwise.

PART THREE

Adaptations to acts adopted by the institutions

Article 29

The acts listed in Annex I to this Act shall be adapted as specified in that Annex.

Article 30

The adaptations to the acts listed in Annex II to this Act made necessary by accession shall be drawn up in conformity with the guidelines set out in that Annex and in accordance with the procedure and under the conditions laid down in Article 153.

PART FOUR

Transitional measures

Title I

Free movement of goods

Chapter 1

Tariff provisions

Article 31

1. The basic duty to which the successive reductions provided for in Articles 32 and 59 are to be applied shall, for each product, be the duty actually applied on 1 January 1972.

The basic duty used for the moves towards the Common Customs Tariff and the ECSC unified tariff provided for in Articles 39 and 59 shall, for each product, be the duty actually applied by the new Member States on 1 January 1972.

For the purposes of this Act, 'ECSC unified tariff' means the customs nomenclature and the existing customs duties for the products in Annex I to the ECSC Treaty, other than coal.

2. If, after 1 January 1972, any tariff reductions deriving from the Agreement Relating Principally to Chemicals supplementary to the Geneva (1967) Protocol to the General Agreement on Tariffs and Trade become applicable, the reduced duties shall replace the basic duties referred to in paragraph 1.

Article 32

1. Customs duties on imports between the Community as originally constituted and the new Member States and between the new Member States themselves shall be progressively abolished in accordance with the following timetable:

– on 1 April 1973, each duty shall be reduced to 80% of the basic duty;

– the four other reductions of 20% each shall be made on:

1 January 1974,

1 January 1975,

1 January 1976,

1 July 1977.

2. Notwithstanding paragraph 1:

(a) customs duties on imports of coal within the meaning of Annex I to the ECSC Treaty shall be abolished between Member States from the date of accession;

(b) customs duties on imports of products listed in Annex III to this Act shall be abolished on 1 January 1974;

(c) duty-free entry shall, from the date of accession, apply to imports which benefit from the provisions relating to tax exemptions applicable to persons travelling from one Member State to another.

3. As regards the products listed in Annex IV to this Act which are subject to contractual margins of preference between the United Kingdom and certain other countries enjoying Commonwealth preference, the United Kingdom may defer until 1 July 1973 the first of the tariff reductions referred to in paragraph 1.

4. Paragraph 1 shall not preclude the possibility of opening tariff quotas

for certain iron and steel products which are not manufactured or the manufacture of which is inadequate in quantity or quality in the Community as originally constituted.

Article 33

In no case shall customs duties higher than those applied to third countries enjoying most-favoured-nation treatment be applied within the Community.

In the event of the Common Customs Tariff duties being amended or suspended or the new Member States applying Article 41, the Council, acting by a qualified majority on a proposal from the Commission, may take the necessary measures for the maintenance of Community preference.

Article 34

Any new Member State may suspend in whole or in part the levying of duties on products imported from other Member States. It shall inform the other Member States and the Commission thereof.

Article 35

Any charge having equivalent effect to a customs duty on imports, introduced after 1 January 1972 in trade between the Community as originally constituted and the new Member States or between the new Member States themselves, shall be abolished on 1 January 1973.

Any charge having equivalent effect to a customs duty on imports the rate of which on 31 December 1972 is higher than that actually applied on 1 January 1972 shall be reduced to the latter rate on 1 January 1973.

Article 36

1. Charges having equivalent effect to customs duties on imports shall be progressively abolished between the Community as originally constituted and the new Member States and between the new Member States themselves in accordance with the following timetable:

- by 1 January 1974 at the latest, each charge shall be reduced to 60% of the rate applied on 1 January 1972;

- the three other reductions of 20% each shall be made on:

1 January 1975,

1 January 1976,

1 July 1977.

2. Notwithstanding paragraph 1:

(a) charges having equivalent effect to customs duties on imports of coal within the meaning of Annex I to the ECSC Treaty shall be abolished between Member States from the date of accession;

(b) charges having equivalent effect to customs duties on imports on the products listed in Annex III to this Act shall be abolished on 1 January 1974.

Article 37

Customs duties on exports and charges having equivalent effect shall be abolished between the Community as originally constituted and the new Member States and between the new Member States themselves by 1 January 1974 at the latest.

Article 38

1. Without prejudice to the following paragraphs, the provisions concerning the progressive abolition of customs duties shall apply to customs duties of a fiscal nature.

2. The new Member States shall retain the right to replace a customs duty of a fiscal nature or the fiscal element of any such duty by an internal tax which is in conformity with Article 95 of the EEC Treaty. If a new Member State avails itself of this right, any element not so replaced by the internal tax shall constitute the basic duty under Article 31. This element shall be abolished in trade within the Community and brought into line with the Common Customs Tariff under the conditions laid down in Articles 32, 39 and 59.

3. Where the Commission finds that in a new Member State there is serious difficulty in replacing a customs duty of a fiscal nature or the fiscal element of any such duty, it shall authorise that State, following a request made before 1 February 1973, to retain the duty or fiscal element, provided the State abolishes it by 1 January 1976 at the latest. The decision of the Commission shall be taken before 1 March 1973.

The protective element, the amount of which shall be fixed by the Commission before 1 March 1973 after consulting the State concerned, shall constitute the basic duty provided for in Article 31. This element shall be abolished in trade within the Community and brought into line with the Common Customs Tariff under the conditions laid down in Articles 32, 39 and 59.

4. The Commission may authorise the United Kingdom to retain customs duties of a fiscal nature or the fiscal element of such duties on tobacco

for two additional years if by 1 January 1976 it has not proved possible to convert those duties into internal taxes on manufactured tobacco on a harmonised basis in accordance with Article 99 of the EEC Treaty, either because there are no Community provisions in this field on 1 January 1975 or because the time limit set for the implementation of such Community provisions is later than 1 January 1976.

5. The Council Directive of 4 March 1969 on the harmonisation of provisions laid down by law, regulation or administrative action for deferred payment of customs duties, charges having equivalent effect and agricultural levies shall not apply in the new Member States to the customs duties of a fiscal nature referred to in paragraphs 3 and 4 or to the fiscal element of such duties.

6. The Council Directive of 4 March 1969 on the harmonisation of provisions laid down by law, regulation or administrative action in respect of inward processing shall not apply in the United Kingdom to the customs duties of a fiscal nature referred to in paragraphs 3 and 4 or to the fiscal element of such duties.

Article 39

1. For the purpose of the progressive introduction of the Common Customs Tariff and of the ECSC unified tariff, the new Member States shall amend their tariffs applicable to third countries as follows:

(*a*) in the case of tariff headings in respect of which the basic duties do not differ by more than 15% in either direction from the duties in the Common Customs Tariff or the ECSC unified tariff, these latter duties shall be applied from 1 January 1974;

(*b*) in other cases, each new Member State shall, from the same date, apply a duty reducing by 40% the difference between the basic duty and the duty in the Common Customs Tariff or the ECSC unified tariff.

This difference shall be further reduced by 20% on 1 January 1975 and by 20% on 1 January 1976.

The new Member States shall apply in full the Common Customs Tariff and the ECSC unified tariff from 1 July 1977.

2. From 1 January 1974, if any duties in the Common Customs Tariff are altered or suspended, the new Member States shall simultaneously amend or suspend their tariffs in the proportion resulting from the implementation of paragraph 1.

3. The new Member States shall apply the Common Customs Tariff from 1 January 1974 in respect of the products listed in Annex III to this Act.

4. The new Member States shall apply the Common Customs Tariff nomenclature from the date of accession. Denmark and the United Kingdom are, however, authorised to defer their application of the nomenclature until 1 January 1974.[20]

The new Member States may include within this nomenclature existing national subdivisions which are indispensable in order that the progressive alignment of their customs duties with those in the Common Customs Tariff be carried out under the conditions laid down in this Act.

5. With a view to facilitating the progressive introduction of the Common Customs Tariff by the new Member States, the Commission shall determine, if necessary, the provisions whereby new Member States alter their customs duties.

Article 40

In respect of the following products in the Common Customs Tariff:

CCT heading No	Description of goods (ECSC)
73.01	Pig iron, cast iron and spiegeleisen in pigs, blocks, lumps and similar forms
73.02	Ferro-alloys:
	A. Ferro-manganese:
	I. Containing more than 2% by weight of carbon (high carbon ferro-manganese)
73.07	Blooms, billets, slabs and sheet bars (including tinplate bars), of iron or steel; pieces roughly shaped by forging, of iron or steel
	A. Blooms and billets:
	ex I. Rolled billets

Ireland shall, notwithstanding the provisions of Article 39, apply from 1 January 1975 duties reducing by one-third the difference between the rates actually applied on 1 January 1972 and those of the ECSC unified tariff. The difference resulting from the first move towards alignment shall be further reduced by 50% on 1 January 1976.

Ireland shall apply in full the ECSC unified tariff from 1 July 1977.

Article 41

In order to bring their tariffs into line with the Common Customs Tariff and the ECSC unified tariff, the new Member States shall remain free to alter their customs duties more rapidly than is provided for in Article 39(1) and (3). They shall inform the other Member States and the Commission thereof.

Chapter 2

Elimination of quantitative restrictions

Article 42

Quantitative restrictions on imports and exports shall, from the date of accession, be abolished between the Community as originally constituted and the new Member States and between the new Member States themselves.

Measures having equivalent effect to such restrictions shall be abolished by 1 January 1975 at the latest.

Article 43

Notwithstanding Article 42, Member States may, for a period of two years, retain restrictions on exports of waste and scrap metal of iron or steel falling within Common Customs Tariff No 73.03, insofar as these arrangements are not more restrictive than those applied to exports to third countries.

For Denmark the period shall be three years and for Ireland five years.[21]

Article 44

1. The new Member States shall progressively adjust State monopolies of a commercial character within the meaning of Article 37(1) of the EEC Treaty so as to ensure that by 31 December 1977 no discrimination regarding the conditions under which goods are procured and marketed exists between nationals of Member States.

The original Member States shall have equivalent obligations in relation to the new Member States.

2. From the beginning of 1973 the Commission shall make recommendations as to the manner in which and the timetable according to which the adjustment provided for in this Article must be carried out, it being understood that the manner and timetable must be the same for the new Member States and the original Member States.

Chapter 3

Other provisions

Article 45

1. The Commission shall, before 1 April 1973 and with due regard for the provisions in force, in particular those relating to Community transit, determine the methods of administrative cooperation designed to ensure that goods fulfilling the requisite conditions benefit from the abolition of customs duties and charges having equivalent effect and quantitative restrictions and measures having equivalent effect.

2. The Commission shall, before the expiry of that time limit, lay down the provisions applicable to trade within the Community in goods obtained in the Community in the manufacture of which have been incorporated:

- products on which the customs duties or charges having equivalent effect which were applicable to them in the Community as originally constituted or in a new Member State have not been levied, or which have benefited from a total or partial drawback of such duties or charges;

- agricultural products which do not fulfil the conditions required for admission to free movement in the Community as originally constituted or in a new Member State.

In adopting these provisions, the Commission shall take into account the rules laid down in this Act for the elimination of customs duties between the Community as originally constituted and the new Member States and between the new Member States themselves, and for the progressive introduction by the new Member States of the Common Customs Tariff and the provisions relating to the common agricultural policy.

Article 46

1. Save as otherwise provided in this Act, the provisions in force with regard to customs legislation for trade with third countries shall apply under the same conditions to trade within the Community, for such time as customs duties are levied in that trade.

For the purpose of establishing the customs value in respect of that trade, the customs territory to be taken into consideration shall be that defined by the provisions existing in the Community and in the new Member States on 31 December 1972.

2. The Member States apply the Common Customs Tariff nomenclature

in trade within the Community from the date of accession. Denmark and the United Kingdom are, however, authorised to defer their application of this nomenclature until 1 January 1974.[22]

The new Member States may include within this nomenclature existing national subdivisions which are indispensable in order that the progressive elimination of their customs duties within the Community be carried out under the conditions laid down in this Act.

Article 47

1. Where the compensatory amounts referred to in Article 55(1)(a) are levied in trade between the Community as originally constituted and the new Member States and between the new Member States themselves on imports of primary products considered as having been used in the manufacture of goods covered by Regulation No 170/67/EEC on the common system of trade for ovalbumin and lactalbumin and Regulation (EEC) No 1059/69 determining the system of trade applicable to certain goods processed from agricultural products, a compensatory amount, calculated on the basis of the said amounts and in accordance with the rules laid down by the above Regulations for calculating either the charge or the variable component applicable to the goods under consideration, shall be applied on importation of those goods.

When these same goods are imported from third countries into the new Member States, the charge laid down by Regulation No 170/67/EEC and the variable component laid down by Regulation (EEC) No 1059/69 shall be reduced or increased, as the case may be, by the compensatory amount under the same conditions as those laid down in Article 55(1)(b).

2. Article 61(2) shall apply for the determination of the customs duty constituting the fixed component of the charge applicable in the new Member States to goods covered by Regulation (EEC) No 1059/69.

Each fixed component applied in trade between the Community as originally constituted and the new Member States and between the new Member States themselves shall be abolished in accordance with Article 32(1).

Each fixed component applied by the new Member States to imports from third countries shall be brought into line with the Common Customs Tariff in accordance with Article 39.

3. The new Member States shall, for the goods covered by Regulations No 170/67/EEC and (EEC) No 1059/69, apply in full the Common Customs Tariff nomenclature by 1 February 1973 at the latest.

4. The new Member States shall abolish customs duties and charges

having equivalent effect, other than those provided for in paragraphs 1 and 2, on 1 February 1973.

On the same date, the new Member States shall abolish the measures having equivalent effect to quantitative restrictions in trade between themselves and with the Community as originally constituted.

5. The Council shall, acting by a qualified majority on a proposal from the Commission, adopt provisions to implement this Article, taking account, in particular, of the special situations which may result from the implementation for the same goods of the first subparagraph of paragraph 1 and of Article 97.

Article 48

1. The provisions of this Title shall not prevent Ireland from applying to products originating in the United Kingdom arrangements enabling customs duties and protective elements contained in customs duties of a fiscal nature to be eliminated more rapidly, in accordance with the Anglo-Irish Free Trade Area Agreement, signed on 14 December 1965, and related Agreements.

2. The provisions adopted pursuant to Article 45(2) shall apply from 1 January 1974 in the context of the customs arrangements in force between Ireland and the United Kingdom.

Article 49

1. Protocols Nos 8 to 15 annexed to this Act shall not preclude any alteration to or suspension of duties decided under Article 28 of the EEC Treaty.

2. The Protocols annexed to the Agreement on the determination of part of the Common Customs Tariff in respect of the products in List G annexed to the EEC Treaty are hereby revoked, with the exception of Protocol No XVII.

Title II

Agriculture

Chapter 1

General provisions

Article 50

Save as otherwise provided in this Title, the rules provided for in this Act shall apply to agricultural products.

Article 51

1. This Article shall apply to prices in respect of which Chapters 2 and 3 refer to this Article.

2. Before the first move towards price alignment referred to in Article 52, the prices to be applied in each new Member State shall be fixed in accordance with the rules provided for in the common organisation of the market in the sector in question at a level which allows producers in that sector to obtain returns equivalent to those obtained under the previous national system.

3. In respect of the United Kingdom, those prices shall, however, be fixed at a level such that the application of the Community rules results in a level of market prices comparable with the level recorded in the Member State concerned during a representative period preceding the implementation of the Community rules.[23]

Article 52

1. If the application of the provisions of this Title results in a price level different from that of the common prices, the prices in respect of which Chapters 2 and 3 refer to this Article shall be aligned with the level of the common prices in six stages.

2. Subject to paragraph 4, the moves towards alignment shall be carried out each year at the beginning of the marketing year according to the following provisions:

(a) when the price of a product in a new Member State is lower than the common price, the price in that Member State shall, at the time of each move towards alignment, be increased successively by a sixth, a fifth, a quarter, a third and a half of the difference between the price level in that new Member State and the common price level which are applicable before each move towards alignment; the price resulting from this calculation shall be increased proportionately to any rise in the common price for the following market year.

(b) when the price of a product in a new Member State is higher than the common price, the difference between the price level applicable before each move towards alignment in the new Member State and the common price level applicable for the next marketing year shall be reduced successively by a sixth, a fifth, a quarter, a third and a half.

3. In the interest of the smooth functioning of the process of integration, the Council, acting in accordance with the procedure laid down in Article 43(2) of the EEC Treaty, may decide that, notwithstanding paragraph 2, the price of one or more products in one or more of the new Member States shall for one marketing year depart from the prices resulting from the application of paragraph 2.

This departure may not exceed 10% of the amount of the price move to be made.

In that event, the price level for the following marketing year shall be that which would have resulted from applying paragraph 2 if the departure had not been decided upon. A further departure from this price level may, however, be decided upon for that marketing year in accordance with the conditions in the preceding subparagraphs.

4. The common prices shall be applied in the new Member States by 1 January 1978 at the latest.

Article 53

If the difference between the price level of a product in a new Member State and the common price level is found to be minimal, the Council, acting in accordance with the procedure laid down in Article 43(2) of the EEC Treaty, may decide that the common price shall be applied in that new Member State in respect of the product concerned.

Article 54

1. For such time as there is a difference in the United Kingdom between prices obtained under the national system of guaranteed prices and market prices resulting from the application of the mechanisms of the common agricultural policy and the provisions of this Title, that Member State is authorised to retain production subsidies.

2. The United Kingdom shall, for each of the products to which paragraph 1 applies, endeavour to abolish these subsidies as soon as possible during the period referred to in Article 9(2).

3. These subsidies may not have the effect of raising the returns of producers above the level which would have resulted from the application to these returns of the rules for the alignment of prices laid down in Article 52.

4. The Council, acting in accordance with the procedure laid down in Article 43(2) of the EEC Treaty, shall adopt the rules necessary for the application of this Article with a view to ensuring the proper functioning of the common agricultural policy and in particular of the common organisation of the market.

Article 55

1. The differences in price levels shall be compensated as follows:

(a) in trade between the new Member States themselves and with the Community as originally constituted, compensatory amounts shall be levied by the importing State or granted by the exporting State;

(b) in trade between the new Member States and third countries, levies or other import charges applied under the common agricultural policy and export refunds shall be reduced or increased, as the case may be, by the compensatory amounts applicable in trade with the Community as originally constituted. Customs duties may not, however, be reduced by the compensatory amount.

2. For products in respect of which prices are fixed in accordance with Articles 51 and 52, the compensatory amounts applicable in trade between the Community as originally constituted and the new Member States, and between those States and third countries, shall be equal to the difference between the prices fixed for the new Member State concerned and the common prices.

For the other products, the compensatory amounts shall be determined in the cases provided for in Chapters 2 and 3 and in accordance with the rules which they lay down.

3. The compensatory amounts applicable in trade between the new Member States shall be determined by direct reference to the compensatory amounts fixed for each of those States in accordance with paragraph 2.

4. No compensatory amount shall, however, be fixed if the application of paragraphs 2 and 3 results in a minimal amount.

5. For products in respect of which the duty in the Common Customs Tariff is bound under the General Agreement on Tariffs and Trade, the binding shall be taken into account.

6. The compensatory amount levied or granted by a Member State in accordance with paragraph 1(a) may not exceed the total amount levied by that same Member State on imports from third countries.

The Council, acting by a qualified majority on a proposal from the Commission, may derogate from this rule, in particular in order to avoid deflections of trade and distortions of competition.

Article 56

If the world market price for a product is higher than the price used in calculating the import charge introduced under the common agricultural policy, less the compensatory amount deducted from the import charge in accordance with Article 55, or if the refund on exports to third countries is less than the compensatory amount, or if no refund is applicable, appropriate measures may be taken with a view to ensuring the proper functioning of the common organisation of the market.

Article 57

In fixing the level of the various elements of the price and intervention system, except for the prices referred to in Articles 51 and 70, account shall be taken for the new Member States, to the extent necessary for the proper functioning of the Community rules, of the difference in prices expressed by the compensatory amount.

Article 58

The compensatory amounts granted shall be financed by the Community from the Guarantee Section of the European Agricultural Guidance and Guarantee Fund.

Article 59

The following provisions shall apply to products the importation of which from third countries into the Community as originally constituted is subject to customs duties:

1. Customs duties on imports shall be progressively abolished between the Community as originally constituted and the new Member States and between the new Member States themselves in five stages. The first reduction, which shall reduce the customs duties to 80% of the basic duty, and the four other reductions of 20% each, shall be made in accordance with the following timetable:

(a) for products covered by the common organisation of the market in beef and veal: at the start of each marketing year, the first reduction taking place in 1973;

(*b*) for products covered by Regulation No 23 on the progressive establishment of a common organisation of the market in fruit and vegetables, by Regulation (EEC) No 234/68 on the establishment of a common organisation of the market in live trees and other plants, bulbs, roots and the like, cut flowers and ornamental foliage, and by Regulation (EEC) No 865/68 on the establishment of a common organisation of the market in products processed from fruit and vegetables: on 1 January each year, the first reduction taking place on 1 January 1974;

(*c*) for other agricultural products: in accordance with the timetable laid down in Article 32(1), the first reduction, however, taking place on 1 July 1973.

2. For the purpose of the progressive introduction of the Common Customs Tariff, each new Member State shall reduce the difference between the basic duty and the duty in the Common Customs Tariff by successive amounts of 20%. These moves towards alignment shall be made on the dates laid down in paragraph 1 for the products in question. For the products referred to in paragraph 1(c), the moves towards alignment shall follow the timetable laid down in Article 39(1).

However, in the case of tariff headings in respect of which the basic duties do not differ by more than 15% in either direction from the duties in the Common Customs Tariff, the latter duties shall be applied from the date of the first move towards alignment for each category of products in question.

3. In respect of the second, third and fourth reductions or moves towards alignment, the Council, acting by a qualified majority on a proposal from the Commission, may decide that, in respect of one or more of the new Member States, the duties applicable to one or more of the products referred to in paragraph 1(b) shall, for one year, depart from the duties resulting from the application of paragraph 1 or, as the case may be, paragraph 2.

This departure may not exceed 10% of the amount of the modification to be made under paragraph 1 or 2.

In that event, the duties to be applied for the following year shall be those which would have resulted from applying paragraph 1 or, as the case may be, paragraph 2, if the departure had not been decided upon. However, for that year, a further departure from those duties may be decided upon in accordance with the conditions set out in the above subparagraphs.

On 1 January 1978, the customs duties on these products shall be abolished and the new Member States shall apply in full the Common Customs Tariff.

4. In respect of products covered by a common organisation of the market, the new Member States may, in accordance with the procedure laid down in Article 26 of Regulation No 120/67/EEC on the common organisation of the market in cereals or, as the case may be, laid down in the corresponding Articles of the other Regulations on the establishment of a common organisation of agricultural markets, be authorised to abolish the customs duties referred to in paragraph 1, or to align duties as provided for in paragraph 2, or both, at a more rapid rate than that laid down in the preceding paragraphs or to suspend in whole or in part the customs duties on products imported from other Member States.

In respect of other products, no authorisation shall be required for the introduction of the measures referred to in the preceding subparagraph.

The customs duties resulting from an accelerated alignment shall not be less than the customs duties on imports of the same products from other Member States.

Each new Member State shall inform the other Member States and the Commission of the measures taken.

Article 60

1. In respect of products covered, on the date of accession, by a common organisation of the market, the system applicable in the Community as originally constituted in respect of customs duties and charges having equivalent effect and quantitative restrictions and measures having equivalent effect shall, subject to Articles 55 and 59, apply in the new Member States from 1 February 1973.

2. In respect of products not covered, on the date of accession, by a common organisation of the market, the provisions of Title I concerning the progressive abolition of charges having equivalent effect to customs duties and of quantitative restrictions and measures having equivalent effect shall not apply to those charges, restrictions and measures if they form part of a national market organisation on the date of accession.

This provision shall apply only to the extent necessary to ensure the maintenance of the national organisation and until the common organisation of the market for these products is implemented.

3. The new Member States shall apply the Common Customs Tariff nomenclature by 1 February 1973 at the latest, in respect of agricultural products covered by a common organisation of the market.

To the extent that no difficulties arise in the application of the Community rules and, in particular, in the functioning of the common organisation of markets and of the transitional mechanisms provided for in this Title, the Council, acting by a qualified majority on a proposal from the Commission, may authorise a new Member State to include within this nomenclature such existing national subdivisions as would be indispensable for carrying out the progressive moves towards alignment with the Common Customs Tariff or the elimination of the duties in the Community under the conditions laid down in this Act.

Article 61

1. The component for protection of the processing industry which is used in calculating the charge on imports from third countries of products covered by the common organisation of the markets in cereals, rice and products processed from fruit and vegetables shall be levied on imports from the new Member States into the Community as originally constituted.

2. For imports into the new Member States, the amount of that component shall be determined by separating out, from the total protection applied on 1 January 1972, the component or components designed to ensure the protection of the processing industry.

Such component or components shall be levied on imports from other Member States; they shall replace, as regards the charge on imports from third countries, the Community protective component.

3. Article 59 shall apply to the component referred to in paragraphs 1 and 2. The reductions or alignments in question shall, however, in respect of cereal and rice products be made at the beginning of the marketing year fixed for the basic product concerned.

Article 62

1. The Council, acting by a qualified majority on a proposal from the Commission, shall adopt the provisions necessary for implementing this Title.

2. The Council, acting unanimously on a proposal from the Commission after consulting the European Parliament, may make the necessary adaptations to the provisions of Chapters 2, 3 and 4 of this Title, if made necessary as a result of a change in Community rules.

Article 63

1. If transitional measures are necessary to facilitate the passage from the existing arrangements in the new Member States to those resulting

from the application of the common organisation of the markets as provided for in this Title, particularly if for certain products the implementation to the new arrangements on the scheduled date meets with appreciable difficulties, such measures shall be adopted in accordance with the procedure provided for in Article 26 of Regulation No 120/67/EEC or, as the case may be, in the corresponding Articles of the other Regulations on the common organisation of agricultural markets. Such measures may be taken during the period up to 31 January 1974, but their application may not extend beyond that date.

2. The Council may, acting unanimously on a proposal from the Commission after consulting the European Parliament, extend the time limit in paragraph 1 up to 31 January 1975.

Article 64

The provisions of this Title shall not affect the degree of freedom of trade in agricultural products which results from the Anglo-Irish Free Trade Area Agreement, signed on 14 December 1965, and related Agreements.

Chapter 2

Provisions relating to certain common organisations of markets

Section 1

Fruit and vegetables

Article 65

1. A compensatory amount shall be fixed for fruit and vegetables in respect of which:

(a) the new Member State concerned applied, during 1971, quantitative restrictions or measures having equivalent effect;

(b) a common basic price is fixed; and

(c) the producer price in that new Member State appreciably exceeds the basic price applicable in the Community as originally constituted during the period preceding the application of the Community system to the new Member States.

2. The producer price referred to in paragraph 1(c) shall be calculated by applying to the national data of the new Member State concerned the principles set out in Article 4(2) of Regulation No 159/66/EEC laying

down additional provisions in respect of the common organisation of the market in fruit and vegetables.

3. The compensatory amount shall apply only during the period for which the basic price is in force.

Article 66

1. Until the first move towards alignment, the compensatory amount applicable in trade between a new Member State in which the conditions referred to in Article 65(1) are fulfilled and the Community as originally constituted, another new Member State, with the exception of those referred to in the following subparagraph, or third countries, shall be equal to the difference between the prices referred to in Article 65(1)(c).

In trade between two new Member States in which the conditions referred to in Article 65(1) are fulfilled, the compensatory amount shall be equal to the difference between their respective producer prices. The compensatory amount shall not be applied if this difference is insignificant.

The differences referred to in the above subparagraphs shall be adjusted, to the extent necessary, by the incidence of customs duties.

2. Where subsequent compensatory amounts are fixed, the compensatory amount shall be reduced by one-fifth of the original amount on 1 January every year, beginning on 1 January 1974.

Article 52(3) shall apply by analogy. The compensatory amount shall be abolished on 1 January 1978.

Article 67

For the purpose of determining entry prices, the price quotations recorded in the new Member States shall be reduced by:

(a) the compensatory amount, if any;

(b) the duties applicable to imports into those Member States from third countries instead of the duties of the Common Customs Tariff.

Article 68

The provisions relating to the common quality standards shall apply to the marketing of home produce in the United Kingdom only from:

(a) 1 February 1974, in respect of artichokes, asparagus, Brussels sprouts, ribbed celery, witloof chicory, garlic and onions;

(b) 1 February 1975, in respect of beans, roundheaded cabbages, carrots, lettuces, curled-leaved endives and broad-leaved (Batavian) endives, shelling peas, spinach and strawberries.

Section 2

Wine

Article 69

Until 31 December 1975, Ireland and the United Kingdom are authorised to retain the use of composite names including the word wine for the designation of certain beverages in respect of which the use of such names is incompatible with Community rules. This derogation shall not, however, apply to products exported to the Member States of the Community as originally constituted.

Section 3

Oilseeds

Article 70

1. Article 52 shall apply to the derived intervention prices for oilseeds.

2. The intervention prices applicable in the new Member States until the first move towards alignment shall be fixed in accordance with the rules provided for within the common organisation of the market, account being taken of the normal relationship which should exist between the income to be obtained from oilseeds and that obtained from the production of the products which compete in crop rotation with oilseeds.

Article 71

The amount of aid in respect of oilseeds harvested in a new Member State shall be adjusted by the compensatory amount applicable in that State, increased by the incidence of the customs duties applied therein.

Article 72

In trade in oilseeds, the compensatory amount shall be applied only to refunds granted on exports to third countries of oilseeds harvested in a new Member State.

Section 4

Cereals

Article 73

Articles 51 and 52 shall apply to the derived intervention prices for cereals.

Article 74

The compensatory amounts applicable in trade between the Community as originally constituted and the new Member States and between those States and third countries shall be fixed as follows:

1. The compensatory amount applicable until the first move towards alignment in the case of cereals for which no derived intervention price is fixed for the new Member States shall be derived from the compensatory amount applicable in the case of a competing cereal for which a derived intervention price is fixed, account being taken of the relationship existing between the threshold prices of the cereals in question. However, if the relationship between the threshold prices differs appreciably from that between the prices recorded on the market of the new Member State concerned, the latter relationship may be taken into consideration.

The subsequent compensatory amounts shall be fixed on the basis of those referred to in the first subparagraph and according to the rules in Article 52 for the alignment of prices.

2. The compensatory amount for the products specified in Article 1(c) and (d) of Regulation No 120/67/EEC shall be derived from the compensatory amount for the cereals to which they relate with the help of the coefficients or rules used in determining the levy, or the variable component of the levy, on those products.

Section 5

Pigmeat

Article 75

1. The compensatory amount per kilogramme of pig carcase shall be calculated on the basis of the compensatory amounts applicable to the quantity of feed grain required for the production in the Community of one kilogramme of pigmeat.

2. The compensatory amount for the products, other than pig carcases,

specified in Article 1(1) of Regulation No 121/67/EEC on the common organisation of the market in pigmeat shall be derived from the compensatory amount referred to in paragraph 1 with the help of the coefficients used in calculating the levy.

Article 76

1. Until 31 December 1975, products which do not correspond to the provisions of point 23 of Annex I to Directive No 64/433/EEC, on health protection questions in intra-Community trade in fresh meat, may be bought in by intervention agencies in Denmark, Ireland and the United Kingdom.

2. Until 31 October 1974, the United Kingdom is authorised not to apply the Community scale of classification for pig carcases.

Section 6

Eggs

Article 77

1. The compensatory amount per kilogramme of eggs in shell shall be calculated on the basis of the compensatory amounts applicable to the quantity of feed grain required for the production in the Community of one kilogramme of eggs in shell.

2. The compensatory amount per hatching egg shall be calculated on the basis of the compensatory amounts applicable to the quantity of feed grain required for the production in the Community of one hatching egg.

3. The compensatory amount for the products specified in Article 1(1)(b) of Regulation No 122/67/EEC on the common organisation of the market in eggs shall be derived from the compensatory amount for eggs in shell with the help of the coefficients used in calculating the levy.

Article 78

With regard to egg-marketing standards, Ireland and the United Kingdom may retain on their markets a system of grading in four and five weight-categories respectively, on condition that the marketing of eggs which comply with Community standards shall not be subject to restrictions because of different systems of grading.

Section 7

Poultrymeat

Article 79

1. The compensatory amount per kilogramme of slaughtered poultry shall be calculated on the basis of the compensatory amounts applicable to the quantity of feed grain, differentiated according to species of poultry, which is required for the production in the Community of one kilogramme of slaughtered poultry.

2. The compensatory amount applicable per chick shall be calculated on the basis of the compensatory amounts applicable to the quantity of feed grain required for the production in the Community of one chick.

3. The compensatory amount for the products specified in Article 1(2)(d) of Regulation No 123/67/EEC on the common organisation of the market in poultrymeat shall be derived from the compensatory amount for slaughtered poultry with the help of the coefficients used in calculating the levy.

Section 8

Rice

Article 80

The compensatory amounts applicable in trade between the Community as originally constituted and the new Member States and between those States and third countries shall be fixed as follows:

1. The compensatory amount applicable until the first move towards alignment for round-grained husked rice, long-grained husked rice and broken rice shall be established on the basis of the difference between the threshold price and the market prices recorded on the market of the new Member State concerned during a reference period.

The subsequent compensatory amounts shall be fixed on the basis of those provided for in the first subparagraph and according to the rules in Article 52 for the alignment of prices.

2. The compensatory amount for paddy rice, semi-milled rice, wholly-milled rice and the products specified in Article 1(1)(c) of Regulation No 359/67/EEC on the common organisation of the market in rice shall, for each of those products, be derived from the compensatory amount for the product referred to in paragraph 1 to which it relates with the help of the coefficients used in determining the levy or the variable component of the levy.

Section 7

Sugar

Article 81

Articles 51 and 52 shall apply to the derived intervention price for white sugar, the intervention price for raw sugar and to the minimum price for beet.

Article 82

The compensatory amounts applicable in trade between the Community as originally constituted and the new Member States and between those States and third countries shall:

(a) in the case of the products, other than fresh beet, in Article 1(1)(b) of Regulation No 1009/67/EEC on the common organisation of the market in sugar, be derived from the compensatory amount for the primary product in question, in accordance with the rules in force for calculating the levy;

(b) in the case of the products in Article 1(1)(d) of Regulation No 1009/67/EEC, be derived from the compensatory amount for the primary product in question, in accordance with the rules in force for calculating:

— the levy, in respect of the compensatory amount applicable to imports,

— the refund, in respect of the compensatory amount applicable to exports.

Article 83

The amount referred to in Article 25(3) of Regulation No 1009/67/EEC shall, in the new Member States, be adjusted by the compensatory amount calculated in accordance with Article 55(2).

Section 10

Live trees and other plants, bulbs, roots and the like, cut flowers and ornamental foliage

Article 84

The provisions relating to common quality standards shall be applicable to the marketing of home produce in the United Kingdom only from 1 February 1974 and, in respect of cut flowers, only from 1 February 1975.

Section 11

Milk and milk products

Article 85

Articles 51 and 52 shall apply to the intervention prices for butter and skimmed-milk powder.

Article 86

In trade between the Community as originally constituted and the new Member States, and between those States and third countries, compensatory amounts shall be fixed as follows:

1. For pilot products other than those referred to in Article 85, the compensatory amount applicable until the first move towards alignment shall be determined on the basis of the difference between the representative market price level of the new Member State concerned and the representative market price level of the Community as originally constituted over a representative period preceding the introduction of the Community rules in the new Member State in question.

In fixing the compensatory amounts applicable from the first move towards alignment, account shall taken of the amount fixed in accordance with the first subparagraph or paragraph 3 and the rules for alignment of prices in Article 52.

2. For products other than pilot products, the compensatory amounts shall be derived from the compensatory amount for the pilot product of the group to which the product concerned belongs, in accordance with the rules in force for calculating the levy.

3. If the first subparagraph of paragraph 1 and paragraph 2 cannot be applied or if their application results in compensatory amounts leading to abnormal price relationships, the compensatory amount shall be calculated on the basis of the compensatory amounts applicable for butter and skimmed milk powder.

Article 87

1. If a system providing for a different valuation of milk according to its use existed in a new Member State before accession, and if the application of Article 86 leads to difficulties on the market, the compensatory amount applicable until the first move towards alignment for one or more products falling within Common Customs Tariff heading No 04.01 shall be fixed on the basis of the difference between market prices.

When subsequent compensatory amounts are fixed, the compensatory amount shall be reduced annually at the beginning of the marketing year by one-sixth of the original amount and shall be abolished on 1 January 1978.

2. Appropriate measures shall be adopted to avoid distortions of competition which might result from the application of paragraph 1, either in respect of the products in question or in respect of other milk products, and to take account of possible changes in the common price.

Article 88

1. Ireland is authorised to grant a subsidy on the direct consumption of butter to the extent necessary to allow, during the transitional period, the price paid by the consumer to be progressively adjusted to the price level obtaining in the Community as originally constituted.

In the event of Ireland making use of the authorisation referred to in the first subparagraph, it shall grant a subsidy of the same amount on the consumption of butter imported from the other Member States.

2. This subsidy shall be abolished in six stages coinciding with the stages for aligning the price of butter.

Article 89

1. Until 31 December 1975 in the United Kingdom and until 31 December 1977 in Ireland, the supply to consumers as whole milk of milk with a fat content of less than 3.5% is authorised.

Milk sold as whole milk pursuant to the first subparagraph must not, however, have been subjected to any skimming. Furthermore, the provisions in respect of whole milk shall apply to such milk.

2. Denmark is authorised to maintain until 31 December 1977 the exclusive milk supply licences which existed in certain areas at the date of accession. Licences which expire before 1 January 1978 may not be renewed.

Section 12

Beef and veal

Article 90

Articles 51 and 52 shall apply to the guide prices for adult bovine animals and calves.

Article 91

1. The compensatory amount for calves and adult bovine animals calculated in accordance with Article 55 shall be corrected to the extent necessary, by the incidence of customs duties.

If the incidence of the customs duty applicable to trade between the Community as originally constituted and the new Member States and between the new Member States themselves is higher than the compensatory amount calculated in accordance with Article 55, the customs duty shall be suspended at a level such that its incidence corresponds to the compensatory amount.

2. If the third subparagraph of Article 10(1) of Regulation (EEC) No 805/68 on the common organisation of the market in beef and veal, or if Article 11(1) of that Regulation, is applied, the appropriate measure shall be adopted in order to maintain Community preference and avoid deflections of trade.

3. The compensatory amount for the products referred to in the Annex to Regulation (EEC) No 805/68 shall be fixed taking account of the provisions laid down in the preceding paragraphs and with the help of the rules laid down for fixing the levies applicable to those products.

Article 92

In respect of the products specified in Article 1(b) and (c) of Regulation (EEC) No 805/68, the refund on exports to third countries by the new Member States shall be corrected by the incidence of the difference between the customs duties on the products listed in the Annex to the said Regulation to imports from third countries into the Community as originally constituted on the one hand and into the new Member States on the other.

Article 93

For such time as the United Kingdom, pursuant to Article 54, retains production subsidies for slaughter cattle, Ireland is authorised, in order to avoid distortion of the Irish cattle market, to retain the measures relating to the export of beef and veal which it applied before accession, in correlation with the system of subsidies applied in the United Kingdom.

Section 13

Products processed from fruit and vegetables

Article 94

Compensatory amounts shall be determined on the basis of the compensatory amounts fixed for sugar, glucose, or glucose syrup, as the case may be, and in accordance with the rules applicable for calculating:

- the levy, in respect of the compensatory amount applicable to imports,

- the refund, in respect of the compensatory amount applicable to exports.

Section 14

Flax

Article 95

1. The amount of aid for flax shall, for the new Member States, be fixed on the basis of the difference between the income to be obtained by flax producers and the return resulting from the foreseeable market price for this product.

2. The income to be received by flax producers shall be established taking into account the price of competing products in the crop rotation in the new Member State in question and the relationship in the Community as originally constituted between the income resulting from flax production and that resulting from the production of competing products.

Section 15

Seeds

Article 96

When an aid is granted for seed production, the amount of the aid may be fixed, in respect of the new Member States, at a level different from that fixed for the Community as originally constituted if the income of producers in a new Member State was previously appreciably different from the income of producers in the Community as originally constituted.

In that event, the amount of aid in respect of the new Member State must take account of the income previously received by seed producers and of the need to avoid any distortion of production patterns, and the need to align that amount gradually with the Community amount.

Section 16

Agricultural products exported in the form of goods not covered by Annex II to the EEC Treaty

Article 97

Compensatory amounts shall be determined on the basis of the compensatory amounts fixed for the basic products and in accordance with the rules applicable for the calculation of the refunds provided for in Regulation (EEC) No 204/69, establishing the general rules concerning the granting of export refunds and the rules for fixing the amounts thereof, with respect to certain agricultural products exported in the form of goods not covered by Annex II to the Treaty.

Chapter 3

Provisions relating to fisheries

Section 1

Common organisation of the market

Article 98

Articles 51 and 52 shall apply to the guide price for fisheries products. The moves towards price alignment shall be made at the beginning of the fishing year, and for the first time on 1 February 1973.

Article 99

The compensatory amounts shall be corrected, to the extent necessary, by the incidence of the customs duties.

Section 2

Fishing rights

Article 100

1. Notwithstanding the provisions of Article 2 of Regulation (EEC) No 2141/70 on the establishment of a common structural policy for the

fishing industry, the Member States of the Community are authorised, until 31 December 1982, to restrict fishing in waters under their sovereignty or jurisdiction, situated within a limit of six nautical miles, calculated from the base lines of the coastal Member State, to vessels which fish traditionally in those waters and which operate from ports in that geographical coastal area; however, vessels from other regions of Denmark may continue to fish in the waters of Greenland until 31 December 1977 at the latest.

Member States may not, in so far as they avail themselves of this derogation, adopt provisions dealing with conditions for fishing in those waters which are less restrictive than those applied in practice at the time of accession.

2. The provisions laid down in the preceding paragraph and in Article 101 shall not prejudice the special fishing rights which each of the original Member States and the new Member States might have enjoyed on 31 January 1971 in regard to one or more other Member States; the Member States may exercise these rights for such time as derogations continue to apply in the areas concerned. As regards the waters of Greenland, however, the special rights shall expire on the dates laid down for these rights.

3. If a Member State extends its fishing limits in certain areas to 12 nautical miles, the existing fishing activities within 12 nautical miles must be so pursued that there is no retrograde change by comparison with the situation on 31 January 1971.

4. In order to permit a satisfactory overall balance of fishing operations to be established within the Community during the period referred to in the first paragraph, the Member States need not make full use of the opportunities presented by the provisions of the first subparagraph of paragraph 1 in certain areas of the maritime waters under their sovereignty or jurisdiction.

The Member States shall inform the Commission of the measures which they adopt for this purpose; on a report from the Commission, the Council shall examine the situation and, in the light thereof, shall where necessary, address recommendations to the Member States.

Article 101[24]

The limit of six nautical miles referred to in Article 100 shall be extended to 12 nautical miles for the following areas:

1. *Denmark*
–   the Faroe Islands

- Greenland
- the west coast, from Thyborøn to Blaavandshuk.

2. *France*

The coasts of the *départements* of Manche, Ille-et-Vilaine, Côtes-du-Nord, Finistère and Morbihan.

3. *Ireland*

- the north and west coasts, from Lough Foyle to Cork Harbour in the south-west
- the east coast, from Carlingford Lough to Carnsore Point, for crustaceans and molluscs (shellfish).

4. *United Kingdom*

- the Shetlands and the Orkneys
- the north and east of Scotland, from Cape Wrath to Berwick
- the north-east of England, from the river Coquet to Flamborough Head
- the south-west from Lyme Regis to Hartland Point (including 12 nautical miles around Lundy Island)
- County Down.

Article 102

From the sixth year after accession at the latest, the Council, acting on a proposal from the Commission, shall determine conditions for fishing with a view to ensuring protection of the fishing grounds and conservation of the biological resources of the sea.

Article 103

Before 31 December 1982, the Commission shall present a report to the Council on the economic and social development of the coastal areas of the Member States and the state of stocks. On the basis of that report, and of the objectives of the common fisheries policy, the Council, acting on a proposal from the Commission, shall examine the provisions which could follow the derogations in force until 31 December 1982.

Chapter 4

Other provisions

Section 1

Veterinary measures

Article 104

Directive No 64/432/EEC on veterinary health inspection questions in intra-Community trade in bovine animals and swine shall be applied account being taken of the following provisions:

1. Until 31 December 1977, the new Member States are authorised to retain, in compliance with the general rules of the EEC Treaty, their national rules on imports of bovine animals and swine for breeding, store and slaughter with the exception, in the case of Denmark, of slaughter cattle.

Adjustments will be sought, within the framework of those national rules, to ensure the progressive development of trade; to this end, those rules will be examined by the Standing Veterinary Committee.

2. Until 31 December 1977, the Member States into which cattle are imported shall grant to the Member States from which cattle are exported the derogation provided for in Article 7(1)(A)(a) of the Directive.

3. Until 31 December 1977, the new Member States are authorised to retain the methods applied in their territory for declaring a herd of cattle officially free of tuberculosis or brucellosis within the meaning of Article 2 of the Directive, subject to the application of the provisions of the Directive relating to the presence of animals vaccinated against brucellosis. The provisions relating to the tests laid down for animals traded within the Community shall continue to apply, subject to paragraphs 4 and 6.

4. Until 31 December 1977, exports of cattle from Ireland to the United Kingdom may be carried out:

(*a*) by way of derogation from the provisions of the Directive relating to brucellosis; however, the provisions relating to the test laid down for animals traded within the Community shall continue to apply to exports of uncastrated cattle;

(*b*) by way of derogation from the provisions of the Directive relating to tuberculosis, provided that, at the time of export, a declaration is made certifying that the exported animal comes from a herd declared officially free of tuberculosis according to the methods in force in Ireland;

(c) by way of derogation from the provisions of the Directive relating to the obligation to separate breeding and store cattle on the one hand and slaughter cattle on the other.

5. Until 31 December 1975, Denmark is authorised to use 'alttuberculin' by way of derogation from the provisions in Annex B to the Directive.

6. Until the implementation of the Community provisions concerning trade within the Member States, in respect of the matters governed by the Directive, Ireland and the United Kingdom are authorised to retain their national rules governing trade between Ireland and Northern Ireland.

The Member States concerned may take appropriate measures in order to limit this derogation exclusively to the trade referred to above.

Article 105

Directive No 64/433/EEC on health protection questions in intra-Community trade in fresh meat shall apply, account being taken of the following provisions:

Until 31 December 1977, Ireland and the United Kingdom in respect of Northern Ireland, are authorised to retain for the import of fresh meat their national rules relating to protection against foot-and-mouth disease, while complying with the general provisions of the EEC Treaty.[25]

Article 106

Before the expiry of the time limits referred to in Articles 104 and 105, a review of the situation in the Community as a whole and in its various parts will be carried out in the light of developments in the veterinary field.

By 1 July 1976 at the latest, the Commission shall submit a report to the Council and, in so far as is necessary, appropriate proposals taking account of these developments.

Section 2

Miscellaneous provisions

Article 107

The acts listed in Annex V to this Act shall apply in respect of the new Member States under the conditions laid down in that Annex.

Title III

External relations

Chapter 1

Agreements of the Communities with certain third countries

Article 108

1. From the date of accession, the new Member States shall apply the provisions of the agreements referred to in paragraph 3, taking into account the transitional measures and adjustments which may appear necessary and which will be the subject of protocols to be concluded with the co-contracting third countries and annexed to those agreements.

2. These transitional measures, which will take into account the corresponding measures adopted within the Community and which may not extend beyond the period of validity thereof, shall be designed to ensure the progressive application by the Community of a single system for its relations with the co-contracting third countries as well as the identity of the rights and obligations of the Member States.

3. Paragraphs 1 and 2 shall apply to the agreements concluded with Greece, Turkey, Tunisia, Morocco, Israel, Spain and Malta.

Paragraphs 1 and 2 shall also apply to agreements which the Community concludes with other third counties in the Mediterranean region before the entry into force of this Act.

Chapter 2

Relations with the Associated African and Malagasy States and with certain developing Commonwealth countries

Article 109

1. The arrangements resulting from the Convention of Association between the European Economic Community and the African and Malagasy States associated with that Community, signed on 29 July 1969, and from the Agreement establishing an Association between the European Economic Community and the United Republic of Tanzania, the Republic of Uganda and the Republic of Kenya, signed on 24 September 1969, shall not apply in relations between the new Member

States and the States associated with the Community under the above acts.

The new Member States need not accede to the Agreement on products within the competence of the European Coal and Steel Community, signed on 29 July 1969.

2. Subject to the provisions of Articles 110 and 111, products originating in the Associated States referred to in paragraph 1 shall, on importation into the new Member States, be subject to the arrangements applied to those products before accession.

3. Subject to the provisions of Articles 110 and 111, products originating in the independent Commonwealth countries listed in Annex VI to this Act shall, on importation into the Community, be subject to the arrangements applied to those products before accession.

Article 110

For those products listed in Annex II to the EEC Treaty which are subject to a common organisation of the market and for those products subject on importation into the Community to specific rules as a result of the implementation of the common agricultural policy, which originate in the Associated States referred to in Article 109(1) or in the independent Commonwealth countries referred to in Article 109(3), the new Member States shall apply on importation the Community rules under the conditions laid down in this Act and subject to the following provisions:

(a) where the Community rules provide for the levying of customs duties on imports from third countries, the new Member States shall, subject to the provisions of Article 111, apply the tariff arrangements which they applied before accession;

(b) as regards protective components other than customs duties, the Council shall, acting by a qualified majority on a proposal from the Commission, determine, should it prove necessary, adaptations to Community rules designed to ensure that those products are imported under conditions similar to those existing before accession.

Article 111

Where alignment with the Common Customs Tariff leads to the reduction of a customs duty in a new Member State, the reduced customs duty shall apply to imports covered by Articles 109 and 110.

Article 112

1. Products imported into the United Kingdom before the dates determined under Article 115 which originate in the independent Commonwealth countries referred to in Article 109(3) shall not, when they are re-exported to another new Member State or to the Community as originally constituted, be considered to be in free circulation within the meaning of Article 10 of the EEC Treaty.

2. Products imported into the Community as originally constituted during that same period which originated in the Associated States referred to in Article 109(1) shall not, when re-exported to another Member State, be considered to be in free circulation in the Community as originally constituted, within the meaning of Article 10 of the EEC Treaty.

3. Where there is no risk of deflection of trade, and in particular in the event of minimal disparities in the import arrangement, the Commission may derogate from paragraphs 1 and 2.

Article 113

1. From accession, the new Member States shall communicate to the original Member States and the Commission the provisions concerning the arrangements which they apply to imports of products originating in or coming from the independent Commonwealth countries referred to in Article 109(3) or the Associated States referred to in Article 109(1).

2. From accession, the Commission shall communicate to the new Member States the internal or conventional provisions concerning arrangements applicable to imports into the Community as originally constituted of products originating in or coming from the independent Commonwealth countries referred to in Article 109(3) or the Associated States referred to in Article 109(1).

Article 114

When the Council takes decisions and when the Committee of the European Development Fund gives opinions within the framework of the Internal Agreement on measures to be taken and procedures to be followed for the implementation of the Convention of Association between the European Economic Community and the African and Malagasy States associated with that Community, signed on 29 July 1969, of the Internal Agreement on the financing and administration of Community aid, signed on 29 July 1969, and of the Internal Agreement on measures to be taken and procedures to be followed for the implementation of the Agreement establishing an Association between the European Economic Community and the United Republic of

Tanzania, the Republic of Uganda and the Republic of Kenya, signed on 24 September 1969, only the votes of the original Member States shall be counted, as the case may be, either in accordance with the weighted voting in force before accession for calculating a qualified majority or in accordance with Article 13(3) of the above-mentioned Internal Agreement on the financing and administration of Community aid.

Article 115

1. Articles 109 to 114 shall apply until 31 January 1975.

2. However, imports originating in any independent Commonwealth country referred to in Article 109(3) which has, before that date, established its relations with the Community on a basis other than association shall be subject in the new Member States from the date of entry into force of its agreement with the Community and in respect of matters not covered by that agreement, to the third country arrangements applicable to those imports taking into account the transitional provisions of this Act.

3. The Council may, acting unanimously after consulting the Commission, decide to defer the date laid down in paragraph 1 in the event of implementation of the transitional provisions laid down in the second paragraph of Article 62 of the Convention of Association between the European Economic Community and the African and Malagasy States associated with that Community, signed on 29 July 1969, or in the second paragraph of Article 36 of the Agreement establishing an Association between the European Economic Community and the United Republic of Tanzania, the Republic of Uganda and the Republic of Kenya, signed on 24 September 1969, for the period during which such transitional provisions are being implemented.

Chapter 3

Relations with Papua New Guinea

Article 116

1. Articles 109(3) and 110 to 113 apply until 31 December 1977 to products originating in or coming from Papua New Guinea imported into the United Kingdom.

2. These arrangements may be reviewed, in particular if that territory becomes independent before 1 January 1978. The Council shall, acting by a qualified majority on a proposal from the Commission, adopt, if the need arises, such provisions as are appropriate and may prove necessary.

Title IV

Association of overseas countries and territories

Article 117

1. The association of the non-European territories maintaining special relations with the United Kingdom and of the Anglo-French Condominium of the New Hebrides, listed in Article 24(2), shall take effect on 1 February 1975 at the earliest upon a decision of the Council taken under Article 136 of the EEC Treaty.[26]

2. The new Member States need not accede to the Agreement on trade with overseas countries and territories in products within the province of the European Coal and Steel Community, signed on 14 December 1970.

Article 118

The provisions of the third part of Protocol No 22 on relations between the European Economic Community and the Associated African and Malagasy States and the independent developing Commonwealth countries situated in Africa, the Indian Ocean, the Pacific Ocean and the Caribbean shall apply both to the overseas countries and territories referred to in Article 117 and to the non-European countries and territories maintaining special relations with the original Member States.

Article 119

1. The arrangements resulting from the Council Decision of 29 September 1970 on the association of the overseas countries and territories with the European Economic Community shall not apply in relations between those countries and territories and the new Member States.

2. Products originating in the countries and territories associated with the Community shall, on importation into the new Member States, be subject to the arrangements applied to those products before accession.

Products originating in the non-European territories maintaining special relations with the United Kingdom and in the Anglo-French Condominium of the New Hebrides, listed in Article 24(2), shall, on importation into the Community, be subject to the arrangements applied to those products before accession.[27]

Articles 110 to 114 shall apply.

3. This Article shall apply until 31 January 1975. If Article 115(3) is

applied, this date may be deferred in accordance with the procedure and under the conditions laid down in that Article.

Title V

Capital movements

Article 120

1. The new Member States may, under the conditions and within the time limits in Articles 121 to 126, defer the liberalisation of capital movements provided for in the First Council Directive of 11 May 1960 for the implementation of Article 67 of the EEC Treaty and in the Second Council Directive of 18 December 1962 adding to and amending the First Directive for the implementation of Article 67 of the EEC Treaty.

2. Appropriate consultations shall take place in due course between the new Member States and the Commission about procedures for applying measures of liberalisation or relaxation, the implementation of which may be deferred under the following provisions.

Article 121

1. Denmark may:

(a) for a period of two years after accession, defer the liberalisation of purchases by non-residents of bonds denominated in Danish kroner and dealt in on the stock exchange in Denmark, including physical transfers of the securities in question;

(b) for a period of five years after accession, defer the liberalisation of purchases by persons resident in Denmark of foreign securities dealt in on the stock exchange and of repurchases from abroad of Danish securities dealt in on the stock exchange denominated entirely or partly in foreign currency, including physical transfers of the securities in question.

2. From the date of accession, Denmark will proceed to a progressive liberalisation of the operations referred to in paragraph 1(a).

Article 122

1. Ireland may:

(a) for a period of two years after accession, defer the liberalisation of direct investments in Member States by persons resident in Ireland and the liberalisation of the liquidation of direct investments in Member States by persons resident in Ireland;

(*b*) for a period of 30 months after accession, defer the liberalisation of the following capital movements of a personal nature:

- transfers of capital belonging to persons resident in Ireland who are emigrating, other than transfers connected with freedom of movement for workers which shall be liberalised from the date of accession;

- gifts and endowments, dowries, succession duties and real estate investments other than those connected with freedom of movement for workers which shall be liberalised from the date of accession;

(*c*) for a period of five years after accession, defer the liberalisation of the operations set out in List B annexed to the Directives referred to in Article 120 and carried out by persons resident in Ireland.

2. Recognising that it is desirable to proceed, from the date of accession, to a substantial relaxation in the rules concerning the operations referred to in paragraph 1(a), Ireland will endeavour to take appropriate measures to this end.

Article 123

[Text ommitted][28]

Article 124

1. The United Kingdom may:

(*a*) for a period of two years after accession, defer the liberalisation of direct investments in Member States by persons resident in the United Kingdom and the liberalisation of the liquidation of direct investments in Member States by persons resident in the United Kingdom;

(*b*) for a period of 30 months after accession, defer the liberalisation of the following capital movements of a personal nature:

- transfers of capital belonging to persons resident in the United Kingdom who are emigrating, other than transfers connected with freedom of movement for workers which shall be liberalised from the date of accession;

- gifts and endowments, dowries, succession duties, and real estate investments other than those connected with freedom of movement for workers which shall be liberalised from the date of accession;

(c) for a period of five years after accession, defer the liberalisation of the operations set out in List B annexed to the Directives referred to in Article 120, and carried out by persons resident in the United Kingdom.

2. From the date of accession, the United Kingdom will proceed to a substantial relaxation in the rules concerning the operations referred to in paragraph 1(a).

Article 125

The new Member States will, circumstances permitting, carry out the liberalisation of capital movements referred to in Articles 121 to 124 before the expiry of the time limits laid down in those Articles.

Article 126

For the purpose of implementing the provisions of this Title, the Commission may consult the Monetary Committee and submit appropriate proposals to the Council.

Title VI

Financial provisions

Article 127

The Decision of 21 April 1970 on the replacement of financial contributions from Member States by the Communities' own resources, hereinafter referred to as the 'Decision of 21 April 1970',[29] shall be applied, account being taken of the following provisions.

Article 128

The revenue referred to in Article 2 of the Decision of 21 April 1970 shall also include:

(a) among those designated as agricultural levies, the revenue from any compensatory amount levied on imports under Articles 47 and 55, and from the fixed components applied in trade between the Community as originally constituted and the new Member States and between the new Member States themselves under Article 61;

(b) among those designated as customs duties, the customs duties levied by the new Member States in trade with non-member States, and also customs duties levied in trade between the Community as originally constituted and the new Member States and between the new Member States themselves.

Article 129

1. The financial contributions from Member States referred to in Article 3(2) of the Decision of 21 April 1970 shall be apportioned as follows:

- for the new Member States:

  Denmark   2.46%

  Ireland   0.61%

  United Kingdom   19.32%;

- and for the original Member States, in accordance with the scale laid down in Article 3(2) of the Decision of 21 April 1970, after the financial contributions of the new Member States specified above have been deducted.[30]

2. For 1973, the basis for calculating the variations referred to in Article 3(3), of the Decision of 21 April 1970 shall be:

- for the new Member States, the percentage referred to in paragraph 1;

- for the original Member States, their relative share for the preceding year, account being taken of the percentages for the new Member States specified above.

Article 130

The Communities' own resources and also the financial contributions and, where appropriate, the contributions referred to in Article 4(2), (3) and (4) of the Decision of 21 April 1970 shall be due from the new Member States to the following extent only:

- 45.0% in 1973,

- 56.0% in 1974,

- 67.5% in 1975,

- 79.5% in 1976,

- 92.0% in 1977.

Article 131

1. From 1 January 1978, the Communities' own resources and, where appropriate, the financial contributions referred to in Article 4(2), (3) and (4) of the Decision of 21 April 1970, shall be due from the new Member States, in full, subject to the following provisions:

(a) the increase in the relative share to be paid by each new Member

State under the head of the Communities' own resources and of the financial contributions for 1978 in comparison with the relative share due for 1977, shall not exceed two-fifths of the difference between the relative share due under the head of the Communities' own resources and of the financial contributions for 1977 and the relative share which each new Member State would have had to pay under the same head for the same year, if this relative share had been calculated in accordance with the arrangements laid down for the original Member States from 1978 by the Decision of 21 April 1970;

(b) for 1979, the increase in the relative share of each new Member State in comparison with 1978 shall not exceed that for 1978 in comparison with 1977.

2. The Commission shall carry out the calculations necessary for the application of this Article.

Article 132

Until 31 December 1979, that part of the Communities' budget which is not covered as a result of applying Articles 130 and 131 shall be incorporated into the amount apportioned for the original Member States in accordance with Article 129. The total amount thus determined shall be apportioned among the original Member States in accordance with the Decision of 21 April 1970.

Title VII

Other provisions

Article 133

The acts listed in Annex VII to this Act shall apply in respect of the new Member States under the conditions laid down in that Annex.

Article 134

1. During the five years following accession, the Commission will examine, with the Governments concerned, whether existing measures arising from provisions laid down by law, regulation or administrative action in force in the new Member States, which had they been introduced after accession would have fallen within the scope of Article 67 of the ECSC Treaty, could, by comparison with the measures in force in the original Member States, give rise to serious distortions in conditions of competition in the coal and steel industries whether within the common market or in export markets. The Commission may, after consulting the Council, propose to the Governments concerned any

action which it considers appropriate to correct such measures or to offset their effects.

2. Until 31 December 1977, the prices charged by undertakings for sales of steel on the Irish market, reduced to their equivalent at the point chosen for their price list, may not be below the prices shown in the price list in question for comparable transactions, save when authorisation has been given by the Commission, in agreement with the Government of Ireland, without prejudice to the last subparagraph of Article 60(2)(b) of the ECSC Treaty.

3. If Decision No 1/64 of the High Authority of 15 January 1964 prohibiting alignment on quotations for steel products and pig iron from State-trading countries or territories is extended after accession, that prohibition shall not apply until 31 December 1975 to products for the Danish market.[31]

Article 135

1. If, before 31 December 1977, difficulties arise which are serious and liable to persist in any sector of the economy or which could bring about serious deterioration in the economic situation of a given area, a new Member State may apply for authorisation to take protective measures in order to rectify the situation and adjust the sector concerned to the economy of the common market.

2. On application by the State concerned, the Commission shall, by emergency procedure, determine without delay the protective measures which it considers necessary, specifying the circumstances and the manner in which they are to be put into effect.

3. The measures authorised under paragraph 2 may involve derogations from the rules of the EEC Treaty and of this Act to such an extent and for such periods as are strictly necessary in order to attain the objective referred to in paragraph 1. Priority shall be given to such measures as will least disturb the functioning of the common market.

4. In the same circumstances and according to the same procedure, any original Member State may apply for authorisation to take protective measures in regard to one or more new Member States.

Article 136

1. If, before 31 December 1977, the Commission, on application by a Member State or by any other interested party, finds that dumping is being practised between the Community as originally constituted and the new Member States or between the new Member States themselves,

it shall address recommendations to the person or persons with whom such practices originate for the purpose of putting an end to them.

Should the practices continue, the Commission shall authorise the injured Member State or States to take protective measures, the conditions and details of which the Commission shall determine.

2. For the application of this Article to the products listed in Annex II to the EEC Treaty, the Commission shall evaluate all relevant factors, in particular the level of prices at which these products are imported into the market in question from elsewhere, account being taken of the provisions of the EEC Treaty relating to agriculture in particular Article 39.

Article 137

1. Notwithstanding Article 136, Ireland may, until 31 December 1977, take the necessary measures in cases of extreme urgency. It shall forthwith notify such measures to the Commission, which may decide to abolish or modify them.

2. This provision shall not apply to the products in Annex II to the EEC Treaty.

Article 138

Notwithstanding the second paragraph of Article 95 of the EEC Treaty, Denmark may retain until 30 June 1974 the special excise duties on table wines imported in bottles or other similar containers.

PART FIVE

Provisions relating to the implementation of this Act

Title I

Setting up of the institutions

Article 139

1. The Parliaments of the new Member States shall, upon accession, designate their delegates to the European Parliament.

2. The European Parliament shall meet at the latest one month after accession. It shall make such adaptations to its rules of procedure as are made necessary by accession.

Article 140

1. Upon accession, the office of President of the Council shall be held by the member of the Council who would have held that office in accordance with the original text of Article 2 of the Treaty establishing a Single Council and a Single Commission of the European Communities. On expiry of this term of office, the office of President shall then be held in the order of Member States laid down in the Article referred to above as amended by Article 11.

2. The Council shall make such adaptations to its rules of procedure as are made necessary by accession.

Article 141

1. The President, the Vice-Presidents and the members of the Commission shall be appointed upon accession. The Commission shall take up its duties on the fifth day after its members have been appointed. The terms of office of the members in office at the time of accession shall terminate at the same time.

2. The Commission shall make such adaptations to its rules of procedure as are made necessary by accession.

Article 142

1. Upon accession, new judges shall be appointed to the Court of Justice in order to bring the number of judges up to nine as provided for in Article 17 of this Act.[32]

2. The term of office of one of the judges appointed in accordance with paragraph 1 shall expire on 6 October 1976. That judge shall be chosen by lot. The term of office of the other judge shall expire on 6 October 1979.[32]

3. Upon accession, a third Advocate-General shall be appointed. His term of office shall expire on 6 October 1979.[33]

4. The Court shall make such adaptations to its rules of procedure as are made necessary by accession. The rules of procedure as adapted shall require the unanimous approval of the Council.

5. In order to give judgment in cases pending before the Court on 1 January 1973 in respect of which oral proceedings have started before that date, the full Court and the Chambers shall be composed as before accession and shall apply the rules of procedure in force on 31 December 1972.

Article 143[34]

Upon accession, the Economic and Social Committee shall be enlarged by the appointment of 42 members representing the various categories of economic and social activity in the new Member States. The terms of office of the members thus appointed shall expire at the same time as those of the members in office at the time of accession.

Article 144

Upon accession, the Consultative Committee of the European Coal and Steel Community shall be enlarged by the appointment of additional members. The terms of office of the members thus appointed shall expire at the same time as those of the members in office at the time of accession.

Article 145

Upon accession, the members of the Scientific and Technical Committee shall be appointed in accordance with the procedure laid down in Article 134 of the Euratom Treaty. The Committee shall take up its duties on the fifth day after its members have been appointed. The terms of office of the members in office at the time of accession shall expire at that time.

Article 146

Upon accession, the Monetary Committee shall be enlarged by the appointment of members representing the new Member States. Their terms of office shall expire at the same time as those of the members in office at the time of accession.

Article 147

Adaptations to the Rules of the Committees established by the original Treaties and to their rules of procedure, necessitated by accession, shall be made as soon as possible after accession.

Article 148

1. The terms of office of the new members of the Committees listed in Annex VII shall expire at the same time as those of the members in office at the time of accession.

2. Upon accession, the membership of the Committees listed in Annex IX shall be completely renewed.

Title II

Applicability of the acts of the institutions

Article 149

From accession, the new Member States shall be considered as being addressees of and as having received notification of directives and decisions within the meaning of Article 189 of the EEC Treaty and of Article 161 of the Euratom Treaty, and of recommendations and decisions within the meaning of Article 14 of the ECSC Treaty, provided that those directives, recommendations and decisions have been notified to all the original Member States.

Article 150

The application in each new Member State of the acts listed in Annex X to this Act shall be deferred until the dates specified in that list.

Article 151

1. The following shall be deferred until 1 February 1973:

(a) the application to the new Member States of the Community rules established for production of and trade in agricultural products and for trade in certain goods processed from agricultural products which are the subject of special arrangements;

(b) the application to the Community as originally constituted of the amendments made to these rules by this Act, including those arising from Article 153.

2. Paragraph 1 shall not apply to the adaptations referred to in Part II, point A, of Annex I, referred to in Article 29 of this Act.

3. Until 31 January 1973, the arrangements applicable to trade between, on the one hand, a new Member State and, on the other hand, the Community as originally constituted, the other new Member States or third countries shall be those applied before accession.

Article 152

The new Member States shall put into effect the measures necessary for them to comply from the date of accession with the provisions of directives and decisions within the meaning of Article 189 of the EEC Treaty and of Article 161 of the Euratom Treaty, and with recommendations and decisions within the meaning of Article 14 of the

ECSC Treaty, unless a time limit is provided for in the list in Annex XI or in any other provisions of this Act.

Article 153

1. Adaptations to the acts of the institutions of the Communities not included in this Act or its Annexes, made by the institutions before accession in accordance with the procedure in paragraph 2 to bring those acts into line with the provisions of this Act, in particular those of Part Four, shall enter into force on accession.

2. The Council, acting by a qualified majority on a proposal from the Commission, or the Commission, according to which of these two institutions adopted the original act, shall to this end draw up the necessary texts.

Article 154

Notwithstanding Article 3(3), the principles concerning the general arrangements for regional aid, elaborated within the framework of the application of Articles 92 to 94 of the EEC Treaty and contained in the communication of the Commission of 23 June 1971 and also in the resolution of the Representatives of the Governments of the Member States, meeting in Council, of 20 October 1971, shall apply to the new Member States on 1 July 1973 at the latest.

These texts will be supplemented to take account of the new situation of the Community after accession, so that all the Member States are in the same situation in regard to them.

Article 155[35]

The texts of the acts of the institutions of the Communities adopted before accession and drawn up by the Council or the Commission in the Danish and English languages shall, from the date of accession, be authentic under the same conditions as the texts drawn up in the four original languages. They shall be published in the *Official Journal of the European Communities* if the texts in the original languages were so published.

Article 156

Agreements, decisions and concerted practices in existence at the time of accession which come within the scope of Article 65 of the ECSC Treaty by reason of accession must be notified to the Commission within three months of accession. Only agreements and decisions which have been notified shall remain provisionally in force until a decision has been taken by the Commission.

Article 157

Provisions laid down by law, regulation or administrative action designed to ensure the protection of the health of the workers and the general public in the territories of the new Member States against the dangers arising from ionizing radiations shall, in accordance with Article 33 of the Euratom Treaty, be communicated by those States to the Commission within three months of accession.

Title III

Final provisions

Article 158

Annexes I to XI, Protocols Nos 1 to 30 and the Exchange of Letters on Monetary Questions, which are attached to this Act, shall form an integral part thereof.

Article 159[36]

The Government of the French Republic shall transmit a certified copy of the Treaty establishing the European Coal and Steel Community and the Treaties amending that Treaty to the Governments of the Kingdom of Denmark, Ireland and the United Kingdom of Great Britain and Northern Ireland.

Article 160[37]

The Government of the Italian Republic shall transmit a certified copy of the Treaty establishing the European Economic Community, the Treaty establishing the European Atomic Energy Community and the Treaties amending or supplementing them in the Dutch, French, German and Italian languages to the Governments of the Kingdom of Denmark, Ireland and the United Kingdom of Great Britain and Northern Ireland.

The texts of the Treaty establishing the European Economic Community and the Treaty establishing the European Atomic Energy Community, and the Treaties amending or supplementing them, drawn up in the Danish, English, Irish and Norwegian languages, shall be annexed to this Act. The texts drawn up in the Danish, English and Irish languages shall be authentic under the same conditions as the original texts of the Treaties referred to above.

Article 161

A certified copy of the international agreements deposited in the archives of the Secretariat of the Council of the European Communities shall be transmitted to the Governments of the new Member States by the Secretary-General.

ANNEXES

Annex I[38]

List referred to in Article 29 of the Act of Accession

Annex II[39]

List referred to in Article 30 of the Act of Accession

Annex III[40]

List of the products referred to in Articles 32, 36 and 39 of the Act of Accession (Euratom)

Annex IV[40]

List of the products referred to in Article 32 of the Act of Accession

(Commonwealth products which are subject to contractual margins of preference in the United Kingdom)

Annex V[40]

List referred to in Article 107 of the Act of Accession

Annex VI[41]

List of the countries referred to in Article 109 of the Act of Accession and in Protocol No 22

Annex VII[42]

List referred to in Article 133 of the Act of Accession

Annex VIII[41]

List of committees referred to in Article 148(1) of the Act of Accession

Annex IX[41]

List of committees referred to in Article 148(2) of the Act of Accession

Annex X[42]

List referred to in Article 150 of the Act of Accession

Annex XI[42]

List referred to in Article 152 of the Act of Accession

PROTOCOLS

Protocol No 1

on the Statute of the European Investment Bank

Part One

Adjustments to the Statute of the European Investment Bank

Article 1[43]

The following shall be substituted for Article 3 of the Protocol on the Statute of the Bank:

'*Article 3*

In accordance with Article 129 of this Treaty, the following shall be members of the Bank:

- the Kingdom of Belgium;
- the Kingdom of Denmark;
- the Federal Republic of Germany;
- the French Republic;
- Ireland;
- the Italian Republic;
- the Grand Duchy of Luxembourg;
- the Kingdom of the Netherlands;
- the United Kingdom of Great Britain and Northern Ireland.'

Article 2[44]

The following shall be substituted for the first subparagraph of Article 4(1) of the Protocol on the Statute of the Bank:

'1. the capital of the Bank shall be 2 025 million units of account, subscribed by the Member States as follows:

Germany	450 million
France	450 million
United Kingdom	450 million
Italy	360 million
Belgium	118.5 million
Netherlands	118.5 million
Denmark	60 million
Ireland	15 million
Luxembourg	3 million'

Article 3

The following shall be substituted for Article 5 of the Protocol on the Statute of the Bank:

'Article 5

1. The subscribed capital shall be paid up by Member States to the extent of 20% of the amounts laid down in Article 4(1).

2. In the event of an increase in the subscribed capital, the Board of Governors, acting unanimously, shall fix the percentage to be paid up and the arrangements for payment.

3. The Board of Directors may require payment of the balance of the subscribed capital, to such extent as may be required for the Bank to meet its obligations towards those who have made loans to it.

Each Member State shall make this payment in proportion to its share of the subscribed capital in the currencies required by the Bank to meet these obligations.'

Article 4

The following shall be substituted for subparagraphs (a) and (c) of Article 9(3) of the Protocol on the Statute of the Bank:

'(a) decide whether to increase the subscribed capital in accordance with Article 4(3) and Article 5(2);

(c) exercise the powers provided in Articles 11 and 13 in respect of the appointment and the compulsory retirement of the members of the Board of Directors and of the Management Committee, and those powers provided in the second subparagraph of Article 13(1);'

Article 5

The following shall be substituted for Article 10 of the Protocol on the Statute of the Bank:

'Article 10

Save as otherwise provided in this Statute, decisions of the Board of Governors shall be taken by a majority of its members. This majority must represent at least 40% of the subscribed capital. Voting by the Board of Governors shall be in accordance with the provisions of Article 148 of this Treaty.'

Article 6[45]

The following shall be substituted for subparagraphs 1 to 5 of Article 11(2) of the Protocol on the Statute of the Bank:

'2. The Board of Directors shall consist of 18 directors and 10 alternates.

The directors shall be appointed by the Board of Governors for five years as shown below:

- 3 directors nominated by the Federal Republic of Germany;
- 3 directors nominated by the French Republic;
- 3 directors nominated by the Italian Republic;
- 3 directors nominated by the United Kingdom of Great Britain and Northern Ireland;
- 1 director nominated by the Kingdom of Belgium;
- 1 director nominated by the Kingdom of Denmark;
- 1 director nominated by Ireland;
- 1 director nominated by the Grand Duchy of Luxembourg;
- 1 director nominated by the Kingdom of the Netherlands;
- 1 director nominated by the Commission.

The alternates shall be appointed by the Board of Governors for five years as shown below:

- 2 alternates nominated by the Federal Republic of Germany;
- 2 alternates nominated by the French Republic;

-   2 alternates nominated by the Italian Republic;

-   2 alternates nominated by the United Kingdom of Great Britain and Northern Ireland;

-   1 alternate nominated by common accord of the Benelux countries;

-   1 alternate nominated by the Commission.

The appointments of the directors and the alternates shall be renewable.

Alternates may take part in the meetings of the Board of Directors. Alternates nominated by a State, or by common accord of several States, or by the Commission, may replace directors nominated by that State, by one of those States or by the Commission respectively. Alternates shall have no right of vote except where they replace one director or more than one director or where they have been delegated for this purpose in accordance with Article 12(1).'

Article 7

The following shall be substituted for Article 12(1) of the Protocol on the Statute of the Bank:

'1. Each director shall have one vote on the Board of Directors. He may delegate his vote in all cases, according to procedures to be laid down in the rules of procedure of the Bank.'

Article 8[46]

The following sentence shall be substituted for the second sentence of Article 12(2) of the Protocol on the Statute of the Bank:

'A qualified majority shall require 12 votes in favour.'

Article 9

The following shall be substituted for Article 13(1) of the Protocol on the Statute of the Bank:

'1. The Management Committee shall consist of a President and four Vice-Presidents appointed for six years by the Board of Governors on a proposal from the Board of Directors. Their appointments shall be renewable.

The Board of Governors, acting unanimously, may vary the number of members on the Management Committee.'

Part Two

Other provisions

1. The new Member States shall, not later than two months from the date of accession, make the payments laid down in paragraph 1 of the amended Article 5 of the Statute of the Bank set out in Article 3 of this Protocol. These payments shall be made out in their respective national currencies. One-fifth of the payment shall be in cash and four-fifths in the form of non-interest-bearing government notes, maturing in four equal instalments, nine months, sixteen months, twenty-three months and thirty months respectively from the date of accession. Part or all of the government notes may be redeemed before their due date by agreement between the Bank and the new Member State concerned. The cash payments, and the proceeds of the government notes when repaid, shall be freely convertible.

2. Article 7 of the Statute of the Bank shall apply to all payments made by the new Member States in their respective national currencies under this Article. Any necessary adjustments relating to outstanding government notes shall be made at the date of maturity or advance redemption of these notes.

Article 11

1. The new Member States shall contribute towards the statutory reserve and those provisions equivalent to reserves, as at 31 December of the year prior to accession, as stated in the Bank's approved balance sheet, the amounts corresponding to the following percentages of these reserves:

United Kingdom	30%
Denmark	4%
Ireland	1%[47]

2. The amounts of the payments under this Article shall be calculated in units of account after the Bank's annual balance sheet for the year prior to accession has been approved.

3. These amounts shall be paid in five equal instalments not later than two months, nine months, sixteen months, twenty-three months and thirty months after accession. Each of these five instalments shall be paid in the freely convertible national currency of each new Member State.

Article 12

1. Upon accession, the Board of Governors shall increase the Board of Directors by appointing:

- 3 directors nominated by the United Kingdom of Great Britain and Northern Ireland;
- 1 director nominated by the Kingdom of Denmark;
- 1 director nominated by Ireland;
- 1 director nominated by the Grand Duchy of Luxembourg;
- 2 alternates nominated by the United Kingdom of Great Britain and Northern Ireland[48].

2. The terms of office of the directors and alternates thus appointed shall expire at the end of the annual meeting of the Board of Governors during which the annual report for the 1977 financial year is examined.

3. At the end of the annual meeting during which the annual report for the 1972 financial year is examined, the Board of Governors shall appoint for a term of office of five years:

- 3 directors nominated by the Federal Republic of Germany;
- 3 directors nominated by the French Republic;
- 3 directors nominated by the Italian Republic;
- 1 director nominated by the Kingdom of Belgium;
- 1 director nominated by the Kingdom of the Netherlands;
- 1 director nominated by the Commission;
- 2 alternates nominated by the Federal Republic of Germany;
- 2 alternates nominated by the French Republic;
- 2 alternates nominated by the Italian Republic;
- 1 alternate nominated by common accord of the Benelux countries;
- 1 alternate nominated by the Commission.

Article 13

Upon accession, the membership of the Management Committee shall be increased by the appointment of an additional Vice-President. His term of office shall expire at the same time as those of the members of the Management Committee who hold office on the date of accession.

Protocol No 2

on the Faroe Islands

[Text omitted]

Protocol No 3

on the Channel Islands and the Isle of Man

Article 1

1. The Community rules on customs matters and quantitative restrictions, in particular those of the Act of Accession, shall apply to the Channel Islands and the Isle of Man under the same conditions as they apply to the United Kingdom. In particular, customs duties and charges having equivalent effect between those territories and the Community as originally constituted and between those territories and the new Member States shall be progressively reduced in accordance with the timetable laid down in Articles 32 and 36 of the Act of Accession. The Common Customs Tariff and the ECSC unified tariff shall be progressively applied in accordance with the timetable laid down in Articles 39 and 59 of the Act of Accession, the account being taken of Articles 109, 110 and 119 of that Act.

2. In respect of agricultural products and products processed therefrom which are the subject of a special trade regime, the levies and other import measures laid down in Community rules and applicable by the United Kingdom shall be applied to third countries.

Such provisions of Community rules, in particular those of the Act of Accession, as are necessary to allow free movement and observance of normal conditions of competition in trade in these products shall also be applicable.

The Council, acting by a qualified majority on a proposal from the Commission, shall determine the conditions under which the provisions referred to in the preceding subparagraphs shall be applicable to these territories.

Article 2

The rights enjoyed by Channel Islanders or Manxmen in the United Kingdom shall not be affected by the Act of Accession. However, such persons shall not benefit from Community provisions relating to the free movement of persons and services.

Article 3

The provisions of the Euratom Treaty applicable to persons or undertakings within the meaning of Article 196 of that Treaty shall apply to those persons or undertakings when they are established in the aforementioned territories.

Article 4

The authorities of these territories shall apply the same treatment to all natural and legal persons of the Community.

Article 5

If, during the application of the arrangements defined in this Protocol, difficulties appear on either side in relations between the Community and these territories, the Commission shall without delay propose to the Council such safeguard measures as it believes necessary, specifying their terms and conditions of application.

The Council shall act by a qualified majority within one month.

Article 6[49]

In this Protocol, Channel Islander or Manxman shall mean any citizen of the United Kingdom and Colonies who holds that citizenship by virtue of the fact that he, a parent or grandparent was born, adopted, naturalised or registered in the island in question; but such a person shall not for this purpose be regarded as a Channel Islander or Manxman if he, a parent or a grandparent was born, adopted, naturalised or registered in the United Kingdom. Nor shall he be so regarded if he has at any time been ordinarily resident in the United Kingdom for five years.

The administrative arrangements necessary to identify these persons will be notified to the Commission.

Protocol No 4

on Greenland[50]

[Text omitted]

Protocol No 5

on Svalbard (Spitzbergen)[51]

[Text omitted]

Protocol No 6

on certain quantitative restrictions relating to Ireland[52]

I. *Ireland*

1. The quantitative restrictions on imports in force in Ireland for the following products shall be progressively abolished by the opening of the following global quotas:

Period	Stockings* CCT heading No ex 60.03 & ex 60.04	Springs for vehicles ** CCT heading No ex 73.35	Sparking plugs and metal component parts CCT heading No ex 85.08 D	Brushes and brooms of a value of not less than £1.50 per dozen CCT heading No ex 96.01 & ex 96.02	Brushes and brooms valued at less than £1.50 per dozen CCT heading No ex 96.01 & ex 96.02
	pairs		items	items	items
1 January 1973 to 30 June 1973	2 000 000	50 000	300 000	130 000	600 000
1 July 1973 to 30 June 1974	5 000 000	150 000	900 000	460 000	1 600 000
1 July 1974 to 30 June 1975	6 000 000	200 000	1 250 000	660 000	2 200 000

* The quota is applicable to tights and stockings other than knee-length stockings entirely or mainly made of silk or man-made fibres, of a value of not more than £2.50 per dozen pairs.

** The quota is applicable to laminated springs of iron or steel, for use as parts of vehicles, and to leaves for these springs.

These restrictions shall be abolished on 1 July 1975.

2. Ireland is authorised to retain for superphosphates (CCT heading No 31.03 A I) an import quota for countries other than the United Kingdom. The volume of this quota shall be fixed with reference to Irish production recorded in 1970 at:

3% of this production volume in 1973,

6% of this production volume in 1974,

half of 8% of this production volume for the first half of 1975.

This quota shall be abolished on 1 July 1975.

3. Ireland is authorised to retain until 1 July 1975 quantitative restrictions on exports of the following products to other Member States:

CCT heading No	Description of goods
ex 41.01	Raw hides and skins (fresh, salted, dried, pickled or limed), whether or not split, including sheepskins in the wool: — Raw hides and skins of sheep (fresh, salted, dried, pickled or limed), whether or not split, including sheepskins in the wool
44.01	Fuel wood, in logs, in billets, in twigs or in faggots; wood waste, including sawdust
44.03	Wood in the rough, whether or not stripped of its bark or merely roughed down
44.04	Wood, roughly squared or half-squared, but not further manufactured
44.05	Wood sawn lengthwise, sliced or peeled, but not further prepared, of a thickness exceeding 5 mm
ex 74.01	Copper matte; unwrought copper (refined or not); copper waste and scrap: — Copper waste and scrap
ex 75.01	Nickel mattes, nickel speiss and other intermediate products of nickel metallurgy; unwrought nickel (excluding electro-plating anodes); nickel waste and scrap: — Nickel waste and scrap
76.01	Unwrought aluminium; aluminium waste and scrap: B. Waste and scrap
78.01	Unwrought lead (including argentiferous lead); lead waste and scrap B. Waste and scrap
79.01	Unwrought zinc; zinc waste and scrap: B. Waste and scrap

II. Norway[53]

Protocol No 7

on imports of motor vehicles and the motor vehicle assembly industry in Ireland

Article 1

Ireland is authorised to retain, until 1 January 1985, the system applicable to assembly and import of motor vehicles (hereinafter referred to as the 'Scheme') applied in accordance with the provisions of the Motor Vehicles (Registration of Importers) Act, 1968 (hereinafter referred to as the 'Act').

Article 2

1. From the date of accession, all the importers-assemblers of makes of vehicles manufactured in the Community who have been registered under the Act, and who continue to fulfil the conditions of registration, shall be authorised to import from other Member States and without restriction fully built-up vehicles of makes manufactured in other Member States.

2. From 1 January 1974, Ireland shall, within the framework of the tariff reductions which it is to carry out in accordance with the provisions of Article 32 of the Act of Accession, apply non-discriminatory tariff treatment to the vehicles imported by the importers-assemblers referred to in paragraph 1.

3. Ireland shall retain the right to replace the fiscal element contained in the customs duties applied to motor vehicles and parts thereof by internal taxes in accordance with Article 95 of the EEC Treaty and Article 38 of the Act of Accession. In particular these taxes must not entail any discrimination between the rates applied to:

- parts manufactured in Ireland and parts imported from other Member States;

- vehicles assembled in Ireland and fully built-up vehicles imported from other Member States;

- parts manufactured in Ireland or imported from other Member States and vehicles assembled in Ireland or imported from other Member States.

Article 3

1. The tariff treatment referred to in Article 2(2) shall, from 1 January 1974, also apply to a global quota which Ireland shall open, from the date of accession, to the other Member States in respect of vehicles originating in the Community other than those covered by special treatment under the Scheme.

2. This quota shall be fixed annually on the basis of a percentage of the number of vehicles assembled in Ireland during the previous year. This percentage is to be 3% in 1973 and shall increase each year by one point to reach 14% in 1984.

Ireland may allocate the amount of this quota between the following categories of vehicles:

I. *Private vehicles*

(a) with a cylinder capacity less than or equal to 1 500 cc;

(b) with a cylinder capacity greater than 1 500 cc.

II. *Commercial vehicles*

(a) with a tare weight less than or equal to 3.5 tonnes;

(b) with a tare weight greater than 3.5 tonnes.

The tare weight shall be established in accordance with the rules for the classification of vehicles for the purposes of the road tax in Ireland.

3. Within this allocation, Ireland may fix the quotas as follows:

Category I – Private vehicles: 85% of the global quota, allocated as follows:

     I. (a) (up to 1 500 cc)   75%

     I. (b) (over 1 500 cc)   25%

Category II – Commercial vehicles: 15% of the global quota, allocated as follows:

     II. (a) (up to 3.5 tonnes)   75%

     II. (b) (over 3.5 tonnes)   25%

4. If, during the period of application of the quota system, it becomes clear that this quota has not been used to the full, for reasons connected with its allocation in the manner described above, the Commission may, after consulting the Irish Government, determine the appropriate measures to be taken by the Irish Government in order to facilitate the full use of the global quota.

Article 4

Where the application of this Protocol, and of Article 2(1) in particular, gives rise to distortions in competition between importers-assemblers established in Ireland likely to jeopardise a phased transition from the system applied at the time of accession to a system which is in accordance with the EEC Treaty, the Commission may authorise the Irish Government to take appropriate measures to redress the situation. These measures may not call into question the final date for the abolition of the Scheme.

Article 5

Ireland shall carry out all additional adjustments to the Scheme with a view to facilitating the transition from the system applied at the time of accession to a system which is in accordance with the EEC Treaty.

Protocol No 8

on phosphorus (CCT subheading No 28.04 C IV)

[Text omitted]

Protocol No 9

on aluminium oxide and hydroxide (alumina) (CCT subheading No 28.20 A)

[Text omitted]

Protocol No 10

on tanning extracts of wattle (mimosa) (CCT subheading No 32.01 A) and tanning extracts of chestnut (CCT subheading No ex 32.01 C)

1. By 1 January 1974 at the latest, the autonomous duty in the Common Customs Tariff on tanning extracts of wattle (mimosa) (CCT subheading No 32.01 A) shall be suspended at a level of 3% for an indefinite period.

2. Ireland and the United Kingdom shall apply from 1 July 1973 a nil duty on imports of tanning extracts of wattle (mimosa) (CCT subheading No 32.01 A) and tanning extracts of chestnut (CCT subheading No ex 32.01 C) from the Community as originally constituted.

Protocol No 11

on plywood (CCT heading No ex 44.15)

1. In respect of the following products:

ex 44.15 Plywood of coniferous species, without the addition of other substances, of a thickness greater than 9 mm, of which the faces are not further prepared than the peeling process,

ex 44.15 Plywood of coniferous species, without the addition of other substances, sanded, and of a thickness greater than 18.5 mm,

two autonomous nil duty Community tariff quotas shall be opened from 1 January 1974. The volume of these quotas shall be decided annually when it is established that all possibilities of supply on the internal market of the Community will be exhausted during the period for which the quotas are open.

2. The Council shall re-examine the situation in the event of a significant change occurring in nil duty imports of plywood into Ireland and the United Kingdom from Finland or in the system of tariff preferences applied by the Community to certain products originating in the developing countries.

3. Denmark, Ireland and the United Kingdom shall, from 1 April 1973, apply a nil duty to imports of plywood from the Community as originally constituted.

Protocol No 12

on wood pulp (CCT subheading No 47.01 A II)

[Text omitted]

Protocol No 13

on newsprint (CCT subheading No 48.01 A)

[Text omitted]

Protocol No 14

on unwrought lead (CCT subheading No 78.01 A)

[Text omitted]

Protocol No 15

on unwrought zinc (CCT subheading No 79.01 A)

[Text omitted]

Protocol No 16

on markets and trade in agricultural products

[Text omitted]

Protocol No 17

on the import of sugar by the United Kingdom from the exporting countries and territories referred to in the Commonwealth Sugar Agreement

[Text omitted]

Protocol No 18

on the import of New Zealand butter and cheese into the United Kingdom

[Text omitted]

Protocol No 19

on spirituous beverages obtained from cereals

[Text omitted]

Protocol No 20

on Norwegian agriculture[54]

[Text omitted]

Protocol No 21

on the fisheries regime for Norway[55]

[Text omitted]

Protocol No 22

on relations between the European Economic Community and the Associated African and Malagasy States and also the independent developing Commonwealth countries situated in Africa, the Indian Ocean, the Pacific Ocean and the Caribbean

[Text omitted]

Protocol No 23

on the application by the new Member States of the generalised tariff preference scheme applied by the European Economic Community

1. The new Member States are authorised to defer until 1 January 1974 the application of the generalised tariff preference scheme applied by the European Economic Community to products originating in the developing countries.

2. However, in respect of products falling under Regulations (EEC) Nos 2796/71, 2797/71, 2798/71 and 2799/71, Ireland is authorised until 31 December 1975 to apply, *vis-a-vis* countries benefiting from generalised preferences, customs duties equal to the duties applied in respect of the same products *vis-a-vis* Member States other than the United Kingdom.

Protocol No 24

on the participation of the new Member States in the funds of the European Coal and Steel Community[56]

The contributions of the new Member States to the funds of the European Coal and Steel Community shall be fixed as follows:

United Kingdom	57 000 000 ua
Denmark	635 500 ua
Ireland	77 500 ua

Payment of these contributions shall take place in three equal annual instalments beginning on accession.

Each instalment shall be paid in the freely convertible national currency of each new Member State.

Protocol No 25

on the exchange of information with Denmark in the field of nuclear energy

[Text omitted]

Protocol No 26

on the exchange of information with Ireland in the field of nuclear energy

Article 1

1. From the date of accession, such information as has been communicated to Member States, persons and undertakings, in accordance with Article 13 of the Euratom Treaty, shall be placed at the disposal of Ireland, which shall give it limited distribution within its territory under the conditions laid down in that Article.

2. From the date of accession, Ireland shall place at the disposal of the European Atomic Energy Community information obtained in the nuclear field in Ireland, which is given limited distribution, in so far as strictly commercial applications are not involved. The Commission shall communicate this information to Community undertakings under the conditions laid down in the abovementioned Article.

3. This information shall mainly concern studies for the development of a power reactor and work on radioisotopes and their application in medicine, including the problems of radiation protection.

Article 2

1. In those sectors in which Ireland places information at the disposal of the Community, the competent authorities shall grant upon request licences on commercial terms to Member States, persons and undertakings of the Community where they possess exclusive rights to patents filed in Member States of the Community and in so far as they have no obligation or commitment in respect of third parties to grant or offer to grant an exclusive or partially exclusive licence to the rights in these patents.

2. Where an exclusive or partially exclusive licence has been granted, Ireland shall encourage and facilitate the granting of sublicences on commercial terms to Member States, persons and undertakings of the Community by the holders of such licences.

Such exclusive or partially exclusive licences shall be granted on a normal commercial basis.

Protocol No 27

on the exchange of information with Norway in the field of nuclear energy[57]

[Text omitted]

Protocol No 28

on the exchange of information with the United Kingdom in the field of nuclear energy

[Text omitted]

Protocol No 29

on the agreement with the International Atomic Energy Agency[58]

The Kingdom of Denmark and Ireland undertake to accede, under conditions to be established therein, to the Agreement between certain original Member States jointly with the European Atomic Energy Community, on the one hand, and the International Atomic Energy Agency, on the other hand, on the application in the territories of certain Member States of the Community of the guarantees provided for in the Treaty on the Non-Proliferation of Nuclear Weapons.

Protocol No 30

on Ireland

The High Contracting Parties,

desiring to settle certain special problems of concern to Ireland, and

having agreed the following provisions,

recall that the fundamental objectives of the European Economic Community include the steady improvement of the living standards and working conditions of the peoples of the Member States and the harmonious development of their economies by reducing the differences existing between the various regions and the backwardness of the less-favoured regions;

take note of the fact that the Irish Government has embarked upon the implementation of a policy of industrialisation and economic development designed to align the standards of living in Ireland with those of the other European nations and to eliminate underemployment while progressively evening out regional differences in levels of development;

recognise it to be in their common interest that the objectives of this policy be so attained;

agree to recommend to this end that the Community institutions implement all the means and procedures laid down by the EEC Treaty, particularly by making adequate use of the Community resources intended for the realisation of the Community's above-mentioned objectives;

recognise in particular that, in the application of Articles 92 and 93 of the EEC Treaty, it will be necessary to take into account the objectives of economic expansion and the raising of the standard of living of the population.

FINAL ACT

The plenipotentiaries of

His Majesty the King of the Belgians,

Her Majesty the Queen of Denmark,

The President of the Federal Republic of Germany,

The President of the French Republic,

The President of Ireland,

The President of the Italian Republic,

His Royal Highness the Grand Duke of Luxembourg,

Her Majesty the Queen of the Netherlands,

His Majesty the King of Norway,

Her Majesty the Queen of the United Kingdom of Great Britain and Northern Ireland

and the Council of the European Communities represented by its President,

assembled at Brussels on the twenty-second day of January one thousand nine hundred and seventy-two on the occasion of the signature of the Treaty concerning the accession of the Kingdom of Denmark, Ireland, the Kingdom of Norway and the United Kingdom of

Great Britain and Northern Ireland to the European Economic Community and the European Atomic Energy Community,

have placed on record the fact that the following texts have been drawn up and adopted within the Conference between the European Communities and the States which have applied for accession to those Communities:

I. the Treaty concerning the accession of the Kingdom of Denmark, Ireland, the Kingdom of Norway and the United Kingdom of Great Britain and Northern Ireland to the European Economic Community and to the European Atomic Energy Community;

II. the Act concerning the Conditions of Accession and the Adjustments to the Treaties;

III. the texts listed below which are annexed to the Act concerning the Conditions of Accession and the Adjustments to the Treaties:

A. Annex I   List referred to in Article 29 of the Act of
                     Accession,

    Annex II   List referred to in Article 30 of the Act of
                     Accession,

    Annex III   List of products referred to in Articles 32, 36 and
                     39 of the Act of Accession (Euratom),

    Annex IV   List of products referred to in Article 32 of the Act
                     of Accession (Commonwealth products which are
                     subject to contractual margins of preference in
                     the United Kingdom),

    Annex V   List referred to in Article 107 of the Act of
                     Accession,

    Annex VI   List of countries referred to in Article 109 of the
                     Act of Accession and in Protocol No 22,

    Annex VII   List referred to in Article 133 of the Act of
                     Accession,

    Annex VIII   List referred to in Article 148(1) of the Act of
                     Accession,

    Annex IX   List referred to in Article 148(2) of the Act of
                     Accession,

    Annex X   List referred to in Article 150 of the Act of
                     Accession,

    Annex XI   List referred to in Article 152 of the Act of
                     Accession;

B. Protocol No 1   on the Statute of the European Investment Bank,

Protocol No 2   on the Faroe Islands,

Protocol No 3   on the Channel Islands and the Isle of Man,

Protocol No 4   on Greenland,

Protocol No 5   on Svalbard (Spitzbergen),

Protocol No 6   on certain quantitative restrictions relating to Ireland and Norway,

Protocol No 7   on imports of motor vehicles and the motor vehicle assembly industry in Ireland,

Protocol No 8   on phosphorus (CCT subheading No 28.04 C IV),

Protocol No 9   on aluminium oxide and hydroxide (alumina) (CCT subheading No 28.20 A),

Protocol No 10   on tanning extracts of wattle (mimosa) (CCT subheading No 32.01 A) and tanning extracts of chestnut (CCT subheading No ex 32.01 C),

Protocol No 11   on plywood (CCT heading No ex 44.15),

Protocol No 12   on wood pulp (CCT subheading No 47.01 A II),

Protocol No 13   on newsprint (CCT subheading No 48.01 A),

Protocol No 14   on unwrought lead (CCT subheading No 78.01 A),

Protocol No 15   on unwrought zinc (CCT subheading No 79.01 A),

Protocol No 16   on markets and trade in agricultural products,

Protocol No 17   on the import of sugar by the United Kingdom from the exporting countries and territories referred to in the Commonwealth Sugar Agreement,

Protocol No 18   on the import of New Zealand butter and cheese into the United Kingdom,

Protocol No 19   on spirituous beverages obtained from cereals,

Protocol No 20   on Norwegian agriculture,

Protocol No 21   on the fisheries regime for Norway,

Protocol No 22   on relations between the European Economic Community and the Associated African and Malagasy States and also the independent developing Commonwealth countries situated in Africa, the Indian Ocean, the Pacific Ocean and the Caribbean,

Protocol No 23   on the application by the new Member States of the generalised tariff preference scheme applied by the European Economic Community,

Protocol No 24   on the participation of the new Member States in the funds of the European Coal and Steel Community,

Protocol No 25   on the exchange of information with Denmark in the field of nuclear energy,

Protocol No 26   on the exchange of information with Ireland in the field of nuclear energy,

Protocol No 27   on the exchange of information with Norway in the field of nuclear energy,

Protocol No 28   on the exchange of information with the United Kingdom in the field of nuclear energy,

Protocol No 29   on the agreement with the International Atomic Energy Agency,

Protocol No 30   on Ireland;

C. Exchange of Letters on Monetary Questions;

D. The texts of the Treaty establishing the European Economic Community and of the Treaty establishing the European Atomic Energy Community, together with the Treaties amending or supplementing them, in the Danish, English, Irish and Norwegian languages.

The plenipotentiaries have taken note of the Decision of the Council of the European Communities of 22 January 1972 concerning the accession of the Kingdom of Denmark, Ireland, the Kingdom of Norway and the United Kingdom of Great Britain and Northern Ireland to the European Coal and Steel Community.

Furthermore, the plenipotentiaries and the Council have adopted the Declarations listed below and annexed to this Final Act:

1. Joint Declaration on the Court of Justice,

2. Joint Declaration on the Sovereign Base Areas of the United Kingdom of Great Britain and Northern Ireland in Cyprus,

3. Joint Declaration on the fisheries sector,

4. Joint Declaration of Intent on the development of trade relations with Ceylon, India, Malaysia, Pakistan and Singapore,

5. Joint Declaration on the free movement of workers.

The plenipotentiaries and the Council have also taken note of the following Declaration to this Final Act:

Declaration by the Government of the Federal Republic of Germany on the application to Berlin of the Decision concerning Accession to the European Coal and Steel Community and of the Treaty of Accession to the European Economic Community and to the European Atomic Energy Community.

The plenipotentiaries and the Council have also taken note of the arrangement regarding the procedure for adopting certain decisions and other measures to be taken during the period preceding accession which has been reached within the Conference between the European Communities and the States which have applied for accession to those Communities and which is annexed to this Final Act.

Finally, the following declarations have been made and are annexed to this Final Act:

1. Declaration by the Government of the United Kingdom of Great Britain and Northern Ireland on the definition of the term 'nationals',

2. Declarations on the economic and industrial development of Ireland,

3. Declaration on liquid milk, pigmeat and eggs,

4. Declaration on the system for fixing Community farm prices,

5. Declarations on hill farming.

In witness whereof the undersigned plenipotentiaries have signed this Final Act.

Done at Brussels this twenty-second day of January in the year one thousand nine hundred and seventy-two.

[List omitted]

Declarations

Joint declaration
on the Court of Justice

Such additional measures as may prove necessary following the accession of the new Member States should be taken by the Council which, at the request of the Court, may increase the number of Advocates-General to four and adjust the provisions of the third paragraph of Article 132 of the ECSC Treaty, the third paragraph of Article 165 of the EEC Treaty and the third paragraph of Article 137 of the Euratom Treaty accordingly.

Joint declaration
on the Sovereign Base Areas of the United Kingdom of Great Britain and Northern Ireland in Cyprus

The arrangements applicable to relations between the European Economic Community and the Sovereign Base Areas of the United Kingdom of Great Britain and Northern Ireland in Cyprus will be defined within the context of any agreement between that Community and the Republic of Cyprus.

Joint declaration
on the fisheries sector

1. The institutions of the European Economic Community will examine the problems of the fish meal and fish oils sector with a view to adopting measures which might prove necessary in that sector with respect to the raw material used. These measures should meet the need for protection and rational use of the sea's biological resources while avoiding the creation or retention of insufficiently profitable production units.

2. The application of common marketing standards for certain fresh or chilled fish must not have the effect of excluding any marketing method and, conversely, no marketing method should hinder the application of the said standards; it is in this spirit that the problems which could arise may be settled when the time comes by the institutions of the European Economic Community.

3. The European Economic Community is aware of the importance of Norwegian exports of fish products to third countries, which are subject like other Community exports to Regulation (EEC) No 2142/70.

4. It is understood that the Norwegian law on 'the marketing of fish coming from processing industries' of 18 December 1970 will be the subject, as soon as possible, of a detailed study with a view to examining the conditions under which it might be applied, having regard to the provisions of Community law.

Joint declaration of intent
on the development of trade relations with Ceylon, India, Malaysia, Pakistan and Singapore

[Text omitted]

Joint declaration
on the free movement of workers

The enlargement of the Community could give rise to certain difficulties for the social situation in one or more Member States as regards the application of the provisions relating to the free movement of workers.

The Member States declare that they reserve the right, should difficulties of that nature arise, to bring the matter before the institutions of the Community in order to obtain a solution to this problem in accordance with the provisions of the Treaties establishing the European Communities and the provisions adopted in application thereof.

Declaration
by the Government of the Federal Republic of Germany on the application to Berlin of the Decision concerning Accession to the European Coal and Steel Community and of the Treaty of Accession to the European Economic Community and to the European Atomic Energy Community

Declaration[59]
by the Government of the United Kingdom of Great Britain and Northern Ireland on the definition of the term 'nationals'

In view of the entry into force of the British Nationality Act 1981, the Government of the United Kingdom of Great Britain and Northern Ireland makes the following Declaration which will replace, as from 1 January 1983, that made at the time of signature of the Treaty of Accession by the United Kingdom to the European Communities:

'As to the United Kingdom of Great Britain and Northern Ireland, the terms 'nationals', 'nationals of Member States' or 'nationals of Member States and overseas countries and territories' wherever used in the Treaty establishing the European Economic Community, the Treaty establishing the European Atomic Energy Community or the Treaty establishing the European Coal and Steel Community or in any of the Community acts deriving from those Treaties, are to be understood to refer to:

(a) British citizens;

(b) persons who are British subjects by virtue of Part IV of the British Nationality Act 1981 and who have the right of abode in the United Kingdom and are therefore exempt from United Kingdom immigration control;

(c) British Dependent Territories citizens who acquire their citizenship from a connection with Gibraltar.'

The reference in Article 6 of the third Protocol to the Act of Accession of 22 January 1972, on the Channel Islands and the Isle of Man, to 'any citizen of the United Kingdom and Colonies' is to be understood as referring to 'any British citizen'.

Declarations
on the economic and industrial development of Ireland

At the 6th Ministerial Meeting in the negotiations between the Community and Ireland, held on 19 October 1971, Mr A. Moro, Minister for Foreign Affairs of the Italian Republic, made, on behalf of the Community delegation, the declaration appearing under I hereinafter.

Mr P. J. Hillery, Minister for Foreign Affairs of Ireland, replied, on behalf of the Irish delegation, with the declaration appearing under II hereinafter.

I. *Declaration made by Mr A. Moro, Minister for Foreign Affairs of the Italian Republic on behalf of the Community delegation*

I

1. The Irish delegation has stressed that the Irish Government is faced with serious economic and social imbalances of a regional and structural nature. This delegation has stated that these imbalances should be remedied in order to achieve a degree of harmonisation consistent with the objectives of the Community and particularly with the realisation of economic and monetary union. The Irish delegation has asked the Community to undertake to employ its means to support the Irish Government's programmes aimed at eliminating these imbalances and to take full account of Ireland's special problems in this field in the development of a major Community regional policy at a later date.

2. The Irish delegation has submitted documents to the Community delegation indicating the general direction and the instruments of the Irish regional programmes. The Irish delegation has also explained how the Irish exporting industries are supported by tax relief. In this respect it is also a question of measures the aim of which is to do away with economic and social imbalances by the development of industry.

II

1. The Community delegation emphasises in this connection that – as follows from the Preamble to the Treaty of Rome – the essential

objectives of the Community consist in the constant improvement of the living and working conditions of the peoples of the Member States, and the harmonious development of the economies of these States by reducing the differences existing between the various regions and the backwardness of the less-favoured regions.

2. The common policies and the various instruments created by the Community in the economic and social sectors are a positive realisation of the abovementioned objective and are furthermore likely to develop. The European Social Fund has been directed along new lines. The European Investment Bank is constantly expanding the field of its activities. At the present time, the institutions of the Community are engaged in discussions to decide the Community instruments, which it is possible to introduce, and according to what procedures, in order to achieve the objectives of the regional policy.

The aids granted by the States, including those granted by way of tax exemptions, are subject to the rules laid down in Articles 92 to 94 of the EEC Treaty. With regard to State aids for regional purposes it should be stressed that, under the terms of Article 92(3)(a) 'aid to promote the economic development of areas where the standard of living is abnormally low or where there is serious under-employment' may be considered to be compatible with the common market. Experience shows that this provision is flexible enough for the Community authorities to be able to take into consideration the special requirements of the underdeveloped regions.

Tax exemptions – in common with all other aids existing in Ireland at the time of accession – will be studied by the Commission in the normal framework of the permanent examination of existing aids. If this examination were to reveal that it would not be possible to retain any particular aid in its existing form, it will fall to the Commission under the rules of the Treaty to establish the appropriate time limits and transitional procedures.

3. Having regard to the abovementioned special problems with which Ireland is confronted, the Community delegation proposes to annex to the Act of Accession a protocol on the economic and industrial development of Ireland.

II. *Declaration made by Mr P. J. Hillery, Minister for Foreign Affairs of Ireland, on behalf of the Irish delegation*

I am pleased to record the Irish delegation's acceptance of the proposed Protocol concerning Ireland which has been the subject of discussions between our two delegations and the background to which has been so clearly set out in your introductory statement. The text adopted will enable the Irish Government to proceed with their plans for economic and social development in the knowledge that the Community, through its institutions and agencies, will be ready to cooperate with us in the pursuit of the objectives which we have set ourselves.

I have on a number of occasions in the course of the negotiations, drawn attention to the problems posed by differences in the level of economic development in an entity such as the enlarged Community. I have endeavoured also to explain to you the difficulties which a country such as Ireland, situated on the periphery of the enlarged Community, must overcome in order to approximate its level of economic development to that of the other Member States. I am fully aware of the Community's will and purpose to achieve the aims set out in the EEC Treaty of ensuring the constant improvement of the living and working conditions of the peoples of the Member States and the harmonious development of their economies. The Protocol on which we have reached agreement today is a convincing demonstration of the Community's determination to give real content to these fundamental aims. This Protocol will be an instrument of practical value in enabling my country to play a full part within the enlarged Community in achieving these aims. Its effectiveness for this purpose will be greatly enhanced by the development of a comprehensive Community regional policy. In this connection may I say that I am heartened by the efforts being made to deal with this important issue as part of the evolution of the Community.

In Irish circumstances, the effectiveness of development measures, whether at the national or at Community level, must be judged by progress in the reduction of unemployment and emigration and the raising of living standards. This is essentially a matter of providing for our growing work force the necessary job opportunities without which a substantial proportion of our most valuable economic resources will remain unused or be lost through emigration and the pace of economic development will be retarded.

My Government will be gratified that our discussions today have shown that Ireland's accession to the Community will enable them to maintain the drive towards the realisation of their aims as recited in the Protocol. I have particularly in mind here the continuing growth of industry which is central to our general aim of economic expansion. It is of vital importance to us that progress in this area be maintained through the application of effective measures of industrial promotion. I understand that like any other incentive scheme, our industrial incentives will come up for examination under Community rules after accession. I note with satisfaction that you recognise the necessity for an incentive policy in Ireland but that questions may arise about the particular forms our scheme of incentives has taken while we have been outside the Community.

I would like to draw your attention to the fact that the question would arise in this connection of the commitments which we had previously entered into. We shall, of course, have to honour these commitments but we shall be ready to discuss in all its aspects the changeover to whatever new incentive system is devised and we shall collaborate in solving these problems in an appropriate way.

I am fully satisfied from what you have said about the flexible nature of the relevant Treaty provisions that in the examination of our incentives the Community institutions will take full account of our special problems. I am also satisfied in the light of the identity of aims of both the Irish Government and the Community that if adjustment of these incentives is called for, the Irish Government will be able to maintain the growth of Irish industry, and achieve a continuous improvement in the level of employment and living standards.

Finally, may I say in conclusion that I appreciate the sympathy and understanding which the Community has shown in its approach to and examination of the questions of our regional problems and industrial incentives which are of the greatest importance to my country. The agreement which we have reached augurs well for our future cooperation within the enlarged Community in pursuit of the fundamental aims of the Treaty. I see in this future cooperation the means by which we in Ireland can best achieve our national economic objectives.

Declaration
on liquid milk, pigmeat and eggs

[U.K./Community delegations]

Declaration
on the system for fixing Community farm prices

[Text omitted]

Declaration

on hill farming

[Text omitted]

FOOTNOTES

1. Text as amended by Article 1 of the Adaptation Decision.
2. Third indent as amended by Article 3 of the Adaptation Decision.
3. Text as amended by Article 4 of the Adaptation Decision.
4. Text as amended by Article 5 of the Adaptation Decision.
5. Text as amended by Article 6 of the Adaptation Decision.
6. Text as amended by Article 7 of the Adaptation Decision.
7. Text as amended by Article 8 of the Adaptation Decision.
8. Article 10(1) first subparagraph of the Treaty establishing a Single Council and a Single Commission of the European Communities, modified by the Council Decision of 1 January 1973 altering the number of members of the Commission (OJ No L 2, 1.1.73, p.28) states:
   'The Commission shall consist of 13 members, who shall be chosen on the grounds of their general competence and whose independence is beyond doubt.'
9. Text as amended by Article 9 of the Adaptation Decision.
10. Article 32a, first paragraph, of the ECSC Treaty, Article 166, first paragraph, of the EEC Treaty and Article 138, first paragraph, of the Euratom Treaty, modified by Article 1 of the Council Decision of 1 January 1973 increasing the number of Advocates-General (OJ No L 2, 1.1.73, p.29), state:
    'The Court of Justice shall be assisted by four Advocates General.'
11. Text as amended by Article 10 of the Adaptation Decision.
12. Article 32b, third paragraph, of the ECSC Treaty, Article 167, third paragraph, of the EEC Treaty and Article 139, third paragraph, of the Euratom Treaty, modified by Article 2 of the Council Decision of 1 January 1973 increasing the number of Advocates-General (OJ No L 2, 1.1.73, p.29), state:
    'Every three years there shall be a partial replacement of the Advocates-General. Two Advocates-General shall be replaced on each occasion.'
13. Text as amended by Article 11 of the Adaptation Decision.
14. Text as amended by Article 12 of the Adaptation Decision.
15. Text as amended by Article 13 of the Adaptation Decision.
16. Text as amended by Article 14 of the Adaptation Decision.
17. Paragraph (1) as amended by Article 15(1) of the Adaptation Decision.
18. Paragraph (3) as amended by Article 15(2) of the Adaptation Decision.
19. Text as amended by Article 16 of the Adaptation Decision.
20. Paragraph (4), first subparagraph as amended by Article 17 of the Adaptation Decision.
21. Second paragraph as amended by Article 18 of the Adaptation Decision.
22. Paragraph (2), first subparagraph as amended by Article 19 of the Adaptation Decision.
23. Paragraph (3) as amended by Article 20 of the Adaptation Decision.
24. Text as amended by Article 21 of the Adaptation Decision
25. Second paragraph as amended by Article 22 of the Adaptation Decision.
26. Paragraph (1) as amended by Article 23 of the Adaptation Decision.

27. Paragraph (2), second subparagraph as amended by Article 24 of the Adaptation Decision.
28. Provisions having lapsed by virtue of Article 25 of the Adaptation Decision.
29. Editorial Note: The Decision of 21 April 1970, was repealed by the Decision of 7 May 1985 (see in this connection Office for Official Publications of the European Communities, documents concerning the Accessions to the European Communities, Luxembourg, 1988, Volume I p.995).
30. Paragraph (1) as amended by Article 26 of the Adaptation Decision.
31. Paragraph (3) as amended by Article 27 of the Adaptation Decision.
32. Paragraphs (1) and (2) as amended by Article 28 of the Adaptation Decision.
33. Article 32a, first paragraph, of the ECSC Treaty, Article 166, first paragraph, of the EEC Treaty and Article 138, first paragraph, of the Euratom Treaty, modified by Article 1 of the Council Decision of 1 January 1973 increasing the number of Advocates-General (OJ No L 2, 1.1.73, p.29), state:
'The Court of Justice shall be assisted by four Advocates-General.'
34. Text as amended by Article 29 of the Adaptation Decision.
35. Text as amended by Article 30 of the Adaptation Decision.
36. Text as amended by Article 31 of the Adaptation Decision.
37. Text as amended by Article 32 of the Adaptation Decision.
38. Editorial Note: For the text of this Annex, see OJ No L 73 27.3.72, p.47. For the amendments that have been made to the text of this Annex consequent on the failure of Norway to accede, see Article 33 of the Adaptation Decision.
39. Editorial Note: For the text of this Annex see the same Official Journal as for Annex I (i.e. footnote no 38 above), p.122. The entries, time-limits and dates appearing in the text of this Annex and concerning the Kingdom of Norway have lapsed by virtue of Article 34 of the Adaptation Decision.
40. Editorial Note: For the text of these three Annexes, see the same Official Journal as for Annex I (pp. 128, 131 and 135 respectively).
41. Editorial Note: For the text of these three Annexes, see the same Official Journal as for Annex I (pp.137 and 146 respectively).
42. Editorial Note: For the text of these three Annexes, see the same Official Journal as for Annex I (pp.137, 148 and 151 respectively).
The entries, time-limits and dates appearing in the text of this Annex and concerning the Kingdom of Norway have lapsed by virtue of Article 34 of the Adaptation Decision.
43. Text as amended by Article 35 of the Adaptation Decision.
44. Text as amended by Article 36 of the Adaptation Decision.
45. Text as amended by Article 37 of the Adaptation Decision.
46. Text as amended by Article 38 of the Adaptation Decision.
47. Paragraph (1) as amended by Article 39 of the Adaptation Decision.
48. Paragraph (1) as amended by Article 40 of the Adaptation Decision.
49. Editorial Note: See in this connection the 'Declaration by the Government of the United Kingdom of Great Britain and Northern Ireland on the definition of the term "nationals",' reproduced in Office for Official Publications of the European Communities, documents concerning the Accessions to the European Communities, Luxembourg, 1988, Volume I, p. 103.
50. Protocol repealed by Article 3(2) of the Greenland Treaty (see Office for Official Publications of the European Communities, documents concerning the Accessions to the European Communities, Luxembourg, 1988, Volume I, p.979 *et seq*).
51. Provisions having lapsed by virtue of Article 41 of the Adaptation Decision.
52. Title of Protocol No 6 as amended by Article 42(1) of the Adaptation Decision.
53. Provisions having lapsed by virtue of Article 42(2) of the Adaptation Decision.

54. Provisions having lapsed by virtue of Article 43 of the Adaptation Decision.
55. Provisions having lapsed by virtue of Article 44 of the Adaptation Decision.
56. Text as amended by Article 45 of the Adaptation Decision.
57. Provisions having lapsed by virtue of Article 46 of the Adaptation Decision.
58. Text as amended by Article 47 of the Adaptation Decision.
59. Editorial Note: This Declaration which appears in OJ No C 23 of 28.1.83 has replaced, from 1 January 1983, that which was made at the time of signature of the Treaty concerning the accession of the United Kingdom of Great Britain and Northern Ireland to the European Communities.

COMMISSION OPINION

of 19 January 1972

on the application for accession to the European Communities by the Kingdom of Denmark, Ireland, the Kingdom of Norway and the United Kingdom of Great Britain and Northern Ireland

(Translation)

The Commission of the European Communities,

Having regard to Article 98 of the Treaty establishing the European Coal and Steel Community, Article 237 of the Treaty establishing the European Economic Community and Article 205 of the Treaty establishing the European Atomic Energy Community;

Whereas the Kingdom of Denmark, Ireland, the Kingdom of Norway and the United Kingdom of Great Britain and Northern Ireland have applied to become members of these Communities;

Whereas in its Opinions of 29 September 1967 and 1 October 1969 the Commission has already been able to express its views on certain essential aspects of the problems arising in connection with these applications;

Whereas the terms for the admission of these States and the adjustments necessitated by their accession have been negotiated in a Conference between the Communities and the applicant States; and whereas singleness of Community representation was ensured with due regard for the institutional dialogue provided for by the Treaties;

Whereas, on the completion of these negotiations, it is apparent that the provisions so agreed are fair and proper; and whereas, this being so, the Community's enlargement, while preserving its internal cohesion and dynamism, will enable it to take a fuller part in the development of international relations;

Whereas in joining the Communities the applicant States accept without reserve the Treaties and their political objectives, all decisions taken since their entry into force, and the action that has been agreed in respect of the development and reinforcement of the Communities;

Whereas it is an essential feature of the legal system set up by the Treaties establishing the Communities that certain of their provisions and certain acts of the Community institutions are directly applicable, that Community law takes precedence over any national provisions conflicting with it, and that procedures exist for ensuring the uniform interpretation of this law; and whereas accession to the Communities entails recognition of the binding force of these rules, observance of which is indispensable to guarantee the effectiveness and unity of Community law,

Hereby delivers a favourable opinion

on the accession to the European Communities of the Kingdom of Denmark, Ireland, the Kingdom of Norway and the United Kingdom of Great Britain and Northern Ireland.

This Opinion is addressed to the Council.

Brussels, 19 January 1972

For the Commission

The President

Franco M. Malfatti

COUNCIL DECISION

of 22 January 1972

concerning the accession of the Kingdom of Denmark, Ireland, the Kingdom of Norway, and the United Kingdom of Great Britain and Northern Ireland to the European Coal and Steel Community

The Council of the European Communities,

Having regard to Article 98 of the Treaty establishing the European Coal and Steel Community,

Whereas the Kingdom of Denmark, Ireland, the Kingdom of Norway and the United Kingdom of Great Britain and Northern Ireland have applied to accede to the European Coal and Steel Community,

Having regard to the Opinion of the Commission,

Whereas the conditions of accession to be determined by the Council have been negotiated with the aforementioned States,

Has decided as follows:

Article 1

1. The Kingdom of Denmark, Ireland, the Kingdom of Norway and the United Kingdom of Great Britain and Northern Ireland may become members of the European Coal and Steel Community by acceding, under the conditions laid down in this Decision, to the Treaty establishing that Community, as amended or supplemented.

2. The conditions of accession and the adjustments to the Treaty establishing the European Coal and Steel Community necessitated thereby are set out in the Act annexed to this Decision. The provisions of that Act concerning the European Coal and Steel Community shall form an integral part of this Decision.

3. The provisions concerning the rights and obligations of the Member States and the powers and jurisdiction of the institutions of the Communities as set out in the Treaty referred to in paragraph 1 shall apply in respect of this Decision.

Article 2

The instruments of accession of the Kingdom of Denmark, Ireland, the Kingdom of Norway and the United Kingdom of Great Britain and Northern Ireland to the European Coal and Steel Community will be deposited with the Government of the French Republic on 1 January 1973.

Accession will take effect on 1 January 1973, provided that all the instruments of accession have been deposited on that date and that all the instruments of ratification of the Treaty concerning Accession to the European Economic Community and the European Atomic Energy Community have been deposited before that date.

If, however, the States referred to in the first paragraph of this Article have not all deposited their instruments of accession and ratification in due time, accession shall take effect for the other acceding States. In this case, the Council of the European Communities, acting unanimously, shall decide immediately upon such resulting adjustments as have become indispensable, to Article 3 of this Decision, and Articles 12, 13, 16, 17, 19, 20, 22, 142, 155 and 160 of the Act concerning the Conditions of Accession and the Adjustments to the Treaties; acting unanimously, it may also declare that those provisions of the aforementioned Act which refer expressly to a State which has not deposited its instruments of accession and ratification have lapsed, or it may adjust them.

The Government of the French Republic will transmit a certified copy of the instrument of accession of each acceding State to the Governments of the Member States and of the other acceding States.

Article 3[1]

This Decision drawn up in the Danish, Dutch, English, French, German, Irish, Italian and Norwegian languages, the Danish, Dutch, English, French, German, Irish and Italian texts all being equally authentic, shall be communicated to the Member States of the European Coal and Steel Community, the Kingdom of Denmark, Ireland, the Kingdom of Norway and the United Kingdom of Great Britain and Northern Ireland.

Done at Brussels, 22 January 1972

For the Council

The President

G. Thorn

FOOTNOTE

1. Text as amended by Article 2 of the Adaptation Decision.

COUNCIL DECISION

of 22 January 1972

on the accession of the Kingdom of Denmark, Ireland, the Kingdom of Norway and the United Kingdom of Great Britain and Northern Ireland to the European Economic Community and to the European Atomic Energy Community

(*Translation*)

The Council of the European Communities,

Having regard to Article 237 of the Treaty establishing the European Economic Community and Article 205 of the Treaty establishing the European Atomic Energy Community,

Whereas the Kingdom of Denmark, Ireland, the Kingdom of Norway and the United Kingdom of Great Britain and Northern Ireland have applied to accede to the European Economic Community and to the European Atomic Energy Community,

Having obtained the Opinion of the Commission,

Has decided

to accept these applications for accession; the conditions of admission and the adjustments to the Treaties necessitated thereby are to be the subject of an agreement between the Member States and the Applicant States.

Done at Brussels, 22 January 1972

For the Council

The President

G. Thorn

PART D

AMENDMENTS OF THE CONSTITUTION ACTS

THIRD AMENDMENT OF THE CONSTITUTION ACT, 1972

An Act To Amend The Constitution

[*8th June*, 1972]

Whereas by virtue of Article 46 of the Constitution any provision of the Constitution may be amended in the manner provided by that Article:

And whereas it is proposed to amend Article 29 of the Constitution:

Be it therefore enacted by the Oireachtas as follows:

1. Amendment of Article 29 of the Constitution

Article 29 of the Constitution is hereby amended as follows:

(*a*) the subsection set out in Part I of the Schedule to this Act shall be added to section 4 of the Irish text,

(*b*) the subsection set out in Part II of the Schedule to this Act shall be added to section 4 of the English text.

2. Citation

1. The amendment of the Constitution effected by this Act shall be called the Third Amendment of the Constitution.

1. This Act may be cited as the Third Amendment of the Constitution Act, 1972.

Schedule

Part I

[Part I is the Irish language version of Part II below]

Part II

3° The State may become a member of the European Coal and Steel Community (established by Treaty signed at Paris on the 18th day of April, 1951), the European Economic Community (established by Treaty signed in Rome on the 25th day of March, 1957) and the European Atomic Energy Community (established by Treaty signed at Rome on the 25th day of March, 1957). No provision of this Constitution invalidates laws enacted, acts done or measures adopted by the State necessitated by the obligations of membership of the Communities or prevents laws enacted, acts done or measures adopted by the Communities, or institutions thereof, from having the force of law in the State.

TENTH AMENDMENT OF THE CONSTITUTION ACT, 1987

An Act to Amend The Constitution

[*22nd June* 1987]

Whereas by virtue of Article 46 of the Constitution any provision of the Constitution may be amended in the manner provided by that Article:

And whereas it is proposed to amend Article 29 of the Constitution:

Be it therefore enacted by the Oireachtas as follows:

1. Amendment of Article 29 of the Constitution

Article 29 of the Constitution is hereby amended as follows:

(*a*) the sentence set out in Part I of the Schedule to this Act shall be inserted in subsection 3° of section 4 of the Irish text after the first sentence,

(*b*) the sentence set out in Part II of the Schedule to this Act shall be inserted in subsection 3° of section 4 of the English text after the first sentence.

2. Citation

1. The amendment of the Constitution effected by this Act shall be called the Tenth Amendment of the Constitution.

2. This Act may be cited as the Tenth Amendment of the Constitution Act, 1987.

Schedule

Part I

[Part I is the Irish language version of Part II below]

Part II

The State may ratify the Single European Act (signed on behalf of the Member States of the Communities at Luxembourg on the 17th day of February, 1986, and at The Hague on the 28th day of February, 1986).

ELEVENTH AMENDMENT OF THE CONSTITUTION ACT, 1992

An Act to amend the Constitution

[16*th* July, 1992]

Whereas by virtue of Article 46 of the Constitution any provision of the Constitution may be amended in the manner provided by that Article:

And whereas it is proposed to amend Article 29 of the Constitution:

Be it therefore enacted by the Oireachtas as follows:

1. Amendment of Article 29 of the Constitution

Article 29.4 of the Constitution is hereby amended as follows:

(*a*) by the repeal of the third sentence in subsection 3° of section 4 of the Irish text and by the insertion of the text set out in Part I of the Schedule to this Act;

(*b*) by the repeal of the third sentence in subsection 3° of section 4 of the English text and by the insertion of the text set out in Part II of the Schedule to this Act.

2. Citation

1. The amendment of the Constitution effected by this Act shall be called the Eleventh Amendment of the Constitution.

2. This Act may be cited as the Eleventh Amendment of the Constitution Act, 1992.

Schedule

Part I

[Part I is the Irish language version of Part II below]

Part II

4° The State may ratify the Treaty on European Union signed at Maastricht on the 7th day of February, 1992, and may become a member of that Union.

5° No provision of this Constitution invalidates laws enacted, acts done or measures adopted by the State which are necessitated by the obligations of membership of the European Union or of the Communities, or prevents laws enacted, acts done or measures adopted by the European Union or by the Communities or by institutions thereof, or by bodies competent under the Treaties establishing the Communities, from having the force of law in the State.

6° The State may ratify the Agreement relating to Community Patents drawn up between the Member States of the Communities and done at Luxembourg on the 15th day of December, 1989.

THIRTEENTH AMENDMENT OF THE CONSTITUTION ACT, 1992

An Act to amend the Constitution

[23rd December, 1992]

Whereas by virtue of Article 46 of the Constitution any provision of the Constitution may be amended in the manner provided by this Article:

And whereas it is proposed to amend Article 40.3 of the Constitution:

Be it therefore enacted by the Oireachtas as follows:

1. Amendment of Article 40.3 of the Constitution

Article 40.3 of the Constitution is hereby amended by the insertion –

(a) in subsection 3° of the Irish text, of a second paragraph the text of which is set out in Part I of the Schedule to this Act;

(b) in subsection 3° of the English text, of a second paragraph the text of which is set out in Part II of the Schedule to this Act.

2. Citation

1. The amendment of the Constitution effected by this Act shall be called the Thirteenth Amendment of the Constitution.

2. This Act may be cited as the Thirteenth Amendment of the Constitution Act, 1992.

Schedule

Part I

[Part I is the Irish language version of Part II below]

Part II

This subsection shall not limit freedom to travel between the State and another state.

FOURTEENTH AMENDMENT OF THE CONSTITUTION ACT, 1992

An Act to amend the Constitution

[23rd December, 1992]

Whereas by virtue of Article 46 of the Constitution any provision of the Constitution may be amended in the manner provided by that Article:

And whereas it is proposed to amend Article 40.3 of the Constitution:

Be it therefore enacted by the Oireachtas as follows:

1. Amendment of Article 40.3 of the Constitution

Article 40.3 of the Constitution is hereby amended by the addition thereto, immediately before section 4 –

(a) in subsection 3° of the Irish text, of a paragraph the text of which is set out in Part I of the Schedule to this Act;

(b) in subsection 3° of the English text, of a paragraph the text of which is set out in Part II of the Schedule to this Act.

2. Citation

1. The amendment of the Constitution effected by this Act shall be called the Fourteenth Amendment of the Constitution.

2. This Act may be cited as the Fourteenth Amendment of the Constitution Act, 1992.

Schedule

Part I

[Part I is the Irish language version of Part II below]

Part II

This subsection shall not limit freedom to obtain or make available, in the State, subject to such conditions as may be laid down by law, information relating to services lawfully available in another state.

PART E

EUROPEAN COMMUNITIES ACTS
1972-1993

EUROPEAN COMMUNITIES ACT, 1972

An Act to make provision with respect to membership of the State of the European Communities

[6th December, 1972]

Be it enacted by the Oireachtas as follows:

1. Definitions

1. In this Act:

'the European Communities' means the European Economic Community, the European Coal and Steel Community and the European Atomic Energy Community;

'the treaties governing the European Communities' means

(a) 'the ECSC Treaty", that is to say, the Treaty establishing the European Coal and Steel Community, signed at Paris on the 18th day of April, 1951,

(b) 'the EEC Treaty', that is to say, the Treaty establishing the European Economic Community, signed at Rome on the 25th day of March, 1957,

(c) 'the Euratom Treaty', that is to say, the Treaty establishing the European Atomic Energy Community, signed at Rome on the 25th day of March, 1957,

(d) the Convention on certain Institutions common to the European Communities, signed at Rome on the 25th day of March, 1957,

(e) the Treaty establishing a single Council and a single Commission of the European Communities, signed at Brussels on the 8th day of April, 1965,

(f) the Treaty amending certain Budgetary Provisions of the Treaties establishing the European Communities and of the Treaty establishing a single Council and a single Commission of the European Communities, signed at Luxembourg on the 22nd day of April, 1970,

(g) the Treaty relating to the accession of Ireland to the European Economic Community and to the European Atomic Energy Community, signed at Brussels on the 22nd day of January, 1972, (*h*) the decision, of the 22nd day of January, 1972, of the Council of the European Communities relating to the accession of Ireland to the European Coal and Steel Community,

as supplemented or amended by treaties or other acts of which the dates of entry into force are dates not later than the 1st day of January, 1973.

(2)(*a*) In the foregoing subsection 'treaties or other acts of which the dates of entry into force are dates not later than the 1st day of January, 1973' does not include a treaty or other act of which the date of entry into force is later than the 22nd day of January, 1972, unless the Government have, not later than the 1st day of January, 1973, by order declared that this section applies to it.

(*b*) Where an order under this section is proposed to be made, a draft thereof shall be laid before each House of the Oireachtas and the order shall not be made until a resolution approving of the draft has been passed by each such House.

2. General provision

From the 1st day of January, 1973, the treaties governing the European Communities and the existing and future acts adopted by the institutions of those Communities shall be binding on the State and shall be part of the domestic law thereof under the conditions laid down in those treaties.

3. Power to make regulations

1. A Minister of State may make regulations for enabling section 2 of this Act to have full effect.

2. Regulations under this section may contain such incidental, supplementary and consequential provisions as appear to the Minister making the regulations to be necessary for the purposes of the regulations (including provisions repealing, amending or applying, with or without modification, other law, exclusive of this Act).

3. Regulations under this section shall not create an indictable offence.

4. Regulations under this section may be made before the 1st day of January, 1973, but regulations so made shall not come into operation before that day.

4. Effect and confirmation of regulations

1. Regulations under this Act shall have statutory effect and, unless they are confirmed by Act of the Oireachtas passed within six months after

they are made or are regulations merely revoking wholly regulations previously made under this Act, they shall cease to have statutory effect on the expiration of that period, but without prejudice to the validity of anything previously done thereunder.

2. If when regulations under this Act are made, or at any time thereafter and before the regulations are confirmed or cease to have statutory effect, Dáil Éireann stands adjourned for a period of more than ten days and if, during the adjournment, at least one-third of the members of Dáil Éireann by notice in writing to the Ceann Comhairle require Dáil Éireann to be summoned, the Ceann Comhairle shall summon Dáil Éireann to meet on a day named by him being neither more than twenty-one days after the receipt by him of the notice nor less than ten days after the issue of the summons.

5. Report to Houses of Oireachtas

The Government shall make a report twice yearly to each House of the Oireachtas on developments in the European Communities.

6. Short title

This Act may be cited as the European Communities Act, 1972.

EUROPEAN COMMUNITIES (AMENDMENT) ACT, 1973

An Act to amend the European Communities Act, 1972

[4th August, 1973]

Be it enacted by the Oireachtas as follows:

1. Amendment of European Communities Act, 1972

1. The European Communities Act, 1972, is hereby amended by the substitution for section 4 of the following section:

'(1) (a) Regulations under this Act shall have statutory effect.

(b) If the Joint Committee on the Secondary Legislation of the European Communities recommends to the Houses of the Oireachtas that any regulations under this Act be annulled and a resolution annulling the regulations is passed by both such Houses within one year after the regulations are made, the regulations shall be annulled accordingly and shall cease to have statutory effect, but without prejudice to the validity of anything previously done thereunder.

(2) (a) If when regulations under this Act are made, or at any time within one year thereafter and while the regulations have statutory effect, Dáil Éireann stands adjourned for a period of more than ten days and if, during the adjournment, at least one-third of the members of Dáil Éireann by notice in writing to the Ceann Comhairle require Dáil Éireann to be summoned, the Ceann Comhairle shall summon Dáil Éireann to meet on a day named by him being neither more than twenty-one days after the receipt by him of the notice nor less then ten days after the issue of the summons.

(b) If when regulations under this Act are made, or at any time within one year thereafter and while the regulations have statutory effect, Seanad Éireann stands adjourned for a period of more than ten days and if, during the adjournment, at least one-third of the members of Seanad Éireann by notice in writing to the Cathaoirleach require Seanad Éireann to be summoned, the Cathaoirleach shall summon Seanad Éireann to meet on a day named by him being neither more than twenty-one days after the receipt by him of the notice nor less than ten days after the issue of the summons.

(c) Paragraphs (a) and (b) of this subsection shall not apply to regulations in relation to which a resolution for their annulment has been refused by either House of the Oireachtas.'

1. This section shall have effect in relation to regulations under the European Communities Act, 1972, other than regulations confirmed by the European Communities (Confirmation of Regulations) Act, 1973, and regulations that ceased to have statutory effect before the passing of this Act.

2. Short title

This Act may be cited as the European Communities (Amendment) Act, 1973.

EUROPEAN COMMUNITIES (AMENDMENT) ACT, 1986

An Act to amend the European Communities Act, 1972, so as to provide that certain provisions of the Single European Act hereinafter specified shall be part of the domestic law of the State and to provide for other connected matters

[23rd December, 1986]

Be it enacted by the Oireachtas as follows:

1. Amendment of European Communities Act, 1972

The European Communities Act, 1972, is hereby amended by the insertion, in the definition of 'the treaties governing the European Communities' in section 1(1) after paragraph (n) (inserted by the European Communities (Amendment) (No.2) Act, 1985), of the following paragraph:

'and

(o) the following provisions of the Single European Act (done at Luxembourg on the 17th day of February, 1986, and at The Hague on the 28th day of February, 1986), namely, Article 3.1; Title II; Articles 31 and 32; and, in so far as they relate to the said Article 3.1, the said Title II and the said Articles 31 and 32, Articles 33 and 34.'

2. Construction of references to Assembly of European Communities

References to the Assembly of the European Communities in any Act passed or statutory instrument made before the commencement of this Act shall be construed as references to the European Parliament.

3. Short title, collective citation, construction and commencement

(1) This Act may be cited as the European Communities (Amendment) Act, 1986.

(2) The European Communities Acts, 1972 to 1985, and this Act may be cited together as the European Communities Acts, 1972 to 1986, and shall be construed together as one Act.

(3) This Act shall come into operation on such date as the Minister for Foreign Affairs appoints by order.

EUROPEAN COMMUNITIES (AMENDMENT) ACT, 1992

An Act to amend the European Communities Act, 1972, and to provide for other connected matters

[11th November, 1992]

1. Amendment of section 1 of European Communities Act, 1972

(1) Section 1 of the European Communities Act, 1972, is hereby amended by the insertion, in the definition of 'the treaties governing the European Communities' in section 1(1) after paragraph (o) (inserted by the European Communities (Amendment) Act, 1986), of the following paragraph:

'and

(p) the following provisions of the Treaty on European Union, namely, Titles II, III and IV; in Title VII, Articles L, M and P, and the other provisions of that Title in so far as they relate to any of the treaties governing the European Communities as defined by this subsection; together with the Protocols (whether expressed to be annexed to the Treaty establishing the European Community, or to the said Treaty on European Union and the Treaties establishing the European Communities), done at Maastricht on the 7th day of February, 1992.'

(2) The text of the definition of 'the treaties governing the European Communities' in the said section 1, as amended by subsection (1) of this section and by previous amendments, is set out in the Table to this section.

Table

'the treaties governing the European Communities' means –

(a) 'the ECSC Treaty', that is to say, the Treaty establishing the European Coal and Steel Community, signed at Paris on the 18th day of April, 1951,

(b) 'the EEC Treaty', that is to say, the Treaty establishing the European Economic Community, signed at Rome on the 25th day of March, 1957,

(c) 'the Euratom Treaty', that is to say, the Treaty establishing the European Atomic Energy Community, signed at Rome on the 25th day of March, 1957,

(d) the Convention on certain Institutions common to the European Communities, signed at Rome on the 25th day of March, 1957,

(e) the Treaty establishing a single Council and a single Commission of the European Communities, signed at Brussels on the 8th day of April, 1965,

(f) the Treaty amending certain Budgetary Provisions of the Treaties establishing the European Communities and of the Treaty establishing a single Council and a single Commission of the European Communities, signed at Luxembourg on the 22nd day of April, 1970,

(g) the Treaty relating to the accession of Ireland to the European Economic Community and to the European Atomic Energy Community, signed at Brussels on the 22nd day of January, 1972,

(h) the decision, of the 22nd day of January, 1972, of the Council of the European Communities relating to the accession of Ireland to the European Coal and Steel Community,

as supplemented or amended by treaties or other acts of which the dates of entry into force are dates not later than the 1st day of January, 1973, and

(i) the Treaty amending certain financial provisions of the treaties establishing the European Communities and of the Treaty establishing a single Council and a single Commission of the European Communities, signed at Brussels on the 22nd day of July, 1975, and

(j) the Treaty relating to the accession of the Hellenic Republic to the European Economic Community and to the European Atomic Energy Community, signed at Athens on the 28th day of May, 1979, and

(k) the decision, of the 24th day of May, 1979, of the Council of the European Communities relating to the accession of the Hellenic Republic to the European Coal and Steel Community, and

(l) the Treaty amending, with regard to Greenland, the Treaties establishing the European Communities, signed at Brussels on the 12th day of March, 1984, and

(m) the Treaty concerning the accession of the Kingdom of Spain and the Portuguese Republic to the European Economic Community and to the European Atomic Energy Community, signed at Lisbon and Madrid on the 12th day of June, 1985, and

(*n*) the decision, of the 11th day of June, 1985, of the Council of the European Communities relating to the accession of the Kingdom of Spain and the Portuguese Republic to the European Coal and Steel Community, and

(*o*) the following provisions of the Single European Act (done at Luxembourg on the 17th day of February, 1986, and at The Hague on the 28th day of February, 1986), namely, Article 3.1; Title II; Articles 31 and 32; and, in so far as they relate to the said Article 3.1, the said Title II and the said Articles 31 and 32, Articles 33 and 34, and

(*p*) the following provisions of the Treaty on European Union, namely, Titles II, III and IV; in Title VII, Articles L, M and P, and the other provisions of that Title in so far as they relate to any of the treaties governing the European Communities as defined by this subsection; together with the Protocols (whether expressed to be annexed to the Treaty establishing the European Community, or to the said Treaty on European Union and the Treaties establishing the European Communities), done at Maastricht on the 7th day of February, 1992.

2. Amendment of section 2 of European Communities Act, 1972

Section 2 of the European Communities Act, 1972, is hereby amended by the insertion after 'those Communities', of the words 'and by bodies competent under the said treaties'.

3. Short title, collective citation, construction and commencement

(1) This Act may be cited as the European Communities (Amendment) Act, 1992.

(2) The European Communities Acts, 1972 to 1986, and this Act may be cited together as the European Communities Acts, 1972 to 1992, and shall be construed together as one Act.

(3) This Act shall come into operation on such day as may be appointed by order made by the Minister for Foreign Affairs.

EUROPEAN COMMUNITIES (AMENDMENT) ACT, 1993

An Act to amend the European Communities Act, 1972, and to provide for other connected matters

[20th July, 1993]

Be it enacted by the Oireachtas as follows:

1. Interpretation

(1) In this Act:

'the Act of 1972' means the European Communities Act, 1972;

'EEA Agreement' means the Agreement on the European Economic Area signed in Oporto on the 2nd day of May, 1992, as adjusted by the Protocol to that Agreement done at Brussels on the 17th day of March, 1993.

(2) In this Act, a reference to any enactment shall, unless the context otherwise requires, be construed as a reference to that enactment as amended, adapted or extended by or under any subsequent enactment including this Act.

2. Amendment of section 1 of Act of 1972

(1) Subsection (1) of section 1 of the Act of 1972 is hereby amended by:

(a) the substitution in paragraph (l) of '13th' for '12th', and

(b) the insertion, in the definition of 'the treaties governing the European Communities' after paragraph (p) (inserted by the European Communities (Amendment) Act, 1992) of the following:

'and

(q) the Act amending the Protocol on the Statute of the European Investment Bank, empowering the Board of Governors to establish a European Investment Fund, signed at Brussels on the 25th day of March, 1993, together with the Treaty amending certain provisions of the Protocol on the Statute of the European Investment Bank, signed at Brussels on the 10th day of July, 1975.'

(2) The text of the definition of 'the treaties governing the European Communities' in the said section 1, as amended by subsection (1) of this section and by previous amendments, is set out in the Table to this section.

Table

'the treaties governing the European Communities' means –

(a) 'the ECSC Treaty', that is to say, the Treaty establishing the European Coal and Steel Community, signed in Paris on the 18th day of April, 1951,

(b) 'the EEC Treaty', that is to say, the Treaty establishing the European Economic Community, signed at Rome on the 25th day of March, 1957,

(c) 'the Euratom Treaty', that is to say, the Treaty establishing the European Atomic Energy Community, signed at Rome on the 25th day of March, 1957,

(d) The Convention on certain Institutions common to the European Communities, signed at Rome on the 25th day of March, 1957,

(e) the Treaty establishing a single Council and a single Commission of the European Communities, signed at Brussels on the 8th day of April, 1965,

(f) The Treaty amending certain Budgetary Provisions of the Treaties establishing the European Communities and of the Treaty establishing a single Council and a single Commission of the European Communities, signed at Luxembourg on the 22nd day of April, 1970,

(g) the Treaty relating to the accession of Ireland to the European Economic Community and to the European Atomic Energy Community, signed at Brussels on the 22nd day of January, 1972,

(h) the decision, on the 22nd day of January, 1972, of the Council of the European Communities relating to the accession of Ireland to the European Coal and Steel Community,

as supplemented or amended by treaties or other acts of which the dates of entry into force are dates not later than the 1st day of January, 1973, and

(i) the Treaty amending certain financial provisions of the treaties establishing the European Communities and of the Treaty establishing a single Council and a single Commission of the European Communities, signed at Brussels on the 22nd day of July, 1975, and

(j) the Treaty relating to the accession of the Hellenic Republic to the European Economic Community and to the European Atomic Energy Community, signed at Athens on the 28th day of May, 1979, and

(k) the decision, of the 24th day of May, 1979, of the Council of the European Communities relating to the accession of the Hellenic Republic to the European Coal and Steel Community, and

(l) the Treaty amending, with regard to Greenland, the Treaties establishing the European Communities, signed at Brussels on the 13th day of March, 1984, and

(m) the Treaty concerning the accession of the Kingdom of Spain and the Portuguese Republic to the European Economic Community and to the European Atomic Energy Community, signed at Lisbon and Madrid on the 12th day of June, 1985, and

(n) the decision, of the 11th day of June, 1985, of the Council of the European Communities relating to the accession of the Kingdom of Spain and the Portuguese Republic to the European Coal and Steel Community, and

(o) the following provisions of the Single European Act (done at Luxembourg on the 17th day of February, 1986, and at The Hague on the 28th day of February, 1986), namely, Article 3.1; Title II; Articles 31 and 32; and, in so far as they relate to the said Article 3.1, the said Title II and the said Articles 31 and 32, Articles 33 and 34, and

(p) the following provisions of the Treaty on European Union, namely, Titles II, III and IV; in Title VII, Articles L, M and P, and the other provisions of that Title in so far as they relate to any of the treaties governing the European Communities as defined by this subsection; together with the Protocols (whether expressed to be annexed to the Treaty establishing the European Community, or to the said Treaty on European Union and the Treaties establishing the European Communities), done at Maastricht on the 7th day of February, 1992, and

(q) the Act amending the Protocol on the Statute of the European Investment Bank, empowering the Board of Governors to establish a European Investment Fund, signed at Brussels on the 25th day of March, 1993, together with the Treaty amending certain provisions of the Protocol on the Statute of the European Investment Bank, signed at Brussels on the 10th day of July, 1975.

3. Amendment of section 2 of Act of 1972

Section 2 of the Act of 1972 is hereby amended by the insertion of the following subsection:

'(2) Without prejudice to subsection (1) of this section, from the coming into force of the EEA Agreement, the provisions of that

Agreement and the Acts to be adopted by institutions established by that Agreement which, pursuant to the treaties governing the European Communities, will be binding on the State and an integral part of the legal order of those Communities, shall have the force of law in the State on the conditions laid down in those treaties and in that Agreement.',

and accordingly the said section 2 as originally enacted shall be subsection (1) of the said section 2.

4. Adaptations to take account of EEA Agreement

(1) Without prejudice to the future exercise of the powers conferred by section 3 of the Act of 1972, any regulations made under the said section 3 which are in force immediately before the coming into operation of section 3 of this Act, and any enactment, or instrument made under an enactment, which implements obligations of the State under the treaties governing the European Communities, shall, as far as practicable, be construed as if, on the coming into operation of section 3 of this Act, they were adapted as required by or under the EEA Agreement.

(2) Without prejudice to the generality of subsection (1) of this section, in any regulations made under section 3 of the Act of 1972, and in any enactment, or instrument made under an enactment, any reference to the Member States of the European Communities or to any person who is affected by the treaties governing those Communities shall, in so far as may be necessary to give effect to the obligations of the State pursuant to the EEA Agreement, be construed as including a reference to those States (not being Member States of the said Communities) which are contracting parties to the EEA Agreement and any person who is affected by the EEA Agreement.

5. Regulations under Act of 1972

(1) Without prejudice to the future exercise of the powers conferred by section 3 of the Act of 1972, all regulations made under section 3 of the Act of 1972 prior to the passing of this Act are hereby confirmed as on and from the date upon which they purported to come into operation.

(2) Subsection (1) of this section shall operate to confirm regulations or any provision of any regulation to the extent only that such confirmation is in accordance with the Constitution.

(3) Nothing in subsection (1) or (2) of this section shall be construed to mean that but for this Act, any regulations or provision of regulations would for any reason be invalid having regard to the provisions of the Constitution or otherwise.

(4) Notwithstanding section 10(4) of the Petty Sessions (Ireland) Act, 1851, proceedings in respect of offences committed after the passing of this Act under regulations (whether made before or after such passing) under the Act of 1972 may be instituted at any time within two years from the date of the commission of the offence.

(5) Subsection (1) of this section shall apply to all regulations made under section 3 of the Act of 1972 prior to the passing of this Act subject to any adaptation, amendment or revocation thereof whether by regulations made under the said section 3 or by any Act of the Oireachtas or instrument thereunder.

6. Amendment of section 4 of Act of 1972

(1) On and from such day as the Minister for Foreign Affairs shall by order appoint, section 4 (inserted by the European Communities (Amendment) Act, 1973) of the Act of 1972 shall stand amended by the substitution for 'Joint Committee on Secondary Legislation of the European Communities' of 'Joint Committee on Foreign Affairs'.

(2) An order shall not be made under subsection (1) of this section before the establishment by both Houses of the Oireachtas of a Joint Committee to be known as the 'Joint Committee on Foreign Affairs'.

7. Short title, collective citation, construction and commencement

(1) This Act may be cited as the European Communities (Amendment) Act, 1993.

(2) The European Communities Acts, 1972 to 1992, and this Act may be cited together as the European Communities Acts, 1972 to 1993, and shall be construed together as one Act.

(3) Sections 2 and 3 of this Act shall come into operation on such day or days as may be appointed by order or orders made by the Minister for Foreign Affairs.

PART F

SECONDARY LEGISLATION

COMPETITION LAW

(a) EC

REGULATION NO 17

First Regulation implementing Articles 85 and 86 of the Treaty

(OJ No 204, 21.2.62, p.87)

The Council of the European Economic Community,

Having regard to the Treaty establishing the European Economic Community, and in particular Article 87 thereof;

Having regard to the proposal from the Commission;

Having regard to the Opinion of the Economic and Social Committee;

Having regard to the Opinion of the European Parliament;

Whereas, in order to establish a system ensuring that competition shall not be distorted in the common market, it is necessary to provide for balanced application of Articles 85 and 86 in a uniform manner in the Member States;

Whereas in establishing the rules for applying Article 85(3) account must be taken of the need to ensure effective supervision and to simplify administration to the greatest possible extent;

Whereas it is accordingly necessary to make it obligatory, as a general principle, for undertakings which seek application of Article 85(3) to notify to the Commission their agreements, decisions and concerted practices;

Whereas, on the one hand, such agreements, decisions and concerted practices are probably very numerous and cannot therefore all be examined at the same time and, on the other hand, some of them have special features which may make them less prejudicial to the development of the common market;

Whereas there is consequently a need to make more flexible arrangements for the time being in respect of certain categories of agreement, decision and concerted practice without prejudging their validity under Article 85;

Whereas it may be in the interest of undertakings to know whether any agreements, decisions or practices to which they are party, or propose to become party, may lead to action on the part of the Commission pursuant to Article 85(1) or Article 86;

Whereas, in order to secure uniform application of Articles 85 and 86 in the common market, rules must be made under which the Commission, acting in close and constant liaison with the competent authorities of the Member States, may take the requisite measures for applying those Articles;

Whereas for this purpose the Commission must have the cooperation of the competent authorities of the Member States and be empowered, throughout the common market, to require such information to be supplied and to undertake such investigations as are necessary to bring to light any agreement, decision or concerted practice prohibited by Article 85(1) or any abuse of a dominant position prohibited by Article 86;

Whereas, in order to carry out its duty of ensuring that the provisions of the Treaty are applied, the Commission must be empowered to address to undertakings or associations of undertakings recommendations and decisions for the purpose of bringing to an end infringements of Articles 85 and 86;

Whereas compliance with Articles 85 and 86 and the fulfilment of obligations imposed on undertakings and associations of undertakings under this Regulation must be enforceable by means of fines and periodic penalty payments;

Whereas undertakings concerned must be accorded the right to be heard by the Commission, third parties whose interests may be affected by a decision must be given the opportunity of submitting their comments beforehand, and it must be ensured that wide publicity is given to decisions taken;

Whereas all decisions taken by the Commission under this Regulation are subject to review by the Court of Justice under the conditions specified in the Treaty; whereas it is moreover desirable to confer upon the Court of Justice, pursuant to Article 172, unlimited jurisdiction in respect of decisions under which the Commission imposes fines or periodic penalty payments;

Whereas this Regulation may enter into force without prejudice to any other provisions that may hereafter be adopted pursuant to Article 87;

Has adopted this Regulation:

Article 1

Basic provision

Without prejudice to Articles 6, 7 and 23 of this Regulation, agreements, decisions and concerted practices of the kind described in Article 85(1) of the Treaty and the abuse of a dominant position in the market, within the meaning of Article 86 of the Treaty, shall be prohibited, no prior decision to that effect being required.

Article 2

Negative clearance

Upon application by the undertakings or associations of undertakings concerned, the Commission may certify that, on the basis of the facts in its possession, there are no grounds under Article 85(1) or Article 86 of the Treaty for action on its part in respect of an agreement, decision or practice.

Article 3

Termination of infringements

1. Where the Commission, upon application or upon its own initiative, finds that there is infringement of Article 85 or Article 86 of the Treaty, it may by decision require the undertakings or associations of undertakings concerned to bring such infringement to an end.

2. Those entitled to make application are:

(a) Member States;

(b) natural or legal persons who claim a legitimate interest.

3. Without prejudice to the other provisions of this Regulation, the Commission may, before taking a decision under paragraph 1, address to the undertakings or associations of undertakings concerned recommendations for termination of the infringement.

Article 4

Notification of new agreements, decisions and practices

1. Agreements, decisions and concerted practices of the kind described in Article 85(1) of the Treaty which come into existence after the entry into force of this Regulation and in respect of which the parties seek application of Article 85(3) must be notified to the Commission. Until

they have been notified, no decision in application of Article 85(3) may be taken.

2. Paragraph 1 shall not apply to agreements, decisions or concerted practices where:

(1) the only parties thereto are undertakings from one Member State and the agreements, decisions or practices do not relate either to imports or to exports between Member States;

(2) not more than two undertakings are party thereto, and the agreements only:

    (a) restrict the freedom of one party to the contract in determining the prices or conditions of business upon which the goods which he has obtained from the other party to the contract may be resold; or

    (b) impose restrictions on the exercise of the rights of the assignee or user of industrial property rights – in particular patents, utility models, designs or trade marks – or of the person entitled under a contract to the assignment, or grant, of the right to use a method of manufacture or knowledge relating to the use and to the application of industrial processes;

(3) they have as their sole object:

    (a) the development or uniform application of standards or types; or

    (b) joint research for improvement of techniques, provided the results are accessible to all parties thereto and may be used by each of them.

These agreements, decisions and practices may be notified to the Commission.

Article 5

Notification of existing agreements, decisions and practices

1. Agreements, decisions and concerted practices of the kind described in Article 85(1) of the Treaty which are in existence at the date of entry into force of this Regulation and in respect of which the parties seek application of Article 85(3) shall be notified to the Commission before 1 August 1962.

2. Paragraph 1 shall not apply to agreements, decisions or concerted practices falling within Article 4(2); these may be notified to the Commission.

Article 6

Decisions pursuant to Article 85(3)

1. Whenever the Commission takes a decision pursuant to Article 85(3) of the Treaty, it shall specify therein the date from which the decision shall take effect. Such date shall not be earlier than the date of notification.

2. The second sentence of paragraph 1 shall not apply to agreements, decisions or concerted practices falling within Article 4(2) and Article 5(2), nor to those falling within Article 5(1) which have been notified within the time limit specified in Article 5(1).

Article 7

Special provisions for existing agreements, decisions and practices

1. Where agreements, decisions and concerted practices in existence at the date of entry into force of this Regulation and notified before 1 August 1962 do not satisfy the requirements of Article 85(3) of the Treaty and the undertakings or associations of undertakings concerned cease to give effect to them or modify them in such manner that they no longer fall within the prohibition contained in Article 85(1) or that they satisfy the requirements of Article 85(3), the prohibition contained in Article 85(1) shall apply only for a period fixed by the Commission. A decision by the Commission pursuant to the foregoing sentence shall not apply as against undertakings and associations of undertakings which did not expressly consent to the notification.

2. Paragraph 1 shall apply to agreements, decisions and concerted practices falling within Article 4(2) which are in existence at the date of entry into force of this Regulation if they are notified before 1 January 1964.

Article 8

Duration and revocation of decisions under Article 85(3)

1. A decision in application of Article 85(3) of the Treaty shall be issued for a specified period and conditions and obligations may be attached thereto.

2. A decision may on application be renewed if the requirements of Article 85(3) of the Treaty continue to be satisfied.

3. The Commission may revoke or amend its decision or prohibit specified acts by the parties:

(a) where there has been a change in any of the facts which were basic to the making of the decision;

(b) where the parties commit a breach of any obligation attached to the decision;

(c) where the decision is based on incorrect information or was induced by deceit;

(d) where the parties abuse the exemption from the provisions of Article 85(1) of the Treaty granted to them by the decision.

In cases to which subparagraphs (b), (c) or (d) apply, the decision may be revoked with retroactive effect.

Article 9

Powers

1. Subject to review of its decision by the Court of Justice, the Commission shall have sole power to declare Article 85(1) inapplicable pursuant to Article 85(3) of the Treaty.

2. The Commission shall have power to apply Article 85(1) and Article 86 of the Treaty; this power may be exercised notwithstanding that the time limits specified in Article 5(1) and in Article 7(2) relating to notification have not expired.

3. As long as the Commission has not initiated any procedure under Articles 2, 3 or 6, the authorities of the Member States shall remain competent to apply Article 85(1) and Article 86 in accordance with Article 88 of the Treaty; they shall remain competent in this respect notwithstanding that the time limits specified in Article 5(1) and in Article 7(2) relating to notification have not expired.

Article 10

Liaison with the authorities of the Member States

1. The Commission shall forthwith transmit to the competent authorities of the Member States a copy of the applications and notifications together with copies of the most important documents lodged with the Commission for the purpose of establishing the existence of infringements of Articles 85 or 86 of the Treaty or of obtaining negative clearance or a decision in application of Article 85(3).

2. The Commission shall carry out the procedure set out in paragraph 1 in close and constant liaison with the competent authorities of the

Member States; such authorities shall have the right to express their views upon that procedure.

3. An Advisory Committee on Restrictive Practices and Monopolies shall be consulted prior to the taking of any decision following upon a procedure under paragraph 1, and of any decision concerning the renewal, amendment or revocation of a decision pursuant to Article 85(3) of the Treaty.

4. The Advisory Committee shall be composed of officials competent in the matter of restrictive practices and monopolies. Each Member State shall appoint an official to represent it who, if prevented from attending, may be replaced by another official.

5. The consultation shall take place at a joint meeting convened by the Commission; such meeting shall be held not earlier than fourteen days after dispatch of the notice convening it. The notice shall, in respect of each case to be examined, be accompanied by a summary of the case together with an indication of the most important documents, and a preliminary draft decision.

6. The Advisory Committee may deliver an opinion notwithstanding that some of its members or their alternates are not present. A report of the outcome of the consultative proceedings shall be annexed to the draft decision. It shall not be made public.

Article 11

Requests for information

1. In carrying out the duties assigned to it by Article 89 and by provisions adopted under Article 87 of the Treaty, the Commission may obtain all necessary information from the Governments and competent authorities of the Member States and from undertakings and associations of undertakings.

2. When sending a request for information to an undertaking or association of undertakings, the Commission shall at the same time forward a copy of the request to the competent authority of the Member State in whose territory the seat of the undertaking or association of undertakings is situated.

3. In its request the Commission shall state the legal basis and the purpose of the request and also the penalties provided for in Article 15(1)(b) for supplying incorrect information.

4. The owners of the undertakings or their representatives and, in the case of legal persons, companies or firms, or of associations having no

legal personality, the persons authorised to represent them by law or by their constitution shall supply the information requested.

5. Where an undertaking or association of undertakings does not supply the information requested within the time limit fixed by the Commission, or supplies incomplete information, the Commission shall by decision require the information to be supplied. The decision shall specify what information is required, fix an appropriate time limit within which it is to be supplied and indicate the penalties provided for in Article 15(1)(b) and Article 16(1)(c) and the right to have the decision reviewed by the Court of Justice.

6. The Commission shall at the same time forward a copy of its decision to the competent authority of the Member State in whose territory the seat of the undertaking or association of undertakings is situated.

Article 12

Inquiry into sectors of the economy

1. If in any sector of the economy the trend of trade between the Member States, price movements, inflexibility of prices or other circumstances suggest that in the economic sector concerned competition is being restricted or distorted within the common market, the Commission may decide to conduct a general inquiry into that economic sector and in the course thereof may request undertakings in the sector concerned to supply the information necessary for giving effect to the principles formulated in Articles 85 and 86 of the Treaty and for carrying out the duties entrusted to the Commission.

2. The Commission may in particular request every undertaking or association of undertakings in the economic sector concerned to communicate to it all agreements, decisions and concerted practices which are exempt from notification by virtue of Article 4(2) and Article 5(2).

3. When making inquiries pursuant to paragraph 2, the Commission shall also request undertakings or groups of undertakings whose size suggests that they occupy a dominant position within the common market or a substantial part thereof to supply to the Commission such particulars of the structure of the undertakings and of their behaviour as are requisite to an appraisal of their position in the light of Article 86 of the Treaty.

4. Article 10(3) to (6) and Articles 11, 13 and 14 shall apply correspondingly.

Article 13

Investigations by the authorities of the Member States

1. At the request of the Commission, the competent authorities of the Member States shall undertake the investigations which the Commission considers to be necessary under Article 14(1), or which it has ordered by decision pursuant to Article 14(3). The officials of the competent authorities of the Member States responsible for conducting these investigations shall exercise their powers upon production of an authorisation in writing issued by the competent authority of the Member State in whose territory the investigation is to be made. Such authorisation shall specify the subject matter and purpose of the investigation.

2. If so requested by the Commission or by the competent authority of the Member State in whose territory the investigation is to be made, the officials of the Commission may assist the officials of such authorities in carrying out their duties.

Article 14

Investigating powers of the Commission

1. In carrying out the duties assigned to it by Article 89 and by provisions adopted under Article 87 of the Treaty, the Commission may undertake all necessary investigations into undertakings and associations of undertakings. To this end the officials authorised by the Commission are empowered:

(a) to examine the books and other business records;

(b) to take copies of or extracts from the books and business records;

(c) to ask for oral explanations on the spot;

(d) to enter any premises, land and means of transport of undertakings.

2. The officials of the Commission authorised for the purpose of these investigations shall exercise their powers upon production of an authorisation in writing specifying the subject matter and purpose of the investigation and the penalties provided for in Article 15(1)(c) in cases where production of the required books or other business records is incomplete. In good time before the investigation, the Commission shall inform the competent authority of the Member State in whose territory the same is to be made of the investigation and of the identity of the authorised officials.

3. Undertakings and associations of undertakings shall submit to

investigations ordered by decision of the Commission. The decision shall specify the subject matter and purpose of the investigation, appoint the date on which it is to begin and indicate the penalties provided for in Article 15(1)(c) and Article 16(1)(d) and the right to have the decision reviewed by the Court of Justice.

4. The Commission shall take decisions referred to in paragraph 3 after consultation with the competent authority of the Member State in whose territory the investigation is to be made.

5. Officials of the competent authority of the Member State in whose territory the investigation is to be made may, at the request of such authority or of the Commission, assist the officials of the Commission in carrying out their duties.

6. Where an undertaking opposes an investigation ordered pursuant to this Article, the Member State concerned shall afford the necessary assistance to the officials authorised by the Commission to enable them to make their investigation. Member States shall, after consultation with the Commission, take the necessary measures to this end before 1 October 1962.

Article 15

Fines

1. The Commission may by decision impose on undertakings or associations of undertakings fines of from 100 to 5000 units of account where, intentionally or negligently:

(a) they supply incorrect or misleading information in an application pursuant to Article 2 or in a notification pursuant to Articles 4 or 5; or

(b) they supply incorrect information in response to a request made pursuant to Article 11(3) or (5) or to Article 12, or do not supply information within the time limit fixed by a decision taken under Article 11(5); or

(c) they produce the required books or other business records in incomplete form during investigations under Article 13 or 14, or refuse to submit to an investigation ordered by decision issued in implementation of Article 14(3).

2. The Commission may by decision impose on undertakings or associations of undertakings fines of from 1000 to 1 000 000 units of account, or a sum in excess thereof but not exceeding 10% of the turnover in the preceding business year of each of the undertakings

participating in the infringement where, either intentionally or negligently:

(a) they infringe Article 85(1) or Article 86 of the Treaty; or

(b) they commit a breach of any obligation imposed pursuant to Article 8(1).

In fixing the amount of the fine, regard shall be had both to the gravity and to the duration of the infringement.

3. Article 10(3) to (6) shall apply.

4. Decisions taken pursuant to paragraphs 1 and 2 shall not be of a criminal law nature.

5. The fines provided for in paragraph 2(a) shall not be imposed in respect of acts taking place:

(a) after notification to the Commission and before its decision in application of Article 85(3) of the Treaty, provided they fall within the limits of the activity described in the notification;

(b) before notification and in the course of agreements, decisions or concerted practices in existence at the date of entry into force of this Regulation, provided that notification was effected within the time limits specified in Article 5(1) and Article 7(2).

6. Paragraph 5 shall not have effect where the Commission has informed the undertakings concerned that after preliminary examination it is of opinion that Article 85(1) of the Treaty applies and that application of Article 85(3) is not justified.

Article 16

Periodic penalty payments

1. The Commission may by decision impose on undertakings or associations of undertakings periodic penalty payments of from 50 to 1000 units of account per day, calculated from the date appointed by the decision, in order to compel them:

(a) to put an end to an infringement of Article 85 or 86 of the Treaty, in accordance with a decision taken pursuant to Article 3 of this Regulation;

(b) to refrain from any act prohibited under Article 8(3);

(c) to supply complete and correct information which it has requested by decision taken pursuant to Article 11(5);

(*d*) to submit to an investigation which it has ordered by decision taken pursuant to Article 14(3).

2. Where the undertakings or associations of undertakings have satisfied the obligation which it was the purpose of the periodic penalty payment to enforce, the Commission may fix the total amount of the periodic penalty payment at a lower figure than that which would arise under the original decision.

3. Article 10(3) to (6) shall apply.

Article 17

Review by the Court of Justice

The Court of Justice shall have unlimited jurisdiction within the meaning of Article 172 of the Treaty to review decisions whereby the Commission has fixed a fine or periodic penalty payment; it may cancel, reduce or increase the fine or periodic penalty payment imposed.

Article 18

Unit of account

For the purposes of applying Articles 15 to 17 the unit of account shall be that adopted in drawing up the budget of the Community in accordance with Articles 207 and 209 of the Treaty.

Article 19

Hearing of the parties and of third persons

1. Before taking decisions as provided for in Articles 2, 3, 6, 7, 8, 15 and 16, the Commission shall give the undertakings or associations of undertakings concerned the opportunity of being heard on the matters to which the Commission has taken objection.

2. If the Commission or the competent authorities of the Member States consider it necessary, they may also hear other natural or legal persons. Applications to be heard on the part of such persons shall, where they show a sufficient interest, be granted.

3. Where the Commission intends to give negative clearance pursuant to Article 2 or take a decision in application of Article 85(3) of the Treaty, it shall publish a summary of the relevant application or notification and invite all interested third parties to submit their observations within a time limit which it shall fix being not less than one month. Publication

shall have regard to the legitimate interest of undertakings in the protection of their business secrets.

Article 20

Professional secrecy

1. Information acquired as a result of the application of Articles 11, 12, 13 and 14 shall be used only for the purpose of the relevant request or investigation.

2. Without prejudice to the provisions of Articles 19 and 21, the Commission and the competent authorities of the Member States, their officials and other servants shall not disclose information acquired by them as a result of the application of this Regulation and of the kind covered by the obligation of professional secrecy.

3. The provisions of paragraphs 1 and 2 shall not prevent publication of general information or surveys which do not contain information relating to particular undertakings or associations of undertakings.

Article 21

Publication of decisions

1. The Commission shall publish the decisions which it takes pursuant to Articles 2, 3, 6, 7 and 8.

2. The publication shall state the names of the parties and the main content of the decision; it shall have regard to the legitimate interest of undertakings in the protection of their business secrets.

Article 22

Special provisions

1. The Commission shall submit to the Council proposals for making certain categories of agreement, decision and concerted practice falling within Article 4(2) or Article 5(2) compulsorily notifiable under Article 4 or 5.

2. Within one year from the date of entry into force of this Regulation, the Council shall examine, on a proposal from the Commission, what special provisions might be made for exempting from the provisions of this Regulation agreements, decisions and concerted practices falling within Article 4(2) or Article 5(2).

Article 23

Transitional provisions applicable to decisions of authorities of the Member States

1. Agreements, decisions and concerted practices of the kind described in Article 85(1) of the Treaty to which, before the entry into force of this Regulation, the competent authority of a Member State has declared Article 85(1) to be inapplicable pursuant to Article 85(3) shall not be subject to compulsory notification under Article 5. The decision of the competent authority of the Member State shall be deemed to be a decision within the meaning of Article 6; it shall cease to be valid upon expiration of the period fixed by such authority but in any event not more than three years after the entry into force of this Regulation. Article 8(3) shall apply.

2. Applications for renewal of decisions of the kind described in paragraph 1 shall be decided upon by the Commission in accordance with Article 8(2).

Article 24

Implementing provisions

The Commission shall have power to adopt implementing provisions concerning the form, content and other details of applications pursuant to Articles 2 and 3 and of notifications pursuant to Articles 4 and 5, and concerning hearings pursuant to Article 19(1) and (2).

This Regulation shall be binding in its entirety and directly applicable in all Member States.

Done at Brussels, 6 February 1962.

For the Council

The President

M. Couve de Murville

CORRIGENDUM

Corrigendum to Council Regulation (EEC) No 4064/89 of 21 December 1989 on the control of concentrations between undertakings

Given that certain errors appear in the various language versions of the abovementioned Regulation, the entire text shall be published as below in the form of a corrected version replacing the version of the Regulation published in OJ No L 395, 30.12.89, p.1.

Council Regulation (EEC) No 4064/89 of 21 December 1989 on the control of concentrations between undertakings

The Council of the European Communities,

Having regard to the Treaty establishing the European Economic Community, and in particular Articles 87 and 235 thereof,

Having regard to the proposal from the Commission[1],

Having regard to the opinion of the European Parliament[2],

Having regard to the opinion of the Economic and Social Committee[3],

(1) Whereas, for the achievement of the aims of the Treaty establishing the European Economic Community, Article 3(f) gives the Community the objective of instituting 'a system ensuring that competition in the common market is not distorted';

(2) Whereas this system is essential for the achievement of the internal market by 1992 and its further development;

(3) Whereas the dismantling of internal frontiers is resulting and will continue to result in major corporate reorganisations in the Community, particularly in the form of concentrations;

(4) Whereas such a development must be welcomed as being in line with the requirements of dynamic competition and capable of increasing the competitiveness of European industry, improving the conditions of growth and raising the standard of living in the Community;

(5) Whereas, however, it must be ensured that the process of reorganisation does not result in lasting damage to competition; whereas Community law must therefore include provisions governing those concentrations which may significantly impede effective competition in the common market or in a substantial part of it;

(6) Whereas Articles 85 and 86, while applicable, according to the case-

law of the Court of Justice, to certain concentrations, are not, however, sufficient to control all operations which may prove to be incompatible with the system of undistorted competition envisaged in the Treaty;

(7) Whereas a new legal instrument should therefore be created in the form of a Regulation to permit effective control of all concentrations from the point of view of their effect on the structure of competition in the Community and to be the only instrument applicable to such concentrations;

(8) Whereas this Regulation should therefore be based not only on Article 87 but, principally, on Article 235 of the Treaty, under which the Community may give itself the additional powers of action necessary for the attainment of its objectives, including with regard to concentrations on the markets for agricultural products listed in Annex II to the Treaty;

(9) Whereas the provisions to be adopted in this Regulation should apply to significant structural changes the impact of which on the market goes beyond the national borders of any one Member State;

(10) Whereas the scope of application of this Regulation should therefore be defined according to the geographical area of activity of the undertakings concerned and be limited by quantitative thresholds in order to cover those concentrations which have a Community dimension; whereas, at the end of an initial phase of the application of this Regulation, these thresholds should be reviewed in the light of the experience gained;

(11) Whereas a concentration with a Community dimension exists where the combined aggregate turnover of the undertakings concerned exceeds given levels worldwide and within the Community and where at least two of the undertakings concerned have their sole or main fields of activities in different Member States or where, although the undertakings in question act mainly in one and the same Member State, at least one of them has substantial operations in at least one other Member State; whereas that is also the case where the concentrations are effected by undertakings which do not have their principal fields of activities in the Community but which have substantial operations there;

(12) Whereas the arrangements to be introduced for the control of concentrations should, without prejudice to Article 90(2) of the Treaty, respect the principle of non-discrimination between the public and the private sectors; whereas, in the public sector, calculation of the turnover of an undertaking concerned in a concentration needs, therefore, to take account of undertakings making up an economic unit with an independent power of decision, irrespective of the way in which their

capital is held or of the rules of administrative supervision applicable to them;

(13) Whereas it is necessary to establish whether concentrations with a Community dimension are compatible or not with the common market from the point of view of the need to maintain and develop effective competition in the common market; whereas, in so doing, the Commission must place its appraisal within the general framework of the achievement of the fundamental objectives referred to in Article 2 of the Treaty, including that of strengthening the Community's economic and social cohesion, referred to in Article 130a;

(14) Whereas this Regulation should establish the principle that a concentration with a Community dimension which creates or strengthens a position as a result of which effective competition in the common market or in a substantial part of it is significantly impeded is to be declared incompatible with the common market;

(15) Whereas concentrations which, by reason of the limited market share of the undertakings concerned, are not liable to impede effective competition may be presumed to be compatible with the common market; whereas, without prejudice to Articles 85 and 86 of the Treaty, an indication to this effect exists, in particular, where the market share of the undertakings concerned does not exceed 25% either in the common market or in a substantial part of it;

(16) Whereas the Commission should have the task of taking all the decisions necessary to establish whether or not concentrations with a Community dimension are compatible with the common market, as well as decisions designed to restore effective competition;

(17) Whereas to ensure effective control undertakings should be obliged to give prior notification of concentrations with a Community dimension and provision should be made for the suspension of concentrations for a limited period, and for the possibility of extending or waiving a suspension where necessary; whereas in the interests of legal certainty the validity of transactions must nevertheless be protected as much as necessary;

(18) Whereas a period within which the Commission must initiate proceedings in respect of a notified concentration and periods within which it must give a final decision on the compatibility or incompatibility with the common market of a notified concentration should be laid down;

(19) Whereas the undertakings concerned must be afforded the right to be heard by the Commission when proceedings have been initiated; whereas the members of the management and supervisory bodies and

the recognised representatives of the employees of the undertakings concerned, and third parties showing a legitimate interest, must also be given the opportunity to be heard;

(20) Whereas the Commission should act in close and constant liaison with the competent authorities of the Member States from which it obtains comments and information;

(21) Whereas, for the purposes of this Regulation, and in accordance with the case-law of the Court of Justice, the Commission must be afforded the assistance of the Member States and must also be empowered to require information to be given and to carry out the necessary investigations in order to appraise concentrations;

(22) Whereas compliance with this Regulation must be enforceable by means of fines and periodic penalty payments; whereas the Court of Justice should be given unlimited jurisdiction in that regard pursuant to Article 172 of the Treaty;

(23) Whereas it is appropriate to define the concept of concentration in such a manner as to cover only operations bringing about a lasting change in the structure of the undertakings concerned; whereas it is therefore necessary to exclude from the scope of this Regulation those operations which have as their object or effect the coordination of the competitive behaviour of undertakings which remain independent, since such operations fall to be examined under the appropriate provisions of the Regulations implementing Articles 85 and 86 of the Treaty; whereas it is appropriate to make this distinction specifically in the case of the creation of joint ventures;

(24) Whereas there is no coordination of competitive behaviour within the meaning of this Regulation where two or more undertakings agree to acquire jointly control of one or more other undertakings with the object and effect of sharing amongst themselves such undertakings or their assets;

(25) Whereas this Regulation should still apply where the undertakings concerned accept restrictions directly related and necessary to the implementation of the concentration;

(26) Whereas the Commission should be given exclusive competence to apply this Regulation, subject to review by the Court of Justice;

(27) Whereas the Member States may not apply their national legislation on competition to concentrations with a Community dimension, unless this Regulation makes provision therefor; whereas the relevant powers of national authorities should be limited to cases where, failing intervention by the Commission, effective competition is likely to be

significantly impeded within the territory of a Member State and where the competition interests of that Member State cannot be sufficiently protected otherwise by this Regulation; whereas the Member States concerned must act promptly in such cases; whereas this Regulation cannot, because of the diversity of national law, fix a single deadline for the adoption of remedies;

(28) Whereas, furthermore, the exclusive application of this Regulation to concentrations with a Community dimension is without prejudice to Article 223 of the Treaty, and does not prevent the Member States from taking appropriate measures to protect legitimate interests other than those pursued by this Regulation, provided that such measures are compatible with the general principles and other provisions of Community law;

(29) Whereas concentrations not covered by this Regulation come, in principle, within the jurisdiction of the Member States; whereas, however, the Commission should have the power to act, at the request of a Member State concerned, in cases where effective competition could be significantly impeded within that Member State's territory;

(30) Whereas the conditions in which concentrations involving Community undertakings are carried out in non-member countries should be observed, and provision should be made for the possibility of the Council giving the Commission an appropriate mandate for negotiation with a view to obtaining non-discriminatory treatment for Community undertakings;

(31) Whereas this Regulation in no way detracts from the collective rights of employees as recognised in the undertakings concerned,

Has adopted this Regulation:

Article 1

Scope

1. Without prejudice to Article 22 this Regulation shall apply to all concentrations with a Community dimension as defined in paragraph 2.

2. For the purposes of this Regulation, a concentration has a Community dimension where:

(a) the combined aggregate worldwide turnover of all the undertakings concerned is more than ECU 5 000 million; and

(b) the aggregate Community-wide turnover of each of at least two of the undertakings concerned is more than ECU 250 million, unless each of the undertakings concerned achieves more than two-thirds of its aggregate Community-wide turnover within one and the same Member State.

3. The thresholds laid down in paragraph 2 will be reviewed before the end of the fourth year following that of the adoption of this Regulation by the Council acting by a qualified majority on a proposal from the Commission.

Article 2

Appraisal of concentrations

1. Concentrations within the scope of this Regulation shall be appraised in accordance with the following provisions with a view to establishing whether or not they are compatible with the common market.

In making this appraisal, the Commission shall take into account:

(a) the need to maintain and develop effective competition within the common market in view of, among other things, the structure of all the markets concerned and the actual or potential competition from undertakings located either within or outwith the Community;

(b) the market position of the undertakings concerned and their economic and financial power, the alternatives available to suppliers and users, their access to supplies or markets, any legal or other barriers to entry, supply and demand trends for the relevant goods and services, the interests of the intermediate and ultimate consumers, and the development of technical and economic progress provided that it is to consumers' advantage and does not form an obstacle to competition.

2. A concentration which does not create or strengthen a dominant position as a result of which effective competition would be significantly impeded in the common market or in a substantial part of it shall be declared compatible with the common market.

3. A concentration which creates or strengthens a dominant position as a result of which effective competition would be significantly impeded in the common market or in a substantial part of it shall be declared incompatible with the common market.

Article 3

Definition of concentration

1. A concentration shall be deemed to arise where:

(a)   two or more previously independent undertakings merge, or (*b*) – one or more persons already controlling at least one undertaking, or

– one or more undertakings

acquire, whether by purchase of securities or assets, by contract or by any other means, direct or indirect control of the whole or parts of one or more other undertakings.

2. An operation, including the creation of a joint venture, which has as its object or effect the coordination of the competitive behaviour of undertakings which remain independent shall not constitute a concentration within the meaning of paragraph 1(b).

The creation of a joint venture performing on a lasting basis all the functions of an autonomous economic entity, which does not give rise to coordination of the competitive behaviour of the parties amongst themselves or between them and the joint venture, shall constitute a concentration within the meaning of paragraph 1(b).

3. For the purposes of this Regulation, control shall be constituted by rights, contracts or any other means which, either separately or in combination and having regard to the considerations of fact or law involved, confer the possibility of exercising decisive influence on an undertaking, in particular by:

(*a*) ownership or the right to use all or part of the assets of an undertaking;

(*b*) rights or contracts which confer decisive influence on the composition, voting or decisions of the organs of an undertaking.

4. Control is acquired by persons or undertakings which:

(*a*) are holders of the rights or entitled to rights under the contracts concerned; or

(*b*) while not being holders of such rights or entitled to rights under such contracts, have the power to exercise the rights deriving therefrom.

5. A concentration shall not be deemed to arise where:

(*a*) credit institutions or other financial institutions or insurance companies, the normal activities of which include transactions and dealing in securities for their own account or for the account of others, hold on a temporary basis securities which they have acquired in an undertaking with a view to reselling them, provided that they do not exercise voting rights in respect of those securities with a view to determining the competitive behaviour of that undertaking or provided that they exercise such voting rights only with a view to preparing the disposal of all or part of that undertaking or of its assets or the disposal of those securities and that any such disposal takes place within one year of the date of acquisition; that period may be extended by the Commission on request where such institutions or companies can show that the disposal was not reasonably possible within the period set;

(b) control is acquired by an office-holder according to the law of a Member State relating to liquidation, winding up, insolvency, cessation of payments, compositions or analogous proceedings;

(c) the operations referred to in paragraph 1(b) are carried out by the financial holding companies referred to in Article 5(3) of the Fourth Council Directive 78/660/EEC of 25 July 1978 on the annual accounts of certain types of companies[4], as last amended by Directive 84/569/EEC[5], provided however that the voting rights in respect of the holding are exercised, in particular in relation to the appointment of members of the management and supervisory bodies of the undertakings in which they have holdings, only to maintain the full value of those investments and not to determine directly or indirectly the competitive conduct of those undertakings.

Article 4

Prior notification of concentrations

1. Concentrations with a Community dimension defined in this Regulation shall be notified to the Commission not more than one week after the conclusion of the agreement, or the announcement of the public bid, or the acquisition of a controlling interest. That week shall begin when the first of those events occurs.

2. A concentration which consists of a merger within the meaning of Article 3(1)(a) or in the acquisition of joint control within the meaning of Article 3(1)(b) shall be notified jointly by the parties to the merger or by those acquiring joint control as the case may be. In all other cases, the notification shall be effected by the person or undertaking acquiring control of the whole or parts of one or more undertakings.

3. Where the Commission finds that a notified concentration falls within the scope of this Regulation, it shall publish the fact of the notification, at the same time indicating the names of the parties, the nature of the concentration and the economic sectors involved. The Commission shall take account of the legitimate interest of undertakings in the protection of their business secrets.

Article 5

Calculation of turnover

1. Aggregate turnover within the meaning of Article 1(2) shall comprise the amounts derived by the undertakings concerned in the preceding financial year from the sale of products and the provision of services falling within the undertakings' ordinary activities after deduction of sales rebates and of value added tax and other taxes directly related to turnover. The aggregate turnover of an undertaking concerned shall not include the sale of products or the provision of services between any of the undertakings referred to in paragraph 4.

Turnover, in the Community or in a Member State, shall comprise products sold and services provided to undertakings or consumers, in the Community or in that Member State as the case may be.

2. By way of derogation from paragraph 1, where the concentration consists in the acquisition of parts, whether or not constituted as legal entities, of one or more undertakings, only the turnover relating to the parts which are the subject of the transaction shall be taken into account with regard to the seller or sellers.

However, two or more transactions within the meaning of the first subparagraph which take place within a two-year period between the same persons or undertakings shall be treated as one and the same concentration arising on the date of the last transaction.

3. In place of turnover the following shall be used:

(a) for credit institutions and other financial institutions, as regards Article 1(2)(a), one-tenth of their total assets.

As regards Article 1(2)(b) and the final part of Article 1(2), total Community-wide turnover shall be replaced by one-tenth of total assets multiplied by the ratio between loans and advances to credit institutions and customers in transactions with Community residents and the total sum of those loans and advances.

As regards the final part of Article 1(2), total turnover within one Member State shall be replaced by one-tenth of total assets multiplied by the ratio between loans and advances to credit institutions and customers in transactions with residents of that Member State and the total sum of those loans and advances;

(b) for insurance undertakings, the value of gross premiums written which shall comprise all amounts received and receivable in respect of insurance contracts issued by or on behalf of the insurance undertakings, including also outgoing reinsurance premiums, and after deduction of taxes and parafiscal contributions or levies charged by reference to the amounts of individual premiums or the total volume of premiums; as regards Article 1(2)(b) and the final part of Article 1(2), gross premiums received from Community residents and from residents of one Member State respectively shall be taken into account.

4. Without prejudice to paragraph 2, the aggregate turnover of an undertaking concerned within the meaning of Article 1(2) shall be calculated by adding together the respective turnovers of the following:

(*a*) the undertaking concerned;

(*b*) those undertakings in which the undertaking concerned, directly or indirectly:

- owns more than half the capital or business assets, or

- has the power to exercise more than half the voting rights, or

- has the power to appoint more than half the members of the supervisory board, the administrative board or bodies legally representing the undertakings, or

- has the right to manage the undertakings' affairs;

(*c*) those undertakings which have in the undertaking concerned the rights or powers listed in (b);

(*d*) those undertakings in which an undertaking as referred to in (c) has the rights or powers listed in (b);

(*e*) those undertakings in which two or more undertakings as referred to in (a) to (d) jointly have the rights or powers listed in (b).

5. Where undertakings concerned by the concentration jointly have the rights or powers listed in paragraph 4(b), in calculating the aggregate turnover of the undertakings concerned for the purposes of Article 1(2):

(*a*) no account shall be taken of the turnover resulting from the sale of products or the provision of services between the joint undertaking and each of the undertakings concerned or any other undertaking connected with any one of them, as set out in paragraph 4(b) to (e);

(*b*) account shall be taken of the turnover resulting from the sale of products and the provision of services between the joint undertaking and any third undertakings. This turnover shall be apportioned equally amongst the undertakings concerned.

Article 6

Examination of the notification and initiation of proceedings

1. The Commission shall examine the notification as soon as it is received.

(a) Where it concludes that the concentration notified does not fall within the scope of this Regulation, it shall record that finding by means of a decision.

(b) Where it finds that the concentration notified, although falling within the scope of this Regulation, does not raise serious doubts as to its compatibility with the common market, it shall decide not to oppose it and shall declare that it is compatible with the common market.

(c) If, on the other hand, it finds that the concentration notified falls within the scope of this Regulation and raises serious doubts as to its compatibility with the common market, it shall decide to initiate proceedings.

2. The Commission shall notify its decision to the undertakings concerned and the competent authorities of the Member States without delay.

Article 7

Suspension of concentrations

1. For the purposes of paragraph 2 a concentration as defined in Article 1 shall not be put into effect either before its notification or within the first three weeks following its notification.

2. Where the Commission, following a preliminary examination of the notification within the period provided for in paragraph 1, finds it necessary in order to ensure the full effectiveness of any decision taken later pursuant to Article 8(3) and (4), it may decide on its own initiative to continue the suspension of a concentration in whole or in part until it takes a final decision, or to take other interim measures to that effect.

3. Paragraphs 1 and 2 shall not prevent the implementation of a public bid which has been notified to the Commission in accordance with Article 4(1), provided that the acquirer does not exercise the voting rights attached to the securities in question or does so only to maintain the full value of those investments and on the basis of a derogation granted by the Commission under paragraph 4.

4. The Commission may, on request, grant a derogation from the obligations imposed in paragraphs 1, 2 or 3 in order to prevent serious

damage to one or more undertakings concerned by concentration or to a third party. That derogation may be made subject to conditions and obligations in order to ensure conditions of effective competition. A derogation may be applied for and granted at any time, even before notification or after the transaction.

5. The validity of any transaction carried out in contravention of paragraph 1 or 2 shall be dependent on a decision pursuant to Article 6(1)(b) or Article 8(2) or (3) or on a presumption pursuant to Article 10(6).

This Article shall, however, have no effect on the validity of transactions in securities including those convertible into other securities admitted to trading on a market which is regulated and supervised by authorities recognized by public bodies, operates regularly and is accessible directly or indirectly to the public, unless the buyer and seller knew or ought to have known that the transaction was carried out in contravention of paragraph 1 or 2.

Article 8

Powers of decision of the Commission

1. Without prejudice to Article 9, all proceedings initiated pursuant to Article 6(1)(c) shall be closed by means of a decision as provided for in paragraphs 2 to 5.

2. Where the Commission finds that, following modification by the undertakings concerned if necessary, a notified concentration fulfils the criterion laid down in Article 2(2), it shall issue a decision declaring the concentration compatible with the common market.

It may attach to its decision conditions and obligations intended to ensure that the undertakings concerned comply with the commitments they have entered into *vis-à-vis* the Commission with a view to modifying the original concentration plan. The decision declaring the concentration compatible shall also cover restrictions directly related and necessary to the implementation of the concentration.

3. Where the Commission finds that a concentration fulfils the criterion laid down in Article 2(3), it shall issue a decision declaring that the concentration is incompatible with the common market.

4. Where a concentration has already been implemented, the Commission may, in a decision pursuant to paragraph 3 or by separate decision, require the undertakings or assets brought together to be separated or the cessation of joint control or any other action that may be appropriate in order to restore conditions of effective competition.

5. The Commission may revoke the decision it has taken pursuant to paragraph 2 where:

(a) the declaration of compatibility is based on incorrect information for which one of the undertakings is responsible or where it has been obtained by deceit; or

(b) the undertakings concerned commit a breach of an obligation attached to the decision.

6. In the cases referred to in paragraph 5, the Commission may take a decision under paragraph 3, without being bound by the deadline referred to in Article 10(3).

Article 9

Referral to the competent authorities of the Member States

1. The Commission may, by means of a decision notified without delay to the undertakings concerned and the competent authorities of the other Member States, refer a notified concentration to the competent authorities of the Member State concerned in the following circumstances.

2. Within three weeks of the date of receipt of the copy of the notification a Member State may inform the Commission, which shall inform the undertakings concerned, that a concentration threatens to create or to strengthen a dominant position as a result of which effective competition would be significantly impeded on a market, within that Member State, which presents all the characteristics of a distinct market, be it a substantial part of the common market or not.

3. If the Commission considers that, having regard to the market for the products or services in question and the geographical reference market within the meaning of paragraph 7, there is such a distinct market and that such a threat exists, either:

(a) it shall itself deal with the case in order to maintain or restore effective competition on the market concerned; or

(b) it shall refer the case to the competent authorities of the Member State concerned with a view to the application of that State's national competition law.

If, however, the Commission considers that such a distinct market or threat does not exist it shall adopt a decision to that effect which it shall address to the Member State concerned.

4. A decision to refer or not to refer pursuant to paragraph 3 shall be taken:

(a) as a general rule within the six-week period provided for in Article 10(1), second subparagraph, where the Commission, pursuant to Article 6(1)(b), has not initiated proceedings; or

(b) within three months at most of the notification of the concentration concerned where the Commission has initiated proceedings under Article 6(1)(c), without taking the preparatory steps in order to adopt the necessary measures under Article 8(2), second subparagraph, (3) or (4) to maintain or restore effective competition on the market concerned.

5. If within the three months referred to in paragraph 4(b) the Commission, despite a reminder from the Member State concerned, has not taken a decision on referral in accordance with paragraph 3 nor has taken the preparatory steps referred to in paragraph 4(b), it shall be deemed to have taken a decision to refer the case to the Member State concerned in accordance with paragraph 3(b).

6. The publication of any report or the announcement of the findings of the examination of the concentration by the competent authority of the Member State concerned shall be effected not more than four months after the Commission's referral.

7. The geographical reference market shall consist of the area in which the undertakings concerned are involved in the supply and demand of products or services, in which the conditions of competition are sufficiently homogeneous and which can be distinguished from neighbouring areas because, in particular, conditions of competition are appreciably different in those areas. This assessment should take account in particular of the nature and characteristics of the products or services concerned, of the existence of entry barriers of consumer preferences, of appreciable differences of the undertakings' market shares between the area concerned and neighbouring areas or of substantial price differences.

8. In applying the provisions of this Article, the Member State concerned may take only the measures strictly necessary to safeguard or restore effective competition on the market concerned.

9. In accordance with the relevant provisions of the Treaty, any Member State may appeal to the Court of Justice, and in particular request the application of Article 186, for the purpose of applying its national competition law.

10. This Article will be reviewed before the end of the fourth year following that of the adoption of this Regulation.

Article 10

Time limits for initiating proceedings and for decisions

1. The decisions referred to in Article 6(1) must be taken within one month at most. That period shall begin on the day following that of the receipt of a notification or, if the information to be supplied with the notification is incomplete, on the day following that of the receipt of the complete information.

That period shall be increased to six weeks if the Commission receives a request from a Member State in accordance with Article 9(2).

2. Decisions taken pursuant to Article 8(2) concerning notified concentrations must be taken as soon as it appears that the serious doubts referred to in Article 6(1)(c) have been removed, particularly as a result of modifications made by the undertakings concerned, and at the latest by the deadline laid down in paragraph 3.

3. Without prejudice to Article 8(6), decisions taken pursuant to Article 8(3) concerning notified concentrations must be taken within not more than four months of the date on which proceedings are initiated.

4. The period set by paragraph 3 shall exceptionally be suspended where, owing to circumstances for which one of the undertakings involved in the concentration is responsible, the Commission has had to request information by decision pursuant to Article 11 or to order an investigation by decision pursuant to Article 13.

5. Where the Court of Justice gives a judgment which annuls the whole or part of a Commission decision taken under this Regulation, the periods laid down in this Regulation shall start again from the date of the judgment.

6. Where the Commission has not taken a decision in accordance with Article 6(1)(b) or (c) or Article 8(2) or (3) within the deadlines set in paragraphs 1 and 3 respectively, the concentration shall be deemed to have been declared compatible with the common market, without prejudice to Article 9.

Article 11

Requests for information

1. In carrying out the duties assigned to it by this Regulation, the

Commission may obtain all necessary information from the Governments and competent authorities of the Member States, from the persons referred to in Article 3(1)(b), and from undertakings and associations of undertakings.

2. When sending a request for information to a person, an undertaking or an association of undertakings, the Commission shall at the same time send a copy of the request to the competent authority of the Member State within the territory of which the residence of the person or the seat of the undertaking or association of undertakings is situated.

3. In its request the Commission shall state the legal basis and the purpose of the request and also the penalties provided for in Article 14(1)(c) for supplying incorrect information.

4. The information requested shall be provided, in the case of undertakings, by their owners or their representatives and, in the case of legal persons, companies or firms, or of associations having no legal personality, by the persons authorised to represent them by law or by their statutes.

5. Where a person, an undertaking or an association of undertakings does not provide the information requested within the period fixed by the Commission or provides incomplete information, the Commission shall by decision require the information to be provided. The decision shall specify what information is required, fix an appropriate period within which it is to be supplied and state the penalties provided for in Articles 14(1)(c) and 15(1)(a) and the right to have the decision reviewed by the Court of Justice.

6. The Commission shall at the same time send a copy of its decision to the competent authority of the Member State within the territory of which the residence of the person or the seat of the undertaking or association of undertakings is situated.

Article 12

Investigations by the authorities of the Member States

1. At the request of the Commission, the competent authorities of the Member States shall undertake the investigations which the Commission considers to be necessary under Article 13(1), or which it has been ordered by decision pursuant to Article 13(3). The officials of the competent authorities of the Member States responsible for conducting those investigations shall exercise their powers upon production of an authorisation in writing issued by the competent authority of the Member State within the territory of which the investigation is to be

carried out. Such authorisation shall specify the subject matter and purpose of the investigation.

2. If so requested by the Commission or by the competent authority of the Member State within the territory of which the investigation is to be carried out, officials of the Commission may assist the officials of that authority in carrying out their duties.

Article 13

Investigative powers of the Commission

1. In carrying out the duties assigned to it by this Regulation, the Commission may undertake all necessary investigations into undertakings and associations of undertakings.

To that end the officials authorised by the Commission shall be empowered:

(a) to examine the books and other business records;

(b) to take or demand copies of or extracts from the books and business records;

(c) to ask of oral explanations on the spot;

(d) to enter any premises, land and means of transport of undertakings.

2. The officials of the Commission authorised to carry out the investigations shall exercise their powers on production of an authorisation in writing specifying the subject matter and purpose of the investigation and the penalties provided for in Article 14(1)(d) in cases where production of the required books or other business records is incomplete. In good time before the investigation, the Commission shall inform, in writing, the competent authority of the Member State within the territory of which the investigation is to be carried out of the investigation and of the identities of the authorised officials.

3. Undertakings and associations of undertakings shall submit to investigations ordered by decision of the Commission. The decision shall specify the subject matter and purpose of the investigation, appoint the date on which it shall begin and state the penalties provided for in Articles 14(1)(d) and 15(1)(b) and the right to have the decision reviewed by the Court of Justice.

4. The Commission shall in good time and in writing inform the competent authority of the Member State within the territory of which the investigation is to be carried out of its intention of taking a decision

pursuant to paragraph 3. It shall hear the competent authority before taking its decision.

5. Officials of the competent authority of the Member State within the territory of which the investigation is to be carried out may, at the request of that authority or of the Commission, assist the officials of the Commission in carrying out their duties.

6. Where an undertaking or association of undertakings opposes an investigation ordered pursuant to this Article, the Member State concerned shall afford the necessary assistance to the officials authorised by the Commission to enable them to carry out their investigation. To this end the Member States shall, after consulting the Commission, take the necessary measures within one year of the entry into force of this Regulation.

Article 14

Fines

1. The Commission may by decision impose on the persons referred to in Article 3(1)(b), undertakings or associations of undertakings fines of from ECU 1 000 to 50 000 where intentionally or negligently:

(a) they fail to notify a concentration in accordance with Article 4;

(b) they supply incorrect or misleading information in a notification pursuant to Article 4;

(c) they supply incorrect information in response to a request made pursuant to Article 11 or fail to supply information within the period fixed by a decision taken pursuant to Article 11;

(d) they produce the required books or other business records in incomplete form during investigations under Article 12 or 13, or refuse to submit to an investigation ordered by decision taken pursuant to Article 13.

2. The Commission may by decision impose fines not exceeding 10% of the aggregate turnover of the undertakings concerned within the meaning of Article 5 on the persons or undertakings concerned where, either intentionally or negligently, they:

(a) fail to comply with an obligation imposed by decision pursuant to Articles 7(4) or 8(2), second subparagraph;

(b) put into effect a concentration in breach of Article 7(1) or disregard a decision taken pursuant to Article 7(2);

(c) put into effect a concentration declared incompatible with the common market by decision pursuant to Article 8(3) or do not take the measures ordered by decision pursuant to Article 8(4).

3. In setting the amount of a fine, regard shall be had to the nature and gravity of the infringement.

4. Decisions taken pursuant to paragraphs 1 and 2 shall not be of criminal law nature.

Article 15

Periodic penalty payments

1. The Commission may by decision impose on the persons referred to in Article 3(1)(b), undertakings or associations of undertakings concerned periodic penalty payments of up to ECU 25 000 for each day of delay calculated from the date set in the decision, in order to compel them:

(a) to supply complete and correct information which it has requested by decision pursuant to Article 11;

(b) to submit to an investigation which it has ordered by decision pursuant to Article 13.

2. The Commission may by decision impose on the persons referred to in Article 3(1)(b) or on undertakings periodic penalty payments of up to ECU 100 000 for each day of delay calculated from the date set in the decision, in order to compel them:

(a) to comply with an obligation imposed by decision pursuant to Article 7(4) or Article 8(2), second subparagraph, or

(b) to apply the measures ordered by decision pursuant to Article 8(4).

3. Where the persons referred to in Article 3(1)(b), undertakings or associations of undertakings have satisfied the obligation which it was the purpose of the periodic penalty payment to enforce, the Commission may set the total amount of the periodic penalty payments at a lower figure than that which would arise under the original decision.

Article 16

Review by the Court of Justice

The Court of Justice shall have unlimited jurisdiction within the meaning of Article 172 of the Treaty to review decisions whereby the Commission has fixed a fine or periodic penalty payments; it may cancel, reduce or increase the fine or periodic penalty payments imposed.

Article 17

Professional secrecy

1. Information acquired as a result of the application of Articles 11, 12, 13 and 18 shall be used only for the purposes of the relevant request, investigation or hearing.

2. Without prejudice to Articles 4(3), 18 and 20, the Commission and the competent authorities of the Member States, their officials and other servants shall not disclose information they have acquired through the application of this Regulation of the kind covered by the obligation of professional secrecy.

3. Paragraphs 1 and 2 shall not prevent publication of general information or of surveys which do not contain information relating to particular undertakings or associations of undertakings.

Article 18

Hearing of the parties and of third persons

1. Before taking any decision provided for in Articles 7(2) and (4), Article 8(2), second subparagraph, and (3) to (5) and Articles 14 and 15, the Commission shall give the persons, undertakings and associations of undertakings concerned the opportunity, at every stage of the procedure up to the consultation of the Advisory Committee, of making known their views on the objections against them.

2. By way of derogation from paragraph 1, a decision to continue the suspension of a concentration or to grant a derogation from suspension as referred to in Article 7(2) or (4) may be taken provisionally, without the persons, undertakings or associations of undertakings concerned being given the opportunity to make known their views beforehand, provided that the Commission gives them that opportunity as soon as possible after having taken its decision.

3. The Commission shall base its decision only on objections on which the parties have been able to submit their observations. The rights of the defence shall be fully respected in the proceedings. Access to the file shall be open at least to the parties directly involved, subject to the legitimate interest of undertakings in the protection of their business secrets.

4. In so far as the Commission or the competent authorities of the Member States deem it necessary, they may also hear other natural or legal persons. Natural or legal persons showing a sufficient interest and especially members of the administrative or management bodies of the

undertakings concerned or the recognised representatives of their employees shall be entitled, upon application, to be heard.

Article 19

Liaison with the authorities of the Member States

1. The Commission shall transmit to the competent authorities of the Member States copies of notifications within three working days and, as soon as possible, copies of the most important documents lodged with or issued by the Commission pursuant to this Regulation.

2. The Commission shall carry out the procedures set out in this Regulation in close and constant liaison with the competent authorities of the Member States, which may express their views upon those procedures. For the purposes of Article 9 it shall obtain information from the competent authority of the Member State as referred to in paragraph 2 of that Article and give it the opportunity to make known its views at every stage of the procedure up to the adoption of a decision pursuant to paragraph 3 of that Article; to that end it shall give it access to the file.

3. An Advisory Committee on concentrations shall be consulted before any decision is taken pursuant to Article 8(2) to (5), 14 or 15, or any provisions are adopted pursuant to Article 23.

4. The Advisory Committee shall consist of representatives of the authorities of the Member States. Each Member State shall appoint one or two representatives; if unable to attend, they may be replaced by other representatives. At least one of the representatives of a Member State shall be competent in matters of restrictive practices and dominant positions.

5. Consultation shall take place at a joint meeting convened at the invitation of and chaired by the Commission. A summary of the case, together with an indication of the most important documents and a preliminary draft of the decision to be taken for each case considered, shall be sent with the invitation. The meeting shall take place not less than 14 days after the invitation has been sent. The Commission may in exceptional cases shorten that period as appropriate in order to avoid serious harm to one or more of the undertakings concerned by a concentration.

6. The Advisory Committee shall deliver an opinion on the Commission's draft decision, if necessary by taking a vote. The Advisory Committee may deliver an opinion even if some members are absent and unrepresented. The opinion shall be delivered in writing and appended to the draft decision. The Commission shall take the utmost account of

the opinion delivered by the Committee. It shall inform the Committee of the manner in which its opinion has been taken into account.

7. The Advisory Committee may recommend publication of the opinion. The Commission may carry out such publication. The decision to publish shall take due account of the legitimate interest of undertakings in the protection of their business secrets and of the interest of the undertakings concerned in such publication's taking place.

Article 20

Publication of decisions

1. The Commission shall publish the decisions which it takes pursuant to Article 8(2) to (5) in the *Official Journal of the European Communities*.

2. The publication shall state the names of the parties and the main content of the decision; it shall have regard to the legitimate interest of undertakings in the protection of their business secrets.

Article 21

Jurisdiction

1. Subject to review by the Court of Justice, the Commission shall have sole jurisdiction to take the decisions provided for in this Regulation.

2. No Member State shall apply its national legislation on competition to any consideration that has a Community dimension.

The first subparagraph shall be without prejudice to any Member State's power to carry out any enquiries necessary for the application of Article 9(2) or, after referral, pursuant to Article 9(3), first subparagraph, indent (b), or (5), to take measures strictly necessary for the application of Article 9(8).

3. Notwithstanding paragraphs 1 and 2, Member States may take appropriate measures to protect legitimate interests other than those taken into consideration by this Regulation and compatible with the general principles and other provisions of Community law.

Public security, plurality of the media and prudential rules shall be regarded as legitimate interests within the meaning of the first subparagraph.

Any other public interest must be communicated to the Commission by the Member State concerned and shall be recognised by the Commission after an assessment of its compatibility with the general principles and other provisions of Community law before the measures referred to above may be taken. The Commission shall inform the Member State concerned of its decision within one month of that communication.

Article 22

Application of the Regulation

1. This Regulation alone shall apply to concentrations as defined in Article 3.

2. Regulations No 17[6], (EEC) No 1017/68[7], (EEC) No 4056/86[8] and (EEC) No 3975/87[9] shall not apply to concentrations as defined in Article 3.

3. If the Commission finds, at the request of a Member State, that a concentration as defined in Article 3 that has no Community dimension within the meaning of Article 1 creates or strengthens a dominant position as a result of which effective competition would be significantly impeded within the territory of the Member State concerned it may, in so far as the concentration affects trade between Member States, adopt the decisions provided for in Article 8(2), second subparagraph, (3) and (4).

4. Articles 2(1)(a) and (b), 5, 6, 8 and 10 to 20 shall apply. The period within which proceedings may be initiated pursuant to Article 10(1) shall begin on the date of the receipt of the request from the Member State. The request must be made within one month at most of the date on which the concentration was made known to the Member State or effected. This period shall begin on the date of the first of those events.

5. Pursuant to paragraph 3 the Commission shall take only the measures strictly necessary to maintain or store effective competition within the territory of the Member State at the request of which it intervenes.

6. Paragraphs 3 to 5 shall continue to apply until the thresholds referred to in Article 1(2) have been reviewed.

Article 23

Implementing provisions

The Commission shall have the power to adopt implementing provisions concerning the form, content and other details of notifications pursuant to Article 4, time limits pursuant to Article 10, and hearings pursuant to Article 18.

Article 24

Relations with non-member countries

1. The Member States shall inform the Commission of any general difficulties encountered by their undertakings with concentrations as defined in Article 3 in a non-member country.

2. Initially not more than one year after the entry into force of this Regulation and thereafter periodically the Commission shall draw up a report examining the treatment accorded to Community undertakings, in the terms referred to in paragraphs 3 and 4, as regards concentrations in non-member countries. The Commission shall submit those reports to the Council, together with any recommendations.

3. Whenever it appears to the Commission, either on the basis of the reports referred to in paragraph 2 or on the basis of other information, that a non-member country does not grant Community undertakings treatment comparable to that granted by the Community to undertakings from that non-member country, the Commission may submit proposals to the Council for an appropriate mandate for negotiation with a view to obtaining comparable treatment for Community undertakings.

4. Measures taken under this Article shall comply with the obligations of the Community or of the Member States, without prejudice to Article 234 of the Treaty, under international agreements, whether bilateral or multilateral.

Article 25

Entry into force

1. This Regulation shall enter into force on 21 September 1990.

2. This Regulation shall not apply to any concentration which was the subject of an agreement or announcement or where control was acquired within the meaning of Article 4(1) before the date of this Regulation's entry into force and it shall not in any circumstances apply to any concentration in respect of which proceedings were initiated before that date by a Member State's authority with responsibility for competition.

This Regulation shall be binding in its entirety and directly applicable in all Member States.

Done at Brussels, 21 December 1989.

For the Council

The President

E. Cresson

FOOTNOTES

1. OJ No C 130, 19.5.88, p.4.
2. OJ No C 309, 5.12.88, p.55.
3. OJ No C 208, 8.8.88, p.11.
4. OJ No L 222, 14.8.78, p.11.
5. OJ No L 314, 4.12.84, p.28.
6. OJ No 13, 21.2.62, p.204.
7. OJ No L 175, 23.7.68, p.1.
8. OJ No L 378, 31.12.86, p.4.
9. OJ No L 374, 31.12.87, p.1.

COMMISSION REGULATION (EEC) No 2367/90

of 25 July 1990

on the notifications, time limits and hearings provided for in Council Regulation (EEC) No 4064/89 on the control of concentrations between undertakings

(OJ No L 219, 14.8.90, p. 5)

The Commission of the European Communities,

Having regard to the Treaty establishing the European Economic Community,

Having regard to Council Regulation (EEC) No 4064/89 of 21 December 1989 on the control of concentrations between undertakings[1], and in particular Article 23 thereof,

Having regard to Council Regulation No 17 of 6 February 1962, First Regulation implementing Articles 85 and 86 of the Treaty[2], as last amended by the Act of Accession of Spain and Portugal, and in particular Article 24 thereof,

Having regard to Council Regulation (EEC) No 1017/68 of 19 July 1968 applying rules of competition to transport by rail, road and inland waterway[3], as last amended by the Act of Accession of Spain and Portugal, and in particular Article 29 thereof,

Having regard to Council Regulation (EEC) No 4056/86 of 22 December 1986 laying down detailed rules for the application of Articles 85 and 86 of the Treaty to maritime transport[4], and in particular Article 26 thereof,

Having regard to Council Regulation (EEC) No 3975/87 of 14 December 1987 laying down detailed rules for the application of the competition rules to undertakings in air transport[5], and in particular Article 19 thereof,

Having consulted the Advisory Committee on Concentrations, as well as the Advisory Committees on Restrictive Practices and Monopolies in the Transport Industry, in Maritime Transport and in Air Transport,

1. Whereas Article 23 of Regulation (EEC) No 4064/89 empowers the Commission to adopt implementing provisions concerning the form, content and other details of notifications pursuant to Article 4, time limits pursuant to Article 10, and hearings pursuant to Article 18;

2. Whereas Regulation (EEC) No 4064/89 is based on the principle of compulsory notification of concentrations before they are put into effect; whereas, on the one hand, a notification has important legal consequences which are favourable to the parties, while, on the other hand, failure to comply with the obligation to notify renders the parties liable to a fine and may also entail civil law disadvantages for them; whereas it is therefore necessary in the interests of legal certainty to define precisely the subject matter and content of the information to be provided in the notification;

3. Whereas it is for the parties concerned to make full and honest disclosure to the Commission of the facts and circumstances which are relevant for taking a decision on the notified concentration;

4. Whereas in order to simplify and expedite examination of the notification it is desirable to prescribe that a form be used;

5. Whereas since notification sets in motion legal time limits for initiating proceedings and for decisions, the conditions governing such time limits and the time when they became effective must also be determined;

6. Whereas rules must be laid down in the interests of legal certainty for calculating the time limits provided for in Regulation (EEC) No 4064/89; whereas in particular the beginning and end of the period and the circumstances suspending the running of the period must be determined; whereas the provisions should be based on the principles of

Regulation (EEC, Euratom) No 1182/71 of 3 June 1971 determining the rules applicable to periods, dates and time limits[6], subject to certain adaptations made necessary by the exceptionally short legal time limits referred to above;

7. Whereas the provisions relating to the Commission's procedure must be framed in such way as to safeguard fully the right to be heard and the rights of defence;

8. Whereas the Commission will give the parties concerned, if they so request, an opportunity before notification to discuss the intended concentration informally and in strict confidence; whereas in addition it will, after notification, maintain close contact with the parties concerned to the extent necessary to discuss with them any practical or legal problems which it discovers on a first examination of the case and if possible to remove such problems by mutual agreement;

9. Whereas in accordance with the principle of the right to be heard, the parties concerned must be given the opportunity to submit their comments on all the objections which the Commission proposes to take into account in its decisions;

10. Whereas third parties having sufficient interest must also be given the opportunity of expressing their views where they make a written application;

11. Whereas the various persons entitled to submit comments should do so in writing, both in their own interest and in the interest of good administration, without prejudice to their right to request an oral hearing where appropriate to supplement the written procedure; whereas in urgent cases, however, the Commission must be able to proceed immediately to oral hearings of the parties concerned or third parties; whereas in such cases the persons to be heard must have the right to confirm their oral statements in writing;

12. Whereas it is necessary to define the rights of persons who are to be heard, to what extent they should be granted access to the Commission's file and on what conditions they may be represented or assisted;

13. Whereas it is also necessary to define the rules for fixing and calculating the time limits for reply fixed by the Commission;

14. Whereas the Advisory Committee on Concentrations shall deliver its opinion on the basis of a preliminary draft decision; whereas it must therefore be consulted on a case after the inquiry into that case has been completed; whereas such consultation does not, however, prevent the Commission from re-opening an inquiry if need be,

Has adopted this Regulation:

Section I

Notifications

Article 1

Persons entitled to submit notifications

1. Notifications shall be submitted by the persons or undertakings referred to in Article 4(2) of Regulation (EEC) No 4064/89.

2. Where notifications are signed by representatives of persons or of undertakings, such representatives shall produce written proof that they are authorised to act.

3. Joint notifications should be submitted by a joint representative who is authorised to transmit and to receive documents on behalf of all notifying parties.

Article 2

Submission of notification

1. Notifications shall be submitted in the manner prescribed by form CO as shown in Annex I. Joint notification shall be submitted on a single form.

2. Twenty copies of each notification and fifteen copies of the supporting documents shall be submitted to the Commission at the address indicated in form CO.

3. The supporting documents shall be either originals or copies of the originals; in the latter case the notifying parties shall confirm that they are true and complete.

4. Notifications shall be in one of the official languages of the Community. This language shall also be the language of the proceeding for the notifying parties. Supporting documents shall be submitted in their original language. Where the original language is not one of the official languages, a translation into the language of the proceeding shall be attached.

Article 3

Information to be provided

1. Notifications shall contain the information requested by form CO. The information must be correct and complete.

2. Material changes in the facts specified in the notification which the notifying parties know or ought to have known must be communicated to the Commission voluntarily and without delay.

3. Incorrect or misleading information shall be deemed to be incomplete information.

Article 4

Effective date of notifications

1. Subject to paragraph 2 notifications shall become effective on the date on which they are received by the Commission.

2. Subject to paragraph 3, where the information contained in the notification is incomplete in a material respect, the Commission shall without delay inform the notifying parties or the joint representative in writing and shall fix an appropriate time limit for the completion of the information; in such cases, the notification shall become effective on the date on which the complete information is received by the Commission.

3. The Commission may dispense with the obligation to provide any particular information requested by form CO where the Commission considers that such information is not necessary for the examination of the case.

4. The Commission shall without delay acknowledge in writing to the notifying parties or the joint representative receipt of the notification and of any reply to a letter sent by the Commission pursuant to paragraph 2 above.

Article 5

Conversion of notifications

1. Where the Commission finds that the operation notified does not constitute a concentration within the meaning of Article 3 of Regulation (EEC) No 4064/89 it shall inform the notifying parties or the joint representative in writing. In such a case, the Commission may, if requested by the notifying parties, as appropriate and subject to paragraph 2 below, treat the notification as an application within the meaning of Article 2 or a notification within the meaning of Article 4 of Regulation No 17, as an application within the meaning of Article 12 or a notification within the meaning of Article 14 of Regulation (EEC) No 1017/68, as an application within the meaning of Article 12 of Regulation (EEC) No 4056/86 or as an application within the meaning of Article 3(2) or of Article 5 of Regulation (EEC) No 3975/87.

2. In cases referred to in paragraph 1, second sentence, the Commission may require that the information given in the notification be supplemented within an appropriate time limit fixed by it in so far as this is necessary for assessing the operation on the basis of the abovementioned Regulations. The application or notification shall be deemed to fulfil the requirements of such Regulations from the date of the original notification where the additional information is received by the Commission within the time limit fixed.

Section II

Time limits for initiating proceedings and for decisions

Article 6

Beginning of the time limit

1. The periods referred to in Article 10(1) of Regulation (EEC) No 4064/89 shall start at the beginning of the day following the effective date of the notification, within the meaning of Article 4(1) and (2) of this Regulation.

2. The period referred to in Article 10(3) of Regulation (EEC) No 4064/89 shall start at the beginning of the day following the day on which proceedings were initiated.

3. Where the first day of a period is not a working day within the meaning of Article 19, the period shall start at the beginning of the following working day.

Article 7

End of the time limit

1. The period referred to in the first subparagraph of Article 10(1) of Regulation (EEC) No 4064/89 shall end with the expiry of the day which in the month following that in which the period began falls on the same date as the day from which the period runs. Where such a day does not occur in that month, the period shall end with the expiry of the last day of that month.

2. The period referred to in the second sub-paragraph of Article 10(1) of Regulation (EEC) No 4064/89 shall end with the expiry of the day which in the sixth week following that in which the period began is the same day of the week as the day from which the period runs.

3. The period referred to in Article 10(3) of Regulation (EEC) No 4064/89 shall end with the expiry of the day which in the fourth month following that in which the period began falls on the same date as the day from

which the period runs. Where such a day does not occur in that month, the period shall end with the expiry of the last day of that month.

4. Where the last day of the period is not a working day within the meaning of Article 19, the period shall end with the expiry of the following working day.

5. Paragraphs 2 to 4 above shall be subject to the provisions of Article 8.

Article 8

Addition of holidays

Where public holidays or other holidays of the Commission as defined in Article 19 fall within the periods referred to in Article 10(1) and in Article 10(3) of Regulation (EEC) No 4064/89, these periods shall be extended by a corresponding number of days.

Article 9

Suspension of the time limit

1. The period referred to in Article 10(3) of Regulation (EEC) No 4064/89 shall be suspended where the Commission, pursuant to Articles 11(5) or 13(3) of the same Regulation, has to take a decision because:

(a) Information which the Commission has requested pursuant to Article 11(2) of Regulation (EEC) No 4064/89 from an undertaking involved in a concentration is not provided or not provided in full within the time limit fixed by the Commission;

(b) an undertaking involved in the concentration has refused to submit to an investigation deemed necessary by the Commission on the basis of Article 13(1) of Regulation (EEC) No 4064/89 or to cooperate in the carrying out of such an investigation in accordance with the abovementioned provision;

(c) the notifying parties have failed to inform the Commission of material changes in the facts specified in the notification.

2. The period referred to in Article 10(3) of Regulation (EEC) No 4064/89 shall be suspended:

(a) in the cases referred to in subparagraph 1(a) above, for the period between the end of the time limit fixed in the request for information and the receipt of the complete and correct information required by decision;

(b) in the cases referred to in subparagraph 1(b) above, for the period between the unsuccessful attempt to carry out the investigation and the completion of the investigation ordered by decision;

(c) in the cases referred to in subparagraph 1(c) above, for the period between the occurrence of the change in the facts referred to therein and the receipt of the complete and correct information requested by decision or the completion of the investigation ordered by decision.

3. The suspension of the time limit shall begin on the day following that on which the event causing the suspension occurred. It shall end with the expiry of the day on which the reason for suspension is removed. Where such day is not a working day within the meaning of Article 19, the suspension of the time limit shall end with the expiry of the following working day.

Article 10

Compliance with the time limit

The time limits referred to in Article 10(1) and (3) of Regulation (EEC) No 4064/89 shall be met where the Commission has taken the relevant decision before the end of the period. Notification of the decision to the undertakings concerned must follow without delay.

Section III

Hearing of the parties and of third parties

Article 11

Decisions on the suspension of concentrations

1. Where the Commission intends to take a decision under Article 7(2) of Regulation (EEC) No 4064/89 or a decision under Article 7(4) of that Regulation which adversely affects the parties, it shall, pursuant to Article 18(1) of that Regulation, inform the parties concerned in writing of its objections and shall fix a time limit within which they may make known their views.

2. Where the Commission pursuant to Article 18(2) of Regulation (EEC) No 4064/89 has taken a decision referred to in paragraph 1 provisionally without having given the parties concerned the opportunity to make known their views, it shall without delay and in any event before the expiry of the suspension send them the text of the provisional decision and shall fix a time limit within which they may make known their views.

Once the parties concerned have made known their views, the Commission shall take a final decision annulling, amending or confirming the provisional decision. Where the parties concerned have not made known their view within the time limit fixed, the Commission's provisional decision shall become final with the expiry of that period.

3. The parties concerned shall make known their views in writing or orally within the time limit fixed. They may confirm their oral statements in writing.

Article 12

Decisions on the substance of the case

1. Where the Commission intends to take a decision pursuant to Article 8(2), second subparagraph, Article 8(3)(4) and (5) [sic], Article 14 or Article 15 of Regulation (EEC) No 4064/89, it shall, before consulting the Advisory Committee on Concentrations, hold a hearing of the parties concerned pursuant to Article 18 of that Regulation.

2. The Commission shall inform the parties concerned in writing of its objections. The communication shall be addressed to the notifying parties or to the joint representative. The Commission shall, when giving notice of objections, fix a time limit within which the parties concerned may inform the Commission of their views.

3. Having informed the parties of its objections, the Commission shall upon request give the parties concerned access to the file for the purposes of preparing their observations. Documents shall not be accessible in so far as they contain business secrets of other parties concerned or of third parties, or other confidential information including sensitive commercial information the disclosure of which would have a significant adverse effect on the supplier of such information or where they are internal documents of the authorities.

4. The parties concerned shall, within the time limit fixed, make known in writing their views on the Commission's objections. They may in their written comments set out all matters relevant to the case and may attach any relevant documents in proof of the facts set out. They may also propose that the Commission hear persons who may corroborate those facts.

Article 13

Oral hearings

1. The Commission shall afford parties concerned who have so requested in their written comments the opportunity to put forward their arguments orally, if those persons show a sufficient interest or if the Commission proposes to impose a fine or periodic penalty payment on

them. It may also in other cases afford the parties concerned the opportunity of expressing their views orally.

2. The Commission shall summon the persons to be heard to attend on such date as it shall appoint.

3. It shall forthwith transmit a copy of the summons to the competent authorities of the Member States, who may appoint an official to take part in the hearing.

Article 14

Hearings

1. Hearings shall be conducted by persons appointed by the Commission for that purpose.

2. Persons summoned to attend shall either appear in person or be represented by legal representatives or representatives authorised by their constitution. Undertakings and associations of undertakings may be represented by a duly authorised agent appointed from among their permanent staff.

3. Persons heard by the Commission may be assisted by lawyers or university teachers who are entitled to plead before the Court of Justice of the European Communities in accordance with Article 17 of the Protocol on the Statute (EEC) of the Court of Justice, or by other qualified persons.

4. Hearings shall not be public. Persons shall be heard separately or in the presence of other persons summoned to attend. In the latter case, regard shall be had to the legitimate interest of the undertakings in the protection of their business secrets.

5. The statements made by each person heard shall be recorded.

Article 15

Hearing of third parties

1. If natural or legal persons showing a sufficient interest, and especially members of the administrative or management organs of the undertakings concerned or recognised workers' representatives of those undertakings, apply in writing to be heard pursuant to the second sentence of Article 18(4) of Regulation (EEC) No 4064/89, the Commission shall inform them in writing of the nature and subject matter of the procedure and shall fix a time limit within which they may make known their views.

2. The third parties referred to in paragraph 1 above shall make known

their views in writing or orally within the time limit fixed. They may confirm their oral statements in writing.

3. The Commission may likewise afford to any other third parties the opportunity of expressing their views.

Section IV

Miscellaneous provisions

Article 16

Transmission of documents

1. Transmission of documents and summonses from the Commission to the addressees may be effected in any of the following ways:

(a) delivery by hand against receipt;

(b) registered letter with acknowledgement of receipt;

(c) telefax with a request for acknowledgement of receipt;

(d) telex.

2. Subject to Article 18(1), paragraph 1 above also applies to the transmission of documents from the parties concerned or from third parties to the Commission.

3. Where a document is sent by telex or by telefax, it shall be presumed that it has been received by the addressee on the day on which it was sent.

Article 17

Setting of time limits

1. In fixing the time limits provided for in Articles 4(2), 5(2), 11(1) and (2), 12(2) and 15(1), the Commission shall have regard to the time required for preparation of statements and to the urgency of the case. It shall also take account of public holidays in the country of receipt of the Commission's communication.

2. The day on which the addressee received a communication shall not be taken into account for the purpose of fixing time limits.

Article 18

Receipt of documents by the Commission

1. Subject to Article 4(1), notifications must be delivered to the Commission at the address indicated in form CO or have been

dispatched by registered letter before expiry of the period referred to in Article 4(1) of Regulation (EEC) No 4064/89. Additional information requested to complete notifications pursuant to Article 4(2) or to supplement notifications pursuant to Article 5(2) of this Regulation must reach the Commission at the aforesaid or have been dispatched by registered letter before the expiry of the time limit fixed in each case. Written comments on Commission communications pursuant to Articles 11(1) and (2), 12(2) and 15(1) must be delivered to the Commission at the aforesaid address before the time limit fixed in each case.

2. Where the last day of a period referred to in paragraph 1 is a day by which documents must be received and that day is not a working day within the meaning of Article 19, the period shall end with the expiry of the following working day.

3. Where the last day of a period referred to in paragraph 1 is a day by which documents must be dispatched and that day is a Saturday, Sunday or public holiday in the country of dispatch, the period shall end with the expiry of the following working day in that country.

Article 19

Definition of Commission working days

The term 'working days' in Articles 6(3), 7(4), 9(3) and 18(2) means all days other than Saturdays, Sundays, public holidays set out in Annex II and other holidays as determined by the Commission and published in the *Official Journal of the European Communities* before the beginning of each year.

Article 20

Entry into force

This Regulation shall enter into force on 21 September 1990.

This Regulation shall be binding in its entirety and directly applicable in all Member States.

Done at Brussels, 25 July 1990.

For the Commission

Leon Brittan

Vice-President

Annex I

Form CO relating to the notification of a concentration pursuant to Council Regulation (EEC) No 4064/89

A. Introduction

This form specifies the information to be provided by an undertaking or undertakings when notifying the Commission of a concentration with a Community dimension. A 'concentration' is defined in Article 3 and 'Community dimension' by Article 1 of Regulation (EEC) No 4064/89.

Your attention is particularly drawn to Regulation (EEC) No 4064/89 and to Commission Regulation (EEC) No 2367/90. In particular you should note that:

(a) all information requested by this form must be provided. However if, in good faith, you are unable to provide a response to a question or can only respond to a limited extent on the basis of available information, indicate this and give reasons. If you consider that any particular information requested by this form may not be necessary for the Commission's examination of the case, you may ask the Commission to dispense with the obligation to provide that information, under Article 4(3) of Regulation (EEC) No 2367/90;

(b) unless all sections are completed in full or good reasons are given explaining why it has not been possible to complete unanswered questions (for example, because of the unavailability of information on a target company during a contested bid) the notification will be incomplete and will only become effective on the date on which all the information is received. The notification will be deemed to be incomplete if information is incorrect or misleading;

(c) incorrect or misleading information where supplied intentionally or negligently could make you liable to a fine.

B. Who must notify

In the case of a merger (within the meaning of Article 3(1)(a) of Regulation (EEC) No 4064/89 or the acquisition of joint control in an undertaking within the meaning of Article 3(1)(b) of Regulation (EEC) No 4064/89, the notification shall be completed jointly by the parties to the merger or by those acquiring joint control as the case may be.

In the case of the acquisition of a controlling interest in an undertaking by another, the acquirer must complete the notification.

In the case of a public bid to acquire an undertaking, the bidder must complete the notification.

Each party completing the notification is responsible for the accuracy of the information which it provides.

For the purposes of this form 'the parties to the concentration' ('the parties') includes the undertaking in which a controlling interest is being acquired or which is the subject of a public bid.

C. Supporting documentation

The completed notification must be accompanied by the following:

(a) copies of the final or most recent versions of all documents bringing about the concentration, whether by agreement between the parties concerned, acquisition of a controlling interest or a public bid;

(b) in a public bid, a copy of the offer document. If unavailable on notification it should be submitted as soon as possible and not later than when it is posted to shareholders;

(c) copies of the most recent annual reports and accounts of all the parties to the concentration;

(d) copies of reports or analyses which have been prepared for the purposes of the concentration and from which information has been taken in order to provide the information requested in sections 5 and 6;

(e) a list and short description of the contents of all other analyses, reports, studies and surveys prepared by or for any of the notifying parties for the purpose of assessing or analysing the proposed concentration with respect to competitive conditions, competitors (actual and potential), and market conditions. Each item in the list must include the name and position held of the author.

D. How to notify

The notification must be completed in one of the official languages of the European Community. This language shall thereafter be the language of the proceeding for all notifying parties.

The information requested by this form is to be set out using the sections and paragraph numbers of the form.

Supporting documents shall be submitted in their original language; where this is not an official language of the Community they shall be translated, into the language of the proceeding (Article 2(4) of Regulation (EEC) No 2367/90).

The supporting documents may be originals or copies of the originals. In the latter case the notifying party shall confirm that they are true and complete.

The financial data requested in Section 2.4 below must be provided in ECUs at the average conversion rates prevailing for the years or other period in question.

Twenty copies of each notification and fifteen copies of all supporting documents must be provided.

The notification should be sent to:

> Commission of the European Communities,
> Directorate General for Competition (DG IV),
> Merger Task Force (Cort. 150),
> 200, rue de la Loi,
> B-1049 Brussels;

or be delivered by hand during normal Commission working hours at the following address:

> Commission of the European Communities,
> Directorate General for Competition (DG IV),
> Merger Task Force,
> 150, avenue de Cortenberg,
> B-1040 Brussels.

E. Secrecy

Article 214 of the Treaty and Article 17(2) of Regulation (EEC) No 4064/89 require the Commission and the Member States, their officials and other servants not to disclose information they have acquired through the application of the Regulation of the kind covered by the obligation of professional secrecy. The same principle must also apply to protect confidentiality as between notifying parties.

If you believe that your interests would be harmed if any of the information you are asked to supply was to be published or otherwise divulged to other parties, submit this information separately with each page clearly marked 'Business secrets'. You should also give reasons why this information should not be divulged or published.

In the case of mergers or joint acquisitions, or in other cases where the notification is completed by more than one of the parties, business secrets may be submitted under separate cover, and referred to in the notification as an annex. In such cases the notification will be considered complete on receipt of all the annexes.

F. References

All references contained in this form are to the relevant articles and paragraphs of Council Regulation (EEC) No 4064/89.

Section 1

1.1. *Information on notifying party (or parties)*

Give details of:

1.1.1. name and address of undertaking,

1.1.2. nature of the undertaking's business,

1.1.3. name, address, telephone, fax and/or telex of, and position held by, the person to be contacted.

1.2. *Information on other parties to the concentration*[7, 8]

For each party to the concentration (except the notifying party) give details of:

1.2.1. name and address of undertaking,

1.2.2. nature of the undertaking's business,

1.2.3. name, address, telephone, fax and/or telex of, and in position held by, the person to be contacted.

1.3. *Address for service*

Give an address in Brussels if available to which all communications may be made and documents delivered in accordance with Article 1(4) of Commission Regulation (EEC) No 2367/90.

1.4. *Appointment of representatives*

Article 1(2) of Commission Regulation (EEC) No 2367/90 states that where notifications are signed by representatives of undertakings, such representatives shall produce written proof that they are authorised to act. Such written authorisation must accompany the notification and the following details of the representatives of the notifying party or parties and other parties to the concentration are to be given below:

1.4.1. is this a joint notification?

1.4.2. if 'yes', has a joint representative been appointed?

if 'yes', please give the details requested in 1.4.3 to 1.4.6 below;

if 'no', please give details of the representatives who have been authorised to act for each of the parties to the concentration indicating who they represent;

1.4.3. name of representative;

1.4.4. address of representative;

1.4.5. name of person to be contacted (and address if different from 1.4.4);

1.4.6. telephone, telefax and/or telex.

Section 2

Details of the concentration

2.1. Briefly describe the nature of the concentration being notified. In doing so state:

– whether the proposed concentration is a full legal merger, an acquisition, a concentrative joint venture or a contract or other means conferring direct or indirect control within the meaning of Article 3(3);

– whether the whole or parts of parties are subject to the concentration;

– whether any public offer for the securities of one party by another has the support of the former's supervisory boards of management or other bodies legally representing the party concerned.

2.2. List the economic sectors involved in the concentration.

2.3. Give a brief explanation of the economic and financial details of the concentration. In doing so provide, where relevant, information about the following:

– any financial or other support received from whatever source (including public authorities) by any of the parties and the nature and amount of this support,

– the proposed or expected date of any major events designed to bring about the completion of the concentration,

– the proposed structure of ownership and control after the completion of the concentration.

2.4. For each of the parties, the notifying party shall provide the following data for the last three financial years:

2.4.1. worldwide turnover[9],

2.4.2. Community-wide turnover[9, 10],

2.4.3. turnover in each Member State[9, 10],

2.4.4. the Member State, if any, in which more than two-thirds of Community-wide turnover is achieved[9, 10],

2.4.5 profits before tax worldwide[11],

2.4.6. number of employees worldwide[12].

Section 3

Ownership and control [13]

For each of the parties provide a list of all undertakings belonging to the same group. This list must include:

3.1. all undertakings controlled by the parties, directly or indirectly, within the meaning of Article 3(3);

3.2. all undertakings or persons controlling the parties directly or indirectly within the meaning of Article 3(3);

3.3. for each undertaking or person identified in 3.2 above, a complete list of all undertakings controlled by them directly or indirectly, within the meaning of Article 3(3).

For each entry to the list the nature and means of control shall be specified;

3.4. provide details of acquisitions made during the last three years by the groups identified above, of undertakings active in affected markets as defined in section 5 below.

The information sought in this section may be illustrated by the use of charts or diagrams where this helps to give a better understanding of the pre-concentration structure of ownership and control of the undertakings.

Section 4

Personal and financial links

With respect to each undertaking or person disclosed in response to Section 3 provide:

4.1. a list of all other undertakings which are active on affected markets (affected markets are defined in section 5) in which the undertakings of the group hold individually or collectively 10% or more of the voting rights or issued share capital. In each case state the percentage held;

4.2. a list of all other undertakings which are active on affected markets in which the persons disclosed in response to Section 3 hold 10% or more of the voting rights or issued share capital. In each case state the percentage held;

4.3. a list for each undertaking of the members of their boards of management who are also members of the boards of management or of the supervisory boards of any other undertaking, which is active on affected markets; and (where applicable) for each undertaking a list of the members of their supervisory boards who are also members of the boards of management of any other undertaking which is active on affected markets;

in each case stating the name of the other undertaking and the position held.

Information provided here may be illustrated by the use of charts or diagrams where this helps to give a better understanding.

Section 5

Information on affected markets

The notifying party shall provide the data requested having regard to the following definitions:

PRODUCT MARKETS

A relevant product market comprises all those products and/or services which are regarded as interchangeable or substitutable by the consumer, by reason of the products' characteristics, their prices and their intended use.

A relevant product market may in some cases be composed of a number of individual product groups. An individual product group is a product or small group of products which present largely identical physical or technical characteristics and are fully interchangeable. The difference between products within the group will be small and usually only a matter of brand and/or image. The product market will usually be the classification used by the undertaking in its marketing operations.

RELEVANT GEOGRAPHIC MARKET

The relevant geographic market comprises the area in which the undertakings concerned are involved in the supply of products or services, in which the conditions of competition are sufficiently homogeneous and which can be distinguished from neighbouring areas because, in particular, conditions of competition are appreciably different in those areas.

Factors relevant to the assessment of the relevant geographic market include the nature and characteristics of the products or services concerned, the existence of entry barriers or consumer preferences, appreciable differences of the undertakings' market shares between neighbouring areas or substantial price differences.

AFFECTED MARKETS

Affected markets consist of relevant product markets or individual product groups, in the Common Market or a Member State or, where different, in any relevant geographic market where:

(a) two or more of the parties (including undertakings belonging to the same group as defined in Section 3) are engaged in business activities in the same product market or individual product group and where the concentration will lead to a combined market share of 10% or more. These are horizontal relationships; or

(b) any of the parties (including undertakings belonging to the same group as defined in Section 3) is engaged in business activities in a product market which is upstream or downstream of a product market or individual product group in which any other party is engaged and any of their market shares is 10% or more, regardless of whether there is or is not any existing supplier/customer relationship between the parties concerned. These are vertical relationships.

I. *Explanation of the affected relevant product markets*

5.1. Describe each affected relevant product market and explain why the products and/or services in these markets are included (and why others are excluded) by reason of their characteristics, their prices and their intended use.

5.2. List the individual product groups defined internally by your undertaking for marketing purposes which are covered by each relevant product market described under 5.1 above.

II. *Market data on affected markets*

For each affected relevant product market and, where different, individual product group, for each of the last three financial years:

(a) for the Community as a whole;

(b) individually for each Member State where the parties (including undertakings belonging to the same group as defined in Section 3) do business;

(c) and where different, for any relevant geographic market,

provide the following:

5.3. an estimate of the value of the market and, where appropriate, of the volume (for example in units shipped or delivered) of the market[14]. If available, include statistics prepared by other sources to illustrate your answers. Also provide a forecast of the evolution of demand on the affected markets;

5.4. the turnover of each of the groups to which the parties belong (as defined in Section 3);

5.5. an estimate of the market share of each of the groups to which the parties belong;

5.6. an estimate of the market share (in value and where appropriate volume) of all competitors having at least 10% of the geographic market under consideration. Provide the name, address and telephone number of these undertakings;

5.7. a comparison of prices charged by the groups to which the parties belong in each of the Member States and a similar comparison of such price levels between the Community and its major trading partners (e.g. the United States, Japan and EFTA);

5.8. an estimate of the value (and where appropriate volume) and source of imports to the relevant geographic market;

5.9. the proportion of such imports that are derived from the groups to which the parties belong;

5.10. an estimate of the extent to which any of these imports are affected by any tariff or non-tariff barriers to trade.

III. *Market data on conglomerate aspects*

In the absence of horizontal or vertical relationships, where any of the parties (including undertakings belonging to the same group as defined in Section 3) holds a market share of 25% or more for any product market or individual product group, provide the following information:

5.11. a description of each relevant product market and explain why the products and/or services in these markets are included (and why others are excluded) by reason of their characteristics, their prices and their intended use;

5.12. a list of the individual product groups defined internally by your undertaking for marketing purposes which are covered by each relevant product market described;

5.13. an estimate of the value of the market and the market shares of each of the groups to which the parties belong for each affected relevant product market and, where different, individual product group, for the last financial year:

(*a*) for the Community as a whole;

(*b*) individually for each Member State where the groups to which the parties belong do business;

(*c*) and where different, for any relevant geographic market.

In each response in Section 5 the notifying party shall explain the basis of the estimates used or assumptions made.

Section 6

General conditions in affected markets

The following information shall be provided in relation to the affected product markets and, where different, affected individual product groups:

RECORD OF MARKET ENTRY

6.1. Over the last five years (or a longer period if this is more appropriate) has there been any significant entry to these markets in the Community? If the answer is 'yes', provide information on these entrants, estimating their current market shares.

6.2. In the opinion of the notifying party are there undertakings (including those at present operating only in extra-Community markets) that could enter the Community's markets? If the answer is 'yes', provide information on these potential entrants.

6.3. In the opinion of the notifying party what is the likelihood of significant market entry over the next five years?

FACTORS INFLUENCING MARKET ENTRY

6.4. Describe the various factors influencing entry into affected markets that exist in the present case, examining entry from both a geographical and product viewpoint. In so doing take account of the following where appropriate:

– the total costs of entry (capital, promotion, advertising, necessary distribution systems, servicing etc.) on a scale equivalent to a significant viable competitor, indicating the market share of such a competitor;

– to what extent is entry to the markets influenced by the requirement of government authorisation or standard setting in any form? Are there any legal or regulatory controls on entry to these markets?

- to what extent is entry to the markets influenced by the availability of raw materials?

- to what extent is entry to the markets influenced by the length of contracts between an undertaking and its suppliers and/or customers?

- describe the importance of licensing patents, know-how and other rights in these markets.

VERTICAL INTEGRATION

6.5. Describe the nature and extent of vertical integration of each of the parties.

RESEARCH AND DEVELOPMENT

6.6. Give an account of the importance of research and development in the ability of a firm operating on the relevant market to compete in the long term. Explain the nature of the research and development in affected markets carried out by the undertakings to the concentration.

In so doing take account of the following where appropriate:

- the research and development intensities[15] for these markets and the relevant research and development intensities for the parties concerned;

- the course of technological development for these markets over an appropriate time period (including developments in products and/or services, production processes, distribution systems etc);

- the major innovations that have been made in these markets over this time period and the undertakings responsible for these innovations;

- the cycle of innovation in these markets and where the parties are in this cycle of innovation;

- describe the extent to which the parties concerned are licensees or licensors of patents, know-how and other rights in affected markets.

DISTRIBUTION AND SERVICE SYSTEMS

6.7. Explain the distribution channels and service networks that exist on the affected markets. In so doing take account of the following where appropriate:

- the distribution systems prevailing on the market and their importance. To what extent is distribution performed by third parties and/or undertakings belonging to the same group as the parties as disclosed in Section 3?

- the service networks (for example maintenance and repair) prevailing and their importance in these markets. To what extent are such services performed by third parties and/or undertakings belonging to the same group as the parties as disclosed in Section 3?

COMPETITIVE ENVIRONMENT

6.8 Give details (names, addresses and contacts) of the five largest suppliers to the notifying parties and their individual share of the purchases of the notifying parties.

6.9. Give details (names, addresses and contacts) of the five largest customers of the notifying parties and their individual share of the sales of the notifying parties.

6.10. Explain the structure of supply and demand in affected markets. This explanation should allow the Commission further to appreciate the competitive environment in which the parties carry out their business. In so doing take account of the following where appropriate:

- the phases of the markets in terms of, for example, take-off, expansion, maturity and decline. In the opinion of the notifying party, where are the affected products in these phases?

- the structure of supply. Give details of the various identifiable categories that comprise the supply side and describe the 'typical supplier' of each category;

- the structure of demand. Give details of the various identifiable groups that comprise the demand side and describe the 'typical customer' of each group;

- whether public authorities, government agencies or state enterprises or similar bodies are important participants as sources of supply or demand. In any instance where this is so give details of this participation;

- the total Community-wide capacity for the last three years. Over the period what proportion of this capacity is accounted for by the parties and what have been their rates of capacity utilisation?

COOPERATIVE AGREEMENTS

6.11. To what extent do cooperative agreements (horizontal and/or vertical) exist in the affected markets?

6.12. Give details of the most important cooperative agreements engaged in by the parties in the affected markets, such as licensing agreements, research and development, specialisation, distribution, long-term supply and exchange of information agreements.

TRADE ASSOCIATIONS

6.13. List the names and addresses of the principal trade associations in the affected markets.

WORLDWIDE CONTEXT

6.14. Describe the worldwide context of the proposed concentration indicating the position of the parties in this market.

Section 7

General matters

7.1. Describe how the proposed concentration is likely to affect the interests of intermediate and ultimate consumers, and the development of technical progress.

7.2. In the event that the Commission finds that the operation notified does not constitute a concentration within the meaning of Article 3 of Regulation (EEC) No 4064/89, do you request that it be treated as an application within the meaning of Article 2 or a notification within the meaning of Article 4 of Regulation No 17, as an application within the meaning of Article 12 or a notification within the meaning of Article 14 of Regulation (EEC) No 1017/68, as an application within the meaning of Article 12 of Regulation (EEC) No 4056/86 or as an application within the meaning of Article 3(2) or Article 5 of Regulation (EEC) No 3975/87?

Section 8

Declaration

The notification must conclude with the following declaration which is to be signed by or on behalf of all the notifying parties.

The undersigned declare that the information given in this notification is correct to the best of their knowledge and belief, that all estimates are identified as such and are their best estimates of the underlying facts and that all the opinions expressed are sincere.

They are aware of the provisions of Article 14(1)b of Regulation (EEC) No 4064/89.

Place and date:

Signatures:

Guidance Note I[16]

Calculation of turnover for credit and other financial institutions

(Article 5(3)(a))

For the calculation of turnover for credit institutions and other financial institutions, we give the following example (proposed merger between bank A and bank B):

I. Consolidated balance sheets

		(in million ECU)
Assets	*Bank A*	*Bank B*
Loans and advances to credit institutions	20 000	1 000
– to credit institutions within the Community:	(10 000)	(500)
– to credit institutions within one (and the same) Member State X:	(5 000)	(500)
Loans and advances to customers	60 000	4 000
– to Community residents:	(30 000)	(2 000)
– to residents of one (and the same) Member State X:	(15 000)	(500)
Other assets:	20 000	1 000
Total assets	100 000	6 000

II. Calculation of turnover

In place of turnover, the following figures shall be used:

	Bank A	Bank B
1. *Aggregate worldwide turnover* is replaced by one-tenth of total assets:	10 000	600

the total sum of which is more than ECU 5 000 million.

2. *Community-wide turnover*

is replaced by, for each bank, one-tenth of total assets multiplied by the ratio between loans and advances to credit institutions and customers within the Community; to the total sum of loans and advances to credit institutions and customers.

	Bank A	Bank B
This is calculated as follows:		
one-tenth of total assets:	10 000	600
which is multiplied for each bank by the ratio between:		
loans and advances to credit institutions and customers	10 000	500
within the Community	30 000	2 000
	40 000	2 500
and		
the total sum of loans and advances to credit institutions	20 000	1 000
and customers	60 000	4 000
	80 000	5 000

For

Bank A: 10 000 multiplied by (40 000: 80 000) = 5 000

Bank B: 600 multiplied by (2 500: 5 000)   =   300

which exceeds ECU 250 million for each of the banks.

3. *Total turnover within one (and the same) Member State* X

	Bank A	Bank B
is replaced by one-tenth of total assets:	10 000	600

which is multiplied for each bank by the ratio between loans and advances to credit institutions and customers within one and the same Member State X; to the total sum of loans and advances to credit institutions and customers.

	Bank A	Bank B
loans and advances to credit institutions and customers	5 000	500
within one (and the same) Member State X	15 000	500
	20 000	1,000
and		
the total sum of loans and advances to credit institutions and customers	80 000	5 000

For

Bank A: 10 000 multiplied by (20 000: 80 000) = 2 500

Bank B: 600 multiplied by (1 000: 5 000)   =   120

Result:

50% of bank A's and 40% of bank B's Community-wide turnover are achieved in one (and the same) Member State X.

III. Conclusion

Since

(a) the aggregate worldwide turnover of bank A plus bank B is more than ECU 5 000 million;

(b) the Community-wide turnover of each of the banks is more than ECU 250 million; and

(c) each of the banks achieve less than two-thirds of its Community-wide turnover in one (and the same) Member State,

the proposed merger would fall under the scope of the Regulation.

Guidance Note II

Calculation of turnover for insurance undertakings

(Article 5(3)(a))

For the calculation of turnover for insurance undertakings, we give the following example (proposed concentration between insurances A and B):

I. Consolidated profit and loss account

(in million ECU)

Income	Insurance A	Insurance B
Gross premiums written	5 000	300
— gross premiums received from Community residents:	(4 500)	(300)
— gross premiums received from residents of one (and the same) Member State X:	(3 600)	(270)
Other income:	500	50
Total income:	5 500	350

II. Calculation of turnover

1. *Aggregate worldwide turnover*

is replaced by the value of gross premiums written worldwide, the sum of which is ECU 5 300 million.

2. *Community-wide turnover*

is replaced, for each insurance undertakings, by the value of gross premiums written with Community residents. For each of the insurance undertakings, this amount is more than ECU 250 million.

3. *Turnover within one (and the same) Member State X*

is replaced, for insurance undertakings, by the value of gross premiums written with residents of one (and the same) Member State X.

For insurance A, it achieves 80% of its gross premiums written with Community residents within Member State X, whereas for insurance B, it achieves 90% of its gross premiums written with Community residents in that Member State X.

III. Conclusion

Since

(a) the aggregate worldwide turnover of insurances A and B, as replaced by the value of gross premiums written worldwide, is more than ECU 5 000 million;

(b) for each of the insurance undertakings, the value of gross premiums written with Community residents is more than ECU 250 million; but

(c) each of the insurance undertakings achieves more than two-thirds of its gross premiums written with Community residents in one (and the same) Member State X,

the proposed concentration would not fall under the scope of the Regulation.

Guidance Note III

Calculation of turnover for joint undertakings

A. *Creation of a joint undertaking* (Article 3(2))

In a case where two (or more) undertakings create a joint undertaking that constitutes a concentration, turnover is calculated for the undertakings concerned.

B. *Existence of a joint undertaking* (Article 5(5))

For the calculation of turnover in case of the existence of a joint undertaking C between two undertakings A and B concerned in a concentration, we give the following example:

I. Profit and loss accounts

(in million ECU)

Turnover	Undertaking A	Undertaking B
Sales revenues worldwide	10 000	2 000
– Community	(8 000)	(1 500)
– Member State Y	(4 000)	(900)

Turnover	Joint undertaking C
Sales revenues worldwide	100
– with undertaking A	(20)
– with undertaking B	(10)
Turnover with third undertakings	70
– Community-wide	(60)
– in Member State Y	(50)

II. Consideration of the joint undertaking

(a) The undertaking C is jointly controlled (in the meaning of Article 3(3) and (4)) by the undertakings A and B concerned by the concentration, irrespective of any third undertaking participating in that undertaking C.

(b) The undertaking C is not consolidated by A and B in their profit and loss accounts.

(c) The turnover of C resulting from operations with A and B shall not be taken into account.

(d) The turnover of C resulting from operations with any third undertaking shall be apportioned equally amongst the undertakings A and B, irrespective of their individual shareholdings in C.

(e) Any joint undertaking existing between one of the undertakings concerned and any third undertaking shall (unless already consolidated) not be taken into account.

III. Calculation of turnover

(a) Undertaking A's aggregate worldwide turnover shall be calculated as follows: ECU 10 000 million and 50% of C's worldwide turnover with third undertakings (i.e. ECU 35 million), the sum of which is ECU 10 035 million.

Undertaking B's aggregate worldwide turnover shall be calculated as follows: ECU 2 000 million and 50% of C's worldwide turnover with third undertakings (i.e. ECU 35 million), the sum of which is ECU 2 035 million.

(b) The aggregate worldwide turnover of the undertakings concerned is ECU 12 070 million.

(c) Undertaking A achieves ECU 4 025 million within Member State Y (50% of C's turnover in this Member State taken into account), and a Community-wide turnover of ECU 8 030 million (including 50% of C's Community-wide turnover);

and undertaking B achieves ECU 925 million within Member State Y (50% of C's turnover in this Member State taken into account), and a Community-wide turnover of ECU 1 530 million (including 50% of C's Community-wide turnover).

IV. Conclusion

Since

(a) the aggregate worldwide turnover of undertakings A and B is more than ECU 5 000 million,

(b) each of the undertakings concerned by the concentration achieves more than ECU 250 million within the Community,

(c) each of the undertakings concerned (undertaking A 50,1% and undertaking B 60,5%) achieves less than two-thirds of its Community-wide turnover in one (and the same) Member State Y,

the proposed concentration would fall under the scope of the Regulation.

Guidance Note IV

Application of the two-thirds rule

(Article 1)

For the application of the two-thirds rule for undertakings, we give the following examples (proposed concentration between undertakings A and B):

I. Consolidated profit and loss accounts

Example 1
(in million ECU)

Turnover	Undertaking A		Undertaking B	
Sales revenues worldwide	10 000		500	
– within the Community:		(8 000)		(400)
– in Member State X:		(6 000)		(200)

Example 2(a)
(in million ECU)

Turnover	Undertaking A		Undertaking B	
Sales revenues worldwide	4 800		500	
– within the Community:		(2 400)		(400)
– in Member State X:		(2 100)		(300)

Example 2(b)

Same figures as in example 2(a), BUT undertaking B achieves ECU 300 million in Member State Y.

II. Application of the two-thirds rule

Example 1

1. *Community-wide turnover*

is, for undertaking A, ECU 8 000 and for undertaking B ECU 400 million.

2. *Turnover in one (and the same) Member State X*

is, for undertaking A (ECU 6 000 million), 75% of its Community-wide turnover and is, for undertaking B (ECU 200 million), 50% of its Community-wide turnover.

3. *Conclusion*

In this case, although undertaking A achieves more than two-thirds of its Community-wide turnover in Member State X, the proposed concentration would fall under the scope of the Regulation due to the fact that undertaking B achieves less than two-thirds of its Community-wide turnover in Member State X.

Example 2(a)

1. Community-wide turnover

of undertaking A is ECU 2 400 million and of undertaking B, ECU 400 million.

2. Turnover in one (and the same) Member State X

is, for undertaking A, ECU 2 100 million (i.e. 87,5% of its Community-wide turnover); and, for undertaking B, ECU 300 million (i.e. 75% of its Community-wide turnover).

3. Conclusion

In this case, each of the undertakings concerned achieves more than two-thirds of its Community-wide turnover in one (and the same) Member State X; the proposed concentration would not fall under the scope of the Regulation.

Example 2(b)

Conclusion

In this case, the two-thirds rule would not apply due to the fact that undertakings A and B achieve more than two-thirds of their Community-wide turnover in different Member States X and Y. Therefore, the proposed concentration would fall under the scope of the Regulation.

FOOTNOTES

1. OJ No L 395, 30.12.89, p. 1.
2. OJ No 13, 21.2.62, p.204.
3. OJ No L 175, 23.7.68, p.1.
4. OJ No L 378, 31.12.86, p.4.
5. OJ No L 374, 31.12.87, p.1.
6. OJ No L 124, 8.6.71, p.1.
7. A concentration is defined in Article 3.
8. This includes the target company in the case of a contested bid, in which case the details should be completed as far as is possible.
9. See Article 5 for the definition of turnover and note the special provisions for credit, insurance, other financial institutions and joint undertakings.
   For insurance undertakings, credit and other financial institutions, Community-residents and residents of a Member State are defined as natural or legal persons having their residence in a Member State, thereby following the respective national legislation. The corporate customer is to be treated as resident in the country in which it is legally incorporated. For the calculation of turnover, the notifying party should also refer to the examples: guidance note I for credit and other financial institutions; guidance note II for insurance undertakings; guidance note III for joint undertakings.
10. See guidance note IV for calculation of turnover in one Member State with respect to Community-wide turnover.

11. 'Profits before tax' shall comprise profit on ordinary activities before tax on profit.
12. 'Employees' shall comprise all persons employed in the enterprise who have a contract of employment and receive remuneration.
13. See Article 3(3) to (5).
14. The value and volume of a market should reflect output less exports plus imports for the geographic market under consideration.
15. Research and development intensity is defined as research and development expenditure as a proportion of turnover.
16. In the following guidance notes, the terms 'institution' or 'undertaking' are used subject to the exact delimitation in each case.

COMMISSION NOTICE

of 3 September 1986

on agreements of minor importance which do not fall under Article 85(1) of the Treaty establishing the European Economic Community[1]

(86/C 231/02)

(OJ No C 231,12.9.86, p.2)

I

1. The Commission considers it important to facilitate cooperation between undertakings where such cooperation is economically desirable without presenting difficulties from the point of view of competition policy, which is particularly true of cooperation between small and medium-sized undertakings. To this end it published the 'Notice concerning agreements, decisions and concerted practices in the field of cooperation between undertakings'[2] listing a number of agreements that by their nature cannot be regarded as restraints of competition. Furthermore, in the Notice concerning its assessment of certain subcontracting agreements[3] the Commission considered that this type of contract which offers opportunities for development, in particular, to small and medium-sized undertakings is not in itself caught by the prohibition in Article 85(1). By issuing the present Notice, the Commission is taking a further step towards defining the field of application of Article 85(1), in order to facilitate cooperation between small and medium-sized undertakings.

2. In the Commission's opinion, agreements whose effects on trade between Member States or on competition are negligible do not fall under the ban on restrictive agreements contained in Article 85(1). Only those agreements are prohibited which have an appreciable impact on

market conditions, in that they appreciably alter the market position, in other words the sales or supply possibilities, of third undertakings and of users.

3. In the present Notice the Commission, by setting quantitative criteria and by explaining their application, has given a sufficiently concrete meaning to the concept 'appreciable' for undertakings to be able to judge for themselves whether the agreements they have concluded with other undertakings, being of minor importance, do not fall under Article 85(1). The quantitative definition of 'appreciable' given by the Commission is, however, no absolute yardstick; in fact, in individual cases even agreements between undertakings which exceed these limits may still have only a negligible effect on trade between Member States or on competition, and are therefore not caught by Article 85(1).

4. As a result of this Notice, there should no longer be any point in undertakings obtaining negative clearance, as defined by Article 2 of Council Regulation No 17[4], for the agreements covered, nor should it be necessary to have the legal position established through Commission decisions in individual cases; notification with this end in view will no longer be necessary for such agreements. However, if it is doubtful whether in an individual case an agreement appreciably affects trade between Member States or competition, the undertakings are free to apply for negative clearance or to notify the agreement.

5. In cases covered by the present Notice the Commission, as a general rule, will not open proceedings under Regulation No 17, either upon application or upon its own initiative. Where, due to exceptional circumstances, an agreement which is covered by the present Notice nevertheless falls under Article 85(1), the Commission will not impose fines. Where undertakings have failed to notify an agreement falling under Article 85(1) because they wrongly assumed, owing to a mistake in calculating their market share or aggregate turnover, that the agreement was covered by the present Notice, the Commission will not consider imposing fines unless the mistake was due to negligence.

6. This Notice is without prejudice to the competence of national courts to apply Article 85(1) on the basis of their own jurisdiction, although it constitutes a factor which such courts may take into account when deciding a pending case. It is also without prejudice to any interpretation which may be given by the Court of Justice of the European Communities.

II

7. The Commission holds the view that agreements between undertakings engaged in the production or distribution of goods or in the

provisions of services generally do not fall under the prohibition of Article 81(1) if:

- the goods or services which are the subject of the agreement (hereinafter referred to as 'the contract products') together with the participation undertakings' other goods or services which are considered by users to be equivalent in view of their characteristics, price and intended use, do not present more than 5% of the total market for such goods or services (hereinafter referred to as 'products') in the area of the common market affected by the agreement and

- the aggregate annual turnover of the participating undertakings does not exceed 200 million ECU.

8. The Commission also holds the view that the said agreements do not fall under the prohibition of Article 85(1) if the abovementioned market share or turnover is exceeded by not more than one tenth during two successive financial years.

9. For the purposes of this Notice, participating undertakings are:

(a) undertakings party to the agreement;

(b) undertakings in which a party to the agreement, directly or indirectly,

- owns more than half the capital or business assets, or

- has the power to exercise more than half the voting rights, or

- has the power to appoint more than half the members of the supervisory board, board of management or bodies legally representing the undertakings, or

- has the right to manage the affairs;

(c) undertakings which directly or indirectly have in or over a party to the agreement the right or powers listed in (b);

(d) undertakings in or over which an undertaking referred to in (c) directly or indirectly has the rights or powers listed in (b).

Undertakings in which several undertakings as referred to in (a) to (d) jointly have, directly or indirectly, the rights or powers set out in (b) shall also be considered to be participating undertakings.

10. In order to calculate the market share, it is necessary to determine the relevant market. This implies the definition of the relevant product market and the relevant geographical market.

11. The relevant product market includes besides the contract products any other products which are identical or equivalent to them. This rule

applies to the products of the participating undertakings as well as to the market for such products. The products in question must be interchangeable. Whether or not this is the case must be judged from the vantage point of the user, normally taking the characteristics, price and intended use of the goods together. In certain cases, however, products can form a separate market on the basis of their characteristics, their price or their intended use alone. This is true especially where consumer preferences have developed.

12. Where the contract products are components which are incorporated into another product by the participating undertakings, reference should be made to the market for the latter product, provided that the components represent a significant part of it. Where the contract products are components which are sold to third undertakings, reference should be made to the market for the components. In cases where both conditions apply, both markets should be considered separately.

13. The relevant geographical market is the area within the Community in which the agreement produces its effects. This area will be the whole common market where the contract products are regularly bought and sold in all Member States. Where the contract products cannot be bought and sold in a part of the common market, or are bought and sold only in limited quantities or at irregular intervals in such a part, that part should be disregarded.

14. The relevant geographical market will be narrower than the whole common market in particular where:

— the nature and characteristics of the contract produce, e.g. high transport costs in relation to the value of the product, restrict its mobility; or

— movement of the contract product within the common market is hindered by barriers to entry to national markets resulting from State intervention, such as quantitative restrictions, severe taxation differentials and non-tariff barriers, e.g. type approvals or safety standard certifications. In such cases the national territory may have to be considered as the relevant geographical market. However, this will only be justified if the existing barriers to entry cannot be overcome by reasonable effort and at an acceptable cost.

15. Aggregate turnover includes the turnover in all goods and services, excluding tax, achieved during the last financial year by the participating undertaking. In cases where an undertaking has concluded similar agreements with various other undertakings in the relevant market, the turnover of all participating undertakings should be taken together. The

aggregate turnover shall not include dealings between participating undertakings.

16. The present Notice shall not apply where in a relevant market competition is restricted by the cumulative effects of parallel networks of similar agreements established by several manufacturers or dealers.

17. The present Notice is likewise applicable to decisions by associations of undertakings and to concerted practices.

FOOTNOTES

1. The present Notice replaces the Commission Notice of 19 December 1977, OJ No C 313, 29.12.77, p.3.
2. OJ No C 75, 29.7.68, p.3, corrected by OJ No C 84, 28.8.68, p.14.
3. OJ No C 1, 3.1.79, p.2.
4. OJ No 13, 21.2.62, p.204.

COMMISSION REGULATION (EEC) No 1983/83

of 22 June 1983

on the application of Article 85(3) of the Treaty to categories of exclusive distribution agreements

(OJ No L 173, 30.6.83, p.1)

The Commission of the European Communities,

Having regard to the Treaty establishing the European Economic Community, and in particular Article 87 thereof,

Having regard to Council Regulation No 19/65/EEC of 2 March 1965 on the application of Article 85(3) of the Treaty to certain categories of agreements and concerned practices[1], as last amended by the Act of Accession of Greece, and in particular Article 1 thereof,

Having published a draft of this Regulation[2],

Having consulted the Advisory Committee on Restrictive Practices and Dominant Positions,

(1) Whereas Regulation No 19/65/EEC empowers the Commission to apply Article 85(3) of the Treaty by regulation to certain categories of bilateral exclusive distribution agreements and analogous concerted practices falling within Article 85(1);

(2) Whereas experience to date makes it possible to define a category of

agreements and concerted practices which can be regarded as normally satisfying the conditions laid down in Article 85(3);

(3) Whereas exclusive distribution agreements of the category defined in Article 1 of this Regulation may fall within the prohibition contained in Article 85(1) of the Treaty; whereas this will apply only in exceptional cases to exclusive agreements of this kind to which only undertakings from one Member State are party and which concern the resale of goods within that Member State; whereas, however, to the extent that such agreements may affect trade between Member States and also satisfy all the requirements set out in this Regulation there is no reason to withhold from them the benefit of the exemption by category;

(4) Whereas it is not necessary expressly to exclude from the defined category those agreements which do not fulfil the conditions of Article 85(1) of the Treaty;

(5) Whereas exclusive distribution agreements lead in general to an improvement in distribution because the undertaking is able to concentrate its sales activities, does not need to maintain numerous business relations with a larger number of dealers and is able, by dealing with only one dealer, to overcome more easily distribution difficulties in international trade resulting from linguistic, legal and other differences;

(6) Whereas exclusive distribution agreements facilitate the promotion of sales of a product and lead to intensive marketing and to continuity of supplies while at the same time rationalising distribution; whereas they stimulate competition between the products of different manufacturers; whereas the appointment of an exclusive distributor who will take over sales promotion, customer services and carrying of stocks is often the most effective way, and sometimes indeed the only way, for the manufacturer to enter a market and compete with other manufacturers already present; whereas this is particularly so in the case of small and medium-sized undertakings; whereas it must be left to the contracting parties to decide whether and to what extent they consider it desirable to incorporate in the agreements terms providing for the promotion of sales;

(7) Whereas, as a rule, such exclusive distribution agreements also allow consumers a fair share of the resulting benefit as they gain directly from the improvement in distribution, and their economic and supply position is improved as they can obtain products manufactured in particular in other countries more quickly and more easily;

(8) Whereas this Regulation must define the obligations restricting competition which may be included in exclusive distribution agreements; whereas the other restrictions on competition allowed under this

Regulation in addition to the exclusive supply obligation produce a clear division of functions between the parties and compel the exclusive distributor to concentrate his sales efforts on the contract goods and the contract territory; whereas they are, where they are agreed only for the duration of the agreement, generally necessary in order to attain the improvement in the distribution of goods sought through exclusive distribution; whereas it may be left to the contracting parties to decide which of these obligations they include in their agreements; whereas further restrictive obligations and in particular those which limit the exclusive distributor's choice of customers or his freedom to determine his prices and conditions of sale cannot be exempted under this Regulation;

(9) Whereas the exemption by category should be reserved for agreements for which it can be assumed with sufficient certainty that they satisfy the conditions of Article 85(3) of the Treaty;

(10) Whereas it is not possible, in the absence of a case-by-case examination, to consider that adequate improvements in distribution occur where a manufacturer entrusts the distribution of his goods to another manufacturer with whom he is in competition; whereas such agreements should, therefore, be excluded from the exemption by category; whereas certain derogations from this rule in favour of small and medium-sized undertakings can be allowed;

(11) Whereas consumers will be assured of a fair share of the benefits resulting from exclusive distribution only if parallel imports remain possible; whereas agreements relating to goods which the user can obtain only from the exclusive distributor should therefore be excluded from the exemption by category; whereas the parties cannot be allowed to abuse industrial property rights or other rights in order to create absolute territorial protection; whereas this does not prejudice the relationship between competition law and industrial property rights, since the sole object here is to determine the conditions for exemption by category;

(12) Whereas, since competition at the distribution stage is ensured by the possibility of parallel imports, the exclusive distribution agreements covered by this Regulation will not normally afford any possibility of eliminating competition in respect of a substantial part of the products in question; whereas this is also true of agreements that allot to the exclusive distributor a contract territory covering the whole of the common market;

(13) Whereas in particular cases in which agreements or concerted practices satisfying the requirements of this Regulation nevertheless have effects incompatible with Article 85(3) of the Treaty, the

Commission may withdraw the benefit of the exemption by category from the undertakings party to them;

(14) Whereas agreements and concerted practices which satisfy the conditions set out in this Regulation need not be notified; whereas an undertaking may nonetheless in a particular case where real doubt exists, request the Commission to declare whether its agreements comply with this Regulation;

(15) Whereas this Regulation does not affect the applicability of Commission Regulation (EEC) No 3604/82 of 23 December 1982 on the application of Article 85(3) of the Treaty to categories of specialisation agreements[3]; whereas it does not exclude the application of Article 86 of the Treaty,

Has adopted this Regulation:

Article 1

Pursuant to Article 85(3) of the Treaty and subject to the provisions of this Regulation, it is hereby declared that Article 85(1) of the Treaty shall not apply to agreements to which only two undertakings are party and whereby one party agrees with the other to supply certain goods for resale within the whole or a defined area of the common market only to that other.

Article 2

1. Apart from the obligation referred to in Article 1 no restriction on competition shall be imposed on the supplier other than the obligation not to supply the contract goods to users in the contract territory.

2. No restriction on competition shall be imposed on the exclusive distributor other than:

(a) the obligation not to manufacture or distribute goods which compete with the contract goods;

(b) the obligation to obtain the contract goods for resale only from the other party;

(c) the obligation to refrain, outside the contract territory and in relation to the contract goods, from seeking customers, from establishing any branch, and from maintaining any distribution depot.

3. Article 1 shall apply notwithstanding that the exclusive distributor undertakes all or any of the following obligations:

(a) to purchase complete ranges of goods or minimum quantities;

(*b*) to sell the contract goods under trademarks, or packed and presented as specified by the other party;

(*c*) to take measures for promotion of sales, in particular:

- to advertise

- to maintain a sales network or stock of goods,

- to provide customer and guarantee services,

- to employ staff having specialised or technical training.

Article 3

Article 1 shall not apply where:

(*a*) manufacturers of identical goods or of goods which are considered by users as equivalent in view of their characteristics, price and intended use enter into reciprocal exclusive distribution agreements between themselves in respect of such goods;

(*b*) manufacturers of identical goods or of goods which are considered by users as equivalent in view of their characteristics, price and intended use enter into a non-reciprocal exclusive distribution agreement between themselves in respect of such goods unless at least one of them has a total annual turnover of no more than 100 million ECU;

(*c*) users can obtain the contract goods in the contract territory only from the exclusive distributor and have no alternative source of supply outside the contract territory;

(*d*) one or both of the parties makes it difficult for intermediaries or users to obtain the contract goods from other dealers inside the common market or, in so far as no alternative source of supply is available there, from outside the common market, in particular where one or both of them:

1. exercises industrial property rights so as to prevent dealers or users from obtaining outside, or from selling in, the contract territory properly marked or otherwise properly marketed contract goods;

2. exercises other rights or takes other measures so as to prevent dealers or users from obtaining outside, or from selling in, the contract territory contract goods.

Article 4

1. Article 3(a) and (b) shall also apply where the goods there referred to

are manufactured by an undertaking connected with a party to the agreement.

2. Connected undertakings are:

(a) undertakings in which a party to the agreement, directly or indirectly:

- owns more than half the capital or business assets, or

- has the power to exercise more than half the voting rights, or

- has the power to appoint more than half the members of the supervisory board, board of directors or bodies legally representing the undertaking, or

- has the right to manage the affairs;

(b) undertakings which directly or indirectly have in or over a party to the agreement the rights or powers listed in (a);

(c) undertakings in which an undertaking referred to in (b) directly or indirectly has the rights or powers listed in (a).

3. Undertakings in which the parties to the agreement or undertakings connected with them jointly have the rights or powers set out in paragraph 2(a) shall be considered to be connected with each of the parties to the agreement.

Article 5

1. For the purpose of Article 3(b), the ECU is the unit of account for drawing up the budget of the Community pursuant to Articles 207 and 209 of the Treaty.

2. Article 1 shall remain applicable where during any period of two consecutive financial years the total turnover referred to in Article 3(b) is exceeded by no more than 10%.

3. For the purpose of calculating total turnover within the meaning of Article 3(b), the turnovers achieved during the last financial year by the party to the agreement and connected undertakings in respect of all goods and services, excluding all taxes and other duties, shall be added together. For this purpose, no account shall be taken of dealings between the parties to the agreement or between these undertakings and undertakings connected with them or between the connected undertakings.

Article 6

The Commission may withdraw the benefit of this Regulation, pursuant to Article 7 of Regulation No 19/65/EEC, when it finds in a particular case that an agreement which is exempted by this Regulation nevertheless has certain effects which are incompatible with the conditions set out in Article 85(3) of the Treaty, and in particular where:

(a) the contract goods are not subject, in the contract territory, to effective competition from identical goods or goods considered by users as equivalent in view of their characteristics, price and intended use;

(b) access by other suppliers to the different stages of distribution within the contract territory is made difficult to a significant extent;

(c) for reasons other than those referred to in Article 3(c) and (d) it is not possible for intermediaries or users to obtain supplies of the contract goods from dealers outside the contract territory on the terms there customary;

(d) the exclusive distributor:

1. without any objectively justified reason refuses to supply in the contract territory categories of purchasers who cannot obtain contract goods elsewhere on suitable terms or applies to them differing prices or conditions of sale;

2. sells the contract goods at excessively high prices.

Article 7

In the period 1 July 1983 to 31 December 1986, the prohibition in Article 85(1) of the Treaty shall not apply to agreements which were in force on 1 July 1983 or entered into force between 1 July and 31 December 1983 and which satisfy the exemption conditions of Regulation No 67/67/EEC[4].

Article 8

This Regulation shall not apply to agreements entered into for the resale of drinks in premises used for the sale and consumption of beer or for the resale of petroleum products in service stations.

Article 9

This Regulation shall apply *mutatis mutandis* to concerted practices of the type defined in Article 1.

Article 10

This Regulation shall enter into force on 1 July 1983.

It shall expire on 31 December 1997.

This Regulation shall be binding in its entirety and directly applicable in all Member States.

Done at Brussels, 22 June 1983.

For the Commission

Frans Andriessen

Member of the Commission

FOOTNOTES

1. OJ No 36, 6.3.65, p.533.
2. OJ No C 172, 10.7.82, p.3.
3. OJ No L 376, 31.12.82, p.33.
4. OJ No 57, 25.3.67, p.849.

COMMISSION REGULATION (EEC) No 1984/83

of 22 June 1983

on the application of Article 85(3) of the Treaty to categories of exclusive purchasing agreements

(OJ No L 173, 30.6.83, p.5)

The Commission of the European Communities,

Having regard to the Treaty establishing the European Economic Community,

Having regard to Council Regulation No 19/65/EEC of 2 March 1965 on the application of Article 85(3) of the Treaty to certain categories of agreements and concerted practices[1], as last amended by the Act of Accession of Greece, and in particular Article 1 thereof,

Having published a draft of this Regulation[2],

Having consulted the Advisory Committee on Restrictive Practices and Dominant Positions,

(1) Whereas Regulation No 19/65/EEC empowers the Commission to apply Article 85(3) of the Treaty by regulation to certain categories of bilateral exclusive purchasing agreements entered into for the purpose of the resale of goods and corresponding concerted practices falling within Article 85[1];

(2) Whereas experience to date makes it possible to define three categories of agreements and concerted practices which can be

regarded as normally satisfying the conditions laid down in Article 85(3); whereas the first category comprises exclusive purchasing agreements of short and medium duration in all sectors of the economy; whereas the other two categories comprise long-term exclusive purchasing agreements entered into for the resale of beer in premises used for the sale and consumption (beer supply agreements) and of petroleum products in filling stations (service-station agreements);

(3) Whereas exclusive purchasing agreements of the categories defined in this Regulation may fall within the prohibition contained in Article 85(1) of the Treaty; whereas this will often be the case with agreements concluded between undertakings from different Member States; whereas an exclusive purchasing agreement to which undertakings from only one Member State are party and which concerns the resale of goods within that Member State may also be caught by the prohibition; whereas this is in particular the case where it is one of a number of similar agreements which together may affect trade between Member States;

(4) Whereas it is not necessary expressly to exclude from the defined categories those agreements which do not fulfil the conditions of Article 85(1) of the Treaty;

(5) Whereas the exclusive purchasing agreements defined in this Regulation lead in general to an improvement in distribution; whereas they enable the supplier to plan the sales of his goods with greater precision and for a longer period and ensure that the reseller's requirements will be met on a regular basis for the duration of the agreement; whereas this allows the parties to limit the risk to them of variations in market conditions and to lower distribution costs;

(6) Whereas such agreements also facilitate the promotion of the sales of a product and lead to intensive marketing because the supplier, in consideration for the exclusive purchasing obligation, is as a rule under an obligation to contribute to the improvement of the structure of the distribution network, the quality of the promotional effort or the sales success; whereas, at the same time, they stimulate competition between the products of different manufacturers; whereas the appointment of several resellers, who are bound to purchase exclusively from the manufacturer and who take over sales promotion, customer services and carrying of stock, is often the most effective way, and sometimes the only way, for the manufacturer to penetrate a market and compete with other manufacturers already present; whereas this is particularly so in the case of small and medium-sized undertakings; whereas it must be left to the contracting parties to decide whether and to what extent they consider it desirable to incorporate in their agreements terms concerning the promotions of sales;

(7) Whereas, as a rule, exclusive purchasing agreements between suppliers and resellers also allow consumers a fair share of the resulting benefit as they gain the advantages of regular supply and are able to obtain the contract goods more quickly and more easily;

(8) Whereas this Regulation must define the obligations restricting competition which may be included in an exclusive purchasing agreement; whereas the other restrictions of competition allowed under this Regulation in addition to the exclusive purchasing obligation lead to a clear division of functions between the parties and compel the reseller to concentrate his sales efforts on the contract goods; whereas they are, where they are agreed only for the duration of the agreement, generally necessary in order to attain the improvement in the distribution of goods sought through exclusive purchasing; whereas further restrictive obligations and in particular those which limit the reseller's choice of customers or his freedom to determine his prices and conditions of sale cannot be exempted under this Regulation;

(9) Whereas the exemption by categories should be reserved for agreements for which it can be assumed with sufficient certainty that they satisfy the conditions of Article 85(3) of the Treaty;

(10) Whereas it is not possible, in the absence of a case-by-case examination, to consider that adequate improvements in distribution occur where a manufacturer imposes an exclusive purchasing obligation with respect to his goods on a manufacturer with whom he is in competition; whereas such agreements should, therefore, be excluded from the exemption by categories; whereas certain derogations from this rule in favour of small and medium-sized undertakings can be allowed;

(11) Whereas certain conditions must be attached to the exemption by categories so that access by other undertakings to the different stages of distribution can be ensured; whereas, to this end, limits must be set to the scope and to the duration of the exclusive purchasing obligation; whereas it appears appropriate as a general rule to grant the benefit of a general exemption from the prohibition on restrictive agreements only to exclusive purchasing agreements which are concluded for a specified product or range of products and for not more than five years;

(12) Whereas, in the case of beer supply agreements and service-station agreements, different rules should be laid down which take account of the particularities of the markets in question;

(13) Whereas these agreements are generally distinguished by the fact that, on the one hand, the supplier confers on the reseller special commercial or financial advantages by contributing to his financing, granting him or obtaining for him a loan on favourable terms, equipping

him with a site or premises for conducting his business, providing him with equipment or fittings, or undertaking other investments for his benefit and that, on the other hand, the reseller enters into a long-term exclusive purchasing obligation which in most cases is accompanied by a ban on dealing in competing products;

(14) Whereas beer supply and service-station agreements, like the other exclusive purchasing agreements dealt with in this Regulation, normally produce an appreciable improvement in distribution in which consumers are allowed a fair share of the resulting benefit;

(15) Whereas the commercial and financial advantages conferred by the supplier on the reseller make it significantly easier to establish, modernise, maintain and operate premises used for the sale and consumption of drinks and service stations; whereas the exclusive purchasing obligation and the ban on dealing in competing products imposed on the reseller incite the reseller to devote all the resources at his disposal to the sale of the contract goods; whereas such agreements lead to durable cooperation between the parties allowing them to improve or maintain the quality of the contract goods and of the services to the customer and sales efforts of the reseller; whereas they allow long-term planning of sales and consequently a cost effective organisation of production and distribution; whereas the pressure of competition between products of different makes obliges the undertakings involved to determine the number and character of premises used for the sale and consumption of drinks and service stations, in accordance with the wishes of customers;

(16) Whereas consumers benefit from the improvements described, in particular because they are ensured supplies of goods of satisfactory quality at fair prices and conditions while being able to choose between the products of different manufacturers;

(17) Whereas the advantages produced by beer supply agreements and service-station agreements cannot otherwise be secured to the same extent and with the same degree of certainty; whereas the exclusive purchasing obligation on the reseller and the non-competition clause imposed on him are essential components of such agreements and thus usually indispensable for the attainment of these advantages; whereas, however, this is true only as long as the reseller's obligation to purchase from the supplier is confined in the case of premises used for the sale and consumption of drinks to beers and other drinks of the types offered by the supplier, and in the case of service stations to petroleum-based fuel for motor vehicles and other petroleum-based fuels; whereas the exclusive purchasing obligation for lubricants and related petroleum-based products can be accepted only on condition that the supplier

provides for the reseller or finances the procurement of specific equipment for the carrying out of lubrication work; whereas this obligation should only relate to products intended for use within the service station;

(18) Whereas, in order to maintain the reseller's commercial freedom and to ensure access to the retail level of distribution on the part of other suppliers, not only the scope but also the duration of the exclusive purchasing obligation must be limited; whereas it appears appropriate to allow drinks suppliers a choice between a medium-term exclusive purchasing agreement covering a range of drinks and a long-term exclusive purchasing agreement for beer; whereas it is necessary to provide special rules for those premises used for the sale and consumption of drinks which the supplier lets to the reseller; whereas, in this case, the reseller must have the right to obtain, under the conditions specified in this Regulation, other drinks, except beer, supplied under the agreement or of the same type but bearing a different trademark; whereas a uniform maximum duration should be provided for service-station agreements, with the exception of tenancy agreements between the supplier and the reseller, which takes account of the long-term character of the relationship between the parties;

(19) Whereas to the extent that Member States provide, by law or administrative measures, for the same upper limit of duration for the exclusive purchasing obligation upon the reseller as in service-station agreements laid down in this Regulation but provide for a permissible duration which varies in proportion to the consideration provided by the supplier or generally provide for a shorter duration than that permitted by this Regulation, such laws or measures are not contrary to the objectives of this Regulation which, in this respect, merely sets an upper limit to the duration of service-station agreements; whereas the application and enforcement of such national laws or measures must therefore be regarded as compatible with the provisions of this Regulation;

(20) Whereas the limitations and conditions provided for in this Regulation are such as to guarantee effective competition on the markets in question; whereas, therefore, the agreements to which the exemption by category applies do not normally enable the participating undertakings to eliminate competition for a substantial part of the products in question;

(21) Whereas, in particular cases in which agreements or concerted practices satisfying the conditions of this Regulation nevertheless have effects incompatible with Article 85(3) of the Treaty, the Commission may

withdraw the benefit of the exemption by category from the undertakings party thereto;

(22) Whereas agreements and concerted practices which satisfy the conditions set out in this Regulation need not be notified; whereas an undertaking may nonetheless, in a particular case where real doubt exists, request the Commission to declare whether its agreements comply with this Regulation;

(23) Whereas this Regulation does not affect the applicability of Commission Regulation (EEC) No 3604/82 of 23 December 1982 on the application of Article 85(3) of the Treaty to categories of specialisation agreements[3]; whereas it does not exclude the application of Article 86 of the Treaty,

Has adopted the Regulation:

TITLE I

General Provisions

Article 1

Pursuant to Article 85(3) of the Treaty, and subject to the conditions set out in Articles 2 to 5 of this Regulation, it is hereby declared that Article 85(1) of the Treaty shall not apply to agreements to which only two undertakings are party and whereby one party, the reseller, agrees with the other, the supplier, to purchase certain goods specified in the agreement for resale only from the supplier or from a connected undertaking or from another undertaking which the supplier has entrusted with the sale of his goods.

Article 2

1. No other restriction of competition shall be imposed on the supplier than the obligation not to distribute the contract goods or goods which compete with the contract goods in the reseller's principal sales area and at the reseller's level of distribution.

2. Apart from the obligation described in Article 1, no other restriction of competition shall be imposed on the reseller than the obligation not to manufacture or distribute goods which compete with the contract goods.

3. Article 1 shall apply notwithstanding that the reseller undertakes any or all of the following obligations:

(a) to purchase complete ranges of goods;

(b) to purchase minimum quantities of goods which are subject to the exclusive purchasing obligation;

(c) to sell the contract goods under trademarks, or packed and presented as specified by the supplier;

(d) to take measures for the promotion of sales, in particular:

  – to advertise,

  – to maintain a sales network or stock of goods,

  – to provide customer and guarantee services,

  – to employ staff having specialised or technical training.

Article 3

Article 1 shall not apply where:

(a) manufacturers of identical goods or of goods which are considered by users as equivalent in view of their characteristics, price and intended use enter into reciprocal exclusive purchasing agreements between themselves in respect of such goods;

(b) manufacturers of identical goods or of goods which are considered by users as equivalent in view of their characteristics, price and intended use enter into a non-reciprocal exclusive purchasing agreement between themselves in respect of such goods, unless at least one of them has a total annual turnover of no more than 100 million ECU;

(c) the exclusive purchasing obligation is agreed for more than one type of goods where these are neither by their nature nor according to commercial usage connected to each other;

(d) the agreement is concluded for an indefinite duration or for a period of more than five years.

Article 4

1. Article 3(a) and (b) shall also apply where the goods there referred to are manufactured by an undertaking connected with a party to the agreement.

2. Connected undertakings are:

(a) undertakings in which a party to the agreement, directly or indirectly:

  – owns more than half the capital or business assets, or

  – has the power to exercise more than half the voting rights, or

– has the power to appoint more than half the members of the supervisory board, board of directors or bodies legally representing the undertaking, or

  – has the right to manage the affairs;

(b) undertakings which directly or indirectly have in or over a party to the agreement the rights or powers listed in (a);

(c) undertakings in which an undertaking referred to in (b) directly or indirectly has the rights or powers listed in (a).

3. Undertakings in which the parties to the agreement or undertaking connected with them jointly have the rights or powers set out in paragraph 2(a) shall be considered to be connected with each of the parties to the agreement.

Article 5

1. For the purpose of Article 3(b), the ECU is the unit of account used for drawing up the budget of the Community pursuant to Articles 207 and 209 of the Treaty.

2. Article 1 shall remain applicable where during any period of two consecutive financial years the total turnover referred to in Article 3(b) is exceeded by no more than 10%.

3. For the purpose of calculating total turnover within the meaning of Article 3(b), the turnovers achieved during the last financial year by the party to the agreement and connected undertakings in respect of all goods and services, excluding all taxes and other duties, shall be added together. For this purpose, no account shall be taken of dealings between the parties to the agreement or between these undertakings and undertakings connected with them or between the connected undertakings.

TITLE II

Special provisions for beer supply agreements

Article 6

1. Pursuant to Article 85(3) of the Treaty, and subject to Articles 7 to 9 of this Regulation, it is hereby declared that Article 85(1) of the Treaty shall not apply to agreements to which only two undertakings are party and whereby one party, the reseller, agrees with the other, the supplier, in consideration for according special commercial or financial advantages, to purchase only from the supplier, an undertaking connected with the

supplier or another undertaking entrusted by the supplier with the distribution of his goods, certain beers, or certain beers and certain other drinks, specified in the agreement for resale in premises used for the sale and consumption of drinks and designated in the agreement.

2. The declaration in paragraph 1 shall also apply where exclusive purchasing obligations of the kind described in paragraph 1 are imposed on the reseller in favour of the supplier by another undertaking which is itself not a supplier.

Article 7

1. Apart from the obligation referred to in Article 6, no restriction on competition shall be imposed on the reseller other than:

(a) the obligation not to sell beers and other drinks which are supplied by other undertakings and which are of the same type as the beers or other drinks supplied under the agreement in the premises designated in the agreement;

(b) the obligation, in the event that the reseller sells in the premises designated in the agreement beers which are supplied by other undertakings and which are of a different type from the beers supplied under the agreement, to sell such beers only in bottles, cans or other small packages, unless the sale of such beers in draught form is customary or is necessary to satisfy a sufficient demand from consumers;

(c) the obligation to advertise goods supplied by other undertakings within or outside the premises designated in the agreement only in proportion to the share of these goods in the total turnover realised in the premises.

2. Beers or other drinks of the same type are those which are not clearly distinguishable in view or their composition, appearance and taste.

Article 8

1. Article 6 shall not apply where:

(a) the supplier or a connected undertaking imposes on the reseller exclusive purchasing obligations for goods other than drinks or for services;

(b) the supplier restricts the freedom of the reseller to obtain from an undertaking of his choice either services or goods for which neither an exclusive purchasing obligation nor a ban on dealing in competing products may be imposed;

(c) the agreement is concluded for an indefinite duration or for a period of more than five years and the exclusive purchasing obligation relates to specified beers and other drinks;

(d) the agreement is concluded for an indefinite duration or for a period of more than 10 years and the exclusive purchasing obligation relates only to specified beers;

(e) the supplier obliges the reseller to impose the exclusive purchasing obligation on his successor for a longer period than the reseller would himself remain tied to the supplier.

2. Where the agreement relates to premises which the supplier lets to the reseller or allows the reseller to occupy on some other basis in law or in fact, the following provisions shall also apply:

(a) notwithstanding paragraphs (1)(c) and (d), the exclusive purchasing obligations and bans on dealing in competing products specified in this Title may be imposed on the reseller for the whole period for which the reseller in fact operates the premises;

(b) the agreement must provide for the reseller to have the right to obtain:

- drinks, except beer, supplied under the agreement from other undertakings where these undertakings offer them on more favourable conditions which the supplier does not meet,

- drinks, except beer, which are of the same type as those supplied under the agreement but which bear different trade marks, from other undertakings where the supplier does not offer them.

Article 9

Articles 2(1) and (3), 3(a) and (b), 4 and 5 shall apply *mutatis mutandis*.

TITLE III

Special provisions for service-station agreements

Article 10

Pursuant to Article 85(3) of the Treaty and subject to Articles 11 to 13 of this Regulation, it is hereby declared that Article 85(1) of the Treaty shall not apply to agreements to which only two undertakings are party and whereby one party, the reseller, agrees with the other, the supplier, in consideration for the according of special commercial or financial advantages, to purchase only from the supplier, an undertaking connected with the supplier or another undertaking entrusted by the supplier with the distribution of his goods, certain petroleum-based motor-vehicle fuels or certain petroleum-based motor-vehicle and other fuels specified in the agreement for resale in a service station designated in the agreement.

Article 11

Apart from the obligation referred to in Article 10, no restriction on competition shall be imposed on the reseller other than:

(a) the obligation not to sell motor-vehicle fuel and other fuels which are supplied by other undertakings in the service station designated in the agreement;

(b) the obligation not to use lubricants or related petroleum-based products which are supplied by other undertakings within the service station designated in the agreement where the supplier or a connected undertaking has made available to the reseller, or financed, a lubrication bay or other motor-vehicle lubrication equipment;

(c) the obligation to advertise goods supplied by other undertakings within or outside the service station designated in the agreement only in proportion to the share of these goods in the total turnover realised in the service station;

(d) the obligation to have equipment owned by the supplier or a connected undertaking or financed by the supplier or a connected undertaking serviced by the supplier or an undertaking designated by him.

Article 12

1. Article 10 shall not apply where:

(a) the supplier or a connected undertaking imposes on the reseller exclusive purchasing obligations for goods other than motor-vehicle and other fuels or for services, except in the case of the obligations referred to in Article 11(b) and (d);

(b) the supplier restricts the freedom of the reseller to obtain, from an undertaking of his choice, goods or services, for which under the provisions of this Title neither an exclusive purchasing obligation nor a ban on dealing in competing products may be imposed;

(c) the agreement is concluded for an indefinite duration or for a period of more than 10 years;

(d) the supplier obliges the reseller to impose the exclusive purchasing obligation on his successor for a longer period than the reseller would himself remain tied to the supplier.

2. Where the agreement relates to a service station which the supplier lets to the reseller, or allows the reseller to occupy on some other basis, in law or in fact, exclusive purchasing obligations or prohibitions of competition indicated in this Title may, notwithstanding paragraph 1(c), be imposed on the reseller for the whole period for which the reseller in fact operates the premises.

Article 13

Articles 2(1) and (3), 3(a) and (b), 4 and 5 of this Regulation shall apply *mutatis mutandis*.

TITLE IV

Miscellaneous provisions

Article 14

The Commission may withdraw the benefit of this Regulation, pursuant to Article 7 of Regulation No 19/65/EEC, when it finds in a particular case that an agreement which is exempted by this Regulation nevertheless has certain effects which are incompatible with the conditions set out in Article 85(3) of the Treaty, and in particular where:

(a) the contract goods are not subject, in a substantial part of the common market, to effective competition from identical goods or goods considered by users as equivalent in view of their characteristics, price and intended use;

(b) access by other suppliers to the different stages of distribution in a substantial part of the common market is made difficult to a significant extent;

(c) the supplier without any objectively justified reason:

1. refuses to supply categories of resellers who cannot obtain the contract goods elsewhere on suitable terms or applies to them differing prices or conditions of sale;

2. applies less favourable prices or conditions of sale to resellers bound by an exclusive purchasing obligation as compared with other resellers at the same level of distribution.

Article 15

1. In the period 1 July 1983 to 31 December 1986, the prohibition in Article 85(1) of the Treaty shall not apply to agreements of the kind described in Article 1 which either were in force on 1 July 1983 or entered into force between 1 July and 31 December 1983 and which satisfy the exemption conditions under Regulation No 67/67/EEC[4].

2. In the period 1 July 1983 to 31 December 1986, the prohibitions in Article 85(1) of the Treaty shall not apply to agreements of the kinds described in Articles 6 and 10 which either were in force on 1 July 1983 or entered into force between 1 July and 31 December 1983 and which satisfy the exemption conditions of Regulation No 67/67/EEC.

3. In the case of agreements of the kinds described in Articles 6 and 10, which were in force on 1 July 1983 and which expire after 31 December 1988, the prohibition in Article 85(1) of the Treaty shall not apply in the period from 1 January 1989 to the expiry of the agreement but at the latest to the expiry of this Regulation to the extent that the supplier releases the reseller, before 1 January 1989, from all obligations which would prevent the application of the exemption under Titles II and III.

Article 16

This Regulation shall not apply to agreements by which the supplier undertakes with the reseller to supply only to the reseller certain goods for resale, in the whole or in a defined part of the Community, and the reseller undertakes with the supplier to purchase these goods only from the supplier.

Article 17

This Regulation shall not apply where the parties or connected undertakings, for the purpose of resale in one and the same premises used for the sale and consumption of drinks or service station, enter into agreements both of the kind referred to in Title I and of a kind referred to in Title II or III.

Article 18

This Regulation shall apply *mutatis mutandis* to the categories of concerted practices defined in Articles 1, 6 and 10.

Article 19

This Regulation shall enter into force on 1 July 1983 . It shall expire on 31 December 1997.

This Regulation shall be binding in its entirety and directly applicable in all Member States.

Done at Brussels, 22 June 1983.

For the Commission

Frans Andriessen

Member of the Commission

FOOTNOTES

1. OJ No 36, 6.3.65, p.533.
2. OJ No C 172, 10.7.82, p.7.
3. OJ No L 376, 31.12.82, p.33.
4. OJ No 57, 25.3.67, p.849.

COMMISSION REGULATION (EEC) No 4087/88

of 30 November 1988

on the application of Article 85(3) of the Treaty to categories of franchise agreements

(OJ No L 359, 28.12.88, p.46)

The Commission of the European Communities,

Having regard to the Treaty establishing the European Economic Community,

Having regard to Council Regulation No 19/65/EEC of 2 March 1965 on the application of Article 85(3) of the Treaty to certain categories of agreements and concerted practices[1], as last amended by the Act of Accession of Spain and Portugal, and in particular Article 1 thereof,

Having published a draft of this Regulation[2],

Having consulted the Advisory Committee on Restrictive Practices and Dominant Positions,

Whereas:

(1) Regulation No 19/65/EEC empowers the Commission to apply Article 85(3) of the Treaty by Regulation to certain categories of bilateral exclusive agreements falling within the scope of Article 85(1) which either have as their object the exclusive distribution or exclusive

purchase of goods, to include restrictions imposed in relation to the assignment or use of industrial property rights.

(2) Franchise agreements consist essentially of licences of industrial or intellectual property rights relating to trade marks or signs and know-how, which can be combined with restrictions relating to supply or purchase of goods.

(3) Several types of franchise can be distinguished according to their object: industrial franchise concerns the manufacturing of goods, distribution franchise concerns the sale of goods, and service franchise concerns the supply of services.

(4) It is possible on the basis of the experience of the Commission to define categories of franchise agreements which fall under Article 85(1) but can normally be regarded as satisfying the conditions laid down in Article 85(3). This is the case for franchise agreements whereby one of the parties supplies goods or provides services to end users. On the other hand industrial franchise agreements should not be covered by this Regulation. Such agreements, which usually govern relationships between producers, present different characteristics than the other types of franchise. They consist of manufacturing licences based on patents and/or technical know-how, combined with trade-mark licences. Some of them may benefit from other block exemptions if they fulfil the necessary conditions.

(5) This Regulation covers franchise agreements between two undertakings, the franchisor and the franchisee, for the retailing of goods or the provision of services to end users, or a combination of these activities, such as the processing or adaptation of goods to fit specific needs of their customers. It also covers cases where the relationship between franchisor and franchisees is made through a third undertaking, the master franchisee. It does not cover wholesale franchise agreements because of the lack of experience of the Commission in that field.

(6) Franchise agreements as defined in this Regulation can fall under Article 85(1). They may in particular affect intra-Community trade where they are concluded between undertakings from different Member States or where they form the basis of a network which extends beyond the boundaries of a single Member State.

(7) Franchise agreements as defined in this Regulation normally improve the distribution of goods and/or the provision of services as they give franchisors the possibility of establishing a uniform network with limited investments, which may assist the entry of new competitors on the market, particularly in the case of small and medium-sized undertakings,

thus increasing interbrand competition. They also allow independent traders to set up outlets more rapidly and with higher chance of success than if they had to do so without the franchisor's experience and assistance. They have therefore the possibility of competing more efficiently with large distribution undertakings.

(8) As a rule, franchise agreements also allow consumers and other end users a fair share of the resulting benefit, as they combine the advantage of a uniform network with the existence of traders personally interested in the efficient operation of their business. The homogeneity of the network and the constant cooperation between the franchisor and the franchisees ensures a constant quality of the products and services. The favourable effect of franchising on interbrand competition and the fact that consumers are free to deal with any franchisee in the network guarantees that a reasonable part of the resulting benefits will be passed on to the consumers.

(9) This Regulation must define the obligations restrictive of competition which may be included in franchise agreements. This is the case in particular for the granting of an exclusive territory to the franchisees combined with the prohibition on actively seeking customers outside that territory, which allows them to concentrate their efforts on their allotted territory. The same applies on the granting of an exclusive territory to a master franchisee combined with the obligation not to conclude franchise agreements with third parties outside that territory. Where the franchisees sell or use in the process of providing services, goods manufactured by the franchisor or according to its instructions and or bearing its trade mark, an obligation on the franchisees not to sell, or use in the process of the provision of services, competing goods, makes it possible to establish a coherent network which is identified with the franchised goods. However, this obligation should only be accepted with respect to the goods which form the essential subject-matter of the franchise. It should notably not relate to accessories or spare parts for these goods.

(10) The obligations referred to above thus do not impose restrictions which are not necessary for the attainment of the abovementioned objectives. In particular, the limited territorial protection granted to the franchisees is indispensable to protect their investment.

(11) It is desirable to list in the Regulation a number of obligations that are commonly found in franchise agreements and are normally not restrictive of competition and to provide that if, because of the particular economic or legal circumstances, they fall under Article 85(1), they are also covered by the exemption. This list, which is not exhaustive, includes, in particular, clauses which are essential either to preserve the

common identity and reputation of the network or to prevent the know-how made available and the assistance given by the franchisor from benefiting competitors.

(12) The Regulation must specify the conditions which must be satisfied for the exemption to apply. To guarantee that competition is not eliminated for a substantial part of the goods which are the subject of the franchise, it is necessary that parallel imports remain possible. Therefore, cross deliveries between franchisees should always be possible. Furthermore, where a franchise network is combined with another distribution system, franchisees should be free to obtain supplies from authorised distributors. To better inform consumers, thereby helping to ensure that they receive a fair share of the resulting benefits, it must be provided that the franchisee shall be obliged to indicate its status as an independent undertaking, by any appropriate means which does not jeopardise the common identity of the franchised network. Furthermore, where the franchisees have to honour guarantees for the franchisor's goods, this obligation should also apply to goods supplied by the franchisor, other franchisees or other agreed dealers.

(13) The Regulation must also specify restrictions which may not be included in franchise agreements if these are to benefit from the exemption granted by the Regulation, by virtue of the fact that such provisions are restrictions falling under Article 85(1) for which there is no general presumption that they will lead to the positive effects required by Article 85(3). This applies in particular to market sharing between competing manufacturers, to clauses unduly limiting the franchisee's choice of suppliers or customers, and to cases where the franchisee is restricted in determining its prices. However, the franchisor should be free to recommend prices to the franchisees, where it is not prohibited by national laws and to the extent that it does not lead to concerted practices for the effective application of these prices.

(14) Agreements which are not automatically covered by the exemption because they contain provisions that are not expressly exempted by the Regulation and not expressly excluded from exemption may nonetheless generally be presumed to be eligible for application of Article 85(3). It will be possible for the Commission rapidly to establish whether this is the case for a particular agreement. Such agreements should therefore be deemed to be covered by the exemption provided for in this Regulation where they are notified to the Commission and the Commission does not oppose the application of the exemption within a specified period of time.

(15) If individual agreements exempted by this Regulation nevertheless have effects which are incompatible with Article 85(3), in particular as

interpreted by the administrative practice of the Commission and the case law of the Court of Justice, the Commission may withdraw the benefit of the block exemption. This applies in particular where competition is significantly restricted because of the structure of the relevant market.

(16) Agreements which are automatically exempted pursuant to this Regulation need not be notified. Undertakings may nevertheless in a particular case request a decision pursuant to Council Regulation No 17[3] as last amended by the Act of Accession of Spain and Portugal.

(17) Agreements may benefit from the provisions either of this Regulation or of another Regulation, according to their particular nature and provided that they fulfil the necessary conditions of application. They may not benefit from a combination of the provisions of this Regulation with those of another block exemption Regulation,

Has adopted this Regulation:

Article 1

1. Pursuant to Article 85(3) of the Treaty and subject to the provisions of this Regulation, it is hereby declared that Article 85(1) of this Treaty shall not apply to franchise agreements to which two undertakings are party, which include one or more of the restrictions listed in Article 2.

2. The exemption provided for in paragraph 1 shall also apply to master franchise agreements to which two undertakings are party, Where applicable, the provisions of this Regulation concerning the relationship between franchisor and franchisee shall apply *mutatis mutandis* to the relationship between franchisor and master franchisee and between master franchisee and franchisee.

3. For the purposes of this Regulation:

(a) 'franchise' means a package of industrial or intellectual property rights relating to trade marks, trade names, shop signs, utility models, designs, copyrights, know-how or patents, to be exploited for the resale of goods or the provision of services to end users;

(b) 'franchise agreements' means an agreement whereby one undertaking, the franchisor, grants the other, the franchisee, in exchange for direct or indirect financial consideration, the right to exploit a franchise for the purposes of marketing specified types of goods and/or services; it includes at least obligations relating to:

– the use of a common name or shop sign and a uniform presentation of contract premises and/or means of transport,

- the communication by the franchisor to the franchisee of know-how,
- the continuing provision by the franchisor to the franchisee of commercial or technical assistance during the life of the agreement;

(c) 'master franchise agreement' means an agreement whereby one undertaking, the franchisor, grants the other, the master franchisee, in exchange of direct or indirect financial consideration, the right to exploit a franchise for the purposes of concluding franchise agreements with third parties, the franchisees;

(d) 'franchisor's goods' means goods produced by the franchisor or according to its instructions, and/or bearing the franchisor's name or trade mark;

(e) 'contract premises' means the premises used for the exploitation of the franchise or, when the franchise is exploited outside those premises, the base from which the franchisee operates the means of transport used for the exploitation of the franchise (contract means of transport);

(f) 'know-how' means a package of non-patented practical information, resulting from experience and testing by the franchisor, which is secret, substantial and identified;

(g) 'secret' means that the know-how, as a body or in the precise configuration and assembly of its components, is not generally known or easily accessible; it is not limited in the narrow sense that each individual component of the know-how should be totally unknown or unobtainable outside the franchisor's business;

(h) 'substantial' means that the know-how includes information which is of importance for the sale of goods or the provision of services to end users, and in particular for the presentation of goods for sale, the processing of goods in connection with the provision of services, methods of dealing with customers, and administration and financial management; the know-how must be useful for the franchisee by being capable, at the date of conclusion of the agreement, of improving the competitive position of the franchisee, in particular by improving the franchisee's performance or helping it to enter a new market;

(i) 'identified' means that the know-how must be described in a sufficiently comprehensive manner so as to make it possible to verify that it fulfils the criteria of secrecy and substantiality; the description of the know-how can either be set out in the franchise agreement or in a separate document or recorded in any other appropriate form.

Article 2

The exemption provided for in Article 1 shall apply to the following restrictions of competition:

(a) an obligation on the franchisor, in a defined area of the common market, the contract territory, not to:

- grant the right to exploit all or part of the franchise to third parties,

- itself exploit the franchise, or itself market the goods or services which are the subject-matter of the franchise under a similar formula;

- itself supply the franchisor's goods to third parties;

(b) an obligation on the master franchisee not to conclude franchise agreements with third parties outside its contract territory;

(c) an obligation on the franchisee to exploit the franchise only from the contract premises;

(d) an obligation on the franchisee to refrain, outside the contract territory, from seeking customers for the goods or the services which are the subject-matter of the franchise;

(e) an obligation on the franchisee not to manufacture, sell or use in the course of the provision of services, goods competing with the franchisor's goods which are the subject-matter of the franchise; where the subject-matter of the franchise is the sale or use in the course of the provision of services both certain types of goods and spare parts or accessories therefor, that obligation may not be imposed in respect of these spare parts or accessories.

Article 3

1. Article 1 shall apply notwithstanding the presence of any of the following obligations on the franchisee, in so far as they are necessary to protect the franchisor's industrial or intellectual property rights or to maintain the common identity and reputation of the franchised network:

(a) to sell, or use in the course of the provision of services, exclusively goods matching minimum objective quality specifications laid down by the franchisor;

(b) to sell, or use in the course of the provision of services, goods which are manufactured only by the franchisor or by third parties designed by it, where it is impracticable, owing to the nature of the goods which are the subject-matter of the franchise, to apply objective quality specifications;

(c) not to engage, directly or indirectly, in any similar business in a territory where it would compete with a member of the franchised network, including the franchisor; the franchisee may be held to this obligation after termination of the agreement, for a reasonable period which may not exceed one year, in the territory where it has exploited the franchise;

(d) not to acquire financial interests in the capital of a competing undertaking, which would give the franchisee the power to influence the economic conduct of such undertaking;

(e) to sell the goods which are the subject-matter of the franchise only to end users, to other franchisees and to resellers within other channels of distribution supplied by the manufacturer of these goods or with its consent;

(f) to use its best endeavours to sell the goods or provide the services that are the subject-matter of the franchise; to offer for sale a minimum range of goods, achieve a minimun turnover, plan its orders in advance, keep minimum stocks and provide customer and warranty services;

(g) to pay to the franchisor a specified proportion of its revenue for advertising and itself carry out advertising for the nature of which it shall obtain the franchisor's approval.

2. Article 1 shall apply notwithstanding the presence of any of the following obligations on the franchisee:

(a) not to disclose to third parties the know-how provided by the franchisor; the franchisee may be held to this obligation after termination of the agreement;

(b) to communicate to the franchisor any experience gained in exploiting the franchise and to grant it, and other franchisees, a non-exclusive licence for the know-how resulting from that experience;

(c) to inform the franchisor of infringements of licensed industrial or intellectual property rights, to take legal action against infringers or to assist the franchisor in any legal actions against infringers:

(d) not to use know-how licensed by the franchisor for purposes other than the exploitation of the franchise; the franchisee may be held to this obligation after termination of the agreement;

(e) to attend or have its staff attend training courses arranged by the franchisor;

(f) to apply the commercial methods devised by the franchisor, including any subsequent modification thereof, and use the licensed industrial or intellectual property rights;

(g) to comply with the franchisor's standards for the equipment and presentation of the contract premises and/or means of transport;

(h) to allow the franchisor to carry out checks of the contract premises and/or means of transport, including the goods sold and the services provided, and the inventory and accounts of the franchisee;

(i) not without the franchisor's consent to change the location of the contract premises;

(j) not without the franchisor's consent to assign the rights and obligations under the franchise agreement.

3. In the event that, because of particular circumstances, obligations referred to in paragraph 2 fall within the scope of Article 85(1), they shall also be exempted even if they are not accompanied by any of the obligations exempted by Article 1.

Article 4

The exemption provided for in Article 1 shall apply on condition that:

(a) the franchisee is free to obtain goods that are the subject-matter of the franchise from other franchisees; where such goods are also distributed through another network of authorised distributors, the franchisee must be free to obtain the goods from the latter;

(b) where the franchisor obliges the franchisee to honour guarantees for the franchisor's goods, that obligation shall apply in respect of such goods supplied by any member of the franchised network or other distributors which give a similar guarantee, in the common market;

(c) the franchisee is obliged to indicate its status as an independent undertaking; this indication shall however not interfere with the common identity of the franchised network resulting in particular from the common name or shop sign and uniform appearance of the contract premises and/or means of transport.

Article 5

The exemption granted by Article 1 shall not apply where:

(a) undertakings producing goods or providing services which are identical or are considered by users as equivalent in view of their characteristics, price and intended use, enter into franchise agreements in respect of such goods or services;

(*b*) without prejudice to Article 2(e) and Article 3(1)(b), the franchisee is prevented from obtaining supplies of goods of a quality equivalent to those offered by the franchisor;

(*c*) without prejudice to Article 2(e), the franchisee is obliged to sell, or use the process of providing services, goods manufactured by the franchisor or third parties designated by the franchisor and the franchisor refuses, for reasons other than protecting the franchisor's industrial or intellectual property rights, or maintaining the common identity and reputation of the franchised network, to designate as authorised manufacturers third parties proposed by the franchisee;

(*d*) the franchisee is prevented from continuing to use the licensed know-how after termination of the agreement where the know-how has become generally known or easily accessible, other than by breach of an obligation by the franchisee;

(*e*) the franchisee is restricted by the franchisor, directly or indirectly, in the determination of sale prices for the goods or services which are the subject-matter of the franchise, without prejudice to the possibility for the franchisor of recommending sale prices;

(*f*) the franchisor prohibits the franchisee from challenging the validity of the industrial and intellectual property rights which form part of the franchise, without prejudice to the possibility for the franchisor of terminating the agreement in such a case;

(*g*) franchisees are obliged not to supply within the common market the goods or services which are the subject-matter of the franchise to end users because of their place of residence.

Article 6

1. The exemption provided for in Article 1 shall also apply to franchise agreements which fulfil the conditions laid down in Article 4 and include obligations restrictive of competition which are not covered by Articles 2 and 3(3) and do not fall within the scope of Article 5, on condition that the agreements in question are notified to the Commission in accordance with the provisions of Commission Regulation No 27[4] and that the Commission does not oppose such exemption within a period of six months.

2. The period of six months shall run from the date on which the notification is received by the Commission. Where, however, the notification is made by registered post, the period shall run from the date shown on the postmark of the place of posting.

3. Paragraph 1 shall apply only if:

(a) express reference is made to this Article in the notification or in a communication accompanying it; and

(b) the information furnished with the notification is complete and in accordance with the facts.

4. The benefit of paragraph 1 can be claimed for agreements notified before the entry into force of this Regulation by submitting a communication to the Commission referring expressly to this Article and to the notification. Paragraphs 2 and 3(b) shall apply *mutatis mutandis*.

5. The Commission may oppose exemption. It shall oppose exemption if it receives a request to do so from a Member State within three months of the forwarding to the Member State of the notification referred to in paragraph 1 or the communication referred to in paragraph 4. This request must be justified on the basis of considerations relating to the competition rules of the Treaty.

6. The Commission may withdraw its opposition to the exemption at any time. However, where that opposition was raised at the request of a Member State, it may be withdrawn only after consultation of the advisory Committee on Restrictive Practices and Dominant Positions.

7. If the opposition is withdrawn because the undertakings concerned have shown that the conditions of Article 85(3) are fulfilled, the exemption shall apply from the date of the notification.

8. If the opposition is withdrawn because the undertakings concerned have amended the agreement so that the conditions of Article 85(3) are fulfilled, the exemption shall apply from the date on which the amendments take effect.

9. If the Commission opposes exemption and its opposition is not withdrawn, the effects of the notification shall be governed by the provisions of Regulation No 17 .

Article 7

1. Information acquired pursuant to Article 6 shall be used only for the purposes of this Regulation.

2. The Commission and the authorities of the Member States, their officials and other servants shall not disclose information acquired by them pursuant to this Regulation of a kind that is covered by the obligation of professional secrecy.

3. Paragraphs 1 and 2 shall not prevent publication of general information or surveys which do not contain information relating to particular undertakings or associations of undertakings.

Article 8

The Commission may withdraw the benefit of this Regulation, pursuant to Article 7 of Regulation No 19/65/EEC, where it finds in a particular case that an agreement exempted by this Regulation nevertheless has certain effects which are incompatible with the conditions laid down in Article 85(3) of the EEC Treaty, and in particular where territorial protection is awarded to the franchisee and:

(a) access to the relevant market or competition therein is significantly restricted by the cumulative effect of parallel networks of similar agreements established by competing manufacturers or distributors;

(b) the goods or services which are the subject-matter of the franchise do not face, in a substantial part of the common market, effective competition from goods or services which are identical or considered by users as equivalent in view of their characteristics, price and intended use;

(c) the parties, or one of them, prevent end users, because of their place of residence, from obtaining, directly or through intermediaries, the goods or services which are the subject-matter of the franchise within the common market, or use differences in specifications concerning those goods or services in different Member States, to isolate markets;

(d) franchisees engage in concerted practices relating to the sale prices of the goods or services which are the subject-matter of the franchise;

(e) the franchisor uses its rights to check the contract premises and means of transport, or refuses its agreement to requests by the franchisee to move the contract premises or assign its rights and obligations under the franchise agreement, for reasons other than protecting the franchisor's industrial or intellectual property rights, maintaining the common identity and reputation of the franchised network or verifying that the franchisee abides by its obligations under the agreement.

Article 9

This Regulation shall enter into force on 1 February 1989.

It shall remain in force until 31 December 1999.

This Regulation shall be binding in its entirety and directly applicable in all Member States.

Done at Brussels, 30 November 1988.

For the Commission

Peter Sutherland

Member of the Commission

EDITORIAL NOTE

Some typographical errors in OJ corrected.

FOOTNOTES

1. OJ No 36, 6.3.65, p 533.
2. OJ No C 229, 27.8.87, p.3.
3. OJ No 13, 21.2.62, p.204.
4. OJ No 35, 10.5.62, p 1118.

COMMISSION REGULATION (EEC) No 556/89

of 30 November 1988

on the application of Article 85(3) of the Treaty to certain categories of know-how licensing agreements

(OJ No L 61, 4.3.89, p.1)

The Commission of the European Communities,

Having regard to the Treaty establishing the European Economic Community,

Having regard to Council Regulation No 19/65/EEC of 2 March 1965 on the application of Article 85(3) of the Treaty to certain categories of agreements and concerted practices[1], as last amended by the Act of Accession of Spain and Portugal, and in particular to Article 1 thereof,

Having published a draft of this Regulation[2],

After consulting the Advisory Committee on Restrictive Practices and Dominant Positions,

Whereas:

(1) Regulation No 19/65/EEC empowers the Commission to apply Article 85(3) of the Treaty by Regulation to certain categories of bilateral agreements and concerted practices falling within the scope of Article 85(1) which include restrictions imposed in relation to the acquisition or

use of industrial property rights, in particular patents, utility models, designs or trade marks, or to the rights arising out of contrasts for assignment of, or the right to use, a method of manufacture or knowledge relating to the use or application of industrial processes.

The increasing economic importance of non-patented technical information (e.g. descriptions of manufacturing processes, recipes, formulae, designs or drawings), commonly termed 'know-how', the large number of agreements currently being concluded by undertakings including public research facilities solely for the exploitation of such information (so-called 'pure' know-how licensing agreements) and the fact that the transfer of know-how is, in practice, frequently irreversible make it necessary to provide greater legal certainty with regard to the status of such agreements under the competition rules, thus encouraging the dissemination of technical knowledge in the Community. In the light of experience acquired so far, it is possible to define a category of such know-how licensing agreements covering all or part of the common market which are capable of falling within the scope of Article 85(1) but which can normally be regarded as satisfying the conditions laid down in Article 85(3), where the licensed know-how is secret, substantial and identified in any appropriate form ('the know-how'). These definitional requirements are only intended to ensure that the communication of the know-how provides a valid justification for the application of the present Regulation and in particular for the exemption of obligations which are restrictive of competition.

A list of definitions for the purposes of this Regulation is set out in Article 1.

(2) As well as pure know-how agreements, mixed know-how and patent licensing agreements play an increasingly important role in the transfer of technology. It is therefore appropriate to include within the scope of this Regulation mixed agreements which are not exempted by Commission Regulation (EEC) No 2349/84 (Article 1, 2 or 4)[3] and in particular the following:

– mixed agreements in which the licensed patents are not necessary for the achievement of the objects of the licensed technology containing both patented and non-patented elements; this may be the case where such patents do not afford affective protection against the exploitation of the technology by third parties;

– mixed agreements which, regardless of whether or not the licensed patents are necessary, for the achievement of the objects of the licensed technology, contain obligations which restrict the exploitation of the relevant technology by the licensor or the licensee in Member States without patent protection, in so far and as long as such obligations are based in whole or in part on the exploitation of the licensed know-how and fulfil the other conditions set out in this Regulation.

It is also appropriate to extend the scope of this Regulation to pure or mixed agreements containing ancillary provisions relating to trade marks and other intellectual property rights where there are no obligations restrictive of competition other than those also attached to the know-how and exempted under the present Regulation.

However, such agreements, too, can only be regarded as fulfilling the conditions of Article 85(3) for the purposes of this Regulation where the licensed technical knowledge is secret, substantial and identified.

(3) The provisions of the present Regulation are not applicable to agreements covered by Regulation (EEC) No 2349/84 on patent licensing agreements.

(4) Where such pure or mixed know-how licensing agreements contain not only obligations relating to territories within the common market but also obligations relating to non-member countries, the presence of the latter does not prevent the present Regulation from applying to the obligations relating to territories within the common market.

However, where know-how licensing agreements for non-member countries or for territories which extend beyond the frontiers of the Community have effects within the common market which may fall within the scope of Article 85(1), such agreements should be covered by the Regulation to the same extent as would agreements for territories within the common market.

(5) It is not appropriate to include within the scope of the Regulation agreements solely for the purpose of sale, except where the licensor undertakes for a preliminary period before the licensee himself commences production using the licensed technology to supply the contract products for sale by the licensee. Also excluded from the scope of the Regulation are agreements relating to marketing know-how communicated in the context of franchising arrangements[4] or to know-how agreements entered into in connection with arrangements such as joint ventures or patent pools and other arrangements in which the licensing of the know-how occurs in exchange for other licences not related to improvements to or new applications of that know-how, as such agreements pose different problems which cannot at present be dealt with in one Regulation (Article 5).

(6) Exclusive licensing agreements, i.e. agreements in which the licensor undertakes not to exploit the licensed technology in the licensed territory himself or to grant further licenses there, may not be in

themselves incompatible with Article 85(1) where they are concerned with the introduction and protection of a new technology in the licensed territory, by reason of the scale of the research which has been undertaken and of the increase in the level of competition, in particular interbrand competition, and in the competitiveness of the undertakings concerned resulting from the dissemination of innovation within the Community.

In so far as agreements of this kind fall in other circumstances within the scope of Article 85(1), it is appropriate to include them in Article 1, in order that they may also benefit from the exemption.

(7) Both these and the other obligations listed in Article 1 encourage the transfer of technology and thus generally contribute to improving the production of goods and to promoting technical progress, by increasing the number of production facilities and the quality of goods produced in the common market and expanding the possibilities of further development of the licensed technology. This is true, in particular, of an obligation on the licensee to use the licensed product only in the manufacture of its own products, since it gives the licensor an incentive to disseminate the technology in various applications while reserving the separate sale of the licensed product to himself or other licensees. It is also true of obligations on the licensor and on the licensee to refrain not only from active but also from passive competition, in the licensed territory, in the case of the licensor, and in the territories reserved for the licensor or other licensees in the case of the licensee. The users of technologically new or improved products requiring major investment are often not final consumers but intermediate industries which are well informed about prices and alternative sources of supply of the products within the Community. Hence, protection against active competition only would not afford the parties and other licensees the security they needed, especially during the initial period of exploitation of the licensed technology when they would be investing in tooling up and developing a market for the product and in effect increasing demand.

In view of the difficulty of determining the point at which know-how can be said to be no longer secret, and the frequent licensing of a continuous stream of know-how, especially where technology in the industry is rapidly evolving, it is appropriate to limit to a fixed number of years the periods of territorial protection, of the licensor and the licensee from one another, and as between licensees, which are automatically covered by the exemption. Since, as distinguished from patent licenses, know-how licenses are frequently negotiated after the goods or services incorporating the licensed technology have proved successful on the market, it is appropriate to take for each licensed territory the date of signature of the first license agreement entered into for that territory by the licensor in respect of the same technology as the starting point for the permitted periods of territorial protection of the licensor and licensee from one another. As to the protection of a licensee from manufacture, use, active or passive sales by other licensees the starting point should be the date of signature of the first license agreement entered into by the licensor within the EEC. The exemption of the territorial protection shall apply for the whole duration of such allowed periods as long as the know-how remains secret and substantial, irrespective of when the Member States in question joined the Community and provided that each of the licensees, the restricted as well as the protected one, manufactures the licensed product himself or has it manufactured.

Exemption under Article 85(3) of longer periods of territorial protection, in particular to protect expensive and risky investments or where the parties were not already competitors before the grant of the licence, can only be granted by individual decision. On the other hand, parties are free to extend the term of their agreement to exploit any subsequent improvements and to provide for the payment of additional royalties. However, in such cases, further periods of territorial protection, starting from the date of licensing of the improvements in the EEC, may be allowed only by individual decision, in particular where the improvements to or new applications of the licensed technology are substantial and secret and not of significantly less importance than the technology initially granted or require new expensive and risky investment.

(8) However, it is appropriate in cases where the same technology is protected in some Member States by necessary patents within the meaning of recital 9 of Regulation (EEC) No 2349/84 to provide with respect to those Member States an exemption under this Regulation for the territorial protection of the licensor and licensee from one another and as between licensees against manufacture, use and active sales in each other's territory for the full life of the patents existing in such Member States.

(9) The obligations listed in Article 1 also generally fulfil the other conditions for the application of Article 85(3). Consumers will as a rule be allowed a fair share of the benefit resulting from the improvement in the supply of goods on the market. Nor do the obligations impose restrictions which are not indispensable to the attainment of the abovementioned objectives. Finally, competition at the distribution stage is safeguarded by the possibility of parallel imports, which may not be hindered by the parties in any circumstances. The exclusivity obligations covered by the Regulation thus do not normally entail the possibility of eliminating competition in respect of a substantial part of

the products in question. This also applies in the case of agreements which grant exclusive licences for a territory covering the whole of the common market where there is the possibility of parallel imports from third countries, or where there are other competing technologies on the market, since then the territorial exclusivity may lead to greater market integration and stimulate Community-wide interbrand competition.

(10) It is desirable to list in the Regulation a number of obligations that are commonly found in know-how licensing agreements but are normally not restrictive of competition and to provide that in the event that because of the particular economic or legal circumstances they should fall within Article 85(1), they also would be covered by the exemption. This list, in Article 2, is not exhaustive.

(11) The Regulation must also specify what restrictions or provisions may not be included in know-how licensing agreements if these are to benefit from the block exemption. The restrictions, which are listed in Article 3, may fall under the prohibition of Article 85(1), but in their case there can be no general presumption that they will lead to the positive effects required by Article 85(3), as would be necessary for the granting of a block exemption, and consequently an exemption can be granted only on an individual basis.

(12) Agreements which are not automatically covered by the exemption because they contain provisions that are not expressly exempted by the Regulation and not expressly excluded from exemption, including those listed in Article 4(2) of the Regulation, may nonetheless generally be presumed to be eligible for application of the block exemption. It will be possible for the Commission rapidly to establish whether this is the case for a particular agreement. Such agreements should therefore be deemed to be covered by the exemption provided for in this Regulation where they are notified to the Commission and the Commission does not oppose the application of the exemption within a specified period of time.

(13) If individual agreements exempted by this Regulation nevertheless have effects which are incompatible with Article 85(3), the Commission may withdraw the benefit of the block exemption (Article 7).

(14) The list in Article 2 includes among others obligations on the licensee to cease using the licensed know-how after the termination of the agreement ('post-term use ban') (Article 2(1)(3)) and to make improvements available to the licensor ('grant-back clause') (Article 2(1)(4)). A post-term use ban may be regarded as a normal feature of the licensing of know-how as otherwise the licensor would be forced to transfer his know-how in perpetuity and this could inhibit the transfer of technology. Moreover, undertakings by the licensee to grant back to the

licensor a licence for improvements to the licensed know-how and/or patents are generally not restrictive of competition if the licensee is entitled by the contract to share in future experience and inventions made by the licensor and the licensee retains the right to disclose experience acquired or grant licences to third parties where to do so would not disclose the licensor's know-how.

On the other hand, a restrictive effect on competition arises where the agreement contains both a post-term use ban and an obligation on the licensee to make his improvements to the know-how available to the licensor, even on a non-exclusive and reciprocal basis, and to allow the licensor to continue using them even after the expiry of the agreement. This is so because in such a case the licensee has no possibility of inducing the licensor to authorise him to continue exploiting the originally licensed know-how, and hence the licensee's own improvements as well, after the expiry of the agreement.

(15) The list in Article 2 also includes an obligation on the licensee to keep paying royalties until the end of the agreement independently of whether or not the licensed know-how has entered into the public domain through the action of third parties (Article 2(1)(7)). As a rule, parties do not need to be protected against the foreseeable financial consequences of an agreement freely entered into and should therefore not be restricted in their choice of the appropriate means of financing the technology transfer. This applies especially where know-how is concerned since here there can be no question of an abuse of a legal monopoly and, under the legal systems of the Member States, the licensee may have a remedy in an action under the applicable national law. Furthermore, provisions for the payment of royalties in return for the grant of a whole package of technology throughout an agreed reasonable period independently of whether or not the know-how has entered into the public domain, are generally in the interest of the licensee in that they prevent the licensor demanding a high initial payment up front with a view to diminishing his financial exposure in the event of premature disclosure. Parties should be free, in order to facilitate payment by the licensee, to spread the royalty payments for the use of the licensed technology over a period extending beyond the entry of the know-how into the public domain. Moreover, continuous payments should be allowed throughout the term of the agreement in cases where both parties are fully aware that the first sale of the product will necessarily disclose the know-how. Nevertheless, the Commission may, where it was clear from the circumstances that the licensee would have been able and willing to develop the know-how himself in a short period of time, in comparison with which the period of continuing

payments is excessively long, withdraw the benefit of the exemption under Article 7 of this Regulation.

Finally, the use of methods of royalties calculation which are unrelated to the exploitation of the licensed technology or the charging of royalties on products whose manufacture at no stage includes the use of any of the licensed patents or secret techniques would render the agreement ineligible for the block exemption (Article 3(5)). The licensee should also be freed from his obligation to pay royalties, where the know-how becomes publicly known through the action of the licensor. However, the mere sale of the product by the licensor or an undertaking connected with him does not constitute such an action (Article 2(1)(7) and Article 3(5)).

(16) An obligation on the licensee to restrict his exploitation of the licensed technology to one or more technical fields of application ('fields of use') or to one or more product markets is also not caught by Article 85(1) (Article 2(1)(8)). This obligation is not restrictive of competition since the licensor can be regarded as having the right to transfer the know-how only for a limited purpose. Such a restriction must however not constitute a disguised means of customer sharing.

(17) Restrictions which give the licensor an unjustified competitive advantage, such as an obligation on the licensee to accept quality specifications, other licences or goods and services that the licensee does not want from the licensor, prevent the block exemption from being applicable. However, this does not apply where it can be shown that the licensee wanted such specifications, licences, goods or services for reasons of his own convenience (Article 3(3)).

(18) Restrictions whereby the parties share customers within the same technological field of use or the same product market, either by an actual prohibition on supplying certain classes of customer or an obligation with an equivalent effect, would also render the agreement ineligible for the block exemption (Article 3(6)).

This does not apply to cases where the know-how licence is granted in order to provide a single customer with a second source of supply. In such a case, a prohibition on the licensee from supplying persons other than the customer concerned may be indispensable for the grant of a licence to the second supplier since the purpose of the transaction is not to create an independent supplier in the market. The same applies to limitations on the quantities the licensee may supply to the customer concerned. It is also reasonable to assume that such restrictions contribute to improving the production of goods and to promoting technical progress by furthering the dissemination of technology. However, given the present state of experience of the Commission with respect to such clauses and the risk in particular that they might deprive the second supplier of the possibility of developing his own business in the fields covered by the agreement it is appropriate to make such clauses subject to the opposition procedure (Article 4(2)).

(19) Besides the clauses already mentioned, the list of restrictions precluding application of the block exemption in Article 3 also includes restrictions regarding the selling prices of the licensed product or the quantities to be manufactured or sold, since they limit the extent to which the licensee can exploit the licensed technology and particularly since quantity restrictions may have the same effect as export bans (Article 3(7) and (8)). This does not apply where a licence is granted for use of the technology in specific production facilities and where both a specific know-how is communicated for the setting-up, operation and maintenance of these facilities and the licensee is allowed to increase the capacity of the facilities or to set up further facilities for its own use on normal commercial terms. On the other hand, the licensee may lawfully be prevented from using the licensor's specific know-how to set up facilities for third parties, since the purpose of the agreement is not to permit the licensee to give other producers access to the licensor's know-how while it remains secret (Article 2(1)(12)).

(20) To protect both the licensor and the licensee from being tied into agreements whose duration may be automatically extended beyond their initial term as freely determined by the parties, through a continuous stream of improvements communicated by the licensor, it is appropriate to exclude agreements with such a clause from the block exemption (Article 3(10)). However, the parties are free at any time to extend their contractual relationship by entering into new agreements concerning new improvements.

(21) The Regulation should apply with retroactive effort to know-how licensing agreements in existence when the Regulation comes into force where such agreements already fulfil the conditions for application of the Regulation or are modified to do so (Articles 8 to 10). Under Article 4(3) of Regulation No 19/65/EEC, the benefit of these provisions may not be claimed in actions pending at the date of entry into force of this Regulation, nor may it be relied on as grounds for claims for damages against third parties.

(22) Agreements which come within the terms of Articles 1 and 2 and which have neither the object nor the effect of restricting competition in any other way need no longer be notified. Nevertheless, undertakings will still have the right to apply in individual cases for negative clearance under Article 2 of Council Regulation No 17[5] or for exemption under Article 85(3),

Has adopted this Regulation:

Article 1

(1) Pursuant to Article 85(3) of the Treaty and subject to the provisions of this Regulation, it is hereby declared that Article 85(1) of the Treaty shall not apply to pure know-how licensing agreements and to mixed know-how and patent licensing agreements not exempted by Regulation (EEC) No 2349/84, including those agreements containing ancillary provisions relating to trademarks or other intellectual property rights, to which only two undertakings are party and which include one or more of the following obligations:

1. an obligation on the licensor not to license other undertakings to exploit the licensed technology in the licensed territory;

2. an obligation on the licensor not to exploit the licensed technology in the licensed territory himself;

3. an obligation on the licensee not to exploit the licensed technology in territories within the common market which are reserved for the licensor;

4. an obligation on the licensee not to manufacture or use the licensed product, or use the licensed process, in territories within the common market which are licensed to other licensees;

5. an obligation on the licensee not to pursue an active policy of putting the licensed product on the market in the territories within the common market which are licensed to other licensees, and in particular not to engage in advertising specifically aimed at those territories or to establish any branch or maintain any distribution depot there;

6. an obligation on the licensee not to put the licensed product on the market in the territories licensed to other licensees within the common market;

7. an obligation on the licensee to use only the licensor's trademark or the get-up determined by the licensor to distinguish the licensed product during the term of the agreement, provided that the licensee is not prevented from identifying himself as the manufacturer of the licensed products;

8. an obligation on the licensee to limit his production of the licensed product to the quantities he requires in manufacturing his own products and to sell the licensed product only as an integral part of or a replacement part for his own products or otherwise in connection with the sale of his own products, provided that such quantities are freely determined by the licensee.

(2) The exemption provided for the obligations referred to in paragraph 1(1), (2) and (3) shall extend for a period not exceeding for each licensed territory within the EEC 10 years from the date of signature of the first licence agreement entered into by the licensor for that territory in respect of the same technology.

The exemption provided for the obligations referred to in paragraph 1(4) and (5) shall extend for a period not exceeding 10 years from the date of signature of the first licence agreement entered into by the licensor within the EEC in respect of the same technology.

The exemption provided for the obligation referred to in paragraph 1(6) shall extend for a period not exceeding five years from the date of signature of the first licence agreement entered into by the licensor within the EEC in respect of the same technology.

(3) The exemption provided for in paragraph 1 shall apply only where the parties have identified in any appropriate form the initial know-how and any subsequent improvements to it, which become available to the parties and are communicated to the other party pursuant to the terms of the agreement and for the purpose thereof, and only for as long as the know-how remains secret and substantial.

(4) In so far as the obligations referred to in paragraph 1(1) to (5) concern territories including Member States in which the same technology is protected by necessary patents, the exemption provided for in paragraph 1 shall extend for those Member States as long as the licensed product or process is protected in those Member States by such patents, where the duration of such protection exceeds the periods specified in paragraph 2.

(5) The exemption of restrictions on putting the licensed product on the market resulting from the obligations referred to in paragraph 1(2), (3), (5) and (6) shall apply only if the licensee manufactures or proposes to manufacture the licensed product himself or has it manufactured by a connected undertaking or by a subcontractor.

(6) The exemption provided for in paragraph 1 shall also apply where in a particular agreement the parties undertake obligations of the types referred to in that paragraph but with a more limited scope than is permitted by the paragraph.

(7) For the purposes of the present Regulation the following terms shall have the following meanings:

1. 'know-how' means a body of technical information that is secret, substantial and identified in any appropriate form;

2. the term 'secret' means that the know-how package as a body or in

the precise configuration and assembly of its components is not generally known or easily accessible, so that part of its value consists in the lead-time the licensee gains when it is communicated to him; it is not limited in the narrow sense that each individual component of the know-how should be totally unknown or unobtainable outside the licensor's business;

3. the term 'substantial' means that the know-how includes information which is of importance for the whole or a significant part of (i) a manufacturing process or (ii) a product or service, or (iii) for the development thereof and excludes information which is trivial. Such know-how must thus be useful, i.e. can reasonably be expected at the date of conclusion of the agreement to be capable of improving the competitive position of the licensee, for example by helping him to enter a new market or giving him an advantage in competition with other manufacturers or providers of services who do not have access to the licensed secret know-how or other comparable secret know-how;

4. the term 'identified' means that the know-how is described or recorded in such a manner as to make it possible to verify that it fulfils the criteria of secrecy and substantiality and to ensure that the licensee is not unduly restricted in his exploitation of his own technology. To be identified the know-how can either be set out in the licence agreement or in a separate document or recorded in any other appropriate form at the latest when the know-how is transferred or shortly thereafter, provided that the separate document or other record can be made available if the need arises;

5. 'pure know-how licensing agreements' are agreements whereby one undertaking, the licensor, agrees to communicate the know-how, with or without an obligation to disclose any subsequent improvements, to another undertaking, the licensee, for exploitation in the licensed territory;

6. 'mixed know-how and patent licensing agreements' are agreements not exempted by Regulation (EEC) No 2349/84 under which a technology containing both non-patented elements and elements that are patented in one or more Member States is licensed;

7. the terms 'licensed know-how' or 'licensed technology' mean the initial and any subsequent know-how communicated directly or indirectly by the licensor to a licensee by means of pure or mixed know-how and patent licensing agreements; however, in the case of mixed know-how and patent licensing agreements the term 'licensed technology' also includes any patents for which a licence is granted besides the communication of the know-how;

8. the term 'the same technology' means the technology as licensed to the first licensee and enhanced by any improvements made thereto subsequently, irrespective of whether and to what extent such improvements are exploited by the parties or the other licensees and irrespective of whether the technology is protected by necessary patents in any Member States;

9. 'the licensed products' are goods or services the production or provision of which requires the use of the licensed technology;

10. the term 'exploitation' refers to any use of the licensed technology in particular in the production, active or passive sales in a territory even if not coupled with manufacture in that territory, or leasing of the licensed products;

11. 'the licensed territory' is the territory covering all or at least part of the common market where the licensee is entitled to exploit the licensed technology;

12. 'territory reserved for the licensor' means territories in which the licensor has not granted any licences and which he has expressly reserved for himself;

13. 'connected undertakings' means:

   (a) undertakings in which a party to the agreement, directly or indirectly;

      — owns more than half the capital or business assets, or

      — has the power to exercise more than half the voting rights, or

      — has the power to appoint more than half the members of the supervisory board, board of directors or bodies legally representing the undertaking, or

      — has the right to manage the affairs of the undertaking;

   (b) undertakings which directly or indirectly have in or over a party to the agreement the rights or powers listed in (a);

   (c) undertakings in which an undertaking referred to in (b) directly or indirectly has the rights or powers listed in (a);

   (d) undertakings in which the parties to the agreement or undertakings connected with them jointly have the rights or powers listed in (a): such jointly controlled undertakings are considered to be connected with each of the parties to the agreement.

Article 2

(1) Article 1 shall apply notwithstanding the presence in particular of any of the following obligations, which are generally not restrictive of competition:

1. an obligation on the licensee not to divulge the know-how communicated by the licensor; the licensee may be held to this obligation after the agreement has expired;

2. an obligation on the licensee not to grant sub-licences or assign the licence;

3. an obligation on the licensee not to exploit the licensed know-how after termination of the agreement in so far and as long as the know-how is still secret;

4. an obligation on the licensee to communicate to the licensor any experience gained in exploiting the licensed technology and to grant him a non-exclusive license in respect of improvements to or new applications of that technology, provided that:

    (a) the licensee is not prevented during or after the term of the agreement from freely using his own improvements, in so far as these are severable from the licensor's know-how, or licensing them to third parties where licensing to third parties does not disclose the know-how communicated by the licensor that is still secret; this is without prejudice to an obligation on the licensee to seek the licensor's prior approval to such licensing provided that approval may not be withheld unless there are objectively justifiable reasons to believe that licensing improvements to third parties will disclose the licensor's know-how, and

    (b) the licensor has accepted an obligation, whether exclusive or not, to communicate his own improvements to the licensee and his right to use the licensee's improvements which are not severable from the licensed know-how does not extend beyond the date on which the licensee's right to exploit the licensor's know-how comes to an end, except for termination of the agreement for breach by the licensee; this is without prejudice to an obligation on the licensee to give the licensor the option to continue to use the improvements after that date, if at the same time he relinquishes the post-term use ban or agrees, after having had an opportunity to examine the licensee's improvements, to pay appropriate royalties for their use;

5. an obligation on the licensee to observe minimum quality specifications for the licensed product or to procure goods or

services from the licensor or from an undertaking designated by the licensor, in so far as such quality specifications, products or services are necessary for:

(a) a technically satisfactory exploitation of the licensed technology, or

(b) for ensuring that the production of the licensee conforms to the quality standards that are respected by the licensor and other licensees,

and to allow the licensor to carry out related checks;

6. obligations:

(a) to inform the licensor of misappropriation of the know-how or of infringements of the licensed patents, or

(b) to take or to assist the licensor in taking legal action against such misappropriation or infringements,

provided that these obligations are without prejudice to the licensee's right to challenge the validity of the licensed patents or to contest the secrecy of the licensed know-how except where he himself has in some way contributed to its disclosure;

7. an obligation on the licensee, in the event of the know-how becoming publicly known other than by action of the licensor, to continue paying until the end of the agreement the royalties in the amounts, for the periods and according to the methods freely determined by the parties, without prejudice to the payment of any additional damages in the event of the know-how becoming publicly known by the action of the licensee in breach of the agreement;

8. an obligation on the licensee to restrict his exploitation of the licensed technology to one or more technical fields of application covered by the licensed technology or to one or more product markets;

9. an obligation on the licensee to pay a minimum royalty or to produce a minimum quantity of the licensed product or to carry out a minimum number of operations exploiting the licensed technology;

10. an obligation on the licensor to grant the licensee any more favourable terms that the licensor may grant to another undertaking after the agreement is entered into;

11. an obligation on the licensee to mark the licensed product with the licensor's name;

12. an obligation on the licensee not to use the licensor's know-how to

construct facilities for third parties; this is without prejudice to the right of the licensee to increase the capacity of its facilities or to set up additional facilities for its own use on normal commercial terms, including the payment of additional royalties.

(2) In the event that, because of particular circumstances, the obligations referred to in paragraph 1 fall within the scope of Article 85(1), they shall also be exempted even if they are not accompanied by any of the obligations exempted by Article 1.

(3) The exemption provided for in paragraph 2 shall also apply where in an agreement the parties undertake obligations of the types referred to in paragraph 1 but with a more limited scope than is permitted by that paragraph.

Article 3

Articles 1 and 2(2) shall not apply where:

1. the licensee is prevented from continuing to use the licensed know-how after the termination of the agreement where the know-how has meanwhile become publicly known, other than by the action of the licensee in breach of the agreement;

2. the licensee is obliged either:

(*a*) to assign in whole or in part to the licensor rights to improvements to or new applications of the licensed technology;

(*b*) to grant the licensor an exclusive licence for improvements to or new applications of the licensed technology which would prevent the licensee during the currency of the agreement and/or thereafter from using his own improvements in so far as these are severable from the licensor's know-how, or from licensing them to third parties, where such licensing would not disclose the licensor's know-how that is still secret; or

(*c*) in the case of an agreement which also includes a post-term use ban, to grant back to the licensor, even on a non-exclusive and reciprocal basis, licences for improvements which are not severable from the licensor's know-how, if the licensor's right to use the improvements is of a longer duration than the licensee's right to use the licensor's know-how, except for termination of the agreement for breach by the licensee;

3. the licensee is obliged at the time the agreement is entered into to accept quality specifications or further licences or to procure goods or services which he does not want, unless such licences, quality specifications, goods or services are necessary for a technically

satisfactory exploitation of the licensed technology or for ensuring that the production of the licensee conforms to the quality standards that are respected by the licensor and other licensees;

4. the licensee is prohibited from contesting the secrecy of the licensed know-how or from challenging the validity of licensed patents within the common market belonging to the licensor or undertakings connected with him, without prejudice to the right of the licensor to terminate the licensing agreement in the event of such a challenge;

5. the licensee is charged royalties on goods or services which are not entirely or partially produced by means of the licensed technology or for the use of know-how which has become publicly known by the action of the licensor or an undertaking connected with him;

6. one party is restricted within the same technological field of use or within the same product market as to the customers he may serve, in particular by being prohibited from supplying certain classes of user, employing certain forms of distribution or, with the aim of sharing customers, using certain types of packaging for the products, save as provided in Article 1(1)(7) and Article 4(2);

7. the quantity of the licensed products one party may manufacture or sell or the number of operations exploiting the licensed technology he may carry out are subject to limitations, save as provided in Article 1(1)(8) and Article 4(2);

8. one party is restricted in the determination of prices, components of prices or discounts for the licensed products;

9. one party is restricted from competing with the other party, with undertakings connected with the other party or with other undertakings within the common market in respect of research and development, production or use of competing products and their distribution, without prejudice to an obligation on the licensee to use his best endeavours to exploit the licensed technology and without prejudice to the right of the licensor to terminate the exclusivity granted to the licensee and cease communicating improvements in the event of the licensee's engaging in any such competing activities and to require the licensee to prove that the licensed know-how is not used for the production of goods and services other than those licensed;

10. the initial duration of the licensing agreement is automatically prolonged by the inclusion in it of any new improvements communicated by the licensor, unless the licensee has the right to refuse such improvements or each party has the right to terminate the agreement at the expiry of the initial term of the agreement and at least every three years thereafter;

11. the licensor is required, albeit in separate agreements, for a period exceeding that permitted under Article 1(2) not to license other undertakings to exploit the same technology in the licensed territory, or a party is required for periods exceeding those permitted under Articles 1(2) or 1(4) not to exploit the same technology in the territory of the other party or of other licensees;

12. one or both of the parties are required:

(a) to refuse without any objectively justified reason to meet demand from users or resellers in their respective territories who would market products in other territories within the common market;

(b) to make it difficult for users or resellers to obtain the products from other resellers within the common market, and in particular to exercise intellectual property rights or take measures so as to prevent users or resellers from obtaining outside, or from putting on the market in the licensed territory products which have been lawfully put on the market within the common market by the licensor or with his consent;

or do so as a result of a concerted practice between them.

Article 4

(1) The exemption provided for in Articles 1 and 2 shall also apply to agreements containing obligations restrictive of competition which are not covered by those Articles and do not fall within the scope of Article 3, on condition that the agreements in question are notified to the Commission in accordance with the provisions of Commission Regulation No 27[6] and that the Commission does not oppose such exemption within a period of six months.

(2) Paragraph 1 shall in particular apply to an obligation on the licensee to supply only a limited quantity of the licensed product to a particular customer, where the know-how licence is granted at the request of such a customer in order to provide him with a second source of supply within a licensed territory.

This provision shall also apply where the customer is the licensee and the licence, in order to provide a second source of supply, provides for the customer to make licensed products or have them made by a sub-contractor.

(3) The period of six months shall run from the date on which the notification is received by the Commission. Where, however, the notification is made by registered post, the period shall run from the date shown on the postmark of the place of posting.

(4) Paragraphs 1 and 2 shall apply only if:

(a) express reference is made to this Article in the notification or in a communication accompanying it; and

(b) the information furnished with the notification is complete and in accordance with the facts.

(5) The benefit of paragraphs 1 and 2 may be claimed for agreements notified before the entry into force of this Regulation by submitting a communication to the Commission referring expressly to this Article and to the notification. Paragraphs 3 and 4(b) shall *apply mutatis mutandis*.

(6) The Commission may oppose the exemption. It shall oppose exemption if it receives a request to do so from a Member State within three months of the transmission to the Member State of the notification referred to in paragraph 1 or of the communication referred to in paragraph 5. This request must be justified on the basis of considerations relating to the competition rules of the Treaty.

(7) The Commission may withdraw the opposition to the exemption at any time. However, where the opposition was raised at the request of a Member State and this request is maintained, it may be withdrawn only after consultation of the Advisory Committee on Restrictive Practices and Dominant Positions.

(8) If the opposition is withdrawn because the undertakings concerned have shown that the conditions of Article 85(3) are fulfilled, the exemption shall apply from the date of notification.

(9) If the opposition is withdrawn because the undertakings concerned have amended the agreement so that the conditions of Article 85(3) are fulfilled, the exemption shall apply from the date on which the amendments take effect.

(10) If the Commission opposes exemption and the opposition is not withdrawn, the effects of the notification shall be governed by the provisions of Regulation No 17.

Article 5

(1) This Regulation shall not apply to :

1. agreements between members of a patent or know-how pool which relate to the pooled technologies;

2. know-how licensing agreements between competing undertakings which hold interests in a joint venture, or between one of them and the joint venture, if the licensing agreements relate to the activities of the joint venture;

3. agreements under which one party grants the other a know-how licence and the other party, albeit in separate agreements or through connected undertakings, grants the first party a patent, trademark or know-how licence or exclusive sales rights, where the parties are competitors in relation to the products covered by those agreements;

4. agreements including the licensing of intellectual property rights other than patents (in particular trademarks, copyright and design rights) or the licensing of software except where these rights or the software are of assistance in achieving the object of the licensed technology and there are no obligations restrictive of competition other than those also attached to the licensed know-how and exempted under the present Regulation.

(2) However, this Regulation shall apply to reciprocal licences of the types referred to in paragraph 1(3) where the parties are not subject to any territorial restriction within the common market on the manufacture, use or putting on the market of the products covered by the agreements or on the use of the licensed technologies.

Article 6

This Regulation shall also apply to:

1. pure know-how agreements or mixed agreements where the licensor is not the developer of the know-how or the patentee but is authorised by the developer or the patentee to grant a licence or a sub-licence;

2. assignments of know-how or of know-how and patents where the risk associated with exploitation remains with the assignor, in particular where the sum payable in consideration of the assignment is dependent upon the turnover attained by the assignee in respect of products made using the know-how or the patents, the quantity of such products manufactured or the number of operations carried out employing the know-how or the patents;

3. pure know-how agreements or mixed agreements in which rights or obligations of the licensor or the licensee are assumed by undertakings connected with them.

Article 7

The Commission may withdraw the benefit of this Regulation, pursuant to Article 7 of Regulation No 19/65/EEC, where it finds in a particular case that an agreement exempted by this Regulation nevertheless has certain effects which are incompatible with the conditions laid down in Article 85(3) of the Treaty, and in particular where:

1. such effects arise from an arbitration award;

2. the effect of the agreement is to prevent the licensed products from being exposed to effective competition in the licensed territory from identical products or products considered by users as equivalent in view of their characteristics, price and intended use;

3. the licensor does not have the right to terminate the exclusivity granted to the licensee at the latest five years from the date the agreement was entered into and at least annually thereafter if, without legitimate reason, the licensee fails to exploit the licensed technology or to do so adequately;

4. without prejudice to Article 1(1)(6), the licensee refuses, without objectively valid reason, to meet unsolicited demand from users or resellers in the territory of other licensees;

5. one or both of the parties:

    (a) without objectively justified reason, refuse to meet demand from users or resellers in their respective territories who would market the products in other territories within the common market; or

    (b) make it difficult for users or resellers to obtain the products from other resellers within the common market, and in particular where they exercise intellectual property rights or take measures so as to prevent resellers or users from obtaining outside, or from putting on the market in the licensed territory, products which have been lawfully put on the market within the common market by the licensor or with his consent;

6. the operation of the post-term use ban referred to in Article 2(1)(3) prevents the licensee from working an expired patent which can be worked by all other manufacturers;

7. the period for which the licensee is obliged to continue paying royalties after the know-how has become publicly known by the action of third parties, as referred to in Article 2(1)(7), substantially exceeds the lead time acquired because of the head-start in production and marketing and this obligation is detrimental to competition in the market;

8. the parties were already competitors before the grant of the licence and obligations on the licensee to produce a minimum quantity or to use his best endeavours as referred to in Article 2(1)(9) and Article 3(9) have the effect of preventing the licensee from using competing technologies.

Article 8

(1) As regards agreements existing on 13 March 1962 and notified before 1 February 1963 and agreements, whether notified or not, to which Article 4(2)(2)(b) of Regulation No 17 applies, the declaration of inapplicability of Article 85(1) of the Treaty contained in this Regulation shall have retroactive effect from the time at which the conditions for application of this Regulation were fulfilled.

(2) As regards all other agreements notified before this Regulation entered into force, the declaration of inapplicability of Article 85(1) of the Treaty contained in this Regulation shall retroactive effect from the time at which the conditions for application of this Regulation were fulfilled, or from the date of notification, whichever is the later.

Article 9

If agreements existing on 13 March 1962 and notified before 1 February 1963 or agreements to which Article 4(2)(2)(b) of Regulation No 17 applies and notified before 1 January 1967 are amended before 1 July 1989 so as to fulfil the conditions for application of this Regulation, and if the amendment is communicated to the Commission before 1 October 1989 the prohibition in Article 85(1) of the Treaty shall not apply in respect of the period prior to the amendment. The communication shall take effect from the time of its receipt by the Commission. Where the communication is sent by registered post, it shall take effect from the date shown on the postmark of the place of posting.

Article 10

(1) As regards agreements to which Article 85 of the Treaty applies as a result of the accession of the United Kingdom, Ireland and Denmark, Articles 8 and 9 shall apply except that the relevant dates shall be 1 January 1973 instead of 13 March 1962 and 1 July 1973 instead of 1 February 1963 and 1 January 1967.

(2) As regard agreements to which Article 85 of the Treaty applies as a result of the accession of Greece, Articles 8 and 9 shall apply except that the relevant dates shall be 1 January 1981 instead of 13 March 1962 and 1 July 1981 instead of 1 February 1963 and 1 January 1967.

(3) As regards agreements to which Article 85 of the Treaty applies as a result of the accession of Spain and Portugal, Articles 8 and 9 shall apply except that the relevant dates shall be 1 January 1986 instead of 13 March 1962 and 1 July 1986 instead of 1 February 1963 and 1 January 1967.

Article 11

(1) Information acquired pursuant to Article 4 shall be used only for the purposes of the Regulation.

(2) The Commission and the authorities of the Member States, their officials and other servants shall not disclose information acquired by them pursuant to this Regulation of the kind covered by the obligation of professional secrecy.

(3) The provisions of paragraphs 1 and 2 shall not prevent publication of general information or surveys which do not contain information relating to particular undertakings or associations of undertakings.

Article 12

This Regulation shall enter into force on 1 April 1989.

It shall apply until 31 December 1999.

This Regulation shall be binding in its entirety and directly applicable in all Member States.

Done at Brussels, 30 November 1988.

For the Commission

Peter Sutherland

Member of the Commission

FOOTNOTES

1. OJ No 36, 6.3.65, p.533.
2. OJ No C 214, 12.8.87, p.2.
3. OJ No L 219, 16.8.84, p.15.
4. Commission Regulation (EEC) No 4087/88 of 30 November 1988 on the application of Article 85(3) of the Treaty to categories of franchising agreements (OJ No L 359, 28.12.88, p.46).
5. OJ No 13, 21.2.62, p.204.
6. OJ No 35, 10.5.62, p.1118.

COMMISSION NOTICE REGARDING THE CONCENTRATIVE AND COOPERATIVE OPERATIONS UNDER COUNCIL REGULATION (EEC) No 4064/89

of 21 December 1989

on the control of concentrations between undertakings[1]

(90/C 203/06)

(OJ No C 203, 14.8.90, p.10)

I. Introduction

1. Article 3(1) of Council Regulation (EEC) No 4064/89 ('the Regulation') contains an exhaustive list of the factual circumstances which fall to be considered as concentrations. In accordance with the 23rd recital, this term refers only to operations that lead to a lasting change in the structures of the participating undertakings.

By contrast, the Regulation does not deal with operations whose object or effect is the coordination of the competitive activities of undertakings that remain independent of each other. Situations of this kind are cooperative in character. Accordingly, they fall to be assessed under the provisions of Regulations (EEC) No 17[2], (EEC) No 1017/68[3], No 4056/86[4] or No 3975/87[5]. The same applies to an operation which includes both a lasting structural change and the coordination of competitive behaviour, where the two are inseparable.

If the structural change can be separated from the coordination of competitive behaviour, the former will be assessed under the Regulation and the latter, to the extent that it does not amount to an ancillary restriction within the meaning of Article 8(2), second subparagraph of the Regulation, falls to be assessed under the new Regulations implementing Articles 85 and 86 of the EEC Treaty.

2. The purpose of this notice is to define as clearly as possible, in the interests of legal certainty, concentrative and cooperative situations. This is particularly important in the case of joint ventures. The same issue is raised in other forms of association between undertakings such as unilateral or reciprocal shareholdings and common directorships, and of certain operations involving more than one undertaking, such as unilateral or reciprocal transfers of undertakings or parts of undertakings, or joint acquisition of an undertaking with a view to its

division. In all these cases, operations may not fall within the scope of the Regulation, where their object or effect is the coordination of the competitive behaviour of the undertakings concerned.

3. This notice sets out the main considerations which will determine the Commission's view to what extent the aforesaid operations are or are not caught by the Regulation. It is not concerned with the assessment of these operations, whether under the Regulation or any other applicable provisions, in particular Articles 85 and 86 of the EEC Treaty.

4. The principles set out in this notice will be followed and further developed by the Commission's practice in individual cases. As the operations considered are generally of a complex nature, this notice cannot provide a definitive answer to all conceivable situations.

5. This notice is without prejudice to the interpretation which may be given by the Court of Justice or the Court of First Instance of the European Communities.

II. Joint Ventures within Article 3 of the Regulation

6. The Regulation in Article 3(2) refers to two types of joint venture: those which have as their object or effect the coordination of the competitive behaviour of undertakings which remain independent (referred to as 'cooperative joint ventures') and those which perform on a lasting basis all the functions of an autonomous economic entity and which do not give rise to coordination amongst themselves or between them and the joint venture (referred to as 'concentrative joint ventures'). The latter are concentrations and as such are caught by the Regulation. Cooperative joint ventures fall to be considered under other regulations implementing Articles 85 and 86[6].

A. Concept of joint venture

7. To define the term 'joint venture' within the meaning of Article 3(2), it is necessary to refer to the provision of Article 3(1)(b) of the Regulation. According to the latter, JVs are undertakings that are jointly controlled by several other undertakings, the parent companies. In the context of the Regulation the term JV thus implies several characteristics:

1. Undertaking

8. A JV must be an undertaking. That is to be understood as an organised assembly of human and material resources, intended to pursue a defined economic purpose on a long-term basis.

2. Control by other undertakings

9. In the context of the Regulation, a JV is controlled by other

undertakings. Pursuant to Article 3(3) of the Regulation, control means the possibility of exercising, directly or indirectly, a decisive influence on the activities of the JV; whether this condition is fulfilled can only be decided by reference to all the legal and factual circumstances of the individual case.

10. Control of a JV can be based on legal, contractual or other means, within which the following elements are especially important:

- ownership or rights to the use of all or some of the JV's assets,
- influence over the composition, voting or decisions of the managing or supervisory bodies of the JV,
- voting rights in the managing or supervisory bodies of the JV,
- contracts concerning the running of the JV's business.

3. Joint control

11. A JV under the Regulation is jointly controlled. Joint control exists where the parent companies must agree on decisions concerning the JV's activities, either because of the rights acquired in the JV or because of contracts or other means establishing the joint control. Joint control may be provided for in the JV's constitution (memorandum or articles of association). However, it need not be present from the beginning, but may also be established later, in particular by taking a share in an existing undertaking.

12. There is no joint control where one of the parent companies can decide alone on the JV's commercial activities. This is generally the case where one company owns more than half the capital or assets of the undertaking, has the right to appoint more than half of the managing or supervisory bodies, controls more than half of the votes in one of those bodies, or has the sole right to manage the undertaking's business. Where the other parent companies either have completely passive minority holdings or, while able to have a certain influence on the undertaking, cannot, individually or together, determine its behaviour, a relative majority of the capital or of the votes or seats on the decision-making bodies will suffice to control the undertaking.

13. In many cases, the joint control of the JV is based on agreements or concentration between the parent companies. Thus, a majority shareholder in a JV often extends to one or more minority shareholders a contractual right to take part in the control of the JV. If two undertakings each hold half of a JV, even if there is no agreement between them, both parent companies will be obliged permanently to cooperate so as to avoid reciprocal blocking votes on decisions affecting the JV's activity. The same applies to JVs with three or more parents,

where each of them has a right of veto. A JV can even be controlled by a considerable number of undertakings that can together muster a majority of the capital or the seats or votes on the JV's decision-making bodies. However, in such cases, joint control can be presumed only if the factual and legal circumstances – especially a convergence of economic interests – support the notion of a deliberate common policy of the parent companies in relation to the JV.

14. If one undertaking's holding in another is, by its nature or its extent, insufficient to establish sole control, and if there is no joint control together with third parties, then there is no concentration within the meaning of Article 3(1)(b) of the Regulation. Articles 85 or 86 of the EEC Treaty may however be applicable on the basis of Regulation (EEC) No 17 or other implementing Regulation (see III.1).

B. Concentrative joint ventures

15. For a joint venture to be regarded as concentrative it must fulfil all the conditions of Article 3(2), subparagraph 2, which lays down a positive condition and a negative condition.

1. Positive condition: joint venture performing on a lasting basis all the functions of an autonomous economic entity

16. To fulfil this condition, a JV must first of all act as an independent supplier and buyer on the market. JVs that take over from their parents only specific partial responsibilities are not to be considered as concentrations where they are merely auxiliaries to the commercial activities of the parent companies. This is the case where the JV supplies its products or services exclusively to its parent companies, or when it meets its own needs wholly from them. The independent market presence can even be insufficient if the JV achieves the majority of its supplies or sales with third parties, but remains substantially dependent on its parents for the maintenance and development of its business.

17. A JV exists on a lasting basis if it intended and able to carry on its activity for an unlimited, or at least for a long, time. If this is not the case there is generally no long-term change in the structures of the parent companies. More important than the agreed duration are the human and material resources of the JV. They must be of such nature and quantity as to ensure the JV's existence and independence in the long term. This is generally the case where the parent companies invest substantial financial resources in the JV, transfer an existing undertaking or business to it, or give it substantial technical or commercial know-how, so that after an initial starting-up period it can support itself by its own means.

18. A decisive question for assessing the autonomous character of the JV

is whether it is in a position to exercise its own commercial policy. This requires, within the limits of its company objects, that it plans, decides and acts independently. In particular, it must be free to determine its competitive behaviour autonomously and according to its own economic interests. If the JV depends for its business on facilities that remain economically integrated with the parent companies' businesses, that weakens the case for the autonomous nature of the JV.

19. The JV's economic independence will not be contested merely because the parent companies reserve to themselves the right to take certain decisions that are important for the development of the JV, namely those concerning alterations of the objects of the company, increases or reductions of capital, or the application of profits. However, if the commercial policy of the JV remains in the hands of the parent undertakings, the JV may take on the aspect of an instrument of the parent undertakings' market interests. Such a situation will usually exist where the JV operates in the market of the parent undertakings. It may also exist where the JV operates in markets neighbouring, or upstream or downstream of, those of the parent undertakings.

2. Negative condition: absence of coordination of competitive behaviour

20. Subject to what is said in the first paragraph of this notice a JV can only be considered to be concentrative within the meaning of Article 3(2), subparagraph 2 of the Regulation, if it does not have as its object or effect the coordination of the competitive behaviour of undertakings that remain independent of each other. There must not be such coordination either between the parent companies themselves or between any or all of them on the one hand and the JV on the other hand. Such coordination must not be an object of the establishment or operation of the JV, nor may it be the consequence thereof. The JV is not to be regarded as concentrative if as a result of the agreement to set up the JV or as a result of its existence or activities it is reasonably foreseeable that the competitive behaviour of a parent or of the JV on the relevant market will be influenced. Conversely, there will normally be no foreseeable coordination when all the parent companies withdraw entirely and permanently from the JV's market and do not operate on markets neighbouring those of the JV's.

21. Not every cooperation between parent companies with regard to the JV prevents a JV from being considered concentrative. Even concentrative JVs generally represent a means for parent companies to pursue common or mutually complementary interests. The establishment and joint control of a JV is, therefore, inconceivable without an understanding between the parent companies as concerns

the pursuit of those interests. Irrespective of its legal form, such a concordance of interests is an essential feature of a JV.

22. As regards the relations of the parent undertakings, or any one of them, with the JV, the risk of coordination within the meaning of Article 3(2) will not normally arise where the parent undertakings are not active in the markets of the JV or in neighbouring or upstream or downstream markets. In other cases, the risk of coordination will be relatively small where the parents limit the influence they exercise on the JV's strategic decisions, such as those concerning the future direction of investment, and when they express their financial, rather than their market-oriented, interests. The membership of the JV's managing and supervisory bodies is also important. Common membership of the JV's and the parent companies' decision-making bodies may be an obstacle to the development of the JV's autonomous commercial policy.

23. The dividing line between the concordance of interests in a JV and a coordination of competitive behaviour that is incompatible with the notion of concentration cannot be laid down for all conceivable kinds of case. The decisive factor is not the legal form of the relationship between the parent companies and between them and the JV. The direct or indirect, actual or potential effects of the establishment and operation of the JV on market relationships, have determinant importance.

24. In assessing the likelihood of coordination of competitive behaviour, it is useful to consider some of the different situations which often occur:

(a) JVs that take over pre-existing activities of the parent companies;

(b) JVs that undertake new activities on behalf of the parent companies;

(c) JVs that enter the parent companies' markets;

(d) JVs that enter upstream, downstream or neighbouring markets.

(a) JVs that take over pre-existing activities of the parent companies

25. There is normally no risk of coordination where the parent companies transfer the whole of certain business activities to the JV and withdraw permanently from the JV's market so that they remain neither actual nor potential competitors – of each other nor of the JV. In this context, the notion of potential competition is to be interpreted realistically, according to the Commission's established practice[7]. A presumption of a competitive relationship requires not only that one or more of the parent companies could re-enter the JV's market at any time: this must be a realistic option and represent a commercially reasonable course in the light of all objective circumstances.

26. Where the parent companies transfer their entire business activities to the JV, and thereafter act only as holding companies, this amounts to complete merger from the economic viewpoint.

27. Where the JV takes on only some of the activities that the parent companies formerly carried on independently, this can also amount to a concentration. In this case, the establishment and operation of the JV must not lead to a coordination of the parent companies' competitive behaviour in relation to other activities which they retain. Coordination of competitive behaviour between any or all of the parent companies and the JV must also be excluded. Such coordination is likely where there are close economic links between the areas of activity of the JV on one side and of the parent companies on the other. This applies to upstream, downstream and neighbouring product markets.

28. The withdrawal of the parent companies need not be simultaneous with the establishment of the JV. It is possible – so far as necessary – to allow the parent companies a short transitional period to overcome any starting-up problems of the JV, especially bottlenecks in production or supplies. This period should not normally exceed one year.

29. It is even possible for the establishment of a JV to represent a concentration situation where the parent companies remain permanently active on the JV's product or service market. In this case, however, the parent companies' geographic market must be different from that of the JV. Moreover, the markets in question must be so widely separated, or must present structures so different, that, taking account of the nature of the goods or services concerned and of the cost of (first or renewed) entry by either into the other's market, competitive interaction may be excluded.

30. If the parent companies' markets and the JV's are in different parts of the Community or neighbouring third countries, there is a degree of probability that either, if it has the necessary human and material resources, could extend its activities from the one market to the other. Where the territories are adjacent or very close to each other, this may even be assumed to be the case. At least in this last case, the actual allocation of markets gives reason to suppose that it follows from a coordination of competitive behaviour between parent companies and the JV.

(b) JVs that undertake new activities on behalf of the parent companies

31. There is normally no risk of coordination in the sense described above where the JV operates on a product or service market which the parent companies individually have not entered and will not enter in the foreseeable future, because they lack the organisational, technical or

financial means or because, in the light of all the objective circumstances, such a move would not represent a commercially reasonable course. An individual market entry will also be unlikely where, after establishing the JV, the parent companies no longer have the means to make new investments in the same field, or where an additional individual operation on the JV's market would not make commercial sense. In both cases there is no competitive relationship between the parent companies and the JV. Consequently, there is no possibility of coordination of their competitive behaviour. However, this assessment is only true if the JV's market is neither upstream nor downstream of, nor neighbouring, that of the parent companies.

32. The establishment of a JV to operate in the same product or service market as the parent companies but in another geographic market involves the risk of coordination if there is competitive interaction between the parent companies' geographic market and that of the JV.

(c) JVs that enter the parent companies' market

33. Where the parent companies, or one of them, remain active on the JV's market or remain potential competitors of the JV, a coordination of competitive behaviour between the parent companies or between them and the JV must be presumed. So long as this presumption is not rebutted, the Commission will take it that the establishment of the JV does not fall under Article 3(2), subparagraph 2 of the Regulation.

(d) JVs that operate in upstream, downstream or neighbouring markets

34. If the JV is operating in a market that is upstream or downstream of that of the parent companies, then, in general, coordination of purchasing or, as the case may be, sales policy between the parent companies is likely where they are competitors on the upstream or downstream market.

35. If the parent companies are not competitors, it remains to be examined whether there is a real risk of coordination of competitive behaviour between the JV and any of the parents. This will normally be the case where the JV's sales or purchases are made in substantial measure with the parent companies.

36. It is not possible to lay down general principles regarding the likelihood of coordination of competitive behaviour in cases where the parent companies and the JV are active in neighbouring markets. The outcome will depend in particular on whether the JV's and the parent companies' products are technically or economically linked, whether they are both components of another product or are otherwise mutually complementary, and whether the parent companies could realistically

enter the JV's market. If there are no concrete opportunities for competitive interaction of this kind, the Commission will treat the JV as concentrative.

III. Other links between undertakings

1. *Minority shareholdings*

37. The taking of a minority shareholding in an undertaking can be considered a concentration within the meaning of Article 3(1)(b) of the Regulation if the new shareholder acquires the possibility of exercising a decisive influence on the undertaking's activity. If the acquisition of a minority shareholding brings about a situation in which there is an undertaking jointly controlled by two or more others, the principles described above in relation to JVs apply.

38. As long as the threshold of individual or joint decisive influence has not been reached, the Regulation is not in any event applicable. Accordingly, the assessment under competition law will be made only in relation to the criteria laid down in Articles 85 and 86 of the EEC Treaty and on the basis of the usual procedural rules for restrictive practices and abuses of dominant position[8].

39. There may likewise be a risk of coordination where an undertaking acquires a majority or minority interest in another in which a competitor already has a minority interest. If so, this acquisition will be assessed under Articles 85 and 86 of the EEC Treaty.

2. *Cross-shareholding*

40. In order to bring their autonomous and hitherto separate undertakings or groups closer together, company owners often cause them to exchange shareholdings in each other. Such reciprocal influences can serve to establish or to secure industrial or commercial cooperation between the undertakings or groups. But they may also result in establishing a 'single economic entity'. In the first case, the coordination of competitive behaviour between independent undertakings is predominant; in the second, the result may be a concentration. Consequently, reciprocal directorships and crossshareholdings can only be evaluated in relation to their foreseeable effects in each case.

41. The Commission considers that two or more undertakings can also combine without setting up a parent-subsidiary relationship and without either losing its legal personality. Article 3(1) of the Regulation refers not only to legal, but also to economic concentrations. The condition for the recognition of a concentration in the form of a combined group is,

however, that the undertakings or groups concerned are not only subject to a permanent, single economic management, but are also amalgamated into a genuine economic unit, characterised internally by profit and loss compensation between the various undertakings within the groups and externally by joint liability.

3. *Representation on controlling bodies of other undertakings*

42. Common membership of managing or supervisory boards of various undertakings is to be assessed in accordance with the same principles as cross-shareholdings.

43. The representation of one undertaking on the decision-making bodies of another is usually the consequence of an existing shareholding. It reinforces the influence of the investing undertaking over the activities of the undertaking in which it holds a share, because it affords it the opportunity of obtaining information on the activities of a competitor or of taking an active part in its commercial decisions.

44. Thus, common membership of the respective boards may be the vehicle for the coordination of the competitive behaviour of the undertakings concerned, or for a concentration of undertakings within the meaning of the Regulation. This will depend on the circumstances of the individual case, among which the economic link between the shareholding and the personal connection must always be examined. This is equally true of unilateral and reciprocal relationships between undertakings.

45. Personal connections not accompanied by shareholdings are to be judged according to the same criteria as shareholding relationships between undertakings. A majority of seats on the managing or supervisory board of an undertaking will normally imply control of the latter; a minority of seats at least a degree of influence over its commercial policy, which may further entail a coordination of behaviour. Reciprocal connections justify a presumption that the undertakings concerned are coordinating their business conduct. A very wide communality of membership of the respective decision-making bodies – that is, up to half of the members or more – may be an indication of a concentration.

4. *Transfers of undertakings or parts of undertakings*

46. A transfer of assets or shares falls within the definition of a concentration, according to Article 3(1)(b) of the Regulation, if it results in the acquirer gaining control of all or of part of one or more undertakings. However, the situation is different where the transfer conferring control over part of an undertaking is linked with an

agreement to coordinate the competitive behaviour of the undertakings concerned, or where it necessarily leads to or is accompanied by coordination of the business conduct of undertakings which remain independent. Cases of this kind are not covered by the Regulation: they must be examined according to Articles 85 and 86 of the EEC Treaty and under the appropriate implementing Regulations.

47. The practical application of this rule requires a distinction between unilateral and reciprocal arrangements. A unilateral acquisition of assets or shares strongly suggests that the Regulation is applicable. The contrary needs to be demonstrated by clear evidence of the likelihood of coordination of the parties' competitive behaviour. A reciprocal acquisition of assets or shares, by contrast, will usually follow from an agreement between the undertakings concerned as to their investments, production or sales, and thus serves to coordinate their competitive behaviour. A concentration situation does not exist where a reciprocal transfer of assets or shares forms part of a specialisation or restructuring agreement or other type of coordination. Coordination presupposes in any event that the parties remain at least potential competitors after the exchange has taken place.

5. Joint acquisition of an undertaking with a view to its division

48. Where several undertakings jointly acquire another, the principles for the assessment of a joint venture are applicable, provided that within the acquisition operation, the period of joint control goes beyond the very short term. In this case the Regulation may or may not be applicable, depending on the concentrative or cooperative nature of the JV. If, by contrast, the sole object of the agreement is to divide up the assets of the undertaking and this agreement is put into effect immediately after the acquisition, then, in accordance with the 24th recital, the Regulation applies.

FOOTNOTES

1. OJ No L 395, 30.12.89, p.1.
2. OJ No 13, 21.2.62, p.204.
3. OJ No L 175, 23.7.68, p.1.
4. OJ No L 378, 31.12.86, p.4.
5. OJ No L 374, 31.21.87, p.1.
6. See footnotes 2 to 5 above.
7. See the Thirteenth Report (1983) on Competition Policy, point 55.
8. Judgment of the Court of Justice of the European Communities in Joined Cases 142 and 156/84 BAT and Reynolds ECR 1987, pp. 4566 and 4577.

COMMISSION REGULATION (EEC) No 417/85

of 19 December 1984

on the application of Article 85(3) of the Treaty to categories of specialisation agreements

(OJ No L 53, 22.2.85, p.1)

The Commission of the European Communities,

Having regard to the Treaty establishing the European Economic Community,

Having regard to Council Regulation (EEC) No 2821/71 of 20 December 1971 on the application of Article 85(3) of the Treaty to categories of agreements, decisions and concerted practices[1], as last amended by the Act of Accession of Greece, and in particular Article 1 thereof,

Having published a draft of this Regulation[2],

Having consulted the Advisory Committee on Restrictive Practices and Dominant Positions,

Whereas:

(1) Regulation (EEC) No 2821/71 empowers the Commission to apply Article 85(3) of the Treaty by Regulation to certain categories of agreements, decisions and concerted practices falling within the scope of Article 85(1) which relate to specialisation, including agreements necessary for achieving it.

(2) Agreements on specialisation in present or future production may fall within the scope of Article 85(1).

(3) Agreements on specialisation in production generally contribute to improving the production or distribution of goods, because undertakings concerned can concentrate on the manufacture of certain products and thus operate more efficiently and supply the products more cheaply. It is likely that, given effective competition, consumers will receive a fair share of the resulting benefit.

(4) Such advantages can arise equally from agreements whereby each participant gives up the manufacture of certain products in favour of another participant and from agreements whereby the participants undertake to manufacture certain products or have them manufactured only jointly.

(5) The Regulation must specify what restrictions of competition may be

included in specialisation agreements. The restrictions of competition that are permitted in the Regulation in addition to reciprocal obligations to give up manufacture are normally essential for the making and implementation of such agreements. These restrictions are therefore, in general, indispensable for the attainment of the desired advantages for the participating undertakings and consumers. It may be left to the parties to decide which of these provisions they include in their agreements.

(6) The exemption must be limited to agreements which do not give rise to the possibility of eliminating competition in respect of a substantial part of the products in question. The Regulation must therefore apply only as long as the market share and turnover of the participating undertakings do not exceed a certain limit.

(7) It is, however, appropriate to offer undertakings which exceed the turnover limit set in the Regulation a simplified means of obtaining the legal certainty provided by the block exemption. This must allow the Commission to exercise effective supervision as well as simplifying its administration of such agreements.

(8) In order to facilitate the conclusion of long-term specialisation agreements, which can have a bearing on the structure of the participating undertakings, it is appropriate to fix the period of validity of the Regulation at 13 years. If the circumstances on the basis of which the Regulation was adopted should change significantly within this period, the Commission will make the necessary amendments.

(9) Agreements, decisions and concerted practices which are automatically exempted pursuant to this Regulation need not be notified. Undertakings may none the less in an individual case request a decision pursuant to Council Regulation No 17[3], as last amended by the Act of Accession of Greece,

Has adopted this Regulation:

Article 1

Pursuant to Article 85(3) of the Treaty and subject to the provisions of this Regulation, it is hereby declared that Article 85(1) of the Treaty shall not apply to agreements on specialisation whereby, for the duration of the agreement, undertakings accept reciprocal obligations:

(a) not to manufacture certain products or to have them manufactured, but to leave it to other parties to manufacture the products or have them manufactured; or

(b) to manufacture certain products or have them manufactured only jointly.

Article 2

1. Apart from the obligations referred to in Article 1, no restrictions of competition may be imposed on the parties other than:

(a) an obligation not to conclude with third parties specialisation agreements relating to identical products or to products considered by users to be equivalent in view of their characteristics, price and intended use;

(b) an obligation to procure products which are the subject of the specialisation exclusively from another party, a joint undertaking or an undertaking jointly charged with their manufacture, except where they are obtainable on more favourable terms elsewhere and the other party, the joint undertaking or the undertaking charged with manufacture is not prepared to offer the same terms;

(c) an obligation to grant other parties the exclusive right to distribute products which are the subject of the specialisation provided that intermediaries and users can also obtain the products from other suppliers and the parties do not render it difficult for intermediaries or users thus to obtain the products.

2. Article 1 shall also apply where the parties undertake obligations of the types referred to in paragraph 1 but with a more limited scope than is permitted by that paragraph.

3. Article 1 shall apply notwithstanding that any of the following obligations, in particular, are imposed:

(a) an obligation to supply other parties with products which are the subject of the specialisation and in so doing to observe minimum standards of quality;

(b) an obligation to maintain minimum stocks of products which are the subject of the specialisation and of replacement parts for them;

(c) an obligation to provide customer and guarantee services for products which are the subject of the specialisation.

Article 3

1. Article 1 shall apply only if:

(a) the products which are the subject of the specialisation together with the participating undertakings' other products which are considered by users to be equivalent in view of their characteristics, price and intended use do not represent more than 20% of the market for such products in the common market or a substantial part thereof;

(*b*) the aggregate annual turnover of all the participating undertakings does not exceed 500 million ECU.

2. Article 1 shall continue to apply if the market share referred to in paragraph 1(a) or the turnover referred to in paragraph 1(b) is exceeded during any period of two consecutive financial years by not more than one-tenth.

3. Where one of the limits laid down in paragraphs 1 and 2 is exceeded, Article 1 shall continue to apply for a period of six months following the end of the financial year during which it was exceeded.

Article 4

1. The exemption provided for in Article 1 shall also apply to agreements involving participating undertakings whose aggregate turnover exceeds the limits laid down in Article 3(1)(b) and (2), on condition that the agreements in question are notified to the Commission in accordance with the provisions of Commission Regulation No 27[4], and that the Commission does not oppose such exemption within a period of six months.

2. The period of six months shall run from the date on which the notification is received by the Commission. Where, however, the notification is made by registered post, the period shall run from the date shown on the postmark of the place of posting.

3. Paragraph 1 shall apply only if:

(*a*) express reference is made to this Article in the notification or in a communication accompanying it; and

(*b*) the information furnished with the notification is complete and in accordance with the facts.

4. The benefit of paragraph 1 may be claimed for agreements notified before the entry into force of this Regulation by submitting a communication to the Commission referring expressly to this Article and to the notification. Paragraphs 2 and 3(b) shall apply *mutatis mutandis*.

5. The Commission may oppose the exemption. It shall oppose exemption if it receives a request to do so from a Member State within three months of the forwarding to the Member State of the notification referred to in paragraph 1 or of the communication referred to in paragraph 4. This request must be justified on the basis of considerations relating to the competition rules of the Treaty.

6. The Commission may withdraw the opposition to the exemption at any time. However, where the opposition was raised at the request of a Member State and this request is maintained, it may be withdrawn only after consultation of the Advisory Committee on Restrictive Practices and Dominant Positions.

7. If the opposition is withdrawn because the undertakings concerned have shown that the conditions of Article 85(3) are fulfilled, the exemption shall apply from the date of notification.

8. If the opposition is withdrawn because the undertakings concerned have amended the agreement so that the conditions of Article 85(3) are fulfilled, the exemption shall apply from the date on which the amendments take effect.

9. If the Commission opposes exemption and the opposition is not withdrawn, the effects of the notification shall be governed by the provisions of Regulation No 17.

Article 5

1. Information acquired pursuant to Article 4 shall be used only for the purposes of this Regulation.

2. The Commission and the authorities of the Member States, their officials and other servants shall not disclose information acquired by them pursuant to this Regulation of a kind that is covered by the obligation of professional secrecy.

3. Paragraphs 1 and 2 shall not prevent publication of general information or surveys which do not contain information relating to particular undertakings or associations of undertakings.

Article 6

For the purpose of calculating total annual turnover within the meaning of Article 3(1)(b), the turnovers achieved during the last financial year by the participating undertakings in respect of all goods and services excluding tax shall be added together. For this purpose, no account shall be taken of dealings between the participating undertakings or between these undertakings and a third undertaking jointly charged with manufacture.

Article 7

1. For the purposes of Article 3(1)(a) and (b) and Article 6, participating undertakings are:

(a) undertakings party to the agreement;

(b) undertakings in which a party to the agreement, directly or indirectly:

- owns more than half the capital or business assets,

- has the power to exercise more than half the voting rights,

- has the power to appoint at least half the members of the supervisory board, board of management or bodies legally representing the undertakings, or

- has the right to manage the affairs;

(c) undertakings which directly or indirectly have in or over a party to the agreement the rights or powers listed in (b);

(d) undertakings in or over which an undertaking referred to in (c) directly or indirectly has the rights or powers listed in (b).

2. Undertakings in which the undertakings referred to in paragraph 1 (a) to (d) directly or indirectly jointly have the rights or powers set out in paragraph 1(b) shall also be considered to be participating undertakings.

Article 8

The Commission may withdraw the benefit of this Regulation, pursuant to Article 7 of Regulation (EEC) No 2821/75, where it finds in a particular case that an agreement exempted by this Regulation nevertheless has effects which are incompatible with the conditions set out in Article 85(3) of the Treaty, and in particular where:

(a) the agreement is not yielding significant results in terms of rationalisation or consumers are not receiving a fair share of the resulting benefit; or

(b) the products which are the subject of the specialisation are not subject in the common market or a substantial part thereof to effective competition from identical products or products considered by users to be equivalent in view of their characteristics, price and intended use.

Article 9

This Regulation shall apply *mutatis mutandis* to decisions of associations of undertakings and concerted practices.

Article 10

1. This Regulation shall enter into force on 1 March 1985. It shall apply until 31 December 1997.

2. Commission Regulation (EEC) No 3604/82[5] is hereby repealed.

This Regulation shall be binding in its entirety and directly applicable in all Member States.

Done at Brussels, 19 December 1984.

For the Commission

Frans Andriessen

Member of the Commission

FOOTNOTES

1. OJ No L 285, 29.12.71, p.26.
2. OJ No C 211, 11.8.84, p.2.
3. OJ No 13, 21.2.62, p.204.
4. OJ No 35, 10.5.62, p.1118.
5. OJ No 376, 31.12.82, p.33.

COMMISSION REGULATION (EEC) No 418/85

of 19 December 1984

on the application of Article 85(3) of the Treaty to categories of research and development agreements

(OJ No L 53, 22.2.85, p.5)

The Commission of the European Communities,

Having regard to the Treaty establishing the European Economic Community,

Having regard to Council Regulation (EEC) No 2821/71 of 20 December 1971 on the application of Article 85(3) of the Treaty to categories of agreements, decisions and concerted practices[1], as last amended by the Act of Accession of Greece, and in particular Article 1 thereof,

Having published a draft of this Regulation[2],

Having consulted the Advisory Committee on Restrictive Practices and Dominant Positions,

Whereas:

(1) Regulation (EEC) No 2821/71 empowers the Commission to apply Article 85(3) of the Treaty by Regulation to certain categories of

agreements, decisions and concerted practices falling within the scope of Article 85(1) which have as their object the research and development of products or processes up to the stage of industrial application, and exploitation of the results, including provisions regarding industrial property rights and confidential technical knowledge.

(2) As stated in the Commission's 1968 notice concerning agreements, decisions and concerted practices in the field of cooperation between enterprises[3], agreements on the joint execution of research work or the joint development of the results of the research, up to but not including the stage of industrial application, generally do not fall within the scope of Article 85(1) of the Treaty. In certain circumstances, however, such as where the parties agree not to carry out other research and development in the same field, thereby forgoing the opportunity of gaining competitive advantages over the other parties, such agreements may fall within Article 85(1) and should therefore not be excluded from this Regulation.

(3) Agreements providing for both joint research and development and joint exploitation of the results may fall within Article 85(1) because the parties jointly determine how the products developed are manufactured or the processes developed are applied or how related intellectual property rights or know-how are exploited.

(4) Cooperation in research and development and in the exploitation of the results generally promotes technical and economic progress by increasing the dissemination of technical knowledge between the parties and avoiding duplication of research and development work, by stimulating new advances through the exchange of complementary technical knowledge, and by rationalising the manufacture of the products or application of the processes arising out of the research and development. These aims can be achieved only where the research and development programme and its objectives are clearly defined and each of the parties is given the opportunity of exploiting any of the results of the programme that interest it; where universities or research institutes participate and are not interested in the industrial exploitation of the results, however, it may be agreed that they may use the said results solely for the purpose of further research.

(5) Consumers can generally be expected to benefit from the increased volume and effectiveness of research and development through the introduction of new or improved products or services or the reduction of prices brought about by new or improved processes.

(6) This Regulation must specify the restrictions of competition which may be included in the exempted agreements. The purpose of the permitted restrictions is to concentrate the research activities of the

parties in order to improve their chances of success, and to facilitate the introduction of new products and services onto the market. These restrictions are generally necessary to secure the desired benefits for the parties and consumers.

(7) The joint exploitation of results can be considered as the natural consequence of joint research and development. It can take different forms ranging from manufacture to the exploitation of intellectual property rights or know-how that substantially contributes to technical or economic progress. In order to attain the benefits and objectives described above and to justify the restrictions of competition which are exempted, the joint exploitation must relate to products or processes for which the use of the results of the research and development is decisive. Joint exploitation is not therefore justified where it relates to improvements which were not made within the framework of a joint research and development programme but under an agreement having some other principal objective, such as the licensing of intellectual property rights, joint manufacture or specialisation, and merely containing ancillary provisions on joint research and development.

(8) The exemption granted under the Regulation must be limited to agreements which do not afford the undertakings the possibility of eliminating competition in respect of a substantial part of the products in question. In order to guarantee that several independent poles of research can exist in the common market in any economic sector, it is necessary to exclude from the block exemption agreements between competitors whose combined share of the market for products capable of being improved or replaced by the results of the research and development exceeds a certain level at the time the agreement is entered into.

(9) In order to guarantee the maintenance of effective competition during joint exploitation of the results, it is necessary to provide that the block exemption will cease to apply if the parties' combined shares of the market for the products arising out of the joint research and development become too great. However, it should be provided that the exemption will continue to apply, irrespective of the parties' market shares, for a certain period after the commencement of joint exploitation, so as to await stabilisation of their market shares, particularly after the introduction of an entirely new product, and to guarantee a minimum period of return on the generally substantial investments involved.

(10) Agreements between undertakings which do not fulfil the market share conditions laid down in the Regulation may, in appropriate cases, be granted an exemption by individual decision, which will in particular

take account of world competition and the particular circumstances prevailing in the manufacture of high technology products.

(11) It is desirable to list in the Regulation a number of obligations that are commonly found in research and development agreements but that are normally not restrictive of competition and to provide that, in the event that, because of the particular economic or legal circumstances, they should fall within Article 85(1), they also would be covered by the exemption. This list is not exhaustive.

(12) The Regulation must specify what provisions may not be included in agreements if these are to benefit from the block exemption by virtue of the fact that such provisions are restrictions falling within Article 85(1) for which there can be no general presumption that they will lead to the positive effects required by Article 85(3).

(13) Agreements which are not automatically covered by the exemption because they include provisions that are not expressly exempted by the Regulation and are not expressly excluded from exemption are none the less capable of benefiting from the general presumption of compatibility with Article 85(3) on which the block exemption is based. It will be possible for the Commission rapidly to establish whether this is the case for a particular agreement. Such an agreement should therefore be deemed to be covered by the exemption provided for in this Regulation where it is notified to the Commission and the Commission does not oppose the application of the exemption within a specified period of time.

(14) Agreements covered by this Regulation may also take advantage of provisions contained in other block exemption Regulations of the Commission, and in particular Regulation (EEC) No 417/85[4] on specialisation agreements, Regulation (EEC) No 1983/83[5] on exclusive distribution agreements, Regulation (EEC) No 1984/83[6] on exclusive purchasing agreements and Regulation (EEC) No 2349/84[7] on patent licensing agreements, if they fulfil the conditions set out in these Regulations. The provisions of the aforementioned Regulations are, however, not applicable in so far as this Regulation contains specific rules.

(15) If individual agreements exempted by this Regulation nevertheless have effects which are incompatible with Article 85(3), the Commission may withdraw the benefit of the block exemption.

(16) The Regulation should apply with retroactive effect to agreements in existence when the Regulation comes into force where such agreements already fulfil its conditions or are modified to do so. The benefits of these provisions may not be claimed in actions pending at the date of

entry into force of this Regulation, nor may it be relied on as grounds for claims for damages against third parties.

(17) Since research and development cooperation agreements are often of a long-term nature, especially where the cooperation extends to the exploitation of the results, it is appropriate to fix the period of validity of the Regulation at 13 years. If the circumstances on the basis of which the Regulation was adopted should change significantly within this period, the Commission will make the necessary amendments.

(18) Agreements which are automatically exempted pursuant to this Regulation need not be notified. Undertakings may nevertheless in a particular case request a decision to Council Regulation No 17[8], as last amended by the Act of Accession of Greece,

Has adopted this Regulation:

Article 1

1. Pursuant to Article 85(3) of the Treaty and subject to the provisions of this Regulation, it is hereby declared that Article 85(1) of the Treaty shall not apply to agreements entered into between undertakings for the purpose of:

(a) joint research and development of products or processes and joint exploitation of the results of that research and development;

(b) joint exploitation of the results of research and development of products or processes jointly carried out pursuant to a prior agreement between the same undertakings; or

(c) joint research and development of products or processes excluding joint exploitation of the results, in so far as such agreements fall within the scope of Article 85(1).

2. For the purposes of this Regulation:

(a) *research and development of products or processes* means the acquisition of technical knowledge and the carrying out of theoretical analysis, systematic study or experimentation, including experimental production, technical testing of products or processes, the establishment of the necessary facilities and the obtaining of intellectual property rights for the results;

(b) *contract processes* means processes arising out of the research and development;

(c) *contract products* means products or services arising out of the research and development or manufactured or provided applying the contract processes;

(d) *exploitation of the results* means the manufacture of the contract products or the application of the contract processes or the assignment or licensing of intellectual property rights or the communication of know-how required for such manufacture or application;

(e) *technical knowledge* means technical knowledge which is either protected by an intellectual property right or is secret (know-how).

3. Research and development of the exploitation of the results are carried out *jointly* where:

(a) the work involved is:

  – carried out by a joint team, organisation or undertaking,

  – jointly entrusted to a third party, or

  – allocated between the parties by way of specialisation in research, development or production;

(b) the parties collaborate in any way in the assignment or the licensing of intellectual property rights or the communication of know-how, within the meaning of paragraph 2(d), to third parties.

Article 2

The exemption provided for in Article 1 shall apply on condition that:

(a) the joint research and development work is carried out within the framework of a programme defining the objectives of the work and the field in which it is to be carried out;

(b) all the parties have access to the results of the work;

(c) where the agreement provides only for joint research and development, each party is free to exploit the results of the joint research and development and any pre-existing technical knowledge necessary therefor independently;

(d) the joint exploitation relates only to results which are protected by intellectual property rights or constitute know-how which substantially contributes to technical or economic progress and that the results are decisive for the manufacture of the contract products or the application of the contract processes;

(e) any joint undertaking or third party charged with manufacture of the contract products is required to supply them only to the parties;

(f) undertakings charged with manufacture by way of specialisation in production are required to fulfil orders for supplies from all the parties.

Article 3

1. Where the parties are not competing manufacturers of products capable of being improved or replaced by the contract products, the exemption provided for in Article 1 shall apply for the duration of the research and development programme and, where the results are jointly exploited, for five years from the time the contract products are first put on the market within the common market.

2. Where two or more of the parties are competing manufacturers within the meaning of paragraph 1, the exemption provided for in Article 1 shall apply for the period specified in paragraph 1 only if, at the time the agreement is entered into, the parties' combined production of the products capable of being improved or replaced by the contract products does not exceed 20% of the market for such products in the common market or a substantial part thereof.

3. After the end of the period referred to in paragraph 1, the exemption provided for in Article 1 shall continue to apply as long as the production of the contract products together with the parties' combined production of other products which are considered by users to be equivalent in view of their characteristics, price and intended use does not exceed 20% of the total market for such products in the common market or a substantial part thereof. Where contract products are components used by the parties of the manufacture of other products, reference shall be made to the markets for such of those latter products for which the components represent a significant part.

4. The exemption provided for in Article 1 shall continue to apply where the market share referred to in paragraph 3 is exceeded during any period of two consecutive financial years by not more than one tenth.

5. Where market shares referred to in paragraphs 3 and 4 are exceeded, the exemption provided for in Article 1 shall continue to apply for a period of six months following the end of the financial year during which it was exceeded.

Article 4

1. The exemption provided for in Article 1 shall also apply to the following restrictions of competition imposed on the parties:

(a) an obligation not to carry out independently research and development in the field to which the programme relates or in a closely connected field during the execution of the programme;

(b) an obligation not to enter into agreements with third parties on research and development in the field to which the programme relates or in a closely connected field during the execution of the programme;

(c) an obligation to procure the contract products exclusively from parties, joint organisations or undertakings or third parties, jointly charged with their manufacture;

(d) an obligation not to manufacture the contract products or apply the contract processes in territories reserved for other parties;

(e) an obligation to restrict the manufacture of the contract products or application of the contract processes to one or more technical fields of application, except where two or more of the parties are competitors within the meaning of Article 3 at the time the agreement is entered into;

(f) an obligation not to pursue, for a period of five years from the time the contract products are first put on the market within the common market, an active policy of putting the products on the market in territories reserved for other parties, and in particular not to engage in advertising specifically aimed at such territories or to establish any branch or maintain any distribution depot there for the distribution of the products, provided that users and intermediaries can obtain the contract products from other suppliers and the parties do not render it difficult for intermediaries and users to thus obtain the products;

(g) an obligation on the parties to communicate to each other any experience they may gain in exploiting the results and to grant each other non-exclusive licences for inventions relating to improvements or new applications.

2. The exemption provided for in Article 1 shall also apply where in a particular agreement the parties undertake obligations of the types referred to in paragraph 1 but with a more limited scope than is permitted by that paragraph.

Article 5

1. Article 1 shall apply notwithstanding that any of the following obligations, in particular, are imposed on the parties during the currency of the agreement:

(a) an obligation to communicate patented or non-patented technical knowledge necessary for the carrying out of the research and development programme for the exploitation of its results;

(b) an obligation not to use any know-how received from another party for purposes other than carrying out the research and development programme and the exploitation of its results;

(c) an obligation to obtain and maintain in force intellectual property rights for the contract products or processes;

(d) an obligation to preserve the confidentiality of any know-how received or jointly developed under the research and development programme; this obligation may be imposed even after the expiry of the agreement;

(e) an obligation:

   (i) to inform other parties of infringements of their intellectual property rights,

   (ii) to take legal action against infringers, and

   (iii) to assist in any such legal action or share with the other parties in the cost thereof;

(f) an obligation to pay royalties or render services to other parties to compensate for unequal contributions to the joint research and development or unequal exploitation of its results;

(g) an obligation to share royalties received from third parties with other parties;

(h) an obligation to supply other parties with minimum quantities of contract products and to observe minimum standards of quality.

2. In the event that, because of particular circumstances, the obligations referred to in paragraph 1 fall within the scope of Article 85(1), they also shall be covered by the exemption. The exemption provided for in this paragraph shall also apply where in a particular agreement the parties undertake obligations of the types referred to in paragraph 1 but with a more limited scope than is permitted by that paragraph.

Article 6

The exemption provided for in Article 1 shall not apply where the parties, by agreement, decision or concerted practice:

(a) are restricted in their freedom to carry out research and development independently or in cooperation with third parties in a field unconnected with that to which the programme relates or, after its completion, in the field to which the programme relates or in a connected field;

(b) are prohibited after completion of the research and development programme from challenging the validity of intellectual property rights which the parties hold in the common market and which are relevant to the programme or, after the expiry of the agreement, from challenging the validity of intellectual property rights which the parties hold in the common market and which protect the results of the research and development;

(c) are restricted as to the quantity of the contract products they may manufacture or sell or as to the number of operations employing the contract process they may carry out;

(d) are restricted in their determination of prices, components of prices or discounts when selling the contract products to third parties;

(e) are restricted as to the customers they may serve, without prejudice to Article 4(1)(e);

(f) are prohibited from putting the contract products on the market or pursuing an active sales policy for them in territories within the common market that are reserved for other parties after the end of the period referred to in Article 4(1)(f);

(g) are prohibited from allowing third parties to manufacture the contract products or apply the contract processes in the absence of joint manufacture;

(h) are required:

– to refuse without any objectively justified reason to meet demand from users or dealers established in their respective territories who would market the contract products in other territories within the common market, or

– to make it difficult for users or dealers to obtain the contract products from other dealers within the common market, and in particular to exercise intellectual property rights or take measures so as to prevent users or dealers from obtaining, or from putting on the market within the common market, products which have been lawfully put on the market within the common market by another party or with its consent.

Article 7

1. The exemption provided for in this Regulation shall also apply to agreements of the kinds described in Article 1 which fulfil the conditions laid down in Articles 2 and 3 and which contain obligations restrictive of competition which are not covered by Articles 4 and 5 and do not fall within the scope of Article 6, on condition that the agreements in question are notified to the Commission in accordance with the

provisions of Commission Regulation No 27[9], and that the Commission does not oppose such exemption within a period of six months.

2. The period of six months shall run from the date on which the notification is received by the Commission. Where, however, the notification is made by registered post, the period shall run from the date shown on the postmark of the place of posting.

3. Paragraph 1 shall apply only if:

(a) express reference is made to this Article in the notification or in a communication accompanying it, and

(b) the information furnished with the notification is complete and in accordance with the facts.

4. The benefit of paragraph 1 may be claimed for agreements notified before the entry into force of this Regulation by submitting a communication to the Commission referring expressly to this Article and to the notification. Paragraphs 2 and 3(b) shall apply *mutatis mutandis*.

5. The Commission may oppose the exemption. It shall oppose exemption if it receives a request to do so from a Member State within three months of the forwarding to the Member State of the notification referred to in paragraph 1 or of the communication referred to in paragraph 4. This request must be justified on the basis of considerations relating to the competition rules of the Treaty.

6. The Commission may withdraw the opposition to the exemption at any time. However, where the opposition was raised at the request of a Member State and this request is maintained, it may be withdrawn only after consultation of the Advisory Committee on Restrictive Practices and Dominant Positions.

7. If the opposition is withdrawn because the undertakings concerned have shown that the conditions of Article 85(3) are fulfilled, the exemption shall apply from the date of notification.

8. If the opposition is withdrawn because the undertakings concerned have amended the agreement so that the conditions of Article 85(3) are fulfilled, the exemption shall apply from the date on which the amendments take effect.

9. If the Commission opposes exemption and the opposition is not withdrawn, the effects of the notification shall be governed by the provisions of Regulation No 17.

Article 8

1. Information acquired pursuant to Article 7 shall be used only for the purposes of this Regulation.

2. The Commission and the authorities of the Member States, their officials and other servants shall not disclose information acquired by them pursuant to this Regulation of a kind that is covered by the obligation of professional secrecy.

3. Paragraphs 1 and 2 shall not prevent publication of general information or surveys which do not contain information relating to particular undertakings or associations of undertakings.

Article 9

1. The provisions of this Regulation shall also apply to rights and obligations which the parties create for undertakings connected with them. The market shares held and the actions and measures taken by connected undertakings shall be treated as those of the parties themselves.

2. Connected undertakings for the purposes of this Regulation are:

(a) undertakings in which a party to the agreement, directly or indirectly:

- owns more than half the capital or business assets,

- has the power to exercise more than half the voting rights,

- has the power to appoint more than half the members of the supervisory board, board of directors or bodies legally representing the undertakings, or

- has the right to manage the affairs;

(b) undertakings which directly have in or over a party to the agreement the rights or powers listed in (a);

(c) undertakings in or over which an undertaking referred to in (b) directly or indirectly has the rights or powers listed in (a);

3. Undertakings in which the parties to the agreement or undertakings connected with them jointly have, directly or indirectly, the rights or powers set out in paragraph 2(a) shall be considered to be connected with each of the parties to the agreement.

Article 10

The Commission may withdraw the benefit of this Regulation, pursuant to Article 7 of Regulation (EEC) No 2821/71, where it finds in a particular case that an agreement exempted by this Regulation nevertheless has certain effects which are incompatible with the conditions laid down in Article 85(3) of the Treaty, and in particular where:

(a) the existence of the agreement substantially restricts the scope for third parties to carry out research and development in the relevant field because of the limited research capacity available elsewhere;

(b) because of the particular structure of supply, the existence of the agreement substantially restricts the access of third parties to the market for the contract products;

(c) without any objectively valid reason, the parties do not exploit the results of the joint research and development;

(d) the contract products are not subject in the whole or a substantial part of the common market to effective competition from identical products or products considered by users as equivalent in view of their characteristics, price and intended use.

Article 11

1. In the case of agreements notified to the Commission before 1 March 1985, the exemption provided for in Article 1 shall have retroactive effect from the time at which the conditions for application of this Regulation were fulfilled or, where the agreement does not fall within Article 4(2)(3)(b) of Regulation No 17, not earlier than the date of notification.

2. In the case of agreements existing on 13 March 1962 and notified to the Commission before 1 February 1963, the exemption shall have retroactive effect from the time at which the conditions for application of this Regulation were fulfilled.

3. Where agreements which were in existence on 13 March 1962 and which were notified to the Commission before 1 February 1963, or which are covered by Article 4(2)(3)(b) of Regulation No 17 and were notified to the Commission before 1 January 1967, are amended before 1 September 1985 so as to fulfil the conditions for application of this Regulation, such amendment being communicated to the Commission before 1 October 1985, the prohibition laid down in Article 85(1) of the Treaty shall not apply in respect of the period prior to the amendment. The communication of amendments shall take effect from the date of their receipt by the Commission. Where the communication is sent by registered post, it shall take effect from the date shown on the postmark of the place of posting.

4. In the case of agreements to which Article 85 of the Treaty applies as a result of the accession of the United Kingdom, Ireland and Denmark,

paragraphs 1 to 3 shall apply except that the relevant dates shall be 1 January 1973 instead of 13 March 1962 and 1 July 1973 instead of 1 February 1963 and 1 January 1967.

5. In the case of agreements to which Article 85 of the Treaty applies as a result of the accession of Greece, paragraphs 1 to 3 shall apply except that the relevant dates shall be 1 January 1981 instead of 13 March 1962 and 1 July 1981 instead of 1 February 1963 and 1 January 1967.

Article 12

This Regulation shall apply *mutatis mutandis* to decisions of associations of undertakings.

Article 13

This Regulation shall enter force on 1 March 1985.

It shall apply until 31 December 1997.

This Regulation shall be binding in its entirety and directly applicable in all Member States.

Done at Brussels, 19 December 1984.

For the Commission

Frans Andriessen

Member of the Commission

FOOTNOTES

1. OJ No L 285, 29.12.71, p.46.
2. OJ No C 16, 21.1.84, p.3.
3. OJ No C 75, 29.7.68, p.3, corrected by OJ No C 84, 28.8.68, p.14.
4. See OJ No L 53, 22.2.85, p.1.
5. OJ No L 173, 30.6.83, p.1.
6. OJ No L 173, 30.6.83, p.5.
7. OJ No L 219, 16.8.84, p.15.
8. OJ No 13, 21.2.62, p.204.
9. OJ No 35, 10.5.62, p.1118.

COMMISSION REGULATION (EEC) NO 2349/84

of 23 July 1984

on the application of Article 85(3) of the Treaty to certain categories of patent licensing agreements

(OJ No L 219, 16.8.84, p.15)

The Commission of the European Communities

Having regard to the Treaty establishing the European Economic Community,

Having regard to Council Regulation No 19/65/EEC of 2 March 1965 on the application of Article 85(3) of the Treaty to certain categories of agreements and concerted practices[1], as last amended by the Act of Accession of Greece, and in particular Article 1 thereof,

Having published a draft of this Regulation[2],

After consulting the Advisory Committee on Restrictive Practices and Dominant Positions,

Whereas:

(1) Regulation No 19/65/EEC empowers the Commission to apply Article 85(3) of the Treaty by Regulation to certain categories of agreements and concerted practices falling within the scope of Article 85(1) to which only two undertakings are party and which include restrictions imposed in relation to the acquisition or use of industrial property rights, in particular patents, utility models, designs or trade marks, or to the rights arising out of contracts for assignment of, or the right to use, a method of manufacture or knowledge relating to the use or application of industrial processes.

(2) Patent licensing agreements are agreements whereby one undertaking, the holder of a patent (the licensor), permits another undertaking (the licensee) to exploit the patented invention by one or more of the means of exploitation afforded by patent law, in particular manufacture, use or putting on the market.

(3) In the light of experience acquired so far, it is possible to define a category of patent licensing agreements which are capable of falling within the scope of Article 85(1), but which can normally be regarded as satisfying the conditions laid down in Article 85(3). To the extent that patent licensing agreements to which undertakings in only one Member State are party and which concern only one or more patents for that

Member State are capable of affecting trade between Member States, it is appropriate to include them in the exempted category.

(4) The present Regulation applies to licences issued in respect of national patents of the Member States, Community patents[3], or European patents[4] granted for Member States, licences in respect of utility models or 'certificats d'utilité' issued in the Member States, and licences in respect of inventions for which a patent application is made within one year. Where such patent licensing agreements contain obligations relating not only to territories within the common market but also obligations relating to non-member countries, the presence of the latter does not prevent the present Regulation from applying to the obligations relating to territories within the common market.

(5) However, where licensing agreements for non-member countries or for territories which extend beyond the frontiers of the Community have effects within the common market which may fall within the scope of Article 85(1), such agreements should be covered by the Regulation to the same extent as would agreements for territories within the common market.

(6) The Regulation should also apply to agreements concerning the assignment and acquisition of the rights referred to in point 4 above where the risk associated with exploitation remains with the assignor, patent licensing agreements in which the licensor is not the patentee but is authorised by the patentee to grant the licence (as in the case of sub-licences) and patent licensing agreements in which the parties' rights or obligations are assumed by connected undertakings.

(7) The Regulation does not apply to agreements concerning sales alone, which are governed by the provisions of Commission Regulation (EEC) No 1983/83 of 22 June 1983 concerning the application of Article 85(3) of the Treaty to categories of exclusive distribution agreements[5].

(8) Since the experience so far acquired is inadequate, it is not appropriate to include within the scope of the Regulation patent pools, licensing agreements entered into in connection with joint ventures, reciprocal licensing or distribution agreements, or licensing agreements in respect of plant breeder's rights. Reciprocal agreements which do not involve any territorial restrictions within the common market should, however, be so included.

(9) On the other hand, it is appropriate to extend the scope of the Regulation to patent licensing agreements which also contain provisions assigning, or granting the right to use, non-patented technical knowledge, since such mixed agreements are commonly concluded in order to allow the transfer of a complex technology containing both

patented and non-patented elements. Such agreements can only be regarded as fulfilling the conditions of Article 85(3) for the purposes of this Regulation where the communicated technical knowledge is secret and permits a better exploitation of the licensed patents (know-how). Provisions concerning the provision of know-how are covered by the Regulation only in so far as the licensed patents are necessary for achieving the objects of the licensed technology and as long as at least one of the licensed patents remains in force.

(10) It is also appropriate to extend the scope of the Regulation to patent licensing agreements containing ancillary provisions relating to trade-marks, subject to ensuring that the trade-mark licence is not used to extend the effects of the patent licence beyond the life of the patents. For this purpose it is necessary to allow the licensee to identify himself within the 'licensed territory', i.e. the territory covering all or part of the common market where the licensor holds patents which the licensee is authorised to exploit, as the manufacturer of the 'licensed product', i.e. the product which is the subject matter of the licensed patent or which has been obtained directly from the process which is the subject matter of the licensed patent, to avoid his having to enter into a new trade-mark agreement with the licensor when the licensed patents expire in order not to lose the goodwill attaching to the licensed product.

(11) Exclusive licensing agreements, i.e. agreements in which the licensor undertakes not to exploit the 'licensed invention', i.e. the licensed patented invention and any know-how communicated to the licensee, in the licensed territory himself or to grant further licenses there, are not in themselves incompatible with Article 85(1) where they are concerned with the introduction and protection of a new technology in the licensed territory, by reason of the scale of the research which has been undertaken and of the risk that is involved in manufacturing and marketing a product which is unfamiliar to users in the licensed territory at the time the agreement is made. This may also be the case where the agreements are concerned with the introduction and protection of a new process for manufacturing a product which is already known. In so far as in other cases agreements of this kind may fall within the scope of Article 85(1), it is useful for the purposes of legal certainty to include them in Article 1, in order that they may also benefit from the exemption. However, the exemption of exclusive licensing agreements and certain export bans imposed on the licensor and his licensees is without prejudice to subsequent developments in the case law of the Court of Justice regarding the status of such agreements under Article 85(1).

(12) The obligations listed in Article 1 generally contribute to improving the production of goods and to promoting technical progress; they make patentees more willing to grant licences and licensees more inclined to

undertake the investment required to manufacture, use and put on the market a new product or to use a new process, so that undertakings other than the patentee acquire the possibility of manufacturing their products with the aid of the latest techniques and of developing those techniques further. The result is that the number of production facilities and the quantity and quality of goods produced in the common market are increased. This is true, in particular, of obligations on the licensor and on the licensee not to exploit the licensed invention in, and in particular not to export the licensed product into, the licensed territory in the case of the licensor and the 'territories reserved for the licensor', that is to say, territories within the common market in which the licensor has patent protection and has not granted any licences, in the case of the licensee. This is also true both of the obligation of the licensee not to conduct an active policy of putting the product in the market (i.e. a prohibition of active competition as defined in Article 1(1)(5)) in the territories of other licensees for a period which may equal the duration of the licence and also the obligation of the licensee not to put the licensed product on the market in the territories of other licensees for a limited period of a few years (i.e. a prohibition not only of active competition but also of 'passive competition' whereby the licensee of a territory simply responds to requests which he has not solicited from users or resellers established in the territories of other licensees – Article 1(1)(6)). However, such obligations may be permitted under the Regulation only in respect of territories in which the licensed product is protected by 'parallel patents', that is to say, patents covering the same invention, within the meaning of the case law of the Court of Justice, and as long as the patents remain in force.

(13) Consumers will as a rule be allowed a fair share of the benefit resulting from this improvement in the supply of goods on the market. To safeguard this effect, however, it is right to exclude from the application of Article 1 cases where the parties agree to refuse to meet demand from users or resellers within their respective territories who would resell for export, or to take other steps to impede parallel imports, or where the licensee is obliged to refuse to meet unsolicited demand from the territory of other licensees (passive sales). The same applies where such action is the result of a concerted practice between the licensor and the licensee.

(14) The obligations referred to above thus do not impose restrictions which are not indispensable to the attainment of the abovementioned objectives.

(15) Competition at the distribution stage is safeguarded by the possibility of parallel imports and passive sales. The exclusivity obligations covered by the Regulation thus do not normally entail the

possibility of eliminating competition in respect of a substantial part of the products in question. This is so even in the case of agreements which grant exclusive licences for a territory covering the whole of the common market.

(16) To the extent that in their agreements the parties undertake obligations of the type referred to in Articles 1 and 2 but which are of more limited scope and thus less restrictive of competition than is permitted by those Articles, it is appropriate that these obligations should also benefit under the exemptions provided for in the Regulation.

(17) If in a particular case an agreement covered by this Regulation is found to have effects which are incompatible with the provisions of Article 85(3) of the Treaty, the Commission may withdraw the benefit of the block exemption from the undertakings concerned, in accordance with Article 7 of Regulation No 19/65/EEC.

(18) It is not necessary expressly to exclude from the category defined in the Regulation agreements which do not fulfil the conditions of Article 85(1). Nevertheless it is advisable, in the interests of legal certainty for the undertakings concerned, to list in Article 2 a number of obligations which are not normally restrictive of competition, so that these also may benefit from the exemption in the event that, because of particular economic or legal circumstances, they should exceptionally fall within the scope of Article 85(1). The list of such obligations given in Article 2 is not exhaustive.

(19) The Regulation must also specify what restrictions or provisions may not be included in patent licensing agreements if these are to benefit from the block exemption. The restrictions listed in Article 3 may fall under the prohibition of Article 85(1); in these cases there can be no general presumption that they will lead to the positive effects required by Article 85(3), as would be necessary for the granting of a block exemption.

(20) Such restrictions include those which deny the licensee the right enjoyed by any third party to challenge the validity of the patent or which automatically prolong the agreement by the life of any new patent granted during the life of the licensed patents which are in existence at the time the agreement is entered into. Nevertheless, the parties are free to extend their contractual relationship by entering into new agreements concerning such new patents, or to agree the payment of royalties for as long as the licensee continues to use know-how communicated by the licensor which has not entered into the public domain, regardless of the duration of the original patents and of any new patents that are licensed.

(21) They also include restrictions on the freedom of one party to compete with the other and in particular to involve himself in techniques

other than those licensed, since such restrictions impede technical and economic progress. The prohibition of such restrictions should however be reconciled with the legitimate interest of the licensor in having his patented invention exploited to the full and to this end to require the licensee to use his best endeavours to manufacture and market the licensed product.

(22) Such restrictions include, further, an obligation on the licensee to continue to pay royalties after all the licensed patents have expired and the communicated know-how has entered into the public domain, since such an obligation would place the licensee at a disadvantage by comparison with his competitors, unless it is established that this obligation results from arrangements for spreading payments in respect of previous use of the licensed invention.

(23) They also include restrictions imposed on the parties regarding prices, customers or marketing of the licensed products or regarding the quantities to be manufactured or sold, especially since restrictions of the latter type may have the same effect as export bans.

(24) Finally, they include restrictions to which the licensee submits at the time the agreement is made because he wishes to obtain the licence, but which give the licensor an unjustified competitive advantage, such as an obligation to assign to the licensor any improvements the licensee may make to the invention, or to accept other licences or goods and services that the licensee does not want from the licensor.

(25) It is appropriate to offer to parties to patent licensing agreements containing obligations which do not come within the terms of Articles 1 and 2 and yet do not entail any of the effects restrictive of competition referred to in Article 3 a simplified means of benefiting, upon notification, from the legal certainty provided by the block exemption (Article 4). This procedure should at the same time allow the Commission to ensure effective supervision as well as simplifying the administrative control of agreements.

(26) The Regulation should apply with retroactive effect to patent licensing agreements in existence when the Regulation comes into force where such agreements already fulfil the conditions for application of the Regulation or are modified to do so (Articles 6 to 8). Under Article 4(3) of Regulation No 19/65/EEC, the benefit of these provisions may not be claimed in actions pending at the date of entry into force of this Regulation, nor may it be relied on as grounds for claims for damages against third parties.

(27) Agreements which come within the terms of Articles 1 and 2 and which have neither the object nor the effect of restricting competition in

any other way need no longer be notified. Nevertheless, undertakings will still have the right to apply in individual cases for negative clearance under Article 2 of Council Regulation No 17[6] or for exemption under Article 85(3).

Has adopted this Regulation:

Article 1

1. Pursuant to Article 85(3) of the Treaty and subject to the provisions of this Regulation, it is hereby declared that Article 85(1) of the Treaty shall not apply to patent licensing agreements, and agreements combining the licensing of patents and the communication of know-how, to which only two undertakings are party and which include one or more of the following obligations:

1. an obligation on the licensor not to license other undertakings to exploit the licensed territory, covering all or part of the common market, in so far and as long as one of the licensed patents remains in force;

2. an obligation on the licensor not to exploit the licensed invention in the licensed territory himself in so far and as long as one of the licensed patents remains in force;

3. an obligation on the licensee not to exploit the licensed invention in territories within the common market which are reserved for the licensor, in so far and as long as the patented product is protected in those territories by parallel patents;

4. an obligation on the licensee not to manufacture or use the licensed product, or use the patented process or the communicated know-how, in territories within the common market which are licensed to other licensees, in so far and as long as the licensed product is protected in those territories by parallel patents;

5. an obligation on the licensee not to pursue an active policy of putting the product on the market in the territories within the common market which are licensed to other licensees, and in particular not to engage in advertising specifically aimed at those territories or to establish any branch or maintain any distribution depot there, in so far and as long as the licensed product is protected in those territories by parallel patents;

6. an obligation on the licensee not to put the licensed product on the market in the territories licensed to other licensees within the common market for a period not exceeding five years from the date when the product is first put on the market within the common

market by the licensor or one of his licensees, in so far as and for as long as the product is protected in these territories by parallel patents;

7. an obligation on the licensee to use only the licensor's trade mark or the get-up determined by the licensor to distinguish the licensed product, provided that the licensee is not prevented from identifying himself as the manufacturer of the licensed product.

2. The exemption of restrictions on putting the licensed product on the market resulting from the obligations referred to in paragraph 1(2),(3),(5) and (6) shall apply only if the licensee manufactures the licensed product himself or has it manufactured by a connected undertaking or by a subcontractor.

3. The exemption provided for in paragraph 1 shall also apply where in a particular agreement the parties undertake obligations of the types referred to in that paragraph but with a more limited scope than is permitted by the paragraph.

Article 2

1. Article 1 shall apply notwithstanding the presence in particular of any of the following obligations, which are generally not restrictive of competition:

1. an obligation on the licensee to procure goods or services from the licensor or from an undertaking designated by the licensor, in so far as such products or services are necessary for a technically satisfactory exploitation of the licensed invention;

2. an obligation on the licensee to pay a minimum royalty or to produce a minimum quantity of the licensed product or to carry out a minimum number of operations exploiting the licensed invention;

3. an obligation on the licensee to restrict his exploitation of the licensed invention to one or more technical fields of application covered by the licensed patent;

4. an obligation on the licensee not to exploit the patent after termination of the agreement in so far as the patent is still in force;

5. an obligation on the licensee not to grant sub-licences or assign the licence;

6. an obligation on the licensee to mark the licensed product with an indication of the patentee's name, the licensed patent or the patent licensing agreement;

7. an   obligation   on   the   licensee   not   to   divulge   know-how

products or services are necessary for a technically satisfactory exploitation of the licensed invention;

10. without prejudice to Article 1(1)(5), the licensee is required, for a period exceeding that permitted under Article 1(1)(6), not to put the licensed product on the market in territories licensed to other licensees within the common market or does not do so as a result of a concerted practice between the parties;

11. one or both of the parties are required:

(a) to refuse without any objectively justified reason to meet demand from users or resellers in their respective territories who would market products in other territories within the common market;

(b) to make it difficult for users or resellers to obtain the products from other resellers within the common market, and in particular to exercise industrial or commercial property rights or take measures so as to prevent users or resellers from obtaining outside, or from putting on the market in, the licensed territory products which have been lawfully put on the market within the common market by the patentee or with his consent;

or do so as a result of a concerted practice between them.

Article 4

1. The exemption provided for in Articles 1 and 2 shall also apply to agreements containing obligations restrictive of competition which are not covered by those Articles and do not fall within the scope of Article 3, on condition that the agreements in question are notified to the Commission in accordance with the provisions of Commission Regulation No 27[7], as last amended by Regulation (EEC) No 1699/75[8], and that the Commission does not oppose such exemption within a period of six months.

2. The period of six months shall run from the date on which the notification is received by the Commission. Where, however, the notification is made by registered post, the period shall run from the date shown on the postmark of the place of posting.

3. Paragraph 1 shall apply only if:

(a) express reference is made to this Article in the notification or in a communication accompanying it; and

(b) the information furnished with the notification is complete and in accordance with the facts.

4. The benefit of paragraph 1 may be claimed for agreements notified

before the entry into force of this Regulation by submitting a communication to the Commission referring expressly to this Article and to the notification. Paragraphs 2 and 3(b) shall apply *mutatis mutandis*.

5. The Commission may oppose the exemption. It shall oppose exemption if it receives a request to do so from a Member State within three months of the transmission to the Member State of the notification referred to in paragraph 1 or of the communication referred to in paragraph 4. This request must be justified on the basis of considerations relating to the competition rules of the Treaty.

6. The Commission may withdraw the opposition to the exemption at any time. However, where the opposition was raised at the request of a Member State and this request is maintained, it may be withdrawn only after consultation of the Advisory Committee on Restrictive Practices and Dominant Positions.

7. If the opposition is withdrawn because the undertakings concerned have shown that the conditions of Article 85(3) are fulfilled, the exemption shall apply from the date of notification.

8. If the opposition is withdrawn because the undertakings concerned have amended the agreement so that the conditions of Article 85(3) are fulfilled, the exemption shall apply from the date on which the amendments take effect.

9. If the Commission opposes exemption and the opposition is not withdrawn, the effects of the notification shall be governed by the provisions of Regulation No 17.

Article 5

1. This Regulation shall not apply:

1. to agreements between members of a patent pool which relate to the pooled patents;

2. to patent licensing agreements between competitors who hold interests in a joint venture or between one of them and the joint venture, if the licensing agreements relate to the activities of the joint venture;

3. to agreements under which the parties, albeit in separate agreements or through connected undertakings, grant each other reciprocal patent or trade-mark licences or reciprocal sales rights for unprotected products or exchange know-how, where the parties are competitors in relation to the products covered by those agreements;

4. to licensing agreements in respect of plant breeder's rights.

2. However, this Regulation shall apply to reciprocal licences of the types referred to in paragraph 1(3) where the parties are not subject to any territorial restriction within the common market on the manufacture, use or putting on the market of the products covered by these agreements or on the use of the licensed processes.

Article 6

1. As regards agreements existing on 13 March 1962 and notified before 1 February 1963 and agreements, whether notified or not, to which Article 4(2)(2)(b) of Regulation No 17 applies, the declaration of inapplicability of Article 85(1) of the Treaty contained in this Regulation shall have retroactive effect from the time at which the conditions for application of this Regulation were fulfilled.

2. As regards all other agreements notified before this Regulation entered into force, the declaration of inapplicability of Article 85(1) of the Treaty contained in this Regulation shall have retroactive effect from the time at which the conditions for application of this Regulation were fulfilled, or from the date of notification, whichever is the later.

Article 7

If agreements existing on 13 March 1962 and notified before 1 February 1963 or agreements to which Article 4(2)(2)(b) of Regulation No 17 applies and notified before 1 January 1967 are amended before 1 April 1985 so as to fulfil the conditions for application of this Regulation, and if the amendment is communicated to the Commission before 1 July 1985 the prohibition in Article 85(1) of the Treaty shall not apply in respect of the period prior to the amendment. The communication shall take effect from the time of its receipt by the Commission. Where the communication is sent by registered post, it shall take effect from the date shown on the postmark of the place of posting.

Article 8

1. As regards agreements to which Article 85 of the Treaty applies as a result of the accession of the United Kingdom, Ireland and Denmark, Articles 6 and 7 shall apply except that the relevant dates shall be 1 January 1973 instead of 13 March 1962 and 1 July 1973 instead of 1 February 1963 and 1 January 1967.

2. As regards agreements to which Article 85 of the Treaty applies as a result of the accession of Greece, Articles 6 and 7 shall apply except that the relevant dates shall be 1 January 1981 instead of 13 March 1962 and 1 July 1981 instead of 1 February 1963 and 1 January 1967.

Article 9

The Commission may withdraw the benefit of this Regulation, pursuant to Article 7 of Regulation No 19/65/EEC, where it finds in a particular case that an agreement exempted by this Regulation nevertheless has certain effects which are incompatible with the conditions laid down in Article 85(3) of the Treaty, and in particular where:

1. such effects arise from an arbitration award;

2. the licensed products or the services provided using a licensed process are not exposed to effective competition in the licensed territory from identical products or services considered by users as equivalent in view of their characteristics, price and intended use;

3. the licensor does not have the right to terminate the exclusivity granted to the licensee at the latest five years from the date the agreement was entered into and at least annually thereafter if, without legitimate reason, the licensee fails to exploit the patent or to do so adequately;

4. without prejudice to Article 1(1)(6), the licensee refuses, without objectively valid reason, to meet unsolicited demand from users or resellers in the territory of other licensees;

5. one or both of the parties:

    (a) without any objectively justified reason, refuse to meet demand from users or resellers in their respective territories who would market the products in other territories within the common market; or

    (b) make it difficult for users or resellers to obtain the products from other resellers within the common market, and in particular where they exercise industrial or commercial property rights or take measures so as to prevent resellers or users from obtaining outside, or from putting on the market in, the licensed territory products which have been lawfully put on the market within the common market by the patentee or with his consent.

Article 10

1. This Regulation shall apply to:

(a) patent applications;

(b) utility models;

(c) applications for registration of utility models;

(d) 'certificats d'utilité' and 'certificats d'addition' under French law; and

(e) applications for 'certificats d'utilité' and 'certificats d'addition' under French law;

equally as it applies to patents.

2. This Regulation shall also apply to agreements relating to the exploitation of an invention if an application within the meaning of paragraph 1 is made in respect of the invention for the licensed territory within one year from the date when the agreement was entered into.

Article 11

This Regulation shall also apply to:

1. patent licensing agreements where the licensor is not the patentee but is authorised by the patentee to grant a licence or a sub-licence;

2. assignments of a patent or of a right to a patent where the sum payable in consideration of the assignment is dependent upon the turnover attained by the assignee in respect of the patented products, the quantity of such products manufactured or the number of operations carried out employing the patented invention;

3. patent licensing agreements in which rights or obligations of the licensor or the licensee are assumed by undertakings connected with them.

Article 12

1. 'Connected undertakings' for the purposes of this Regulation means:

(a) undertakings in which a party to the agreement, directly or indirectly:

   - owns more than half the capital or business assets, or

   - has the power to exercise more than half the voting rights, or

   - has the power to appoint more than half the members of the supervisory board, board of directors or bodies legally representing the undertaking, or

   - has the right to manage the affairs of the undertaking;

(b) undertakings which directly or indirectly have in or over a party to the agreement the rights or powers listed in (a);

(c) undertakings in which an undertaking referred to in (b) directly or indirectly has the rights or powers listed in (a).

2. Undertakings in which the parties to the agreement or undertakings connected with them jointly have the rights or powers set out in paragraph 1(a) shall be considered to be connected with each of the parties to the agreement.

Article 13

1. Information acquired pursuant to Article 4 shall be used only for the purposes of this Regulation.

2. The Commission and the authorities of the Member States, their officials and other servants shall not disclose information acquired by them pursuant to this Regulation of the kind covered by the obligation of professional secrecy.

3. The provisions of paragraphs 1 and 2 shall not prevent publication of general information or surveys which do not contain information relating to particular undertakings or associations of undertakings.

Article 14

This Regulation shall enter into force on 1 January 1985.

It shall apply until 31 December 1994.

This Regulation shall be binding in its entirety and directly applicable in all Member States.

Done at Brussels, 23 July 1984.

For the Commission

Frans Andriessen

Member of the Commission

FOOTNOTES

1. OJ No 36, 6.3.65, p.533.
2. OJ No C 58, 3.3.79, p.12.
3. Convention for the European patent for the common market (Community Patent Convention) of 15 December 1975 (OJ No L 17, 26.1.76, p.1).
4. Convention on the grant of European patents of 5 October 1973.
5. OJ No L 173, 30.6.83, p.1.
6. OJ No 13, 21.2.62, p.204.
7. OJ No 35, 10.5.62, p.1118.
8. OJ No L 172, 3.7.75, p.11.

(b) Ireland

COMPETITION ACT, 1991

Schedule

An Act to prohibit, by analogy with Articles 85 and 86 of the Treaty establishing the European Economic Community, and in the interests of the common good, the prevention, restriction or distortion of competition and the abuse of dominant positions in trade in the State, to establish a Competition Authority, to amend the Mergers, Take-overs and Monopolies (Control) Act, 1978, and to provide for other matters connected with the matters aforesaid.

[22nd July, 1991]

Be it enacted by the Oireachtas as follows:

Part I

Preliminary

1. Short title

This Act may be cited as the Competition Act, 1991.

2. Commencement

(1) This Act shall come into operation on such day or days as may be fixed therefor by order or orders of the Minister, either generally or with reference to a particular purpose or provision, and different days may be so fixed for different purposes and different provisions of this Act.

(2) An order under subsection (1) may as respects the repeal effected by *section* 22 of the provisions of the Act of 1972 fix different days for the repeal of different provisions of that Act or for the repeal for different purposes of any provision of that Act.

3. Interpretation

(1) In this Act, unless the context otherwise requires:

'the Act of 1972' means the Restrictive Practices Act, 1972;

'the Act of 1978' means the Mergers, Take-overs and Monopolies (Control) Act, 1978;

'the Act of 1987' means the Restrictive Practices (Amendment) Act, 1987;

'authorised officer' means a person appointed under section 20;

'the Authority' means the Competition Authority established by section 10;

'the Court' means the High Court, or in the case of an appeal, the Supreme Court;

'the Minister' means the Minister for Industry and Commerce;

'prescribed' means prescribed by regulations made by the Minister;

'undertaking' means a person being an individual, a body corporate or an unincorporated body of persons engaged for gain in the production, supply or distribution of goods or the provision of a service.

(2) In this Act a reference to a section or Schedule is to a section of, or Schedule to, this Act unless it is indicated that a reference to some other provision is intended.

(3) In this Act a reference to a subsection or paragraph is to the subsection or paragraph of the provision in which the reference occurs, unless it is indicated that reference to another provision is intended.

(4) In this Act a reference to any other enactment is to that enactment as amended by any other enactment including this Act.

Part II

Rules of Competition

4. Anti-competitive agreements, decisions and concerted practices

(1) Subject to the provisions of this section, all agreements between undertakings, decisions by associations of undertakings and concerted practices which have as their object or effect the prevention, restriction or distortion of competition in trade in any goods or services in the State or in any part of the State are prohibited and void, including in particular, without prejudice to the generality of this subsection, those which–

(a) directly or indirectly fix purchase or selling prices or any other trading conditions;

(b) limit or control production, markets, technical development or investment;

(c) share markets or sources of supply;

(*d*) apply dissimilar conditions to equivalent transactions with other trading parties thereby placing them at a competitive disadvantage;

(*e*) make the conclusion of contracts subject to acceptance by the other parties of supplementary obligations which by their nature or according to commercial usage have no connection with the subject of such contracts.

(2) The Competition Authority established by this Act ('the Authority') may in accordance with section 8 grant a licence for the purposes of this section in the case of–

(*a*) any agreement or category of agreements,

(*b*) any decision or category of decisions,

(*c*) any concerted practice or category of concerted practices, which in the opinion of the Authority, having regard to all relevant market conditions, contributes to improving the production or distribution of goods or provision of services or to promoting technical or economic progress, while allowing consumers a fair share of the resulting benefit and which does not–

(i) impose on the undertakings concerned terms which are not indispensable to the attainment of those objectives;

(ii) afford undertakings the possibility of eliminating competition in respect of a substantial part of the products or services in question.

(3) (*a*) A licence under subsection (2) shall, while it is in force, and in accordance with its terms, permit the doing of acts which would otherwise be prohibited and void under subsection (1).

(*b*) Where a licence under subsection (2) covers a category of agreements, decisions or concerted practices, any agreements, decisions or concerted practices (as the case may be) within that category which comply with the terms of the licence need not be notified under section 7 to benefit from the licence while it is in force.

(4) The Authority may certify that in its opinion, on the basis of the facts in its possession, an agreement, decision or concerted practice notified under section 7 does not offend against subsection (1).

(5) Before granting a licence or issuing a certificate under this section, the Authority may invite any Minister of the Government concerned with the matter to offer such observations as he may wish to make.

(6) On granting a licence or issuing a certificate under this section, the Authority shall forthwith give notice in the prescribed manner to every

body to which it relates stating the terms and the date thereof and the reasons therefor and cause the notice to be published in Iris Oifigiúil and cause notice of the grant of the licence or issue of the certificate, as the case may be, to be published in one daily newspaper published in the State.

(7) The prohibition in subsection (1) shall not prevent the Court, in exercising any jurisdiction conferred on it by this Act concerning an agreement, decision or concerted practice which contravenes that prohibition and which creates or, but for this Act, would have created legal relations between the parties thereto, from applying, where appropriate, any relevant rules of law as to the severance of those terms of that agreement, decision or concerted practice which contravene that prohibition from those which do not.

(8) In respect of an agreement, decision or concerted practice such as is referred to in subsection (7) a court of competent jurisdiction may make such order as to recovery, restitution or otherwise between the parties to such agreement, decision or concerted practice as may in all the circumstances seem just, having regard in particular to any consideration or benefit given or received by such parties on foot thereof.

5. Abuse of dominant position

(1) Any abuse by one or more undertakings of a dominant position in trade for any goods or services in the State or in a substantial part of the State is prohibited.

(2) Without prejudice to the generality of subsection (1), such abuse may, in particular, consist in –

(a) directly or indirectly imposing unfair purchase or selling prices or other unfair trading conditions;

(b) limiting production, markets or technical development to the prejudice of consumers;

(c) applying dissimilar conditions to equivalent transactions with other trading parties, thereby placing them at a competitive disadvantage;

(d) making the conclusion of contracts subject to the acceptance by other parties of supplementary obligations which by their nature or according to commercial usage have no connection with the subject of such contracts.

6. Right of action

(1) Any person who is aggrieved in consequence of any agreement, decision, concerted practice or abuse which is prohibited under section

4 or 5 shall have a right of action for relief under this section against any undertaking which is or has at any material time been a party to such agreement, decision or concerted practice or has been guilty of such abuse.

(2) (*a*) Subject to paragraph (*b*), an action under this section shall be brought in the High Court.

(*b*) An action under this section may be brought in the Circuit Court in respect of any abuse which is prohibited under section 5 but any relief by way of damages, including exemplary damages, shall not, except by consent of the necessary parties in such form as may be provided for by rules of court, be in excess of the limit of the jurisdiction of the Circuit Court in an action founded on tort.

(3) The following reliefs, or any of them, may be granted to the plaintiff in an action under this section:

(*a*) relief by way of injunction or declaration,

(*b*) subject to subsection (6), damages, including exemplary damages.

(4) The Minister shall have a right of action, in respect of an agreement, decision or concerted practice or an abuse which is prohibited under section 4 or 5, for the reliefs specified in subsection (3)(*a*).

(5) (*a*) Where in proceedings under this section it is finally decided by the Court that an agreement, decision or concerted practice which is in question infringes the prohibition in section 4(1), any certificate in force under section 4(4) in relation to that agreement, decision or concerted practice shall thereupon cease to have force and effect as from the date of the order of the Court and the Court shall cause a certified copy of the said order to be served on the Authority.

(*b*) The Authority shall, as soon as may be, cause notice of the fact that, pursuant to paragraph (a), its certificate has ceased to have force and effect to be published in *Iris Oifigiúil*.

(6) Where there is or has been in force a certificate pursuant to section 4(4) in relation to an agreement, decision or concerted practice, and that certificate has not been revoked under section 8(6)(*b*), a claimant shall not be entitled to damages pursuant to this section for a contravention of the prohibition in section 4(1) in any proceedings under this section commenced after the issue of that certificate for loss suffered in consequence of that agreement, decision or concerted practice in respect of the period during which the certificate is or has been in force, but this subsection shall not prejudice any right to damages for a contravention of the prohibition in section 5.

(7) This section shall not apply to any agreement, decision or concerted practice to which section 7(2) applies which has been duly notified to the Authority until the Authority has decided to grant or refuse to grant a licence under section 4(2), or to issue a certificate or not to issue a certificate under section 4(4), in relation thereto and any appeal to the Court under section 9 in relation to the licence or the certificate has been concluded.

(8) The Authority shall as soon as may be cause to be published in I*ris Oifigiúil* any decision of the Authority referred to in subsection (7) and a copy of any such notice shall be *prima facie* evidence of the making and content of such decision and of the date thereof in any action under this section.

7. Notification of agreements, decisions and concerted practices to Authority

(1) Every agreement, decision and concerted practice of a kind described in section 4(1) which comes into existence after the commencement of that section in respect of which the parties thereto request a licence under section 4(2) or a certificate under section 4(4) of that section shall be notified to the Authority.

(2) Every agreement, decision and concerted practice of a kind described in section 4(1) which is in existence at the commencement of that section and in respect of which the parties seek a licence under section 4(2) or a certificate under section 4(4) shall be notified to the Authority within one year of such commencement.

(3) A licence under section 4(2) or a certificate under section 4(4) shall not be granted until the agreement, decision or concerted practice (as the case may be) has been notified to the Authority but any such licence may in the case of an agreement, decision or concerted practice to which subsection (1) applies be made retrospective to the date of notification under that subsection.

(4) A notification in accordance with this section shall be accompanied by such fee as may be prescribed.

(5) For the purpose of the exercise of its functions in relation to licences under section 4(2) and certificates under section 4(4) the Authority may accept such observations or submissions from persons claiming to be interested as it may think proper.

(6) The functions of the Authority under this Act shall be carried out in accordance with such procedures, if any, as may be prescribed.

8. Licence of Authority under section 4(2) and certificate of Authority under section 4(4)

(1) A licence of the Authority under section 4(2) shall be granted for a specified period subject to such conditions as may be attached to and specified in the licence.

(2) The Authority may from time to time, on the application of a party to a request under section 7, extend the period of a licence if it is of opinion that the requirements of section 4(2) continue to be fulfilled and the Authority shall, as soon as may be, cause to be published in Iris Oifigiúil notice of any such extension.

(3) Where the Authority is of the opinion that, having regard to the requirements of section 4(2) and to the basis upon which a licence under that subsection was granted –

(a) there has been a material change in any of the circumstances on which the decision was based,

(b) any party commits a breach of any obligation attached to the decision,

(c) the licence was based on materially incorrect or misleading information, or

(d) any party abuses the permission granted to it by the licence,

the Authority may revoke or amend the licence and, without prejudice to the generality of this subsection, may in particular insert in a licence conditions the effect of which is to prohibit specific acts by any party thereto which would otherwise be authorised pursuant to such a licence.

(4) The Authority shall as soon as may be cause to be published in Iris Oifigiúil notice of every revocation or amendment of a licence under section 4(2).

(5) Every licence under section 4(2) shall have effect in accordance with its terms, subject to any amendment thereof including any conditions inserted therein under subsection (3) of this section.

(6) The Authority may revoke a certificate under *section* 4(4) where it is of opinion that –

(a) there has been a material change in any of the circumstances on which the certificate was based, or

(b) the certificate was based on materially incorrect or misleading information.

(7) The Authority shall as soon as may be cause to be published in *Iris Oifigiúil* notice of every revocation under subsection (6).

9. Appeal to High Court

(1) Any undertaking or association of undertakings concerned, or any other person aggrieved by a licence or a certificate of the Authority under section 4(2) or (4), or the Minister, may appeal to the High Court within 28 days of publication pursuant to this Act of the licence or certificate and on the hearing of any such appeal the Court may confirm, amend or revoke the licence so appealed against, or, in the case of such a certificate, may cancel or refuse to cancel the certificate.

(2) The right of appeal in relation to a licence under section 4(2) includes the right to appeal against the insertion or exclusion of conditions attaching to any exemption granted.

(3) The Court may order that a licence or certificate in respect of which an appeal has been brought under this section shall be suspended pending the hearing and conclusion of the appeal.

(4) Any undertaking or association of undertakings concerned or the Minister may within 28 days of the notification or publication pursuant to this Act of a revocation or amendment by the Authority, pursuant to section 8(3), of a licence under section 4(2), or of a revocation by the Authority, pursuant to section 8(6), of a certificate under section 4(4), appeal to the High Court.

(5) The Court may extend the time specified in subsection (1) or (4) in any case where it seems just and convenient to do so.

Part III

The Competition Authority

10. Establishment of Competition Authority

(1) There shall be a body to be known as the Competition Authority to exercise the functions assigned to it by this Act.

(2) The Authority shall stand established on such day as the Minister may by order appoint.

(3) The Authority shall in particular discharge any function of the Fair Trade Commission under the Act of 1972 not completed at the commencement of this section and, accordingly, sections 7 and 8 of the Act of 1978 are amended by the substitution of references to the Authority for references to the Fair Trade Commission.

(4) The provisions of the Schedule shall have effect in relation to the Authority.

11. Studies and analyses by Authority

The Authority may, at the request of the Minister, study and analyse and, when requested by the Minister, report to him the results of any such study or analysis, any practice or method of competition affecting the supply and distribution of goods or the provision of services. A study or analysis may consist of, or include, a study or analysis of any development outside the State.

12. Reports

(1) The Authority shall submit to the Minister an annual report of its activities within four months of the end of each year.

(2) The Minister shall lay before each House of the Oireachtas a copy of every such report within four months of receiving the report.

Part IV

Mergers, Take-overs and Monopolies

13. Construction with Act of 1978

This Part shall be construed as one with the Act of 1978 and with the other Parts of this Act.

14. Investigation of abuse of dominant position

(1) Where the Minister is of the opinion that there is, contrary to section 5, an abuse of a dominant position he may request the Authority to carry out an investigation and the Authority shall comply with the request.

(2) Where the Authority holds an investigation pursuant to a request under subsection (1) it shall report thereon to the Minister and the report shall state whether in the opinion of the Authority –

(a) a dominant position exists, and

(b) if it does, whether that dominant position is being abused.

(3) The Minister, having considered a report of the Authority under subsection (2), may, if the interests of the common good so warrant, after consultation with any other Minister of the Government concerned, by order either:

(a) prohibit the continuance of the dominant position except on conditions specified in the order, or

(b) require the adjustment of the dominant position, in a manner and within a period specified in the order, by a sale of assets or otherwise as he may specify.

(4) An order under this section shall state the reasons for making the order.

(5) The Minister may by order revoke an order under this section and may, with the agreement of every enterprise concerned, amend an order under this section.

(6) An order under this section shall not have effect unless and until it is confirmed by a resolution of each House of the Oireachtas.

(7) References in sections 12 and 13 of the Act of 1978 to section 11 of that Act shall be construed as references to this section and the expression 'monopoly' shall be construed as a reference to an abuse of a dominant position.

(8) Compliance with an order under this section shall be a good defence to an action under section 6 in respect of any period after such compliance, in so far as such action is in respect of any matter which is the subject of such compliance.

(9) A right of action for relief under section 6 includes a right of action for contravention of an order under this section.

(10) The Minister shall publish a report under subsection (2), with due regard to commercial confidentiality, within two months of its being furnished to him by the Authority.

(11) Sections 10 and 11 of the Act of 1978 are hereby repealed.

15. Definitions in Act of 1978

(1) 'Service' in section 1(1) of the Act of 1978 shall not include the owning and transfer of land where this activity is the sole activity of the enterprise in which control is being sought.

(2) Section 1(3) of the Act of 1978 is hereby amended by the substitution for paragraph (c) of the following:

'(c) Without prejudice to paragraph (b), where an enterprise (in this paragraph referred to as 'the first enterprise'), whether by means of acquisition or otherwise, obtains the right in another enterprise (in this paragraph referred to as 'the second enterprise') which is a body corporate –

(i) to appoint or remove a majority of the board or committee of management of the second enterprise, or

(ii) to shares of the second enterprise which carry voting rights, except where the voting rights in the second enterprise which are controlled by the first enterprise –

(I) are not after the acquisition more than 25 per cent of the total of such voting rights, or

(II) are before the acquisition more than one half of the total of such voting rights,

the said enterprises shall be deemed to have been brought under common control.'

(3) Section 1(3)(e) of the Act of 1978 is hereby amended by the insertion after 'acquisition' at the end of the paragraph of 'and the value of those assets or the value of the turnover generated therefrom, exceeds the thresholds referred to in section 2(1)(a).'

16. Notification of proposed merger or take-over

The Act of 1978 is hereby amended by the substitution, for section 5, of the following section:

'5. (1) Each of the enterprises involved in a proposed merger or take-over shall notify the Minister in writing of the proposal, and provide full details thereof within the specified period of the offer capable of acceptance having been made, the effect of which would bring the enterprises under common control.

(2) Where, having received a notification under this section from each of the enterprises involved, the Minister is of opinion that in order to consider for the purposes of this Act a proposed merger or take-over he requires further information he may, within one month of the date of receipt by him of the notification, or of the last of such notifications, as the case may be, request such further information in writing from any one or more of the enterprises concerned, each of which shall provide the information within a period to be stated to them by the Minister in writing.

(3) (a) Where there is a contravention of subsection (1) or (2) the person in control of an enterprise failing to notify the Minister within the specified period or failing to supply the information requested within the period stated by the Minister shall be guilty of an offence and shall be liable –

(i) on summary conviction, to a fine not exceeding £1,000 and, for continued contravention, to a daily default fine not exceeding £100, or

(ii) on conviction on indictment, to a fine not exceeding £200,000 and, for continued contravention to a daily default fine not exceeding £20,000.

(*b*) Where a person is liable to a daily default fine he shall be guilty of contravening the provision on every day on which the contravention continues after the specified period has elapsed.

(*c*) For the purposes of this subsection the person in control of an enterprise is –

(i) in the case of a body corporate, any officer of the body corporate who knowingly and wilfully authorises or permits the contravention,

(ii) in the case of a partnership, each partner who knowingly and wilfully authorises or permits the contravention,

(iii) in the case of any other form of enterprise, any individual in control of that enterprise who knowingly and wilfully authorises or permits the contravention.

(4) For the purposes of this section the specified period shall be one month, or such other period as the Minister may specify.

(5) A notification for the purposes of subsection (1) shall not be valid where any information provided or statement made under subsection (1) or (2) is false or misleading.'.

17. Amendment of sections 6, 7 and 8 of the Act of 1978

(1) Section 6 of the Act of 1978 is hereby amended by the insertion after 'section 3' of 'or section 7'.

(2) The Act of 1978 is hereby amended by the substitution of the following for section 7:

'7. Upon receipt of a notification under section 5 the Minister shall –

(*a*) as soon as practicable inform the enterprises which made the notification and any other enterprise involved which enquires of him that he has decided not to make an order under section 9 in relation to the proposed merger or take-over, or

(*b*) within 30 days of the commencement of the relevant period refer the notification to the Authority for investigation.'

(3) Section 8(1) of the Act of 1978 is hereby amended by the insertion after the word 'date' of 'not being less than 30 days after the reference'.

(4) Section 8 of the Act of 1978 is hereby amended by the substitution for subsection (2) of the following:

'(2) (a) A report of the Authority under subsection (1) shall state its opinion as to whether or not the proposed merger or take-over concerned would be likely to prevent or restrict competition or restrain trade in any goods or services and would be likely to operate against the common good.

(b) The Authority shall give its views on the likely effect of the proposed merger or take-over on the common good in respect of:

(i) continuity of supplies or services,

(ii) level of employment,

(iii) regional development,

(iv) rationalisation of operations in the interests of greater efficiency,

(v) research and development,

(vi) increased production,

(vii) access to markets,

(viii) shareholders and partners,

(ix) employees,

(x) consumers.'

(5) The Minister shall publish any such report, with due regard to commercial confidentiality, within two months of its being furnished to him by the Authority.

(6) The Schedule to the Act of 1978 is hereby repealed.

18. Amendment of section 9 of the Act of 1978

Section 9(1)(a) of the Act of 1978 is hereby amended by the insertion after 'so warrant', of the following, 'which shall include, but is not confined to, the criteria in section 8'.

19. Control of concentrations

(1) The transmission to the Minister by the Commission of the European Communities of a copy of a notification made under Council Regulation

(EEC) No 4064/89 on the control of concentrations between undertakings shall constitute a notification under section 5 of the Act of 1978 (as inserted by section16 of this Act).

(2) The relevant period in respect of such a notification shall not commence until the Commission of the European Communities makes a decision under either Article 9 or 21(3) of that Regulation.

Part V

General

20. Authorised officers

The Minister and the Authority with the consent of the Minister may appoint persons to be authorised officers for the purposes of this Act.

21. Powers of authorised officers

(1) For the purpose of obtaining any information necessary for the exercise by the Authority or the Minister of any of their functions under this Act, an authorised officer may, on production of a warrant issued by a Justice of the District Court expressly authorising him to do so –

(a) enter and inspect premises at or vehicles in or by means of which any activity in connection with the business of supplying or distributing goods or providing a service, or in connection with the organisation or assistance of persons engaged in any such business, is carried on,

(b) require the person who carries on such activity and any person employed in connection therewith to produce to the authorised officer any books, documents or records relating to such activity which are in that person's power or control, and to give to the authorised officer such information as he may reasonably require in regard to any entries in such books, documents and records,

(c) inspect and copy or take extracts from any such books, documents and records,

(d) require a person mentioned in paragraph (b) to give to the authorised officer any information he may require in regard to the persons carrying on such activity (including in particular, in the case of an unincorporated body of persons, information in regard to the membership thereof and its committee of management or other controlling authority) or employed in connection therewith,

(e) require a person mentioned in paragraph (b) to give to the authorised officer any information which the officer may reasonably require in regard to such activity.

(2) A Justice of the District Court may issue a warrant under subsection (1), if satisfied by information on oath that it is proper for him to do so for the purposes of that subsection.

(3) A person who obstructs or impedes an authorised officer in the exercise of a power conferred by this section or does not comply with a requirement under this section shall be guilty of an offence and shall be liable on summary conviction to a fine not exceeding £1,000 or imprisonment for a period not exceeding twelve months or, at the discretion of the Court, to both such fine and imprisonment.

22. Repeals

The provisions of the Act of 1972 and every order made under that Act and sections 5 and 6 and sections 8 to 23 of the Act of 1987 are hereby repealed.

23. Regulations

(1) The Minister may by regulations provide for any matter referred to in this Act as prescribed or to be prescribed.

(2) Every regulation made by the Minister under this section shall be laid before each House of the Oireachtas as soon as may be after it is made and, if a resolution annulling the regulation is passed by either House within the next 21 days on which that House has sat after the regulation is laid before it, the regulation shall be annulled accordingly, but without prejudice to the validity of anything previously done thereunder.

24. Expenses

Any expenses incurred by the Minister in the administration of this Act shall, to such extent as may be sanctioned by the Minister for Finance, be paid out of moneys provided by the Oireachtas

Schedule

Competition Authority

1. (1) The permanent members of the Authority shall consist of a chairman and not less than two and not more than four other members each of whom shall be appointed by the Minister.

(2) Whenever it appears to the Minister that a permanent member is temporarily unable to discharge his duties, the Minister may appoint a temporary member to act in his place during such inability or for such shorter period as the Minister thinks proper.

(3) The Minister may also appoint additional temporary members for such period and on such terms and conditions as he may specify in the appointment.

2. (1) The term of office of a permanent member shall be fixed by the Minister when appointing him and shall not exceed five years.

(2) An outgoing permanent member shall be eligible for reappointment.

(3) Each member shall hold office on such conditions as may be fixed by the Minister after consultation with the Minister for Finance.

(4) A member may be paid such remuneration as the Minister with the consent of the Minister for Finance determines.

(5) The Civil Service Commissioners Act, 1956 and the Civil Service Regulation Acts, 1956 and 1958, shall not apply to the office of member.

3. If a member is personally interested in a particular matter with which the Authority is dealing, he shall inform the Minister accordingly and shall not act as a member during the consideration of the matter, unless the Minister, being of opinion that the member's interest is not such as to interfere with the impartial performance of his duties, authorises him to act.

4. (1) The Minister may remove from office a member who has become incapable through ill-health of performing efficiently his duties as such member or whose removal appears to the Minister to be necessary in the interests of the effective and economical performance of the functions of the Authority.

(2) Where the Minister removes a member from office he shall lay before each House of the Oireachtas a statement in writing of the reasons for such removal.

(3) A member may resign his office.

(4) Where a member of the Authority is –

(a) nominated as a member of Seanad Éireann, or

(b) elected as member of either House of the Oireachtas or of the European Parliament, or

(c) regarded pursuant to section 15 (inserted by the European Assembly Elections Act, 1984) of the European Assembly Elections Act, 1977, as having been elected to the European Parliament to fill a vacancy,

he shall thereupon cease to be a member of the Authority.

(5) A person who is, for the time being, entitled under the Standing Orders of either House of the Oireachtas to sit therein or who is a member of the European Parliament shall be disqualified from being a member of the Authority.

(6) A member shall be disqualified from holding and shall cease to hold office if he is adjudged bankrupt or makes a composition or arrangement with his creditors, or is sentenced by a court of competent jurisdiction to suffer imprisonment or penal servitude or ceases to be ordinarily resident in the State.

5. (1) The Minister shall, with the consent of the Minister for Finance, as soon as may be make and carry out a scheme for the granting of pensions, gratuities or other allowances to or in respect of members of the Authority ceasing to hold office other than members in respect of whom an award under the Superannuation Acts, 1934 to 1963, may be made.

(2) A scheme under this paragraph may provide that the termination of the appointment of a member of the Authority during the member's term of office shall not preclude the award to him of a pension, gratuity or other allowance.

(3) The Minister may, with the consent of the Minister for Finance, amend a scheme made by him under this paragraph.

6. (1) The quorum for a meeting of the Authority shall be –

(a) three permanent members unless the Minister otherwise authorises,

(b) three permanent members for decisions on requests for a licence or certificate under section 4.

(2) The Authority may act notwithstanding vacancies in its membership.

(3) Subject to this Act, the Authority may regulate its own procedure.

(4) The Authority may, with the consent of the Minister, appoint officers of the Minister to be authorised officers for the purposes of this Act.

7. (1) The Authority may, for the purposes of its functions under this Act and the Act of 1978, do all or any of the following things –

(a) summon witnesses to attend before it,

(b) examine on oath (which any member is hereby authorised to administer) the witnesses attending before it,

(c) require any such witness to produce to the Authority any document in his power or control,

(d) perform such of its functions as it deems proper through or by any officer of the Minister duty authorised by it in that behalf.

(2) A witness before the Authority shall be entitled to the same immunities and privileges as if he were a witness before the High Court.

(3) A summons shall be signed by at least one member.

(4) Any person who –

(a) on being duly summoned as a witness before the Authority makes default in attending, or

(b) being in attendance as a witness refuses to take an oath legally required by the Authority to be taken, or to produce any document in his power or control legally required by the Authority to be produced by him, or to answer any question to which the Authority may legally require an answer, or

(c) does any other thing which would, if the Authority were a court, having power to commit for contempt of court, be contempt of such court,

shall be guilty of an offence and shall be liable on summary conviction to a fine not exceeding £1,000 or imprisonment for a period not exceeding six months or, at the discretion of the court, to both such fine and imprisonment.

8. Any person may make a submission to the Authority in the manner prescribed by its rules in relation to the subject matter of any investigation.

9. (1) No person shall disclose information available to him by virtue of the powers of obtaining information conferred by this Act or by any other enactment conferring functions on the Authority or through being present at a meeting of the Authority held in private.

(2) Subparagraph (1) shall not apply to –

(i) a communication made by a member of the Authority in the execution of his functions under this Act, or

(ii) the disclosure of information in a report of the Authority or for the purpose of legal proceedings under this Act or pursuant to an order of a court of competent jurisdiction for the purposes of any proceedings in that court.

(3) If any person contravenes this paragraph he shall be guilty of an offence and shall be liable on summary conviction to a fine not exceeding £1,000 or imprisonment for a period not exceeding six months or, at the discretion of the court, to both such fine and imprisonment.

10. (1) The Minister, with the consent of the Minister for Finance, may appoint such officers and servants as he thinks necessary to assist the Authority in the performance of its functions.

(2) The officers and servants so appointed shall hold office on such terms and receive such remuneration as the Minister for Finance determines.

11. The Authority shall be entitled, in any proceedings, to the same privilege in respect of a communication to or by the Authority, any member of the Authority or any of its officers or servants as any Minister of the Government.

MERGERS, TAKE-OVERS AND MONOPOLIES (CONTROL) ACT, 1978

An Act to provide for the control by the Minister for Industry, Commerce and Energy in the interests of the common good of certain take-overs, mergers and monopolies, to extend the Restrictive Practices Act, 1972, and to provide for other matters connected with the aforesaid matters.

[3rd July, 1978]

Be it enacted by the Oireachtas as follows:

1. Interpretation

(1) In this Act–

'the Act of 1972' means the Restrictive Practices Act, 1972;

'the Commission' means the Restrictive Practices Commission;

'conditional order' means an order under section 9 prohibiting a proposed merger or take-over except on conditions specified in the order;

'enterprise' means –

(i) a person or partnership engaged for profit in the supply or distribution of goods or the provision of services, including –

   (a) a society, including a credit union, registered under the Industrial and Provident Societies Acts, 1893 to 1971,

   (b) a society registered under the Friendly Societies Acts, 1896 to 1977, and

   (c) a society established under the Building Societies Act, 1976; or

(ii) a holding company within the meaning of section 155 of the Companies Act, 1963;

'the Examiner' means the Examiner of Restrictive Practices;

'the Minister' means the Minister for Industry, Commerce and Energy;

'monopoly' means an enterprise or two or more enterprises under common control, which supply or provide, or to which is supplied or provided, not less than one-half of goods or services of a particular kind supplied or provided in the State in a particular year, according to the most recent information available on an annual basis, but does not include any enterprise at least 90 per cent. of whose output is exported from the State or any enterprise at least 90 per cent. of whose output comprises components for products which are exported from the State:

'the scheduled criteria' means the matters specified in the Schedule to this Act;

'service' includes any professional service, but does not include –

(i) any service provided by the holder of a licence under section 9 of the Central Bank Act, 1971,

(ii) any service provided by a trustee savings bank certified under the Trustee Savings Banks Acts, 1863 to 1965,

(iii) any service provided under a contract of employment,

(iv) the supplying of electricity,

(v) any transport service provided or operated by Córas Iompair Éireann,

(vi) any air service or service ancillary thereto,

(vii) any transport service provided by the holder of a licence under the Road Transport Act, 1932, or the Road Transport Act, 1933,

(viii) any service provided by a harbour authority within the meaning of the Harbours Act, 1946, or by a pilotage authority constituted under the Pilotage Act, 1913, or

(ix) any service provided by a local authority within the meaning of section 2 of the Local Government Act, 1941.

(2) For the purposes of this Act, a merger or take-over shall be deemed to be proposed when an offer capable of acceptance is made.

(3) (a) For the purposes of this Act, but subject to section 3, a merger or take-over shall be taken to exist when two or more enterprises, at least one of which carries on business in the State, come under common control.

(b) Enterprises shall be deemed to be under common control if the decision as to how or by whom each shall be managed can be made either by the same person, or by the same group of persons acting in concert.

(c) Without prejudice to paragraph (b), the acquisition by an enterprise (in this paragraph referred to as 'the first enterprise') in another (in this paragraph referred to as 'the second enterprise') which is a body corporate –

(i) of the right to appoint or remove a majority of the board or committee of management of the second enterprise, or

(ii) of shares of the second enterprise which carry voting rights, except where the voting rights in the second enterprise which are controlled by the first enterprise –

(A) are not after the acquisition more than 30 per cent. of the total of such voting rights,

or

(B) are before the acquisition more than one-half of the total of such voting rights,

shall be deemed to bring those enterprises under common control.

(d) For the purposes of paragraph (c) –

(i) 'voting rights' do not include voting rights which arise only in specified circumstances; and

(ii) voting rights shall be deemed to be controlled by an enterprise when it can determine how the votes concerned shall be cast.

(e) Subject to section 3, where the assets, including goodwill, (or a substantial part of the assets) of an enterprise are acquired by another enterprise, the acquisition shall be deemed to constitute a merger or take-over for the purposes of this Act if upon the acquisition a result of the acquisition is to place the second-mentioned enterprise in a position to replace (or substantially to replace) the first-mentioned enterprise in the business in which that enterprise was engaged immediately before the acquisition.

(f) This subsection does not apply to a case where enterprises come under common control (or are deemed to come under common control) either because the person referred to in paragraph (b) is a receiver or liquidator acting as such or because the person making an acquisition referred to in paragraph (c) is an underwriter or jobber acting as such, or because the person making an acquisition referred to in paragraph (e) is a receiver or liquidator acting as such.

(g) This subsection does not apply to two or more bodies corporate, each of which is a wholly-owned subsidiary of the same body corporate.

(4) In this Act a reference to a section is to a section of this Act unless it is indicated that reference to some other enactment is intended.

(5) In this Act a reference to a subsection, paragraph, subparagraph or clause is to the subsection, paragraph, subparagraph or clause of the provision in which the reference occurs, unless it is indicated that reference to some other provision is intended.

2. Application of

(1) (a) This Act shall apply to a proposed merger or take-over if in the most recent financial year the value of the gross assets of each of two or more of the enterprises to be involved in the proposal is not less then £1,250,000 or the turnover of each of those two or more enterprises is not less than £2,500,000.

(b) For the purposes of this subsection, 'turnover' does not include any payment in respect of value-added tax on sales or in respect of duty of excise.

(2) This Act shall apply to a monopoly where in the most recent financial

year the monopoly's sales or purchases of the goods or services concerned exceed £1,500,000.

(3) This Act shall not apply to enterprises coming under common control where this occurs solely as a result of a testamentary disposition or an intestacy.

(4) The Minister may from time to time by order amend subsection (1) or subsection (2) by the substitution for an amount mentioned in that subsection of another amount, not being in any case a smaller amount than the amount for which it is substituted.

(5) (a) Where he is of opinion that the exigencies of the common good so warrant, the Minister may by order declare that, notwithstanding subsection (1), this Act shall apply to a proposed merger or take-over of a particular class specified in the order and, upon the making of such an order, this Act shall apply to a proposed merger or take-over of that class.

    (b) The Minister may by order amend or revoke an order under this subsection.

(6) Every order under this section shall have effect on and from the date on which it is made and shall be laid before each House of the Oireachtas as soon as may be after it is made and, if a resolution confirming the order is not passed by each such House within the next 21 days after each House has sat after the order is laid before it, the order shall lapse, but without prejudice to the validity of anything previously done thereunder.

3. Limitation on commencement of merger or take-over

(1) In relation to a proposed merger or take-over, title to any shares or assets concerned shall not pass until –

    (a) the Minister, in pursuance of section 7(a), has stated in writing that he has decided not to make an order under section 9 in relation to the proposed merger or take-over, or

    (b) the Minister has stated in writing that he has made a conditional order in relation to the proposed merger or take-over, or

    (c) the relevant period within the meaning of section 6 has elapsed without the Minister's having made an order under section 9 in relation to the proposed merger or take-over,

whichever first occurs.

(2) A statement under subsection (1)(a) shall cease to have effect at the end of the period of 12 months beginning on the date of the statement

if the enterprises the subject of the proposed merger or take-over referred to in the statement have not come under common control during that period.

4. Right of purported vendor of shares to damages

Where a purported sale of shares is rendered invalid under section 3, the purported vendor shall be entitled to recover from the purported purchaser any damages the purported vendor suffers by reason only of invalidity, unless the purported purchaser satisfies the court that before the purported sale he had notified the purported vendor of circumstances relating to the proposed sale which gave rise to the possibility of such an invalidity.

5. Notification of proposed mergers and take-overs to Minister

(1) Where a merger or take-over is proposed each of the enterprises involved and having knowledge of the existence of the proposal shall notify the Minister in writing of the proposal as soon as may be.

(2) Where, having received a notification under this section, the Minister is of opinion that in order to consider for the purposes of this Act a proposed merger or take-over he requires further information he may, within one month of the date of receipt by him of the notification, request such further information in writing from any one or more of the enterprises concerned.

(3) (a) Where there is a contravention of subsection (1) the person in control of an enterprise failing to notify the Minister shall be guilty of an offence and shall be liable on summary conviction to a fine not exceeding £500 or on conviction on indictment to a fine not exceeding £5,000.

   (b) For the purposes of this subsection the person in control of an enterprise shall be –

   (i) in the case of a body corporate, any officer of the body corporate who knowingly and wilfully authorises or permits the contravention,

   (ii) in the case of a partnership, each partner who knowingly and wilfully authorises or permits the contravention.

6. Relevant period for purpose of section 3

(1) For the purpose of section 3, the relevant period in relation to a particular merger or take-over shall be the period of three months

beginning on the date on which the Minister first receives a notification under section 5(1) or, where the Minister requests further information under section 5(2), the date of receipt by him of such information.

(2) Where a person involved in a proposed merger or take-over which is being investigated by the Examiner under section 8 applies, by virtue of that section, to the High Court for a declaration under section 15 of the Act of 1972, the period beginning on the date of the application and ending on the date of the decision of the High Court, or (where that decision is appealed) the date of the decision of the Supreme Court, on the application shall, notwithstanding any other provision of this section, not be reckoned in calculating the relevant period for the purposes of this section.

7. Reference to Examiner of proposed merger or take-over

Upon receipt of a notification under section 5 the Minister shall as soon as practicable either –

(a) inform the enterprises which made the notification and any other enterprise involved which enquires of him that he has decided not to make an order under section 9 in relation to the proposed merger or take-over, or

(b) refer the notification to the Examiner for investigation in relation to the scheduled criteria and inform those enterprises of such reference.

8. Report by Examiner to Minister

(1) As soon as practicable after a reference to him under section 7, the Examiner shall investigate the proposal so referred and shall, before such date, if any, as the Minister specifies, furnish the Minister with a report of his investigation.

(2) A report of the Examiner under subsection (1) shall state his opinion as to whether or not the proposed merger or take-over concerned would operate against the common good in respect of the scheduled criteria.

(3) Section 15 of the Act of 1972, which relates to inspection of premises and records, shall for the purposes of an investigation under this section apply to a person authorised in writing by the Examiner.

9. Order by Minister prohibiting proposed merger or take-over

(1) (a) The Minister, having considered a report of the Examiner under section 8(1), may, if he thinks that the exigencies of the common

good so warrant, after consultation with any other Minister of the Government appearing to him to be concerned, by order prohibit a proposed merger or take-over either absolutely or except on conditions specified in the order.

(b) The conditions referred to in paragraph (a) shall include a condition requiring the proposed merger or take-over to be effected within 12 months of the making of the order.

(2) An order under this section shall state the reasons for making the order and, in the case of a conditional order, may have retrospective effect.

(3) Before making an order under this section the Minister shall have regard to any relevant international obligations of the State.

(4) The Minister may by order revoke an order under this section and may, with the agreement of the enterprise or enterprises concerned, amend an order under this section.

(5) Every order under this section shall be laid before each House of the Oireachtas as soon as may be after it is made and, if a resolution annulling the order is passed by either such House within the next twenty-one days on which that House has sat after the order is laid before it, the order shall be annulled accordingly, but without prejudice to the validity of anything previously done thereunder.

10. Commission's enquiry and report on monopoly

(1) (a) Where the Minister is of opinion that an enquiry should be held into an apparent monopoly –

(i) he may request the Commission through the Examiner to hold such an enquiry, and

(ii) the Commission shall comply with the request.

(b) The following provisions shall apply in relation to a request under subsection (1)(a):

(i) where the Minister so directs, a request shall be transmitted forthwith by the Examiner to the Commission;

(ii) a request may be accompanied by such report, if any, as the Minister may provide, and the report shall be transmitted by the Examiner to the Commission with the request;

(iii) nothing in this subsection shall be construed as preventing the Examiner from making available to the Commission any relevant information in his possession.

(2) Where the Examiner states in a report under section 16(1) of the Act of 1972 that he is of opinion that a monopoly exists which should be the subject of an enquiry by the Commission, or where the Commission holds an enquiry pursuant to a request under subsection (1), a report of the Commission under section 5 of the Act of 1972 of an enquiry held under that section shall state whether in the opinion of the Commission –

(a) a monopoly exists,

(b) if it does, it prevents or restricts competition or endangers the continuity of supplies or services or restrains trade or the provision of any service, or is likely to do any of these things,

(c) any interference or likely interference with competition, the provision of services or the continuity of supplies or services or any restraint of trade or of the provision of a service such as are mentioned in paragraph (b) is or would be unfair or operates or would operate against the common good.

(3) Any enquiry held by the Commission by virtue of this section shall be deemed to be an enquiry under section 5 of the Act of 1972.

11. Order by Minister relating to monopoly

(1) The Minister, having considered a report of the Commission (being a report referred to in section 10), may, if he thinks that the exigencies of the common good so warrant, after consultation with any other Minister of the Government appearing to him to be concerned, by order either –

(a) prohibit the continuance of the monopoly except on conditions specified in the order, or

(b) require the division, in a manner and within a period specified in the order, of the monopoly by a sale of assets or as otherwise so specified.

(2) An order under this section shall state the reasons for making the order.

(3) Before making an order under this section the Minister shall have regard to any relevant international obligations of the State.

(4) The Minister may by order revoke an order under this section and may, with the agreement of the enterprise or enterprises concerned, amend an order under this section.

(5) An order under this section shall not have effect unless it is confirmed by Act of the Oireachtas but, upon being so confirmed, it shall have the force of law in accordance with its terms.

12. Appeal to High Court against orders of Minister

(1) Where the Minister makes an order under section 9(1) or 11(1), an appeal on a point of law may be made to the High Court against the order within one month of the coming into effect of the order by any enterprise referred to in the order.

(2) Where the High Court allows an appeal under this section, the Minister shall by order amend or revoke (as may be appropriate) the order the subject of the appeal as soon as practicable.

(3) Where pursuant to subsection (2) the Minister makes an order following an appeal, section 9(5) (in the case of an appeal against an order under section 9(1)) or section 11(5) (in the case of an appeal against an order under section 11(1)) shall not apply to the order under subsection (2).

(4) An appeal against a decision of the High Court under this section shall not lie to the Supreme Court.

13. Provisions relating to orders under section 9 or 11

(1) (a) It shall be lawful for a court of competent jurisdiction to grant an injunction on the motion of the Minister or of any other person to enforce compliance with the terms of an order under section 9 or 11 for the time being in force.

   (b) This subsection shall not affect any other right of the Minister or other person to bring proceedings (whether civil or criminal) for the enforcement of compliance with the terms of an order under section 9 or 11.

(2) A person who contravenes (whether by act or omission) a provision of an order under section 9 or 11 for the time being in force shall be guilty of an offence under this section and shall be liable –

   (a) on summary conviction, to a fine not exceeding £500 (together with, in the case of a continuing offence, a fine not exceeding £100 for every day on which the offence is continued) or, at the discretion of the court, to imprisonment for a term not exceeding six months, or to both such fine and such imprisonment, or

   (b) on conviction on indictment, to a fine not exceeding £5,000 (together with, in the case of a continuing offence, a fine not exceeding £500 for every day on which the offence is continued) or, at the discretion of the court, to imprisonment for a term not exceeding two years or to both such fine and such imprisonment.

(3) (a) Where a person is convicted of an offence under this section by

reason of his failure, neglect or refusal to comply with a provision in an order requiring him to perform a specified act within a specified period or before a specified date, and the act remains, after the date of conviction, unperformed by him, the person shall be guilty of an offence and shall be liable on summary conviction to a fine not exceeding £100, or on conviction on indictment to a fine not exceeding £500, for each day, after the date of the first-mentioned conviction, on which the act remains unperformed by him or, at the discretion of the court, to imprisonment for a term not exceeding six months.

(b) An offence under this section shall be a continuing offence and, accordingly, fresh proceedings in respect thereof may be taken from time to time.

(4) Every person who aids, abets or assists another person, or conspires with another person, to do anything (whether by way of act or of omission), the doing of which is an offence by virtue of subsection (2) or (3) shall himself be guilty of an offence under this section and shall be liable on conviction to the penalties specified in subsection (2) or (3).

(5) (a) Summary proceedings in relation to an offence under this section may be prosecuted by the Minister.

(b) Notwithstanding section 10(4) of the Petty Sessions (Ireland) Act, 1851, summary proceedings for an offence under this section may be instituted within twelve months from the latest day on which the offence was committed.

(6) Where an offence under this section which is committed by a body corporate or by a person purporting to act on behalf of a body corporate or an unincorporated body of persons is proved to have been so committed with the consent or connivance of, or to be attributable to any neglect on the part of, any person who is a director, manager, secretary, member of the committee of management or other controlling authority of any such body, or who is any other similar officer of any such body, that person shall also be guilty of the offence and shall be liable to be proceeded against and punished accordingly.

14. Application of certain statutory provisions relating to amalgamation

(1) Nothing in the Companies Acts, 1963 to 1977, the Industrial and Provident Societies Acts, 1893 to 1971, the Building Societies Act, 1976, or the Friendly Societies Acts, 1896 to 1977, shall be construed as relieving an enterprise of the obligation to comply with section 5.

(2) An order under section 201 or 203 of the Companies Act, 1963, shall

not be made in respect of a proposed amalgamation (being a proposed merger or take-over to which this Act applies) until either –

(a) the Minister has stated in writing that he has decided not to make an order under section 9 in relation to the proposed amalgamation, or

(b) the Minister has stated in writing that he has made a conditional order in relation to the proposed amalgamation, or

(c) the relevant period within the meaning of section 6 has elapsed without the Minister's having made an order under section 9 in relation to the proposed amalgamation,

whichever first occurs.

(3) (a) a copy of a special resolution under section 53 of the Act of 1893, providing for the amalgamation of, or the transfer of engagements between, two or more societies registered under that Act (being a proposed merger or take-over to which this Act applies) shall not be registered under section 56 of the Act of 1893 until either –

(i) the Minister has stated in writing that he has decided not to make an order under section 9 in relation to the proposed amalgamation or transfer of engagements, or

(ii) the Minister has stated in writing that he has made a conditional order in relation to the proposed amalgamation or transfer of engagements, or

(iii) the relevant period within the meaning of section 6 has elapsed without the Minister's having made an order under section 9 in relation to the proposed amalgamation or transfer of engagements,

whichever first occurs.

(b) In this subsection 'the Act of 1893' means the Industrial and Provident Societies Act, 1893.

(4) (a) A copy of a special resolution under section 70 of the Act of 1896, providing for the amalgamation of, or the transfer of engagements between, two or more societies registered under that Act (being a proposed merger or take-over to which this Act applies) shall not be registered under section 75 of the Act of 1896 until either –

(i) the Minister has stated in writing that he has decided not to make an order under section 9 in relation to the proposed amalgamation or transfer of engagements, or

(ii) the Minister has stated in writing that he has made a conditional order in relation to the proposed amalgamation or transfer of engagements, or

(iii) the relevant period within the meaning of section 6 has elapsed without the Minister's having made an order under section 9 in relation to the proposed amalgamation or transfer of engagements,

whichever first occurs.

(b) In this subsection 'the Act of 1896' means the Friendly Societies Act, 1896.

(5) (a) A union of two or more societies which are registered under the Act of 1976, a transfer of engagements between two such societies or an undertaking by one such society to fulfill the engagements of another such society (being in each case a proposed merger or take-over to which this Act applies) shall not be registered under section 25(2), 26(2) or section 27(6) of the Act of 1976 until either –

(i) the Minister has stated in writing that he has decided not to make an order under section 9 in relation to the proposed union, transfer or undertaking, or

(ii) the Minister has stated in writing that he has made a conditional order in relation to the proposed union, transfer or undertaking, or

(iii) the relevant period within the meaning of section 6 has elapsed without the Minister having made an order under section 9 in relation to the proposed union, transfer or undertaking,

whichever first occurs.

(b) In this subsection 'the Act of 1976' means the Building Societies Act, 1976.

15. Annual report by Minister

(1) The Minister shall furnish to each House of the Oireachtas an annual report stating the number and the nature of investigations under section 8.

(2) It shall be lawful for the Minister to omit from an annual report under this section any information the publication of which would in his

opinion materially injure the legitimate interests of an enterprise, if the information is not essential to the full understanding of the investigation to which it relates, and a statement indicating the general character of information so omitted shall be included in the report.

16. Amendment of Second Schedule to Act of 1972

Paragraph 8 of the Second Schedule to the Act of 1972 is hereby amended by the insertion in subparagraph (1) after 'under section 14' and in subparagraph (2) after 'under this Act' of 'or under the Mergers, Take-overs and Monopolies (Control) Act, 1978', and that paragraph as so amended is set out in the Table to this section.

Table

8. (1) No person shall disclose information available to him through being present at an investigation held by the Examiner under section 14 or under the Mergers, Take-overs and Monopolies (Control) Act, 1978.

   (2) Subparagraph (1) does not apply to a communication made by the Examiner or an authorised officer in the execution of his duties under this Act or under the Mergers, Take-overs and Monopolies (Control) Act, 1978, or to the disclosure of information in a report by the Examiner or for the purpose of legal proceedings under this Act or under the Mergers, Take-overs and Monopolies (Control) Act, 1978.

   (3) If any person contravenes this paragraph he shall be guilty of an offence and shall be liable on summary conviction to a fine not exceeding one hundred pounds or imprisonment for a period not exceeding six months or, at the discretion of the court, to both such fine and imprisonment.

17. Expenses

Any expenses incurred by the Minister in the administration of this Act shall, to such extent as may be sanctioned by the Minister for Finance, be paid out of moneys provided by the Oireachtas.

18. Short title

This Act may be cited as the Mergers, Take-overs and Monopolies (Control) Act, 1978.

Schedule

Criteria for purposes of sections 7(b) and 8(2)

(*a*) The extent to which the proposed merger or take-over would be likely to prevent or restrict competition or to restrain trade or the provision of any service.

(*b*) The extent to which the proposed merger or take-over would be likely to endanger the continuity of supplies or services.

(*c*) The extent to which the proposed merger or take-over would be likely to affect employment and would be compatible with national policy in relation to employment.

(*d*) The extent to which the proposed merger or take-over is in accordance with national policy for regional development.

(*e*) The extent to which the proposed merger or take-over is in harmony with the policy of the Government relating to the rationalisation, in the interests of greater efficiency, of operations in the industry or business concerned.

(*f*) Any benefits likely to be derived from the proposed take-over or merger and relating to research and development, technical efficiency, increased production, efficient distribution of products and access to markets.

(*g*) The interests of shareholders and partners in the enterprises involved.

(*h*) The interests of employees in the enterprises involved.

(*i*) The interests of the consumer.

Acts referred to

[List omitted]

EDITORIAL NOTE

Amendment to Section 2 (1): S.I. 239/1985; S.I. 135/1993 not included in this volume.

LABOUR LAW
(a) Health and Safety

COUNCIL DIRECTIVE

of 12 June 1989

on the introduction of measures to encourage improvements in the safety and health of workers at work

(89/391/EEC)

(OJ No L 183, 29.6.89, p.1)

The Council of the European Communities,

Having regard to the Treaty establishing the European Economic Community, and in particular Article 118a thereof,

Having regard to the proposal from the Commission[1], drawn up after consultation with the Advisory Committee on Safety, Hygiene and Health Protection at Work.

In cooperation with the European Parliament[2],

Having regard to the opinion of the Economic and Social Committee[3],

Whereas Article 118a of the Treaty provides that the Council shall adopt, by means of Directives, minimum requirements for encouraging improvements, especially in the working environment, to guarantee a better level of protection of the safety and health of workers;

Whereas this Directive does not justify any reduction in levels of protection already achieved in individual Member States, the Member State being committed, under the Treaty, to encouraging improvements in conditions in this area and to harmonising conditions while maintaining the improvements made;

Whereas it is known that workers can be exposed to the effects of dangerous environmental factors at the work place during the course of their working life;

Whereas, pursuant to Article 118a of the Treaty, such Directives must avoid imposing administrative, financial and legal constraints which would hold back the creation and development of small and medium-sized undertakings;

Whereas the communication from the Commission on its programme concerning safety, hygiene and health at work[4] provides for the adoption of Directives designed to guarantee the safety and health of workers;

Whereas the Council, in its resolution of 21 December 1987 on safety, hygiene and health at work[5], took note of the Commission's intention to submit to the Council in the near future a Directive on the organisation of the safety and health of workers at the work place;

Whereas in February 1988 the European Parliament adopted four resolutions following the debate on the internal market and worker protection; whereas these resolutions specifically invited the Commission to draw up a framework Directive to serve as a basis for more specific Directives covering all the risks connected with safety and health at the work place;

Whereas Member States have a responsibility to encourage improvements in the safety and health of workers on their territory; whereas taking measures to protect the health and safety of workers at work also helps; in certain cases, to preserve the health and possibly the safety of persons residing with them;

Whereas Member States' legislative systems covering safety and health at the work place differ widely and need to be improved; whereas national provisions on the subject, which often include technical specifications and/or self-regulatory standards, may result in different levels of safety and health protection and allow competition at the expense of safety and health;

Whereas the incidence of accidents at work and occupational diseases is still too high; whereas preventive measures must be introduced or improved without delay in order to safeguard the safety and health of workers and ensure a higher degree of protection;

Whereas, in order to ensure an improved degree of protection, workers and/or their representatives must be informed of the risks to their safety and health and of the measures required to reduce or eliminate these risks; whereas they must also be in a position to contribute, by means of balanced participation in accordance with national laws and/or practices, to seeing that the necessary protective measures are taken;

Whereas information, dialogue and balanced participation on safety and health at work must be developed between employers and workers and/or their representatives by means of appropriate procedures and instruments, in accordance with national laws and/or practices;

Whereas the improvements of workers' safety, hygiene and health at work is an objective which should not be subordinated to purely economic considerations;

Whereas employers shall be obliged to keep themselves informed of the latest advances in technology and scientific findings concerning work-place design, account being taken of the inherent dangers in their undertaking, and to inform accordingly the workers' representatives exercising participation rights under this Directive, so as to be able to guarantee a better level of protection of workers' health and safety;

Whereas the provisions of this Directive apply, without prejudice to more stringent present or future Community provisions, to all risks, and in particular to those arising from the use at work of chemical, physical and biological agents covered by Directive 80/1107/EEC[6], as last amended by Directive 88/642/EEC[7];

Whereas, pursuant to Decision 74/325/EEC[8], the Advisory Committee on Safety, Hygiene and Health Protection at Work is consulted by the Commission on the drafting of proposals in this field;

Whereas a Committee composed of members nominated by the Member States needs to be set up to assist the Commission in making the technical adaptations to the individual Directives provided for in this Directive.

Has adopted this Directive:

Section I

General provisions

Article 1

Object

1. The object of this Directive is to introduce measures to encourage improvements in the safety and health of workers at work.

2. To that end it contains general principles concerning the prevention of occupational risks, the protection of safety and health, the elimination of risk and accident factors, the informing, consultation, balanced participation in accordance with national laws and/or practices and training of workers and their representatives, as well as general guidelines for the implementation of the said principles.

3. This Directive shall be without prejudice to existing or future national and Community provisions which are more favourable to protection of the safety and health of workers at work.

Article 2

Scope

1. This Directive shall apply to all sectors of activity, both public and private (industrial, agricultural, commercial, administrative, service, educational, cultural, leisure, etc.).

2. This Directive shall not be applicable where characteristics peculiar to certain specific public service activities, such as the armed forces or the police, or to certain specific activities in the civil protection services inevitably conflict with it.

In that event, the safety and health of workers must be ensured as far as possible in the light of the objectives of this Directive.

Article 3

Definitions

For the purposes of this Directive, the following terms shall have the following meanings:

(a) worker: any person employed by an employer, including trainees and apprentices but excluding domestic servants;

(b) employer: any natural or legal person who has an employment relationship with the worker and has responsibility for the undertaking and/or establishment;

(c) workers' representative with specific responsibility for the safety and health of workers: any person elected, chosen or designated in accordance with national laws and/or practices to represent workers where problems arise relating to the safety and health protection of workers at work;

(d) prevention: all the steps or measures taken or planned at all stages of work in the undertaking to prevent or reduce occupational risks.

Article 4

1. Member States shall take the necessary steps to ensure that employers, workers and workers' representatives are subject to the legal provisions necessary for the implementation of this Directive.

2. In particular, Member States shall ensure adequate controls and supervision.

Section II

Employers' obligations

Article 5

General provision

1. The employer shall have a duty to ensure the safety and health of workers in every aspect related to the work.

2. Where, pursuant to Article 7(3), an employer enlists competent external services or persons, this shall not discharge him from his responsibilities in this area.

3. The workers' obligations in the field of safety and health at work shall not affect the principle of the responsibility of the employer.

4. This Directive shall not restrict the option of Member States to provide for the exclusion or the limitation of employers' responsibility where occurrences are due to unusual and unforeseeable circumstances, beyond the employers' control, or to exceptional events, the consequences of which could not have been avoided despite the exercise of all due care.

Member States need not exercise the option referred to in the first subparagraph.

Article 6

General obligations on employers

1. Within the context of his responsibilities, the employer shall take the measures necessary for the safety and health protection of workers, including prevention of occupational risks and provision of information and training, as well as provision of the necessary organisation and means.

The employer shall be alert to the need to adjust these measures to take account of changing circumstances and aim to improve existing situations.

2. The employer shall implement the measures referred to in the first subparagraph of paragraph 1 on the basis of the following general principles of prevention:

(*a*) avoiding risks;

(*b*) evaluating the risks which cannot be avoided;

(c) combating the risks at source;

(d) adapting the work to the individual, especially as regards the design of work places, the choice of work equipment and the choice of working and production methods, with a view, in particular, to alleviating monotonous work and work at a predetermined work-rate and to reducing their effect on health;

(e) adapting to technical progress;

(f) replacing the dangerous by the non-dangerous or the less dangerous;

(g) developing a coherent overall prevention policy which covers technology, organisation of work, working conditions, social relationships and the influence of factors related to the working environment;

(h) giving collective protective measures priority over individual protective measures;

(i) giving appropriate instructions to the workers.

3. Without prejudice to the other provisions of this Directive, the employer shall, taking into account the nature of the activities of the enterprise and/or establishment:

(a) evaluate the risks to the safety and health of workers, *inter alia* in the choice of work equipment, the chemical substances or preparations used, and the fitting-out of work places.

Subsequent to this evaluation and as necessary, the preventive measures and the working and production methods implemented by the employer must:

— assure an improvement in the level of protection afforded to workers with regard to safety and health,

— be integrated into all the activities of the undertaking and/or establishment and at all hierarchical levels;

(b) where he entrusts tasks to a worker, take into consideration the worker's capabilities as regards health and safety;

(c) ensure that the planning and introduction of new technologies are the subject of consultation with the workers and/or their represent-atives, as regards the consequences of the choice of equipment, the working conditions and the working environment for the safety and health of workers;

(d) take appropriate steps to ensure that only workers who have received adequate instructions may have access to areas where there is serious and specific danger.

4. Without prejudice to the other provisions of this Directive, where several undertakings share a work place, the employers shall cooperate in implementing the safety, health and occupational hygiene provisions and, taking into account the nature of the activities, shall coordinate their actions in matters of the protection and prevention of occupational risks, and shall inform one another and their respective workers and/or workers' representatives of these risks.

5. Measures related to safety, hygiene and health at work may in no circumstances involve the workers in financial cost.

Article 7

Protective and preventive services

1. Without prejudice to the obligations referred to in Articles 5 and 6, the employer shall designate one or more workers to carry out activities related to the protection and prevention of occupational risks for the undertaking and/or establishment.

2. Designated workers may not be placed at any disadvantage because of their activities related to the protection and prevention of occupational risks.

Designated workers shall be allowed adequate time to enable them to fulfil their obligations arising from this Directive.

3. If such protective and preventive measures cannot be organised for lack of competent personnel in the undertaking and/or establishment, the employer shall enlist competent external services or persons.

4. Where the employer enlists such services or persons, he shall inform them of the factors known to affect, or suspected of affecting, the safety and health of the workers and they must have access to the information referred to in Article 10(2).

5. In all cases:

- the workers designated must have the necessary capabilities and the necessary means,
- the external services or persons consulted must have the necessary aptitudes and the necessary personal and professional means, and
- the workers designated and the external services or persons consulted must be sufficient in number

to deal with the organisation of protective and preventive measures, taking into account the size of the undertaking and/or establishment and/or the hazards to which the workers are exposed and their distribution throughout the entire undertaking and/or establishment.

6. The protection from, and prevention of, the health and safety risks which form the subject of this Article shall be the responsibility of one or more workers, of one service or of separate services whether from inside or outside the undertaking and/or establishment.

The worker(s) and/or agency(ies) must work together whenever necessary.

7. Member States may define, in the light of the nature of the activities and size of the undertakings, the categories of undertakings in which the employer, provided he is competent, may himself take responsibility for the measures referred to in paragraph 1.

8. Member States shall define the necessary capabilities and aptitudes referred to in paragraph 5.

They may determine the sufficient number referred to in paragraph 5.

Article 8

First aid, fire-fighting and evacuation of workers, serious and imminent danger

1. The employer shall:

- take the necessary measures for first aid, fire-fighting and evacuation of workers, adapted to the nature of the activities and the size of the undertaking and/or establishment and taking into account other persons present,

- arrange any necessary contacts with external services, particularly as regards first aid, emergency medical care, rescue work and fire-fighting.

2. Pursuant to paragraph 1, the employer shall, *inter alia*, for first aid, fire-fighting and the evacuation of workers, designate the workers required to implement such measures.

The number of such workers, their training and the equipment available to them shall be adequate, taking account of the size and/or specific hazards of the undertaking and/or establishment.

3. The employer shall:

(*a*) as soon as possible, inform all workers who are, or may be, exposed to serious and imminent danger of the risk involved and of the steps taken or to be taken as regards protection;

(*b*) take action and give instructions to enable workers in the event of serious, imminent and unavoidable danger to stop work and/or immediately to leave the work place and proceed to a place of safety;

(c) save in exceptional cases for reasons duly substantiated, refrain from asking workers to resume work in a working situation where there is still a serious and imminent danger.

4. Workers who, in the event of serious, imminent and unavoidable danger, leave their workstation and/or a dangerous area may not be placed at any disadvantage because of their action and must be protected against any harmful and unjustified consequences, in accordance with national laws and/or practices.

5. The employer shall ensure that all workers are able, in the event of serious and imminent danger to their own safety and/or that of other persons, and where the immediate superior responsible cannot be contacted, to take the appropriate steps in the light of their knowledge and the technical means at their disposal, to avoid the consequences of such danger.

Their actions shall not place them at any disadvantage, unless they acted carelessly or there was negligence on their part.

Article 9

Various obligations on employers

1. The employer shall:

(a) be in possession of an assessment of the risks to safety and health at work, including those facing groups of workers exposed to particular risks;

(b) decide on the protective measures to be taken and, if necessary, the protective equipment to be used;

(c) keep a list of occupational accidents resulting in a worker being unfit for work for more than three working days;

(d) draw up, for the responsible authorities and in accordance with national laws and/or practices, reports on occupational accidents suffered by his workers.

2. Member States shall define, in the light of the nature of the activities and size of the undertakings, the obligations to be met by the different categories of undertakings in respect of the drawing-up of the documents provided for in paragraph 1(a) and (b) and when preparing the documents provided for in paragraph 1(c) and (d).

Article 10

Worker information

1. The employer shall take appropriate measures so that workers and/or their representatives in the undertaking and/or establishment receive, in accordance with national laws and/or practices which may take account, *inter alia*, of the size of the undertaking and/or establishment, all the necessary information concerning:

(a) the safety and health risks and protective and preventive measures and activities in respect of both the undertaking and/or establishment in general and each type of workstation and/or job;

(b) the measures taken pursuant to Article 8(2).

2. The employer shall take appropriate measures so that employers of workers from any outside undertakings and/or establishments engaged in work in his undertaking and/or establishment receive, in accordance with national laws and/or practices, adequate information concerning the points referred to in paragraph 1(a) and (b) which is to be provided to the workers in question.

3. The employer shall take appropriate measures so that workers with specific functions in protecting the safety and health of workers, or workers' representatives with specific responsibility for the safety and health of workers shall have access, to carry out their functions and in accordance with national laws and/or practices, to:

(a) the risk assessment and protective measures referred to in Article 9(1)(a) and (b);

(b) the list and reports referred to in Article 9(1)(c) and (d);

(c) the information yielded by protective and preventive measures, inspection agencies and bodies responsible for safety and health.

Article 11

Consultation and participation of workers

1. Employers shall consult workers and/or their representatives and allow them to take part in discussions on all questions relating to safety and health at work.

This presupposes:

– the consultation of workers,

– the right of workers and/or their representatives to make proposals,

– balanced participation in accordance with national laws and/or practices.

2. Workers or workers' representatives with specific responsibility for the safety and health of workers shall take part in a balanced way, in accordance with national laws and/or practices, or shall be consulted in advance and in good time by the employer with regard to:

(a) any measure which may substantially affect safety and health;

(b) the designation of workers referred to in Articles 7(1) and 8(2) and the activities referred to in Article 7(1);

(c) the information referred to in Articles 9(1) and 10;

(d) the enlistment, where appropriate, of the competent services or persons outside the undertaking and/or establishment, as referred to in Article 7(3);

(e) the planning and organisation of the training referred to in Article 12.

3. Workers' representatives with specific responsibility for the safety and health of workers shall have the right to ask the employer to take appropriate measures and to submit proposals to him to that end to mitigate hazards for workers and/or to remove sources of danger.

4. The workers referred to in paragraph 2 and the workers' representatives referred to in paragraphs 2 and 3 may not be placed at a disadvantage because of their respective activities referred to in paragraphs 2 and 3.

5. Employers must allow workers' representatives with specific responsibility for the safety and health of workers adequate time off work, without loss of pay, and provide them with the necessary means to enable such representatives to exercise their rights and functions deriving from this Directive.

6. Workers and/or their representatives are entitled to appeal, in accordance with national law and/or practice, to the authority responsible for safety and health protection at work if they consider that the measures taken and the means employed by the employer are inadequate for the purposes of ensuring safety and health at work.

Workers' representatives must be given the opportunity to submit their observations during inspection visits by the competent authority.

Article 12

Training of workers

1. The employer shall ensure that each worker receives adequate safety and health training, in particular in the form of information and instructions specific to his workstation or job:

- on recruitment,

- in the event of a transfer or a change of job,

- in the event of the introduction of new work equipment or a change in equipment,

- in the event of the introduction of any new technology.

The training shall be:

- adapted to take account of new or changed risks, and

- repeated periodically if necessary.

2. The employer shall ensure that workers from outside undertakings and/or establishments engaged in work in his undertaking and/or establishment have in fact received appropriate instructions regarding health and safety risks during their activities in his undertaking and/or establishment.

3. Workers' representatives with a specific role in protecting the safety and health of workers shall be entitled to appropriate training.

4. The training referred to in paragraphs 1 and 3 may not be at the workers' expense or at that of the workers' representatives.

The training referred to in paragraph 1 must take place during working hours.

The training referred to in paragraph 3 must take place during working hours or in accordance with national practice either within or outside the undertaking and/or the establishment.

Section III

Workers' obligations

Article 13

1. It shall be the responsibility of each worker to take care as far as possible of his own safety and health and that of other persons affected

by his acts or omissions at work in accordance with his training and the instructions given by his employer.

2. To this end, workers must in particular, in accordance with their training and the instructions given by their employer:

(*a*) make correct use of machinery, apparatus, tools, dangerous substances, transport equipment and other means of production;

(*b*) make correct use of the personal protective equipment supplied to them and, after use, return it to its proper place;

(*c*) refrain from disconnecting, changing or removing arbitrarily safety devices fitted, e.g. to machinery, apparatus, tools, plant and buildings, and use such safety devices correctly;

(*d*) immediately inform the employer and/or the workers with specific responsibility for the safety and health of workers of any work situation they have reasonable grounds for considering represents a serious and immediate danger to safety and health and of any shortcomings in the protection arrangements;

(*e*) cooperate, in accordance with national practice, with the employer and/or workers with specific responsibility for the safety and health of workers, for as long as may be necessary to enable any tasks or requirements imposed by the competent authority to protect the safety and health of workers at work to be carried out;

(*f*) cooperate, in accordance with national practice, with the employer and/or workers with specific responsibility for the safety and health of workers, for as long as may be necessary to enable the employer to ensure that the working environment and working conditions are safe and pose no risk to safety and health within their field of activity.

Section IV

Miscellaneous provisions

Article 14

Health surveillance

1. To ensure that workers receive health surveillance appropriate to the health and safety risks they incur at work, measures shall be introduced in accordance with national law and/or practices.

2. The measures referred to in paragraph 1 shall be such that each worker, if he so wishes, may receive health surveillance at regular intervals.

3. Health surveillance may be provided as part of a national health system.

Article 15

Risk groups

Particularly sensitive risk groups must be protected against the dangers which specifically affect them.

Article 16

Individual Directives – Amendments – General scope of this Directive

1. The Council, acting on a proposal from the Commission based on Article 118a of the Treaty, shall adopt individual Directives, *inter alia*, in the areas listed in the Annex.

2. This Directive and, without prejudice to the procedure referred to in Article 17 concerning technical adjustments, the individual Directives may be amended in accordance with the procedure provided for in Article 118a of the Treaty.

3. The provisions of this Directive shall apply in full to all the areas covered by the individual Directives, without prejudice to more stringent and/or specific provisions contained in these individual Directives.

Article 17

Committee

1. For the purely technical adjustments to the individual Directives provided for in Article 16(1) to take account of:

– the adoption of Directives in the field of technical harmonisation and standardisation, and/or

– technical progress, changes in international regulations or specifications, and new findings,

the Commission shall be assisted by a committee composed of the representatives of the Member States and chaired by the representatives of the Commons.

2. The representatives of the Commission shall submit to the committee a draft of the measures to be taken.

The committee shall deliver its opinion on the draft within a time limit which the chairman may lay down according to the urgency of the matter.

The opinion shall be delivered by the majority laid down in Article 148(2) of the Treaty in the case of decisions which the Council is required to adopt on a proposal from the Commission.

The votes of the representatives of the Member States within the committee shall be weighted in the manner set out in that Article. The chairman shall not vote.

3. The Commission shall adopt the measures envisaged if they are in accordance with the opinion of the committee.

If the measures envisaged are not in accordance with the opinion of the committee, or if no opinion is delivered, the Commission shall, without delay, submit to the Council a proposal relating to the measures to be taken. The Council shall act by a qualified majority.

If, on the expiry of three months from the date of the referral to the Council, the Council has not acted, the proposed measures shall be adopted by the Commission.

Article 18

Final provisions

1. Member States shall, bring into force the regulations and administrative provisions necessary to comply with this Directive by 31 December 1992.

They shall forthwith inform the Commission thereof.

2. Member States shall communicate to the Commission the texts of the provisions of national law which they have already adopted or adopt in the field covered by this Directive.

3. Member States shall report to the Commission every five years on the practical implementation of the provisions of this Directive, indicating the points of view of employers and workers.

The Commission shall inform the European Parliament, the Council, the Economic and Social Committee and the Advisory Committee on Safety, Hygiene and Health Protection at Work.

4. The Commission shall submit periodically to the European Parliament, the Council and the Economic and Social Committee a report on the implementation of this Directive, taking into account paragraphs 1 to 3.

Article 19

This Directive is addressed to the Member States.

Done at Luxembourg, 12 June 1989.

For the Council

The President

M. Chaves Gonzales

Annex

List of areas referred to in Article 16(1)

- Work places
- Work equipment
- Personal protective equipment
- Work with visual display units
- Handling of heavy loads involving risk of back injury
- Temporary or mobile work sites
- Fisheries and agriculture

FOOTNOTES

1. OJ No C 141, 30.5.88, p.1.
2. OJ No C 326, 19.12.88, p.102, and OJ No C 158, 26.6.89.
3. OJ No C 175, 4.7.88, p.22.
4. OJ No C 28, 3.2.88, p.3.
5. OJ No C 28, 3.2.88, p.1.
6. OJ No L 327, 3.12.80, p.8.
7. OJ No L 356, 24.12.88, p.74.
8. OJ No L 185, 9.7.74, p.15.

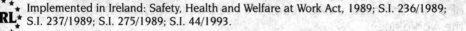

Implemented in Ireland: Safety, Health and Welfare at Work Act, 1989; S.I. 236/1989; S.I. 237/1989; S.I. 275/1989; S.I. 44/1993.

COUNCIL DIRECTIVE

of 30 November 1989

concerning the minimum safety and health requirements for the workplace (first individual directive within the meaning of Article 16(1) of Directive 89/391/EEC)

(89/654/EEC)

(OJ No L 393, 30.12.89, p.1)

The Council of the European Communities,

Having regard to the Treaty establishing the European Economic Community, and in particular Article 118a thereof,

Having regard to the proposal from the Commission[1], submitted after consulting the Advisory Committee on Safety, Hygiene and Health Protection at Work,

In cooperation with the European Parliament[2],

Having regard to the opinion of the Economic and Social Committee[3],

Whereas Article 118a of the Treaty provides that the Council shall adopt, by means of directives, minimum requirements for encouraging improvements, especially in the working environment, to ensure a better level of protection of the safety and health of workers;

Whereas, under the terms of that Article, those directives are to avoid imposing administrative, financial and legal constraints in a way which would hold back the creation and development of small and medium-sized undertakings;

Whereas the communication from the Commission on its programme concerning safety, hygiene and health at work[4] provides for the adoption of a directive designed to guarantee the safety and health of workers at the workplace;

Whereas, in its resolution of 21 December 1987 on safety, hygiene and health at work[5], the Council took note of the Commission's intention of submitting to the Council in the near future minimum requirements concerning the arrangement of the place of work;

Whereas compliance with the minimum requirements designed to guarantee a better standard of safety and health at work is essential to ensure the safety and health of workers;

Whereas this Directive is an individual directive within the meaning of Article 16(1) of Council Directive 89/391/EEC of 12 June 1989 on the introduction of measures to encourage improvements in the safety and health of workers at work[6]; whereas the provisions of the latter are therefore fully applicable to the workplace without prejudice to more stringent and/or specific provisions contained in the present Directive;

Whereas this Directive is a practical contribution towards creating the social dimension of the internal market;

Whereas, pursuant to Decision 74/325/EEC[7], as last amended by the 1985 Act of Accession, the Advisory Committee on Safety, Hygiene and Health Protection at Work is consulted by the Commission on the drafting of proposals in this field,

Has adopted this Directive:

Section 1

General provisions

Article 1

Subject

1. This Directive, which is the first individual directive within the meaning of Article 16(1) of Directive 89/391/EEC, lays down minimum requirements for safety and health at the workplace, as defined in Article 2.

2. This Directive shall not apply to:

(a) means of transport used outside the undertaking and/or the establishment, or workplaces inside means of transport;

(b) temporary or mobile work sites;

(c) extractive industries;

(d) fishing boats;

(e) fields, woods and other land forming part of an agricultural or forestry undertaking but situated away from the undertaking's buildings.

3. The provisions of Directive 89/391/EEC are fully applicable to the whole scope referred to in paragraph 1, without prejudice to more restrictive and/or specific provisions contained in this Directive.

Article 2

Definition

For the purposes of this Directive, 'workplace' means the place intended to house workstations on the premises of the undertaking and/or establishment and any other place within the area of the undertaking and/or establishment to which the worker has access in the course of his employment.

Section II

Employers' obligations

Article 3

Workplaces used for the first time

Workplaces used for the first time after 31 December 1992 must satisfy the minimum safety and health requirements laid down in Annex I.

Article 4

Workplaces already in use

Workplaces already in use before 1 January 1993 must satisfy the minimum safety and health requirements laid down in Annex II at the latest three years after that date.

However, as regards the Portuguese Republic, workplaces used before 1 January 1993 must satisfy, at the latest four years after that date, the minimum safety and health requirements appearing in Annex II.

Article 5

Modifications to workplaces

When workplaces undergo modifications, extensions and/or conversions after 31 December 1992, the employer shall take the measures necessary to ensure that those modifications, extensions and/or conversions are in compliance with the corresponding minimum requirements laid down in Annex I.

Article 6

General requirements

To safeguard the safety and health of workers, the employer shall see to it that:

– traffic routes to emergency exits and the exits themselves are kept clear at all times,

– technical maintenance of the workplace and of the equipment and devices, and in particular those referred to in Annexes I and II, is carried out and any faults found which are liable to affect the safety and health of workers are rectified as quickly as possible,

– the workplace and the equipment and devices, and in particular those referred to in Annex I, point 6, and Annex II, point 6, are regularly cleaned to an adequate level of hygiene,

– safety equipment and devices intended to prevent or eliminate hazards, and in particular those referred to in Annexes I and II, are regularly maintained and checked.

Article 7

Information of workers

Without prejudice to Article 10 of Directive 89/391/EEC, workers and/or their representatives shall be informed of all measures to be taken concerning safety and health at the workplace.

Article 8

Consultation of workers and workers' participation

Consultation and participation of workers and/or of their representatives shall take place in accordance with Article 11 of Directive 89/391/EEC on the matters covered by this Directive, including the Annexes thereto.

Section III

Miscellaneous provisions

Article 9

Amendments to the Annexes

Strictly technical amendments to the Annexes as a result of:

– the adoption of Directives on technical harmonisation and standardisation of the design, manufacture or construction of parts of workplaces, and/or

– technical progress, changes in international regulations or specifications and knowledge with regard to workplaces, shall be adopted in accordance with the procedure laid down in Article 17 of Directive 89/391/EEC.

Article 10

Final provisions

1. Member States shall bring into force the laws, regulations and administrative provisions necessary to comply with this Directive by 31 December 1992. They shall forthwith inform the Commission thereof.

However, the date applicable for the Hellenic Republic shall be 31 December 1994.

2. Member States shall communicate to the Commission the texts of the provisions of national law which they have already adopted or adopt in the field governed by this Directive.

3. Member States shall report to the Commission every five years on the practical implementation of the provisions of this Directive, indicating the points of view of employers and workers.

The Commission shall inform the European Parliament, the Council, the Economic and Social Committee and the Advisory Council on Safety, Hygiene and Health Protection at Work.

4. The Commission shall submit periodically to the European Parliament, the Council and the Economic and Social Committee a report on the implementation of this Directive, taking into account paragraphs 1 to 3.

Article 11

This Directive is addressed to the Member States.

Done at Brussels, 30 November 1989.

For the Council

The President

J.P. Soisson

Annex I

Minimum safety and health requirements for workplaces used for the first time, as referred to in Article 3 of the Directive

1. *Preliminary note*

The obligations laid down in this Annex apply whenever required by the features of the workplace, the activity, the circumstances or a hazard.

2. *Stability and solidity*

Buildings which house workplaces must have a structure and solidity appropriate to the nature of their use.

3. *Electrical installations*

Electrical installations must be designed and constructed so as not to present a fire or explosion hazard; persons must be adequately protected against the risk of accidents caused by direct or indirect contact.

The design, construction and choice of material and protection devices must be appropriate to the voltage, external conditions and the competence of persons with access to parts of the installation.

4. *Emergency routes and exits*

4.1. Emergency routes and exits must remain clear and lead as directly as possible to the open air or to a safe area.

4.2. In the event of danger, it must be possible for workers to evacuate all workstations quickly and as safely as possible.

4.3. The number, distribution and dimensions of the emergency routes and exits depend on the use, equipment and dimensions of the workplaces and the maximum number of persons that may be present.

4.4. Emergency doors must open outwards.

Sliding or revolving doors are not permitted if they are specifically intended as emergency exits.

Emergency doors should not be so locked or fastened that they cannot be easily and immediately opened by any person who may require to use them in an emergency.

4.5. Specific emergency routes and exits must be indicated by signs in accordance with the national regulations transposing Directive 77/576/EEC[8] into law.

Such signs must be placed at appropriate points and be made to last.

4.6. Emergency doors must not be locked.

The emergency routes and exits, and the traffic routes and doors giving access to them, must be free from obstruction so that they can be used at any time without hindrance.

4.7. Emergency routes and exits requiring illumination must be provided with emergency lighting of adequate intensity in case the lighting fails.

5. Fire detection and fire fighting

5.1. Depending on the dimensions and use of the buildings, the equipment they contain, the physical and chemical properties of the substances present and the maximum potential number of people present, workplaces must be equipped with appropriate fire-fighting equipment and, as necessary, with fire detectors and alarm systems.

5.2. Non-automatic fire-fighting equipment must be easily accessible and simple to use.

The equipment must be indicated by signs in accordance with the national regulations transposing Directive 77/576/EEC into law.

Such signs must be placed at appropriate points and be made to last.

6. Ventilation of enclosed workplaces

6.1. Steps shall be taken to see to it that there is sufficient fresh air in enclosed workplaces, having regard to the working methods used and the physical demands placed on the workers.

If a forced ventilation system is used, it shall be maintained in working order.

Any breakdown must be indicated by a control system where this is necessary for workers' health.

6.2. If air-conditioning or mechanical ventilation installations are used, they must operate in such a way that workers are not exposed to draughts which cause discomfort.

Any deposit or dirt likely to create an immediate danger to the health of workers by polluting the atmosphere must be removed without delay.

7. Room temperature

7.1. During working hours, the temperature in rooms containing workplaces must be adequate for human beings, having regard to the working methods being used and the physical demands placed on the workers.

7.2. The temperature in rest areas, rooms for duty staff, sanitary facilities, canteens and first aid rooms must be appropriate to the particular purpose of such areas.

7.3. Windows, skylights and glass partitions should allow excessive effects of sunlight in workplaces to be avoided, having regard to the nature of the work and of the workplace.

8. Natural and artificial room lighting

8.1. Workplaces must as far as possible receive sufficient natural light and be equipped with artificial lighting adequate for the protection of workers' safety and health.

8.2. Lighting installations in rooms containing workplaces and in passageways must be placed in such a way that there is no risk of accident to workers as a result of the type of lighting fitted.

8.3. Workplaces in which workers are especially exposed to risks in the event of failure of artificial lighting must be provided with emergency lighting of adequate intensity.

9. Floors, walls, ceilings and roofs of rooms

9.1. The floors of workplaces must have no dangerous bumps, holes or slopes and must be fixed, stable and not slippery.

Workplaces containing workstations must be adequately insulated, bearing in mind the type of undertaking involved and the physical activity of the workers.

9.2. The surfaces of floors, walls and ceilings in rooms must be such that they can be cleaned or refurbished to an appropriate standard of hygiene.

9.3. Transparent or translucent walls, in particular all-glass partitions, in rooms or in the vicinity of workplaces and traffic routes must be clearly indicated and made of safety material or be shielded from such places or traffic routes to prevent workers from coming into contact with walls or being injured should the walls shatter.

9.4. Access to roofs made of materials of insufficient strength must not be permitted unless equipment is provided to ensure that the work can be carried out in a safe manner.

10. Windows and skylights

10.1. It must be possible for workers to open, close, adjust or secure windows, skylights and ventilators in a safe manner. When open, they must not be positioned so as to constitute a hazard to workers.

10.2. Windows and skylights must be designed in conjunction with equipment or otherwise fitted with devices allowing them to be cleaned without risk to the workers carrying out this work or to workers present in and around the building.

11. Doors and gates

11.1. The position, number and dimensions of doors and gates, and the materials used in their construction, are determined by the nature and use of the rooms or areas.

11.2. Transparent doors must be appropriately marked at a conspicuous level.

11.3. Swing doors and gates must be transparent or have see-through panels.

11.4. If transparent or translucent surfaces in doors and gates are not made of safety material and if there is a danger that workers may be injured if a door or gate should shatter, the surfaces must be protected against breakage.

11.5. Sliding doors must be fitted with a safety device to prevent them from being derailed and falling over.

11.6. Doors and gates opening upwards must be fitted with a mechanism to secure them against falling back.

11.7. Doors along escape routes must be appropriately marked.

It must be possible to open them from the inside at any time without special assistance.

It must be possible to open the doors when the workplaces are occupied.

11.8. Doors for pedestrians must be provided in the immediate vicinity of any gates intended essentially for vehicle traffic, unless it is safe for pedestrians to pass through; such doors must be clearly marked and left permanently unobstructed.

11.9. Mechanical doors and gates must function in such a way that there is no risk of accident to workers.

They must be fitted with easily identifiable and accessible emergency shut-down devices and, unless they open automatically in the event of a power failure, it must also be possible to open them manually.

12. *Traffic routes – danger areas*

12.1. Traffic routes, including stairs, fixed ladders and loading bays and ramps, must be located and dimensioned to ensure easy, safe and appropriate access for pedestrians or vehicles in such a way as not to endanger workers employed in the vicinity of these traffic routes.

12.2. Routes used for pedestrian traffic and/or goods traffic must be dimensioned in accordance with the number of potential users and the type of undertaking.

If means of transport are used on traffic routes, a sufficient safety clearance must be provided for pedestrians.

12.3. Sufficient clearance must be allowed between vehicle traffic routes and doors, gates, passages for pedestrians, corridors and staircases.

12.4. Where the use and equipment of rooms so requires for the protection of workers, traffic routes must be clearly identified.

12.5. If the workplaces contain danger areas in which, owing to the nature of the work, there is a risk of the worker or objects falling, the places must be equipped, as far as possible, with devices preventing unauthorised workers from entering those areas.

Appropriate measures must be taken to protect workers authorised to enter danger areas.

Danger areas must be clearly indicated.

13. *Specific measures for escalators and travelators*

Escalators and travelators must function safely.

They must be equipped with any necessary safety devices.

They must be fitted with easily identifiable and accessible emergency shut-down devices.

14. *Loading bays and ramps*

14.1. Loading bays and ramps must be suitable for the dimensions of the loads to be transported.

14.2. Loading bays must have at least one exit point.

Where technically feasible, bays over a certain length must have an exit point at each end.

14.3. Loading ramps must as far as possible be safe enough to prevent workers from falling off.

15. Room dimensions and air space in rooms – freedom of movement at the workstation

15.1. Workrooms must have sufficient surface area, height and air space to allow workers to perform their work without risk to their safety, health or well-being.

15.2. The dimensions of the free unoccupied area at the workstation must be calculated to allow workers sufficient freedom of movement to perform their work.

If this is not possible for reasons specific to the workplace, the worker must be provided with sufficient freedom of movement near his workstation.

16. Rest rooms

16.1. Where the safety or health of workers, in particular because of the type of activity carried out or the presence of more than a certain number of employees, so require, workers must be provided with an easily accessible rest room.

This provision does not apply if the workers are employed in offices or similar workrooms providing equivalent relaxation during breaks.

16.2. Rest rooms must be large enough and equipped with an adequate number of tables and seats with backs for the number of workers.

16.3. In rest rooms appropriate measures must be introduced for the protection of non-smokers against discomfort caused by tobacco smoke.

16.4. If working hours are regularly and frequently interrupted and there is no rest room, other rooms must be provided in which workers can stay during such interruptions, wherever this is required for the safety or health of workers.

Appropriate measures should be taken for the protection of non-smokers against discomfort caused by tobacco smoke.

17. Pregnant women and nursing mothers

Pregnant women and nursing mothers must be able to lie down to rest in appropriate conditions.

18. *Sanitary equipment*

18.1. *Changing rooms and lockers*

18.1.1. Appropriate changing rooms must be provided for workers if they have to wear special work clothes and where, for reasons of health or propriety, they cannot be expected to change in another room.

Changing rooms must be easily accessible, be of sufficient capacity and be provided with seating.

18.1.2. Changing rooms must be sufficiently large and have facilities to enable each worker to lock away his clothes during working hours.

If circumstances so require (e.g. dangerous substances, humidity, dirt), lockers for work clothes must be separate from those for ordinary clothes.

18.1.3. Provision must be made for separate changing rooms or separate use of changing rooms for men and women.

18.1.4. If changing rooms are not required under 18.1.1, each worker must be provided with a place to store his clothes.

18.2. *Showers and washbasins*

18.2.1. Adequate and suitable showers must be provided for workers if required by the nature of the work or for health reasons.

Provision must be made for separate shower rooms or separate use of shower rooms for men and women.

18.2.2. The shower rooms must be sufficiently large to permit each worker to wash without hindrance in conditions of an appropriate standard of hygiene.

The showers must be equipped with hot and cold running water.

18.2.3. Where showers are not required under the first subparagraph of 18.2.1, adequate and suitable washbasins with running water (hot water if necessary) must be provided in the vicinity of the workstations and the changing rooms.

Such washbasins must be separate for, or used separately by, men and women when so required for reasons of propriety.

18.2.4. Where the rooms housing the showers or washbasins are separate from the changing rooms, there must be easy communication between the two.

18.3. *Lavatories and washbasins*

Separate facilities must be provided in the vicinity of workstations, rest rooms, changing rooms and rooms housing showers or washbasins, with an adequate number of lavatories and washbasins.

Provision must be made for separate lavatories or separate use of lavatories for men and women.

19. First aid rooms

19.1. One or more first aid rooms must be provided where the size of the premises, type of activity being carried out and frequency of accidents so dictate.

19.2. First aid rooms must be fitted with essential first aid installations and equipment and be easily accessible to stretchers.

They must be signposted in accordance with the national regulations transposing Directive 77/576/EEC into law.

19.3. In addition, first aid equipment must be available in all places where working conditions require it.

This equipment must be suitably marked and easily accessible.

20. Handicapped workers

Workplaces must be organised to take account of handicapped workers, if necessary.

This provision applies in particular to the doors, passageways, staircases, showers, washbasins, lavatories and workstations used or occupied directly by handicapped persons.

21. Outdoor workplaces (special provisions)

21.1. Workstations, traffic routes and other areas or installations outdoors which are used or occupied by the workers in the course of their activity must be organised in such a way that pedestrians and vehicles can circulate safely.

Sections 12, 13 and 14 also apply to main traffic routes on the site of the undertaking (traffic routes leading to fixed workstations), to traffic routes used for the regular maintenance and supervision of the undertaking's installations and to loading bays.

Section 12 is also applicable to outdoor workplaces.

21.2. Workplaces outdoors must be adequately lit by artificial lighting if daylight is not adequate.

21.3. When workers are employed at workstations outdoors, such workstations must as far as possible be arranged so that workers:

(*a*) are protected against inclement weather conditions and if necessary against falling objects;

(*b*) are not exposed to harmful noise levels nor to harmful external influences such as gases, vapours or dust;

(*c*) are able to leave their workstations swiftly in the event of danger or are able to be rapidly assisted;

(*d*) cannot slip or fall.

Annex II

Minimum health and safety requirements for workplaces already in use, as referred to in Article 4 of the Directive

1. *Preliminary note*

The obligations laid down in this Annex apply wherever required by the features of the workplace, the activity, the circumstances or a hazard.

2. *Stability and solidity*

Buildings which have workplaces must have a structure and solidity appropriate to the nature of their use.

3. *Electrical installations*

Electrical installations must be designed and constructed so as not to present a fire or explosion hazard; persons must be adequately protected against the risk of accidents caused by direct or indirect contact.

Electrical installations and protection devices must be appropriate to the voltage, external conditions and the competence of persons with access to parts of the installation.

4. *Emergency routes and exits*

4.1. Emergency routes and exits must remain clear and lead as directly as possible to the open air or to a safe area.

4.2. In the event of danger, it must be possible for workers to evacuate all workstations quickly and as safely as possible.

4.3. There must be an adequate number of escape routes and emergency exits.

4.4. Emergency exit doors must open outwards.

Sliding or revolving doors are not permitted if they are specifically intended as emergency exits.

Emergency doors should not be locked or fastened that they cannot be easily and immediately opened by any person who may require to use them in an emergency.

4.5. Specific emergency routes and exits must be indicated by signs in accordance with the national regulations transposing Directive 77/576/EEC into law.

Such signs must be placed at appropriate points and be made to last.

4.6. Emergency doors must not be locked.

The emergency routes and exits, and the traffic routes and doors giving access to them, must be free from obstruction so that they can be used at any time without hindrance.

4.7. Emergency routes and exits requiring illumination must be provided with emergency lighting of adequate intensity in case the lighting fails.

5. *Fire detection and fire fighting*

5.1. Depending on the dimensions and use of the buildings, the equipment they contain, the physical and chemical characteristics of the substances present and the maximum potential number of people present, workplaces must be equipped with appropriate fire-fighting equipment, and, as necessary, fire detectors and an alarm system.

5.2. Non-automatic fire-fighting equipment must be easily accessible and simple to use.

It must be indicated by signs in accordance with the national regulations transposing Directive 77/576/EEC into law.

Such signs must be placed at appropriate points and be made to last.

6. *Ventilation of enclosed workplaces*

Steps shall be taken to see to it that there is sufficient fresh air in enclosed workplaces, having regard to the working methods used and the physical demands placed on the workers.

If a forced ventilation system is used, it shall be maintained in working order.

Any breakdown must be indicated by a control system where this is necessary for the workers' health.

7. *Room temperature*

7.1. During working hours, the temperature in rooms containing workplaces must be adequate for human beings, having regard to the working methods being used and the physical demands placed on the workers.

7.2. The temperature in rest areas, rooms for duty staff, sanitary facilities, canteens and first aid rooms must be appropriate to the particular purpose of such areas.

8. *Natural and artificial room lighting*

8.1. Workplaces must as far as possible receive sufficient natural light and be equipped with artificial lighting adequate for workers' safety and health.

8.2. Workplaces in which workers are especially exposed to risks in the event of failure of artificial lighting must be provided with emergency lighting of adequate intensity.

9. *Doors and gates*

9.1. Transparent doors must be appropriately marked at a conspicuous level.

9.2. Swing doors and gates must be transparent or have see-through panels.

10. *Danger areas*

If the workplaces contain danger areas in which, owing to the nature of the work, there is a risk of the worker or objects falling, the places must be equipped, as far as possible, with devices preventing unauthorised workers from entering those areas.

Appropriate measures must be taken to protect workers authorised to enter danger areas.

Danger areas must be clearly indicated.

11. *Rest rooms and rest areas*

11.1. Where the safety or health of workers, in particular because of the type of activity carried out or the presence of more than a certain number of employees, so require, workers must be provided with an easily accessible rest room or appropriate rest area.

This provision does not apply if the workers are employed in offices or similar workrooms providing equivalent relaxation during breaks.

11.2. Rest rooms and rest areas must be equipped with tables and seats with backs.

11.3. In rest rooms and rest areas appropriate measures must be introduced for the protection of non-smokers against discomfort caused by tobacco smoke.

12. *Pregnant women and nursing mothers*

Pregnant women and nursing mothers must be able to lie down to rest in appropriate conditions.

13. *Sanitary equipment*

13.1. *Changing rooms and lockers*

13.1.1. Appropriate changing rooms must be provided for workers if they have to wear special work clothes and where, for reasons of health or propriety, they cannot be expected to change in another room.

Changing rooms must be easily accessible and of sufficient capacity.

13.1.2. Changing rooms must have facilities to enable each worker to lock away his clothes during working hours.

If circumstances so require (e.g. dangerous substances, humidity, dirt), lockers for work clothes must be separate from those for ordinary clothes.

13.1.3. Provision must be made for separate changing rooms or separate use of changing rooms for men and women.

13.2. *Showers, lavatories and washbasins*

13.2.1. Workplaces must be fitted out in such a way that workers have in the vicinity:

– showers, if required by the nature of their work,

– special facilities equipped with an adequate number of lavatories and washbasins.

13.2.2. The showers and washbasins must be equipped with running water (hot water if necessary).

13.2.3. Provision must be made for separate showers or separate use of showers for men and women.

Provision must be made for separate lavatories or separate use of lavatories for men and women.

14. *First aid equipment*

Workplaces must be fitted with first aid equipment.

The equipment must be suitably marked and easily accessible.

15. *Handicapped workers*

Workplaces must be organised to take account of handicapped workers, if necessary.

This provision applies in particular to the doors, passageways, staircases, showers, washbasins, lavatories and workstations used or occupied directly by handicapped persons.

16. *Movement of pedestrians and vehicles*

Outdoor and indoor workplaces must be organised in such a way that pedestrians and vehicles can circulate in a safe manner.

17. *Outdoor workplaces (special provisions)*

When workers are employed at workstations outdoors, such workstations must as far as possible be organised so that workers:

(a) are protected against inclement weather conditions and if necessary against falling objects;

(b) are not exposed to harmful noise levels nor to harmful external influences such as gases, vapours or dust;

(c) are able to leave their workstations swiftly in the event of danger or are able to be rapidly assisted;

(d) cannot slip or fall.

FOOTNOTES

1. OJ No C 141, 30.5.88, p.6, OJ No C 115, 8.5.89, p.34 and OJ No C 284, 10.11.89, p.8.
2. OJ No C 326, 19.12.88, p.123 and OJ No C 256, 9.10.88, p.51.
3. OJ No C 175, 4.7.88, p.28.
4. OJ No C 28, 3.2.88, p.3.
5. OJ No C 28, 3.2.88, p.1.
6. OJ No L 183, 29.6.89, p.1.
7. OJ No L 185, 9.7.74, p.15.
8. OJ No L 229, 7.9.77, p.12.

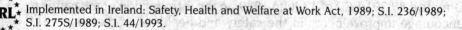 Implemented in Ireland: Safety, Health and Welfare at Work Act, 1989; S.I. 236/1989; S.I. 275S/1989; S.I. 44/1993.

COUNCIL DIRECTIVE

of 25 June 1991

supplementing the measures to encourage improvements in the safety and health at work of workers with a fixed-duration employment relationship or a temporary employment relationship

(91/383/EEC)

(OJ No L 206, 29.7.91, p.19)

The Council of the European Communities,

Having regard to the Treaty establishing the European Economic Community, and in particular Article 118a thereof,

Having regard to the proposal from the Commission[1],

In cooperation with the European Parliament[2],

Having regard to the opinion of the Economic and Social Committee[3],

Whereas Article 118a of the Treaty provides that the Council shall adopt, by means of Directives, minimum requirements for encouraging improvements, especially in the working environment to guarantee a better level of protection of the safety and health of workers;

Whereas, pursuant to the said Article, Directives must avoid imposing administrative, financial and legal constraints which would hold back the creation and development of small and medium-sized undertakings;

Whereas recourse to forms of employment such as fixed-duration employment and temporary employment has increased considerably;

Whereas research has shown that in general workers with a fixed-duration employment relationship or temporary employment relationship are, in certain sectors, more exposed to the risk of accidents at work and occupational diseases than other workers;

Whereas these additional risks in certain sectors are in part linked to certain particular modes of integrating new workers into the undertaking; whereas these risks can be reduced through adequate provision of information and training from the beginning of employment;

Whereas the Directives on health and safety at work, notably Council Directive 89/391/EEC of 12 June 1989 on the introduction of measures to encourage improvements in the safety and health of workers at work[4], contain provisions intended to improve the safety and health of workers in general;

Whereas the specific situation of workers with a fixed-duration employment relationship or a temporary employment relationship and the special nature of the risks they face in certain sectors calls for special additional rules, particularly as regards the provision of information, the training and the medical surveillance of the workers concerned;

Whereas this Directive constitutes a practical step within the framework of the attainment of the social dimension of the internal market,

Has adopted this Directive:

Section 1

Scope and object

Article 1

Scope

This Directive shall apply to :

1. employment relationships governed by a fixed-duration contract of employment concluded directly between the employer and the worker, where the end of the contract is established by objective conditions such as: reaching a specific date, completing a specific task or the occurrence of a specific event;

2. temporary employment relationships between a temporary employment business which is the employer and the worker, where the latter is assigned to work for and under the control of an undertaking and/or establishment making use of his services.

Article 2

Object

1. The purpose of this Directive is to ensure that workers with an employment relationship as referred to in Article 1 are afforded, as regards safety and health at work, the same level of protection as that of other workers in the user undertaking and/or establishment.

2. The existence of an employment relationship as referred to in Article 1 shall not justify different treatment with respect to working conditions inasmuch as the protection of safety and health at work are involved, especially as regards access to personal protective equipment.

3. Directive 89/391/EEC and the individual Directives within the meaning of Article 16(1) thereof shall apply in full to workers with an employment relationship as referred to in Article 1, without prejudice to more binding and/or more specific provisions set out in this Directive.

Section II

General Provisions

Article 3

Provision of information to workers

Without prejudice to Article 10 of Directive 89/391/EEC, Member States shall take the necessary steps to ensure that:

1. before a worker with an employment relationship as referred to in Article 1 takes up any activity, he is informed by the undertaking and/or establishment making use of his services of the risks which he faces;

2. such information:

- covers, in particular, any special occupational qualifications or skills or special medical surveillance required, as defined in national legislation, and

- states clearly any increased specific risks, as defined in national legislation, that the job may entail.

Article 4

Workers' training

Without prejudice to Article 12 of Directive 89/391/EEC, Member States shall take the necessary measures to ensure that, in the cases referred to in Article 3, each worker receives sufficient training appropriate to the particular characteristics of the job, account being taken of his qualifications and experience.

Article 5

Use of workers' services and medical surveillance of workers

1. Member States shall have the option of prohibiting workers with an employment relationship as referred to in Article 1 from being used for certain work as defined in national legislation which would be particularly dangerous to their safety or health, and in particular for

certain work which requires special medical surveillance, as defined in national legislation.

2. Where Member States do not avail themselves of the option referred to in paragraph 1, they shall, without prejudice to Article 14 of Directive 89/391/EEC, take the necessary measures to ensure that workers with an employment relationship as referred to in Article 1 who are used for work which requires special medical surveillance, as defined in national legislation, are provided with appropriate special medical surveillance.

3. It shall be open to Member States to provide that the appropriate special medical surveillance referred to in paragraph 2 shall extend beyond the end of the employment relationship of the worker concerned.

Article 6

Protection and prevention services

Member States shall take the necessary measures to ensure that workers, services or persons designated, in accordance with Article 7 of Directive 89/391/EEC, to carry out activities related to protection from and prevention of occupational risks are informed of the assignment of workers with an employment relationship as referred to in Article 1, to the extent necessary for the workers, services or persons designated to be able to carry out adequately their protection and prevention activities for all the workers in the undertaking and/or establishment.

Section III

Special Provisions

Article 7

Temporary employment relationships: information

Without prejudice to Article 3, Member States shall take the necessary steps to ensure that:

1. before workers with an employment relationship as referred to in Article 1(2) are supplied, a user undertaking and/or establishment shall specify to the temporary employment business, *inter alia*, the occupational qualifications required and the specific features of the job to be filled;

2. the temporary employment business shall bring all these facts to the attention of the workers concerned.

Member States may provide that the details to be given by the user undertaking and/or establishment to the temporary employment business in accordance with point 1 of the first subparagraph shall appear in a contract of assignment.

Article 8

Temporary employment relationships: responsibility

Member States shall take the necessary steps to ensure that:

1. without prejudice to the responsibility of the temporary employment business as laid down in national legislation, the user undertaking and/or establishment is/are responsible, for the duration of the assignment, for the conditions governing performance of the work;

2. for the application of point 1, the conditions governing the performance of the work shall be limited to those connected with safety, hygiene and health at work.

Section IV

Miscellaneous Provisions

Article 9

More favourable provisions

This Directive shall be without prejudice to existing or future national or Community provisions which are more favourable to the safety and health protection of workers with an employment relationship as referred to in Article 1.

Article 10

Final provisions

1. Member States shall bring into force the laws, regulations and administrative provisions necessary to comply with this Directive by 31 December 1992 at the latest. They shall forthwith inform the Commission thereof.

When Member States adopt these measures, the latter shall contain a reference to this Directive or shall be accompanied by such reference on the occasion of their official publication. The methods of making such a reference shall be laid down by the Member States.

2. Member States shall forward to the Commission the texts of the

provisions of national law which they have already adopted or adopt in the field covered by this Directive.

3. Member States shall report to the Commission every five years on the practical implementation of this Directive, setting out the point of view of workers and employers.

The Commission shall bring the report to the attention of the European Parliament, the Council, the Economic and Social Committee and the Advisory Committee on Safety, Hygiene and Health Protection at Work.

4. The Commission shall submit to the European Parliament, the Council and the Economic and Social Committee a regular report on the implementation of this Directive, due account being taken of paragraphs 1,2 and 3.

Article 11

This Directive is addressed to the Member States.

Done at Luxembourg, 25 June 1991.

For the Council

The President

J.-C. Juncker

FOOTNOTES

1. OJ No C 224, 8.9.90, p.4.
2. OJ No C 295, 26.11.90, p.106 and OJ No C 158, 17.6.91.
3. OJ No C 332, 31.12.90, p.167.
4. OJ No L 183, 29.6.89, p.1.

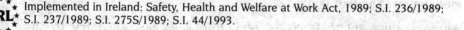 Implemented in Ireland: Safety, Health and Welfare at Work Act, 1989; S.I. 236/1989; S.I. 237/1989; S.I. 275S/1989; S.I. 44/1993.

COUNCIL DIRECTIVE 92/85/EEC

of 19 October 1992

on the introduction of measures to encourage improvements in the safety and health at work of pregnant workers and workers who have recently given birth or are breastfeeding (tenth individual Directive within the meaning of Article 16(1) of Directive 89/391/EEC)

(OJ No L 348, 28.11.92, p.1)

The Council of the European Communities,

Having regard to the Treaty establishing the European Economic Community, and in particular Article 118a thereof,

Having regard to the proposal from the Commission, drawn up after consultation with the Advisory Committee on Safety, Hygiene and Health Protection at Work[1],

In cooperation with the European Parliament[2],

Having regard to the opinion of the Economic and Social Committee[3],

Whereas Article 118a of the Treaty provides that the Council shall adopt, by means of directives, minimum requirements for encouraging improvements, especially in the working environment, to protect the safety and health of workers;

Whereas this Directive does not justify any reduction in levels of protection already achieved in individual Member States, the Member States being committed, under the Treaty, to encouraging improvements in conditions in this area and to harmonising conditions while maintaining the improvements made;

Whereas, under the terms of Article 118a of the Treaty, the said directives are to avoid imposing administrative, financial and legal constraints in a way which would hold back the creation and development of small and medium-sized undertakings;

Whereas, pursuant to Decision 74/325/EEC[4], as last amended by the 1985 Act of Accession, the Advisory Committee on Safety, Hygiene and Health Protection at Work is consulted by the Commission on the drafting of proposals in this field;

Whereas the Community Charter of the fundamental social rights of workers, adopted at the Strasbourg European Council on 9 December

1989 by the Heads of State or Government of 11 Member States, lays down, in paragraph 19 in particular, that:

'Every worker must enjoy satisfactory health and safety conditions in his working environment. Appropriate measures must be taken in order to achieve further harmonisation of conditions in this area while maintaining the improvements made';

Whereas the Commission, in its action programme for the implementation of the Community Charter of the fundamental social rights of workers, has included among its aims the adoption by the Council of a Directive on the protection of pregnant women at work;

Whereas Article 15 of Council Directive 89/391/EEC of 12 June 1989 on the introduction of measures to encourage improvements in the safety and health of workers at work[5] provides that particularly sensitive risk groups must be protected against the dangers which specifically affect them;

Whereas pregnant workers, workers who have recently given birth or who are breastfeeding must be considered a specific risk group in many respects, and measures must be taken with regard to their safety and health;

Whereas the protection of the safety and health of pregnant workers, workers who have recently given birth or workers who are breastfeeding should not treat women on the labour market unfavourably nor work to the detriment of directives concerning equal treatment for men and women;

Whereas some types of activities may pose a specific risk, for pregnant workers, workers who have recently given birth or workers who are breastfeeding, of exposure to dangerous agents, processes or working conditions; whereas such risks must therefore be assessed and the result of such assessment communicated to female workers and/or their representatives;

Whereas, further, should the result of this assessment reveal the existence of a risk to the safety or health of the female worker, provision must be made for such worker to be protected;

Whereas pregnant workers and workers who are breastfeeding must not engage in activities which have been assessed as revealing a risk of exposure, jeopardising safety and health, to certain particularly dangerous agents or working conditions;

Whereas provision should be made for pregnant workers, workers who have recently given birth or workers who are breastfeeding not to be required to work at night where such provision is necessary from the point of view of their safety and health;

Whereas the vulnerability of pregnant workers, workers who have recently given birth or who are breastfeeding makes it necessary for them to be granted the right to maternity leave of at least 14 continuous weeks, allocated before and/or after confinement, and renders necessary the compulsory nature of maternity leave of at least two weeks, allocated before and/or after confinement;

Whereas the risk of dismissal for reasons associated with their condition may have harmful effects on the physical and mental state of pregnant workers, workers who have recently given birth or who are breastfeeding; whereas provision should be made for such dismissal to be prohibited;

Whereas measures for the organisation of work concerning the protection of the health of pregnant workers, workers who have recently given birth or workers who are breastfeeding would serve no purpose unless accompanied by the maintenance of rights linked to the employment contract, including maintenance of payment and/or entitlement to an adequate allowance;

Whereas, moreover, provision concerning maternity leave would also serve no purpose unless accompanied by the maintenance of rights linked to the employment contract and/or entitlement to an adequate allowance;

Whereas the concept of an adequate allowance in the case of maternity leave must be regarded as a technical point of reference with a view to fixing the minimum level of protection and should in no circumstances be interpreted as suggesting an analogy between pregnancy and illness,

Has adopted this Directive.

Section I

Purpose and Definitions

Article 1

Purpose

1. The purpose of this Directive, which is the tenth individual Directive within the meaning of Article 16(1) of Directive 89/391/EEC, is to implement measures to encourage improvements in the safety and health at work of pregnant workers and workers who have recently given birth or who are breastfeeding.

2. The provisions of Directive 89/391/EEC, except for Article 2(2) thereof, shall apply in full to the whole area covered by paragraph 1, without prejudice to any more stringent and/or specific provisions contained in this Directive.

3. This Directive may not have the effect of reducing the level of protection afforded to pregnant workers, workers who have recently given birth or who are breastfeeding as compared with the situation which exists in each Member State on the date on which this Directive is adopted.

Article 2

Definitions

For the purposes of this Directive:

(a) *pregnant worker* shall mean a pregnant worker who informs her employer of her condition, in accordance with national legislation and/or national practice;

(b) *worker who has recently given birth* shall mean a worker who has recently given birth within the meaning of national legislation and/or national practice and who informs her employer of her condition, in accordance with that legislation and/or practice;

(c) *worker who is breastfeeding* shall mean a worker who is breastfeeding within the meaning of national legislation and/or national practice and who informs her employer of her condition, in accordance with that legislation and/or practice.

Section II

General provisions

Article 3

Guidelines

1. In consultation with the Member States and assisted by the Advisory Committee on Safety, Hygiene and Health Protection at Work, the Commission shall draw up guidelines on the assessment of the chemical, physical and biological agents and industrial processes considered hazardous for the safety or health of workers within the meaning of Article 2.

The guidelines referred to in the first subparagraph shall also cover movements and postures, mental and physical fatigue and other types of physical and mental stress connected with the work done by workers within the meaning of Article 2.

2. The purpose of the guidelines referred to in paragraph 1 is to serve as a basis for the assessment referred to in Article 4(1).

To this end, Member States shall bring these guidelines to the attention of all employers and all female workers and/or their representatives in the respective Member State.

Article 4

Assessment and information

1. For all activities liable to involve a specific risk of exposure to the agents, processes or working conditions of which a non-exhaustive list is given in Annex I, the employer shall assess the nature, degree and duration of exposure, in the undertaking and/or establishment concerned, of workers within the meaning of Article 2, either directly or by way of the protective and preventive services referred to in Article 7 of Directive 89/391/EEC, in order to:

– assess any risks to the safety or health and any possible effect on the pregnancys (sic) or breastfeeding of workers within the meaning of Article 2,

– decide what measures should be taken.

2. Without prejudice to Article 10 of Directive 89/391/EEC, workers within the meaning of Article 2 and workers likely to be in one of the situations referred to in Article 2 in the undertaking and/or establishment concerned and/or their representatives shall be informed of the results of the assessment referred to in paragraph 1 and of all measures to be taken concerning health and safety at work.

Article 5

Action further to the results of the assessment

1. Without prejudice to Article 6 of Directive 89/391/EEC, if the results of the assessment referred to in Article 4(1) reveal a risk to the safety or health or an effect on the pregnancy or breastfeeding of a worker within the meaning of Article 2, the employer shall take the necessary measures to ensure that, by temporarily adjusting the working conditions and/or the working hours of the worker concerned, the exposure of that worker to such risks is avoided.

2. If the adjustment of her working conditions and/or working hours is not technically and/or objectively feasible, or cannot reasonably be

required on duly substantiated grounds, the employer shall take the necessary measures to move the worker concerned to another job.

3. If moving her to another job is not technically and/or objectively feasible or cannot reasonably be required on duly substantiated grounds, the worker concerned shall be granted leave in accordance with national legislation and/or national practice for the whole of the period necessary to protect her safety or health.

4. The provisions of this Article shall apply *mutatis mutandis* to the case where a worker pursuing an activity which is forbidden pursuant to Article 6 becomes pregnant or starts breastfeeding and informs her employer thereof.

Article 6

Cases in which exposure is prohibited

In addition to the general provisions concerning the protection of workers, in particular those relating to the limit values for occupational exposure:

1. pregnant workers within the meaning of Article 2(a) may under no circumstances be obliged to perform duties for which the assessment has revealed a risk of exposure, which would jeopardise safety or health, to the agents and working conditions listed in Annex II, Section A;

2. workers who are breastfeeding, within the meaning of Article 2(c), may under no circumstances be obliged to perform duties for which the assessment has revealed a risk of exposure, which would jeopardise safety or health, to the agents and working conditions listed in Annex II, Section B.

Article 7

Night work

1. Member States shall take the necessary measures to ensure that workers referred to in Article 2 are not obliged to perform night work during their pregnancy and for a period following childbirth which shall be determined by the national authority competent for safety and health, subject to submission, in accordance with the procedures laid down by the Member States, of a medical certificate stating that this is necessary for the safety and health of the worker concerned.

2. The measures referred to in paragraph 1 must entail the possibility, in accordance with national legislation and/or national practice, of:

(a) transfer to daytime work; or

(b) leave from work or extension of maternity leave where such a transfer is not technically and/or objectively feasible or cannot reasonably be required on duly substantiated grounds.

Article 8

Maternity leave

1. Member States shall take the necessary measures to ensure that workers within the meaning of Article 2 are entitled to a continuous period of maternity leave of at least 14 weeks allocated before and/or after confinement in accordance with national legislation and/or practice.

2. The maternity leave stipulated in paragraph 1 must include compulsory maternity leave of at least two weeks allocated before and/or after confinement in accordance with national legislation and/or practice.

Article 9

Time off for ante-natal examinations

Member States shall take the necessary measures to ensure that pregnant workers within the meaning of Article 2(a) are entitled to, in accordance with national legislation and/or practice, time off, without loss of pay, on order to attend ante-natal examinations, if such examinations have to take place during working hours.

Article 10

Prohibition of dismissal

In order to guarantee workers, within the meaning of Article 2, the exercise of their health and safety protection rights as recognised under this Article, it shall be provided that:

1. Member States shall take the necessary measures to prohibit the dismissal of workers, within the meaning of Article 2, during the period from the beginning of their pregnancy to the end of the maternity leave referred to in Article 8(1), save in exceptional cases not connected with their condition which are permitted under national legislation and/or practice and, where applicable, provided that the competent authority has given its consent;

2. if a worker, within the meaning of Article 2, is dismissed during the

period referred to in point 1, the employer must cite duly substantiated grounds for her dismissal in writing;

3. Member States shall take the necessary measures to protect workers, within the meaning of Article 2, from consequences of dismissal which is unlawful by virtue of point 1.

Article 11

Employment rights

In order to guarantee workers within the meaning of Article 2 the exercise of their health and safety protection rights as recognised in this Article, it shall be provided that:

1. in the cases referred to in Article 5, 6 and 7, the employment rights relating to the employment contract, including the maintenance of a payment to, and/or entitlement to an adequate allowance for, workers within the meaning of Article 2, must be ensured in accordance with national legislation and/or national practice;

2. in the case referred to in Article 8, the following must be ensured:

(a) the rights connected with the employment contract of workers within the meaning of Article 2, other than those referred to in point (b) below;

(b) maintenance of a payment to, and/or entitlement to an adequate allowance for, workers within the meaning of Article 2;

3. the allowance referred to in point 2(b) shall be deemed adequate if it guarantees income at least equivalent to that which the worker concerned would receive in the event of a break in her activities on grounds connected with her state of health, subject to any ceiling laid down under national legislation;

4. Member States may make entitlement to pay or the allowance referred to in points 1 and 2(b) conditional upon the worker concerned fulfilling the conditions of eligibility for such benefits laid down under national legislation.

These conditions may under no circumstances provide for periods of previous employment in excess of 12 months immediately prior to the presumed date of confinement.

Article 12

Defence of rights

Member States shall introduce into their national legal systems such measures as are necessary to enable all workers who should themselves wronged by failure to comply with the obligations arising from this Directive to pursue their claims by judicial process (and/or, in accordance with national laws and/or practices) by recourse to other competent authorities (sic).

Article 13

Amendments to the Annexes

1. Strictly technical adjustments to Annex I as a result of technical progress, changes in international regulations or specifications and new findings in the area covered by this Directive shall be adopted in accordance with the procedure laid down in Article 17 of Directive 89/391/EEC.

2. Annex II may be amended only in accordance with the procedure laid down in Article 118a of the Treaty.

Article 14

Final provisions

1. Member States shall bring into force the laws, regulations and administrative provisions necessary to comply with this Directive not later than two years after the adoption thereof or ensure, at the latest two years after adoption of this Directive, that the two sides of industry introduce the requisite provisions by means of collective agreements, with Member States being required to make all the necessary provisions to enable them at all times to guarantee the results laid down by this Directive. They shall forthwith inform the Commission thereof.

2. When Member States adopt the measures referred to in paragraph 1, they shall contain a reference of this Directive or shall be accompanied by such reference on the occasion of their official publication. The method of making such a reference shall be laid down by the Member States.

3. Member States shall communicate to the Commission the texts of the essential provisions of national law which they have already adopted or adopt in the field governed by this Directive.

4. Member States shall report to the Commission every five years on the

practical implementation of the provisions of this Directive, indicating the points of view of the two sides of industry.

However, Member States shall report for the first time to the Commission on the practical implementation of the provisions of this Directive, indicating the points of view of the two sides of industry, four years after its adoption.

The Commission shall inform the European Parliament, the Council, the Economic and Social Committee and the Advisory Committee on Safety, Hygiene and Health Protection at Work.

5. The Commission shall periodically submit to the European Parliament, the Council and the Economic and Social Committee a report on the implementation of this Directive, taking into account paragraphs 1, 2 and 3.

6. The Council will re-examine this Directive, on the basis of an assessment carried out on the basis of the reports referred to in the second subparagraph of paragraph 4 and, should the need arise, of a proposal, to be submitted by the Commission at the latest five years after adoption of the Directive.

Article 15

This Directive is addressed to the Member States.

Done at Luxembourg, 19 October 1992.

For the Council

The President

D. Curry

Annex I

Non-exhaustive list of agents, processes and working conditions

referred to in Article 4(1)

A. Agents

1. *Physical agents* where these are regarded as agents causing foetal lesions and/or likely to disrupt placental attachment, and in particular:

(*a*) shocks, vibration or movement;

(b) handling of loads entailing risks, particularly of a dorsolumbar nature;

(c) noise;

(d) ionizing radiation[6]

(e) non-ionising radiation;

(f) extremes of cold or heat;

(g) movements and postures, travelling – either inside or outside the establishment – mental and physical fatigue and other physical burdens connected with the activity of the worker within the meaning of Article 2 of the Directive.

2. Biological agents

Biological agents of risk groups 2, 3 and 3 (sic) within the meaning of Article 2(d) numbers 2, 3 and 4 of Directive 90/679/EEC[7], in so far as it is known that these agents or the therapeutic measures necessitated by such agents endanger the health of pregnant women and the unborn child and in so far as they do not yet appear in Annex II.

3. Chemical agents

The following chemical agents in so far as it is known that they endanger the health of pregnant women and the unborn child and in so far as they do not yet appear in Annex II:

(a) substances labelled R 40, R 45, R 46, and R 47 under Directive 67/548/EEC[8] in so far as they do not yet appear in Annex II;

(b) chemical agents in Annex I to Directive 90/394/EEC[9];

(c) mercury and mercury derivatives;

(d) antimitotic drugs;

(e) carbon monoxide;

(f) chemical agents of known and dangerous percutaneous absorption.

B. Processes

Industrial processes listed in Annex I to Directive 90/394/EEC.

C. Working conditions

Underground mining work.

Annex II

Non-exhaustive list of agents and working conditions referred to in Article 6

A. Pregnant workers within the meaning of Article 2(a)

1. *Agents*

   (a) Physical agents

   Work in hyperbaric atmosphere, e.g. pressurised enclosures and underwater diving.

   (b) Biological agents

   The following biological agents:

   – toxoplasma,

   – rubella virus,

   unless the pregnant workers are proved to be adequately protected against such agents by immunisation.

   (c) Chemical agents

   Lead and lead derivatives in so far as these agents are capable of being absorbed by the human organism.

2. *Working conditions*

Underground mining work.

B. Workers who are breastfeeding within the meaning of Article 2(c)

1. *Agents*

(a) Chemical agents

Lead and lead derivatives in so far as these agents are capable of being absorbed by the human organism.

2. *Working conditions*

Underground mining work.

Statement of the Council and the Commission concerning Article 11(3) of Directive 92/85/EEC, entered in the minutes of the 1608th meeting of the Council (Luxembourg, 19 October 1992)

The Council and the Commission stated that:

'In determining the level of the allowances referred to in Article 11(2)(b) and (3), reference shall be made, for purely technical reasons, to the allowance which a worker would receive in the event of a break in her activities on grounds connected with her state of health. Such a reference is not intended in any way to imply that pregnancy and childbirth be equated with sickness. The national social security legislation of all Member States provides for an allowance to be paid during an absence from work due to sickness. The link with such allowance in the chosen formulation is simply intended to serve as a concrete, fixed reference amount in all Member States for the determination of the minimum amount of maternity allowance payable. In so far as allowances are paid in individual Member States which exceed those provided for in the Directive, such allowances are, of course, retained. This is clear from Article 1(3) of the Directive.'

FOOTNOTES

1. OJ No C 281, 9.11.90, p.3; and OJ No C 25, 1.2.91, p.9.
2. OJ No C 19, 28.1.91, p.177; and OJ No C 150, 15.6.92, p.99.
3. OJ No C 41, 18.2.91, p.29.
4. OJ No L 185, 9.7.74, p.15.
5. OJ No L 183, 29.6.89, p.1.
6. See Directive 80/836/Euratom (OJ No L 246, 17.9.80, p.1).
7. OJ No L 374, 31.12.90, p.1.
8. OJ No L 196, 16.8.67, p.1. Directive as last amended by Directive 90/517/EEC (OJ No L 287, 19.10.90, p.37).
9. OJ No L 196, 26.7.90, p.1.

 Implemented in Ireland: To be implemented by 10.10.1994.

(b) Employment Law

COUNCIL DIRECTIVE

of 14 February 1977

on the approximation of the laws of the Member States relating to the safeguarding of employees' rights in the event of transfers of undertakings, businesses or parts of businesses

(77/187/EEC)

(OJ No L 61, 5.3.77, p.26)

The Council of the European Communities,

Having regard to the Treaty establishing the European Economic Community, and in particular Article 100 thereof,

Having regard to the proposal from the Commission,

Having regard to the opinion of the European Parliament[1],

Having regard to the opinion of the Economic and Social Committee[2],

Whereas economic trends are bringing in their wake, at both national and Community level, changes in the structure of undertakings, through transfers of undertakings, businesses or parts of businesses to other employers as a result of legal transfers or mergers;

Whereas it is necessary to provide for the protection of employees in the event of a change of employer, in particular, to ensure that their rights are safeguarded;

Whereas differences still remain in the Member States as regards the extent of the protection of employees in this respect and these differences should be reduced;

Whereas these differences can have a direct effect on the functioning of the common market;

Whereas it is therefore necessary to promote the approximation of laws in this field while maintaining the improvement described in Article 117 of the Treaty,

Has adopted this Directive:

Section I

Scope and definitions

Article 1

1. This Directive shall apply to the transfer of an undertaking, business or part of a business to another employer as a result of a legal transfer or merger.

2. This Directive shall apply where and in so far as the undertaking, business or part of the business to be transferred is situated within the territorial scope of the Treaty.

3. This Directive shall not apply to sea-going vessels.

Article 2

For the purposes of this Directive:

(a) 'transferor' means any natural or legal person who, by reason of a transfer within the meaning of Article 1(1), ceases to be the employer in respect of the undertaking, business or part of the business;

(b) 'transferee' means any natural or legal person who, by reason of a transfer within the meaning of Article 1(1), becomes the employer in respect of the undertaking, business or part of the business;

(c) 'representatives of the employees' means the representatives of the employees provided for by the laws or practice of the Member States, with the exception of members of administrative, governing or supervisory bodies of companies who represent employees on such bodies in certain Member States.

Section II

Safeguarding of employees' rights

Article 3

1. The transferor's rights and obligations arising from a contract of employment or from an employment relationship existing on the date of a transfer within the meaning of Article 1(1) shall, by reason of such transfer, be transferred to the transferee.

Member States may provide that, after the date of transfer within the meaning of Article 1(1) and in addition to the transferee, the transferor shall continue to be liable in respect of obligations which arose from a contract of employment or an employment relationship.

2. Following the transfer within the meaning of Article 1(1), the transferee shall continue to observe the terms and conditions agreed in any collective agreement on the same terms applicable to the transferor under that agreement, until the date of termination or expiry of the collective agreement or the entry into force or application of another collective agreement.

Member States may limit the period for observing such terms and conditions, with the proviso that it shall not be less than one year.

3. Paragraphs 1 and 2 shall not cover employees' rights to old-age, invalidity or survivors' benefits under supplementary company or inter-company pension schemes outside the statutory social security schemes in Member States.

Member States shall adopt the measures necessary to protect the interests of employees and of persons no longer employed in the transferor's business at the time of the transfer within the meaning of Article 1(1) in respect of rights conferring on them immediate or prospective entitlement to old-age benefits, including survivors' benefits, under supplementary schemes referred to in the first subparagraph.

Article 4

1. The transfer of an undertaking, business or part of a business shall not in itself constitute grounds for dismissal by the transferor or the transferee. This provision shall not stand in the way of dismissals that may take place for economic, technical or organisational reasons entailing changes in the workforce.

Member States may provide that the first subparagraph shall not apply to certain specific categories of employees who are not covered by the laws or practice of the Member States in respect of protection against dismissal.

2. If the contract of employment or the employment relationship is terminated because the transfer within the meaning of Article 1(1) involves a substantial change in working conditions to the detriment of the employee, the employer shall be regarded as having been responsible for termination of the contract of employment or of the employment relationship.

Article 5

1. If the business preserves its autonomy, the status and function, as laid down by the laws, regulations or administrative provisions of the Member States, of the representatives or of the representation of the

employees affected by the transfer within the meaning of Article 1(1) shall be preserved.

The first subparagraph shall not apply if, under the laws, regulations, administrative provisions or practice of the Member States, the conditions necessary for the re-appointment of the representatives of the employees or for the reconstitution of the representation of the employees are fulfilled.

2. If the term of office of the representatives of the employees affected by a transfer within the meaning of Article 1(1) expires as a result of the transfer, the representatives shall continue to enjoy the protection provided by the laws, regulations, administrative provisions or practice of the Member States.

Section III

Information and consultation

Article 6

1. The transferor and the transferee shall be required to inform the representatives of their respective employees affected by a transfer within the meaning of Article 1(1) of the following:

- the reasons for the transfer,
- the legal, economic and social implications of the transfer for the employees,
- measures envisaged in relation to the employees.

The transferor must give such information to the representatives of his employees in good time before the transfer is carried out.

The transferee must give such information to the representatives of his employees in good time, and in any event before his employees are directly affected by the transfer as regards their conditions of work and employment.

2. If the transferor or the transferee envisages measures in relation to his employees, he shall consult his representatives of the employees in good time on such measures with a view to seeking agreement.

3. Member States whose laws, regulations or administrative provisions provide that representatives of the employees may have recourse to an arbitration board to obtain a decision on the measures to be taken in relation to employees may limit the obligations laid down in paragraphs 1 and 2 to cases where the transfer carried out gives rise to a change in

the business likely to entail serious disadvantages for a considerable number of the employees.

The information and consultations shall cover at least the measures envisaged in relation to the employees.

The information must be provided and consultations take place in good time before the change in the business as referred to in the first subparagraph is effected.

4. Member States may limit the obligations laid down in paragraphs 1, 2 and 3 to undertakings or businesses which, in respect of the number of employees, fulfil the conditions for the election or designation of a collegiate body representing the employees.

5. Member States may provide that where there are no representatives of the employees in an undertaking or business, the employees concerned must be informed in advance when a transfer within the meaning of Article 1(1) is about to take place.

Section IV

Final provisions

Article 7

This Directive shall not affect the right of Member States to apply or introduce laws, regulations or administrative provisions which are more favourable to employees.

Article 8

1. Member States shall bring into force the laws, regulations and administrative provisions needed to comply with this Directive within two years of its notification and shall forthwith inform the Commission thereof.

2. Member States shall communicate to the Commission the texts of the laws, regulations and administrative provisions which they adopt in the field covered by this Directive.

Article 9

Within two years following expiry of the two-year period laid down in Article 8, Member States shall forward all relevant information to the Commission in order to enable it to draw up a report on the application of this Directive for submission to the Council.

Article 10

This Directive is addressed to the Member States.

Done at Brussels, 14 February 1977.

For the Council

The President

J. Silkin

FOOTNOTES

1. OJ No C 95, 28.4.75, p. 17.
2. OJ No C 255, 7.11.75, p. 25.

 Implemented in Ireland: S.I. 306/1980.

COUNCIL DIRECTIVE

of 20 October 1980

on the approximation of the laws of the Member States relating to the protection of employees in the event of the insolvency of their employer

(80/987/EEC)

(OJ No L 283, 20.10.80, p. 23)

The Council of the European Communities,

Having regard to the Treaty establishing the European Economic Community, and in particular Article 100 thereof,

Having regard to the proposal from the Commission[1],

Having regard to the opinion of the European Parliament[2],

Having regard to the opinion of the Economic and Social Committee[3],

Whereas it is necessary to provide for the protection of employees in the event of the insolvency of their employer, in particular in order to guarantee payment of their outstanding claims, while taking account of the need for balanced economic and social development in the Community;

Whereas differences still remain between the Member States as regards the extent of the protection of employees in this respect; whereas efforts should be directed towards reducing these differences, which can have a direct effect on the functioning of the common market;

Whereas the approximation of laws in this field should, therefore, be promoted while the improvement within the meaning of Article 117 of the Treaty is maintained;

Whereas as a result of the geographical situation and the present job structures in that area, the labour market in Greenland is fundamentally different from that of the other areas of the Community;

Whereas to the extent that the Hellenic Republic is to become a member of the European Economic Community on 1 January 1981 in accordance with the Act concerning the Conditions of Accession of the Hellenic Republic and the Adjustments to the Treaties, it is appropriate to stipulate in the Annex to the Directive under the heading 'Greece', those categories of employees whose claims may be excluded in accordance with Article 1(2) of the Directive,

Has adopted this Directive:

Section I

Scope and definitions

Article 1

1. This Directive shall apply to employees' claims arising from contracts of employment or employment relationships and existing against employers who are in a state of insolvency within the meaning of Article 2(1).

2. Member States may, by way of exception, exclude claims by certain categories of employee from the scope of this Directive, by virtue of the special nature of the employee's contract of employment or employment relationship or of the existence of other forms of guarantee offering the employee protection equivalent to that resulting from this Directive.

The categories of employee referred to in the first subparagraph are listed in the Annex.

3. This Directive shall not apply to Greenland. This exception shall be re-examined in the event of any development in the job structures in that region.

Article 2

1. For the purposes of this Directive, an employer shall be deemed to be in a state of insolvency:

(a) where a request has been made for the opening of proceedings involving the employer's assets, as provided for under the laws, regulations and administrative provisions of the Member State concerned, to satisfy collectively the claims of creditors and which make it possible to take into consideration the claims referred to in Article 1(1), and

(b) where the authority which is competent pursuant to the said laws, regulations and administrative provisions has:

   – either decided to open the proceedings,

   – or established that the employer's undertaking or business has been definitively closed down and that the available assets are insufficient to warrant the opening of the proceedings.

2. This Directive is without prejudice to national law as regards the definition of the terms 'employee', 'employer', 'pay', 'right conferring immediate entitlement' and 'right conferring prospective entitlement'.

Section II

Provisions concerning guarantee institutions

Article 3

1. Member States shall take the measures necessary to ensure that guarantee institutions guarantee, subject to Article 4, payment of employees' outstanding claims resulting from contracts of employment or employment relationships and relating to pay for the period prior to a given date.

2. At the choice of the Member States, the date referred to in paragraph 1 shall be:

– either that of the onset of the employer's insolvency;

– or that of the notice of dismissal issued to the employee concerned on account of the employer's insolvency;

– or that of the onset of the employer's insolvency or that on which the contract of employment or the employment relationship with the employee concerned was discontinued on account of the employer's insolvency.

Article 4

1. Member States shall have the option to limit the liability of guarantee institutions, referred to in Article 3.

2. When Member States exercise the option referred to in paragraph 1, they shall:

- in the case referred to in Article 3(2), first indent, ensure the payment of outstanding claims relating to pay for the last three months of the contract of employment or employment relationship occurring within a period of six months preceding the date of the onset of the employer's insolvency;

- in the case referred to in Article 3(2), second indent, ensure the payment of outstanding claims relating to pay for the last three months of the contract of employment or employment relationship preceding the date of the notice of dismissal issued to the employee on account of the employer's insolvency;

- in the case referred to in Article 3(2), third indent, ensure the payment of outstanding claims relating to pay for the last 18 months of the contract of employment or employment relationship preceding the date of the onset of the employer's insolvency or the date on which the contract of employment or the employment relationship with the employee was discontinued on account of the employer's insolvency. In this case, Member States may limit the liability to make payment to pay corresponding to a period of eight weeks or to several shorter periods totalling eight weeks.

3. However, in order to avoid the payment of sums going beyond the social objective of this Directive, Member States may set a ceiling to the liability for employees' outstanding claims.

When Member States exercise this option, they shall inform the Commission of the methods used to set the ceiling.

Article 5

Member States shall lay down detailed rules for the organisation, financing and operation of the guarantee institutions, complying with the following principles in particular:

(a) the assets of the institutions shall be independent of the employers' operating capital and be inaccessible to proceedings for insolvency;

(b) employers shall contribute to financing, unless it is fully covered by the public authorities;

(c) the institutions' liabilities shall not depend on whether or not obligations to contribute to financing have been fulfilled.

Section III

Provisions concerning social security

Article 6

Member States may stipulate that Articles 3, 4 and 5 shall not apply to contributions due under national statutory social security schemes or under supplementary company or inter-company pension schemes outside the national statutory social security schemes.

Article 7

Member States shall take the measures necessary to ensure that non-payment of compulsory contributions due from the employer, before the onset of his insolvency, to their insurance institutions under national statutory social security schemes does not adversely affect employees' benefit entitlement in respect of these insurance institutions inasmuch as the employees' contributions were deducted at source from the remuneration paid.

Article 8

Member States shall ensure that the necessary measures are taken to protect the interests of employees and of persons having already left the employer's undertaking or business at the date of the onset of the employer's insolvency in respect of rights conferring on them immediate or prospective entitlement to old-age benefits, including survivors' benefits, under supplementary company or inter-company pension schemes outside the national statutory social security schemes.

Section IV

General and final provisions

Article 9

This Directive shall not affect the option of Member States to apply or introduce laws, regulations or administrative provisions which are more favourable to employees.

Article 10

This Directive shall not affect the option of Member States:

(a) to take the measures necessary to avoid abuses;

(b) to refuse or reduce the liability referred to in Article 3 or the guarantee obligation referred to in Article 7 if it appears that fulfilment of the obligation is unjustifiable because of the existence of special links between the employee and the employer and of common interests resulting in collusion between them.

Article 11

1. Member States shall bring into force the laws, regulations and administrative provisions necessary to comply with this Directive within 36 months of its notification. They shall forthwith inform the Commission thereof.

2. Member States shall communicate to the Commission the texts of the laws, regulations and administrative provisions which they adopt in the field governed by this Directive.

Article 12

Within 18 months of the expiry of the period of 36 months laid down in Article 11(1), Member States shall forward all relevant information to the Commission in order to enable it to draw up a report on the application of this Directive for submission to the Council.

Article 13

This Directive is addressed to the Member States.

Done at Luxembourg, 20 October 1980.

For the Council

The President

J. Santer

Annex

Categories of employee whose claims may be excluded from the scope of this Directive, in accordance with Article 1(2)

I. Employees having a contract of employment, or an employment relationship, of a special nature

A. GREECE

The master and the members of a crew of a fishing vessel, if and to the extent that they are remunerated by a share in the profits or gross earnings of the vessel.

B. IRELAND

1. Out-workers (i.e. persons doing piece-work in their own homes), unless they have a written contract of employment.

2. Close relatives of the employer, without a written contract of employment, whose work has to do with a private dwelling or farm in, or on, which the employer and the close relatives reside.

3. Persons who normally work for less than 18 hours a week for one or more employers and who do not derive their basic means of subsistence from the pay for this work.

4. Persons engaged in share fishing on a seasonal, casual or part-time basis.

5. The spouse of the employer.

C. NETHERLANDS

Domestic servants employed by a natural person and working less than three days a week for the natural person in question.

D. UNITED KINGDOM

1. The master and the members of the crew of a fishing vessel who are remunerated by a share in the profits or gross earnings of the vessel.

2. The spouse of the employer.

II. Employees covered by other forms of guarantee

A. GREECE

The crews of sea-going vessels.

B. IRELAND

1. Permanent and pensionable employees of local or other public authorities or statutory transport undertakings.

2. Pensionable teachers employed in the following: national schools, secondary schools, comprehensive schools, teachers' training colleges.

3. Permanent and pensionable employees of one of the voluntary hospitals funded by the Exchequer.

C. ITALY

1. Employees covered by benefits laid down by law guaranteeing that

their wages will continue to be paid in the event that the undertaking is hit by an economic crisis.

2. The crews of sea-going vessels.

D. UNITED KINGDOM

1. Registered dock workers other than those wholly or mainly engaged in work which is not dock work.

2. The crews of sea-going vessels.

FOOTNOTES

1. OJ No C 135, 9.6.78, p.2.
2. OJ No C 39, 12.2.79, p.26.
3. OJ No C 105, 26.4.79, p.15.

IRL Implemented in Ireland: See Protection of Employees (Employers' Insolvency) Act, 1984; S.I. 50/1984; S.I. 356/1984; S.I. 123/1985; S.I. 235/1985; S.I. 50/1986; S.I. 48/1988; S.I. 17/1990.

COUNCIL DIRECTIVE

of 14 October 1991

on an employer's obligation to inform employees of the conditions applicable to the contract or employment relationship

(91/533/EEC)

(OJ No L 288, 18.10.91, p. 32)

The Council of the European Communities,

Having regard to the Treaty establishing the European Economic Community, and in particular Article 100 thereof,

Having regard to the proposal from the Commission[1],

Having regard to the opinion of the European Parliament[2],

Having regard to the opinion of the Economic and Social Committee[3],

Whereas the development, in the Member States, of new forms of work has led to an increase in the number of types of employment relationship;

Whereas, faced with this development, certain Member States have considered it necessary to subject employment relationships to formal requirements; whereas these provisions are designed to provide employees with improved protection against possible infringements of their rights and to create greater transparency on the labour market;

Whereas the relevant legislation of the Member States differs considerably on such fundamental points as the requirement to inform employees in writing of the main terms of the contract or employment relationship;

Whereas differences in the legislation of Member States may have a direct effect on the operation of the common market;

Whereas Article 117 of the Treaty provides for the Member States to agree upon the need to promote improved working conditions and an improved standard of living for workers, so as to make possible their harmonisation while the improvement is being maintained;

Whereas point 9 of the Community Charter of Fundamental Social Rights for Workers, adopted at the Strasbourg European Council on 9 December 1989 by the Heads of State and Government of 11 Member States, states:

'The conditions of employment of every worker of the European Community shall be stipulated in laws, a collective agreement or a contract of employment, according to arrangements applying in each country.';

Whereas it is necessary to establish at Community level the general requirement that every employee must be provided with a document containing information on the essential elements of his contract or employment relationship;

Whereas, in view of the need to maintain a certain degree of flexibility in employment relationships, Member States should be able to exclude certain limited cases of employment relationship from this Directive's scope of application;

Whereas the obligation to provide information may be met by means of a written contract, a letter of appointment or one or more other documents or, if they are lacking, a written statement signed by the employer;

Whereas, in the case of expatriation of the employee, the latter must, in addition to the main terns of his contract or employment relationship, be supplied with relevant information connected with his secondment;

Whereas, in order to protect the interests of employees with regard to obtaining a document, any change in the main terms of the contract or employment relationship must be communicated to them in writing;

Whereas it is necessary for Member States to guarantee that employees can claim the rights conferred on them by this Directive;

Whereas Member States are to adopt the laws, regulations and legislative provisions necessary to comply with this Directive or are to ensure that both sides of industry set up the necessary provisions by agreement, with Member States being obliged to take the necessary steps enabling them at all times to guarantee the results imposed by this Directive,

Has adopted this Directive:

Article 1

Scope

1. This Directive shall apply to every paid employee having a contract or employment relationship defined by the law in force in a Member State and/or governed by the law in force in a Member State.

2. Member States may provide that this Directive shall not apply to employees having a contract or employment relationship:

(a) – with a total duration not exceeding one month, and/or

   – with a working week not exceeding eight hours; or

(b) of a casual and/or specific nature provided, in these cases, that its non-application is justified by objective considerations.

Article 2

Obligation to provide information

1. An employer shall be obliged to notify an employee to whom this Directive applies, hereinafter referred to as 'the employee', of the essential aspects of the contract or employment relationship.

2. The information referred to in paragraph 1 shall cover at least the following:

(a) the identities of the parties;

(b) the place or work; where there is no fixed or main place of work, the principle that the employee is employed at various places and the registered place of business or, where appropriate, the domicile of the employer;

(c) (i) the title, grade, nature or category of the work for which the employee is employed; or

(ii) a brief specification or description of the work;

(d) the date of commencement of the contract or employment relationship;

(e) in the case of a temporary contract or employment relationship, the expected duration thereof;

(f) the amount of paid leave to which the employee is entitled or, where this cannot be indicated when the information is given, the procedures for allocating and determining such leave;

(g) the length of the periods of notice to be observed by the employer and the employee should their contract or employment relationship be terminated or, where this cannot be indicated when the information is given, the method for determining such periods of notice;

(h) the initial basic amount, the other component elements and the frequency of payment of the remuneration to which the employee is entitled;

(i) the length of the employee's normal working day or week;

(j) where appropriate:

(i) the collective agreements governing the employee's conditions of work;

or

(ii) in the case of collective agreements concluded outside the business by special joint bodies or institutions, the name of the competent body or joint institution within which the agreements were concluded.

3. The information referred to in paragraph 2(f), (g), (h) and (i) may, where appropriate, be given in the form of a reference to the laws, regulations and administrative or statutory provisions or collective agreements governing those particular points.

Article 3

Means of information

1. The information referred to in Article 2(2) may be given to the employee, not later than two months after the commencement of employment, in the form of:

(a) a written contract of employment; and/or

(b) a letter of engagement; and/or

(c) one or more other written documents, where one of these documents contains at least all the information referred to in Article 2(2)(a), (b), (c), (d), (h) and (i).

2. Where none of the documents referred to in paragraph 1 is handed over to the employee within the prescribed period, the employer shall be obliged to give the employee, not later than two months after the commencement of employment, a written declaration signed by the employer and containing at least the information referred to in Article 2(2).

Where the document(s) referred to in paragraph 1 contain only part of the information required, the written declaration provided for in the first subparagraph of this paragraph shall cover the remaining information.

3. Where the contract or employment relationship comes to an end before expiry of a period of two months as from the date of the start of work, the information provided for in Article 2 and in this Article must be made available to the employee by the end of this period at the latest.

Article 4

Expatriate employees

1. Where an employee is required to work in a country or countries other than the Member State whose law and/or practice governs the contract or employment relationship, the document(s) referred to in Article 3 must be in his/her possession before his/her departure and must include at least the following additional information:

(a) the duration of the employment abroad;

(b) the currency to be used for the payment of remuneration;

(c) where appropriate, the benefits in cash or kind attendant on the employment abroad;

(d) where appropriate, the conditions governing the employee's repatriation.

2. The information referred to in paragraph 1(b) and (c) may, where appropriate, be given in the form of a reference to the laws, regulations and administrative or statutory provisions or collective agreements governing those particular points.

3. Paragraphs 1 and 2 shall not apply if the duration of the employment

outside the country whose law and/or practice governs the contract or employment relationship is one month or less.

Article 5

Modification of aspects of the contract or employment relationship

1. Any change in the details referred to in Articles 2(2) and 4(1) must be the subject of a written document to be given by the employer to the employee at the earliest opportunity and not later than one month after the date of entry into effect of the change in question.

2. The written document referred to in paragraph 1 shall not be compulsory in the event of a change in the laws, regulations and administrative or statutory provisions or collective agreements cited in the documents referred to in Article 3, supplemented, where appropriate, pursuant to Article 4(1).

Article 6

Form and proof of the existence of a contract or employment relationship and procedural rules

This Directive shall be without prejudice to national law and practice concerning:

- the form of the contract or employment relationship,
- proof as regards the existence and content of a contract or employment relationship,
- the relevant procedural rules.

Article 7

More favourable provisions

This Directive shall not affect Member States' prerogative to apply or to introduce laws, regulations or administrative provisions which are more favourable to employees or to encourage or permit the application of agreements which are more favourable to employees.

Article 8

Defence of rights

1. Member States shall introduce into their national legal systems such measures as are necessary to enable all employees who consider themselves wronged by failure to comply with the obligations arising

from this Directive to pursue their claims by judicial process after possible recourse to other competent authorities.

2. Member States may provide that access to the means of redress referred to in paragraph 1 are subject to the notification of the employer by the employee and the failure by the employer to reply within 15 days of notification.

However, the formality of prior notification may in no case be required in the cases referred to in Article 4, neither for workers with a temporary contract or employment relationship, nor for employees not covered by a collective agreement or by collective agreements relating to the employment relationship.

Article 9

Final provisions

1. Member States shall adopt the laws, regulations and administrative provisions necessary to comply with this Directive no later than 30 June 1993 or shall ensure by that date that the employers' and workers' representatives introduce the required provisions by way of agreement, the Member States being obliged to take the necessary steps enabling them at all times to guarantee the results imposed by this Directive.

They shall forthwith inform the Commission thereof.

2. Member States shall take the necessary measures to ensure that, in the case of employment relationships in existence upon entry into force of the provisions that they adopt, the employer gives the employee, on request, within two months of receiving that request; any of the documents referred to in Article 3, supplemented, where appropriate, pursuant to Article 4(1).

3. When Member States adopt the measures referred to in paragraph 1, such measures shall contain a reference to this Directive or shall be accompanied by such reference on the occasion of their official publication. The methods of making such a reference shall be laid down by the Member States.

4. Member States shall forthwith inform the Commission of the measures they take to implement this Directive.

Article 10

This Directive is addressed to the Member States.

Done at Luxembourg, 14 October 1991.

For the Council

The President

B. de Vries

FOOTNOTES

1. OJ No C 24, 31.1.91, p.3.
2. OJ No C 240, 16.9.91, p.21.
3. OJ No C 159, 17.6.91, p.32.

 IRL Implemented in Ireland: Terms of Employment (Information) Act, 1994; S.I. 96S/1994.

COUNCIL DIRECTIVE

of 17 February 1975

on the approximation of the laws of the Member States relating to collective redundancies

(75/129/EEC)

(OJ No L 48, 22.2.75, p.29)

The Council of the European Communities,

Having regard to the Treaty establishing the European Economic community, and in particular Article 100 thereof;

Having regard to the proposal from the Commission;

Having regard to the opinion of the European Parliament[1];

Having regard to the opinion of the Economic and Social Committee[2];

Whereas it is important that greater protection should be afforded to workers in the event of collective redundancies while taking into account the need for balanced economic and social development within the Community;

Whereas, despite increasing convergence, differences still remain between the provisions in force in the Member States of the Community concerning the practical arrangements and procedures for such redundancies and the measures designed to alleviate the consequences of redundancy for workers;

Whereas these differences can have a direct effect on the functioning of the common market;

Whereas the Council Resolution of 21 January 1974[3] concerning a social action programme makes provision for a Directive on the approximation of Member States' legislation on collective redundancies;

Whereas this approximation must therefore be promoted while the improvement is being maintained within the meaning of Article 117 of the Treaty,

Has adopted this Directive:

Section I

Definitions and scope

Article 1

1. For the purposes of this Directive:

(a) 'collective redundancies' means dismissals effected by an employer for one or more reasons not related to the individual workers concerned where, according to the choice of the Member States, the number of redundancies is:

either, over a period of 30 days:

(1) at least 10 in establishments normally employing more than 20 and less than 100 workers;

(2) at least 10% of the number of workers in establishments normally employing at least 100 but less than 300 workers;

(3) at least 30 in establishments normally employing 300 workers or more;

or, over a period of 90 days, at least 20, whatever the number of workers normally employed in the establishments in question;

(b) 'workers' representatives' means the workers' representatives provided for by the laws or practices of the Member States.

2. This Directive shall not apply to:

(a) collective redundancies affected under contracts of employment concluded for limited periods of time or for specific tasks except where such redundancies take place prior to the date of expiry or the completion of such contracts;

(b) workers employed by public administrative bodies or by establishments governed by public law (or, in Member States where this concept is unknown, by equivalent bodies);

(c) the crews of sea-going vessels;

(d) workers affected by the termination of an establishment's activities where that is the result of a judicial decision.

Section II

Consultation procedure

Article 2

1. Where an employer is contemplating collective redundancies, he shall begin consultations with the workers' representatives with a view to reaching an agreement.

2. These consultations shall, at least, cover ways and means of avoiding collective redundancies or reducing the number of workers affected, and mitigating the consequences.

3. To enable the workers' representatives to make constructive proposals the employer shall supply them with all relevant information and shall in any event give in writing the reasons for the redundancies, the number of workers to be made redundant, the number of workers normally employed and the period over which the redundancies are to be effected.

The employer shall forward to the competent public authority a copy of all the written communications referred to in the preceding subparagraph.

Section III

Procedure for collective redundancies

Article 3

1. Employers shall notify the competent public authority in writing of any projected collective redundancies.

This notification shall contain all relevant information concerning the projected collective redundancies and the consultations with workers' representatives provided for in Article 2, and particularly the reasons for the redundancies, the number of workers to be made redundant, the number of workers normally employed and the period over which the redundancies are to be effected.

2. Employers shall forward to the workers' representatives a copy of the notification provided for in paragraph 1.

The workers' representatives may send any comments they may have to the competent public authority.

Article 4

1. Projected collective redundancies notified to the competent public authority shall take effect not earlier than 30 days after the notification referred to in Article 3(1) without prejudice to any provisions governing individual rights with regard to notice of dismissal. Member States may grant the competent public authority the power to reduce the period provided for in the preceding subparagraph.

2. The period provided for in paragraph 1 shall be used by the competent public authority to seek solutions in the problems raised by the projected collective redundancies.

3. Where the initial period provided for in paragraph 1 is shorter than 60 days, Member States may grant the competent public authority the power to extend the initial period to 60 days following notification where the problems raised by the projected collective redundancies are not likely to be solved within the initial period.

Member States may grant the competent public authority wider powers of extension.

The employer must be informed of the extension and the grounds for it before expiry of the initial period provided for in paragraph 1.

Section IV

Final provisions

Article 5

This Directive shall not affect the right of Member States to apply or to introduce laws, regulations or administrative provisions which are more favourable to workers.

Article 6

1. Member States shall bring into force the laws, regulations and administrative provisions needed in order to comply with this Directive within two years following its notification and shall forthwith inform the Commission thereof.

2. Member States shall communicate to the Commission the texts of the laws, regulations and administrative provisions which they adopt in the field covered by this Directive.

Article 7

Within two years following expiry of the two year period laid down in Article 6, Member States shall forward all relevant information to the Commission to enable it to draw up a report for submission to the Council on the application of this Directive.

Article 8

This Directive is addressed to the Member States.

Done at Brussels, 17 February 1975.

For the Council

The President

R. Ryan

FOOTNOTES

1. OJ No C 19, 12.4.73, p.10.
2. OJ No C 100, 22.11.73, p.11.
3. OJ No C 13, 12.2.74, p.1.

 IRL Implemented in Ireland: Protection of Employment Act, 1977; S.I. 140/1977; S.I. 50/1986.

COUNCIL DIRECTIVE 92/56/EEC

of 24 June 1992

amending Directive 75/129/EEC on the approximation of the laws of the Member States relating to collective redundancies

(OJ No L 245, 26.8.92, p.3)

The Council of the European Communities,

Having regard to the Treaty establishing the European Economic Community, and in particular Article 100 thereof,

Having regard to the proposal from the Commission[1],

Having regard to the opinion of the European Parliament[2],

Having regard to the opinion of the Economic and Social Committee[3],

Whereas the Community Charter of the Fundamental Social Rights of Workers, adopted at the Regulation Council meeting held in Strasbourg on 9 December 1989 by the Heads of State or Government of eleven Member States, states *inter alia* in point 7, first paragraph, first sentence, and second paragraph; in point 17, first paragraph; and in point 18, third indent:

'7. The completion of the internal market must lead to an improvement in the living and working conditions of workers in the European Community (...).

The improvement must cover, where necessary, the development of certain aspects of employment regulations such as procedures for collective redundancies and those regarding bankruptcies.

17. Information, consultation and participation for workers must be developed along appropriate lines, taking account of the practices in force in the various Member States.

(...)

18. Such information, consultation and participation must be implemented in due time, particularly in the following cases:

(– ...)

(– ...)

– in cases of collective redundancy procedures;

(– ...)';

Whereas, in order to calculate the number of redundancies provided for in the definition of collective redundancies within the meaning of Council Directive 75/129/EEC of 17 February 1975 on the approximation of the laws of the Member States relating to collective redundancies[4], other forms of termination of employment contracts on the initiative of the employer should be equated to redundancies, provided that there are at least five redundancies;

Whereas it should be stipulated that Directive 75/129/EEC applies in principle also to collective redundancies resulting where the establishment's activities are terminated as a result of a judicial decision;

Whereas the Member States should be given the option of stipulating that workers' representatives may call on experts on grounds of the technical complexity of the matters which are likely to be the subject of the informing and consulting;

Whereas the provisions of Directive 75/129/EEC should be clarified and supplemented as regards the employer's obligations regarding the informing and consulting of workers' representatives;

Whereas it is necessary to ensure that employers' obligations as regards information, consultation and notification apply independently of the fact that the decision on collective redundancies emanates from the employer or from an undertaking which controls that employer;

Whereas Member States should ensure that workers' representatives and/or workers have at their disposal administrative and/or judicial procedures in order to ensure that the obligations laid down in Directive 75/129/EEC are fulfilled,

Has adopted this Directive:

Article 1

Directive 75/129/EEC is hereby amended as follows:

1. Article 1 shall be amended as follows:

(*a*) the following subparagraph shall be added to paragraph 1:

'For the purpose of calculating the number of redundancies provided for in the first subparagraph of point (a), terminations of an employment contract which occur to the individual workers concerned shall be assimilated to redundancies, provided that there are at least five redundancies.';

(*b*) subparagraph 2(d) shall be deleted.

2. Section II shall be replaced by the following:

'Section II

Information and consultation

Article 2

1. Where an employer is contemplating collective redundancies, he shall begin consultations with the workers' representatives in good time with a view to reaching an agreement.

2. These consultations shall, at least, cover ways and means of avoiding collective redundancies or reducing the number of workers affected, and of mitigating the consequences by recourse to accompanying social measures aimed, *inter alia*, at aid for redeploying or retraining workers made redundant.

Member States may provide that the workers' representatives may call upon the services of experts in accordance with national legislation and/or practice.

3. To enable workers' representatives to make constructive proposals, the employers shall in good time during the course of the consultations:

(a) supply them with all relevant information and

(b) in any event notify them in writing of:

   (i) the reasons for the projected redundancies;

   (ii) the number of categories of workers to be made redundant;

   (iii) the number and categories of workers normally employed;

   (iv) the period over which the projected redundancies are to be effected;

   (v) the criteria proposed for the selection of the workers to be made redundant in so far as national legislation and/or practice confers the power therefor upon the employer;

   (vi) the method for calculating any redundancy payments other than those arising out of national legislation and/or practice.

The employer shall forward to the competent public authority a copy of, at least, the elements of the written communication which are provided for in the first subparagraph, point (b), subpoints (i) to (v).

4. The obligations laid down in paragraphs 1, 2 and 3 shall apply irrespective of whether the decision regarding collective redundancies is being taken by the employer or by an undertaking controlling the employer.

In considering alleged breaches of the information, consultation and notification requirements laid down by this Directive, account shall not be taken of any defence on the part of the employer on the ground that the necessary information has not been provided to the employer by the undertaking which took the decision leading to collective redundancies.';

3. in Article 3(1) the following subparagraph shall be added after the first subparagraph:

'However, Member States may provide that in the case of planned collective redundancies arising from termination of the establishment's activities as a result of a judicial decision, the employer shall be obliged to notify the competent public authority in writing only if the latter so requests.';

4. in Article 4, the following paragraph shall be added after paragraph 3:

'4. Member States need not apply this Article to collective redundancies arising from termination of the establishment's activities where this is the result of a judicial decision.';

5. the following phrase shall be inserted at the end of Article 5:

'or to promote or to allow the application of collective agreements more favourable to workers.';

6. the following text shall be inserted after Article 5:

'*Article 5a*

Member States shall ensure that judicial and/or administrative procedures for the enforcement of obligations under this Directive are available to the workers' representatives and/or workers.'

Article 2

1. Member States shall bring into force the laws, regulations and administrative provisions necessary to comply with this Directive at the latest two years after its adoption or shall ensure, at the latest two years after adoption, that the employers' and workers' representatives introduce the required provisions by way of agreement, the Member States being obliged to take the necessary steps enabling them at all times to guarantee the results imposed by this Directive.

They shall immediately inform the Commission thereof.

2. When Member States adopt the provisions referred to in paragraph 1, such provisions shall contain a reference to this Directive or shall be accompanied by such reference at the time of their official publication. The procedure for such reference shall be adopted by Member States.

3. Member States shall forward to the Commission the text of any fundamental provisions of national law already adopted or being adopted in the area governed by this Directive.

Article 3

This Directive is addressed to the Member States.

Done at Luxembourg, 24 June 1992.

For the Council

The President

José da Silva Peneda

FOOTNOTES

1. OJ No C 310, 30.11.91, p.5 and OJ No C 117, 8.5.92, p.10.
2. OJ No C 94, 13.4.92, p.157.
3. OJ No C 79, 30.3.92, p.12.
4. OJ No L 48, 22.2.75, p.29.

RL Implemented in Ireland: Not yet implemented in Ireland (13.7.1994)
(Editorial note: draft bill prepared).

COUNCIL DIRECTIVE 93/104/EEC

of 23 November 1993

concerning certain aspects of the organisation of working time

(OJ No L 307, 13.12.93, p.18)

The Council of the European Union,

Having regard to the Treaty establishing the European Community, and in particular Article 118a thereof,

Having regard to the proposal from the Commission[1],

In cooperation with the European Parliament[2],

Having regard to the opinion of the Economic and Social Committee[3],

Whereas Article 118a of the Treaty provides that the Council shall adopt, by means of directives, minimum requirements for encouraging improvements, especially in the working environment, to ensure a better level of protection of the safety and health of workers;

Whereas, under the terms of that Article, those directives are to avoid imposing administrative, financial and legal constraints in a way which would hold back the creation and development of small and medium-sized undertakings;

Whereas the provisions of Council Directive 89/391/EEC of 12 June 1989 on the introduction of measures to encourage improvements in the safety and health of workers at work[4] are fully applicable to the areas covered by this Directive without prejudice to more stringent and/or specific provisions contained therein;

Whereas the Community Charter of the Fundamental Social Rights of Workers, adopted at the meeting of the European Council held at

Strasbourg on 9 December 1989 by the Heads of State or of Government
of 11 Member States, and in particular points 7, first subparagraph, 8
and 19, first subparagraph, thereof, declared that:

'7. The completion of the internal market must lead to an
improvement in the living and working conditions of workers in the
European Community. This process must result from an
approximation of these conditions while the improvement is being
maintained, as regards in particular the duration and organisation of
working time and forms of employment other than open-ended
contracts, such as fixed-term contracts, part-time working,
temporary work and seasonal work.

8. Every worker in the European Community shall have a right to a
weekly rest period and to annual paid leave, the duration of which
must be progressively harmonised in accordance with national
practices.

19. Every worker must enjoy satisfactory health and safety
conditions in his working environment. Appropriate measures must
be taken in order to achieve further harmonisation of conditions in
this area while maintaining the improvements made.';

Whereas the improvement of workers' safety, hygiene and health at work
is an objective which should not be subordinated to purely economic
considerations;

Whereas this Directive is a practical contribution towards creating the
social dimension of the internal market;

Whereas laying down minimum requirements with regard to the
organisation of working time is likely to improve the working conditions
of workers in the Community;

Whereas, in order to ensure the safety and health of Community workers,
the latter must be granted minimum daily, weekly and annual periods of
rest and adequate breaks; whereas it is also necessary in this context to
place a maximum limit on weekly working hours;

Whereas account should be taken of the principles of the International
Labour Organisation with regard to the organisation of working time,
including those relating to night work;

Whereas, with regard to the weekly rest period, due account should be
taken of the diversity of cultural, ethnic, religious and other factors in the
Member States; whereas, in particular, it is ultimately for each Member
State to decide whether Sunday should be included in the weekly rest
period, and if so to what extent;

Whereas research has shown that the human body is more sensitive at night to environmental disturbances and also to certain burdensome forms of work organisation and that long periods of night work can be detrimental to the health of workers and can endanger safety at the workplace;

Whereas there is a need to limit the duration of periods of night work, including overtime, and to provide for employers who regularly use night workers to bring this information to the attention of the competent authorities if they so request;

Whereas it is important that night workers should be entitled to a free health assessment prior to their assignment and thereafter at regular intervals and that whenever possible they should be transferred to day work for which they are suited if they suffer from health problems;

Whereas the situation of night and shift workers requires that the level of safety and health protection should be adapted to the nature of their work and that the organisation and functioning of protection and prevention services and resources should be efficient;

Whereas specific working conditions may have detrimental effects on the safety and health of workers; whereas the organisation of work according to a certain pattern must take account of the general principle of adapting work to the worker;

Whereas, given the specific nature of the work concerned, it may be necessary to adopt separate measures with regard to the organisation of working time in certain sectors or activities which are excluded from the scope of this Directive;

Whereas, in view of the question likely to be raised by the organisation of working time within an undertaking, it appears desirable to provide for flexibility in the application of certain provisions of this Directive, whilst ensuring compliance with the principles of protecting the safety and health of workers;

Whereas it is necessary to provide that certain provisions may be subject to derogations implemented, according to the case, by the Member States or the two sides of industry; whereas, as a general rule, in the event of a derogation, the workers concerned must be given equivalent compensatory rest periods,

Has adopted this Directive:

Section I

Scope and definitions

Article 1

Purpose and scope

1. This Directive lays down minimum safety and health requirements for the organisation of working time.

2. This Directive applies to:

(*a*) minimum periods of daily rest, weekly rest and annual leave, to breaks and maximum weekly working time; and

(*b*) certain aspect of night work, shift work and patterns of work.

3. This Directive shall apply to all sectors of activity, both public and private, within the meaning of Article 2 of Directive 89/391/EEC, without prejudice to Article 17 of this Directive, with the exception of air, rail, road, sea, inland waterway and lake transport, sea fishing, other work at sea and the activities of doctors in training;

4. The provisions of Directive 89/391/EEC are fully applicable to the matters referred to in paragraph 2, without prejudice to more stringent and/or specific provisions contained in this Directive.

Article 2

Definitions

For the purposes of this Directive, the following definitions shall apply:

1. 'working time' shall mean any period during which the worker is working, at the employer's disposal and carrying out his activity or duties, in accordance with national laws and/or practice;

2. 'rest period' shall mean any period which is not working time;

3. 'night time' shall mean any period of not less than seven hours, as defined by national law, and which must include in any case the period between midnight and 5 a.m.;

4. 'night worker' shall mean:

(*a*) on the one hand, any worker, who, during night time, works at least three hours of his daily working time as a normal course; and

(b) on the other hand, any worker who is likely during night time to work a certain proportion of his annual working time, as defined at the choice of the Member State concerned:

(i) by national legislation, following consultation with the two sides of industry; or

(ii) by collective agreements or agreements concluded between the two sides of industry at national or regional level;

5. 'shift work' shall mean any method of organising work in shifts whereby workers succeed each other at the same work stations according to a certain pattern, including a rotating pattern, and which may be continuous or discontinuous, entailing the need for workers to work at different times over a given period of days or weeks;

6. 'shift worker' shall mean any worker whose work schedule is part of shift work.

Section II

Minimum rest periods – other aspects of the organisation of working time

Article 3

Daily rest

Member States shall take the measures necessary to ensure that every worker is entitled to a minimum daily rest period of 11 consecutive hours per 24-hour period.

Article 4

Breaks

Member States shall take the measures necessary to ensure that, where the working day is longer than six hours, every worker is entitled to a rest break, the details of which, including duration and the terms on which it is granted, shall be laid down in collective agreements or agreements between the two sides of industry or, failing that, by national legislation.

Article 5

Weekly rest period

Member States shall take the measures necessary to ensure that, per each seven-day period, every worker is entitled to a minimum uninterrupted rest period of 24 hours plus the 11 hours' daily rest referred to in Article 3.

The minimum rest period referred to in the first subparagraph shall in principle include Sunday.

If objective, technical or work organisation conditions so justify, a minimum rest period of 24 hours may be applied.

Article 6

Maximum weekly working time

Member States shall take the measures necessary to ensure that, in keeping with the need to protect the safety and health of workers:

1. the period of weekly working time is limited by means of laws, regulations or administrative provisions or by collective agreements or agreements between the two sides of industry;

2. the average working time for each seven-day period, including overtime, does not exceed 48 hours.

Article 7

Annual leave

1. Member States shall take the measures necessary to ensure that every worker is entitled to paid annual leave of at least four weeks in accordance with the conditions for entitlement to, and granting of, such leave laid down by national legislation and/or practice.

2. The minimum period of paid annual leave may not be replaced by an allowance in lieu, except where the employment relationship is terminated.

Section III

Night work – shift work – patterns of work

Article 8

Length of night work

Members shall take the measures necessary to ensure that:

1. normal hours of work for night workers do not exceed an average of eight hours in any 24-hour period;

2. night workers whose work involves special hazards or heavy physical

or mental strain do not work more then eight hours in any period of 24 hours during which they perform night work.

For the purposes of the aforementioned, work involving special hazards or heavy physical or mental strain shall be defined by national legislation and/or practice or by collective agreements or agreements concluded between the two sides of industry, taking account of the specific effects and hazards of night work.

Article 9

Health assessment and transfer of night workers to day work

1. Member States shall take the measures necessary to ensure that:

(a) night workers are entitled to a free health assessment before their assignment and thereafter at regular intervals:

(b) night workers suffering from health problems recognised as being connected with the fact that they perform night work are transferred whenever possible to day work to which they are suited.

2. The free health assessment referred to in paragraph 1(a) must comply with medical confidentiality.

3. The free health assessment referred to in paragraph 1(a) may be conducted with the national health system.

Article 10

Guarantees for night-time working

Member States may make the work of certain categories of night workers subject to certain guarantees, under conditions laid down by national legislation and/or practice, in the case of workers who incur risks to their safety or health linked to night-time working.

Article 11

Notification of regular use of night workers

Member States shall take the measures necessary to ensure that an employer who regularly uses night workers brings this information to the attention of the competent authorities if they so request.

Article 12

Safety and health protection

Member States shall take the measures necessary to ensure that:

1. night workers and shift workers have safety and health protection appropriate to the nature of their work;

2. appropriate protection and prevention services or facilities with regard to the safety and health of night workers and shift workers are equivalent to those applicable to other workers and are available at all times.

Article 13

Pattern of work

Member States shall take the measures necessary to ensure that an employer who intends to organise work according to a certain pattern takes account of the general principle of adapting work to the worker, with a view, in particular, to alleviating monotonous work and work at a predetermined work-rate, depending on the type of activity, and of safety and health requirements, especially as regard breaks during working time.

Section IV

Miscellaneous provisions

Article 14

More specific Community provisions

The provisions of this Directive shall not apply where other Community instruments contain more specific requirement concerning certain occupations or occupational activities.

Article 15

More favourable provisions

This Directive shall not affect Member States' right to apply or introduce laws, regulations or administrative provisions more favourable to the protection of the safety and health of workers or to facilitate or permit the application of collective agreements or agreements concluded between the two sides of industry which are more favourable to the protection of the safety and health of workers.

Article 16

Reference periods

Member States may lay down:

1. for the application of Article 5 (weekly rest period), a reference period not exceeding 14 days;

2. for the application of Article 6 (maximum weekly working time), a reference period not exceeding four months.

   The periods of paid annual leave, granted in accordance with Article 7, and the periods of sick leave shall not be included or shall be neutral in the calculation of the average;

3. for the application of Article 8 (length of night work), a reference period defined after consultation of the two sides of industry or by collective agreements or agreements concluded between the two sides of industry at national or regional level.

   If the minimum weekly rest period of 24 hours required by Article 5 falls within that reference period, it shall not be included in the calculation of the average.

Article 17

Derogations

1. With due regard for the general principles of the protection of the safety and health of workers, Member States may derogate from Article 3, 4, 5, 6, 8 or 16 when, on account of the specific characteristics of the activity concerned, the duration of the working time is not measured and/or predetermined or can be determined by the workers themselves, and particularly in the case of:

(a) managing executives or other persons with autonomous decision-taking powers;

(b) family workers; or

(c) workers officiating at religious ceremonies in churches and religious communities.

2. Derogations may be adopted by means of laws, regulations or administrative provisions or by means of collective agreements or agreements between the two sides of industry provided that the workers concerned are afforded equivalent periods of compensatory rest or that, in exceptional cases in which it is not possible, for objective reasons, to

grant such equivalent periods of compensatory rest, the workers concerned are afforded appropriate protection:

2.1. from Articles 3, 4, 5, 8 and 16:

   (a) in the case of activities where the worker's place of work and his place of residence are distant from one another or where the worker's different places of work are distant from one another;

   (b) in the case of security and surveillance activities requiring a permanent presence in order to protect property and persons, particular security guards and caretakers or security firms;

   (c) in the case of activities involving the need for continuity of service or production, particularly:

      (i) services relating to the reception, treatment and/or care provided by hospitals or similar establishments, residential institutions and prisons;

      (ii) dock or airport workers;

      (iii) press, radio, television, cinematographic production, postal and telecommunications services, ambulance, fire and civil protection services;

      (iv) gas, water and electricity production, transmission and distribution, household refuse collection and incineration plants;

      (v) industries in which work cannot be interrupted on technical grounds;

      (vi) research and development activities;

      (vii) agriculture;

   (d) where there is a foreseeable surge of activity, particularly in:

      (i) agriculture;

      (ii) tourism;

      (iii) postal services;

2.2. from Articles 3, 4, 5, 8 and 16:

   (a) in the circumstances described in Article 5(4) of Directive 89/391/EEC;

   (b) in cases of accident or imminent risk of accident;

2.3. from Articles 3 and 5:

   (a) in the case of shift work activities, each time the worker changes shift and cannot take daily and/or weekly rest periods between the end of one shift and the start of the next one;

(*b*) in the case of activities involving periods of work split up over the day, particularly those of cleaning staff.

3. Derogations may be made from Articles 3, 4, 5, 8 and 16 by means of collective agreements or agreements concluded between the two sides of industry at national or regional level or, in conformity with the rules laid down by them, by means of collective agreements or agreements concluded between the two sides of industry at a lower level.

Member States in which there is no statutory system ensuring the conclusion of collective agreements or agreements concluded between the two sides of industry at national or regional level, on the matters covered by this Directive, or those Member States in which there is a specific legislative framework for this purpose and within the limits thereof, may, in accordance with national legislation and/or practice, allow derogations from Articles 3, 4, 5, 8 and 16 by way of collective agreements or agreements concluded between the two sides of industry at the appropriate collective level.

The derogations provided for in the first and second subparagraphs shall be allowed on condition that equivalent compensating rest periods are granted to the workers concerned or, in exceptional cases where it is not possible for objective reasons to grant such periods, the workers concerned are afforded appropriate protection.

Member States may lay down rules:

– for the application of this paragraph by the two sides of industry, and

– for the extension of the provisions of collective agreements or agreements concluded in conformity with this paragraph to other workers in accordance with national legislation and/or practice.

4. The option to derogate from point 2 of Article 16, provided in paragraph 2, points 2.1 and 2.2 and in paragraph 3 of this Article, may not result in the establishment of a reference period exceeding six months.

However, Member States shall have the option, subject to compliance with the general principles relating to the protection of the safety and health of workers, of allowing, for objective or technical reasons or reasons concerning the organisation of work, collective agreements or agreements concluded between the two sides of industry to set reference periods in no event exceeding 12 months.

Before the expiry of a period of seven years from the date referred to in

Article 18(1)(a), the Council shall, on the basis of a Commission proposal accompanied by an appraisal report, re-examine the provisions of this paragraph and decide what action to take.

Article 18

Final provisions

1. (a) Member States shall adopt the laws, regulations and administrative provisions necessary to comply with this Directive by 23 November 1996, or shall ensure by that date that the two sides of industry establish the necessary measures by agreement, with Member States being obliged to take any necessary steps to enable them to guarantee at all times that the provisions laid down by this Directive are fulfilled.

   (b) (i) However, a Member State shall have the option not to apply Article 6, while respecting the general principles of the protection of the safety and health of workers, and provided it takes the necessary measures to ensure that:

   – no employer requires a worker to work more than 48 hours over a seven-day period, calculated as an average for the reference period referred to in point 2 of Article 16, unless he has first obtained such work,

   – no worker is subjected to any detriment by his employer because he is not willing to give his agreement to perform such work,

   – the employer keeps up-to-date records of all workers who carry out such work,

   – the records are placed at the disposal of the competent authorities, which may, for reasons connected with the safety and/or health of workers, prohibit or restrict the possibility of exceeding the maximum weekly working hours,

   – the employer provides the competent authorities at their request with information on cases in which agreement has been given by workers to perform work exceeding 48 hours over a period of seven days, calculated as an average for the reference period referred to in point 2 of Article 16.

   Before the expiry of a period of seven years from the date referred to in (a), the Council shall, on the basis of a Commission proposal accompanied by an appraisal report, re-examine the provisions of this point (i) and decide on what action to take.

(ii) Similarly, Member States shall have the option, as regards the application of Article 7, of making use of a transitional period of not more than three years from the date referred to in (a), provided that during that transitional period:

- every worker receives three weeks' paid annual leave in accordance with the conditions of the entitlement to, and granting of, such leave laid down by national legislation and/or practice, and

- the three-week period of paid annual leave may not be replaced by an allowance in lieu, except where the employment relationship is terminated.

(c) Member States shall forthwith inform the Commission thereof.

2. When Member States adopt the measures referred to in paragraph 1, they shall contain a reference to this Directive or shall be accompanied by such reference on the occasion of their official publication. The methods of making such a reference shall be laid down by the Member States.

3. Without prejudice to the right of Member States to develop, in the light of changing circumstances, different legislative, regulatory or contractual provisions in the field of working time, as long as the minimum requirements provided for in this Directive are complied with, implementation of this Directive shall not constitute valid grounds for reducing the general level of protection afforded to workers.

4. Member States shall communicate to the Commission the texts of the provisions of national law already adopted or being adopted in the field governed by this Directive.

5. Member States shall report to the Commission every five years on the practical implementation of the provisions of this Directive, indicating the viewpoints of the two sides of industry.

The Commission shall inform the European Parliament, the Council, the Economic and Social Committee and the Advisory Committee on Safety, Hygiene and Health Protection at Work thereof.

6. Every five years the Commission shall submit to the European Parliament, the Council and the Economic and Social Committee a report on the application of this Directive taking into account paragraphs 1, 2, 3, 4 and 5.

Article 19

This Directive is addressed to the Member States.

Done at Brussels, 23 November 1993.

For the Council

The President

M. Smet

FOOTNOTES

1. OJ No C 254, 9.10.90, p.4.
2. OJ No C 72, 18.3.91, p.95; and Decision of 27 October 1993, OJ No C 312, 22.11.93, p.125.
3. OJ No C 60, 8.3.91, p.26.
4. OJ No L 183, 29.6.89, p.1.

✴IRL✴ Implemented in Ireland: To be implemented by 23.11.1996.

(c) Equality

COUNCIL DIRECTIVE

of 10 February 1975

on the approximation of the laws of the Member States relating to the application of the principle of equal pay for men and women

(75/117/EEC)

(OJ No L 45, 19.2.75, p.19)

The Council of the European Communities,

Having regard to the Treaty establishing the European Economic Community, and in particular Article 100 thereof;

Having regard to the proposal from the Commission;

Having regard to the opinion of the European Parliament[1];

Having regard to the opinion of the Economic and Social Committee[2];

Whereas implementation of the principle that men and women should receive equal pay contained in Article 119 of the Treaty is an integral part of the establishment and functioning of the common market;

Whereas it is primarily the responsibility of the Member States to ensure the application of this principle by means of appropriate laws, regulations and administrative provisions;

Whereas the Council resolution of 21 January 1974[3] concerning a social action programme, aimed at making it possible to harmonise living and working conditions while the improvement is being maintained and at achieving a balanced social and economic development of the Community, recognised that priority should be given to action taken on behalf of women as regards access to employment and vocational training and advancement, and as regards working conditions, including pay;

Whereas it is desirable to reinforce the basic laws by standards aimed at facilitating the practical application of the principle of equality in such a way that all employees in the Community can be protected in these matters;

Whereas differences continue to exist in the various Member States despite the efforts made to apply the resolution of the conference of the Member States of 30 December 1961 on equal pay for men and women and whereas, therefore, the national provisions should be approximated as regards application of the principle of equal pay,

Has adopted this Directive:

Article 1

The principle of equal pay for men and women outlined in Article 119 of the Treaty, hereinafter called 'principle of equal pay', means, for the same work or for work to which equal value is attributed, the elimination of all discrimination on grounds of sex with regard to all aspects and conditions of remuneration.

In particular, where a job classification system is used for determining pay, it must be based on the same criteria for both men and women and so drawn up as to exclude any discrimination on grounds of sex.

Article 2

Member States shall introduce into their national legal systems such measures as are necessary to enable all employees who consider themselves wronged by failure to apply the principle of equal pay to pursue their claims by judicial process after possible recourse to other competent authorities.

Article 3

Member States shall abolish all discrimination between men and women arising from laws, regulations or administrative provisions which is contrary to the principle of equal pay.

Article 4

Member States shall take the necessary measures to ensure that provisions appearing in collective agreements, wage scales, wage agreements or individual contracts of employment which are contrary to the principle of equal pay shall be, or may be declared, null and void or may be amended.

Article 5

Member States shall take the necessary measures to protect employees against dismissal by the employer as a reaction to a complaint within the undertaking or to any legal proceedings aimed at enforcing compliance with the principle of equal pay.

Article 6

Member States shall, in accordance with their national circumstances and legal systems, take the measures necessary to ensure that the principle of equal pay is applied. They shall see that effective means are available to take care that this principle is observed.

Article 7

Member States shall take care that the provisions adopted pursuant to this Directive, together with the relevant provisions already in force, are brought to the attention of employees by all appropriate means, for example at their place of employment.

Article 8

1. Member States shall put into force the laws, regulations and administrative provisions necessary in order to comply with this Directive within one year of its notification and shall immediately inform the Commission thereof.

2. Member States shall communicate to the Commission the texts of the laws, regulations and administrative provisions which they adopt in the field covered by this Directive.

Article 9

Within two years of the expiry of the one-year period referred to in Article 8, Member States shall forward all necessary information to the Commission to enable it to draw up a report on the application of this Directive for submission to the Council.

Article 10

This Directive is addressed to the Member States.

Done at Brussels, 10 February 1975.

For the Council

The President

G. FitzGerald

FOOTNOTES

1. OJ No C 55, 13.5.74, p.43.
2. OJ No C 88, 26.7.74, p.7.
3. OJ No C 13, 12.2.74, p.1.

RL Implemented in Ireland: Anti-discrimination (Pay) Act, 1974, Employment Equality Act, 1977.

COUNCIL DIRECTIVE

of 9 February 1976

on the implementation of the principle of equal treatment for men and women as regards access to employment, vocational training and promotion, and working conditions

(76/207/EEC)

(OJ No L 39, 14.2.76, p. 40)

The Council of the European Communities,

Having regard to the Treaty establishing the European Economic Community, and in particular Article 235 thereof,

Having regard to the proposal from the Commission,

Having regard to the opinion of the European Parliament[1],

Having regard to the opinion of the Economic and Social Committee[2],

Whereas the Council, in its resolution of 21 January 1974 concerning a social action programme[3], included among the priorities action for the purpose of achieving equality between men and women as regards access to employment and vocational training and promotion and as regards working conditions, including pay;

Whereas, with regard to pay, the Council adopted on 10 February 1975 Directive 75/117/EEC on the approximation of the laws of the Member States relating to the application of the principle of equal pay for men and women[4];

Whereas Community action to achieve the principle of equal treatment for men and women in respect of access to employment and vocational training and promotion and in respect of other working conditions also appears to be necessary; whereas, equal treatment for male and female workers constitutes one of the objectives of the Community, in so far as the harmonisation of living and working conditions while maintaining their improvement are *inter alia* to be furthered; whereas the Treaty does not confer the necessary specific powers for this purpose;

Whereas the definition and progressive implementation of the principle of equal treatment in matters of social security should be ensured by means of subsequent instruments,

Has adopted this Directive:

Article 1

1. The purpose of this Directive is to put into effect in the Member States the principle of equal treatment for men and women as regards access to employment, including promotion, and to vocational training and as regards working conditions and, on the conditions referred to in paragraph 2, social security. This principle is hereinafter referred to as 'the principle of equal treatment.'

2. With a view to ensuring the progressive implementation of the principle of equal treatment in matters of social security, the Council, acting on a proposal from the Commission, will adopt provisions defining its substance, its scope and the arrangements for its application.

Article 2

1. For the purposes of the following provisions, the principle of equal treatment shall mean that there shall be no discrimination whatsoever on grounds of sex either directly or indirectly by reference in particular to marital or family status.

2. This Directive shall be without prejudice to the right of Member States to exclude from its field of application those occupational activities and, where appropriate, the training leading thereto, for which, by reason of their nature or the context in which they are carried out, the sex of the worker constitutes a determining factor.

3. This Directive shall be without prejudice to provisions concerning the protection of women, particularly as regards pregnancy and maternity.

4. This Directive shall be without prejudice to measures to promote equal opportunity for men and women, in particular by removing existing inequalities which affect women's opportunities in the areas referred to in Article 1(1).

Article 3

1. Application of the principle of equal treatment means that there shall be no discrimination whatsoever on grounds of sex in the conditions, including selection criteria, for access to all jobs or posts, whatever the sector or branch of activity, and to all levels of the occupational hierarchy.

2. To this end, Member States shall take the measures necessary to ensure that:

(a) any laws, regulations and administrative provisions contrary to the principle of equal treatment shall be abolished;

(b) any provisions contrary to the principle of equal treatment which are included in collective agreements, individual contracts of employment, internal rules of undertakings or in rules governing the independent occupations and professions shall be, or may be declared, null and void or may be amended;

(c) those laws, regulations and administrative provisions contrary to the principle of equal treatment when the concern for protection which originally inspired them is no longer well founded shall be revised; and that where similar provisions are included in collective agreements labour and management shall be requested to undertake the desired revision.

Article 4

Application of the principle of equal treatment with regard to access to all types and to all levels of vocational guidance, vocational training, advanced vocational training and retraining, means that Member States shall take all necessary measures to ensure that:

(a) any laws, regulations and administrative provisions contrary to the principle of equal treatment shall be abolished;

(b) any provisions contrary to the principle of equal treatment which are included in collective agreements, individual contracts of employment, internal rules of undertakings or in rules governing the independent occupations and professions shall be, or may be declared, null and void or may be amended;

(c) without prejudice to the freedom granted in certain Member States to certain private training establishments, vocational guidance, vocational training, advanced vocational training and retraining shall be accessible on the basis of the same criteria and at the same levels without any discrimination on grounds of sex.

Article 5

1. Application of the principle of equal treatment with regard to working conditions, including the conditions governing dismissal, means that men and women shall be guaranteed the same conditions without discrimination on grounds of sex.

2. To this end, Member States shall take the measures necessary to ensure that:

(a) any laws, regulations and administrative provisions contrary to the principle of equal treatment shall be abolished;

(b) any provisions contrary to the principle of equal treatment which are included in collective agreements, individual contracts of employment, internal rules of undertakings or in rules governing the independent occupations and professions shall be, or may be declared, null and void or may be amended;

(c) those laws, regulations and administrative provisions contrary to the principle of equal treatment when the concern for protection which originally inspired them is no longer well founded shall be revised; and that where similar provisions are included in collective agreements labour and management shall be requested to undertake the desired revision.

Article 6

Member States shall introduce into their national legal systems such measures as are necessary to enable all persons who consider themselves wronged by failure to apply to them the principle of equal treatment within the meaning of Articles 3, 4 and 5 to pursue their claims by judicial process after possible recourse to other competent authorities.

Article 7

Member States shall take the necessary measures to protect employees against dismissal by the employer as a reaction to a complaint within the undertaking or to any legal proceedings aimed at enforcing compliance with the principle of equal treatment.

Article 8

Member States shall take care that the provisions adopted pursuant to this Directive, together with the relevant provisions already in force, are brought to the attention of employees by all appropriate means, for example at their place of employment.

Article 9

1. Member States shall put into force the laws, regulations and administrative provisions necessary in order to comply with this Directive within 30 months of its notification and shall immediately inform the Commission thereof.

However, as regards the first part of Article 3(2)(c) and the first part of Article 5(2)(c), Member States shall carry out a first examination and if necessary a first revision of the laws, regulations and administrative provisions referred to therein within four years of notification of this Directive.

2. Member States shall periodically assess the occupational activities referred to in Article 2(2) in order to decide, in the light of social developments, whether there is justification for maintaining the exclusions concerned. They shall notify the Commission of the results of this assessment.

3. Member States shall also communicate to the Commission the texts of laws, regulations and administrative provisions which they adopt in the field covered by this Directive.

Article 10

Within two years following expiry of the 30-month period laid down in the first subparagraph of Article 9(1), Member States shall forward all necessary information to the Commission to enable it to draw up a report on the application of this Directive for submission to the Council.

Article 11

This Directive is addressed to the Member States.

Done at Brussels, 9 February 1976.

For the Council

The President

G. Thorn

FOOTNOTES

1. OJ No C 111, 20.5.75, p.14.
2. OJ No C 286, 15.12.75, p.8.
3. OJ No C 13, 12.2.74, p.1.
4. OJ No L 45, 19.2.75, p.19.

 IRL Implemented in Ireland: Employment Equality Act, 1977; (amendments) S.I. 334/1977; S.I. 302/1982; S.I. 176/1985; S.I. 331/1985; S.I. 112/1987; S.I. 153/1991.

COUNCIL DIRECTIVE

of 19 December 1978

on the progressive implementation of the principle of equal treatment for men and women in matters of social security

(79/7/EEC)

(OJ No L 6, 10.1.79, p.24)

The Council of the European Communities,

Having regard to the Treaty establishing the European Economic Community, and in particular Article 235 thereof,

Having regard to the proposal from the Commission[1],

Having regard to the opinion of the European Parliament[2],

Having regard to the opinion of the Economic and Social Committee[3],

Whereas Article 1(2) of Council Directive 76/207/EEC of 9 February 1976 on the implementation of the principle of equal treatment for men and women as regards access to employment, vocational training and promotion, and working conditions[4] provides that, with a view to ensuring the progressive implementation of the principle of equal treatment in matters of social security, the Council, acting on a proposal from the Commission, will adopt provisions defining its substance, its scope and the arrangements for its application; whereas the Treaty does not confer the specific powers required for this purpose;

Whereas the principle of equal treatment in matters of social security should be implemented in the first place in the statutory schemes which provide protection against the risks of sickness, invalidity, old age, accidents at work, occupational diseases and unemployment, and in social assistance in so far as it is intended to supplement or replace the abovementioned schemes;

Whereas the implementation of the principle of equal treatment in matters of social security does not prejudice the provisions relating to the protection of women on the ground of maternity; whereas, in this respect, Member States may adopt specific provisions for women to remove existing instances of unequal treatment,

Has adopted this Directive:

Article 1

The purpose of this Directive is the progressive implementation, in the field of social security and other elements of social protection provided for in Article 3, of the principle of equal treatment for men and women in matters of social security, hereinafter referred to as 'the principle of equal treatment'.

Article 2

This Directive shall apply to the working population – including self-employed persons, workers and self-employed persons whose activity is interrupted by illness, accident or involuntary unemployment and persons seeking employment – and to retired or invalided workers and self-employed persons.

Article 3

1. This Directive shall apply to:

(a) statutory schemes which provide protection against the following risks:

- sickness,
- invalidity,
- old age,
- accidents at work and occupational diseases,
- unemployment;

(b) social assistance, in so far as it is intended to supplement or replace the schemes referred to in (a).

2. This Directive shall not apply to the provisions concerning survivors' benefits nor to those concerning family benefits, except in the case of family benefits granted by way of increases of benefits due in respect of the risks referred to in paragraph 1(a).

3. With a view to ensuring implementation of the principle of equal treatment in occupational schemes, the Council, acting on a proposal from the Commission, will adopt provisions defining its substance, its scope and the arrangements for its application.

Article 4

1. The principle of equal treatment means that there shall be no discrimination whatsoever on ground of sex either directly, or indirectly by reference in particular to marital or family status, in particular as concerns:

- the scope of the schemes and the conditions of access thereto,
- the obligation to contribute and the calculation of contributions,
- the calculation of benefits including increases due in respect of a spouse and for dependants and the conditions governing the duration and retention of entitlement to benefits.

2. The principle of equal treatment shall be without prejudice to the provisions relating to the protection of women on the grounds of maternity.

Article 5

Member States shall take the measures necessary to ensure that any laws, regulations and administrative provisions contrary to the principle of equal treatment are abolished.

Article 6

Member States shall introduce into their national legal systems such measures as are necessary to enable all persons who consider themselves wronged by failure to apply the principle of equal treatment to pursue their claims by judicial process, possibly after recourse to other competent authorities.

Article 7

1. This Directive shall be without prejudice to the right of Member States to exclude from its scope:

(a) the determination of pensionable age for the purposes of granting old-age and retirement pensions and the possible consequences thereof for other benefits;

(b) advantages in respect of old-age pension schemes granted to persons who have brought up children; the acquisition of benefit entitlements following periods of interruption of employment due to the bringing up of children;

(c) the granting of old-age or invalidity benefit entitlements by virtue of the derived entitlements of a wife;

(d) the granting of increases of long-term invalidity, old-age, accidents at work and occupational disease benefits for a dependent wife;

(e) the consequences of the exercise, before the adoption of this Directive, of a right of option not to acquire rights or incur obligations under a statutory scheme.

2. Member States shall periodically examine matters excluded under paragraph 1 in order to ascertain, in the light of social developments in the matter concerned, whether there is justification for maintaining the exclusions concerned.

Article 8

1. Member States shall bring into force the laws, regulations and administrative provisions necessary to comply with this Directive within six years of its notification. They shall immediately inform the Commission thereof.

2. Member States shall communicate to the Commission the text of laws, regulations and administrative provisions which they adopt in the field covered by this Directive, including measures adopted pursuant to Article 7(2).

They shall inform the Commission of their reasons for maintaining any existing provisions on the matters referred to in Article 7(1) and of the possibilities for reviewing them at a later date.

Article 9

Within seven years of notification of this Directive, Member States shall forward all information necessary to the Commission to enable it to draw up a report on the application of this Directive for submission to the Council and to propose such further measures as may be required for the implementation of the principle of equal treatment.

Article 10

This Directive is addressed to the Member States.

Done at Brussels, 19 December 1978.

For the Council

The President

H. -D. Genscher

FOOTNOTES

1. OJ No C 34, 11.2.77, p.3.
2. OJ No C 299, 12.12.77, p.13.
3. OJ No C 180, 28.7.77, p.36.
4. OJ No L 39, 14.2.76, p.40.

IRL Implemented in Ireland: Social Welfare (No 2) Act, 1986, section 6; S.I. 173/1976; S.I. 365/1986; Social Welfare Act, 1988.

COUNCIL DIRECTIVE

of 24 July 1986

on the implementation of the principle of equal treatment for men and women in occupational social security schemes

(86/378/EEC)

(OJ No L 225, 12.8.86, p.40)

The Council of the European Communities,

Having regard to the Treaty establishing the European Economic Community, and in particular Articles 100 and 235 thereof,

Having regard to the proposal from the Commission[1],

Having regard to the opinion of the European Parliament[2],

Having regard to the opinion of the Economic and Social Committee[3],

Whereas the Treaty provides that each Member State shall ensure the application of the principle that men and women should receive equal pay for equal work; whereas 'pay' should be taken to mean the ordinary basic or minimum wage or salary and any other consideration, whether in cash or in kind, which the worker receives, directly or indirectly, from his employer in respect of his employment;

Whereas, although the principle of equal pay does indeed apply directly in cases where discrimination can be determined solely on the basis of the criteria of equal treatment and equal pay, there are also situations in which implementation of this principle implies the adoption of additional measures which more clearly define its scope;

Whereas Article 1(2) of Council Directive 76/207/EEC of 9 February 1976 on the implementation of the principle of equal treatment for men and women as regards access to employment, vocational training and promotion, and working conditions[4] provides that, with a view to ensuring the progressive implementation of the principle of equal treatment in matters of social security, the Council, acting on a proposal from the Commission, will adopt provisions defining its substance, its scope and the arrangements for its application; whereas the Council adopted to this end Directive 79/7/EEC of 19 December 1978 on the progressive implementation of the principle of equal treatment for men and women in matters of social security[5];

Whereas Article 3(3) of Directive 79/7/EEC provides that, with a view to ensuring implementation of the principle of equal treatment in occupational schemes, the Council, acting on a proposal from the Commission, will adopt provisions defining its substance, its scope and the arrangements for its application;

Whereas the principle of equal treatment should be implemented in occupational social security schemes which provide protection against the risks specified in Article 3(1) of Directive 79/7/EEC as well as those which provide employees with any other consideration in cash or in kind within the meaning of the Treaty;

Whereas implementation of the principle of equal treatment does not prejudice the provisions relating to the protection of women by reason of maternity,

Has adopted this Directive:

Article 1

The object of this Directive is to implement, in occupational social security schemes, the principle of equal treatment for men and women, hereinafter referred to as 'the principle of equal treatment'.

Article 2

1. 'Occupational social security schemes' means schemes not governed by Directive 79/7/EEC whose purpose is to provide workers, whether employees or self-employed, in an undertaking or group of undertakings, area of economic activity or occupational sector or group of such sectors with benefits intended to supplement the benefits provided by statutory social security schemes or to replace them, whether membership of such schemes is compulsory or optional.

2. This Directive does not apply to:

(a) individual contracts,

(b) schemes having only one member,

(c) in the case of salaried workers, insurance schemes offered to participants individually to guarantee them:

 – either additional benefits, or

 – a choice of date on which the normal benefits will start, or a choice between several benefits.

Article 3

This Directive shall apply to members of the working population including self-employed persons, persons whose activity is interrupted by illness, maternity, accident or involuntary unemployment and persons seeking employment, and to retired and disabled workers.

Article 4

This Directive shall apply to:

(a) occupational schemes which provide protection against the following risks:

 – sickness,

 – invalidity,

 – old age, including early retirement,

 – industrial accidents and occupational diseases,

 – unemployment;

(b) occupational schemes which provide for other social benefits, in cash or in kind, and in particular survivors' benefits and family allowances, if such benefits are accorded to employed persons and thus constitute a consideration paid by the employer to the worker by reason of the latter's employment.

Article 5

1. Under the conditions laid down in the following provisions, the principle of equal treatment implies that there shall be no discrimination on the basis of sex, either directly or indirectly, by reference in particular to marital or family status, especially as regards:

- the scope of the schemes and the conditions of access to them;
- the obligation to contribute and the calculation of contributions;
- the calculation of benefits, including supplementary benefits due in respect of a spouse or dependants, and the conditions governing the duration and retention of entitlement to benefits.

2. The principle of equal treatment shall not prejudice the provisions relating to the protection of women by reason of maternity.

Article 6

1. Provisions contrary to the principle of equal treatment shall include those based on sex, either directly or indirectly, in particular by reference to marital or family for:

(a) determining the persons who may participate in an occupational scheme;

(b) fixing the compulsory or optional nature of participation in an occupational scheme;

(c) laying down different rules as regards the age of entry into the scheme or the minimum period of employment or membership of the scheme required to obtain the benefits thereof;

(d) laying down different rules, except as provided for in subparagraphs (h) and (i), for the reimbursement of contributions where a worker leaves a scheme without having fulfilled the conditions guaranteeing him a deferred right to long-term benefits;

(e) setting different conditions for the granting of benefits of restricting such benefits to workers of one or other of the sexes;

(f) fixing different retirement ages;

(g) suspending the retention or acquisition of rights during periods of maternity leave or leave for family reasons which are granted by law or agreement and are paid by the employer;

(h) setting different levels of benefit, except insofar as may be necessary to take account of actuarial calculation factors which differ according to sex in the case of benefits designated as contribution-defined;

(i) setting different levels of worker contribution;

setting different levels of employer contribution in the case of benefits designated as contribution-defined, except with a view to making the amount of those benefits more nearly equal;

(j) laying down different standards or standards applicable only to workers of a specified sex, except as provided for in subparagraphs (h) and (i), as regards the guarantee or retention of entitlement to deferred benefits when a worker leaves a scheme.

2. Where the granting of benefits within the scope of this Directive is left to the discretion of the scheme's management bodies, the latter must take account of the principle of equal treatment.

Article 7

Member States shall take all necessary steps to ensure that:

(a) provisions contrary to the principle of equal treatment in legally compulsory collective agreements, staff rules of undertakings or any other arrangements relating to occupational schemes are null and void, or may be declared null and void or amended;

(b) schemes containing such provisions may not be approved or extended by administrative measures.

Article 8

1. Member States shall take all necessary steps to ensure that the provisions of occupational schemes contrary to the principle of equal treatment are revised by 1 January 1993.

2. This Directive shall not preclude rights and obligations relating to a period of membership of an occupational scheme prior to revision of that scheme from remaining subject to the provisions of the scheme in force during that period.

Article 9

Member States may defer compulsory application of the principle of equal treatment with regard to:

(a) determination of pensionable age for the purposes of granting old-age or retirement pensions, and the possible implications for other benefits:

– either until the date on which such equality is achieved in statutory schemes,

– or, at the latest, until such equality is required by a directive.

(b) survivors' pensions until a directive requires the principle of equal treatment in statutory social security schemes in that regard;

(c) the application of the first subparagraph of Article 6(1)(i) to take account of the different actuarial calculation factors, at the latest until the expiry of the thirteen-year period as from the notification of this Directive.

Article 10

Member States shall introduce into their national legal systems such measures as are necessary to enable all persons who consider themselves injured by failure to apply the principle of equal treatment to pursue their claims before the courts, possibly after bringing the matters before other competent authorities.

Article 11

Member States shall take all the necessary steps to protect worker against dismissal where this constitutes a response on the part of the employer to a complaint made at undertaking level or to the institution of legal proceedings aimed at enforcing compliance with the principle of equal treatment.

Article 12

1. Member States shall bring into force such laws, regulations and administrative provisions as are necessary in order to comply with this Directive at the latest three years after notification thereof[6]. They shall immediately inform the Commission thereof.

2. Member States shall communicate to the Commission at the latest five years after notification of this Directive all information necessary to enable the Commission to draw up a report on the application of this Directive for submission to the Council.

Article 13

This Directive is addressed to the Member States.

Done at Brussels, 24 July 1986.

For the Council

The President

A. Clark

FOOTNOTES

1. OJ No C 134, 21.5.83, p.7.
2. OJ No C 117, 30.4.84, p.169.
3. OJ No C 35, 9.2.84, p.7.
4. OJ No L 39, 14.2.76, p.40.
5. OJ No L 6, 10.1.79, p.24.
6. This Directive was notified to the Member States on 30 July 1986.

 Implemented in Ireland: Pensions Act, 1990; Social Welfare Act, 1992; S.I. 365/1992.

COUNCIL DIRECTIVE

of 11 December 1986

on the application of the principle of equal treatment between men and women engaged in an activity, including agriculture, in a self-employed capacity, and on the protection of self-employed women during pregnancy and motherhood

(86/613/EEC)

(OJ No L 359, 19.12.86, p. 56)

The Council of the European Communities,

Having regard to the Treaty establishing the European Economic Community, and in particular Articles 100 and 235 thereof,

Having regard to the proposal from the Commission[1],

Having regard to the opinion of the European Parliament[2],

Having regard to the opinion of the Economic and Social Committee[3],

Whereas, in its resolution of 12 July 1982 on the promotion of equal opportunities for women[4], the Council approved the general objectives of the Commission communication concerning a new Community action programme on the promotion of equal opportunities for women (1982 to 1985) and expressed the will to implement appropriate measures to achieve them;

Whereas action 5 of the programme referred to above concerns the application of the principle of equal treatment to self-employed women and to women in agriculture;

Whereas the implementation of the principle of equal pay for men and women workers, as laid down in Article 119 of the Treaty, forms an integral part of the establishment and functioning of the common market;

Whereas on 10 February 1975 the Council adopted Directive 75/117/EEC on the approximation of the laws of the Member States relating to the application of the principle of equal pay for men and women[5];

Whereas, as regards other aspects of equality of treatment between men and women, on 9 February 1976 the Council adopted Directive 76/207/EEC on the implementation of the principle of equal treatment for men and women as regards access to employment, vocational training and promotion, and working conditions[6] and on 19 December 1978 Directive 79/7/EEC on the progressive implementation of the principle of equal treatment for men and women in matters of social security[7];

Whereas, as regards persons engaged in a self-employed capacity, in an activity in which their spouses are also engaged, the implementation of the principle of equal treatment should be pursued through the adoption of detailed provisions designed to cover the specific situation of these persons;

Whereas differences persist between the Member States in this field, whereas, therefore it is necessary to approximate national provisions with regard to the application of the principle of equal treatment;

Whereas in certain respects the Treaty does not confer the powers necessary for the specific actions required;

Whereas the implementation of the principle of equal treatment is without prejudice to measures concerning the protection of women during pregnancy and motherhood,

Has adopted this Directive:

Section I

Aims and scope

Article 1

The purpose of this Directive is to ensure, in accordance with the following provisions, application in the Member States of the principle of equal treatment as between men and women engaged in an activity in a self-employed capacity, or contributing to the pursuit of such an activity, as regards those aspects not covered by Directives 76/207/EEC and 79/7/EEC.

Article 2

This Directive covers:

(a) self-employed workers, i.e. all persons pursuing a gainful activity for their own account, under the conditions laid down by national law, including farmers and members of the liberal professions;

(b) their spouses, not being employees or partners, where they habitually, under the conditions laid down by national law, participate in the activities of the self-employed worker and perform the same tasks or ancillary tasks.

Article 3

For the purposes of this Directive the principle of equal treatment implies the absence of all discrimination on grounds of sex, either directly or indirectly, by reference in particular to marital or family status.

Section II

Equal treatment between self-employed male and female workers – position of the spouses without professional status of self-employed workers – protection of self-employed workers or wives of self-employed workers during pregnancy and motherhood

Article 4

As regards self-employed persons, Member States shall take the measures necessary to ensure the elimination of all provisions which are contrary to the principle of equal treatment as defined in Directive 76/207/EEC, especially in respect of the establishment, equipment or extension of a business or the launching or extension of any other form of self-employed activity including financial facilities.

Article 5

Without prejudice to the specific conditions for access to certain activities which apply equally to both sexes, Member States shall take the measures necessary to ensure that the conditions for the formation of a company between spouses are not more restrictive than the conditions for the formation of a company between unmarried persons.

Article 6

Where a contributory social security system for self-employed workers exists in a Member State, that Member State shall take the necessary measures to enable the spouses referred to in Article 2(b) who are not protected under the self-employed worker's social security scheme to join a contributory social security scheme voluntarily.

Article 7

Member States shall undertake to examine under what conditions recognition of the work of the spouses referred to in Article 2(b) may be encouraged and, in the light of such examination, consider any appropriate steps for encouraging such recognition.

Article 8

Member States shall undertake to examine whether, and under what conditions, female self-employed workers and the wives of self-employed workers may, during interruptions in their occupational activity owing to pregnancy or motherhood,

- have access to services supplying temporary replacements or existing national social services, or
- be entitled to cash benefits under a social security scheme or under any other public social protection system.

Section III

General and final provisions

Article 9

Member States shall introduce into their national legal systems such measures as are necessary to enable all persons who consider themselves wronged by failure to apply the principle of equal treatment in self-employed activities to pursue their claims by judicial process, possibly after recourse to other competent authorities.

Article 10

Member States shall ensure that the measures adopted pursuant to this Directive, together with the relevant provisions already in force, are brought to the attention of bodies representing self-employed workers and vocational training centres.

Article 11

The Council shall review this Directive, on a proposal from the Commission, before 1 July 1993.

Article 12

1. Member States shall bring into force the laws, regulations and administrative provisions necessary to comply with this Directive not later than 30 June 1989.

However, if a Member State which, in order to comply with Article 5 of this Directive, has to amend its legislation on matrimonial rights and obligations, the date on which such Member State must comply with Article 5 shall be 30 June 1991.

2. Member States shall immediately inform the Commission of the measures taken to comply with this Directive.

Article 13

Member States shall forward to the Commission, not later than 30 June 1991, all the information necessary to enable it to draw up a report on the application of this Directive for submission to the Council.

Article 14

This Directive is addressed to the Member States.

Done at Brussels, 11 December 1986.

For the Council

The President

A. Clark

FOOTNOTES

1. OJ No C 113, 27.4.84, p.4.
2. OJ No C 172, 2.7.84, p.90.
3. OJ No C 343, 24.12.84, p.1.
4. OJ No C 186, 21.7.82, p.3.
5. OJ No L 45, 19.2.75, p.19.
6. OJ No L 39, 14.2.75, p.40.
7. OJ No L 6, 10.1.79, p.24.

 Implemented in Ireland: Social Welfare Act, 1988.

FOUR FREEDOMS

(a) Free Movement of Persons

REGULATION (EEC) No 1612/68
OF THE COUNCIL

of 15 October 1968

on freedom of movement for workers within
the Community

(OJ No L 257/2, 19.10.68, p.475)

The Council of the European Communities,

Having regard to the Treaty establishing the European Economic Community, and in particular Article 49 thereof;

Having regard to the proposal from the Commission;

Having regard to the opinion of the European Parliament[1];

Having regard to the opinion of the Economic and Social Committee[2];

Whereas freedom of movement for workers should be secured within the Community by the end of the transitional period at the latest; whereas the attainment of this objective entails the abolition of any discrimination based on nationality between workers of the Member States as regards employment, remuneration and other conditions of work and employment, as well as the right of such workers to move freely within the Community in order to pursue activities as employed persons subject to any limitations justified on grounds of public policy, public security or public health;

Whereas by reason in particular of the early establishment of the customs union and in order to ensure the simultaneous completion of the principal foundations of the Community, provisions should be adopted to enable the objectives laid down in Articles 48 and 49 of the Treaty in the field of freedom of movement to be achieved and to perfect measures adopted successively under Regulation No 15[3] on the first steps for attainment of freedom of movement and under Council Regulation No 38/54/EEC[4] of 25 March 1964 on freedom of movement for workers within the Community;

Whereas freedom of movement constitutes a fundamental right of workers and their families; whereas mobility of labour within the Community must be one of the means by which the worker is guaranteed the possibility of improving his living and working conditions and promoting his social advancement, while helping to satisfy the requirements of the economies of the Member States; whereas the right of all workers in the Member States to pursue the activity of their choice within the Community should be affirmed;

Whereas such right must be enjoyed without discrimination by permanent, seasonal and frontier workers and by those who pursue their activities for the purpose of providing services;

Whereas the right of freedom of movement, in order that it may be exercised, by objective standards, in freedom and dignity, requires that equality of treatment shall be ensured in fact and in law in respect of all matters relating to the actual pursuit of activities as employed persons and to eligibility for housing, and also that obstacles to the mobility of workers shall be eliminated, in particular as regards the worker's right to be joined by his family and the conditions for the integration of that family into the host country;

Whereas the principle of non-discrimination between Community workers entails that all nationals of Member States have the same priority as regards employment as is enjoyed by national workers;

Whereas it is necessary to strengthen the machinery for vacancy clearance, in particular by developing direct co-operation between the central employment services and also between the regional services, as well as by increasing and co-ordinating the exchange of information in order to ensure in a general way a clearer picture of the labour market; whereas workers wishing to move should also be regularly informed of living and working conditions; whereas, furthermore, measures should be provided for the case where a Member State undergoes or foresees disturbances on its labour market which may seriously threaten the standard of living and level of employment in a region or an industry; whereas for this purpose the exchange of information, aimed at discouraging workers from moving to such a region or industry, constitutes the method to be applied in the first place but, where necessary, it should be possible to strengthen the results of such exchange of information by temporarily suspending the above-mentioned machinery, any such decision to be taken at Community level;

Whereas close links exist between freedom of movement for workers, employment and vocational training, particularly where the latter aims at putting workers in a position to take up offers of employment from other regions of the Community; whereas such links make it necessary that the problems arising in this connection should no longer be studied in isolation but viewed as inter-dependent, account also being taken of the problems of employment at the regional level; and whereas it is therefore necessary to direct the efforts of Member States toward co-ordinating their employment policies at Community level;

Whereas the Council, by its Decision of 15 October 1968[5] made Articles 48 and 49 of the Treaty and also the measures taken in implementation thereof applicable to the French overseas departments;

Has adopted this Regulation:

Part I

Employment and workers' families

Title I

Eligibility for employment

Article 1

1. Any national of a Member State, shall, irrespective of his place of residence, have the right to take up an activity as an employed person, and to pursue such activity, within the territory of another Member State in accordance with the provisions laid down by law, regulation or administrative action governing the employment of nationals of that State.

2. He shall, in particular, have the right to take up available employment in the territory of another Member State with the same priority as nationals of that State.

Article 2

Any national of a Member State and any employer pursuing an activity in the territory of a Member State may exchange their applications for and offers of employment, and may conclude and perform contracts of employment in accordance with the provisions in force laid down by law, regulation or administrative action, without any discrimination resulting therefrom.

Article 3

1. Under this Regulation, provisions laid down by law, regulation or administrative action or administrative practices of a Member State shall not apply:

– where they limit application for and offers of employment, or the right of foreign nationals to take up and pursue employment or subject these to conditions not applicable in respect of their own nationals; or

– where, though applicable irrespective of nationality, their exclusive or principal aim or effect is to keep nationals of other Member States away from the employment offered.

This provision shall not apply to conditions relating to linguistic knowledge required by reason of the nature of the post to be filled.

2. There shall be included in particular among the provisions or practices of a Member State referred to in the first subparagraph of paragraph 1 those which:

(a) prescribe a special recruitment procedure for foreign nationals;

(b) limit or restrict the advertising of vacancies in the press or through any other medium or subject it to conditions other than those applicable in respect of employers pursuing their activities in the territory of that Member State;

(c) subject eligibility for employment to conditions of registration with employment offices or impede recruitment of individual workers, where persons who do not reside in the territory of that State are concerned.

Article 4

1. Provisions laid down by law, regulation or administrative action of the Member States which restrict by number or percentage the employment of foreign nationals in any undertaking, branch of activity or region, or at a national level, shall not apply to nationals of the other Member States.

2. When in a Member State the granting of any benefit to undertakings is subject to a minimum percentage of national workers being employed, nationals of the other Member States shall be counted as national workers, subject to the provisions of the Council Directive of 15 October 1963.[6]

Article 5

A national of a Member State who seeks employment in the territory of another Member State shall receive the same assistance there as that afforded by the employment offices in that State to their own nationals seeking employment.

Article 6

1. The engagement and recruitment of a national of one Member State

for a post in another Member State shall not depend on medical, vocational or other criteria which are discriminatory on grounds of nationality by comparison with those applied to nationals of the other Member State who wish to pursue the same activity.

2. Nevertheless, a national who holds an offer in his name from an employer in a Member State other than that of which he is a national may have to undergo a vocational test, if the employer expressly requests this when making his offer of employment.

Title II

Employment and equality of treatment

Article 7

1. A worker who is a national of a Member State may not, in the territory of another Member State, be treated differently from national workers by reason of his nationality in respect of any conditions of employment and work, in particular as regards remuneration, dismissal, and should he become unemployed, reinstatement or re-employment;

2. He shall enjoy the same social and tax advantages as national workers.

3. He shall also, by virtue of the same right and under the same conditions as national workers, have access to training in vocational schools and retraining centres.

4. Any clause of a collective or individual agreement or of any other collective regulation concerning eligibility for employment, employment, remuneration and other conditions of work or dismissal shall be null and void in so far as it lays down or authorises discriminatory conditions in respect of workers who are nationals of the other Member States.

Article 8

1. A worker who is a national of a Member State and who is employed in the territory of another Member State shall enjoy equality of treatment as regards membership of trade unions and the exercise of rights attaching thereto, including the right to vote; he may be excluded from taking part in the management of bodies governed by public law and from holding an office governed by public law. Furthermore, he shall have the right of eligibility for workers' representative bodies in the undertaking. The provisions of this Article shall not affect laws or regulations in certain Member States which grant more extensive rights to workers coming from the other Member States.

2. This Article shall be reviewed by the Council on the basis of a proposal from the Commission which shall be submitted within not more than two years.

Article 9

1. A worker who is a national of a Member State and who is employed in the territory of another Member State shall enjoy all the rights and benefits accorded to national workers in matters of housing, including ownership of the housing he needs.

2. Such worker may, with the same right as nationals, put his name down on the housing lists in the region in which he is employed, where such lists exist; he shall enjoy the resultant benefits and priorities.

If his family has remained in the country whence he came, they shall be considered for this purpose as residing in the said region, where national workers benefit from a similar presumption.

Title III

Workers' families

Article 10

1. The following shall, irrespective of their nationality, have the right to install themselves with a worker who is a national of one Member State and who is employed in the territory of another Member State:

(a) his spouse and their descendants who are under the age of 21 years or are dependants;

(b) dependent relatives in the ascending line of the worker and his spouse.

2. Member States shall facilitate the admission of any member of the family not coming within the provisions of paragraph 1 if dependent on the worker referred to above or living under his roof in the country whence he comes.

3. For the purposes of paragraphs 1 and 2, the worker must have available for his family housing considered as normal for national workers in the region where he is employed; this provision, however must not give rise to discrimination between national workers and workers from the other Member States.

Article 11

Where a national of a Member State is pursuing an activity as an employed or self-employed person in the territory of another Member State, his spouse and those of the children who are under the age of 21 years or dependent on him shall have the right to take up any activity as an employed person throughout the territory of that same State, even if they are not nationals of any Member State.

Article 12

The children of a national of a Member State who is or has been employed in the territory of another Member State shall be admitted to that State's general educational, apprenticeship and vocational training courses under the same conditions as the nationals of that State, if such children are residing in its territory.

Member States shall encourage all efforts to enable such children to attend these courses under the best possible conditions.

Part II

Clearance of vacancies and applications for employment

Title I

Co-operation between the Member States and with the Commission

Article 13

1. The Member States or the Commission shall instigate or together undertake any study of employment or unemployment which they consider necessary for securing freedom of movement for workers within the Community.

The central employment services of the Member States shall co-operate closely with each other and with the Commission with a view to acting jointly as regards the clearing of vacancies and applications for employment within the Community and the resultant placing of workers in employment.

2. To this end the Member States shall designate specialist services which shall be entrusted with organising work in the fields referred to above and co-operating with each other and with the departments of the Commission.

The Member States shall notify the Commission of any change in the designation of such services; the Commission shall publish details thereof for information in the *Official Journal of the European Communities*.

Article 14

1. The Member States shall send to the Commission information on problems arising in connection with the freedom of movement and employment of workers and particulars of the state and development of employment by region and by branch of activity.

2. In co-operation with the Technical Committee, the Commission shall determine the manner in which the information referred to in paragraph 1 shall be drawn up and intervals at which it shall be communicated. To assess the state of their labour markets, the Member States shall use uniform criteria established by the Commission in accordance with the results of the work of the Technical Committee carried out in pursuance of Article 33(d), after having obtained the Opinion of the Advisory Committee.

3. In accordance with the procedure laid down by the Commission in agreement with the Technical Committee, the specialist service of each Member State shall send to the specialist services of the other Member States and to the European Co-ordination Office such information concerning living and working conditions and the state of the labour market as is likely to be of guidance to workers from the other Member States. Such information shall be brought up to date regularly.

The specialist services of the other Member States shall ensure that wide publicity is given to such information, in particular by circulating it among the appropriate employment services and by all suitable means of communication for informing the workers concerned.

Title II

Machinery for vacancy clearance

Article 15

1. At least once a month the specialist service of each Member State shall send to the specialist services of the other Member States and to the European Co-ordination Office a return showing by occupation and by region:

(a) vacancies unfilled or unlikely to be filled by manpower from the national labour market;

(b) applicants for employment who have declared themselves actually ready and able to accept employment in another country.

The specialist service of each Member State shall forward such information to the appropriate employment services and agencies.

2. The returns referred to in paragraph 1 shall be circulated according to a uniform system to be established by the European Co-ordination Office in collaboration with the Technical Committee, within eighteen months following the entry into force of this Regulation.

Article 16

1. Any vacancy communicated to the employment services of a Member State which cannot be filled from the national labour market and which, on the basis of the returns referred to in Article 15, can be cleared within the Community, shall be notified to the competent employment services of the Member State which has indicated that it has manpower available in the same occupation.

2. Such services shall forward to the services of the first Member State the details of suitable applications. For a period of 18 days from receipt of the communication of the vacancy to the services of the second Member State, such applications shall be submitted to employers with the same priority as that granted to national workers over nationals of non-Member States. During the above-mentioned period, vacancies shall be notified to non-Member States only if the Member State having such vacancies considers that for the occupations corresponding to such vacancies there are insufficient workers available who are nationals of the Member States.

3. The provisions of paragraph 1 shall not apply to vacancies offered to workers who are nationals of non-Member States where:

(a) such an offer is made to a named worker and is of a special nature in view of:

(i) the requirement of specialist qualifications or the confidential nature of the post offered or previous occupational ties;

(ii) the existence of family ties either between the employer and the worker asked for, or between the latter and a worker who has been employed regularly for at least a year in the undertaking.

Items (i) and (ii) shall be applied in accordance with the provisions set out in the Annex;

(b) such vacancies are for the recruitment of homogeneous groups of seasonal workers of whom at least one named member has been offered a vacancy;

(c) such vacancies are offered by employers to workers resident in regions adjacent to either side of the frontier between a Member State and a non-Member State;

(*d*)   vacancies are offered expressly to workers from non-Member States by the employer for reasons connected with the smooth running of the undertaking, where the employment services, having intervened for the purposes of securing the employment of national workers or workers from the other Member States of the Community, are of the opinion that such reasons are justified.

Article 17

1. The provisions of Article 16 shall be implemented by the specialist services. However, in so far as they have been authorised by the central services and in so far as the organisation of the employment services of a Member State and the placing techniques employed make it possible:

(*a*)   the regional employment services of the Member States shall:

(i)   on the basis of the returns referred to in Article 15, on which appropriate action will be taken, directly bring together and clear vacancies and applications for employment;

(ii) establish direct relations for clearance:

– of vacancies offered to a named worker;

– of individual applications for employment sent either to a specific employment service or to an employer pursuing his activity within the area covered by such a service;

– where the clearing operations concern seasonal workers who must be recruited as quickly as possible;

(*b*)   the services territorially responsible for the border regions of two or more Member States shall regularly exchange data relating to vacancies and applications for employment outstanding in their area and, acting in accordance with their arrangements with the other employment services of their countries, shall directly bring together and clear vacancies and applications for employment;

(*c*)   official employment services which specialise in certain occupations or specific categories of persons shall cooperate directly with each other.

2. The Member States concerned shall forward to the Commission the list, drawn up by common accord, of services referred to in paragraph 1; the Commission shall publish such list, and any amendment thereto, in the *Official Journal of the European Communities*.

Article 18

Adoption of recruiting procedures as applied by the implementing bodies provided for under agreements concluded between two or more Member States shall not be obligatory.

Title III

Measures for controlling the balance of the labour market

Article 19

1. Twice a year, on the basis of a report from the Commission drawn up from information supplied by the Member States, the latter and the Commission shall together analyse:

– the results of Community arrangements for vacancy clearance;

– the number of placings of nationals of non-Member States;

– the foreseeable developments in the state of the labour market and, as far as possible, the movements of manpower within the Community.

2. The Member States shall examine with the Commission all the possibilities of giving priority to nationals of Member States when filling employment vacancies in order to achieve a balance between vacancies and applications for employment within the Community. They shall adopt all measures necessary for this purpose.

Article 20

1. When a Member State undergoes or foresees disturbances on its labour market which could seriously threaten the standard of living or level of employment in a given region or occupation, that State shall inform the Commission and the other Member States thereof and shall supply them with all relevant particulars.

2. The Member States and the Commission shall take all suitable measures to inform Community workers so that they shall not apply for employment in that region or occupation.

3. Without prejudice to the application of the Treaty and of the Protocols annexed thereto, the Member State referred to in paragraph 1 may request the Commission to state that, in order to restore to normal the situation in that region or occupation, the operation of the clearance machinery provided for in Articles 15, 16 and 17 should be partially or totally suspended.

The Commission shall decide on the suspension as such and on the duration thereof not later than two weeks after receiving such request. Any Member State may, within a strict time limit of two weeks, request the Council to annul or amend any such decision. The Council shall act on any such request within two weeks.

4. Where such suspension does take place, the employment services of the other Member States which have indicated that they have workers available shall not take any action to fill vacancies notified directly to them by employers in the Member States referred to in paragraph 1.

Title IV

European Co-ordination Office

Article 21

The European Office for Co-ordinating the Clearance of Vacancies and Applications for Employment, established within the Commission (called in this Regulation the 'European Co-ordination Office'), shall have the general task of promoting vacancy clearance at Community level. It shall be responsible in particular for all the technical duties in this field which, under the provisions of this Regulation, are assigned to the Commission, and especially for assisting the national employment services.

It shall summarise the information referred to in Articles 14 and 15 and the data arising out of the studies and research carried out pursuant to Article 13, so as to bring to light any useful facts about foreseeable developments on the Community labour market; such facts shall be communicated to the specialist services of the Member States and to the Advisory and Technical Committees.

Article 22

1. The European Co-ordination Office shall be responsible, in particular, for:

(a) co-ordinating the practical measures necessary for vacancy clearance at Community level and for analysing the resulting movements of workers;

(b) contributing to such objectives by implementing, in co-operation with the Technical Committee, joint methods of action at administrative and technical levels;

(c) carrying out, where a special need arises, and in agreement with the specialist services, the bringing together of vacancies and applications for employment for clearance by these specialist services.

2. It shall communicate to the specialist services vacancies and

applications for employment sent directly to the Commission, and shall be informed of the action taken thereon.

Article 23

The Commission may, in agreement with the competent authority of each Member State, and in accordance with the conditions and procedures which it shall determine on the basis of the Opinion of the Technical Committee, organise visits and assignments for officials of other Member States, and also advanced programmes for specialist personnel.

Part III

Committees for ensuring close co-operation between the Member States in matters concerning the freedom of movement of workers and their employment

Title I

The Advisory Committee

Article 24

The Advisory Committee shall be responsible for assisting the Commission in the examination of any questions arising from the application of the Treaty and measures taken in pursuance thereof, in matters concerning the freedom of movement of workers and their employment.

Article 25

The Advisory Committee shall be responsible in particular for:

(a) examining problems concerning freedom of movement and employment within the framework of national manpower policies, with a view to co-ordinating the employment policies of the Member States at Community level, thus contributing to the development of the economies and to an improved balance of the labour market;

(b) making a general study of the effects of implementing this Regulation and any supplementary measures;

(c) submitting to the Commission any reasoned proposals for revising this Regulation;

(d) delivering, either at the request of the Commission or on its own initiative, reasoned opinions on general questions or on questions of principle, in particular on exchange of information concerning developments in the labour market, on the movement of workers between Member States, on programmes or measures to develop vocational guidance and vocational training which are likely to increase the possibilities of freedom of movement and employment, and on all forms of assistance to workers and their families, including social assistance and the housing of workers.

Article 26

1. The Advisory Committee shall be composed of six members of each Member State, two of whom shall represent the government, two the trade unions and two the employers' associations.

2. For each of the categories referred to in paragraph 1, one alternate member shall be appointed by each Member State.

3. The term of office of the members and their alternates shall be two years. Their appointments shall be renewable.

On expiry of their term of office, the members and their alternates shall remain in office until replaced or until their appointments are renewed.

Article 27

The members of the Advisory Committee and their alternates shall be appointed by the Council which shall endeavour, when selecting representatives of trade unions and employers' associations, to achieve adequate representation on the Committee of the various economic sectors concerned.

The list of members and their alternates shall be published by the Council for information in the *Official Journal of the European Communities*.

Article 28

The Advisory Committee shall be chaired by a member of the Commission or his alternate. The Chairman shall not vote. The Committee shall meet at least twice a year. It shall be convened by its Chairman, either on his own initiative, or at the request of at least one third of the members. Secretarial services shall be provided for the Committee by the Commission.

Article 29

The Chairman may invite individuals or representatives of bodies with wide experience in the field of employment or movement of workers to take part in meetings as observers or as experts. The Chairman may be assisted by expert advisers.

Article 30

1. An opinion delivered by the Committee shall not be valid unless two-thirds of the members are present.

2. Opinions shall state the reasons on which they are based; they shall be delivered by an absolute majority of the votes validly cast; they shall be accompanied by a written statement of the views expressed by the minority, when the latter so requests.

Article 31

The Advisory Committee shall establish its working methods by rules of procedure which shall enter into force after the Council, having received an opinion from the Commission, has given its approval. The entry into force of any amendment that the Committee decides to make thereto shall be subject to the same procedure.

Title II

The Technical Committee

Article 32

The Technical Committee shall be responsible for assisting the Commission to prepare, promote and follow up all technical work and measures for giving effect to this Regulation and any supplementary measures.

Article 33

The Technical Committee shall be responsible in particular for:

(a) promoting and advancing co-operation between the public authorities concerned in the Member States on all technical questions relating to freedom of movement of workers and their employment;

(b) formulating procedures for the organisation of the joint activities of the public authorities concerned;

(c) facilitating the gathering of information likely to be of use to the Commission and for the studies and research provided for in this Regulation, and encouraging exchange of information and experience between the administrative bodies concerned;

(d) investigating at a technical level the harmonisation of the criteria by which Member States assess the state of their labour markets.

Article 34

1. The Technical Committee shall be composed of representatives of the Governments of the Member States. Each Government shall appoint as member of the Technical Committee one of the members who represent it on the Advisory Committee.

2. Each government shall appoint an alternate from among its other representatives – members or alternates – on the Advisory Committee.

Article 35

The Technical Committee shall be chaired by a member of the Commission or his representative. The Chairman shall not vote. The Chairman and the members of the Committee may be assisted by expert advisers.

Secretarial services shall be provided for the Committee by the Commission.

Article 36

The proposals and opinions formulated by the Technical Committee shall be submitted to the Commission, and the Advisory Committee shall be informed thereof. Any such proposals and opinions shall be accompanied by a written statement of the views expressed by the various members of the Technical Committee, when the latter so request.

Article 37

The Technical Committee shall establish its working methods by rules of procedure which shall enter into force after the Council, having received an opinion from the Commission, has given its approval. The entry into force of any amendment which the Committee decides to make thereto shall be subject to the same procedure.

Part IV

Transitional and final provisions

Title I

Transitional provisions

Article 38

Until the adoption by the Commission of the uniform system referred to in Article 15(2), the European Co-ordination Office shall propose any measures likely to be of use in drawing up and circulating the returns referred to in Article 15(1).

Article 39

The rules of procedure of the Advisory Committee and the Technical Committee in force at the time of entry into force of this Regulation shall continue to apply.

Article 40

Until the entry into force of the measures to be taken by Member States in pursuance of the Council Directive of 15 October 1968[7] and where, under the measures taken by the Member States in pursuance of the Council Directive of 25 March 1964[8] the work permit provided for in Article 22 of Regulation No 38/64/EEC is necessary to determine the period of validity and extension of the residence permit, written confirmation of engagement from the employer or a certificate of employment stating the period of employment may be substituted for such work permit. Any written confirmation by the employer or certificate of employment showing that the worker has been engaged for an indefinite period shall have the same effect as that of a permanent work permit.

Article 41

If, by reason of the abolition of the work permit, a Member State can no longer compile certain statistics on the employment of foreign nationals, such Member State may, for statistical purposes, retain the work permit in respect of nationals of the other Member States until new statistical methods are introduced, but no later than 31 December 1969. The work permit must be issued automatically and must be valid until the actual abolition of work permits in such Member State.

Title II

Final provisions

Article 42

1. This Regulation shall not affect the provisions of the Treaty establishing the European Coal and Steel Community which relate to workers with recognised qualifications in coalmining or steelmaking, nor those of the Treaty establishing the European Atomic Energy Community which deal with eligibility for skilled employment in the field of nuclear energy, nor any measures taken in pursuance of those Treaties.

Nevertheless, this Regulation shall apply to categories of workers referred to in the first subparagraph and to members of their families in so far as their legal position is not governed by the above-mentioned Treaties or measures.

2. This Regulation shall not affect measures taken in accordance with Article 51 of the Treaty.

3. This Regulation shall not affect the obligations of Member States arising out of:

– special relations or future agreements with certain non-European countries or territories, based on institutional ties existing at the time of the entry into force of this Regulation; or

– agreements in existence at the time of the entry into force of this Regulation with certain non-European countries or territories, based on institutional ties between them.

Workers from such countries or territories who, in accordance with this provision, are pursuing activities as employed persons in the territory of one of those Member States may not invoke the benefit of the provisions of this Regulation in the territory of the other Member States.

Article 43

Member States shall, for information purposes, communicate to the Commission the texts of agreements, conventions or arrangements concluded between them in the manpower field between the date of their being signed and that of their entry into force.

Article 44

The Commission shall adopt measures pursuant to this Regulation for its implementation. To this end it shall act in close co-operation with the central public authorities of the Member States.

Article 45

The Commission shall submit to the Council proposals aimed at abolishing, in accordance with the conditions of the Treaty, restrictions on eligibility for employment of workers who are nationals of Member States, where the absence of mutual recognition of diplomas, certificates or other evidence of formal qualifications may prevent freedom of movement for workers.

Article 46

The administrative expenditure of the Committees referred to in Part III shall be included in the budget of the European Communities in the section relating to the Commission.

Article 47

This Regulation shall apply to the territories of the Member States and to their nationals, without prejudice to Articles 2, 3, 10 and 11.

Article 48

Regulation No 38/64/EEC shall cease to have effect when this Regulation enters into force.

This Regulation shall be binding in its entirety and directly applicable in all Member States.

Done at Luxembourg, 15 October 1968.

For the Council

The President

G. Sedati

Annex

For the purposes of Article 16(3)(a):

(1) The expression 'specialist' indicates a high or uncommon qualification referring to a type of work or a trade requiring specific technical knowledge; it shall refer in particular to foremen in the case of seasonal workers recruited in groups.

(2) The expression 'confidential nature of the post' refers to employment which in the host country customarily involves special relations of trust between the employer and the worker.

(3) The expression 'previous occupational ties' applies when an employer applies for the engagement in the territory of a Member State of a worker whom he has already employed in that same territory for at least twelve months during the last four years.

(4) The expression 'family ties' means ties of marriage or relationship to the second degree between an employer and a worker, and ties of relationship to the first degree between two workers.

EDITORIAL NOTE

For amendments see OJ of the ECs Directory of Community Legislation in force and other acts of the Community Institutions Volume I – as at 1.12.1993, page 499.

FOOTNOTES

1. OJ No 268, 6.11.67, p.9.
2. OJ No 298, 7.12.67, p.10.
3. OJ No 57, 26.8.61, p.1073.
4. OJ No 62, 17.4.64, p.965.
5. OJ No L 257, 19.10.68, p.1.
6. OJ No 159, 2.11.63, p.2661.
7. OJ No L 257, 19.10.68, p.13.
8. OJ No 62, 17.4.64, p.981.

COUNCIL REGULATION (EEC) No 312/76

of 9 February 1976

amending the provisions relating to the trade union rights of workers contained in Regulation (EEC) No 1612/68 on freedom of movement for workers within the Community

(OJ No L 39, 14.2.76, p.2)

The Council of the European Communities,

Having regard to the Treaty establishing the European Economic Community, and in particular Article 49 thereof,

Having regard to the proposal from the Commission,

Having regard to the opinion of the European Parliament[1],

Having regard to the opinion of the Economic and Social Committee[2],

Whereas it should be specified in Article 8 of Council Regulation (EEC) No 1612/68 of 15 October 1968 on freedom of movement for workers within the Community[3], that workers who are nationals of one Member State and who are employed in the territory of another Member State shall also enjoy equality of treatment as regards the exercise of trade union rights with respect to eligibility for the administration or management posts of a trade union,

Has adopted this Regulation:

Article 1

Article 8 of Regulation (EEC) No 1612/68 shall be amended as follows:

1. The following shall be added to the first sentence of paragraph 1 after 'including the right to vote':

> 'and to be eligible for the administration or management posts of a trade union.'

2. Paragraph 2 is hereby deleted.

Article 2

This Regulation shall enter into force on the third day following that of its publication in the *Official Journal of the European Communities*.

This Regulation shall be binding in its entirety and directly applicable in all Member States.

Done at Brussels, 9 February 1976.

For the Council

The President

G. Thorn

FOOTNOTES

1. OJ No C 280, 8.12.75, p.43
2. OJ No C 12, 17.1.76, p.2.
3. OJ No L 257, 19.10.68, p.2.

COUNCIL REGULATION (EEC) No 2434/92

of 27 July 1992

amending Part II of Regulation (EEC) No 1612/68 on freedom of movement for workers within the Community

(OJ No L 245, 26.8.92, p.1)

The Council of the European Communities,

Having regard to the Treaty establishing the European Economic Community, and in particular Article 49 thereof,

Having regard to the proposal from the Commission[1],

In cooperation with the European Parliament[2],

Having regard to the opinion of the Economic and Social Committee[3],

Whereas freedom of movement for workers within the Community constitutes a fundamental right established by the Treaty;

Whereas to give effect to freedom of movement for workers who are nationals of Member States it is necessary to strengthen the mechanism for clearing vacancies and applications for employment provided for in Regulation (EEC) No 1612/68[4];

Whereas the principle of non-discrimination between Community workers implies the recognition, in fact and in law, of the right of all nationals of the Member States to enjoy the same priority on the labour market as that enjoyed by nationals in each Member State; whereas this equality of priority should apply under the mechanism for clearing vacancies and applications for employment;

Whereas it is important to ensure the greatest possible transparency of the Community labour market, especially when determining vacancies and applications for employment which are the subject of Community clearance,

Has adopted this Regulation:

Article 1

Regulation (EEC) No 1612/86 is hereby amended as follows:

1. does not concern the English text;

2. in Article 14:

– in paragraph 1 the words 'by region and by branch of activity' shall be deleted,

– paragraph 2 shall be replaced by the following:

'2. The Commission, taking the utmost account of the opinion of the Technical Committee, shall determine the manner in which the information referred to in paragraph 1 is to be drawn up.',

– in the first sentence of paragraph 3 the words 'in agreement with the Technical Committee' shall be replaced by 'taking the utmost account of the opinion of the Technical Committee',

– does not concern the English text;

3. Article 15 shall be replaced by the following:

'*Article* 15

1. The specialist service of each Member State shall regularly send to the specialist services of the other Member States and to the European Coordination Office:

(*a*) details of vacancies which could be filled by nationals of other Member States;

(*b*) details of vacancies addressed to non-Member States;

(*c*) details of applications for employment by those who have formally expressed a wish to work in another Member State;

(*d*) information, by region and by branch of activity, on applicants who have declared themselves actually willing to accept employment in another country.

The specialist service of each Member State shall forward this information to the appropriate employment services and agencies as soon as possible.

2. The details of vacancies and applications referred to in paragraph 1 shall be circulated according to a uniform system to be established by the European Coordination Office in collaboration with the Technical Committee.

If necessary, the European Coordination Office may adapt this system in collaboration with the Technical Committee.'

4. Article 16 shall be replaced by the following:

'*Article* 16

1. Any vacancy within the meaning of Article 15 communicated to the employment services of a Member State shall be notified to and

processed by the competent employment services of the other Member States concerned.

Such services shall forward to the services of the first Member State the details of suitable applications.

2. The applications for employment referred to in Article 15(1)(c) shall be responded to by the relevant services of the Member State within a reasonable period, not exceeding one month.

3. The employment services shall grant workers who are nationals of the Member States the same priority as the relevant measures grant to nationals *vis-à-vis* workers from non-Member States';

5.   in Article 17(1):

-   does not concern the English text,

-   the word 'returns' in subparagraph (a)(i) shall be replaced by 'details',

-   subparagraph (b) shall be replaced by the following:

'(b) the services territorially responsible for the border regions of two or more Member States shall regularly exchange data relating to vacancies and applications for employment in their area and, acting in accordance with their arrangements with the other employment services of their countries, shall directly bring together and clear vacancies and applications for employment.

If necessary, the services territorially responsible for border regions shall also set up cooperation and service structures to provide:

-   users with as much practical information as possible on the various aspects of mobility, and

-   management and labour, social services (in particular public, private or those of public interest) and all institutions concerned, with a framework of coordinated measures relating to mobility;'

6. in Article 19:

-   paragraph 1 shall be replaced by the following:

'1. On the basis of a report from the Commission drawn up from information supplied by the Member States, the latter and the Commission shall at least once a year analyse jointly the results of Community arrangements regarding vacancies and applications';

– the following shall be added:

'3. Every two years the Commission shall submit a report to the European Parliament, the Council and the Economic and Social Committee on the implementation of Part II of this Regulation, summarising the information required and the data obtained from the studies and research carried out and highlighting any useful points with regard to developments on the Community's labour market';

7. Article 20 shall deleted;

8. the Annex shall be deleted.

Article 2

This Regulation shall enter into force on the day following its publication in the *Official Journal of the European Communities*.

This Regulation shall be binding in its entirety and directly applicable to all Member States.

Done at Brussels, 27 July 1992.

For the Council

The President

N. Lamont

FOOTNOTES

1. OJ No C 254, 28.9.91, p.9 and OJ No C 107, 28.4.92, p.10.
2. OJ No C 94, 13.4.92, p.202 and Decision of 8 July 1992 (OJ No C 241, 21.9.92, p.41).
3. OJ No C 40, 17.2.92, p.1.
4. OJ No L 257, 19.10.68, p.2. Last amended by Regulation (EEC) No 312/76 (OJ No L 39, 14.2.76, p.2).

COMMISSION DECISION

of 22 October 1993

on the implementing of Council Regulation (EEC) No 1612/68 on freedom of movement for workers within the Community as regards, in particular, a network entitled Eures (European Employment Services)

(93/569/EEC)

(OJ No L 274, 6.11.93, p.32)

The Commission of the European Communities,

Having regard to the Treaty establishing the European Economic Community,

Having regard to Council Regulation (EEC) No 1612/68 of 15 October 1968 on freedom of movement for workers within the Community[1], as last amended by Regulation (EEC) No 2434/92[2], and in particular Articles 14, 15, 16, 17, 19, 21, 22 and 44 thereof,

Having regard to the opinion of the Technical Committee on freedom of movement for workers,

Whereas the objectives defined in Regulation (EEC) No 1612/68 are:

– to develop cooperation between Member States and in particular between the employment services of the Member States and the Commission,

– to exchange job vacancies and applications at Community level,

– to ensure the exchange of information on working and living conditions between the Member States,

– to coordinate and follow up the resultant exchange of information at the appropriate European level;

Whereas the SEDOC system (European system for the international clearing of vacancies and applications for employment) currently in force no longer corresponds to the requirements of the labour market in Europe and hence needs to be adapted; whereas it is therefore necessary to repeal the Commission Decisions of 8 December and 14 December 1972,

Has adopted this Decision:

Article 1

The Commission, the employment services of the Member States and any further national partners which they may have, shall create a European network of services, designated Eures (European Employment Services) responsible for developing the exchange of information and cooperation provided for in Part II of Regulation (EEC) No 1612/68.

The designation Eures is a acronym which belongs exclusively to the Commission and is illustrated by a standard logo so that it can be identified by the public concerned. Use of this logo, which is defined by a graphic design scheme, shall require prior authorization by the Commission.

The elements making up this network and its operations, as well as the relevant measures for its implementation, are set out in Annexes I, II, III and IV.

Article 2

The Commission shall designate, within the Directorate-General of Employment, Social Affairs and Industrial Relations, the service responsible for the European Coordination Office established under the terms of Article 21 of Regulation (EEC) No 1612/68 and for implementing the Eures network.

Article 3

The Commission Decisions of 8 and 14 December 1972 are repealed.

Article 4

The Decision is addressed to the Member States.

Done at Brussels, 22 October 1993.

For the Commission

Padraig Flynn

Member of the Commission

Annex I

1. General Description of the Eures network

1.1. *Definition*

Eures is a network made up of the national employment services, their eventual partners and the Commission, and is responsible for exchanging information specified by Regulation (EEC) No 1612/68, and providing the information to potential users. It is based on a computer system and a uniform exchange defined by the present decision.

1.2 *Members*

- The employment services of the Member States.

- The Commission of the European Communities, through the European Coordination Office defined in Articles 21 and 22 of Regulation (EEC) No 1612/68.

- Public or private partners of the employment services operating under national legal provisions in the field of employment and approved by them, who have signed an agreement with the Commission.

- The social and economic partners designated by conventions establishing a crossborder Eures.

1.3 *Information to be exchanged*

- Information (in accordance with Article 15 of Regulation (EEC) No 1612/68) on vacancies and applications for employment in another Member State.

- Information on the state and trends of the labour market broken down by regions, sectors of activity, and, if necessary by level of worker qualification (Article 14(1) of Regulation (EEC) No 1612/68).

- Information on living and working conditions in the Member States (Article 14(3) of Regulation (EEC) No 1612/68).

1.4 *The information exchange system*

A computer system and a uniform procedure for exchanging information are part of the network.

Members of the Eures network have access to this system via national computer systems within the employment services or by using specific workstations that are directly linked to the Eures computer system.

2. Structure and procedure for exchanging information

To exercise the right to freedom of movement within the Community, workers need access to information on available jobs and living and working conditions in the Member States of the Community. Employers must also, in order to satisfy their needs with regard to recruitment, be able to advertise their vacancies and access applications from different Member States of the Community.

2.1. *Advertising and Processing vacancies in the Eures network (Articles 15 and 16 of Regulation (EEC) No 1612/68)*

2.1.1. Definition

The circulation of vacancies in the Member States is at the centre of the Eures network information exchange system.

Regulation (EEC) No 1612/68 provides for the circulation of information concerning 'vacancies which could be filled by nationals of other Member States'.

These vacancies, hereafter called 'Euro-vacancies' are defined as follows: 'vacancies more likely to be filled if advertised at Community level, as more quality applications shall be received'. A non-exhaustive list of these categories of vacancies is given in Annex II.

2.1.2. Processing in the Eures-network

2.1.2.1. Processing of Euro-vacancies requires:

- rapid circulation of information between the local employment service which receives the employer's offer, and potential applicants in all Member States of the Community,

- full responsibility of that local service for advertising it and processing subsequent applications,

- sufficient information on vacancies, thus allowing potential candidates to apply where appropriate, and avoiding superfluous journeys,

- that the overall responsibility falls on the employment services and their partners who belong to the network.

2.1.2.2. To this end the members of the Eures network take it upon themselves:

- in the case of vacancies advertised to other Member States:

- to inform employers of Eures, persuading them to advertise their vacancies and accept applications of European level,

- to advertise vacancies through Eures,

  - either because they are Euro-vacancies,

  - or because an employer requests that the vacancy be advertised at Community level,

- to withdraw advertised vacancies when they have been cancelled or filled,

- to provide supplementary information on the vacancies advertised, to allow potential applicants to make decisions, setting in motion the placement process. A contact person must be designated to supply this information,

- to receive and process applications from the different employment services and their partners relating to the vacancies advertised,

- to inform the originating service of the results of the placement process, within a time limit to be laid down by the members of the Eures network,

- in the case of vacancies from other Member States:

  - to direct the vacancies received towards the local addressee(s), if indicated by the source service,

  - to process these vacancies in at least the same way as national vacancies with comparable features.

2.1.2.3. The information disseminated concerning vacancies contains two parts:

- the first part contains the data corresponding to the criteria listed in Annex III. These data are classified in a particular order and coded at Community level. Coding is done automatically with the aid of conversion tables, whose creation and updating are the responsibility of the employment services of the Member States and their partners,

- a second part, describing the vacancy, complementary to the first part, and drawn up in free text.

2.1.2.4. The transmission and follow-up procedures for applications will be established by the European Coordination Office in cooperation with the Technical Committee and the members of the Eures network.

2.2. Advertising and Processing vacancies addressed to non-Member States (Article 15(1)(b) of Regulation (EEC) No 1612/68)

2.2.1. Definition

Article 15(1)(b) of Regulation (EEC) No 1612/68 provides for the advertising of vacancies from Member States to non-Member States, while obliging national employment services and their network partners to advertise these vacancies within the Eures network at the same time.

This advertising within Eures should permit:

- transparency of the European labour market,

- [equality of priority for workers who are nationals of Member States][3].

2.2.2. Processing these vacancies, in the context of the Eures network

This processing is identical to that described in Chapter 2.1.2:

- the firms advertising the vacancies are informed of the advertising of their vacancies at Community level,

- they are required to give priority to applications from Community nationals of the Member States,

- if the vacancies apply to seasonal workers, they can be transmitted in accordance with special needs, i.e. establishing lists that include essential information for global use.

2.3. Advertising and processing applications (Article 15(1)(c) of Regulation (EEC) No 1612/68)

The advertising of vacancies within the European community via the Eures network satisfies the basic information needs of potentially-mobile European citizens, and of businesses which wish to widen their range of potential recruitees.

The advertising of applications for employment is also an important concern. This advertising enables people to advertise their wish to be mobile, even in the absence of corresponding vacancies.

2.3.1. Definition

Efficiency within the Eures network requires that only information genuinely useful to citizens and businesses will be circulated.

Employers are particularly interested by requests for mobility from those with the relevant qualifications, experience and linguistic knowledge. A non-exhaustive list of such requests is given at Annex IV.

2.3.2. *Processing of applications for employment in the Eures network*

The employment services and their partners must:

2.3.2.1. in the case of applications for employment addressed to other Member States:

– inform Eures users and others of the two possibilities offered to them:

– to reply to vacancies advertised through Eures,

– in the absence of a vacancy that suits them, to advertise their readiness to go to another Member State,

– enter their application for employment in the Eures network using the system designed for this purpose and to direct it to the desired Member State(s),

– inform the applicant of any responses to his application, within a period not exceeding one month (Article 16(2) of Regulation (EEC) No 1612/68),

– update, in line with procedures yet to be defined, the information transmitted concerning the applicants;

2.3.2.2. in the case of applications for employment coming from other Member States:

– direct these applications towards the local service(s), possibly already indicated by the source employment service,

– treat the applications as at least as equivalent to national or regional applications,

– inform the source service of the results, within a period not exceeding one month (Article 16(2) of Regulation (EEC) No 1612/68)

A computer system for disseminating applications for employment in the context of Eures must be created once the system for processing the vacancies described in this decision has been perfected. In the meantime, each employment service and its potential partners must, in agreement with the Commission of the European Communities, propose a means of disseminating and processing applications with a Community dimension so as to guarantee the points mentioned above.

2.4. *Advertising through Eures of information, by region and branch of activity, on applicants willing to accept employment in another country (Article 15(1)(d) of Regulation (EEC) No 1612/68)*

2.4.1. Definition

The possibility offered to employment services of the Member States by the Eures network to advertise Euro-vacancies and applications and also to choose the services to which these data are targeted, provides ...[4] useful information to the advertising services. It allows these services to identify the services in the Member States where they may [have][4] a high quantity of potential applications.

2.4.2. Preparation and processing of the information

The information referred to in Article 15(1)(d) of Regulation (EEC) No 1612/68 is determined by each Member State systematically evaluating mobility needs. In particular all applicants for employment who are registered with the employment services and their possible partners shall be asked about their willingness to accept, if relevant, employment in another Member State.

These data shall be presented by region and branch of activity (NACE nomenclature). The branch of activity is that in which employment is sought, or failing this, that of the applicant's last job.

These data shall be transmitted regularly to the Commission, which shall be responsible for circulating them to all members of the Eures network. The evaluation methodology used by the employment services shall be notified to the European Coordination Office.

2.5. *General information and information on working and living conditions (Articles 14, 19 and 21 of Regulation (EEC) No 1612/68)*

2.5.1. The objective of the database and nature of the information

The objective of the database is to provide answers to questions on worker mobility, by providing users of the Eures network with information on working and living conditions in the different Member States.

The database facilitates the free movement of workers through the information it provides, notably as regards:

- the labour markets and their evolution in the Member States and also in the regions, as well as the services offered by the employment services,

- working conditions, including relevant legislation,

- information on job-seeking, such as advertisements, job-seeking strategies, *curriculum vitae*, standards relating to interviews, recruitment procedures, and counselling services,

- living conditions, including accommodation, education, taxation, cost of living, health, recreation,

- the programmes and services of the European Community, particularly those that facilitate mobility,

- the transfers of rights and procedures in the field of social security,

- opportunities and procedures for self-employed persons,

- training opportunities,

- comparability of qualifications,

- administrative procedures linked to mobility,

- useful addresses and contacts for more specialised information.

The information shall be presented in a user-friendly manner in all official languages.

2.5.2. *The users of the database*

Access to the general information database is available to:

- members of the Eures network,

- other bodies or individuals approved by the Eures members.

The access conditions are to be negotiated and will be the subject of an agreement between the parties.

2.5.3. *Organisation and functioning of the database*

General management of the database is the responsibility of the Commission and the other members of the Eures network.

The managers will hold meetings regularly, at least once a year.

2.5.4. *Collecting and supplying the information*

The Commission coordinates the collection and presentation of the information in the following manner:

- the employment services and other partners transmit to the Commission all information they consider relevant and which responds to particular questions raised,

- other competent institutions in the Member States may be requested to provide information, where relevant,

- Euro-advisers shall provide information,
- the Commission itself shall provide information,
- the Commission collects and prepares all this information for the database.

2.5.5. *Verification of the information*

If the information provided to the database does not come from the Commission or other institutions of the Member States, it shall be verified with the Member State concerned as follows:

- the information is addressed to the Member State concerned for verification at an appropriate level,
- the employment service receives a copy of the information,
- after six weeks the information will be put into the system.

Nonetheless, the Commission may include information yet to be verified in the database, provided its status is clearly indicated.

The verification procedure is designed purely to establish the accuracy of the information.

Information contained in the database does not necessarily reflect the position or opinion of the Commission.

2.5.6. *Evaluation of the information*

The objective of evaluating the information is:

- to ensure that the information contained in the database corresponds to the overall objective of facilitating worker mobility,
- to ensure that the information is clearly presented.

Evaluation is carried out through systematic consultation at least once every 12 months, with an evaluation group or independent experts.

2.5.7. *Updating the information*

It is the responsibility of each Member State and its institutions to supply any changes necessary as regards the data base information. However, the Commission will ensure regular monitoring:

- by requesting supplementary information and/or information on changes from the Euro-advisers,
- by requesting information and updates in regular collaboration with the evaluation group,

  – by specifying, if necessary, other ways of obtaining information about changes, depending on the circumstances.

All new information must be verified as set out at point 2.5.5.

2.6. *Ethical rules concerning the use of the Eures network*

The information on vacancies and applications for employment advertised in the context of the Eures network is introduced under the explicit responsibility of the source services, which must thus check beforehand that this information complies with the rules relating to non-discrimination of racial, sexual, political or religious nature in the Member States.

In the case of applications for employment advertised in the network, candidates for mobility must expressly ask for information concerning them to be advertised.

Access and use of the Eures network is free of charge both to workers and employers.

The database information will be available either wholly or in part to the network members as agreed with whoever provides the information.

3. *The computer system established for the Eures network*

Article 15(2) of Regulation (EEC) No 1612/68 quoted above provides for the circulation of details on vacancies and applications within a uniform system.

This uniform system shall use computer resources already available to the Member States' employment services and their partners, plus a computer system established by the Commission of the European Communities, to transfer data between the relevant services of the Member States as well as to manage data information.

The format of the messages concerning vacancies and applications advertised by the system, electronic thereof and the procedures for accessing this information will be subject to a uniform procedure, the details of which will be defined at a later stage, through agreement between the employment services of the Member States and the European Coordination Office.

The system established by the Commission will have the following functions:

  – exchange of details on vacancies and applications between the employment services of the Member States,

- access to a database maintained and managed by the Commission relating to general information and working and living conditions,

- access to the electronic mail service, permitting the exchange of informal information with a view to facilitating placement.

A key aspect of the computer system shall be the European Coordination Office, which will permit the monitoring and evaluation of information flows and the production of statistics relating to the state of the labour market.

If they wish, the employment services and their partners may integrate the process of introducing details on Euro-vacancies and applications in their national computer systems.

In the absence of such measures, terminals are installed at key points within employment services and their partners providing direct access to the abovementioned system.

4. **The role of members of the Eures network**

4.1. *Employment services*

The information, advisory and placement tasks which the Member States have entrusted to the employment services and their partners, mean that the employment services have a key role within the Eures network.

In order for Eures to be fully effective, this means that all employment services be associated with the Eures network.

However, Regulation (EEC) No 1612/68 provides that specialist services designated by each Member State may have a particular role.

These services are based on the national network of agents known as 'Euro-advisers', who have received appropriate professional training under the aegis of the Commission. Their function, status and working tools are described below.

4.1.1. *Function of the Euro-advisers*

The decision to move from one country to another, to be confronted by new living and working conditions, requires information, counselling and specific assistance specially designed for mobile workers.

An employer's intention to recruit at European level, or to extend its production activities or services to another country within the Community, also needs specialist advice.

Supplying this advice and information on the European labour market, is the role of the Euro-advisers. Depending on the tasks entrusted to them at national level, they may also support or carry out placement operations at Community level.

4.1.2. *Status of the Euro-advisers at national and Community level*

The Euro-advisers work in the framework of their institution, which chooses them, and determines their numbers, their workplace, and their mode of activity (full or part-time). Their institutions, within their national and Eures frameworks, determine tasks which are the responsibility of the Euro-advisers.

The Euro-advisers cooperate at national level and with the services concerned with problems of employment and/or vocational training, and are in direct contact with the workers and employers who are potential Eures users.

The Euro-advisers also belong to a Community network. To this end they have contacts with the national institutions which are active in the Community and regularly participate in working meetings where they can exchange information and expertise.

They undergo basic training and continuous training, organised under the aegis of the Commission of the European Communities, in liaison with the national services.

The national institutions communicate to the Commission all changes within the national Euro-adviser network as regards:

-   the names, title and work address of the persons concerned,

-   their geographical and sectoral field of activity.

4.1.3. *The Euro-advisers' working conditions*

The national institutions with the Commission's financial and technical support provide their Euro-advisers with the necessary resources for carrying out their tasks. This concerns in particular:

-   workplace equipment, which will allow them to access the Eures computer system, either directly or via the national system,

-   tools necessary for information guidance and counselling at national and European levels.

4.2. *Other members of the network* (Article 17 of Regulation (EEC) No 1612/68)

Various organisations are active in the field of employment in the Member States and participate in the exchange of information in the context of the Eures-network.

Their activities must be authorised by the Member States and must fall within the scope of the objectives defined by Regulation (EEC) No 1612/68.

5. **Specific forms of the Eures network (Article 17)**

Although the majority of the employment services are national, and may have an exclusive or almost exclusive legal framework as concerns job placement, regions are increasing their role in employment matters, as are organisations separate from the employment services and often specialising in certain professions or categories of employees.

5.1. *Regional services* (*Article 17(a)(i) and (ii)*)

Regional services of two or more neighbouring Member States, with the authorisation of their central employment services, may organise direct exchanges of information between themselves within the provisions of Regulation (EEC) No 1612/68.

These exchanges should however occur within the framework of the Eures network as laid down in this Decision.

At cross-border level, these regional services, in accordance with their capabilities and the approval of their central services, may if necessary (Article 17(b)) create cooperation structures between their services with a view:

- to ensure circulation of information concerning vacancies and applications between the border regions concerned, with a view to informing the public,

- to provide similar information concerning living and working conditions in the regions concerned,

- to draw up an inventory of vocational training opportunities and to make it accessible to the public,

- to set up a framework for dialogue and consultation between management and labour in the domain of employment.

The economic and social partners, and in general all institutions concerned with employment problems and vocational training in the border regions concerned, shall contribute to the functioning of these cooperation structures mentioned above.

5.2. *Services specialising in certain professions or categories of employees*

These organisations within the different Member States, once they are operating within a recognised legal framework and with the agreement of the employment services, may establish direct cooperation with each other.

This cooperation, inasmuch as it involves exchange of information as foreseen by the Regulation (EEC) No 1612/68, should be coordinated or integrated with the Eures network as set out by this Decision.

6. **Promotion of the Eures network-communication**

The effectiveness of the Eures network requires that potential users (individuals and businesses), plus employees of the employment services and their partners are all aware of what the network has to offer.

For this reason both internal and external long-term communication strategies must be developed.

The employment services and their partners are responsible for preparing this plan and for developing it in close liaison with the Commission. The Commission proposes an overall strategy, designed to ensure the consistency and cohesion of the network *vis-à-vis* its users.

In particular, the Commission proposes, in order to support the national communication actions:

- seminars for all Euro-advisers,
- booklets and updates on the network's activity,
- promotional material for the network.

7. **Coordination and management of the Eures network**

7.1. *The European Coordination Office (Articles 21 and 22 of Regulation (EEC) No 1612/68)*

The constant development of the Eures network as well as the motivation of members and partners in this network justifies the creation of a coordination and technical support structure known as the European Coordination Office.

This office, established within the Commission, is responsible in particular for:

- promoting, at Community level, the clearing of vacancies and applications by coordinating the necessary technical operations,
- analysing movement of workers and providing information on likely market trends within the Community,
- contributing to establish, in collaboration with the Technical Committee on Free Movement, the national employment services and their partners, the means necessary at administrative and technical level for achieving the objectives laid down in the Regulation (EEC) No 1612/68.

7.2. *The Technical Committee on Free Movement (Article 32 et seq. Regulation (EEC) No 1612/68)*

The Technical Committee, which is composed of representatives of the governments of the Member States, is responsible for helping the Commission to prepare, promote and monitor all technical work and measures giving effect to the Regulation referred to by this Decision.

7.3. *The working party of the members of the Eures network*

The work of the Commission and that of the Technical Committee for Free Movement on the maintenance and development of Eures, in accordance with the needs of the final users must be explained and supported by those operating the network in the Member States.

A working party consisting of representatives of the Commission, the employment services and their partners shall therefore be established.

It may also be widened to include:

– representatives of Eures partner organisations at Community level and in the crossborder structures (Eures Crossborder),

– all experts outside the Eures network who are capable of contributing to development of the network.

The meetings of this working party are organised at the Commission's initiative or at the express request of the members of the Eures network or the Technical Committee on Free Movement.

Annex II

Non-exhaustive list of the types of vacancies with a Community dimension

– Vacancies for managers, engineers, senior technicians etc. in which the applicants must have a level of study or training of at least three years after the leaving certificate, or equivalent experience.

– Vacancies in certain economic sectors with strong international links (for example tourism, hotel business, transport).

– Vacancies involving the practical use of several languages.

– Vacancies, necessitating work experience in countries other than that in which the post is available.

– Vacancies which are unfilled due to the lack of qualified applicants within the Member State concerned.

- Vacancies which the employment service believe can be filled by workers available in another Member State.

- All vacancies where the employer formally requests circulation of details at European level.

COUNCIL DIRECTIVE

of 15 October 1968

on the abolition of restrictions on movement and residence within the Community for workers of Member States and their families

(68/360/EEC)

(OJ No L 257, 19.10.68, p.13)

The Council of the European Communities,

Having regard to the Treaty establishing the European Economic Community, and in particular Article 49 thereof;

Having regard to the proposal from the Commission;

Having regard to the opinion of the European Parliament[1];

Having regard to the opinion of the Economic and Social Committee[2];

Whereas Council Regulation (EEC) No 1612/68[3] fixed the provisions governing freedom of movement for workers within the Community; whereas, consequently, measures should be adopted for the abolition of restrictions which still exist concerning movement and residence within the Community, which conform to the rights and privileges accorded by the said Regulation to nationals of any Member State who move in order to pursue activities as employed persons and to members of their families;

Whereas the rules applicable to residence should, as far as possible, bring the position of workers from other Member States and members of their families into line with that of nationals;

Whereas the co-ordination of special measures relating to the movement and residence of foreign nationals, justified on grounds of public policy, public security or public health, is the subject of the Council Directive of 25 February 1964[4], adopted in application of Article 56(2) of the Treaty;

Has adopted this Directive:

Article 1

Member States shall, acting as provided in this Directive, abolish restrictions on the movement and residence of nationals of the said States and of members of their families to whom Regulation (EEC No 1612/68) applies.

Article 2

1. Member States shall grant the nationals referred to in Article 1 the right to leave their territory in order to take up activities as employed persons and to pursue such activities in the territory of another Member State. Such right shall be exercised simply on production of a valid identity card or passport. Members of the family shall enjoy the same right as the national on whom they are dependent.

2. Member States shall, acting in accordance with their laws, issue to such nationals, or renew, an identity card or passport, which shall state in particular the holder's nationality.

3. The passport must be valid at least for all Member States and for countries through which the holder must pass when travelling between Member States. Where a passport is the only document on which the holder may lawfully leave the country, its period of validity shall be not less than five years.

4. Member States may not demand from the nationals referred to in Article 1 any exit visa or any equivalent document.

Article 3

1. Member States shall allow the persons referred to in Article 1 to enter their territory simply on production of a valid identity card or passport.

2. No entry visa or equivalent document may be demanded save from members of the family who are not nationals of a Member State. Member States shall accord to such persons every facility for obtaining any necessary visas.

Article 4

1. Member States shall grant the right of residence in their territory to

the persons referred to in Article 1 who are able to produce the documents listed in paragraph 3.

2. As proof of the right of residence, a document entitled 'Residence Permit for a National of a Member State of the EEC' shall be issued. This document must include a statement that it has been issued pursuant to Regulation (EEC) No 1612/68 and to the measures taken by the Member States for the implementation of the present Directive. The text of such statement is given in the Annex to this Directive.

3. For the issue of a Residence Permit for a National of a Member State of the EEC, Member States may require only the production of the following documents;

– by the worker:

(a) the document with which he entered their territory;

(b) a confirmation of engagement from the employer or a certificate of employment;

– by the members of the worker's family:

(c) the document with which they entered the territory;

(d) a document issued by the competent authority of the State of origin or the State whence they came, proving their relationship;

(e) in the cases referred to in Article 10(1) and (2) of Regulation (EEC) No 1612/68, a document issued by the competent authority of the State of origin or the State whence they came, testifying that they are dependent on the worker or that they live under his roof in such country.

4. A member of the family who is not a national of a Member State shall be issued with a residence document which shall have the same validity as that issued to the worker on whom he is dependent.

Article 5

Completion of the formalities for obtaining a residence permit shall not hinder the immediate beginning of employment under a contract concluded by the applicants.

Article 6

1. The residence permit:

(a) must be valid throughout the territory of the Member State which issued it;

(b) must be valid for at least five years from the date of issue and be automatically renewable.

2. Breaks in residence not exceeding six consecutive months and absence on military service shall not affect the validity of a residence permit.

3. Where a worker is employed for a period exceeding three months but not exceeding a year in the service of an employer in the host State or in the employ of a person providing services, the host Member State shall issue him a temporary residence permit, the validity of which may be limited to the expected period of the employment.

Subject to the provisions of Article 8(1)(c), a temporary residence permit shall be issued also to a seasonal worker employed for a period of more than three months. The period of employment must be shown in the documents referred to in paragraph 4(3)(b).

Article 7

1. A valid residence permit may not be withdrawn from a worker solely on the grounds that he is no longer in employment, either because he is temporarily incapable of work as a result of illness or accident, or because he is involuntarily unemployed, this being duly confirmed by the competent employment office.

2. When the residence permit is renewed for the first time, the period of residence may be restricted, but not to less than twelve months, where the worker has been involuntarily unemployed in the Member State for more than twelve consecutive months.

Article 8

1. Member States shall, without issuing an residence permit, recognise the right of residence in their territory of:

(a) a worker pursuing an activity as an employed person, where the activity is not expected to last for more than three months. The document with which the person concerned entered the territory and a statement by the employer on the expected duration of the employment shall be sufficient to cover his stay; a statement by the employer shall not, however, be required in the case of workers coming within the provisions of the Council Directive of 25 February 1964[5] on the attainment of freedom of establishment and freedom to provide services in respect of the activities of intermediaries in commerce, industry and small craft industries;

(b) a worker who, while having his residence in the territory of a Member

State to which he returns as a rule, each day or at least once a week, is employed in the territory of another Member State. The competent authority of the State where he is employed may issue such worker with a special permit valid for five years and automatically renewable;

(c) a seasonal worker who holds a contract of employment stamped by the competent authority of the Member State on whose territory he has come to pursue his activity.

2. In all cases referred to in paragraph 1, the competent authorities of the host Member State may require the worker to report his presence in the territory.

Article 9

1. The residence documents granted to nationals of a Member State of the EEC referred to in this Directive shall be issued and renewed free of charge or on payment of an amount not exceeding the dues and taxes charged for the issue of identity cards to nationals.

2. The visa referred to in Article 3(2) and the stamp referred to in Article 8(1)(c) shall be free of charge.

3. Member States shall take the necessary steps to simplify as much as possible the formalities and procedure for obtaining the documents mentioned in paragraph 1.

Article 10

Member States shall not derogate from the provisions of this Directive save on grounds of public policy, public security or public health.

Article 11

1. This Directive shall not affect the provisions of the Treaty establishing the European Coal and Steel Community which relate to workers with recognised skills in coal mining and steel making, or the provisions of the Treaty establishing the European Atomic Energy Community which deal with the right to take up skilled employment in the field of nuclear energy, or any measures taken in implementation of those Treaties.

2. Nevertheless, this Directive shall apply to the categories of workers referred to in paragraph 1, and to members of their families, in so far as their legal position is not governed by the abovementioned Treaties or measures.

Article 12

1. Member States shall, within nine months of notification of this Directive, bring into force the measures necessary to comply with its provisions and shall forthwith inform the Commission thereof.

2. They shall notify the Commission of amendments made to provisions imposed by law, regulation or administrative action for the simplification of the formalities and procedure for issuing such documents as are still necessary for the entry, exit and residence of workers and members of their families.

Article 13

1. The Council Directive of 25 March 1964[6] on the abolition of restrictions on movement and on residence within the Community of workers and their families shall continue to have effect until this Directive is implemented by the Member States.

2. Residence permits issued pursuant to the Directive referred to in Paragraph 1 shall remain valid until the date on which they next expire.

Article 14

This Directive is addressed to the Member States.

Done at Luxembourg, 15 October 1968.

For the Council

The President

G. Sedati

Annex

Text of the statement referred to in Article 4(2):

'This permit is issued pursuant to Regulation (EEC) No 1612/68 of the Council of the European Communities of 15 October 1968 and to the measures taken in implementation of the Council Directive of 15 October 1968.

In accordance with the provisions of the abovementioned Regulation, the holder of this permit has the right to take up and pursue an activity as an employed person in ...[7] territory under the same conditions as ...[7] workers.'

FOOTNOTES

1. OJ No 268, 6.11.67, p.10.
2. OJ No 298, 7.12.67, p.10.
3. OJ No L 257, 19.10.68, p.2.
4. OJ No 56, 4.4.64, p.850.
5. OJ No 56, 4.4.64, p.869.
6. OJ No 62, 17.4.64, p.981.
7. Belgian, German, French, Italian, Luxembourg, Netherlands, according to the country issuing the permit.

 IRL Implemented in Ireland: S.I. 333/1972; S.I. 128/1975; S.I. 393/1977; S.I. 351/1978.

COUNCIL DIRECTIVE

of 21 May 1973

on the abolition of restrictions on movement and residence within the Community for nationals of Member States with regard to establishment and the provision of services

(73/148/EEC)

(OJ No L 172, 28.6.73, p.14)

The Council of the European Communities,

Having regard to the Treaty establishing the European Economic Community, and in particular Article 54(2) and Article 63(2) thereof;

Having regard to the General Programmes for the abolition of restrictions on freedom of establishment and freedom to provide services[1], and in particular Title II thereof;

Having regard to the proposal from the Commission;

Having regard to the opinion of the European Parliament[2];

Having regard to the opinion of the Economic and Social Committee[3];

Whereas freedom of movement of persons as provided for in the Treaty and the General Programmes for the abolition of restrictions on freedom of establishment and on freedom to provide services entails the abolition of restrictions on movement and residence within the Community for nationals of Member States wishing to establish themselves or to provide services within the territory of another Member State;

Whereas freedom of establishment can be fully attained only if a right of permanent residence is granted to the persons who are to enjoy freedom of establishment; whereas freedom to provide services entails that persons providing and receiving services should have the right of residence for the time during which the services are being provided;

Whereas Council Directive of 25 February 1964[4] on the abolition of restrictions on movement and residence within the Community for nationals of Member States with regard to establishment and provision of services laid down the rules applicable in this area to activities as self-employed persons;

Whereas Council Directive of 15 October 1968[5] on the abolition of restrictions on movement and residence within the Community for workers of Member States and their families, which replaced the Directive of 25 March 1964[6] bearing the same title, has in the meantime amended the rules applicable to employed persons;

Whereas the provisions concerning movement and residence within the Community of self-employed persons and their families should likewise be improved;

Whereas the coordination of special measures concerning the movement and residence of foreign nationals, justified on grounds of public policy, public security or public health, is already the subject of the Council Directive of 25 February 1964[7];

Has adopted this Directive:

Article 1

1. The Member States shall, acting as provided in this Directive, abolish restrictions on the movement and residence of:

(a) nationals of a Member State who are established or who wish to establish themselves in another Member State in order to pursue activities as self-employed persons, or who wish to provide services in that State;

(b) nations of Member States wishing to go to another Member State as recipients of services;

(c) the spouse and the children under twenty-one years of age of such nationals, irrespective of their nationality;

(d) the relatives in the ascending and descending lines of such nationals and of the spouse of such nationals, which relatives are dependent on them, irrespective of their nationality.

2. Member States shall favour the admission of any other member of the family of a national referred to in paragraph 1(a) or (b) or of the spouse of that national, which member is dependent on that national or spouse of that national or who in the country of origin was living under the same roof.

Article 2

1. Member States shall grant the persons referred to in Article 1 the right to leave their territory. Such right shall be exercised simply on production of a valid identity card or passport. Members of the family shall enjoy the same right as the national on whom they are dependent.

2. Member States shall, acting in accordance with their laws, issue to their nationals, or renew, an identity card or passport, which shall state in particular the holder's nationality.

3. The passport must be valid at least for all Member States and for countries through which the holder must pass when travelling between Member States. Where a passport is the only document on which the holder may lawfully leave the country, its period of validity shall be not less than five years.

4. Member States may not demand from the persons referred to in Article 1 any exit visa or any equivalent requirement.

Article 3

1. Member States shall grant to the persons referred to in Article 1 right to enter their territory merely on production of a valid identity card or passport.

2. No entry visa or equivalent requirement may be demanded save in respect of members of the family who do have the nationality of a Member State. Member States shall afford to such persons every facility for obtaining any necessary visas.

Article 4

1. Each Member State shall grant the right of permanent residence to nationals of other Member States who establish themselves within its territory in order to pursue activities as self-employed persons, when the restrictions on these activities have been abolished pursuant to the Treaty.

As proof of the right of residence, a document entitled 'residence permit for a national of a Member State of the European Communities' shall be issued. This document shall be valid for not less than five years from the date of issue and shall be automatically renewable.

Breaks in residence not exceeding six consecutive months and absence on military service shall not affect the validity of a residence permit.

A valid residence permit may not be withdrawn from a national referred to in Article 1(1)(a) solely on the grounds that he is no longer in employment because he is temporarily incapable of work as a result of illness or accident.

Any national of a Member State who is not specified in the first subparagraph but who is authorised under the laws of another Member State to purse an activity within its territory shall be granted a right of abode for a period not less than that of the authorisation granted for the pursuit of the activity in question.

However, any national referred to in subparagraph 1 and to whom the provisions of the preceding subparagraph apply as a result of a change of employment shall retain his residence permit until the date on which it expires.

2. The right of residence for persons providing and receiving services shall be of equal duration with the period during which the services are provided.

Where such period exceeds three months, the Member State in the territory of which the services are performed shall issue a right of abode as proof of the right of residence.

Where the period does not exceed three months, the identity card or passport with which the person concerned entered the territory shall be sufficient to cover his stay. The Member State may, however, require the person concerned to report his presence in the territory.

3. A member of the family who is not a national of a Member State shall be issued with a residence document which shall have the same validity as that issued to the national on whom he is dependent.

Article 5

The right of residence shall be effective throughout the territory of the Member State concerned.

Article 6

An applicant for a residence permit or right of abode shall not be required by a Member State to produce anything other than the following, namely:

(a) the identity card or passport with which he or she entered its territory;

(b) proof that he or she comes within one of the classes of person referred to in Articles 1 and 4.

Article 7

1. The residence documents granted to nationals of a Member State shall be issued and renewed free of charge or on payment of an amount not exceeding the dues and taxes charged for the issue of identity cards to nationals. These provisions shall also apply to documents and certificates required for the issue and renewal of such residence documents.

2. The visas referred to in Article 3(2) shall be free of charge.

3. Member States shall take the necessary steps to simplify as much as possible the formalities and the procedure for obtaining the documents mentioned in paragraph 1.

Article 8

Member States shall not derogate from the provisions of this Directive save on grounds of public policy, public security or public health.

Article 9

1. Member States shall, within six months of notification of this Directive, bring into force the measures necessary to comply with its provisions and shall forthwith inform the Commission thereof.

2. They shall notify the Commission of amendments made to provisions imposed by law, regulation or administrative action for the simplification with regard to establishment and the provision of services of the formalities and procedure for issuing such documents as are still necessary for the movement and residence of persons referred to in Article 1.

Article 10

1. The Council Directive of 25 February 1964 on the abolition of restrictions on movement and residence within the Community for nationals of Member States with regard to establishment and the provision of services shall remain applicable until this Directive is implemented by the Member States.

2. Residence documents issued pursuant to the Directive referred to in paragraph 1 shall remain valid until the date on which they next expire.

Article 11

This Directive is addressed to the Member States.

Done at Brussels, 21 May 1973.

For the Council

The President

E. Glinne

FOOTNOTES

1. OJ No 2, 15.1.62, pp.32 and 36.
2. OJ No C 19, 28.2.72, p.5.
3. OJ No C 67, 24.6.72, p.7.
4. OJ No 56, 4.4.64, p.845.
5. OJ No L 257, 19.10.68, p.13.
6. OJ No 62, 17.4.64, p.981.
7. OJ No 56, 4.4.64, p.850.

IRL Implemented in Ireland: S.I. 393/1977; S.I. 165/1981; S.I. 39/1985; S.I. 441/1985.

(b) Right to Remain

REGULATION (EEC) No 1251/70 OF THE COMMISSION

of 29 June 1970

on the right of workers to remain in the territory of a Member State after having been employed in that State

(OJ No L 142, 30.6.70, p.24)

The Commission of the European Communities,

Having regard to the Treaty establishing the European Economic Community, and in particular Article 48(3)(d) thereof, and Article 2 of the Protocol on the Grand Duchy of Luxembourg;

Having regard to the Opinion of the European Parliament[1];

Whereas Council Regulation (EEC) No 1612/68[2] of 15 October 1968 and Council Directive No 68/360/EEC of 15 October 1968[3] enabled freedom of movement for workers to be secured at the end of a series of measures to be achieved progressively; whereas the right of residence acquired by workers in active employment has as a corollary the right, granted by the Treaty to such workers, to remain in the territory of a Member State after having been employed in that State; whereas it is important to lay down the conditions for the exercise of such right;

Whereas the said Council Regulation and Council Directive contain the appropriate provisions concerning the right of workers to reside in the territory of a Member State for the purposes of employment; whereas the right to remain, referred to in Article 48(3)(d) of the Treaty, is interpreted therefore as the right of the worker to maintain his residence in the territory of a Member State when he ceases to be employed there;

Whereas the mobility of labour in the Community requires that workers may be employed successively in several Member States without thereby being placed at a disadvantage;

Whereas it is important, in the first place, to guarantee to the worker residing in the territory of a Member State the right to remain in that territory when he ceases to be employed in that State because he has reached retirement age or by reason of permanent incapacity to work; whereas, however, it is equally important to ensure that right for the worker who, after a period of employment and residence in the territory of a Member State, works as an employed person in the territory of another Member State, while still retaining his residence in the territory of the first State;

Whereas, to determine the conditions under which the right to remain arises, account should be taken of the reasons which have led to the termination of employment in the territory of the Member State concerned and, in particular, of the difference between retirement, the normal and foreseeable end of working life, and incapacity to work which leads to a premature and unforeseeable termination of activity; whereas special conditions must be laid down where termination of activity is the result of an accident at work or occupational disease, or where the worker's spouse is or was a national of the Member State concerned;

Whereas the worker who has reached the end of his working life should have sufficient time in which to decide where he wishes to establish his final residence;

Whereas the exercise by the worker of the right to remain entails that such right shall be extended to members of his family; whereas in the case of the death of the worker during his working life, maintenance of

the right of residence of the members of his family must also be recognised and be the subject of special conditions;

Whereas persons to whom the right to remain applies must enjoy equality of treatment with national workers who have ceased their working lives;

Has adopted this Regulation:

Article 1

The provisions of this Regulation shall apply to nationals of a Member State who have worked as employed persons in the territory of another Member State and to members of their families, as defined in Article 10 of Council Regulation (EEC) No 1612/68 on freedom of movement for workers within the Community.

Article 2

1. The following shall have the right to remain permanently in the territory of a Member State:

(a) a worker who, at the time of termination of his activity, has reached the age laid down by the law of that Member State for entitlement to an old-age pension and who has been employed in that State for at least the last twelve months and has resided there continuously for more than three years;

(b) a worker who, having resided continuously in the territory of that State for more than two years, ceases to work there as an employed person as a result of permanent incapacity to work. If such incapacity is the result of an accident at work or an occupational disease entitling him to a pension for which an institution of that State is entirely or partially responsible, no condition shall be imposed as to length of residence;

(c) a worker who, after three years' continuous employment and residence in the territory of that State, works as an employed person in the territory of another Member State, while retaining his residence in the territory of the first State, to which he returns, as a rule, each day or at least once a week.

Periods of employment completed in this way in the territory of the other Member State shall, for the purposes of entitlement to the rights referred to in subparagraphs (a) and (b), be considered as having been completed in the territory of the State of residence.

2. The conditions as to length of residence and employment laid down in paragraph 1(a) and the condition as to length of residence laid down

in paragraph 1(b) shall not apply if the worker's spouse is a national of the Member State concerned or has lost the nationality of that State by marriage to that worker.

Article 3

1. The members of a worker's family referred to in Article 1 of this Regulation who are residing with him in the territory of a Member State shall be entitled to remain there permanently if the worker has acquired the right to remain in the territory of that State in accordance with Article 2, and to do so even after his death.

2. If, however, the worker dies during his working life and before having acquired the right to remain in the territory of the State concerned, members of his family shall be entitled to remain there permanently on condition that:

- the worker, on the date of his decease, had resided continuously in the territory of that Member State for at least 2 years; or

- his death resulted from an accident at work or an occupational disease; or

- the surviving spouse is a national of the State of residence or lost the nationality of that State by marriage to that worker.

Article 4

1. Continuity of residence as provided for in Articles 2(1) and 3(2) may be attested by any means of proof in use in the country of residence. It shall not be affected by temporary absences not exceeding a total of three months per year, nor by longer absences due to compliance with the obligations of military service.

2. Periods of involuntary unemployment, duly recorded by the competent employment office, and absences due to illness or accident shall be considered as periods of employment within the meaning of Article 2(1).

Article 5

1. The person entitled to the right to remain shall be allowed to exercise it within two years from the time of becoming entitled to such right pursuant to Article 2(1)(a) and (b) and Article 3. During such period he may leave the territory of the Member State without adversely affecting such right.

2. No formality shall be required on the part of the person concerned in respect of the exercise of the right to remain.

Article 6

1. Persons coming under the provisions of this Regulation shall be entitled to a residence permit which:

(a) shall be issued and renewed free of charge or on payment of a sum not exceeding the dues and taxes payable by nationals for the issue or renewal of identity documents;

(b) must be valid throughout the territory of the Member State issuing it;

(c) must be valid for at least five years and be renewable automatically.

2. Periods of non-residence not exceeding six consecutive months shall not affect the validity of the residence permit.

Article 7

The right to equality of treatment, established by Council Regulation (EEC) No 1612/68, shall apply also to persons coming under the provisions of this Regulation.

Article 8

1. This Regulation shall not affect any provisions laid down by law, regulation or administrative action of one Member State which would be more favourable to nationals of other Member States.

2. Member States shall facilitate re-admission to their territories of workers who have left those territories after having resided there permanently for a long period and having been employed there and who wish to return there when they have reached retirement age or are permanently incapacitated for work.

Article 9

1. The Commission may, taking account of developments in the demographic situation of the Grand Duchy of Luxembourg, lay down, at the request of that State, different conditions from those provided for in this Regulation, in respect of the exercise of the right to remain in Luxembourg territory.

2. Within two months after the request supplying all appropriate details has been put before it, the Commission shall take a decision, stating the reasons on which it is based.

It shall notify the Grand Duchy of Luxembourg of such decision and inform the other Member States thereof;

This Regulation shall be binding in its entirety and directly applicable in all Member States.

Done at Brussels, 29 June 1970.

For the Commission

The President

Jean Rey

FOOTNOTES

1. OJ No C 65, 5.6.70, p.16.
2. OJ No L 257, 19.10.68, p.2.
3. OJ No L 257, 19.10.68, p.13.

COUNCIL DIRECTIVE

of 18 May 1972

extending to workers exercising the right to remain in the territory of a Member State after having been employed in that State the scope of the Directive of 25 February 1964 on coordination of special measures concerning the movement and residence of foreign nationals which are justified on grounds of public policy, public security or public health

(72/194/EEC)

(OJ No L 121, 26.5.72, p.32)

The Council of the European Communities,

Having regard to the Treaty establishing the European Economic Community, and in particular Articles 49 and 56(2) thereof;

Having regard to the proposal from the Commission;

Having regard to the opinion of the European Parliament;

Having regard to the opinion of the Economic and Social Committee;

Whereas the Council Directive of 25 February 1964[1] coordinated special measures concerning the movement and residence of foreign nationals which are justified on grounds of public policy, public security or public health and whereas Commission Regulation (EEC) No 1251/70[2] of 29

June 1970 on the right of workers to remain in the territory of a Member State after having been employed in that State laid down conditions for the exercise of such right;

Whereas the Directive of 25 February 1964 should continue to apply to persons to whom that Regulation applies;

Has adopted the following Directive:

Article 1

The Council Directive of 25 February 1964 on coordination of special measures concerning the movement and residence of foreign nationals which are justified on grounds of public policy, public security or public health shall apply to nationals of Member States and members of their families who pursuant to Regulation (EEC) No 1251/70, exercise the right to remain in the territory of a Member State

Article 2

Member States shall put into force the measures necessary to comply with this Directive within six months of its notification and shall forthwith inform the Commission thereof.

Article 3

This Directive is addressed to the Member States.

Done at Brussels, 18 May 1972.

For the Council

The President

M. Mart

FOOTNOTES

1. OJ No 56, 4.4.64, p.850.
2. OJ No L 142, 30.6.70, p.24.

RL Implemented in Ireland: S.I. 393/1977; S.I. 165/1981; S.I. 39/1985; S.I. 441/1985.

COUNCIL DIRECTIVE

of 17 December 1974

concerning the right of nationals of a Member State to remain in the territory of another Member State after having pursued therein an activity in a self-employed capacity

(75/34/EEC)

(OJ No L 14, 20.1.75, p.10)

The Council of the European Communities,

Having regard to the Treaty establishing the European Economic Community, and in particular Article 235 thereof;

Having regard to the general programme for the abolition of restrictions on freedom of establishment[1], and in particular Title II thereof;

Having regard to the proposal from the Commission;

Having regard to the opinion of the European Parliament[2];

Having regard to the opinion of the Economic and Social Committee[3];

Whereas pursuant to Council Directive No 73/148/EEC[4] of 21 May 1973 on the abolition of restrictions on movement and residence within the Community for nationals of Member States with regard to establishment and the provision of services, each Member State grants the right of permanent residence to nationals of other Member States who establish themselves within its territory in order to pursue activities as self-employed persons, when the restrictions on these activities have been abolished pursuant to the Treaty;

Whereas it is normal for a person to prolong a period of permanent residence in the territory of a Member State by remaining there after having pursued an activity there; whereas the absence of a right so to remain in such circumstances is an obstacle to the attainment of freedom of establishment; whereas, as regards employed persons, the conditions under which such a right may be exercised have already been laid down by Regulation (EEC) No 1251/70[5];

Whereas Article 48(3)(d) of the Treaty recognises the right of workers to remain in the territory of a Member State after having been employed in that State; whereas Article 54(2) does not expressly provide a similar right for self-employed persons; whereas, nevertheless, the nature of

establishment, together with attachments formed to the countries in which they have pursued their activities, means that such persons have a definite interest in enjoying the same right to remain as that granted to workers; whereas in justification of this measure reference should be made to the Treaty provision enabling it to be taken;

Whereas freedom of establishment within the Community requires that nationals of Member State may pursue self-employed activities in several Member States in succession without thereby being placed at a disadvantage;

Whereas a national of a Member State residing in the territory of another Member State should be guaranteed the right to remain in that territory when he ceases to pursue an activity as a self-employed person in that State because he has reached retirement age or by reason of permanent incapacity to work; whereas such a right should also be guaranteed to the national of a Member State who, after a period of activity in a self-employed capacity and residence in the territory of a second Member State, pursues an activity in the territory of a third Member State, while still retaining his residence in the territory of the second State;

Whereas, to determine the conditions under which the right to remain arises, account should be taken of the reasons which have led to the termination of activity in the territory of the Member State concerned and, in particular, of the difference between retirement, the normal and foreseeable end of working life, and permanent incapacity to work which leads to a premature and unforeseeable termination of activity; whereas special conditions must be laid down where the spouse is or was a national of the Member State concerned, or where termination of activity is the result of an accident at work or occupational illness;

Whereas a national of a Member State who has reached the end of his working life, after working in a self-employed capacity in the territory of another Member State, should have sufficient time in which to decide where he wishes to establish his final residence;

Whereas the exercise of the right to remain by a national of a Member State working in a self-employed capacity entails extension of such right to the members of his family; whereas in the case of the death of a national of a Member State working in a self-employed capacity during his working life the right of residence of the members of his family must also be recognised and be the subject of special conditions;

Whereas persons to whom the right to remain applies must enjoy equality of treatment with nationals of the State concerned who have reached the end of their working lives,

Has adopted this Directive:

Article 1

Member States shall, under the conditions laid down in this Directive abolish restrictions on the right to remain in their territory in favour of nationals of another Member State who have pursued activities as self-employed persons in their territory, and members of their families, as defined in Article 1 of Directive 73/148/EEC.

Article 2

1. Each Member State shall recognise the right to remain permanently in its territory of:

(a) any person who, at the time of termination of his activity, has reached the age laid down by the law of that State for entitlement to an old-age pension and who has pursued his activity in that State for at least the previous twelve months and has resided there continuously for more than three years.

Where the law of that Member State does not grant the right to an old-age pension to certain categories of self-employed workers, the age requirement shall be considered as satisfied when the beneficiary reaches 65 years of age;

(b) any person who, having resided continuously in the territory of that State for more than two years, ceases to pursue his activity there as a result of permanent incapacity to work.

If such incapacity is the result of an accident at work or an occupational illness entitling him to a pension which is payable in whole or in part by an institution of that State no condition shall be imposed as to length of residence;

(c) any person who, after three years' continuous activity and residence in the territory of that State, pursues his activity in the territory of another Member State, while retaining his residence in the territory of the first State, to which he returns, as a rule, each day or at least once a week.

Periods of activity so completed in the territory of the other Member State shall, for the purposes of entitlement to the rights referred to in (a) and (b), be considered as having been completed in the territory of the State of residence.

2. The conditions as to length of residence and activity laid down in paragraph 1(a) and the condition as to length of residence laid down in paragraph 1(b) shall not apply if the spouse of the self-employed person

is a national of the Member State concerned or has lost the nationality of that State by marriage to that person.

Article 3

1. Each Member State shall recognise the right of the members of the self-employed person's family referred to in Article 1 who are residing with him in the territory of that State to remain there permanently, if the person concerned has acquired the right to remain in the territory of that State in accordance with Article 2. This provision shall continue to apply even after the death of the person concerned.

2. If, however, the self-employed person dies during his working life and before having acquired the right to remain in the territory of the State concerned, that State shall recognise the right of the members of his family to remain there permanently on condition that:

- the person concerned, on the date of his decease, had resided continuously in its territory for at least two years; or

- his death resulted from an accident at work or an occupational illness; or

- the surviving spouse is a national of that State or lost such nationality by marriage to the person concerned.

Article 4

1. Continuity of residence as provided for in Articles 2(1) and 3(2) may be attested by any means of proof in use in the country of residence. It may not be affected by temporary absences not exceeding a total of three months per year, nor by longer absences due to compliance with the obligations of military service.

2. Periods of inactivity due to circumstances outside the control of the person concerned or of inactivity owing to illness or accident must be considered as periods of activity within the meaning of Article 2(1).

Article 5

1. Member States shall allow the person entitled to the right to remain to exercise such right within two years from the time of becoming entitled thereto pursuant to Article 2(1)(a) and (b) and Article 3. During this period the beneficiary must be able to leave the territory of the Member State without adversely affecting such right.

2. Member States shall not require the person concerned to comply with any particular formality in order to exercise the right to remain.

Article 6

1. Member States shall recognise the right of persons having the right to remain in their territory to a residence permit, which must:

(a) be issued and renewed free of charge or on payment of a sum not exceeding the dues and taxes payable by nationals for the issue or renewal of identity cards;

(b) be valid throughout the territory of the Member State issuing it;

(c) be valid for five years and renewable automatically.

2. Periods of non-residence not exceeding six consecutive months and longer absences due to compliance with the obligations of military service may not affect the validity of a residence permit.

Article 7

Member States shall apply to persons having the right to remain in their territory the right of equality of treatment recognised by the Council Directives on the abolition of restrictions on freedom of establishment pursuant to Title III of the general programme which provides for such abolition.

Article 8

1. This Directive shall not affect any provisions laid down by law, regulation or administrative action of any Member State which would be more favourable to nationals of other Member States.

2. Member States shall facilitate re-admission to their territories of self-employed persons who left those territories after having resided there permanently for a long period while pursuing an activity there and who wish to return when they have reached retirement age as defined in Article 2(1)(a) or are permanently incapacitated for work.

Article 9

Member States may not derogate from the provisions of this Directive save on grounds of public policy, public security or public health.

Article 10

1. Member States shall, within twelve months of notification of this Directive, bring into force the measures necessary to comply with its provisions and shall forthwith inform the Commission thereof.

2. Following notification of this Directive, Member States shall further ensure that the Commission is informed, in sufficient time for it to

submit its comments, of all proposed laws, regulations or administrative provisions which they intend to adopt in the field covered by this Directive.

Article 11

This Directive is addressed to the Member States.

Done at Brussels, 17 December 1974.

For the Council

The President

M. Durafour

FOOTNOTES

1. OJ No 2, 15.1.62, p.36.
2. OJ No C 14, 27.3.73, p.20.
3. OJ No C 142, 31.12.72, p.12
4. OJ No L 172, 28.6.73, p.14.
5. OJ No L 142, 30.6.70, p.24.

IRL Implemented in Ireland: S.I. 393/1977; S.I. 165/1981; S.I. 39/1985; S.I. 441/1985.

(c) Social Security

REGULATION (EEC) No 1408/71
OF THE COUNCIL

of 14 June 1971

on the application of social security schemes to employed persons and their families moving within the Community

(OJ No L 149, 5.7.71, p.416)

The Council of the European Communities,

Having regard to the Treaty establishing the European Economic Community, and in particular Articles 2, 7 and 51 thereof;

Having regard to the proposals from the Commission drawn up after consultation with the Administrative Commission on Social Security for Migrant Workers[1];

Having regard to the opinions of the European Parliament[2];

Having regard to the opinions of the Economic and Social Committee[3];

Whereas the need for a general revision of Council Regulation No 3[4] on social security for migrant workers has become progressively more apparent, both in the light of the practical experience of its implementation since 1959 and as a result of amendments made to national legislations;

Whereas the existing provisions for co-ordination can, as a whole, be developed, improved and to some extent simplified at the same time, taking into account the considerable differences existing between national social security legislations;

Whereas it is appropriate at this time to bring together in a single legislative instrument all the basic provisions for implementing Article 51 of the Treaty for the benefit of workers, including frontier workers, seasonal workers and seamen;

Whereas the considerable differences existing between national legislations as regards the persons to whom they apply make it preferable to establish the principle that the Regulation applies to all nationals of Member States insured under social security schemes for employed persons;

Whereas the provisions for co-ordination of national social security legislations fall within the framework of freedom of movement for workers who are nationals of Member States and should, to this end, contribute towards the improvement of their standard of living and conditions of employment, by guaranteeing within the Community firstly equality of treatment for all nationals of Member States under the various national legislations and secondly social security benefits for workers and their dependents regardless of their place of employment or of residence;

Whereas these objectives must be attained in particular by aggregation of all the periods taken into account under the various national legislations for the purpose of acquiring and retaining the right to benefits and of calculating the amount of benefits, and by the provision of benefits for the various categories of persons covered by the Regulation regardless of their place of residence within the Community;

Whereas the provisions for co-ordination adopted for the implementation of Article 51 of the Treaty must guarantee to workers who move within the Community their accrued rights and advantages whilst not giving rise to unjustified overlapping of benefits;

Whereas to this end, persons entitled to benefits for invalidity, old age

and death (pensions) must be able to enjoy all the benefits which have accrued to them in the various Member States; whereas, however, in order to avoid unjustified overlapping of benefits, which could result in particular from the duplication of insurance periods and other periods treated as such, it is necessary to limit the benefits to the greatest amount which would have been due to a worker from one of these States if he had spent all his working life there;

Whereas, in order to secure mobility of labour under improved conditions, it is necessary henceforth to ensure closer co-ordination between the unemployment insurance schemes and the unemployment assistance schemes of all the Member States; whereas it is therefore particularly appropriate, in order to facilitate search for employment in the various Member States, to grant to an unemployed worker, for a limited period, the unemployment benefits provided for by the legislation of the Member State to which he was last subject;

Whereas it seems desirable to improve the system under Regulation No 3 governing family benefits in cases of separated families, both as regards the categories of persons to be entitled to such benefits and as regards the machinery for awarding them;

Whereas, taking into account the problems relating to unemployment, it is appropriate to extend entitlement to family benefits to members of the families of unemployed workers residing in a Member State other than the one which is responsible for payment of the unemployment benefit;

Whereas, moreover, the current restrictions on the granting of family benefits should be abolished, and whereas in order to ensure payment of benefits for the maintenance of the members of separated families, leaving aside those benefits aimed largely at encouraging an increase in population, it would be preferable to lay down rules common to all the Member States and efforts should continue to this end; but in the face of great variations between national legislations a solution should be adopted to take this situation into account: payment of family benefits of the country of employment in respect of five countries, and payment of family allowances of the country of residence of members of the family where the country of employment is France;

Whereas by analogy with the solutions contained in Council Regulation (EEC) 1612/68[5] of 15 October 1968 on freedom of movement for workers within the Community, it is desirable to bring together in an Advisory Committee representatives of workers and employers to examine the problems dealt with by the Administrative Commission;

Whereas the present Regulation may replace the arrangements provided

for in Article 69(4) of the Treaty establishing the European Coal and Steel Community;

Has adopted this Regulation:

Title I

General provisions

Article 1

Definitions

For the purpose of this Regulation:

(a) 'worker' means:

(i) subject to the restrictions set out in Annex V, any person who is insured, compulsorily or on an optional continued basis, for one or more of the contingencies covered by the branches of a social security scheme for employed persons;

(ii) any person who is compulsorily insured for one or more of the contingencies covered by the branches of social security dealt with in this Regulation, under a social security scheme for all residents or for the whole working population if such person:

– can be identified as an employed person by virtue of the manner in which such scheme is administered or financed, or

– failing such criteria, is insured for some other contingency specified in Annex V under a scheme for employed persons, either compulsorily or on an optional continued basis;

(iii) any person who is voluntarily insured for one or more of the contingencies covered by the branches dealt with in this Regulation, under a social security scheme of a Member State for employed persons or for all residents or for certain categories of residents if such person has previously been compulsorily insured for the same contingency under a scheme for employed persons of the same Member State;

(b) 'frontier worker' means any worker employed in the territory of a Member State and residing in the territory of another Member State to which he returns as a rule daily or at least once a week; however, a frontier worker who is posted elsewhere in the territory of the same or another Member State by the undertaking to which he is normally attached and is prevented on account of such posting from returning daily or at least once a week to the place where he resides shall

nevertheless retain the status of frontier worker for a period not exceeding four months;

(c) 'seasonal worker' means any worker who goes to the territory of a Member State other than the one in which he is resident to do work there of a seasonal nature for an undertaking or an employer of that State for a period which may on no account exceed eight months, and who stays in the territory of the said State for the duration of his work; work of a seasonal nature shall be taken to mean work which, being dependent on the succession of the seasons, automatically recurs each year;

(d) 'refugee' shall have the meaning assigned to it in Article 1 of the Convention on the Status of Refugees, signed at Geneva on 28 July 1951;

(e) 'stateless person' shall have the meaning assigned to it in Article 1 of the Convention on the Status of Stateless Persons, signed in New York on 28 September 1954;

(f) 'member of the family' means any person defined or recognised as a member of the family or designated as a member of the household by the legislation under which benefits are provided or, in the cases referred to in Article 22(1)(a) and Article 39, by the legislation of the Member State in whose territory such person resides; where, however, the said legislations regard as a member of the family or a member of the household only a person living under the same roof as the worker, this condition shall be considered satisfied if the person in question is mainly dependent on that worker;

(g) 'survivor' means any person defined or recognised as such by the legislation under which the benefits are granted; where, however, the said legislation regards as a survivor only a person who was living under the same roof as the deceased worker, this condition shall be considered satisfied if such person was mainly dependent on the deceased worker;

(h) 'residence' means habitual residence;

(i) 'stay' means temporary residence;

(j) 'legislation' means all the laws, regulations, and other provisions and all other present or future implementing measures of each Member State relating to the branches and schemes of social security covered by Article 4(1) and (2);

This term excludes provisions of existing or future industrial agreements, whether or not they have been the subject of a decision by the authorities rendering them compulsory or extending their

scope. However, where such industrial agreements serve to implement an insurance requirement under the laws or regulations referred to in the preceding subparagraph, this restriction may at any time be lifted by a declaration by the Member State concerned, specifying the schemes of such a kind to which this Regulation applies. Notification shall be given of such declaration, which shall be published in accordance with the provisions of Article 96. The provisions of the preceding subparagraph shall not have the effect of exempting from application of this Regulation the schemes to which Regulation No 3 has been applied;

(k) 'social security convention' means any bilateral or multilateral instrument which binds or will bind two or more Member States exclusively, and any other multilateral instrument which binds or will bind at least two Member States and one or more other States in the field of social security, for all or part of the branches and schemes set out in Article 4(1) and (2), together with agreements, of whatever kind, concluded pursuant to the said instruments;

(l) 'competent authority' means, in respect of each Member State, the Minister, Ministers or other equivalent authority responsible for social security schemes throughout or in any part of the territory of the State in question;

(m) 'Administrative Commission' means the Commission referred to in Article 80;

(n) 'institution' means, in respect of each Member State, the body or authority responsible for administering all or part of the legislation;

(o) 'competent institution' means:

(i) the institution with which the person concerned is insured at the time of the application for benefit, or

(ii) the institution from which the person concerned is entitled or would be entitled to benefits if he or a member or members of his family were resident in the territory of the Member State in which the institution is situated, or

(iii) the institution designated by the competent authority of the Member State concerned, or

(iv) in the case of a scheme relating to an employer's liability in respect of the benefits set out in Article 4(1), either the employer or the insurer involved or, in default thereof, a body or authority designated by the competent authority of the Member State concerned;

(p) 'institution of the place of residence' and 'institution of the place of

stay' mean respectively the institution which is competent to provide benefits in the place where the person concerned resides and the institution which is competent to provide benefits in the place where the person concerned is staying, under the legislation administered by that institution or, where no such institution exists, the institution designated by the competent authority of the Member State in question;

(q) 'competent State' means the Member State in whose territory the competent institution is situated;

(r) 'insurance periods' means contribution periods or periods of employment as defined or recognised as insurance periods by the legislation under which they were completed or considered as completed, and all periods treated as such, where they are regarded by the said legislation as equivalent to insurance periods;

(s) 'periods of employment' means periods defined or recognised as such by the legislation under which they were completed, and all periods treated as such, where they are regarded by the said legislation as equivalent to periods of employment;

(t) 'benefits' and 'pensions' mean all benefits and pensions, including all elements thereof payable out of public funds, revalorisation increases and supplementary allowances, subject to the provisions of Title III, as also lump-sum benefits which may be paid in lieu of pensions, and payments made by way of reimbursement of contributions;

(u) (i) 'family benefits' means all benefits in kind or in cash intended to meet family expenses under the legislation provided for in Article 4(1)(h), excluding the special childbirth allowances mentioned in Annex I;

(ii) 'family allowances' means periodical cash benefits granted exclusively by reference to the number and, where appropriate, the age of members of the family;

(v) 'death grants' means any once-for-all payment, in the event of death, exclusive of the lump-sum benefits referred to in subparagraph (t).

Article 2

Persons covered

1. This Regulation shall apply to workers who are or have been subject to the legislation of one or more Member States and who are nationals of one of the Member States or who are stateless persons or refugees

residing within the territory of one of the Member States, as also to the members of their families and their survivors.

2. In addition, this Regulation shall apply to the survivors of workers who have been subject to the legislation of one or more Member States, irrespective of the nationality of such workers, where their survivors are nationals of one of the Member States, or stateless persons or refugees residing within the territory of one of the Member States.

3. This Regulation shall apply to civil servants and to persons who, in accordance with the legislation applicable, are treated as such, where they are or have been subject to the legislation of a Member State to which this Regulation applies.

Article 3

Equality of treatment

1. Subject to the special provisions of this Regulation, persons resident in the territory of one of the Member States to whom this Regulation applies shall be subject to the same obligations and enjoy the same benefits under the legislation of any Member State as the nationals of that State.

2. The provisions of paragraph 1 shall apply to the right to elect members of the organs of social security institutions or to participate in their nomination, but shall not affect the legislative provisions of any Member State relating to eligibility or methods of nomination.

3. Save as provided in Annex II, social security conventions which remain in force pursuant to Article 7(2)(c) and conventions concluded pursuant to Article 8(1), shall apply to all persons to whom this Regulation applies.

Article 4

Matters covered

1. This Regulation shall apply to all legislation concerning the following branches of social security:

(a) sickness and maternity benefits;

(b) invalidity benefits, including those intended for the maintenance or improvement of earning capacity;

(c) old-age benefits;

(d) survivors' benefits;

(e) benefits in respect of accidents at work and occupational diseases;

(f) death grants;

(g) unemployment benefits;

(h) family benefits.

2. This Regulation shall apply to all general and special social security schemes, whether contributory or non-contributory, and to schemes concerning the liability of an employer or ship owner in respect of the benefits referred to in paragraph 1.

3. The provisions of Title III of this Regulation shall not, however, affect the legislative provisions of any Member State concerning a ship owner's liability.

4. This Regulation shall not apply to social and medical assistance, to benefit schemes for victims of war or its consequences, or to special schemes for civil servants and persons treated as such.

Article 5

Declarations of Member States on the scope of this Regulation

The Member States shall specify the legislation and schemes referred to in Article 4(1) and (2), the minimum benefits referred to in Article 50 and the benefits referred to in Articles 77 and 78 in declarations to be notified and published in accordance with Article 96.

Article 6

Social security conventions replaced by this Regulation

Subject to the provisions of Articles 7, 8 and 46(4) this Regulation shall, as regards persons and matters which it covers, replace the provisions of any social security convention binding either;

(a) two or more Member States exclusively, or

(b) at least two Member States and one or more other States, where settlement of the cases concerned does not involve any institution of one of the latter States.

Article 7

International provisions not affected by this Regulation

1. This Regulation shall not affect obligations arising from:

(a) any convention adopted by the International Labour Conference

which, after ratification by one or more Member States, has entered into force;

(b) the European Interim Agreements on Social Security of 11 December 1953 concluded between the Member States of the Council of Europe.

2. The provisions of Article 6 notwithstanding, the following shall continue to apply:

(a) the Agreement of 27 July 1950 concerning social security for Rhine boatmen, revised on 13 February 1961;

(b) the European Convention of 9 July 1956 concerning social security for workers in international transport;

(c) the social security conventions listed in Annex II.

Article 8

Conclusion of conventions between Member States

1. Two or more Member States may, as need arises, conclude conventions with each other based on the principles and in the spirit of this Regulation.

2. Each Member State shall notify, in accordance with Article 96(1), any convention concluded with another Member State pursuant to paragraph 1.

Article 9

Admission to voluntary or optional continued insurance

1. The legislative provisions of any Member State which make admission to voluntary or optional continued insurance conditional upon residence in the territory of that State shall not apply to workers to whom this Regulation applies and who are resident in the territory of another Member State, provided that at some time in their past working life they were subject to the legislation of the first State.

2. Where, under the legislation of a Member State, admission to voluntary or optional continued insurance is conditional upon completion of insurance periods, any such periods completed under the legislation of another Member State shall be taken into account, to the extent required, as if they were completed under the legislation of the first State.

Article 10

Waiving of residence clauses – Effect of compulsory insurance on reimbursement of contributions

1. Save as otherwise provided in this Regulation, invalidity, old-age or survivors' cash benefits, pensions for accidents at work or occupational diseases and death grants acquired under the legislation of one or more Member States shall not be subject to any reduction, modification, suspension, withdrawal or confiscation by reason of the fact that the recipient resides in the territory of a Member State other than that in which the institution responsible for payment is situated.

The preceding subparagraph shall also apply to lump-sum benefits granted in cases of remarriage of a surviving spouse who was entitled to a survivor's pension.

2. Where under the legislation of a Member State reimbursement of contributions is conditional upon the person concerned having ceased to be subject to compulsory insurance, this condition shall not be considered satisfied as long as the person concerned is subject to compulsory insurance as a worker under the legislation of another Member State.

Article 11

Revalorisation of benefits

Rules for revalorisation provided by the legislation of a Member State shall apply to benefits due under that legislation by virtue of the provisions of this Regulation.

Article 12

Prevention of overlapping of benefits

1. This Regulation can neither confer nor maintain the right to several benefits of the same kind for one and the same period of compulsory insurance. However, this provision shall not apply to benefits in respect of invalidity, old age, death (pensions) or occupational disease which are awarded by the institutions of two or more Member States, in accordance with Article 41, Article 43(2) and (3), Articles 46, 50 and 51 or Article 60(1)(b).

2. The legislative provisions of a Member State for reduction, suspension or withdrawal of benefit in cases of overlapping with other social security benefits or other income may be invoked even though the right to such benefits was acquired under the legislation of another Member State or

such income arises in the territory of another Member State. However, this provision shall not apply when the person concerned receives benefits of the same kind in respect of invalidity, old age, death (pensions) or occupational disease which are awarded by the institutions of two or more Member States in accordance with Articles 46, 50, 51 or Article 60(1)(b).

3. The legislative provisions of a Member State for reduction, suspension or withdrawal of benefit in the case of a person in receipt of invalidity benefits or anticipatory old-age benefits pursuing a professional or trade activity may be invoked against such person even though he is pursuing his activity in the territory of another Member State.

4. An invalidity pension payable under Netherlands legislation shall, in a case where the Netherlands institution is bound under Article 57(3)(c) or Article 60(2)(a) to contribute also to the cost of benefits for occupational disease granted under the legislation of another Member State, be reduced by the amount payable to the institution of the other Member State which is responsible for granting the benefits for occupational disease.

Title II

Determination of the legislation applicable

Article 13

General rules

1. A worker to whom this Regulation applies shall be subject to the legislation of a single Member State only. That legislation shall be determined in accordance with the provisions of this Title.

2. Subject to the provisions of Articles 14 to 17:

(a) a worker employed in the territory of one Member State shall be subject to the legislation of that State even if he resides in the territory of another Member State or if the registered office or place of business of the undertaking or individual employing him is situated in the territory of another Member State;

(b) a worker employed on board a vessel flying the flag of a Member State shall be subject to the legislation of that State;

(c) civil servants and persons treated as such shall be subject to the legislation of the Member State to which the administration employing them is subject;

(d) a worker called up or recalled for service in the armed forces of a

Member State shall retain the status of worker, and shall be subject to the legislation of that State; if entitlement under that legislation is subject to the completion of insurance periods before entry into or release from such service, insurance periods completed under the legislation of any other Member State shall be taken into account, to the extent necessary, as if they were insurance periods completed under the legislation of the first State.

Article 14

Special rules

1. Article 13(2)(a) shall apply subject to the following exceptions or circumstances:

(a) (i) A worker employed in the territory of a Member State by an undertaking to which he is normally attached who is posted by that undertaking to the territory of another Member State to perform work there for that undertaking shall continue to be subject to the legislation of the first Member State, provided that the anticipated duration of that work does not exceed twelve months and that he is not sent to replace another worker who has completed his term of posting;

  (ii) if the duration of the work to be done extends beyond the duration originally anticipated, owing to unforeseeable circumstances, and exceeds twelve months, the legislation of the first State shall continue to apply until the completion of such work, provided that the competent authority of the State in whose territory the worker is posted or the body designated by that authority gives its consent; such consent must be requested before the end of the initial twelve month period. Such consent cannot, however, be given for a period exceeding twelve months;

(b) a worker employed in international transport in the territory of two or more Member States as a member of travelling or flying personnel and who is working for an undertaking which, for hire or reward or on own account, operates transport services for passengers or goods by rail, road, air or inland waterway and has its registered office or place of business in the territory of a Member State, shall be subject to the legislation of the latter State, with the following restrictions:

  (i) where the said undertaking has a branch or permanent representation in the territory of a Member State other than that in which it has its registered office or place of business, a worker employed by such branch or agency shall be subject to the

legislation of the Member State in whose territory such branch or permanent representation is situated;

(ii) where a worker is employed principally in the territory of the Member State in which he resides, he shall be subject to the legislation of that State, even if the undertaking which employs him has no registered office or place of business or branch or permanent representation in that territory;

(c) a worker, other than one employed in international transport, who normally pursues his activity in the territory of two or more Member States shall be subject:

(i) to the legislation of the Member State in whose territory he resides, if he pursues his activity partly in that territory or if he is attached to several undertakings or several employers who have their registered offices or places of business in the territory of different Member States;

(ii) to the legislation of the Member State in whose territory is situated the registered office or place of business of the undertaking or individual employing him, if he does not reside in the territory of any of the Member States where he is pursuing his activity;

(d) a worker who is employed in the territory of one Member State by an undertaking which has its registered office or place of business in the territory of another Member State and which straddles the common frontier of these States shall be subject to the legislation of the Member State in whose territory the undertaking has its registered office or place of business.

2. Article 13(2)(b) shall apply subject to the following exceptions and circumstances:

(a) a worker employed by an undertaking to which he is normally attached, either in the territory of a Member State or on board a vessel flying the flag of a Member State, who is posted by that undertaking on board a vessel flying the flag of another Member State to perform work there for that undertaking shall, subject to the conditions provided in paragraph 1(a), continue to be subject to the legislation of the first Member State;

(b) a worker who, while not being habitually employed at sea, is employed in the territorial waters or in a port of a Member State on a vessel flying the flag of another Member State, but is not a member of the crew, shall be subject to the legislation of the first State;

(c) a worker employed on board a vessel flying the flag of a Member

State and remunerated for such employment by an undertaking or a person whose registered office of place of business is in the territory of another Member State shall be subject to the legislation of the latter State if he is resident in the territory of that State; the undertaking or person paying the remuneration shall be considered as the employer for the purposes of the said legislation.

3. The legislative provisions of a Member State under which a pensioner who is pursuing a professional or trade activity is not subject to compulsory insurance in respect of such activity shall also apply to a pensioner whose pension was acquired under the legislation of another Member State.

Article 15

Rules concerning voluntary insurance or optional continued insurance

1. The provisions of Articles 13 and 14 shall not apply to voluntary insurance or optional continued insurance.

2. Where application of the legislations of two or more Member States entails overlapping of insurance:

- under a compulsory insurance scheme and one or more voluntary or optional continued insurance schemes, the person concerned shall be subject exclusively to the compulsory insurance schemes;

- under two or more voluntary or optional continued insurance schemes, the person concerned may join only the voluntary or optional continued insurance scheme for which he has opted.

3. However, in respect of invalidity, old age and death (pensions), the person concerned may join the voluntary or optional continued insurance scheme of a Member State, even if he is compulsorily subject to the legislation of another Member State, to the extent that such overlapping is explicitly or implicitly admitted in the first Member State.

The person concerned who applies to join a voluntary or optional continued insurance scheme in a Member State whose legislation provides, in addition to such insurance, for complementary optional insurance may only join the latter.

Article 16

Special rules regarding persons employed by diplomatic missions and consular posts, and auxiliary staff of the European Communities

1. Article 13(2)(a) shall apply to persons employed by diplomatic

missions and consular posts and to the private domestic staff of agents of such missions or posts.

2. However, workers covered by paragraph 1 who are nationals of the Member State which is the accrediting or sending State may opt to be subject to the legislation of that State. Such right of option may be renewed at the end of each calendar year and shall not have retrospective effect.

3. Auxiliary staff of the European Communities may opt to be subject to the legislation of the Member State in whose territory they are employed, to the legislation of the Member State to which they were last subject or to the legislation of the Member State whose nationals they are, in respect of provisions other than those relating to family allowances, the granting of which is governed by the conditions of employment applicable to such staff. This right of option, which may be exercised once only, shall take effect from the date of entry into employment.

Article 17

Exceptions to the provisions of Articles 13 to 16

Two or more Member States or the competent authorities of those States may, by common agreement, provide for exceptions to the provisions of Articles 13 to 16 in the interest of certain workers or categories of workers.

Title III

Special provisions relating to the various categories of benefits

Chapter 1

Sickness and maternity

Section 1

Common provisions

Article 18

Aggregation of insurance periods

1. The competent institution of a Member State whose legislation makes the acquisition, retention or recovery of the right to benefits conditional upon the completion of insurance periods shall, to the extent necessary,

take account of insurance periods completed under the legislation of any other Member State as if they were periods completed under its own legislation.

2. The provisions of paragraph 1 shall apply to seasonal workers, even in respect of periods prior to any break in insurance exceeding the period allowed by the legislation of the competent State, provided however that the worker concerned has not ceased to be insured for a period exceeding four months.

Section 2

Workers and members of their families

Article 19

Residence in a Member State other than the competent State – General rules

1. A worker residing in the territory of a Member State other than the competent State, who satisfies the conditions of the legislation of the competent State for entitlement to benefits, taking account where appropriate of the provisions of Article 18, shall receive in the State in which he is resident:

(a) benefits in kind provided on behalf of the competent institution by the institution of the place of residence in accordance with the legislation administered by that institution as though he were insured with it;

(b) cash benefits provided by the competent institution in accordance with the legislation which it administers. However, by agreement between the competent institution and the institution of the place of residence, such benefits may be provided by the latter institution on behalf of the former, in accordance with the legislation of the competent State.

2. The provisions of paragraph 1(a) shall apply by analogy to members of the family who are residing in the territory of a Member State other than the competent State, where they are not entitled to such benefits under the legislation of the State in whose territory they reside.

Article 20

Frontier workers and members of their families – Special rules

A frontier worker may also obtain benefits in the territory of the competent State. Such benefits shall be provided by the competent

institution in accordance with the legislation of that State, as though the worker were resident there. Members of his family may receive benefits in kind under the same conditions; however, receipt of such benefits shall, except in urgent cases, be conditional upon an agreement between the States concerned or between the competent authorities of those States or, in its absence, on prior authorisation by the competent institution.

Article 21

Stay in or transfer of residence to the competent State

1. A worker and members of his family referred to in Article 19 who are staying in the territory of the competent State shall receive benefits in accordance with the legislation of that State as though they were resident there even if they have already received benefits for the same case of sickness or maternity before their stay. This provision shall not, however, apply to frontier workers and members of their families.

2. A worker and members of his family referred to in Article 19 who transfer their residence to the territory of the competent State, shall receive benefits in accordance with the legislation of that State, even if they have already received benefits for the same case of sickness or maternity before transferring their residence.

Article 22

Stay outside the competent State – Return to or transfer of residence to another Member State during sickness or maternity – Need to go to another Member State in order to receive appropriate treatment

1. A worker who satisfies the conditions of the legislation of the competent State for entitlement to benefits, taking account where appropriate of the provisions of Article 18, and:

(a) whose condition necessitates immediate benefits during a stay in the territory of another Member State, or

(b) who, having become entitled to benefits chargeable to the competent institution, is authorised by that institution to return to the territory of the Member State where he resides, or to transfer his residence to the territory of another Member State, or

(c) who is authorised by the competent institution to go to the territory of another Member State to receive there the treatment appropriate to his condition, shall be entitled:

(i) to benefits in kind provided on behalf of the competent

institution by the institution of the place of stay or residence in accordance with the legislation which it administers, as though he were insured with it; the length of the period during which benefits are provided shall be governed however by the legislation of the competent State;

(ii) to cash benefits provided by the competent institution in accordance with the legislation which it administers. However, by agreement between the competent institution and the institution of the place of stay or residence, such benefits may be provided by the latter institution on behalf of the former, in accordance with the legislation of the competent State.

2. The authorisation required under paragraph 1(b) may be refused only if it is established that movement of the person concerned would be prejudicial to his state of health or the receipt of medical treatment.

The authorisation required under paragraph 1(c) may not be refused where the treatment in question cannot be provided for the person concerned within the territory of the Member State in which he resides.

3. The provisions of paragraphs 1 and 2 shall apply to members of a worker's family in respect of benefits in kind.

4. The fact that the provisions of paragraph 1 apply to a worker shall not affect the right to benefit of members of his family.

Article 23

Calculation of cash benefits

1. The competent institution of a Member State whose legislation provides that the calculation of cash benefits shall be based on an average wage or salary, shall determine that average wage or salary exclusively by reference to wages or salaries confirmed as having been paid during the periods completed under the said legislation.

2. The competent institution of a Member State whose legislation provides that the calculation of cash benefits shall be based on a standard wage or salary, shall take account exclusively of the standard wage or salary or, where appropriate, of the average of the standard wages or salaries for the periods completed under the said legislation.

3. The competent institution of a Member State under whose legislation the amount of cash benefits varies with the number of members of the family, shall also take into account the members of the family of the person concerned who are resident in the territory of another Member State as if they were resident in the territory of the competent State.

Article 24

Substantial benefits in kind

1. Where the right of a worker or a member of his family to a prosthesis, a major appliance or other substantial benefits in kind has been recognised by the institution of a Member State before he becomes insured with the institution of another Member State, the said worker shall receive such benefits at the expense of the first institution, even if they are granted after he becomes insured with the second institution.

2. The Administrative Commission shall draw up the list of benefits to which the provisions of paragraph 1 apply.

Section 3

Unemployed persons and members of their families

Article 25

1. An unemployed person, to whom Article 69(1) and the second sentence of Article 71(1)(b)(ii) apply, and who satisfies the conditions of the legislation of the competent State for entitlement to benefits in kind and in cash, taking account where appropriate of the provisions of Article 18, shall receive for the period provided under Article 69(1)(c):

(a) benefits in kind provided on behalf of the competent institution by the institution of the Member State in which he seeks employment in accordance with the legislation of the latter institution, as though he were insured with it;

(b) cash benefits provided by the competent institution in accordance with the legislation which it administers. However, by agreement between the competent institution and the institution of the Member State in which the unemployed person seeks employment, benefits may be provided by the latter institution on behalf of the former institution in accordance with the legislation of the competent State. Unemployment benefits under Article 69(1) shall not be granted for the period during which cash benefits are received.

2. A totally unemployed person to whom the provisions of Article 71(1)(a)(ii) or the first sentence of Article 71(1)(b)(ii) apply shall receive benefits in kind and in cash in accordance with the legislation of the Member State in whose territory he resides, as though he had been subject to that legislation during his last employment, taking account where appropriate of the provisions of Article 18; the cost of such benefits shall be met by the institution of the country of residence.

3. Where an unemployed person satisfies the conditions of the legislation of the Member State which is responsible for the cost of unemployment benefits for entitlement to benefits in kind, taking account where appropriate of the provisions of Article 18, the members of his family shall receive such benefits, irrespective of the Member State in whose territory they reside or are staying. Such benefits shall be provided by the institution of the place of residence or of stay, in accordance with the legislation which it administers on behalf of the competent institution of the Member State which is responsible for the cost of unemployment benefits.

4. Without prejudice to any legislative provisions of a Member State which permit an extension of the period during which sickness benefits may be granted, the period provided for in paragraph 1 may, in cases of *force majeure*, be extended by the competent institution within the limit fixed by the legislation administered by the institution.

Section 4

Pension claimants and members of their families

Article 26

Right to benefits in kind in cases of cessation of the right to benefits from the institution which was last competent

1. A worker, members of his family or his survivors who, during the investigation of a claim, cease to be entitled to benefits in kind under the legislation of the Member State last competent, shall nevertheless receive such benefits under the following conditions: benefits in kind shall be provided in accordance with the legislation of the Member State in whose territory the person or persons concerned reside, provided that they are entitled to such benefits under that legislation or would be entitled to them under the legislation of another Member State if they were residing in the territory of that State, taking account where appropriate of the provisions of Article 18.

2. A pension claimant who is entitled to benefits in kind under the legislation of a Member State which obliges the person concerned to pay sickness insurance contributions himself during the investigation of his pension claim shall cease to be entitled to benefits in kind at the end of the second month for which he has not paid the contributions due.

3. Benefits in kind provided pursuant to paragraph 1 shall be chargeable to the institution which has collected contributions pursuant to paragraph 2; where no contributions are payable under paragraph 2, the

institution responsible for the cost of the benefits in kind shall, after awarding the pension pursuant to Article 28, refund the amount of the benefits provided to the institution of the place of residence.

Section 5

Pensioners and members of their families

Article 27

Pensions payable under the legislation of several States where a right to benefits in kind is enjoyed in the country of residence

A pensioner who is entitled to draw pensions under the legislation of two or more Member States and who is entitled to benefits in kind under the legislation of the Member State in whose territory he resides, taking account where appropriate of the provisions of Article 18 and Annex V, shall, with the members of his family, receive such benefits from the institution of the place of residence and at the expense of that institution as though he were a pensioner whose pension was payable solely under the legislation of the latter State.

Article 28

Pensions payable under the legislation of one or more States where no right to benefits in kind is enjoyed in the country of residence

1. A pensioner who is entitled to draw a pension or pensions under the legislation of one or more Member States and who is not entitled to benefits in kind under the legislation of the Member State in whose territory he resides, shall nevertheless receive such benefits for himself and members of his family if, taking account where appropriate of the provisions of Article 18 and Annex V, he would be entitled thereto under the legislation of the Member State, or of at least one of the Member States, competent in respect of pensions if he were resident in the territory of such State. The benefits shall be provided on behalf of the institution referred to in paragraph 2 by the institution of the place of residence as though the person concerned were a pensioner under the legislation of the State in whose territory he resides and were entitled to benefits in kind.

2. In the cases covered by paragraph 1, the cost of benefits in kind shall be borne by the institution determined according to the following rules:

(a) where the pensioner is entitled to the said benefits under the legislation of a single Member State, the cost shall be borne by the competent institution of that State;

(b) where the pensioner is entitled to the said benefits under the legislations of two or more Member States, the cost thereof shall be borne by the competent institution of the Member State under whose legislation the pensioner has completed the longest period of insurance; should the application of this rule result in several institutions being responsible for the cost of benefits, cost shall be borne by the institution with which the pensioner was last insured.

Article 29

Residence of members of the family in a State other than the one in which the pensioner resides – Transfer of residence to the State where the pensioner resides

1. Members of the family of a pensioner entitled to draw a pension or pensions under the legislation of one or more Member States who reside in the territory of a Member State other than the one in which the pensioner resides shall where he is entitled under the legislation of a Member State to benefits in kind, receive such benefits as though the pensioner were resident in the same territory as them. Such benefits shall be provided by the institution of the place of residence of the members of the family, in accordance with the legislation which that institution administers and shall be chargeable to the institution of the pensioner's place of residence.

2. Members of the family referred to in paragraph 1 who transfer their residence to the territory of the Member State where the pensioner resides, shall receive benefits under the legislation of that State, even if they have already received benefits for the same case of sickness or maternity before transferring their residence.

Article 30

Substantial benefits in kind

The provisions of Article 24 shall apply by analogy to pensioners.

Article 31

A pensioner and/or member of his family staying in a State other than the State in which they reside

A pensioner entitled to draw a pension or pensions under the legislation of one or more Member States who is also entitled to benefits in kind under the legislation of one of those States shall, with members of his

family, receive such benefits while staying in the territory of a Member State other than the one in which they reside. Such benefits shall be provided by the institution of the place of stay in accordance with the legislation which it administers and shall be chargeable to the institution of the pensioner's place of residence.

Article 32

Special provisions concerning responsibility for the cost of benefits provided for former frontier workers, members of their families or their survivors

The cost of benefits with which a pensioner who is a former frontier worker or the survivor of a frontier worker is provided under Article 27, and the cost of benefits with which members of his family are provided under Article 27 or 31 shall, where the frontier worker was working as such for the three months immediately preceding the date on which the pension became payable on the date of his death, be divided equally between the institution of the pensioner's place of residence and that with which he was last insured.

Article 33

Contributions payable by pensioners

The institution responsible for payment of a pension, and belonging to a Member State whose legislation provides for deductions from pensions in respect of contributions payable by a pensioner to cover benefits in kind, shall be authorised to make such deductions from the pension payable by such institution, calculated in accordance with the legislation concerned, to the extent that the cost of the benefits in kind under Articles 27, 28, 31 and 32 are to be borne by an institution of the said Member State.

Article 34

General provision

The provisions of Articles 27 to 33 shall not apply to a pensioner or to members of his family who are entitled to benefits in kind under the legislation of a Member State as a result of pursuing a professional or trade activity. In such a case the person concerned shall for the purposes of this Chapter, be considered as a worker or as a member of a worker's family.

Section 6

Miscellaneous provisions

Article 35

Scheme applicable where there are a number of schemes in the country of residence or stay – Previous illness – Maximum period during which benefits are granted

1. Where the legislation of the country of stay or residence contains several sickness or maternity insurance schemes, the provisions applicable under Articles 19, 21(1), 22, 25, 26, 28(1), 29(1) or 31 shall be those of the scheme covering manual workers in the steel industry. Where, however, the said legislation includes a special scheme for workers in mines and similar undertakings, the provisions of such scheme shall apply to that category of workers and members of their families provided the institution of the place of stay or residence to which application is made is competent to administer such scheme.

2. Where, under the legislation of a Member State, the granting of benefits is conditional upon the origin of the illness, that condition shall apply neither to workers nor to the members of their families to whom this Regulation applies, regardless of the Member State in whose territory they reside.

3. Where the legislation of a Member State fixes a maximum period for the granting of benefits, the institution which administers that legislation may, where appropriate, take account of the period during which the benefits have already been provided by the institution of another Member State for the same case of sickness or maternity.

Section 7

Reimbursement between institutions

Article 36

1. Without prejudice to the provisions of Article 32, benefits in kind provided pursuant to this Chapter by the institution of one Member State on behalf of the institution of another Member State shall be fully refunded.

2. The refunds referred to in paragraph 1 shall be determined and made in accordance with the procedure provided for by the implementing regulation referred to in Article 97, either on production of proof of actual expenditure or on the basis of lump-sum payments.

In the latter case, the lump-sum payments shall be such as to ensure that the refund is as close as possible to actual expenditure.

3. Two or more Member States, or the competent authorities of those States, may provide for other methods of reimbursement or may waive all reimbursement between institutions under their jurisdiction.

Chapter 2

Invalidity

Section 1

Workers subject only to legislations under which the amount of invalidity benefits is independent of the duration of insurance periods

Article 37

General provisions

1. A worker who has been successively or alternately subject to the legislations of two or more Member States and who has completed insurance periods exclusively under legislations according to which the amount of invalidity benefits is independent of the duration of insurance periods, shall receive benefits in accordance with Article 39. This Article shall not affect pension increases or supplements in respect of children, granted in accordance with the provisions of Chapter 8.

2. Annex III lists legislations of the kind mentioned in paragraph 1 which are in force in the territory of each of the Member States concerned.

Article 38

Aggregation of insurance periods

1. The competent institution of a Member State whose legislation makes the acquisition, retention or recovery of the right to benefit conditional upon the completion of insurance periods shall take account to the extent necessary of insurance periods completed under the legislation of any other Member States, as though they had been completed under its own legislation.

2. Where the legislation of a Member State makes the granting of certain benefits conditional upon the insurance periods having been completed ... [6] in a specific employment, insurance periods completed under the legislations of other Member States shall be taken into account for the granting of these benefits only if completed under a

corresponding scheme or, failing this, in the same occupation or, where appropriate, in the same employment. If, account having been taken of the periods thus completed, the person concerned does not satisfy the conditions for receipt of these benefits, these periods shall be taken into account for the granting of the benefits under the general scheme or, failing this, under the scheme applicable to manual or clerical workers, as appropriate.

Article 39

Award of benefits

1. The institution of the Member State whose legislation was applicable at the time when incapacity for work followed by invalidity occurred, shall determine, in accordance with that legislation, whether the person concerned satisfies the conditions for entitlement to benefits, taking account where appropriate of the provisions of Article 38.

2. A person who satisfies the conditions referred to in paragraph 1 shall obtain the benefits exclusively from the said institution, in accordance with the legislation which it administers.

3. A person who does not satisfy the conditions referred to in paragraph 1 shall receive the benefits to which he is still entitled under the legislation of another Member State, taking account where appropriate of the provisions of Article 38.

4. If the legislation applicable under paragraph 2 or 3 provides that the amount of the benefits shall be determined taking into account the existence of members of the family other than the children, the competent institution shall also take into consideration the members of the family of the person concerned who are residing in the territory of another Member State, as if they were residing in the territory of the competent State.

Section 2

Workers subject either only to legislations under which the amount of invalidity benefit depends on the duration of insurance periods or to legislations of this type and of the type referred to in Section I

Article 40

General provisions

1. A worker who has been successively or alternately subject to the legislations of two or more Member States, of which at least one is not

of the type referred to in Article 37(1), shall receive benefits under the provisions of Chapter 3, which shall apply by analogy, taking into account the provisions of paragraph 3.

2. However, a worker who suffers incapacity for work followed by invalidity while subject to a legislation listed in Annex III, shall receive benefits in accordance with Article 37(1) on two conditions:

– that he satisfies the conditions of that legislation or other legislations of the same type, taking account where appropriate of the provisions of Article 38, but without having recourse to insurance periods completed under legislations not listed in Annex III, and

– that he does not satisfy the conditions for entitlement to benefits under a legislation not listed in Annex III.

3. A decision taken by an institution of a Member State concerning the degree of invalidity of a claimant shall be binding on the institution of any other Member State concerned, provided that that concordance between the legislations of these States on conditions relating to the degree of invalidity is acknowledged in Annex IV.

Section 3

Aggravation of invalidity

Article 41

1. In the case of aggravation of an invalidity for which a worker is receiving benefits under the legislation of a single Member State, the following provisions shall apply:

(a) if the person concerned has not been subject to the legislation of another Member State since receiving benefits, the competent institution of the first State shall be bound to grant the benefits, taking the aggravation into account, in accordance with the legislation which it administers;

(b) if the person concerned has been subject to the legislation of one or more other Member States since receiving benefits, the benefits shall be granted to him, taking the aggravation into account, in accordance with Article 37(1) or Article 40(1) or (2) as appropriate;

(c) if the total amount of the benefit or benefits payable under subparagraph (b) is lower than the amount of the benefit which the person concerned was receiving at the expense of the institution previously liable for payment, such institution shall be bound to pay him a supplement equal to the difference between the two amounts;

(d) if, in the case referred to in subparagraph (b), the institution responsible for the initial incapacity is a Netherlands institution, and if:

(i) the illness which caused the aggravation is the same as the one which gave rise to the granting of benefits under Netherlands legislation;

(ii) this illness is an occupational disease within the meaning of the legislation of the Member State to which the person concerned was last subject and entitles him to payment of the supplement referred to in Article 60(1)(b); and

(iii) the legislation or legislations to which the person concerned has been subject since receiving benefits is a legislation, or are legislations, listed in Annex III,

the Netherlands institution shall continue to provide the initial benefit after the aggravation occurs, and the benefit due under the legislation of the last Member State to which the person concerned was subject shall be reduced by the amount of the Netherlands benefit;

(e) if, in the case referred to in subparagraph (b), the person concerned is not entitled to benefits at the expense of an institution of another Member State, the competent institution of the first State shall be bound to grant the benefits, according to the legislation of that State, taking into account the aggravation and, where appropriate, the provisions of Article 38.

2. In cases of aggravation of an invalidity for which a worker is receiving benefits under the legislations of two or more Member States, the benefits shall be granted to him, taking the aggravation into account, in accordance with the provisions of Article 40(1).

Section 4

Resumption of provisions of benefits after suspension or withdrawal – Conversion of invalidity benefits into old age benefits

Article 42

Determination of the institution responsible for the provision of benefits where provision of invalidity benefits is resumed

1. If provision of benefits is to be resumed after their suspension such provision shall, without prejudice to Article 43, be the responsibility of

the institution or institutions which were responsible for provision of the benefits at the time of their suspension.

2. If, after withdrawal of benefits, the condition of the person concerned warrants the granting of further benefits, they shall be granted in accordance with the provisions of Article 37(1) or Article 40(1) or (2), as appropriate.

Article 43

Conversion of invalidity benefits into old age benefits

1. Invalidity benefits shall be converted into old age benefits, where appropriate, under the conditions laid down by the legislation or legislations under which they were granted, and in accordance with the provisions of Chapter 3.

2. Any institution of a Member State which is responsible for providing invalidity benefits shall, where a person receiving invalidity benefits can, by virtue of Article 49, establish a claim to old age benefits under the legislation of other Member States, continue to provide such person with the invalidity benefits to which he is entitled under the legislation which it administers until the provisions of paragraph 1 become applicable as regards that institution.

3. However, if in the case referred to in paragraph 2 the invalidity benefits have been granted pursuant to Article 39, the institution remaining responsible for providing those benefits may apply Article 49(1)(a) as if the recipient of the said benefits satisfied the conditions of the legislation of the Member State concerned for entitlement to old age benefits, by substituting for the theoretical amount referred to in Article 46(2)(a) the amount of the invalidity benefits due from the said institution.

Chapter 3

Old age and death (pensions)

Article 44

General provisions for the award of benefits when a worker has been subject to the legislation of two or more Member States

1. The rights to benefits of a worker who has been subject to the legislation of two or more Member States, or of his survivors, shall be determined in accordance with the provisions of this Chapter.

2. Subject to the provisions of Article 49, when a claim for the award of a benefit is lodged, such award must be made having regard to all the legislations to which the worker has been subject. Exception shall be made to this rule if the person concerned expressly asks for postponement of the award of old age benefits to which he would be entitled under the legislation of one or more Member States, provided that the periods completed under that legislation or those legislations are not taken into account for the purpose of acquiring the right to benefit in another Member State.

3. This Chapter shall not apply to increases in or supplements to pensions in respect of children, or to orphans' pensions granted pursuant to Chapter 8.

Article 45

Consideration of insurance periods completed under the legislations to which a worker has been subject for the acquisition, retention or recovery of the right to benefits

1. An institution of a Member State whose legislation makes the acquisition, retention or recovery of the right to benefits conditional upon the completion of insurance period shall take into account, to the extent necessary, insurance periods completed under the legislation of any Member State as though they had been competed under the legislation which it administers.

2. Where the legislation of a Member State makes the granting of certain benefits conditional upon the insurance periods having been completed in an occupation subject to a special scheme or, where appropriate, in a specific employment, periods completed under the legislations of other Member States shall be taken into account for the granting of such benefits only if completed under such a scheme or, failing this, in the same occupation or, where appropriate, in the same employment. If, taking into account periods thus completed, the person concerned does not satisfy the conditions for receipt of these benefits, those periods shall be taken into account for the granting of benefits under the general scheme or, failing this, under the scheme applicable to manual or clerical workers, as appropriate.

3. Where the legislation of a Member State which makes the granting of benefits conditional upon a worker being subject to its legislation at the time when the risk materialises has no requirements as to the length of insurance periods either for entitlement to or calculation of benefits, any worker who is no longer subject to that legislation shall for the purposes of this Chapter, be deemed to be still so subject at the time when the risk materialises, if at that time he is subject to the legislation of another

Member State or, failing this, can establish a claim to benefits under the legislation of another Member State. However, this latter condition shall be deemed to be satisfied in the case referred to in Article 48(1).

Article 46

Award of benefits

1. Where a worker has been subject to the legislation of a Member State and where he satisfies its conditions for entitlement to benefits, without application of the provisions of Article 45 being necessary, the competent institution of that Member State shall, in accordance with the legislation which it administers, determine the amount of benefit corresponding to the total length of the insurance periods to be taken into account in pursuance of such legislation.

This institution shall also calculate the amount of benefit which would be obtained by applying the rules laid down in paragraph (2)(a) and (b). Only the higher of these two amounts shall be taken into consideration.

2. Where a worker has been subject to the legislation of a Member State and does not satisfy the conditions for entitlement to benefits unless account is taken of the provisions of Article 45, the competent institution of that Member State shall apply the following rules:

(a) the institution shall calculate the theoretical amount of benefit that the person concerned could claim if all the insurance periods completed under the legislations of the Member States to which he has been subject had been completed in the State in question and under the legislation administered by it on the date the benefit is awarded. If, under that legislation, the amount of the benefit does not depend on the length of the insurance periods, then that amount shall be taken as the theoretical amount referred to in this subparagraph;

(b) the institution shall then establish the actual amount of the benefit on the basis of the theoretical amount referred to in the preceding subparagraph and in the ratio which the length of the insurance periods completed before the materialisation of the risk under the legislation administered by that institution, bears to the total length of the insurance periods completed before materialisation of the risk under the legislations of all the Member States concerned;

(c) if the total length of the insurance periods completed under the legislations of all the Member States concerned before the materialisation of the risk is longer than the maximum period required by the legislation of one of these States for receipt of full benefit, the competent institution of that State shall, when applying

the provisions of this paragraph, take into consideration this maximum period instead of the total length of the periods completed; this method of calculation must not result in the imposition on that institution of the costs of a benefit greater than the full benefit provided for by the legislation which it administers;

(d) the procedure for taking into account duplicate periods when applying the rules of calculation laid down in this paragraph, shall be laid down in the implementing Regulation referred to in Article 97.

3. The person concerned shall be entitled to the total sum of the benefits calculated in accordance with the provisions of paragraphs 1 and 2, within the limit of the highest theoretical amount of benefits calculated according to paragraph 2(a).

Where the amount referred to in the preceding subparagraph is exceeded, any institution applying paragraph 1 shall adjust its benefit by an amount corresponding to the proportion which the amount of the benefit concerned bears to the total of the benefits determined in accordance with paragraph 1.

4. When in a case of invalidity, old age or survivors' pensions, the total of the benefits due from two or more Member States, under the provisions of a multilateral social security convention referred to in Article 6(b), is lower than the total which would be due from such Member States under paragraphs 1 and 3, the person concerned shall benefit from the provisions of this Chapter.

Article 47

Additional provisions for the calculation of benefits

1. For the calculation of the theoretical amount referred to in Article 46(2)(a), the following rules shall apply:

(a) where, under the legislation of a Member State, benefits are calculated on the basis of an average wage or salary, an average contribution, an average increase or on the ratio which existed, during the insurance periods, between the claimant's gross wage or salary and the average gross wage or salary of all insured persons other than apprentices, such average figures or ratios shall be determined by the competent institution of that State solely on the basis of the insurance periods completed under the legislation of the said State, or the gross wage or salary received by the person concerned during those periods only;

(b) where, under the legislation of a Member State, benefits are calculated on the basis of the amount of wages or salaries,

contributions or increases, the competent institution shall determine the wages or salaries, contributions and increases to be taken into account in respect of insurance periods completed under the legislations of other Member States on the basis of the average wages or salaries, contributions or increases recorded in respect of the insurance periods completed under the legislation which it administers;

(c) where, under the legislation of a Member State, benefits are calculated on the basis of a standard wage or salary or a fixed amount, the competent institution shall consider the wage or salary or fixed amount to be taken into account by it in respect of insurance periods completed under the legislations of other Member States as being equal to the standard wage or salary or fixed amount or, where appropriate, to the average of the standard wages or salaries or fixed amounts corresponding to the insurance periods completed under the legislation which it administers;

(d) where, under the legislation of a Member State, benefits are calculated for some periods on the basis of the amount of wages or salaries and, for other periods, on the basis of a standard wage or salary or a fixed amount, the competent institution shall, in respect of insurance periods completed under the legislations of other Member States, take into account the wages or salaries or fixed amounts determined in accordance with the provisions of (b) or (c) or, as appropriate, the average of these wages or salaries or amounts; where benefits are calculated on the basis of a standard wage or salary or a fixed amount for all the periods completed under the legislation which it administers, the competent institution shall consider the wage or salary to be taken into account in respect of the insurance periods completed under the legislations of other Member States as being equal to the notional wage or salary corresponding to that standard wage or salary or fixed amount.

2. The legislative provisions of a Member State concerning the revalorisation of the factors taken into account for the calculation of benefits shall apply, as appropriate, to the factors to be taken into account by the competent institution of that State, in accordance with the provisions of paragraph 1, in respect of the insurance periods completed under the legislations of other Member States.

3. If, under the legislation of a Member State, the amount of benefits is determined taking into account the existence of members of the family other than children, the competent institution of that State shall also take into consideration the members of the family of the person concerned who are residing in the territory of the competent State.

Article 48

Insurance periods of less than one year

1. Notwithstanding the provisions of Article 46(2), if the total length of the insurance periods completed under the legislation of a Member State does not amount to one year, and if under that legislation no right to benefits is acquired by virtue only of those periods the institution of that State shall not be bound to award benefits in respect of such periods.

2. The competent institution of each of the other Member States concerned shall take into account the periods referred to in paragraph 1, for the purposes of applying the provisions of Article 46(2) excepting those of subparagraph (b).

3. If the effect of applying the provisions of paragraph 1 would be to relieve them of their obligations all the institutions of the States concerned, benefits shall be awarded exclusively under the legislation of the last of those States whose conditions are satisfied, as if all the insurance periods completed and taken into account in accordance with Article 45(1) and (2) had been completed under the legislation of that State.

Article 49

Calculation of benefits when the person concerned does not simultaneously satisfy the conditions laid down by all the legislations under which insurance periods have been completed

1. If, at a given time, the person concerned does not satisfy the conditions laid down for the provision of benefits by all the legislations of the Member States to which he has been subject, taking into account where appropriate the provisions of Article 45, but satisfies the conditions of one or more of them only, the following provisions shall apply:

(a) each of the competent institutions administering a legislation whose conditions are satisfied shall calculate the amount of the benefit due, in accordance with the provisions of Article 46;

(b) however:

(i) if the person concerned satisfies the conditions of at least two legislations without having recourse to insurance periods completed under the legislations whose conditions are not satisfied, these periods shall not be taken into account for the purposes of Article 46(2);

(ii) if the person concerned satisfies the conditions of one legislation only without having recourse to insurance periods completed under the legislations whose conditions are not satisfied, the amount of the benefit due shall be calculated only in accordance with the provisions of the legislation whose conditions are satisfied, taking account of the periods completed under that legislation only.

2. The benefit or benefits awarded under one or more of the legislations in question, in the case referred to in paragraph 1, shall be recalculated automatically in accordance with Article 46, as and when the conditions required by one or more of the other legislations to which the person concerned had been subject are satisfied, taking into account as appropriate the provisions of Article 45.

3. A recalculation shall automatically be made in accordance with paragraph 1, and without prejudice to Article 40(2), when the conditions required by one or more of the legislations concerned are no longer satisfied.

Article 50

Award of a supplement when the total of benefits due under the legislations of the various Member States does not amount to the minimum laid down by the legislation of the State in whose territory the recipient resides

A recipient of benefits to whom this Chapter applies may not, in the State in whose territory he resides and under whose legislation a benefit is due to him, be awarded a benefit which is less than the minimum benefit fixed by that legislation for an insurance period equal to all the insurance periods taken into account for the payment in accordance with the preceding Articles. The competent institution of that State shall, if necessary, pay him throughout the period of his residence in its territory a supplement equal to the difference between the total of the benefits due under this Chapter and the amount of the minimum benefit.

Article 51

Revalorisation and recalculation of benefits

1. If, by reason of an increase in the cost of living or changes in the level of wages or salaries or other reasons for adjustment, the benefits of the States concerned are altered by fixed percentage or amount, such percentage or amount must be applied directly to the benefits determined under Article 46, without the need for a recalculation in accordance with the provisions of that Article.

2. On the other hand, if the method of determining, or the rules for calculating benefits should be altered, a recalculation shall be carried out in accordance with Article 46.

Chapter 4

Accidents at work and occupational diseases

Section 1

Right to benefits

Article 52

Residence in a Member State other than the competent State – General rules

A worker who sustains an accident at work or contracts an occupational disease, and who is residing in the territory of a Member State other than the competent State, shall receive in the State in which he is residing:

(a) benefits in kind, provided on behalf of the competent institution by the institution of his place of residence in accordance with the legislation which it administers as if he were insured with it;

(b) cash benefits provided by the competent institution in accordance with the legislation which it administers. However, by agreement between the competent institution and the institution of the place of residence, these benefits may be provided by the latter institution on behalf of the former in accordance with the legislation of the competent State.

Article 53

Frontier workers – Special rule

A frontier worker may also obtain benefits in the territory of the competent State. Such benefits shall be provided by the competent institution in accordance with the legislation of that State, as if the worker were residing there.

Article 54

Stay in or transfer of residence to the competent State

1. A worker covered by Article 52 who is staying in the territory of the competent State shall receive benefits in accordance with the legislation

of that State, even if he has already received benefits before his stay. This provision shall not, however, apply to frontier workers.

2. A worker covered by Article 52 who transfers his place of residence to the territory of the competent State shall receive benefits in accordance with the legislation of that State, even if he has already received benefits before transferring his residence.

Article 55

Stay outside the competent State – Return to or transfer of residence to another Member State after sustaining an accident or contracting an occupational disease – Need to go to another Member State in order to receive appropriate treatment

1. A worker who sustains an accident at work or contracts an occupational disease and:

(a) who is staying in the territory of a Member State other than the competent State, or

(b) who, after having become entitled to benefits at the expense of the competent institution, is authorised by that institution to return to the territory of the Member State where he is resident, or to transfer his place of residence to the territory of another Member State, or

(c) who is authorised by the competent institution to go to the territory of another Member State in order to receive there the treatment appropriate to his condition,

shall be entitled:

(i) to benefits in kind provided on behalf of the competent institution by the institution of the place of stay or residence in accordance with the legislation administered by that institution as though he were insured with it, the period during which benefits are provided shall, however, be governed by the legislation of the competent State;

(ii) to cash benefits provided by the competent institution in accordance with the legislation which it administers. However, by agreement between the competent institution and the institution of the place of stay or residence, those benefits may be provided by the latter institution on behalf of the former institution, in accordance with the legislation of the competent State.

2. The authorisation required under paragraph 1(b) may be refused only if it is established that movement of the person concerned would be prejudicial to his state of health or to the medical treatment being given.

The authorisation required under paragraph 1(c) may not be refused where the treatment in question cannot be given to the person concerned in the territory of the Member State in which he resides.

Article 56

Accidents while travelling

An accident while travelling which occurs in the territory of a Member State other than the competent State shall be deemed to have occurred in the territory of the competent State.

Article 57

Benefits for an occupational disease where the person concerned has been exposed to the same risk in several Member States

1. When a person who has contracted an occupational disease has, under the legislation of two or more Member States, pursued an activity likely to cause that disease, the benefits that he or his survivors may claim shall be awarded exclusively under the legislation of the last of these States whose conditions are satisfied, taking into account, where appropriate, the provisions of paragraphs 2 and 3.

2. If, under the legislation of a Member State, the granting of benefits in respect of an occupational disease is subject to the conditions that the disease in question was first diagnosed within its territory, such condition shall be deemed to be fulfilled if the disease was first diagnosed in the territory of another Member State.

3. In case of sclerogenic pneumoconiosis, the following provisions shall apply:

(a) if under the legislation of a Member State the granting of benefits in respect of an occupational disease is subject to the condition that the disease in question was diagnosed within a specific time limit following cessation of the last activity which was likely to cause such a disease, the competent institution of that State, in examining the time at which such activity was pursued shall take into account, to the extent necessary, similar activities pursued under the legislation of any other Member State, as if they had been pursued under the legislation of the first State;

(b) if under the legislation of a Member State the granting of benefits in respect of an occupational disease is subject to the condition that the activity likely to cause the disease in question was pursued for a certain length of time, the competent institution of that State shall take into account, to the extent necessary, periods during which such

activity was pursued under the legislation of any other Member State, as if it had been pursued under the legislation of the first State;

(c) the cost of cash benefits including pensions shall be divided between the competent institutions of the Member States in whose territories the person concerned pursued an activity likely to cause the disease. This division shall be carried out in the ratio which the length of old age insurance periods completed under the legislation of each of the States bears to the total length of the old age insurance periods completed under the legislations of all those States at the date on which the benefits commenced.

4. The Council shall determine unanimously, on a proposal from the Commission, the occupational diseases to which the provisions of paragraph 3 shall be extended.

Article 58

Calculation of cash benefits

1. The competent institution of a Member State whose legislation provides that the calculation of cash benefits shall be based on an average wage or salary shall determine such average wage or salary exclusively by reference to wages or salaries recorded during the periods completed under the said legislation.

2. The competent institution of a Member State whose legislation provides that the calculation of cash benefits shall be based on a standard wage or salary shall determine such average wage or salary exclusively by reference where appropriate, the average of the standard wages or salaries corresponding to the periods completed under the said legislation.

3. The competent institution of a Member State whose legislation provides that the amount of cash benefits shall vary with the number of members in the family shall take into account also the members of the family of the person concerned who are residing in the territory of another Member State, as if they were residing in the territory of the competent State.

Article 59

Costs of transporting a person who has sustained an accident at work or is suffering from an occupational disease

1. The competent institution of a Member State whose legislation provides for meeting the costs of transporting a person who has sustained an accident at work or is suffering from an occupational

disease, either to his place of residence or to a hospital, shall meet such costs to the corresponding place in the territory of another Member State where the person resides, provided that that institution gives prior authorisation for such transport, duly taking into account the reasons justifying it. Such authorisation shall not be required in the case of a frontier worker.

2. The competent institution of a Member State whose legislation provides for the costs of transporting the body of a person killed in an accident at work to the place of burial shall, in accordance with the legislation which it administers, meet such costs to the corresponding place in the territory of another Member State where the person was residing at the time of the accident.

Section 2

Aggravation of an occupational disease for which the benefit has been awarded

Article 60

1. In the event of aggravation of an occupational disease for which a worker has received or is receiving benefit under the legislation of a Member State, the following rules shall apply:

(a) if the worker has not, while in receipt of benefits, been in employment under the legislation of another Member State likely to cause or aggravate the disease in question, the competent institution of the first Member State shall be bound to meet the cost of the benefits under the legislation which it administers taking into account the aggravation;

(b) if the worker, while in receipt of benefits, has been in such employment under the legislation of another Member State, the competent institution of the first State shall be bound to meet the cost of the benefits under the legislation which it administers without taking into account the aggravation. The competent institution of the second Member State shall grant a supplement to the worker, the amount of which shall be determined according to the legislation which it administers and shall be equal to the difference between the amount of benefits due after the aggravation and the amount which would have been due prior to the aggravation under the legislation which it administers if the disease in question had occurred under the legislation of that State;

(c) if in cases covered by subparagraph (b) a worker suffering from sclerogenic pneumoconiosis or from a disease determined under Article 57(4) is not entitled to benefits under the legislation of the

second State, the competent institution of the first State shall be bound to provide benefits under the legislation which it administers, taking into account the aggravation. The institution of the second State shall, however, meet the cost of the difference between the amount of cash benefits, including pensions, due from the competent institution of the first State, taking into account the aggravation and the amount of the corresponding benefits which were due prior to the aggravation.

2. In the event of aggravation of an occupational disease giving rise to the application of Article 57(3)(c), the following provisions shall apply:

(a) the competent institution which granted the benefits pursuant to Article 57(1) shall be bound to provide benefits under the legislation which it administers, taking into account the aggravation;

(b) the cost of cash benefits, including pensions, shall continue to be divided between the institutions which shared the costs of former benefits in accordance with Article 57(3)(c). Where, however, the person has again pursued an activity likely to cause or to aggravate the occupational disease in question, either under the legislation of one of the Member States in which he had already pursued an activity of the same nature or under the legislation of another Member State, the competent institution of such State shall meet the cost of the difference between the amount of benefits due, taking account of the aggravation, and the amount of benefits due prior to the aggravation.

Section 3

Miscellaneous provisions

Article 61

Rules for taking into account the special features of certain legislations

1. If there is no insurance against accidents at work or occupational diseases in the territory of the Member State in which a worker happens to be, or if such insurance exists but there is no institution responsible for providing benefits in kind, those benefits shall be provided by the institution of the place of stay or residence responsible for providing benefit in kind in the event of illness.

2. Where the legislation of the competent State makes wholly cost-free benefits in kind conditional upon use of the medical service organised by the employer, benefits in kind provided in the cases referred to in Articles 52 and 55(1) shall be deemed to have been provided by such a medical service.

3. Where the legislation of the competent State includes a scheme relating to the obligations of the employer, benefits in kind provided in the cases referred to in Articles 52 and 55(1) shall be deemed to have been provided at the request of the competent institution.

4. Where the nature of the scheme of the competent State relating to compensation for accidents at work is not that of compulsory insurance, the provision of benefits in kind shall be made directly by the employer or by the insurer involved.

5. Where the legislation of a Member State expressly or by implication provides that accidents at work or occupational diseases which have occurred or have been confirmed previously shall be taken into consideration in order to assess the degree of incapacity, the competent institution of that State shall also take into consideration accidents at work or occupational diseases which have occurred or have been confirmed previously under the legislation of another Member State, as if they had occurred or had been confirmed under the legislation which it administers.

Article 62

Scheme applicable where there are several schemes in the country of stay or residence – Maximum duration of benefits

1. If the legislation of the country of stay or residence has several insurance schemes, the provisions applicable to workers covered by Article 52 or 55(1) shall be those of the scheme for manual workers in the steel industry. However, if the said legislation includes a special scheme for workers in mines and similar undertakings, the provisions of that scheme shall apply to that category of workers where the institution of the place of stay or residence to which they submit their claim is competent to administer that scheme.

2. If the legislation of a Member State fixes a maximum period during which benefits may be granted, the institution which administers that legislation may take into account any period during which the benefits have already been provided by the institution of another Member State.

Section 4

Reimbursements between institutions

Article 63

1. The competent institutions shall be obliged to reimburse the amount

of benefits in kind provided on their behalf pursuant to Articles 52 and 55(1).

2. The reimbursements referred to in paragraph 1 shall be determined and made in accordance with the procedures laid down by the implementing Regulation referred to in Article 97, on proof of actual expenditure.

3. Two or more Member States, or the competent authorities of such States, may provide for other methods of reimbursement or waive reimbursement between the institutions coming under their jurisdiction.

Chapter 5

Death grants

Article 64

Aggregation of insurance periods

The competent institution of a Member State whose legislation makes the acquisition, retention of recovery of the right to death grants subject to the completion of insurance periods shall take account, to the extent necessary, of insurance periods completed under the legislation of any other Member State as though they had been completed under the legislation which it administers.

Article 65

Right to grants where death occurs in, or where the person entitled resides in, a Member State other than the competent State

1. When a worker, a pensioner or a pension claimant, or a member of his family, dies in the territory of a Member State other than the competent State, the death shall be deemed to have occurred in the territory of the competent State.

2. The competent institution shall be obliged to award death grants payable under the legislation which it administers, even if the person entitled resides in the territory of a Member State other than the competent State.

3. The provisions of paragraphs 1 and 2 shall also apply when the death is the result of an accident at work or an occupational disease.

Article 66

Provision of benefits in the event of the death of a pensioner who had resided in a Member State other than the one whose institution was responsible for providing benefits in kind

In the event of the death of a pensioner who was entitled to draw a pension or pensions under the legislation of one or more Member States, when such pensioner was residing in the territory of a Member State other than the one whose institution was responsible for providing him with benefits in kind under Article 28, the death grants payable under the legislation administered by that institution shall be provided by the institution at its own expense as though the pensioner had been residing in the territory of the Member State of that institution at the time of his death.

The provisions of the preceding paragraph shall apply by analogy to the members of a pensioner's family.

Chapter 6

Unemployment

Section 1

Common provisions

Article 67

Aggregation of periods of insurance or employment

1. The competent institution of a Member State whose legislation makes the acquisition, retention or recovery of the right to benefits subject to the completion of insurance periods shall take into account, to the extent necessary, periods of insurance or employment completed under the legislation of any other Member State, as though they were periods completed under the legislation which it administers, provided, however, that the periods of employment would have been counted as insurance periods had they been completed under that legislation.

2. The competent institution of a Member State whose legislation makes the acquisition, retention or recovery of the right to benefits subject to the completion of periods of employment shall take into account, to the extent necessary, periods of insurance or employment completed under the legislation of any other Member State, as though they were periods of employment completed under the legislation which it administers.

3. Except in the cases referred to in Article 71(1)(a)(ii) and (b)(ii), application of the provisions of paragraphs 1 and 2 shall be subject to the condition that the person concerned should have completed lastly:

– in the case of paragraph 1, periods of insurance,

– in the case of paragraph 2, periods of employment,

in accordance with the provisions of the legislation under which the benefits are claimed.

4. Where the length of the period during which benefits may be granted depends on the length of periods of insurance or employment, the provisions of paragraph 1 or 2 shall apply, as appropriate.

Article 68

Calculation of benefits

1. The competent institution of a Member State whose legislation provides that the calculation of benefits should be based on the amount of the previous wage or salary shall take into account exclusively the wage or salary received by the person concerned in respect of his last employment in the territory of that State. However, if the person concerned had been in his last employment in that territory for less than four weeks, the benefits shall be calculated on the basis of the normal wage or salary corresponding, in the place where the unemployed person is residing or staying, to an equivalent or similar employment to his last employment in the territory of another Member State.

2. The competent institution of a Member State whose legislation provides that the amount of benefits varies with the number of members of the family, shall take into account also members of the family of the person concerned who are residing in the territory of another Member State, as though they were residing in the territory of the competent State. This provision shall not apply if, in the country of residence of the members of the family, another person is entitled to unemployment benefits for the calculation of which the members of the family are taken into consideration.

Section 2

Unemployed persons going to a Member State other than the competent State

Article 69

Conditions and limits for the retention of the right to benefits

1. A worker who is wholly unemployed and who satisfies the conditions of the legislation of a Member State for entitlement to benefits and who goes to one or more other Member States in order to seek employment there shall retain his entitlement to such benefits under the conditions and within the limits hereinafter indicated:

(a) before his departure, he must have been registered with the employment services of the competent State as a person seeking work and must have remained available for at least four weeks after becoming unemployed. However, the competent services or institutions may authorise his departure before such time has expired;

(b) he must register as a person seeking work with the employment services of each of the Member States to which he goes and be subject to the control procedure organised therein. This condition shall be considered satisfied for the period before registration if the person concerned registered within seven days of the date when he ceased to be available to the employment services of the State he left. In exceptional cases, this period may be extended by the competent services or institutions;

(c) entitlement to benefits shall continue for a maximum period of three months from the date when the person concerned ceased to be available to the employment services of the State which he left, provided that the total duration of the benefits does not exceed the duration of the period of benefits he was entitled to under the legislation of that State. In the case of a seasonal worker such duration shall, moreover, be limited to the period remaining until the end of the season for which he was engaged.

2. If the person concerned returns to the competent State before the expiry of the period during which he is entitled to benefits under paragraph 1(c), he shall continue to be entitled to benefits under the legislation of that State; he shall lose all entitlement to benefits under the legislation of the competent State if he does not return there before the expiry of that period. In exceptional cases, this time limit may be extended by the competent services or institutions.

3. The provisions of paragraph 1 may be invoked only once between two periods of employment.

4. Where the competent State is Belgium, an unemployed person who returns there after the expiry of the three month period laid down in paragraph 1(c), shall not requalify for benefits in that country until he has been employed there for at least three months.

Article 70

Provision of benefits and reimbursements

1. In the cases referred to in Article 69(1), benefits shall be provided by the institution of each of the States to which an unemployed person goes to seek employment.

The competent institution of the Member State to whose legislation a worker was subject at the time of his last employment shall be obliged to reimburse the amount of such benefits.

2. The reimbursements referred to in paragraph 1 shall be determined and made in accordance with the procedure laid down by the implementing Regulation referred to in Article 97, on proof of actual expenditure, or by lump sum payments.

3. Two or more Member States, or the competent authorities of those States, may provide for other methods of reimbursement or payment, or may waive all reimbursement between the institutions coming under their jurisdiction.

Section 3

Unemployed persons who, during their last employment, were residing in a Member State other than the competent State

Article 71

1. An unemployed person who, during his last employment, was residing in the territory of a Member State other than the competent State shall receive benefits in accordance with the following provisions:

(a) (i) a frontier worker who is partially or intermittently unemployed in the undertaking which employs him, shall receive benefits in accordance with the legislation of the competent State as if he were residing in the territory of that State; these benefits shall be provided by the competent institution;

(ii) a frontier worker who is wholly unemployed shall receive benefits in accordance with the legislation of the Member State in whose territory he resides as though he had been subject to that legislation while last employed the institution of the place of residence shall provide such benefits at its own expense;

(b) (i) a worker, other than a frontier worker who is partially, intermittently or wholly unemployed and who remains available to his employer or to the employment services in the territory of the competent State shall receive benefits in accordance with the legislation of that State as though he were residing in its territory; these benefits shall be provided by the competent institution;

(ii) a worker, other than a frontier worker, who is wholly unemployed and who makes himself available for work to the employment services in the territory of the Member State in which he resides, or who returns to that territory, shall receive benefits in accordance with the legislation of that State as if he had last been employed there; the institution of the place of residence shall provide such benefits at its own expense. However, if such worker has become entitled to benefits at the expense of the competent institution of the Member State to whose legislation he was last subject, he shall receive benefits under the provisions of Article 69. Receipt of benefits under the legislation of the State in which he resides shall be suspended for any period during which the unemployed person may, under Article 69, make a claim for benefits under the legislation to which he was last subject.

2. An unemployed person may not claim benefits under the legislation of the Member State in whose territory he resides while he is entitled to benefits under paragraph 1(a)(i) or (b)(i).

Chapter 7

Family benefits and family allowances for employed and unemployed persons

Section 1

Common Provision

Article 72

Aggregation of periods of employment

Where the legislation of one Member State makes acquisition of the right to benefits conditional upon the completion of periods of employment,

the competent institution of that State shall take into account, to the extent necessary, periods of employment completed in the territory of any other Member State, as if they had been completed under its own legislation.

Section 2

Workers and unemployed workers whose families reside in a Member State other than the competent State

Article 73

Workers

1. A worker subject to the legislation of a Member State other than France shall be entitled to the family benefits provided for by the legislation of the first Member State for members of his family residing in the territory of another Member State, as though they were residing in the territory of the first State.

2. A worker subject to French legislation shall be entitled, in respect of members of his family residing in the territory of a Member State other than France, to the family allowances provided for by the legislation of such Member State; the worker must satisfy the conditions regarding employment on which French legislation bases entitlement to such benefits.

3. However, a worker who is subject to French legislation by virtue of the provisions of Article 14(1)(a) shall be entitled to the family benefits provided for by French legislation and set out in Annex V in respect of members of his family who accompany him to the territory of the Member State where he is posted.

Article 74

Unemployed persons

1. An unemployed person drawing unemployment benefits under the legislation of a Member State other than France shall be entitled to the family benefits provided for by the legislation of the first Member State for members of his family residing in the territory of another Member State as though they were residing in the territory of the first State.

2. An unemployed person drawing unemployment benefits under French legislation shall be entitled, in respect of members of his family residing in the territory of a Member State other than France, to the family

allowances provided for by the legislation of the State in whose territory those members of the family are residing.

Article 75

Provisions of benefits and reimbursements

1. (a) Family benefits shall be provided, in the cases referred to in Article 73(1) and (3), by the competent institution of the State to whose legislation the worker is subject and, in the case referred to in Article 74(1), by the competent institution of the State under whose legislation the unemployed worker is receiving unemployment benefits. They shall be provided in accordance with the provisions administered by such institutions, whether the natural or legal person to whom such benefits are payable is staying, residing or situated in the territory of the competent State or in that of another Member State;

   (b) however, if the family benefits are not applied by the person to whom they should be provided for the maintenance of the members of the family, the competent institution shall discharge its legal obligations by providing the said benefits to the natural or legal person actually maintaining the members of the family, on application by and through the agency of the institution of their place of residence or of the institution or body appointed to that end by the competent authority of their country of residence;

   (c) two or more Member States may agree, in accordance with Article 8, that the competent institution shall provide the family benefits due under the legislation of one or more of those States to the natural or legal person actually maintaining the members of the family, either directly, or through the agency of the institution of their place of residence.

2. (a) Family allowances shall be provided, in the cases referred to in Articles 73(2) and 74(2), by the institution of the place of residence of the members of the family, in accordance with the legislation administered by that institution;

   (b) however, if, under that legislation, the allowances must be provided to the worker, the institution referred to in the preceding subparagraph shall pay such allowances to the natural or legal person actually maintaining the members of the family in their place of residence or, where appropriate, directly to the members of the family;

(c) the competent institution shall reimburse the full amount of the allowances provided in accordance with the preceding subparagraphs. The reimbursements shall be determined and made in accordance with the procedures laid down by the implementing Regulation referred to in Article 97.

Article 76

Rules of priority in cases of overlapping entitlement to family benefits or family allowances in pursuance of Articles 73 and 74 by reason of the pursuit of a professional or trade activity in the country of residence of the members of the family

Entitlement to family benefits or family allowances under Articles 73 and 74 shall be suspended if, by reason of the pursuit of a professional or trade activity, family benefits or family allowances are also payable under the legislation of the Member State in whose territory the members of the family are residing.

Chapter 8

Benefits for dependent children of pensioners and for orphans

Article 77

Dependent children of pensioners

1. The term 'benefits', for the purposes of this Article, shall mean family allowances for persons receiving pensions for old age, invalidity or an accident at work or occupational disease, and increases or supplements to such pensions in respect of the children of such pensioners, with the exception of supplements granted under insurance schemes for accidents at work and occupational diseases.

2. Benefits shall be granted in accordance with the following rules, irrespective of the Member State in whose territory the pensioner or the children are residing:

(a) to a pensioner who draws a pension under the legislation of one Member State only, in accordance with the legislation of the Member State responsible for the pension;

(b) to a pensioner who draws pensions under the legislation of more than one Member State:

   (i) in accordance with the legislation of whichever of these States he

resides in provided that, taking into account where appropriate Article 79(1)(a), a right to one of the benefits referred to in paragraph 1 is acquired under the legislation of that State, or

(ii) in other cases, in accordance with that legislation under which he has completed the longest insurance period, provided that, taking into account where appropriate Article 79(1)(a), a right to one of the benefits referred to in paragraph (i) is acquired under such legislation; if no right to benefit is acquired under such legislation, the conditions for the acquisition of such right under the legislations of the other States concerned shall be examined in decreasing order of the length of insurance periods completed under the legislation of those States.

Article 78

Orphans

1. The term 'benefits', for the purposes of this Article, means family allowances and, where appropriate, supplementary or special allowances for orphans and orphans' pensions except those granted under insurance schemes for accidents at work and occupational diseases.

2. Orphans' benefits shall be granted in accordance with the following rules, irrespective of the Member State in whose territory the orphan or the natural or legal person actually maintaining him is resident or situated;

(a) for the orphan of a deceased worker who was subject to the legislation of one Member State only in accordance with the legislation of that State;

(b) for the orphan of a deceased worker who was subject to the legislation of several Member States:

(i) in accordance with the legislation of the Member State in whose territory the orphan resides provided that, taking into account where appropriate Article 79(1)(a), a right to one of the benefits referred to in paragraph 1 is acquired under the legislation of that State, or

(ii) in other cases, in accordance with the legislation of the Member State under which the deceased worker had completed the longest insurance period provided that, taking into account where appropriate Article 79(1)(a), the right to one of the benefits referred to in paragraph 1 is acquired under the legislation of that State; if no right is acquired under that

legislation, the conditions for the acquisition of such right under the legislations of the other States in question shall be examined in decreasing order of the length of insurance periods completed under the legislation of these States.

However, the legislation of the Member State applicable in respect of provision of the benefits referred to in Article 77 for a pensioner's children shall remain applicable after the death of the said pensioner in respect of the provision of the benefits to his orphans.

Article 79

Provisions common to benefits for dependent children of pensioners and for orphans

1. Benefits, within the meaning of Articles 77 and 78, shall be provided in accordance with the legislation determined by applying the provisions of those Articles by the institution responsible for administering such legislation and at its expense as if the pensioner or the deceased worker had been subject only to the legislation of the competent State.

However:

(a) if that legislation provides that the acquisition, retention or recovery of the right to benefits shall be dependent on the length of periods of insurance or employment, such lengths shall be determined taking account where necessary of Articles 45 or 72 as appropriate;

(b) if that legislation provides that the amount of benefits shall be calculated on the basis of the amount of the pension, or shall depend on the length of insurance periods, the amount of these benefits shall be calculated on the basis of the theoretical amount determined in accordance with Article 46(2).

2. In a case where the effect of applying the rule laid down in Articles 77(2)(b)(ii) and 78(2)(b)(ii) would be to make several Member States responsible, the length of the insurance periods being equal, benefits within the meaning of Article 77 or Article 78, as the case may be, shall be granted in accordance with the legislation of the Member State to which the worker was last subject.

3. The right to benefits due under paragraph 2 and under Articles 77 and 78 shall be suspended if the children become entitled to family benefits or family allowances under the legislation of a Member State by virtue of the pursuit of a professional or trade activity. In such a case, the persons concerned shall be considered as members of the family of a worker.

Title IV

Administrative commission on social security for migrant workers

Article 80

Composition and working methods

1. There shall be attached to the Commission of the European Communities, an Administrative Commission on Social Security for Migrant Workers (hereinafter called 'Administrative Commission') made up of a government representative of each of the Member States, assisted, where necessary, by expert advisers. A representative of the Commission of the European Communities shall attend the meetings of the Administrative Commission in an advisory capacity.

2. The Administrative Commission shall be assisted in technical matters by the International Labour Office under the terms of the agreements concluded to that end between the European Economic Community and the International Labour Organisation.

3. The rules of the Administrative Commission shall be drawn up by mutual agreement among its members.

Decisions on questions of interpretation referred to in Article 81(a) shall be unanimous. They shall be given the necessary publicity.

4. Secretarial services shall be provided for the Administrative Commission by the Commission of the European Communities.

Article 81

Tasks of the Administrative Commission

The Administrative Commission shall have the following duties:

(a) to deal with all administrative questions and questions of interpretation arising from this Regulation and subsequent regulations, or from any agreement or arrangement concluded thereunder, without prejudice to the right of the authorities, institutions and persons concerned to have recourse to the procedures and tribunals provided for by the legislations of Member States, by this Regulation or by the Treaty;

(b) to carry out all translations of documents relating to the implementation of this Regulation at the request of the competent authorities, institutions and courts of the Member States, and in

particular translations of claims submitted by persons who may be entitled to benefit under this Regulation;

(c) to foster and develop co-operation between Member States in social security matters, particularly in respect of health and social measures of common interest;

(d) to foster and develop co-operation between Member States with a view to expediting, taking into account developments in administrative management techniques, the award of benefits, in particular those due under this Regulation for invalidity, old age and death (pensions);

(e) to assemble the factors to be taken into consideration for drawing up accounts relating to the costs to be borne by the institutions of the Member States under this Regulation and to adopt the annual accounts between the said institutions;

(f) to undertake any other function coming within its competence under the provisions of this and of subsequent Regulations or any agreement or arrangement made thereunder;

(g) to submit proposals to the Commission of the European Economic Communities for working out subsequent Regulations and for the revision of this and subsequent Regulations.

Title V

Advisory Committee on Social Security for Migrant Workers

Article 82

Establishment, composition and working methods

1. An Advisory Committee on Social Security for Migrant Workers (hereinafter called the 'Advisory Committee') is hereby established, with thirty-six members comprising, from each Member State:

(a) two representatives of the government, of whom one at least must be a member of the Administrative Commission;

(b) two representatives of trade unions;

(c) two representatives of employers' organisations.

For each of the categories referred to above, an alternate member shall be appointed for each Member State.

2. Members of the Advisory Committee and their alternates shall be

appointed by the Council which shall endeavour, when selecting representatives of trade unions and employers' organisations, to achieve adequate representation on the Committee of the various sectors concerned.

The list of members and their alternates shall be published by the Council in the *Official Journal of the European Communities*.

3. The term of office for members and alternates shall be two years. Their appointments may be renewed. On expiry of their term of office, members and alternates shall remain in office until they are replaced or until their appointments are renewed.

4. The Advisory Committee shall be chaired by a member of the Commission or his representative. The Chairman shall not vote.

5. The Advisory Committee shall meet at least once each year. It shall be convened by its Chairman, either on his own initiative or on written application to him by at least one third of the members. Such application must include concrete proposals concerning the agenda.

6. Acting on a proposal from its Chairman, the Advisory Committee may decide, in exceptional circumstances, to take advice from any persons or representatives of organisations with extensive experience in social security matters. Furthermore, the Committee shall receive technical assistance from the International Labour Office under the same conditions as the Administrative Commission, under the terms of the agreement concluded between the European Economic Community and the International Labour Organisation.

7. The opinions and proposals of the Advisory Committee must state the reasons on which they are based. They shall be delivered by an absolute majority of the votes validly cast.

The Committee shall, by a majority of its members, draw up its rules of procedure which shall be approved by the Council, after receiving the Opinion of the Commission.

8. Secretarial services shall be provided for the Advisory Committee by the Commission of the European Communities.

Article 83

Tasks of the Advisory Committee

The Advisory Committee shall be empowered, at the request of the Commission of the European Communities or of the Administrative Commission on its own initiative:

(a) to examine general questions or questions of principle and problems arising from the implementation of the Regulation adopted within the framework of the provisions of Article 51 of the Treaty;

(b) to formulate opinions on the subject for the Administrative Commission and proposals for any revision of the Regulations.

Title VI

Miscellaneous provisions

Article 84

Co-operation between competent authorities

1. The competent authorities of Member States shall communicate to each other all information regarding:

(a) measures taken to implement this Regulation;

(b) changes in their legislation which are likely to affect the implementation of this Regulation.

2. For the purposes of implementing this Regulation, the authorities and institutions of Member States shall lend their good offices and act as though implementing their own legislation. The administrative assistance furnished by the said authorities and institutions shall, as a rule, be free of charge. However, the competent authorities of the Member States may agree to certain expenses being reimbursed.

3. The authorities and institutions of Member States may, for the purpose of implementing this Regulation, communicate directly with one another and with the persons concerned or their representatives.

4. The authorities, institutions and tribunals of one Member State may not reject claims or other documents submitted to them on the grounds that they are written in an official language of another Member State. They shall have recourse where appropriate to the provisions of Article 81(b).

Article 85

Exemptions from or reductions of taxes – Exemption from authentication

1. Any exemption from or reduction of taxes, stamp duty, notarial or registration fees provided for in the legislation of one Member State in respect of certificates or documents required to be produced for the

purposes of the legislation of that State shall be extended to similar documents required to be produced for the purposes of the legislation of another Member State or of this Regulation.

2. All statements, documents and certificates of any kind whatsoever required to be produced for the purposes of this Regulation shall be exempt from authentication by diplomatic or consular authorities.

Article 86

Claims, declarations or appeals submitted to an authority, institution or court of a Member State other than the competent State

Any claim, declaration or appeal which should have been submitted, in order to comply with the legislation of one Member State, within a specified period to an authority, institution or court of that State shall be admissible if it is submitted within the same period to a corresponding authority, institution, or court of another Member State. In such a case the authority, institution, or court receiving the claim, declaration or appeal shall forward it without delay to the competent authority, institution or court of the former State either directly or through the competent authorities of the Member State concerned. The date on which such claims, declarations or appeals were submitted to the authority, institution or court of the second State shall be considered as the date of their submission to the competent authority, institution or court.

Article 87

Medical examinations

1. Medical examinations provided for by the legislation of one Member State may be carried out at the request of the competent institution, in the territory of another Member State, by the institution of the place of stay or residence of the person entitled to benefits, under conditions laid down in the implementing Regulation referred to in Article 97 or, failing these, under conditions agreed upon between the competent authorities of the Member States concerned.

2. Medical examinations carried out under the conditions laid down in paragraph 1 shall be considered as having been carried out in the territory of the competent State.

Article 88

Transfers from one Member State to another of sums of money payable pursuant to this Regulation

Subject to the provisions of Article 106 of the Treaty, money transfers effected pursuant to this Regulation shall be made in accordance with the relevant agreements in force between the Member States concerned at the time of transfer. Where no such agreements are in force between two Member States, the competent authorities of the said States or the authorities responsible for international payments shall, by mutual agreement, determine the measures necessary for effecting such transfers.

Article 89

Special procedures for implementing certain legislations

Special procedures for implementing the legislations of certain Member States are set out in Annex V.

Article 90

Housing allowances and family benefits introduced after the entry into force of this Regulation

Housing allowances and, in the case of Luxembourg, family benefits introduced after the entry into force of this Regulation for demographic reasons shall not be granted to persons resident in the territory of a Member State other than the competent State.

Article 91

Contributions chargeable to employers or undertakings not established in the competent State

An employer shall not be bound to pay increased contributions by reason of the fact that his place of business or the registered office or place of business of his undertaking is in the territory of a Member State other than the competent State.

Article 92

Collection of contributions

1. Contributions payable to an institution of one Member State may be collected in the territory of another Member State in accordance with the administrative procedure and with the guarantees and privileges applicable to the collection of contributions payable to the corresponding institution of the latter State.

2. The procedure for the implementation of paragraph 1 shall be governed, in so far as is necessary, by the implementing Regulation referred to in Article 97 or by means of agreements between Member States. Such implementing procedure may also cover procedure for enforcing payment.

Article 93

Rights of institutions responsible for benefits against liable third parties

1. If a person receives benefits under the legislation of one Member State in respect of an injury resulting from an occurrence in the territory of another State, any rights of the institution responsible for benefits against a third party bound to compensate for the injury shall be governed by the following rules:

(*a*) where the institution responsible for benefits is, by virtue of the legislation which it administers, subrogated to the rights which the recipient has against the third party, such subrogation shall be recognised by each Member State;

(*b*) where the said institution has direct rights against the third party, such rights shall be recognised by each Member State.

2. If a person receives benefits under the legislation of one Member State in respect of an injury resulting from an occurrence in the territory of another Member State, the provisions of the said legislation which determine in which cases the civil liability of employers or of their employees is to be excluded shall apply with regard to the said person or to the institution responsible for benefits.

The provisions of paragraph 1 shall also apply to any rights of the institution responsible for benefit against an employer or his employees in cases where their liability is not excluded.

Title VII

Transitional and final provisions

Article 94

Miscellaneous provisions

1. No right shall be acquired under this Regulation for a period prior to the date of its entry into force.

2. All insurance periods and, where appropriate, all periods of employment or residence completed under the legislation of a Member

State before the date of entry into force of this Regulation shall be taken into consideration for the determination of rights to benefits under this Regulation.

3. Subject to the provisions of paragraph 1, a right shall be acquired under this Regulation though relating to a contingency which materialised prior to the date of entry into force of this Regulation.

4. Any benefit which has not been awarded or which has been suspended by reason of the nationality or place of residence of the person concerned shall, on the application of the person concerned, be awarded or resumed with effect from the entry into force of this Regulation provided that the rights previously determined have not given rise to a lump sum payment.

5. The rights of a person to whom a pension was awarded prior to the entry into force of this Regulation may, on the application of the person concerned, be reviewed, taking into account the provisions of this Regulation. This provision shall also apply to the other benefits referred to in Article 78.

6. If an application referred to in paragraph 4 or 5 is submitted within two years from the date of entry into force of this Regulation, the rights acquired under this Regulation shall have effect from that date, and the provisions of the legislation of any Member State concerning the forfeiture or limitation of rights may not be invoked against the persons concerned.

7. If an application referred to in paragraph 4 or 5 is submitted after the expiry of the two-year period following the entry into force of this Regulation, rights which have not been forfeited or are not barred by limitation shall have effect from the date on which the application was submitted, except where more favourable provisions of the legislation of any Member State apply.

8. In cases of sclerogenic pneumoconiosis, Article 57(3)(c) shall apply to cash benefits for an occupational disease the expense of which, in the absence of an agreement between the institutions concerned, could not be divided between those institutions before the date of entry into force of this Regulation.

9. The implementation of Article 73(2) shall not have the effect of reducing any rights existing at the date of entry into force of this Regulation. As regards persons who at that date are receiving more favourable benefits by virtue of bilateral agreements concluded with France, those agreements shall continue to apply to such persons for as long as they are subject to French legislation. Account shall not be taken of interruptions lasting less than one month, nor of periods in which

unemployment or sickness benefit is drawn. The procedure for implementing those provisions shall be laid down by the implementing Regulation referred to in Article 97.

Article 95

Annexes to this Regulation

The Annexes to this Regulation may be amended by a Regulation adopted by the Council on a proposal from the Commission, at the request of one or more Member States concerned, and after receiving the Opinion of the Administrative Commission.

Article 96

Notifications pursuant to certain provisions

1. The notifications referred to in Articles 1(j), 5 and 8(2) shall be addressed to the President of the Council of the European Communities. They shall indicate the date of entry into force of the laws and schemes in question or, in the case of the notifications referred to in Article 1(j), the date from which this Regulation shall apply to the schemes mentioned in the declarations of the Member States.

2. Notifications received in accordance with paragraph 1 shall be published in the *Official Journal of the European Communities.*

Article 97

Implementing regulation

A further regulation shall lay down the procedure for implementing this Regulation.

Article 98

Re-examination of the problem of payment of family benefits

Before 1 January 1973 the Council shall, on a proposal from the Commission, re-examine the whole problem of payment of family benefits to members of families who are not residing in the territory of the competent State, in order to reach a uniform solution for all Member States.

Article 99

Entry into force

This Regulation shall enter into force on the first day of the seventh month following the publication in the *Official Journal of the European Communities* of the implementing Regulation referred to in Article 97.

These two Regulations shall repeal the following Regulations:

- Council Regulation No 3 concerning social security for migrant workers,

- Council Regulation No 4 laying down implementing procedures and supplementary provisions in respect of Regulation No 3[7], and

- Council Regulation No 36/63/EEC of 2 April 1963 concerning social security for frontier workers[8].

However, the provisions of Articles 82 and 83 concerning the setting up of the Advisory Committee, shall enter into force on the day of publication of the implementing regulation referred to in Article 97.

This Regulation shall be binding in its entirety and directly applicable in all Member States.

Done at Luxembourg, 14 June 1971.

For the Council

The President

M. Cointat

Annex I

(Article 1(u) of the Regulation)

Special childbirth allowances excluded from the scope of the Regulation in pursuance of Article 1(u)

A. BELGIUM

Childbirth allowances

B. GERMANY

None

C. FRANCE

(a) Prenatal allowances

(b) Maternity allowances under the social security code (code de la sécurité sociale)

D. ITALY

None

E. LUXEMBOURG

Childbirth allowances

F. NETHERLANDS

None

Annex II

(Articles 7(2)(c) and 3(3) of the Regulation)

Provisions of social security conventions remaining applicable notwithstanding Article 6 of the Regulation – Provisions of social security conventions which do not apply to persons to whom the Regulation applies

General comments

1. In so far as the provisions contained in this Annex provide for references to the provisions of other conventions, references shall be replaced by references to the corresponding provisions of this Regulation, unless the provisions of the conventions in question are themselves contained in this Annex.

2. The termination clause provided for in a social security convention, some of whose provisions are contained in this Annex shall continue to apply as regards those provisions.

A

Provisions of social security conventions remaining applicable notwithstanding Article 6 of the Regulation

(Article 7(2)(c) of the Regulation)

1. BELGIUM – GERMANY

(a) Articles 3 and 4 of the Final Protocol of 7 December 1957 to the General Convention of the same date, in the version appearing in the Supplementary Protocol of 10 November 1960;

(b) Supplementary Agreement No 3 of 7 December 1957 to the General Convention of the same date, in the version appearing in the Supplementary Protocol of 10 November 1960 (payment of pensions payable in respect of the period preceding the entry into force of the General Convention).

2. BELGIUM – FRANCE

(a) Articles 13, 16 and 23 of the Supplementary Agreement of 17 January 1948 to the General Convention of the same date (workers in mines and similar undertakings);

(b) Exchange of Letters of 27 February 1953 (application of Article 4(2) of the General Convention of 17 January 1948);

(c) Exchange of Letters of 29 July 1953 on allowances to elderly employed persons.

3. BELGIUM – ITALY

Article 29 of the Convention of 30 April 1948.

4. BELGIUM – LUXEMBOURG

Articles 3, 4, 5, 6 and 7 of the Convention of 16 November 1959, in the version appearing in the Convention of 12 February 1964 (frontier workers).

5. BELGIUM – NETHERLANDS

None.

6. GERMANY – FRANCE

(a) Article 11(1), the second paragraph of Article 16, and Article 19 of the General convention of 10 July 1950;

(b) Article 9 of Supplementary Agreement No 1 of 10 July 1950 to the General Convention of the same date (workers in mines and similar undertakings);

(c) Supplementary Agreement No 4 of 10 July 1950 to the General Convention of the same date, in the version appearing in the added section No 2 of 18 June 1955;

(d) Titles I and III of added section No 2 of 18 June 1955;

(e) Points 6, 7 and 8 of the General Protocol of 10 July 1950 to the General Convention of the same date;

(f) Titles II, III and IV of the Agreement of 20 December 1963 (social security in the Saar).

7. GERMANY – ITALY

(a) Articles 3(2), 23(2), 26 and 36(3) of the Convention of 5 May 1953 (social insurance);

(b) Supplementary Agreement of 12 May 1953 to the Convention of 5 May 1953 (payment of pensions payable in respect of the period preceding the entry into force of the Convention).

8. GERMANY – LUXEMBOURG

Articles 4, 5, 6 and 7 of the Treaty of 11 July 1959 (settlement of the dispute between Germany and Luxembourg) and Article 11(2)(b) of the Convention of 14 July 1960 (sickness and maternity benefits for persons who have opted for the application of the legislation of the country whence they come).

9. GERMANY – NETHERLANDS

(a) Article 3(2) of the Convention of 29 March 1951;

(b) Articles 2 and 3 of Supplementary Agreement No 4 of 21 December 1956 to the Convention of 29 March 1951 (settlement of rights acquired under the German social security insurance scheme by Netherlands workers between 13 May 1940 and 1 September 1945).

10. FRANCE – ITALY

(a) Articles 20 and 24 of the General Convention of 31 March 1948;

(b) Exchange of Letters of 3 March 1956 (sickness benefits for seasonal workers employed in agriculture).

11. FRANCE – LUXEMBOURG

Articles 11 and 14 of the Supplementary Agreement of 12 November 1949 to the General Convention of the same date (workers in mines and similar undertakings).

12. FRANCE – NETHERLANDS

Article 11 of the Supplementary Agreement of 1 June 1954 to the General Convention of 7 January 1950 (workers in mines and similar undertakings).

13. ITALY – LUXEMBOURG

Article 18(2) and Article 24 of the General Convention of 29 May 1951.

14. ITALY – NETHERLANDS

Article 21(2) of the General Convention of 28 October 1952.

15. LUXEMBOURG – NETHERLANDS

None.

B

Provisions of conventions which do not apply to all persons to whom the Regulation applies

(Article 3(3) of the Regulation)

1. BELGIUM – GERMANY

(a) Articles 3 and 4 of the Final Protocol of 7 December 1957 to the General Convention of the same date, in the version appearing in the Supplementary Protocol of 10 November 1960;

(b) Supplementary Agreement No 3 of 7 December 1957 to the General Convention of the same date, in the version appearing in the Supplementary Protocol of 10 November 1960 (payment of pensions payable in respect of the period preceding the entry into force of the General Convention).

2. BELGIUM – FRANCE

(a) Exchange of Letters of 29 July 1953 on allowances to elderly employed persons;

(b) Article 23 of the Supplementary Agreement of 17 January 1948 to the General Convention of the same date (workers in mines and similar undertakings);

(c) Exchange of Letters of 27 February 1953 (application of Article 4(2) of the General Convention of 17 January 1948).

3. BELGIUM – ITALY

None.

4. BELGIUM – LUXEMBOURG

None.

5. BELGIUM – NETHERLANDS

None.

6. GERMANY – FRANCE

(a) Articles 16(2) and 19 of the General Convention of 10 July 1950;

(b) Supplementary Agreement No 4 of 10 July to the General Convention of the same date, in the version appearing in the added Section No 2 of 18 June 1955;

(c) Titles I and III of added Section No 2 of 18 June 1955;

(d) Points 6, 7 and 8 of the General Protocol of 10 July 1950 to the General Convention of the same date;

(e) Titles II, III and IV of the Agreement of 20 December 1963 (social security in the Saar).

7. GERMANY – ITALY

(a) Articles 3(2) and 26 of the Convention of 5 May 1953 (social insurance);

(b) The Supplementary Agreement of 12 May 1953 to the Convention of 5 May 1953 (payment of pensions payable in respect of the period preceding the entry into force of the Convention).

8. GERMANY – LUXEMBOURG

Articles 4, 5, 6 and 7 of the Treaty of 11 June 1959 (settlement of the dispute between Germany and Luxembourg).

9. GERMANY – NETHERLANDS

(a) Article 3(2) of the Convention of 29 March 1951;

(b) Articles 2 and 3 of Supplementary Agreement No 4 of 21 December 1956 to the Convention of 29 March 1951 (settlement of rights acquired under the German social security insurance scheme by Netherlands workers between 13 May 1940 and 1 September 1945).

10. FRANCE – ITALY

(a) Articles 20 and 24 of the General Convention of 31 March 1948;

(b) Exchange of Letters of 3 March 1956 (sickness benefits for seasonal workers employed in agriculture).

11. FRANCE – LUXEMBOURG

None.

12. FRANCE – NETHERLANDS

None.

13. ITALY – LUXEMBOURG

None.

14. ITALY – NETHERLANDS

None.

15. LUXEMBOURG – NETHERLANDS

None.

Annex III

(*Article 37(2) of the Regulation*)

Legislations referred to in Article 37(1) of the Regulation under which the amount of invalidity benefits is independent of the length of insurance periods

A. BELGIUM

The legislations relating to the general invalidity scheme, to the special invalidity scheme for miners and to the special scheme for mariners in the merchant navy.

B. GERMANY

None.

C. FRANCE

All legislations on invalidity insurance, except for the legislation concerning the invalidity insurance of the social security scheme for miners.

D. ITALY

None.

E. LUXEMBOURG

None.

F. NETHERLANDS

The law of 18 February 1966 on insurance against incapacity for work.

Annex IV

(*Article* 40(3) *of the Regulation*)

Concordance between the legislations of Member States on conditions relating to the degree of invalidity

BELGIUM

Member States	Schemes administered by Member States' institutions who have taken a decision recognising the degree of invalidity	Schemes administered by Belgium institutions on which the decision is binding in cases of concordance			
		General scheme	Miners' scheme		Mariners' scheme
			General invalidity	Occupational invalidity	
FRANCE	1. General scheme: – Group III (constant attendance) – Group II – Group I	Concordance	Concordance	Concordance	Concordance
	2. Agricultural scheme: – total, general invalidity – two-thirds general invalidity – constant attendance	Concordance	Concordance	Concordance	Concordance
	3. Miners' scheme: – partial, general invalidity – constant attendance	Concordance	Concordance	Concordance	Concordance
	– occupational invalidity	No concordance	No concordance	No concordance	No concordance
	4. Mariners' scheme: – general invalidity – constant attendance	Concordance	Concordance	Concordance	Concordance
	– occupational invalidity	No concordance	No concordance	No concordance	No concordance
ITALY	1. General scheme: – invalidity – manual workers – invalidity – clerical staff	Concordance	Concordance	Concordance	Concordance
	2. Mariners' scheme: Unfitness for seafaring	No concordance	No concordance	No concordance	No concordance
LUXEMBOURG	Workers' – Invalidity – manual workers Invalidity – clerical staff	Concordance	Concordance	Concordance	Concordance

FRANCE

Schemes administered by French institutions on which the decision is binding in cases of concordance

Member States	Schemes administered by Member States' institutions having taken a decision recognising the degree of invalidity	General scheme			Agricultural scheme			Miners' scheme			Mariners' scheme		
		Group I	Group II	Group III Constant attendance	2/3 invalidity	Total invalidity	Constant attendance	2/3 General invalidity	Constant attendance	Occupational invalidity	2/3 general invalidity	Total occupational invalidity	Constant attendance
BELGIUM	1. General scheme	Concordance	No concordance	No concordance	Concordance	No concordance	No concordance	Concordance	No concordance	No concordance	No concordance	No concordance	No concordance
	2. Miners' scheme: – partial general invalidity	Concordance	No concordance	No concordance	Concordance	No concordance	No concordance	Concordance	No concordance	No concordance	No concordance	No concordance	No concordance
	– occupational invalidity	No concordance	No concordance	No concordance	No concordance	No concordance	No concordance	No concordance	No concordance	Concordance[2]	No concordance	No concordance	No concordance
	3. Mariners' scheme	Concordance[1]	No concordance	No concordance	Concordance[1]	No concordance	No concordance	Concordance[1]	No concordance	No concordance	No concordance	No concordance	No concordance
ITALY	1. General scheme: – invalidity – manual workers	Concordance	No concordance	No concordance	Concordance	No concordance	No concordance	Concordance	No concordance	No concordance	No concordance	No concordance	No concordance
	– invalidity – clerical staff	No concordance	No concordance	No concordance	No concordance	No concordance	No concordance	No concordance	No concordance	No concordance	No concordance	No concordance	No concordance
	2. Mariners' schemes:	No concordance	No concordance	No concordance	No concordance	No concordance	No concordance	No concordance	No concordance	No concordance	No concordance	No concordance	No concordance
LUXEMBOURG	Invalidity – manual workers	Concordance	No concordance	No concordance	Concordance	No concordance	No concordance	Concordance	No concordance	No concordance	No concordance	No concordance	No concordance
	Invalidity – clerical staff	No concordance	No concordance	No concordance	No concordance	No concordance	No concordance	No concordance	No concordance	No concordance	No concordance	No concordance	No concordance

1. In so far as the invalidity recognised by the Belgian institution is general invalidity.
2. Only if the Belgian institution has recognised that the worker is unfit for work underground or at ground level.

ITALY

Member States	Schemes administered by Member States' institutions who have taken a decision recognising the degree of invalidity	Schemes administered by Italian institutions on which the decision is binding in cases of concordance		
		General scheme		Mariners' Unfitness for navigation
		Manual workers	Clerical staff	
BELGIUM	1. General scheme	Concordance	Concordance	No concordance
	2. Miners' scheme:			
	– partial general invalidity	Concordance	Concordance	No concordance
	– occupational invalidity	No concordance	No concordance	No concordance
	3. Mariners' scheme:			
	– unfitness for seafaring	No concordance	No concordance	No concordance
FRANCE	1. General scheme:			
	– Group III (constant attendance)			
	– Group II	Concordance	Concordance	No concordance
	– Group I			
	2. Agricultural scheme:			
	– total general invalidity			
	– partial general invalidity	Concordance	Concordance	No concordance
	– constant attendance			
	3. Miners' scheme:			
	– partial general invalidity			
	– constant attendance	Concordance	Concordance	No concordance
	– occupational invalidity	No concordance	No concordance	No concordance
	4. Mariners' scheme:			
	– partial general invalidity			
	– constant attendance	No concordance	No concordance	No concordance
	– occupational invalidity			
LUXEM-BOURG	Invalidity – manual workers	Concordance	Concordance	No concordance
	Invalidity – clerical staff	No concordance	No concordance	

LUXEMBOURG

Member States	Schemes administered by institutions of Member States which have taken a decision recognising the degree of invalidity	Schemes administered by Luxembourg institutions on which the decision is binding in cases of concordance	
		Workers' Invalidity – manual workers	Invalidity – clerical workers
BELGIUM	1. General scheme	Concordance	Concordance
	2. Miners' scheme:		
	– partial general invalidity	Concordance	Concordance
	– occupational invalidity	No concordance	No concordance
	3. Mariners' scheme	Concordance[1]	Concordance[1]
FRANCE	1. General scheme:		
	– Group III (constant attendance)		
	– Group II	Concordance	Concordance
	– Group I		
	2. Agricultural scheme:		
	– total general invalidity		
	– 2/3 general invalidity	Concordance	Concordance
	– constant attendance		
	3. Miners' scheme:		
	– 2/3 general invalidity	Concordance	Concordance
	– constant attendance		
	– occupational invalidity	No concordance	No concordance
	4. Mariners' scheme:		
	– partial general invalidity	Concordance	Concordance
	– constant attendance		
	– occupational invalidity	No concordance	No concordance
ITALY	1. General scheme:		
	– invalidity – manual workers	Concordance	Concordance
	– invalidity – clerical staff	No concordance	
	2. Mariners' scheme:		
	– unfitness for seafaring		

1. In so far as the invalidity recognised by the Belgian institution is general invalidity.

Annex V

(Article 89 of the Regulation)

Special procedures for applying the legislations of certain Member States

A. BELGIUM

1. The provisions of Article 1(a)(i) of the Regulation shall not apply to self-employed persons or to other persons receiving medical treatment under the law of 9 August 1963 on the establishment and organisation of a compulsory sickness and invalidity insurance scheme, unless they receive the same protection as employed persons in respect of such treatment.

2. For the application of the provisions of Chapters 7 and 8 of Title III of the Regulation by the competent Belgian institution, a child shall be considered to have been brought up in the Member State in whose territory he resides.

3. For the purposes of Article 46(2) of the Regulation, old-age insurance periods completed under Belgian legislation before 1 January 1945 shall also be considered as insurance periods completed under the Belgian legislation on the general invalidity scheme and the mariners' scheme.

B. GERMANY

1. (a) Where no provision is already made under German legislation for accident insurance, German institutions shall also provide compensation, in accordance with that legislation, for accidents at work (and occupational diseases) which occurred in Alsace-Lorraine before 1 January 1919, the responsibility for the cost of which has not been assumed by French institutions in pursuance of the Decision of the Council of the League of Nations of 21 June 1921 (*Reichsgesetzblatt, p.* 1289) where the person concerned or his survivors are residing in a Member State;

   (b) Article 10 of the Regulation shall not affect the provisions under which accidents (and occupational diseases) occurring outside the territory of the Federal Republic of Germany, and periods completed outside that territory, do not give rise to payment of benefits, or only give rise to payment of benefits under certain conditions, when those entitled to them reside outside the territory of the Federal Republic of Germany.

2. (a) In order to determine whether periods considered by German legislation as interrupted periods (*Ausfallzeiten*) or supplementary

periods (*Zurechnungszeiten*) should be taken into account as such, compulsory contributions paid under the legislation of another Member State and insurance under the pensions' insurance scheme of another Member State shall be treated as compulsory contributions paid under German legislation and as insurance under the German pension insurance scheme.

When calculating the number of calendar months which have elapsed between the date of entry into the insurance scheme and the materialisation of the risk, periods taken into consideration under the legislation of another Member State which fall between those two dates shall not be taken into account, neither shall periods during which the person concerned has been in receipt of a pension.

(b) Subparagraph (a) shall not apply to the standard interrupted period (*pauschale Ausfallzeit*). This shall be determined exclusively on the basis of insurance periods completed in Germany.

(c) The taking into account of an additional period (*Zurechnungszeit*) in pursuance of German legislation on pension insurance for miners shall, moreover, be subject to the condition that the last contribution paid under German legislation was paid into the pension insurance for miners.

(d) For the purpose of taking into account German substitute periods (*Ersatzzeiten*), only German national legislation shall apply.

(e) By way of derogation from the provision laid down in subparagraph (d), the following provision shall apply to persons insured under the German pension insurance scheme who were residing in German territories under Netherlands administration during the period from 1 January 1948 to 31 July 1963; for the purpose of taking into account German substitute periods (*Ersatzzeiten*) within the meaning of Article 1251(2) of the German social security law (RVO) or corresponding provisions, payment of contributions to Netherlands insurance schemes during that period shall be treated as equivalent to having been employed or having pursued an activity coming under compulsory insurance within the meaning of German legislation.

3. Where payments to be made into German sickness insurance funds are concerned, compulsory payment of the contributions referred to in Article 26(2) of the Regulation shall be suspended until a decision is made concerning pensions claims.

4. In order to determine whether a child is receiving an orphan's pension,

receipt of one or the benefits referred to in Article 78 or of another family benefit granted under French legislation for a minor residing in France shall be treated as the receipt of an orphan's pension under German legislation.

5. If application of this Regulation or of subsequent social security Regulations involves exceptional expenses for certain sickness insurance institutions, such expenses may be partially or totally reimbursed. The Federal Association of Regional Sickness Funds, in its function of liaison agency (sickness insurance) shall decide on such reimbursement by common agreement with the other Central Associations of Sickness Funds. The resources needed for effecting such reimbursements shall be provided by taxes imposed on all sickness insurance institutions in proportion to the average number of members during the preceding year, including retired persons.

6. If the competent institution for granting family benefits in accordance with Title III Chapter 7 of the Regulation is a German institution, a person compulsorily insured against the risk of unemployment or a person who, as a result of such insurance, obtains cash benefits under sickness insurance or comparable benefits shall be considered as a worker (Article 1(a) of the Regulation).

C. FRANCE

1. (a) The allowance for elderly employed persons shall be granted under the conditions laid down for French workers by French legislation, to all workers who are nationals of other Member States and who, at the time of making their claim, were residing in French territory.

   (b) The same shall apply to refugees and stateless persons.

   (c) The provisions of the Regulation shall not affect the provisions of French legislation under which only periods of work as employed persons or periods treated as such which are completed in the territories of the European departments and the overseas departments (Guadeloupe, Guiana, Martinique and Réunion) of the French Republic shall be taken into consideration for acquisition of the right to the allowance for elderly employed persons.

2. The special allowance and cumulative indemnity provided for by the special legislation for social security in the mines shall be provided only for workers employed in French mines.

3. Law No 65-655 of 10 July 1965 which grants to French nationals who are pursuing, or who have pursued, a professional or trade activity

abroad the right to join the voluntary old-age insurance scheme, shall apply to nationals of other Member States under the following conditions:

- the professional or trade activity giving rise to voluntary insurance under the French system should not be, or have been, pursued either on French territory or on the territory of the Member State of which the worker is a national;

- the worker must produce evidence, when making his claim, either that he has resided in France for at least ten consecutive years, or that he has been continuously subject to French legislation on a compulsory or optional basis for the same length of time.

4. Within the meaning of Article 73(3) of the Regulation, the expression 'family benefits' shall include:

(a) prenatal allowances provided for in Article L 516 of the Social Security Code;

(b) the family allowances provided for in Articles L 524 and L 531 of the Social Security Code;

(c) the compensatory allowance for scheduled taxes provided for in Article L 532 of the Social Security Code;

However, this benefit can only be paid if the wage or salary received during the period of the posting is subject to tax on income in France;

(d) the single wage or salary allowance provided for in Article L 533 of the Social Security Code.

D. ITALY

None.

E. LUXEMBOURG

By way of derogation from Article 94(2) of the Regulation, insurance periods or periods treated as such completed before 1 January 1946 under Luxembourg legislation for invalidity, old-age or death pension insurance shall only be taken into consideration for the purpose of applying this legislation to the extent that rights in the process of being acquired should be maintained until 1 January 1959 or subsequently recovered in accordance with that legislation alone, or in accordance with bilateral conventions in force or to be concluded. Where several bilateral conventions apply, the insurance periods or periods treated as such dating the farthest back shall be taken into consideration.

F. NETHERLANDS

1. *Sickness insurance for old-age pensioners*

(a) A person receiving an old-age pension under Netherlands legislation and a pension under the legislation of another Member State shall, for the purposes of Article 27 and/or 28, be considered to be entitled to benefits in kind if, taking into account Article 9 where appropriate, he satisfies the conditions required for entitlement to voluntary sickness insurance for elderly persons.

(b) The contribution for voluntary sickness insurance for elderly persons shall amount, in respect of the persons concerned who are residing in one of the other Member States, to half of the average costs incurred in the Netherlands for medical treatment for an elderly person and members of his family.

2. *Application of Netherlands legislation on general old-age insurance*

(a) Insurance periods before 1 January 1957 during which a recipient, not satisfying the conditions permitting him to have such periods treated as insurance periods, resided in the territory of the Netherlands after the age of 15 or during which, whilst residing in the territory of another Member State, he pursued an activity as an employed person in the Netherlands for an employer established in that country, shall also be considered as insurance periods completed in application of Netherlands legislation for general old-age insurance.

(b) Periods to be taken into account in pursuance of subparagraph (a) above shall not be taken into account if they coincide with periods taken into account for the calculation of the pension payable under the legislation of another Member State in respect of old-age insurance.

(c) As regards a married woman whose husband is entitled to a pension under Netherlands legislation on general old-age insurance, periods of the marriage preceding the date when she reached the age of sixty-five years and during which she resided in the territory of one or more Member States shall also be taken into account as insurance periods, in so far as those periods coincide with insurance periods completed by her husband under that legislation and with those to be taken into account in pursuance of subparagraph (a).

(d) Periods to be taken into account in pursuance of subparagraph (c) shall not be taken into account where they coincide with periods taken into account for calculating a pension payable to the married woman in question under the old-age insurance legislation of

another Member State or with periods during which she received an old-age pension in pursuance of such legislation.

(e) As regards a woman who has been married and whose husband has been subject to Netherlands legislation on old-age insurance, or is deemed to have completed insurance periods in pursuance of subparagraph (a), the provisions of the two preceding subparagraphs shall apply by analogy.

(f) The periods referred to in subparagraphs (a) and (c) shall only be taken into account for calculation of the old-age pension if the person concerned has resided for six years in the territory of one or more Member States after the age of fifty-nine years and for as long as that person is residing in the territory of one of those Member States.

3. *Application of Netherlands legislation on general insurance for widows and orphans*

(a) For the purposes of Article 46(2) of the Regulation, periods before 1 October 1959 during which the worker resided in the territory of the Netherlands after the age of fifteen years or during which, whilst residing in the territory of another Member State, he pursued an activity as an employed person in the Netherlands for an employer established in that country shall also be considered as insurance periods completed under Netherlands legislation relating to general insurance for widows and orphans.

(b) Periods to be taken into account in pursuance of subparagraph (a) shall not be taken into account where they coincide with insurance periods completed under the legislation of another State in respect of survivors' pensions.

4. *Application of Netherlands legislation on insurance against incapacity for work*

(a) For the purposes of Article 46(2) of the Regulation, periods of paid employment and periods treated as such completed under Netherlands legislation before 1 July 1967 shall also be considered as insurance periods completed under Netherlands legislation on insurance against incapacity for work.

(b) The periods to be taken into account in pursuance of subparagraph (a) shall be considered as insurance periods completed under a legislation of the type referred to in Article 37(1) of the Regulation.

FOOTNOTES

1 OJ No 194, 28.10.66, p.3333 and OJ No C 95, 21.9.68, p.18.
2. OJ No C 10 14.2.68, p.30 and OJ No C 135, 14.12.68, p.4.

3. OJ No 64, 5.4.67, p,1009 and OJ No C 21, 20,2.69, p.18
4. OJ No 30, 16.12.58, p.561.
5. OJ No 259, 19.10.68, p.2.
6. Editorial note: Amended to reflect consolidated version of this Regulation in OJ No C 325, 10.12.92, p.19 which is a more up-to-date translation.
7. OJ No 30, 16.12.58, p.597.
8. OJ No 62, 20.4.63, p.1314.

COUNCIL REGULATION (EEC) No 1390/81

of 12 May 1981

extending to self-employed persons and members of their families Regulation (EEC) No 1408/71 on the application of social security schemes to employed persons and their families moving within the Community

(OJ No L 143, 29.5.81, p.1)

The Council of the European Communities,

Having regard to the Treaty establishing the European Economic Community, and in particular Articles 2, 7, 51 and 235 thereof,

Having regard to the proposal from the Commission drawn up after consultation of the Administrative Commission on Social Security for Migrant Workers[1],

Having regard to the opinion of the European Parliament[2],

Having regard to the opinion of the Economic and Social Committee[3],

Whereas, in order to attain freedom of movement for employed persons and eliminate the obstacles that would, in the sphere of social security, result from the application of national legislations only, the Council adopted, on the basis of Article 51 of the Treaty, Regulation (EEC) No 1408/71 on the application of social security schemes to employed persons and their families moving within the Community[4], as last amended by Regulation (EEC) No 196/81[5], fixing the rules for coordinating social security schemes for employed persons;

Whereas freedom of movement for persons, which is one of the cornerstones of the Community, is not confined to employed persons but also extends to self-employed persons in the framework of the freedom of establishment and the freedom to supply services;

Whereas the coordination of the social security schemes applicable to self-employed persons is necessary to attain one of the objectives of the

Community; whereas the Treaty has not provided the necessary specific powers for this purpose;

Whereas, in pursuance of the Treaty, any discrimination on grounds of nationality with regard to establishment and the provision of services has been prohibited since the end of the transitional period;

Whereas, in the sphere of social security, the application of national legislations only would not afford sufficient protection to self-employed persons moving within the Community; whereas, in order to make the freedom of establishment and the freedom to provide services fully effective, the social security schemes for self-employed persons should be coordinated;

Whereas Regulation (EEC) No 1408/71, even though it applies to employed persons, already covers certain categories of self-employed persons; whereas, for reasons of equity, it would be appropriate to apply, to the largest possible extent, the same rules to self-employed persons as are laid down for employed persons;

Whereas there are grounds for making the necessary adaptations to Regulation (EEC) No 1408/71 to make it possible to apply the provisions of that Regulation to self-employed persons and their families moving within the Community to the largest possible extent that is compatible with the nature of their occupation and the characteristics of the special social security schemes that cover them;

Whereas the adjustments to be made to Regulation (EEC) No 1408/71 call for adjustments to certain of the Annexes to that Regulation;

Whereas, in particular, it is necessary to stipulate in an Annex, what the terms 'employed person' and 'self-employed person', introduced in Regulation (EEC) No 1408/71, mean when the person concerned is insured under a social security scheme which applies to all residents or to certain categories of resident or to the entire working population of a Member State; whereas it seems preferable to define these expressions and the expression 'member of the family' in a separate Annex; whereas two further Annexes are needed, to indicate the special arrangements for self-employed persons excluded from the scope of the Regulation and for instances in which a person is subject simultaneously to the legislation of two Member States,

Has adopted this Regulation

Article 1

Regulation EEC No 1408/71 shall be amended as follows:

1. The title shall be replaced by the following:

'COUNCIL REGULATION (EEC) No 1408/71

of 14 June 1971

on the application of social security schemes to employed persons, to self-employed persons and to their families moving within the Community'

2. In Article 1:

(a) subparagraphs (a) and (b) be replaced by the following:

'(a) 'employed person' and 'self-employed person' mean respectively:

(i) any person who is insured, compulsorily or on an optional continued basis, for one or more of the contingencies covered by the branches of a social security scheme for employed or self-employed persons;

(ii) any person who is compulsorily insured for one or more of the contingencies covered by the branches of social security dealt with in this Regulation, under a social security scheme for all residents or for the whole working population, if such person:

— can be identified as an employed or self-employed person by virtue of the manner in which such scheme is administered or financed, or,

— failing such criteria, is insured for some other contingency specified in Annex I under a scheme for employed or self-employed persons, or under a scheme referred to in (iii), either compulsorily or on an optional continued basis, or, where no such scheme exists in the Member State concerned, complies with the definition given in Annex I;

(iii) any person who is compulsorily insured for several of the contingencies covered by the branches dealt with in this Regulation, under a standard social security scheme for the whole rural population in accordance with the criteria laid down in Annex I;

(iv) any person who is voluntarily insured for one or more of the contingencies covered by the branches dealt with in this Regulation, under a social security scheme of a Member State for employed or self-employed persons or for all residents or for certain categories of residents:

> – if such person carries out an activity as an employed or self-employed person, or
>
> – if such person has previously been compulsorily insured for the same contingency under a scheme for employed or self-employed persons of the same Member State;

(b) 'frontier worker' means any employed or self-employed person who pursues his occupation in the territory of a Member State and resides in the territory of another Member State to which he returns as a rule daily or at least once a week; however, a frontier worker who is posted elsewhere in the territory of the same or another Member State by the undertaking to which he is normally attached, or who engages in the provision of services elsewhere in the territory of the same or another Member State, shall retain the status of frontier worker for a period not exceeding four months, even if he is prevented, during that period, from returning daily or at least once a week to the place where he resides;'

(b) in subparagraph (c), first line, 'any worker' shall be replaced by 'any employed person';

(c) subparagraph (f) shall be replaced by the following:

'(f) 'member of the family' means any person defined or recognised as a member of the family or designated as a member of the household by the legislation under which benefits are provided or, in the cases referred to in Article 22(1)(a) and Article 31, by the legislation of the Member State in whose territory such person resides, where, however, the said legislations regard as a member of the family or a member of the household only a person living under the same roof as the employed or self-employed person, this condition shall be considered satisfied if the person in question is mainly dependent on that person. Where a Member State's legislation on sickness or maternity benefits in kind does not enable members of the family to be distinguished from the other persons to whom it applies, the term 'member of the family' shall have the meaning given to it in Annex I;'

(d) in subparagraph (g), sixth and eighth lines, 'deceased worker' shall be replaced by 'deceased';

(e) in subparagraph (j) the following subparagraph shall be inserted after the last subparagraph:

'The term 'legislation' also excludes provisions governing special schemes for self-employed persons the creation of which is left to the initiatives of those concerned or which apply only to a part of the territory of the Member State concerned, irrespective of whether or not the authorities decided to make them compulsory or extend their scope. The special schemes in question are specified in Annex II;'

(f) in the first and second lines of paragraph (r), the words 'periods of contribution or periods of employment' shall be replaced by the words 'periods of contribution or periods of employment or self-employment';

(g) paragraph (s) shall be replaced by the following:

'(s) 'periods of employment' and 'periods of self-employment' mean periods so defined or recognised by the legislation under which they were completed, and all periods treated as such, where they are regarded by the said legislation as equivalent to periods of employment or of self-employment;'

(h) in the last line of paragraph (u)(i) 'Annex I' shall be replaced by 'Annex II'.

3. In Article 2:

(a) in the first line of paragraph 1, 'to workers' shall be replaced by 'to employed or self-employed persons';

(b) paragraph 2:

- in line 2, 'workers' shall be replaced by 'employed or self-employed persons',

- in line 4, 'such workers' shall be replaced by 'such employed or self-employed persons'.

4. In Article 3(3) in the first line, 'Annex II' shall be replaced by 'Annex III'.

5. In the last line of Article 7(2)(c), 'Annex II' shall be replaced by 'Annex III'.

6. Article 9(1) shall be replaced by the following:

'1. The provisions of the legislation of any Member State which make admission to voluntary or optional continued insurance conditional upon residence in the territory of that State shall not apply to persons resident in the territory of another Member State, provided that at some time in their past working life they were subject to the

legislation of the first State as employed or as self-employed persons.'

7. In the sixth line of Article 10(2), 'as a worker' shall be replaced by 'as an employed or self-employed person'.

8. Articles 13 and 14 shall be replaced by the following:

'*Article 13*

General rules

1. Subject to Article 14(c), persons to whom this Regulation applies shall be subject to the legislation of a single Member State only. That legislation shall be determined in accordance with the provisions of this Title.

2. Subject to Articles 14 to 17:

(*a*) a person employed in the territory of one Member State shall be subject to the legislation of that State even if he resides in the territory of another Member State or if the registered office or place of business of the undertaking or individual employing him is situated in the territory of another Member State;

(*b*) a person who is self-employed in the territory of one Member State shall be subject to the legislation of that State even if he resides in the territory of another Member State;

(*c*) a person employed on board a vessel flying the flag of a Member State shall be subject to the legislation of that State;

(*d*) civil servants and persons treated as such shall be subject to the legislation of the Member State to which the administration employing them is subject;

(*e*) a person called up or recalled for service in the armed forces, or for civilian service, of a Member State shall be subject to the legislation of that State. If entitlement under that legislation is subject to the completion of periods of insurance before entry into or after release from such military or civilian service, periods of insurance completed under the legislation of any other Member State shall be taken into account, to the extent necessary, as if they were periods of insurance completed under the legislation of the first State. The employed or self-employed person called up or recalled for service in the armed forces or for civilian service shall retain the status of employed or self-employed person.

Article 14

Special rules applicable to persons, other than mariners, engaged in paid employment

Article 13(2)(a) shall apply subject to the following exceptions and circumstances:

1. (*a*) A person employed in the territory of a Member State by an undertaking to which he is normally attached who is posted by that undertaking to the territory of another Member State to perform work there for that undertaking shall continue to be subject to the legislation of the first Member State, provided that the anticipated duration of that work does not exceed 12 months and that he is not sent to replace another person who has completed his term of posting;

   (*b*) if the duration of the work to be done extends beyond the duration originally anticipated, owing to unforeseeable circumstances, and exceeds 12 months, the legislation of the first Member State shall continue to apply until the completion of such work, provided that the competent authority of the Member State in whose territory the person concerned is posted or the body designated by that authority gives its consent; such consent must be requested before the end of the initial 12-month period. Such consent cannot, however, be given for a period exceeding 12 months.

2. A person normally employed in the territory of two or more Member States shall be subject to the legislation determined as follows:

   (*a*) a person who is a member of the travelling or flying personnel of an undertaking which, for hire or reward or on its own account, operates international transport services for passengers or goods by rail, road, air or inland waterway and has its registered office or place of business in the territory of a Member State, shall be subject to the legislation of the latter State, with the following restrictions:

   (i) where the said undertaking has a branch or permanent representation in the territory of a Member State other than that in which it has its registered office or place of business, a person employed by such branch or permanent representation shall be subject to the legislation of the Member State in whose territory such branch or permanent representation is situated;

(ii) where a person is employed principally in the territory of the Member State in which he resides, he shall be subject to the legislation of that State, even if the undertaking which employs him has no registered office or place of business or branch or permanent representation in that territory;

(b) a person other than that referred to in (a) shall be subject:

(i) to the legislation of the Member State in whose territory he resides, if he pursues his activity partly in that territory or if he is attached to several undertakings or several employers who have their registered offices or places of business in the territory of different Member States;

(ii) to the legislation of the Member State in whose territory is situated the registered office or place of business of the undertaking or individual employing him, if he does not reside in the territory of any of the Member States where he is pursuing his activity.

3. A person who is employed in the territory of one Member State by an undertaking which has its registered office or place of business in the territory of another Member State and which straddles the common frontier of these States shall be subject to the legislation of the Member State in whose territory the undertaking has its registered office or place of business.

Article 14a

Special rules applicable to persons, other than mariners, who are self-employed

Article 13(2)(b) shall apply subject to the following exceptions and circumstances:

1. (a) A person normally self-employed in the territory of a Member State and who performs work in the territory of another Member State shall continue to be subject to the legislation of the first Member State, provided that the anticipated duration of the work does not exceed 12 months;

(b) if the duration of the work to be done extends beyond the duration originally anticipated, owing to unforeseeable circumstances, and exceeds 12 months, the legislation of the first Member State shall continue to apply until the completion of such work, provided that the competent authority of the Member State in whose territory the person concerned has entered to perform the work in question or the body appointed by that authority gives its consent; such consent must be

requested before the end of the initial 12-month period. Such consent cannot, however, be given for a period exceeding 12 months.

2. A person normally self-employed in the territory of two or more Member States shall be subject to the legislation of the Member State in whose territory he resides if he pursues any part of his activity in the territory of that Member State. If he does not pursue any activity in the territory of the Member State in which he resides, he shall be subject to the legislation of the Member State in whose territory he pursues his main activity. The criteria used to determine the principal activity are laid down in the regulation referred to in Article 97.

3. A person who is self-employed in an undertaking which has its registered office or place of business in the territory of one Member State and which straddles the common frontier of two Member States shall be subject to the legislation of the Member State in whose territory the undertaking has its registered office or place of business.

4. If the legislation to which a person should be subject in accordance with paragraphs 2 or 3 does not enable that person, even on a voluntary basis, to join a pension scheme, the person concerned shall be subject to the legislation of the other Member State which would apply apart from these particular provisions or, should the legislations of two or more Member States apply in this way, he shall be subject to the legislation decided on by common agreement amongst the Member States concerned or their competent authorities.

Article 14b

Special rules applicable to mariners

Article 13(2)(c) shall apply subject to the following exceptions and circumstances:

1. A person employed by an undertaking to which he is normally attached, either in the territory of a Member State or on board a vessel flying the flag of a Member State, who is posted by that undertaking on board a vessel flying the flag of another Member State to perform work there for that undertaking shall, subject to the conditions provided in Article 14(1), continue to be subject to the legislation of the first Member State.

2. A person normally self-employed, either in the territory of a

Member State or on board a vessel flying the flag of a Member State and who performs work on his own account on board a vessel flying the flag of another Member State shall, subject to the conditions provided in Article 14a(1), continue to be subject to the legislation of the first Member State.

3. A person who, while not being normally employed at sea, performs work in the territorial waters or in a port of a Member State on a vessel flying the flag of another Member State within those territorial waters or in that port, but is not a member of the crew of the vessel, shall be subject to the legislation of the first Member State.

4. A person employed on board a vessel flying the flag of a Member State and remunerated for such employment by an undertaking or a person whose registered office or place of business is in the territory of another Member State shall be subject to the legislation of the latter State if he is resident in the territory of that State; the undertaking or person paying the remuneration shall be considered as the employer for the purposes of the said legislation.

Article 14c

Special rules applicable to persons employed simultaneously in the territory of one Member State and self-employed in the territory of another Member State

1. A person who is employed simultaneously in the territory of one Member State and self-employed in the territory of another Member State shall be subject:

(a) to the legislation of the Member State in the territory of which he is engaged in paid employment, subject to subparagraph (b);

(b) in the instances referred to in Annex VII, to the legislation of each of these Member States, as regards the activity pursued in its territory.

2. The detailed rules for implementing subparagraph (b) of paragraph 1 shall be laid down in a Regulation to be adopted by the Council on a proposal from the Commission.

Article 14d

Miscellaneous provisions

1. The person referred to in Article 14(2) and (3), Article 14a(2), (3) and (4) and Article 14c(1)(a) shall be treated, for the purposes of application of the legislation laid down in accordance with these

provisions, as if he pursued all his professional activity or activities in the territory of the Member State concerned.

2. The provisions of the legislation of a Member State under which a pensioner who is pursuing a professional activity is not subject to compulsory insurance in respect of such activity shall also apply to a pensioner whose pension was acquired under the legislation of another Member State, unless the person concerned expressly asks to be so subject by applying to the institution designated by the competent authority of the first Member State and named in Annex 10 to the Regulation referred to in Article 97.'

9. Article 15(1) shall be replaced by the following:

'1. Articles 13 to 14d shall not apply to voluntary insurance or to optional continued insurance unless, in respect of one of the branches referred to in Article 4, there exists in any Member State only a voluntary scheme of insurance.'

10. Article 17 shall be replaced by the following:

'*Article* 17

Exceptions to Articles 13 *to* 16

Two or more Member States, the competent authorities of those States or the bodies designated by those authorities may, by common agreement, provide for exceptions to the provisions of Articles 13 to 16 in the interests of certain categories of employed or self-employed persons, or of certain such persons.'

11. Article 18(2), in the fifth line, 'worker concerned' shall be replaced by 'person concerned'.

12. In the heading of section 2, 'Workers' shall be replaced by 'Employed or self-employed persons'.

13. In the first line of Article 19(1), 'A worker' shall be replaced by 'An employed or self-employed person' and in the eighth line of the second subparagraph of Article 19(2), 'the worker' shall be replaced by 'the employed or self-employed person'.

14. In the fifth line of Article 20, 'the worker' shall be replaced by 'the person concerned'.

15. In the first line of Article 21(1), in the second line of the second subparagraph of Article 21(2) and in the first line of Article 21(4), 'the worker' or 'a worker' shall be replaced by 'the employed or self-employed person' or 'an employed or self-employed person', as the case may be.

16. In Article 22:

(a) in the first line of paragraph 1, 'a worker' shall be replaced by 'an employed or self-employed person';

(b) in the second line of the first subparagraph of paragraph 3, 'of a worker's' shall be replaced by 'of an employed or self-employed person's';

(c) in the third line of the second subparagraph of paragraph 3 and in the fourth line of (a) in the second subparagraph of paragraph 3, 'the worker' shall be replaced by 'the employed or self-employed person';

(d) in the second line of paragraph 4, 'a worker' shall be replaced by 'an employed or self-employed person'.

17. In Article 23, paragraphs 1 and 2 shall be replaced by the following:

'1. The competent institution of a Member State whose legislation provides that the calculation of cash benefits shall be based on average earnings, shall determine such average earnings exclusively by reference to earnings confirmed as having been paid during the periods completed under the said legislation.

2. The competent institution of a Member State whose legislation provides that the calculation of cash benefits shall be based on standard earnings, shall take account exclusively of the standard earnings or, where appropriate, of the average of standard earnings for the periods completed under the said legislation'.

18. In Article 24(1):

– in the first line, 'a worker' shall be replaced by 'an employed or self-employed person',

– in the sixth line, 'the said worker' shall be replaced by 'the said employed or self-employed person'.

19. In Article 25:

(a) in the first line of paragraph 1 'an unemployed person' shall be replaced by 'an unemployed person who was formerly employed or self-employed';

(b) in the first line of paragraph 2, 'who was formerly employed and' shall be added after 'A totally unemployed person'.

20. In the first line of Article 26(1) 'a worker' shall be replaced by 'an employed or self-employed person'.

21. Article 34 shall be replaced by the following:

'*Article* 34

General provisions

1. For the purpose of Articles 28, 28a, 29 and 31, a pensioner who is in receipt of two or more pensions due under the legislation of a single Member State shall be regarded as a pensioner entitled to draw a pension under the legislation of one Member State, within the meaning of these provisions.

2. Articles 27 to 33 shall not apply to a pensioner or to members of his family who are entitled to benefits under the legislation of a Member State as a result of pursuing a professional or trade activity. In such a case, the person concerned shall, for the purposes of the implementation of this Chapter, be considered as an employed or self-employed person or as a member of an employed or self-employed person's family'.

22. In Article 35:

(*a*) Paragraphs 1 and 2 shall be replaced by the following:

'1. Subject to paragraph 2, where the legislation of the country of stay or residence contains several sickness or maternity insurance schemes, the provision applicable under Articles 19, 21(1), 22, 25, 26, 28(1), 29(1) or 31 shall be those of the scheme covering manual workers in the steel industry. Where, however, the said legislation includes a special scheme for workers in mines and similar undertakings, the provisions of such scheme shall apply to that category of workers and members of their families provided the institution of the place of stay or residence to which application is made is competent to administer such scheme.

2. Where the legislation of the country of stay or residence includes one or more special schemes, covering all or most occupational categories of self-employed persons, which grant benefits in kind less favourable than those granted to employed persons, the provisions applicable to the person concerned and to the members of his family pursuant to Article 19(1)(a) and (2), Article 22(1) under (i) and 3, Article 28(1)(a) and Article 31(a) shall be those of the scheme or schemes determined by the implementing Regulation referred to in Article 97:

(*a*) where, in the competent State, the person concerned is insured under a special scheme for self-employed persons which also grants less favourable benefits in kind than those granted to employed persons, or

(*b*) where a person in receipt of one or more pensions is, under the pensions legislation of the competent Member State or Member States, entitled only to the benefits in kind provided for by a special scheme for self-employed persons which also grants less-favourable benefits in kind than those granted to employed persons.';

(*b*) paragraphs 2 and 3 shall become paragraphs 3 and 4 respectively;

(*c*) in the fourth line of the new paragraph 3, 'workers' shall be replaced by 'employed or self-employed persons'.

23. In the heading of Section 1, Chapter 2 of Title III, the word 'workers' shall be replaced by 'employed or self-employed persons'.

24. In Article 37:

(*a*) in the first line of paragraph 1, 'a worker' shall be replaced by 'an employed or self-employed person';

(*b*) in the first line of paragraph 2, 'Annex III' shall be replaced by 'Annex IV'.

25. (*a*) Article 38(2) shall read as follows:

'2. Where the legislation of a Member State makes the granting of certain benefits conditional upon the periods of insurance having been completed only in an occupation which is subject to a special scheme for employed persons or, where appropriate, in a specific employment, periods of insurance completed under the legislations of other Member States shall be taken into account for the granting of these benefits only if completed under a corresponding scheme or, failing this, in the same occupation or, where appropriate, in the same employment. If, account having been taken of the periods thus completed, the person concerned does not satisfy the conditions for receipt of these benefits, these periods shall be taken into account for the granting of the benefits, under the general scheme or, failing this, under the scheme applicable to manual or clerical workers, as appropriate.';

(*b*) the following paragraph shall be added:

'3. Where the legislation of a Member State makes the granting of certain benefits conditional upon the periods of insurance having been completed only in an occupation subject to a special scheme for self-employed persons, periods of insurance completed under the legislations of other Member States shall

be taken into account for the granting of these benefits only if completed under a corresponding scheme or, failing this, in the same occupation.

If, account having been taken of the periods thus completed, the person concerned does not satisfy the conditions for receipt of these benefits, these periods shall be taken into account for the granting of the benefits under the general scheme or, failing this, under the scheme applicable to manual or clerical workers, as appropriate, in so far as they have been completed under a scheme other than the abovementioned corresponding scheme and provided that the person concerned has also been insured under this general scheme or, failing this, under the scheme applicable to manual or clerical workers, as appropriate.'

26. Article 39(3) shall be replaced by the following :

'3. A person who is not entitled to benefits under paragraph 1 shall receive the benefits to which he is still entitled under the legislation of another Member State, taking account, where appropriate, of the provisions of Article 38'.

27. In the heading of Section 2, Chapter 2 or Title III, the word 'workers' shall be replaced by 'employed or self-employed persons'.

28. In Article 40:

(a) in the first line of paragraph 1, 'a worker' shall be replaced by 'an employed or self-employed person';

(b) in the first line of paragraph 2, 'a worker' shall be replaced by 'an employed or self-employed person'; 'Annex III' shall be replaced by 'Annex IV':

 — in the third line,

 — in the last line of the first indent,

 — in the last line of the second indent;

(c) in paragraph 3(a):

 — in the second line, 'Annex III' shall be replaced by 'Annex IV',

 — in the fifth line, 'where a worker' shall be replaced by 'where an employed or self-employed person';

(d) in the last line of paragraph 4, 'Annex IV' shall be replaced by 'Annex V'.

29. In Article 41:

(*a*) in the second line of paragraph 1, 'a worker' shall be replaced by 'an employed or self-employed person';

(*b*) in the last line of paragraph 1(d)(iii), 'Annex III' shall be replaced by 'Annex IV';

(*c*) in the second line of paragraph 2, 'a worker' shall be replaced by 'an employed or self-employed person'.

30. In Article 44:

(*a*) in the title, 'a worker' shall be replaced by 'an employed or self-employed person';

(*b*) in the first line of paragraph 1, 'of a worker' shall be replaced by 'of an employed or self-employed person';

(*c*) in the fourth line of paragraph 2, 'the worker' shall be replaced by 'the employed or self-employed person'.

31. In Article 45:

(*a*) in the heading, 'a worker' shall be replaced by 'an employed or self-employed person';

(*b*) paragraph 2:

– in the third line 'only' shall be added after 'completed',

– in the fourth line 'for employed persons' shall be added after 'special scheme';

(*c*) the following paragraph shall be added :

'3. Where the legislation of a Member State makes the granting of certain benefits conditional upon the periods of insurance having been completed only in an occupation subject to a special scheme for self-employed persons, periods completed under the legislations of other Member States shall be taken into account for the granting of such benefits only if completed under a corresponding scheme or, failing this, in the same occupation.

If, taking into account the periods thus completed, the person concerned does not satisfy the conditions for receipt of these benefits, those periods shall be taken into account for the granting of the benefits under the general scheme or, failing this, under the scheme applicable to manual or clerical workers, as appropriate, in so far as they have been completed under a scheme other than the abovementioned corresponding scheme and provided that the person concerned has also been insured under this general scheme

or, failing this, under the scheme applicable to manual or clerical workers, as appropriate.';

(d) paragraph 3 shall become paragraph 4 and shall read as follows:

'4. Where the legislation of a Member State which makes the granting of benefits conditional upon an employed person being subject to its legislation at the time when the risk materialises has no requirements as to the length of insurance periods either for entitlement to or calculation of benefits, any employed person who is no longer subject to that legislation shall for the purposes of this Chapter, be deemed to be still so subject at the time when the risk materialises, if at that time he is subject to the legislation of another Member State or, failing this, can establish a claim to benefits under the legislation of another Member State. However, this latter condition shall be deemed to be satisfied in the case referred to in Article 48(1).';

(e) the following paragraphs shall be added:

'5. Paragraph 4 shall apply to self-employed persons in order to determine whether the conditions for entitlement to survivors' benefits have been satisfied.

6. Where the legislation of a Member State which makes granting of invalidity benefits conditional upon the person concerned being subject to that legislation at the time when the risk materialises has no requirements as to the length of insurance periods either for the entitlement to or the calculation of benefits, any self-employed person who is no longer subject to that legislation shall, for the purposes of this Chapter, be deemed to be still so subject at the time when the risk materialises, if at that time he is subject to the legislation of another Member State.'

32. In Article 46:

(a) in the first line of the first subparagraph of paragraph 1, 'a worker' shall be replaced by 'an employed or self-employed person';

(b) in the first line of paragraph 2, 'a worker' shall be replaced by 'an employed or self-employed person';

(c) in the sixth line of paragraph 2(a), 'worker' shall be replaced by 'employed or self-employed person'.

33. Article 47(1) shall be replaced by the following:

'1. For the calculation of the theoretical amount referred to in Article 46(2)(a), the following rules shall apply:

(*a*) where, under the legislation of a Member State, benefits are calculated on the basis of average earnings, an average contribution, an average increase or on the ratio which existed, during the periods of insurance, between the claimant's gross earnings and the average gross earnings of all insured persons other than apprentices, such average figures or ratios shall be determined by the competent institution of that State solely on the basis of the periods of insurance completed under the legislation of the said State, or the gross earnings received by the person concerned during those periods only;

(*b*) where, under the legislation of a Member State, benefits are calculated on the basis of the amount of earnings, contributions or increases, the competent institution of that State shall determine the earnings, contributions and increases to be taken into account in respect of the periods of insurance or residence completed under the legislation of other Member States on the basis of the average earnings, contributions or increases recorded in respect of the periods of insurance completed under the legislation which it administers;

(*c*) where, under the legislation of a Member State, benefits are calculated on the basis of standard earnings or a fixed amount, the competent institution of that State shall consider the standard earnings or the fixed amount to be taken into account by it in respect of periods of insurance or residence completed under the legislations of other Member States as being equal to the standard earnings or fixed amount or, where appropriate, to the average of the standard earnings or the fixed amount corresponding to the periods of insurance completed under its own legislation;

(*d*) where, under the legislation of a Member State, benefits are calculated for some periods on the basis of the amount of earnings, and, for other periods, on the basis of standard earnings or a fixed amount, the competent institution of that State shall, in respect of periods of insurance or residence completed under the legislations of other Member States, take into account the earnings or fixed amounts determined in accordance with the provisions of (b) or (c) above or, as appropriate, the average of these earnings or fixed amounts; where benefits are calculated on the basis of standard earnings or a fixed amount for all the periods completed under the legislation which it administers, the competent institution shall consider the earnings to be taken into account in respect of the periods of insurance or residence completed under the

legislations of other Member States as being equal to the notional earnings corresponding to the standard earnings or fixed amount.'

34. In the first line of Article 52, 'a worker' shall be replaced by 'an employed or self-employed person'.

35. In the last line of Article 53, 'worker' shall be replaced by 'person concerned'.

36. In the first lines of paragraphs 1 and 2 of Article 54, 'a worker' shall be replaced by 'an employed or self-employed person'.

37. In the first line of Article 55(1), 'A worker' shall be replaced by 'An employed or self-employed person'.

38. Article 58(1) and (2) shall be replaced by the following:

'1. The competent institution of a Member State whose legislation provides that the calculation of cash benefits shall be based on average earnings shall determine such average earnings exclusively by reference to earnings confirmed as having been paid during the periods completed under the said legislation.

2. The competent institution of a Member State whose legislation provides that the calculation of cash benefits shall be based on standard earnings shall take account exclusively of the standard earnings or, where appropriate, of the average of standard earnings for the periods completed under the said legislation.'

39. Article 60(1) shall be replaced by the following :

'1. In the event of aggravation of an occupational disease for which an employed or self-employed person has received or is receiving benefit under the legislation of a Member State, the following rules shall apply:

(a) if the person concerned has not, while in receipt of benefits, been engaged in an occupation under the legislation of another Member State likely to cause or aggravate the disease in question, the competent institution of the first Member State shall be bound to meet the cost of the benefits under the provisions of the legislation which it administers taking into account the aggravation;

(b) if the person concerned, while in receipt of benefits, has pursued such an activity under the legislation of another Member State, the competent institution of the first Member State shall be bound to meet the cost of the benefits under the legislation which it administers without taking into account the aggravation.

The competent institution of the second Member State shall grant a supplement to the person concerned, the amount of which shall be equal to the difference between the amount of benefits due after the aggravation and the amount which would have been due prior to the aggravation under the legislation which it administers if the disease in question had occurred under the legislation of that Member State;

(c) if, in the case covered by subparagraph (b), an employed or self-employed person suffering from sclerogenic pneumoconiosis or from a disease determined under Article 57(4) is not entitled to benefits under the legislation of the second Member State, the competent institution of the first Member State shall be bound to provide benefits under the legislation which it administers, taking into account the aggravation. The competent institution of the second Member State shall, however, meet the cost of the difference between the amount of cash benefits, including pensions, due from the competent institution of the first Member State, taking into account the aggravation, and the amount of the corresponding benefits which were due prior to the aggravation.'

40. In the third line of Article 61(1) 'a worker' shall be replaced by 'the person concerned'.

41. In the third line of Article 62(1), 'workers' shall be replaced by 'employed or self-employed persons'.

42. In the first line of Article 65(1), 'when a worker' shall be replaced by 'when an employed or self-employed person'.

43. In Article 67(1) and (2) the words 'completed under the legislation of any other Member State' shall be replaced by the words 'completed as an employed person under the legislation of any other Member State.'

44. In the first line of Article 69(1), 'a worker' shall be replaced by 'an employed or self-employed person'.

45. In the second line of the second subparagraph of Article 70(1), 'a worker' shall be replaced by 'an employed or self-employed person'.

46. In Article 71(1):

(a) in the first line, 'an unemployed person who' shall be replaced by 'an unemployed person who was formerly employed and who';

(b) in the first line of (b)(i) and in the first line of (b)(ii), 'a worker' shall be replaced by 'an employed person';

(c) in the 11th line of (b)(ii), 'such worker' shall be replaced by 'such employed person'.

47. In Title III:

(a) the title of Chapter 7 shall be replaced by the following:

'FAMILY BENEFITS AND FAMILY ALLOWANCES';

(b) the title of Section 1 of Chapter 7 shall be replaced by the following:

*'Provision common to benefits for employed,
self-employed and unemployed persons'*;

(c) in the title of Section 2 of Chapter 7 'Workers and unemployed workers' shall be replaced by 'Employed and unemployed persons'.

48. The title of Article 72 shall read 'Aggregation of periods of insurance, employment or self-employment' and, in the Article itself, 'periods of insurance or employment' shall be replaced by 'periods of insurance, employment or self-employment'.

49. In Article 73:

(a) the title shall be replaced by the following:

'Employed persons';

(b) in the first line of both paragraphs 1 and 2 and in the sixth line of paragraph 2, 'a worker' shall be replaced by 'an employed person';

(c) paragraph 3 shall be replaced by the following:

'3. However, an employed person who is subject to French legislation by virtue of Article 14(1) shall be entitled to the family benefits set out in Annex VI in respect of members of his family who accompany him to the territory of the Member State where he is working.'

50. In the first line of Article 74(1) and of Article 74(2), 'an unemployed person drawing' shall be replaced by 'an unemployed person who was formerly employed and who draws.'

51. In Article 75:

(a) in the fourth line of paragraph 1(a), 'the worker' shall be replaced by the 'employed person' and, in the seventh line, 'the unemployed worker' shall be replaced by 'the unemployed person';

(b) in the second line of paragraph 2(b), 'to the worker' shall be replaced by 'to the employed person'.

52. In Article 78:

(a) in the first line of both paragraph 2(a) and (b), 'deceased worker' shall be replaced by 'deceased employed or self-employed person';

(b) in the third line of paragraph 2(b)(ii), 'deceased worker' shall be replaced by 'the deceased'.

53. In Article 79:

(a) paragraph 1:

  – in the sixth line of the first subparagraph, the word 'worker' shall be deleted,

  – in the fourth line of (a) of the second subparagraph, 'self-employment' shall be inserted between 'employment' and 'or residence';

(b) in the last line of paragraph 2, 'the worker' shall be replaced by 'the pensioner or the deceased';

(c) in the last line of paragraph 3, 'of a worker' shall be replaced by 'of an employed or self-employed person'.

54. In Article 89, 'Annex V' shall be replaced by 'Annex VI'.

55. In Article 93(2), in the sixth line of the first subparagraph, 'or of their employees' shall be replaced by 'or of the persons employed by them'. In the third line of the second subparagraph, 'or his employees' shall be replaced by 'or the persons employed by him'.

56. Annexes I to V shall become Annexes II to VI and the following Annex shall be inserted:

'Annex I

Persons covered by the Regulation

I. *Employed persons and/or self-employed persons*

(Article 1(a)(ii) and (iii) of the Regulation

A. BELGIUM

Does not apply.

B. DENMARK

1. Any person who, from the fact of pursuing an activity as an employed person, is subject to legislation on accidents at work and occupational diseases, shall be considered an employed person within the meaning of Article 1(a)(ii) of the Regulation.

2. Any person who, pursuant to the law on daily cash benefits in the event of sickness or maternity, is entitled to such benefits on the basis of an earned income other than a wage or salary shall be considered a self-employed person within the meaning of Article 1(a)(ii) of the Regulation.

C. GERMANY

If the competent institution for granting family benefits in accordance with Title III, Chapter 7, of the Regulation is a German institution, than within the meaning of Article 1(a)(ii) of the Regulation:

(a) 'employed person' means any person compulsorily insured against unemployment or any person who, as a result of such insurance, obtains cash benefits under sickness insurance or comparable benefits;

(b) 'self-employed person' means any person pursuing a self-employed activity who is bound:

- to join, or pay contributions in respect of, an old-age insurance within a scheme for self-employed persons, or

- to join a scheme within the framework of compulsory pension insurance.

D. FRANCE
Does not apply.

E. GREECE

1. Persons insured under the OGA scheme who pursue exclusively activities as employed persons or who are or have been subject to the legislation of another Member State and who consequently are or have been 'workers' within the meaning of Article 1(a)(iii) of the Regulation.

2. For the purposes of granting the national family allowances, persons referred to in Article 1(a)(i) and (iii) of the Regulation are considered as workers within the meaning of Article 1(a)(ii) of the Regulation.

F. IRELAND

1. Any person who is compulsorily or voluntarily insured pursuant to the provisions of Sections 5 and 37 of the Social Welfare (Consolidation) Act 1981 shall be considered an employed person within the meaning of Article 1(a)(ii) of the Regulation.

2. Any person who is pursuing a professional or trade activity without a contract of employment or who has retired from such activity shall be considered a self-employed person within the meaning of Article 1(a)(ii) of the Regulation. As regards sickness benefits in kind, the person concerned must also be entitled to such benefits under Section 45 or Section 46 of the Health Act 1970.

G. ITALY

Does not apply.

H. LUXEMBOURG

Does not apply.

I. NETHERLANDS

Any person pursuing an activity or occupation without a contract of employment shall be considered a self-employed person within the meaning of Article 1(a)(ii) of the Regulation.

J. UNITED KINGDOM

Any person who is an 'employed earner' or a 'self-employed earner' within the meaning of the legislation of Great Britain or of the legislation of Northern Ireland shall be regarded respectively as an employed person or a self-employed person within the meaning of Article 1(a)(ii) of the Regulation. Any person in respect of whom contributions are payable as an 'employed person' or a 'self-employed person' in accordance with the legislation of Gibraltar shall be regarded respectively as an employed person or a self-employed person within the meaning of Article 1(a)(ii) of the Regulation.

II. *Members of the family*

(Article 1(f), second sentence, of the Regulation)

A. BELGIUM

Does not apply.

B. DENMARK

For the purpose of determining entitlement to benefits in kind pursuant to Article 22(1)(a) and Article 31 of the Regulation, 'member of the family' means any person regarded as a member of the family under the Law on the Public Health Service.

C. GERMANY

Does not apply.

D. FRANCE

Does not apply.

E. GREECE

Does not apply.

F. IRELAND

For the purpose of determining entitlement of benefits in kind pursuant to Article 22(1)(a) and Article 31 of the Regulation, 'member of the family' means any person regarded as a dependent of the employed or self-employed person for the purposes of the Health Acts 1947 to 1970.

G. ITALY

Does not apply.

H. LUXEMBOURG

Does not apply.

I. NETHERLANDS

Does not apply.

J. UNITED KINGDOM

For the purpose of determining entitlement to benefits in kind pursuant to Articles 22(1)(a) and 31 of the Regulation, the expression 'member of the family' shall mean:

(a) as regards the legislation of either Great Britain or Northern Ireland, any person regarded as a dependant within the meaning of the Social Security Act 1975 or, as the case may be, the Social Security (Northern Ireland) Act 1975, and

(b) as regards the legislation of Gibraltar, any person regarded as a dependant within the meaning of the Group Practice Medical Scheme Ordinance 1973.'

57. In Annex II:

(a) the title shall be replaced by the following :

'Annex II

(Article 1(u) of the Regulation)

I. Special childbirth allowances excluded from the scope of the Regulation in pursuance of Article 1(u)';

(b) the following shall be added:

'II. Special schemes for self-employed persons excluded from the scope of the Regulation pursuant to Article 1(j), second subparagraph

A. BELGIUM
Does not apply.

B. DENMARK
Does not apply.

C. GERMANY

Insurance and welfare institutions for doctors, dentists, veterinary surgeons, dispensing chemists, barristers and counsel, patent agents, notaries public, auditors, tax consultants and advisers, sea pilots and architects, set up pursuant to legislation of the Länder, and other insurance and welfare institutions, in particular welfare funds and the system for extended fee-sharing.[6]

D. FRANCE

1. Self-employed persons outside the agricultural sphere:

(a) The supplementary old-age insurance schemes and the invalidity and death insurance schemes for self-employed persons, such as are mentioned in Articles L 658, L 659, L 663-11, L 663-12, L 682 and L 683-1 of the Social Security Code.

(b) The additional benefits referred to in Article 9 of Law No 66.509 of 12 July 1966.

2. Self-employed persons in agriculture:

The types of insurance set out in Articles 1049 and 1234.19 of the Rural Code, concerning, on the one hand, sickness, maternity and old-age and, on the other, accidents at work and occupational diseases of self-employed persons in agriculture.

E. GREECE
Does not apply.

F. IRELAND

Does not apply.

G. ITALY

Does not apply.

H. LUXEMBOURG

Does not apply.

I. NETHERLANDS

Does not apply.

J. UNITED KINGDOM

Does not apply.'

58. In part A, point 7, BELGIUM – LUXEMBOURG, of Annex III, the present text shall become subparagraph (a) and the following shall be inserted:

'(b) Exchange of letters of 10 and 12 July 1968 concerning self-employed persons.'

59. In Annex IV:

(a) point A shall be replaced by the following:

'A. BELGIUM

The legislation relating to the general invalidity scheme, to the special invalidity scheme for miners and to the special scheme for sailors in the Merchant Navy and the legislation concerning insurance against incapacity for work for self-employed persons.'

(b) point D shall be replaced by the following:

'D. FRANCE

1. Employed persons

All legislation on invalidity insurance, except for the legislation concerning the invalidity insurance of the social security scheme for miners.

2. Self-employed persons

The legislation on invalidity insurance for self-employed workers.'

60. Annex VI shall be replaced by the following:

'Annex VI

(*Article* 89 *of the Regulation*)

Special procedures for applying the legislations of certain Member States

A. BELGIUM

1. Persons whose entitlement to sickness insurance benefits in kind derives from the provisions of the Belgian compulsory sickness and invalidity scheme applicable to self-employed persons shall be eligible under the provisions of Title III, Chapter 1, of the Regulation, including Article 35(1) under the following conditions:

(*a*) in the event that they are temporarily resident in the territory of a Member State other than Belgium, the persons concerned shall be entitled:

   (i) to the benefits in kind provided for under the legislation of the Member State of temporary residence in respect of hospitalisation care;

   (ii) to reimbursement in respect of other benefits in kind provided for under the Belgian scheme by the relevant Belgian institution at the rate provided for under the legislation of the State of temporary residence;

(*b*) in the event that they are permanently resident in the territory of a Member State other than Belgium, the persons concerned shall be entitled to the benefits in kind provided for under the legislation of the Member State of permanent residence provided that they pay the relevant Belgian institution the appropriate additional contribution provided for under Belgian regulations.

2. For the application of the provisions of Chapters 7 and 8 of Title III of the Regulation by the competent Belgian institution, a child shall be considered to have been brought up in the Member State in whose territory he resides.

3. For the purposes of Article 46(2) of the Regulation, periods of old-age insurance completed under Belgian legislation before 1 January 1945 shall also be considered as periods of insurance completed under the Belgian legislation on the general invalidity scheme and the mariners' scheme.

4. In applying Article 40(3)(a)(ii), account shall only be taken of periods during which the employed or self-employed person was incapable of work within the meaning of Belgian legislation.

5. For the purposes of Article 46(2) of the Regulation, periods of old-age insurance completed by self-employed persons under Belgian legislation, prior to the entry into force of the legislation on the incapacity for work of self-employed persons, shall be considered as periods completed under the latter legislation.

6. In order to establish whether the requirements imposed by Belgian legislation for entitlement to unemployment benefits are fulfilled, account shall be taken of days accepted as equivalent within the meaning of the said legislation only in so far as the days worked which preceded them were days of paid employment.

B. DENMARK

1. Completed periods of insurance, employment or self-employment in a Member State other than Denmark shall be taken into account for admission to membership of an approved unemployment insurance fund in the same way as if they were periods of employment or self-employment completed in Denmark.

2. Employed persons, self-employed persons, applicants for pensions and pensioners with members of their family referred to in Articles 19, 22(1) and (3), 25(1) and (3), 26(1), 28a, 29 and 31 of the Regulation, resident or staying in Denmark shall be entitled to benefits in kind on the same terms as those laid down by Danish legislation for persons whose income does not exceed the level indicated in Article 3 of Law No 311 of 9 June 1971 concerning the Public Health Service, where the cost of the said benefits shall be borne by the institution of a Member State other than Denmark.

3. The provisions of Article 1(1), No 2 of the Law on old age pensions, Article 1(1), No 2, of the Law on invalidity pensions and Article 2(1), No 2, of the Law on widows' pensions and allowances are not applicable to employed or self-employed persons or their survivors whose residence is in the territory of a Member State other than Denmark.

4. The provisions of the Danish legislation governing old-age and widows' pensions are applicable to the widow of an employed or self-employed person subject to the Danish legislation, even if she has not resided in Denmark.

5. The terms of the Regulation shall be without prejudice to the provisional rules under the Danish Laws of 7 June 1972 on the pension rights of Danish nationals having their effective residence in Denmark for a specified period immediately preceding the date of the application. However, a pension shall be granted under those conditions laid down for Danish nationals to nationals of other

Member States having their effective residence in Denmark during the year immediately preceding the date of application.

6. (*a*) The periods during which a frontier worker residing within the territory of a Member State other than Denmark has pursued his professional or trade activity in Denmark are to be considered as periods of residence for the purposes of Danish legislation. The same shall apply to periods in which a frontier worker is posted to or provides services in a Member State other than Denmark.

(*b*) The periods during which a seasonal worker residing within the territory of a Member State other than Denmark has pursued his occupation in Denmark are to be considered as periods of residence for the purposes of Danish legislation. The same applies to periods during which a seasonal worker is posted to the territory of a Member State other than Denmark.

7. In order to determine whether the conditions of a right to maternity benefits laid down in Chapter 12 of the Law on the daily cash benefits for sickness or maternity are satisfied in the case where the person concerned was not subject to the Danish legislation throughout the whole period referred to in Article 34(1) or (2) of the aforementioned Law:

(*a*) account shall be taken of the periods of insurance completed, as appropriate, under the legislation of a Member State other than Denmark, during the course of the said period of reference during which the person concerned was not subject to the Danish legislation, as if those periods completed were under the latter legislation; and

(*b*) the person concerned shall be deemed to have received during the periods taken into account an average salary equal to that of the average salary confirmed as having been paid during the periods completed under the Danish legislation for the said period of reference.

8. For the purpose of applying Article 12(2) of the Regulation to Danish legislation, invalidity, old-age and widows' pensions shall be regarded as benefits of the same kind.

9. For the purpose of applying Article 67 of the Regulation, unemployment benefits for self-employed persons insured in Denmark shall be calculated in accordance with Danish legislation.

C. GERMANY

1. (*a*) Where no provision is already made under German legislation for accident insurance, German institutions shall also provide

compensation, in accordance with that legislation, for accidents at work (and occupational diseases) which occurred in Alsace-Lorraine before 1 January 1919, the responsibility for the cost of which has not been assumed by French institutions in pursuance of the Decision of the Council of the League of Nations of 21 June 1921, where the person concerned or his survivors are residing in a Member State;

(b) the provisions of Article 10 of the Regulation shall not affect the provisions under which accidents (and occupational diseases) occurring outside the territory of the Federal Republic of Germany, and periods completed outside that territory, do not give rise to payment of benefits, or only give rise to payment of benefits under certain conditions, when those entitled to them reside outside the territory of the Federal Republic of Germany.[7]

2. (a) In order to determine whether periods considered by German legislation as interrupted periods or supplementary periods should be taken into account as such, compulsory contributions paid under the legislation of another Member State and insurance under the insurance scheme of another Member State shall be treated as compulsory contributions paid under German legislation and as insurance under the German pension insurance scheme. This provision shall not apply to old-age insurance for farmers of the Federal Republic of Germany or to corresponding special schemes in the other Member States.

When calculating the number of calendar months which have elapsed between the date of entry into the insurance scheme and the materialisation of the risk, periods taken into consideration under the legislation of another Member State which fall between those two dates shall not be taken into account, neither shall periods during which the person concerned has been in receipt of a pension;

(b) the provisions of subparagraph (a) shall not apply to the standard interrupted period. This shall be determined exclusively on the basis of insurance periods completed in Germany;

(c) the taking into account of a supplementary period in pursuance of German legislation on pension insurance for miners shall, moreover, be subject to the condition that the last contribution paid under German legislation was paid into the pension insurance for miners;

(d) for the purpose of taking into account German substitute periods, only German national legislation shall apply;

(e) by way of derogation from the provision laid down in subparagraph (d), the following provision shall apply to persons insured under the German pension insurance scheme who were residing in German territories under Netherlands administration during the period 1 January 1948 to 31 July 1963 for the purpose of taking into account German substitute periods within the meaning of Article 1251(2) of the German social security law (RVO) or corresponding provisions, payment of contributions to Netherlands insurance schemes during that period shall be treated as equivalent to having been employed or having pursued an activity coming under compulsory insurance within the meaning of German legislation.[8]

3. Where payments to be made into German sickness insurance funds are concerned, compulsory payment of the contributions referred to in Article 26(2) of the Regulation shall be suspended until a decision is made concerning pension claims.

4. In order to determine whether a child is receiving an orphan's pension, receipt of one of the benefits referred to in Article 78 or of another family benefit granted under French legislation for a minor residing in France shall be treated as the receipt of an orphan's pension under German legislation.

5. If application of this Regulation or of subsequent social security Regulations involves exceptional expenses for certain sickness insurance institutions, such expenses may be partially or totally reimbursed. The National Federation of Local Sickness Funds, in its function as liaison body shall decide on such reimbursement by common agreement with the other Central Associations of Sickness Funds. The resources needed for effecting such reimbursements shall be provided by taxes imposed on all sickness insurance institutions in proportion to the average number of members during the preceding year, including retired persons.

6. For the purposes of the Regulation, the lump-sum payment for following a course of medical treatment on the occasion of confinement granted under German legislation to female insured persons and to members of the families of insured persons shall be considered as a benefit in kind.

7. Article 1233 of the insurance code (RVO) and Article 10 of the clerical staff insurance law (AVG), as amended by the pension reform law of 16 October 1972, which govern voluntary insurance under German pension insurance schemes, shall apply to nationals of the other Member States and to stateless persons and refugees residing

in the territory of the other Member States, according to the following rules.

Where the general conditions are fulfilled, voluntary contributions to the German pension insurance scheme may be paid:

(a) if the person concerned has his domicile or residence in the territory of the Federal Republic of Germany;

(b) if the person concerned has his domicile or residence in the territory of another Member State and at any time previously belonged compulsorily or voluntarily to a German pension insurance scheme;

(c) if the person concerned is a national of another Member State, has his domicile or residence in the territory of a third State and has paid contributions for German pension insurance for at least 60 months, or was eligible for voluntary insurance under the transitional provisions previously in force and is not compulsorily or voluntarily insured under the legislation of another Member State.

8. The Regulation shall not affect Article 51a(2) of the manual workers pension reform law (ArVNG) or Article 49a(2) of the clerical staff pension reform law (AnVNG), as amended by the pension reform law of 16 October 1972. The persons who, under paragraph 8(b) and (c), may join voluntary insurance, may pay contributions only in respect of periods for which they have not yet paid contributions under the legislation of another Member State.

9. Where the costs of benefits in kind which are granted by German institutions of the place of residence to pensioners or members of their family who are insured with competent institutions of other Member States must be refunded on the basis of monthly lump sums, such costs shall, for the purpose of financial equalisation among German institutions of sickness insurance for pensioners, be treated as expenditure on the German sickness insurance scheme for pensioners. The lump sums refunded to the German institutions of the place of residence by the competent institutions of other Member States shall be regarded as receipts which must be taken into account in the aforementioned financial equalisation.

10. In the case of self-employed persons, the award of unemployment assistance shall be conditional on the person concerned having, before reporting himself unemployed, worked for at least a year mainly as a self-employed person in the territory of the Federal Republic of Germany, and not having simply left that work temporarily.

11. Periods of insurance completed under the legislation of another Member State, under a special old-age insurance scheme for farmers or, if no such scheme exists, as farmers under the general scheme, shall be taken into account to satisfy the conditions of minimum length of insurance required for the person to be subject to contribution within the meaning of Article 27 of the law on old-age insurance for farmers, always providing that:

(a) the declaration on which the obligation to pay contributions is based shall have been lodged within the prescribed time; and

(b) before lodging the declaration, the person concerned shall have been last subject to contribution under the old-age insurance scheme for farmers in the territory of the Federal Republic of Germany.

12. Periods of compulsory insurance completed under the legislation of another Member State, either under a special scheme for craftsmen or, if no such scheme exists, under a special scheme for self-employed persons or under the general scheme, are counted towards the completion of the 216 months of compulsory insurance required to establish the right to voluntary withdrawal from the pension insurance scheme for craftsmen.

D. FRANCE

1. (a) The allowance for elderly employed persons, together with the allowance for elderly self-employed persons, and the agricultural old-age allowance shall be granted, under the conditions laid down for French workers by French legislation, to all employed or self-employed persons who are nationals of other Member States and who, at the time of making their claim, are resident in French territory.

(b) The same shall apply to refugees and stateless persons.

(c) The provisions of the Regulation shall not affect the provisions of French legislation under which only periods of work as employed persons or periods treated as such or, as appropriate, periods of work as self-employed persons in the territories of the European Departments and the Overseas Departments (Guadeloupe, Guyana, Martinique and Réunion) of the French Republic shall be taken into consideration for acquisition of the right to the allowance for elderly employed persons.

2. The special allowance and cumulative indemnity provided for by the special legislation for social security in the mines shall be provided only for workers employed in French mines.

3. Law No 65-555 of 10 July 1965 which grants to French nationals, who are pursuing, or who have pursued, a professional or trade activity abroad, the right to join the voluntary old-age insurance scheme, shall apply to nationals of other Member States under the following conditions:

– the professional or trade activity giving rise to voluntary insurance under the French system should not be, or have been, pursued either on French territory or on the territory of the Member State of which the employed or self-employed person is a national,

– the employed or self-employed person must produce evidence, when making his claim, either that he has resided in France for at least 10 years, consecutive or not, or that he has been continuously subject to French legislation on a compulsory or optional basis for the same length of time.

4. Within the meaning of Article 73(3) of the Regulation, the expression 'family benefits' shall include:

(a) prenatal allowances provided for in Article L 516 of the Social Security Code;

(b) the family allowances provided for in Articles L 524 and L 531 of the Social Security Code;

(c) the compensatory allowance for scheduled taxes provided for in Article L 532 of the Social Security Code;

However, this benefit can only be paid if the wage or salary received during the period of the posting is subject to tax on income in France;

(d) the single wage or salary allowance provided for in Article L 533 of the Social Security Code.

5. For the calculation of the theoretical amount referred to in Article 46(2)(a) of the Regulation, in schemes in which old-age pensions are calculated on the basis of retirement points, the competent institution shall take into account, in respect of each of the years of insurance completed under the legislation of any other Member State, the number of retirement points arrived at by dividing the number of retirement points acquired under the legislation it applies by the number of years corresponding to these points.

E. GREECE

1. Notwithstanding Annex I, Section I, Part E, point 1, Article 22(1)(a) of the Regulation applies to an OGA-insured person whose state of

health necessitates immediate care before he begins the employment which he has come to take up in a Member State other than Greece.

2. Article 10(1) of the Regulation does not affect the provision of Article 2(4) of Decree Law No 4577/66 whereby the payment of pensions awarded by IKA to persons of Greek nationality or origin coming from Egypt or Turkey is suspended if the pension-holder resides abroad without valid reason for more than six months.

F. IRELAND

1. Employed or self-employed persons, unemployed persons, pension claimants and pensioners, together with members of their families, referred to in Articles 19(1), 22(1) and (3), 25(1) and (3), 26(1), 28a, 29 and 31 of the Regulation, who are residing or staying in Ireland, shall be entitled free of charge to all medical treatment provided for by Irish legislation where the cost of this treatment is payable by the institution of a Member State other than Ireland.

2. The members of the family of an employed or self-employed person who is subject to the legislation of a Member State other than Ireland and who satisfies the conditions laid down by that legislation for entitlement to benefits, account being taken, where appropriate, of Article 18 of the Regulation, shall be entitled free of charge, if they are resident in Ireland, to all medical treatment provided for by Irish legislation.

The cost of such benefits shall be payable by the institution with which the employed or self-employed person is insured.

However, where the spouse of the employed or self-employed person or the person looking after the children pursues a professional or trade activity in Ireland, benefits for members of the family shall remain payable by the Irish institution to the extent that entitlement to such benefits is granted solely under the provisions of Irish legislation.

3. If an employed person subject to Irish legislation has left the territory of a Member State to proceed, in the course of his employment, to the territory of another Member State and sustains an accident before arriving there, his entitlement to benefit in respect of the said accident shall be established:

(a) as if this accident had occured on the territory of Ireland; and

(b) without taking into consideration his absence from the territory of Ireland, when determining whether, by virtue of his employment, he was insured under the said legislation.

4. For the purpose of applying Article 12(2) of the Regulation to Irish legislation, invalidity, old-age and widows' pensions shall be regarded as benefits of the same kind.

5. For the purpose of calculating the earnings for the granting of the pay-related benefit payable under Irish legislation with sickness, maternity and unemployment benefits, an amount equal to the average weekly wage in that year of male or female employed persons, as applicable, shall, notwithstanding Articles 23(1) and 68(1) of the Regulation, be credited to the employed person in respect of each week of employment completed as an employed person under the legislation of another Member State during the relevant income tax year.

6. In applying Article 40(3)(a)(ii), account shall only be taken of periods during which the employed or self-employed person was incapable of work within the meaning of Irish legislation.

7. For the purposes of Article 44(2), an employed person shall be deemed to have expressly asked for postponement of the award of an old-age pension to which he would be entitled under the legislation of Ireland if, where retirement is a condition for receiving the old-age pension, he has not retired.

8. Until 31 December 1983, for the purpose of applying Irish legislation to benefits other than family benefits and sickness and maternity benefits in kind, periods other than periods completed as an employed person shall not be reckonable.

G. ITALY

None.

H. LUXEMBOURG

1. By way of derogation from Article 94(2) of the Regulation, periods of insurance or periods treated as such completed before 1 January 1946 under Luxembourg legislation for invalidity, old-age or death pension insurance shall only be taken into consideration for the purpose of applying this legislation to the extent that rights in the process of being acquired should be maintained until 1 January 1959 or subsequently recovered in accordance with that legislation alone, or in accordance with bilateral conventions in force or to be concluded. Where several bilateral conventions apply, the periods of insurance or periods treated as such dating the farthest back shall be taken into consideration.

2. For the purpose of granting the fixed part of Luxembourg pensions, periods of insurance completed under Luxembourg

legislation by employed or self-employed persons not residing in Luxembourg territory shall, as from 1 October 1972, be treated as periods of residence.

I. NETHERLANDS

1. *Insurance for medical expenses*

(a) As regards entitlement to benefits in kind, Title III, Chapter 1 of the Regulation shall apply only to persons who are entitled to benefits in kind through compulsory insurance, voluntary insurance or elderly persons' insurance, which insurance schemes are covered by the law on sickness funds[9].

(b) A person receiving an old-age pension under Netherlands legislation and a pension under the legislation of another Member State shall, for the purposes of Article 27 and/or Article 28, be considered to be entitled to benefits in kind if, taking into account Article 9, where appropriate, he satisfies the conditions required for admission to sickness insurance schemes for elderly persons or to voluntary insurance schemes laid down in the law on sickness fund insurance.

This provision also applies to a married woman whose husband is receiving an old-age pension for married persons under Netherlands legislation and satisfies the conditions required for admission to sickness insurance schemes for elderly persons or to voluntary insurance schemes laid down in the law on sickness fund insurance.

(c) A person receiving an old-age pension under Netherlands legislation who resides in another Member State shall, if he is insured under the sickness insurance schemes for elderly persons or under the voluntary insurance schemes laid down in the law on sickness fund insurance, pay for himself and, if appropriate, for members of his family, a contribution based on half of the average costs incurred in the Netherlands for medical treatment for an elderly person and members of his family. A reduction of this contribution shall be granted, the costs thereof being borne by the compulsory insurance scheme provided for in the law on sickness fund insurance, corresponding to the part of the reduction, the costs whereof are borne by the said scheme, that is granted to persons residing in the Netherlands who are covered by the sickness insurance schemes for elderly persons and whose contributions are fixed on the same basis.

(d) A person who is not receiving an old-age pension under Netherlands legislation and, if he is married, whose spouse is not

receiving an old-age pension for married persons under Netherlands legislation shall, if he resides in another Member State and if he is insured under the voluntary insurance scheme laid down in the Law on sickness fund insurance, pay for himself and, if appropriate, for each member of his family who has reached the age of 16 years an amount of contribution which corresponds to the average of the contributions fixed by the sickness funds in the Netherlands for voluntary insured persons residing in the Netherlands. The contribution shall be rounded up to the nearest multiple of one guilder.

2. *Application of Netherlands legislation on general old-age insurance*

(a) Periods of insurance before 1 January 1957 during which a recipient, not satisfying the conditions permitting him to have such periods treated as periods of insurance, resided in the territory of the Netherlands after the age of 15 or during which, whilst residing in the territory of another Member State, he pursued an activity as an employed person in the Netherlands for an employer established in that country, shall also be considered as periods of insurance completed in application of Netherlands legislation for general old-age insurance.

(b) Periods to be taken into account in pursuance of subparagraph (a) above shall not be taken into account if they coincide with periods taken into account for the calculation of the pension payable under the legislation of another Member State in respect of old-age insurance.

(c) As regards a married woman whose husband is entitled to a pension under Netherlands legislation on general old-age insurance, periods of the marriage preceding the date when she reached the age of sixty-five years and during which she resided in the territory of one or more Member States shall also be taken into account as insurance periods, in so far as those periods coincide with periods of insurance completed by her husband under that legislation and with those to be taken into account in pursuance of subparagraph (a).

(d) Periods to be taken into account in pursuance of subparagraph (c) shall not be taken into account where they coincide with periods taken into account for calculating a pension payable to the married woman in question under the old-age insurance legislation of another Member State or with periods during which she received an old-age pension in pursuance of such legislation.

(e) As regards a woman who has been married and whose husband has been subject to Netherlands legislation on old-age

insurance, or is deemed to have completed periods of insurance in pursuance of subparagraph (a), the provisions of the two preceding subparagraphs shall apply *mutatis mutandis*.

(f) The periods referred to in subparagraph (a) and (c) shall only be taken into account for calculation of the old-age pension if the person concerned has resided for six years in the territory of one or more Member States after the age of 59 years and for as long as that person is residing in the territory of one of those Member States.

3. *Application of Netherlands legislation on general insurance for widows and orphans*

(a) For the purposes of the provisions of Article 46(2) of the Regulation, periods before 1 October 1959 during which the employed or self-employed person resided in the territory of the Netherlands after the age of 15 years or during which, whilst residing in the territory of another Member State, he pursued an activity as an employed person in the Netherlands for an employer established in that country shall also be considered as periods of insurance completed under Netherlands legislation relating to general insurance for widows and orphans.

(b) Periods to be taken into account in pursuance of the provisions of subparagraph (a) shall not be taken into account where they coincide with periods of insurance completed under the legislation of another State in respect of survivors' pension.

4. *Application of the Netherlands legislation on insurance against incapacity for work*

For the purposes of applying Article 46(2) of the Regulation, Netherlands institutions will respect the following provisions:

(a) if, when incapacity for work or the resultant invalidity occurred, the person concerned was an employed person within the meaning of Article 1(a) of the Regulation, the competent institution shall fix the amount of cash benefits in accordance with the provisions of the law of 18 February 1966 on insurance against incapacity for work (WAO), taking account of:

– insurance periods completed under the abovementioned law of 18 February 1966 (WAO),

– insurance periods completed after the age of 15 under the law of 11 December 1975 on incapacity for work (AAW), provided that they do not coincide with insurance periods

completed by the person concerned under the abovementioned law of 18 February 1966 (WAO), and

- periods of paid work and equivalent periods completed in the Netherlands before 1 July 1967;

(b) if, when incapacity for work and the resultant invalidity occurred, the person concerned was not an employed person within the meaning of Article 1(a)[10] of the Regulation, the competent institution shall fix the amount of cash benefits in accordance with the provisions of the law of 11 December 1975 on incapacity for work (AAW), taking account of:

- insurance periods completed by the person concerned after the age of 15 under the abovementioned law of 11 December 1975 (AAW),

- insurance periods completed under the law of 18 February 1966 on insurance against incapacity for work (WAO), provided that they do not coincide with insurance periods completed under the abovementioned law of 11 December 1975 (AAW), and

- periods of paid work and equivalent periods completed in the Netherlands before 1 July 1967.

5. *Application of certain transitional provisions*

Article 45(1) shall not apply to the assessment of entitlement to benefits under the transitional provisions of the legislations on general old-age insurance (Article 46), on general insurance for widows and orphans and on general insurance against incapacity for work.

J. UNITED KINGDOM

1. When a person who is normally resident in Gibraltar, or who has been required, since he last arrived in Gibraltar, to pay contributions under the legislation of Gibraltar as an employed person, applies, as a result of incapacity to work, maternity or unemployment, for exemption from the payment of contributions over a certain period, and asks for contributions for that period to be credited to him, any period during which that person has been working in the territory of a Member State other than the United Kingdom shall, for the purposes of his application, be regarded as a period during which he has been employed in Gibraltar and for which he has paid contributions as an employed person in accordance with the legislation of Gibraltar.

2. For the purposes of the provisions of Title III, Chapter 3, of the Regulation, where, in accordance with United Kingdom legislation, a woman applies for an old-age pension:

(a) on the basis of her husband's insurance or

(b) on the basis of her personal insurance, and where, because the marriage has ended as a result of the death of the husband, or for other reasons, the contributions paid by the latter are taken into account for the determination of pension rights,

any reference to a period of insurance completed by her shall be considered, for the purposes of establishing the annual average of the contributions paid by her husband or credited to him, to include reference to a period of insurance completed by the husband.

3. (a) If unemployment benefit provided under United Kingdom legislation is paid to a person pursuant to Article 71(1)(a)(ii) or (b)(ii) of the Regulation, then for the purpose of satisfying the conditions imposed by United Kingdom legislation in relation to child benefit concerning a period of presence within Great Britain or, as the case may be, Northern Ireland, periods of insurance, employment or self-employment completed by that person under the legislation of another Member State shall be regarded as periods of presence in Great Britain or, as the case may be, Northern Ireland.

(b) If, pursuant to Title II of the Regulation, United Kingdom legislation is applicable in respect of an employed or self-employed person who does not satisfy the condition imposed by United Kingdom legislation in relation to child benefit concerning:

(i) presence within Great Britain or, as the case may be, Northern Ireland, he shall be regarded, for the purpose of satisfying such condition, as being so present;

(ii) a period of presence within Great Britain, or, as the case may be, Northern Ireland, periods of insurance, employment or self-employment completed by the said worker under the legislation of another Member State shall, for the purpose of satisfying such conditions, be regarded as periods of presence in Great Britain or, as the case may be, Northern Ireland.

(c) In respect of claims to family allowances under the legislation of Gibraltar the foregoing provisions of subparagraph (a) and (b) shall apply by analogy.

4. Any employed or self-employed person subject to United Kingdom

legislation in accordance with the provisions of Title II of the Regulation shall be treated for the purposes of entitlement to the attendance allowance:

(a) as if his place of birth were within the territory of the United Kingdom, if his place of birth is within the territory of another Member State, and;

(b) as if he had been normally resident in the United Kingdom and had been present there during any period of insurance, employment or self-employment that he may have completed within the territory or under the legislation of another Member State.

5. In the event of an employed person subject to United Kingdom legislation being the victim of an accident after leaving the territory of one Member State while travelling, in the course of his employment, to the territory of another Member State, but before arriving there, his entitlement to benefits in respect of that accident shall be established:

(a) as if the accident had occurred within the territory of the United Kingdom; and

(b) for the purpose of determining whether he was an employed earner under the legislation of Great Britain or the legislation of Northern Ireland or an employed person under the legislation of Gibraltar, by disregarding his absence from those territories.

6. The Regulation does not apply to those provisions of United Kingdom legislation which are intended to bring into force any social security agreement concluded between the United Kingdom and a third State.

7. Wherever required by United Kingdom legislation for the purposes of determining entitlement to benefits, nationals of any Member State born in a third State are to be considered nationals of the United Kingdom born in a third State.

8. For the purposes of Title III, Chapter 3, of the Regulation no account shall be taken of graduated contributions paid by the insured person under United Kingdom legislation or of graduated retirement benefits payable under that legislation. The amount of the graduated benefits shall be added to the amount of the benefit due under the United Kingdom legislation as determined in accordance with the said chapter. The total of these two amounts shall constitute the benefit actually due to the person concerned.

9. For the purpose of applying Article 12(2) of the Regulation to the

legislation of the United Kingdom, invalidity, old-age and widow's pensions shall be regarded as benefits of the same kind.

10. For the purpose of applying the Non-Contributory Social Insurance Benefit and Unemployment Insurance Ordinance (Gibraltar), any person to whom this Regulation is applicable shall be deemed to be domiciled in Gibraltar if he resides in a Member State.

11. For the purposes of Articles 10, 27, 28, 28a, 29, 30 and 31 of the Regulation, the attendance allowance granted to an employed or self-employed person under United Kingdom legislation shall be considered as an invalidity benefit.

12. For the purposes of Article 10(1) of the Regulation any beneficiary under United Kingdom legislation who is staying in the territory of another Member State shall, during that stay, be considered as if he resided in the territory of that other Member State.

13. (1) For the purpose of calculating an earnings factor with a view to determining the right to benefits under United Kingdom legislation, subject to paragraph 15, each week during which an employed or self-employed person has been subject to the legislation of another Member State and which commenced during the relevant income tax year within the meaning of United Kingdom legislation shall be taken into account in the following way:

    (a) (i) for each week of insurance, employment, or residence as an employed person the person concerned shall be deemed to have paid contributions as an employed earner on the basis of earnings equivalent to two-thirds of that year's upper earnings limit;

        (ii) for each week of insurance, self-employment or residence as a self-employed person the person concerned shall be deemed to have paid Class 2 contributions as a self-employed earner;

    (b) for each full week during which he has completed a period treated as a period of insurance, employment, self-employment or residence, the person concerned shall be deemed to have had a contribution credited to him, but only to the extent required to bring his total earnings factor that year to the level required to make that year a reckonable year within the meaning of the United Kingdom legislation governing the crediting of contributions.

(2) For the purpose of converting an earnings factor into periods of

insurance the earnings factor achieved in the relevant income tax year within the meaning of United Kingdom legislation shall be divided by that year's lower earnings limit. The result shall be expressed as a whole number, any remaining fraction being ignored. The figure so calculated shall be treated as representing the number of weeks of insurance completed under United Kingdom legislation during that year provided that such figure shall not exceed the number of weeks during which in that year the person was subject to that legislation.

14. In applying Article 40(3)(a)(ii), account shall only be taken of periods during which the employed or self-employed person was incapable of work within the meaning of United Kingdom legislation.

15. (1) For the purpose of calculating, under Article 46(2)(a) of the Regulation, the theoretical amount of that part of the pension which consists of an additional component under United Kingdom legislation:

(a) the expression 'earnings, contributions or increases' in Article 47(1)(b) of the Regulation shall be construed as meaning surpluses in earnings factors as defined in the Social Security Pensions Act 1975 or, as the case may be, the Social Security Pensions (Northern Ireland) Order 1975;

(b) an average of the surpluses in earning factors shall be calculated in accordance with Article 47(1)(b) of the Regulation as construed in subparagraph (a) above by dividing the aggregated surpluses recorded under United Kingdom legislation by the number of income tax years within the meaning of United Kingdom legislation (including part income tax years) completed under that legislation since 6 April 1978 which occur within the relevant period of insurance.

(2) The expression 'periods of insurance or residence' in Article 46(2) of the Regulation shall be construed, for the purpose of assessing the amount of that part of the pension which consists of an additional component under United Kingdom legislation, as meaning periods of insurance or residence which have been completed since 6 April 1978.'

61. The following Annex shall be added:

'Annex VII

(Implementation of subparagraph (b) of Article 14c(1))

Instances in which a person shall be simultaneously subject to the legislation of two Member States

1. Where he is self-employed in Belgium and gainfully employed in any other Member State except Luxembourg. For Luxembourg the exchange of letters of 10 and 12 July 1968 between Belgium and Luxembourg shall be applicable.

2. Where a person resident in Denmark is self-employed in Denmark and gainfully employed in any other Member State.

3. Where he is self-employed in farming in Germany and gainfully employed in any other Member State.

4. Where he is self-employed in France and gainfully employed in any other Member State except Luxembourg.

5. Where he is self-employed in farming in France and gainfully employed in Luxembourg.

6. Where he is self-employed in Greece and gainfully employed in any other Member State.

7. Where he is self-employed in Italy and gainfully employed in any other Member State.'

Article 2

1. No right shall be acquired under this Regulation in respect of a period prior to the date of its entry into force.

2. All insurance periods and, where appropriate, all periods of employment, of self-employment or of residence completed under the legislation of a Member State before the date of entry into force of this Regulation shall be taken into consideration for the determination of rights to benefits under this Regulation.

3. Subject to paragraph 1, a right shall be acquired under this Regulation through relating to a contingency which materialised prior to the date of entry into force of this Regulation.

4. Any benefit which has not been awarded or which has been suspended by reason of the nationality or place of residence of the person concerned shall, on the application of the person concerned, be awarded or resumed with effect from the entry into force of this Regulation provided that the rights previously determined have not given rise to a lump sum payment.

5. The rights of a person to whom a pension was awarded prior to the entry into force of this Regulation may, on the application of the person concerned, be reviewed, taking into account the provisions of this Regulation. This provision shall also apply to the other benefits referred to in Article 78 of Regulation (EEC) No 1408/71.

6. If an application referred to in paragraph 4 or 5 is submitted within two years from the date of entry into force of this Regulation, the rights acquired under this Regulation shall have effect from that date, and the provisions of the legislation of any Member State concerning the forfeiture or limitation of rights may not be invoked against the persons concerned.

7. If the application referred to in paragraph 4 or 5 is submitted after the expiry of the two-year period following the date of entry into force of this Regulation, rights which have not been forfeited or are not barred by limitation shall have effect from the date on which the application was submitted, except where more favourable provisions of the legislation of any Member State apply.

Article 3

Unless the Member States concerned decide otherwise, the agreements concluded pursuant to Article 36(3), Article 63(3) and Article 70(3) of Regulation (EEC) No 1408/71, prior to the entry into force of this Regulation, shall not apply to the persons to whom the scope of Regulation (EEC) No 1408/71 has been extended by virtue of this Regulation.

Article 4

This Regulation shall enter into force on the first day of the seventh month following the publication in the *Official Journal of the European Communities* of the Regulation adapting Regulation (EEC) No 574/72[11] with a view to applying it to self-employed persons and to their families.

This Regulation shall be binding in its entirety and directly applicable in all Member States.

Done at Brussels, 12 May 1981

For the Council

The President

G. Braks

EDITORIAL NOTE

See consolidated version of Regulation (EEC) No 1408/71 of 15.6.1971 in OJ No C 325, 10.12.92, p.91; and consolidated version of Regulation (EEC) No 574/72 of 21.3.1972 in OJ No C 325, 10.12.92, p.96.

FOOTNOTES

1. OJ No C 14, 18.1.78, p.15.
2. OJ No C 131, 5.6.78, p.45.
3. OJ No C 269, 13.11.78, p.40.
4. OJ No L 149, 5.7.71, p.2.
5. OJ No L 24, 28.1.81, p.3.
6. Editorial note: German terms omitted – see OJ No L 143, 29.5.81, p.16.
7. Editorial note: German terms omitted – see OJ No L 143, 29.5.81, p.19.
8. Editorial note: German terms omitted – see OJ No L 143, 29.5.81, p.20.
9. Editorial note: Dutch terms omitted – see OJ No L 143, 29.5.81 p.25.
10. Editorial note: correction made to allow for typing error in original.
11. OJ No L 74, 27.3.72, p.1.

COUNCIL REGULATION (EEC) No 2195/91

of 25 June 1991

amending Regulation (EEC) No 1408/71 on the application of social security schemes to employed persons, self-employed persons and members of their families moving within the Community and Regulation (EEC) No 574/72 laying down the procedure for implementing Regulation (EEC) No 1408/71

(OJ No L 206, 29.7.91, p.2)

The Council of the European Communities,

Having regard to the Treaty establishing the European Economic Community, and in particular Articles 51 and 235, thereof,

Having regard to the proposal from the Commission, drawn up after consulting the Administrative Commission on Social Security for Migrant Workers[1],

Having regard to the opinion of the European Parliament[2],

Having regard to the opinion of the Economic and Social Committee[3],

Whereas it is necessary to amend Regulations (EEC) No 1408/71[4] and No 574/72[5] as updated by Regulation (EEC) No 2001/83[6], as last amended

by Regulation (EEC) No 3427/89[7]; whereas certain of these amendments are connected with changes made by the Member States in their social security legislation, while others are of a technical nature and are intended to improve these Regulations in the light of experience gained from implementing them;

Whereas the amendments made to Article 57 of Regulation (EEC) No 1408/71 by Regulation (EEC) No 2332[8] make it necessary to alter Article 12(4) of Regulation (EEC) No 1408/71;

Whereas it has proved necessary, following the judgment delivered by the Court of Justice in Case 302/84 (Ten Holder) on 12 June 1986, to insert a new subparagraph (f) in Article 13(2) of Regulation (EEC) No 1408/71 in order to determine what legislation is applicable to persons to whom one Member State's legislation ceases to be applicable without the legislation of another Member State becoming applicable to them, in accordance with one of the rules laid down in the previous subparagraphs of the same Article 13(2) or one of the exceptions provided for in Articles 14 to 17 of Regulation (EEC) No 1408/71; whereas this amendment also makes it necessary to alter Article 17 of the same Regulation;

Whereas a new provision must be inserted in Regulation (EEC) No 1408/71 to exempt pensioners from the legislation of the State of residence when they are already entitled to sickness insurance, maternity and family benefits under the legislation of another Member State;

Whereas it has proved necessary to supplement Article 39 of Regulation (EEC) No 1408/71 in order to specify the wages or salaries to be taken into account in the case of frontier-zone workers for the application of the legislation of those Member States in which the calculation of invalidity benefits is based on wages or salaries;

Whereas it has proved necessary, following the judgment delivered by the Court of Justice in Case 58/87 (Rebmann) of 29 July 1988, to insert a new paragraph in Article 45 of Regulation (EEC) No 1408/71 providing that the Member State in which the worker resides shall take account for pensions purposes of periods of full unemployment completed by this worker in respect of which benefits have been paid by that State under Article 71(1)(a)(ii) and (b)(ii) of Regulation (EEC) No 1408/71;

Whereas it has also proved necessary, for Member States whose legislation provides for the calculation of old-age benefits to be based on wages or salaries, to supplement Article 47 of Regulation (EEC) No 1408/71 by specifying the wage or salary to be taken into account where

the frontier-zone worker has not completed any period of occupation in the country of residence;

Whereas a loophole has been found in Regulation (EEC) No 1408/71 in respect of the unemployed persons who were formerly employed as mentioned in Article 71(1)(a)(ii) and (b)(ii) who reside in the territory of the same Member State as the members of their families; whereas this loophole should be remedied by inserting a provision to the effect that the Member State of residence which provides sickness and maternity benefits under Articles 25(2) and 39(5) of Regulation (EEC) No 1408/71 shall also pay family benefits to the person concerned;

Whereas it seems necessary, following the addition, by this Regulation, of an eighth paragraph to Article 45 of Regulation (EEC) No 1408/71, to give the person concerned the right to ask for benefits awarded under the former system to be reviewed in his favour;

Whereas Annex I to Regulation (EEC) No 1408/71 must be amended as a result of the transfer of responsibility for medical services in Gibraltar;

Whereas Annex IV to Regulation (EEC) No 1408/71 must be amended because of the introduction in the united Kingdom of a severe disablement allowance, the value of which does not depend on the length of periods of insurance;

Whereas section 'A. Belgium' to Regulation (EEC) No 1408/71 should be amended in order to solve the problem of conversion into Belgian francs of income received by self-employed persons in a foreign currency;

Whereas certain entries in section 'C. Germany' of Annex VI to Regulation (EEC) No 1408/71 must be amended to take account of several changes of form and substance made in German sickness insurance and pensions insurance legislation; whereas account should in particular be taken of a special feature of German legislation whereby recognition of a pension insurance period depends only on the person concerned residing in Germany; whereas, in order to protect migrant workers, the instances in which that condition is deemed to be fulfilled by workers who raise their children in another Member State should be specified;

Whereas, following the insertion by this Regulation of a new Article 13(2)(f) in Regulation (EEC) No 1408/71, section 'G. Ireland' and section 'L. United Kingdom' of Annex VI to Regulation (EEC) No 1408/71 should be amended to clarify the implementation of this new provision with respect to these two States;

Whereas section 'I. Luxembourg' of Annex VI to Regulation (EEC) No 1408/71 must be amended to take account of the changes made in

Luxembourg legislation on old-age, invalidity and survivor's pension insurance;

Whereas section 'J. Netherlands' of Annex VI to Regulation (EEC) No 1408/71 must be amended because of changes in the arrangements for collection of contributions and the abolition of the age limit for the obligation to contribute to social insurance; whereas point 1(b) of the same section also needs to be amended in the interests of clarity;

Whereas section 'L. United Kingdom' of Annex VI to Regulation (EEC) No 1408/71 should be amended as a result of the abolition of the British maternity allowance, the introduction of a new lump-sum benefit for widows, the change in the manner of calculating earnings giving rise to Class 1 national insurance contributions and the introduction of the severe disablement allowance;

Whereas Article 4(10)(a) and (b) of Regulation (EEC) 574/72 should be amended in order to take account of the fact that the former paragraph 2 of Article 14d of Regulation (EEC) No 1408/71 has become paragraph 3 by virtue of Article 1 of Regulation (EEC) No 3811/86[9] and to include a reference to Article 8 and to the new Article 10b of Regulation (EEC) No 574/72 inserted by this Regulation;

Whereas, following the insertion by this Regulation into Regulation (EEC) No 1408/71 of a new Article 13(2)(f) stipulating that persons to whom the legislation of a Member State ceases to apply without the legislation of another Member State becoming applicable to them shall be subject to the legislation of the Member State in whose territory they reside, a provision is required stipulating when, and under what conditions, this legislation ceases to be applicable;

Whereas a reference to Article 14d(1) of Regulation (EEC) No 1408/71 must be inserted in Article 107(1)(a) of Regulation (EEC) No 574/72 for the purposes of stipulating the conversion rate to be applied for collection of contributions under this provision when it is necessary to convert into national currency the earnings received by an employed or self-employed person in the currency of another Member State;

Whereas section 'L. United Kingdom' of Annex to Regulation (EEC) 574/72 should be amended as a result of the division of the Department of Health and Social Security in Great Britain into two separate departments;

Whereas Annex 2 to Regulation (EEC) No 574/72 should be amended in order to take account of organisational changes in Denmark in involving the division of the Danish National Social Security Office, and of the transfer of responsibility for Gibraltar's medical services and the division

of the Department of Health and Social Security in Great Britain into two separate departments;

Whereas Annex 3 to Regulation (EEC) No 574/72 should be amended in order to take account of the division of the Danish National Social Security Office, of the fact that as from 1 January 1991 the German accident insurance bodies will have sole responsibility for benefits for accidents at work or occupational diseases in Germany and of the transfer of responsibility for Gibraltar's medical services and the division of the Department of Health and Social Security in Great Britain into two separate departments;

Whereas Annex 4 to Regulation (EEC) No 574/72 must be amended to take account of the new function assigned to the Belgian Accidents at Work Fund, which is to act as the liaison body of accidents at work, the division of the Danish National Social Security Office, the change in the name of the German liaison body for sickness insurance and the division of the Department of Health and Social Security in Great Britain into two separate departments;

Whereas Annex 5 to Regulation (EEC) No 574/72 must be amended because of the change in the Agreement of 7 February 1964 between the Netherlands and Belgium on family and childbirth allowances and in order to take account of the changes in the Agreement of 20 July 1978 between Germany and Luxembourg, which no longer covers benefits in kind for accidents at work and occupational diseases;

Whereas the sections on Belgium, France, Greece, Ireland and the United Kingdom of Annex 10 to Regulation (EEC) 574/72 should be amended in order to indicate the institutions designated by the competent authorities for implementation of Articles 14c of Regulation (EEC) No 1408/71 and 12a(7) and (8) of Regulation (EEC) No 574/72 for those States;

Whereas sections 'B. Denmark' and 'C. Germany' of Annex 10 to Regulation (EEC) No 574/72 should be amended as necessary to take account of the division of the Danish National Social Security Office and the need to delete, in point 2(c) of section 'C. Germany' of Annex 10 to Regulation (EEC) No 574/72, the reference to Article 14c(1) of Regulation (EEC) No 1408/71, following the amendments made by Regulation (EEC) No 3811/86;

Whereas section 'C. Germany' of Annex 10 to Regulation (EEC) No 574/72 must be amended to take account of the fact that as from 1 January 1991 the German accident insurance bodies will have sole responsibility for benefits in respect of accidents at work or occupational diseases in Germany, of the fact that the former paragraph

2 of Article 14d of Regulation (EEC) No 1408/71 has become paragraph 3 and of the change in the name of the German liaison body for sickness insurance;

Whereas the former paragraph 2 of Article 14d of Regulation (EEC) No 1408/71 has become the new paragraph 3 and the references to this provision must therefore be corrected in sections 'F. Greece' and 'I. Luxembourg' of Annex 10 to Regulation (EEC) No 574/72;

Whereas section 'F. Greece' of Annex 10 to Regulation (EEC) No 574/72 must be amended to take account of the transfer of competence between the Greek social security institutions for mariners;

Whereas section 'J. Netherlands' and section 'L. United Kingdom' of Annex 10 to Regulation (EEC) No 574/72 must be amended following the changes in the responsibilities of the Netherlands Social Insurance Council and the division of the Department of Health and Social Security in Great Britain into two separate departments,

Has adopted this Regulation:

Article 1[10]

12. Annex VI shall be amended as follows:

(a) the following entry shall be added to section 'A. Belgian':

'8. For the purposes of applying Articles 14a(2), (3) and (4), 14c(a) and 14d of Regulation (EEC) No 1408/71, business revenues in the reference year which serve as a basis for determining the contributions due by virtue of the social arrangements for self-employed persons shall be calculated using the mean annual rate for the year during which this income was received.

The rate of conversion is the annual mean of the conversion rates published in the *Official Journal of the European Communities* pursuant to Article 107(5) of Regulation (EEC) No 574/72';

(b) in section 'C. Germany'

(i) point 6 shall be deleted with effect from 1 January 1989;

(ii) point 13 shall be deleted with effect from 1 January 1989:

'13. For the purposes of applying German legislation on compulsory sickness insurance of pensioners as provided for in Article 5(1)(ii) of Volume V of the Social Insurance Code (Fünftes Buch Sozialgesetzbuch – SGB V) and Article 56 of the Sickness Insurance Reform Law (Gesundheitsreformgesetz), periods of insurance or residence completed under the legislation of

another Member State during which the person concerned was entitled to sickness benefits in kind are taken into account, in so far as is necessary, as periods of insurance completed under German legislation provided they do not overlap with periods of insurance completed under that legislation.';

(iii) point 14 shall be replaced by the following with effect from 1 January 1989:

'14. For the grant of cash benefits pursuant to Article 47(1) of Volume V of the German Social Insurance Code (SGB V) and Articles 200(2) and 561(1) of the German Law on Social Insurance (Reichsversicherungsordnung – RVO), the German institutions shall determine the net remuneration to be taken into account for the calculation of the benefits as though the insured persons resided in the Federal Republic of Germany.';

(iv) the following entries shall be added with effect from 1 January 1989:

'17. For the grant of benefits to persons requiring in-depth and constant care under Articles 53 *et seq.* of Volume V of the German Social Insurance Code (SGB V), the institution of the place of residence shall, for the provision of assistance in the form of benefits in kind, take account of periods of insurance, employment or residence completed under the legislation of another Member State as if they were periods completed under the legislation applicable to that institution.

18. A person in receipt of a pension under German legislation and a pension under the legislation of another Member State shall be deemed, for the purposes of applying Article 27 of the Regulation, to be entitled to sickness and maternity benefits in kind if, under Article 8(1), point 4, of Volume V of the German Social Insurance Code (SGB V), that person is exempted from compulsory sickness insurance (Krankenversicherung).';

(v) the following entry shall be added with effect from 1 January 1986:

'19. A period of insurance for child-rearing under German legislation is valid even for a period during which the employed person concerned brought up the child in another Member State provided that person was unable to engage in occupational activity by virtue of Article 6(1) of the Protection of Mothers Law (Mutterschutzgesetz) or took parental leave under Article 15 of the Federal Child-rearing Allowance Law (Bundeserziehungs-

geldgesetz) and did 'not engage in any minor (geringfügig) employment within the meaning of Article 8 of SGB IV.';

(c) the following entry shall be added to section 'G. Ireland':

'10. A period of subjection to Irish legislation in accordance with Article 13(2)(f) of the Regulation may not:

(i) be taken into account under that provision as a period of subjection to Irish legislation for the purposes of Title III of the Regulation;

nor

(ii) make Ireland the competent State for the provision of benefits provided for in Articles 18, 38 or 39(1) of the Regulation.';

(d) in section 'I. Luxembourg':

(i) point 1 shall be replaced by the following with effect from 1 January 1988:

'1. Notwithstanding Article 94(2) of the Regulation, periods of insurance or periods treated as such completed by employed persons or self-employed persons under Luxembourg legislation for invalidity, old-age or death pension insurance either before 1 January 1946 or before an earlier date stipulated by a bilateral convention shall be taken into consideration for the purpose of applying this legislation only if the person concerned demonstrates that he has competed six months of insurance under the Luxembourg scheme after the date in question. Where several bilateral conventions apply, periods of insurance or periods treated as such shall be taken into consideration as from the earliest of these dates.';

(ii) the following entry shall be added with effect from 1 January 1988:

'4. For the purpose of taking the insurance period provided for in Article 171(7) of the Social Insurance Code (Code des Assurances Sociales) into account, the Luxembourg institution shall recognise periods of insurance completed by the person concerned under the legislation of any other Member State as if they were periods completed under the legislation which it administers. Application of the foregoing provision shall be subject to the condition that the person concerned last completed insurance periods under Luxembourg legislation.';

(e) in section 'J. Netherlands':

(i) in point 1(b), the words 'at the time at which the aforementioned Article is applicable to him' shall be deleted with effect from 1 November 1989;

(ii) in point 2, the following shall be added with effect from 1 January 1990:

'(i) For the purposes of Article 46(2) of the Regulation, only periods of insurance completed after the age of 15 years under the Netherlands General Law on Old-Age Insurance (AOW) shall be taken into account as periods of insurance;';

(iii) in point 3, (a) shall be replaced by the following with effect from 1 January 1990:

'(a)(i) for the purposes of Article 46(2) of the Regulation, only periods of insurance completed after the age of 15 years under the Netherlands General Law on Insurance for Widows and Orphans (AWW) shall be taken into account as periods of insurance;

(ii) for the purposes of the provisions of Article 46(2) of the Regulation, periods before 1 October 1959 during which the employed or self-employed person resided in the territory of the Netherlands after the age of 15 years or during which, whilst residing in the territory of another Member State, he pursued an activity as an employed person in the Netherlands for an employer established in that country shall also be considered as periods of insurance completed and under Netherlands legislation relating to general insurance for widows and orphans.';

(f) in section 'L. United Kingdom':

(i) in point 3(b), after the words 'if, pursuant to Title II of the Regulation', the following words shall be added: 'excluding Article 13(2)(f)';

(ii) point 4 shall be replaced by the following with effect from 1 April 1988:

'4. The widow's payment provided under United Kingdom shall be treated, for the purposes of Chapter 3 of the Regulation, as a survivor's pension.';

(iii) in point 5, after the words 'in accordance with Title II of the Regulation', the following words shall be added: 'excluding Article 13(2)(f)';

(iv) point 13.1 shall be replaced by the following:

'13.1. For the purposes of calculating an earnings factor with a view to determining the right to benefits under United Kingdom legislation, subject to point 15, each week during which an employed or self-employed person has been subject to the legislation of another Member State and which commenced during the relevant income tax year within the meaning of United Kingdom legislation shall be taken into account in the following way:

(a) periods between 6 April 1975 and 5 April 1987:

  (i) for each week of insurance, employment or residence as an employed person, the person concerned shall be deemed to have paid contributions as an employed earner on the basis of earnings equivalent to two-thirds of that year's upper earnings limit;

  (ii) for each week of insurance, self-employment or residence as a self-employed person the person concerned shall be deemed to have paid class 2 contributions as a self-employed earner;

(b) periods from 6 April 1987 onwards:

  (i) for each week of insurance, employment or residence as an employed person, the person concerned shall be deemed to have received, and paid contributions as an employed earner for, weekly earnings equivalent to two-thirds of that week's upper earnings limit;

  (ii) for each week of insurance, self-employment or residence as a self-employed person the person concerned shall be deemed to have paid class 2 contributions as a self-employed earner;

(c) for each full week during which he has completed a period treated as a period of insurance, employment, self-employment or residence, the person concerned shall be deemed to have had contributions or earnings credited to him as appropriate, but only to the extend required to bring his total earnings factor for that tax year to the level required to make that tax year a reckonable year within the meaning of the United Kingdom legislation governing the crediting of contributions or earnings.';

(v) point 13.2(a) shall be replaced by the following:

'(a) if in any income tax year starting on or after 6 April 1975, an

employed person has completed periods of insurance, employment or residence exclusively in a Member State other than the United Kingdom, and the application of paragraph (1)(a)(i) or paragraph 1(b)(i) results in that year being counted as a qualifying year within the meaning of United Kingdom legislation for the purposes of Article 46(2)(a) of the Regulation, he shall be deemed to have been insured for 52 weeks in that year in that other Member State;'

(vi) the following entries shall be added:

'17. For the purposes of entitlement to severe disablement allowance any employed or self-employed person who is, or has been, subject to United Kingdom legislation in accordance with Title II of the Regulation, excluding Article 13(2)(f):

(a) shall, for the entire period during which he was employed or self-employed and subject to United Kingdom legislation whilst present or resident in another Member State, be treated as having been present or resident in the United Kingdom;

(b) shall be entitled to have periods of insurance as an employed or self-employed person completed in the territory and under the legislation of anther Member State treated as periods of presence or residence in the United Kingdom.

18. A period of subjection to United Kingdom legislation in accordance with Article 13(2)(f) of the Regulation may not:

(i) be taken into account under that provision as a period of subjection to United Kingdom legislation for the purposes of Title III of the Regulation,

nor

(ii) make the United Kingdom the competent State for the provision of the benefits provided for in Articles 18, 38 or 39(1) of the Regulation.

19. Subject to any conventions concluded with individual Member States, for the purposes of Article 13(2)(f) of the Regulation and Article 10b of the Implementing Regulation, United Kingdom legislation shall cease to apply at the end of the day on the latest of the following three days to any person previously subject to United Kingdom legislation as an employed or self-employed person:

(a) the day on which residence is transferred to the Member State referred to in Article 13(2)(f);

(b) the day of cessation of the employment or self-employment, whether permanent or temporary, during which that person was subject to United Kingdom legislation;

(c) the last day of any period of receipt of United Kingdom sickness or maternity benefit (including benefits in kind for which the United Kingdom is the competent State) or unemployment benefit which

   (i) began before the date of transfer or residence to another Member State or, if later,

   (ii) immediately followed employment or self-employment in another Member State while that person was subject to United Kingdom legislation.

20. The fact that person has become subject to the legislation of another Member State in accordance with Article 13(2)(f) of the Regulation, Article 10b of the Implementing Regulation and point 19 above, shall not prevent:

(a) the application to him by the United Kingdom as the competent State of the provisions relating to employed or self-employed persons of Title III, Chapter 1 and Chapter 2, Section 1 or Article 40(2) of the Regulation if he remains an employed or self-employed person for those purposes and was last so insured under the legislation of the United Kingdom;

(b) his treatment as an employed or self-employed person for the purposes of Chapter 7 and 8 of Title III of the Regulation or Articles 10 or 10a of the Implementing Regulation, provided United Kingdom benefit under Chapter 1 of Title III is payable to him in accordance with paragraph (a).'

Article 2

Regulation (EEC) No 574/72 is hereby amended as follows:

1. In Article 4(10):

(i) under (a), with effect from 1 January 1987, the words 'Article 14d(2)' shall be replaced by the words 'Article 14d(3)' and the following words shall be inserted after the word 'Regulation': 'Article 14c';

(ii) under (b), after the words 'Article 6(1)', the following words shall be inserted: 'Article 8, Article 10b'.

2. The following Article shall be inserted in Title III:

'*Article* 10*b*

Formalities pursuant to Article 13(2)(f) *of the Regulation*

The date and conditions on which the legislation of a Member State ceases to be applicable to a person referred to in Article 13(2)(f) of the Regulation shall be determined in accordance with that legislation. The institution designated by the competent authority of the Member State whose legislation becomes applicable to this person shall apply to the institution designated by the competent authority of the former Member State with a request to specify this date.'

3. In Article 107(1)(a), after the words 'Article 12(2), (3) and (4)' the words 'Article 14d(1)' shall be added.

4. In Annex 1, section 'L. United Kingdom':

 (i) point 1 shall be replaced by the following with effect from 25 July 1988:

   '1. Secretary of State for Social Security, London';

 (ii) the following point shall be inserted with effect from 25 July 1988:

   '1.a Secretary of State for Health, London';

(iii) point 6 shall be replaced by the following with effect from 1 April 1988:

   '6. Director of the Gibraltar Health Authority.'

5. Annex 2 shall be amended as follows:

(*a*) in section 'B. Denmark' with effect from 1 July 1989:

   (i) in point 2(a), the words 'Sikringsstyrelsen (National Social Security Office)' shall be replaced by the words 'Socialministeriet (Ministry for Social Affairs)';

   (ii) in point 3(a), the words 'Sikringsstyrelsen (National Social Security Office)' shall be replaced by the words 'Socialministeriet (Ministry for Social Affairs)';

   (iii) in point 4(a) the words 'Sikringsstyrelsen (National Social Security Office)' shall be replaced by the words 'Arbejdsskadestyrelsen (National Office for Accidents at Work and Occupational Diseases)';

(*b*) in section 'L. United Kingdom':

(i) in point 1, the entry concerning Gibraltar shall be replaced by: 'Gibraltar Health Authority' with effect from 1 April 1988;

(ii) in point 2, in the entry concerning Great Britain, the words 'Health and ...' shall be deleted with effect from 25 July 1988.

6. Annex 3 shall be amended as follows:

(a) in section 'B. Denmark', with effect from 1 July 1989:

in part I – *Institutions of the place of residence*:

(i) in points (b) and (c)(i) the words 'Sikringsstyrelsen (National Social Security Office)' shall be replaced by the words 'Socialministeriet (Ministry of Social Affairs)';

(ii) in point (d)(i) the words 'Sikringsstyrelsen (National Social Security Office)' shall be replaced by the words 'Arbejdsskadestyrelsen (National Office for Accidents at Work and Occupational Diseases)';

(iii) in point (e) the words 'Sikringsstyrelsen (National Social Security Office)' shall be replaced by the words 'Socialministeriet (Ministry of Social Affairs)'.

in part II – *Institutions of the place of stay*, in point (b)(i), the words 'Sikringsstyrelsen (National Social Security Office)' shall be replaced by the words 'Arbejdsskadestyrelsen (National Office for Accidents at Work and Occupational Diseases)'.

(b) in section 'C. Germany' point 2 shall be replaced by the following with effect from 1 January 1991:

'2. **Accident insurance:**

In all cases, the Hauptverband der gewerblichen Berufsgenossenschaften (Federation of Professional and Trade Associations in Industry), St Augustin';

(c) in section 'L. United Kingdom':

(i) in point 1, the entry for Gibraltar shall be replaced by: 'Gibraltar: Gibraltar Health Authority' with effect from 1 April 1988;

(ii) in point 2, in the entry for Great Britain, the words 'Health and ...' shall be deleted with effect from 25 July 1988;

(iii) in Point 3, in the entry for Great Britain, the words 'Health and...' shall be deleted with effect from 25 July 1988;

7. Annex 4 shall be amended as follows:

(a) in section 'A. Belgium', point 4 shall be replaced by the following with effect from 1 January 1988:

'4. **Accidents at work and occupational diseases**

(a) Accidents at work:

fonds des accidents du travail (Accidents at Work Fund), Brussels;

(b) Occupational diseases:

ministère de la prévoyance sociale (Ministry of Social Welfare), Brussels';

(b) in section 'B. Denmark' with effect from 1 July 1989:

(i) in points 1, 2, 3, 5, 6 and 7 the words 'Sikringsstyrelsen (National Social Security Office)' shall be replaced by the words 'Socialministeriet (Ministry of Social Affairs)';

(ii) in point 4, the words 'Sikringsstyrelsen (National Social Security Office)' shall be replaced by the words 'Arbejdsskadestyrelsen (National Office for Accidents at Work and Occupational Diseases)';

(c) in section 'C. Germany', point 1, the words 'Bundesverband der Ortskrankenkassen' (National Federation of Local Sickness Funds)' shall be replaced by the words 'AOK-Bundesverband (National Federation of Local Sickness Funds)' with effect from 1 January 1991;

(d) in section 'L. United Kingdom', in the entry for Great Britain the words 'Health and . . .' shall be deleted, with effect from 25 July 1988;

8. Annex 5 shall be amended as follows:

(a) in section '9. Belgium – Netherlands' in the first line of entry (a), the reference to Article 6 shall be deleted with effect from 1 April 1985;

(b) in section '27. Germany – Luxembourg', entry (e) shall be deleted with effect from 1 January 1989.

9. In Annex 6, section 'F. Greece' shall be replaced by the following:

'F. Greece

Pension insurance for employed and self-employed persons (sickness, old age and death):

Direct payment'.

10. Annex 10 shall be amended as follows:

(a) in section 'A. Belgium', the following entry shall be inserted:

'3.a For the purposes of applying Article 14c of the Regulation and Article 12a of the Implementing Regulation:

Employed persons:

office national de sécurité sociale (National Social Security Office), Brussels;

Self-employed persons:

institut national d'assurances sociales pour travailleurs indépendants (National Social Insurance Institute for the Self-Employed), Brussels';

(b) in section 'B. Denmark' with effect from 1 July 1989:

(i) in points 1, 2, 3, 6 and 7 the words Sikringsstyrelsen (National Social Security Office)' shall be replaced by the words 'Socialministeriet (Ministry for Social Affairs)';

(ii) point 7 shall be replaced by the following:

'7. For the purposes of applying Article 110 of the Implementing Regulation:

(a) benefits in pursuance of Chapters 1 to 3 and Chapters 5, 7 and 8 of Title III of the Regulation:

Socialministeriet (Ministry for Social Affairs), København;

(b) benefits in pursuance of Chapter 4 of Title III of the Regulation:

Arbejdsskadestyrelsen (National Office for Accidents at Work and Occupational Diseases), København;

(c) benefits in pursuance of Chapter 6 of Title III of the Regulation:

Direktoratet for Arbejdsloshedsforsikringen (Unemployment Insurance Office), København;

(c) in section 'C. Germany':

(i) in point 2(c), first sentence, the reference '(1)' after the words 'Article 14c' shall be deleted with effect from 1 January 1987;

(ii) point 2(c)(ii) shall be replaced by the following with effect from 1 January 1989:

'(ii) Persons not insured with sickness insurance:

employed persons: Bundesversicherungsanstalt für Angestellte (Federal Insurance Office for Clerical Staff), Berlin;

for manual workers: the competent pension insurance institution for manual workers';

(iii) in point 3, the words 'Bundesverband der Ortskrankenkassen (National Federation of Local Sickness Funds)' shall be replaced by the words 'AOK-Bundesverband (National Federation of Local Sickness Funds)' with effect from 1 January 1991;

(iv) point 8 shall be replaced by the following with effect from 1 January 1991:

'8. For the purposes of applying:

(a) Article 36 of the Regulation and Article 102(2) of the implementing Regulation:

'AOK-Bundesverband (National Federation of Local Sickness Funds), Bonn 2;

(b) Article 63 of the Regulation and Article 102(2) of the implementing Regulation:

Hauptverband der gewerblichen Berufsgenossenschaften (Federation of Professional and Trade Associations), St Augustin;

(c) Article 75 of the Regulation and Article 102(2) of the implementing Regulation:

Bundesanstalt für Arbeit (Federal Labour Office), Nürnberg';

(v) in point 9(a), the words 'Bundesverband der Ortskrankenkassen (National Federation of Local Sickness Funds)' shall be replaced by the words 'AOK-Bundesverband (National Federation of Local Sickness Funds)' with effect from 1 January 1991;

(vi) point 9(b) shall be replaced by the following with effect from 1 January 1991:

'(b) refund of benefits in kind incorrectly provided to workers on presentation of the certified statement provided for in Article 62(2) of the implementing Regulation:

Hauptverband der gewerblichen Berufsgenossenschaften (Federation of Professional and Trade Associations), St Augustin'.

(vii) in point 10, the words 'For the purposes of applying Article 14d(2) of the Regulation' shall be replaced by the words 'For the purposes of applying Article 14d(3) of the Regulation' with effect from 1 January 1987;

(d) in section 'E. France' the following entry shall be inserted:

'4.a For the purposes of applying Article 14c of the Regulation and Article 12a(7) and (8) of the implementing Regulation:

(a) Article 12a(7) of the implementing Regulation:

(i) employment in France and non-agricultural self-employment in another Member State:

caisse mutuelle régionale (Regional Mutual Benefit Fund);

(ii) employment in France and agricultural self-employment in another Member State:

caisse de mutualité sociale agricole (Agricultural Social Insurance Mutual Benefit Fund);

(b) Article 12a(8) of the implementing Regulation:

(i) non-agricultural self-employment in France:

caisse mutuelle régionale (Regional Mutual Benefit Fund);

(ii) agricultural self-employment in France:

caisse de mutualité sociale agricole (Agricultural Social Insurance Mutual Benefit Fund);

(c) in the case of non-agricultural self-employment in France and employment in Luxembourg, form E 101 shall be issued to the person concerned who shall submit it to the Regional Mutual Benefit Fund';

(e) in section 'F. Greece':

(i) the following entry shall be inserted:

'4.a For the purposes of applying Articles 14c of Regulation (EEC) No 1408/71 and 12a of Regulation (EEC) No 574/72:

(a) in general:

Ίδρυμα Κοινωνικών Ασφαλίσεων (ΙΚΑ), Αθήνα (Social Insurance Institute, Athens);

(b) for mariners:

Ναυτικό Απομαχικό Ταμειό (ΝΑΤ), Πειραιάς (Mariners' Retirement Fund, Piraeus)';

(ii) in point 5, the words 'For the purposes of applying Article 14d(2)' shall be replaced by the words 'For the purposes of applying Article 14d(3)' with effect from 1 January 1987;

(iii) point 9 shall be amended as follows:

– the first sentence shall be replaced by the following:

'For the purposes of applying Article 102(2) of the implementing Regulation';

– subparagraph (b) shall be replaced by the following:

(b) Benefits for mariners:

Οίκοβ Ναυτου, Πειραιάς (Seamen's Home, Piraeus)';

(iv) the following entry shall be added:

'9a.For the purposes of applying Article 110 of the implementing Regulation:

(a) Family allowances, unemployment:

Οργανισμός, Απασχολησεως Εργτιυκού Δυναμικού (ΟΑΕΔ), Αθήνα (Labour Employment Office, Athens);

(b) benefits for mariners:

Ναυτικό Απομαςικο Ταμείο (ΝΑΤ), Πειραιάς (Mariners' Retirement Fund, Piraeus)';

(c) other benefits:

Ιδρυμα Κοινωνικών Ασφαλίσεων (ΙΚΑ), Αθήνα (Social Insurance Institute, Athens)';

(f) in section 'G. Ireland', the words 'For the purposes of applying Article 14(c) of the Regulation' shall be inserted at the beginning of point 1;

(g) in section 'I. Luxembourg', in point 1, the words 'For the purposes of applying Article 14d(2)' shall be replaced by the words 'For the purposes of applying Article 14d(3)' with effect from 1 January 1987;

(h) in section 'J. Netherlands', in point 1, the words 'For the purposes of applying Article 17 of the Regulation' shall be added at the beginning, with effect from 1 April 1990;

(i) in section 'L. United Kingdom':

(i) point 1 shall be replaced by the following:

'1. For the purposes of applying Articles 14c, 14d(3), 17, 36 and 63 of the Regulation and Articles 6(1), 8, 11(1), 11a(1), 12a, 13(2) and (3), 14(1), (2) and (3), 38(1), 70(1), 80(2), 81, 82(2), 91(2), 102(2), 109, 110 and 113(2) of the implementing Regulation:

Great Britain:

Department of Social Security (Overseas Branch), Newcastle-upon-Tyne NE98 1YX);

Northern Ireland (excluding Articles 36 and 63 of the Regulation and Articles 102(2) and 113(2) of the implementing Regulation, for which see Great Britain):

Department of Health and Social Services (Overseas Branch), Belfast BT1 5DP';

(ii) point 2 shall be replaced as follows:

'2 For the purposes of applying Articles 85(2), 86(2) and 89(1) of the implementing Regulation:

Great Britain:

Department of Social Security, Child Benefit Centre, Newcastle-upon-Tyne NE88 1AA;

Northern Ireland:

Department of Health and Social Services (Overseas Branch), Belfast BT1 5DP'.

Article 3

This Regulation shall enter into force on the day of its publication in the *Official Journal of the European Communities*.

This Regulation shall be binding in its entirety and directly applicable to all Member States.

Done at Luxembourg, 25 June 1991.

For the Council

The President

J.-C. Juncker

FOOTNOTES

1. OJ No C 221, 5.9.90, p.3.
2. OJ No C 19, 28.1.91, p.579.

3. OJ No C 41, 18.2.91, p.34.
4. OJ No L 149, 5.7.91, p.2.
5. OJ No L 74, 27.3.72, p.1.
6. OJ No L 230, 22.8.83, p.6.
7. OJ No L 331, 16.11.89, p.1.
8. OJ No L 224, 2.8.89, p.1.
9. OJ No L 355, 16.12.86, p.5.
10. Editorial note: Article 1 (1) to (11), details omitted.

(d) Persons (Independent means, retired, students)

COUNCIL DIRECTIVE

of 28 June 1990

on the right of residence

(90/364/EEC)

(OJ No L 180, 13.7.90, p.26)

The Council of the European Communities,

Having regard to the Treaty establishing the European Economic Community, and in particular Article 235 thereof,

Having regard to the proposal from the Commission[1],

Having regard to the opinion of the European Parliament[2],

Having regard to the opinion of the Economic and Social Committee[3],

Whereas Article 3(c) of the Treaty provides that the activities of the Community shall include, as provided in the Treaty, the abolition, as between Member States, of obstacles to freedom of movement for persons;

Whereas Article 8a of the Treaty provides that the internal market must be established by 31 December 1992; whereas the internal market comprises an area without internal frontiers in which the free movement of goods, persons, services and capital is ensured in accordance with the provisions of the Treaty;

Whereas national provisions on the right of nationals of the Member States to reside in a Member State other than their own must be harmonised to ensure such freedom of movement;

Whereas beneficiaries of the right of residence must not become an unreasonable burden on the public finances of the host Member State;

Whereas this right can only be genuinely exercised if it is also granted to members of the family;

Whereas the beneficiaries of this Directive should be covered by administrative arrangements similar to those laid down in particular in Directive 68/360/EEC[4] and Directive 64/221/EEC[5];

Whereas the Treaty does not provide, for the action concerned, powers other than those of Article 235,

Has adopted this Directive:

Article 1

1. Member States shall grant the right of residence to nationals of Member States who do not enjoy this right under other provisions of Community law and to members of their families as defined in paragraph 2, provided that they themselves and the members of their families are covered by sickness insurance in respect of all risks in the host Member State and have sufficient resources to avoid becoming a burden on the social assistance system of the host Member State during their period of residence.

The resources referred to in the first subparagraph shall be deemed sufficient where they are higher than the level of resources below which the host Member State may grant social assistance to its nationals, taking into account the personal circumstances of the applicant and, where appropriate, the personal circumstances of persons admitted pursuant to paragraph 2.

Where the second subparagraph cannot be applied in a Member State, the resources of the applicant shall be deemed sufficient if they are higher than the level of the minimum social security pension paid by the host Member State.

2. The following shall, irrespective of their nationality, have the right to install themselves in another Member State with the holder of the right of residence:

(a) his or her spouse and their descendants who are dependants;

(b) dependent relatives in the ascending line of the holder of the right of residence and his or her spouse.

Article 2

1. Exercise of the right of residence shall be evidenced by means of the

issue of a document known as a 'Residence permit for a national of a Member State of the EEC', the validity of which may be limited to five years on a renewable basis. However, the Member States may, when they deem it to be necessary, require revalidation of the permit at the end of the first two years of residence. Where a member of the family does not hold the nationality of a Member State, he or she shall be issued with a residence document of the same validity as that issued to the national on whom he or she depends.

For the purpose of issuing the residence permit or document, the Member State may require only that the applicant present a valid identity card or passport and provide proof that he or she meets the conditions laid down in Article 1.

2. Articles 2, 3, 6(1)(a) and (2) and Article 9 of Directive 68/360/EEC shall apply *mutatis mutandis* to the beneficiaries of this Directive.

The spouse and the dependent children of a national of a Member State entitled to the right of residence within the territory of a Member State shall be entitled to take up any employed or self-employed activity anywhere within the territory of that Member State, even if they are not nationals of a Member State.

Member States shall not derogate from the provisions of this Directive save on grounds of public policy, public security or public health. In that event, Directive 64/221/EEC shall apply.

3. This Directive shall not affect existing law on the acquisition of second homes.

Article 3

The right of residence shall remain for as long as beneficiaries of that right fulfil the conditions laid down in Article 1.

Article 4

The Commission shall, not more than three years after the date of implementation of this Directive, and at three-yearly intervals thereafter, draw up a report on the application of this Directive and submit it to the European Parliament and the Council.

Article 5

Member States shall bring into force the laws, regulations and administrative provisions necessary to comply with this Directive not later than 30 June 1992. They shall forthwith inform the Commission thereof.

Article 6

This Directive is addressed to the Member States.

Done at Luxembourg, 28 June 1990.

For the Council

The President

M. Geoghegan-Quinn

FOOTNOTES

1. OJ No C 191, 28.7.89, p.5; and OJ No C 26, 3.2.90, p.22.
2. OJ No C 175, 16.7.90, p.84.
3. OJ No C 329, 30.12.89, p.25.
4. OJ No L 257, 19.10.68, p.13.
5. OJ No 56, 4.4.64, p.850.

RL* Implemented in Ireland: S.I. 109S/1993.

COUNCIL DIRECTIVE

of 28 June 1990

on the right of residence for employees and self-employed persons who have ceased their occupational activity

(90/365/EEC)

(OJ No L 180, 13.7.90, p.28)

The Council of the European Communities,

Having regard to the Treaty establishing the European Economic Community, and in particular Article 235 thereof,

Having regard to the proposal from the Commission[1],

Having regard to the opinion of the European Parliament[2],

Having regard to the opinion of the Economic and Social Committee[3],

Whereas Article 3(c) of the Treaty provides that the activities of the Community shall include, as provided in the Treaty, the abolition, as between Member States, of obstacles to freedom of movement for persons;

Whereas Article 8a of the Treaty provides that the internal market must be established by 31 December 1992; whereas the internal market comprises an area without internal frontiers in which the free movement of goods, persons, services and capital is ensured, in accordance with the provisions of the Treaty;

Whereas Articles 48 and 52 of the Treaty provide for freedom of movement for workers and self-employed persons, which entails the right of residence in the Member States in which they pursue their occupational activity; whereas it is desirable that this right of residence also be granted to persons who have ceased their occupational activity even if they have not exercised their right to freedom of movement during their working life;

Whereas beneficiaries of the right of residence must not become an unreasonable burden on the public finances of the host Member State;

Whereas under Article 10 of Regulation (EEC) No 1408/71[4], as amended by Regulation (EEC) No 1390/81[5], recipients of invalidity or old age cash benefits or pensions for accidents at work or occupational diseases are entitled to continue to receive these benefits and pensions even if they reside in the territory of a Member State other than that in which the institution responsible for payment is situated;

Whereas this right can only be genuinely exercised if it is also granted to members of the family;

Whereas the beneficiaries of this Directive should be covered by administrative arrangements similar to those laid down in particular by Directive 68/630/EEC[6] and Directive 64/221/EEC[7];

Whereas the Treaty does not provide, for the action concerned, powers other than those of Article 235,

Has adopted this Directive:

Article 1

1. Member States shall grant the right of residence to nationals of Member States who have pursued an activity as an employee or self-employed person and to members of their families as defined in paragraph 2, provided that they are recipients of an invalidity or early retirement pension, or old age benefits, or of a pension in respect of an industrial accident or disease of an amount sufficient to avoid becoming a burden on the social security system of the host Member State during their period of residence and provided they are covered by sickness insurance in respect of all risks in the host Member State.

The resources of the applicant shall be deemed sufficient where they are

higher than the level of resources below which the host Member State may grant social assistance to its nationals, taking into account the personal circumstances of persons admitted pursuant to paragraph 2.

Where the second subparagraph cannot be applied in a Member State, the resources of the applicant shall be deemed sufficient if they are higher than the level of the minimum social security pension paid by the host Member State.

2. The following shall, irrespective of their nationality, have the right to install themselves in another Member State with the holder of the right of residence:

(a) his or her spouse and their descendants who are dependants;

(b) dependent relatives in the ascending line of the holder of the right of residence and his or her spouse.

Article 2

1. Exercise of the right of residence shall be evidenced by means of the issue of a document known as a 'Residence permit for a national of a Member State of the EEC', whose validity may be limited to five years on a renewable basis. However, the Member States may, when they deem it to be necessary, require revalidation of the permit at the end of the first two years of residence. Where a member of the family does not hold the nationality of a Member State, he or she shall be issued with a residence document of the same validity as that issued to the national on whom he or she depends.

For the purpose of issuing the residence permit or document, the Member State may require only that the applicant present a valid identity card or passport and provide proof that he or she meets the conditions laid down in Article 1.

2. Articles 2, 3, 6(1)(a) and (2) and Article 9 of Directive 68/360/EEC shall apply *mutatis mutandis* to the beneficiaries of this Directive.

The spouse and the dependent children of a national of a Member State entitled to the right of residence within the territory of a Member State shall be entitled to take up any employed or self-employed activity anywhere within the territory of that Member State, even if they are not nationals of a Member State.

Member States shall not derogate from the provisions of this Directive save on grounds of public policy, public security or public health. In that event, Directive 64/221/EEC shall apply.

3. This Directive shall not affect existing law on the acquisition of second homes.

Article 3

The right of residence shall remain for as long as beneficiaries of that right fulfil the conditions laid down in Article 1.

Article 4

The Commission shall, not more than three years after the date of implementation of this Directive, and at three-yearly intervals thereafter, draw up a report on the application of this Directive and submit it to the European Parliament and the Council.

Article 5

Member States shall bring into force the laws, regulations and administrative provisions necessary to comply with this Directive not later than 30 June 1992. They shall forthwith inform the Commission thereof.

Article 6

This Directive is addressed to the Member States.

Done at Luxembourg, 28 June 1990.

For the Council

The President

M. Geoghegan-Quinn

FOOTNOTES

1. OJ No C 191, 28.7.89, p.3; and OJ No C 26, 3.2.90, p.19.
2. OJ No C 175, 16.7.90, p.90.
3. OJ No C 329, 30.12.89, p.25.
4. OJ No L 149, 5.7.71, p.2.
5. OJ No L 143, 29.5.81, p.1.
6. OJ No L 257, 19.10.68, p.13.
7. OJ No 56, 4.4.64, p.850.

 Implemented in Ireland: S.I. 109/1993.

COUNCIL DIRECTIVE 93/96/EEC

of 29 October 1993

on the right of residence of students

(OJ No L 317, 18.12.93, p.59)

The Council of the European Communities,

Having regard to the Treaty establishing the European Economic Community, and in particular the second paragraph of Article 7 thereof,

Having regard to the proposal from the Commission[1],

In cooperation with the European Parliament[2],

Having regard to the opinion of the Economic and Social Committee[3],

Whereas Article 3(c) of the Treaty provides that the activities of the Community shall include, as provided in the Treaty, the abolition, as between Member States, of obstacles to freedom of movement for persons;

Whereas Article 8a of the Treaty provides that the internal market must be established by 31 December 1992; whereas the internal market comprises an area without internal frontiers in which the free movement of goods, persons, services and capital is ensured in accordance with the provisions of the Treaty;

Whereas, as the Court of Justice has held, Articles 128 and 7 of the Treaty prohibit any discrimination between nationals of the Member States as regards access to vocational training in the Community; whereas access by a national of one Member State to vocational training in another Member State implies, for that national, a right of residence in that other Member State;

Whereas, accordingly, in order to guarantee access to vocational training, the conditions likely to facilitate the effective exercise of that right of residence should be laid down;

Whereas the right of residence for students forms part of a set of related measures designed to promote vocational training;

Whereas beneficiaries of the right of residence must not become an unreasonable burden on the public finances of the host Member State;

Whereas, in the present state of Community law, as established by the case law of the Court of Justice, assistance granted to students, does not fall within the scope of the Treaty within the meaning of Article 7 thereof;

Whereas the right of residence can only be genuinely exercised if it is also granted to the spouse and their dependent children;

Whereas the beneficiaries of this Directive should be covered by administrative arrangements similar to those laid down in particular in Council Directive 68/360/EEC of 15 October 1968 on the abolition of restrictions on movement and residence within the Community for workers of Member States and their families[4] and Council Directive 64/221/EEC of 25 February 1964 on the coordination of special measures concerning the movement and residence of foreign nationals which are justified on grounds of public policy, public security or public health[5];

Whereas this Directive does not apply to students who enjoy the right of residence by virtue of the fact that they are or have been effectively engaged in economic activity or are members of the family of a migrant worker;

Whereas, by judgment of 7 July 1992 in Case C-295/90, the Court of Justice annulled Council Directive 90/366/EEC of 28 June 1990 on the right of residence for students[6], while maintaining the effects of the annulled Directive until the entry into force of a directive adopted on the appropriate legal basis;

Whereas the effects of Directive 90/366/EEC should be maintained during the period up to 31 December 1993, the date by which Member States are to have adopted the laws, regulations and administrative provisions necessary to comply with this Directive,

Has adopted this Directive:

Article 1

In order to lay down conditions to facilitate the exercise of the right of residence and with a view to guaranteeing access to vocational training in a non-discriminatory manner for a national of a Member State who has been accepted to attend a vocational training course in another Member State, the Member States shall recognise the right of residence for any student who is a national of a Member State and who does not enjoy that right under other provisions of Community law, and for the student's spouse and their dependent children, where the student assures the relevant national authority, by means of a declaration or by such alternative means as the student may choose that are at least equivalent, that he has sufficient resources to avoid becoming a burden on the social assistance system of the host Member State during their period of residence, provided that the student is enrolled in a recognised educational establishment for the principal purpose of following a vocational training course there and that is covered by sickness insurance in respect of all risks in the host Member State.

Article 2

1. The right of residence shall be restricted to the duration of the course of studies in question.

The right of residence shall be evidenced by means of the issue of a document known as a 'residence permit for a national of a Member State of the Community', the validity of which may be limited to the duration of the course of studies or to one year where the course lasts longer; in the latter event is shall be renewable annually. Where a member of the family does not hold the nationality of a Member State, he or she shall be issued with a residence document of the same validity as that issued to the national on whom he or she depends.

For the purpose of issuing the residence permit or document, the Member State may require only that the applicant present a valid identity card or passport and provide proof that he or she meets the conditions laid down in Article 1.

2. Articles 2, 3 and 9 of Directive 68/360/EEC shall apply *mutatis mutandis* to the beneficiaries of this Directive.

The spouse and the dependent children of a national of a Member State entitled to the right of residence within the territory of a Member State shall be entitled to take up any employed or self-employed activity anywhere within the territory of that Member State, even if they are not nationals of a Member State.

Member States shall not derogate from the provisions of this Directive save on grounds of public policy, public security or public health; in that event, Articles 2 to 9 of Directive 64/221/EEC shall apply.

Article 3

This Directive shall not establish any entitlement to the payment of maintenance grants by the host Member State on the part of students benefiting from the right of residence.

Article 4

The right of residence shall remain for as long as beneficiaries of that right fulfil the conditions laid down in Article 1.

Article 5

The Commission shall, not more than three years after the date of implementation of this Directive, and at three-yearly intervals thereafter, draw up a report on the application of this Directive and submit it to the European Parliament and the Council.

The Commission shall pay particular attention to any difficulties to which the implementation of Article 1 might give rise in the Member States; it shall, if appropriate, submit proposals to the Council with the aim of remedying such difficulties.

Article 6

Member States shall bring into force the laws, regulations and administrative provisions necessary to comply with this Directive not later than 31 December 1993. They shall forthwith inform the Commission thereof.

For the period preceding that date, the effects of Directive 90/366/EEC shall be maintained.

When Member States adopt those measures, they shall contain a reference to this Directive or shall be accompanied by such a reference on the occasion of their official publication. The methods of making such references shall be laid down by the Member States.

Article 7

This Directive is addressed to the Member States.

Done at Brussels, 29 October 1993.

For the Council

The President

R. Urbain

FOOTNOTES

1. OJ No C 166, 17.6.93, p.16.
2. OJ No C 255, 20.9.93, p.70 and OJ No C 315, 22.11.93.
3. OJ No C 304, 10.11.93, p.1.
4. OJ No L 257, 19.10.68, p.13. Directive as last amended by the Act of Accession of 1985.
5. OJ No 56, 4.4.64, p. 850.
6. OJ No L 180, 13.7.90, p. 30.

 Implemented in Ireland: Not yet implemented in Ireland (13.7.1994 – editorial note).

(e) Exclusion

COUNCIL DIRECTIVE

of 25 February 1964

on the co-ordination of special measures concerning the movement and residence of foreign nationals which are justified on grounds of public policy, public security or public health

(64/221/EEC)

(OJ No 56, 4.4.64, p. 850)

The Council of the European Economic Community,

Having regard to the Treaty establishing the European Economic Community, and in particular Article 56(2) thereof;

Having regard to Council Regulation No 15 of 16 August 1961[1] on initial measures to bring about free movement of workers within the Community, and in particular Article 47 thereof;

Having regard to Council Directive of 16 August 1961[2] on administrative procedures and practices governing the entry into and employment and residence in a Member State of workers and their families from other Member States of the Community;

Having regard to the General Programmes[3] for the abolition of restrictions on freedom of establishment and on freedom to provide services, and in particular Title II of each such programme;

Having regard to the Council Directive of 25 February 1964[4] on the abolition of restrictions on movement and residence within the Community for nationals of Member States with regard to establishment and the provision of services;

Having regard to the proposal from the Commission;

Having regard to the opinion of the European Parliament[5];

Having regard to the opinion of the Economic and Social Committee[6];

Whereas co-ordination of provisions laid down by law, regulation or administrative action which provide for special treatment for foreign nationals on grounds of public policy, public security or public health should in the first place deal with the conditions for entry and residence of nationals of Member States moving within the Community either in

order to purse activities as employed or self-employed persons, or as recipients of services;

Whereas such co-ordination presupposes in particular an approximation of the procedures followed in each Member State when invoking grounds of public policy, public security or public health in matters connected with the movement or residence of foreign nationals;

Whereas, in each Member State, nationals of other Member States should have adequate legal remedies available to them in respect of the decisions of the administration in such matters;

Whereas it would be of little practical use to compile a list of diseases and disabilities which might endanger public health, public policy or public security and it would be difficult to make such a list exhaustive; whereas it is sufficient to classify such diseases and disabilities in groups;

Has adopted this Directive:

Article 1

1. The provisions of this Directive shall apply to any national of a Member State who resides in or travels to another Member State of the Community, either in order to pursue an activity as an employed or self-employed person, or as a recipient of services.

2. These provisions shall apply also to the spouse and to members of the family who come within the provisions of the regulations and directives adopted in this field in pursuance of the Treaty.

Article 2

1. This Directive relates to all measures concerning entry into their territory, issue or renewal of residence permits, or expulsion from their territory, taken by Member States on grounds of public policy, public security or public health.

2. Such grounds shall not be invoked to service economic ends.

Article 3

1. Measures taken on grounds of public policy or of public security shall be based exclusively on the personal conduct of the individual concerned.

2. Previous criminal convictions shall not in themselves constitute grounds for the taking of such measures.

3. Expiry of the identity card or passport used by the person concerned

to enter the host country and to obtain a residence permit shall not justify expulsion from the territory.

4. The State which issued the identity card or passport shall allow the holder of such document to re-enter its territory without any formality even if the document is no longer valid or the nationality of the holder is in dispute.

Article 4

1. The only diseases or disabilities justifying refusal of entry into a territory or refusal to issue a first residence permit shall be those listed in the Annex to this Directive.

2. Diseases or disabilities occurring after a first residence permit has been issued shall not justify refusal to renew the residence permit or expulsion from the territory.

3. Member States shall not introduce new provisions or practices which are more restrictive than those in force at the date of notification of this Directive.

Article 5

1. A decision to grant or to refuse a first residence permit shall be taken as soon as possible and in any event not later than six months from the date of application for the permit.

The person concerned shall be allowed to remain temporarily in the territory pending a decision either to grant or to refuse a residence permit.

2. The host country may, in cases where this is considered essential, request the Member State of origin of the applicant, and if need be other Member States, to provide information concerning any previous police record. Such enquires shall not be made as a matter of routine. The Member State consulted shall give its reply within two months.

Article 6

The person concerned shall be informed of the grounds of public policy, public security, or public health upon which the decision taken in his case is based, unless this is contrary to the interests of the security of the State involved.

Article 7

The person concerned shall be officially notified of any decision to refuse the issue or renewal of a residence permit or to expel him from

the territory. The period allowed for leaving the territory shall be stated in this notification. Save in cases of urgency, this period shall be not less than fifteen days if the person concerned has not yet been granted a residence permit and not less than one month in all other cases.

Article 8

The person concerned shall have the same legal remedies in respect of any decision concerning entry, or refusing the issue or renewal of a residence permit, or ordering expulsion from the territory, as are available to nationals of the State concerned in respect of acts of the administration.

Article 9

1. Where there is no right of appeal to a court of law, or where such appeal may be only in respect of the legal validity of the decision, or where the appeal cannot have suspensory effect, a decision refusing renewal of a residence permit or ordering the expulsion of the holder of a residence permit from the territory shall not be taken by the administrative authority, save in cases of urgency, until an opinion has been obtained from a competent authority of the host country before which the person concerned enjoys such rights of defence and of assistance or representation as the domestic law of that country provides for.

This authority shall not be the same as that empowered to take the decision refusing renewal of the residence permit or ordering expulsion.

2. Any decision refusing the issue of a first residence permit or ordering expulsion of the person concerned before the issue of the permit shall, where that person so requests, be referred for consideration to the authority whose prior opinion is required under paragraph I. The person concerned shall then be entitled to submit his defence in person, except where this would be contrary to the interests of national security.

Article 10

1. Member States shall within six months of notification of this Directive put into force the measures necessary to comply with its provisions and shall forthwith inform the Commission thereof.

2. Member States shall ensure that the texts of the main provisions of national law which they adopt in the field governed by this Directive are communicated to the Commission.

Article 11

This Directive is addressed to the Member States.

Done at Brussels, 25 February 1964.

For the Council

The President

H. Fayat

Annex

A. Diseases which might endanger public health:

1. Diseases subject to quarantine listed in International Health Regulation No 2 of the World Health Organisation of 25 May 1951;

2. Tuberculosis of the respiratory system in an active state or showing a tendency to develop;

3. Syphilis;

4. Other infectious diseases or contagious parasitic diseases if they are the subject of provisions for the protection of nationals of the host country.

B. Diseases and disabilities which might threaten public policy or public security:

1. Drug addiction;

2. Profound mental disturbance; manifest conditions of psychotic disturbance with agitation, delirium, hallucinations or confusion.

FOOTNOTES

1. OJ No 57, 26.8.61, p. 1073.
2. OJ No 89, 13.12.61, p. 1513.
3. OJ No 2, 15.1.62, pp. 32 and 36.
4. OJ No 56, 4.4.64, p. 845.
5. OJ No 134, 14.12.62, p. 2861.
6. OJ No 56, 4.4.64 p. 856.

 Implemented in Ireland: S.I. 393/1977.

COUNCIL DIRECTIVE

of 17 December 1974

extending the scope of Directive No 64/221/EEC on the coordination of special measures concerning the movement and residence of foreign nationals which are justified on grounds of public policy, public security or public health to include nationals of a Member State who exercise the right to remain in the territory of another Member State after having pursued therein an activity in a self-employed capacity.

(75/35/EEC)

(OJ No L 14, 20.1.75, p.14)

The Council of the European Communities,

Having regard to the Treaty establishing the European Economic Community, and in particular Article 56(2) and Article 235 thereof;

Having regard to the proposal from the Commission;

Having regard to the opinion of the European Parliament[1];

Having regard to the opinion of the Economic and Social Committee[2];

Whereas Directive No 64/221/EEC[3] coordinated special measures concerning the movement and residence of foreign nationals which are justified on grounds of public policy, public security or public health and whereas Directive No 75/34/EEC[4] laid down conditions for the exercise of the right of nationals of a Member State to remain in the territory of another Member State after having pursued therein an activity in a self-employed capacity;

Whereas Directive No 64/221/EEC should therefore apply to persons to whom Directive No 75/34/EEC applies,

Has adopted this Directive:

Article 1

Directive No 64/221/EEC shall apply to nationals of Member States and members of their families who have the right to remain in the territory of a Member State pursuant to Directive No 75/34/EEC.

Article 2

Member States shall, within twelve months of notification of this Directive, bring into force the measures necessary to comply with its provisions and shall forthwith inform the Commission thereof.

Article 3

This Directive is addressed to the Member States.

Done at Brussels, 17 December 1974.

For the Council

The President

M. Durafour

FOOTNOTES

1. OJ No C 14, 27.3.73, p.21.
2. OJ No C 142, 31.12.72, p.10.
3. OJ No 56, 4.4.64, p.850-64.
4. OJ No L 14, 20.1.75, p.10.

IRL Implemented in Ireland: S.I. 393/1977.

(f) Recognition of Qualifications

COUNCIL DIRECTIVE

of 21 December 1988

on a general system for the recognition of higher-education diplomas awarded on completion of professional education and training of at least three years' duration

(89/48/EEC)

(OJ No L 19, 24.1.89, p. 16)

The Council of the European Communities,

Having regard to the Treaty establishing the European Economic Community, and in particular Articles 49, 57(1) and 66 thereof,

Having regard to the proposal from the Commission[1],

In cooperation with the European Parliament[2],

Having regard to the opinion of the Economic and Social Committee[3],

Whereas, pursuant to Article 3(c) of the Treaty the abolition, as between Member States, of obstacles to freedom of movement for persons and services constitutes one of the objectives of the Community; whereas, for nationals of the Member States, this means in particular the possibility of pursuing a profession, whether in a self-employed or employed capacity, in a Member State other than that in which they acquired their professional qualifications;

Whereas the provisions so far adopted by the Council, and pursuant to which Member States recognise mutually and for professional purposes higher-education diplomas issued within their territory, concern only a few professions; whereas the level and duration of the education and training governing access to those professions have been regulated in a similar fashion in all the Member States or have been the subject of the minimal harmonisation needed to establish sectoral systems for the mutual recognition of diplomas;

Whereas, in order to provide a rapid response to the expectations of nationals of Community countries who hold higher-education diplomas awarded on completion of professional education and training issued in a Member State other than that in which they wish to pursue their profession, another method of recognition of such diplomas should also be put in place such as to enable those concerned to pursue all those professional activities which in a host Member State are dependent on the completion of post-secondary education and training, provided they hold such a diploma preparing them for those activities awarded on completion of a course of studies lasting at least three years and issued in another Member State;

Whereas this objective can be achieved by the introduction of a general system for the recognition of higher-education diplomas awarded on completion of professional education and training of at least three years' duration;

Whereas, for those professions for the pursuit of which the Community has not laid down the necessary minimum level of qualification, Member States reserve the option of fixing such a level with a view to guaranteeing the quality of services provided in their territory; whereas, however, they may not, without infringing their obligations laid down in Article 5 of the Treaty, require a national of a Member State to obtain those qualifications which in general they determine only by reference to diplomas issued under their own national education systems, where the

person concerned has already acquired all or part of those qualifications in another Member State; whereas, as a result, any host Member State in which a profession is regulated is required to take account of qualifications acquired in another Member State and to determine whether those qualifications correspond to the qualifications which the Member State concerned requires;

Whereas collaboration between the Member States is appropriate in order to facilitate their compliance with those obligations; whereas, therefore, the means of organising such collaboration should be established;

Whereas the term 'regulated professional activity' should be defined so as to take account of differing national sociological situations; whereas the term should cover not only professional activities access to which is subject, in a Member State, to the possession of a diploma, but also professional activities, access to which is unrestricted when they are practised under a professional title reserved for the holders of certain qualifications; whereas the professional associations and organisations which confer such titles on their members and are recognised by the public authorities cannot invoke their private status to avoid application of the system provided for by this Directive;

Whereas it is also necessary to determine the characteristics of the professional experience or adaptation period which the host Member State may require of the person concerned in addition to the higher-education diploma, where the person's qualifications do not correspond to those laid down by national provisions;

Whereas an aptitude test may also be introduced in place of the adaptation period; whereas the effect of both will be to improve the existing situation with regard to the mutual recognition of diplomas between Member States and therefore to facilitate the free movement of persons within the Community; whereas their function is to assess the ability of the migrant, who is a person who has already received his professional training in another Member State, to adapt to this new professional environment; whereas, from the migrant's point of view, an aptitude test will have the advantage of reducing the length of the practice period; whereas, in principle, the choice between the adaptation period and the aptitude test should be made by the migrant; whereas, however, the nature of certain professions is such that Member States must be allowed to prescribe, under certain conditions, either the adaptation period or the test; whereas, in particular, the differences between the legal systems of the Member States, whilst they may vary in extent from one Member State to another, warrant special provisions since, as a rule, the education or training attested by the diploma,

certificate or other evidence of formal qualifications in a field of law in the Member State of origin does not cover the legal knowledge required in the host Member State with respect to the corresponding legal field;

Whereas, moreover, the general system for the recognition of higher-education diplomas is intended neither to amend the rules, including those relating to professional ethics, applicable to any person pursuing a profession in the territory of a Member State nor to exclude migrants from the application of those rules; whereas that system is confined to laying down appropriate arrangements to ensure that migrants comply with the professional rules of the host Member State;

Whereas Articles 49,57(1) and 66 of the Treaty empower the Community to adopt provisions necessary for the introduction and operation of such a system;

Whereas the general system for the recognition of higher-education diplomas is entirely without prejudice to the application of Article 48(4) and Article 55 of the Treaty;

Whereas such a system, by strengthening the right of a Community national to use his professional skills in any Member State, supplements and reinforces his right to acquire such skills wherever he wishes;

Whereas this system should be evaluated, after being in force for a certain time, to determine how efficiently it operates and in particular how it can be improved or its field of application extended,

Has adopted this Directive:

Article 1

For the purposes of this Directive the following definitions shall apply:

(a) diploma: any diploma, certificate or other evidence of formal qualifications or any set of such diplomas, certificates or other evidence:

- which has been awarded by a competent authority in a Member State, designated in accordance with its own laws, regulations or administrative provisions;

- which shows that the holder has successfully completed a post-secondary course of at least three years' duration, or of an equivalent duration part-time, at a university or establishment of higher education or another establishment of similar level and, where appropriate, that he has successfully completed the professional training required in addition to the post-secondary course, and

- which shows that the holder has the professional qualifications required for the taking up or pursuit of a regulated profession in that Member State,

provided that the education and training attested by the diploma, certificate or other evidence of formal qualifications were received mainly in the Community, or the holder thereof has three years' professional experience certified by the Member State which recognised a third-country diploma, certificate or other evidence of formal qualifications.

The following shall be treated in the same way as a diploma, within the meaning of the first subparagraph: any diploma, certificate or other evidence of formal qualifications or any set of such diplomas, certificates or other evidence awarded by a competent authority in a Member State if it is awarded on the successful completion of education and training received in the Community and recognised by a competent authority in that Member State as being of an equivalent level and if it confers the same rights in respect of the taking up and pursuit of a regulated profession in that Member State;

(b) host Member State: any Member State in which a national of a Member State applies to pursue a profession subject to regulation in that Member State, other than the State in which he obtained his diploma or first pursued the profession in question;

(c) a regulated profession: the regulated professional activity or range of activities which constitute this profession in a Member State;

(d) regulated professional activity: a professional activity, in so far as the taking up or pursuit of such activity or one of its modes of pursuit in a Member State is subject, directly or indirectly by virtue of laws, regulations or administrative provisions, to the possession of a diploma. The following in particular shall constitute a mode of pursuit of a regulated professional activity:

- pursuit of an activity under a professional title, in so far as the use of such a title is reserved to the holders of a diploma governed by laws, regulations or administrative provisions,

- pursuit of a professional activity relating to health, in so far as remuneration and/or reimbursement for such an activity is subject by virtue of national social security arrangements to the possession of a diploma.

Where the first subparagraph does not apply, a professional activity shall be deemed to be a regulated professional activity if it is

pursued by the members of an association or organisation the purpose of which is, in particular, to promote and maintain a high standard in the professional field concerned and which, to achieve that purpose, is recognised in a special form by a Member State and:

- awards a diploma to its members,

- ensures that its members respect the rules of professional conduct which it prescribes, and

- confers on them the right to use a title or designatory letters, or to benefit from a status corresponding to that diploma.

A non-exhaustive list of associations or organisations which, when this Directive is adopted, satisfy the conditions of the second subparagraph is contained in the Annex. Whenever a Member State grants the recognition referred to in the second subparagraph to an association or organisation, it shall inform the Commission thereof, which shall publish this information in the *Official Journal of the European Communities*;

(e) professional experience: the actual and lawful pursuit of the profession concerned in a Member State;

(f) adaptation period: the pursuit of a regulated profession in the host Member State under the responsibility of a qualified member of that profession, such period of supervised practice possibly being accompanied by further training. This period of supervised practice shall be the subject of an assessment. The detailed rules governing the adaptation period and its assessment as well as the status of a migrant person under supervision shall be laid down by the competent authority in the host Member States;

(g) aptitude test: a test limited to the professional knowledge of the applicant, made by the competent authorities of the host Member State with the aim of assessing the ability of the applicant to pursue a regulated profession in that Member State.

In order to permit this test to be carried out, the competent authorities shall draw up a list of subjects which, on the basis of a comparison of the education and training required in the Member State and that received by the applicant, are not covered by the diploma or other evidence of formal qualifications possessed by the applicant.

The aptitude test must take account of the fact that the applicant is a qualified professional in the Member State of origin or the Member State from which he comes. It shall cover subjects to be selected from those on the list, knowledge of which is essential in order to be

able to exercise the profession in the host Member State. The test may also include knowledge of the professional rules applicable to the activities in question in the host Member State. The detailed application of the aptitude test shall be determined by the competent authorities of that State with due regard to the rules of Community law.

The status, in the host Member State, of the applicant who wishes to prepare himself for the aptitude test in that State shall be determined by the competent authorities in that State.

Article 2

This Directive shall apply to any national of a Member State wishing to pursue a regulated profession in a host Member State in a self-employed capacity or as an employed person.

This Directive shall not apply to professions which are the subject of a separate Directive establishing arrangements for the mutual recognition of diplomas by Member States.

Article 3

Where, in a host Member State, the taking up or pursuit of a regulated profession is subject to possession of a diploma, the competent authority may not, on the grounds of inadequate qualifications, refuse to authorise a national of a Member State to take up or pursue that profession on the same conditions as apply to its own nationals:

(a) if the applicant holds the diploma required in another Member State for the taking up or pursuit of the profession in question in its territory, such diploma having been awarded in a Member State; or

(b) if the applicant has pursued the profession in question full-time for two years during the previous ten years in another Member State which does not regulate that profession, within the meaning of Article 1(c) and the first subparagraph of Article 1(d), and possesses evidence of one or more formal qualifications:

– which have been awarded by a competent authority in a Member State, designated in accordance with the laws, regulations or administrative provisions of such State,

– which show that the holder has successfully completed a post-secondary course of at least three years' duration, or of an equivalent duration part-time, at a university or establishment of higher education or another establishment of similar level of a Member State and, where appropriate, that he has successfully

completed the professional training required in addition to the post-secondary course and

- which have prepared the holder for the pursuit of his profession.

The following shall be treated in the same way as the evidence of formal qualifications referred to in the first subparagraph: any formal qualifications or any set of such formal qualifications awarded by a competent authority in a Member State if it is awarded on the successful completion of training received in the Community and is recognised by that Member State as being of an equivalent level, provided that the other Member States and the Commission have been notified of this recognition.

Article 4

1. Notwithstanding Article 3, the host Member State may also require the applicant:

(a) to provide evidence of professional experience, where the duration of the education and training adduced in support of his application, as laid down in Article 3(a) and (b), is at least one year less than that required in the host Member State. In this event, the period of professional experience required:

- may not exceed twice the shortfall in duration of education and training where the shortfall relates to post-secondary studies and/or to a period of probationary practice carried out under the control of a supervising professional person and ending with an examination,

- may not exceed the shortfall where the shortfall relates to professional practice acquired with the assistance of a qualified member of the profession.

In the case of diplomas within the meaning of the last subparagraph of Article 1(a), the duration of education and training recognised as being of an equivalent level shall be determined as for the education and training defined in the first subparagraph of Article 1(a).

When applying these provisions, account must be taken of the professional experience referred to in Article 3(b).

At all events, the professional experience required may not exceed four years;

(b) to complete an adaptation period not exceeding three years or take an aptitude test:

- where the matters covered by the education and training he has

received as laid down in Article 3(a) and (b), differ substantially from those covered by the diploma required in the host Member State, or

- where, in the case referred to in Article 3(a), the profession regulated in the host Member State comprises one or more regulated professional activities which are not in the profession regulated in the Member State from which the applicant originates or comes and that difference corresponds to specific education and training required in the host Member State and covers matters which differ substantially from those covered by the diploma adduced by the applicant, or

- where, in the case referred to in Article 3(b), the profession regulated in the host Member State comprises one or more regulated professional activities which are not in the profession pursued by the applicant in the Member State from which he originates or comes, and that difference corresponds to specific education and training required in the host Member State and covers matters which differ substantially from those covered by the evidence of formal qualifications adduced by the applicant.

Should the host Member State make use of this possibility, it must give the applicant the right to choose between an adaptation period and an aptitude test. By way of derogation from this principle, for professions whose practice requires precise knowledge of national law and in respect of which the provision of advice and/or assistance concerning national law is an essential and constant aspect of the professional activity, the host Member State may stipulate either an adaptation period or an aptitude test. Where the host Member State intends to introduce derogations for other professions as regards an applicant's right to choose, the procedure laid down in Article 10 shall apply.

2. However, the host Member State may not apply the provisions of paragraph 1(a) and (b) cumulatively.

Article 5

Without prejudice to Articles 3 and 4, a host Member State may allow the applicant, with a view to improving his possibilities of adapting to the professional environment in that State, to undergo there, on the basis of equivalence, that part of his professional education and training represented by professional practice, acquired with the assistance of a qualified member of the profession, which he has not undergone in his Member State of origin or the Member State from which he has come.

Article 6

1. Where the competent authority of a host Member State requires of persons wishing to take up a regulated profession proof that they are of good character or repute or that they have not been declared bankrupt, or suspends or prohibits the pursuit of that profession in the event of serious professional misconduct or a criminal offence, that State shall accept as sufficient evidence, in respect of nationals of Member States wishing to pursue that profession in its territory, the production of documents issued by competent authorities in the Member State of origin or the Member State from which the foreign national comes showing that those requirements are met.

Where the competent authorities of the Member State of origin or of the Member State from which the foreign national comes do not issue the documents referred to in the first subparagraph, such documents shall be replaced by a declaration on oath – or, in States where there is no provision for declaration on oath, by a solemn declaration – made by the person concerned before a competent judicial or administrative authority or, where appropriate, a notary or qualified professional body of the Member State of origin or the Member State from which the person comes; such authority or notary shall issue a certificate attesting the authenticity of the declaration on oath or solemn declaration.

2. Where the competent authority of a host Member State requires of nationals of that Member State wishing to take up or pursue a regulated profession a certificate of physical or mental health, that authority shall accept as sufficient evidence in this respect the production of the document required in the Member State of origin or the Member State from which the foreign national comes.

Where the Member State of origin or the Member State from which the foreign national comes does not impose any requirements of this nature on those wishing to take up or pursue the profession in question, the host Member State shall accept from such nationals a certificate issued by a competent authority in that State corresponding to the certificates issued in the host Member State.

3. The competent authorities of host Member States may require that the documents and certificates referred to in paragraphs 1 and 2 are presented no more than three months after their date of issue.

4. Where the competent authority of a host Member State requires nationals of that Member State wishing to take up or pursue a regulated profession to take an oath or make a solemn declaration and where the form of such oath or declaration cannot be used by nationals of other Member States, that authority shall ensure that an appropriate and

equivalent form of oath or declaration is offered to the person concerned.

Article 7

1. The competent authorities of host Member States shall recognise the right of nationals of Member States who fulfil the conditions for the taking up and pursuit of a regulated profession in their territory to use the professional title of the host Member State corresponding to that profession.

2. The competent authorities of host Member States shall recognise the right of nationals of Member States who fulfil the conditions for the taking up and pursuit of a regulated profession in their territory to use their lawful academic title and, where appropriate, the abbreviation thereof deriving from their Member State of origin or the Member State from which they come, in the language of that State. Host Member State may require this title to be followed by the name and location of the establishment or examining board which awarded it.

3. Where a profession is regulated in the host Member State by an association or organisation referred to in Article 1(d), nationals of Member States shall only be entitled to use the professional title or designatory letters conferred by that organisation or association on proof of membership.

Where the association or organisation makes membership subject to certain qualification requirements, it may apply these to nationals of other Member States who are in possession of a diploma within the meaning of Article 1(a) or a formal qualification within the meaning of Article 3(b) only in accordance with this Directive, in particular Articles 3 and 4.

Article 8

1. The host Member State shall accept as proof that the conditions laid down in Articles 3 and 4 are satisfied the certificates and documents issued by the competent authorities in the Member States, which the person concerned shall submit in support of his application to pursue the profession concerned.

2. The procedure for examining an application to pursue a regulated profession shall be completed as soon as possible and the outcome communicated in a reasoned decision of the competent authority in the host Member State not later than four months after presentation of all the documents relating to the person concerned. A remedy shall be

available against this decision, or the absence thereof, before a court or tribunal in accordance with the provisions of national law.

Article 9

1. Member States shall designate, within the period provided for in Article 12, the competent authorities empowered to receive the applications and take the decisions referred to in this Directive.

They shall communicate this information to the other Member States and to the Commission.

2. Each Member State shall designate a person responsible for coordinating the activities of the authorities referred to in paragraph 1 and shall inform the other Member States and the Commission to that effect. His role shall be to promote uniform application of this Directive to all the professions concerned. A coordinating group shall be set up under the aegis of the Commission, composed of the coordinators appointed by each Member State or their deputies and chaired by a representative of the Commission.

The task of this group shall be:

– to facilitate the implementation of this Directive,

– to collect all useful information for its application in the Member States.

The group may be consulted by the Commission on any changes to the existing system that may contemplated (sic).

3. Member States shall take measures to provide the necessary information on the recognition of diplomas within the framework of this Directive. They may be assisted in this task by the information centre on the academic recognition of diplomas and periods of study established by the Member States within the framework of the Resolution of the Council and the Ministers of Education meeting within the Council of 9 February 1976[4], and, where appropriate, the relevant professional associations or organisations. The Commission shall take the necessary initiatives to ensure the development and coordination of the communication of the necessary information.

Article 10

1. If, pursuant to the third sentence of the second subparagraph of Article 4(1)(b), a Member State proposes not to grant applicants the right to choose between an adaptation period and an aptitude test in respect of a profession within the meaning of this Directive, it shall immediately communicate to the Commission the corresponding draft

provision. It shall at the same time notify the Commission of the grounds which make the enactment of such a provision necessary.

The Commission shall immediately notify the other Member States of any draft it has received; it may also consult the coordinating group referred to in Article 9(2) of the draft.

2. Without prejudice to the possibility for the Commission and the other Member States of making comments on the draft, the Member State may adopt the provision only if the Commission has not taken a decision to the contrary within three months.

3. At the request of a Member State or the Commission, Member States shall communicate to them, without delay, the definitive text of a provision arising from the application of this Article.

Article 11

Following the expiry of the period provided for in Article 12, Member States shall communicate to the Commission, every two years, a report on the application of the system introduced.

In addition to general remarks, this report shall contain a statistical summary of the decisions taken and a description of the main problems arising from application of the Directive.

Article 12

Member States shall take the measures necessary to comply with this Directive within two years of its notification[5]. They shall forthwith inform the Commission thereof.

Member States shall communicate to the Commission the texts of the main provisions of national law which they adopt in the field governed by this Directive.

Article 13

Five years at the latest following the date specified in Article 12, the Commission shall report to the European Parliament and the Council on the state of application of the general system for the recognition of higher-education diplomas awarded on completion of professional education and training of at least three years' duration.

After conducting all necessary consultations, the Commission shall, on this occasion, present its conclusions as to any changes that need to be made to the system as it stands. At the same time the Commission shall, where appropriate, submit proposals for improvements in the present system in the interest of further facilitating the freedom of movement,

right of establishment and freedom to provide services of the persons covered by this Directive.

Article 14

This Directive is addressed to the Member States.

Done at Brussels, 21 December 1988.

For the Council

The President

V. Papandreou

Annex

List of professional associations or organisations which satisfy the conditions of the second subparagraph of Article 1(d)

Ireland[6]

1. The Institute of Chartered Accountants in Ireland[7]

2. The Institute of Certified Public Accountants in Ireland[7]

3. The Association of Certified Accountants[7]

4. Institution of Engineers of Ireland

5. Irish Planning Institute

United Kingdom

1. Institute of Chartered Accountants in England and Wales

2. Institute of Chartered Accountants of Scotland

3. Institute of Chartered Accountants in Ireland

4. Chartered Association of Certified Accountants

5. Chartered Institute of Loss Adjusters

6. Chartered Institute of Management Accountants

7. Institute of Chartered Secretaries and Administrators

8. Chartered Insurance Institute

9. Institute of Actuaries

10. Faculty of Actuaries

11. Chartered Institute of Bankers

12. Institute of Bankers in Scotland

13. Royal Institution of Chartered Surveyors

14. Royal Town Planning Institute

15. Chartered Society of Physiotherapy

16. Royal Society of Chemistry

17. British Psychological Society

18. Library Association

19. Institute of Chartered Foresters

20. Chartered Institute of Building

21. Engineering Council

22. Institute of Energy

23. Institution of Structural Engineers

24. Institution of Civil Engineers

25. Institution of Mining Engineers

26. Institution of Mining and Metallurgy

27. Institution of Electrical Engineers

28. Institution of Gas Engineers

29. Institution of Mechanical Engineers

30. Institution of Chemical Engineers

31. Institution of Production Engineers

32. Institution of Marine Engineers

33. Royal Institution of Naval Architects

34. Royal Aeronautical Society

35. Institute of Metals

36. Chartered Institution of Building Services Engineers

37. Institute of Measurement and Control

38. British Computer Society

Statement by the Council and the Commission

Re Article 9(1)

'The Council and the Commission agree that professional bodies and higher-education establishments should be consulted or be involved in an appropriate way in the decision-making process'

FOOTNOTES

1. OJ No C 217, 28.8.85, p.3, and OJ No C 143, 10.6.86, p.7.
2. OJ No C 345, 31.12.85, p.80, and OJ No C 309, 5.12.88.
3. OJ No C 75, 3.4.86, p.5.
4. OJ No C 38, 19.2.76, p.1.
5. This Directive was notified to Member States on 4 January 1989.
6. Irish nationals are also members of the following United Kingdom chartered bodies:
   Institute of Chartered Accountants in England and Wales
   Institute of Chartered Accountants of Scotland
   Institute of Actuaries
   Faculty of Actuaries
   The Chartered Institute of Management Accountants
   Institute of Chartered Secretaries and Administrators
   Royal Town Planning Institute
   Royal Institution of Chartered Surveyors
   Chartered Institute of Building.
7. For the purposes of the activity of auditing only.

 Implemented in Ireland: S.I. 1/1991.

COUNCIL DIRECTIVE 92/51/EEC

of 18 June 1992

on a second general system for the recognition of professional education and training to supplement Directive 89/48/EEC

(OJ No L 209, 24.7.92, p. 25)

The Council of the European Communities,

Having regard to the Treaty establishing the European Economic Community, particularly Articles 49, 57(1) and 66 thereof,

Having regard to the proposal from the Commission[1],

In cooperation with the European Parliament[2],

Having regard to the opinion of the Economic and Social Committee[3],

(1) Whereas, pursuant to Article 8a of the Treaty, the internal market shall comprise an area without internal frontiers and whereas, pursuant to

Article 3(c) of the Treaty, the abolition, as between Member States, of obstacles to freedom of movement for persons and services constitutes one of the objectives of the Community; whereas, for nationals of the Member States, this means in particular the possibility of pursuing a profession, whether in a self-employed or employed capacity, in a Member State other than that in which they acquired their professional qualifications;

(2) Whereas, for those professions for the pursuit of which the Community has not laid down the necessary minimum level of qualification, Member States reserve the option of fixing such a level with a view to guaranteeing the quality of services provided in their territory; whereas, however, they may not, without disregarding their obligations laid down in Articles 5, 48, 52 and 59 of the Treaty, require a national of a Member State to obtain those qualifications which in general they determine only by reference to those issued under their own national education and training systems, where the person concerned has already acquired all or part of those qualifications in another Member State; whereas, as a result, any host Member State in which a profession is regulated is required to take account of qualifications acquired in another Member State and to determine whether those qualifications correspond to the qualifications which the Member State concerned requires;

(3) Whereas Council Directive 89/48/EEC of 21 December 1988 on a general system for the recognition of higher education diplomas awarded on completion of professional education and training of at least three years' duration[4] facilitates compliance with such obligations; whereas, however, it is limited to higher education;

(4) Whereas, in order to facilitate the pursuit of all those professional activities which in a host Member State are dependent on the completion of a certain level of education and training, a second general system should be introduced to complement the first;

(5) Whereas the complementary general system must be based on the same principles and contain *mutatis mutandis* the same rules as the initial general system;

(6) Whereas this Directive is not applicable to those regulated professions which are covered by specific Directives principally concerned with introducing mutual recognition of training courses completed before entry into professional life;

(7) Whereas neither is it applicable, furthermore, to those activities covered by specific Directives principally intended to introduce recognition of technical skills based on experience acquired in another

Member State; whereas certain of those Directives apply solely to the pursuit of activities in a self-employed capacity; whereas, in order to ensure that the pursuit of such activities as an employed person does not fall within the scope of this Directive, whereby the pursuit of the same activity would be subject to different legal recognition arrangements depending on whether it was pursued in a self-employed capacity or as an employed person, those Directives should be made applicable to persons pursuing the activities in question as employed persons;

(8) Whereas the complementary general system is entirely without prejudice to the application of Article 48(4) and Article 55 of the Treaty;

(9) Whereas this complementary system must cover the levels of education and training not covered by the initial general system, namely that corresponding to other post-secondary education and training courses and other equivalent education and training, and that corresponding to long or short secondary courses, possibly complemented by professional training or experience;

(10) Whereas, where in most Member States pursuit of a given regulated profession is subject to either very short training or the possession of certain personal attributes or merely general knowledge, the normal mechanisms for recognition under this Directive may be excessively cumbersome; whereas in such cases there should be provision for simplified mechanisms;

(11) Whereas account should also be taken of the professional training system in the United Kingdom whereby standards for levels of performance for all professional activities are established via the 'National Framework of Vocational Qualifications';

(12) Whereas in some Member States there are only relatively few regulated professions; whereas, however, training for professions which are not regulated may be specifically geared to the pursuit of the profession, with the structure and level of training being monitored or approved by the competent authorities of the Member State concerned; whereas this provides guarantees equivalent to those provided in connection with a regulated profession;

(13) Whereas the competent authorities of the host Member State should be allowed to determine, in accordance with the relevant provisions of Community law, the detailed rules necessary for implementation of the adaptation period and the aptitude test;

(14) Whereas, since it covers two levels of education and training and since the initial general system covers a third level, the complementary general system must lay down whether and under what conditions a

person possessing a certain level of education and training may pursue, in another Member State, a profession the qualifications for which are regulated at a different level;

(15) Whereas, for the pursuit of certain professions, certain Member States require the possession of a diploma within the meaning of Directive 89/48/EEC, while for the same profession other Member States require the completion of professional education or training with a different structure; whereas certain kinds of education and training, while not of a post-secondary nature of minimum duration within the meaning of this Directive, nevertheless result in a comparable professional level and prepare the person for similar responsibilities and activities; whereas such education and training should therefore be classed in the same category as that attested by a diploma; whereas such education and training is very varied and this classification can be achieved only by listing the courses in question; whereas such classification would, where appropriate, establish the recognition of equivalence between such education and training and that covered by Directive 89/48/EEC; whereas some regulated education and training should also be classed at diploma level in a second list;

(16) Whereas, in view of the constantly changing organisation of professional training, there should be a procedure for amending those lists;

(17) Whereas, since it covers occupations the pursuit of which is dependent on the possession of professional or vocational education and training qualifications of secondary level and generally requires manual skills, the complementary general system must also provide for the recognition of such qualifications even where they have been acquired solely through professional experience in a Member State which does not regulate such professions;

(18) Whereas the aim of this general system, like the first general system, is to eliminate obstacles to the taking up and pursuit of regulated professions; whereas work carried out pursuant to Council Decision 85/368/EEC of 16 July 1985 on the comparability of vocational training qualifications between the Member States of the European Community[5], while pursuing a different objective from the elimination of legal obstacles to freedom of movement, namely that of improving the transparency of the labour market, must be used, where appropriate, in the application of this Directive, particularly where it could provide information on the subject, content and duration of professional training;

(19) Whereas professional bodies and professional educational and

training establishments should, where appropriate, be consulted or be involved in an appropriate way in the decision-making process;

(20) Whereas, like the initial system, such a system, by strengthening the right of a Community national to use his occupational skills in any Member State, supplements and reinforces his right to acquire such skills wherever he wishes;

(21) Whereas the two systems should be evaluated, after a certain period of application, in order to determine how efficiently they operate and, in particular, how they can both be improved,

Has adopted this Directive:

Chapter I

Definitions

Article 1

For the purposes of this Directive, the following definitions shall apply:

(a) *diploma*: any evidence of education and training or any set of such evidence:

    – which has been awarded by a competent authority in a Member State, designated in accordance with the laws, regulations or administrative provisions of that State,

    – which shows that the holder has successfully completed:

      (i) either a post-secondary course other than that referred to in the second indent of Article 1(a) of Directive 89/48/EEC, of at least one year's duration or of equivalent duration on a part-time basis, one of the conditions of entry of which is, as a general rule, the successful completion of the secondary course required to obtain entry to university or higher education, as well as the professional training which may be required in addition to that post-secondary course;

      (ii) or one of the education and training courses in Annex C, and:

    – which shows that the holder has the professional qualifications required for the taking up or pursuit of a regulated profession in that Member State,

    provided that the education and training attested by this evidence was received mainly in the Community, or outside the Community at teaching establishments which provide education and training in accordance with the laws, regulations or administrative provisions of

pursue a regulated profession in a host Member State in a self-employed capacity or as an employed person.

This Directive shall apply to neither professions which are the subject of a specific Directive establishing arrangements for the mutual recognition of diplomas by Member States, nor activities covered by a Directive listed in Annex A.

The Directives listed in Annex B shall be made applicable to the pursuit as an employed person of the activities covered by those Directives.

Chapter III

System for recognition where a host Member State requires possession of a diploma within the meaning of this Directive or Directive 89/48/EEC

Article 3

Without prejudice to Directive 89/48/EEC, where, in a host Member State, the taking up or pursuit of a regulated profession is subject to possession of a diploma, as defined in this Directive or in Directive 89/48/EEC, the competent authority may not, on the grounds of inadequate qualifications, refuse to authorise a national of a Member State to take up or pursue that profession on the same conditions as those which apply to its own nationals:

(a) if the applicant holds the diploma, as defined in this Directive or in Directive 89/48/EEC, required in another Member State for the taking up or pursuit of the profession in question in its territory, such diploma having been awarded in a Member State; or

(b) if the applicant has pursued the profession in question full-time for two years, or for an equivalent period on a part-time basis, during the previous 10 years in another Member State which does not regulate that profession within the meaning of either Article 1(e) and the first subparagraph of Article 1(f) of this Directive or Article 1(c) and the first subparagraph of Article 1(d) of Directive 89/48/EEC, and possesses evidence of education and training which:

- has been awarded by a competent authority in a Member State, designated in accordance with the laws, regulations or administrative provisions of that State, and

- either shows that the holder has successfully completed a post-secondary course, other than that referred to in the second indent of Article 1(a) of Directive 89/48/EEC, of at least one year's duration, or of equivalent duration on a part-time basis,

one of the conditions of entry of which is, as a general rule, the successful completion of the secondary course required to obtain entry to university or higher education, as well as any professional training which is an integral part of that post-secondary course,

- — or attests to regulated education and training referred to in Annex D, and

- — has prepared the holder for the pursuit of his profession.

However, the two years' professional experience referred to above may not be required where the evidence of education and training held by the applicant and referred to in this point is awarded on completion of regulated education and training.

The following shall be treated in the same way as the evidence of education and training referred to in the first subparagraph of this point: any evidence of education and training or any set of such evidence awarded by a competent authority in a Member State if it is awarded on the completion of education and training received in the Community and is recognised by that Member State as being of an equivalent level, provided that the other Member States and the Commission have been notified of this recognition.

By way of derogation from the first subparagraph of this Article, the host Member State is not required to apply this Article where the taking up or pursuit of a regulated profession is subject in its country to possession of a diploma as defined in Directive 89/48/EEC, one of the conditions for the issue of which shall be the completion of a post-secondary course of more than four years' duration.

Article 4

1. Notwithstanding Article 3, the host Member State may also require the applicant:

(a) to provide evidence of professional experience, where the duration of the education and training adduced in support of his application, as laid down in points (a) and (b) of the first subparagraph of Article 3, is at least one year less than that required in the host Member State. In this event, the period of professional experience required may not exceed:

- — twice the shortfall in duration of education and training where the shortfall relates to a post-secondary course and/or to a period of probationary practice carried out under the control of a supervising professional person and ending with an examination,

- the shortfall where the shortfall relates to professional practice acquired with the assistance of a qualified member of the profession concerned.

In the case of diplomas within the meaning of the second subparagraph of Article 1(a), the duration of education and training recognised as being of an equivalent level shall be determined as for the education and training defined in the first subparagraph of Article 1(a).

When these provisions are applied, account must be taken of the professional experience referred to in point (b) of the first subparagraph of Article 3.

In any event, the professional experience required may not exceed four years.

Professional experience may not, however, be required of an applicant holding a diploma attesting to a post-secondary course as referred to in the second indent of Article 1(a) or a diploma as defined in Article 1(a) of Directive 89/48/EEC who wishes to pursue his profession in a host Member State which requires the possession of a diploma or evidence of education and training attesting to one of the courses of education and training as referred to in Annexes C and D;

(b) to complete an adaptation period not exceeding three years or take an aptitude test where:

- the theoretical and/or practical matters covered by the education and training which he has received as laid down in points (a) or (b) of the first subparagraph of Article 3 differ substantially from those covered by the diploma, as defined in this Directive or in Directive 89/48/EEC, required in the host Member State, or

- in the case referred to in point (a) of the first subparagraph of Article 3, the profession regulated in the host Member State comprises one or more regulated professional activities which do not form part of the profession regulated in the Member State from which the applicant originates or comes and that difference corresponds to specific education and training required in the host Member State and covers theoretical and/or practical matters which differ substantially from those covered by the diploma, as defined in this Directive or in Directive 89/48/EEC, adduced by the applicant, or

- in the case referred to in point (b) of the first subparagraph of Article 3, the profession regulated in the host Member State comprises one or more regulated professional activities which do

not form part of the profession pursued by the applicant in the Member State from which he originates or comes, and that difference corresponds to specific education and training required in the host Member State and covers theoretical and/or practical matters which differ substantially from those covered by the evidence of education and training adduced by the applicant.

Should the Member State make use of this possibility, it must give the applicant the right to choose between an adaptation period and an aptitude test. Where the host Member State, which requires a diploma as defined in Directive 89/48/EEC or in this Directive, intends to introduce derogations from an applicant's right to choose, the procedure laid down in Article 14 shall apply.

By way of derogation from the second subparagraph of this point, the host Member State may reserve the right to choose between the adaptation period and the aptitude test if

– a profession is involved the pursuit of which requires a precise knowledge of national law and in respect of which the provision of advice and/or assistance concerning national law is an essential and constant feature of the professional activity, or

– where the host Member State makes access to the profession or its pursuit subject to the possession of a diploma as defined in Directive 89/48/EEC, one of the conditions for the award of which is the completion of a post-secondary course of at least three years' duration or an equivalent period on a part-time basis and the applicant holds either a diploma as defined in this Directive or evidence of education and training within the meaning of point (b) of the first subparagraph of Article 3 and not covered by Article 3(b) of Directive 89/48/EEC.

2. However, the host Member State may not apply the provisions of paragraph 1(a) and (b) cumulatively.

Chapter IV

System for recognition where a host Member State requires possession of a diploma and the applicant is the holder of a certificate or has received corresponding education and training

Article 5

Where, in a host Member State, the taking up or pursuit of a regulated

profession is subject to possession of a diploma, the competent authority may not, on the grounds of inadequate qualifications, refuse to authorise a national of a Member State to take up or pursue that profession on the same conditions as those which apply to its own nationals:

(a) if the applicant holds the certificate required in another Member State for the taking up or pursuit of the same profession in its territory, such certificate having been awarded in a Member State; or

(b) if the applicant has pursued the same profession full-time for two years during the previous 10 years in another Member State which does not regulate that profession, within the meaning of Article 1(e) and the first subparagraph of Article 1(f), and possesses evidence of education and training:

- which was awarded by a competent authority in a Member State, designated in accordance with the laws, regulations or administrative provisions of that State, and

- which shows that the holder, after having followed a secondary course, has completed:

  either a course of professional education or training other than courses referred to in point (a), provided at an educational or training establishment or on the job, or in combination at an educational or training establishment and on the job and complemented, where appropriate, by the probationary or professional practice which is an integral part of that training course,

  or the probationary or professional practice which is an integral part of that secondary course, or

- which shows that the holder, after having followed a secondary course of a technical or vocational nature has completed, where necessary:

  either a course of professional education or training as referred to in the previous indent,

  or the period of probationary or professional practice which is an integral part of that secondary course of a technical or vocational nature and

- which has prepared the holder for the pursuit of this profession.

However, the two years' professional experience referred to above may not be required where the evidence of education and training

held by the applicant and referred to in this point is awarded on completion of regulated education and training.

Nevertheless, the host Member State may require the applicant to undergo an adaptation period not exceeding three years or take an aptitude test. The host Member State must give the applicant the right to choose between an adaptation period and an aptitude test.

Where the host Member State intends to introduce derogations from an applicant's right to choose, the procedure laid down in Article 14 shall apply.

Chapter V

System for recognition where a host Member State requires possession of a certificate

Article 6

Where, in the host Member State, the taking up or pursuit of a regulated profession is subject to possession of a certificate, the competent authority may not, on the grounds of inadequate qualifications, refuse to authorise a national of a Member State to take up or pursue that profession on the same conditions as those which apply to its own nationals:

(a) if the applicant holds the diploma, as defined in this Directive or in Directive 89/48/EEC, or the certificate required in another Member State for the taking up or pursuit of the profession in question in its territory, such diploma having been awarded in a Member State; or

(b) if the applicant has pursued the profession in question full-time for two years or for an equivalent period on a part-time basis during the previous 10 years in another Member State which does not regulate that profession, within the meaning of Article 1(e) and the first subparagraph of Article 1(f), and possesses evidence of education and training:

– which has been awarded by a competent authority in a Member State, designated in accordance with the laws, regulations or administrative provisions of that State, and

– which shows that the holder has successfully completed a post-secondary course other than that referred to in the second indent of Article 1(a) of Directive 89/48/EEC, of at least one year's duration or of equivalent duration on a part-time basis, one of the conditions of entry of which is, as a general rule, the completion of the secondary course required to obtain entry to

university or higher education, as well as any professional training which is an integral part of that post-secondary course, or

– which shows that the holder, after having followed a secondary course, has completed:

either a course of education or training for a profession other than courses referred to in point (a), provided at an educational establishment or on the job, or in combination at an educational establishment and on the job and complemented, where appropriate, by the probationary or professional practice which is an integral part of that training course,

or the probationary or professional practice which is an integral part of that secondary course, or

– which shows that the holder, after having followed a secondary course of a technical or vocational nature has completed, where necessary:

either a course of education or training for a profession as referred to in the previous indent,

or the period of probationary or professional practice which is an integral part of that secondary course of a technical or vocational nature and

– which has prepared the holder for the pursuit of this profession.

However, the two years' professional experience referred to above may not be required where the evidence of education and training held by the applicant and referred to in this point is awarded on completion or regulated education and training.

(c) if the applicant who does not hold any diploma, certificate or other evidence of education and training within the meaning of Article 3(b) or of point (b) of this Article has pursued the profession in question full-time for three consecutive years, or for an equivalent period on a part-time basis, during the previous 10 years in another Member State which does not regulate that profession within the meaning of Article 1(e) and the first subparagraph of Article 1(f).

The following shall be treated in the same way as the evidence of education and training referred to under (b) in the first subparagraph: any evidence of education and training or any set of such evidence awarded by a competent authority in a Member State if it is awarded on the completion of education and training received in the Community and is recognised by that Member State as being of an equivalent level,

provided that the other Member States and the Commission have been notified of this recognition.

Article 7

Without prejudice to Article 6, a host Member State may also require the applicant to:

(*a*) complete an adaptation period not exceeding two years or to take an aptitude test when the education and training which he received in accordance with points (a) or (b) of the first subparagraph of Article 5 relates to theoretical or practical matters differing substantially from those covered by the certificate required in the host Member State, or where there are differences in the fields of activity characterised in the host Member State by specific education and training relating to theoretical or practical matters differing substantially from those covered by the applicant's evidence of formal qualifications.

Should the host Member State make use of this possibility, it must give the applicant the right to choose between an adaptation period and an aptitude test. Where the host Member State which requires a certificate intends to introduce derogations as regards an applicant's right to choose, the procedure laid down in Article 14 shall apply;

(*b*) undergo an adaptation period not exceeding two years or take an aptitude test where, in the instance referred to in point (c) of the first subparagraph of Article 6, he does not hold a diploma, certificate or other evidence of education and training. The host Member State may reserve the right to choose between an adaptation period and an aptitude test.

Chapter VI

Special systems for recognition of other qualifications

Article 8

Where, in the host Member State, the taking up or pursuit of a regulated profession is subject to possession of an attestation of competence, the competent authority may not, on the grounds of inadequate qualifications, refuse to authorise a national of a Member State to take up or pursue that profession on the same conditions as those which apply to its own nationals:

(*a*) if the applicant holds the attestation of competence required in another Member State for the taking up or pursuit of the same

profession in its territory, such attestation having been awarded in a Member State; or

(b) if the applicant provides proof of qualifications obtained in other Member States,

and giving guarantees, in particular in the matter of health, safety, environmental protection and consumer protection, equivalent to those required by the laws, regulations or administrative provisions of the host Member State.

If the applicant does not provide proof of such an attestation or of such qualifications the laws, regulations or administrative provisions of the host Member State shall apply.

Article 9

Where, in the host Member State, the taking up or pursuit of a regulated profession is subject only to possession of evidence of education attesting to general education at primary or secondary school level, the competent authority may not, on the grounds of inadequate qualifications, refuse to authorise a national of a Member State to take up or pursue that profession on the same conditions as those which apply to its own nationals if the applicant possesses formal qualifications of the corresponding level, awarded in another Member State.

This evidence of formal qualifications must have been awarded by a competent authority in that Member State, designated in accordance with its own laws, regulations or administrative provisions.

Chapter VII

Other measures to facilitate the effective exercise of the right of establishment, freedom to provide services and freedom of movement of employed persons

Article 10

1. Where the competent authority of the host Member State requires of persons wishing to take up a regulated profession proof that they are of good character or repute or that they have not been declared bankrupt, or suspends or prohibits the pursuit of that profession in the event of serious professional misconduct or a criminal offence, that State shall accept as sufficient evidence, in respect of nationals of Member States wishing to pursue that profession in its territory, the production of documents issued by competent authorities in the Member State of

origin or the Member State from which the foreign national comes showing that those requirements are met.

Where the competent authorities of the Member State of origin or of the Member State from which the foreign national comes do not issue the documents referred to in the first subparagraph, such documents shall be replaced by a declaration on oath – or, in Member States where there is no provision for declaration on oath, by a solemn declaration – made by the person concerned before a competent judicial or administrative authority or, where appropriate, a notary or qualified professional body of the Member State of origin or the Member State from which the person comes; such authority or notary shall issue written confirmation attesting the authenticity of the declaration on oath or solemn declaration.

2. Where the competent authority of the host Member State requires of nationals of that Member State wishing to take up or pursue a regulated profession a statement of physical or mental health, that authority shall accept as sufficient evidence in this respect the production of the document required in the Member State of origin or the Member State from which the foreign national comes.

Where the Member State of origin or the Member State from which the foreign national comes does not impose any requirements of this nature on those wishing to take up or pursue the profession in question, the host Member State shall accept from such nationals a statement issued by a competent authority in that State corresponding to the statement issued in the host Member State.

3. The competent authority of the host Member State may require that the documents and statements referred to in paragraphs 1 and 2 are presented no more than three months after their date of issue.

4. Where the competent authority of the host Member State requires nationals of that Member State wishing to take up or pursue a regulated profession to take an oath or make solemn declaration and where the form of such oath or declaration cannot be used by nationals of other Member States, that authority shall ensure that an appropriate and equivalent form of oath or declaration is offered to the person concerned.

Article 11

1. The competent authorities of host Member States shall recognise the right of nationals of Member States who fulfil the conditions for the taking up and pursuit of a regulated profession in their territory to use the professional title of the host Member State corresponding to that profession.

2. The competent authority of the host Member State shall recognise the

right of nationals of Member States who fulfil the conditions for the taking up and pursuit of a regulated profession in the territory to use their lawful academic title and, where appropriate, the abbreviation thereof deriving from their Member State of origin or the Member State from which they come, in the language of that State. The host Member State may require this title to be followed by the name and location of the establishment or examining board which awarded it.

3. Where a profession is regulated in the host Member State by an association or organisation referred to in Article 1(f), nationals of Member States shall be entitled to use the professional title or designatory letters conferred by that organisation or association only on proof of membership.

Where the association or organisation makes membership subject to certain qualification requirements, it may apply these to nationals of other Member States who are in possession of a diploma within the meaning of Article 1(a), a certificate within the meaning of Article 1(b) or evidence of education and training or qualification within the meaning of point (b) of the first subparagraph of Article 3, point (b) of the first subparagraph of Article 5 or Article 9 in accordance only with this Directive, in particular Articles 3, 4 and 5.

Article 12

1. The host Member State shall accept as means of proof that the conditions laid down in Articles 3 to 9 are satisfied the documents issued by the competent authorities in the Member States, which the person concerned shall submit in support of his application to pursue the profession concerned.

2. The procedure for examining an application to pursue a regulated profession shall be completed as soon as possible and the outcome communicated in a reasoned decision of the competent authority in the host Member State not later than four months after presentation of all the documents relating to the person concerned. A remedy shall be available against this decision or the absence thereof, before a court or tribunal in accordance with the provisions of national law.

Chapter VIII

Procedure for coordination

Article 13

1. Member States shall designate, within the period provided for in Article 17, the competent authorities empowered to receive the

applications and take the decisions referred to in this Directive. They shall communicate this information to the other Member States and to the Commission.

2. Each Member State shall designate a person responsible for coordinating the activities of the authorities referred to in paragraph 1 and shall inform the other Member States and the Commission to that effect. His role shall be to promote uniform application of this Directive to all the professions concerned. This coordinator shall be a member of the coordinating group set up under the aegis of the Commission by Article 9(2) of Directive 89/48/EEC.

The coordinating group set up under the aforementioned provision of Directive 89/48/EEC shall also be required to:

– facilitate the implementation of this Directive,

– collect all useful information for its application in the Member States, particularly information relating to the establishment of an indicative list of regulated professions and to the disparities between the qualifications awarded in the Member States with a view to assisting the competent authorities of the Member States in their task of assessing whether substantial differences exist.

The group may be consulted by the Commission on any changes to the existing system which may be contemplated.

3. The Member States shall take measures to provide the necessary information on the recognition of diplomas and certificates and on other conditions governing the taking up of the regulated professions within the framework of this Directive. To carry out this task they may call upon the existing information networks and, where appropriate, the relevant professional associations or organisations. The Commission shall take the necessary initiatives to ensure the development and coordination of the communication of the necessary information.

Chapter IX

Procedure for derogating from the right to choose between adaptation period and aptitude test

Article 14

1. If, pursuant to the second sentence of the second subparagraph of Article 4(1)(b), the third subparagraph of Article 5, or the second sentence of the second subparagraph of Article 7(a), a Member State proposes not to grant applicants the right to choose between an adaptation period and an aptitude test, it shall immediately

communicate to the Commission the corresponding draft provision. It shall at the same time notify the Commission of the grounds which make the enactment of such a provision necessary.

The Commission shall immediately notify the other Member States of any draft which it has received; it may also consult the coordinating group referred to in Article 13(2) on the draft.

2. Without prejudice to the possibility for the Commission and the other Member States to make comments on the draft, the Member State may adopt the provision only if the Commission has not taken a decision to the contrary within three months.

3. At the request of a Member State or the Commission, Member States shall communicate to them, without delay, the definitive text of any provision arising from the application of this Article.

Chapter X

Procedure for amending Annexes C and D

Article 15

1. The lists of education and training courses set out in Annexes C and D may be amended on the basis of a reasoned request from any Member State concerned to the Commission. All appropriate information and in particular the text of the relevant provisions of national law shall accompany the request. The Member State making the request shall also inform the other Member States.

2. The Commission shall examine the education and training course in question and those required in the other Member States. It shall verify in particular whether the qualification resulting from the course in question confers on the holder:

– a level of professional education or training of a comparably high level to that of the post-secondary course referred to in point (i) of the second indent of the first subparagraph of Article 1(a),

– a similar level of responsibility and activity.

3. The Commission shall be assisted by a committee composed of the representatives of the Member States and chaired by the representative of the Commission.

4. The representative of the Commission shall submit to the committee a draft of the measures to be taken. The committee shall deliver its opinion on the draft within a time limit which the chairman may lay down according to the urgency of the matter. The opinion shall be delivered by the majority laid down in Article 148(2) of the Treaty in the case of

decisions which the Council is required to adopt on a proposal from the Commission. The votes of the representatives of the Member States within the committee shall be weighted in the manner set out in that Article. The chairman shall not vote.

5. The Commission shall adopt measures which shall apply immediately. However, if these measures are not in accordance with the opinion of the committee, they shall be communicated by the Commission to the Council forthwith. In that event, the Commission shall defer for a period of two months the application of the measures which it has decided.

6. The Council, acting by a qualified majority, may take a different decision within the time limit referred to in the previous paragraph.

7. The Commission shall inform the Member State concerned of the decision and shall, where appropriate, publish the amended list in the *Official Journal of the European Communities*.

Chapter XI

Other provisions

Article 16

Following the expiry of the period provided for in Article 17, Member States shall communicate to the Commission, every two years, a report on the application of the system introduced.

In addition to general remarks, this report shall contain a statistical summary of the decisions taken and a description of the main problems arising from the application of this Directive.

Article 17

1. Member States shall adopt the laws, regulations and administrative provisions necessary for them to comply with this Directive before 18 June 1994. They shall forthwith inform the Commission thereof.

When Member States adopt these measures, the latter shall include a reference to this Directive or be accompanied by such reference at the time of their official publication. The methods of making such a reference shall be laid down by the Member States.

2. Member States shall communicate to the Commission the texts of the main provisions of national law which they adopt in the field governed by this Directive.

Article 18

Five years at the latest following the date specified in Article 17, the

Commission shall report to the European Parliament, the Council and the Economic and Social Committee on the progress of the application of this Directive.

After conducting all necessary consultations, the Commission shall present its conclusions as to any changes which need to be made to this Directive. At the same time the Commission shall, where appropriate, submit proposals for improving the existing rules in the interest of facilitating freedom of movement, right of establishment and freedom to provide services.

Article 19

This Directive is addressed to the Member States.

Done at Luxembourg, 18 June 1992.

For the Council

The President

Vitor Martins

FOOTNOTES

1. OJ No C 263, 16.10.89, p.1 and OJ No C 217, 1.9.90, p.4.
2. OJ No C 149, 18.6.90, p.149 and OJ No C 150 15.6.92.
3. OJ No C 75, 26.3.90, p.11.
4. OJ No L 19, 24.1.89, p.16.
5. OJ No L 199, 31.7.85, p.56.

IRL Implemented in Ireland: (Not implemented by original date, 18.6.94, due to amending Directive adopted in April 1994 – not published as of 13.7.94. New implemented date October 1994 – editorial note.)

COUNCIL RECOMMENDATION

21 December 1988

concerning nationals of Member States who hold a diploma conferred in a third State

(89/49/EEC)

(OJ No L 19, 24.1.89, p.24)

The Council of the European Communities,

Approving Council Directive 89/48/EEC of 21 December 1988 on a

general system for the recognition of higher-education diplomas awarded on completion of professional education and training of at least three years' duration[1];

Noting that this Directive refers only to diplomas, certificates and other evidence of formal qualifications awarded in Member States to nationals of Member States;

Anxious, however, to take account of the special position of nationals of Member States who hold diplomas, certificates or other evidence of formal qualifications awarded in third States and who are thus in a position comparable to one of those described in Article 3 of the Directive,

Hereby recommends:

that the Governments of the Member States should allow the persons referred to above to take up and pursue regulated professions within the Community by recognising these diplomas, certificates and other evidence of formal qualifications in their territories.

Done at Brussels, 21 December 1988.

For the Council

The President

V. Papandreou

FOOTNOTE

1. See OJ No L 19, 24.1.89, p.16.

COUNCIL DECISION

of 16 July 1985

on the comparability of vocational training qualifications between the Member States of the European Community

(85/368/EEC)

(OJ No L 199, 31.7.85, p.56)

The Council of the European Communities,

Having regard to the Treaty establishing the European Economic Community, and in particular Article 128 thereof,

Having regard to Council Decision 63/266/EEC of 2 April 1963 laying down general principles for implementing a common vocational training policy[1], and in particular the eighth principle thereof,

Having regard to the proposal from the Commission, as amended on 17 July 1984,

Having regard to the opinion of the European Parliament[2],

Having regard to the opinion of the Economic and Social Committee[3],

Whereas the eighth principle of Decision 63/266/EEC is to make it possible to achieve the mutual recognition of certificates and other documents confirming completion of vocational training;

Whereas the Council resolution of 6 June 1974[4] on the mutual recognition of diplomas, certificates and other evidence of formal qualifications requires lists of such qualifications recognised as being equivalent to be drawn up;

Whereas the absence of the said mutual recognition is a factor inhibiting freedom of movement for workers within the Community, insofar as it restricts the possibility for workers seeking employment in one Member State to rely on vocational qualifications which they have obtained in another Member State;

Whereas there is a very substantial degree of diversity in the vocational training systems in the Community; whereas these systems are constantly requiring adaptation to the new situations brought about by the impact of technological change on employment and job content;

Whereas the Council resolution of 11 July 1983 concerning vocational training policies in the European Community in the 1980s[5] affirmed the need for a convergence of policies in the vocational training field, whilst recognising the diversity of training systems in the Member States, and the need for Community action to be flexible;

Whereas it has been possible for the Commission to establish as a reference point, with the help of the Advisory Committee for Vocational Training, a structure of levels of training which represents a first step towards the achievement of the aims laid down in the eighth principle of Decision 63/266/EEC, but whereas this structure does not reflect all the training systems being developed in the Member States;

Whereas for the skilled-worker level within this structure, and for selected priority groups of occupations, it has been possible to arrive at

practical job descriptions and to identify the corresponding vocational training qualifications in the various Member States;

Whereas consultation with the vocational sectors concerned has provided evidence that these results can provide firms, workers and public authorities with valuable information concerning the comparability of vocational training qualifications;

Whereas the same basic methodology could be applied to other occupations or groups of occupations on advice from the Advisory Committee for Vocational Training and with the collaboration of employers, workers and the public authorities in the vocational sectors concerned;

Whereas it is therefore essential to make rapid progress towards the comparability of vocational training qualifications for all skilled workers, and to extend the work to other levels of training as quickly as possible;

Whereas it is advisable to have all the necessary opinions, in particular that of the Advisory Committee for Vocational Training, and the technical assistance of the European Centre for the Development of Vocational Training, and to enable the Member States and the Commission to act in accordance with existing procedures;

Whereas the Advisory Committee for Vocational Training delivered an opinion at its meeting on 18 and 19 January 1983;

Whereas paragraph 21 of the report of the Committee on a People's Europe of 29 and 30 March 1985 should be taken into account,

Has adopted this Decision:

Article 1

The aim of enabling workers to make better use of their qualifications, in particular for the purposes of obtaining suitable employment in another Member State, shall require, for features of job descriptions mutually agreed by the Member States on behalf of workers, within the meaning of Article 128 of the Treaty, expedited common action by the Member States and the Commission to establish the comparability of vocational training qualifications in the Community and improved information on the subject.

Article 2

1. The Commission, in close cooperation with the Member States, shall undertake work to fulfil the aims set out in Article 1 on the comparability of vocational training qualifications between the various Member States, in respect of specific occupations or groups of occupations.

2. The work may use as a reference the structure of training levels drawn up by the Commission with the help of the Advisory Committee for Vocational Training.

The text of the said structure is attached to this Decision for information purposes.

3. The work referred to in paragraph 2 shall first and foremost concentrate on the occupational qualifications of skilled workers in mutually agreed occupations or group of occupations.

4. The scope of this Decision may subsequently be extended to permit work to be undertaken, on a proposal from the Commission, at other levels of training.

5. The SEDOC register, used in connection with the European System for the international clearing of vacancies and applications for employment, shall, whenever possible, be used as the common frame of reference for vocational classifications.

Article 3

The following working procedure shall be employed by the Commission in establishing the comparability of vocational training qualifications in close cooperation with the Member States and the organisations of workers and employers at Community level:

–   selection of the relevant occupations or groups of occupations on a proposal from the Member States or the competent employer or worker organisations at Community level;

–   drawing up mutually agreed Community job descriptions for the occupations or groups of occupations referred to in the first indent;

–   matching the vocational training qualifications recognised in the various Member States with the job descriptions referred to in the second indent;

–   establishing tables incorporating information on:

    (a) the SEDOC and national classification codes;

    (b) the level of vocational training;

    (c) for each Member State, the vocational title and corresponding vocational training qualifications;

    (d) the organisations and institutions responsible for dispensing vocational training;

    (e) the authorities and organisations competent to issue or to

> validate diplomas, certificates, or other documents certifying that vocational training has been acquired;

- publication of the mutually agreed Community job descriptions and the comparative tables in the *Official Journal of the European Communities*;

- establishment, within the meaning of Article 4(3), of a standard information sheet for each occupation or group of occupations, to be published in the *Official Journal of the European Communities*;

- dissemination of information on the established comparabilities to all appropriate bodies at national, regional and local levels, as well as throughout the occupational sectors concerned.

This action could be supported by the creation of a Community-wide data base, if experience shows the need for such a base.

Article 4

1. Each Member State shall designate a coordination body, based wherever possible on existing structures, which shall be responsible for ensuring – in close collaboration with the social partners and the occupational sectors concerned – the proper dissemination of information to all interested bodies. The Member States shall also designate the body responsible for contacts with the coordination bodies in other Member States and with the Commission.

2. The coordination bodies of the Member States shall be competent to establish appropriate arrangements with regard to vocational training information for their competent national, regional or local bodies as well as for their own nationals wishing to work in other Member States and for workers who are nationals of other Member States, on established cases of comparable vocational qualifications.

3. The bodies referred to in paragraph 2 may supply on request in all Member States an information sheet drawn up in accordance with the model provided for in the sixth indent of Article 3, which the worker may present to the employer together with his national certificate.

4. The Commission is to continue studying the introduction of the European vocational training pass advocated by the Committee for a People's Europe in paragraph 21 of its report of 29 and 30 March 1985.

5. The Commission shall give the bodies referred to in paragraph 2, on request, all necessary assistance and advice concerning the preparation and setting up of the arrangements provided for in paragraph 2,

including the adaptation and checking of the relevant technical documents.

Article 5

The Commission shall, in close liaison with the national coordination bodies designated by the Member States,

- review and update at appropriate, regular intervals, in close cooperation with the Member States and the organisations of workers and employers at Community level, the mutually agreed Community job descriptions and the comparative tables relating to the comparability of vocational training qualifications,

- where necessary, formulate proposals for a more efficient operation of the system including other measures likely to improve the situation as regards the comparability of vocational qualification certificates,

- where necessary, assist in the case of technical difficulties encountered by the national authorities or specialised bodies concerned.

Article 6

Each Member State shall submit to the Commission, for the first time two years after adoption of this Decision, and therefore every four years, a national report on the implementation of this Decision and the results obtained.

The Commission shall, at appropriate intervals, submit a report on its own work and on the application of this Decision in the Member States.

Article 7

The Decision is addressed to the Member States and the Commission.

Done at Brussels, 16 July 1985.

For the Council

The President

M. Fischbach

Annex

Training-level structure referred to in Article 2(2)

Level 1

Training providing access to this level: compulsory education and professional initiation

This professional initiation is acquired at an educational establishment, in an out-of-school training programme, or at the undertaking. The volume of theoretical knowledge and practical capabilities involved is very limited.

This form of training must primarily enable the holder to perform relatively simple work and may be fairly quickly acquired.

Level 2

Training providing access to this level: compulsory education and vocational training (including, in particular, apprenticeships)

This level corresponds to a level where the holder is fully qualified to engage in a specific activity, with the capacity to use the instruments and techniques relating thereto.

This activity involves chiefly the performance of work which may be independent within the limits of the relevant techniques.

Level 3

Training providing access to this level: compulsory education and/or vocational training and additional technical training or technical educational training or other secondary-level training

This form of training involves a greater fund of theoretical knowledge than level 2. Activity involves chiefly technical work which can be performed independently and/or entail executive and coordination duties.

Level 4

Training providing access to this level: secondary training (general or vocational) and post-secondary technical training

This form of training involves high-level technical training acquired at or outside educational establishments. The resultant qualification covers a higher level of knowledge and of capabilities. It does not generally

require mastery of the scientific bases of the various areas concerned. Such capabilities and knowledge make it possible in a generally autonomous or in an independent way to assume design and/or management and/or administrative responsibilities.

Level 5

Training providing access to this level: secondary training (general or vocational) and complete higher training

This form of training generally leads to an autonomously pursued vocational activity – as an employee or as self-employed person – entailing a mastery of the scientific bases of the occupation. The qualifications required for engaging in a vocational activity may be integrated at these various levels.

FOOTNOTES

1. OJ No 63, 20.4.63, p.1338.
2. OJ No C 77, 19.3.84, p.11.
3. OJ No C 35, 9.2.84, p.12.
4. OJ No C 98, 20.8.74, p.1.
5. OJ No C 193, 20.7.83, p.2.

COUNCIL DIRECTIVE

of 22 March 1977

to facilitate the effective exercise by lawyers of freedom to provide services

(77/249/EEC)

(OJ No L 78, 26.3.77, p.17)

The Council of the European Communities,

Having regard to the Treaty establishing the European Economic Community, and in particular Articles 57 and 66 thereof,

Having regard to the proposal from the Commission,

Having regard to the opinion of the European Parliament[1],

Having regard to the opinion of the Economic and Social Committee[2],

Whereas, pursuant to the Treaty, any restriction on the provision of services which is based on nationality or on conditions of residence has been prohibited since the end fo the transitional period;

Whereas this Directive deals only with measures to facilitate the effective pursuit of the activities of lawyers by way of provisison of services; whereas more detailed measures will be necessary to facilitate the effective exercise of the right of establishment;

Whereas if lawyers are to exercise effectively the freedom to provide services host Member State must recognise as lawyers those persons practising the profession in the various Member States;

Whereas, since this Directive solely concerns provision of services and does not contain provisions on the mutual recognition of diplomas, a person to whom the Directive applies must adopt the professional title used in the Member State in which he is established, hereinafter referred to as 'the Member State from which he comes',

Has adopted this Directive:

Article 1

1. This Directive shall apply, within the limits and under the conditions laid down herein, to the activities of lawyers pursued by way of provision of services.

Notwithstanding anything contained in this Directive, Member States may reserve to prescribed categories of lawyers the preparation of formal documents for obtaining title to administer estates of deceased persons, and the drafting of formal documents creating or transferring interests in land.

2. 'lawyer' means any person entitled to pursue his professional activities under one of the following designations:

Belgium:	advocat – advocaat
Denmark:	advokat
Germany:	rechtsanwalt
France:	avocat
Ireland:	barrister
	solicitor
Italy:	avvocato
Luxembourg:	avocat-avoue
Netherlands:	advocaat
United Kingdom:	advocate
	barrister
	solicitor.

Article 2

Each Member State shall recognise as a lawyer for the purpose of

pursuing the activities specified in Article 1(1) any person listed in paragraph 2 of that Article.

Article 3

A person referred to in Article 1 shall adopt the professional title used in the Member State from which he comes, expressed in the language or one of the languages, of that State, with an indication of the professional organisation by which he is authorised to practise or the court of law before which he is entitled to practise pursuant to the laws of that State.

Article 4

1. Activities relating to the representation of a client in legal proceedings or before public authorities shall be pursued in each host Member State under the conditions laid down for lawyers established in that State, with the exception of any conditions requiring residence, or registration with a professional organisation, in that State.

2. A lawyer pursuing these activities shall observe the rules of professional conduct of the host Member State, without prejudice to his obligations in the Member State from which he comes.

3. When these activities are pursued in the United Kingdom, 'rules of professional conduct of the host Member State' means the rules of professional conduct applicable to solicitors, where such activities are not reserved for barristers and advocates. Otherwise the rules of professional conduct applicable to the latter shall apply. However, barristers from Ireland shall always be subject to the rules of professional conduct applicable in the United Kingdom to barristers and advocates.

When these activities are pursued in Ireland 'rules of professional conduct of the host Member State' means, in so far as they govern the oral presentation of a case in court, the rules of professional conduct applicable to barristers. In all other cases the rules of professional conduct applicable to solicitors shall apply. However, barristers and advocates from the United Kingdom shall always be subject to the rules of professional conduct appplicable in Ireland to barristers.

4. A lawyer pursuing activities other than those referred to in paragraph 1 shall remain subject to the conditions and rules of professional conduct of the Member State from which he comes without prejudice to respect for the rules, whatever their source, which govern the profession in the host member state, especially those concerning the incompatibility of the exercise of the activities of a lawyer with the exercise of other activities in that State, professional secrecy, relations with other lawyers, the prohibition on the same lawyer acting for parties with mutually conflicting interests, and publicity. The latter rules are

applicable only if they are capable of being observed by a lawyer who is not established in the host Member State and to the extent to which their observance is objectively justified to ensure, in that State, the proper exercise of a lawyer's activities, the standing of the profession and respect for the rules concerning incompatibility.

Article 5

For the pursuit of activities relating to the representation of a client in legal proceedings, a Member State may require lawyers to whom Article 1 applies:

- to be introduced, in accordance with local rules or customs, to the presiding judge and, where appropriate, to the president of the relevant bar in the host Member State;
- to work in conjunction with a lawyer who practices before the judicial authority in question and who would, where necessary, be answerable to that authority, or with an 'avoue' or 'procuratore' practising before it.

Article 6

Any Member State may exclude lawyers who are in the salaried employment of a public or private undertaking from pursuing activities relating to the representation of that undertaking in legal proceedings in so far as lawyers established in that State are not permitted to pursue those activities.

Article 7

1. The competent authority of the host Member State may request the person providing the services to establish his qualifications as a lawyer.

2. In the event of non-compliance with the obligations referred to in Article 4 and in force in the host Member State, the competent authority of the latter shall determine in accordance with its own rules and procedures the consequences of such non-compliance, and to this end may obtain any appropriate professional information concerning the person providing services. It shall notify the competent authority of the Member State from which the person comes of any decision taken. Such exchanges shall not affect the confidential nature of the information supplied.

Article 8

1. Member States shall bring into force the measures necessary to comply with this Directive within two years of its notification and shall forthwith inform the Commission thereof.

2. Member States shall communicate to the Commission the texts of the

main provisions of national law which they adopt in the field covered by this Directive.

Article 9

This Directive is addressed to the Member States.

Done at Brussels, 22 March 1977.

For the Council

The President

Judith Hart

FOOTNOTES

1. OJ No C 103, 5.10.72, p.19 and OJ No C 53, 8.3.76, p.33.
2. OJ No 36, 28.3.70, p.37 and OJ No C 50, 4.3.76, p.17.

IRL Implemented in Ireland: S.I. 58/1979; S.I. 197/1981; S.I. 226/1986.

(g) Capital

COUNCIL DIRECTIVE

of 24 June 1988

for the implementation of Article 67 of the Treaty

(88/361/EEC)

(OJ No L 178, 8.7.88, p.5)

The Council of the European Communities,

Having regard to the Treaty establishing the European Economic Community, and in particular Articles 69 and 70(1) thereof,

Having regard to the proposal from the Commission, submitted following consultation with the Monetary Committee[1],

Having regard to the opinion of the European Parliament[2],

Whereas Article 8a of the Treaty stipulates that the internal market shall comprise an area without internal frontiers in which the free movement of capital is ensured, without prejudice to the other provisions of the Treaty;

Whereas Member States should be able to take the requisite measures to regulate bank liquidity; whereas these measures should be restricted to this purpose;

Whereas Member States should, if necessary, be able to take measures to restrict, temporarily and within the framework of appropriate Community procedures, short-term capital movements which, even where there is no appreciable divergence in economic fundamentals, might seriously disrupt the conduct of their monetary and exchange-rate policies;

Whereas, in the interests of transparency, it is advisable to indicate the scope, in accordance with the arrangements laid down in this Directive, of the transitional measures adopted for the benefit of the Kingdom of Spain and the Portuguese Republic by the 1985 Act of Accession in the field of capital movements;

Whereas the Kingdom of Spain and the Portuguese Republic may, under the terms of Articles 61 to 66 and 222 to 232 respectively of the 1985 Act of Accession, postpone the liberalisation of certain capital movements in derogation from the obligations set out in the First Council Directive of 11 May 1960 for the implementation of Article 67 of the Treaty[3], as last amended by Directive 86/566/EEC[4]; whereas Directive 86/566/EEC also proves for transitional arrangements to be applied for the benefit of those two Member States in respect of their obligations to liberalise capital movements; whereas it is appropriate for those two Member States to be able to postpone the application of the new liberalisation obligations resulting from this Directive;

Whereas the Hellenic Republic and Ireland are faced, albeit to differing degrees, with difficult balance-of-payments situations and high levels of external indebtedness; whereas the immediate and complete liberalisation of capital movements by those two Member States would make it more difficult for them to continue to apply the measures they have taken to improve their external positions and to reinforce the capacity of their financial systems to adapt to the requirements of an integrated financial market in the Community; whereas it is appropriate, in accordance with Article 8c of the Treaty, to grant to those two Member States, in the light of their specific circumstances, further time in which to comply with the obligations arising from this Directive;

Whereas, since the full liberalisation of capital movements could in some Member States, and especially in border areas, contribute to difficulties in the market for secondary residences; whereas existing national leglislation regulating these purchases should not be affected by the entry into effect of this Directive;

Whereas advantage should be taken of the period adopted for bringing this Directive into effect in order to enable the Commission to submit proposals designed to eliminate or reduce risks of distortion, tax evasion and tax avoidance resulting from the diversity of national systems for taxation and to permit the Council to take a position on such proposals;

Whereas, in accordance with Article 70(1) of the Treaty, the Community shall endeavour to attain the highest possible degree of liberalisation in respect of the movement of capital between its residents and those of third countries;

Whereas large-scale short-term capital movements to or from third countries may seriously disturb the monetary or financial situation of Member States or cause serious stresses on the exchange markets; whereas such developments may prove harmful for the cohesion of the European Monetary System, for the smooth operation of the internal market and for the progressive achievement of economic and monetary union; whereas it is therefore appropriate to create the requisite conditions for concerted action by Member States should this prove necessary;

Whereas this Directive replaces Council Directive 72/156/EEC of 21 March 1972 on regulating international capital flows and neutralising their undesirable effects on domestic liquidity[5]; whereas Directive 72/156/EEC should accordingly be repealed,

Has adopted this Directive:

Article 1

1. Without prejudice to the following provisions, Member States shall abolish restrictions on movements of capital taking place between persons resident in Member States. To facilitate application of this Directive, capital movements shall be classified in accordance with the Nomenclature in Annex I.

2. Transfers in respect of capital movements shall be made on the same exchange rate conditions as those governing payments relating to current transactions.

Article 2

Member States shall notify the Committee of Governors of the Central Banks, the Monetary Committee and the Commission, by the date of their entry into force at the latest, of measures to regulate bank liquidity which have a specific impact on capital transactions carried out by credit institutions with non-residents.

Such measures shall be confined to what is necessary for the purposes of domestic monetary regulation. The Monetary Committee and the Committee of Governors of the Central Banks shall provide the Commission with opinions on this subject.

Article 3

1. Where short-term capital movements of exceptional magnitude impose severe strains on foreign-exchange markets and lead to serious disturbances in the conduct of a Member State's monetary and exchange rate policies, being reflected in particular in substantial variations in domestic liquidity, the Commission may, after consulting the Monetary Committee and the Committee of Governors of the Central Banks, authorise that Member State to take, in respect of the capital movements listed in Annex II, protective measures the conditions and details of which the Commission shall determine.

2. The Member State concerned may itself take the protective measures referred to above, on grounds of urgency, should these measures be necessary. The Commission and the other Member States shall be informed of such measures by the date of their entry into force at the latest. The Commission, after consulting the Monetary Committee and the Committee of Governors of the Central Banks, shall decide whether the Member State concerned may continue to apply these measures or whether it should amend or abolish them.

3. The decisions taken by the Commission under paragraphs 1 and 2 may be revoked or amended by the Council acting by a qualified majority.

4. The period of application of protective measures taken pursuant to this Article shall not exceed six months.

5. Before 31 December 1992, the Council shall examine, on the basis of a report from the Commission, after delivery of an opinion by the Monetary Committee and the Committee of Governors of the Central Banks, whether the provisions of this Article remain appropriate, as regards their principle and details, to the requirements which they were intended to satisfy.

Article 4

This Directive shall be without prejudice to the right of Member States to take all requisite measures to prevent infringements of their laws and regulations, *inter alia* in the field of taxation and prudential supervision of financial institutions, or to lay down procedures for the declaration of capital movements for purposes of administrative or statistical information.

Application of those measures and procedures may not have the effect of impeding capital movements carried out in accordance with Community law.

Article 5

For the Kingdom of Spain and the Portuguese Republic, the scope, in accordance with the Nomenclature of capital movements contained in Annex I, of the provisions of the 1985 Act of Accession in the field of capital movements shall be as indicated in Annex III.

Article 6

1. Member States shall take the measures necessary to comply with this Directive no later than 1 July 1990. They shall forthwith inform the Commission thereof. They shall also make known, by the date of their entry into force at the latest, any new measure or any amendment made to the provisions governing the capital movements listed in Annex I.

2. The Kingdom of Spain and the Portuguese Republic, without prejudice for these two Member States to Articles 61 to 66 and 222 to 232 of the 1985 Act of Accession, and the Hellenic Republic and Ireland may temporarily continue to apply restrictions to the capital movements listed in Annex IV, subject to the conditions and the time limits laid down in that Annex.

If, before expiry of the time limit set for the liberalisation of the capital movements referred to in Lists III and IV of Annex IV, the Portuguese Republic or the Hellenic Republic considers that it is unable to proceed with liberalisation, in particular because of difficulties as regards its balance of payments or because the national financial system is insufficiently adapted, the Commission, at the request of one or other of these Member States, shall in collaboration with the Monetary Committee, review the economic and financial situation of the Member State concerned. On the basis of the outcome of this review, the Commission shall propose to the Council an extension of the time limit set for liberalisation of all or part of the capital movements referred to. This extension may not exceed three years. The Council shall act in accordance with the procedure laid down in Article 69 of the Treaty.

3. The Kingdom of Belgium and the Grand Duchy of Luxembourg may temporarily continue to operate the dual exchange market under the conditions and for the periods laid down in Annex V.

4. Existing national legislation regulating purchases of secondary residences may be upheld until the Council adopts further provisions in this area in accordance with Article 69 of the Treaty. This provision does not affect the applicability of other provisions of Community law.

5. The Commission shall submit to the Council, by 31 December 1988, proposals aimed at eliminating or reducing risks of distortion, tax evasion and tax avoidance linked to the diversity of national systems for the taxation of savings and for controlling the application of these systems.

The Council shall take a position on these Commission proposals by 30 June 1989. Any tax provisions of a Community nature shall, in accordance with the Treaty, be adopted unanimously.

Article 7

1. In their treatment of transfers in respect of movements of capital to or from third countries, the Member States shall endeavour to attain the same degree of liberalisation as that which applies to operations with residents of other Member States, subject to the other provisions of this Directive.

The provisions of the preceding subparagraph shall not prejudice the application to third countries of domestic rules or Community law, particularly any reciprocal conditions, concerning operations involving establishment, the provisions of financial services and the admission of securities to capital markets.

2. Where large-scale short-term capital movements to or from third countries seriously disturb the domestic or external monetary or financial situation of the Member States, or of a number of them, or cause serious strains in exchange relations within the Community or between the Community and third countries, Member States shall consult with one another on any measure to be taken to counteract such difficulties. This consultation shall take place within the Committee of Governors of the Central Banks and the Monetary Committee on the initiative of the Commission or of any Member State.

Article 8

At least once a year the Monetary Committee shall examine the situation regarding free movement of capital as it results from the application of this Directive. The examination shall cover measures concerning the domestic regulation of credit and financial and monetary markets which could have a specific impact on international capital movements and on all other aspects of this Directive. The Committee shall report to the Commission on the outcome of this examination.

Article 9

The First Directive of 11 May 1960 and Directive 72/156/EEC shall be repealed with effect from 1 July 1990.

Article 10

This Directive is addressed to the Member States.

Done at Luxembourg, 24 June 1988.

For the Council

The President

M. Bangemann

Annex 1

Nomenclature of the Capital Movements referred to in Article 1 of the Directive

In this Nomenclature, capital movements are classified according to the economic nature of the assets and liabilities they concern, denominated either in national currency or in foreign exchange.

The capital movements listed in this Nomenclature are taken to cover:

– all the operations necessary for the purposes of capital movements: conclusion and performance of the transaction and related transfers. The transaction is generally between residents of different Member States although some capital movements are carried out by a single person for his own account (eg transfers of assets belonging to emigrants),

– operations carried out by any natural or legal person[6], including operations in respect of the assets or liabilities of Member States or of other public administrations and agencies, subject to the provisions of Article 68(3) of the Treaty,

– access for the economic operator to all the financial techniques available on the market approached for the purpose of carrying out the operation in question. For example, the concept of acquisition of securities and other financial instruments covers not only spot transactions but also all the dealing techniques available: forward transactions, transactions carrying an option or warrant, swaps against other assets, etc. Similarly, the concept of operations in current and deposit accounts with financial institutions, includes not only the opening and placing of funds on accounts but also forward

foreign exchange transactions, irrespective of whether these are intended to cover an exchange risk or to take an open foreign exchange position,

– operations to liquidate or assign assets built up, repatriation of the proceeds of liquidation thereof[6] or immediate use of such proceeds within the limits of Community obligations,

– operations to repay credits or loans.

This Nomenclature is not an exhaustive list for the notion of capital movements – whence a heading XIII – F. 'Other capital movements – Miscellaneous'. It should not therefore be interpreted as restricting the scope of the principle of full liberalisation of capital movements as referred to in Article I of the Directive.

I – Direct Investments[6]

1. Establishment and extension of branches or new undertakings belonging solely to the person providing the capital, and the acquisition in full of existing undertakings.

2. Participation in new or existing undertaking with a view to establishing or maintaining lasting economic links.

3. Long-term loans with a view to establishing or maintaining lasting economic links.

4. Reinvestment of profits with a view to maintaining lasting economic links.

A – *Direct investments on national territory by non-residents*[6]

B – *Direct investments abroad by residents*[6]

II – Investments in Real Estate

(not included under I)[6]

A – *Investments in real estate on national territory by non-residents*

B – *Investments in real estate abroad by residents*

III – Operations in securities normally dealt in on the capital market (not included under I, IV and V)

(a) *Shares and other securities of a participating nature*[6].

(b) *Bonds*[6].

A – *Transactions in securities on the capital market*

1. Acquisition by non-residents of domestic securities dealt in on a stock exchange[6].

2. Acquisition by residents of foreign securities dealt in on a stock exchange.

3. Acquisition by non-residents of domestic securities not dealt in on a stock exchange[6].

4. Acquisition by residents of foreign securities not dealt in on a stock exchange.

B – *Admission of securities to the capital market[6]*

 (i) *Introduction on a stock exchange[6].*

(ii) *Issue and placing on a capital market.*

   1. Admission of domestic securities to a foreign capital market.

   2. Administration of foreign securities to the domestic capital market.

IV – Operations in units of collective investment undertakings[6]

(*a*) Units of undertakings for collective investment in securities normally dealt in on the capital market (shares, other equities and bonds).

(*b*) Units of undertakings for collective investment in securities or instruments normally dealt in on the money market.

(*c*) Units of undertakings for collective investment in other assets.

A – *Transactions in units of collective investment undertakings*

1. Acquisition by non-residents of units of national undertakings dealt in on a stock exchange.

2. Acquisition by residents of units of foreign undertakings dealt in on a stock exchange.

3. Acquisition by non-residents of units of national undertakings not dealt in on a stock exchange.

4. Acquisition by residents of units of foreign undertakings not dealt in on a stock exchange.

B – *Administration of units of collective investment undertakings to the capital market*

(i) *Introduction on a stock exchange.*

(ii) *Issue and placing on a capital market.*

1. Admission of units of national collective investment undertakings to a foreign capital market.

2. Admission of units of foreign collective investment undertakings to the domestic capital market.

V – Operations in securities and other instruments normally dealt in on the money market[6]

A – *Transactions in securities and other instruments on the money market*

1. Acquisition by non-residents of domestic money market securities and instruments.

2. Acquisition by residents of foreign money market securities and instruments.

B – *Admission of securities and other instruments to the money market*

(i) *Introduction on a recognised money market.*

(ii) *Issue and placing on a recognised money market.*

1. Admission of domestic securities and instruments to a foreign money market.

2. Admission of foreign securities and instruments to the domestic money market.

VI – Operations in current and deposit accounts with financial institutions[6]

A – *Operations carried out by non-residents with domestic financial institutions*

B – *Operations carried out by residents with foreign financial institutions*

VII – Credits related to commercial transactions or to the provision of services in which a resident is participating[6]

1. Short-term (less than one year).

2. Medium-term (from one to five years).

3. Long-term (five years or more).

A – *Credits granted by non-residents to residents*

B – *Credits granted by residents to non-residents*

VIII – Financial loans and credits (not included under I, VII and XI)[6]

1. Short-term (less than one year).

2. Medium-term (from one to five years).

3. Long-term (five years or more).

A – *Loans and credits granted by non-residents to residents*

B – *Loans and credits granted by residents to non-residents*

IX – Sureties, other guarantees and rights of pledge

A – *Granted by non-residents to residents*

B – *Granted by residents to non-residents*

X – Transfers in performance of Insurance Contracts

A – *Premiums and payments in respect of life assurance*

1. Contracts concluded between domestic life assurance companies and non-residents.

2. Contracts concluded between foreign life assurance companies and residents.

B – *Premiums and payments in respect of credit insurance*

1. Contracts concluded between domestic credit insurance companies and non-residents.

2. Contracts concluded between foreign credit insurance companies and residents.

C – *Other transfers of capital in respect of insurance contracts*

XI – Personal capital movements

A – Loans

B – *Gifts and endowments*

C – *Dowries*

D – *Inheritances and legacies*

E – *Settlement of debts by immigrants in their previous country of residence*

F – *Transfers of assets constituted by residents, in the event of emigration, at the time of their installation or during their period of stay abroad*

G – *Transfers, during their period of stay, of immigrants' savings to their previous country of residence*

XII – Physical import and export of financial assets

A – *Securities*

B – *Means of payment of every kind*

XIII – Other capital movements

A – *Death duties*

B – *Damages (where these can be considered as capital)*

C – *Refunds in the case of cancellation of contracts and refunds of uncalled-for payments (where these can be considered as capital)*

D – *Authors' royalties: patents, designs, trade marks and inventions (assignments and transfers arising out of such assignments)*

E – *Transfers of the monies required for the provision of services (not included under VI)*

F – *Miscellaneous*

Explanatory notes

For the purposes of this Nomenclature and the Directive only, the following expressions have the meanings assigned to them respectively:

Direct investments

Investments of all kinds by natural persons or commercial, industrial or financial undertakings, and which serve to establish or to maintain lasting and direct links between the person providing the capital and the entrepreneur to whom or the undertaking to which the capital is made available in order to carry on an economic activity. This concept must therefore be understood in its widest sense.

The undertakings mentioned under I-1 of the Nomenclature include legally independent undertakings (wholly-owned subsidiaries) and branches.

As regards those undertakings mentioned under I-2 of the Nomenclature which have the status of companies limited by shares, there is participation in the nature of direct investment where the block of shares held by a natural person of another undertaking or any other holder enables the shareholder, either pursuant to the provisions of national laws relating to companies limited by shares or otherwise, to participate effectively in the management of the company or in its control.

Long-term loans of a participating nature, mentioned under I-3 of the Nomenclature, means loans for a period of more than five years which are made for the purpose of establishing or maintaining lasting economic links. The main examples which may be cited are loans granted by a company to its subsidiaries or to companies in which it has a share and loans linked with a profit-sharing arrangement. Loans granted by financial institutions with a view to establishing or maintaining lasting economic links are also included under this heading.

Investments in real estate

Purchases of buildings and land and the construction of buildings by private persons for gain or personal use. This category also includes rights of usufruct, easements and building rights.

Introduction on a stock exchange or on a recognised money market

Access – in accordance with a specified procedure – for securities and other negotiable instruments to dealings, whether controlled officially or unofficially, on an officially recognised stock exchange or in an officially recognised segment of the money market.

Securities dealt in on a stock exchange (quoted or unquoted)

Securities the dealings in which are controlled by regulations, the prices for which are regularly published, either by official stock exchanges (quoted securities) or by other bodies attached to a stock exchange – e.g. committees of banks (unquoted securities).

Issue of securities and other negotiable instruments

Sale by way of an offer to the public.

Placing of securities and other negotiable instruments

The direct sale of securities by the issuer of by (sic) the consortium which the issuer has instructed to sell them, with no offer being made to the public.

Domestic or foreign securities and other instruments

Securities according to the country in which the issuer has his principal place of business. Acquisition by residents of domestic securities and other instruments issued on a foreign market ranks as the acquisition of foreign securities.

Share and other securities of a participating nature

Including rights to subscribe to new issues of shares.

Bonds

Negotiable securities with a maturity of two years or more from issue for which the interest rate and the terms for the repayment of the principal and the payment of interest are determined at the time of issue.

Collective investment undertakings

Undertakings:

– the object of which is the collective investment in transferable securities or other assets of the capital they raise and which operate on the principle of risk-spreading, and

– the units of which are, at the request of holders, under the legal, contractual or statutory conditions governing them, repurchased or redeemed, directly or indirectly, out of those undertakings' assets. Action taken by a collective investment undertaking to ensure that the stock exchange value of its units does not significantly vary from their net asset value shall be regarded as equivalent to such repurchase or redemption.

Such undertakings may be constituted according to law either under the law of contract (as common funds managed by management companies) or trust law (as unit trusts) or under statute (as investment companies).

For the purposes of the Directive, 'common funds' shall also include unit trusts.

Securities and other instruments normally dealt in on the money market

Treasury bills and other negotiable bills, certificates of deposit, bankers' acceptances, commercial paper and other like instruments.

Credits related to commercial transactions or to the provision of services

Contractual trade credits (advances or payments by instalment in respect of work in progress or on order and extended payment terms, whether or not involving subscription to a commercial bill) and their financing by credits provided by credit institutions. This category also includes factoring operations.

Financial loans and credits

Financing of every kind granted by financial institutions, including financing related to commercial transactions or to the provision of services in which no resident is participating.

This category also includes mortgage loans, consumer credit and financial leasing, as well as back-up facilities and other note-issuance facilities.

Residents or non-residents

Natural and legal persons according to the definitions laid down in the exchange control regulations in force in each Member State.

Proceeds of liquidation (of investments, securities, etc)

Proceeds of sale including any capital appreciation, amount of repayments, proceeds of execution of judgments, etc.

Natural or legal persons

As defined by the national rules.

Financial institutions

Banks, savings banks and institutions specialising in the provision of short-term, medium-term and long-term credit, and insurance companies, building societies, investment companies and other instutions of like character.

Credit institutions

Banks, savings banks and institutions specialising in the provision of short-term, medium-term and long-term credit.

Annex II

List of Operations referred to in Article 3 of the Directive

Nature of operation	Heading
Operations in securities and other instruments normally dealt in on the money market	V
Operations in current and deposit accounts with financial institutions	VI
Operations in units of collective investment undertakings	IV-A and B (c)
– undertakings for investment in securities or instruments normally dealt in on the money market	
Financial loans and credits	VIII-A and B-1
– short-term	
Personal capital movements	XI-A
– loans	
Physical import and export of financial assets	XII
– securities normally dealt in on the money market	
– means of payment	
Other capital movements: Miscellaneous	XIII-F
– operations similar to those listed above	short-term

The restrictions which Member States may apply to the capital movements listed above must be defined and applied in such a way as to cause the least possible hindrance to the free movement of persons, goods and services.

*   Council Directive 85/611/EEC on the coordination of laws, regulations and
    administrative provisions relating to undertakings for collective investment in
    transferable securities (UCITS) (OJ No L 375, 31.12.85, p.3).

III. The Hellenic Republic, the Kingdom of Spain, Ireland and the
Portuguese Republic may, until 31 December 1992, continue to apply or
reintroduce restrictions existing at the date of notification of the
Directive on capital movements given in List III below:

List III

Nature of operation	Heading
Operations in securities dealt in on the capital market	
– Admission of securities to the capital market	III-B-1 and 2
– where they are not dealt in on or in the process of introduction to a stock exchange in a Member State	
Operations in units of collective investment undertakings	
– Admission to the capital market of units of collective investment undertakings	IV-B-1 and 2
– undertakings not subject to Directive 85/611/EEC* and the sole object of which is the acquisition of assets that have been liberalised	
Financial loans and credits	VIII-A, B-2 and 3
– medium-term and long-term	

*   Council Directive 85/611/EEC on the coordination of laws, regulations and
    administrative provisions relating to undertakings for collective investment in
    transferable securities (UCITS) (OJ No L 375, 31.12.85, p.3).

IV. The Hellenic Republic, the Kingdom of Spain, Ireland and the
Portuguese Republic may, until 31 December 1992, defer liberalisation of
the capital movements given in List IV below:

List IV

Nature of operation	Heading
Operations in securities and other instruments normally dealt in on the money market	V
Operations in current and deposit accounts with financial institutions	VI
Operations in units of collective undertakings	IV-A and B(c)
— undertakings for investment in securities or instruments normally dealt in on the money market	
Financial loans and credits	VIII-A and B-1
— short term	
Personal capital movements	XI-A
— loans	
Physical import and export of financial assets	XII
— securities normally dealt in on the money market	
— means of payment	
Other capital movements: Miscellaneous	XIII-F

Annex V

Since the dual exchange market system, as operated by the Kingdom of Belgium and the Grand Duchy of Luxembourg, has not had the effect of restricting capital movements but nevertheless constitutes an anomaly in the EMS and should therefore be brought to an end in the interests of effective implementation of the Directive and with a view to strengthening the European Monetary System, these two Member States undertake to abolish it by 31 December 1992. They also undertake to administer the system, until such time as it is abolished, on the basis of procedures which will ensure the *de facto* free movement of capital on such conditions that the exchange rates ruling on the two markets show no appreciable and lasting differences.

FOOTNOTES

1. OJ No 26, 1.2.88 ,p.1.
2. OJ No C 187, 18.7.88.

3.   OJ No 43,12.7.60, p.921.
4.   OJ No L 332, 26.11.86, p.22.
5.   OJ No L 91, 18.4.72, p.13.
6.   See Explanatory notes below.

 Implemented in Ireland: The Exchange Control Acts, 1954-1990; S.I. 134S/1992.

(h) Goods

See S.I. 35/1993 (not included in this volume – editorial note).

COURT OF JUSTICE

COUNCIL DECISION

of 24 October 1988

establishing a Court of First Instance of the European Communities

(OJ No L 319, 25.11.88, p.1)

(88/591/ECSC, EEC, Euratom)

The Council of the European Communities,

Having regard to the Treaty establishing the European Coal and Steel Community, and in particular Article 32d thereof,

Having regard to the Treaty establishing the European Economic Community, and in particular Article 168a thereof,

Having regard to the Treaty establishing the European Atomic Energy Community, and in particular Article 140a thereof,

Having regard to the Protocol on the Statute of the Court of Justice of the European Coal and Steel Community, signed in Paris on 18 April 1951,

Having regard to the Protocol on the Statute of the Court of Justice of the European Economic Community, signed in Brussels on 17 April 1957,

Having regard to the Protocol on the Statute of the Court of Justice of the European Atomic Energy Community, signed in Brussels on 17 April 1957,

Having regard to the Protocol on Privileges and Immunities of the European Communities, signed in Brussels on 8 April 1965,

Having regard to the request of the Court of Justice,

Having regard to the opinion of the Commission,

Having regard to the opinion of the European Parliament[1],

Whereas Article 32d of the ECSC Treaty, Article 168a of the EEC Treaty and Article 140a of the EAEC Treaty empower the Council to attach to the Court of Justice a Court of First Instance called upon to exercise important judicial functions and whose members are independent beyond doubt and possess the ability required for performing such functions;

Whereas the aforesaid provisions empower the Council to give the Court of First Instance jurisdiction to hear and determine at first instance, in accordance with the conditions laid down by the Statutes, certain classes of action or proceeding brought by natural or legal persons, subject to the right of appeal to the Court of Justice on questions of law alone;

Whereas the Council is to determine, pursuant to the aforesaid provisions, the composition of that court and adopt the necessary adjustments and additional provisions to the Statutes of the Court of Justice;

Whereas, in respect of actions requiring close examination of complex facts, the establishment of a second court will improve the judicial protection of individual interests;

Whereas it is necessary, in order to maintain the quality and effectiveness of judicial review in the Community legal order, to enable the Court to concentrate its activities on its fundamental task of ensuring uniform interpretation of Community law;

Whereas it is therefore necessary to make use of the powers granted by Article 32d of the ECSC Treaty, Article 168a of the EEC Treaty and Article 140a of the EAEC Treaty and to transfer to the Court of First Instance jurisdiction to hear and determine at first instance certain classes of action or proceeding which frequently require an examination of complex facts, that is to say actions or proceedings brought by servants of the Communities and also, in so far as the ECSC Treaty is concerned, by undertakings and associations in matters concerning levies, production, prices, restrictive agreements, decisions or practices and concentrations, and so far as the EEC Treaty is concerned, by natural or legal persons in competition matters,

Has decided as follows:

Article 1

A Court, to be called the Court of First Instance of the European Communities, shall be attached to the Court of Justice of the European Communities. Its seat shall be at the Court of Justice.

Article 2

1. The Court of First Instance shall consist of 12 members.

2. The members shall elect the President of the Court of First Instance from among their number for a term of three years. He may be re-elected.

3. The members of the Court of First Instance may be called upon to perform the task of an Advocate-General.

It shall be the duty of the Advocate-General, acting with complete impartiality and independence, to make, in open court, reasoned submissions on certain cases brought before the Court of First Instance in order to assist the Court of First Instance in the performance of its task.

The criteria for selecting such cases, as well as the procedures for designating the Advocates-General, shall be laid down in the Rules of Procedure of the Court of First Instance.

A member called upon to perform the task of Advocate-General in a case may not take part in the judgment of the case.

4. The Court of First Instance shall sit in chambers of three or five judges. The composition of the chambers and the assignment of the cases to them shall be governed by the Rules of Procedure. In certain cases governed by the Rules of Procedure the Court of First Instance may sit in plenary session.

5. Article 21 of the Protocol on Privileges and Immunities of the European Communities and Article 6 of the Treaty establishing a Single Council and a Single Commission of the European Communities shall apply to the members of the Court of First Instance and to its Registrar.

Article 3

[Replaced by of Decision 93/350/Euratom, ECSC, EEC, OJ No L 144, 16.6.93, p.21, Article 1]

Article 4

[Replaced by of Decision 93/350/Euratom, ECSC, EEC, OJ No L 144, 16.6.93, p.21, Article 1]

Article 5

The following provisions shall be inserted after Article 43 of the Protocol on the Statute of the Court of Justice of the European Coal and Steel Community:

'Title IV:

The Court of First Instance of the European Communities

Rules concerning the members of the Court of First Instance and its organisation

Article 44

Articles 2, 3, 4, 6 to 9, 13(1), 17, 18(2) and 19 of this Statute shall apply to the Court of First Instance and its members. The oath referred to in Article 2 shall be taken before the Court of Justice and the decisions referred to in Articles 3, 4 and 7 shall be adopted by that Court after hearing the Court of First Instance.

Registrar and staff

Article 45

The Court of First Instance shall appoint its Registrar and lay down the rules governing his service. Articles 9 and 14 of this Statute shall apply to the Registrar of the Court of First Instance *mutatis mutandis*.

The President of the Court of Justice and the President of the Court of First Instance shall determine, by common accord, the conditions under which officials and other servants attached to the Court of Justice shall render their services to the Court of First Instance to enable it to function. Certain officials or other servants shall be responsible to the Registrar of the Court of First Instance under the authority of the President of the Court of First Instance.

Procedure before the Court of First Instance

Article 46

The procedure before the Court of First Instance shall be governed by Title III of this Statute, with the exception of Articles 41 and 42.

Such further and more detailed provisions as may be necessary shall

be laid down in the Rules of Procedure established in accordance with Article 32d(4) of the Treaty.

Notwithstanding the fourth paragraph of Article 21, the Advocate-General may make his reasoned submissions in writing.

Article 47

Where an application or other procedural document addressed to the Court of First Instance is lodged by mistake with the Registrar of the Court of Justice it shall be transmitted immediately by that Registrar to the Registrar of the Court of First Instance; likewise, where an application or other procedural document addressed to the Court of Justice is lodged by mistake with the Registrar of the Court of First Instance, it shall be transmitted immediately by that Registrar to the Registrar of the Court of Justice.

Where the Court of First Instance finds that it does not have jurisdiction to hear and determine an action in respect of which the Court of Justice has jurisdiction, it shall refer that action to the Court of Justice; likewise, where the Court of Justice finds that an action falls within the jurisdiction of the Court of First Instance, it shall refer that action to the Court of First Instance, whereupon that Court may not decline jurisdiction.

Where the Court of Justice and the Court of First Instance are seised of cases in which the same relief is sought, the same issue of interpretation is raised or the validity of the same act is called in question, the Court of First Instance may, after hearing the parties, stay the proceedings before it until such time as the Court of Justice shall have delivered judgment. Where applications are made for the same act to be declared void the Court of First Instance may also decline jurisdiction in order that the Court of Justice may rule on such applications. In the cases referred to in this subparagraph, the Court of Justice may also decide to stay the proceedings before it; in that event, the proceedings before the Court of First Instance shall continue.

Article 48

Final decisions of the Court of First Instance, decisions disposing of the substantive issues in part only, or disposing of a procedural issue concerning a plea of lack of competence or inadmissibility, shall be notified by the Registrar of the Court of First Instance to all parties as well as all Member States and the Community institutions even if they have not intervened in the case before the Court of First Instance.

Appeals to the Court of Justice

Article 49

An appeal may be brought before the Court of Justice, within two months of the notification of the decision appealed against, against final decisions of the Court of First Instance and decisions of that Court disposing of the substantive issues in part only, or disposing of a procedural issue concerning a plea of lack of competence or inadmissibility.

Such an appeal may be brought by any party which has been unsuccessful, in whole or in part, in its submissions. However, interveners other than the Member States and the Community institutions may bring such an appeal only where the decision of the Court of First Instance directly affects them.

With the exception of cases relating to disputes between the Communities and their servants, an appeal may also be brought by Member States and Community institutions which did not intervene in the proceedings before the Court of First Instance. Such Member States and institutions shall be in the same position as Member States or institutions which intervened at first instance.

Article 50

Any person whose application to intervene has been dismissed by the Court of First Instance may appeal to the Court of Justice within two weeks of the notification of the decision dismissing the application.

The parties to the proceedings may appeal to the Court of Justice against any decision of the Court of First Instance made pursuant to the second or third paragraphs of Article 39 or the third paragraph of Article 92 of the Treaty within two months from their notification.

The appeal referred to in the first two paragraphs of this Article shall be heard and determined under the procedure referred to in Article 33 of this Statute.

Article 51

An appeal to the Court of Justice shall be limited to points of law. It shall lie on the grounds of lack of competence of the Court of First Instance, a breach of procedure before it which adversely affects the interests of the appellant as well as the infringement of Community law by the Court of First Instance.

No appeal shall lie regarding only the amount of the costs or the party ordered to pay them.

Procedure before the Court

Article 52

Where an appeal is brought against a decision of the Court of First Instance, the procedure before the Court of Justice shall consist of a written part and an oral part. In accordance with conditions laid down in the Rules of Procedure the Court of Justice, having heard the Advocate-General and the parties, may dispense with the oral procedure.

Suspensory effect

Article 53

Without prejudice to the second and third paragraphs of Article 39 of the Treaty, an appeal shall not have suspensory effect.

[Second paragraph replaced by Decision 93/350/Euratom, ECSC, EEC, OJ No L 144, 16.6.93, p.21, Article 2]

The decision of the Court of Justice on the appeal

Article 54

If the appeal is well founded, the Court of Justice shall quash the decision of the Court of First Instance. It may itself give final judgment in the matter, where the state of the proceedings so permits, or refer the case back to the Court of First Instance for judgment.

Where a case is referred back to the Court of First Instance, that Court shall be bound by the decision of the Court of Justice on points of law.

When an appeal brought by a Member State or a Community institution, which has not intervened in the proceedings before the Court of First Instance, is well founded the Court of Justice may, if it considers this necessary, state which of the effects of the decision of the Court of First Instance which has been quashed shall be considered as definitive in respect of the parties to the litigation.'

Article 6

The former Articles 44 and 45 of the Protocol on the Statute of the Court

of Justice of the European Coal and Steel Community shall become Articles 55 and 56 respectively.

Article 7

The following provisions shall be inserted after Article 43 of the Protocol on the Statute of the Court of Justice of the European Economic Community:

'Title IV:

The Court of First Instance of the European Communities

Article 44

Articles 2 to 8, and 13 to 16 of this Statute shall apply to the Court of First Instance and its members. The oath referred to in Article 2 shall be taken before the Court of Justice and the decisions referred to in Articles 3, 4 and 6 shall be adopted by that Court after hearing the Court of First Instance.

Article 45

The Court of First Instance shall appoint its Registrar and lay down the rules governing his service. Articles 9, 10 and 13 of this Statute shall apply to the Registrar of the Court of First Instance *mutatis mutandis*.

The President of the Court of Justice and the President of the Court of First Instance shall determine, by common accord, the conditions under which officials and other servants attached to the Court of Justice shall render their services to the Court of First Instance to enable it to function. Certain officials or other servants shall be responsible to the Registrar of the Court of First Instance under the authority of the President of the Court of First Instance.

Article 46

The procedure before the Court of First Instance shall be governed by Title III of this Statute, with the exception of Article 20.

Such further and more detailed provisions as may be necessary shall be laid down in the Rules of Procedure established in accordance with Article 168a(4) of the Treaty.

Notwithstanding the fourth paragraph of Article 18 of this Statute,

the Advocate-General may make his reasoned submissions in writing.

Article 47

Where an application or other procedural document addressed to the Court of First Instance is lodged by mistake with the Registrar of the Court of Justice it shall be transmitted immediately by that Registrar to the Registrar of the Court of First Instance; likewise, where an application or other procedural document addressed to the Court of Justice is lodged by mistake with the Registrar of the Court of First Instance, it shall be transmitted immediately by that Registrar to the Registrar of the Court of Justice.

Where the Court of First Instance finds that it does not have jurisdiction to hear and determine an action in respect of which the Court of Justice has jurisdiction, it shall refer that action to the Court of Justice; likewise, where the Court of Justice finds that an action falls within the jurisdiction of the Court of First Instance, it shall refer that action to the Court of First Instance, whereupon that Court may not decline jurisdiction.

Where the Court of Justice and the Court of First Instance are seised of cases in which the same relief is sought, the same issue of interpretation is raised or the validity of the same act is called in question, the Court of First Instance may, after hearing the parties, stay the proceedings before it until such time as the Court of Justice shall have delivered judgment. Where applications are made for the same act to be declared void, the Court of First Instance may also decline jurisdiction in order that the Court of Justice may rule on such applications. In the cases referred to in this subparagraph, the Court of Justice may also decide to stay the proceedings before it; in that event, the proceedings before the Court of First Instance shall continue.

Article 48

Final decisions of the Court of First Instance, decisions disposing of the substantive issues in part only or disposing of a procedural issue concerning a plea of lack of competence or inadmissibility, shall be notified by the Registrar of the Court of First Instance to all parties as well as all Member States and the Community institutions even if they have not intervened in the case before the Court of First Instance.

Article 49

An appeal may be brought before the Court of Justice, within two

months of the notification of the decision appealed against, against final decisions of the Court of First Instance and decisions of that Court disposing of the substantive issues in part only or disposing of a procedural issue concerning a plea of lack of competence or inadmissibility.

Such an appeal may be brought by any party which has been unsuccessful, in whole or in part, in its submissions. However, interveners other than the Member States and the Community institutions may bring such an appeal only where the decision of the Court of First Instance directly affects them.

With the exception of cases relating to disputes between the Communities and their servants, an appeal may also be brought by Member States and Community institutions which did not intervene in the proceedings before the Court of First Instance. Such Member States and institutions shall be in the same position as Member States or institutions which intervened at first instance.

Article 50

Any person whose application to intervene has been dismissed by the Court of First Instance may appeal to the Court of Justice within two weeks of the notification of the decision dismissing the application.

The parties to the proceedings may appeal to the Court of Justice against any decision of the Court of First Instance made pursuant to Article 185 or 186 or the fourth paragraph of Article 192 of the Treaty within two months from their notification.

The appeal referred to in the first two paragraphs of this Article shall be heard and determined under the procedure referred to in Article 36 of this Statute.

Article 51

An appeal to the Court of Justice shall be limited to points of law. It shall lie on the grounds of lack of competence of the Court of First Instance, a breach of procedure before it which adversely affects the interests of the appellant as well as the infringement of Community law by the Court of First Instance.

No appeal shall lie regarding only the amount of the costs or the party ordered to pay them.

Article 52

Where an appeal is brought against a decision of the Court of First Instance, the procedure before the Court of Justice shall consist of a written part and an oral part. In accordance with conditions laid down in the Rules of Procedure the Court of Justice, having heard the Advocate-General and the parties, may dispense with the oral procedure.

Article 53

Without prejudice to Articles 185 and 186 of the Treaty, an appeal shall not have suspensory effect.

By way of derogation from Article 187 of the Treaty, decisions of the Court of First Instance declaring a regulation to be void shall take effect only as from the date of expiry of the period referred to in the first paragraph of Article 49 of this Statute or, if an appeal shall have been brought within that period, as from the date of dismissal of the appeal, without prejudice, however, to the right of a party to apply to the Court of Justice, pursuant to Articles 185 and 186 of this Treaty, for the suspension of the effects of the regulation which has been declared void or for the prescription of any other interim measure.

Article 54

If the appeal is well founded, the Court shall quash the decision of the Court of First Instance. It may itself give final judgment in the matter, where the state of the proceedings so permits, or refer the case back to the Court of First Instance for judgment.

Where a case is referred back to the Court of First Instance, that Court shall be bound by the decision of the Court of Justice on points of law.

When an appeal brought by a Member State or a Community institution, which has not intervened in the proceedings before the Court of First Instance, is well founded the Court of Justice may, if it considers this necessary, state which of the effects of the decision of the Court of First Instance which has been quashed shall be considered as definitive in respect of the parties to the litigation.'

Article 8

The former Articles 44, 45 and 46 of the Protocol on the Statute of the Court of Justice of the European Economic Community shall become Articles 55, 56 and 57 respectively.

Article 9

The following provisions shall be inserted after Article 44 of the Protocol on the Statute of the Court of Justice of the European Atomic Energy Community:

'Title IV:

The Court of First Instance of the European Communities

Article 45

Articles 2 to 8 and 13 to 16 of this Statute shall apply to the Court of First Instance and its members. The oath referred to in Article 2 shall be taken before the Court of Justice and the decisions referred to in Articles 3, 4 and 6 shall be adopted by that Court after hearing the Court of First Instance.

Article 46

The Court of First Instance shall appoint its Registrar and lay down the rules governing his service. Articles 9, 10 and 13 of this Statute shall apply to the Registrar of the Court of First Instance *mutatis mutandis*.

The President of the Court of Justice and the President of the Court of First Instance shall determine, by common accord, the conditions under which officials and other servants attached to the Court of Justice shall render their services to the Court of First Instance to enable it to function. Certain officials or other servants shall be responsible to the Registrar of the Court of First Instance under the authority of the President of the Court of First Instance.

Article 47

The procedure before the Court of First Instance shall be governed by Title III of this Statute, with the exception of Articles 20 and 21.

Such further and more detailed provisions as may be necessary shall be laid down in the Rules of Procedure established in accordance with Article 140a(4) of the Treaty.

Notwithstanding the fourth paragraph of Article 18 of this Statute, the Advocate-General may make his reasoned submissions in writing.

Article 48

Where an application or other procedural document addressed to

the Court of First Instance is lodged by mistake with the Registrar of the Court of Justice it shall be transmitted immediately by that Registrar to the Registrar of the Court of First Instance; likewise, where an application or other procedural document addressed to the Court of Justice is lodged by mistake with the Registrar of the Court of First Instance, it shall be transmitted immediately by that Registrar to the Registrar of the Court of Justice.

Where the Court of First Instance finds that it does not have jurisdiction to hear and determine an action in respect of which the Court of Justice has jurisdiction, it shall refer that action to the Court of Justice; likewise, where the Court of Justice finds that an action falls within the jurisdiction of the Court of First Instance, it shall refer that action to the Court of First Instance, whereupon that Court may not decline jurisdiction.

Where the Court of Justice and the Court of First Instance are seised of cases in which the same relief is sought, the same issue of interpretation is raised or the validity of the same act is called in question, the Court of First Instance may, after hearing the parties, stay the proceedings before it until such time as the Court of Justice shall have delivered judgment. Where applications are made for the same act to be declared void, the Court of First Instance may also decline jurisdiction in order that the Court of Justice may rule on such applications. In the cases referred to in this subparagraph, the Court of Justice may also decide to stay the proceedings before it; in that event, the proceedings before the Court of First Instance shall continue.

Article 49

Final decisions of the Court of First Instance, decisions disposing of the substantive issues in part only or disposing of a procedural issue concerning a plea of lack of competence or inadmissibility, shall be notified by the Registrar of the Court of First Instance to all parties as well as all Member States and the Community institutions even if they have not intervened in the case before the Court of First Instance.

Article 50

An appeal may be brought before the Court of Justice, within two months of the notification of the decision appealed against, against final decisions of the Court of First Instance and decisions of that Court disposing of the substantive issues in part only or disposing of a procedural issue concerning a plea of lack of competence or inadmissibility.

Such an appeal may be brought by any party which has been unsuccessful, in whole or in part, in its submissions. However, interveners other than Member States and the Community institutions may bring such an appeal only where the decision of the Court of First Instance directly affects them.

With the exception of cases relating to disputes between the Communities and their servants, an appeal may also be brought by Member States and Community institutions which did not intervene in the proceedings before the Court of First Instance. Such Member States and institutions shall be in the same position as Member States or institutions which intervened at first instance.

Article 51

Any person whose application to intervene has been dismissed by the Court of First Instance may appeal to the Court of Justice within two weeks of the notification of the decision dismissing the application.

The parties to the proceedings may appeal to the Court of Justice against any decision of the Court of First Instance made pursuant to Article 157 or 158 or the third paragraph of Article 164 of the Treaty within two months from their notification.

The appeal referred to in the first two paragraphs of this Article shall be heard and determined under the procedure referred to in Article 37 of this Statute.

Article 52

An appeal to the Court of Justice shall be limited to points of law. It shall lie on the grounds of lack of competence of the Court of First Instance, a breach of procedure before it which adversely affects the interests of the appellant as well as the infringement of Community law by the Court of First Instance.

No appeal shall lie regarding only the amount of the costs or the party ordered to pay them.

Article 53

Where an appeal is brought against a decision of the Court of First Instance, the procedure before the Court of Justice shall consist of a written part and an oral part. In accordance with conditions laid down in the Rules of Procedure the Court of Justice, having heard the Advocate-General and the parties, may dispense with the oral procedure.

Article 54

Without prejudice to Articles 157 and 158 of the Treaty, an appeal shall not have suspensory effect.

By way of derogation from Article 159 of the Treaty, decisions of the Court of First Instance declaring a regulation to be void shall take effect only as from the date of expiry of the period referred to in the first paragraph of Article 50 of this Statute or, if an appeal shall have been brought within that period, as from the date of dismissal of the appeal, without prejudice, however, to the right of a party to apply to the Court of Justice, pursuant to Articles 157 and 158 of this Treaty, for the suspension of the effects of the regulation which has been declared void or for the prescription of any other interim measure.

Article 55

If the appeal is well founded, the Court of Justice shall quash the decision of the Court of First Instance. It may itself give final judgment in the matter, where the state of the proceedings so permits, or refer the case back to the Court of First Instance for judgment.

Where a case is referred back to the Court of First Instance, that Court shall be bound by the decision of the Court of Justice on points of law.

When an appeal brought by a Member State or a Community institution, which has not intervened in the proceedings before the Court of First Instance, is well founded the Court of Justice may, if it considers this necessary, state which of the effects of the decision of the Court of First Instance which has been quashed shall be considered as definitive in respect of the parties to the litigation.'

Article 10

The former Articles 45, 46 and 47 of the Protocol on the Statute of the Court of Justice of the European Atomic Energy Community shall become Articles 56, 57 and 58 respectively.

Article 11

The first President of the Court of First Instance shall be appointed for three years in the same manner as its members. However, the Governments of the Member States may, by common accord, decide that the procedure laid down in Article 2(2) shall be applied.

The Court of First Instance shall adopt its Rules of Procedure immediately upon its constitution.

Until the entry into force of the Rules of Procedure of the Court of First Instance, the Rules of Procedure of the Court of Justice shall apply *mutatis mutandis*.

Article 12

Immediately after all members of the Court of First Instance have taken oath, the President of the Council shall proceed to choose by lot the members of the Court of First Instance whose terms of office are to expire at the end of the first three years in accordance with Article 32d(3) of the ECSC Treaty, Article 168a(3) of the EEC Treaty, and Article 140a(3) of the EAEC Treaty.

Article 13

This Decision shall enter into force on the day following its publication in the *Official Journal of the European Communities*, with the exception of Article 3, which shall enter into force on the date of the publication in the *Official Journal of the European Communities* of the ruling by the President of the Court of Justice that the Court of First Instance has been constituted in accordance with law.

Article 14

Cases referred to in Article 3 of which the Court of Justice is seised on the date on which that Article enters into force but in which the preliminary report provided for in Article 44(1) of the Rules of Procedure of the Court of Justice has not yet been presented shall be referred back to the Court of First Instance.

Done at Luxembourg, 24 October 1988.

For the Council

The President

Th. Pangalos

FOOTNOTE

1. OJ No C 187, 18.7.88, p.227.

COUNCIL DECISION

of 8 June 1993

amending Council Decision 88/591/ECSC, EEC, Euratom establishing a Court of First Instance of the European Communities

(93/350/Euratom, ECSC, EEC)

(OJ No L 144, 16.6.93, p.21)

The Council of the European Communities,

Having regard to the Treaty establishing the European Coal and Steel Community, and in particular Article 32d thereof,

Having regard to the Treaty establishing the European Economic Community, and in particular Article 168a thereof,

Having regard to the Treaty establishing the European Atomic Energy Community, and in particular Article 140a thereof,

Having regard to the Protocol on the Statute of the Court of Justice of the European Coal and Steel Community, signed in Paris on 18 April 1951,

Having regard to the request from the Court of Justice,

Having regard to the opinion of the Commission,

Having regard to the opinion of the European Parliament[1],

Whereas the attachment to the Court of Justice of a Court of First Instance by Decision 88/591/ECSC, EEC, Euratom[2] is intended, by the establishment of a second court, in particular in respect of actions requiring close examination of complex facts, to improve the judicial protection of individual interests and to maintain the quality and effectiveness of judicial review in the Community legal order by enabling the Court of Justice to concentrate its activities on its fundamental task, of ensuring uniform interpretation of Community law;

Whereas, with the same end in view, it is appropriate, taking into account past experience to enlarge the jurisdiction transferred to the Court of First Instance to hear and determine at first instance certain classes of action or proceeding brought by natural or legal persons;

Whereas Decision 88/591/ECSC, EEC, Euratom should therefore be amended in consequence,

Has decided as follows:

Article 1

Decision 88/591/ECSC, EEC, Euratom is hereby amended as follows:

1. the following shall be substituted for Article 3(1):

'The Court of First Instance shall exercise at first instance the jurisdiction conferred on the Court of Justice by the Treaties establishing the Communities and by the acts adopted in implementation thereof, save as otherwise provided in an act setting up a body governed by Community law:

(a) in disputes as referred to in Article 179 of the EEC Treaty and Article 152 on the EAEC Treaty;

(b) in actions brought by natural or legal persons pursuant to the second paragraph of Article 33, Article 35, the first and the second paragraphs of Article 40 and Article 42 of the ECSC Treaty;

(c) in actions brought by natural or legal persons pursuant to the second paragraph of Article 173, the third paragraph of Article 175 and Articles 178 and 181 of the EEC Treaty;

(d) in actions brought by natural or legal persons pursuant to the second paragraph of Article 146, the third paragraph of Article 148 and Articles 151 and 153 of the EAEC Treaty.';

2. paragraphs 2 and 3 of Article 3 are hereby repealed;

3. the following shall be substituted for Article 4:

'Article 4

Save as hereinafter provided, Articles 34, 36, 39, 44 and 92 of the ECSC Treaty, Articles 172, 174, 176, 184 to 187 and 192 of the EEC Treaty and Articles 49, 83, 144b, 147, 149, 156 to 159 and 164 of the Euratom Treaty shall apply to the Court of First Instance.'

Article 2

In the Protocol on the Statute of the Court of Justice of the European Coal and Steel Community, as amended by Decision 88/591/ECSC, EEC, Euratom, the following shall be substituted for the second paragraph of Article 53:

'By way of derogation from Article 44 of the Treaty, decisions of the Court of First Instance declaring a general decision or general recommendation to be void shall take effect only as from the date of expiry of the period referred to in the first paragraph of Article 49 of this Statute, or if an appeal shall have been brought within that

period, as from the date of dismissal of the appeal, without prejudice, however, to the right of a party to apply to the Court of Justice pursuant to the second and third paragraphs of Article 39 of the Treaty, for the suspension of the effects of the act which has been declared void or for the prescription of any other interim measure.'

Article 3

This Decision shall enter into force on the first day of the second month following that of its publication in the *Official Journal of the European Communities*; however, in respect of actions brought by natural or legal persons pursuant to the second paragraph of Article 33, Article 35 and the first and second paragraphs of Article 40 of the ECSC Treaty and which concern acts relating to the application of Article 74 of the said Treaty in respect of actions brought by natural or legal persons pursuant to the second paragraph of Article 173, the third paragraph of Article 175 and Article 178 of the EEC Treaty and relating to measures to protect trade within the meaning of Article 113 of that Treaty in the case of dumping and subsidies, its entry into force shall be deferred to a date that the Council shall fix by unanimous decision.

The provisions relating to actions brought under Article 42 of the ECSC Treaty, Article 181 of the EEC Treaty or Article 153 of the EAEC Treaty shall apply only to contracts concluded after the entry into force of this Decision.

Article 4

Cases falling within the scope of Article 3 of Decision 88/591/ECSC, EEC, Euratom, as amended by this Decision, of which the Court of Justice is seised on the date on which this Decision enters into force but in which the preliminary report provided for in Article 44(1) of the Rules of Procedure of the Court of Justice has not yet been presented, shall be referred to the Court of First Instance.

Done at Luxembourg, 8 June 1993.

For the Council

The President

N. Helveg Petersen

FOOTNOTES

1. OJ No C 241, 21.9.92, p.1.
2. OJ No L 319, 25.11.88, p.1. Corrected version published in OJ No C 215, 21.8.89, p.1.

COUNCIL DECISION

of 7 March 1994

amending Decision 93/350/Euratom, ECSC, EEC amending Decision 88/591/ECSC, EEC, Euratom establishing a Court of First Instance of the European Communities

(94/149/ECSC, EC)

(OJ No L 66, 10.3.94, p.29)

The Council of the European Union,

Having regard to Council Decision 93/350/Euratom, ECSC, EEC of 8 June 1993 amending Decision 88/591/ECSC, EEC, Euratom establishing a Court of First Instance of the European Communities[1], and in particular Article 3 thereof,

Whereas, under Decision 88/591/ECSC, EEC, Euratom[2], as thus amended, the Court of First Instance has jurisdiction to hear and determine virtually all the actions brought by natural or legal persons;

Whereas, however, with regard to trade protection measures taken under the Treaties establishing the European Coal and Steel Community and the European Community in the case of dumping and subsidies, the entry into force of Decision 93/350/Euratom, ECSC, EEC was deferred:

Whereas, in the light of developments since then, the date of the entry into force of this part of the abovementioned Decision needs to be determined,

Has decided as follows:

Article 1

The second part of the first sentence of Article 3 of Decision 93/350/Euratom, ECSC, EEC shall be replaced by the following:

'however, in respect of actions brought by natural or legal persons pursuant to the second paragraph of Article 33, Article 35 and the first and second paragraphs of Article 40 of the ECSC Treaty and which concern acts relating to the application of Article 74 of the said Treaty and in respect of actions brought by natural or legal persons pursuant to the fourth paragraph of Article 173, the third paragraph of Article 175 and Article 178 of the EC Treaty and relating to measures to protect trade within the meaning of Article 113 of

that Treaty in the case of dumping and subsidies, its entry into force shall be fixed at 15 March 1994.'

Article 2

This Decision shall enter into force on the day following its publication in the *Official Journal of the European Communities*.

Done at Brussels, 7 March 1994.

For the Council

The President

Th. Pangalos

FOOTNOTES

1. OJ No L 144, 16.6.93, p.21.
2. OJ No L 319, 25.11.88, p.1.

INSTRUCTIONS TO THE REGISTRAR OF THE COURT OF FIRST INSTANCE

of 3 March 1994

(OJ No L 78, 22.3.94, p.32)

The Court of First Instance of the European Communities,

On a proposal from the President of the Court of First Instance,

Having regard to the Rules of Procedure adopted on 2 May 1991 and in particular Article 23 thereof,

Has laid down the following:

Instructions to the Registrar

Article 1

The tasks of the Registrar

The Registrar shall be responsible for the maintenance of the register of the Court and the files of pending cases, for the acceptance, transmission, service and custody of documents, for correspondence with the parties and third parties in relation to pending cases, and for the custody of the seals of the Court. He shall ensure that registry charges are

collected and that sums due to the Court treasury are recovered. He shall be responsible for the publications of the Court.

Article 2

Opening hours of the Registry

1. The offices of the Registry shall be open to the public every working day.

All days other than Saturdays, Sundays and the official holidays on the list referred to in Article 101(2) of the Rules of Procedure shall be working days.

If a working day as referred to in the previous subparagraphs is a holiday for the officials and servants of the institution, arrangements shall be made for a skeleton staff to be on duty at the Registry during the hours in which it is normally open to the public.

2. The Registry shall be open to the public at the following times:

- in the morning, from Monday to Friday, from 9.30 am to 12 noon,
- in the afternoon, from Monday to Thursday, from 2.30 pm to 5.30 pm and, except during the vacations provided for in Article 34(1) of the Rules of Procedure, on Fridays from 2.30 pm to 4.30 pm.

The Registry shall be open to the public half an hour before the commencement of a hearing.

3. When the Registry is closed, procedural documents may be validly lodged with the janitor at the entrances to the Court buildings at any time of the day or night. The janitor shall make a record, which shall constitute good evidence, of the date and time of such lodgment and shall issue a receipt upon request.

Article 3

The register

1. Judgments and orders as well as all the documents placed on the file in cases brought before the Court shall be entered in the register.

2. Entries in the register shall be numbered consecutively; they shall be made in the language of the case and contain the information necessary for identifying the document, in particular the date of registration, the number of the case and the nature of the document.

3. Where a correction is made to the register, a note to that effect shall be made in the margin.

4. The registration number of every document drawn up by the Court shall be noted on its first page.

A note of the registration, indicating the registration number and the date of entry in the register, shall be stamped on the original of every procedural document lodged by the parties and on every copy which is notified to them. This note shall be in the language of the case and signed by the Registrar.

5. When a document is not entered in the register on the same day on which it is lodged, the date of lodgment shall be entered in the register and stamped on the original and on the copies of the procedural document concerned.

6. For the purposes of the application of the previous paragraph, the following dates shall be taken into account, depending on the circumstances: the date on which the procedural document was received by the Registrar or by a Registry official or employee, the date referred to in Article 2(3) or, in the cases provided for in the first paragraph of Article 47 of the EC Statute of the Court of Justice, the first paragraph of Article 47 of the ECSC Statute of the Court of Justice and the first paragraph of Article 48 of the EAEC Statute of the Court of Justice, the date on which the procedural document was lodged with the Registrar of the Court of Justice.

Article 4

The case number

1. When an application initiating proceedings is registered, the case shall be given a serial number preceded by 'T-' and followed by an indication of the year.

Applications for interim measures, applications to intervene, applications for rectification or interpretation of judgments, applications for revision or initiating third-party proceedings, applications for the taxation of costs and applications for legal aid relating to pending cases shall be given the same serial number as the principal action, followed by a note to indicate that the proceedings concerned are special forms of procedure. An action which is preceded by an application for legal aid in connection therewith shall be given the same case number as the latter. Where the Court of Justice refers a case back to the Court of First Instance following an appeal, that case shall keep the number previously given to it when it was before the Court of First Instance.

2. The serial number of the case together with the names of the parties shall be indicated on the procedural documents, in correspondence

relating to the case and, without prejudice to Article 17(4) of these Instructions, in the publications of the Court of First Instance.

Article 5

The file and access to the file

1. The case-file shall contain the originals, including their annexes, of the procedural documents produced by the parties, with the exception of those whose acceptances are refused pursuant to Article 6 of these Instructions, the decisions taken in the case, including any decisions relating to refusal to accept documents, reports for the hearing, minutes of the hearing, notices served by the Registrar and any other documents or correspondence to be taken into consideration in deciding the case.

If in doubt the Registrar shall refer the question whether a document is to be placed on the case-file to the President in order for a decision to be taken.

2. The documents contained in the file shall be given a serial number. Each page of the file shall be numbered consecutively.

3. The lawyers or agents of the parties to a case before the Court or persons duly authorised by them may inspect the original case-file, including administrative files produced before the Court, at the Registry and may request copies or extracts of procedural documents and of the register.

Lawyers or agents of intervening parties once granted leave to intervene and lawyers or agents of all the parties to joined cases shall have the same right of access to case-files, subject to the provisions of paragraph 4 relating to the confidential treatment of certain matters or documents on the file.

No third party, private or public, may have access to the case-file or to the procedural documents without the express authorisation of the President, after the parties have been heard. That authorisation may be granted only upon written request accompanied by a detailed explanation of the third party's legitimate interest in inspecting the file.

4. An application by a party for certain matters or certain documents on the file to be treated confidentially must be made by a separate document. The application must specify the confidential matters or passages, explain why each matter or passage concerned is confidential and be accompanied by a copy of the pages concerned of the pleading or annex in question, with an indication of the matters or passages in respect of which confidential treatment is requested.

If certain matters or certain documents on the file are accorded

confidential treatment, the Registrar shall, where necessary, request the parties to produce, in accordance with the decision of the Court, non-confidential versions of their pleadings together with the number of certified copies required by Article 43(1) of the Rules of Procedure.

The confidential and non-confidential versions of procedural documents shall be kept in separate sections of the file. Access to the confidential section of the file shall be confined to the parties in respect of whom no confidential treatment has been ordered.

5. At the close of the proceedings, the case-file shall be closed and bound. The closed file shall contain a list of the documents on the file, an indication of their number, and a cover page showing the serial number of the case, the parties and the date on which the file was closed.

Article 6

Non-acceptance of documents and regularisation

1. The Registrar shall ensure that the documents placed on the file are in conformity with the provisions of the Statutes of the Court of Justice, with the Rules of Procedure and with these Instructions. If necessary, he shall allow the parties a period of time for making good any formal irregularities in the documents lodged.

2. The Registrar shall refuse to register pleadings or procedural documents which are not provided for by the Rules of Procedure. If in doubt the Registrar shall refer the matter to the President in order for a decision to be taken.

3. Without prejudice to Article 10(3) of these Instructions concerning the use of facsimile transmission, the Registrar shall accept only documents bearing the original signature of the party's lawyer or agent.

The Registrar may request the lodgment of a lawyer's or agent's specimen signature, if necessary certified as a true specimen, in order to enable him to verify that the first paragraph of Article 43(1) of the Rules of Procedure has been complied with.

4. Documents annexed to a pleading or procedural document shall be accepted only if the document in question is mentioned in the body of the pleading or procedural document and appears in a schedule of annexes, as provided for by Article 43(4) of the Rules of Procedure. The schedule of annexes must indicate the annex numbers and the dates and nature of the documents annexed.

If the party concerned fails to make good the irregularity, the Registrar may refuse to accept annexes not in conformity with the provisions of this paragraph.

5. Save in the cases expressly provided for by the Rules of Procedure, the Registrar shall refuse to accept pleadings or procedural documents of the parties drawn up in a language other than the language of the case.

Where documents annexed to a pleading or procedural document are not accompanied by a translation into the language of the case, the Registrar shall require the party concerned to make good the omission if the translation appears necessary for the efficient conduct of the proceedings.

Where an application to intervene originating from a third party other than a Member State is not drawn up in the language of the case, the Registrar shall require the application to be put in order before it is placed on the file and served on the parties. If, however, a version of such an application drawn up in the language of the case is lodged within the period prescribed for this purpose by the Registrar, the date on which the first version, not in the language of the case, was lodged shall be taken as the date on which the document was lodged for the purposes of registration.

6. Each copy of any procedural document which the parties are required to produce by virtue of Article 43(1) of the Rules of Procedure must bear a note, signed by the lawyer or agent of the party concerned, certifying that the copy is a true copy of the original of the document concerned.

7. Where a party challenges the Registrar's refusal to accept a document, the Registrar shall submit the document concerned to the President for a decision on whether it is to be accepted.

Article 7

Presentation of originating applications

1. Where the Registrar considers that an application initiating proceedings is manifestly not in conformity with Article 44(1) of the Rules of Procedure, he shall suspend service of the application in order that the Court may give a decision on the admissibility of the action.

2. For the purposes of the production of the document required by Article 44(3) of the Rules of Procedure certifying that the lawyer acting for a party or assisting the party's agent is entitled to practise before a court of a Member State, reference may be made to a document previously lodged at the Registry of the Court.

3. Documents to be produced by virtue of Article 44(5)(a) and (b) of the Rules of Procedure in the case of an application made by a legal person must include the authority granted to the lawyer, signed by a representative of that legal person authorised for the purpose, as well as

evidence establishing the existence in law of the legal person and the power of the authority's signatory to act in the name of the legal person.

Article 8

Translations

1. The Registrar shall, in accordance with Article 36(1) of the Rules of Procedure, arrange for everything said or written in the course of the proceedings to be translated, at the request of a Judge, an Advocate-General or a party, into the language of the case or, where necessary, into another language as provided for in Article 35(2) of the Rules of Procedure. Where, for the purposes of the efficient conduct of the proceedings, a translation into another language, as provided for in Article 35(1) of the Rules of Procedure, is necessary, the Registrar shall also arrange for such a translation to be made.

2. The Registrar shall prescribe the periods within which institutions which are parties to proceedings are to produce the translations provided for by Article 43(2) of the Rules of Procedure.

Article 9

Service

1. Service shall be effected, in accordance with Article 100 of the Rules of Procedure, either by the dispatch by registered post, with a form for acknowledgement of receipt, of a certified copy of the original of the document to be served or by personal delivery of such copy to the addressee against a receipt. If need be, the certified copy shall be prepared by the Registrar.

The copy of the document shall be accompanied by a letter specifying the case number, the register number and a brief indication of the nature of the document.

2. Provided that the addressee concerned has an address for service in Luxembourg, documents shall be served on the person authorised to accept service.

Where, contrary to the first subparagraph of Article 44(2) of the Rules of Procedure, a party has omitted to state an address for service in Luxembourg, service shall be effected by the posting in Luxembourg of a registered letter addressed to the lawyer or agent of the party concerned.

3. The form for acknowledgment of receipt, the receipt or, where applicable, the proof of posting of the registered letter in Luxembourg

shall be kept in the case-file together with the copy of the letter addressed to the person upon whom service was to be effected.

4. If, owing to the length of a document, only one copy is annexed to a procedural document lodged by a party or if, for other reasons, copies of a document or an object lodged at the Registry cannot be forwarded to the parties, the Registrar shall inform the parties accordingly and indicate to them that the document or object in question is available to them at the Registry.

Article 10

Setting and extension of time limits

1. The Registrar shall prescribe the time limits provided for in the Rules of Procedure, in accordance with the authority accorded to him by the President.

2. Documents received at the Registry after the period prescribed for their lodgment has expired may be accepted only with the authorisation of the President.

3. Where a procedural document is received at the Registry by means of facsimile transmission before the expiry of the period prescribed for its lodgment and the original of the document concerned is then lodged with the required promptness, the Registrar shall accept lodgment of the document as if it had occurred on the date on which the facsimile transmission was received, provided that the time limit is one which may be extended pursuant to Article 103 of the Rules of Procedure.

In particular, originating applications or applications to intervene may not be lodged by means of facsimile transmission.

4. The Registrar may extend the time limits prescribed, in accordance with the authority accorded to him by the President. When necessary, he shall submit to the President proposals for the extension of time limits.

Applications for extensions of time limits must be duly reasoned and be submitted in good time before the expiry of the period prescribed. A time limit may not be extended more than once save for exceptional reasons.

Article 11

Procedures on applications for interim measures

1. In the procedures referred to in Articles 104 to 110 of the Rules of Procedure, applications, written observations, applications to intervene and other procedural documents may be submitted by means of facsimile transmission followed by the sending of the original document.

2. The Registrar may send messages and serve documents by all appropriate means which urgency requires, and in particular by means of facsimile transmission; in the event of facsimile transmission, the Registrar shall nevertheless ensure that the facsimile transmission is followed by a dispatch in the manner prescribed by Article 100 of the Rules of Procedure.

Article 12

Hearings and minutes of hearings

1. Before every public hearing the Registrar shall draw up a cause list in the language of the case. The cause list shall contain the date, hour and place of the hearing, an indication of the cases which will be called and the names of the parties.

The cause list shall be displayed at the entrance to the courtroom.

2. The Registrar shall draw up in the respective language of each case the minutes of every hearing. Those minutes shall contain an indication of the case, the date, hour and place of the hearing, an indication of whether the hearing was in public or *in camera*, the names of the Judges, the Advocate-General and the Registrar present, the names and capacities of the agents, lawyers or advisers of the parties present, the surnames, forenames, status and permanent addresses of the witnesses or experts examined, an indication of the evidence or documents produced at the hearing and, in so far as is necessary, the statements made at the hearing and the decisions pronounced at the hearing by the Court or the President.

3. Minutes of the examination of a witness which reproduce the witness's evidence shall be drawn up by the Registrar in the language in which the witness gave his evidence.

Before signing the minutes and submitting them to the President for his signature the Registrar shall forward the draft minutes to the witness, if necessary by registered post, and request the witness to check them, make any observations which he may wish to make upon them and sign them.

Article 13

Witnesses and experts

1. The Registrar shall take the measures necessary for giving effect to orders requiring the taking of expert opinion or the examination of witnesses.

2. The Registrar shall obtain from witnesses evidence of their expenses

and loss of earnings and from experts a fee note accounting for their expenses and services.

3. The Registrar shall cause sums due to witnesses and experts under the Rules of Procedure to be paid from the Court's treasury. In the event of a dispute concerning such sums, the Registrar shall refer the matter to the President in order for a decision to be taken.

4. The Registrar shall arrange for the costs of examining experts or witnesses' advances by the Court in a case to be demanded from the parties ordered to pay the costs. If necessary, steps pursuant to Article 15(2) shall be taken.

Article 14

Originals of judgments and orders

1. Originals of judgments and orders of the Court shall be kept in chronological order in the archives of the Registry. A certified copy shall be placed on the case file.

At the parties' request, the Registrar shall supply them with a certified copy of the original of a judgment or of an order.

The Registrar may supply uncertified copies of judgments and orders to third parties who so request.

2. Judgments or orders rectifying or interpreting a judgment or an order, judgments given on applications to set aside judgments by default, judgments and orders given in third-party proceedings or on applications for revision and judgments or orders given by the Court of Justice in appeals shall be mentioned in the margin of the judgment or order concerned. A certified copy shall be appended to the original of the judgment or order.

Article 15

Recovery of sums

1. Where sums paid out by way of legal aid or sums advanced to witnesses or experts are recoverable, the Registrar shall, by registered letter, demand payment to those sums from the party which is to bear them in accordance with the Rules of Procedure.

2. If the sums demanded are not paid within the period prescribed by the Registrar, he may request the Court to make an enforceable decision and, if necessary, require its enforcement.

Article 16

Registry charges

1. Where a copy of a procedural document or an extract from the case-file or from the register is supplied to a party at its request, the Registrar shall impose a Registry charge of ECU 3,50 a page for a certified copy and ECU 2,50 a page for an uncertified copy.

2. Where the Registrar arranges for a procedural document or an extract from the case-file to be translated at the request of a party, a Registry charge of ECU 1,25 a line shall be imposed.

3. The charges referred to in this Article shall, as from 1 January 1994, be increased by 10% each time the weighted cost-of-living index published by the Government of the Grand Duchy of Luxembourg is increased by 10%.

Article 17

Publications

1. The Registrar shall cause to be published in the *Official Journal of the European Communities* the composition of the Chambers and the criteria applied in the allocation of cases to them, the election of the President of the Court of First Instance and of the Presidents of Chambers, the appointment of the Registrar and of any Deputy Registrar.

2. The Registrar shall cause to be published in the *Official Journal of the European Communities* notices of proceedings brought and of decisions closing proceedings.

3. The Registrar shall ensure that the case-law of the Court of First Instance is made public and that the *Reports of Cases before the Court of First Instance* are published in the languages referred to in Article 1 of Council Regulation No 1 and in accordance with any arrangements adopted by the Court of First Instance.

4. Where a party request or the Court of its own motion so decides, the names of parties or third parties or other information may be omitted from the publications relating to a case if there is a legitimate interest in keeping the identity of a person or other information confidential.

Article 18

Advice for lawyers and agents

1. At the request of lawyers or agents or, if need be, of his own accord,

the Registrar shall send to lawyers or agents a copy of these Instructions to the Registrar,

2. The Registrar shall draw up notes of advice on the conduct of the written and oral procedure and make them known to lawyers and agents.

3. When requested by lawyers or agents, the Registrar shall provide them with information on the practice followed pursuant to the Rules of Procedure and pursuant to these Instructions to the Registrar in order to ensure the proceedings are conducted efficiently.

Article 19

Derogations from these Instructions

Where the special circumstances of a case and the proper administration of justice require, the Court or the President may derogate from any of these Instructions to the Registrar.

Article 20

Entry into force of these Instructions

These Instructions to the Registrar, which are authentic in the languages referred to in Article 36(2) of the Rules of Procedure, shall be published in the *Official Journal of the European Communities.*

The shall enter into force on the day following their publication.

Done at Luxembourg, 3 March 1994.

[*Signatories omitted*]

EUROPEAN PARLIAMENT

COUNCIL DECISION

concerning the Election of the representatives of the European Parliament by direct universal suffrage

(76/787/ECSC, EEC, Euratom)

(OJ L 278, 8.10.76, p.1)

The Council,

Composed of the representatives of the Member States and acting unanimously,

Having regard to Article 21(3) of the Treaty establishing the European Coal and Steel Community,

Having regard to Article 138(3) of the Treaty establishing the European Economic Community,

Having regard to Article 108(3) of the Treaty establishing the European Atomic Energy Community,

Having regard to the proposal from the European Parliament,

Intending to give effect to the conclusions of the European Council in Rome on 1 and 2 December 1975, that the election of the European Parliament should be held on a single date within the period May/June 1978,

Has laid down the provisions annexed to this Decision which it recommends to the Member States for adoption in accordance with their respective constitutional requirements.

This Decision and the provisions annexed hereto shall be published in the *Official Journal of the European Communities*.

The Member States shall notify the Secretary-General of the Council of the European Communities without delay of the completion of the procedures necessary in accordance with their respective constitutional requirements for the adoption of the provisions annexed to this Decision.

This Decision shall enter into force on the day of its publication in the *Official Journal of the European Communities*.

Done at Brussels on the twentieth day of September in the year one thousand nine hundred and seventy-six.

The President

M. *van der Stoel*

[List omitted]

Act

concerning the election of the representatives of the European Parliament by direct universal suffrage

Article 1

The representatives in the European Parliament of the peoples of the States brought together in the Community shall be elected by direct universal suffrage.

[Article 2

The number of representatives elected in each Member State shall be as follows:

Belgium	25
Denmark	16
Germany	99
Greece	25
Spain	64
France	87
Ireland	15
Italy	87
Luxembourg	6
Netherlands	31
Portugal	25
United Kingdom	87][1]

Article 3

1. Representatives shall be elected for a term of five years.

2. This five-year period shall begin at the opening of the first session following each election.

It may be extended or curtailed pursuant to the second subparagraph of Article 10(2).

3. The term of office of each representative shall begin and end at the same time as the period referred to in paragraph 2.

Article 4

1. Representatives shall vote on an individual and personal basis. They shall not be bound by any instructions and shall not receive a binding mandate.

2. Representatives shall enjoy the privileges and immunities applicable to members of the European Parliament by virtue of the Protocol on the Privileges and Immunities of the European Communities annexed to the

Treaty establishing a Single Council and a Single Commission of the European Communities.

Article 5

The office of representative in the European Parliament shall be compatible with membership of the Parliament of a Member State.

Article 6

1. The office of representative in the European Parliament shall be incompatible with that of:

- member of the Government of a Member State,
- member of the Commission of the European Communities,
- Judge, Advocate-General or Registrar of the Court of Justice of the European Communities,
- member of the Court of Auditors of the European Communities,
- member of the Consultative Committee of the European Coal and Steel Community or member of the Economic and Social Committee of the European Economic Community and of the European Atomic Energy Community,
- member of committees or other bodies set up pursuant to the Treaties establishing the European Coal and Steel Community, the European Economic Community and the European Atomic Energy Community for the purpose of managing the Communities' funds or carrying out a permanent direct administrative task.
- member of the Board of Directors, Management Committee or staff of the European Investment Bank,
- active official or servant of the institutions of the European Communities or of the specialised bodies attached to them.

2. In addition, each Member State may, in the circumstances provided for in Article 7(2), lay down rules at national level relating to incompatibility.

3. Representatives in the European Parliament to whom paragraphs 1 and 2 become applicable in the course of the five-year period referred to in Article 3 shall be replaced in accordance with Article 12.

Article 7

1. Pursuant to Article 21(3) of the Treaty establishing the European Coal and Steel Community, Articles 138(3) of the Treaty establishing the

European Economic Community and 108(3) of the Treaty establishing the European Atomic Energy Community, the European Parliament shall draw up a proposal for a uniform electoral procedure.

2. Pending the entry into force of a uniform electoral procedure and subject to the other provisions of this Act, the electoral procedure shall be governed in each Member State by its national provisions.

Article 8

No one may vote more than once in any election of representatives to the European Parliament.

Article 9

1. Elections to the European Parliament shall be held on the date fixed by each Member State; for all Member States this date shall fall within the same period starting on a Thursday morning and ending on the following Sunday.

2. The counting of votes may not begin until after the close of polling in the Member State whose electors are the last to vote within the period referred to in paragraph 1.

3. If a Member State adopts a double ballot system for elections to the European Parliament, the first ballot must take place during the period referred to in paragraph 1.

Article 10

1. The Council, acting unanimously after consulting the European Parliament, shall determine the period referred to in Article 9(1) for the first elections.

2. Subsequent elections shall take place in the corresponding period in the last year of the five-year period referred to in Article 3.

Should it prove impossible to hold the elections in the Community during that period, the Council acting unanimously shall, after consulting the European Parliament, determine another period which shall be not more than one month before or one month after the period fixed pursuant to the preceding subparagraph.

3. Without prejudice to Article 22 of the Treaty establishing the European Coal and Steel Community, Article 139 of the Treaty establishing the European Economic Community and Article 109 of the Treaty establishing the European Atomic Energy Community, the European Parliament shall meet, without requiring to be convened, on the first

Tuesday after expiry of an interval of one month from the end of the period referred to in Article 9(1).

4. The powers of the outgoing European Parliament shall cease upon the opening of the first sitting of the new European Parliament.

Article 11

Pending the entry into force of the uniform electoral procedure referred to in Article 7(1), the European Parliament shall verify the credentials of representatives. For this purpose it shall take note of the results declared officially by the Member States and shall rule on any disputes which may arise out of the provisions of this Act other than those arising out of the national provisions to which the Act refers.

Article 12

1. Pending the entry into force of the uniform electoral procedure referred to in Article 7(1) and subject to the other provisions of this Act, each Member State shall lay down appropriate procedures for filling any seat which falls vacant during the five-year term of office referred to in Article 3 for the remainder of that period.

2. Where a seat falls vacant pursuant to national provisions in force in a Member State, the latter shall inform the European Parliament, which shall take note of that fact.

In all other cases, the European Parliament shall establish that there is a vacancy and inform the Member State thereof.

Article 13

Should it appear necessary to adopt measures to implement this Act, the Council acting unanimously on a proposal from the European Parliament after consulting the Commission, shall adopt such measures after endeavouring to reach agreement with the European Parliament in a conciliation committee consisting of the Council and representatives of the European Parliament.

Article 14

Article 21(1) and (2) of the Treaty establishing the European Coal and Steel Community, Article 138(1) and (2) of the Treaty establishing the European Economic Community and Article 108(1) and (2) of the Treaty establishing the European Atomic Energy Community shall lapse on the date of the sitting held in accordance with Article 10(3) by the first European Parliament elected pursuant to this Act.

Article 15

This Act is drawn up in the Danish, Dutch, English, French, German, Irish and Italian languages, all the texts being equally authentic.

Annexes I to III shall form an integral part of this Act.

A declaration by the Government of the Federal Republic of Germany is attached hereto.

Article 16

The provisions of this Act shall enter into force on the first day of the month following that during which the last of the notifications referred to in the Decision is received.

Done at Brussels on the twentieth day of September in the year one thousand nine hundred and seventy-six.

[*List omitted*]

Annex I

The Danish authorities may decide on the dates on which the election of members to the European Parliament shall take place in Greenland.

Annex II

The United Kingdom will apply the provisions of this Act only in respect of the United Kingdom.

Annex III

Declaration on Article 13

As regards the procedure to be followed by the Conciliation Committee, it is agreed to have recourse to the provisions of paragraphs 5, 6 and 7 of the procedure laid down in the Joint Declaration of the European Parliament, the Council and the Commission of 4 March 1975.[2, 3]

Declaration by the Government of the Federal Republic of Germany

The Government of the Federal Republic of Germany declares that the Act concerning the election of the members of the European Parliament by direct universal suffrage shall equally apply to *Land* Berlin.

In consideration of the rights and responsibilities of France, the United Kingdom of Great Britain and Northern Ireland, and the United States of

America, the Berlin House of Deputies will elect representatives to those seats within the quota of the Federal Republic of Germany that fall to *Land* Berlin.

EDITORIAL NOTE:
This Act is annexed to Decision 76/787/ECSC, EEC, Euratom OJ No L 2781, 8.10.76, p.1.

FOOTNOTES

1. Article 2 replaced by Decision 93/81/Euratom, ECSC, EEC, OJ No L 33, 9.2.93, p.15.
2. OJ No C 89, 22.4.75.
3. This Joint Declaration is given on OJ L 89, 22.4.75.

COUNCIL DECISION

amending the Act concerning the election of the representatives of the European Parliament by direct universal suffrage, annexed to Council Decision 76/787/ECSC, EEC, Euratom of 20 September 1976

(93/81/Euratom, ECSC, EEC)

(OJ No L 33, 9.2.93, p.15)

The Council,

Having regard to Article 21(3) of the Treaty establishing the European Coal and Steel Community,

Having regard to Article 138(3) of the Treaty establishing the European Economic Community,

Having regard to Article 108(3) of the Treaty establishing the European Atomic Energy Community,

Having regard to the resolution of the European Parliament of 10 June 1992, and in particular point 4 thereof[1],

Intending to give effect to the conclusions of the European Council in Edinburgh on 11 and 12 December 1992 concerning the allocation of the seats of the European Parliament, as from 1994, to take account of the unification of Germany and enlargement in prospect,

Has laid down the following amendments to the Act which is annexed to Council Decision 76/787/ECSC, EEC, Euratom of 20 September 1976[2] and which was amended by Article 10 of the Act of Accession of Spain and Portugal to the European Communities and recommends them to

the Member States for adoption in accordance with their respective constitutional requirements,

Article 1

Article 2 of the Act concerning the election of the representatives of the European Parliament by direct universal suffrage, which is annexed to Council Decision 76/787/ECSC, EEC, Euratom of 20 September 1976 and which was amended by Article 10 of the Act of Accession of Spain and Portugal to the European Communities, shall be replaced by the following:

'Article 2

The number of representatives elected in each Member State shall be as follows:

Belgium	25
Denmark	16
Germany	99
Greece	25
Spain	64
France	87
Ireland	15
Italy	87
Luxembourg	6
Netherlands	31
Portugal	25
United Kingdom	87.'

Article 2

The Member States shall notify the Secretary-General of the Council of the European Communities without delay of the completion of the procedures necessary in accordance with their respective constitutional requirements for the adoption of the provisions of Article 1.

The said provisions shall enter into force on the first day of the month following receipt of the last of these notifications. They shall be applied for the first time at the elections to the European Parliament to be held in 1994.

Article 3

This Decision shall be published in the *Official Journal of the European Communities.*

It shall enter into force on the day of its publication.

Done at Brussels, 1 February 1993.

For the Council

The President

N. Helveg Petersen

FOOTNOTES

1. OJ No C 176, 13.7.92, p.72.
2. OJ No L 278, 8.10.76.

COUNCIL DIRECTIVE 93/109/EC

of 6 December 1993

laying down detailed arrangements for the exercise of the right to vote and stand as a candidate in elections to the European Parliament for citizens of the Union residing in a Member State of which they are not nationals

(OJ No L 329, 30.12.93, p.34)

The Council of the European Union,

Having regard to the Treaty establishing the European Community, and in particular Article 8b(2) thereof,

Having regard to the proposal from the Commission,

Having regard to the opinion of the European Parliament[1],

Whereas the Treaty on European Union marks a new stage in the process of creating an ever closer union among the peoples of Europe; whereas one of its tasks is to organise, in a manner demonstrating consistency and solidarity, relations between the peoples of the Member States; whereas its fundamental objectives include a strengthening of the protection of the rights and interest of the nationals of its Member States through the introduction of a citizenship of the Union;

Whereas to that end Title II of the Treaty on European Union, amending

the Treaty establishing the European Economic Community, with a view to establishing the European Community, introduces a citizenship of the Union for all nationals of the Member States and confers on such nationals on that basis a number of rights;

Whereas the right to vote and to stand as a candidate in elections to the European Parliament in the Member State of residence, laid down in Article 8b(2) of the Treaty establishing the European Community, is an instance of the application of the principle of non-discrimination between nationals and non-nationals and a corollary of the right to move and reside freely enshrined in Article 8(a) of that Treaty;

Whereas Article 8b(2) of the Treaty is concerned only with the possibility of exercising the right of vote and to stand as a candidate in elections to the European Parliament, without prejudice to Article 138(3) of the EC Treaty, which provides for the establishment of a uniform procedure in all Member States for those elections; whereas it essentially seeks to abolish the nationality requirement which currently has to be satisfied in most Member States in order to exercise those rights;

Whereas application of Article 8b(2) of the EC Treaty does not presuppose harmonisation of Member States' electoral systems; whereas, moreover, to take account of the principle of proportionality set out in the third paragraph of Article 3b of the EC Treaty, the content of Community legislation in this sphere must not go beyond what is necessary to achieve the objective of Article 8b(2) of the EC Treaty;

Whereas the purpose of Article 8b(2) of the EC Treaty is to ensure that all citizens of the Union, whether or not they are nationals of the Member State in which they reside, can exercise in that State their right to vote and to stand as a candidate in elections to the European Parliament under the same conditions; whereas the conditions applying to non-nationals, including those relating to period and proof of residence, should therefore be identical to those, if any, applying to nationals of the Member State concerned;

Whereas Article 8b(2) of the EC Treaty provides for the right to vote and to stand as a candidate in elections to the European Parliament in the Member State of residence, without, nevertheless, substituting it for the right to vote and to stand as a candidate in the Member State of which the citizen is a national; whereas the freedom of citizens of the Union to choose the Member State in which to take part in European elections must be respected, while taking care to ensure that this freedom is not abused by people voting or standing as a candidate in more than one country;

Whereas any derogation from the general rules of this Directive must be

warranted, pursuant to Article 8b(2) of the EC Treaty, by problems specific to a Member State; whereas any derogation must, by its very nature, be subject to review;

Whereas such specific problems may arise in a Member State in which the proportion of citizens of the Union of voting age, who reside in it but are not nationals of it, is very significantly above average; whereas derogations are warranted where such citizens form more than 20% of the total electorate; whereas such derogations must be based on the criterion of period of residence;

Whereas citizenship of the Union is intended to enable citizens of the Union to integrate better in their host country and that in this context, it is in accordance with the intentions of the authors of the Treaty to avoid any polarisation between lists of national and non-national candidates;

Whereas this risk of polarisation concerns in particular a Member State in which the proportion of non-national citizens of the Union of voting age exceeds 20% of the total number of citizens of the Union of voting age who reside there and that, therefore, it is important that this Member State may lay down, in compliance with Article 8b of the Treaty, specific provisions concerning the composition of lists of candidates;

Whereas account must be taken of the fact that in certain Member States residents who are nationals of other Member States have the right to vote in elections to the national parliament and certain provisions of this Directive may consequently be dispensed with in those Member States,

Has adopted this Directive:

Chapter I

General provisions

Article 1

1. This Directive lays down the detailed arrangements whereby citizens of the Union residing in a Member State of which they are not nationals may exercise the right to vote and to stand as a candidate there in elections to the European Parliament.

2. Nothing in this Directive shall affect each Member State's provisions concerning the right to vote or to stand as a candidate of its nationals who reside outside its electoral territory.

Article 2

For the purposes of this Directive:

1. 'elections to the European Parliament' means elections by direct universal suffrage to the European Parliament of representatives in accordance with the Act of 20 September 1976[2];

2. 'electoral territory' means the territory of a Member State in which, in accordance with the above Act and, within that framework, in accordance with the electoral law of that Member State, members of the European Parliament are elected by the people of that Member State;

3. 'Member State of residence' means a Member State in which a citizen of the Union resides but of which he is not a national;

4. 'home Member State' means the Member State of which a citizen of the Union is a national;

5. 'Community voter' means any citizen of the Union who is entitled to vote in elections to the European Parliament in his Member State of residence in accordance with this Directive;

6. 'Community national entitled to stand as a candidate' means any citizen of the Union who has the right to stand as a candidate in elections to the European Parliament in his Member State of residence in accordance with this Directive;

7. 'electoral roll' means the official register of all voters entitled to vote in a given constituency or locality, drawn up and kept up to date by the competent authority under the electoral law of the Member State of residence, or the population register if it indicates eligibility to vote;

8. 'reference date' means the day or the days on which citizens of the Union must satisfy, under the law of the Member State of residence, the requirements for voting or for standing as a candidate in that State;

9. 'formal declaration' means a declaration by the person concerned, inaccuracy in which makes that person liable to penalties, in accordance with the national law applicable.

Article 3

Any person who, on the reference date:

(a) is a citizen of the Union within the meaning of the second subparagraph of Article 8(1) of the Treaty;

(b) is not a national of the Member State of residence, but satisfies the same conditions in respect of the right to vote and to stand as a candidate as that State imposes by law on its own nationals,

shall have the right to vote and to stand as a candidate in elections to the European Parliament in the Member State of residence unless deprived of those rights pursuant to Articles 6 and 7.

Where, in order to stand as a candidate, nationals of the Member State of residence must have been nationals for a certain minimum period, citizens of the Union shall be deemed to have met this condition when they have been nationals of a Member State for the same period.

Article 4

1. Community voters shall excise their right to vote either in the Member State of residence or in their home Member State. No person may vote more than once at the same election.

2. No person may stand as a candidate in more than one Member State at the same election.

Article 5

If, in order to vote or to stand as candidates, nationals of the Member State or residence must have spent a certain minimum period as a resident in the electoral territory of that State, Community voters and Community nationals entitled to stand as candidates shall be deemed to have fulfilled that condition where they have resided for an equivalent period in other Member States. This provision shall apply without prejudice to any specific conditions as to length of residence in a given constituency or locality.

Article 6

1. Any citizen of the Union who resides in a Member State of which he is not a national and who, though an individual criminal law or civil law decision, has been deprived of his right to stand as a candidate under either the law of the Member State of residence or the law of his home Member State, shall be precluded from exercising that right in the Member State of residence in elections to the European Parliament.

2. An application from any citizen of the Union to stand as a candidate in elections to the European Parliament in the Member State of residence shall be declared inadmissible where that citizen is unable to provide the attestation referred to in Article 10(2).

Article 7

1. The Member State of residence may check whether the citizens of the Union who have expressed a desire to exercise their right to vote there

have not been deprived of that right in the home Member State through an individual civil law or criminal law decision.

2. For the purposes of paragraph 1 of this Article, the Member State of residence may notify the home Member State of the declaration referred to in Article 9(2). To that end, the relevant and normally available information from the home Member State shall be provided in good time and in an appropriate manner; such information may only include details which are strictly necessary for the implementation of this Article and may only be used for that purpose. If the information provided invalidates the content of the declaration, the Member State of residence shall take the appropriate steps to prevent the person concerned from voting.

3. The home Member State may, in good time and in an appropriate manner, submit to the Member State of residence any information necessary for the implementation of this Article.

Article 8

1. A Community voter exercises his right to vote in the Member State of residence if he has expressed the wish to do so.

2. If voting is compulsory in the Member State of residence, Community voters who have expressed the wish to do so shall be obliged to vote.

Chapter II

Exercise of the right to vote and the right to stand as a candidate

Article 9

1. Member States shall take the necessary measures to enable a Community voter who has expressed the wish for such to be entered on the electoral roll sufficiently in advance of polling day.

2. In order to have his name entered on the electoral roll, a Community voter shall produce the same documents as a voter who is a national. He shall also produce a formal declaration stating:

(a) his nationality and his address in the electoral territory of the Member State of residence;

(b) where applicable, the locality or constituency in his home Member State on the electoral roll of which his name was last entered, and

(c) that he will exercise his right to vote in the Member State of residence only.

3. The Member State of residence may also require a Community voter to:

(a) state in his declaration under paragraph 2 that he has not been deprived of the right to vote in his home Member State;

(b) produce a valid identity document, and

(c) indicate the date from which he has been resident in that State or in another Member State.

4. Community voters who have been entered on the electoral roll shall remain thereon, under the same conditions as voters who are nationals, until such time as they request to be removed or until such time as they are removed automatically because they no longer satisfy the requirements for exercising the right to vote.

Article 10

1. When he submits his application to stand as a candidate, a Community national shall produce the same supporting documents as a candidate who is a national. He shall also produce a formal declaration stating:

(a) his nationality and his address in the electoral territory of the Member State of residence;

(b) that his not standing as a candidate for election to the European Parliament in any other Member State, and

(c) where applicable, the locality or constituency in his home Member State on the electoral roll of which his name was last entered.

2. When he submits his application to stand as a candidate a Community national must also produce an attestation from the competent administrative authorities of his home Member State certifying that he has not been deprived of the right to stand as a candidate in that Member State or that no such disqualification is known to those authorities.

3. The Member State of residence may also require a Community national entitled to stand as a candidate to produce a valid identity document. It may also require him to indicate the date from which he has been a national of a Member State.

Article 11

1. The Member State of residence shall inform the person concerned of the action taken on his application for entry on the electoral roll or of

the decision concerning the admissibility of his application to stand as a candidate.

2. Should a person be refused entry on the electoral roll or his application to stand as a candidate be rejected, the person concerned shall be entitled to legal remedies on the same terms as the legislation of the Member State of residence prescribes for voters and persons entitled to stand as candidates who are its nationals.

Article 12

The Member State of residence shall inform Community voters and Community nationals entitled to stand as candidates in good time and in an appropriate manner of the conditions and detailed arrangements for the exercise of the right to vote and to stand as a candidate in elections in that State.

Article 13

Member States shall exchange the information required for the implementation of Article 4. To that end, the Member State of residence shall, on the basis of the formal declaration referred to in Articles 9 and 10, supply the home Member State, sufficiently in advance of polling day, with information on the latter State's nationals entered on electoral rolls or standing as candidates. The home Member State shall, in accordance with its national legislation, take appropriate measures to ensure that its nationals do not vote more than once or stand as candidates in more than one Member State.

Chapter III

Derogations and transitional provisions

Article 14

1. If on 1 January 1993, in a given Member State, the proportion of citizens of the Union of voting age who reside in it but are not nationals of it exceeds 20% of the total number of citizens of the Union residing there who are of voting age, that Member State may, by way of derogation from Articles 3, 9 and 10:

(a) restrict the right to vote to Community voters who have resided in that Member State for a minimum period, which may not exceed five years;

(b) restrict the right to stand as a candidate to Community nationals entitled to stand as candidates who have resided in that Member State for a minimum period, which may not exceed 10 years.

These provisions are without prejudice to appropriate measures which this Member State may take with regard to the composition of lists of candidates and which are intended in particular to encourage the integration of non-national citizens of the Union.

However, Community voters and Community nationals entitled to stand as candidates who, owing to the fact that they have take up residence outside their home Member State or by reason of the duration of such residence, do not have the right to vote or to stand as candidates in that home State shall not be subject to the conditions as to length of residence set out above.

2. Where, on 1 February 1994, the laws of a Member State prescribe that the nationals of another Member State who reside there have the right to vote for the national parliament of that State and, for that purpose, may be entered on the electoral roll of that State under exactly the same conditions as national voters, the first Member State may, by way of derogation from this Directive, refrain from applying Articles 6 to 13 in respect of such nationals.

3. By 31 December 1997 and thereafter 18 months prior to each election to the European Parliament, the Commission shall submit to the European Parliament and to the Council a report in which it shall check whether the grant to the Member States concerned of a derogation pursuant to Article 8b(2) of the EC Treaty is still warranted and shall propose that any necessary adjustments be made.

Member States which invoke derogations under paragraph 1 shall furnish the Commission with all the necessary background information.

Article 15

For the fourth direct elections to the European Parliament, the following special provisions shall apply:

(a) citizens of the Union who, on 15 February 1994, already have the right to vote in the Member State of residence and whose names appear on the electoral roll in the Member State of residence shall not be subject to the formalities laid down in Article 9;

(b) Member States in which the electoral rolls have been finalised before 15 February 1994 shall take the steps necessary to enable Community voters who wish to exercise their right to vote there to enter names on the electoral roll sufficiently in advance of polling day;

(c) Member States which do not draw up specific electoral rolls but indicate eligibility to vote in the population register and where voting is not compulsory may also apply this system to Community voters who appear on that register and who, having been informed

individually of their rights, have not expressed a wish to exercise their right to vote in their home Member State. They shall forward to the home Member State the document showing the intention expressed by those voters to vote in the Member State of residence;

(d) Member States in which the internal procedure for the nomination of candidates for political parties and groups is governed by law may provide that any such procedures which, in accordance with that law, were opened before 1 February 1994 and the decisions taken within that framework shall remain valid.

Chapter IV

Final provisions

Article 16

The Commission shall submit a report to the European Parliament and the Council by 31 December 1995 on the application of this Directive to the June 1994 elections to the European Parliament. On the basis of the said report the Council, acting unanimously on a proposal from the Commission and after consulting the European Parliament, may adopt provisions amending this Directive.

Article 17

Member States shall adopt the laws, regulations and administrative provisions necessary to comply with this Directive no later than 1 February 1994. They shall forthwith inform the Commission thereof.

When Member States adopt these measures, they shall contain a reference to this Directive or shall be accompanied by such reference on the occasion of their official publication. The methods of making such reference shall be laid down by Member States.

Article 18

This Directive shall enter into force on the day of its publication in the *Official Journal of the European Communities*.

Article 19

This Directive is addressed to the Member States.

Done at Brussels, 6 December 1993

For the Council

The President

W. Claes

FOOTNOTES

1. OJ No C 329, 6.12.93.
2. OJ No L 278, 8.10.76, p.5.

 IRL Implemented in Ireland: European Parliament Elections Act, 1993; S.I. 14S/1994; S.I. 75S/1994; Electoral Act, 1992.

COUNCIL OF EUROPEAN UNION

COUNCIL DECISION

of 8 November 1993

concerning the name to be given to the Council following the entry into force of the Treaty on European Union

(93/591)

(OJ No L 281, 16.11.93, p.18)

The Council shall henceforth be called the 'Council of the European Union' and shall be so designated, in particular in all the acts which it adopts, including those adopted under Titles V and VI of the Treaty on European Union; political declarations which the Council adopts under the common foreign and security policy will thus be made in the name of 'the European Union'.

Done at Brussels, 8 November 1993.

For the Council

The President

W. Claes

ENLARGEMENT

COUNCIL DECISION

of 29 March 1994

concerning the taking of Decision by qualified majority by the Council

(94/C 105/01)

(OJ No C 105, 13.4.94, p.1)

The Council of the European Union,

Decides:

Article 1

If Members of the Council representing a total of 23 to 26 votes indicate their intention to oppose the adoption by the Council of a Decision by qualified majority, the Council will do all in its power to reach, within a reasonable time and without prejudicing obligatory time limits laid down by the Treaties and by secondary law, such as in Articles 189B and 189C of the Treaty establishing the European Community, a satisfactory solution that could be adopted by at least 68 votes. During this period and always respecting the Rules of Procedure of the Council, the President undertakes, with the assistance of the Commission, any initiative necessary to facilitate a wider basis of agreement in the Council. The Members of the Council lend him their assistance.

Article 2

The present Decision shall be published in the *Official Journal of the European Communities*.

Done at Brussels, 29 March 1994.

For the Council

The President

Th. Pangalos

EDITORIAL NOTE

Declarations by the twelve Member States and by the four applicant States omitted. Included in conference minutes as is the Commission statement.

CONVENTIONS RELEVANT TO ARTICLE 220 EC TREATY

JURISDICTION OF COURTS AND ENFORCEMENT OF JUDGMENTS (EUROPEAN COMMUNITIES) ACT, 1988

An Act to give the force of law to the Convention on Jurisdiction and the Enforcement of Judgments in Civil and Commercial Matters (including the Protocol annexed to that Convention) signed at Brussels on the 27th day of September, 1968, the Protocol on the Interpretation of that Convention by the Court of Justice of the European Communities signed at Luxembourg on the 3rd day of June, 1971, and the Conventions providing for the Accession of the State, Denmark, the United Kingdom and the Hellenic Republic to that Convention and that Protocol and to provide for matters consequent upon and otherwise related to the matters aforesaid

[5th March, 1988]

Be it enacted by the Oireachtas as follows:

1. Interpretation

(1) In this Act–

'the 1978 Accession Convention' means the Convention on the accession to the 1968 Convention and the 1971 Protocol of the State, Denmark and the United Kingdom, signed at Luxembourg on the 9th day of October, 1978;

'the 1982 Accession Convention' means the Convention on the accession to the 1968 Convention and the 1971 Protocol (as amended in each case by the 1978 Accession Convention) of the Hellenic Republic, signed at Luxembourg on the 25th day of October, 1982;

'Contracting State' means –

(a) one of the original parties to the 1968 Convention (Belgium, the Federal Republic of Germany, France, Italy, Luxembourg and the Netherlands), or

(b) one of the parties acceding to the 1968 Convention under the 1978 Accession Convention or the 1982 Accession Convention

(the State, Denmark, the United Kingdom and the Hellenic Republic),

being a state in respect of which the 1978 Accession Convention has entered into force in accordance with Article 39 of that Convention or, as may be appropriate, the 1982 Accession Convention has entered into force in accordance with Article 15 of that Convention, and, where the context so allows, 'Contracting State' shall be construed so as to enable this Act to have effect as respects the places as respects which the 1968 Convention has effect by virtue of Article 60;

'the 1968 Convention' means the Convention on jurisdiction and the enforcement of judgments in civil and commercial matters (including the Protocol annexed to that Convention), signed at Brussels on the 27th day of September, 1968;

'the Conventions' means the 1968 Convention, the 1971 Protocol, the 1978 Accession Convention and, on and from the commencement of section 3 of this Act, in so far as it relates to the 1982 Accession Convention, the 1982 Accession Convention;

'court' includes a tribunal;

'enforcement order' means –

(a) an order made by the Master of the High Court under section 5 of this Act for the recognition or enforcement of the whole or part of a judgment, or

(b) an order of the High Court for the recognition or enforcement of the whole or part of an instrument or settlement referred to in Title IV of the 1968 Convention,

and includes an enforcement order made or varied on appeal from a decision of the Master of the High Court or a decision of the High Court;

'the European Communities' has the same meaning as in section 1 of the European Communities Act, 1972;

'the European Court' means the Court of Justice of the European Communities;

'judgment', except in section 2 of this Act but subject to section 6 of this Act, means a judgment or order to which, by virtue of the said ssection 2, this Act applies;

'maintenance creditor' means, in relation to a maintenance order, the person entitled to the payments for which the order provides;

'maintenance debtor' means, in relation to a maintenance order, the person liable to make payments under the order;

'maintenance order' means, subject to section 6 of this Act, a judgment that is a judgment relating to maintenance (within the meaning of the 1968 Convention) in so far, but only in so far, as it provides for the making of periodic payments;

'the Minister' means the Minister for Justice;

'non-contracting state' means any state, country or territory other than a Contracting State;

'the 1971 Protocol' means the Protocol on the interpretation of the 1968 Convention by the European Court, signed at Luxembourg on the 3rd day of June, 1971.

(2) A document purporting to be a copy of a judgment given by a court of a Contracting State shall, for the purposes of this Act, be regarded as being duty authenticated if it purports –

(a) to bear the seal of that court, or

(b) to be certified by a person in his capacity as a judge or officer of that court to be a true copy of a judgment given by that court.

(3)   In this Act, unless the context otherwise requires –

(a) references to, or to any provision of, the 1968 Convention or the 1971 Protocol are references to the 1968 Convention, the 1971 Protocol or the provision, as the case may be, as amended by –

   (i) the 1978 Accession Convention, and

   (ii) after the commencement of section 3 of this Act, in so far as it relates to the 1982 Accession Convention, the 1982 Accession Convention,

(b) any reference to a numbered Article is, unless the context otherwise requires, a reference to the Article so numbered of the 1968 Convention and any reference to a subdivision of a numbered Article shall be construed accordingly.

(4) (a) The Minister for Foreign Affairs may by order declare –

   (i) that any state specified in the order is a Contracting State, or

   (ii) that a declaration (the text of which shall be set out in the order) has been made pursuant to Article 60 or Article IV, or a communication (the text of which shall be set out in the order) has been made pursuant to Article VI, to the

Secretary-General of the Council of the European Communities.

(b) An order that is in force under this subsection shall be evidence –

(i) as respects any declaration under paragraph (a)(i) therein, that any state to which the declaration relates is a Contracting State, and

(ii) as respects any declaration under paragraph (a)(ii) therein, that the declaration pursuant to Article 60 or Article IV, or, as the case may be, the communication pursuant to Article VI, to which the first mentioned declaration relates was made and of its contents.

(c) The Minister for Foreign Affairs may by order amend or revoke an order under this subsection including an order under this paragraph.

2. Application of Act

This Act applies to any judgment or order (by whatever name called) that is a judgment for the purposes of the 1968 Convention.

3. Conventions to have force of law

(1) The Conventions shall have the force of law in the State and judicial notice shall be taken of them.

(2) For convenience of reference there are set out in the First, Second, Third and Fourth Schedules, respectively, to this Act:

(a) the 1968 Convention, as amended by Titles II and III of the 1978 Accession Convention and Titles II and III of the 1982 Accession Convention,

(b) the 1971 Protocol, as amended by Title IV of the 1978 Accession Convention and Title IV of the 1982 Accession Convention,

(c) Titles V and VI of the 1978 Accession Convention,

(d) Titles V and VI of the 1982 Accession Convention,

being texts prepared from the authentic texts in the English language referred to in Articles 37 and 41 of the 1978 Accession Convention and Article 17 of the 1982 Accession Convention.

4. Interpretation of Conventions

(1) Judicial notice shall be taken of –

(a) any ruling or decision of, or expression of opinion by, the European

Court on any question as to the meaning or effect of any provision of the Conventions, and

(b) the reports specified in subsection (2) of this section.

(2) The following reports (which are reproduced in the Official Journal of the European Communities), namely –

(a) the reports by Mr P. Jenard on the 1968 Convention and the 1971 Protocol[1],

(b) the report by Professor Peter Schlosser on the 1978 Accession Convention[2], and

(c) the report by Professor Demetrios Evrigenis and Professor K.D. Kerameus on the accession of the Hellenic Republic to the 1968 Convention and the 1971 Protocol[3],

may be considered by any court when interpreting any provision of the Conventions and shall be given such weight as is appropriate in the circumstances.

5. Applications for recognition and enforcement of Community judgments

An application under Article 31 for the recognition or enforcement in the State of a judgment shall be made to the Master of the High Court and shall be determined by him by order (including an order for the recognition or enforcement of a judgment in part only) in accordance with the Conventions.

6. Enforcement of Community judgments (other than maintenance orders)

(1) Subject to section 8(4) of this Act and to the restriction on enforcement contained in Article 39 –

(a) a judgment, other than a maintenance order, in respect of which an enforcement order has been made, shall, to the extent to which the enforcement of the judgment is authorised by the enforcement order, be of the same force and effect, and

(b) for or as respects the enforcement of the judgment, the High Court shall have the same powers, and proceedings may be taken,

as if the judgment was a judgment of the High Court.

(2) (a) The Master of the High Court may, on application to him in that behalf by the maintenance creditor, by order declare that sums which were payable under an enforceable maintenance order, but were not paid, before the date of the making of the relevant

enforcement order shall be regarded as being payable under a judgment referred to in subsection (1) of this section.

(*b*) The Master of the High Court shall not make a declaration under paragraph (*a*) of this subsection unless he considers that by so doing the enforceable maintenance order concerned would be more effectively enforced as respects the sums concerned.

(*c*) Whenever the Master of the High Court makes a declaration under paragraph (*a*) of this subsection, the sums to which it relates shall be deemed, for the purposes of this Act, to be payable under a judgment referred to in the said subsection (1) and not otherwise.

(3) In this section 'judgment' includes an instrument or settlement referred to in Title IV of the 1968 Convention.

7. Enforcement of Community maintenance orders

(1) In this section 'enforceable maintenance order' means –

(*a*) a maintenance order as regards the enforcement of the whole of which an enforcement order has been made, or

(*b*) in case an enforcement order has been made for the enforcement of a maintenance order in part only, the maintenance order to the extent to which it is so ordered to be enforced.

(2) (*a*) Subject to section 8(4) of this Act and to the restriction on enforcement contained in Article 39, the District Court shall have jurisdiction to enforce an enforceable maintenance order and –

(i) for that purpose,

(ii) for the purposes of section 98(1) of the Defence Act, 1954, and

(iii) subject to the 1968 Convention, for the purpose of the variation or revocation of such an order under section 5 of the Illegitimate Children (Affiliation Orders) Act, 1930, or section 6 of the Family Law (Maintenance of Spouses and Children) Act, 1976,

such an order shall, from the date on which the maintenance order was made, be deemed to be an order made by the District Court under section 3 of the said Illegitimate Children (Affiliation Orders) Act, 1930, or section 5 of the said Family Law (Maintenance of Spouses and Children) Act, 1976, as may be appropriate.

(*b*) Paragraph (*a*) of this subsection shall have effect notwithstanding

that any amount payable under the order concerned exceeds the maximum amount which the District Court has jurisdiction to award under the appropriate enactment mentioned in that paragraph.

(3) Where an enforceable maintenance order is varied by a court in a Contracting State other than the State and an enforcement order has been made as regards the whole or part of the enforceable maintenance order as so varied or as regards the whole or part of the order effecting the variation, as the case may be, the enforceable maintenance order shall, from the date on which the variation takes effect, be enforceable in the State only as so varied.

(4) Where an enforceable maintenance order is revoked by a court in a Contracting State other than the State and an enforcement order has been made as regards the order effecting the revocation, the enforceable maintenance order shall, from the date on which the revocation takes effect, cease to be enforceable in the State except in relation to any sums under the order which were payable, but were not paid, on or before that date.

(5) In the case of an enforceable maintenance order –

(a) any sums which were payable thereunder, but were not paid, before the date of the making of the relevant enforcement order, and

(b) any costs of or incidental to the application for the said enforcement order payable by virtue of section 8(2) of this Act,

shall, subject to section 6(2) of this Act, be regarded as being payable by virtue of an order made under section 3 of the Illegitimate Children (Affiliation Orders) Act, 1930, or section 5 of the Family Law (Maintenance of Spouses and Children) Act, 1976, as may be appropriate.

(6) The jurisdiction vested in the District Court by this section shall be exercised by the justice of the District Court for the time being assigned to the district court district in which the maintenance debtor under the enforceable maintenance order concerned resides.

(7) (a) Any sum payable by virtue of an enforceable maintenance order shall, notwithstanding anything to the contrary therein, be paid by the maintenance debtor concerned to the court clerk for the district court area in which the maintenance debtor for the time being resides for transmission to the maintenance creditor or, where a public authority has been authorised by the maintenance creditor to receive such sum, to that authority.

(*b*) If any sum payable by virtue of an enforceable maintenance order is not duly paid and if the maintenance creditor concerned so requests in writing, the district court clerk concerned shall make an application under section 10 (which relates to the attachment of certain earnings) of the Family Law (Maintenance of Spouses and Children) Act, 1976, or section 8 (which relates to the enforcement of certain maintenance orders) of the Enforcement of Court Orders Act, 1940, in respect of the sum and, for that purpose, the references in the said section 8 (other than subsections (4) and (5)) to the applicant shall be construed as references to the district court clerk.

(*c*) Nothing in this subsection shall affect the right of a maintenance creditor to institute proceedings for the recovery of any sum payable to a district court clerk under paragraph (*a*) of this subsection.

(8) Section 8(7) of the Enforcement of Court Orders Act, 1940, shall not apply to proceedings for the enforcement of an enforceable maintenance order.

(9) A maintenance debtor under an enforceable maintenance order shall give notice to the district court clerk for the district court area in which he has been residing of any change of his address and, if he fails without reasonable cause to do so, he shall be guilty of an offence and shall be liable on summary conviction to a fine not exceeding £500.

(10) In this section a reference to a district court clerk shall, where there are two or more district court clerks for the district court area concerned, be construed as a reference to any of those clerks.

(11) For the purposes of this section, the Dublin Metropolitan District shall be deemed to be a district court area.

8. Provisions in enforcement orders for payment of interest on judgments and payment of costs

(1) Where, on an application for an enforcement order, it is shown –

(*a*) that the relevant judgment provides for the payment of a sum of money, and

(*b*) that, in accordance with the law of the Contracting State in which the judgment was given, interest on that sum is recoverable under the judgment at a particular rate or rates and from a particular date or time,

the order, if made, shall provide that the person by whom the sum aforesaid is payable shall also be liable to pay the interest aforesaid,

apart from any interest on costs recoverable by virtue of subsection (2) of this section, in accordance with the particulars noted in the order, and the amount of the interest shall be recoverable by the applicant concerned as if it was part of the sum aforesaid.

(2) An enforcement order may, at the discretion of the court concerned or the Master of the High Court, as may be appropriate, provide for the payment to the applicant concerned by the respondent concerned of the reasonable costs of or incidental to the application for the order.

(3) A person by whom costs recoverable by virtue of subsection (2) of this section are payable shall be liable to pay interest on the costs as if they were the subject of an order for the payment of costs made by the High Court on the date of the making of the relevant enforcement order.

(4) Interest shall be payable on a sum referred to in subsection (1) of this section only as provided for by this section.

9. Currency of payments under Community maintenance orders

(1) An amount payable in the State under a maintenance order by virtue of an enforcement order shall be paid in the currency of the State and, if the amount is stated in the maintenance order in a currency other than the currency of the State, the payment shall be made on the basis of the exchange rate prevailing, on the date of the making of the enforcement order, between that currency and the currency of the State.

(2) For the purposes of this section, a certificate purporting to be signed by an officer of a bank in the State and to state the exchange rate prevailing on a specified date between a specified currency and the currency of the State shall be admissible as evidence of the facts stated in the certificate.

(3) In this section 'bank' means the holder of a banker's licence within the meaning of the Central Bank Act, 1971.

10. Proof and admissibility of certain judgments and related translations and documents

(1) For the purposes of the Conventions –

(a) a document, duly authenticated, which purports to be a copy of a judgment given by a court of a Contracting State other than the State shall without further proof be deemed to be a true copy of the judgment, unless the contrary is shown; and

(b) the original or a copy of any such document as is mentioned in

Article 46.2 or 47 shall be admissible as evidence of any matter to which it relates.

(2) A document which –

(*a*) purports to be a translation of a judgment given by a court of a Contracting State other than the State or of a document mentioned in Article 46.2, 47 or 50 or containing a settlement referred to in Article 51, and

(*b*) is certified as correct by a person competent to do so,

shall be admissible as evidence of the translation.

11. Provisional, including protective, measures

(1) Where –

(*a*) proceedings have been commenced or are to be commenced in a Contracting State other than the State, and

(*b*) they are (sic) or will be proceedings whose subject-matter is within the scope of the 1968 Convention as determined by Article 1 (whether or not the 1968 Convention has effect in relation to the proceedings),

the High Court may, on application to it pursuant to Article 24, grant provisional, including protective, measures of any kind that the Court has power to grant in proceedings that, apart from this Act, are within its jurisdiction.

(2) On an application under subsection (1) of this section, the High Court may refuse to grant the measures sought if, in the opinion of that Court, the fact that that Court has not jurisdiction, apart from this section, in relation to the subject-matter of the proceedings in question makes it inexpedient for that Court to grant such measures.

(3) Subject to Article 39, an application to the Master of the High Court for the enforcement of a judgment and an application to the High Court for the enforcement of an instrument or settlement referred to in Title IV of the 1968 Convention may include an application for the granting of such protective measures as the High Court has power to grant in proceedings that, apart from this Act, are within its jurisdiction and, where an enforcement order is made in relation to a judgment or such an instrument or settlement, the order shall include a provision granting any such protective measures as aforesaid as are applied for as aforesaid.

12. Provision of certain documents by courts in the State to interested parties

As respects a judgment given by a court in the State, the registrar or clerk of the court shall, at the request of an interested party and subject to any conditions that may be specified by rules of court, give to the interested party –

(a) a copy of the judgment duly authenticated,

(b) a certificate signed by the registrar or clerk of the court stating –

　(i) the nature of the proceedings,

　(ii) the grounds, pursuant to the 1968 Convention, on which the court assumed jurisdiction,

　(iii) the date on which the time for the lodging of an appeal against the judgment will expire or, if it has expired, the date on which it expired,

　(iv) whether notice of appeal against, or, in any case where the defendant does not appear, a notice to set aside, the judgment has been entered,

　(v) where the judgment is for the payment of a sum of money, the rate of interest, if any, payable on the sum and the date from which interest is payable, and

　(vi) such other particulars (if any) as may be specified by rules of court,

and

(c) in case the judgment was given in default of appearance, the original or a copy, certified by the registrar or clerk of the court to be a true copy, of a document establishing that notice of the institution of proceedings was served on the person in default.

13. Domicile for purposes of 1968 Convention and Act

(1) Subject to Article 52, Part I of the Fifth Schedule to this Act shall apply in relation to the text in the English language of the 1968 Convention, and Part II of the said Fifth Schedule shall apply in relation to the text in the Irish language of the 1968 Convention, in order to determine for the purposes of the 1968 Convention and this Act whether an individual is domiciled in the State, in a place in the State or in a state other than a Contracting State.

(2) The seat of a corporation or association shall be treated as its

domicile, and Part III of the said Fifth Schedule shall apply in relation to the text in the English language of the 1968 Convention, and Part IV of the said Fifth Schedule shall apply in relation to the text in the Irish language of the 1968 Convention, in order to determine for the purposes of Article 53 of the 1968 Convention and this Act whether a corporation or association has its seat in the State, in a place in the State or in a state other than the State.

(3) Part V of the said Fifth Schedule shall apply in relation to the text in the English language of the 1968 Convention, and Part VI of the said Fifth Schedule shall apply in relation to the text in the Irish language of the 1968 Convention, in order to determine for the purposes of the 1968 Convention and this Act whether a trust is domiciled in the State.

(4) In this section –

'association' means an unincorporated body of persons;

'corporation' means a body corporate.

14. Venue for certain proceedings instituted in Circuit Court or District Court by virtue of this Act

(1) Subject to Title II of the Convention, the jurisdiction of the Circuit Court as respects proceedings that may be instituted in the State by virtue of Article 2, 8.1, 11 or 14 shall, where, apart from this subsection, that jurisdiction would be determined by reference to the place where the defendant or one of the defendants resides or carries on business, be exercised by the judge of the Circuit Court for the time being assigned to the circuit where the defendant or one of the defendants ordinarily resides or carries on any profession, business or occupation.

(2) The jurisdiction of the Circuit Court and the District Court as respects proceedings that may be instituted in the State by virtue of Article 14 by a plaintiff domiciled in the State may be exercised as follows:

 (i) in the case of the Circuit Court, by the judge of the Circuit Court for the time being assigned to the circuit where the plaintiff or one of the plaintiffs ordinarily resides or carries on any profession, business or occupation, or

(ii) in the case of the District Court, by the justice of the District Court for the time being assigned to the district court district in which the plaintiff or one of the plaintiffs ordinarily resides or carried on any profession, business or occupation.

15. Short title, construction and commencement

(1) This Act may be cited as the Jurisdiction of Courts and Enforcement of Judgments (European Communities) Act, 1988.

(2) The Courts (Supplemental Provisions) Acts, 1961 to 1986, and sections 5 to 8, and 11, 12 and 14 of this Act shall be construed together as one.

(3) (a) This Act, other than section 3 in so far as it relates to the 1982 Accession Convention, shall come into operation on such day or days as the Minister shall fix by order or orders either generally or with reference to any particular purpose or provision and different days may be so fixed for different purposes and different provisions.

(b) Section 3 of this Act shall, in so far as it relates to the 1982 Accession Convention, come into operation on such day or days as the Minister shall fix by order or orders either generally or with reference to any particular purpose or provision and different days may be so fixed for different purposes and different provisions and any day so fixed may be the same day as a day fixed under paragraph (a) of this subsection or a different day.

First Schedule

Text of the 1968 Convention as amended by the 1978 Accession Convention and the 1982 Accession Convention.

CONVENTION

on jurisdiction and the enforcement of judgments in civil and commercial matters

Preamble

The High Contracting Parties to the Treaty establishing the European Economic Community,

Desiring to implement the provisions of Article 220 of that Treaty by virtue of which they undertook to secure the simplification of formalities governing the reciprocal recognition and enforcement of judgments of courts or tribunals;

Anxious to strengthen in the Community the legal protection of persons therein established;

Considering that it is necessary for this purpose to determine the

international jurisdiction of their courts, to facilitate recognition and to introduce an expeditious procedure for securing the enforcement of judgments, authentic instruments and court settlements;

Have decided to conclude this Convention and to this end have designated as their plenipotentiaries:

(*Designations of plenipotentiaries of the original six Contracting States*)

Who, meeting within the Council, having exchanged their Full Powers, found in good and due form,

Have agreed as follows:

Title I

Scope

Article 1

This Convention shall apply in civil and commercial matters whatever the nature of the court or tribunal. It shall not extend, in particular, to revenue, customs or administrative matters.

The Convention shall not apply to:

1. the status or legal capacity of natural persons, rights in property arising out of a matrimonial relationship, wills and succession;

2. bankruptcy, proceedings relating to the winding-up of insolvent companies or other legal persons, judicial arrangements, compositions and analogous proceedings;

3. social security;

4. arbitration.

Title II

Jurisdiction

Section 1

General provisions

Article 2

Subject to the provision of this Convention, persons domiciled in a Contracting State shall, whatever their nationality, be sued in the courts of that State.

Persons who are not nationals of the State in which they are domiciled

shall be governed by the rules of jurisdiction applicable to nationals of that State.

Article 3

Persons domiciled in a Contracting State may be sued in the courts of another Contracting State only by virtue of the rules set out in Sections 2 to 6 of this Title.

In particular the following provisions shall not be applicable as against them:

- in Belgium: Article 15 of the civil code (*Code civil – Burgerlijk Wetboek*) and Article 638 of the judicial code (*Code judiciaire – Gerechtelijk Wetboek*);

- in Denmark: Article 248(2) of the law on civil procedure (*Lov om rettens pleje*) and Chapter 3, Article 3 of the Greenland law on civil procedure (*Lov for Grønland om rettens pleje*);

- in the Federal Republic of Germany: Article 23 of the code of civil procedure (*Zivilproβordnung*);

- in Greece: Article 40 of the code of civil procedure (Πολιτιχης Διχομιας);

- in France: Articles 14 and 15 of the civil code (*Code civil*);

- in Ireland: the rules which enable jurisdiction to be founded on the document instituting the proceedings having been served on the defendant during his temporary presence in Ireland;

- in Italy: Article 2 and Article 4, Nos 1 and 2 of the code of civil procedure (*Codice di procedura civile*);

- in Luxembourg: Articles 14 and 15 of the civil code (*Code civil*);

- in the Netherlands: Articles 126(3) and 127 of the code of civil procedure (*Wetboek van Burgerlijke Rechtsvordering*);

- in the United Kingdom: the rules which enable jurisdiction to be founded on:

  (a) the document instituting the proceedings having been served on the defendant during his temporary presence in the United Kingdom; or

  (b) the presence within the United Kingdom of property belonging to the defendant; or

(*c*) the seizure by the plaintiff of property situated in the United Kingdom.

Article 4

If the defendant is not domiciled in a Contracting State, the jurisdiction of the courts of each Contracting State shall, subject to the provisions of Article 16, be determined by the law of that State.

As against such a defendant, any person domiciled in a Contracting State may, whatever his nationality, avail himself in that State of the rules of jurisdiction there in force, and in particular those specified in the second paragraph of Article 3, in the same way as the nationals of that State.

Section 2

Special jurisdiction

Article 5

A person domiciled in a Contracting State may, in another Contracting State, be sued:

1. in matters relating to a contract, in the courts for the place of performance of the obligation in question;

2. in matters relating to maintenance, in the courts for the place where the maintenance creditor is domiciled or habitually resident or, if the matter is ancillary to proceedings concerning the status of a person, in the court which, according to its own law, has jurisdiction to entertain those proceedings, unless that jurisdiction is based solely on the nationality of one of the parties;

3. in matters relating to tort, delict or quasi-delict, in the courts for the place where the harmful event occurred;

4. as regards a civil claim for damages or restitution which is based on an act giving rise to criminal proceedings, in the court seised of those proceedings, to the extent that that court has jurisdiction under its own law to entertain civil proceedings;

5. as regards a dispute arising out of the operations of a branch, agency or other establishment, in the courts for the place in which the branch, agency or other establishment is situated;

6. in his capacity as settlor, trustee or beneficiary of a trust created by the operation of a statute, or by a written instrument, or created orally

and evidenced in writing, in the courts of the Contracting State in which the trust is domiciled;

7. as regards a dispute concerning the payment of remuneration claimed in respect of the salvage of a cargo or freight, in the court under the authority of which the cargo or freight in question –

(a) has been arrested to secure such payment, or

(b) could have been so arrested, but bail or other security has been given;

provided that this provision shall apply only if it is claimed that the defendant has an interest in the cargo or freight or had such an interest at the time of salvage.

Article 6

A person domiciled in a Contracting State may also be sued:

1. where he is one of a number of defendants, in the courts for the place where any one of them is domiciled;

2. as a third party in an action on a warranty or guarantee or in any other third party proceedings, in the court seised of the original proceedings, unless these were instituted solely with the object of removing him from the jurisdiction of the court which would be competent in his case;

3. on a counter-claim arising from the same contract or facts on which the original claim was based, in the court in which the original claim is pending.

Article 6a

Where by virtue of this Convention a court of a Contracting State has jurisdiction in actions relating to liability arising from the use or operation of a ship, that court, or any other court substituted for this purpose by the internal law of that State, shall also have jurisdiction over claims for limitation of such liability.

Section 3

Jurisdiction in matters relating to insurance

Article 7

In matters relating to insurance, jurisdiction shall be determined by this Section without prejudice to the provisions of Articles 4 and 5.5.

Article 8

An insurer domiciled in a Contracting State may be sued:

1. in the courts of the State where he is domiciled, or

2. in another Contracting State, in the courts for the place where the policy-holder is domiciled, or

3. if he is a co-insurer, in the courts of a Contracting State in which proceedings are brought against the leading insurer.

An insurer who is not domiciled in a Contracting State but has a branch, agency or other establishment in one of the Contracting States shall, in disputes arising out of the operations of the branch, agency or establishment, be deemed to be domiciled in that State.

Article 9

In respect of liability insurance or insurance of immovable property, the insurer may in addition be sued in the courts for the place where the harmful event occurred. The same applies if movable and immovable property are covered by the same insurance policy and both are adversely affected by the same contingency.

Article 10

In respect of liability insurance, the insurer may also, if the law of the court permits it, be joined in proceedings which the injured party has brought against the insured.

The provisions of Articles 7, 8 and 9 shall apply to actions brought by the injured party directly against the insurer, where such direct actions are permitted.

If the law governing such direct actions provides that the policyholder or the insured may be joined as a party to the action, the same court shall have jurisdiction over them.

Article 11

Without prejudice to the provisions of the third paragraph of Article 10, an insurer may bring proceedings only in the courts of the Contracting State in which the defendant is domiciled, irrespective of whether he is the policy-holder, the insured or a beneficiary.

The provisions of this Section shall not affect the right to bring a counterclaim in the court in which, in accordance with this Section, the original claim is pending.

Article 12

The provisions of this Section may be departed from only by an agreement on jurisdiction:

1. which is entered into after the dispute has arisen, or

2. which allows the policy-holder, the insured or a beneficiary to bring proceedings in courts other than those indicated in this Section, or

3. which is concluded between a policy-holder and an insurer, both of whom are at the time of conclusion of the contract domiciled or habitually resident in the same Contracting State, and which has the effect of conferring jurisdiction on the courts of that State even if the harmful event were to occur abroad, provided that such an agreement is not contrary to the law of that State, or

4. which is concluded with a policy-holder who is not domiciled in a Contracting State, except in so far as the insurance is compulsory or relates to immovable property in a Contracting State, or

5. which relates to a contract of insurance in so far as it covers one or more of the risks set out in Article 12a.

Article 12a

The following are the risks referred to in Article 12.5:

1. Any loss of or damage to

(a) sea-going ships, installations situated offshore or on the high seas, or aircraft, arising from perils which relate to their use for commercial purposes,

(b) goods in transit other than passengers' baggage where the transit consists of or includes carriage by such ships or aircraft;

2. Any liability, other than for bodily injury to passengers or loss of or damage to their baggage,

(a) arising out of the use or operation of ships, installations or aircraft as referred to in 1.(a) above in so far as the law of the Contracting State in which such aircraft are registered does not prohibit agreements on jurisdiction regarding insurance of such risks,

(b) for loss or damage caused by goods in transit as described in 1.(b) above;

3. Any financial loss connected with the use or operation of ships,

installations or aircraft as referred to in 1.(*a*) above, in particular loss of freight or charter-hire;

4. Any risk or interest connected with any of those referred to in 1. to 3. above.

Section 4

Jurisdiction over consumer contracts

Article 13

In proceedings concerning a contract concluded by a person for a purpose which can be regarded as being outside his trade or profession, hereinafter called 'the consumer', jurisdiction shall be determined by this Section, without prejudice to the provisions of Articles 4 and 5.5, if it is:

1. a contract for the sale of goods on instalment credit terms, or

2. a contract for a loan repayable by instalments, or for any other form of credit, made to finance the sale of goods, or

3. any other contract for the supply of goods or a contract for the supply of services, and –

(*a*) in the State of the consumer's domicile the conclusion of the contract was preceded by a specified invitation addressed to him or by advertising, and

(*b*) the consumer took in that State the steps necessary for the conclusion of the contract.

Where a consumer enters into a contract with a party who is not domiciled in a Contracting State but has a branch, agency or other establishment in one of the Contracting States, that party shall, in disputes arising out of the operations of the branch, agency or establishment, be deemed to be domiciled in that State.

This Section shall not apply to contracts of transport.

Article 14

A consumer may bring proceedings against the other party to a contract either in the courts of the Contracting State in which that party is domiciled or in the courts of the Contracting State in which he is himself domiciled.

Proceedings may be brought against a consumer by the other party to the contract only in the courts of the Contracting State in which the consumer is domiciled.

These provisions shall not affect the right to bring a counter-claim in the court in which, in accordance with this Section, the original claim is pending.

Article 15

The provisions of this Section may be departed from only by an agreement:

1. which is entered into after the dispute has arisen, or

2. which allows the consumer to bring proceedings in courts other than those indicated in this Section, or

3. which is entered into by the consumer and the other party to the contract, both of whom are at the time of conclusion of the contract domiciled or habitually resident in the same Contracting State, and which confers jurisdiction on the courts of that State, provided that such an agreement is not contrary to the law of that State.

Section 5

Exclusive jurisdiction

Article 16

The following courts shall have exclusive jurisdiction, regardless of domicile:

1. in proceedings which have as their object rights *in rem* in, or tenancies of, immovable property, the courts of the Contracting State in which the property is situated;

2. in proceedings which have as their object the validity of the constitution, the nullity or the dissolution of companies or other legal persons or associations of natural or legal persons, or the decisions of their organs, the courts of the Contracting State in which the company, legal person or association has its seat;

3. in proceedings which have as their object the validity of entries in public registers, the courts of the Contracting State in which the register is kept;

4. in proceedings concerned with the registration or validity of patents, trade marks, designs, or other similar rights required to be deposited or registered, the courts of the Contracting State in which the deposit or registration has been applied for, has taken place or is under the terms of an international convention deemed to have taken place;

5. in proceedings concerned with the enforcement of judgments, the courts of the Contracting State in which the judgment has been or is to be enforced.

Section 6

Prorogation of jurisdiction

Article 17

If the parties, one or more of whom is domiciled in a Contracting State, have agreed that a court or the courts of a Contracting State are to have jurisdiction to settle any disputes which have arisen or which may arise in connection with a particular legal relationship, that court or those courts shall have exclusive jurisdiction. Such an agreement conferring jurisdiction shall be either in writing or evidenced in writing or, in international trade or commerce, in a form which accords with practices in that trade or commerce of which the parties are or ought to have been aware. Where such an agreement is concluded by parties, none of whom is domiciled in a Contracting State, the courts of other Contracting States shall have no jurisdiction over their disputes unless the court or courts chosen have declined jurisdiction.

The court or courts of a Contracting State on which a trust instrument has conferred jurisdiction shall have exclusive jurisdiction in any proceedings brought against a settlor, trustee or beneficiary, if relations between these persons or their rights or obligations under the trust are involved.

Agreements or provisions of a trust instrument conferring jurisdiction shall have no legal force if they are contrary to the provisions of Articles 12 or 15, or if the courts whose jurisdiction they purport to exclude have exclusive jurisdiction by virtue of Article 16.

If an agreement conferring jurisdiction was concluded for the benefit of only one of the parties, that party shall retain the right to bring proceedings in any other court which has jurisdiction by virtue of this Convention.

Article 18

Apart from jurisdiction derived from other provisions of this Convention, a court of a Contracting State before whom a defendant enters an appearance shall have jurisdiction. This rule shall not apply where appearance was entered solely to contest the jurisdiction, or where another court has exclusive jurisdiction by virtue of Article 16.

Section 7

Examination as to jurisdiction and admissibility

Article 19

Where a court of a Contracting State is seised of a claim which is principally concerned with a matter over which the courts of another Contracting State have exclusive jurisdiction by virtue of Article 16, it shall declare of its own motion that it has no jurisdiction.

Article 20

Where a defendant domiciled in one Contracting State is sued in a court of another Contracting State and does not enter an appearance, the court shall declare of its own motion that it has no jurisdiction unless its jurisdiction is derived from the provisions of this Convention.

The court shall stay the proceedings so long as it is not shown that the defendant has been able to receive the document instituting the proceedings or an equivalent document in sufficient time to enable him to arrange for his defence, or that all necessary steps have been taken to this end.

The provisions of the foregoing paragraph shall be replaced by those of Article 15 of the Hague Convention of 15th November, 1965 on the service abroad of judicial and extrajudicial documents in civil or commercial matters, if the document instituting the proceedings or notice thereof had to be transmitted abroad in accordance with that Convention.

Section 8

Lis Pendens – related actions

Article 21

Where proceedings involving the same cause of action and between the same parties are brought in the courts of different Contracting States, any court other than the court first seised shall of its own motion decline jurisdiction in favour of that court.

A court which would be required to decline jurisdiction may stay its proceedings if the jurisdiction of the other court is contested.

Article 22

Where related actions are brought in the courts of different Contracting

States, any court other than the court first seised may, while the actions are pending at first instance, stay its proceedings.

A court other than the court first seised may also, on the application of one of the parties, decline jurisdiction if the law of that court permits the consolidation of related actions and the court first seised has jurisdiction over both actions.

For the purposes of this Article, actions are deemed to be related where they are so closely connected that it is expedient to hear and determine them together to avoid the risk of irreconcilable judgments resulting from separate proceedings.

Article 23

Where actions come within the exclusive jurisdiction of several courts, any court other than the court first seised shall decline jurisdiction in favour of that court.

Section 9

Provisional, including protective, measures

Article 24

Application may be made to the courts of a Contracting State for such provisional, including protective, measures as may be available under the law of that State, even if, under this Convention, the courts of another Contracting State have jurisdiction as to the substance of the matter.

Title III

Recognition and enforcement

Article 25

For the purposes of this Convention, 'judgment' means any judgment given by a court or tribunal of a Contracting State, whatever the judgment may be called, including a decree, order, decision or writ of execution, as well as the determination of costs or expenses by an officer of the court.

Section 1

Recognition

Article 26

A judgment given in a Contracting State shall be recognised in the other Contracting States without any special procedure being required.

Any interested party who raises the recognition of a judgment as the principal issue in a dispute may, in accordance with the procedures provided for in Sections 2 and 3 of this Title, apply for a decision that the judgment be recognised.

If the outcome of proceedings in a court of a Contracting State depends on the determination of an incidental question of recognition that court shall have jurisdiction over that question.

Article 27

A judgment shall not be recognised:

1. if such recognition is contrary to public policy in the State in which recognition is sought;

2. where it was given in default of appearance, if the defendant was not duly served with the document which instituted the proceedings or with an equivalent document in sufficient time to enable him to arrange for his defence;

3. if the judgment is irreconcilable with a judgment given in a dispute between the same parties in the State in which recognition is sought;

4. if the court of the State in which the judgment was given, in order to arrive at its judgment, has decided a preliminary question concerning the status or legal capacity of natural persons, rights in property arising out of a matrimonial relationship, wills or succession in a way that conflicts with a rule of the private international law of the State in which the recognition is sought, unless the same result would have been reached by the application of the rules of private international law of that State;

5. if the judgment is irreconcilable with an earlier judgment given in a non-Contracting State involving the same cause of action and between the same parties, provided that this latter judgment fulfils the conditions necessary for its recognition in the State addressed.

Article 28

Moreover, a judgment shall not be recognised if it conflicts with the provisions of Sections 3, 4 or 5 of Title II, or in a case provided for in Article 59.

In its examination of the grounds of jurisdiction referred to in the foregoing paragraph, the court or authority applied to shall be bound by the findings of fact on which the court of the State in which the judgment was given based its jurisdiction.

Subject to the provisions of the first paragraph, the jurisdiction of the court of the State in which the judgment was given may not be reviewed; the test of public policy referred to in Article 27.1 may not be applied to the rules relating to jurisdiction.

Article 29

Under no circumstances may a foreign judgment be reviewed as to its substance.

Article 30

A court of a Contracting State in which recognition is sought of a judgment given in another Contracting State may stay the proceedings if an ordinary appeal against the judgment has been lodged.

A court of a Contracting State in which recognition is sought of a judgment given in Ireland or the United Kingdom may stay the proceedings if enforcement is suspended in the State in which the judgment was given by reason of an appeal.

Section 2

Enforcement

Article 31

A judgment given in a Contracting State and enforceable in that State shall be enforced in another Contracting State when, on the application of any interested party, the order for its enforcement has been issued here.

However, in the United Kingdom, such a judgment shall be enforced in England and Wales, in Scotland, or in Northern Ireland, when on the application of any interested party, it has been registered for enforcement in that part of the United Kingdom.

Article 32

The application shall be submitted:

- in Belgium, to the *tribunal de première instance* or *rechtbank van eerste aanleg*;
- in Denmark, to the *underret*;
- in the Federal Republic of Germany, to the presiding judge of a chamber of the *Landgericht*;
- in Greece, to the Μονομελες Πρωτοδιειο;
- in France, to the presiding judge of the *tribunal de grande instance*;
- in Ireland, to the High Court;
- in Italy, to the *corte d'appello*;
- in Luxembourg, to the presiding judge of the *tribunal d'arrondissement*;
- in the Netherlands, to the presiding judge of the *arrondissement-srechtbank*,
- in the United Kingdom:

1. in England and Wales, to the High Court of Justice, or in the case of a maintenance judgment to the Magistrates' Court on transmission by the Secretary of State;

2. in Scotland, to the Court of Session, or in the case of a maintenance judgment to the Sheriff Court on transmission by the Secretary of State;

3. in Northern Ireland, to the High Court of Justice, or in the case of a maintenance judgment to the Magistrates' Court on transmission by the Secretary of State.

The jurisdiction of local courts shall be determined by reference to the place of domicile of the party against whom enforcement is sought. If he is not domiciled in the State in which enforcement is sought, it shall be determined by reference to the place of enforcement.

Article 33

The procedure for making the application shall be governed by the law of the State in which enforcement is sought.

The applicant must give an address for service or process within the area of jurisdiction of the court applied to. However, if the law of the State in which enforcement is sought does not provide for the furnishing of such an address, the applicant shall appoint a representative *ad litem*.

The documents referred to in Articles 46 and 47 shall be attached to the application.

Article 34

The court applied to shall give its decision without delay; the party against whom enforcement is sought shall not at this stage of the proceedings be entitled to make any submissions on the application.

The application may be refused only for one of the reasons specified in Articles 27 and 28.

Under no circumstances may the foreign judgment be reviewed as to its substance.

Article 35

The appropriate officer of the court shall without delay bring the decision given on the application to the notice of the applicant in accordance with the procedure laid down by the law of the State in which enforcement is sought.

Article 36

If enforcement is authorised, the party against whom enforcement is sought may appeal against the decision within one month of service thereof.

If that party is domiciled in a Contracting State other than that in which the decision authorising enforcement was given, the time for appealing shall be two months and shall run from the date of service, either on him in person or at his residence. No extension of time may be granted on account of distance.

Article 37

An appeal against the decision authorising enforcement shall be lodged in accordance with the rules governing procedure in contentious matters:

- in Belgium, with the *tribunal de première instance* or *rechtbank van eerste aanleg*;
- in Denmark, with the *landsret*;
- in the Federal Republic of Germany, with the *Oberlandesgericht*;
- in Greece, with the Εφετειο;
- in France, with the *cour d'appel*;

- in Ireland, with the High Court;

- in Italy, with the *corte d'appello*;

- in Luxembourg, with the *Cour supérieure de justice* sitting as a court of civil appeal;

- in the Netherlands, with the *arrondissementsrechtbank*;

- in the United Kingdom:

1. in England and Wales, with the High Court of Justice, or in the case of a maintenance judgment with the Magistrates' Court;

2. in Scotland, with the Court of Session, or in the case of a maintenance judgment with the Sheriff Court;

3. in Northern Ireland, with the High of Court of Justice, or in the case of a maintenance judgment with the Magistrates' Court.

The judgment given on the appeal may be contested only:

- in Belgium, Greece, France, Italy, Luxembourg and in the Netherlands, by an appeal in cassation;

- in Denmark, by an appeal to the *højesteret*, with the leave of the Minister of Justice;

- in the Federal Republic of Germany, by a *Rechtsbeschwerde*;

- in Ireland, by an appeal on a point of law to the Supreme Court;

- in the United Kingdom, by a single further appeal on a point of law.

Article 38

The court with which the appeal under the first paragraph of Article 37 is lodged may, on the application of the appellant, stay the proceedings if an ordinary appeal has been lodged against the judgment in the State in which that judgment was given or if the time for such an appeal has not yet expired; in the latter case, the court may specify the time within which such an appeal is to be lodged.

Where the judgment was given in Ireland or the United Kingdom, any form of appeal available in the State in which it was given shall be treated as an ordinary appeal for the purposes of the first paragraph.

The court may also make enforcement conditional on the provision of such security as it shall determine.

Article 39

During the time specified for an appeal pursuant to Article 36 and until

any such appeal has been determined, no measures of enforcement may be taken other than protective measures taken against the property of the party against whom enforcement is sought.

The decision authorising enforcement shall carry with it the power to proceed to any such protective measures.

Article 40

If the application for enforcement is refused, the applicant may appeal:

- in Belgium, to the *cour d'appel* or *hof van beroep*;
- in Denmark, to the *landsret*;
- in the Federal Republic of Germany, to the *Oberlandesgericht*;
- in Greece, to the Εφετειο;
- in France, to the *cour d'appel*;
- in Ireland, to the High Court;
- in Italy, to the *corte d'appello*;
- in Luxembourg, to the *Cour supérieure de justice* sitting as a court of civil appeal;
- in the Netherlands, to the *gerechtshof*;
- in the United Kingdom:

1. in England and Wales, to the High Court of Justice, or in the case of a maintenance judgment to the Magistrates' Court;

2. in Scotland, to the Court of Session, or in the case of a maintenance judgment to the Sheriff Court;

3. in Northern Ireland, to the High Court of Justice, or in the case of a maintenance judgment to the Magistrates' Court.

The party against whom enforcement is sought shall be summoned to appear before the appellate court. If he fails to appear, the provisions of the second and third paragraphs of Article 20 shall apply even where he is not domiciled in any of the Contracting States.

Article 41

A judgment given on an appeal provided for in Article 40 may be contested only:

- in Belgium, Greece, France, Italy, Luxembourg and in the Netherlands, by an appeal in cassation;

- in Denmark, by an appeal to the *højesteret*, with the leave of the Minister of Justice;

- in the Federal Republic of Germany, by a *Rechtsbeschwerde*;

- in Ireland, by an appeal on a point of law to the Supreme Court;

- in the United Kingdom, by a single further appeal on a point of law.

Article 42

Where a foreign judgment has been given in respect of several matters and enforcement cannot be authorised for all of them, the court shall authorise enforcement for one or more of them.

An applicant may request partial enforcement of a judgment.

Article 43

A foreign judgment which orders a periodic payment by way of a penalty shall be enforceable in the State in which enforcement is sought only if the amount of the payment has been finally determined by the courts of the State in which the judgment was given.

Article 44

An applicant who, in the State in which the judgment was given, has benefited from complete or partial legal aid or exemption from costs or expenses, shall be entitled, in the procedures provided for in Articles 32 to 35, to benefit from the most favourable legal aid or the most extensive exemption from costs or expenses provided for by the law of the State addressed.

An applicant who requests the enforcement of a decision given by an administrative authority in Denmark in respect of a maintenance order may, in the State addressed, claim the benefits referred to in the first paragraph if he presents a statement from the Danish Ministry of Justice to the effect that he fulfils the economic requirements to qualify for the grant of complete or partial legal aid or exemption from costs or expenses.

Article 45

No security, bond or deposit, however described, shall be required of a party who in one Contracting State applies for enforcement of a judgment given in another Contracting State on the ground that he is a foreign national or that he is not domiciled or resident in the State in which enforcement is sought.

Section 3

Common provisions

Article 46

A party seeking recognition or applying for enforcement of a judgment shall produce:

1. a copy of a judgment which satisfies the conditions necessary to establish its authenticity;

2. in the case of a judgment given in default, the original or a certified true copy of the document which establishes that the party in default was served with the document instituting the proceedings or with an equivalent document.

Article 47

A party applying for enforcement shall also produce;

1. documents which establish that, according to the law of the State in which it has been given, the judgment is enforceable and has been served;

2. where appropriate, a document showing that the applicant is in receipt of legal aid in the State in which the judgment was given.

Article 48

If the documents specified in Articles 46.2 and 47.2 are produced, the court may specify a time for their production, accept equivalent documents or, if it considers that it has sufficient information before it, dispense with their production.

If the court so requires, a translation of the documents shall be produced; the translation shall be certified by a person qualified to do so in one of the Contracting States.

Article 49

No legalisation or other similar formality shall be required in respect of the documents referred to in Articles 46 or 47 or the second paragraph of Article 48, or in respect of a document appointing a representative *ad litem*.

Title IV

Authentic instruments and court settlements

Article 50

A document which has been formally drawn up or registered as an authentic instrument and is enforceable in one Contracting State shall, in another Contracting State, have an order for its enforcement issued there, on application made in accordance with the procedures provided for in Article 31 *et seq*. The application may be refused only if enforcement of the instrument is contrary to public policy in the State in which enforcement is sought.

The instrument produced must satisfy the conditions necessary to establish its authenticity in the State of origin.

The provisions of Section 3 of Title III shall apply as appropriate.

Article 51

A settlement which has been approved by a court in the course of proceedings and is enforceable in the State in which it was concluded shall be enforceable in the State in which enforcement is sought under the same conditions as authentic instruments.

Title V

General provisions

Article 52

In order to determine whether a party is domiciled in the Contracting State whose courts are seised of the matter, the court shall apply its internal law.

If a party is not domiciled in the State whose courts are seised of the matter, then, in order to determine whether the party is domiciled in another Contracting State, the court shall apply the law of that State.

The domicile of a party shall, however, be determined in accordance with his national law, by that law, his domicile depends on that of another person or on the seat of an authority.

Article 53

For the purposes of this Convention, the seat of a company or other legal

person or association of natural or legal persons shall be treated as its domicile. However, in order to determine that seat, the court shall apply its rules of private international law.

In order to determine whether a trust is domiciled in the Contracting State whose courts are seised of the matter, the court shall apply its rules of private international law.

Title VI

Transitional provisions

Article 54

The provisions of this Convention shall apply only to legal proceedings instituted and to documents formally drawn up or registered as authentic instruments after its entry into force.

However, judgments given after the date of entry into force of this Convention in proceedings instituted before that date shall be recognised and enforced in accordance with the provisions of Title III if jurisdiction was founded upon rules which accorded with those provided for either in Title II of this Convention or in a convention concluded between the State of origin and the State addressed which was in force when the proceedings were instituted.

Title VII

Relationship to other conventions

Article 55

Subject to the provisions of the second paragraph of Article 54, and of Article 56, this Convention shall, for the States which are parties to it, supersede the following conventions concluded between two or more of them:

– the Convention between Belgium and France on jurisdiction and the validity and enforcement of judgments, arbitration awards and authentic instruments, signed at Paris on 8 July 1899;

– the Convention between Belgium and the Netherlands on jurisdiction, bankruptcy, and the validity and enforcement of judgments, arbitration awards and authentic instruments, signed at Brussels on 28 March 1925;

– the Convention between France and Italy on the enforcement of

judgments in civil and commercial matters, signed at Rome on 3 June 1930;

– the Convention between the United Kingdom and the French Republic providing for the reciprocal enforcement of judgments in civil and commercial matters, with Protocol, signed at Paris on 18 January 1934;

– the Convention between the United Kingdom and the Kingdom of Belgium providing for the reciprocal enforcement of judgments in civil and commercial matters, with Protocol, signed at Brussels on 2 May 1934;

– the Convention between Germany and Italy on the recognition and enforcement of judgments in civil and commercial matters, signed at Rome on 9 March 1936;

– the Convention between the Federal Republic of Germany and the Kingdom of Belgium on the mutual recognition and enforcement of judgments, arbitration awards and authentic instruments in civil and commercial matters, signed at Bonn on 30 June 1958;

– the Convention between the Kingdom of the Netherlands and the Italian Republic on the recognition and enforcement of judgments in civil and commercial matters, signed at Rome on 17 April 1959;

– the Convention between the United Kingdom and the Federal Republic of Germany for the reciprocal recognition and enforcement of judgments in civil and commercial matters, signed at Bonn on 14 July 1960;

– the Convention between the Kingdom of Greece and the Federal Republic of Germany for the reciprocal recognition and enforcement of judgments, settlements and authentic instruments in civil and commercial matters, signed in Athens on 4 November 1961;

– the Convention between the Kingdom of Belgium and the Italian Republic on the recognition and enforcement of judgments and other enforceable instruments in civil and commercial matters, signed at Rome on 6 April 1962;

– the Convention between the Kingdom of the Netherlands and the Federal Republic of Germany on the mutual recognition and enforcement of judgments and other enforceable instruments in civil and commercial matters, signed at The Hague on 30 August 1962;

– the Convention between the United Kingdom and the Republic of Italy for the reciprocal recognition and enforcement of judgments in

civil and commercial matters, signed at Rome on 7 February 1964, with amending Protocol signed at Rome on 14 July 1970;

- the Convention between the United Kingdom and the Kingdom of the Netherlands providing for the reciprocal recognition and enforcement of judgments in civil matters, signed at The Hague on 17 November 1967,

and, in so far as it is in force:

- the Treaty between Belgium, the Netherlands and Luxembourg on jurisdiction, bankruptcy, and the validity and enforcement of judgments, arbitration awards and authentic instruments, signed at Brussels on 24 November 1961.

Article 56

The Treaty and the conventions referred to in Article 55 shall continue to have effect in relation to matters to which this Convention does not apply.

They shall continue to have effect in respect of judgments given and documents formally drawn up or registered as authentic instruments before the entry into force of this Convention.

Article 57

This Convention shall not affect any convention to which the Contracting States are or will be parties and which, in relation to particular matters, govern jurisdiction or the recognition or enforcement of judgments.

This Convention shall not affect the application of provisions which, in relation to particular matters, govern jurisdiction or the recognition or enforcement of judgments and which are or will be contained in acts of the institutions of the European Communities or in national laws harmonised in implementation of such acts.

(*Article 25.2 of the 1978 Accession Convention provides*:

'With a view to its uniform interpretation, paragraph 1 of Article 57 shall be applied in the following manner:

(*a*) the 1968 Convention as amended shall not prevent a court of a Contracting State which is a party to a convention on a particular matter from assuming jurisdiction in accordance with that convention, even where the defendant is domiciled in another Contracting State which is not a party to that convention. The court shall, in any event, apply Article 20 of the 1968 Convention as amended;

(*b*) a judgment given in a Contracting State in the exercise of jurisdiction provided for in a convention on a particular matter shall be recognised and enforced in the other Contracting States in accordance with the 1968 Convention as amended.

Where a convention on a particular matter to which both the State of origin and the State addressed are parties lays down conditions for the recognition or enforcement of judgments, those conditions shall apply. In any event, the provisions of the 1968 Convention as amended which concern the procedures for recognition and enforcement of judgments may be applied.')

Article 58

This Convention shall not affect the rights granted to Swiss nationals by the Convention concluded on 15 June 1869 between France and the Swiss Confederation on jurisdiction and the enforcement of judgments in civil matters.

Article 59

This Convention shall not prevent a Contracting State from assuming, in a convention on the recognition and enforcement of judgments, an obligation towards a third State not to recognise judgments given in other Contracting States against defendants domiciled or habitually resident in the third State where, in cases provided for in Article 4, the judgment could only be founded on a ground of jurisdiction specified in the second paragraph of Article 3.

However, a Contracting State may not assume an obligation towards a third State not to recognise a judgment given in another Contracting State by a court basing its jurisdiction on the presence within that State of property belonging to the defendant, or the seizure by the plaintiff of property situated there:

1. if the action is brought to assert or declare proprietary or possessory rights in that property, seeks to obtain authority to dispose of it, or arises from another issue relating to such property, or,

2. if the property constitutes the security for a debt which is the subject-matter of the action.

Title VIII

Final provisions

Article 60

This Convention shall apply to the European territories of the Contracting States, including Greenland, to the French overseas departments and territories, and to Mayotte.

The Kingdom of the Netherlands may declare at the time of signing or ratifying this Convention or at any later time, by notifying the Secretary-General of the Council of the European Communities, that this Convention shall be applicable to the Netherlands Antilles. In the absence of such declaration, proceedings taking place in the European territory of the Kingdom as a result of appeal in cassation from the judgment of a court in the Netherlands Antilles shall be deemed to be proceedings taking place in the latter court.

Notwithstanding the first paragraph, this Convention shall not apply to:

1. the Faroe Islands, unless the Kingdom of Denmark makes a declaration to the contrary;

2. any European territory situated outside the United Kingdom for the international relations of which the United Kingdom is responsible, unless the United Kingdom makes a declaration to the contrary in respect of any such territory.

Such declarations may be made at any time by notifying the Secretary-General of the Council of the European Communities.

Proceedings brought in the United Kingdom on appeal from courts in one of the territories referred to in subparagraph 2 of the third paragraph shall be deemed to be proceedings taking place in those courts.

Proceedings which in the Kingdom of Denmark are dealt with under the law on civil procedure for the Faroe Islands (*lov for Faerøerne om rettens pleje*) shall be deemed to be proceedings taking place in the courts of the Faroe Islands.

Article 61

This Convention shall be ratified by the signatory States. The instruments of ratification shall be deposited with the Secretary-General of the Council of the European Communities.

Article 62

This Convention shall enter into force on the first day of the third month following the deposit of the instrument of ratification by the last signatory State to take this step.

Article 63

The Contracting States recognise that any State which becomes a member of the European Economic Community shall be required to accept this Convention as a basis for the negotiations between the Contracting States and that State necessary to ensure the implementation of the last paragraph of Article 220 of the Treaty establishing the European Economic Community.

The necessary adjustments may be the subject of a special convention between the Contracting States of the one part and the new Member State of the other part.

Article 64

The Secretary-General of the Council of the European Communities shall notify the signatory States of:

(a) the deposit of each instrument of ratification;

(b) the date of entry into force of this Convention;

(c) any declaration received pursuant to Article 60;

(d) any declaration received pursuant to Article IV of the Protocol;

(e) any communication made pursuant to Article VI of the Protocol.

Article 65

The Protocol annexed to this Convention by common accord of the Contracting States shall form an integral part thereof.

Article 66

This Convention is concluded for an unlimited period.

Article 67

Any Contracting State may request the revision of this Convention. In this event, a revision conference shall be convened by the President of the Council of the European Communities.

Article 68

This Convention, drawn up in a single original in the Dutch, French, German and Italian languages, all four texts being equally authentic, shall be deposited in the archives of the Secretariat of the Council of the European Communities. The Secretary-General shall transmit a certified copy to the Government of each signatory State.

(*Signatures of Plenipotentiaries of the original six Contracting States*)

Annexed Protocol

The High Contracting Parties have agreed upon the following provisions, which shall be annexed to the Convention:

Article I

Any person domiciled in Luxembourg who is sued in a court of another Contracting State pursuant to Article 5.1 may refuse to submit to the jurisdiction of that court. If the defendant does not enter an appearance the court shall declare of its own motion that it has no jurisdiction.

An agreement conferring jurisdiction, within the meaning of Article 17, shall be valid with respect to a person domiciled in Luxembourg only if that person has expressly and specifically so agreed.

Article II

Without prejudice to any more favourable provisions of national laws, persons domiciled in a Contracting State who are being prosecuted in the criminal courts of another Contracting State of which they are not nationals for an offence which was not intentionally committed may be defended by persons qualified to do so, even if they do not appear in person.

However, the court seised of the matter may order appearance in person; in the case of failure to appear, a judgment given in the civil action without the person concerned having had the opportunity to arrange for his defence need not be recognised or enforced in the other Contracting States.

Article III

In proceedings for the issue of an order for enforcement, no charge, duty or fee calculated by reference to the value of the matter in issue may be levied in the State in which enforcement is sought.

Article IV

Judicial and extrajudicial documents drawn up in one Contracting State which have to be served on persons in another Contracting State shall be transmitted in accordance with the procedures laid down in the conventions and agreements concluded between the Contracting States.

Unless the State in which service is to take place objects by declaration to the Secretary-General of the Council of the European Communities, such documents may also be sent by the appropriate public officers of the State in which the document has been drawn up directly to the appropriate public officers of the State in which the addressee is to be found. In this case the officer of the State of origin shall send a copy of the document to the officer of the State addressed who is competent to forward it to the addressee. The document shall be forwarded in the manner specified by the law of the State addressed. The forwarding shall be recorded by a certificate sent directly to the officer of the State of origin.

Article V

The jurisdiction specified in Articles 6.2 and 10 in actions on a warranty or guarantee or in any other third party proceedings may not be resorted to in the Federal Republic of Germany. In that State, any person domiciled in another Contracting State may be sued in the courts in pursuance of Articles 68, 72, 73 and 74 of the code of civil procedure (*Zivilprozeßordnung*) concerning third-party notices.

Judgments given in the other Contracting States by virtue of Article 6.2 or Article 10 shall be recognised and enforced in the Federal Republic of Germany in accordance with Title III. Any effects which judgments given in that State may have on third parties by application of Articles 68, 72, 73 and 74 of the code of civil procedure (*Zivilprozeßordnung*) shall also be recognised in the other Contracting States.

Article Va

In matters relating to maintenance, the expression 'court' includes the Danish administrative authorities.

Article Vb

In proceedings involving a dispute between the master and a member of the crew of a sea-going ship registered in Denmark, in Greece or in Ireland, concerning remuneration or other conditions of service, a court in a Contracting State shall establish whether the diplomatic or consular

officer responsible for the ship has been notified of the dispute. It shall stay the proceedings so long as he has not been notified. It shall of its own motion decline jurisdiction if the officer, having been duly notified, has exercised the powers accorded to him in the matter by a consular convention, or in the absence of such a convention, has, within the time allowed, raised any objection to the exercise of such jurisdiction.

Article Vc

Articles 52 and 53 of this Convention shall, when applied by Article 69(5) of the Convention for the European Patent for the Common Market, signed at Luxembourg on 15 December 1975, to the provisions relating to 'residence' in the English text of that Convention, operate as if 'residence' in that text were the same as 'domicile' in Articles 52 and 53.

Article Vd

Without prejudice to the jurisdiction of the European Patent Office under the Convention on the Grant of European Patents, signed at Munich on 5 October 1973, the courts of each Contracting State shall have exclusive jurisdiction, regardless of domicile, in proceedings concerned with the registration or validity of any European patent granted for that State which is not a Community patent by virtue of the provisions of Article 86 of the Convention for the European Patent for the Common Market, signed at Luxembourg on 15 December 1975.

Article VI

The Contracting States shall communicate to the Secretary-General of the Council of the European Communities the text of any provisions of their laws which amend either those articles of their laws mentioned in the Convention or the lists of courts specified in Section 2 of Title III of the Convention.

Second Schedule

Text of the 1971 Protocol as amended by the 1978 Accession Convention and the 1982 Accession Convention.

Article 1

The Court of Justice of the European Communities shall have jurisdiction to give rulings on the interpretation of the Convention on Jurisdiction and the Enforcement of Judgments in Civil and Commercial Matters and of the Protocol annexed to that Convention, signed at Brussels on 27 September 1968, and also on the interpretation of the present Protocol.

The Court of Justice of the European Communities shall also have jurisdiction to give rulings on the interpretation of the Convention on the accession of the Kingdom of Denmark, Ireland and the United Kingdom of Great Britain and Northern Ireland to the Convention of 27 September 1968 and to this Protocol.

The Court of Justice of the European Communities shall also have jurisdiction to give rulings on the interpretation of the Convention on the accession of the Hellenic Republic to the Convention of 27 September 1968 and to this Protocol, as adjusted by the 1978 Convention.

Article 2

The following courts may request the Court of Justice to give preliminary rulings on questions of interpretation:

1.   –   in Belgium: *la Cour de Cassation – het Hof van Cassatie* and *le Conseil d'État – de Raad van State,*

    –   in Denmark: *højesteret,*

    –   in the Federal Republic of Germany: *die obersten Gerichtshöfe des Bundes,*

    –   in Greece: the αυωτατα διαχαοτοια,

    –   in France: *la Cour de Cassation* and *le Conseil d'État,*

    –   in Ireland: the Supreme Court,

    –   in Italy: *la Corte Suprema di Cassazione,*

    –   in Luxembourg: *la Cour supérieure de Justice* when sitting as *Cour de Cassation,*

    –   in the Netherlands: *de Hoge Raad,*

    –   in the United Kingdom: the House of Lords and courts to which application has been made under the second paragraph of Article 37 or under Article 41 of the Convention;

2. the courts of the Contracting States when they are sitting in an appellate capacity;

3. in the cases provided for in Article 37 of the Convention, the courts referred to in that Article.

Article 3

1. Where a question of interpretation of the Convention or of one of the other instruments referred to in Article 1 is raised in a case pending before one of the courts listed in Article 2.1, that court shall, if it

considers that a decision on the question is necessary to enable it to give judgment, request the Court of Justice to give a ruling thereon.

2. Where such a question is raised before any court referred to in Article 2.2 or 2.3, that court may, under the conditions laid down in paragraph 1, request the Court of Justice to give a ruling thereon.

Article 4

1. The competent authority of a Contracting State may request the Court of Justice to give a ruling on a question of interpretation of the Convention or of one of the other instruments referred to in Article 1 if judgments given by courts of that State conflict with the interpretation given either by the Court of Justice or in a judgment of one of the courts of another Contracting State referred to in Article 2.1 or 2.2. The provisions of this paragraph shall apply only to judgments which have become *res judicata*.

2. The interpretation given by the Court of Justice in response to such a request shall not affect the judgments which gave rise to the request for interpretation.

3. The Procurators-General of the Courts of Cassation of the Contracting States, or any other authority designated by a Contracting State, shall be entitled to request the Court of Justice for a ruling on interpretation in accordance with paragraph 1.

4. The Registrar of the Court of Justice shall give notice of the request to the Contracting States, to the Commission and to the Council of the European Communities; they shall then be entitled within two months of the notification to submit statements of case or written observations to the Court.

5. No fees shall be levied or any costs or expenses awarded in respect of the proceedings provided for in this Article.

Article 5

1. Except where this Protocol otherwise provides, the provisions of the Treaty establishing the European Economic Community and those of the Protocol on the Statute of the Court of Justice annexed thereto, which are applicable when the Court is requested to give a preliminary ruling, shall also apply to any proceedings for the interpretation of the Convention and the other instruments referred to in Article 1.

2. The Rules of Procedure of the Court of Justice shall, if necessary, be adjusted and supplemented in accordance with Article 188 of the Treaty establishing the European Economic Community.

Article 6

This Protocol shall apply to the European territories of the Contracting States, including Greenland, to the French overseas departments and territories, and to Mayotte.

The Kingdom of the Netherlands may declare at the time of signing or ratifying this Protocol or at any later time, by notifying the Secretary-General of the Council of the European Communities, that this Protocol shall be applicable to the Netherlands Antilles.

Notwithstanding the first paragraph, this Protocol shall not apply to:

1. the Faroe Islands, unless the Kingdom of Denmark makes a declaration to the contrary,

2. any European territory situated outside the United Kingdom for the international relations of which the United Kingdom is responsible, unless the United Kingdom makes a declaration to the contrary in respect of any such territory.

Such declarations may be made at any time by notifying the Secretary-General of the Council of the European Communities.

Article 7

This Protocol shall be ratified by the signatory States. The instruments of ratification shall be deposited with the Secretary-General of the Council of the European Communities.

Article 8

This Protocol shall enter into force on the first day of the third month following the deposit of the instrument of ratification by the last signatory State to take this step; provided that it shall at the earliest enter into force at the same time as the Convention of 27th September, 1968 on Jurisdiction and the Enforcement of Judgments in Civil and Commercial Matters.

Article 9

The Contracting States recognise that any State which becomes a member of the European Economic Community, and to which Article 63 of the Convention on Jurisdiction and the Enforcement of Judgments in Civil and Commercial Matters applies, must accept the provisions of this Protocol, subject to such adjustments as may be required.

Article 10

The Secretary-General of the Council of the European Communities shall notify the signatory States of:

(a) the deposit of each instrument of ratification;

(b) the date of entry into force of this Protocol;

(c) any designation received pursuant to Article 4.3;

(d) any declaration received pursuant to Article 6.

Article 11

The Contracting States shall communicate to the Secretary-General of the Council of the European Communities the texts of any provisions of their laws which necessitate an amendment to the list of courts in Article 2.1.

Article 12

This Protocol is concluded for an unlimited period.

Article 13

Any Contracting State may request the revision of this Protocol. In this event, a revision conference shall be convened by the President of the Council of the European Communities.

Article 14

This Protocol, drawn up in a single original in the Dutch, French, German and Italian languages, all four texts being equally authentic, shall be deposited in the archives of the Secretariat of the Council of the European Communities. The Secretary-General shall transmit a certified copy to the Government of each signatory State.

Third Schedule

Titles V and VI of the 1978 Accession Convention

Title V

Transitional Provisions

Article 34

1. The 1968 Convention and the 1971 Protocol, with the amendments made by this Convention, shall apply only to legal proceedings instituted

and to authentic instruments formally drawn up or registered after the entry into force of this Convention in the State of origin and, where recognition or enforcement of a judgment or authentic instrument is sought, in the State addressed.

2. However, as between the six Contracting States to the 1968 Convention, judgments given after the date of entry into force of the Convention in proceedings instituted before that date shall be recognised and enforced in accordance with the provisions of Title III of the 1968 Convention as amended.

3. Moreover, as between the six Contracting States to the 1968 Convention and the three States mentioned in Article 1 of this Convention, and as between those three States, judgments given after the date of entry into force of this Convention between the State of origin and the State addressed in proceedings instituted before that date shall also be recognised and enforced in accordance with the provisions of Title III of the 1968 Convention as amended if jurisdiction was founded upon rules which accorded with the provisions of Title II, as amended, or with provisions of a convention concluded between the State of origin and the State addressed which was in force when the proceedings were instituted.

Article 35

If the parties to a dispute concerning a contract had agreed in writing before the entry into force of this Convention that the contract was to be governed by the law of Ireland or of a part of the United Kingdom, the courts of Ireland or of that part of the United Kingdom shall retain the right to exercise jurisdiction in the dispute.

Article 36

For a period of three years from the entry into force of the 1968 Convention for the Kingdom of Denmark and Ireland respectively, jurisdiction in maritime matters shall be determined in these States not only in accordance with the provisions of that Convention but also in accordance with the provisions of paragraphs 1 to 6 following. However, upon the entry into force of the International Convention relating to the arrest of sea-going ships, signed at Brussels on 10 May 1952, for one of these States, these provisions shall cease to have effect for that State.

1. A person who is domiciled in a Contracting State may be sued in the courts of one of the States mentioned above in respect of a maritime claim if the ship to which the claim relates or any other ship owned by him has been arrested by judicial process within the territory of the latter

State to secure the claim, or could have been so arrested there but bail or other security has been given, and either:

(a)　the claimant is domiciled in the latter State; or

(b)　the claim arose in the latter State; or

(c)　the claim concerns the voyage during which the arrest was made or could have been made; or

(d)　the claim arises out of a collision or out of damage caused by a ship to another ship or to goods or persons on board either ship, either by the execution or non-execution of a manoeuvre or by the non-observance of regulations; or

(e)　the claim is for salvage; or

(f)　the claim is in respect of a mortgage or hypothecation of the ship arrested.

2. A claimant may arrest either the particular ship to which the maritime claim relates, or any other ship which is owned by the person who was, at the time when the maritime claim arose, the owner of the particular ship. However, only the particular ship to which the maritime claim relates may be arrested in respect of the maritime claims set out in subparagraphs (o), (p) or (q) of paragraph 5 of this Article.

3. Ships shall be deemed to be in the same ownership when all the shares therein are owned by the same person or persons.

4. When in the case of a charter by demise of a ship the charterer alone is liable in respect of a maritime claim relating to that ship, the claimant may arrest that ship or any other ship owned by the charterer, but no other ship owned by the owner may be arrested in respect of such claim. The same shall apply to any case in which a person other than the owner of a ship is liable in respect of a maritime claim relating to that ship.

5. The expression 'maritime claim' means a claim arising out of one or more of the following:

(a)　damage caused by any ship either in collision or otherwise;

(b)　loss of life or personal injury caused by any ship or occurring in connection with the operation of any ship;

(c)　salvage;

(d)　agreement relating to the use or hire of any ship whether by charterparty or otherwise;

(e)　agreement relating to the carriage of goods in any ship whether by charterparty or otherwise;

(f) loss of or damage to goods including baggage carried in any ship;

(g) general average;

(h) bottomry;

(i) towage;

(j) pilotage;

(k) goods or materials wherever supplied to a ship for her operation or maintenance;

(l) construction, repair or equipment of any ship or dock charges and dues;

(m) wages of masters, officers or crew;

(n) master's disbursements, including disbursements made by shippers, charterers or agents on behalf of a ship or her owner;

(o) dispute as to the title to or ownership of any ship;

(p) disputes between co-owners of any ship as to the ownership, possession, employment or earnings of that ship;

(q) the mortgage or hypothecation of any ship.

6. In Denmark, the expression 'arrest' shall be deemed as regards the maritime claims referred to in subparagraphs (o) and (p) of paragraph 5 of this Article, to include a *forbud*, where that is the only procedure allowed in respect of such a claim under Articles 646 to 653 of the law on civil procedure (*lov om rettens pleje*).

Title VI

Final provisions

Article 37

The Secretary-General of the Council of the European Communities shall transmit a certified copy of the 1968 Convention and of the 1971 Protocol in the Dutch, French, German and Italian languages to the Governments of the Kingdom of Denmark, Ireland and the United Kingdom of Great Britain and Northern Ireland.

The texts of the 1968 Convention and the 1971 Protocol, drawn up in the Danish, English and Irish languages, shall be annexed to this Convention. The texts drawn up in the Danish, English and Irish languages shall be authentic under the same conditions as the original texts of the 1968 Convention and the 1971 Protocol.

Article 38

This Convention shall be ratified by the signatory States. The instruments of ratification shall be deposited with the Secretary-General of the Council of the European Communities.

Article 39

This Convention shall enter into force, as between the States which shall have ratified it, on the first day of the third month following the deposit of the last instrument of ratification by the original Member States of the Community and one new Member State.

It shall enter into force for each new Member State which subsequently ratifies it on the first day of the third month following the deposit of its instrument of ratification.

Article 40

The Secretary-General of the Council of the European Communities shall notify the signatory States of:

(a) the deposit of each instrument of ratification,

(b) the dates of entry into force of this Convention for the Contracting States.

Article 41

This Convention, drawn up in a single original in the Danish, Dutch, English, French, German, Irish and Italian languages, all seven texts being equally authentic, shall be deposited in the archives of the Secretariat of the Council of the European Communities. The Secretary-General shall transmit a certified copy to the Government of each signatory State.

Fourth Schedule

Titles V and VI of the 1982 Accession Convention

Title V

Transitional provisions

Article 12

1. The 1968 Convention and the 1971 Protocol, as amended by the 1978 Convention and this Convention, shall apply only to legal proceedings instituted and to authentic instruments formally drawn up or registered

after the entry into force of this Convention in the State of origin and, where recognition or enforcement of a judgment or authentic instrument is sought, in the State addressed.

2. However, judgments given after the date of entry into force of this Convention between the State of origin and the State addressed in proceedings instituted before that date shall be recognised and enforced in accordance with the provisions of Title III of the 1968 Convention, as amended by the 1978 Convention and this Convention, if jurisdiction was founded upon rules which accorded with the provisions of Title II of the 1968 Convention, as amended, or with the provisions of a convention which was in force between the State or origin and the State addressed when the proceedings were instituted.

Title VI

Final provisions

Article 13

The Secretary-General of the Council of the European Communities shall transmit a certified copy of the 1968 Convention, of the 1971 Protocol and of the 1978 Convention in the Danish, Dutch, English, French, German, Irish and Italian languages to the government of the Hellenic Republic.

The texts of the 1968 Convention, of the 1971 Protocol and of the 1978 Convention, drawn up in the Greek language, shall be annexed to this Convention. The texts drawn up in the Greek language shall be authentic under the same conditions as the other texts of the 1968 Convention, the 1971 Protocol and the 1978 Convention.

Article 14

This Convention shall be ratified by the signatory States. The instruments of ratification shall be deposited with the Secretary-General of the Council of the European Communities.

Article 15

This Convention shall enter into force, as between the States which have ratified it, on the first day of the third month following the deposit of the last instrument of ratification by the Hellenic Republic and those States which have put into force the 1978 Convention in accordance with Article 39 of that Convention.

It shall enter into force for each Member State which subsequently

ratifies it on the first day of the third month following the deposit of its instrument of ratification.

Article 16

The Secretary-General of the Council of the European Communities shall notify the signatory States of:

(a) the deposit of each instrument of ratification;

(b) the dates of entry into force of this Convention for the Contracting States.

Article 17

This Convention, drawn up in a single original in the Danish, Dutch, English, French, German, Greek, Irish and Italian languages, all eight texts being equally authentic, shall be deposited in the archives of the General Secretariat of the Council of the European Communities. The Secretary-General shall transmit a certified copy to the Government of each signatory State.

Fifth Schedule

Domicile

Part I

1. An individual is domiciled in the State, or in a state other than a Contracting State if, but only if, he is ordinarily resident in the State or in that other state.

2. An individual is domiciled in a place in the State if, but only if, he is domiciled in the State and is ordinarily resident or carries on any profession, business or occupation in that place.

Part III

1. A corporation or association has its seat in the State if, but only if –

(a) it was incorporated or formed under the law of the State, or

(b) its central management and control is exercised in the State.

2. A corporation or association has its seat in a particular place in the State if, but only if, it has its seat in the State and –

(a) it has its registered office or some other official address at that place, or

(b) its central management and control is exercised in that place or it is carrying on business in that place.

3. Subject to *paragraph* 4 of this Part, a corporation or association has its seat in a state other than the State if, but only if –

(a) it was incorporated or formed under the law of that state, or

(b) its central management and control is exercised in that state.

4. A corporation or association shall not be regarded as having its seat in a Contracting State other than the State if –

(a) it has its seat in the State by virtue of *paragraph* 1(a) of this Part, or

(b) it is shown that the courts of that other state would not regard it for the purposes of Article 16.2 as having its seat there.

5. In this Part –

'association' means an unincorporated body of persons;

'business' includes any activity carried on by a corporation or association;

'corporation' means a body corporate;

'official address' means, in relation to a corporation or association, an address which it is required by law to register, notify or maintain for the purpose of receiving notices or other communications.

Part V

A trust is domiciled in the State if, but only if, the law of the State is the system of law with which the trust has its closest and most real connection.

EDITORIAL NOTE

Parts II, IV and VI of the Fifth Schedule, being the Irish translations of Parts I, III and V, have been omitted.

FOOTNOTES

1. OJ No C 59, 5.3.79, p.1.
2. OJ No C 59, 5.3.79, p.71.
3. OJ No C 298, 24.11.86, p.1.

CONTRACTUAL OBLIGATIONS (APPLICABLE LAW) ACT, 1991

An Act to give the force of law to the Convention on the law applicable to contractual obligations signed at Rome on behalf of the State on the 19th day of June, 1980, and the Convention on the accession of the Hellenic Republic to the aforesaid Convention signed at Luxembourg on the 10th day of April, 1984, and to provide for connected matters.

[*8th May*, 1991]

Be it enacted by the Oireachtas as follows:

1. Definitions

In this Act–

'the 1980 Convention' means the Convention on the law applicable to contractual obligations signed at Rome on behalf of the State on the 19th day of June, 1980;

'the 1984 Accession Convention' means the Convention on the accession of the Hellenic Republic to the 1980 Convention signed at Luxembourg on the 10th day of April, 1984;

'the Conventions' means the 1980 Convention and the 1984 Accession Convention;

'the European Communities' has the same meaning as in section 1 of the European Communities Act, 1972;

'the European Court' means the Court of Justice of the European Communities;

'the Minister' means the Minister for Justice.

2. Conventions to have force of law

(1) Subject to subsection (2) of this section, the Conventions shall have force of law in the State and judicial notice shall be taken of them.

(2) Article 7(1) of the 1980 Convention shall not have the force of law in the State.

(3) For convenience of reference there are set out in the First, Second, Third and Fourth Schedules, respectively, to this Act –

(*a*) the text in the English language of the 1980 Convention,

(b) the text in the English language of the 1984 Accession Convention,

(c) the text in the Irish language of the 1980 Convention, and

(d) the text in the Irish language of the 1984 Accession Convention.

3. Interpretation of Conventions

(1) Judicial notice shall be taken of –

(a) any ruling or decision of, or expression of opinion by, the European Court on any question as to the meaning or effect of any provision of the Conventions, and

(b) the report referred to in subsection (2) of this section.

(2) The report by Professor Mario Giuliano and Professor Paul Lagarde on the 1980 Convention (which is reproduced in the Official Journal of the European Communities[1]) may be considered by any court when interpreting any provision of that Convention and shall be given such weight as is appropriate in the circumstances.

4. Short title and commencement

(1) This Act may be cited as the Contractual Obligations (Applicable Law) Act, 1991

(2) (a) This Act, other than section 2 in so far as it relates to the 1984 Accession Convention, shall come into operation on such day or days as the Minister shall fix by order or orders either generally or with reference to any particular purpose or provision and different days may be so fixed for different purposes and for different provisions.

(b) Section 2 of this Act shall in so far as it relates to the 1984 Accession Convention, come into operation on such day or days as the Minister shall fix by order or orders either generally or with reference to any particular purpose or provision and different days may be so fixed for different purposes and different provisions and any day so fixed may be the same day as a day fixed under paragraph (a) of this subsection or a different day.

First Schedule

The text in the English language of the 1980 Convention

CONVENTION ON THE LAW APPLICABLE TO CONTRACTUAL OBLIGATIONS

Preamble

The High Contracting Parties to the Treaty establishing the European Economic Community,

Anxious to continue in the field of private international law the work of unification of law which has already been done within the Community, in particular in the field of jurisdiction and enforcement of judgments,

Wishing to establish uniform rules concerning the law applicable to contractual obligations,

Have agreed as follows:

Title I

Scope of the Convention

Article 1

Scope of the Convention

1. The rules of this Convention shall apply to contractual obligations in any situation involving a choice between the laws of different countries.

2. They shall not apply to:

(a) questions involving the status or legal capacity of natural persons, without prejudice to Article 11;

(b) contractual obligations relating to:

– wills and succession,

– rights in property arising out of a matrimonial relationship,

– rights and duties arising out of a family relationship, parentage, marriage or affinity, including maintenance obligations in respect of children who are not legitimate;

(c) obligations arising under bills of exchange, cheques and promissory notes and other negotiable instruments to the extent that the

obligations under such other negotiable instruments arise out of their negotiable character;

(*d*) arbitration agreements and agreements on the choice of court;

(*e*) questions governed by the law of companies and other bodies corporate or unincorporate such as the creation, by registration or otherwise, legal capacity, internal organisation or winding-up of companies and other bodies corporate or unincorporate and the personal liability of officers and members as such for the obligations of the company or body;

(*f*) the question whether an agent is able to bind a principal, or an organ to bind a company or body corporate or unincorporate, to a third party;

(*g*) the constitution of trusts and the relationship between settlors, trustees and beneficiaries;

(*h*) evidence and procedure, without prejudice to Article 14.

3. The rules of this Convention do not apply to contracts of insurance which cover risks situated in the territories of the Member States of the European Economic Community. In order to determine whether a risk is situated in these territories the court shall apply its internal law.

4. The preceding paragraph does not apply to contracts of re-insurance.

Article 2

Application of law of non-contracting States

Any law specified by this Convention shall be applied whether or not it is the law of a Contracting State.

Title II

Uniform Rules

Article 3

Freedom of choice

1. A contract shall be governed by the law chosen by the parties. The choice must be expressed or demonstrated with reasonable certainty by the terms of the contract or the circumstances of the case. By their choice the parties can select the law applicable to the whole or a part only of the contract.

2. The parties may at any time agree to subject the contract to a law other than that which previously governed it, whether as a result of an earlier choice under this Article or of other provisions of this Convention. Any variation by the parties of the law to be applied made after the conclusion of the contract shall not prejudice its formal validity under Article 9 or adversely affect the rights of third parties.

3. The fact that the parties have chosen a foreign law, whether or not accompanied by the choice of a foreign tribunal, shall not, where all the other elements relevant to the situation at the time of the choice are connected with one country only, prejudice the application of rules of the law of that country which cannot be derogated from by contract, hereinafter called 'mandatory rules'.

4. The existence and validity of the consent of the parties as to the choice of the applicable law shall be determined in accordance with the provisions of Articles 8, 9 and 11.

Article 4

Applicable law in the absence of choice

1. To the extent that the law applicable to the contract has not been chosen in accordance with Article 3, the contract shall be governed by the law of the country with which it is most closely connected. Nevertheless, a severable part of the contract which has a closer connection with another country may by way of exception be governed by the law of that other country.

2. Subject to the provisions of paragraph 5 of this Article, it shall be presumed that the contract is most closely connected with the country where the party who is to effect the performance which is characteristic of the contract has, at the time of conclusion of the contract, his habitual residence, or, in the case of a body corporate or unincorporate, its central administration. However, if the contract is entered into in the course of that party's trade or profession, that country shall be the country in which the principal place of business is situated or, where under the terms of the contract the performance is to be effected through a place of business other than the principal place of business, the country in which that other place of business is situated.

3. Notwithstanding the provisions of paragraph 2 of this Article, to the extent that the subject matter of the contract is a right in immovable property or a right to use immovable property it shall be presumed that the contract is most closely connected with the country where the immovable property is situated.

4. A contract for the carriage of goods shall not be subject to the presumption in paragraph 2. In such a contract if the country in which, at the time the contract is concluded, the carrier has his principal place of business is also the country in which the place of loading or the place of discharge or the principal place of business of the consignor is situated, it shall be presumed that the contract is most closely connected with that country. In applying this paragraph single voyage charterparties and other contracts the main purpose of which is the carriage of goods shall be treated as contracts for the carriage of goods.

5. Paragraph 2 shall not apply if the characteristic performance cannot be determined, and the presumptions in paragraphs 2, 3 and 4 shall be disregarded if it appears from the circumstances as a whole that the contract is more closely connected with another country.

Article 5

Certain consumer contracts

1. This Article applies to a contract the object of which is the supply of goods or services to a person ('the consumer') for a purpose which can be regarded as being outside his trade or profession, or a contract for the provision of credit for that object.

2. Notwithstanding the provisions of Article 3, a choice of law made by the parties shall not have the result of depriving the consumer of the protection afforded to him by the mandatory rules of the law of the country in which he has his habitual residence:

- if in that country the conclusion of the contract was preceded by a specific invitation addressed to him or by advertising, and he had taken in that country all the steps necessary on his part for the conclusion of the contract, or

- if the other party or his agent received the consumer's order in that country, or

- if the contract is for the sale of goods and the consumer travelled from that country to another country and there gave his order, provided that the consumer's journey was arranged by the seller for the purpose of inducing the consumer to buy.

3. Notwithstanding the provisions of Article 4, a contract to which this Article applies shall, in the absence of choice in accordance with Article 3, be governed by the law of the country in which the consumer has his habitual residence if it is entered into in the circumstances described in paragraph 2 of this Article.

4. This Article shall not apply to:

(*a*) a contract of carriage;

(*b*) a contract for the supply of services where the services are to be supplied to the consumer exclusively in a country other than that in which he has his habitual residence.

5. Notwithstanding the provisions of paragraph 4, this Article shall apply to a contract which, for an inclusive price, provides for a combination of travel and accommodation.

Article 6

Individual employment contracts

1. Notwithstanding the provisions of Article 3, in a contract of employment a choice of law made by the parties shall not have the result of depriving the employee of the protection afforded to him by the mandatory rules of the law which would be applicable under paragraph 2 in the absence of choice.

2. Notwithstanding the provisions of Article 4, a contract of employment shall, in the absence of choice in accordance with Article 3, be governed:

(*a*) by the law of the country in which the employee habitually carries out his work in performance of the contract, even if he is temporarily employed in another country; or

(*b*) if the employee does not habitually carry out his work in any one country, by the law of the country in which the place of business through which he was engaged is situated;

unless it appears from the circumstances as a whole that the contract is more closely connected with another country, in which case the contract shall be governed by the law of that country.

Article 7

Mandatory rules

1. When applying under this Convention the law of a country, effect may be given to the mandatory rules of the law of another country with which the situation has a close connection, if and in so far as, under the law of the latter country, those rules must be applied whatever the law applicable to the contract. In considering whether to give effect to these mandatory rules, regard shall be had to their nature and purpose and to the consequences of their application or non-application.

2. Nothing in this Convention shall restrict the application of the rules of

the law of the forum in a situation where they are mandatory irrespective of the law otherwise applicable to the contract.

Article 8

Material validity

1. The existence and validity of a contract, or of any term of a contract, shall be determined by the law which would govern it under this Convention if the contract or term were valid.

2. Nevertheless a party may rely upon the law of the country in which he has his habitual residence to establish that he did not consent if it appears from the circumstances that it would not be reasonable to determine the effect of his conduct in accordance with the law specified in the preceding paragraph.

Article 9

Formal validity

1. A contract concluded between persons who are in the same country is formally valid if it satisfies the formal requirements of the law which governs it under this Convention or of the law of the country where it is concluded.

2. A contract concluded between persons who are in different countries is formally valid if it satisfies the formal requirements of the law of one of those countries.

3. Where a contract is concluded by an agent, the country in which the agent acts is the relevant country for the purposes of paragraphs 1 and 2.

4. An act intended to have legal effect relating to an existing or contemplated contract is formally valid if it satisfies the formal requirements of the law which under this Convention governs or would govern the contract or of the law of the country where the act was done.

5. The provisions of the preceding paragraphs shall not apply to a contract to which Article 5 applies, concluded in the circumstances described in paragraph 2 of Article 5. The formal validity of such a contract is governed by the law of the country in which the consumer has his habitual residence.

6. Notwithstanding paragraphs 1 to 4 of this Article, a contract the subject matter of which is a right in immovable property or a right to use immovable property shall be subject to the mandatory requirements of form of the law of the country where the property is situated if by that

law those requirements are imposed irrespective of the country where the contract is concluded and irrespective of the law governing the contract.

Article 10

Scope of the applicable law

1. The laws applicable to a contract by virtue of Articles 3 to 6 and 12 of this Convention shall govern in particular:

(a) interpretation;

(b) performance;

(c) within the limits of the powers conferred on the court by its procedural law, the consequences of breach, including the assessment of damages in so far as it is governed by rules of law;

(d) the various ways of extinguishing obligations, and prescription and limitation of actions;

(e) the consequences of nullity of the contract.

2. In relation to the manner of performance and the steps to be taken in the event of defective performance regard shall be had to the law of the country in which performance takes place.

Article 11

Incapacity

In a contract concluded between persons who are in the same country, a natural person who would have capacity under the law of that country may invoke his incapacity resulting from another law only if the other party to the contract was aware of this incapacity at the time of the conclusion of the contract or was not aware thereof as a result of negligence.

Article 12

Voluntary assignment

1. The mutual obligations of assignor and assignee under a voluntary assignment of a right against another person ('the debtor') shall be governed by the law which under this Convention applies to the contract between the assignor and assignee.

2. The law governing the right to which the assignment relates shall

determine its assignability, the relationship between the assignee and the debtor, the conditions under which the assignment can be invoked against the debtor and any question whether the debtor's obligations have been discharged.

Article 13

Subrogation

1. Where a person ('the creditor') has a contractual claim upon another ('the debtor'), and a third person has a duty to satisfy the creditor, or has in fact satisfied the creditor in discharge of that duty, the law which governs the third person's duty to satisfy the creditor shall determine whether the third person is entitled to exercise against the debtor the rights which the creditor had against the debtor under the law governing their relationship and, if so, whether he may do so in full or only to a limited extent.

2. The same rule applies where several persons are subject to the same contractual claim and one of them has satisfied the creditor.

Article 14

Burden of proof, etc.

1. The law governing the contract under this Convention applies to the extent that it contains, in the law of contract, rules which raise presumptions of law or determine the burden of proof.

2. A contract or an act intended to have legal effect may be proved by any mode of proof recognised by the law of the forum or by any of the laws referred to in Article 9 under which that contract or act is formally valid, provided that such mode of proof can be administered by the forum.

Article 15

Exclusion of renvoi

The application of the law of any country specified by this Convention means the application of the rules of law in force in that country other than its rules of private international law.

Article 16

'Ordre public'

The application of a rule of the law of any country specified by this Convention may be refused only if such application is manifestly incompatible with the public policy ('ordre public') of the forum.

Article 17

No retrospective effect

This Convention shall apply in a Contracting State to contracts made after the date on which this Convention has entered into force with respect to that State.

Article 18

Uniform interpretation

In the interpretation and application of the preceding uniform rules, regard shall be had to their international character and to the desirability of achieving uniformity in their interpretation and application.

Article 19

States with more than one legal system

1. Where a State comprises several territorial units each of which has its own rules of law in respect of contractual obligations, each territorial unit shall be considered as a country for the purposes of identifying the law applicable under this Convention.

2. A State within which different territorial units have their own rules of law in respect of contractual obligations shall not be bound to apply this Convention to conflicts solely between the laws of such units.

Article 20

Precedence of Community law

This Convention shall not affect the application of provisions which, in relation to particular matters, lay down choice of law rules relating to contractual obligations and which are or will be contained in acts of the institutions of the European Communities or in national laws harmonised in implementation of such acts.

Article 21

Relationship with other conventions

This Convention shall not prejudice the application of international conventions to which a Contracting State is, or becomes, a party.

Article 22

Reservations

1. Any Contracting State may, at the time of signature, ratification, acceptance or approval, reserve the right not to apply:

(a) the provisions of Article 7(1);

(b) the provisions of Article 10(1)(e).

2. Any Contracting State may also, when notifying an extension of the Convention in accordance with Article 27(2), make one or more of these reservations, with its effect limited to all or some of the territories mentioned in the extension.

3. Any Contracting State may at any time withdraw a reservation which it has made; the reservation shall cease to have effect on the first day of the third calendar month after notification of the withdrawal.

Title III

Final provisions

Article 23

1. If, after the date on which this Convention has entered into force for a Contracting State, that State wishes to adopt any new choice of law rule in regard to any particular category of contract within the scope of this Convention, it shall communicate its intention to the other signatory States through the Secretary-General of the Council of the European Communities.

2. Any signatory State may, within six months from the date of the communication made to the Secretary-General, request him to arrange consultations between signatory States in order to reach agreement.

3. If no signatory State has requested consultations within this period or if within two years following the communication made to the Secretary-General no agreement is reached in the course of consultations, the Contracting State concerned may amend its law in the manner indicated. The measures taken by that State shall be brought to the knowledge of

the other signatory States through the Secretary-General of the Council of the European Communities.

Article 24

1. If, after the date on which this Convention has entered into force with respect to a Contracting State, that State wishes to become a party to a multilateral convention whose principal aim or one of whose principal aims is to lay down rules of private international law concerning any of the matters governed by this Convention, the procedure set out in Article 23 shall apply. However, the period of two years, referred to in paragraph 3 of that Article, shall be reduced to one year.

2. The procedure referred to in the preceding paragraph need not be followed if a Contracting State or one of the European Communities is already a party to the multilateral convention, or if its object is to revise a convention to which the State concerned is already a party, or if it is a convention concluded within the framework of the Treaties establishing the European Communities.

Article 25

If a Contracting State considers that the unification achieved by this Convention is prejudiced by the conclusion of agreements not covered by Article 24(1), that State may request the Secretary-General of the Council of the European Communities to arrange consultations between the signatory States of this Convention.

Article 26

Any Contracting State may request the revision of this Convention. In this event a revision conference shall be convened by the President of the Council of the European Communities.

Article 27

1. This Convention shall apply to the European territories of the Contracting States, including Greenland, and to the entire territory of the French Republic.

2. Notwithstanding paragraph 1:

(a) this Convention shall not apply to the Faroe Islands, unless the Kingdom of Denmark makes a declaration to the contrary;

(b) this Convention shall not apply to any European territory situated outside the United Kingdom for the international relations of which the United Kingdom is responsible, unless the United Kingdom makes a declaration to the contrary in respect of any such territory;

(c) this Convention shall apply to the Netherlands Antilles, if the Kingdom of the Netherlands makes a declaration to that effect.

3. Such declarations may be made at any time by notifying the Secretary-General of the Council of the European Communities.

4. Proceedings brought in the United Kingdom on appeal from courts in one of the territories referred to in paragraph 2(b) shall be deemed to be proceedings taking place in those courts.

Article 28

1. This Convention shall be open from 19 June 1980 for signature by the States party to the Treaty establishing the European Economic Community.

2. This Convention shall be subject to ratification, acceptance or approval by the signatory States. The instruments of ratification, acceptance or approval shall be deposited with the Secretary-General of the Council of the European Communities.

Article 29

1. This Convention shall enter into force on the first day of the third month following the deposit of the seventh instrument of ratification, acceptance or approval.

2. This Convention shall enter into force for each signatory State ratifying, accepting or approving at a later date on the first day of the third month following the deposit of its instrument of ratification, acceptance or approval.

Article 30

1. This Convention shall remain in force for 10 years from the date of its entry into force in accordance with Article 29(1), even for States for which it enters into force at a later date.

2. If there has been no denunciation it shall be renewed tacitly every five years.

3. A Contracting State which wishes to denounce shall, not less than six months before the expiration of the period of 10 or five years, as the case may be, give notice to the Secretary-General of the Council of the European Communities. Denunciation may be limited to any territory to which the Convention has been extended by a declaration under Article 27(2).

4. The denunciation shall have effect only in relation to the State which

has notified it. The Convention will remain in force as between all other Contracting States.

Article 31

The Secretary-General of the Council of the European Communities shall notify the States party to the Treaty establishing the European Economic Community of:

(a) the signatures;

(b) the deposit of each instrument of ratification, acceptance or approval;

(c) the date of entry into force of this Convention;

(d) communications made in pursuance of Articles 23, 24, 25, 26, 27 and 30;

(e) the reservations and withdrawals of reservations referred to in Article 22.

Article 32

The Protocol annexed to this Convention shall form an integral part thereof.

Article 33

This Convention, drawn up in a single original in the Danish, Dutch, English, French, German, Irish and Italian languages, these texts being equally authentic, shall be deposited in the archives of the Secretariat of the Council of the European Communities. The Secretary-General shall transmit a certified copy thereof to the Government of each signatory State.

Protocol

The High Contracting Parties have agreed upon the following provision which shall be annexed to the Convention:

Notwithstanding the provisions of the Convention, Denmark may retain the rules contained in Søloven (Statute on Maritime Law) paragraph 169 concerning the applicable law in matters relating to carriage of goods by sea and may revise these rules without following the procedure prescribed in Article 23 of the Convention.

Second Schedule

The text in the English language of the 1984 Accession Convention

Convention

on the accession of the Hellenic Republic to the Convention on the law applicable to contractual obligations, opened for signature in Rome on 19 June 1980.

The High Contracting Parties to the Treaty establishing the European Economic Community,

Considering that the Hellenic Republic, in becoming a Member of the Community, undertook to accede to the Convention on the law applicable to contractual obligations, opened for signature in Rome on 19 June 1980,

Have decided to conclude this Convention, and to this end have designated as their plenipotentiaries:

(*Designations of Plenipotentiaries*)

Who, meeting within the Council, having exchanged their full powers, found in good and due form,

Have agreed as follows:

Article 1

The Hellenic Republic hereby accedes to the Convention on the law applicable to contractual obligations, opened for signature in Rome on 19 June 1980.

Article 2

The Secretary-General of the Council of the European Communities shall transmit a certified copy of the Convention on the law applicable to contractual obligations in the Danish, Dutch, English, French, German, Irish and Italian languages to the Government of the Hellenic Republic.

The text of the Convention on the law applicable to contractual obligations in the Greek language is annexed hereto. The text in the Greek language shall be authentic under the same conditions as the other texts of the Convention on the law applicable to contractual obligations.

Article 3

This Convention shall be ratified by the Signatory States. The instruments of ratification shall be deposited with the Secretary-General of the Council of the European Communities.

Article 4

This Convention shall enter into force, as between the States which have ratified it, on the first day of the third month following the deposit of the last instrument of ratification by the Hellenic Republic and seven States which have ratified the Convention on the law applicable to contractual obligations.

This Convention shall enter into force for each Contracting State which subsequently ratifies it on the first day of the third month following the deposit of its instrument of ratification.

Article 5

The Secretary-General of the Council of the European Communities shall notify the Signatory States of:

(a) the deposit of each instrument of ratification;

(b) the dates of entry into force of this Convention for the Contracting States.

Article 6

This Convention, drawn up in a single original in the Danish, Dutch, English, French, German, Greek, Irish and Italian languages, all eight texts being equally authentic, shall be deposited in the archives of the General Secretariat of the Council of the European Communities. The Secretary-General shall transmit a certified copy to the Government of each Signatory State.

Third Schedule

The text in the Irish language of the 1980 Convention.

Fourth Schedule

**The text in the Irish language of the
1984 Accession Convention.**

FOOTNOTE

1. OJ No C 282, 31.10.80, p.1.

CONSUMER POLICY

COUNCIL DIRECTIVE

of 25 July 1985

on the approximation of the laws, regulations and administrative provisions of the Member States concerning liability for defective products

(85/374/EEC)

(OJ No L 210, 7.8.85, p.29)

The Council of the European Communities,

Having regard to the Treaty establishing the European Economic Community, and in particular Article 100 thereof,

Having regard to the proposal from the Commission[1],

Having regard to the opinion of the European Parliament[2],

Having regard to the opinion of the Economic and Social Committee[3],

Whereas approximation of the laws of the Member States concerning the liability of the producer for damage caused by the defectiveness of his products is necessary because the existing divergences may distort competition and affect the movement of goods within the common market and entail a differing degree of protection of the consumer against damage caused by a defective product to his health or property;

Whereas liability without fault on the part of the producer is the sole means of adequately solving the problem, peculiar to our age of increasing technicality, of a fair apportionment of the risks inherent in modern technological production;

Whereas liability without fault should apply only to movables which have been industrially produced; whereas, as a result, it is appropriate to exclude liability for agricultural products and game, except where they have undergone a processing of an industrial nature which could cause a defect in these products; whereas the liability provided for in this Directive should also apply to movables which are used in the construction of immovables or are installed in immovables;

Whereas protection of the consumer requires that all producers involved in the production process should be made liable, in so far as their finished product, component part or any raw material supplied by them was defective; whereas, for the same reason, liability should extend to importers of products into the Community and to persons who present themselves as producers by affixing their name, trade mark or other distinguishing feature or who supply a product the producer of which cannot be identified;

Whereas, in situations where several persons are liable for the same damage, the protection of the consumer requires that the injured person should be able to claim full compensation for the damage from any one of them;

Whereas, to protect the physical well-being and property of the consumer, the defectiveness of the product should be determined by reference not to its fitness for use but to the lack of the safety which the public at large is entitled to expect; whereas the safety is assessed by excluding any misuse of the product not reasonable under the circumstances;

Whereas a fair apportionment of risk between the injured person and the producer implies that the producer should be able to free himself from liability if he furnishes proof as to the existence of certain exonerating circumstances;

Whereas the protection of the consumer requires that the liability of the producer remains unaffected by acts or omissions of other persons having contributed to cause the damage; whereas, however, the contributory negligence of the injured person may be taken into account to reduce or disallow such liability;

Whereas the protection of the consumer requires compensation for death and personal injury as well as compensation for damage to property; whereas the latter should nevertheless be limited to goods for private use or consumption and be subject to a deduction of a lower threshold of a fixed amount in order to avoid litigation in an excessive number of cases; whereas this Directive should not prejudice compensation for pain and suffering and other non-material damages payable, where appropriate, under the law applicable to the case;

Whereas a uniform period of limitation for the bringing of action for compensation is in the interests both of the injured person and of the producer;

Whereas products age in the course of time, higher safety standards are developed and the state of science and technology progresses; whereas, therefore, it would not be reasonable to make the producer liable for an unlimited period for the defectiveness of his product; whereas, therefore, liability should expire after a reasonable length of time, without prejudice to claims pending at law;

Whereas, to achieve effective protection of consumers, no contractual derogation should be permitted as regards the liability of the producer in relation to the injured person;

Whereas under the legal systems of the Member States an injured party may have a claim for damages based on grounds of contractual liability or on grounds of non-contractual liability other than that provided for in this Directive; in so far as these provisions also serve to attain the objective of effective protection of consumers, they should remain unaffected by this Directive; whereas, in so far as effective protection of consumers in the sector of pharmaceutical products is already also attained in a Member State under a special liability system, claims based on this system should similarly remain possible;

Whereas, to the extent that liability for nuclear injury or damage is already covered in all Member States by adequate special rules, it has been possible to exclude damage of this type from the scope of this Directive;

Whereas, since the exclusion of primary agricultural products and game from the scope of this Directive may be felt, in certain Member States, in view of what is expected for the protection of consumers, to restrict unduly such protection, it should be possible for a Member State to extend liability to such products;

Whereas, for similar reasons, the possibility offered to a producer to free himself from liability if he proves that the state of scientific and technical knowledge at the time when he put the product into circulation was not such as to enable the existence of a defect to be discovered may be felt in certain Member States to restrict unduly the protection of the consumer; whereas it should therefore be possible for a Member State to maintain in its legislation or to provide by new legislation that this exonerating circumstance is not admitted; whereas, in the case of new legislation, making use of this derogation should, however, be subject to a Community stand-still procedure, in order to raise, if possible, the level of protection in a uniform manner throughout the Community;

Whereas, taking into account the legal traditions in most of the Member States, it is inappropriate to set any financial ceiling on the producer's liability without fault; whereas, in so far as there are, however, differing traditions, it seems possible to admit that a Member State may derogate from the principle of unlimited liability by providing a limit for the total liability of the producer for damage resulting from a death or personal injury and caused by identical items with the same defect, provided that this limit is established at a level sufficiently high to guarantee adequate protection of the consumer and the correct functioning of the common market;

Whereas the harmonisation resulting from this cannot be total at the present stage, but opens the way towards greater harmonisation; whereas it is therefore necessary that the Council receive at regular intervals, reports from the Commission on the application of this Directive, accompanied, as the case may be, by appropriate proposals;

Whereas it is particularly important in this respect that a re-examination be carried out of those parts of the Directive relating to the derogations open to the Member States, at the expiry of a period of sufficient length to gather practical experience on the effects of these derogations on the protection of consumers and on the functioning of the common market,

Has adopted this Directive:

Article 1

The producer shall be liable for damage caused by a defect in his product.

Article 2

For the purpose of this Directive 'product' means all movables, with the exception of primary agricultural products and game, even though incorporated into another movable or into an immovable. 'Primary agricultural products' means the products of the soil, of stock-farming and of fisheries, excluding products which have undergone initial processing. 'Product' includes electricity.

Article 3

1. 'Producer' means the manufacturer of a finished product, the

producer of any raw material or the manufacturer of a component part and any person who, by putting his name, trade mark or other distinguishing feature on the product presents himself as its producer.

2. Without prejudice to the liability of the producer, any person who imports into the Community a product for sale, hire, leasing or any form of distribution in the course of his business shall be deemed to be a producer within the meaning of this Directive and shall be responsible as a producer.

3. Where the producer of the product cannot be identified, each supplier of the product shall be treated as its producer unless he informs the injured person, within a reasonable time, of the identity of the producer or of the person who supplied him with the product. The same shall apply, in the case of an imported product, if this product does not indicate the identity of the importer referred to in paragraph 2, even if the name of the producer is indicated.

Article 4

The injured person shall be required to prove the damage, the defect and the causal relationship between defect and damage.

Article 5

Where, as a result of the provisions of this Directive, two or more persons are liable for the same damage, they shall be liable jointly and severally, without prejudice to the provisions of national law concerning the rights of contribution or recourse.

Article 6

1. A product is defective when it does not provide the safety which a person is entitled to expect, taking all circumstances into account, including:

(a) the presentation of the product;

(b) the use to which it could reasonably be expected that the product would be put;

(c) the time when the product was put into circulation.

2. A product shall not be considered defective for the sole reason that a better product is subsequently put into circulation.

Article 7

The producer shall not be liable as a result of this Directive if he proves:

(*a*) that he did not put the product into circulation; or

(*b*) that, having regard to the circumstances, it is probable that the defect which caused the damage did not exist at the time when the product was put into circulation by him or that this defect came into being afterwards; or

(*c*) that the product was neither manufactured by him for sale or any form of distribution for economic purpose nor manufactured or distributed by him in the course of his business; or

(*d*) that the defect is due to compliance of the product with mandatory regulations issued by the public authorities; or

(*e*) that the state of scientific and technical knowledge at the time when he put the product into circulation was not such as to enable the existence of the defect to be discovered; or

(*f*) in the case of a manufacturer of a component, that the defect is attributable to the design of the product in which the component has been fitted or to the instructions given by the manufacturer of the product.

Article 8

1. Without prejudice to the provisions of national law concerning the right of contribution or recourse, the liability of the producer shall not be reduced when the damage is caused both by a defect in product and by the act or omission of a third party.

2. The liability of the producer may be reduced or disallowed when, having regard to all the circumstances, the damage is caused both by a defect in the product and by the fault of the injured person or any person for whom the injured person is responsible.

Article 9

For the purpose of Article 1, 'damage' means:

(*a*) damage caused by death or by personal injuries;

(*b*) damage to, or destruction of, any item of property other than the defective product itself, with a lower threshold of 500 ECU, provided that the item of property:

   (i) is of a type ordinarily intended for private use or consumption, and

   (ii) was used by the injured person mainly for his own private use or consumption.

This Article shall be without prejudice to national provisions relating to non-material damage.

Article 10

1. Member States shall provide in their legislation that a limitation period of three years shall apply to proceedings for the recovery of damages as provided for in this Directive. The limitation period shall begin to run from the day on which the plaintiff became aware, or should reasonably have become aware, of the damage, the defect and the identity of the producer.

2. The laws of Member States regulating suspension or interruption of the limitation period shall not be affected by this Directive.

Article 11

Member States shall provide in their legislation that the rights conferred upon the injured person pursuant to this Directive shall be extinguished upon the expiry of a period of 10 years from the date on which the producer put into circulation the actual product which caused the damage, unless the injured person has in the meantime instituted proceedings against the producer.

Article 12

The liability of the producer arising from this Directive may not, in relation to the injured person, be limited or excluded by a provision limiting his liability or exempting him from liability.

Article 13

This Directive shall not affect any rights which an injured person may have according to the rules of the law of contractual or non-contractual liability or a special liability system existing at the moment when this Directive is notified.

Article 14

This Directive shall not apply to injury or damage arising from nuclear accidents and covered by international conventions ratified by the Member States.

Article 15

1. Each Member State may:

(a) by way of derogation from Article 2, provide in its legislation that within the meaning of Article 1 of this Directive 'product' also means primary agricultural products and game;

(b) by way of derogation from Article 7(e), maintain or, subject to the procedure set out in paragraph 2 of this Article, provide in this legislation that the producer shall be liable even if he proves that the state of scientific and technical knowledge at the time when he put the product into circulation was not such as to enable the existence of a defect to be discovered.

2. A Member State wishing to introduce the measure specified in paragraph 1(b) shall communicate the text of the proposed measure to the Commission. The Commission shall inform the other Member States thereof.

The Member State concerned shall hold the proposed measure in abeyance for nine months after the Commission is informed and provided that in the meantime the Commission has not submitted to the Council a proposal amending this Directive on the relevant matter. However, if within three months of receiving the said information, the Commission does not advise the Member State concerned that it intends submitting such a proposal to the Council, the Member State may take the proposed measure immediately.

If the Commission does submit to the Council such a proposal amending this Directive within the aforementioned nine months, the Member State concerned shall hold the proposed measure in abeyance for a further period of 18 months from the date on which the proposal is submitted.

3. Ten years after the date of notification of this Directive, the Commission shall submit to the Council a report on the effect that rulings by the courts as to the application of Article 7(e) and of paragraph 1(b) of this Article have on consumer protection and the functioning of the common market. In the light of this report the Council, acting on a proposal from the Commission and pursuant to the terms of Article 100 of the Treaty, shall decide whether to repeal Article 7(e).

Article 16

1. Any Member State may provide that a producer's total liability for damage resulting from a death or personal injury and caused by identical items with the same defect shall be limited to an amount which may not be less than 70 million ECU.

2. Ten years after the date of notification of this Directive, the Commission shall submit to the Council a report on the effect on consumer protection and the functioning of the common market of the implementation of the financial limit on liability by those Member States which have used the option provided for in paragraph 1. In the light of this report the Council, acting on a proposal from the Commission and

pursuant to the terms of Article 100 of the Treaty, shall decide whether to repeal paragraph 1.

Article 17

This Directive shall not apply to products put into circulation before the date on which the provisions referred to in Article 19 enter into force.

Article 18

1. For the purposes of this Directive, the ECU shall be that defined by Regulation (EEC) No 3180/78[4], as amended by Regulation (EEC) No 2626/84[5]. The equivalent in national currency shall initially be calculated at the rate obtaining on the date of adoption of this Directive.

2. Every five years the Council, acting on a proposal from the Commission, shall examine and, if need be, revise the amounts in this Directive, in the light of economic and monetary trends in the Community.

Article 19

1. Member States shall bring into force, not later than three years from the date of notification of this Directive, the laws, regulations and administrative provisions necessary to comply with this Directive. They shall forthwith inform the Commission thereof[6].

2. The procedure set out in Article 15(2) shall apply from the date of notification of this Directive.

Article 20

Member States shall communicate to the Commission the texts of the main provisions of national law which they subsequently adopt in the field governed by this Directive.

Article 21

Every five years the Commission shall present a report to the Council on the application of this Directive and, if necessary, shall submit appropriate proposals to it.

Article 22

This Directive is addressed to the Member States.

Done at Brussels, 25 July 1985.

For the Council

The President

J. Poos

FOOTNOTES

1. OJ No C 241, 14.10.76, p.9 and OJ No C 271, 26.10.79, p.3.
2. OJ No C 127, 21.5.79, p.61.
3. OJ No C 114, 7.5.79, p.15.
4. OJ No L 379, 30.12.78, p.1.
5. OJ No L 247, 16.9.84, p.1.
6. This Directive was notified to the Member States on 30 July 1985.

 Implemented in Ireland: Liability for Defective Products Act, 1991; S.I. 316S/1991.

OTHER

Joint Declaration by the European Parliament, the Council, the Representatives of the Member States, meeting within the Council, and the Commission against racism and xenophobia

of 11 June 1986

DECLARATION AGAINST RACISM AND XENOPHOBIA

(OJ No C 158, 25.6.86, p.1)

The European Parliament, the Council, the Representatives of the Member States, meeting within the Council, and the Commission,

Recognising the existence and growth of xenophobic attitudes, movements and acts of violence in the Community which are often directed against immigrants;

Whereas the Community institutions attach prime importance to respect for fundamental rights, as solemnly proclaimed in the Joint Declaration of 5 April 1977, and to the principle of freedom of movement as laid down in the Treaty of Rome;

Whereas respect for human dignity and the elimination of forms of racial discrimination are part of the common cultural and legal heritage of all the Member States;

Mindful of the positive contribution which workers who have their origins in other Member States or in third countries have made, and can continue to make, to the development of the Member State in which they legally reside and of the resulting benefits for the Community as a whole,

1. vigorously condemn all forms of intolerance, hostility and use of force against persons or groups of persons on the grounds of racial, religious, cultural, social or national differences;

2. affirm their resolve to protect the individuality and dignity of every member of society and to reject any form of segregation of foreigners;

3. look upon it as indispensable that all necessary steps be taken to guarantee that this joint resolve is carried through;

4. are determined to pursue the endeavours already made to protect the individuality and dignity of every member of society and to reject any form of segregation of foreigners;

5. stress the importance of adequate and objective information and of making all citizens aware of the dangers of racism and xenophobia, and the need to ensure that all acts or forms of discrimination are prevented or curbed.

Done at Strasbourg, 11 June 1986.

[List omitted]

COUNCIL DECISION

of 24 June 1988

on the system of the Communities' own resources

(88/376/EEC, Euratom)

(OJ No L 185, 15.7.88, p.24)

The Council of the European Communities,

Having regard to the Treaty establishing the European Economic Community, and in particular Articles 199 and 201 thereof,

Having regard to the Treaty establishing the European Atomic Energy Community, and in particular Articles 171(1) and 173 thereof,

Having regard to the proposal from the Commission[1],

Having regard to the opinion of the European Parliament[2],

Having regard to the opinion of the Economic and Social Committee[3],

Whereas Council Decision 85/257/EEC, Euratom of 7 May 1985 on the Communities' system of own resources[4], as last amended by the Single European Act, raised to 1.4% the limit for each Member State on the rate applied to the uniform value-added tax (VAT) base previously set at 1% by the Council Decision of 21 April 1970 on the replacement of financial contributions from Member States by the Communities' own resources[5] hereinafter referred to as 'the Decision of 21 April 1970';

Whereas the resources available within the limit of 1,4% are no longer sufficient to cover the estimates of Community expenditure;

Whereas the Single European Act opens up new possibilities to the Community; whereas Article 8a of the Treaty establishing the European Economic Community provides for the completion of the internal market by 31 December 1992;

Whereas the Community must possess stable and guaranteed revenue enabling it to stabilise the present situation and operate the common policies; whereas this revenue must be based on the expenditure deemed necessary to this end which was determined in the financial estimates in the Interinstitutional Agreement between the European Parliament, the Council and the Commission, which will take effect on 1 July 1988;

Whereas the European Council meeting in Brussels on 11, 12 and 13 February 1988 reached certain conclusions;

Whereas, in accordance with these conclusions, the Community will, by 1992, be assigned a maximum amount of own resources corresponding to 1.2% of the total of the Member States' gross national product for the year at market prices, hereinafter referred to as 'GNP';

Whereas observance of this ceiling requires that the total amount of own resources at the Community's disposal for the period 1988 to 1992 does not in any one year exceed a specified percentage of the sum of the Community's GNP for the year in question; whereas that percentage shall correspond to application of the guidelines established for growth in Community expenditure as laid down in the European Council conclusions concerning budgetary discipline and budget management, and a safety margin of 0.03% of Community GNP aimed at coping with unforeseen expenditure;

Whereas a global ceiling of 1.30% of the Member States' GNP is set for commitment appropriations; whereas an orderly progression of commitment appropriations and payment appropriations must be ensured;

Whereas these ceilings should remain applicable until this Decision is amended;

Whereas, with a view to matching the resources paid by each Member State more closely with its ability to contribute, the composition of Community own resources should be amended and enlarged; whereas it is necessary for this purpose:

- to fix at 1.4% the maximum rate to be applied to each Member State's uniform base for value added tax, limited where appropriate to 55% of its GNP;

- to introduce an additional type of own resource to balance budget revenue and expenditure, based on the sum of Member States' GNP; for this purpose, the Council will adopt a Directive on the harmonisation of the compilation of gross national product at market prices;

Whereas the customs duties on products coming under the Treaty establishing the European Coal and Steel Community should be included in Community own resources;

Whereas the conclusions of the European Council of 25 and 26 June 1984 on the correction of budgetary imbalances continue to apply for the duration of this Decision's validity; whereas the present compensation mechanism must, however, be adjusted to take account of the capping of the VAT base and the introduction of an additional resource and must provide for financing of the correction on the basis of a GNP key whereas this adjustment should ensure that the VAT share of the United Kingdom is replaced by its share of payments under the third and fourth resources (those provided by VAT and GNP respectively) and that the effect on the United Kingdom, in respect of a given year, of the capping of the VAT base and of the introduction of the fourth resource which is not compensated by this change will be offset by an adjustment to the compensation in respect of that year; whereas the contributions of Spain and Portugal should be reduced in accordance with the rebates provided for in Articles 187 and 374 of the 1985 Act of Accession;

Whereas the budgetary imbalances should be corrected in such a way as not to affect the own resources available for the Community's policies;

Whereas the conclusions of the European Council of 11, 12 and 13 February 1988 provided for the creation, in the Community budget, of a monetary reserve, hereinafter referred to as the 'EAGGF monetary reserve', to offset the impact of significant and unforeseen fluctuations in the ECU/dollar parity on the expenditure under the Guarantee Section of the European Agricultural Guidance and Guarantee Fund (EAGGF); whereas that reserve should be covered by specific provisions;

Whereas provisions must be laid down to cover the changeover from the system introduced by Decision 85/257/EEC, Euratom to that arising from this Decision;

Whereas the European Council of 11, 12 and 13 February 1988 provided that this Decision should take effect on 1 January 1988,

Has laid down these provisions, which it recommends to the Member States for adoption:

Article 1

The Communities shall be allocated resources of their own in accordance with the following Articles in order to ensure the financing of their budget.

The budget of the Communities shall, irrespective of their revenue, be financed entirely from the Communities' own resources.

Article 2

1. Revenue from the following shall constitute own resources entered in the budget of the Communities:

(a) levies, premiums, additional or compensatory amounts, additional amounts or factors and other duties established or to be established by the institutions of the Communities in respect of trade with non-member countries within the framework of the common agricultural policy, and also contributions and other duties provided for within the framework of the common organisation of the markets in sugar;

(b) Common Customs Tariff duties and other duties established or to be established by the institutions of the Communities in respect of trade with non-member countries and customs duties on products coming under the Treaty establishing the European Coal and Steel Community;

(c) the application of a uniform rate valid for all Member States to the VAT assessment base which is determined in a uniform manner for Member States according to Community rules; however, the assessment base for any Member State to be taken into account for the purposes of this Decision shall not exceed 55% of its GNP;

(d) the application of a rate – to be determined under the budgetary procedure in the light of the total of all other revenue – to the sum of all the Member States' GNP established in accordance with Community rules to be laid down in a Directive adopted under Article 8(2) of this Decision.

2. Revenue deriving from any new charges introduced within the

framework of a common policy, in accordance with the Treaty establishing the European Economic Community or the Treaty establishing the European Atomic Energy Community, provided the procedure laid down in Article 201 of the Treaty establishing the European Economic Community or in Article 173 of the Treaty establishing the European Atomic Energy Community has been followed, shall also constitute own resources entered in the budget of the Communities.

3. Member States shall retain, by way of collection costs, 10% of the amounts paid under 1(a) and (b).

4. The uniform rate referred to in 1(c) shall correspond to the rate resulting from:

(a) the application of 1.4% to the VAT assessment base for the Member States, and

(b) the deduction of the gross amount of the reference compensation referred to in Article 4(2). The gross amounts shall be the compensation amount adjusted for the fact that the United Kingdom is not participating in the financing of its own compensation and the Federal Republic of Germany's share is reduced by one-third. It shall be calculated as if the reference compensation amount were financed by Member States according to their VAT assessment bases established in accordance with Article 2(1)(c). For 1988, the gross amount of the reference compensation shall be reduced by 780 million ECU.

5. The rate fixed under paragraph 1(d) shall apply to the GNP of each Member State.

6. If, at the beginning of the financial year, the budget has not been adopted, the previous uniform VAT rate and rate applicable to Member States' GNP, without prejudice to whatever provisions may be adopted in accordance with Article 8(2) by reason of the entry of an EAGGF monetary reserve in the budget, shall remain applicable until the entry into force of the new rates.

7. By way of derogation from 1(c), if, on 1 January of the financial year in question, the rules for determining the uniform basis for assessing VAT are not yet applied in all the Member States, the financial contribution which a Member State not yet applying this uniform basis is to make to the budget of the Communities in lieu of VAT shall be determined according to the proportion of its gross national product at market prices to the sum total of the gross national product of the Member States at market prices in the first three years of the five-year period preceding the year in question. This derogation shall cease to have effect

as soon as the rules for determining the uniform basis for assessing VAT are applied in all Member States.

8. For the purposes of applying this Decision, GNP shall mean gross national product for the year at market prices.

Article 3

1. The total amount of own resources assigned to the Communities may not exceed 1.20% of the total GNP of the Community for payment appropriations.

The total amount of own resources assigned to the Communities may not, for any of the years during the 1988 to 1992 period, exceed the following percentages of the total GNP of the Community for the year in question:

- 1988: 1.15,

- 1989: 1.17,

- 1990: 1.18,

- 1991: 1.19,

- 1992: 1.20.

2. The commitment appropriations entered in the general budget of the Communities over the period 1988 to 1992 must follow an orderly progression resulting in a total amount which does not exceed 1.30% of the total GNP of the Community in 1992. A precise ratio between commitment appropriations and payment appropriations shall be maintained to guarantee their compatibility and to enable the ceiling mentioned in paragraph 1 to be observed in subsequent years.

3. The overall ceilings referred to in paragraphs 1 and 2, shall continue to apply until such time as this Decision is amended.

Article 4

The United Kingdom shall be granted a correction in respect of budgetary imbalances. This correction shall consist of a basic amount and an adjustment. The adjustment shall correct the basic amount to a reference compensation amount.

1. The basic amount shall be established by:

(a) calculating the difference, in the preceding financial year, between:

- the percentage share of the United Kingdom in the sum total of the payments referred to in Article 2(1)(c) and (d) made during the financial year, including adjustments at the uniform rate in respect of earlier financial years, and

- the percentage share of the United Kingdom in total allocated expenditure;

(c) multiplying the result by 0.66.

2. The reference compensation shall be the correction resulting from application of (a), (b) and (c) below, corrected by the effects arising for the United Kingdom from the changeover to capped VAT and the payments referred to in Article 2(1)(d).

It shall be established by:

(a) calculating the difference, in the preceding financial year, between:

- the percentage total of VAT payments which would have been made during that financial year, including adjustments in respect of earlier financial years, for the amounts financed by the resources referred to in Article 2(1)(c) and (d) if the uniform VAT rate had been applied to non-capped bases, and

- the percentage share of the United Kingdom in total allocated expenditure;

(b) applying the difference thus obtained to total allocated expenditure;

(c) multiplying the result by 0.66;

(d) subtracting the payments by the United Kingdom taken into account in the first indent of 1(a) from those taken into account in the first indent of 2(a);

(e) subtracting the amount calculated at (d) from the amount calculated at (c).

3. The basic amount shall be adjusted in such a way as to correspond to the reference compensation amount.

Article 5

1. The cost of the correction shall be borne by the other Member States in accordance with the following arrangements:

the distribution of the cost shall first be calculated by reference to each Member State's share of the payments referred to in Article 2(1)(d), the United Kingdom being excluded; it shall then be adjusted in such a way as to restrict the share of the Federal Republic of Germany to two-thirds of the share resulting from this calculation.

2. The correction shall be granted to the United Kingdom by a reduction

in its payments resulting from the application of Article 2(1)(c). The costs borne by the other Member States shall be added to their payments resulting from the application for each Member State of Article 2(1)(c) up to a 1.4% VAT rate and Article 2(1)(d).

3. The Commission shall perform the calculations required for the application of Article 4 and this Article.

4. If, at the beginning of the financial year, the budget has not been adopted, the correction granted to the United Kingdom and the costs borne by the other Member States as entered in the last budget finally adopted shall remain applicable.

Article 6

The revenue referred to in Article 2 shall be used without distinction to finance all expenditure entered in the budget of the Communities. However, the revenue needed to cover in full or in part the EAGGF monetary reserve, entered in the budget of the Communities, shall not be called up from the Member States until the reserve is implemented. Provisions for the operation of that reserve shall be adopted as necessary in accordance with Article 8(2).

The preceding subparagraph shall be without prejudice to the treatment of contributions by certain Member States to supplementary programmes provided for in Article 130l of the Treaty establishing the European Economic Community.

Article 7

Any surplus of the Communities' revenue over total actual expenditure during a financial year shall be carried over to the following financial year. However, any surplus generated by a transfer from EAGGF Guarantee chapters to the monetary reserve shall be regarded as constituting own resources.

Article 8

1. The Community own resources referred to in Article 2(1)(a) and (b) shall be collected by the Member States in accordance with the national provisions imposed by law, regulation or administrative action, which shall, where appropriate, be adapted to meet the requirements of Community rules. The Commission shall examine at regular intervals the national provisions communicated to it by the Member States, transmit to the Member States the adjustments it deems necessary in order to ensure that they comply with Community rules and report to the budget

authority. Member States shall make the resources under Article 2(1)(a) to (d) available to the Commission.

2. Without prejudice to the auditing of the accounts and to checks that they are lawful and regular and as laid down in Article 206a of the Treaty establishing the European Economic Community, such auditing and checks being mainly concerned with the reliability and effectiveness of national systems and procedures for determining the base for own resources accruing from VAT and GNP and without prejudice to the inspection arrangements made pursuant to Article 209(c) of that Treaty, the Council shall, acting unanimously on a proposal from the Commission and after consulting the European Parliament, adopt the provisions necessary to apply this Decision and to make possible the inspection of the collection, the making available to the Commission and payment of the revenue referred to in Articles 2 and 5.

Article 9

The mechanism for the graduated refund of own resources accruing from VAT or GNP-based financial contributions introduced for the Kingdom of Spain and the Portuguese Republic up to 1991 by Articles 187 and 374 of the 1985 Act of Accession shall apply to the own resources accruing from VAT and the GNP-based resource referred to in Article 2(1)(c) and (d) of this Decision. It shall also apply to payments by these two Member States in accordance with Article 5(2) of this Decision. In the latter case the rate of refund shall be that applicable for the year in respect of which the correction is granted.

Article 10

The Commission shall submit, by the end of 1991, a report on the operation of the system, including a re-examination of the correction of budgetary imbalances granted to the United Kingdom, established by this Decision.

Article 11

1. Member States shall be notified of this Decision by the Secretary-General of the Council of the European Communities; it shall be published in the *Official Journal of the European Communities*.

Member States shall notify the Secretary-General of the Council of the European Communities without delay of the completion of the procedures for the adoption of this Decision in accordance with their respective constitutional requirements.

This Decision shall enter into force on the first day of the month following receipt of the last of the notifications referred to in the second subparagraph. It shall take effect on 1 January 1988.

2. (a) Subject to (b) and (c), Decision 85/257/EEC, Euratom shall be repealed as of 1 January 1988. Any references to the Decision of 21 April 1970 or to Decision 85/257/EEC, Euratom shall be construed as references to this Decision.

    (b) Article 3 of Decision 85/257/EEC, Euratom shall continue to apply to the calculation and adjustment of revenue accruing from the application of rates to the uncapped uniform assessment basis for value added tax in 1987 and earlier years. For 1988 the deduction in favour of the United Kingdom in respect of previous financial years shall be calculated in accordance with points (b)(i), (ii) and (iii) of Article 3(3) of the said Decision. The distribution of the cost of financing it shall be calculated in accordance with Article 5(1) of this Decision. The amounts corresponding to the deduction and the distribution of the cost of financing it shall be dealt with in accordance with Article 5(2) of this Decision. When Article 2(7) has to be applied, the value added tax payments shall be replaced by financial contributions in the calculations referred to in this paragraph for any Member State concerned; this system shall also apply to the payment of adjustments of corrections for earlier years.

    (c) Article 4(2) of Decision 85/257/EEC, Euratom shall continue to apply to the financial contributions needed to finance the completion of the supplementary programme for the operation of the HFR (high-flux reactor) reactor of 1984 to 1987.

Done at Luxembourg, 24 June 1988.

For the Council

The President

M. Bangemann

FOOTNOTES

1. OJ No C 102, 16.4.88, p.8.
2. OJ No C 187, 18.7.88, p.72.
3. OJ No C 175, 4.7.88.
4. OJ No L 128, 14.5.85, p.15.
5. OJ No L 94, 28.4.70, p.19.

JOINT DECLARATION BY THE EUROPEAN PARLIAMENT, THE COUNCIL AND THE COMMISSION ON FUNDAMENTAL RIGHTS

of 5 April 1977

(OJ No C 103, 27.4.77, p.1)

The European Parliament, the Council and the Commission,

Whereas the Treaties establishing the European Communities are based on the principles of respect for the law;

Whereas, as the Court of Justice has recognised, that law comprises, over and above the rules embodied in the treaties and secondary Community legislation, the general principles of law and in particular the fundamental rights, principles and rights on which the constitutional law of the Member States is based;

Whereas, in particular, all the Member States are Contracting Parties to the European Convention for the Protection of Human Rights and Fundamental Freedoms signed in Rome on 4 November 1950,

Have adopted the following declaration:

1. The European Parliament, the Council and the Commission stress the prime importance they attach to the protection of fundamental rights, as derived in particular from the constitutions of the Member States and the European Convention for the Protection of Human Rights and Fundamental Freedoms.

2. In the exercise of their powers and in pursuance of the aims of the European Communities they respect and will continue to respect these rights.

Done at Luxembourg on the fifth day of April in the year one thousand nine hundred and seventy-seven.

[List omitted]

PART G

COMPARISON OF EC/EEC TREATY ARTICLES

COMPARISON OF EC TREATY AND EEC TREATY ARTICLES

EUROPEAN COMMUNITY (EC)	EUROPEAN ECONOMIC COMMUNITY (EEC)	EUROPEAN COMMUNITY (EC)	EUROPEAN ECONOMIC COMMUNITY (EEC)
Article	Article	Article	Article
1 amended	1	21	21
2 amended	2	22	22
3 amended	3	23	23
3a new	–	24	24
3b new	–	25	25
4 amended	4	26	26
4a new	–	27	27
4b new	–	28	28
5	5	29	29
–	6 deleted	30	30
6 amended	7	31	31
7	8	32	32
7 a	8 a	33	33
7 b	8 b	34	34
7 c	8 c	35	35
8 new	–	36	36
8a new	–	37	37
8b new	–	38	38
8c new	–	39	39
8d new	–	40	40
8e new	–	41	41
9	9	42	42
10	10	43	43
11	11	44	44
12	12	45	45
13	13	46	46
14	14	47	47
15	15	48	48
16	16	49 amended	49
17	17	50	50
18	18	51	51
19	19	52	52
20	20	53	53

EUROPEAN COMMUNITY (EC)	EUROPEAN ECONOMIC COMMUNITY (EEC)	EUROPEAN COMMUNITY (EC)	EUROPEAN ECONOMIC COMMUNITY (EEC)
Article	*Article*	*Article*	*Article*
54 amended	54	82	82
55	55	83	83
56 amended	56	84	84
57 amended	57	85	85
58	58	86	86
59	59	87	87
60	60	88	88
61	61	89	89
62	62	90	90
63	63	91	91
64	64	92 amended	92
65	65	93	93
66	66	94 amended	94
67	67	95	95
68	68	96	96
69	69	97	97
70	70	98	98
71	71	99 amended	99
72	72	100 amended	100
73	73	100a amended	100a
73a new	–	100b	100b
73b new	–	100c new	–
73c new	–	100d new	–
73d new	–	101	101
73e new	–	102	102
73f new	–	102a new	102a deleted
73g new	–	103 new	103 deleted
73h new	–	103a new	–
74	74	104 new	104 deleted
75 amended	75	104a new	–
76	76	104b new	–
77	77	104c new	–
78	78	105 new	105 deleted
79	79	105a new	–
80	80	106 new	106 deleted
81	81	107 new	107 deleted

EUROPEAN COMMUNITY (EC) Article	EUROPEAN ECONOMIC COMMUNITY (EEC) Article	EUROPEAN COMMUNITY (EC) Article	EUROPEAN ECONOMIC COMMUNITY (EEC) Article
108 new	108 deleted	129 new	129 see E.C.T. Article 198d
108a new	–		
109 new	109 deleted		
109a new	–	129a new	–
109b new	–	129b new	–
109c new	–	129c new	–
109d new	–	129d new	–
109e new	–	130 new	130 see E.C.T. Article 198e
109f new	–		
109g new	–	130a amended	130a
109h new	–	130b amended	130b
109i new	–	130c new	–
109j new	–	130d new	130d deleted
109k new	–	130e amended	130e
109l new	–	130f amended	130f
109m new	–	130g	130g
110	110	130h new	130h deleted
–	111 repealed	130i new	130i deleted
112	112	130j new	–
113 amended	113	–	130k deleted
–	114 repealed	130k	130l
115 amended	115	130l	130m
–	116 repealed	130m	130n
117	117	130n	130o
118	118	130o new	–
118a amended	118a	130p new	130p deleted
119	119	–	130q deleted
120	120	130r amended	130r
121	121	130s amended	130s
122	122	130t amended	130t
123 amended	123	130u new	–
124	124	130v new	–
125 new	125 deleted	130w new	–
126 new	126 deleted	130x new	–
127 new	127 deleted	130y new	–
128 new	128 deleted	131	131

EUROPEAN COMMUNITY (EC)	EUROPEAN ECONOMIC COMMUNITY (EEC)	EUROPEAN COMMUNITY (EC)	EUROPEAN ECONOMIC COMMUNITY (EEC)
Article	*Article*	*Article*	*Article*
132	132	154 new	154 repealed by Merger Treaty
133	133		
134	134		
135	135	155	155
136	136	156 new	156 repealed by Merger Treaty
136 a	136 a		
137 amended	137	157 new	157 repealed by Merger Treaty
138 amended	138		
138a new	–		
138b new	–	158 new	158 repealed by Merger Treaty
138c new	–		
138d new	–	159 new	159 repealed by Merger Treaty
138e new	–		
139	139		
140	140	160 new	160 repealed by Merger Treaty
141	141		
142	142		
143	143	161 new	161 repealed by Merger Treaty
144 amended	144		
145	145		
146 new	146 repealed by Merger Treaty	162 new	162 repealed by Merger Treaty
147 new	147 repealed by Merger Treaty	163 new	163 repealed by Merger Treaty
148	148	164	164
–	149 repealed see E.C.T. Article189a-c	165 amended	165
		166	166
		167	167
150	150	168	168
151 new	151 repealed by Merger Treaty	168a amended	168a
		169	169
152	152	170	170
153	153	171 amended	171
		172 amended	172
		173 amended	173

EUROPEAN COMMUNITY (EC)	EUROPEAN ECONOMIC COMMUNITY (EEC)	EUROPEAN COMMUNITY (EC)	EUROPEAN ECONOMIC COMMUNITY (EEC)
Article	*Article*	*Article*	*Article*
174	174	199 amended	199
175 amended	175	–	200 repealed
176 amended	176	201 new	201 deleted
177 amended	177	201a new	–
178	178	202	202
179	179	203	203
180 amended	180	204	204
181	181	205 amended	205
182	182	205a	205a
183	183	206 new	206 deleted see E.C.T. Article188a-c
184 amended	184		
185	185		
186	186	–	206a repealed see E.C.T. Article188a-c
187	187		
188	188		
188a new	–	–	206b repealed see E.C.T. Article188a-c
188b new	–		
188c new	–		
189 amended	189		
189a new	–	207	207
189b new	–	208	208
189c new	–	209 amended	209
190 amended	190	209a new	–
191 amended	191	210	210
192	192	211	211
193	193	–	212 repealed by Merger Treaty
194 amended	194		
195	195		
196 amended	196	213	213
197	197	214	214
198 amended	198	215 amended	215
198a new	–	216	216
198b new	–	217	217
98c new	–	–	218 repealed by Merger Treaty
8d new	–		
new	–	219	219

EUROPEAN COMMUNITY (EC)	EUROPEAN ECONOMIC COMMUNITY (EEC)	EUROPEAN COMMUNITY (EC)	EUROPEAN ECONOMIC COMMUNITY (EEC)
Article	*Article*	*Article*	*Article*
220	220	–	236 repealed. See Article N TEU
221	221		
222	222		
223	223	–	237 repealed. See Article O TEU
224	224		
225	225		
226	226		
227 amended	227	238 amended	238
228 new	228 deleted	239	239
228a new	–	240	240
229	229	241	241
230	230	242	242
231 amended	231	243	243
232	232	244	244
233	233	245	245
234	234	246	246
235	235	247	247
		248	248